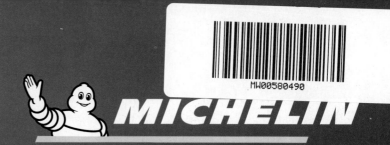

Road Atlas

USA   CANADA   MEXICO

Legend .... Cover flap

Key to Map Pages.. Inside front cover

How to Use this Atlas 2

Listing of State and City Maps 3

United States Interstate Map 4–5

Canada Highway Map 6–7

Michelin Scenic Drives 8–11, 301–302

Maps 12–187

    United States 12–155

    BONUS MAPS! Washington DC to Boston
    Large-Scale Northeast Corridor Maps........................... 144–151

    Canada 156–183

    Mexico 184–187

Index with City and Local Maps 188–283

    United States 188–276

    Canada 277–282

    Mexico 283

City to City Distance Chart............................... 284–285

Distances and Driving Times across North America 286–287

Tourism and Border Crossing Information 288

Parks Index with GPS Coordinates 289–300

    United States 289–297

    Canada 298–300

NORTH AMERICA

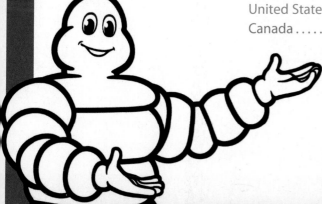

ROAD MAPS are organized geographically. *United States, Canada, and Mexico road maps are organized in a grid layout, starting in the northwest of each country. To find your way, use either the* **Key to Map Pages** *inside the front cover, the* **Listing of State and City Maps** *on page 3, or the* **index** *in the back of the atlas.*

COUNTRY COLORS
Colors represent countries throughout the atlas.
Red → Canada
Green → Mexico
Blue → United States
Purple → United States (Northeast Corridor)

MAP SCALES
Scale bars are shown at a constant length throughout the atlas for quick and easy scale comparison between regions.

DRIVING DISTANCES
Use this chart to check driving distances between major cities within each map. Refer to distance and driving time information at the back of the atlas for travel over greater distances.

LOCATOR MAPS
A quick glance at this miniature map lets you check which states and/or provinces are shown on each page.

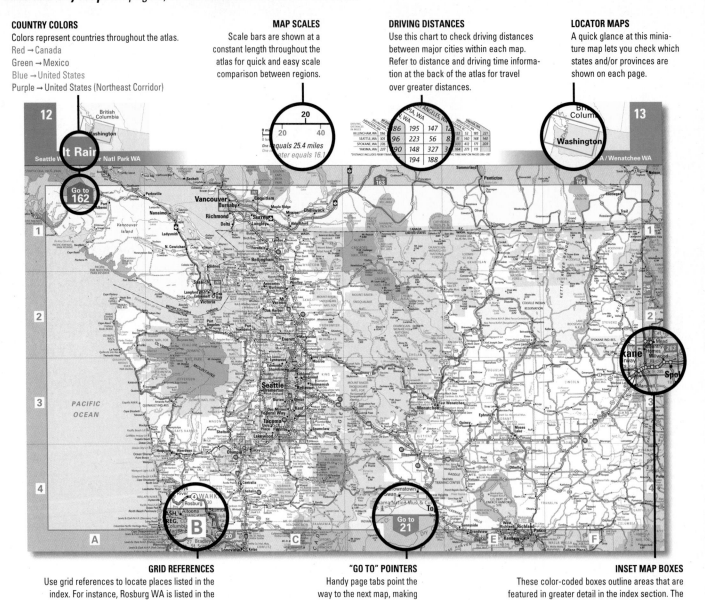

GRID REFERENCES
Use grid references to locate places listed in the index. For instance, Rosburg WA is listed in the index with "12" and "B4", indicating that the town may be found on page 12 in grid square B4.

"GO TO" POINTERS
Handy page tabs point the way to the next map, making navigation a breeze.

INSET MAP BOXES
These color-coded boxes outline areas that are featured in greater detail in the index section. The tab with "263" (above) indicates that a detailed map of Spokane may be found on page 263 (below).

HOW THE INDEX WORKS
Cities and towns are listed alphabetically, with separate indexes for the United States, Canada, and Mexico. Figures after entries indicate page number and grid reference. Entries in bold color indicate cities with detailed inset maps. The U.S. index also includes counties and parishes, which are shown in bold black type.

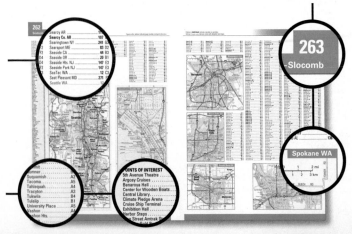

INSET MAP INDEXES
Many inset maps have their own indexes. Metro area inset map indexes list cities and towns; downtown inset map indexes list points of interest.

UNITED STATES   pages **12–155**

ALABAMA (AL).......119–120, 127–128, 135–137
  Birmingham.............................. 195
  Huntsville................................ 221
  Mobile................................... 236
  Montgomery.............................. 236
ALASKA (AK).........................154–155
  Anchorage............................... 189
  Juneau.................................. 223
ARIZONA (AZ)....................46–48, 53–55
  Flagstaff................................. 213
  Phoenix.................................. 249
  Phoenix Downtown....................... 249
  Tucson................................... 268
  Yuma.................................... 276
ARKANSAS (AR)......106–108, 116–118, 124–126
  Fayetteville.............................. 212
  Hot Springs.............................. 219
  Little Rock............................... 227
CALIFORNIA (CA)..... 28–29, 36–37, 44–46, 52–54
  Bakersfield............................... 192
  Fresno................................... 214
  Los Angeles.............................. 228
  Los Angeles Downtown.................... 230
  Monterey Bay............................ 236
  Oxnard/Ventura.......................... 247
  Palm Springs............................. 247
  Sacramento.............................. 255
  San Diego................................ 258
  San Diego Downtown..................... 258
  San Francisco Bay Area................... 259
  San Francisco Downtown................. 260
  Santa Barbara............................ 260
  Stockton................................. 265
COLORADO (CO)............32–34, 40–42, 48–50
  Colorado Springs......................... 205
  Denver................................... 209
  Denver Downtown........................ 209
  Fort Collins.............................. 213
  Pueblo................................... 252
CONNECTICUT (CT)..............94–95, 148–150
  Hartford................................. 218
  New Haven/Bridgeport.................... 238
  Stamford................................ 264
  Waterbury............................... 273
DELAWARE (DE)..........103–104, 114, 145–146
  Dover.................................... 211
  Wilmington.............................. 274
DISTRICT OF COLUMBIA (DC)...103–104, 114, 144
  Washington.............................. 270
  Washington Downtown.................... 272
FLORIDA (FL)........................135–143
  Daytona Beach........................... 208
  Fort Myers............................... 214
  Jacksonville.............................. 222
  Key West................................. 224
  Melbourne/Titusville..................... 232
  Miami/Fort Lauderdale.................... 233
  Miami Downtown......................... 233
  Orlando.................................. 246
  Panama City.............................. 247
  Pensacola................................ 247
  Tallahassee............................... 265
  Tampa/St. Petersburg..................... 266
GEORGIA (GA).......120–121, 128–130, 137–139
  Atlanta................................... 190
  Atlanta Downtown........................ 191
  Augusta.................................. 191
  Columbus................................ 205
  Macon................................... 231
  Savannah................................ 261
HAWAII (HI)........................152–153
  Honolulu................................ 219
IDAHO (ID).................14–15, 22–24, 30–31
  Boise.................................... 196
  Idaho Falls............................... 221
  Pocatello................................ 250
ILLINOIS (IL)....... 73–75, 87–89, 97–99, 108–109
  Chicago.................................. 203
  Chicago Downtown....................... 202
  Peoria................................... 247

Quad Cities (Davenport IA)................ 208
Rockford.................................. 255
Springfield................................ 264
INDIANA (IN)..............89–90, 99–100, 109
  Evansville................................ 212
  Fort Wayne............................... 214
  Indianapolis.............................. 221
  Indianapolis Downtown................... 222
  South Bend............................... 263
IOWA (IA).................27, 35, 72–74, 86–88
  Cedar Rapids............................. 200
  Davenport/Quad Cities................... 208
  Des Moines............................... 210
KANSAS (KS)...........42–43, 50–51, 96, 106
  Kansas City.............................. 224
  Topeka................................... 267
  Wichita.................................. 273
KENTUCKY (KY)..............99–101, 108–111
  Frankfort................................ 214
  Lexington................................ 227
  Louisville................................ 230
LOUISIANA (LA)...............124–126. 132–135
  Baton Rouge............................. 194
  Lafayette................................. 225
  New Orleans.............................. 239
  New Orleans Downtown................... 239
  Shreveport............................... 263
MAINE (ME)..........................81–85
  Augusta.................................. 191
  Portland................................. 251
MARYLAND (MD).........102–104, 114, 144–146
  Annapolis................................ 189
  Baltimore................................ 193
  Baltimore Downtown...................... 194
  Washington DC........................... 270
MASSACHUSETTS (MA)....94–95, 150–151
  Boston................................... 197
  Boston Downtown......................... 197
  New Bedford/Fall River................... 238
  Springfield................................ 264
  Worcester................................ 275
MICHIGAN (MI).........65, 68–71, 75–77, 89–90
  Ann Arbor............................... 190
  Detroit.................................. 210
  Detroit Downtown........................ 210
  Flint..................................... 213
  Grand Rapids............................. 215
  Kalamazoo............................... 223
  Lansing.................................. 225
MINNESOTA (MN)..........19, 27, 64–67, 72–73
  Duluth................................... 211
  Minneapolis/St. Paul..................... 235
  Minneapolis Downtown................... 236
MISSISSIPPI (MS).....118–119, 125–127, 133–135
  Biloxi/Gulfport.......................... 195
  Jackson.................................. 222
  Vicksburg................................ 269
MISSOURI (MO)..........86–87, 96–98, 106–108
  Branson.................................. 198
  Jefferson City............................ 223
  Kansas City.............................. 224
  St. Louis................................. 256
  St. Louis Downtown...................... 256
  Springfield................................ 264
MONTANA (MT).....................14–17, 22–25
  Billings.................................. 194
  Great Falls............................... 215
  Helena................................... 218
  Missoula................................. 236
NEBRASKA (NE)...........33–35, 42–43, 86, 96
  Lincoln.................................. 227
  Omaha................................... 245
NEVADA (NV)..........29–31, 37–38, 45–46, 53
  Carson City.............................. 199
  Las Vegas................................ 226
  Las Vegas Strip.......................... 226
  Reno..................................... 253
NEW HAMPSHIRE (NH).........81–82, 84, 94–95
  Concord.................................. 206
  Manchester.............................. 231
NEW JERSEY (NJ).......93–94, 104–105, 145–148
  Atlantic City............................. 191

Newark (New York NY).................... 240
Trenton.................................. 268
NEW MEXICO (NM)...............48–49, 55–57
  Albuquerque............................. 189
  Las Cruces............................... 226
  Santa Fe................................. 260
NEW YORK (NY)......78–81, 92–95, 105, 147–149
  Albany/Schenectady/Troy................. 188
  Buffalo/Niagara Falls..................... 198
  New York................................ 240
  Manhattan/New York...................... 242
  Rochester................................ 254
  Syracuse................................. 265
NORTH CAROLINA (NC)....111–113, 115, 120–123
  Asheville................................. 190
  Charlotte................................. 201
  Fayetteville.............................. 213
  Greensboro/Winston-Salem............... 216
  Raleigh/Durham/Chapel Hill.............. 253
  Wilmington.............................. 275
NORTH DAKOTA (ND)...........17–19, 25–27
  Bismarck................................. 196
  Fargo.................................... 211
OHIO (OH).................90–91, 100–102
  Akron.................................... 188
  Canton................................... 199
  Cincinnati................................ 204
  Cleveland................................ 204
  Cleveland Downtown...................... 205
  Columbus................................ 206
  Dayton................................... 208
  Toledo................................... 267
  Youngstown/Warren....................... 276
OKLAHOMA (OK)...........49–51, 59, 106, 116
  Oklahoma City........................... 244
  Tulsa.................................... 269
OREGON (OR)...................20–22, 28–30
  Eugene................................... 212
  Portland................................. 251
  Salem.................................... 257
PENNSYLVANIA (PA)...91–94, 102–104, 146–147
  Allentown/Bethlehem..................... 189
  Erie..................................... 212
  Harrisburg............................... 218
  Lancaster................................ 225
  Philadelphia.............................. 248
  Philadelphia Downtown................... 248
  Pittsburgh............................... 250
  Pittsburgh Downtown..................... 250
  Scranton/Wilkes-Barre.................... 261
  York..................................... 275
RHODE ISLAND (RI)...............95, 149–151
  Newport.................................. 239
  Providence............................... 251
SOUTH CAROLINA (SC)........121–123, 130–131
  Charleston............................... 200
  Columbia................................. 205
  Greenville/Spartanburg................... 217
  Myrtle Beach............................. 237
SOUTH DAKOTA (SD)..........25–27, 33–35
  Pierre.................................... 249
  Rapid City............................... 253
  Sioux Falls............................... 263
TENNESSEE (TN).............108–111, 118–121
  Chattanooga.............................. 201
  Knoxville................................ 225
  Memphis................................. 232
  Nashville................................. 237
TEXAS (TX)......49–51, 56–63, 116, 124, 132–133
  Amarillo................................. 189
  Austin................................... 192
  Corpus Christi............................ 206
  Dallas/Fort Worth........................ 207
  Dallas Downtown......................... 207
  El Paso.................................. 211
  Houston.................................. 220
  Houston Downtown....................... 220
  Lubbock.................................. 231
  McAllen.................................. 232
  San Antonio.............................. 257
  San Antonio Downtown................... 257
  Waco..................................... 269

UTAH (UT)..................31–32, 38–40, 46–48
  Ogden................................... 244
  Provo.................................... 252
  Salt Lake City............................ 257
VERMONT (VT)....................81–82, 94
  Burlington................................ 199
  Montpelier............................... 237
VIRGINIA (VA)..........102–104, 110–115, 144
  Charlottesville............................ 201
  Norfolk/Hampton Roads.................. 243
  Richmond................................ 254
  Roanoke................................. 254
  Washington DC........................... 270
  Williamsburg............................. 269
WASHINGTON (WA)................12–14, 20–22
  Olympia.................................. 245
  Seattle/Tacoma........................... 262
  Seattle Downtown........................ 262
  Spokane.................................. 263
  Yakima................................... 275
WEST VIRGINIA (WV)...91, 101–103, 111–112, 144
  Charleston............................... 200
  Huntington............................... 221
WISCONSIN (WI)..........64–65, 67–69, 73–75
  Green Bay................................ 216
  Madison.................................. 231
  Milwaukee............................... 234
  Milwaukee Downtown.................... 234
  Racine/Kenosha.......................... 252
WYOMING (WY)...........23–25, 31–33
  Casper................................... 199
  Cheyenne................................ 202
PUERTO RICO (PR)....................... 187
  San Juan................................. 276

CANADA   pages **155–183**

ALBERTA (AB)............155, 157–160, 164–165
  Calgary.................................. 277
  Edmonton................................ 277
BRITISH COLUMBIA (BC).......155–158, 162–164
  Vancouver............................... 282
  Victoria.................................. 282
MANITOBA (MB)..................161, 166–168
  Winnipeg................................ 282
NEW BRUNSWICK (NB).................177–181
  Fredericton............................... 277
  Saint John................................ 280
NEWFOUNDLAND & LABRADOR (NL)....182–183
  St. John's................................ 280
NORTHWEST TERRITORIES (NT)............ 155
NOVA SCOTIA (NS)................180–182
  Halifax................................... 277
NUNAVUT (NU)........................ 6–7
ONTARIO (ON)....................167–174
  Hamilton................................ 278
  London................................... 278
  Niagara Falls (Buffalo NY)................ 198
  Ottawa.................................. 279
  Sudbury.................................. 281
  Toronto.................................. 281
  Toronto Downtown........................ 281
  Windsor (Detroit MI)..................... 210
PRINCE EDWARD ISLAND (PE)..........179–182
  Charlottetown............................ 277
QUÉBEC (QC).............171, 174–179, 182–183
  Gatineau (Ottawa ON).................... 279
  Montréal................................. 279
  Québec.................................. 280
  Sherbrooke............................... 281
SASKATCHEWAN (SK)........159–161, 165–166
  Regina................................... 280
  Saskatoon................................ 280
YUKON (YT).......................... 155

MEXICO   pages **184–187**

Cancún.................................... 283
Guadalajara................................ 283
México.................................... 283
Monterrey................................. 283

0 mi   125   250   375

0 km   125   250   375   500

One inch equals 217 miles
One centimeter equals 138 kilometers

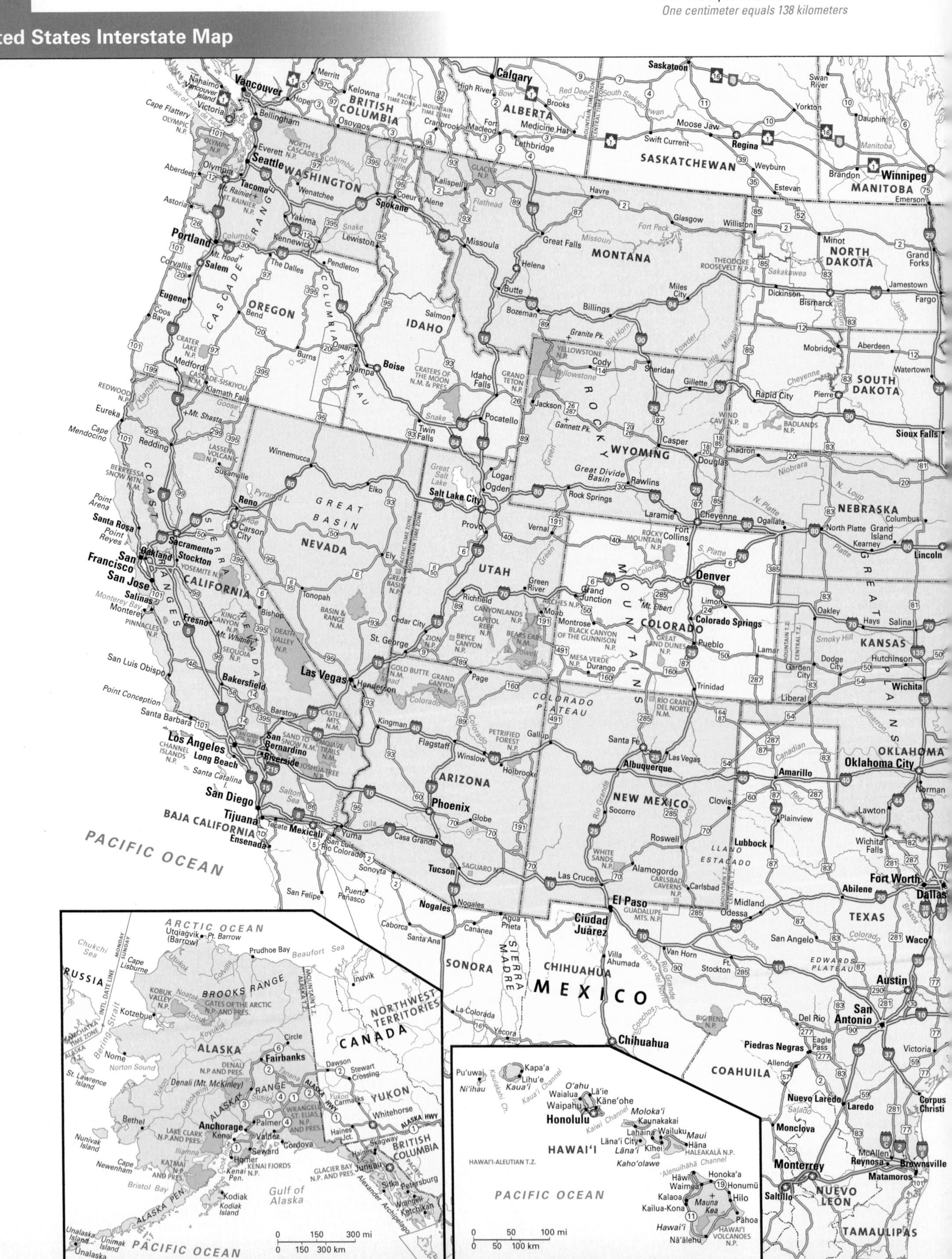

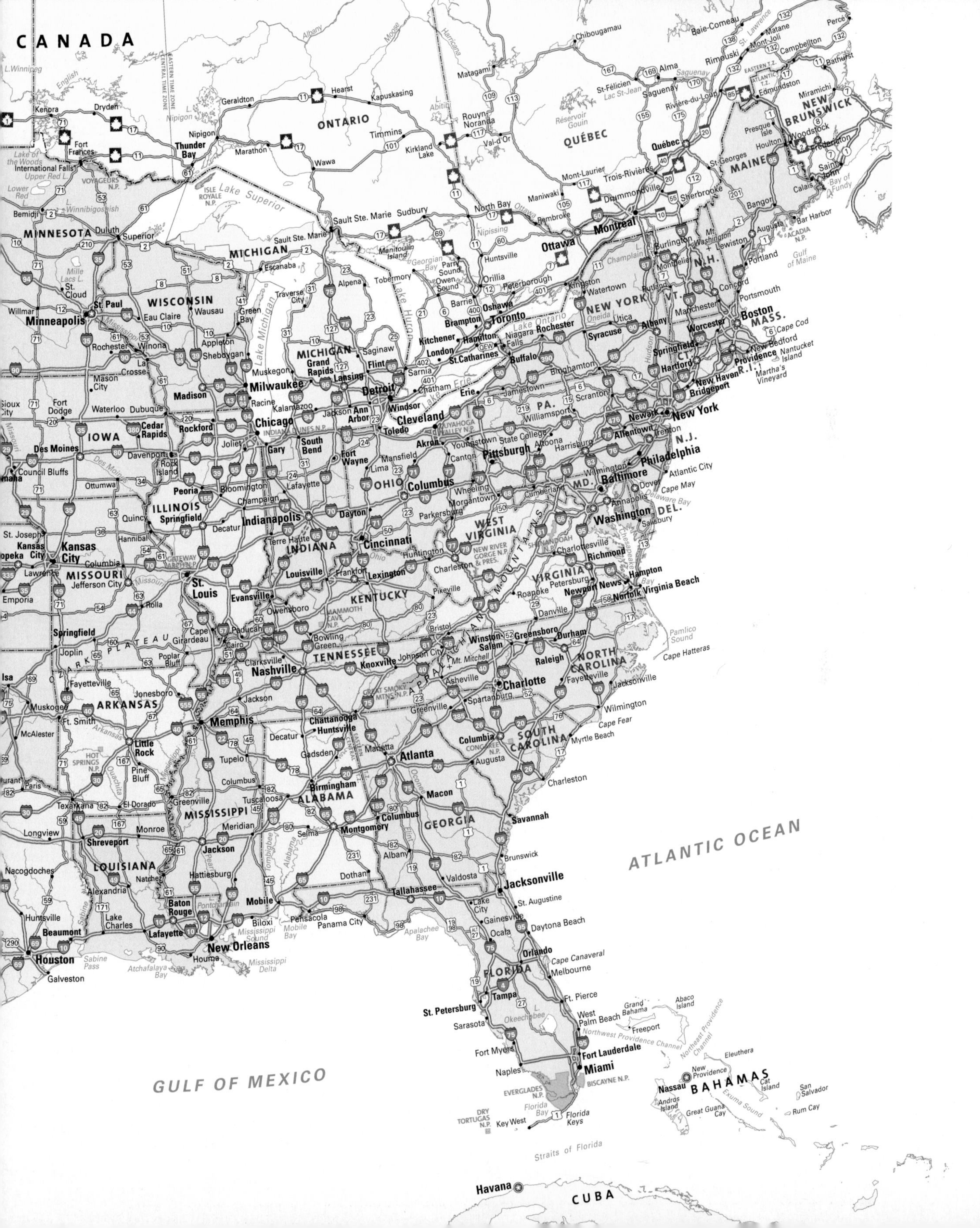
CANADA
ONTARIO
QUÉBEC
NEW BRUNSWICK
MAINE
N.H.
VT.
MASS.
R.I.
CT.
NEW YORK
PA.
N.J.
DEL.
MD.
WEST VIRGINIA
VIRGINIA
NORTH CAROLINA
SOUTH CAROLINA
GEORGIA
FLORIDA
ALABAMA
MISSISSIPPI
LOUISIANA
ARKANSAS
TENNESSEE
KENTUCKY
OHIO
INDIANA
ILLINOIS
MISSOURI
IOWA
MINNESOTA
WISCONSIN
MICHIGAN
Lake Superior
Lake Michigan
Lake Huron
Lake Erie
Lake Ontario
ATLANTIC OCEAN
GULF OF MEXICO
Straits of Florida
BAHAMAS
CUBA
Havana
Montreal
Ottawa
Toronto
Québec
Boston
New York
Philadelphia
Baltimore
Washington
Pittsburgh
Cleveland
Detroit
Chicago
Milwaukee
Minneapolis
St. Paul
Des Moines
Kansas City
St. Louis
Indianapolis
Columbus
Cincinnati
Louisville
Nashville
Memphis
Atlanta
Charlotte
Richmond
Norfolk
Virginia Beach
Jacksonville
Orlando
Tampa
Miami
New Orleans
Houston
Jackson
Birmingham
Montgomery
Shreveport
Little Rock
APPALACHIAN MOUNTAINS
OZARK PLATEAU

6

One inch equals 250 miles/Un pouce équivaut à 250 milles
One cm equals 159 km/Un cm équivaut à 159 km

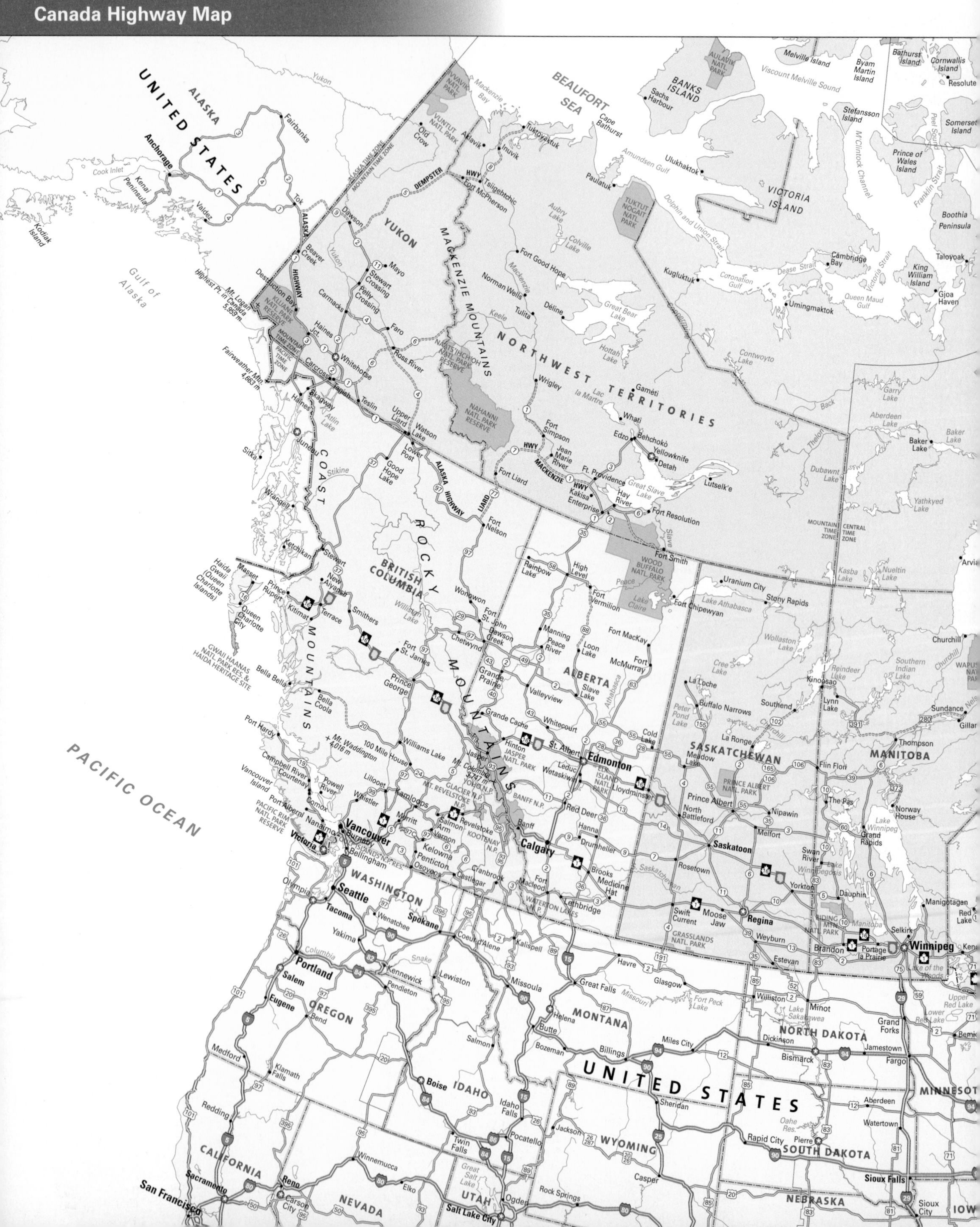

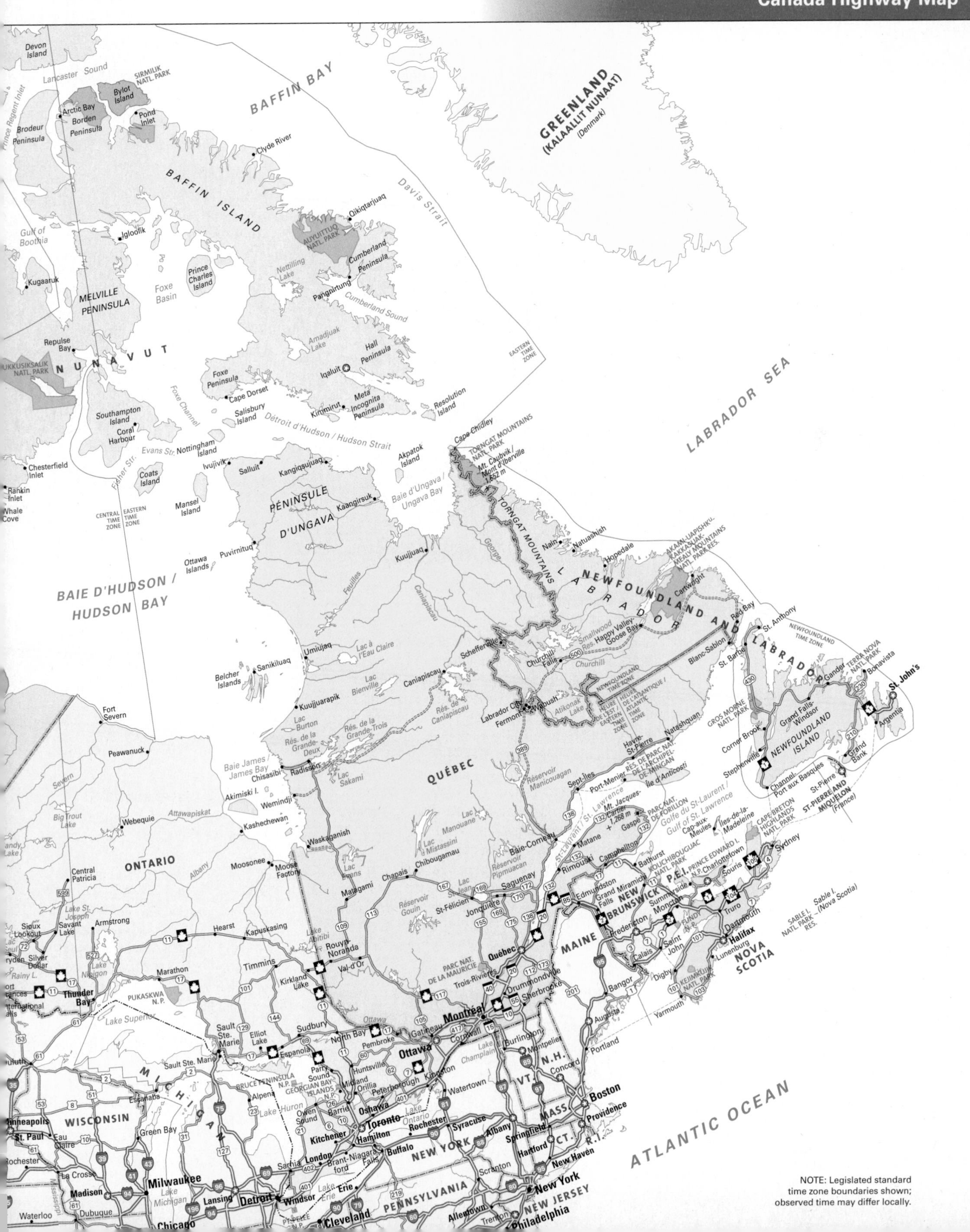

NOTE: Legislated standard
time zone boundaries shown;
observed time may differ locally.

Experience the thrill of the open roads of North America with these great Scenic Drives from Michelin. The famous star ratings highlight natural and cultural attractions along the way.

★★★ **Worth a special journey**
★★ **Worth a detour**
★ **Worth a visit**

Michelin Scenic Drives are indicated by a green and yellow dashed line (▄▄▄▄▄) on corresponding atlas maps for easy reference. The following 16 drives are also plotted for your use.

North Coast/Mendocino★★ ....Maps 259, 36
Napa Valley/Sonoma★★ .... Map 36
Willamette Valley★ ....Maps 251, 20, 257, 212
Florida Panhandle★ ....Maps 265, 137, 136, 247
Coastal Carolinas★★ ....Maps 115, 123, 275, 237, 131, 200, 261
San Juan Country★★ .... Map 40
Snake River Valley★ .... Maps 221, 23, 22, 196, 30
Hill Country★★ ....Maps 192, 61, 60, 257
Southern New Mexico★ .....Maps 211, 56, 226, 48, 49, 57
New Jersey Pine Barrens★ .....Maps 191, 147, (105, 104)
Litchfield Hills★★ ....Maps 148, 94
Hudson River Valley★★★ ....Maps 240, 148, 94
Thompson Canyon★ ....Maps 282, 163
Alberta Badlands★★★ ....Maps 277, 164, 165
Saint John River Valley★★ ....Maps 277, 180, 178
Annapolis Valley/Atlantic Shore★★.Maps 180, 181, 277
Blue Heron Drive★★ ....Maps 277, 181

ABBREVIATIONS

N	North	NL	National Lakeshore
E	East	NM	National Memorial/
S	South		National Monument
W	West	NMP	National Military Park
NE	Northeast	NP	National Park
NW	Northwest	NPR	National Park Reserve
SE	Southeast	NRA	National
SW	Southwest		Recreation Area
Hwy.	Highway	NWR	National Wildlife
Pkwy.	Parkway		Refuge
Rte.	Route	PP	Provincial Park
Mi	Miles	SHP	State Historical Park
Km	Kilometers	SHS	State Historic Site
Sq Ft	Square Feet	SP	State Park
NHS	National Historic	SR	State Reserve
	Site	VC	Visitor Center

For detailed coverage of the attractions, and for where to dine and stay overnight, see Michelin's North America **Regional Atlas Series**, designed for the way you drive, and Michelin's **Green Guide** and **Short Stays** collections, the ultimate guidebooks for the independent traveler.

NORTHWEST

Anchorage/Fairbanks/Denali★★★
892 miles/1,436 kilometers
Maps 189, 154, 155

From **Anchorage★**, Alaska's largest city, take Rte. 1 (Glenn Hwy. and Tok Cutoff) N and then E through the broad Matanuska Valley to the small town of **Tok**. The route passes agricultural communities, the **Matanuska Glacier** and the Wrangell Mountains before heading up the Copper River Basin. From Tok, take the Alaska Hwy. (Rte. 2) NW to **Fairbanks★**, a friendly town with a frontier feel. The road passes the **Trans-Alaska Pipeline** and **Big Delta SHP** then parallels the Tanana River. From Fairbanks, opt for Rte. 3 W which crosses the river at Nenana, then veers S to **Denali NP★★★**, home of spruce forests, grassy tundra, grizzlies, moose and North America's highest peak, **Mount McKinley** (20,320ft). Return S to Anchorage via Rtes. 3 and 1.

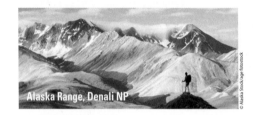
Alaska Range, Denali NP
© Alaska Stock/age fotostock

Badlands★★★
164 miles/264 kilometers
Maps 253, 26

From **Rapid City★**, South Dakota, drive SE on Rte. 44 through Farmingdale and Scenic, then east to Interior to enter **Badlands NP★★★**. Take Rte. 377 NE 2mi to Cedar Pass and stop at the park's Ben Reifel VC. From there, Cliff **Shelf Nature Trail★★** (.5mi) is popular for its shady juniper trees; **Castle Trail★★★** (4.5mi) is spectacular in early morning when the moonscape valley and pointed spires get first light. Turn left onto Rte. 240, **Badlands Loop Road★★★**, along the northern rim, where prairie grasslands give way to buttes and hoodoos. **Pinnacles Overlook★★** is a sweeping viewpoint to the south.
Drive N to I-90, and cross the Interstate N to Wall. On Main St. visit **Wall Drug★**, a "drug store in name only" with over 20 shops filled

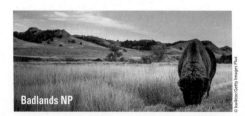
Badlands NP
© kwiktor/Getty Images Plus

with historical photos, 6,000 pairs of cowboy boots, wildlife exhibits and Western art displayed in five dining rooms. In the backyard a roaring, 80ft **Tyrannosaurus** sends toddlers running. Leave Wall on I-90, driving W. Take Exit 67 to Ellsworth Air Force Base, where the **South Dakota Air and Space Museum** displays stealth bombers and other aircraft. Continue W on I-90 back to Rapid City to conclude the tour.

Black Hills★★
244 miles/393 kilometers Maps 253, 26, 25

From **Rapid City★**, drive S on US-16 then US-16A S past Keystone. Take Rte. 244 W to **Mount Rushmore NM★★★**. Continue W on Rte. 244 to the junction of US-16/385. Enroute S to Custer, **Crazy Horse Memorial★** honors the famous Sioux chief. From Custer, head S on US-385 through Pringle to the junction of Rte. 87. Take Rte. 87 N through **Wind Cave NP★★** and into **Custer SP★★★**. Follow **Wildlife Loop Road★★** (access S of Blue Bell, across from Rte. 342 junction) E and N to US-16A. Then travel W to join scenic **Needles Highway★★** (Rte. 87) NW to US-16/385 N. Where US-16 separates, continue N on US-385 to **Deadwood★★**, a former gold camp. Turn left onto US-14A, driving SW through **Lead★**, site of the former **Homestake Gold Mine★★**, to Cheyenne Crossing. Drive N on US-14A to I-90, turning SE back to Rapid City.

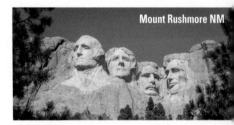
Mount Rushmore NM

Columbia River Gorge★★
83 miles/134 kilometers Maps 251, 20, 21

From **Portland★★**, Oregon's largest city, take I-84 E to Exit 17 in Troutdale. There, head E on the winding **Historic Columbia River Highway★★** (US-30), which skirts the steep cliffs above the river. For great **views★★**, stop at **Vista House at Crown Point**. You'll pass the 620ft **Multnomah Falls★★** and moss-draped **Oneonta Gorge**. At Ainsworth State Park (Exit 35), rejoin I-84 and travel E to Mosier (Exit 69), where US-30, with its hairpin turns, begins again. Continue E on US-30, stopping at **Rowena Crest Viewpoint★★** for grand vistas—and wildflowers. Just past the Western-style town called The Dalles, take US-197 N to conclude the tour at **The Dalles Lock** and **Dam VC★★**.

Grand Tetons/Yellowstone★★★

224 miles/361 kilometers   Map 24

Note: parts of this tour are closed in winter.
From **Jackson★★**, drive N on US-26/191/89
to Moose. Turn left onto Teton Park Rd. to
access **Grand Teton NP★★★** and **Jenny Lake
Scenic Drive★★★**. From Teton Park Rd., drive
N to the junction of US-89/191/287 (**John D.
Rockefeller Jr. Memorial Pkwy.**) and follow
the parkway N into **Yellowstone NP★★★** to
West Thumb. Take Grand Loop Rd. W to **Old
Faithful★★★**, the world's most famous geyser.
Continue N on the Grand Loop Rd., passing
Norris Geyser Basin★★ en route to **Mammoth
Hot Springs★★★**. Turn E on Grand Loop Rd.
to Tower Junction, then S into **Grand Canyon
of the Yellowstone★★★**. Continue S from
Canyon Village through **Hayden Valley★★** to
Yellowstone Lake. Head SW, back to West
Thumb, to conclude the tour.

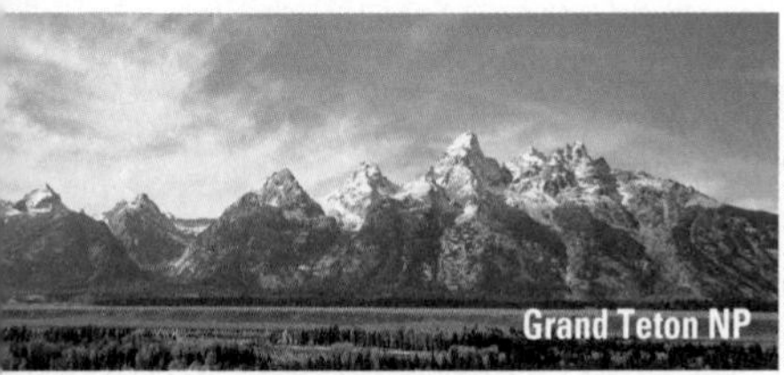
Grand Teton NP

Pacific Coast/Olympic Peninsula★★★

419 miles/675 kilometers   Maps 245, 12

From the state capital of **Olympia**, drive N on
US-101 to Discovery Bay. Detour on Rte. 20
NE to **Port Townsend★★**, a well-preserved
Victorian seaport. From Discovery Bay, head
W on US-101 through **Port Angeles** to the
Heart O' the Hills park entrance for **Olympic
NP★★★** to see **Hurricane Ridge★★★**.
Back on US-101, head E then S to the park
entrance that leads to **Hoh Rain Forest★★★**.
Follow US-101 S, then E after Queets to **Lake
Quinaulte**, home to bald eagles, trumpeter
swans and loons. Continue S on US-101 to
Aberdeen, taking Rte. 105 to the coast. At
Raymond, return to US-101 heading S to **Long
Beach**. Follow Rte. 103 N past the former
cannery town of **Oysterville** to **Leadbetter
Point★** on Willapa Bay, where oysters are still
harvested. Return S to **Ilwaco** and drive E and S
on US-101 to Astoria, Oregon, to end the tour.

The Oregon Coast★★★

368 miles/592 kilometers   Maps 20, 28

Leave **Astoria★**, Oregon's first settlement, via
US-101, heading SW. **Fort Clatsop National
Memorial★★** recalls Lewis and Clark's
historic stay. **Cannon Beach★** boasts a sandy
beach and tall coastal rock. At the farming
community of **Tillamook★**, go west on 3rd
St. to **Cape Meares** to begin **Three Capes**

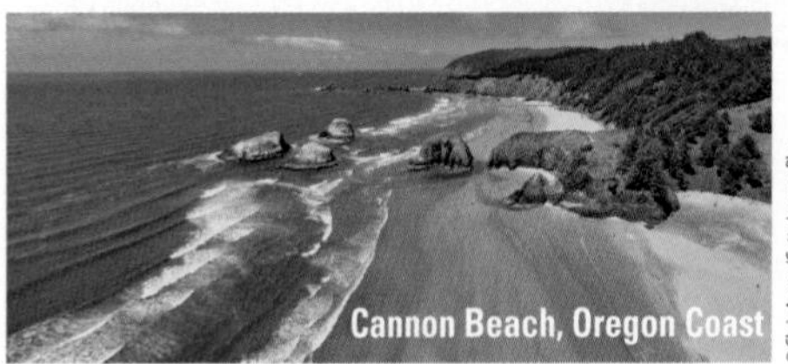
Cannon Beach, Oregon Coast

Scenic Drive★★. Continue S, rejoining US-101
just beyond Pacific City. Drive S on US-101
through **Newport★**, then **Yachats★**, which
neighbors **Cape Perpetua Scenic Area★★**.
From **Florence** to **Coos Bay★** stretches
Oregon Dunes National Recreation Area★★.
At Coos Bay, take Cape Arago Hwy. W to
tour the gardens of **Shore Acres State Park★**.
Drive S on the highway to rejoin US-101. Pass
Bandon★, known for its cheese factory, and
Port Orford, with its fishing fleet. Farther S,
Boardman State Park★ shelters Sitka spruce,
Douglas fir and **Natural Bridge Cove**. End the
tour at **Brookings**.

SOUTHWEST

Big Bend Area★★

581 miles/935 kilometers
Maps 211, 56, 57, 62, 60

Head S from **El Paso★** via I-10, then E to Kent.
Take Rte. 118 S to Alpine, passing **McDonald
Observatory★** (telescope tours) and **Fort
Davis NHS★★**. Continue S to Study Butte
to enter **Big Bend NP★★★**, edged by the
Rio Grande River and spanning 1,252sq mi
of spectacular canyons, lush bottomlands,
sprawling desert and mountain woodlands.
The park has more species of migratory and
resident birds than any other national park.
Travel E to the main VC at Panther Junction in
the heart of the park (US-385 and Rio Grande
Village Dr.). Then take US-385 N to Marathon.
Turn E on US-90 to Langtry, site of **Judge Roy
Bean VC★**. Continue E to **Seminole Canyon
SP★★**, with its 4,000-year-old pictographs.
Farther E, **Amistad NRA★** is popular for water
sports. Continue on US-90 to conclude the
tour in Del Rio.

Canyonlands of Utah★★★

481 miles/774 kilometers   Maps, 39, 40

From **St. George★**, drive NE on I-15 to Exit 16.
Take Rte. 9 E to Springdale, gateway to **Zion
NP★★★**, with its sandstone canyon, waterfalls
and hanging gardens. Continue E on Rte. 9
to Mt. Carmel Junction, turn left onto US-89
and head N to the junction with Rte. 12. Take
Rte. 12 SE to **Bryce Canyon NP★★★**, with its
colored rock formations. Continue SE on Rte.
12 to Cannonville, then S to **Kodachrome Basin
SP★★**, where sandstone chimneys rise from

the desert floor. Return to Cannonville, and
drive NE on Rte. 12 through Boulder to Torrey.
Take Rte. 24 E through **Capitol Reef NP★★**—
with its unpaved driving roads and trails—
then N to I-70. Travel E on I-70 to Exit 182,
then S on US-191 to Rte. 313 into **Canyonlands
NP★★★** to **Grand View Point Overlook**.
Return to US-191, turning S to access **Arches
NP★★★**—the greatest concentration of
natural stone arches in the country. Continue
S on US-191 to **Moab★** to end the tour.

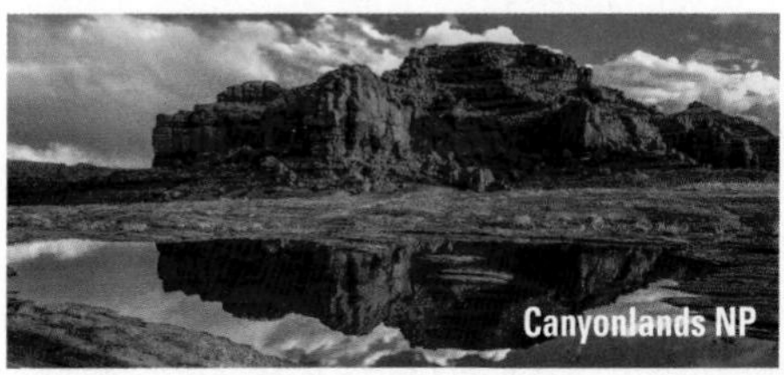
Canyonlands NP

Central Coast/Big Sur★★★

118 miles/190 kilometers   Maps 236, 44

From **Cannery Row★** in **Monterey★★**, take
Prescott Ave. to Rte. 68. Turn right and
continue to Pacific Grove Gate (on your left)
to begin scenic **17-Mile Drive★★**, a private toll
road. Exit at Carmel Gate to reach the upscale
beach town of **Carmel★★**, site of Carmel
mission★★★. The town's Scenic Road winds S
along the beachfront. Leave Carmel by Hwy. 1
S. Short, easy trails at **Point Lobos SR★★** line
the shore. Enjoy the wild beauty of the **Big
Sur★★★** coastline en route to San Simeon,
where **Hearst Castle★★★**, the magnificent
estate of a former newspaper magnate,
overlooks the Pacific Ocean. Continue S on
Hwy. 1 to **Morro Bay**, where the tour ends.

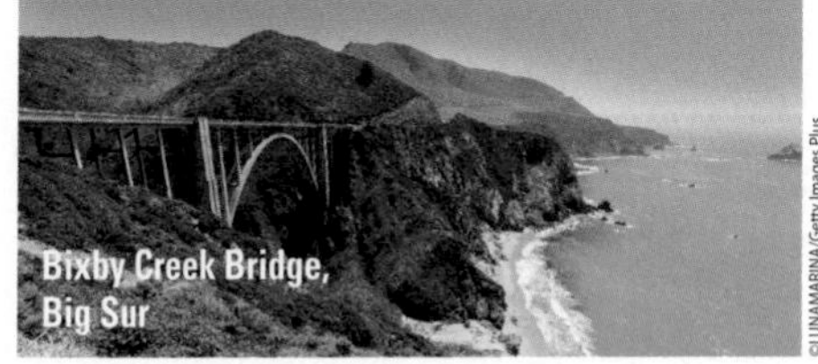
Bixby Creek Bridge, Big Sur

Colorado Rockies★★★

499 miles/803 kilometers
Maps 209, 41, 33, 40

*Note: Rte. 82 S of Leadville to Aspen is
closed mid-Oct to Memorial Day due to
snow.*
From **Golden★★**, W of **Denver★★**, drive
W on US-6 along Clear Creek to Rte. 119,
heading N on the *Peak to Peak Highway★★*
to **Nederland★**. Continue N on Rte. 72, then
follow Rte. 7 N to the town of **Estes Park★★**.
Take US-36 W to enter **Rocky Mountain
NP★★★**. Drive **Trail Ridge Road★★★** (US-34)

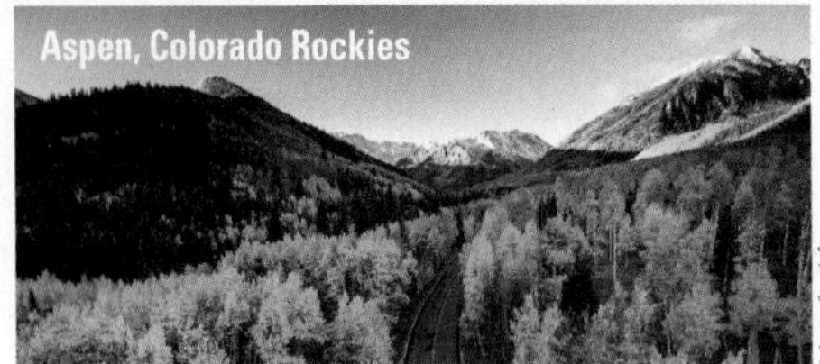

Aspen, Colorado Rockies

S to the town of **Grand Lake★**. Continue S to Granby, turn left on US-40 to I-70 at Empire. Head W on I-70 past **Georgetown★** and through **Eisenhower Tunnel**. You'll pass ski areas Arapahoe Basin, **Keystone Resort★** and **Breckenridge★★**. At Exit 195 for **Copper Mountain Resort★**, take Rte. 91 S to **Leadville★★**, Colorado's former silver capital. Then travel S on US-24 to Rte. 82 W over **Independence Pass★★** to **Aspen★★★**. Head NW to I-70, passing **Glenwood Springs★★** with its **Hot Springs Pool★★**. Drive E on I-70 along **Glenwood Canyon★★** and the Colorado River to **Vail★★**. Continue E on I-70 to the old mining town of **Idaho Springs** to return to Golden via Rte. 119.

Lake Tahoe Loop★★

71 miles/114 kilometers   Map 37

Begin in **Tahoe City** at the intersection of Rtes. 89 and 28. Drive S on Rte. 89. **Ed Z'berg-Sugar Pine Point State Park★** encompasses a promontory topped by **Ehrman Mansion★** and other historic buildings. Farther S, **Emerald Bay State Park★★** surrounds beautiful **Emerald Bay★★**. At the bay's tip stands **Vikingsholm★★**, a mansion that resembles an ancient Nordic castle. At **Tallac Historic Site★★**, preserved summer estates recall Tahoe's turn-of-the-19C opulence. From Tahoe Valley, take Rte. 50 NE. **South Lake Tahoe**, the lake's largest town, offers lodging, dining and shopping. High-rise hotel-casinos characterize neighboring **Stateline** in Nevada. Continue N to Spooner Junction. Then follow Nevada Rte. 28 N to **Sand Harbor** (7mi), where picnic tables and a sandy beach fringe a sheltered cove. Continue through Kings Beach to end the tour at Tahoe City.

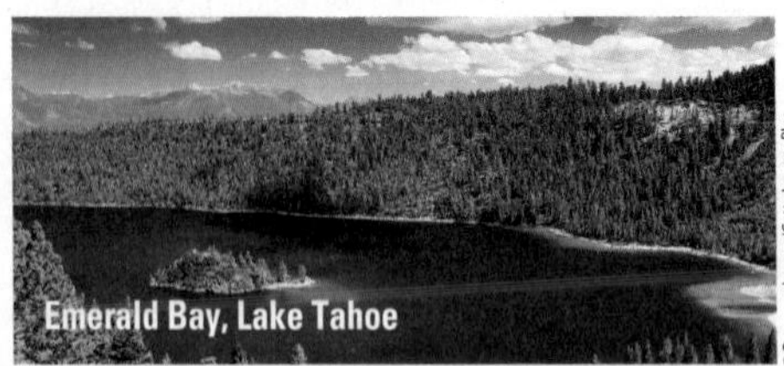

Emerald Bay, Lake Tahoe

Maui's Hana Highway★★

108 miles/174 kilometers   Map 153

Leave **Kahului** on Rte. 36 E toward **Paia**, an old sugar-plantation town. Continue E on Rte. 36, which becomes Rte. 360, the **Hana Highway★★**. The road passes **Ho'okipa**

Beach Park, famous for windsurfing, and **Puohokamoa Falls**, a good picnic stop, before arriving in **Hana**, a little village on an attractive bay. If adventurous, continue S on the Pulaui Highway to **Ohe'o Gulch★★** in **Haleakala NP★★★**, where small waterfalls tumble from the SE flank of the dormant volcano Haleakala. Past the gulch the grave of aviator **Charles Lindbergh** can be found in the churchyard at Palapala Hoomau Hawaiian Church. End the tour at Kipahulu.

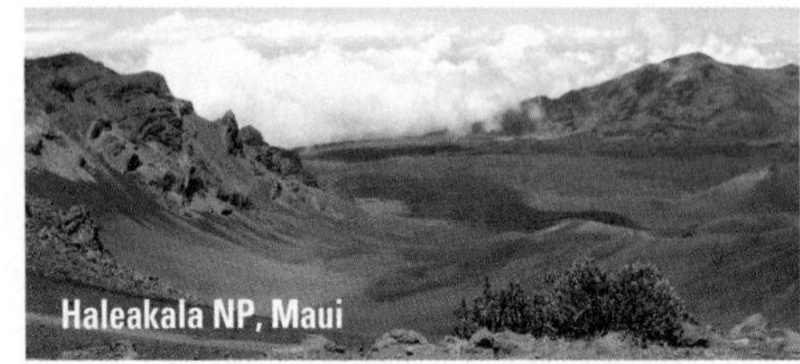

Haleakala NP, Maui

Redwood Empire★★

182 miles/293 kilometers   Maps 36, 28

In **Leggett**, S of the junction of Hwy. 1 and US-101, go N on US-101 to pass through a massive redwood trunk at **Chandelier Drive-Thru Tree Park**. To the N, see breathtaking groves along 31mi **Avenue of the Giants★★★**. **Humboldt Redwoods SP★★** contains **Rockefeller Forest★★**, the world's largest virgin redwood forest. From US-101, detour 4mi to **Ferndale★**, a quaint Victorian village. N. along US-101, **Eureka★** preserves a logging camp cookhouse and other historic sites. The sleepy fishing town of **Trinidad★** is home to a marine research lab. **Patrick's Point SP★★** offers dense forests, agate-strewn beaches and clifftop **view★★**. At **Orick**, enter the **Redwood National and State Parks★★★**, which protect a 379ft-high, 750-year-old **tree★**. The tour ends in Crescent City.

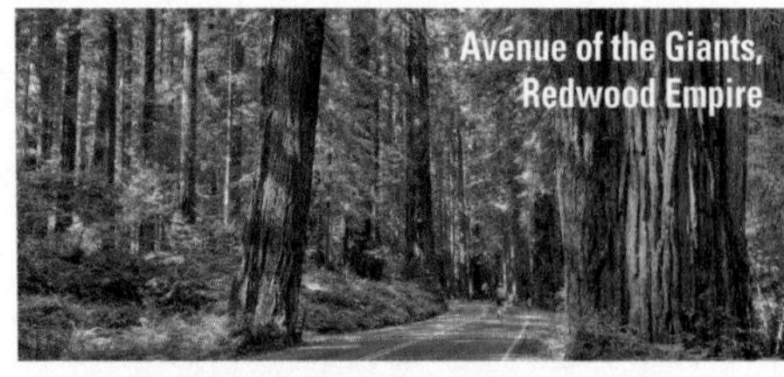

Avenue of the Giants, Redwood Empire

Santa Fe Area★★★

267 miles/430 kilometers
Maps 189, 48, 260, 49

From **Albuquerque★**, drive E on I-40 to Exit 175 and take Rte. 14, the **Turquoise Trail★★**, N to **Santa Fe★★★**. This 52mi back road runs along the scenic Sandia Mountains and passes dry washes, arroyos and a series of revived "ghost towns." Continue N on US-84/285, turning NE onto Rte. 76, the **High Road to Taos★★**. East of Vadito, take Rte. 518 N to Rte. 68 N into the rustic Spanish colonial town

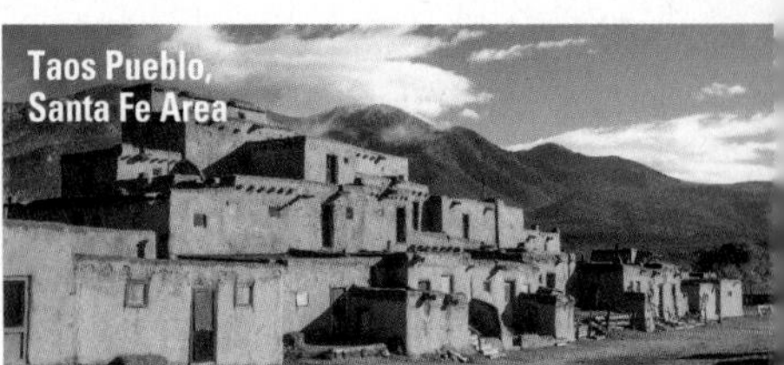

Taos Pueblo, Santa Fe Area

of **Taos★★**, a center for the arts. Head N on US-64 to the junction of Rte. 522. Continue W on US-64 for an 18mi round-trip detour to see the 1,200ft-long, three-span **Rio Grande Gorge Bridge** over the river. Return to Rte. 522 and take this route, part of the **Enchanted Circle★★** Scenic Byway, N to **Questa**, starting point for white-water trips on the Rio Grande. Turn onto Rte. 38, heading E to the old mining town of **Eagle Nest**. There, detour 23mi E on US-64 to **Cimarron**, a Wild West haunt. Back at Eagle Nest, travel SW on US-64, detouring on Rte. 434 S to tiny **Angel Fire**. Return to Taos on US-64 W to end the tour.

Sedona/Grand Canyon NP★★★

482 miles/776 kilometers
Maps 249, 54, 47, 213

Drive N from **Phoenix★** on I-17 to Exit 298 and take Rte. 179 N toward **Sedona★★** in the heart of **Red Rock Country★★★**. The red-rock formations are best accessed by four-wheel-drive vehicle via 12mi **Schnebly Hill Road★** (off Rte. 179, across Oak Creek bridge from US-89A "Y" junction), which offers splendid **views★★★**. Then head N on Rte. 89A through Sedona to begin 14mi drive of **Oak Creek Canyon★★**. Continue N on Rte. 89A and I-17 to **Flagstaff★★**, commercial hub for the region. Take US-180 NW to Rte. 64, which leads N to the **South Rim★★★** of **Grand Canyon NP★★★**. Take the shuttle (or drive, if permitted) along **West Rim Drive★★** to **Hermits Rest★**. Then travel **East Rim Drive★★★** (Rte. 64 E) to **Desert View Watchtower★** for **views★★★** of the canyon. Continue to the junction with US-89 at Cameron. Return S to Flagstaff, then S to Phoenix via I-17.

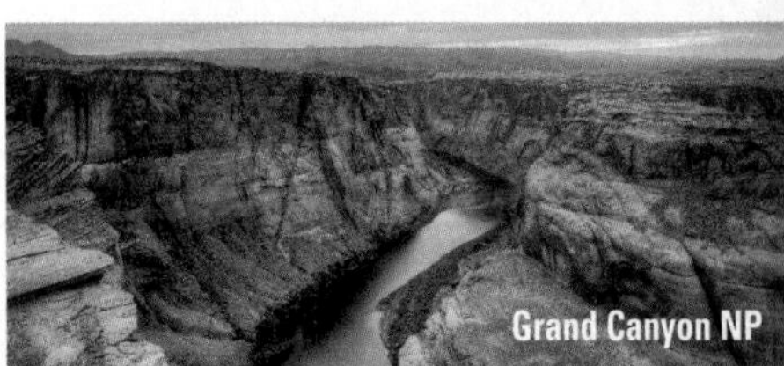

Grand Canyon NP

NORTHEAST

The Berkshires Loop★★★

57 miles/92 kilometers   Map 94

From **Great Barrington**, take US-23 E to Monterey, turning left onto Tyringham Rd., which becomes Monterey Rd., to experience scenic **Tyringham Valley★**. Continue N on Main Rd. to Tyringham Rd., which leads to **Lee**, famous for its marble. Then go NW on US-20 to **Lenox★**, with its inviting inns and restaurants. Detour on Rte. 183 W to **Tanglewood★**, site of a popular summer music festival. Return to Lenox and drive N on US-7 to **Pittsfield**, the commercial capital of the region. Head W on US-20 to enjoy **Hancock Shaker Village★★★**, a museum village that relates the history of a Shaker community established here in 1790. Rte. 41 S passes West Stockbridge, then opt for Rte. 102 SE to **Stockbridge★★** and its picturesque **Main Street★**. Follow US-7 S to the junction with Rte. 23, passing **Monument Mountain★** en route. Return to Great Barrington.

Cape Cod★★★

164 miles/264 kilometers   Maps 151, 95

At US-6 and Rte. 3, cross **Cape Cod Canal** via Sagamore Bridge and turn onto Rte. 6A to tour the Cape's **North Shore★★**. Bear right onto Rte. 130 to reach **Sandwich★**, famous for glass manufacturing. Continue on Rte. 6A E to Orleans. Take US-6 N along **Cape Cod National Seashore★★★**, with its wooded and marshland trails, to reach **Provincetown★★**, a seaside town and longtime LGBTQ retreat offering **dune tours★★** and summer theater. Return to Orleans and take Rte. 28 S through **Chatham★**, then W to Hyannis, where ferries depart for **Nantucket★★★**. Continue to quaint **Falmouth★**. Take Surf Dr., which becomes Oyster Pond Rd. to nearby **Woods Hole**, a world center for marine research and departure point for ferries to **Martha's Vineyard★★**. Take Woods Hole Rd., N to Rte. 28. Cross the canal via Bourne Bridge and head E on US-6 to end the tour at Rte. 3.

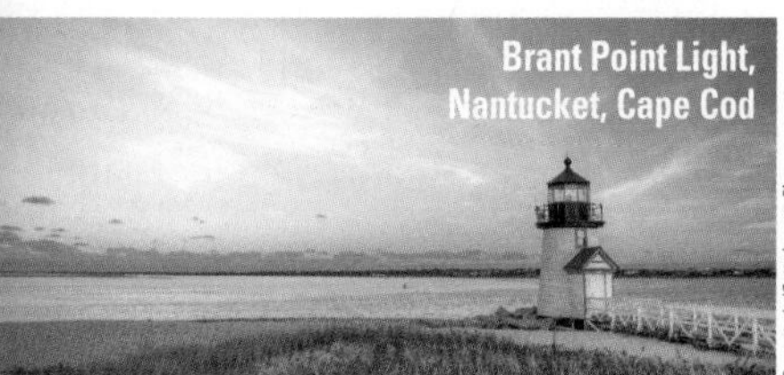
Brant Point Light, Nantucket, Cape Cod

Maine Coast★★

238 miles/383 kilometers
Maps 82, 251, 83

From **Kittery**, drive N on US-1 to **York★**, then along US-1A to see the 18C buildings of **Colonial York★★**. Continue N on coastal US-1A to **Ogunquit★**. Rejoin US-1 and head N to Rte. 9, turn right, and drive to **Kennebunkport**, with its colorful shops. Take Rte. 9A/35 to **Kennebunk**. Then travel N on US-1 to **Portland★★**, Maine's largest city, where the **Old Port★★** brims with galleries and boutiques. Take US-1 N through the outlet town of **Freeport**, then on to **Brunswick**, home of **Bowdoin College**. Turn NE through **Bath★**, **Wiscasset**, **Rockland**, **Camden★★**, **Searsport** and **Bucksport**. At Ellsworth, take Rt. 3 S to enter **Acadia NP★★★** on **Mount Desert Island★★★**, where **Park Loop Road★★★** (closed in winter) parallels open coast. From the top of **Cadillac Mountain★★★**, the **views★★★** are breathtaking. The tour ends at **Bar Harbor★**, a popular charming town just outside Acadia NP.

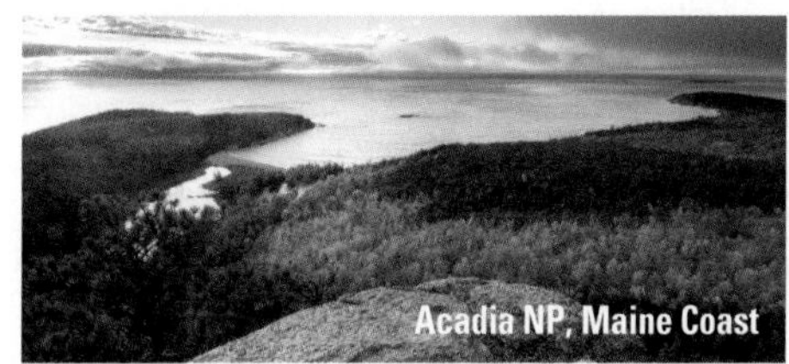
Acadia NP, Maine Coast

Mohawk Valley★

114 miles/184 kilometers
Maps 188, 94, 80

From the state capital of **Albany★**, take I-90 NW to Exit 25 for I-890 into **Schenectady**, founded by Dutch settlers in 1661. Follow Rte. 5 W along the Mohawk River. In Fort Hunter, **Schoharie Crossing SHS★** stretches along a canal towpath. Near Little Falls, **Herkimer Home SHS** (Rte. 169 at Thruway Exit 29A) interprets colonial farm life. Rte. 5 continues W along the Erie Canal to Utica. From Utica, drive W on Rte. 49 to Rome, where the river turns N and peters out. The tour ends in Rome, site of **Fort Stanwix NM★**.

South Shore Lake Superior★

530 miles/853 kilometers
Maps 211, 64, 65, 69

From **Duluth★**, drive SE on I-535/US-53 to the junction of Rte. 13 at Parkland. Follow Rte. 13 E to quaint Bayfield, gateway to **Apostle Islands NL★★**, accessible by boat. Head S to the junction of US-2, and E through Ashland, Ironwood and Wakefield. There, turn left onto Rte. 28, heading NE to Bergland, and turning left onto Rte. 64. Drive N to Silver City and take Rte. M-107 W into **Porcupine Mountains Wilderness SP★**. Return to Rte. 64 and go E to Ontonagon. Take Rte. 38 SE to Greenland,

then follow Rte. 26 NE to Houghton. Cross to Hancock on US-41 and continue NE to Phoenix. Turn left onto Rte. 26 to Eagle River and on to Copper Harbor via **Brockway Mountain Drive★★**. Return S to Houghton via US-41, then travel S and E past Marquette, turning left onto Rte. 28. Head E to Munising, then take County Road H-58 E and N through **Pictured Rocks NL★**. End the tour at Grand Marais.

Villages of Southern Vermont★★

118 miles/190 kilometers   Map 81

Head N from the resort town of **Manchester★** by Rte. 7A. At Manchester Center, take Rte. 11 E past **Bromley Mountain**, a popular ski area, to Peru. Turn left on the backroad to **Weston★**, a favorite tourist stop along Rte. 100. Continue to **Chester**, turning right onto Rte. 35 S to reach **Grafton★**, with its **Old Tavern**. Farther S, Rte. 30 S from Townshend leads to **Newfane** and its lovely **village green★**. Return to Townshend, then travel W, following Rte. 30 through West Townshend, passing **Stratton Mountain** en route to Manchester. S of Manchester by Rte. 7A, the crest of Mt. Equinox is accessible via **Equinox Skyline Drive** (fee). Then continue S on Rte. 7A to end the tour at **Arlington**, known for its trout fishing.

The White Mountains Loop★★★

127 miles/204 kilometers   Map 81

From the all-season resort of Conway, drive N on Rte. 16 to **North Conway★**, abundant with tourist facilities. Continue N on US-302/Rte. 16 through **Glen**, passing **Glen Ellis Falls★** and **Pinkham Notch★★** en route to Glen House. There, drive the Auto Road to the top of **Mount Washington★★★** (or take guided van tour). Head N on Rte. 16 to Gorham, near the Androscoggin River, then W on US-2 to Jefferson Highlands. Travel SW on Rte. 115 to Carroll, then S on US-3 to Twin Mountain. Go SW on US-3 to join I-93. Head S on I-93/Rte.3, passing scenic **Franconia Notch★★★** and **Profile Lake★★**. Bear E on Rte. 3 where it separates from the interstate to visit **The Flume★★**, a natural gorge 90ft deep. Rejoin I-93 S to the intersection with Rte. 112. Head E on Rte. 112 through Lincoln on the **Kancamagus Highway★★★** until it joins Rte. 16 back to Conway.

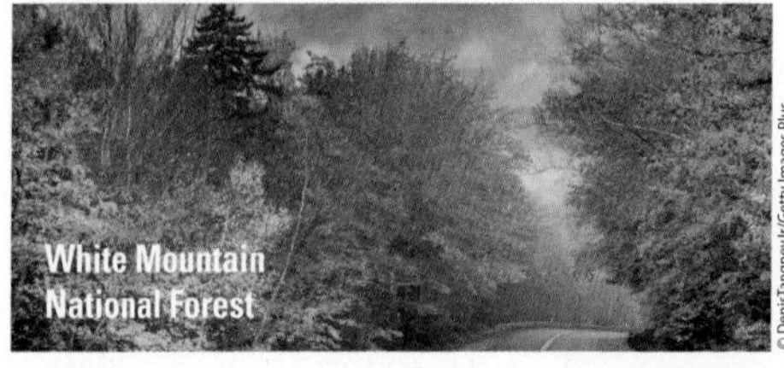
White Mountain National Forest

Michelin Scenic Drives - continues on page 301

British Columbia

Washington

0 mi   20   40
0 km   20   40   60
One inch equals 25.4 miles
One centimeter equals 16.1 kilometers

STRATHCONA PROV. PARK

Go to 162

PACIFIC RIM NATL PARK RESERVE

Tofino
Ucluelet
Bamfield
Port Alberni
Parksville
Nanaimo
Ladysmith
N. Cowichan
Duncan

Vancouver Island

Vancouver
Burnaby
Coquitlam
Maple Ridge
Mission
Chilliwack
Richmond
Surrey
Langley
Delta
Abbotsford
Kent
Blaine
Lynden
Ferndale
Bellingham
Sedro-Woolley
Burlington
Mt. Vernon
Oak Harbor
Anacortes

Sidney
Saanich
Langford
Esquimalt
Oak Bay
Victoria

B.C. WASH.

BRITISH COLUMBIA
CANADA
WASHINGTON
U.S.

OLYMPIC NATL PARK
OLYMPIC NATL. FOR.
OLYMPIC MOUNTAINS

Cape Flattery
Neah Bay
MAKAH IND. RES.
Forks
La Push
Queets
Kalaloch
Clearwater
Taholah
Moclips
Pacific Beach
Ocean Shores
Hoquiam
Aberdeen

Port Angeles
Port Townsend
Sequim

Everett
Marysville
Snohomish
Monroe
Lynnwood
Edmonds
Shoreline
Bothell
Kirkland
Redmond
Sammamish
Bellevue
Seattle
Bremerton
Burien
Renton
North Bend
Des Moines
Federal Way
Kent
Tacoma
Univ. Place
Puyallup
Sumner
Enumclaw
Lakewood
Parkland
Spanaway
Buckley

PACIFIC OCEAN

GRAYS HARBOR
Shelton
Olympia
Lacey
Yelm
Montesano
Elma
Centralia
Chehalis

MT. RAINIER NATL. PARK
Paradise
Longmire
Ashford

MT. ST. HELENS NATL VOLCANIC MON.

Go to 20

Astoria

A   B   C

1   2   3   4

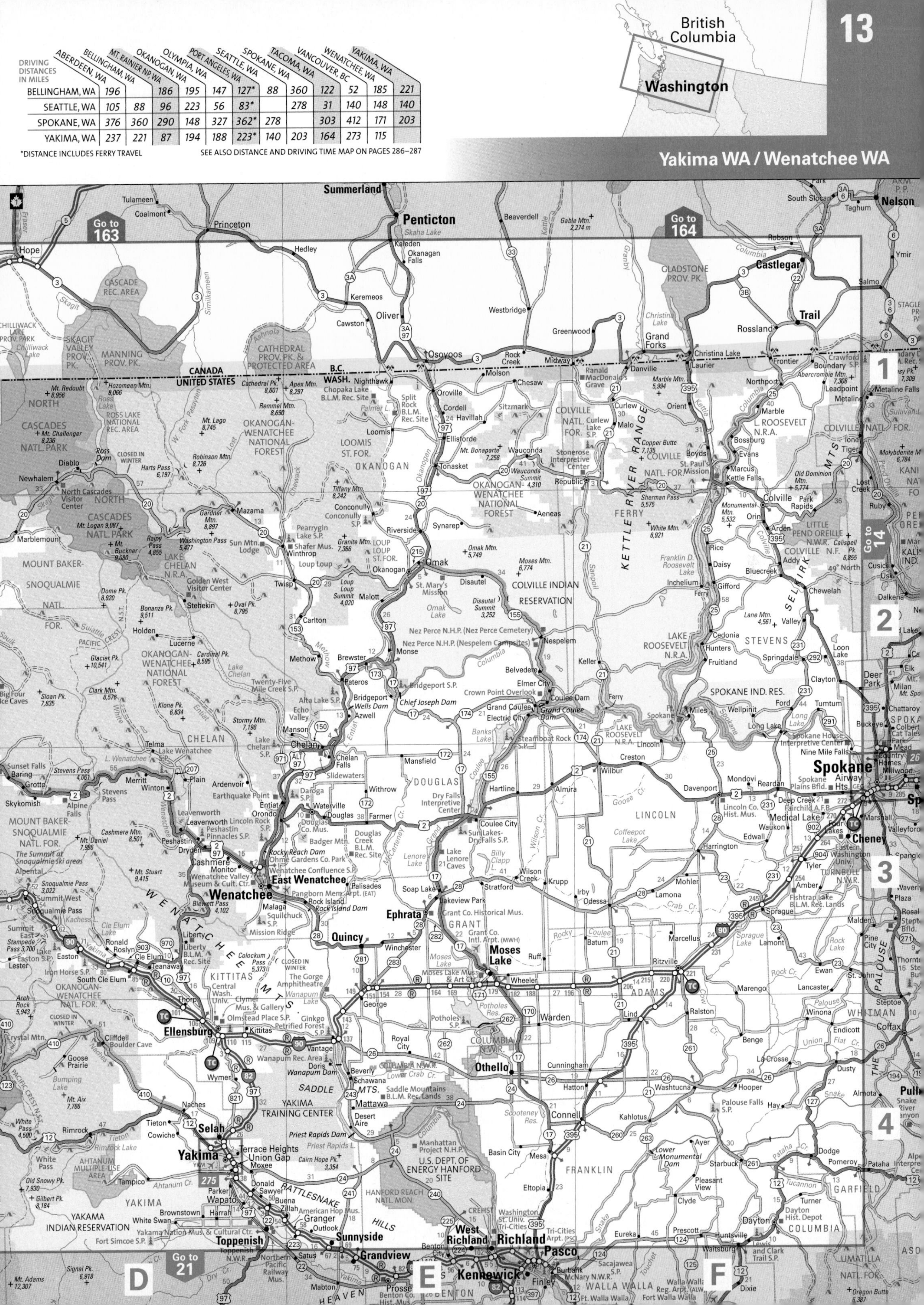

DRIVING DISTANCES IN MILES	ABERDEEN, WA	BELLINGHAM, WA	MT. RAINIER NP, WA	OKANOGAN, WA	OLYMPIA, WA	PORT ANGELES, WA	SEATTLE, WA	SPOKANE, WA	TACOMA, WA	VANCOUVER, BC	WENATCHEE, WA	YAKIMA, WA
BELLINGHAM, WA	196		186	195	147	127*	88	360	122	52	185	221
SEATTLE, WA	105	88	96	223	56	83*		278	31	140	148	140
SPOKANE, WA	376	360	290	148	327	362*	278		303	412	171	203
YAKIMA, WA	237	221	87	194	188	223*	140	203	164	273	115	

*DISTANCE INCLUDES FERRY TRAVEL

SEE ALSO DISTANCE AND DRIVING TIME MAP ON PAGES 286–287

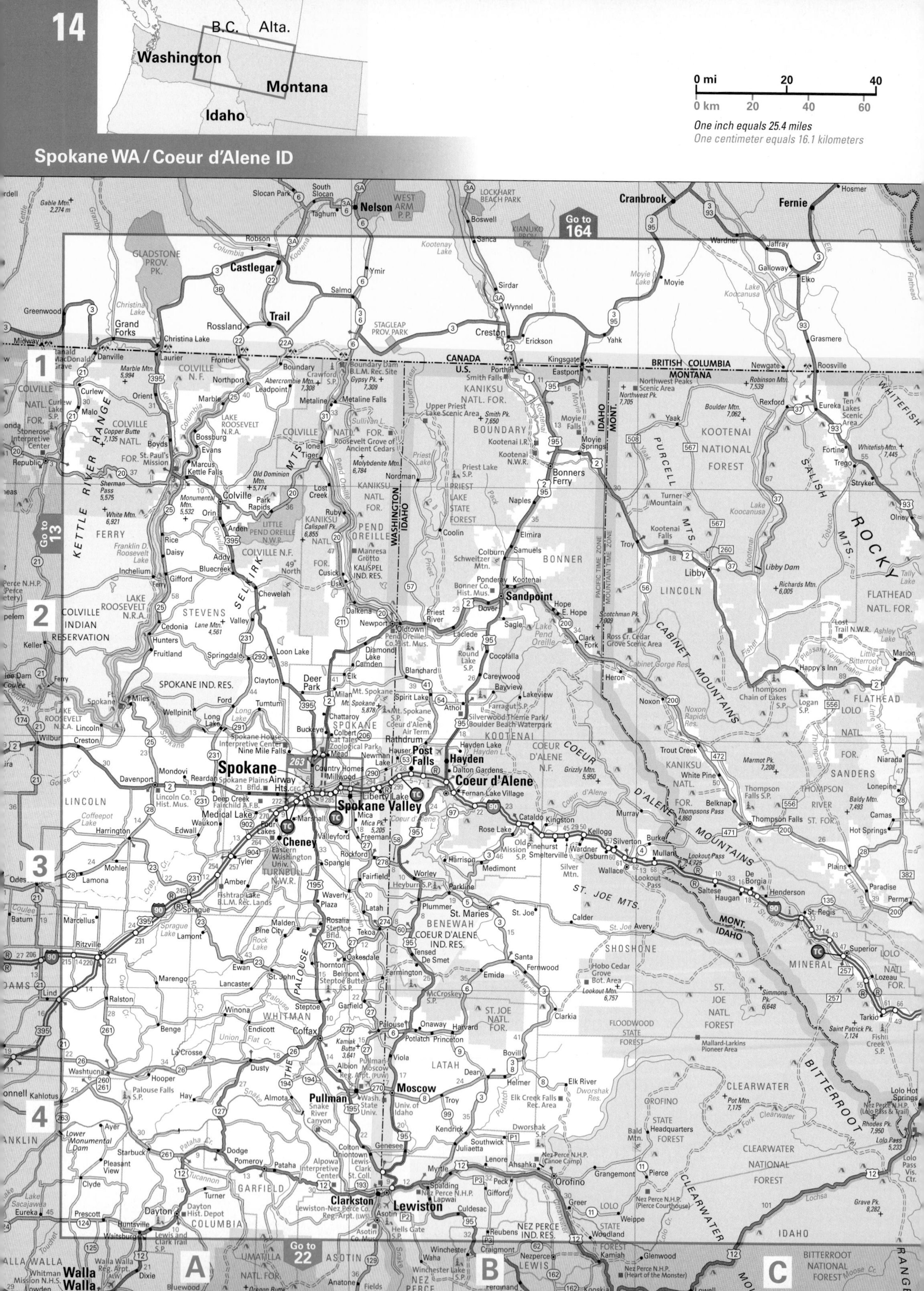
14
B.C.
Alta.
Washington
Montana
Idaho
0 mi 20 40
0 km 20 40 60
One inch equals 25.4 miles
One centimeter equals 16.1 kilometers
Spokane WA / Coeur d'Alene ID
Go to 164
Go to 13
Go to 22
1
2
3
4
A
B
C
Slocan Park
South Slocan
Nelson
WEST ARM P.P.
LOCKHART BEACH PARK
Cranbrook
Fernie
Hosmer
Taghum
Boswell
Sanca
KIANUKO PROV. PK.
Kootenay Lake
Robson
Castlegar
GLADSTONE PROV. PK.
Ymir
Salmo
Sirdar
Wynndel
Moyie Lake
Moyie
Wardner
Jaffray
Galloway
Elko
Lake Koocanusa
Grasmere
Greenwood
Christina Lake
Grand Forks
Rossland
Trail
STAGLEAP PROV. PARK
Creston
Erickson
Yahk
Midway
Danville
Christina Lake
Laurier
Frontier
Boundary
Boundary Dam B.L.M. Rec. Site
CANADA
U.S.
Porthill
Smith Falls
Kingsgate
Eastport
BRITISH COLUMBIA
MONTANA
Newgate
Roosville
Hosmer
Gable Mtn. 2,274 m
Marble Mtn. 5,994
COLVILLE N.F.
Northport
Abercrombie Mtn. 7,308
Crawford S.P.
Gypsy Pk. 7,309
Leadpoint
Metaline
Metaline Falls
Upper Priest Lake Scenic Area
Smith Pk. 7,650
KANIKSU NATL. FOR.
BOUNDARY
Kootenai I.R.
Kootenai N.W.R.
Moyie Falls
Moyie Springs
Bonners Ferry
IDAHO
MONT.
Northwest Peaks Scenic Area
Northwest Pk. 7,705
Robinson Mtn. 7,539
Rexford
Eureka
Ten Lakes Scenic Area
WHITEFISH
Yaak
Boulder Mtn. 7,062
PURCELL MTS.
KOOTENAI NATIONAL FOREST
SALISH MTS.
Fortine
Whitefish Mtn. 7,445
Trego
Stryker
Olney
ROCKY MTS.
Curlew
Malo
Orient
COLVILLE NATL. FOR.
KETTLE RIVER RANGE
Stonerose Interpretive Center
Copper Butte 7,135
Boyds
Bossburg
Evans
Marcus
Kettle Falls
St. Paul's Mission
Republic
Sherman Pass 5,575
LAKE ROOSEVELT N.R.A.
Old Dominion Mtn. 5,774
Ione
Tiger
Sullivan L.
COLVILLE NATL. FOR.
Roosevelt Grove of Ancient Cedars
Molybdenite Mtn. 6,784
Nordman
Priest Lake
Priest Lake S.P.
PRIEST LAKE STATE FOREST
Naples
Colville
Monumental Mtn. 5,532
Park Rapids
Orin
Arden
White Mtn. 6,921
FERRY
Franklin D. Roosevelt Lake
Rice
Daisy
LITTLE PEND OREILLE N.W.R.
COLVILLE N.F.
Addy
49° North
Lost Creek
Ruby
KANIKSU NATL. FOR.
Calispell Pk. 6,855
PEND OREILLE
Manresa Grotto
KALISPEL IND. RES.
Cusick
Usk
WASHINGTON
IDAHO
Coolin
Elmira
Colburn
Samuels
Schweitzer Mtn.
BONNER
Ponderay
Kootenai
Sandpoint
Bonner Co. Hist. Mus.
Dover
Hope
E. Hope
PACIFIC TIME ZONE
MOUNTAIN TIME ZONE
Troy
Kootenai Falls
Turner Mountain
Libby
Libby Dam
Richards Mtn. 6,005
LINCOLN
FLATHEAD NATL. FOR.
Inchelium
Bluecreek
Gifford
Chewelah
SELKIRK MTS.
STEVENS
Lane Mtn. 4,561
Valley
Cedonia
Hunters
Fruitland
Springdale
Loon Lake
COLVILLE INDIAN RESERVATION
Keller
Dalkena
Newport
Oldtown
Pend Oreille Co. Hist. Mus.
Priest River
Laclede
Sagle
Lake Pend Oreille
Clark Fork
Scotchman Pk. 7,009
Ross Cr. Cedar Grove Scenic Area
CABINET MOUNTAINS
Lost Trail N.W.R.
Ashley Lake
Pleasant Valley
Little Bitterroot Lake
Marion
Happy's Inn
Diamond Lake
Camden
Elk
Clayton
Deer Park
Blanchard
Round Lake S.P.
Cocolalla
Careywood
Bayview
Lakeview
Farragut S.P.
Athol
Heron
Noxon
Noxon Rapids Res.
Thompson Chain of Lakes S.P.
Logan S.P.
LOLO
Grand Coulee Dam
Coulee
SPOKANE IND. RES.
Tumtum
Ford
Wellpinit
Long Lake
Miles
Milan
Mt. Spokane
Spirit Lake
Chattaroy
Mt. Spokane 5,878
Mt. Spokane S.P.
Coeur d'Alene Air Term.
Silverwood Theme Park/Boulder Beach Waterpark
SPOKANE
KOOTENAI
Lincoln
Creston
Wilbur
Buckeye
Colbert
Cat Tales Zoological Park
Rathdrum
Spokane House Interpretive Center
Nine Mile Falls
Mead
Hauser
Post Falls
Hayden
Hayden Lake
COEUR D'ALENE N.F.
Grizzly Mtn. 5,950
Trout Creek
KANIKSU NATL. FOR.
White Pine
Marmot Pk. 7,208
Niarada
SANDERS
Spokane
Davenport
Mondovi
Reardan
Spokane Plains Bfld.
Airway Hts.
Country Homes
Millwood
Newman Lake
Dalton Gardens
Coeur d'Alene
Fernan Lake Village
Lincoln Co. Hist. Mus.
Deep Creek
Fairchild A.F.B.
Liberty Lake
Spokane Valley
Thompson Falls S.P.
THOMPSON RIVER
Lonepine
LINCOLN
Coffeepot Lake
Medical Lake
Waukon
Marshall
Mica
Mica Pk. 5,205
Coeur d'Alene L.
Cataldo
Kingston
Rose Lake
Belknap
Thompsons Pass 4,860
Murray
D'ALENE MOUNTAINS
Thompson Falls
Baldy Mtn. 7,493
Camas
Hot Springs
Harrington
Edwall
Four Lakes
Cheney
Valleyford
Freeman
Old Mission S.P.
Pinehurst
Smelterville
Kellogg
Wardner
Osburn
Silverton
Burke
Mullan
Lookout Pass 4,725
Eastern Washington Univ.
Mohler
Lamona
Odessa
Tyler
Amber
Spangle
Rockford
Harrison
Medimont
Silver Mtn.
Wallace
Lookout Pass
TURNBULL N.W.R.
Fishtrap Lake B.L.M. Rec. Lands
Fairfield
Worley
Heyburn S.P.
Parkline
ST. JOE MTS.
Saltese
Haugan
De Borgia
Henderson
Plains
Paradise
Perma
Sprague
Waverly
Plaza
Plummer
St. Maries
St. Joe
Calder
Avery
St. Regis
Batum
Marcellus
Sprague Lake
Lamont
Malden
Pine City
Rosalia
Steptoe Bfld.
Latah
Tekoa
BENEWAH
COEUR D'ALENE IND. RES.
Tensed
De Smet
Santa
Fernwood
SHOSHONE
Hobo Cedar Grove Bot. Area
MONT.
IDAHO
MINERAL
Superior
LOLO NATL. FOR.
Lozeau
Ritzville
Rock Lake
Ewan
Thornton
Oakesdale
St. John
Belmont
Steptoe Butte S.P.
Farmington
Emida
Lookout Mtn. 6,757
ST. JOE NATL. FOREST
Simmons Pk. 6,648
Marengo
Lancaster
Ralston
Lind
ADAMS
PALOUSE
McCroskey S.P.
ST. JOE NATL. FOR.
Clarkia
Tarkio
Winona
WHITMAN
Steptoe
Garfield
Benge
Endicott
Colfax
Union Flat Cr.
Palouse
Onaway
Harvard
Potlatch
Princeton
FLOODWOOD STATE FOREST
Mallard-Larkins Pioneer Area
Saint Patrick Pk. 7,124
Fish Creek S.P.
La Crosse
Kamiak Butte 3,641
Viola
LATAH
Bovill
Deary
Washtucna
Hooper
Dusty
Albion
Pullman-Moscow Reg. Arpt.
Moscow
Helmer
Elk River
Dworshak Res.
BITTERROOT
CLEARWATER
Pot Mtn. 7,175
Kahlotus
Palouse Falls S.P.
Hay
Almota
Pullman
Snake River Canyon
Wash. State Univ.
Univ. of Idaho
Troy
Elk Creek Falls Rec. Area
OROFINO
STATE Headquarters FOREST
Bald Mtn.
Lolo Hot Springs
Nez Perce N.H.P. (Lolo Pass & Trail)
Rhodes Pk. 7,950
Lolo Pass 5,233
Lower Monumental Dam
Ayer
Starbuck
Dodge
Pleasant View
Pomeroy
Pataha
Kendrick
Southwick
Juliaetta
Dworshak S.P.
Colton
Uniontown
Genesee
Alpowa Interpretive Center
Lewis-Clark St. Coll.
Nez Perce N.H.P. (Canoe Camp)
Lenore
Ahsahka
Orofino
Grangemont
Pierce
CLEARWATER NATIONAL FOREST
Clyde
Tucannon
GARFIELD
Myrtle
Spalding
Nez Perce N.H.P.
Lapwai
Peck
Gifford
Lake Sacajawea
Eureka
Prescott
Turner
Dayton
Dayton Hist. Depot
COLUMBIA
Clarkston
Lewiston
Lewiston-Nez Perce Co. Reg. Arpt.
Asotin
Culdesac
Greer
LOLO
Weippe
Nez Perce N.H.P. (Pierce Courthouse)
Lochsa
Grave Pk. 8,282
Lolo Pass Vis. Ctr.
Huntsville
Waitsburg
Lewis and Clark Trail S.P.
Asotin Co. Mus.
Hells Gate S.P.
Reubens
NEZ PERCE IND. RES.
STATE FOREST
Woodland
IDAHO
WALLA WALLA
Walla Walla
Walla Walla Reg. Arpt.
Whitman Mission N.H.S.
Dixie
Lowden
Bluewood
UMATILLA NATL. FOR.
Oregon Butte
ASOTIN
Anatone
Fields Spring
Winchester
Waha
Winchester Lake S.P.
Craigmont
NEZ PERCE
Nezperce
LEWIS
Kamiah
Glenwood
Nez Perce N.H.P. (Heart of the Monster)
Kooskia
Ferdinand
Lowell
BITTERROOT NATIONAL FOREST
RANGE

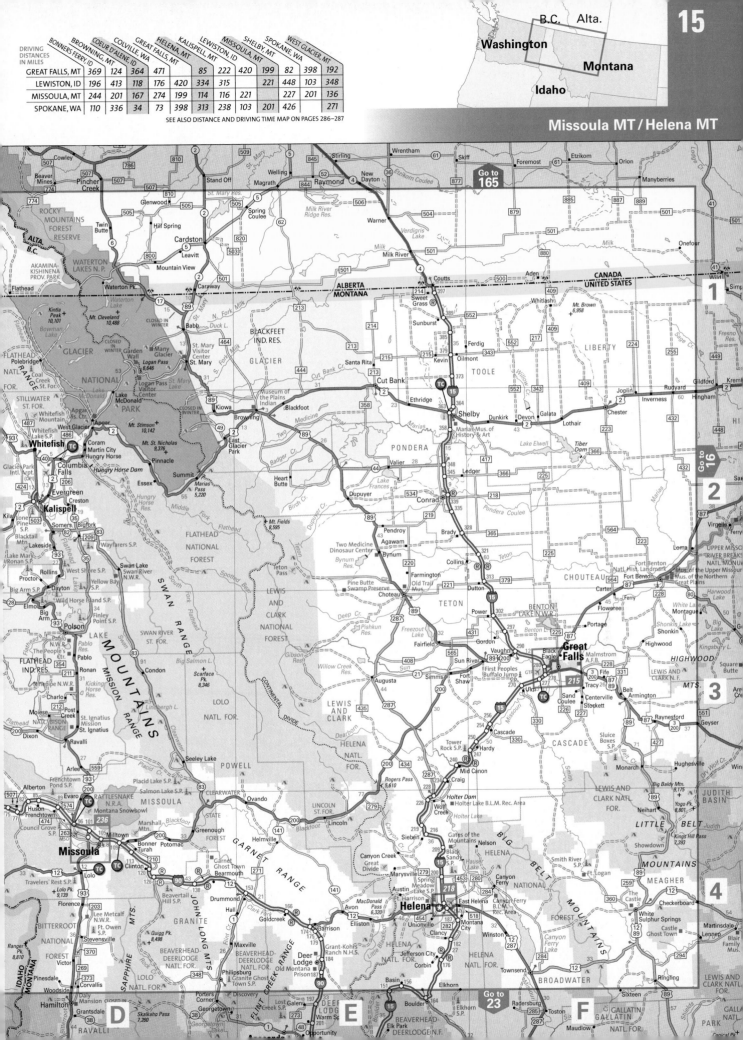

Washington
Montana
Idaho
B.C. Alta.

DRIVING DISTANCES IN MILES	BONNERS FERRY, ID	BROWNING, MT	COEUR D'ALENE, ID	COLVILLE, WA	GREAT FALLS, MT	HELENA, MT	KALISPELL, MT	LEWISTON, ID	MISSOULA, MT	SHELBY, MT	SPOKANE, WA	WEST GLACIER, MT
GREAT FALLS, MT	369	124	364	471		85	222	420	199	82	398	192
LEWISTON, ID	196	413	118	176	420	334	315		221	448	103	348
MISSOULA, MT	244	201	167	274	199	114	116	221		227	201	136
SPOKANE, WA	110	336	34	73	398	313	238	103	201	426		271

SEE ALSO DISTANCE AND DRIVING TIME MAP ON PAGES 286–287

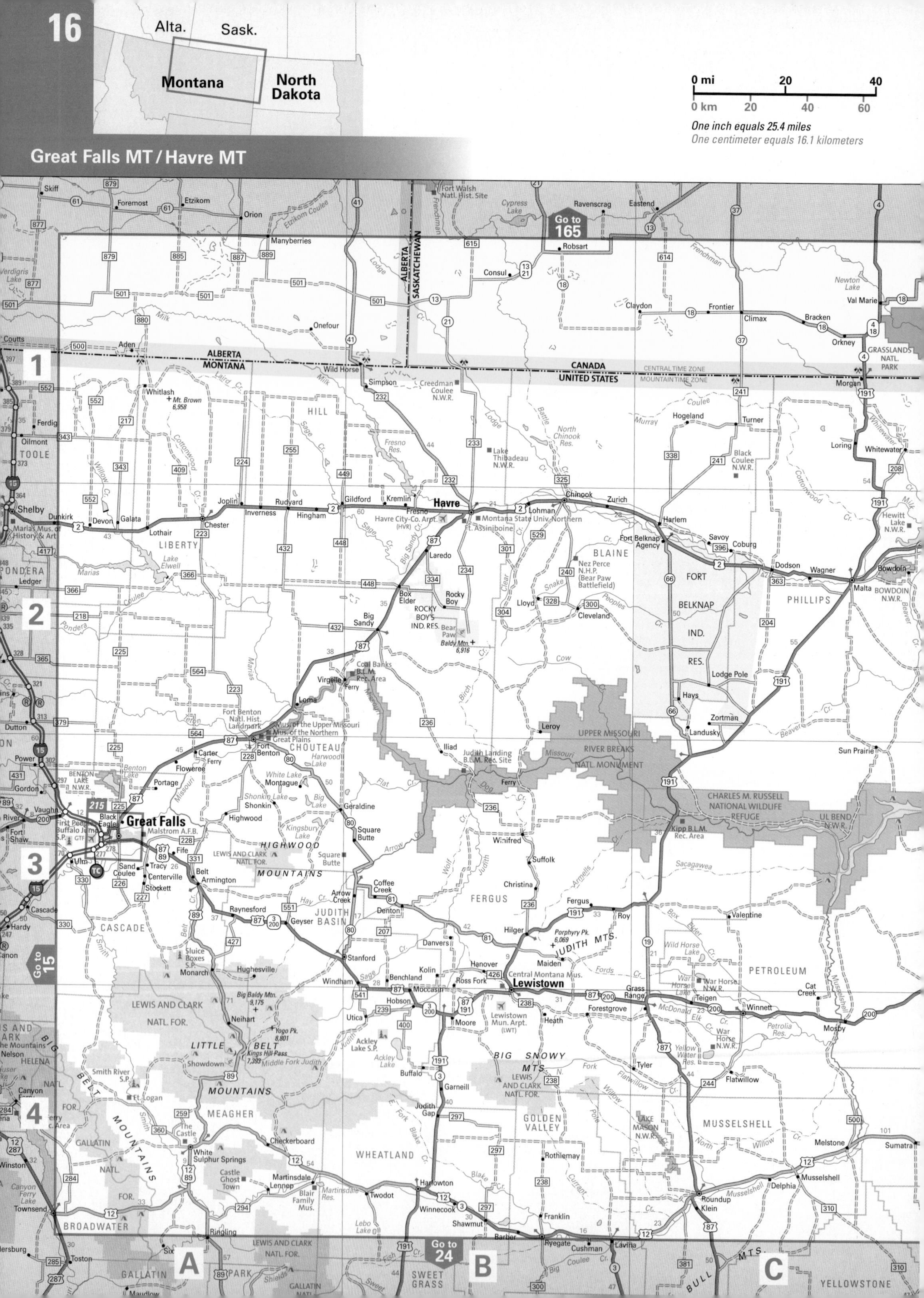

Alta. Sask.

Montana   North Dakota

0 mi   20   40
0 km   20   40   60
One inch equals 25.4 miles
One centimeter equals 16.1 kilometers

Great Falls MT / Havre MT

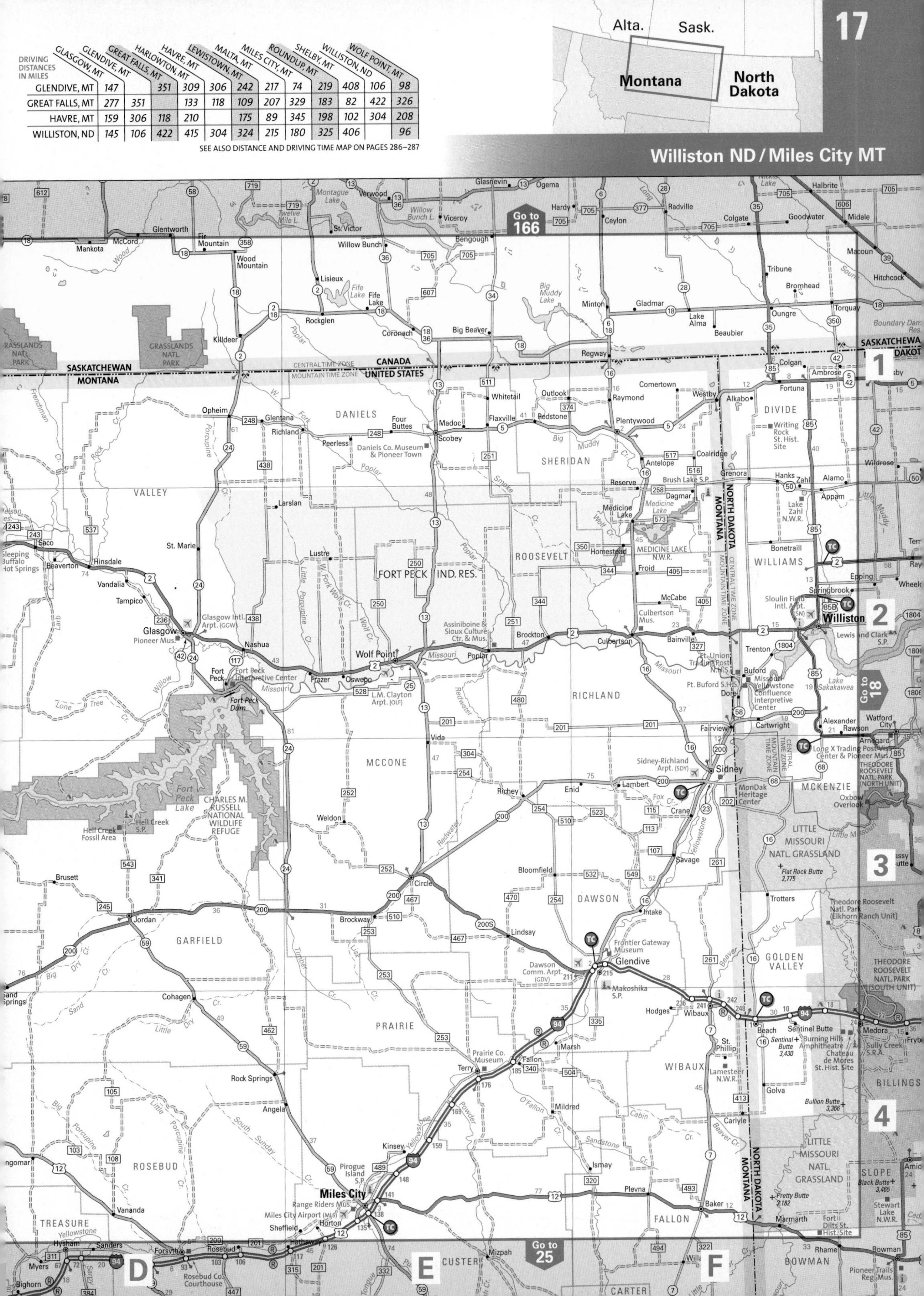

DRIVING DISTANCES IN MILES

	GLASGOW, MT	GLENDIVE, MT	GREAT FALLS, MT	HARLOWTON, MT	HAVRE, MT	LEWISTOWN, MT	MALTA, MT	MILES CITY, MT	ROUNDUP, MT	SHELBY, MT	WILLISTON, ND	WOLF POINT, MT
GLENDIVE, MT	147		351	309	306	242	217	74	219	408	106	98
GREAT FALLS, MT	277	351		133	118	109	207	329	183	82	422	326
HAVRE, MT	159	306	118	210		175	89	345	198	102	304	208
WILLISTON, ND	145	106	422	415	304	324	215	180	325	406		96

SEE ALSO DISTANCE AND DRIVING TIME MAP ON PAGES 286–287

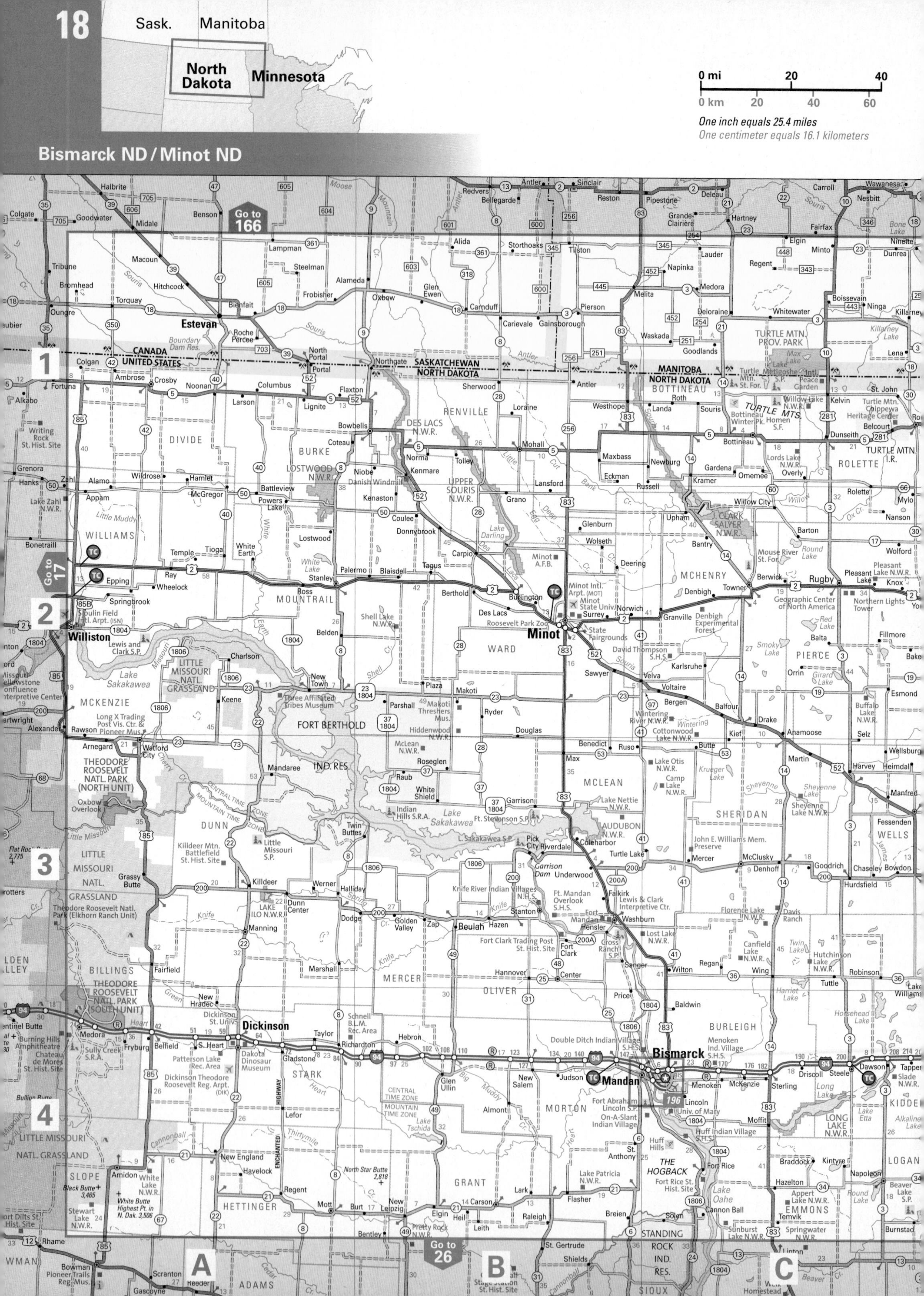
Sask.
Manitoba
North Dakota
Minnesota
0 mi 20 40
0 km 20 40 60
One inch equals 25.4 miles
One centimeter equals 16.1 kilometers
Go to 166
Go to 17
Go to 26
CANADA
UNITED STATES
SASKATCHEWAN
NORTH DAKOTA
MANITOBA
NORTH DAKOTA
Halbrite
Midale
Benson
Colgate
Goodwater
Macoun
Lampman
Steelman
Alida
Storthoaks
Tilston
Tribune
Bromhead
Hitchcock
Alameda
Frobisher
Oxbow
Glen Ewen
Carnduff
Torquay
Bienfait
Estevan
Roche Percee
Boundary Dam Res.
North Portal
Portal
Oungre
Carievale
Gainsborough
Pierson
Melita
Napinka
Lauder
Medora
Deloraine
Waskada
Goodlands
Whitewater
Boissevain
Ninga
Killarney
TURTLE MTN. PROV. PARK
Redvers
Bellegarde
Antler
Sinclair
Reston
Pipestone
Grande-Clairière
Deleau
Hartney
Carroll
Wawanesa
Nesbitt
Elgin
Minto
Fairfax
Ninette
Dunrea
Regent
Colgan
Ambrose
Crosby
Fortuna
Noonan
Columbus
Flaxton
Larson
Lignite
Sherwood
Westhope
Landa
Roth
Souris
Kelvin
St. John
Alkabo
Writing Rock St. Hist. Site
DIVIDE
BURKE
RENVILLE
BOTTINEAU
ROLETTE
Bowbells
Coteau
DES LACS N.W.R.
Loraine
Mohall
Maxbass
Bottineau
Dunseith
Belcourt
TURTLE MTN. I.R.
TURTLE MTS.
Willow Lake N.W.R.
Grenora
Hanks
Zahl
Lake Zahl N.W.R.
Alamo
Wildrose
Hamlet
McGregor
Battleview
Powers Lake
LOSTWOOD N.W.R.
Niobe
Danish Windmill
Norma
Kenmare
Tolley
UPPER SOURIS N.W.R.
Lansford
Eckman
Newburg
Russell
Gardena
Omemee
Overly
Lords Lake N.W.R.
Rolette
Appam
Kenaston
Coulee
Donnybrook
Grano
Willow City
Upham
J. CLARK SALYER N.W.R.
Nanson
Barton
Mylo
WILLIAMS
Bonetraill
Temple
Tioga
White Earth
Lostwood
Glenburn
Wolseth
Carpio
Lake Darling
Minot A.F.B.
Deering
Bantry
Mouse River St. For.
Round Lake
Wolford
Pleasant Lake
Epping
Ray
Wheelock
Stanley
Palermo
Blaisdell
Tagus
Berthold
Burlington
Minot Intl. Arpt. (MOT)
Minot State Univ.
Surrey
Norwich
MCHENRY
Denbigh
Towner
Berwick
Rugby
Knox
Geographic Center of North America
Northern Lights Tower
Springbrook
Ross
MOUNTRAIL
Des Lacs
Roosevelt Park Zoo
Minot
State Fairgrounds
Granville
Denbigh Experimental Forest
Williston
Lewis and Clark S.P.
Sloulin Field Intl. Arpt. (ISN)
Belden
Shell Lake N.W.R.
WARD
David Thompson S.H.S.
Karlsruhe
Balta
PIERCE
Fillmore
Lake Sakakawea
LITTLE MISSOURI NATL. GRASSLAND
Charlson
Keene
New Town
Plaza
Makoti
Sawyer
Velva
Voltaire
Orrin
Esmond
MCKENZIE
Long X Trading Post Vis. Ctr. & Pioneer Mus.
Three Affiliated Tribes Museum
Parshall
Makoti Threshers Mus.
Ryder
Bergen
Balfour
Drake
Anamoose
Buffalo Lake N.W.R.
Alexander
Rawson
FORT BERTHOLD
Hiddenwood N.W.R.
Douglas
Benedict
Ruso
Butte
Kief
Selz
Arnegard
Watford City
McLean N.W.R.
Roseglen
Max
Lake Otis N.W.R.
Camp Lake N.W.R.
Martin
Harvey
Heimdal
Wellsburg
THEODORE ROOSEVELT NATL. PARK (NORTH UNIT)
Mandaree
IND. RES.
Raub
White Shield
MCLEAN
Krueger Lake
Sheyenne Lake N.W.R.
Manfred
Oxbow Overlook
CENTRAL TIME ZONE
MOUNTAIN TIME ZONE
DUNN
Indian Hills S.R.A.
Garrison
Lake Nettie N.W.R.
Ft. Stevenson S.P.
AUDUBON N.W.R.
SHERIDAN
Fessenden
WELLS
Killdeer Mtn. Battlefield St. Hist. Site
Little Missouri S.P.
Twin Buttes
L. Sakakawea S.P.
Pick City
Riverdale
Coleharbor
Turtle Lake
John E. Williams Mem. Preserve
Mercer
McClusky
Denhoff
Goodrich
Chaseley
Bowdon
Hurdsfield
Flat Rock Butte 2,775
LITTLE MISSOURI NATL. GRASSLAND
Grassy Butte
Killdeer
Werner
Halliday
Garrison Dam
Underwood
Knife River Indian Villages N.H.S.
Ft. Mandan Overlook S.H.S.
Falkirk
Lewis & Clark Interpretive Ctr.
Theodore Roosevelt Natl. Park (Elkhorn Ranch Unit)
LAKE ILO N.W.R.
Dunn Center
Dodge
Golden Valley
Zap
Beulah
Hazen
Stanton
Fort Mandan
Washburn
Hensler
Florence Lake N.W.R.
Davis Ranch
Manning
Fort Clark Trading Post St. Hist. Site
Fort Clark
Cross Ranch S.P.
Lost Lake N.W.R.
Canfield Lake N.W.R.
Twin Lake
Hutchinson Lake N.W.R.
Fairfield
BILLINGS
Marshall
MERCER
Hannover
Center
OLIVER
Sanger
Wilton
Regan
Wing
Robinson
Tuttle
THEODORE ROOSEVELT NATL. PARK (SOUTH UNIT)
New Hradec
Dickinson St. Univ.
Price
Baldwin
BURLEIGH
Harriet Lake
Horsehead Lake
Sentinel Butte
Burning Hills Amphitheatre
Chateau de Mores St. Hist. Site
Medora
Sully Creek S.R.A.
Fryburg
Belfield
S. Heart
Dickinson
Taylor
Schnell B.L.M. Rec. Area
Richardton
Hebron
Double Ditch Indian Village S.H.S.
Menoken Ind. Village S.H.S.
Bismarck
Patterson Lake Rec. Area
Dakota Dinosaur Museum
Gladstone
Dickinson Theodore Roosevelt Reg. Arpt. (DIK)
STARK
Glen Ullin
New Salem
Judson
Mandan
Menoken
McKenzie
Driscoll
Steele
Dawson
Sterling
Long Lake
Slade N.W.R.
Bullion Butte
CENTRAL TIME ZONE
MOUNTAIN TIME ZONE
ENCHANTED HIGHWAY
Lefor
Lake Tschida
Almont
MORTON
Fort Abraham Lincoln S.P.
On-A-Slant Indian Village
Lincoln
Univ. of Mary
Huff Indian Village S.H.S.
Moffit
LONG LAKE N.W.R.
Lake Etta
KIDDER
LITTLE MISSOURI NATL. GRASSLAND
New England
Havelock
North Star Butte 2,818
GRANT
St. Anthony
Huff Hills
THE HOGBACK
Fort Rice
Fort Rice St. Hist. Site
Braddock
Kintyre
Napoleon
LOGAN
SLOPE
Amidon
White Lake N.W.R.
Black Butte 3,465
White Butte Highest Pt. in N. Dak. 3,506
Regent
Lake Patricia N.W.R.
Lark
Flasher
Lake Oahe
Hazelton
Appert Lake N.W.R.
Round Lake
Beaver Lake S.P.
HETTINGER
Mott
Burt
New Leipzig
Carson
Raleigh
Breien
Solen
Cannon Ball
EMMONS
Temvik
Springwater N.W.R.
Stewart Lake N.W.R.
Fort Dilts St. Hist. Site
Rhame
Elgin
Heil
Pretty Rock N.W.R.
Bentley
Leith
STANDING ROCK IND. RES.
Sunburst Lake N.W.R.
Burnstad
Bowman
Pioneer Trails Reg. Mus.
Scranton
Gascoyne
Reeder
ADAMS
St. Gertrude
Shields
SIOUX
Linton
Homestead
A
B
C
1
2
3
4

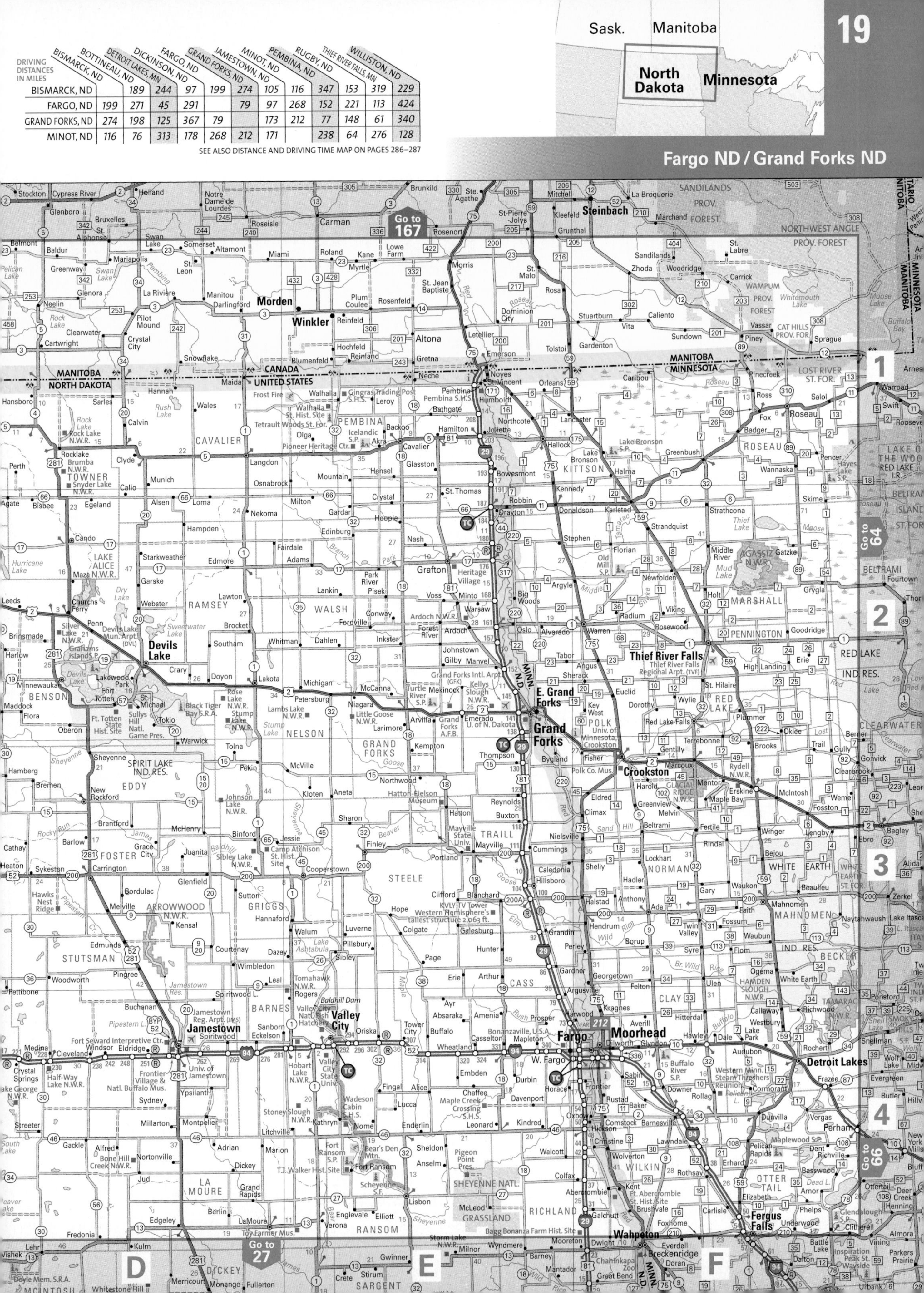

Sask. Manitoba

North Dakota Minnesota

DRIVING DISTANCES IN MILES

	BISMARCK, ND	BOTTINEAU, ND	DETROIT LAKES, MN	DICKINSON, ND	FARGO, ND	GRAND FORKS, ND	JAMESTOWN, ND	MINOT, ND	PEMBINA, ND	RUGBY, ND	THIEF RIVER FALLS, MN	WILLISTON, ND
BISMARCK, ND		189	244	97	199	274	105	116	347	153	319	229
FARGO, ND	199	271	45	291		79	97	268	152	221	113	424
GRAND FORKS, ND	274	198	125	367	79		173	212	77	148	61	340
MINOT, ND	116	76	313	178	268	212	171		238	64	276	128

SEE ALSO DISTANCE AND DRIVING TIME MAP ON PAGES 286–287

Washington

Oregon

0 mi   20   40
0 km   20   40   60

One inch equals 25.4 miles
One centimeter equals 16.1 kilometers

Portland OR / Eugene OR

Go to 12

1

2

3

4

PACIFIC

OCEAN

A   B   C

Go to 28

Washington

Oregon

DRIVING DISTANCES IN MILES	ASTORIA, OR	BEND, OR	BURNS, OR	COOS BAY, OR	EUGENE, OR	KENNEWICK, WA	LA GRANDE, OR	NEWPORT, OR	PORTLAND, OR	SALEM, OR	THE DALLES, OR	WALLA WALLA, WA
BEND, OR	252		142	227	115	245	295	183	158	134	137	276
EUGENE, OR	216	115	257	105		328	377	101	112	65	198	359
KENNEWICK, WA	306	245	256	440	328		111	328	212	264	131	49
PORTLAND, OR	97	158	299	224	112	212	261	116		48	82	243

SEE ALSO DISTANCE AND DRIVING TIME MAP ON PAGES 286-287

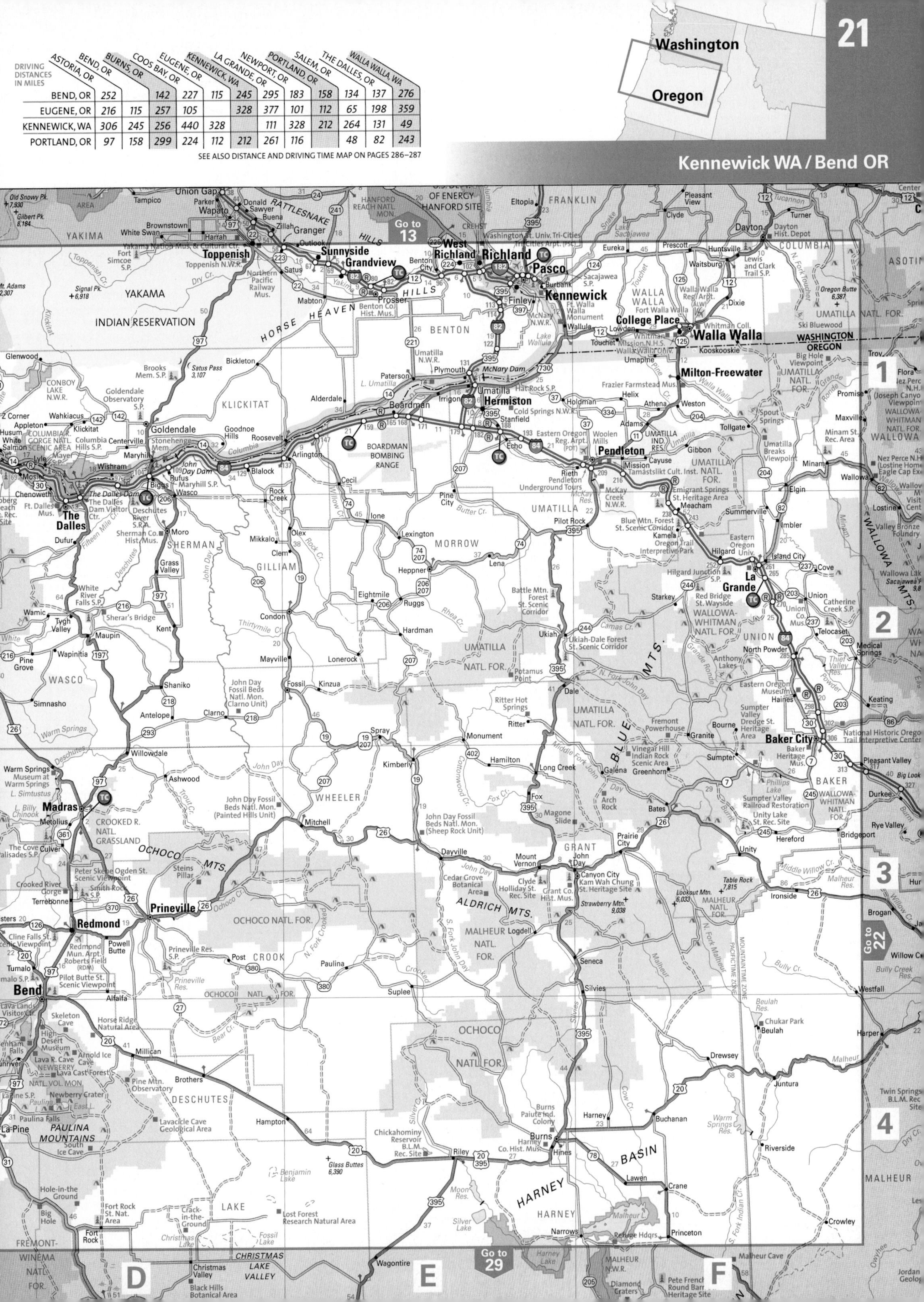

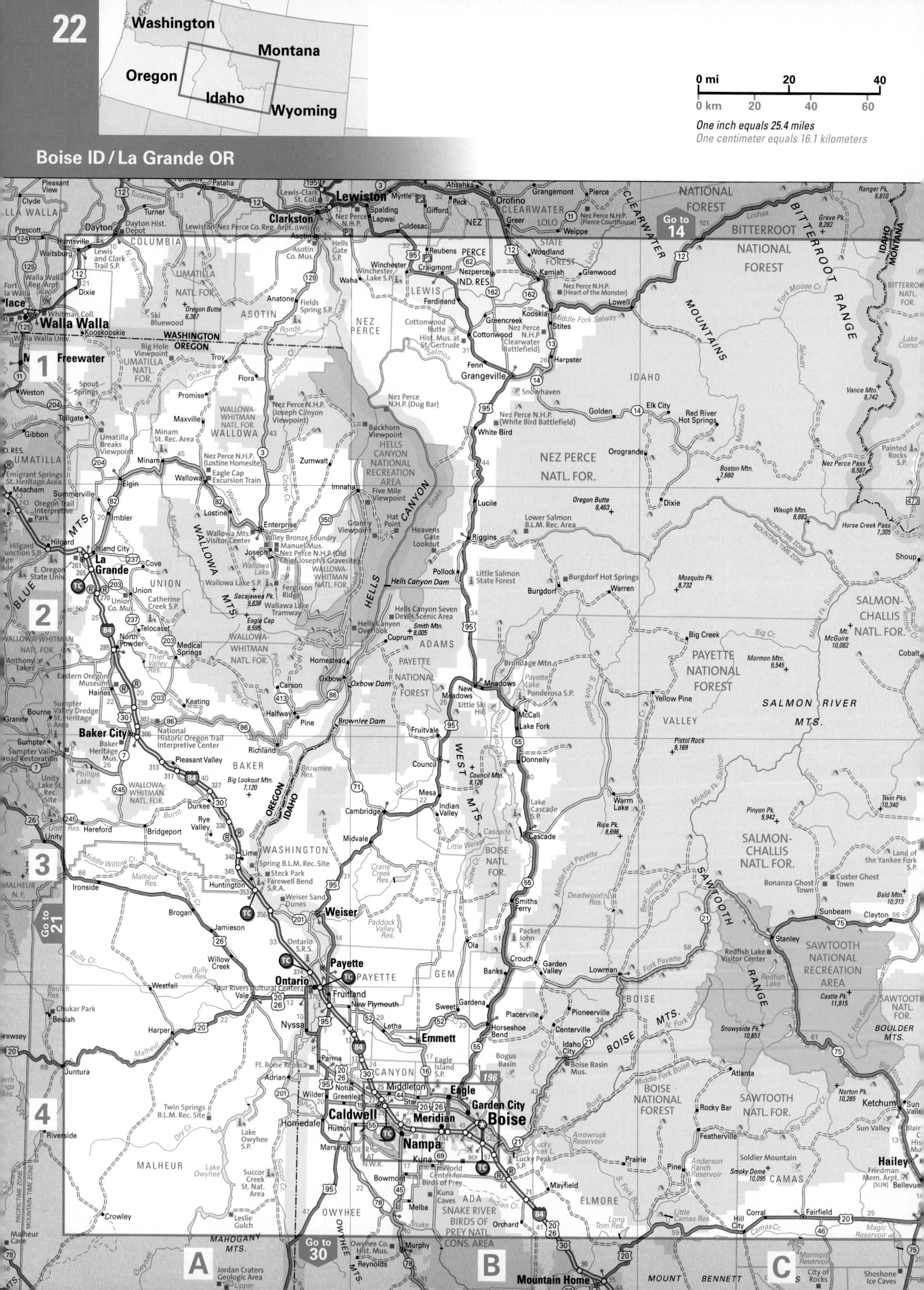

Washington
Montana
Oregon
Idaho
Wyoming

Go to 14
Go to 21
Go to 30

0 mi 20 40
0 km 20 40 60
One inch equals 25.4 miles
One centimeter equals 16.1 kilometers

DRIVING DISTANCES IN MILES	BOISE, ID	BOZEMAN, MT	BUTTE, MT	GRANGEVILLE, ID	HAMILTON, MT	IDAHO FALLS, ID	JACKSON, WY	LA GRANDE, OR	ONTARIO, OR	SALMON, ID	SUN VALLEY, ID	W. YELLOWSTONE, MT
BOISE, ID		485	486	202	339	288	378	170	58	247	163	395
BUTTE, MT	486	81		290	103	203	275	566	541	150	312	162
IDAHO FALLS, ID	288	199	203	483	272		92	455	342	168	153	109
W. YELLOWSTONE, MT	395	90	162	451	264	109	128	562	449	244	252	

SEE ALSO DISTANCE AND DRIVING TIME MAP ON PAGES 286–287

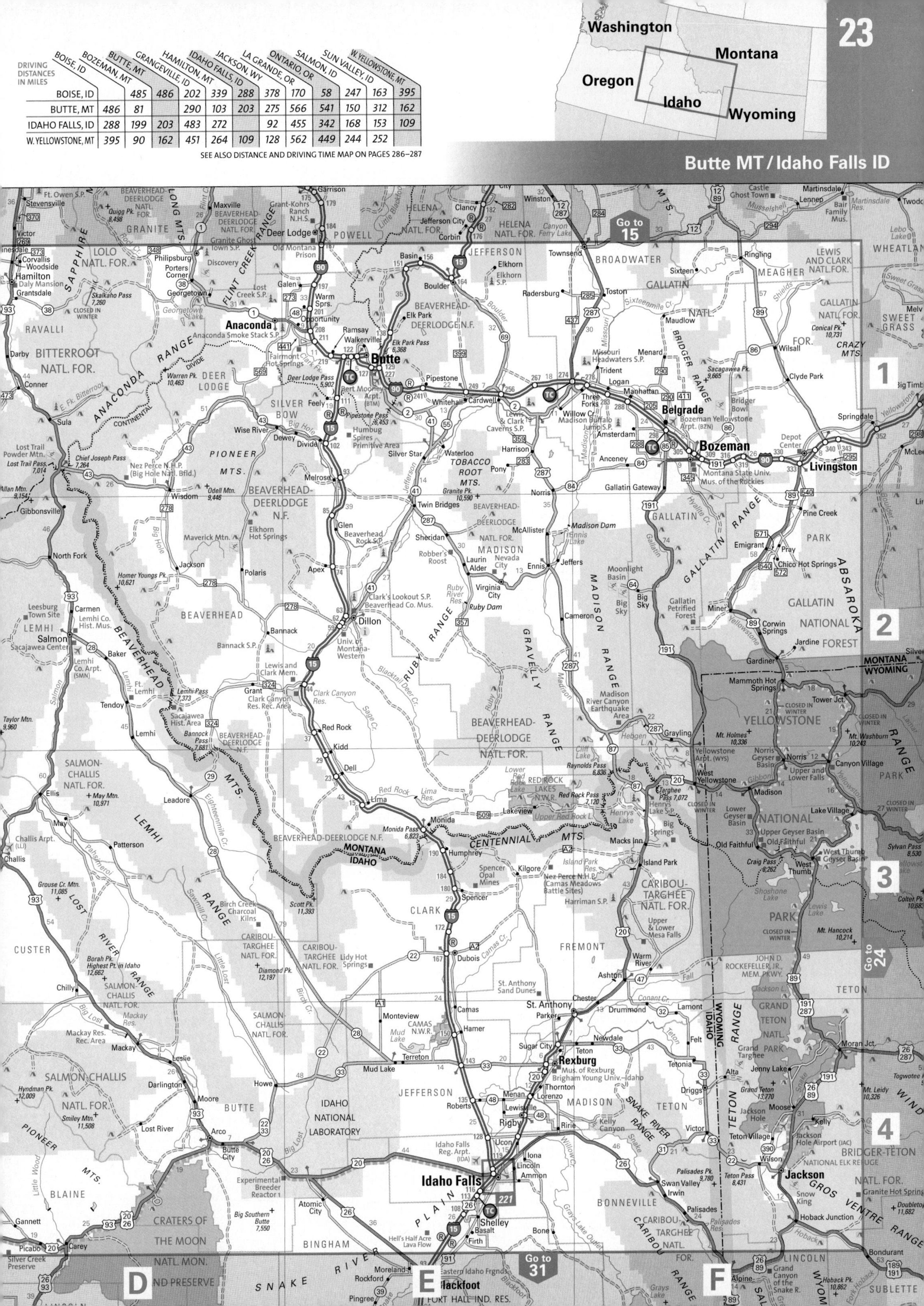

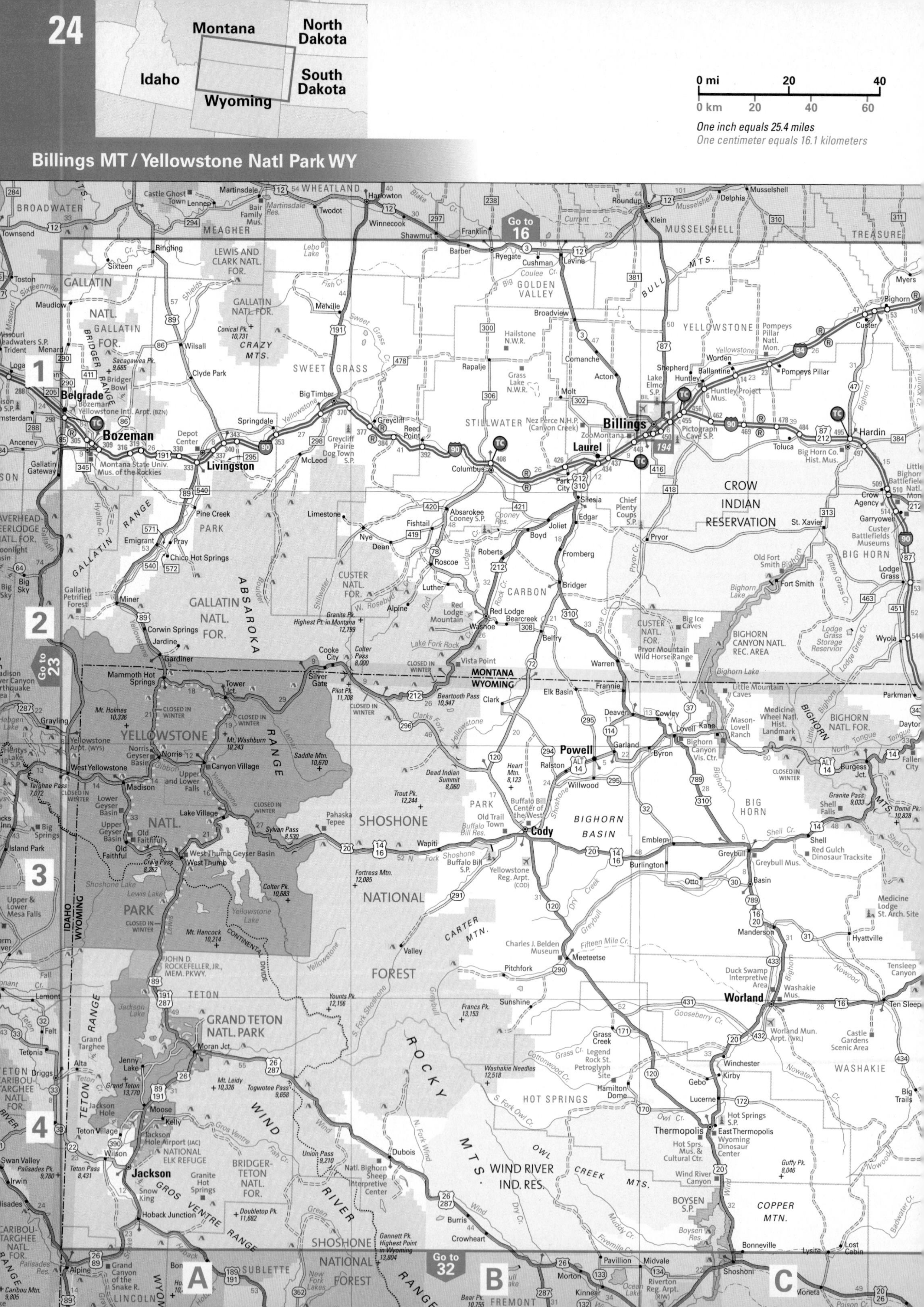

Montana North Dakota
Idaho South Dakota
Wyoming

0 mi   20   40
0 km 20 40 60
One inch equals 25.4 miles
One centimeter equals 16.1 kilometers

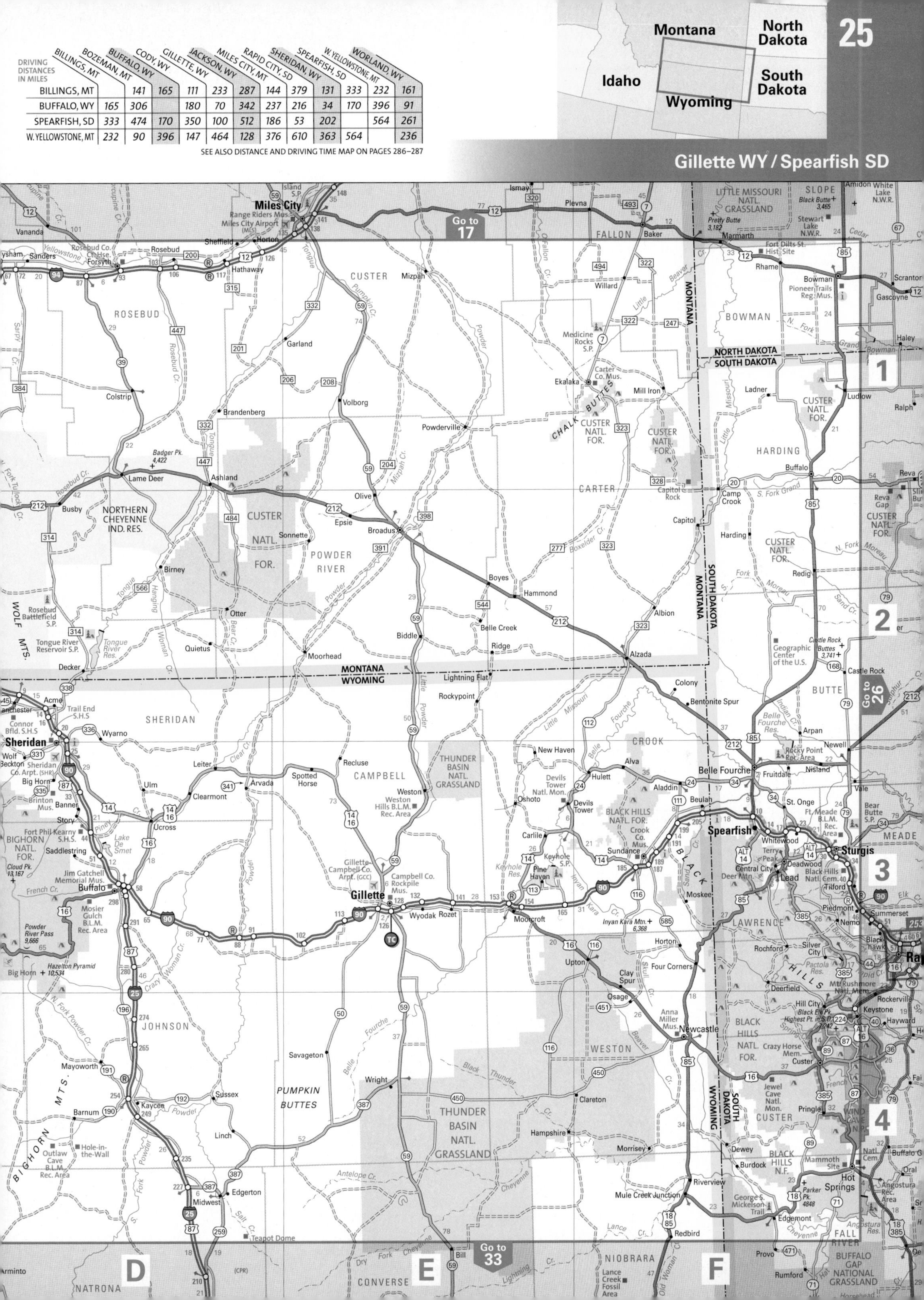

Montana | North Dakota
Idaho | South Dakota
Wyoming

DRIVING DISTANCES IN MILES	BILLINGS, MT	BOZEMAN, MT	BUFFALO, WY	CODY, WY	GILLETTE, WY	JACKSON, WY	MILES CITY, MT	RAPID CITY, SD	SHERIDAN, WY	SPEARFISH, SD	W. YELLOWSTONE, MT	WORLAND, WY
BILLINGS, MT		141	165	111	233	287	144	379	131	333	232	161
BUFFALO, WY	165	306		180	70	342	237	216	34	170	396	91
SPEARFISH, SD	333	474	170	350	100	512	186	53	202		564	261
W. YELLOWSTONE, MT	232	90	396	147	464	128	376	610	363	564		236

SEE ALSO DISTANCE AND DRIVING TIME MAP ON PAGES 286–287

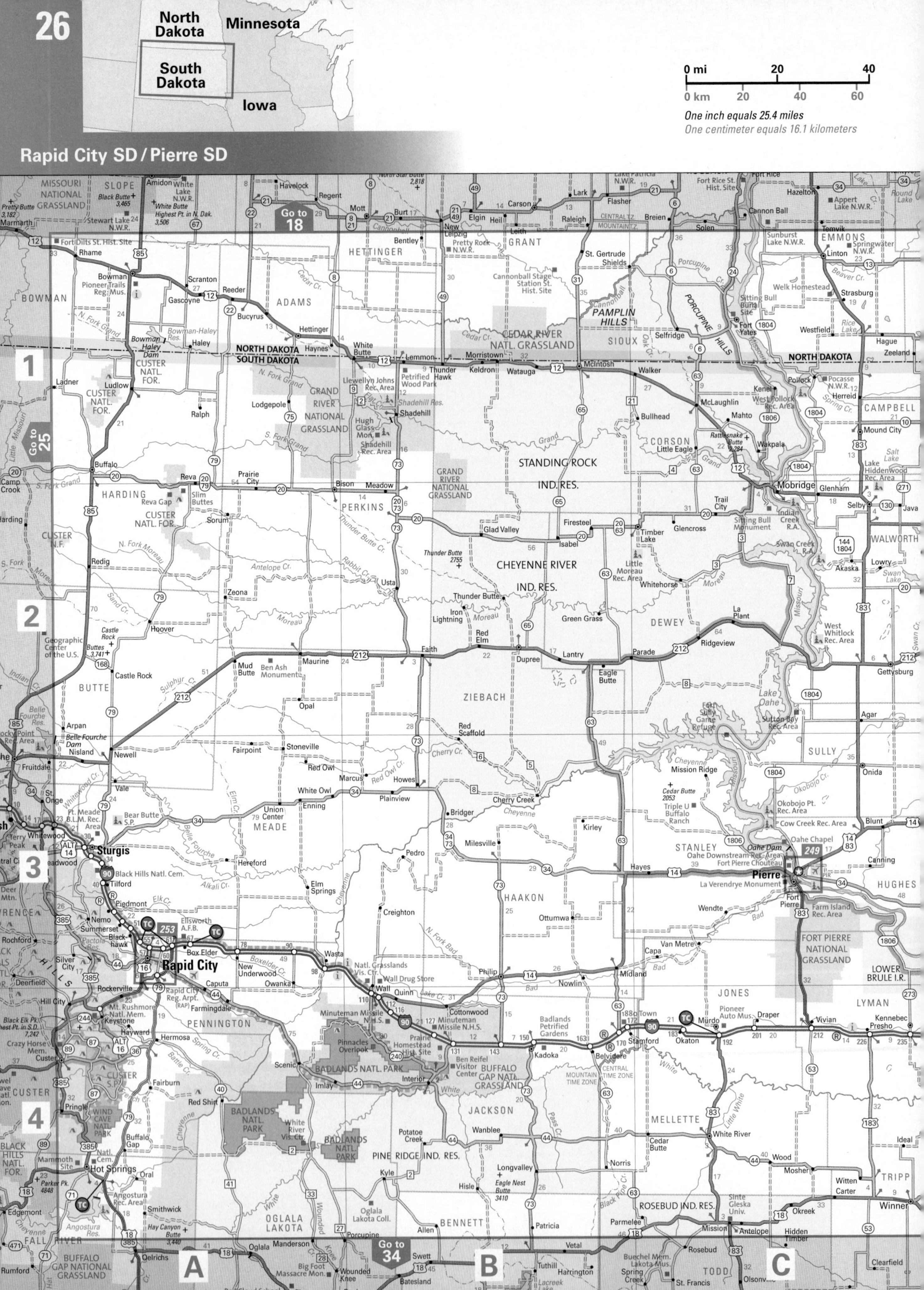

0 mi 20 40
0 km 20 40 60
One inch equals 25.4 miles
One centimeter equals 16.1 kilometers

MISSOURI NATIONAL GRASSLAND

SLOPE

Pretty Butte 3,182
Marmarth
Amidon
White Butte
Black Butte 3,465
White Butte Highest Pt. in N. Dak. 3,506

Havelock
North Star Butte 2,818

Regent
Mott
Carson
Flasher
Lark
Hazelton
Round Lake N.W.R.

Go to 18

Burt
New Leipzig
Elgin Heil
Raleigh
Solen
Breien
Cannon Ball

HETTINGER

GRANT

Bentley
Pretty Rock N.W.R.
St. Gertrude Shields
CENTRAL TZ MOUNTAIN TZ

Sunburst Lake N.W.R.
Appert Lake N.W.R.
Springwater N.W.R.
Linton
Strasburg

Fort Dilts St. Hist. Site
Rhame
Fort Rice St. Hist. Site

Bowman
Pioneer Trails Reg. Mus.
Scranton
Reeder
Cannonball Stage Station St. Hist. Site

EMMONS

BOWMAN

Gascoyne
Bucyrus
Hettinger
ADAMS

PAMPLIN HILLS

Selfridge

Welk Homestead

Sitting Bull Burial Site
Fort 1804
Westfield

Hague
Zeeland

Bowman-Haley Res.
Haley

CEDAR RIVER NATL. GRASSLAND

SIOUX

PORCUPINE HILLS

Rice Lake

Bowman Haley Dam

CUSTER NATL. FOR.

Ladner
Ludlow
N. Fork Grand
Lodgepole

NORTH DAKOTA
SOUTH DAKOTA
Haynes
White Butte
Lemmon
Morristown
McIntosh
Walker

Pollock
Pocasse N.W.R.
Herreid

CAMPBELL

Go to 25

Buffalo
Reva
Ralph
Prairie City

Llewellyn Johns Rec. Area
Thunder Hawk
Keldron
Watauga

Kenel
West Pollock Rec. Area
Mahto

Mound City

Camp Crook

HARDING

Reva Gap
Slim Buttes
Sorum

CUSTER NATL. FOR.

Petrified Wood Park
Shadehill
Hugh Glass Mon.
Shadehill Rec. Area

Bullhead
McLaughlin
1806
1804

Lake Hiddenwood Rec. Area

Harding

Redig

Bison
Meadow

GRAND RIVER NATIONAL GRASSLAND

STANDING ROCK IND. RES.

Little Eagle
Rattlesnake Butte 2,284
Wakpala

83

Selby
Java

CUSTER N.F.

Antelope Cr.

PERKINS

Glad Valley
Firesteel
Isabel

Timber Lake
Glencross

Trail City
Sitting Bull Monument
Indian Creek R.A.

Mobridge
Glenham

271
130

Geographic Center of the U.S.

Castle Rock Buttes 3,741
Zeona

Thunder Butte 2755

CHEYENNE RIVER IND. RES.

Little Moreau Rec. Area
Whitehorse

Swan Creek R.A.
Akaska
Lowry

WALWORTH

Hoover

Thunder Butte

Iron Lightning
Red Elm
Green Grass

DEWEY
La Plant
Ridgeview

West Whitlock Rec. Area

BUTTE

Mud Butte
Maurine
Faith
Dupree
Lantry
Parade

Gettysburg

Castle Rock
Ben Ash Monument

Eagle Butte

1804

Arpan
Belle Fourche Res.
Opal

ZIEBACH

Fort Sully Game Refuge
Sutton Bay Rec. Area
Agar

SULLY

Belle Fourche Dam
Nisland
Newell

Fairpoint
Stoneville
Red Scaffold

Cedar Butte 2053
Triple U Buffalo Ranch
Onida

Rocky Point Rec. Area
Fruitdale

Vale
Red Owl
Marcus
Howes
Cherry Creek

Mission Ridge

Okobojo Pt. Rec. Area
Cow Creek Rec. Area
Blunt

St. Onge
Bear Butte S.P.
White Owl
Plainview

Bridger
Kirley

1806
Oahe Dam
STANLEY
Oahe Chapel
249

Whitewood
Union Center
Enning

Milesville

Hayes
Oahe Downstream Rec. Area
Fort Pierre Chouteau

Canning

Sturgis
Black Hills Natl. Cem.
MEADE
Hereford

HAAKON
Ottumwa
Wendte
Pierre
La Verendrye Monument
Fort Pierre

HUGHES

Tilford
Piedmont
Elm Springs
Creighton

Nemo
Summerset
Black Hawk
Ellsworth A.F.B.
253 TC

Farm Island Rec. Area

Rochford
Silver City
Rapid City
Wasta
Capa
Van Metre
Midland

FORT PIERRE NATIONAL GRASSLAND

LOWER BRULE I.R.

Deerfield
Box Elder
New Underwood
Owanka
Natl. Grasslands Vis. Ctr.
Wall Drug Store

Hill City
Rockerville
Rapid City Reg. Arpt. (RAP)
Farmingdale
Wall
Quinn
Philip
Nowlin

JONES

Crazy Horse Mem.
Mt. Rushmore Natl. Mem.
Keystone
PENNINGTON
Hermosa
Hayward

Minuteman Missile N.H.S.
Cottonwood
Kadoka
Belvidere
Stamford
1880 Town
Pioneer Auto Mus.
Murdo
Draper
Vivian
Kennebec
Presho
LYMAN

Black Elk Pk. Highest Pt. in S.D. 7,242

Pinnacles Overlook
Prairie Homestead Hist. Site
Ben Reifel Visitor Center

Badlands Petrified Gardens
CENTRAL TIME ZONE
MOUNTAIN TIME ZONE
Okaton

WIND CAVE NATL. PARK
Pringle
Fairburn
Red Shirt
Scenic
Imlay
Interior
BADLANDS NATL. PARK
BUFFALO GAP NATL. GRASSLAND
JACKSON

Jewel Cave Natl. Mon.
CUSTER S.P.
Buffalo Gap
White River Vis. Ctr.
Wanblee
MELLETTE
Cedar Butte
White River

183

BLACK HILLS NATL. FOR.
Mammoth Site
Hot Springs
Oral
BADLANDS NATL. PARK
PINE RIDGE IND. RES.
Potato Creek
Kyle
Norris
Mosher
Witten
Carter
Ideal
TRIPP

Parker Pk. 4848
Smithwick
Hay Canyon Butte 3,440
Hisle
Longvalley
Eagle Nest Butte 3410

Wood

Angostura Rec. Area
Angostura Res.
OGLALA LAKOTA
Oglala Lakota Coll.
Allen
Patricia
Parmelee
Sinte Gleska Univ.
Okreek
Winner

Edgemont
FALL RIVER
BUFFALO GAP NATIONAL GRASSLAND
Oelrichs
Oglala
Manderson
Porcupine
BENNETT
ROSEBUD IND. RES.
Mission
Antelope
Hidden Timber

Rumford
Big Foot Massacre Mon.
Wounded Knee
Swett
Vetal
Tuthill
Hartington
53

Go to 34

Red Cloud School
Pine
Batesland
Denby
Lacreek N.W.R.
Spring Creek
St. Francis
TODD
Rosebud
Olsonville
Clearfield
Kevanaha

A   B   C

DRIVING DISTANCES IN MILES	ABERDEEN, SD	BROOKINGS, SD	HOT SPRINGS, SD	HURON, SD	MITCHELL, SD	MOBRIDGE, SD	PIERRE, SD	RAPID CITY, SD	SIOUX FALLS, SD	WAHPETON, ND	WALL, SD	WATERTOWN, SD
ABERDEEN, SD		150	412	90	146	99	160	357	204	154	303	98
PIERRE, SD	160	188	247	115	155	107		193	226	301	138	189
RAPID CITY, SD	357	390	56	313	275	243	193		346	543	55	436
SIOUX FALLS, SD	204	57	401	127	73	303	226	346		210	292	103

SEE ALSO DISTANCE AND DRIVING TIME MAP ON PAGES 286–287

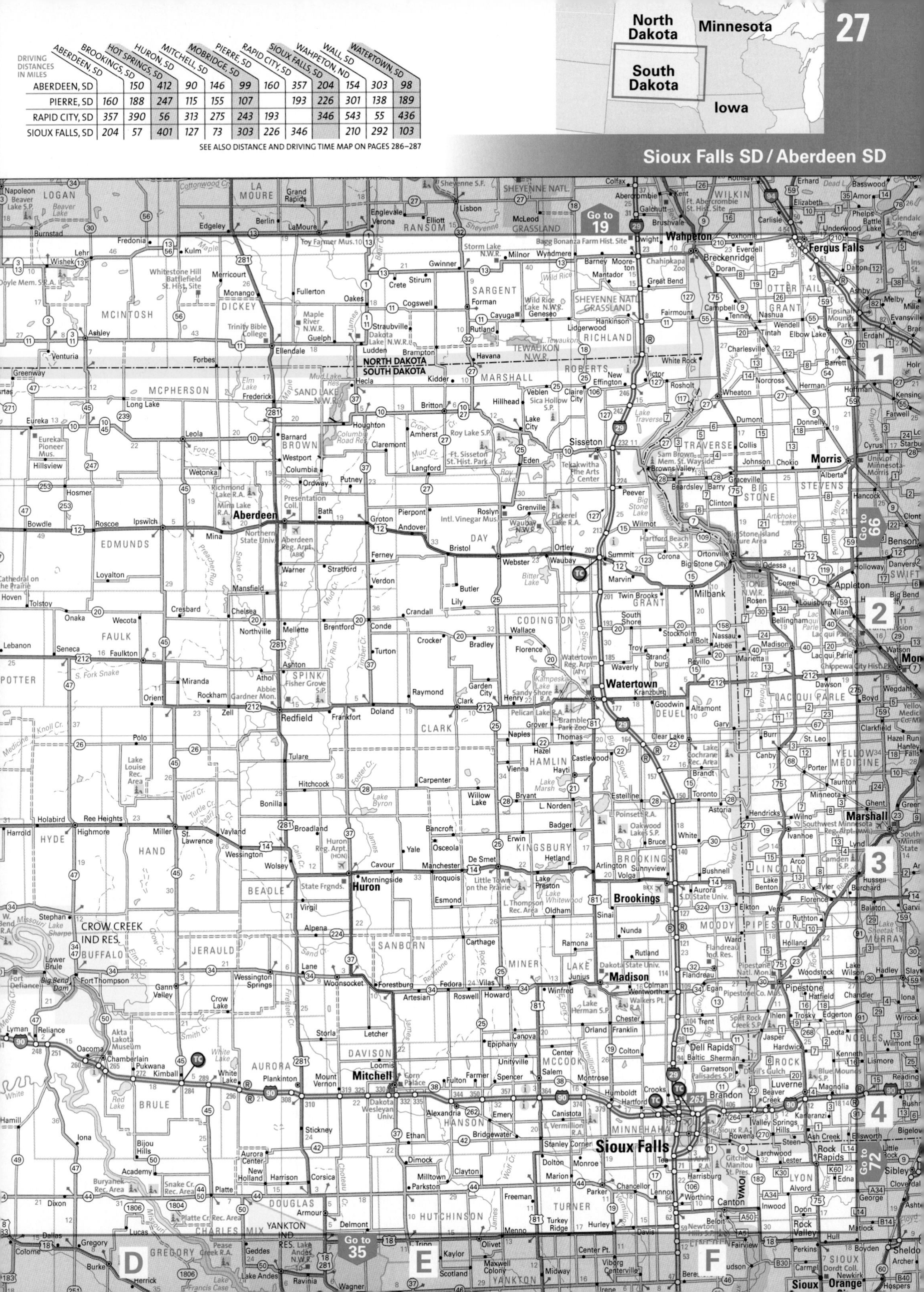

Oregon

California   Nevada

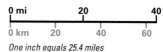

0 mi		20		40
0 km	20	40	60	

One inch equals 25.4 miles
One centimeter equals 16.1 kilometers

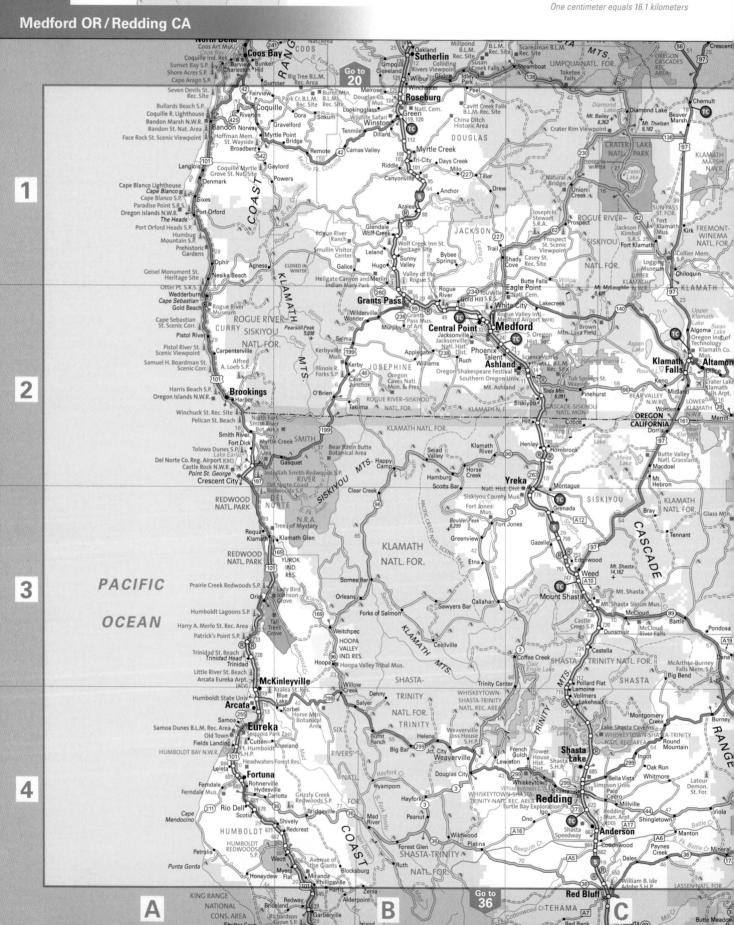

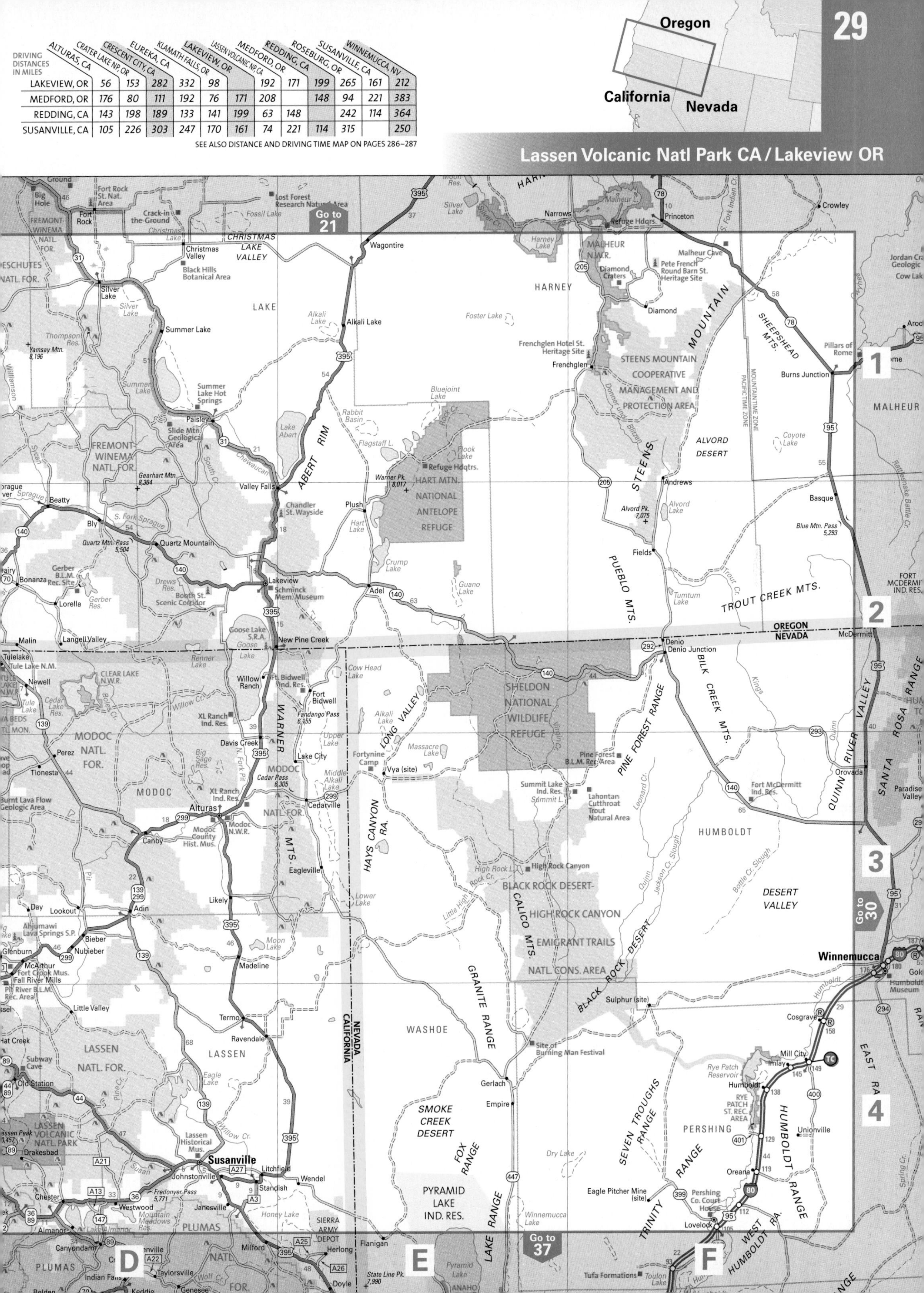

DRIVING DISTANCES IN MILES	ALTURAS, CA	CRATER LAKE NP, OR	CRESCENT CITY, CA	EUREKA, CA	KLAMATH FALLS, OR	LAKEVIEW, OR	LASSEN VOLCANIC NP, CA	MEDFORD, OR	REDDING, CA	ROSEBURG, OR	SUSANVILLE, CA	WINNEMUCCA, NV
LAKEVIEW, OR	56	153	282	332	98		192	171	199	265	161	212
MEDFORD, OR	176	80	111	192	76	171	208		148	94	221	383
REDDING, CA	143	198	189	133	141	199	63	148		242	114	364
SUSANVILLE, CA	105	226	303	247	170	161	74	221	114	315		250

SEE ALSO DISTANCE AND DRIVING TIME MAP ON PAGES 286–287

Oregon
Idaho
Wyoming
Nevada
Utah

0 mi   20   40
0 km   20   40   60
One inch equals 25.4 miles
One centimeter equals 16.1 kilometers

MALHEUR
Crowley
St. Nat. Area
MAHOGANY MTS.
Turnbull Dry Lake
Jordan Craters Geologic Area
Cow Lakes B.L.M. Rec. Site
Upper Cow Lake
Leslie Gulch
Jordan Valley
Arock
Antelope Res.
Antelope Res. B.L.M. Rec. Site
SHEEPSHEAD MTS.
58
78
Pillars of Rome
Burns Junction
Rome
Owyhee Canyon Overlook
Three Forks B.L.M. Rec. Site
Three Forks
Basque
Blue Mtn. Pass 5,293
Coyote Lake
REEK MTS.
55

Reynolds
Silver City
Hayden Pk. 8,403
OWYHEE MTS.
OREGON / IDAHO
FORT McDERMITT IND. RES.
McDermott
OREGON / NEVADA
Little Owyhee
West Little Owyhee
S. Fork Owyhee
Owyhee
DESERT

22 45
95
CANYON
78 127
Melba
Kuna Caves
Indian Cr.
ADA
Mayfield
NATIONAL FOREST
CAMAS
Corral
Fairfield
Hill City
CANYON
Orchard
Murphy
Owyhee Co. Hist. Mus.
Oreana
Grand View
SNAKE RIVER BIRDS OF PREY NATL. CONS. AREA
Go to 22
ELMORE
Long Tom Res.
Anderson Ranch Res.
Mountain Home
Mountain Home A.F.B.
MOUNT BENNETT HILLS
King Hill
Glenns Ferry
Hammett
GOODING
Gooding
Shoshone
Shoshone Ice Caves
Idaho's Mammoth Cave
City of Rocks
Mormon Res.
Magic Res.
20
26
84
90
95
44
59
67
23
51
112 114 120 121 125
129
137
141
11
24 46
147
155
157

Bruneau
Bruneau Dunes S.P.
Hot Spring
Bruneau Canyon Overlook
Three Island Crossing S.P.
Thousand Springs S.P. (Malad Gorge)
Hagerman
HAGERMAN FOSSIL BEDS NATL. MON.
Thousand Springs (Box Canyon)
Thousand Springs S.P. (Niagara Sprs.)
Balanced Rock
Buhl
Filer
Castleford
Wendell
Jerome
Shoshone Falls
TWIN FALLS
Twin Falls
Kimber
Magic Valley Reg. Arpt. (TWF)
Roseworth
Hollister
Rogerson
Idaho Heritage Mus.
Magic Mounta
165
168
173
182
30
93
25
24

OWYHEE
Grasmere
Riddle
51
74

DUCK VALLEY IND. RES.
MOUNTAIN TIME ZONE
PACIFIC TIME ZONE
Owyhee
Mountain City
Jarbidge
HUMBOLDT-TOIYABE NATL. FOR.
North Wildhorse B.L.M. Rec. Area
Matterhorn 10,839
Red Point 8,827
Jackpot
Salmon Falls Creek Falls B.L.M. Rec. Area
Cedar Creek Res.
Salmon Falls Cr. Res. B.L.M. Rec. Area
Three Creek
Magic Hot Springs
225
43
93

Go to 29
HUMBOLDT-TOIYABE NATL. FOR.
Orovada
Paradise Valley
SANTA ROSA RANGE
QUINN RIVER VALLEY
Desert Ranch Res.
Wilson Res. B.L.M. Rec. Area
McAfee Pk. 10,439
Jack Creek
North Fork
Wild Horse B.L.M. Rec. Area
Wild Horse Res.
Charleston (site)
Wild Horse S.R.A.
Contact
SNAKE MTS.
Wilkins (site)
Sun Cr.
Bishop Creek Res.
Thousand Springs Cr.
293
40
95
290
96
226
225
68

HUMBOLDT
DESERT VALLEY
OSGOOD MTS.
Midas
Tuscarora (site)
Willow Creek Res.
Rock Cr.
Kelly Cr.
TUSCARORA MTS.
INDEPENDENCE MOUNTAINS
N. Fork Humboldt
Tabor Cr.
Tabor Creek B.L.M. Rec. Area
ELKO
Wells
Pequop Summit 6,988
140
65
31
95
226
225
333
31
351
80 ALT 93
233
Fort McDermitt Ind. Res.

Winnemucca
Cosgrave
Mill City
Humboldt Mus.
Golconda
Golconda Summit 5,159
Valmy
North Battle Mountain
Dunphy
Carlin
Palisade
Emigrant Pass 6,089
Beowawe
Battle Mountain Ind. Res.
Copper Canyon
Battle Mountain
Crescent Valley
Mt. Lewis 9,680
Mill Creek B.L.M. Rec. Area
Mt. Tobin 9,775
Unionville
EAST RANGE
SONOMA RANGE
TOBIN RANGE
FISH CREEK MTS.
SHOSHONE RANGE
LANDER
CORTEZ MTS.
EUREKA
PERSHING
HUMBOLDT RANGE
Leeville (site)
Calif. Trail Interpretive Ctr.
Elko Reg. Arpt. (EKO)
Northeastern Nev. Mus.
Elko
Deeth
Halleck
Spring Creek
Arthur
Lamoille
Ruby Dome 11,387
South Fork S.R.A.
South Fork Ind. Res.
Lee
Zunino/Jiggs B.L.M. Rec. Site
Jiggs
Ruby Valley
Ruby Mountains Scenic Area
HUMBOLDT-TOIYABE N.F.
HUMBOLDT-TOIYABE N.F.
Franklin Lake
RUBY LAKE N.W.R.
Shantytown
Currie
Goshute Lake
White Horse Pass 6,031
GOSHUTE RANGE
PEQUOP MTS.
ANTELOPE VALLEY
Oasis
Shafter (site)
Silver Zone Pass (site) 5,955
WHITE PINES
Lages
187
176
180
29
294
216
806
229
233
305
50
254
261
306
278
766
276
301
303
298
292
228
21
49
767
50
93
28
232
230
231
352
26
378
387
80
149
145
44
400
158
88
92
80
270
321
Mill Creek
Humboldt
Maggie Cr.
Pine Cr.
Huntington Cr.
RUBY MTS.
SULPHUR SPRING RANGE

A   B   C

Go to 37   Go to 38

PACIFIC TIME ZONE
MOUNTAIN TIME ZONE

1
2
3
4

DRIVING DISTANCES IN MILES

	BRIGHAM CITY, UT	ELKO, NV	EVANSTON, WY	MONTPELIER, ID	MOUNTAIN HOME, ID	OGDEN, UT	POCATELLO, ID	PROVO, UT	SALT LAKE CITY, UT	TWIN FALLS, ID	WELLS, NV	WINNEMUCCA, NV
ELKO, NV	286		314	375	194	267	283	279	232	167	50	127
POCATELLO, ID	107	283	200	87	193	127		205	159	116	233	410
SALT LAKE CITY, UT	56	232	82	145	295	37	159	47		217	182	359
TWIN FALLS, ID	165	167	259	204	86	185	116	264	217		117	294

SEE ALSO DISTANCE AND DRIVING TIME MAP ON PAGES 286–287

Salt Lake City UT / Pocatello ID

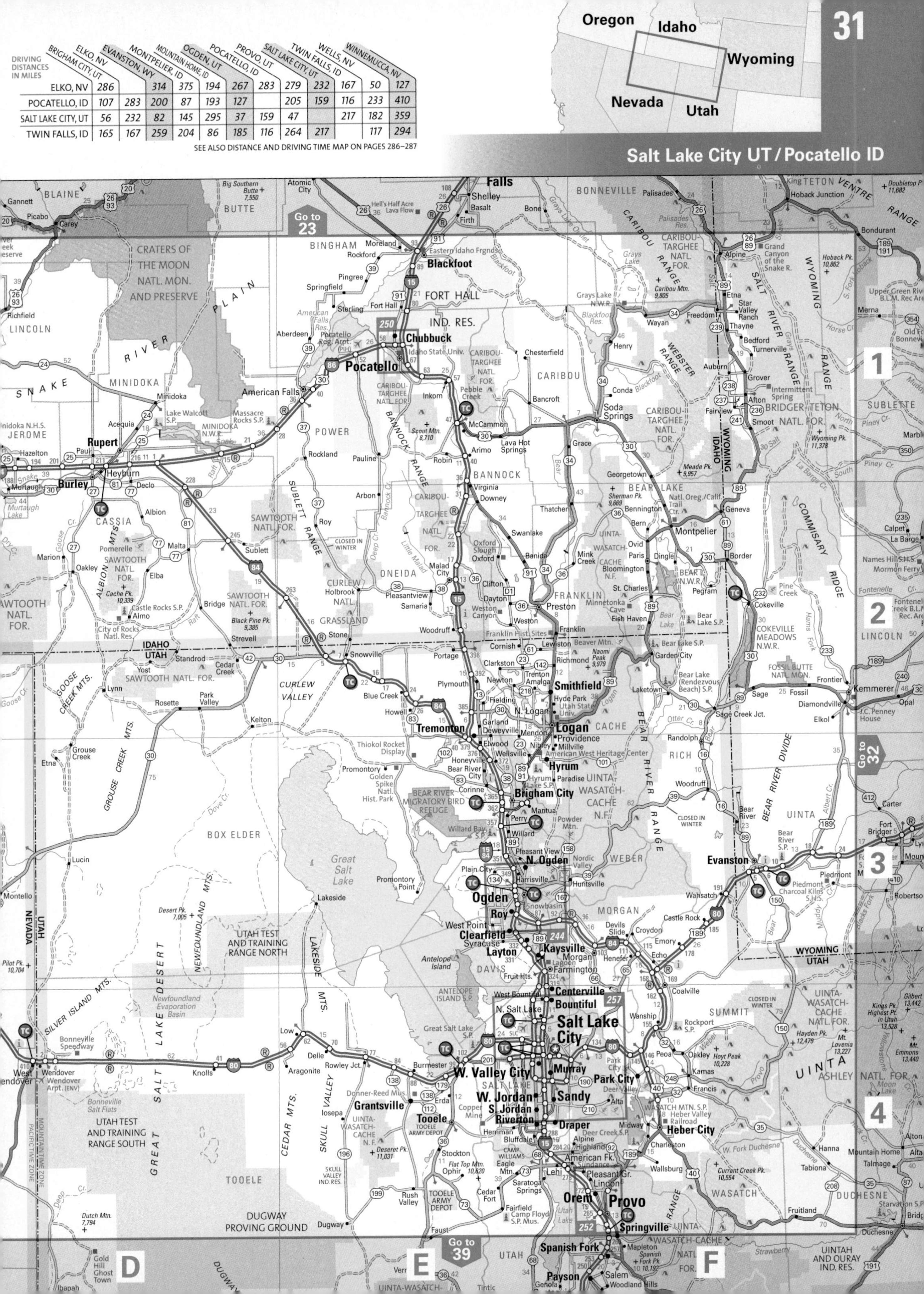

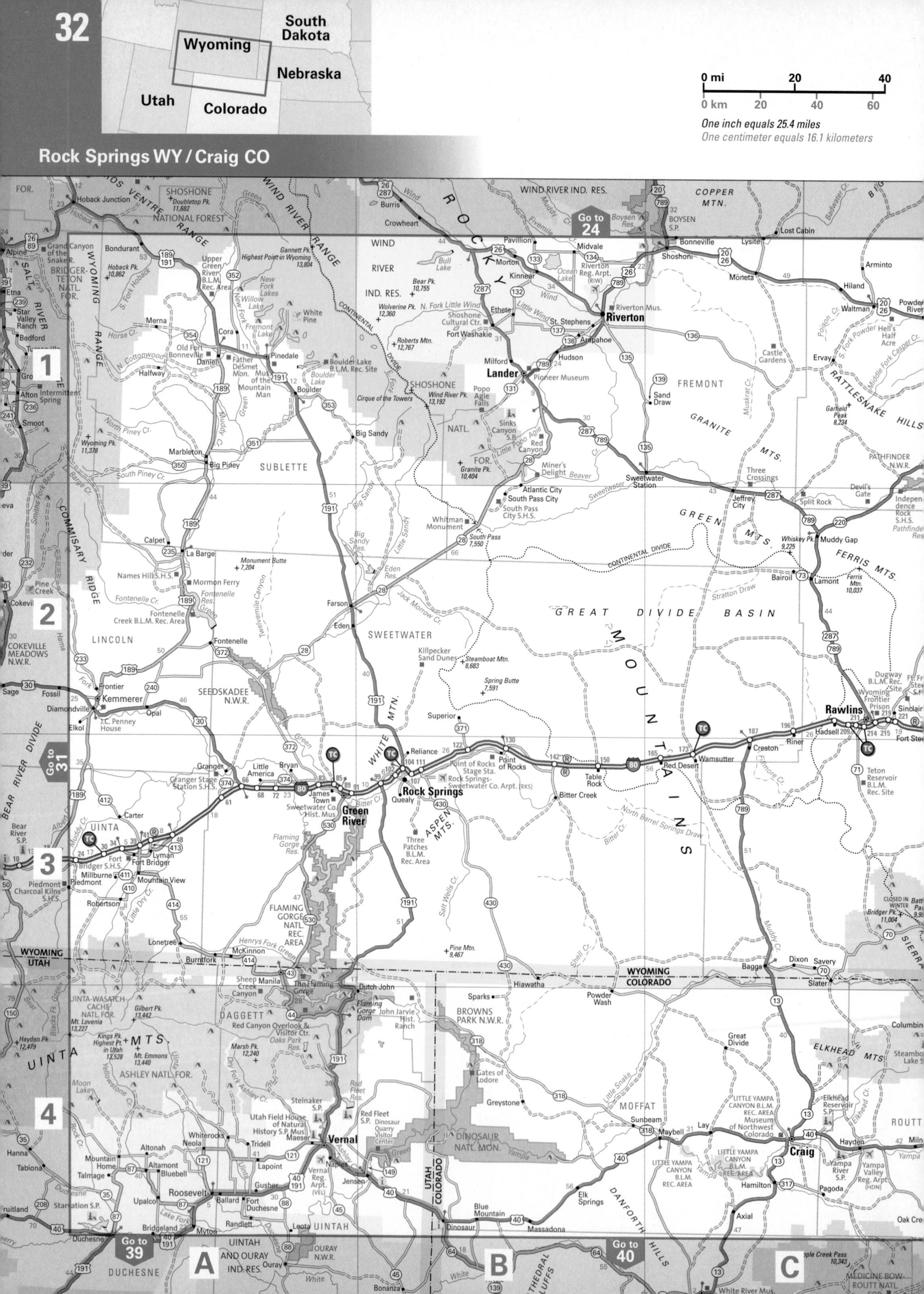

0 mi   20   40
0 km   20   40   60
One inch equals 25.4 miles
One centimeter equals 16.1 kilometers

Cheyenne WY / Fort Collins CO

DRIVING DISTANCES IN MILES	CASPER, WY	CHEYENNE, WY	CRAIG, CO	FORT COLLINS, CO	KEMMERER, WY	LANDER, WY	LARAMIE, WY	PINEDALE, WY	RAWLINS, WY	ROCK SPRINGS, WY	SCOTTSBLUFF, NE	VERNAL, UT
CASPER, WY		175	234	217	297	144	148	271	117	214	173	322
CHEYENNE, WY	175		221	44	342	276	52	355	151	260	111	367
CRAIG, CO	234	221		194	257	221	171	269	117	149	331	123
ROCK SPRINGS, WY	214	260	149	273	86	118	210	98	110		370	111

SEE ALSO DISTANCE AND DRIVING TIME MAP ON PAGES 286–287

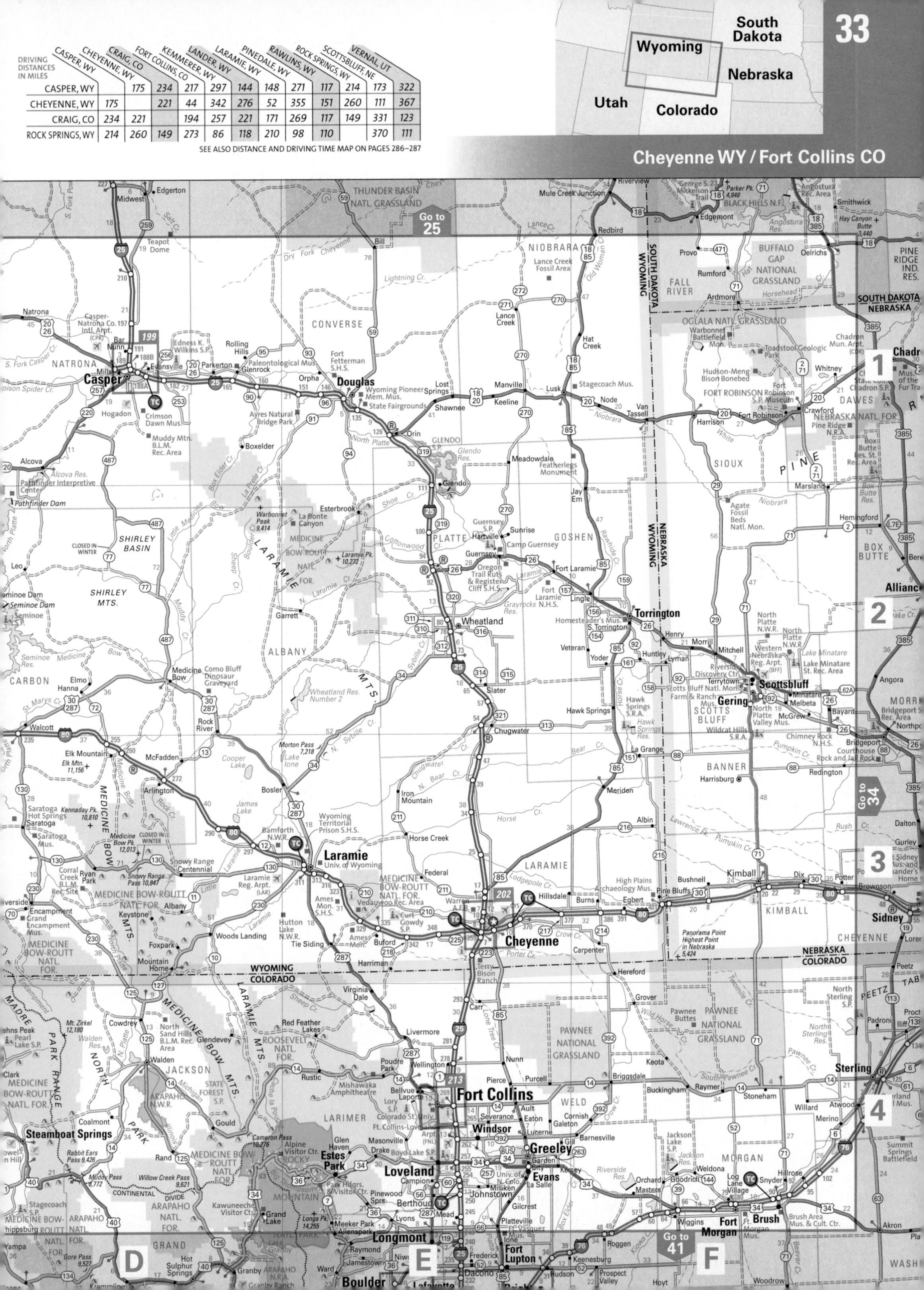

0 mi   20   40
0 km   20   40   60
One inch equals 25.4 miles
One centimeter equals 16.1 kilometers

Go to 26
Go to 33
Go to 42

PINE RIDGE IND. RES.
SHANNON
BENNETT
MELLETTE
TODD
TRIPP
ROSEBUD IND. RES.
SOUTH DAKOTA
NEBRASKA

FALL RIVER
BUFFALO GAP NATL. GRASSLAND
OGLALA NATL. GRASSLAND

Chadron
Crawford
Ft. Robinson
DAWES
PINE RIDGE
SHERIDAN
CHERRY
Valentine
FORT NIOBRARA N.W.R.
BROWN
KEYA PAHA
Ainsworth

BOX BUTTE
Alliance
Hemingford
Berea

SAMUEL R. McKELVIE NATL. FOR.
Merritt Res. St. Rec. Area
VALENTINE N.W.R.

SAND HILLS
SURVEY VALLEY

Scottsbluff
MORRILL
GRANT
HOOKER
THOMAS
BLAINE
Dunning
NEBRASKA NATL. FOR.

SCOTTS BLUFF
BANNER
Bridgeport
GARDEN
ARTHUR
McPHERSON
LOGAN
CUSTER

CRESCENT LAKE N.W.R.

Oshkosh
KEITH
Lake McConaughy
Kingsley Dam
Ogallala
North Platte
LINCOLN

CHEYENNE
Sidney
KIMBALL
DEUEL
PERKINS
Lexington
Cozad
Gothenburg

NEBRASKA
COLORADO

Sterling
LOGAN
SEDGWICK
PHILLIPS
CHASE
HAYES
FRONTIER
GOSPER

WASHINGTON
YUMA
DUNDY
HITCHCOCK
McCook
RED WILLOW
FURNAS

A   B   C
1   2   3   4

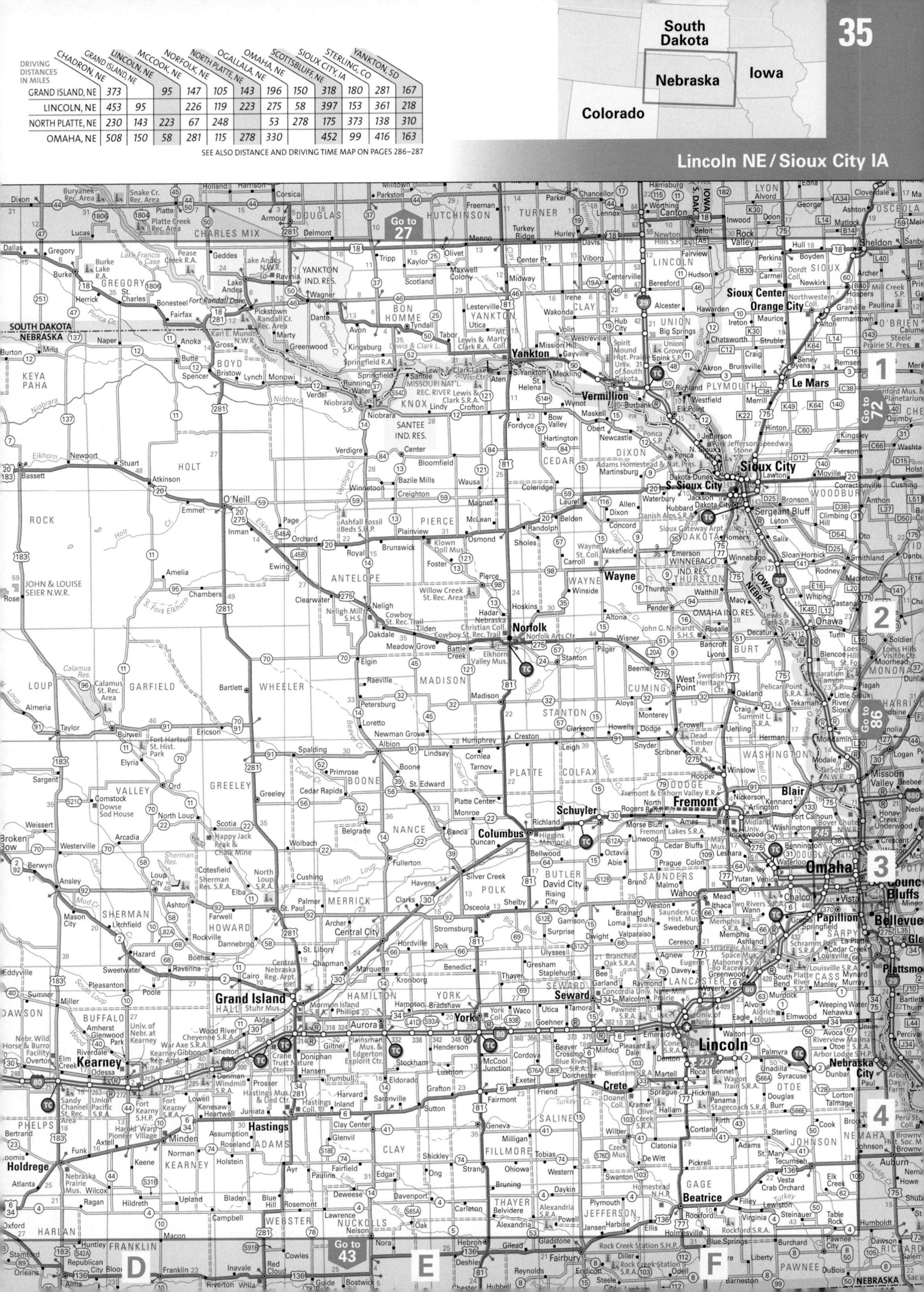

DRIVING DISTANCES IN MILES	CHADRON, NE	GRAND ISLAND, NE	LINCOLN, NE	McCOOK, NE	NORFOLK, NE	NORTH PLATTE, NE	OGALLALA, NE	OMAHA, NE	SCOTTSBLUFF, NE	SIOUX CITY, IA	STERLING, CO	YANKTON, SD
GRAND ISLAND, NE	373		95	147	105	143	196	150	318	180	281	167
LINCOLN, NE	453	95		226	119	223	275	58	397	153	361	218
NORTH PLATTE, NE	230	143	223	67	248		53	278	175	373	138	310
OMAHA, NE	508	150	58	281	115	278	330		452	99	416	163

SEE ALSO DISTANCE AND DRIVING TIME MAP ON PAGES 286–287

California   Nevada

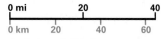

0 mi   20   40
0 km   20   40   60
One inch equals 25.4 miles
One centimeter equals 16.1 kilometers

DRIVING DISTANCES IN MILES	AUSTIN, NV	CHICO, CA	MERCED, CA	RENO, NV	SACRAMENTO, CA	SAN FRANCISCO, CA	SAN JOSE, CA	S. LAKE TAHOE, CA	STOCKTON, CA	TONOPAH, NV	UKIAH, CA	YOSEMITE VIL., CA
RENO, NV	171	164	243		132	217	245	59	177	237	261	199
SACRAMENTO, CA	302	88	118	132		87	115	100	48	329	153	170
SAN FRANCISCO, CA	387	182	131	217	87		43	185	82	352	116	183
YOSEMITE VIL., CA	280	257	79	199	170	183	168	180	123	199	289	

SEE ALSO DISTANCE AND DRIVING TIME MAP ON PAGES 286–287

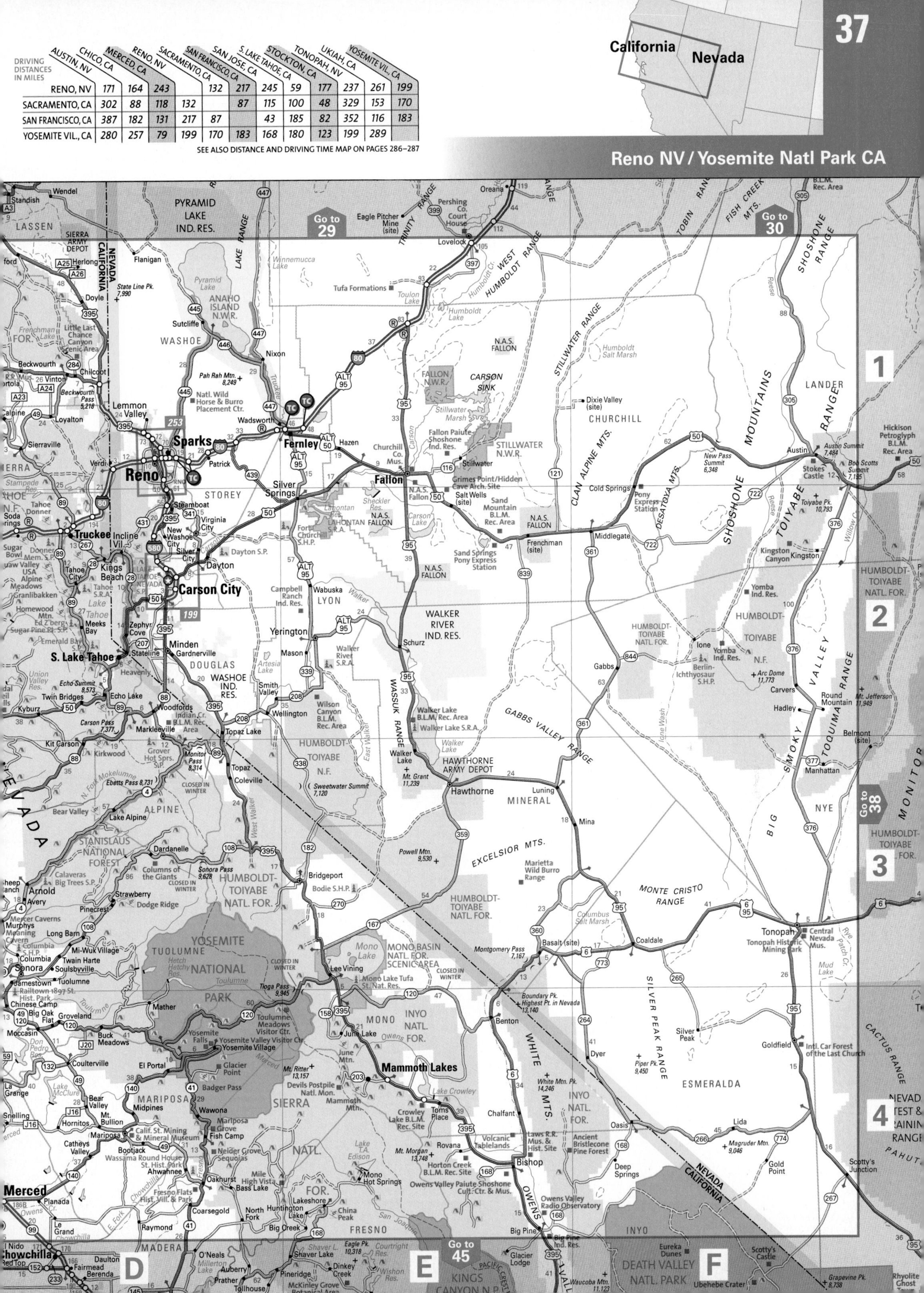

0 mi 20 40
0 km 20 40 60
One inch equals 25.4 miles
One centimeter equals 16.1 kilometers

Go to 30

Go to 45

Go to 46

Go to 37

1
2
3
4

A B C

ELKO
LANDER
EUREKA
WHITE PINE
LINCOLN
NYE
WASHINGTON
DIXIE

NEVADA
UTAH

Ruby Valley
Shantytown
Ruby Lake
Currie
White Horse Pass 6,031
Gold Hill Ghost Town
Dutch Mtn. 7,794
Ibapah
Callao
Goshute Canyon and Cave
Cherry Creek
Lages
Tippett
Goshute
Ibapah Pk. 12,087
Trout Creek
Blue Mass Scenic Area
Tonkin Spring B.L.M. Rec. Area
Newark Lake
Steptoe (site)
Salt Marsh Lake
Gandy
Austin
Austin Summit 7,484
Hickison Petroglyph B.L.M. Rec. Area
Bob Scotts Summit 7,195
Eureka
Eureka Opera House
Eureka Sentinel Mus.
Diamond Pk. 10,614
Robinson Summit 7,539
McGill
North Schell Pk. 11,883
Mt. Moriah 12,050
Eskdale
Stokes Castle
Toiyabe Pk. 10,793
Summit Mtn. 10,461
Little Antelope Summit 7,438
Garnet Hill
Ely Arpt. (ELY)
Nev. Northern Railway Mus.
Sacramento Pass 7,136
Kingston Canyon
Kingston
Potts (site)
Mt. Hamilton 10,745
Ruth
Lane Ely
E. Ely
Cleve Creek B.L.M. Rec. Site
Cave Lake S.P.
Baker
Garrison
Carvers
Duckwater
Illipah Res. B.L.M. Rec. Area
Ward Mtn. B.L.M. Rec. Area
Ward Charcoal Ovens S.H.P.
Connors Pass 7,733
Wheeler Pk. 13,063
Lehman Caves
GREAT BASIN NATL PARK
Pruess Lake
Round Mountain
Mt. Jefferson 11,949
Duckwater Ind. Res.
Currant Mtn. 11,513
Majors Place
Minerva (site)
Shoshone
DESERT EXPERIMENTAL RANGE
Hadley
Belmont (site)
Currant Summit 6,999
Preston
Lund
Manhattan
Currant
Warm Springs Summit 6,293
Lunar Crater Volcanic Field Natl. Natural Landmark
Nyala (site)
Troy Pk. 11,298
Adams-McGill Res.
Sunnyside
Mt. Wilson 9,296
Spring Valley S.P.
Meadow Valley B.L.M. Rec. Site
Hamlin Valley
Warm Springs (site)
Central Nev. Mus.
Tonopah Hist. Mining Park
Michael Heizer's City
BASIN & RANGE NATIONAL MONUMENT
Pioche
Caselton
Ursine
Beryl
Zane
Goldfield
Intl. Car Forest of the Last Church
TONOPAH TEST RANGE
Queen City Summit 5,935
Cathedral Gorge S.P.
Echo Canyon S.P.
Modena
Panaca
Uvada
Newcastle
Enterprise
Pinto
Tempiute (site)
Rachel
Hiko
Caliente
Caliente Railroad Depot
Kershaw-Ryan S.P.
Beaver Dam S.P.
Lost Pk. 7,514
Mountain Meadows Monument
NEVADA TEST & TRAINING RANGE
Ash Springs
Alamo
Rainbow Canyon
Elgin
Elgin Schoolhouse S.H.S.
Gunlock
Gunlock S.P.
Snow Canyon S.P.
PAIUTE IND. RES. Shivwits
Santa Clara
Jacob Hamblin Home
St. George
Scotty's Junction
Grapevine Pk. 8,738
NEVADA NATIONAL SECURITY SITE
DESERT NATL. WILDLIFE REFUGE
PAHRANAGAT N.W.R.

SHOSHONE RANGE, CORTEZ MTS, RUBY RANGE, DIAMOND MTS, SULPHUR SPRING RANGE, FISH CREEK RANGE, BUTTE MOUNTAINS, EGAN RANGE, SCHELL CREEK RANGE, ANTELOPE RANGE, DEEP CREEK RANGE, CONFUSION RANGE, TOQUIMA RANGE, MONITOR RANGE, HOT CREEK RANGE, PANCAKE RANGE, RAILROAD VALLEY, GRANT RANGE, SEAMAN RANGE, SNAKE RANGE, WILSON CREEK RANGE, INDIAN PEAK RANGE, KAWICH RANGE, REVEILLE RANGE, GROOM RANGE, BELTED RANGE, PAHRANAGAT RANGE, CACTUS RANGE, PAHUTE MESA, CLOVER MTS, DELAMAR MTS

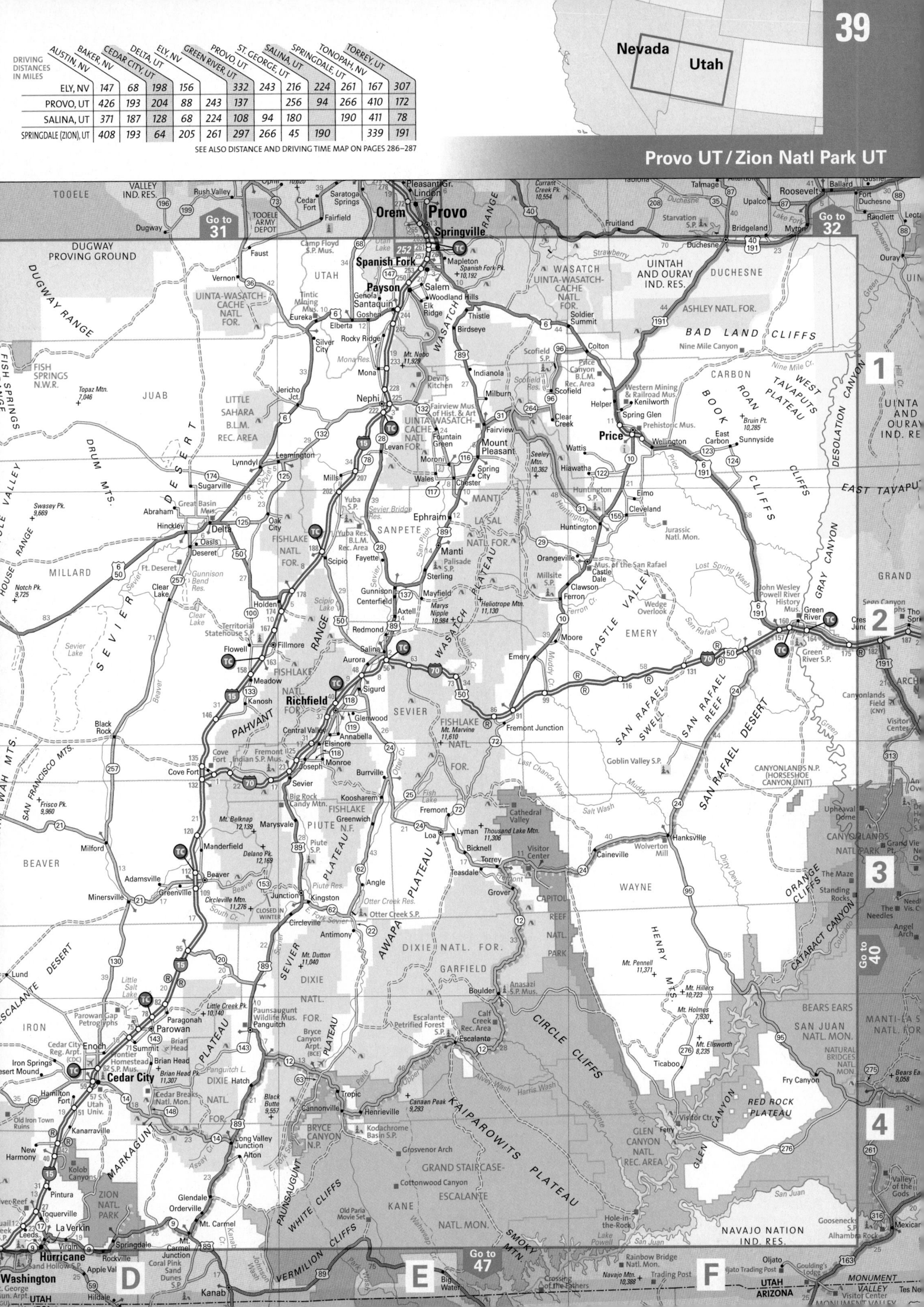

DRIVING DISTANCES IN MILES

	AUSTIN, NV	BAKER, NV	CEDAR CITY, UT	DELTA, UT	ELY, NV	GREEN RIVER, UT	PROVO, UT	ST. GEORGE, UT	SALINA, UT	SPRINGDALE, UT	TONOPAH, NV	TORREY, UT
ELY, NV	147	68	198	156		332	243	216	224	261	167	307
PROVO, UT	426	193	204	88	243	137		256	94	266	410	172
SALINA, UT	371	187	128	68	224	108	94	180		190	411	78
SPRINGDALE (ZION), UT	408	193	64	205	261	297	266	45	190		339	191

SEE ALSO DISTANCE AND DRIVING TIME MAP ON PAGES 286–287

Utah

Colorado

0 mi 20 40
0 km 20 40 60
One inch equals 25.4 miles
One centimeter equals 16.1 kilometers

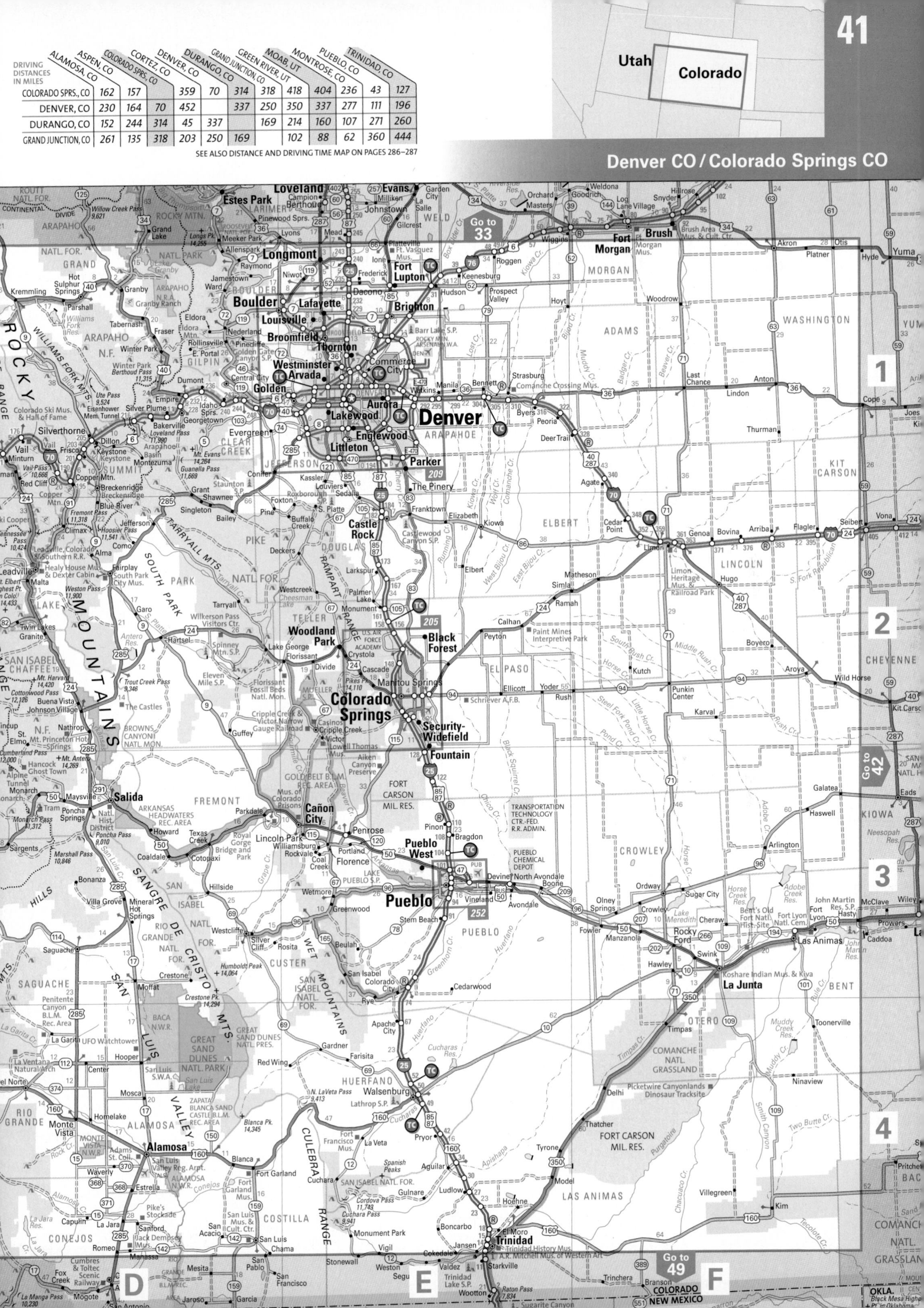

Utah Colorado

DRIVING DISTANCES IN MILES	ALAMOSA, CO	ASPEN, CO	COLORADO SPRS., CO	CORTEZ, CO	DENVER, CO	DURANGO, CO	GRAND JUNCTION, CO	GREEN RIVER, UT	MOAB, UT	MONTROSE, CO	PUEBLO, CO	TRINIDAD, CO
COLORADO SPRS., CO	162	157		359	70	314	318	418	404	236	43	127
DENVER, CO	230	164	70	452		337	250	350	337	277	111	196
DURANGO, CO	152	244	314	45	337		169	214	160	107	271	260
GRAND JUNCTION, CO	261	135	318	203	250	169		102	88	62	360	444

SEE ALSO DISTANCE AND DRIVING TIME MAP ON PAGES 286–287

Garden City KS / Dodge City KS

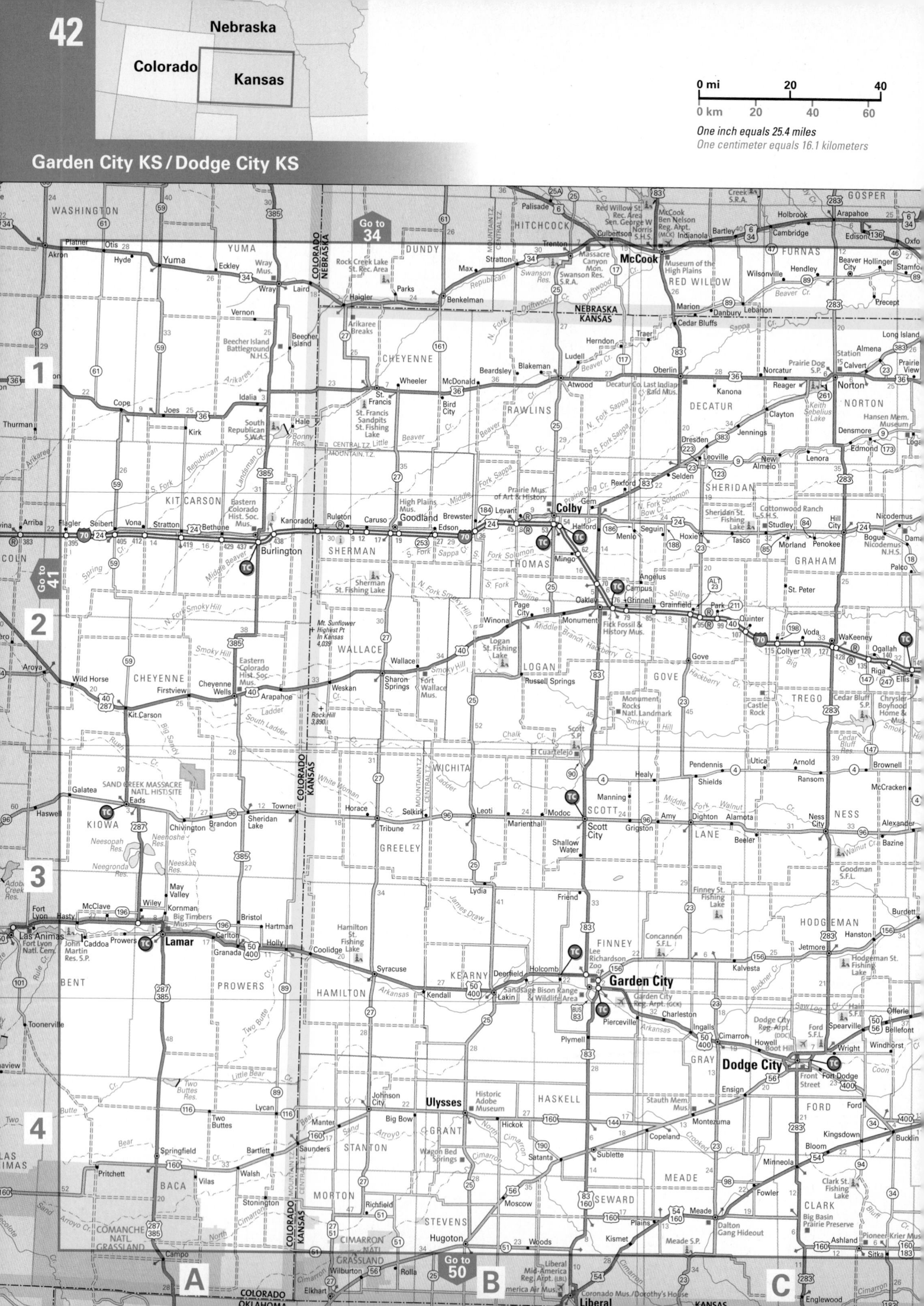

Nebraska
Colorado
Kansas
0 mi 20 40
0 km 20 40 60
One inch equals 25.4 miles
One centimeter equals 16.1 kilometers
Go to 34
Go to 41
Go to 50
McCook
Colby
Goodland
Burlington
Lamar
Garden City
Dodge City
Scott City
Ulysses
Liberal
Hugoton
Norton
Oberlin
WaKeeney
Syracuse
Johnson City
Yuma
Wray
St. Francis
Atwood
Oakley
Ness City
1
2
3
4
A
B
C

DRIVING DISTANCES IN MILES	BURLINGTON, CO	DODGE CITY, KS	EMPORIA, KS	GARDEN CITY, KS	HAYS, KS	LAMAR, CO	MANHATTAN, KS	McCOOK, NE	OAKLEY, KS	SALINA, KS	TOPEKA, KS	WICHITA, KS
GARDEN CITY, KS	167	52	290		139	98	272	167	79	204	311	205
OAKLEY, KS	88	136	293	79	87	156	247	88		179	286	268
SALINA, KS	266	164	118	204	93	335	72	240	179		111	92
WICHITA, KS	354	153	85	205	181	303	131	329	268	92	137	

SEE ALSO DISTANCE AND DRIVING TIME MAP ON PAGES 286–287

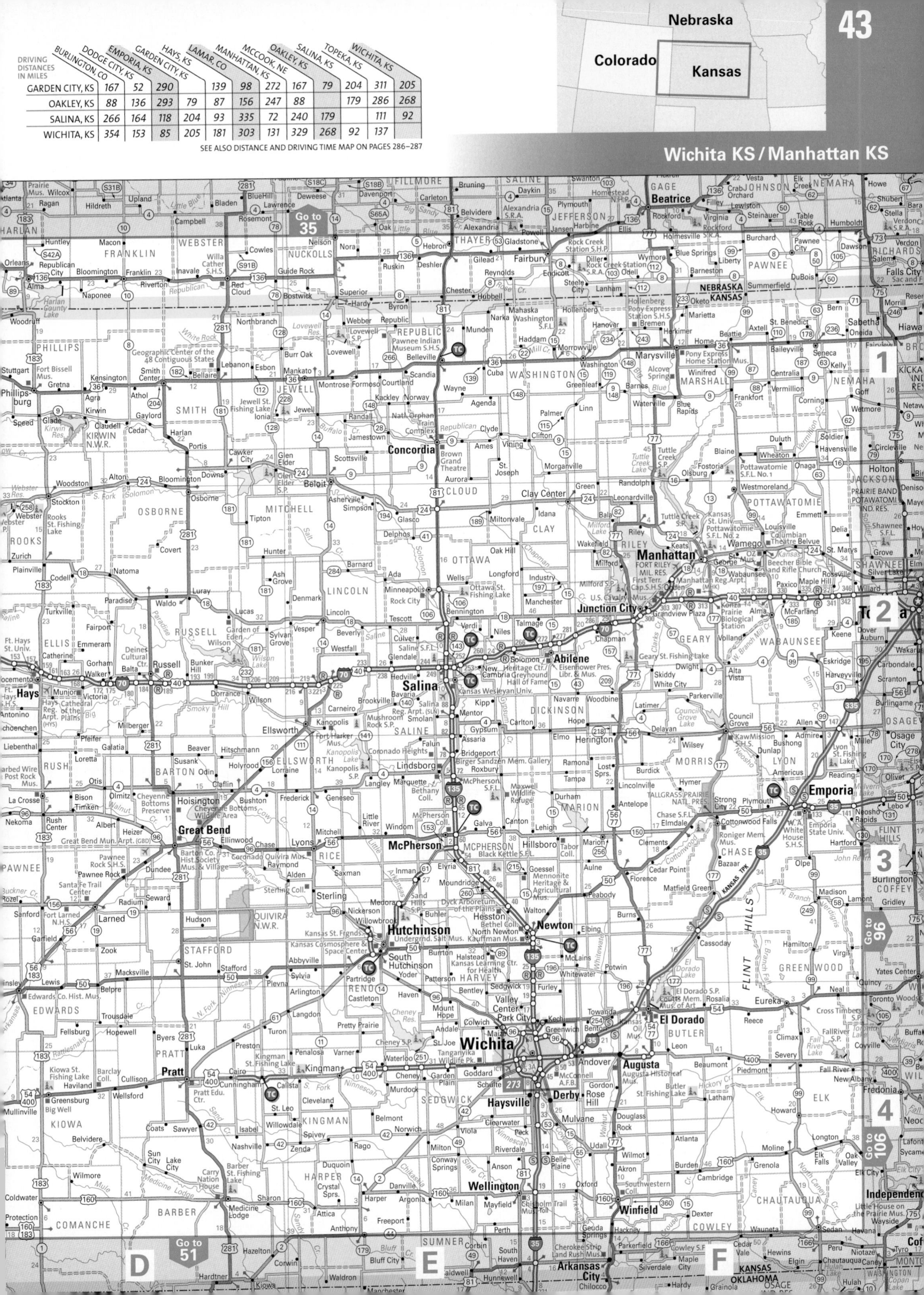

One inch equals 25.4 miles
One centimeter equals 16.1 kilometers

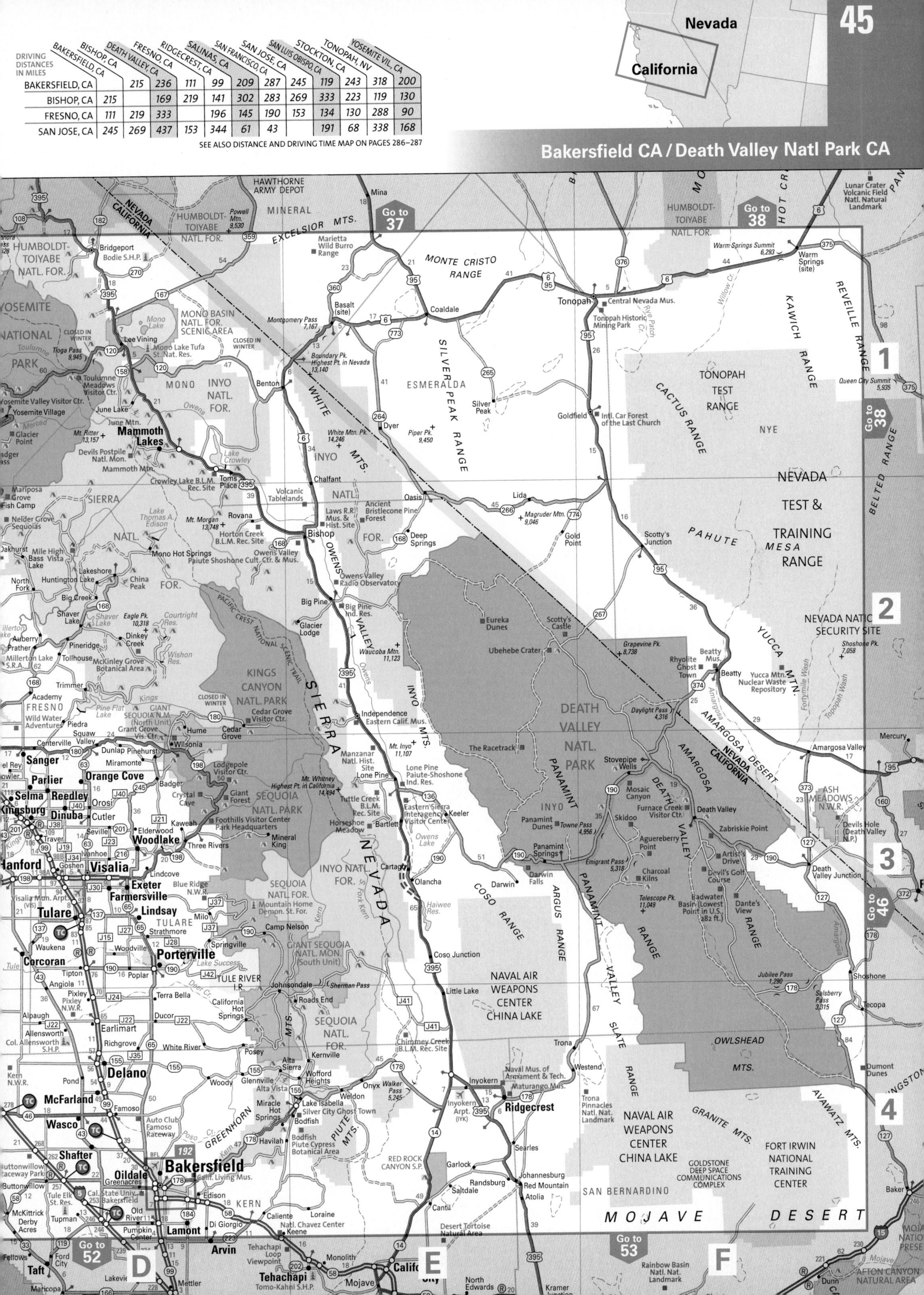

DRIVING DISTANCES IN MILES	BAKERSFIELD, CA	BISHOP, CA	DEATH VALLEY, CA	FRESNO, CA	RIDGECREST, CA	SALINAS, CA	SAN FRANCISCO, CA	SAN JOSE, CA	SAN LUIS OBISPO, CA	STOCKTON, CA	TONOPAH, NV	YOSEMITE VIL, CA
BAKERSFIELD, CA		215	236	111	99	209	287	245	119	243	318	200
BISHOP, CA	215		169	219	141	302	283	269	333	223	119	130
FRESNO, CA	111	219	333		196	145	190	153	134	130	288	90
SAN JOSE, CA	245	269	437	153	344	61	43		191	68	338	168

SEE ALSO DISTANCE AND DRIVING TIME MAP ON PAGES 286–287

Nevada • Utah
California
Arizona

Las Vegas NV / St George UT

0 mi   20   40
0 km   20   40   60
One inch equals 25.4 miles
One centimeter equals 16.1 kilometers

Major places: Las Vegas, North Las Vegas, Henderson, Boulder City, Pahrump, St. George, Washington, Hurricane, Mesquite, Kingman, Bullhead City, Mohave Valley, Lake Havasu City, Needles, Twentynine Palms, Baker, Ludlow

Regions / features: Nevada Test & Training Range, Nevada National Security Site, Desert National Wildlife Refuge, Spring Mountains N.R.A., Red Rock Canyon N.C.A., Nellis Air Force Range Complex, Lake Mead National Recreation Area, Grand Canyon-Parashant National Monument, Gold Butte National Monument, Mojave National Preserve, Joshua Tree National Park, Death Valley Junction, Zion National Park, Grand Canyon National Park, Grand Canyon West & Skywalk, Hoover Dam, Davis Dam, Parker Dam

Grid labels: 1, 2, 3, 4 (left) — A, B, C (bottom)

Go to 38, Go to 45, Go to 53, Go to 54

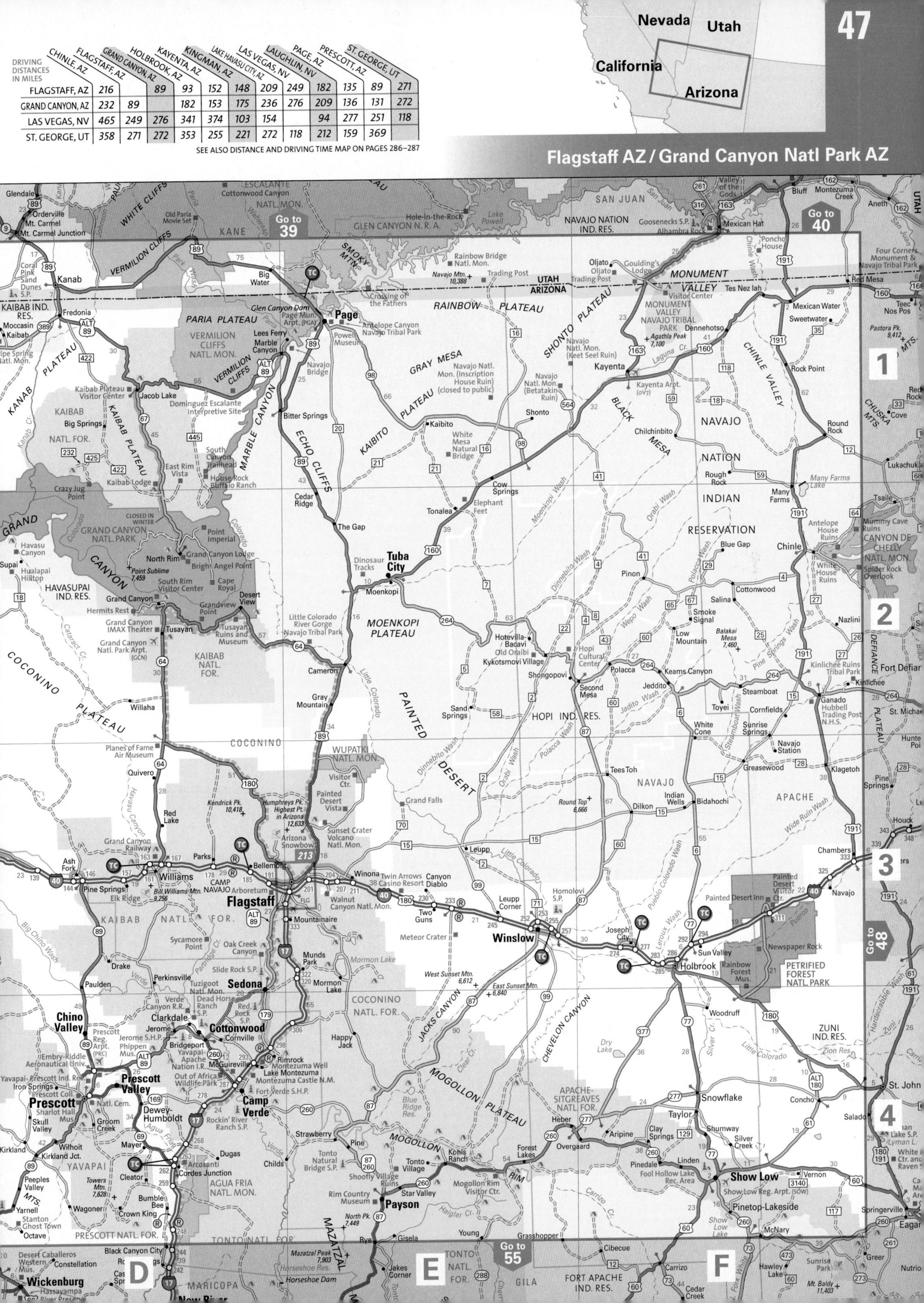

DRIVING DISTANCES IN MILES

	CHINLE, AZ	FLAGSTAFF, AZ	GRAND CANYON, AZ	HOLBROOK, AZ	KAYENTA, AZ	KINGMAN, AZ	LAKE HAVASU CITY, AZ	LAS VEGAS, NV	LAUGHLIN, NV	PAGE, AZ	PRESCOTT, AZ	ST. GEORGE, UT
FLAGSTAFF, AZ	216		89	93	152	148	209	249	182	135	89	271
GRAND CANYON, AZ	232	89		182	153	175	236	276	209	136	131	272
LAS VEGAS, NV	465	249	276	341	374	103	154		94	277	251	118
ST. GEORGE, UT	358	271	272	353	255	221	272	118	212	159	369	

SEE ALSO DISTANCE AND DRIVING TIME MAP ON PAGES 286–287

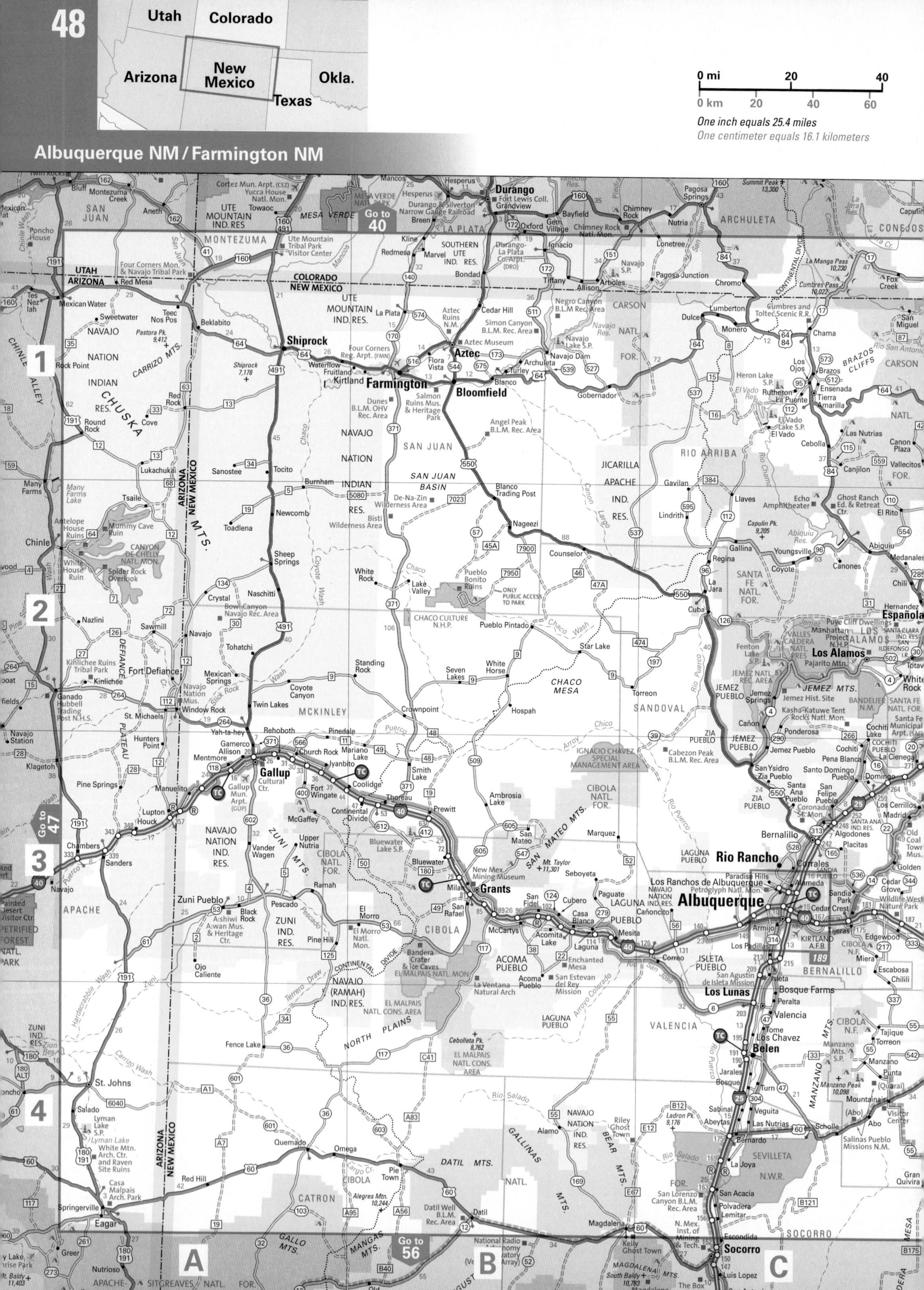

48

Utah
Colorado
Arizona
New Mexico
Okla.
Texas

Albuquerque NM / Farmington NM

0 mi · 20 · 40
0 km · 20 · 40 · 60
One inch equals 25.4 miles
One centimeter equals 16.1 kilometers

DRIVING DISTANCES IN MILES

	ALBUQUERQUE, NM	CLAYTON, NM	CLOVIS, NM	DURANGO, CO	FARMINGTON, NM	GALLUP, NM	SANTA FE, NM	SOCORRO, NM	TAOS, NM	TRINIDAD, CO	TUCUMCARI, NM	VAUGHN, NM
ALBUQUERQUE, NM		266	220	212	181	141	55	77	123	242	174	104
FARMINGTON, NM	181	368	401	50		120	205	263	211	300	355	284
SANTA FE, NM	55	216	213	207	205	197		132	68	192	167	96
TUCUMCARI, NM	174	111	82	386	355	316	167	251	195	198		98

SEE ALSO DISTANCE AND DRIVING TIME MAP ON PAGES 286–287

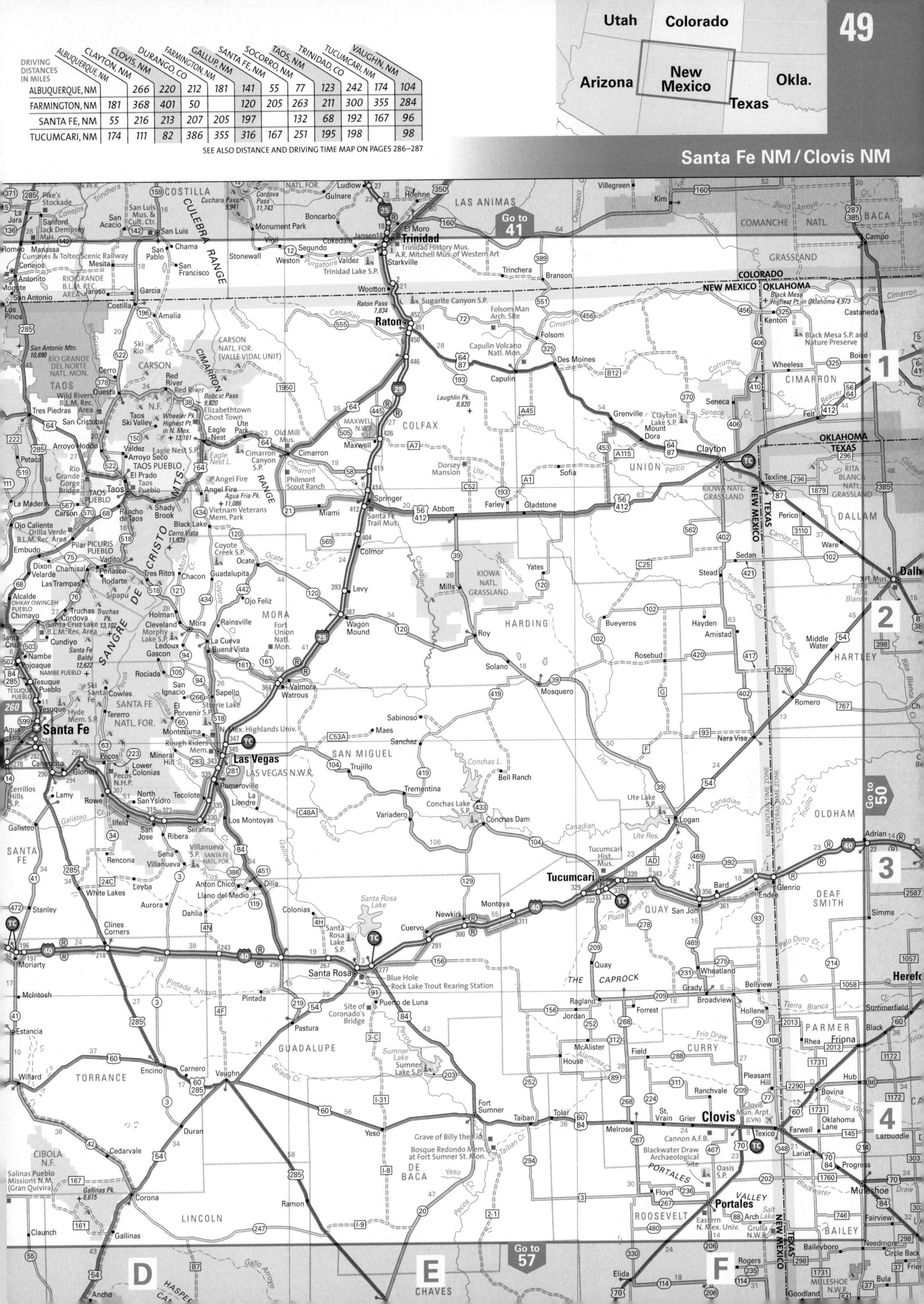

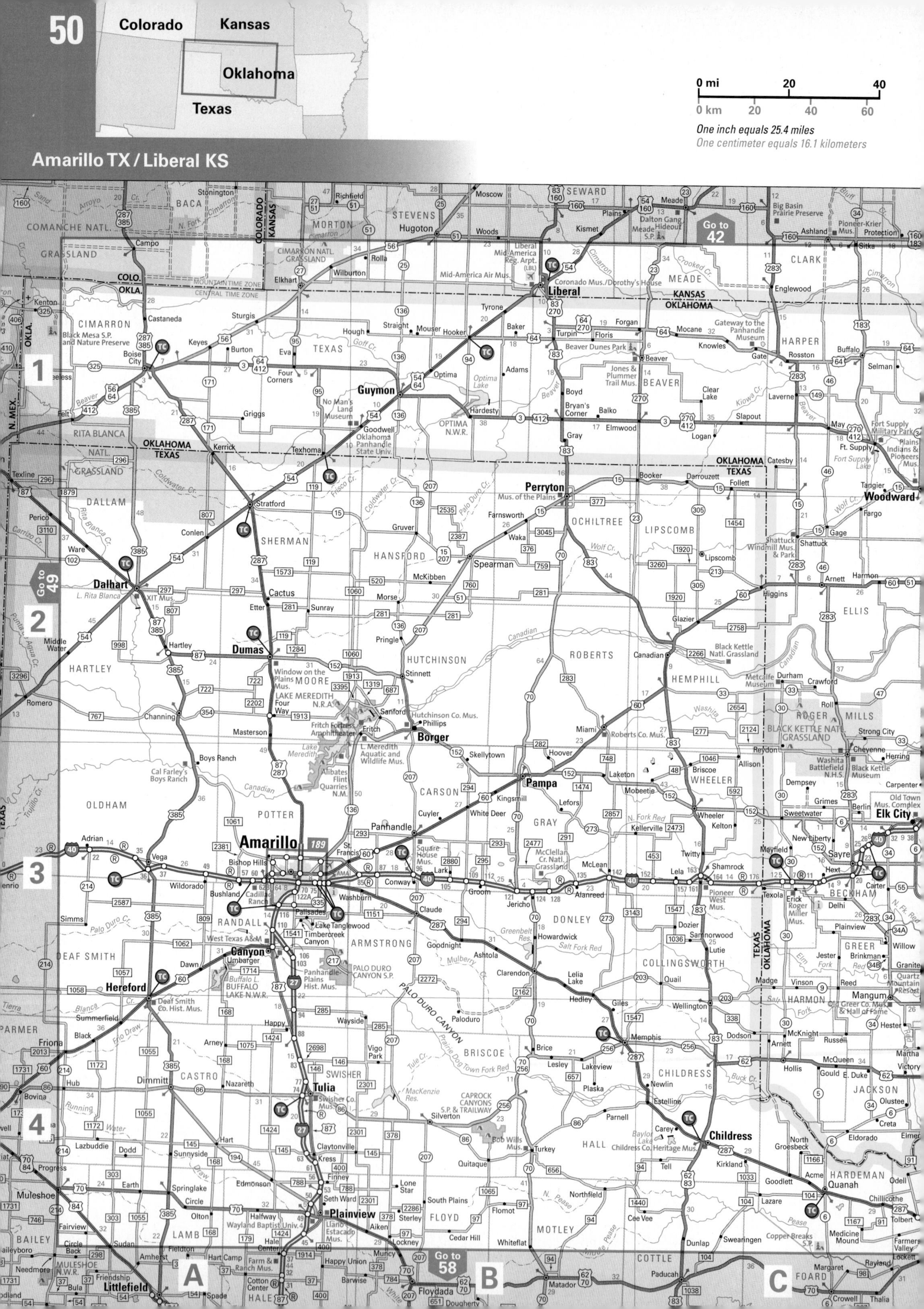

0 mi   20   40

0 km   20   40   60

One inch equals 25.4 miles
One centimeter equals 16.1 kilometers

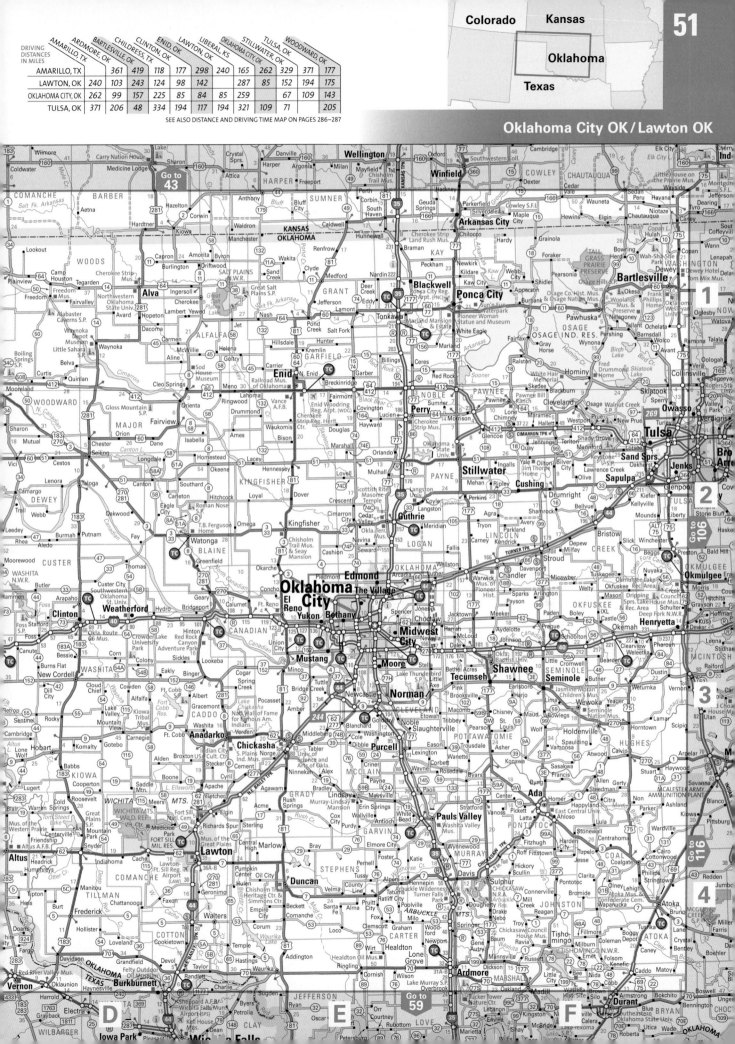

SEE ALSO DISTANCE AND DRIVING TIME MAP ON PAGES 286–287

DRIVING DISTANCES IN MILES	AMARILLO, TX	ARDMORE, OK	BARTLESVILLE, OK	CHILDRESS, TX	CLINTON, OK	ENID, OK	LAWTON, OK	LIBERAL, KS	OKLAHOMA CITY, OK	STILLWATER, OK	TULSA, OK	WOODWARD, OK
AMARILLO, TX		361	419	118	177	298	240	165	262	329	371	177
LAWTON, OK	240	103	243	124	98	142		287	85	152	194	175
OKLAHOMA CITY, OK	262	99	157	225	85	84	85	259		67	109	143
TULSA, OK	371	206	48	334	194	117	194	321	109	71		205

Nev. · California · Arizona · Mexico

0 mi 20 40
0 km 20 40 60
One inch equals 25.4 miles
One centimeter equals 16.1 kilometers

Los Angeles CA / Santa Barbara CA

PACIFIC OCEAN

Bakersfield, Santa Maria, San Luis Obispo, Morro Bay, Atascadero, Pismo Beach, Grover Beach, Lompoc, Santa Barbara, Goleta, Ventura, Oxnard, Camarillo, Thousand Oaks, Simi Valley, Santa Clarita, Lancaster, Palmdale, Los Angeles, Burbank, Pasadena, Glendale, Beverly Hills, Santa Monica, Malibu, Inglewood, Torrance, Long Beach, Anaheim, Santa Ana, Orange, Irvine, Huntington Beach, Newport Beach, Laguna Beach, San Clemente, Pomona, Fullerton, Ridgecrest, California City, Mojave, Tehachapi, Rosamond, Lamont, Arvin

Channel Islands Natl. Park, Santa Cruz Island, Santa Rosa Island, San Miguel I., San Nicolas Island, Santa Catalina Island, Avalon, San Clemente Island, Gulf of Santa Catalina

Go to 44 · Go to 45

1 2 3 4 · A B C

53

San Diego CA / Palm Springs CA

DRIVING DISTANCES IN MILES

	BAKERSFIELD, CA	BARSTOW, CA	BLYTHE, CA	EL CENTRO, CA	LOS ANGELES, CA	NEEDLES, CA	PALM SPRINGS, CA	SAN BERNARDINO, CA	SAN DIEGO, CA	SAN LUIS OBISPO, CA	SANTA BARBARA, CA	YUMA, AZ
LOS ANGELES, CA	111	118	230	234		263	110	62	124	190	97	294
SAN DIEGO, CA	234	181	211	117	124	326	143	111		314	221	177
SANTA BARBARA, CA	150	213	325	330	97	358	205	157	221	93		391
YUMA, AZ	403	294	103	65	294	187	171	225	177	483	391	

SEE ALSO DISTANCE AND DRIVING TIME MAP ON PAGES 286–287

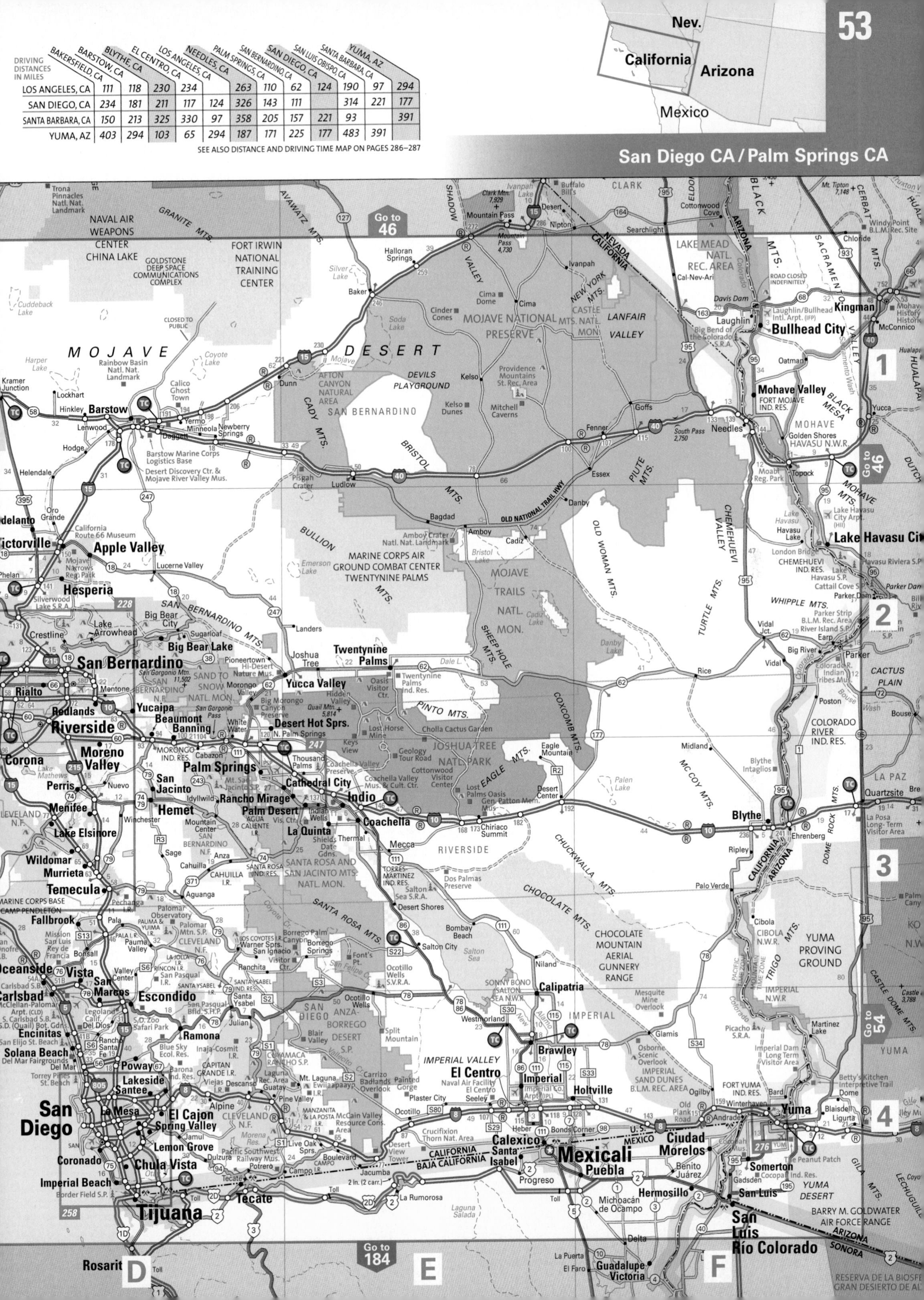

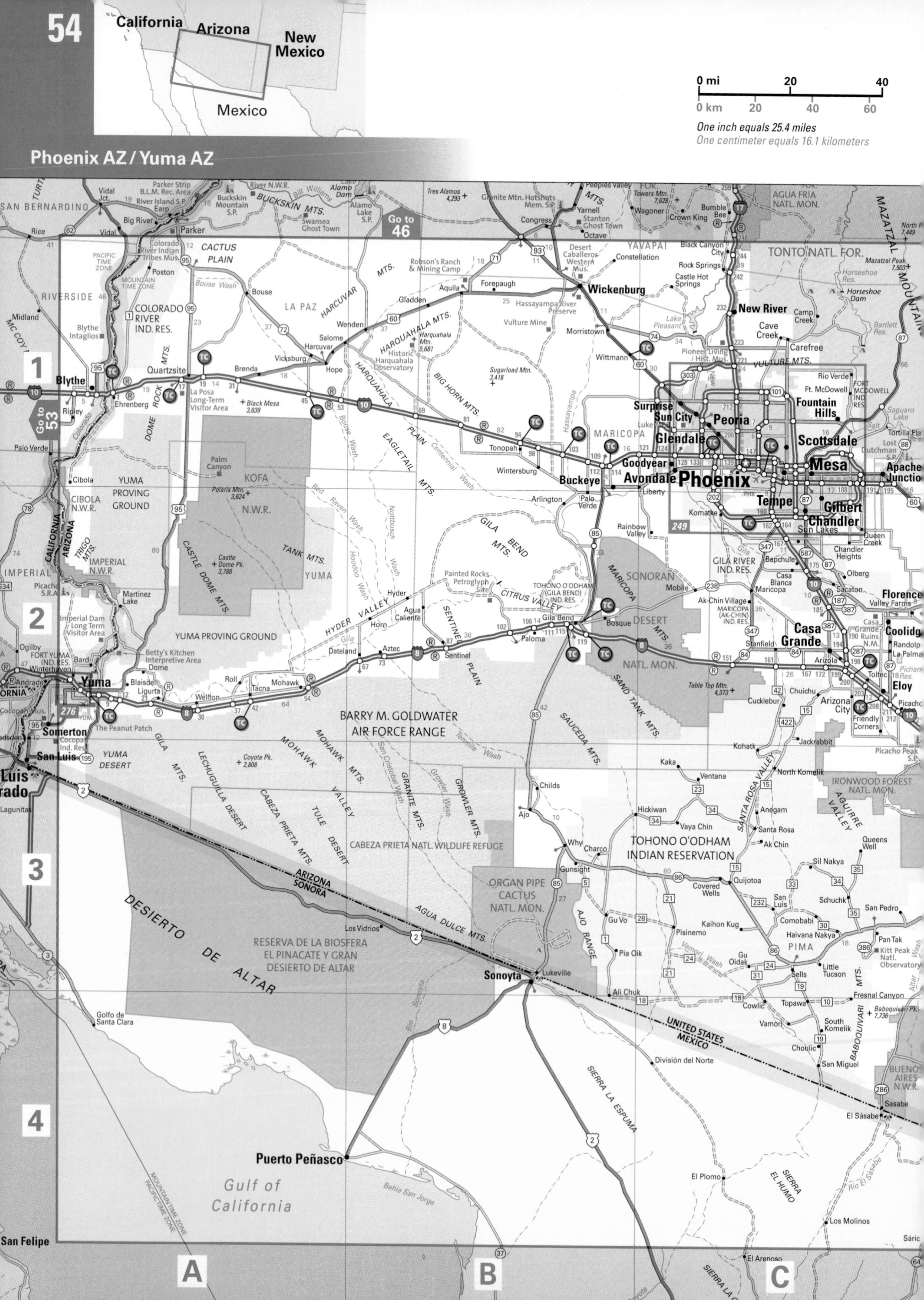
California
Arizona
New Mexico
Mexico
0 mi 20 40
0 km 20 40 60
One inch equals 25.4 miles
One centimeter equals 16.1 kilometers
Go to 46
Go to 53
1
2
3
4
A
B
C
Blythe
Ehrenberg
Quartzsite
Brenda
Parker
Poston
Vidal
Vidal Jct.
Rice
Big River
Earp
Bouse
Salome
Harcuvar
Hope
Vicksburg
Wenden
Aquila
Forepaugh
Congress
Wickenburg
Morristown
Wittmann
Surprise
Sun City
Peoria
Glendale
Goodyear
Avondale
Buckeye
Phoenix
Scottsdale
Mesa
Tempe
Gilbert
Chandler
Fountain Hills
New River
Cave Creek
Carefree
Casa Grande
Coolidge
Florence
Eloy
Arizona City
Gila Bend
Maricopa
Tonopah
Wintersburg
Arlington
Palo Verde
Yuma
Somerton
San Luis
Wellton
Tacna
Mohawk
Dateland
Hyder
Sentinel
Ajo
Why
Gunsight
Lukeville
Sonoyta
Sells
Puerto Peñasco
Gulf of California
San Felipe
Golfo de Santa Clara
Los Vidrios
Bahia San Jorge
El Sásabe
Sasabe
El Plomo
Los Molinos
El Arenoso
Sáric
División del Norte
KOFA N.W.R.
YUMA PROVING GROUND
BARRY M. GOLDWATER AIR FORCE RANGE
CABEZA PRIETA NATL. WILDLIFE REFUGE
ORGAN PIPE CACTUS NATL. MON.
SONORAN DESERT NATL. MON.
TOHONO O'ODHAM INDIAN RESERVATION
GILA RIVER IND. RES.
COLORADO RIVER IND. RES.
IRONWOOD FOREST NATL. MON.
TONTO NATL. FOR.
AGUA FRIA NATL. MON.
RESERVA DE LA BIOSFERA EL PINACATE Y GRAN DESIERTO DE ALTAR
DESIERTO DE ALTAR
UNITED STATES
MEXICO
ARIZONA
SONORA
MARICOPA
YAVAPAI
LA PAZ
PIMA
YUMA
RIVERSIDE
IMPERIAL
SAN BERNARDINO

DRIVING DISTANCES IN MILES	BLYTHE, CA	CASA GRANDE, AZ	DOUGLAS, AZ	EAGAR, AZ	GLOBE, AZ	LORDSBURG, NM	NOGALES, AZ	PHOENIX, AZ	SAFFORD, AZ	SILVER CITY, NM	TUCSON, AZ	YUMA, AZ
LORDSBURG, NM	417	228	101	184	155		185	278	77	45	161	401
PHOENIX, AZ	140	50	237	227	92	278	181		169	322	118	183
TUCSON, AZ	258	68	120	242	106	161	65	118	128	205		241
YUMA, AZ	103	179	360	401	265	401	304	183	368	446	241	

SEE ALSO DISTANCE AND DRIVING TIME MAP ON PAGES 286–287

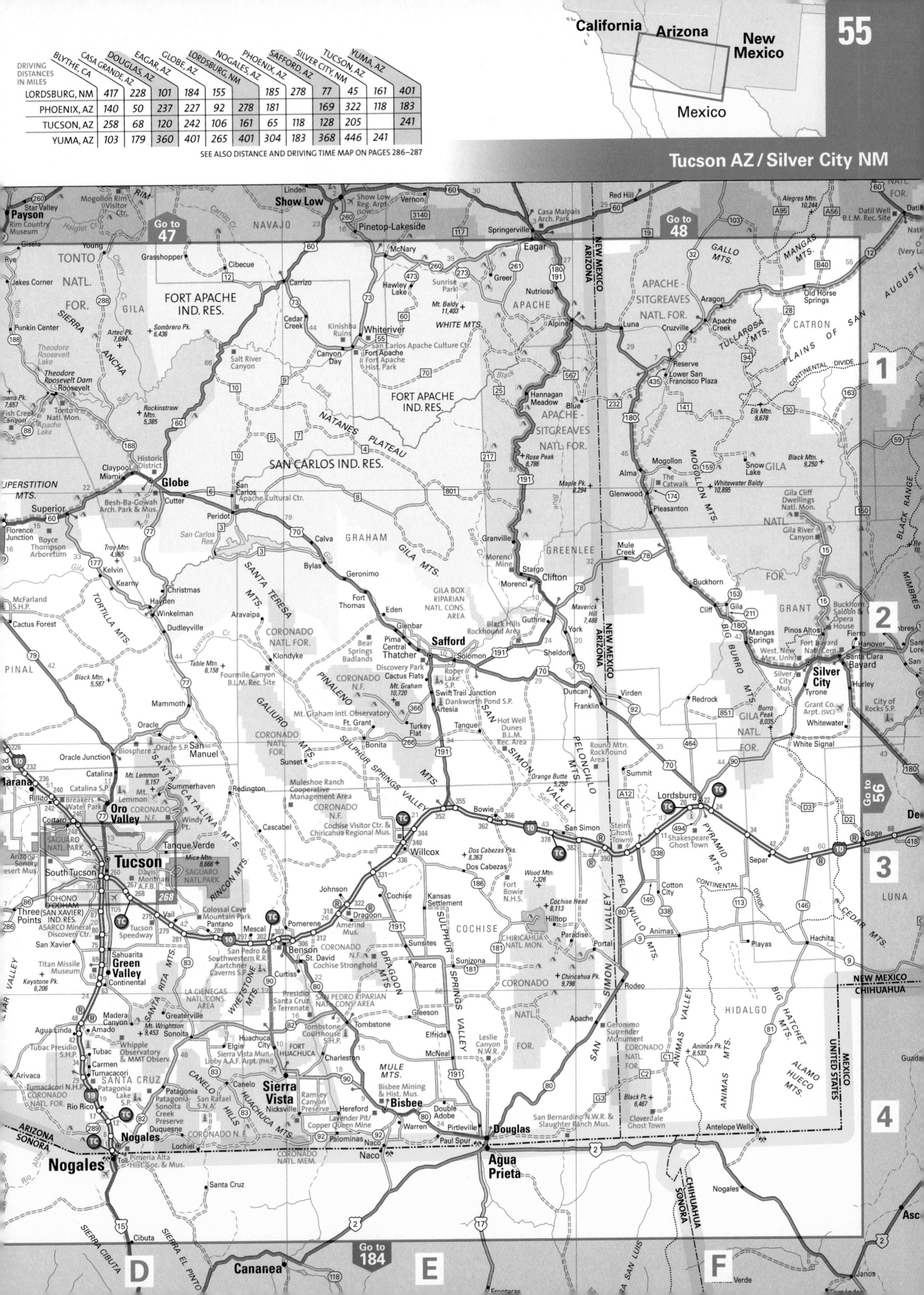

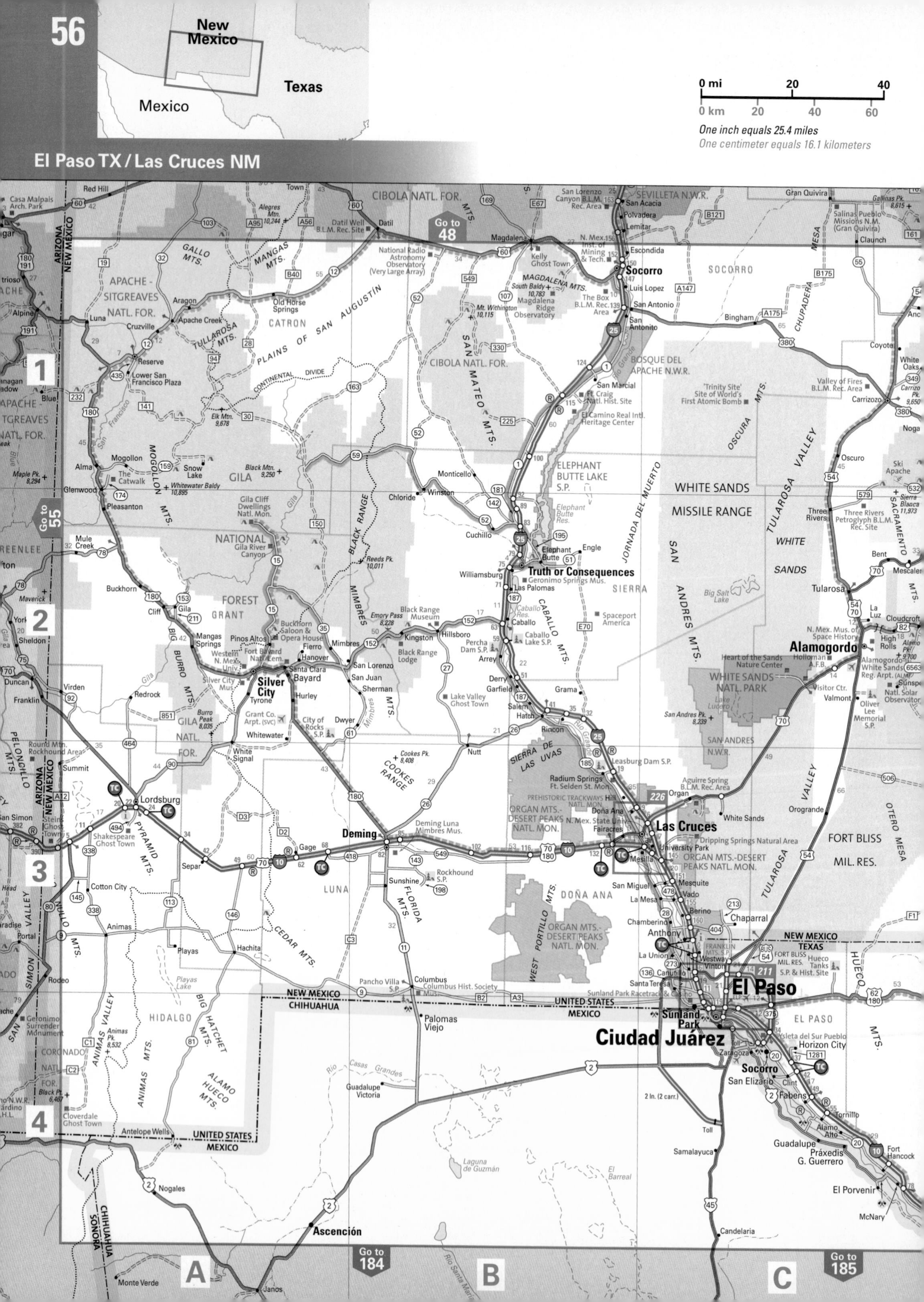

0 mi   20   40
0 km   20   40   60
One inch equals 25.4 miles
One centimeter equals 16.1 kilometers

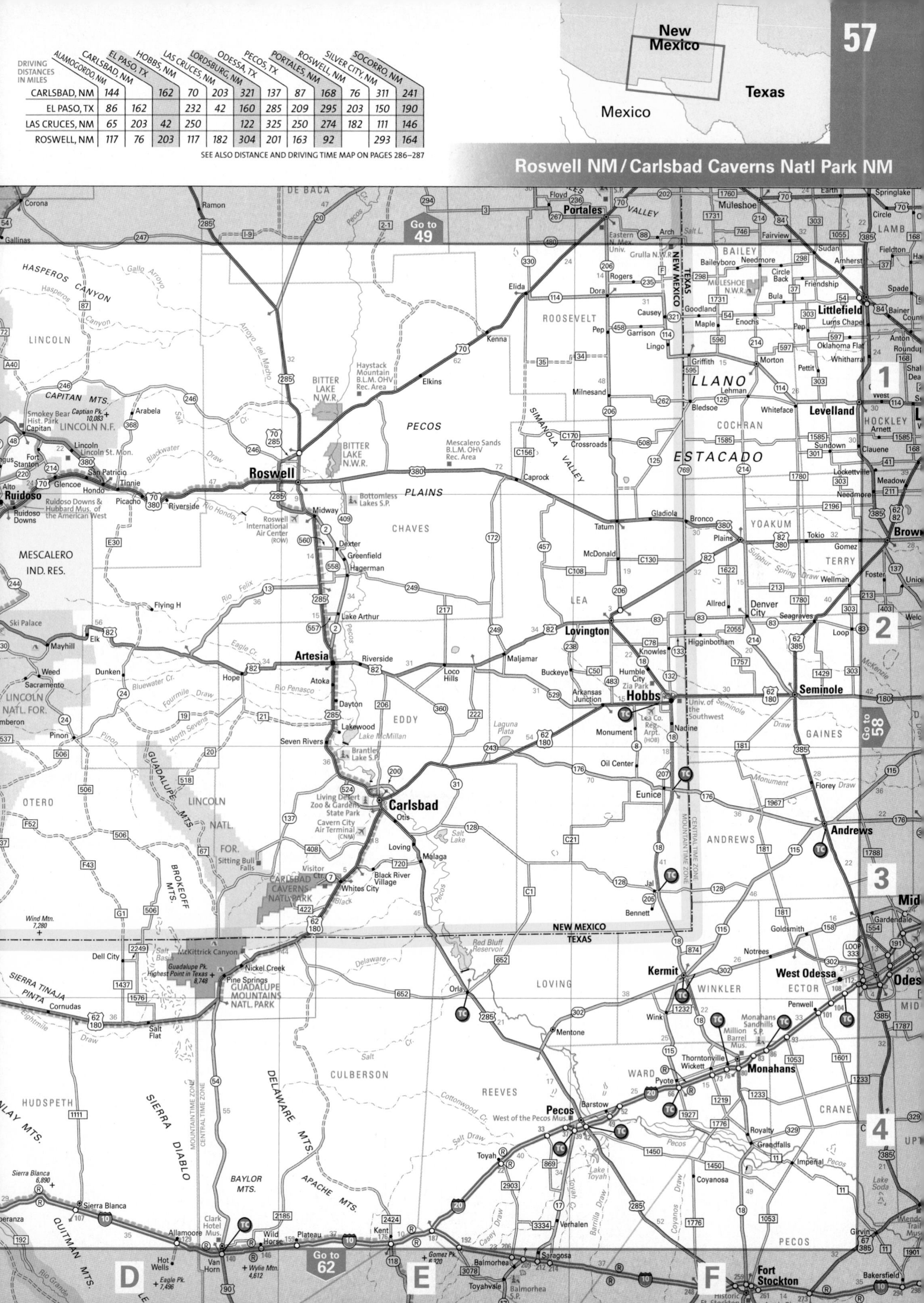

New Mexico

Texas

Mexico

SEE ALSO DISTANCE AND DRIVING TIME MAP ON PAGES 286–287

DRIVING DISTANCES IN MILES	ALAMOGORDO, NM	CARLSBAD, NM	EL PASO, TX	HOBBS, NM	LAS CRUCES, NM	LORDSBURG, NM	ODESSA, TX	PECOS, TX	PORTALES, NM	ROSWELL, NM	SILVER CITY, NM	SOCORRO, NM
CARLSBAD, NM	144		162	70	203	321	137	87	168	76	311	241
EL PASO, TX	86	162		232	42	160	285	209	295	203	150	190
LAS CRUCES, NM	65	203	42	250		122	325	250	274	182	111	146
ROSWELL, NM	117	76	203	117	182	304	201	163	92		293	164

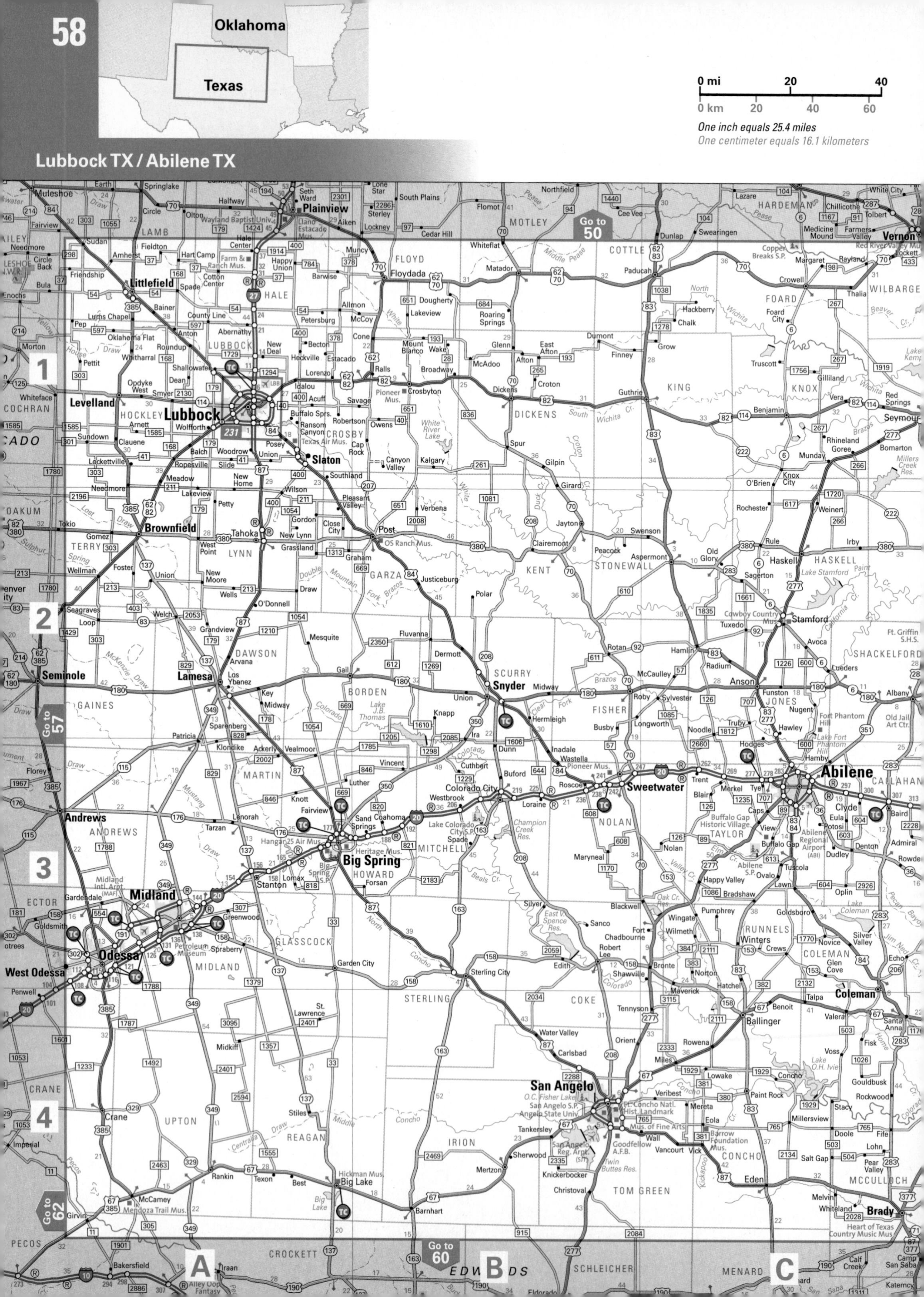

Oklahoma

Texas

0 mi 20 40
0 km 20 40 60
One inch equals 25.4 miles
One centimeter equals 16.1 kilometers

DRIVING DISTANCES IN MILES	ABILENE, TX	BIG SPRING, TX	BROWNWOOD, TX	DALLAS, TX	FORT WORTH, TX	LUBBOCK, TX	ODESSA, TX	SAN ANGELO, TX	SHERMAN, TX	TEMPLE, TX	WACO, TX	WICHITA FALLS, TX
ABILENE, TX		110	78	191	153	166	176	91	249	194	235	144
DALLAS, TX	191	298	190		32	354	364	265	64	130	94	141
LUBBOCK, TX	166	106	247	354	317		142	185	322	358	399	207
WACO, TX	235	343	124	94	87	399	409	219	159	40		201

SEE ALSO DISTANCE AND DRIVING TIME MAP ON PAGES 286–287

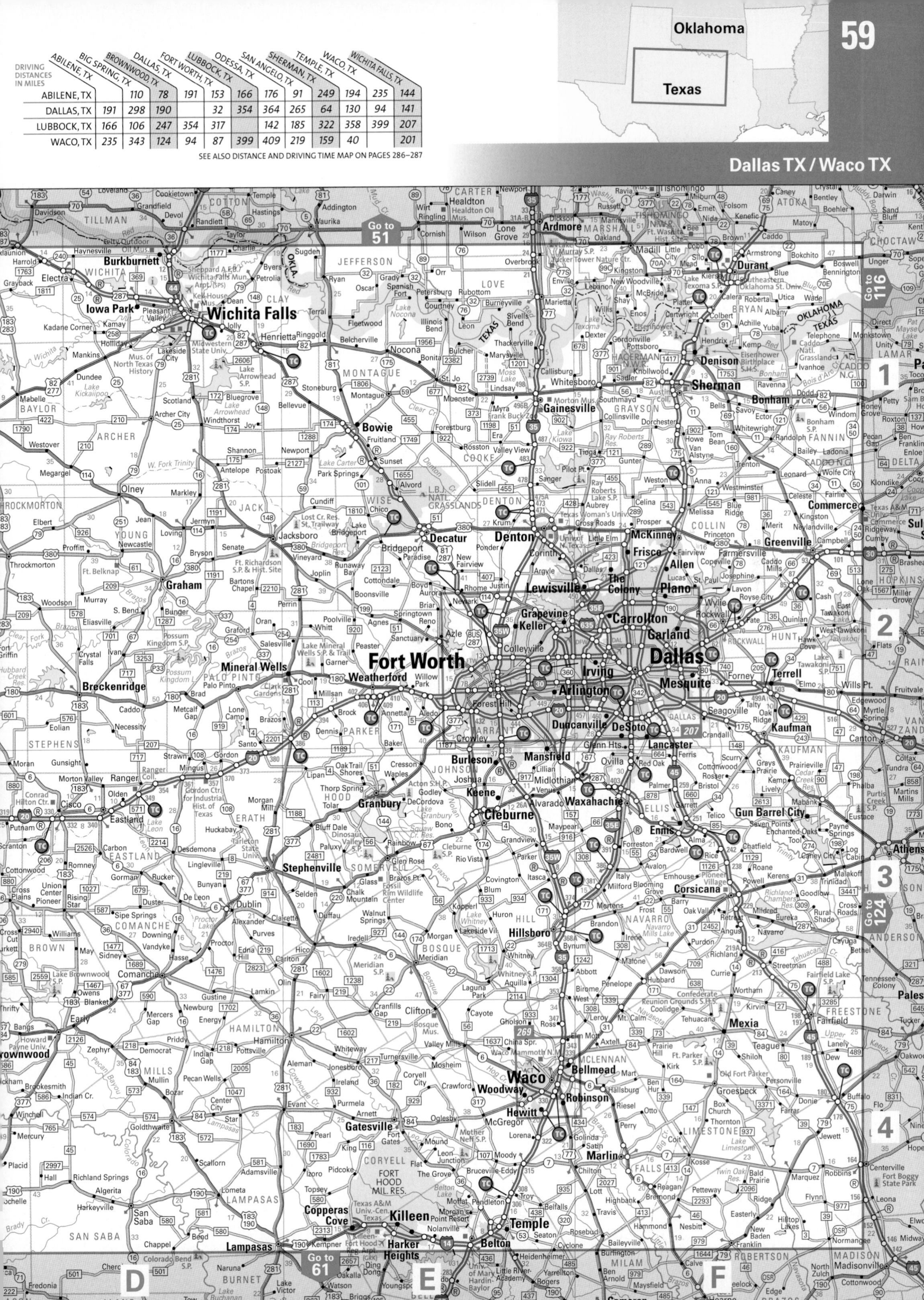

Texas

Mexico

0 mi   20   40
0 km   20   40   60

One inch equals 25.4 miles
One centimeter equals 16.1 kilometers

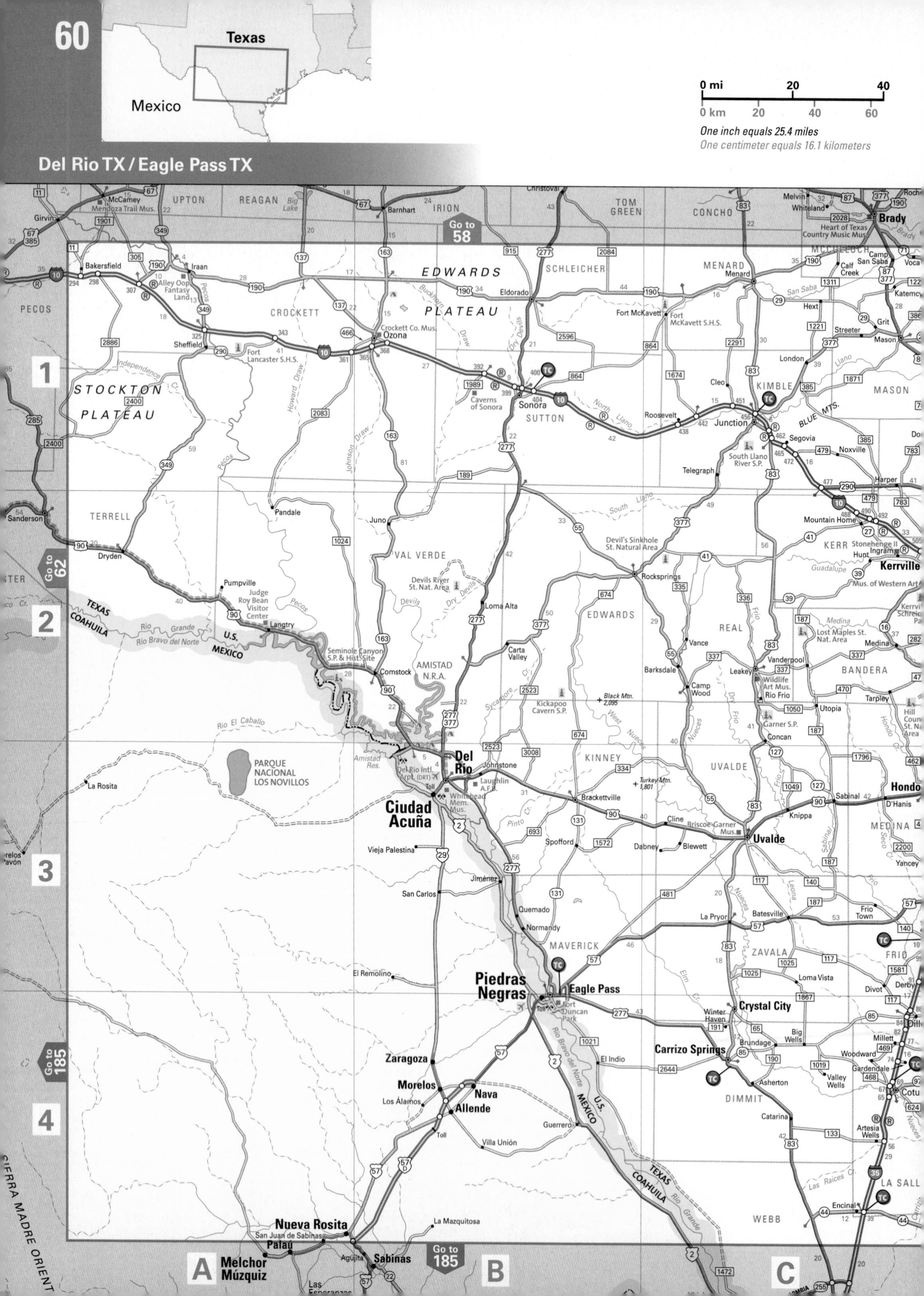

1
2
3
4

A   **B**   **C**

Texas

Mexico

DRIVING DISTANCES IN MILES	AUSTIN, TX	BEEVILLE, TX	COLLEGE STATION, TX	COLUMBUS, TX	DEL RIO, TX	EAGLE PASS, TX	FREDERICKSBURG, TX	SAN ANTONIO, TX	SONORA, TX	TEMPLE, TX	UVALDE, TX	VICTORIA, TX
AUSTIN, TX		136	108	92	229	226	78	78	244	67	159	123
DEL RIO, TX	229	235	322	277		55	178	152	89	295	70	268
SAN ANTONIO, TX	78	110	171	128	152	145	67		172	144	82	118
VICTORIA, TX	123	56	160	87	268	254	186	118	292	187	198	

SEE ALSO DISTANCE AND DRIVING TIME MAP ON PAGES 286–287

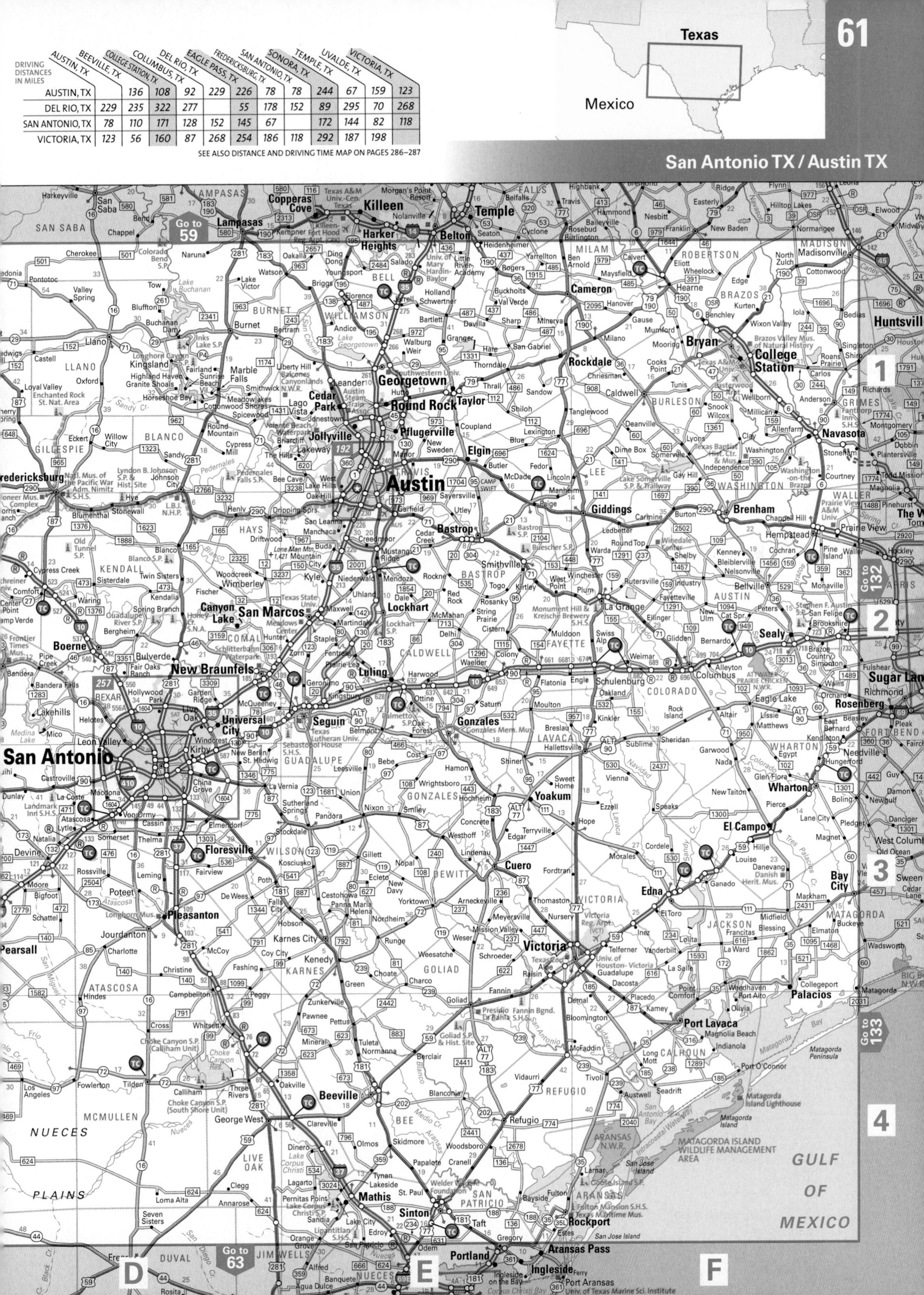

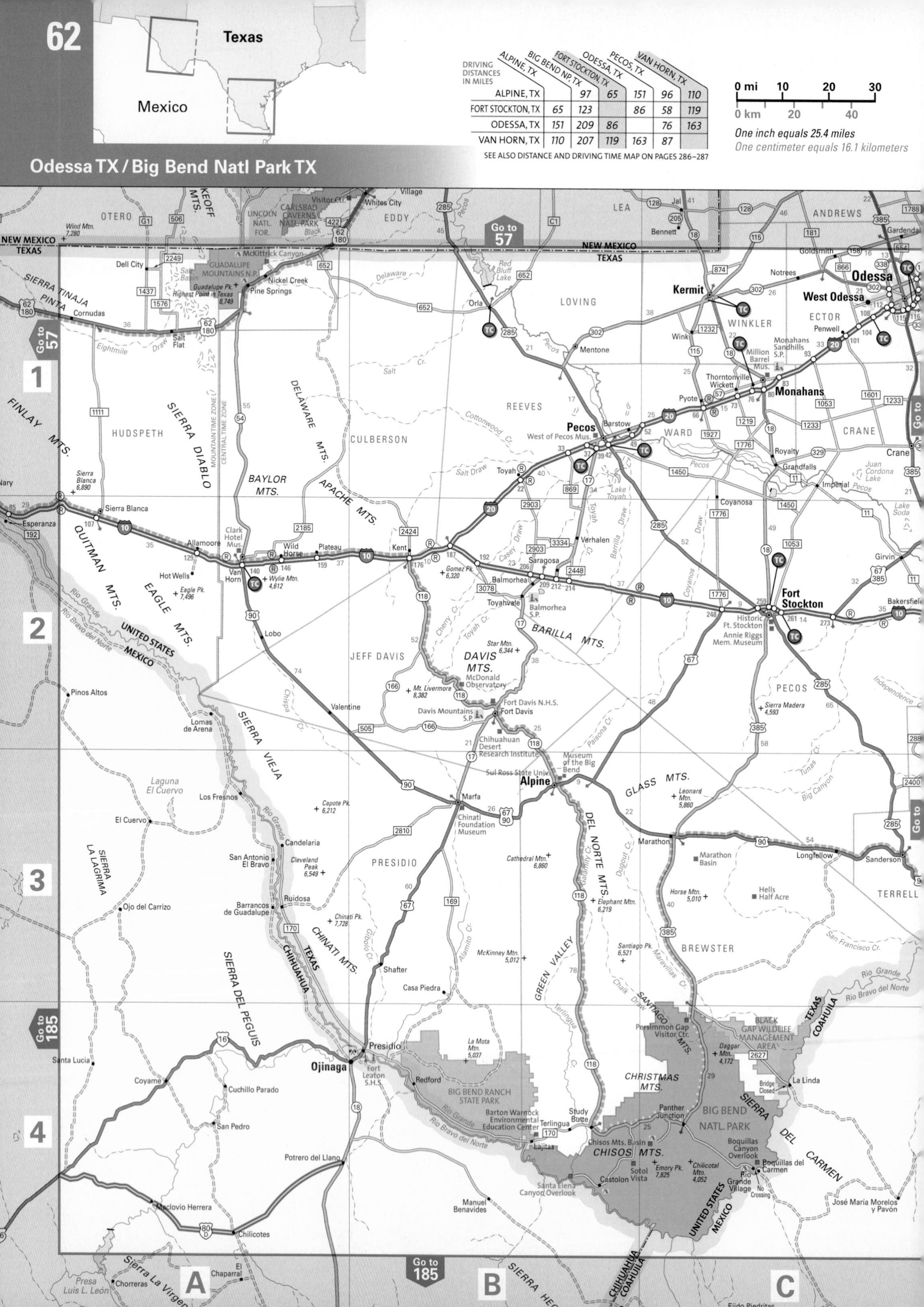

DRIVING DISTANCES IN MILES	ALPINE, TX	BIG BEND NP, TX	FORT STOCKTON, TX	ODESSA, TX	PECOS, TX	VAN HORN, TX
ALPINE, TX		97	65	151	96	110
FORT STOCKTON, TX	65	123		86	58	119
ODESSA, TX	151	209	86		76	163
VAN HORN, TX	110	207	119	163	87	

SEE ALSO DISTANCE AND DRIVING TIME MAP ON PAGES 286–287

0 mi 10 20 30
0 km 20 40

One inch equals 25.4 miles
One centimeter equals 16.1 kilometers

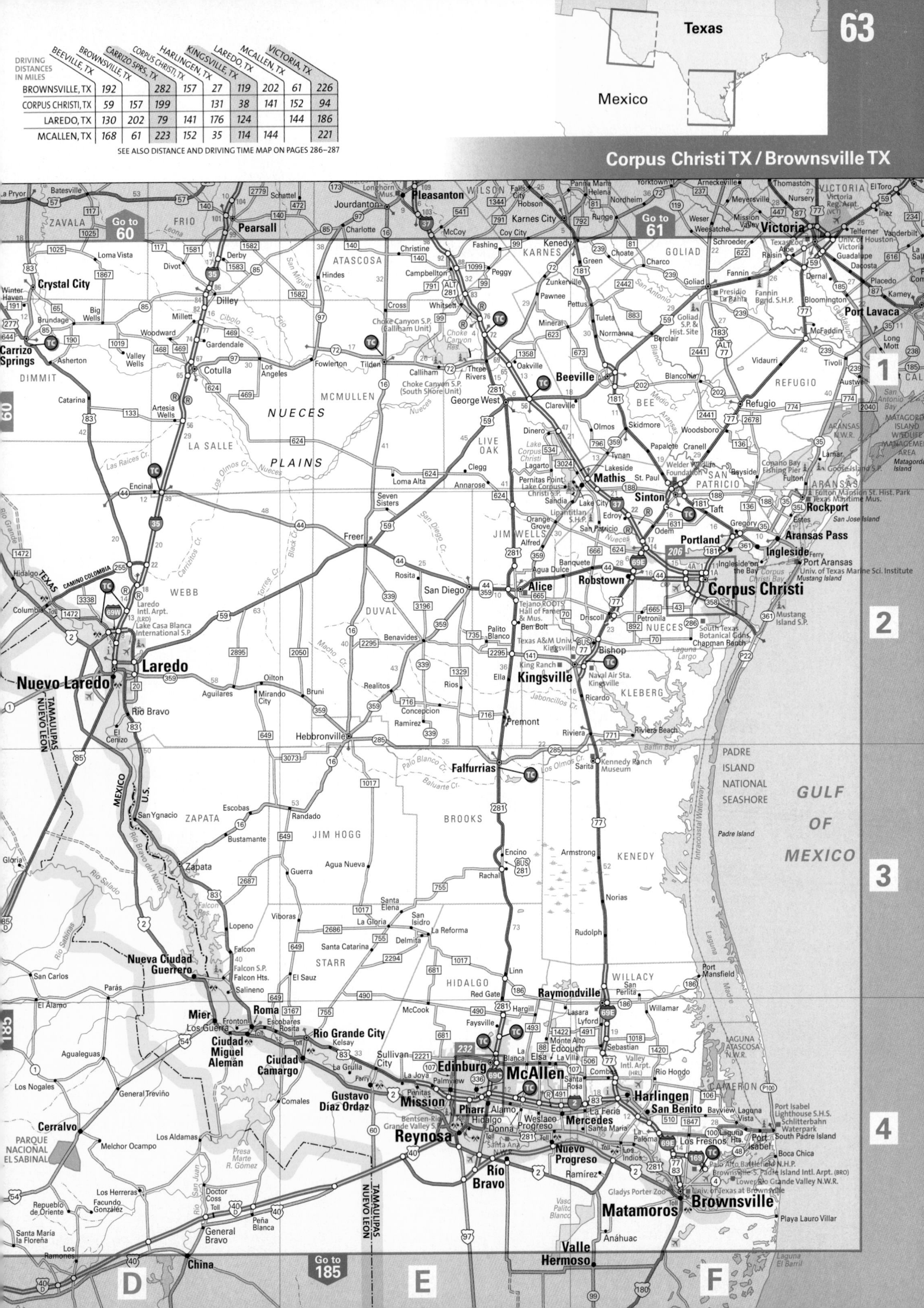

DRIVING DISTANCES IN MILES

	BEEVILLE, TX	BROWNSVILLE, TX	CARRIZO SPRS., TX	CORPUS CHRISTI, TX	HARLINGEN, TX	KINGSVILLE, TX	LAREDO, TX	McALLEN, TX	VICTORIA, TX
BROWNSVILLE, TX	192		282	157	27	119	202	61	226
CORPUS CHRISTI, TX	59	157	199		131	38	141	152	94
LAREDO, TX	130	202	79	141	176	124		144	186
McALLEN, TX	168	61	223	152	35	114	144		221

SEE ALSO DISTANCE AND DRIVING TIME MAP ON PAGES 286–287

Manitoba
Ontario
Minnesota
Michigan
Wisconsin

0 mi 20 40
0 km 20 40 60
One inch equals 25.4 miles
One centimeter equals 16.1 kilometers

Go to 168

Go to 19

Go to 66

Go to 67

International Falls
Fort Frances
Bemidji
Grand Rapids
Hibbing
Virginia
Duluth
Superior
Detroit Lakes
Baxter
Brainerd
Hermantown
Cloquet
Park Rapids

MANITOBA
ONTARIO
MINNESOTA
CANADA
U.S.
WISCONSIN

LAKE OF THE WOODS
Lake of the Woods
VOYAGEURS NATL. PARK
QUETICO PROVINCIAL PARK
SUPERIOR NATIONAL FOREST
CHIPPEWA N.F.
ITASCA
KOOCHICHING
MESABI RANGE
RED LAKE IND. RES.
BOIS FORTE IND. RES.
LEECH LAKE IND. RES.
FOND DU LAC IND. RES.
WHITE EARTH IND. RES.

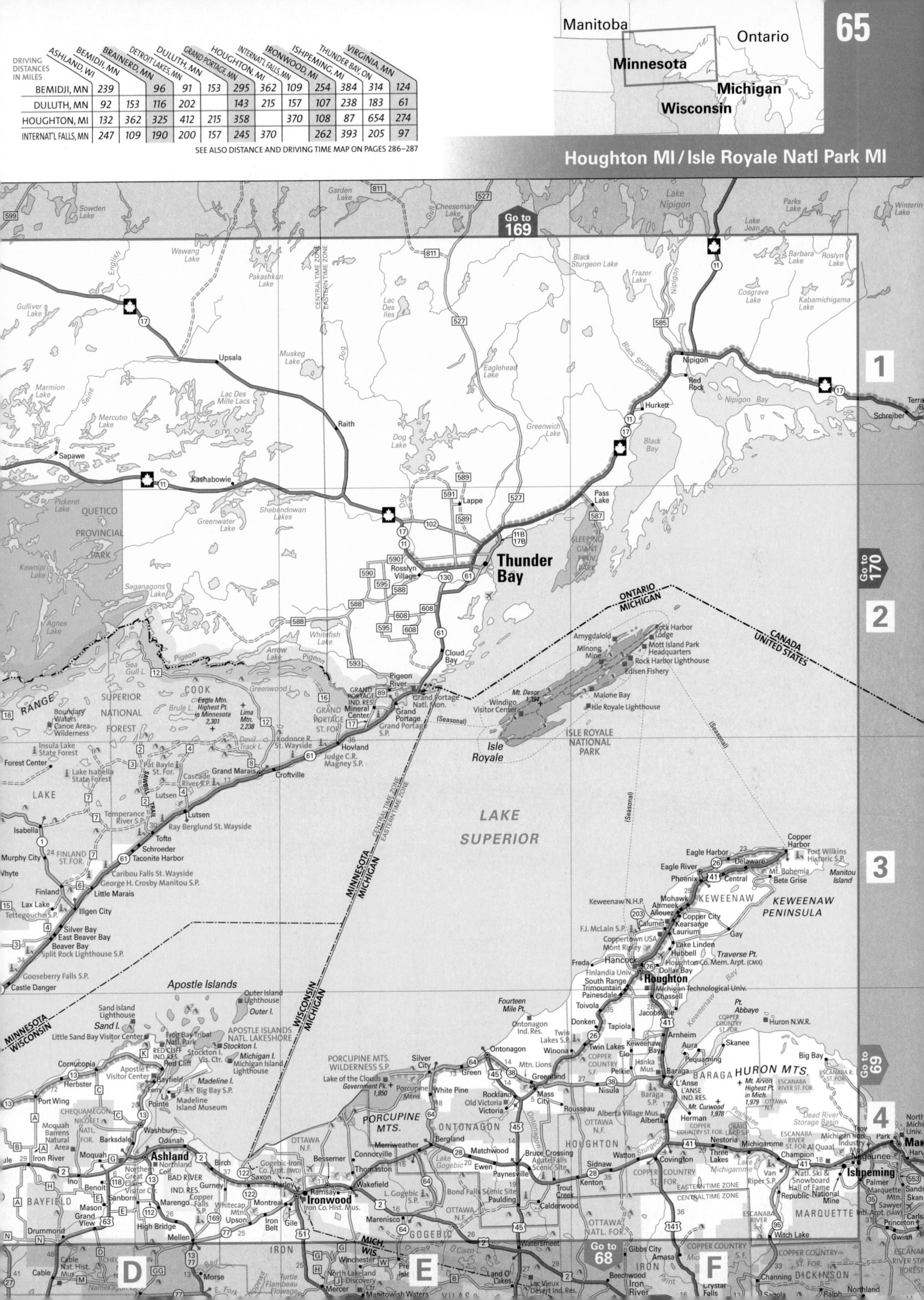

SEE ALSO DISTANCE AND DRIVING TIME MAP ON PAGES 286-287

DRIVING DISTANCES IN MILES	ASHLAND, WI	BEMIDJI, MN	BRAINERD, MN	DETROIT LAKES, MN	DULUTH, MN	GRAND PORTAGE, MN	HOUGHTON, MI	INTERNAT'L FALLS, MN	IRONWOOD, MI	ISHPEMING, MI	THUNDER BAY, ON	VIRGINIA, MN
BEMIDJI, MN	239		96	91	153	295	362	109	254	384	314	124
DULUTH, MN	92	153	116	202		143	215	157	107	238	183	61
HOUGHTON, MI	132	362	325	412	215	358		370	108	87	654	274
INTERNAT'L FALLS, MN	247	109	190	200	157	245	370		262	393	205	97

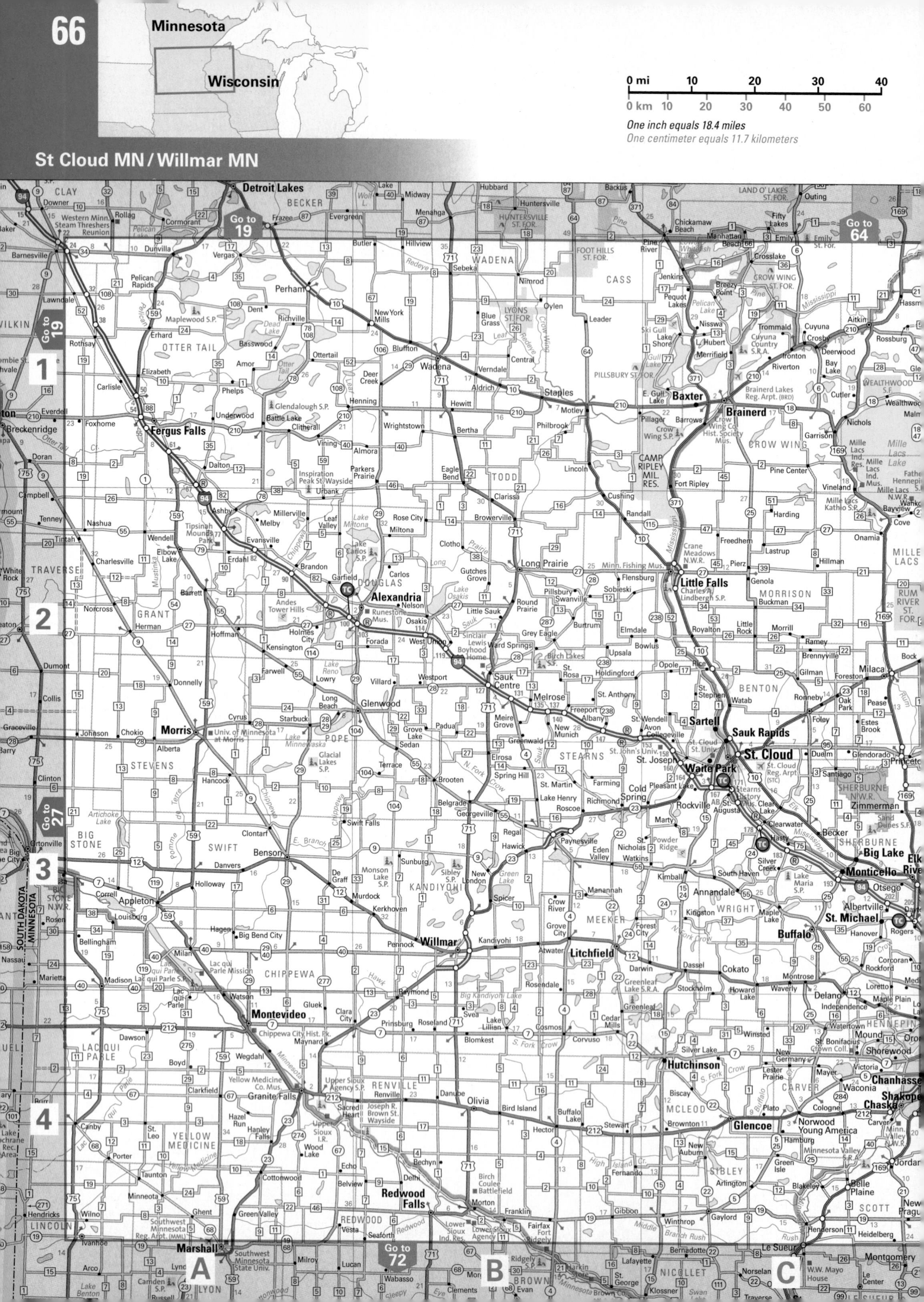

St Cloud MN / Willmar MN

0 mi   10   20   30   40
0 km 10 20 30 40 50 60
One inch equals 18.4 miles
One centimeter equals 11.7 kilometers

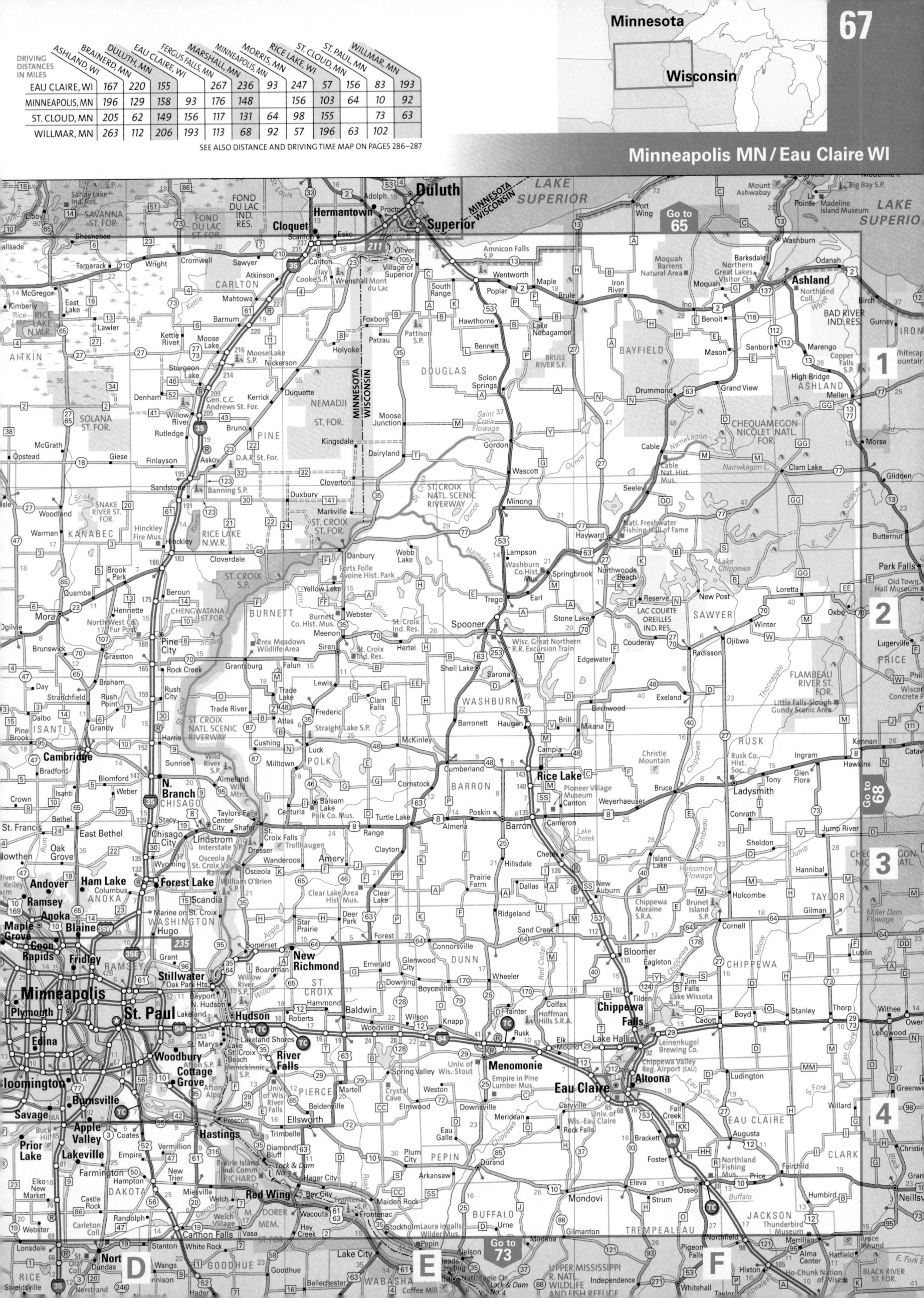

DRIVING DISTANCES IN MILES	ASHLAND, WI	BRAINERD, MN	DULUTH, MN	EAU CLAIRE, WI	FERGUS FALLS, MN	MARSHALL, MN	MINNEAPOLIS, MN	MORRIS, MN	RICE LAKE, WI	ST. CLOUD, MN	ST. PAUL, MN	WILLMAR, MN
EAU CLAIRE, WI	167	220	155		267	236	93	247	57	156	83	193
MINNEAPOLIS, MN	196	129	158	93	176	148		156	103	64	10	92
ST. CLOUD, MN	205	62	149	156	117	131	64	98	155		73	63
WILLMAR, MN	263	112	206	193	113	68	92	57	196	63	102	

SEE ALSO DISTANCE AND DRIVING TIME MAP ON PAGES 286–287

Wisconsin

Michigan

Green Bay WI / Wausau WI

0 mi 10 20 30 40
0 km 10 20 30 40 50 60

One inch equals 18.4 miles
One centimeter equals 11.7 kilometers

Wisconsin

Michigan

DRIVING DISTANCES IN MILES	ESCANABA, MI	GREEN BAY, WI	IRON MOUNTAIN, MI	IRONWOOD, MI	L'ANSE, MI	MANISTIQUE, MI	MARINETTE, WI	MARQUETTE, MI	RHINELANDER, WI	STEVENS POINT, WI	TRAVERSE CITY, MI	WAUSAU, WI
ESCANABA, MI		111	52	178	134	54	57	65	132	185	252	171
GREEN BAY, WI	111		96	202	178	165	54	175	124	87	363	93
MARQUETTE, MI	65	175	79	145	70	86	122		147	238	269	204
WAUSAU, WI	171	93	133	121	176	225	112	204	58	35	423	

SEE ALSO DISTANCE AND DRIVING TIME MAP ON PAGES 286–287

Ontario

Michigan

0 mi — 10 — 20 — 30 — 40
0 km 10 — 20 — 30 — 40 — 50 — 60
One inch equals 18.4 miles
One centimeter equals 11.7 kilometers

LAKE SUPERIOR

Go to 170

Searchmont

PICTURED ROCKS NATIONAL LAKESHORE

Great Lakes Shipwreck Museum
Whitefish Pt. Bird Observatory
Whitefish Point

CANADA U.S.

Sault Ste. Marie

ONTARIO MICHIGAN

Grand Island
GRAND ISLAND NATL. REC. AREA

Au Sable Pt.
Au Train
Christmas
Munising Falls
Melstrand
Miners Castle
Chapel Basin

Au Sable
Grand Sable Dunes
Beaver Basin Overlook
Grand Marais
Deer Park

Muskallonge Lake S.P.

Lower Falls
Paradise
Point Iroquois Light

Heyden

1 Munising
Wetmore
Shingleton
Wagner Falls Scenic Site

Forest Lake
Chatham
Limestone
Traunik

LUCE

LAKE SUPERIOR STATE FOREST

Dollarville
Newberry
McMillan
Seney

TAHQUAMENON FALLS S.P.
Upper Falls

Lake Superior State Univ.

Soo Locks
Sault Ste. Marie
Soo Valley Camp
Echo Bay

Gros Cap

Sugar I.

Echo Lake

Desbarats

Bay Mills Ind. Community
Brimley
Pendills Creek Natl. Fish Hatchery
Raco
Brimley S.P.

Dafter
Rosedale
Bay Mills Ind. Community
Barbeau
Neebish
Richards Landing
Hilton Beach
Kentvale

ALGER

Cleveland Cliffs Basin

SENEY N.W.R.
SCHOOLCRAFT

Germfask

CHIPPEWA

HIAWATHA

Eckerman
Strongs
Hulbert
Soo Junction
McLeods Corner

HIAWATHA NATIONAL FOREST

Kinross
Chippewa Co. Intl. Arpt. (CIU)

HIAWATHA NATIONAL FOREST
Big Spring
Palms Book S.P.
Indian Lake S.P.

Steuben
Blaney Park
Gould City
Curtis
Helmer
Gilchrist
Garnet
Rexton
Trout Lake
Ozark
Fibre
Rudyard
Pickford
Stalwart
Goetzville
Cedarville

Manistique
Thompson
Gulliver
Seul Choix Point Lighthouse
Seul Choix Pt.
Scott Pt.
Naubinway
Epoufette
Brevort
Gould City

MACKINAC NATIONAL FOREST

LAKE SUPERIOR ST. FOR.

SUPERIOR

Cooks
Garden Corners
Nahma
Fayette
Fayette Historic S.P.

Isabella
Garden
Pt. aux Barques

DELTA

Big Bay De Noc
Portage Bay

LAKE SUPERIOR STATE FOREST

Garden I.
Hog I.
Beaver Island Marine Museum
High I.
St. James
Welke Arpt. (6Y8)
Michigan Islands N.W.R.

Moran
Allenville
Sand Dunes
Gros Cap
Father Marquette Natl. Mem.
St. Ignace

Fort Mackinac
Mackinac Island S.P.
Mackinac Island
Les Cheneaux Islands

St. Martin Bay
Hessel

ST. FOR.

Go to 69

Fairport
Pt. Detour
Little Summer I.
Summer I.

LAKE MICHIGAN

North Fox I.
South Fox I.

Beaver Island
MACKINAW ST. FOR.

Sturgeon Bay
WILDERNESS S.P.
Colonial Michilimackinac
Mackinaw City
Historic Mill Creek
Pointe Aux Pins

Straits of Mackinac
Bois Blanc I.

LAKE HURON

MACKINAW ST. FOR.

Cross Village
Bliss
Levering
Carp Lake
Ferry
Cheboygan S.P.

Cheboygan

Good Hart
Pellston Reg. Arpt. (PLN)
Pellston
Brutus
Alverno
Grace
Hammond Bay
Huron Beach

St. Martin I.
Washington I.
Rock Island S.P.
Green Bay N.W.R.

MICHIGAN / WISCONSIN

EMMET

Mackinaw St. For.
Pleasant View
Nub's Nob
Boyne Highlands
Harbor Springs
Petoskey S.P.
Alanson
Indian River
Topinabee
Mullett Lake
Burt Lake
Aloha S.P.
Onaway S.P.
Black Lake
Ocqueoc Falls
Ocqueoc

CHEBOYGAN
Burt Lake S.P.
Afton
Tower
Onaway
Millersburg
Hawks

PRESQUE ISLE

Wequetonsing
Petoskey
Conway
Oden
Epsilon

Petoskey
Bay View
Little Traverse Bay

Mt. McSauba
Bay Shore
Lake Charlevoix
Fisherman's Island S.P.
Charlevoix Mun. Arpt. (CVX)
Charlevoix

WISCONSIN / MICHIGAN

Little Traverse Bay Ind. Res.
Horton Bay
Clarion
Walloon Lake
Wolverine

MACKINAW STATE FOREST

3 Norwood
Ironton
Young
Walloon Lake
Boyne City
Boyne Mtn.
Boyne Falls

OTSEGO
Vanderbilt
Otsego Club
Treetops Resort

Clear Lake S.P.

Grand Traverse Lighthouse
Leelanau S.P.
Cathead Pt.
North Manitou I.
Northport
Omena

Eastport
Ellsworth
East Jordan
Elmira
Gaylord

Johannesburg
Vienna
Atlanta

MONTMORENCY

North Manitou I.
South Manitou I.
Grand Traverse Bay
Leland
Lake Leelanau

CHARLEVOIX

Central Lake
ANTRIM

Torch Lake
Bellaire
Alba

MACKINAW ST. FOR.

Oak Grove
Otsego Lake S.P.
Otsego Lake
Arbutus Beach
Lewiston

SLEEPING BEAR DUNES NATL. LAKESHORE
The Homestead
Glen Haven
Pierce Stocking Scenic Drive
Glen Arbor

Suttons Bay
Peshawbestown
Old Mission Point Lighthouse
Old Mission

Kewadin
Elk Rapids
Clam River
Shanty Creek
Mancelona
Waters

CAMP GRAYLING JOINT MANEUVER TRAINING CTR.

Comins
Fairview

LEELANAU
Maple City
Cedar
L. Leelanau
Spirit of the Woods Museum
Music House Museum
Rapid City
Kalkaska

MACKINAW ST. FOR.

Sleeping Bear Dunes Natl. Lakeshore Visitors Center
Empire

Hickory Hills
Alden
Darragh
Frederic
Lovells

OSCODA

4 BENZIE
Honor
Interlochen
Lake Ann
Traverse City S.P.
Bates
Williamsburg
Acme

Traverse City
Cherry Capital Arpt. (TVC)

Grawn
Grayling
Hartwick Pines S.P.
Hartwick Pines Logging Mus.
Red Oak

KALKASKA

Frankfort
Elberta
Beulah
Benzonia
Benzie Area Hist. Mus.
Center for the Arts
Bendon
Karlin
Interlochen S.P.
Mayfield
South Boardman
Spencer
Hanson Hills
Camp Grayling J.M.T.C.

North Higgins Lake S.P.
Mio
McKinley

PERE MARQUETTE S.F.

Arcadia
Pt. Betsie
Crystal L.
Thompsonville
Copemish
Buckley
Fife Lake
Kingsley
Kalkaska

GRAND TRAVERSE

Pierport
Crystal Mtn.

MANISTEE
WEXFORD
Sherman
Manton
Moorestown
Civilian Conservation Corps Museum
Higgins Lake
Roscommon

CRAWFORD HURON NATL. FOR.

Luzerne

Go to 75
Go to 76

Kaleva
Norwalk
Mesick
Yuma
Meauwataka

MISSAUKEE
Missaukee Mountain
Jennings

PERE MARQUETTE ST. FOR.
Houghton Lake
South Higgins Lake S.P.

St. Helen
Rose City

OGEMAW

Rifle River Rec. Area
South Branch
Curtisville

Ontario

Michigan

DRIVING DISTANCES IN MILES	ALPENA, MI	CHEBOYGAN, MI	GAYLORD, MI	GRAYLING, MI	MACKINAW CITY, MI	MANISTIQUE, MI	MUNISING, MI	PETOSKEY, MI	ROGERS CITY, MI	SAULT STE. MARIE, MI	SUDBURY, ON	TRAVERSE CITY, MI
ALPENA, MI		78	76	95	94	187	215	101	38	148	334	141
MACKINAW CITY, MI	94	16	60	87		95	123	38	58	57	242	106
SAULT STE. MARIE, MI	148	71	114	142	57	120	120	93	112		186	160
TRAVERSE CITY, MI	141	115	65	52	106	198	226	67	135	160	346	

SEE ALSO DISTANCE AND DRIVING TIME MAP ON PAGES 286–287

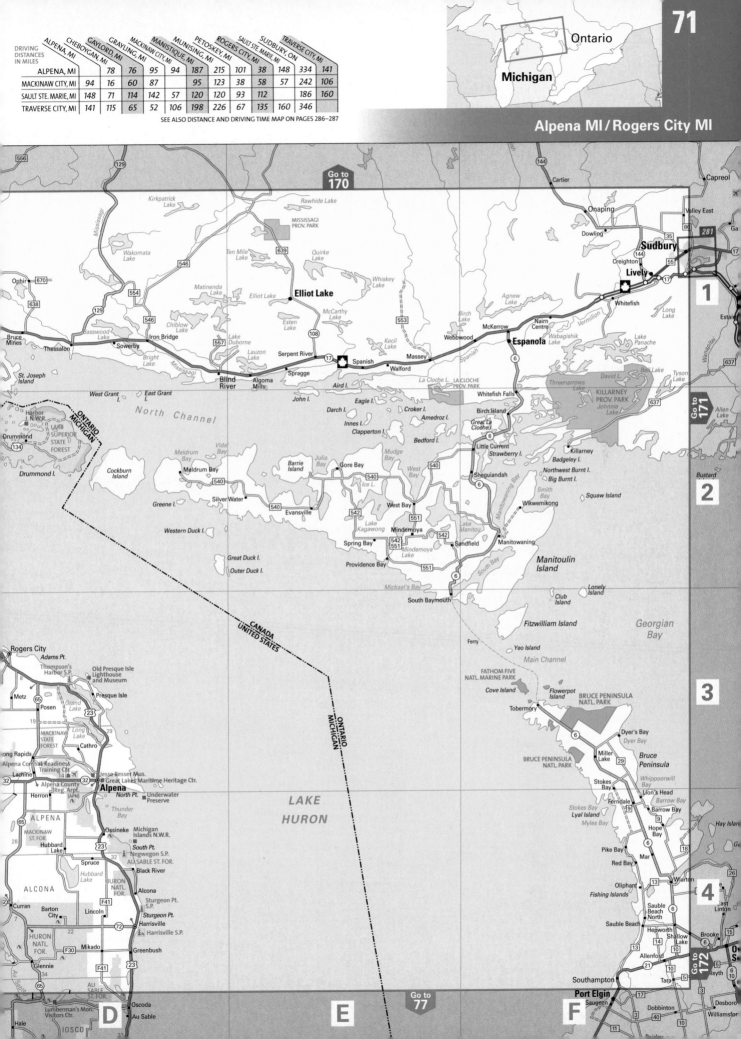

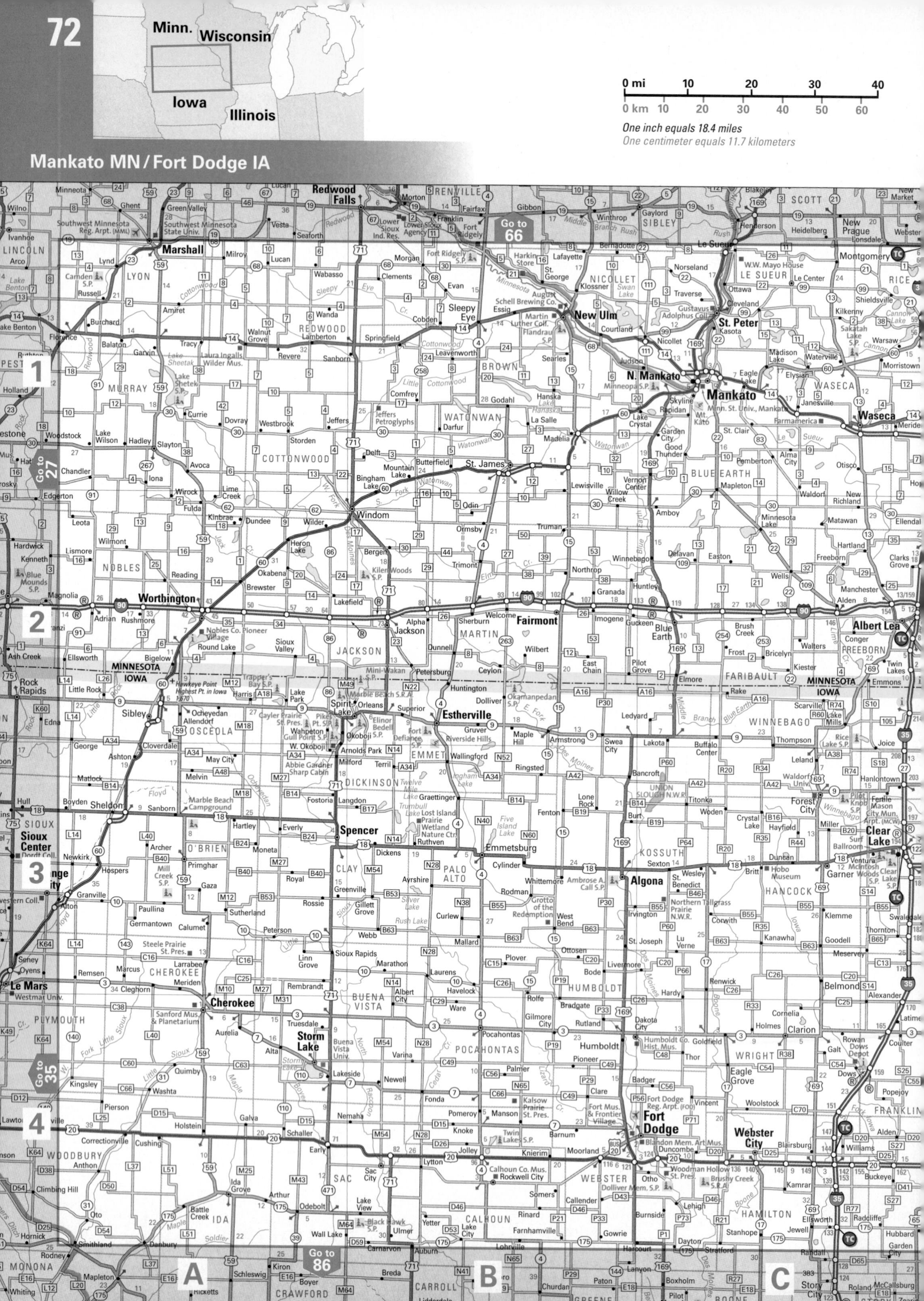
Minn.
Wisconsin
Iowa
Illinois
Mankato MN / Fort Dodge IA
0 mi 10 20 30 40
0 km 10 20 30 40 50 60
One inch equals 18.4 miles
One centimeter equals 11.7 kilometers
Go to 66
Go to 27
Go to 35
Go to 86
Marshall
New Ulm
St. Peter
N. Mankato
Mankato
Waseca
St. James
Windom
Worthington
Fairmont
Jackson
Blue Earth
Albert Lea
Estherville
Spirit Lake
Spencer
Emmetsburg
Algona
Clear Lake
Sioux Center
Le Mars
Cherokee
Storm Lake
Fort Dodge
Webster City
MINNESOTA
IOWA
A
B
C
1
2
3
4

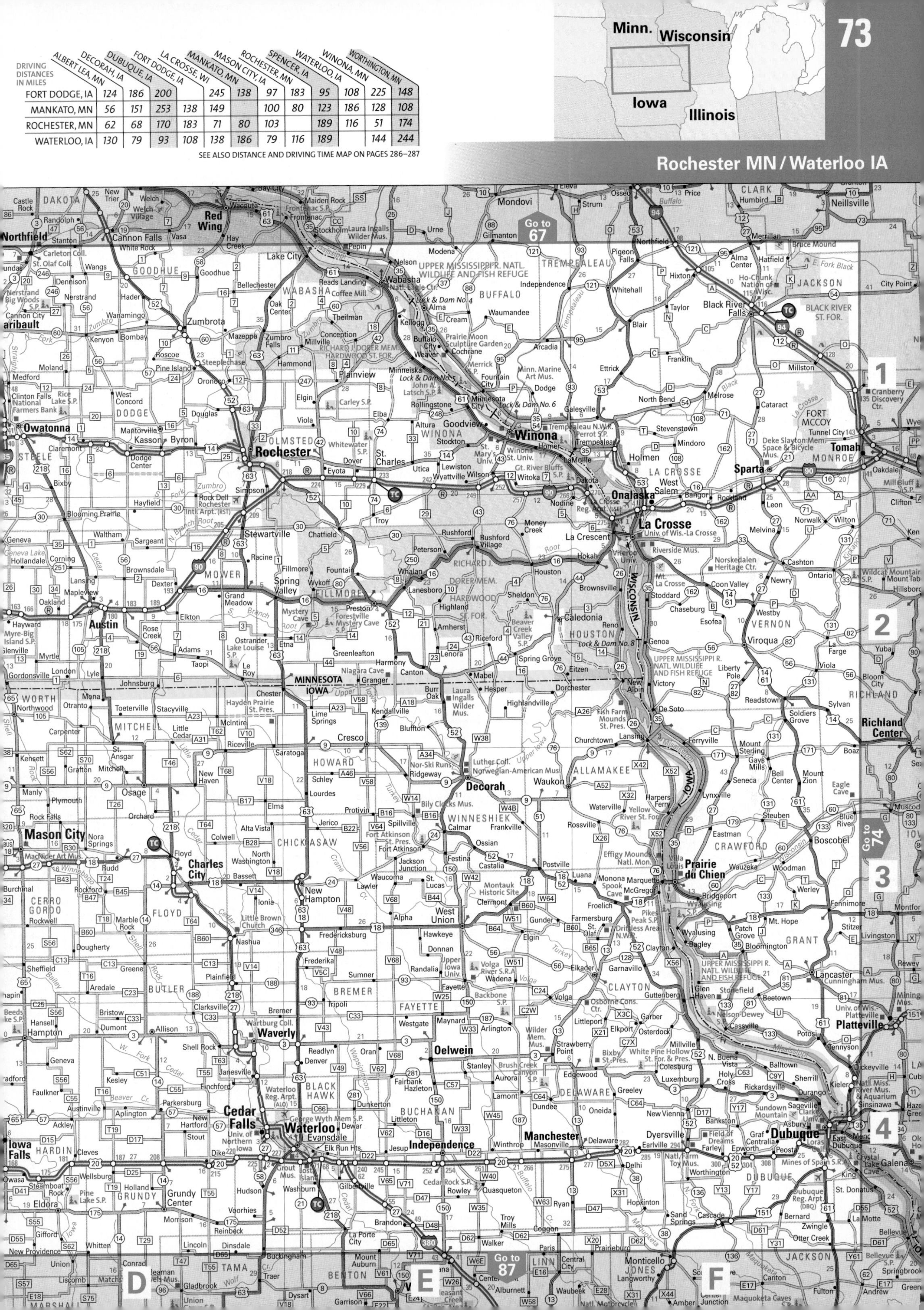

DRIVING DISTANCES IN MILES	ALBERT LEA, MN	DECORAH, IA	DUBUQUE, IA	FORT DODGE, IA	LA CROSSE, WI	MASON CITY, IA	ROCHESTER, MN	SPENCER, IA	WATERLOO, IA	WINONA, MN	WORTHINGTON, MN
FORT DODGE, IA	124	186	200		245	138	97	183	95	108	225	148
MANKATO, MN	56	151	253	138	149		100	80	123	186	128	108
ROCHESTER, MN	62	68	170	183	71	80	103		189	116	51	174
WATERLOO, IA	130	79	93	108	138	186	79	116	189		144	244

SEE ALSO DISTANCE AND DRIVING TIME MAP ON PAGES 286–287

Wisconsin

Michigan

Iowa

Illinois

0 mi   10   20   30   40

0 km   10   20   30   40   50   60

One inch equals 18.4 miles
One centimeter equals 11.7 kilometers

Milwaukee WI / Madison WI

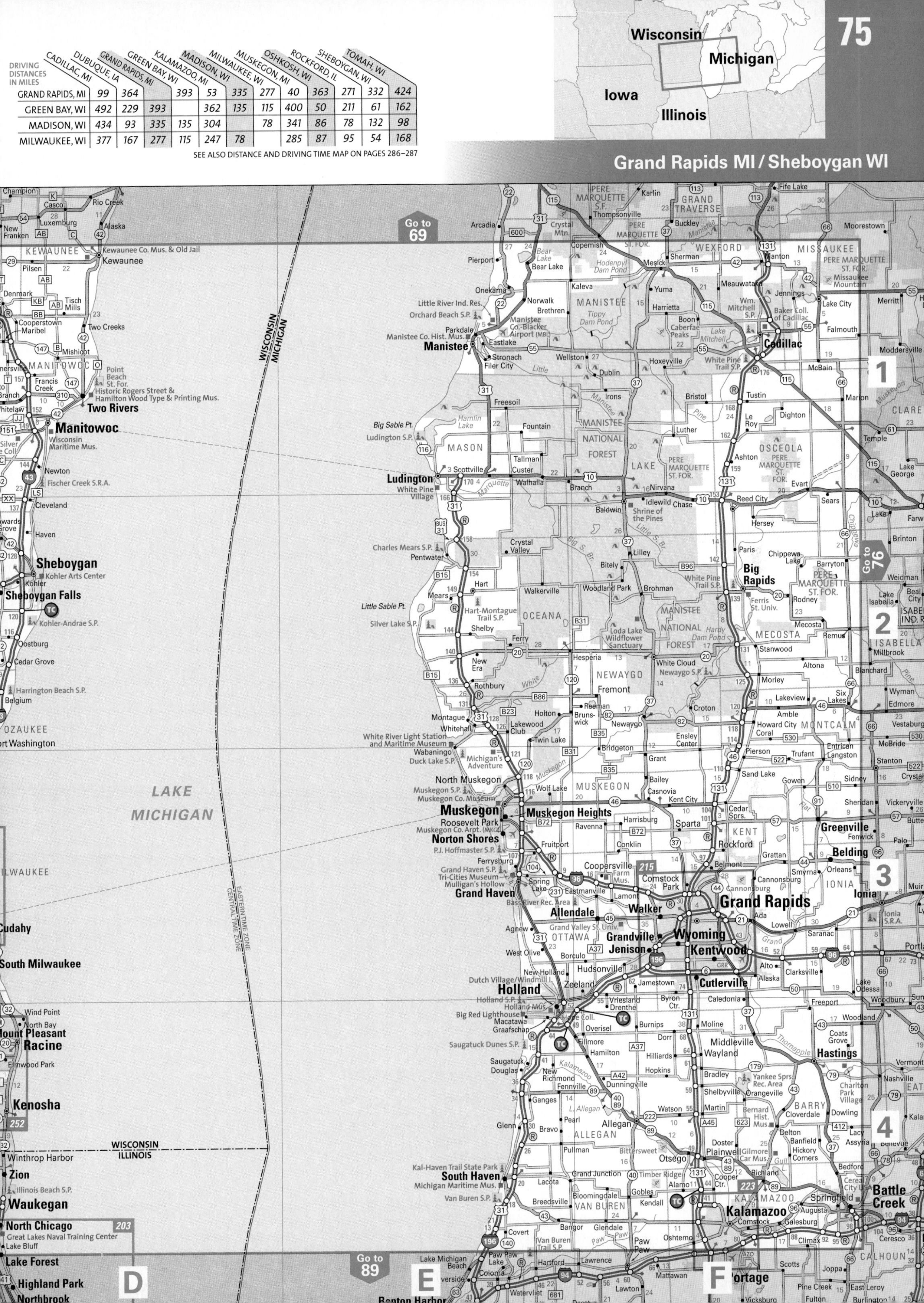

Wisconsin

Michigan

Iowa

Illinois

DRIVING DISTANCES IN MILES	CADILLAC, MI	DUBUQUE, IA	GRAND RAPIDS, MI	GREEN BAY, WI	KALAMAZOO, MI	MADISON, WI	MILWAUKEE, WI	MUSKEGON, MI	OSHKOSH, WI	ROCKFORD, IL	SHEBOYGAN, WI	TOMAH, WI
GRAND RAPIDS, MI	99	364		393	53	335	277	40	363	271	332	424
GREEN BAY, WI	492	229	393		362	135	115	400	50	211	61	162
MADISON, WI	434	93	335	135	304		78	341	86	78	132	98
MILWAUKEE, WI	377	167	277	115	247	78		285	87	95	54	168

SEE ALSO DISTANCE AND DRIVING TIME MAP ON PAGES 286–287

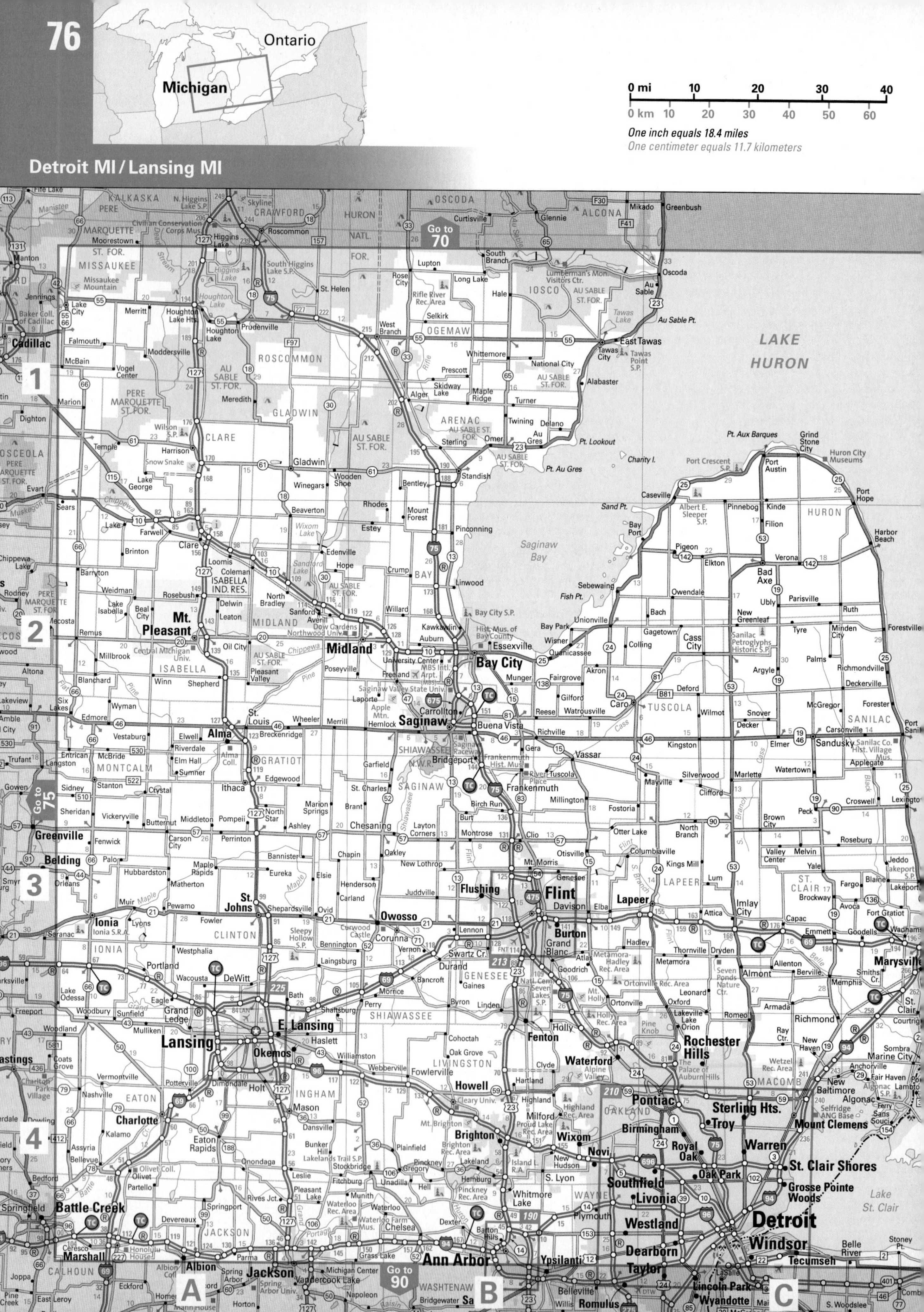

Michigan   Ontario

0 mi   10   20   30   40
0 km 10   20   30   40   50   60
One inch equals 18.4 miles
One centimeter equals 11.7 kilometers

LAKE HURON

Lake St. Clair

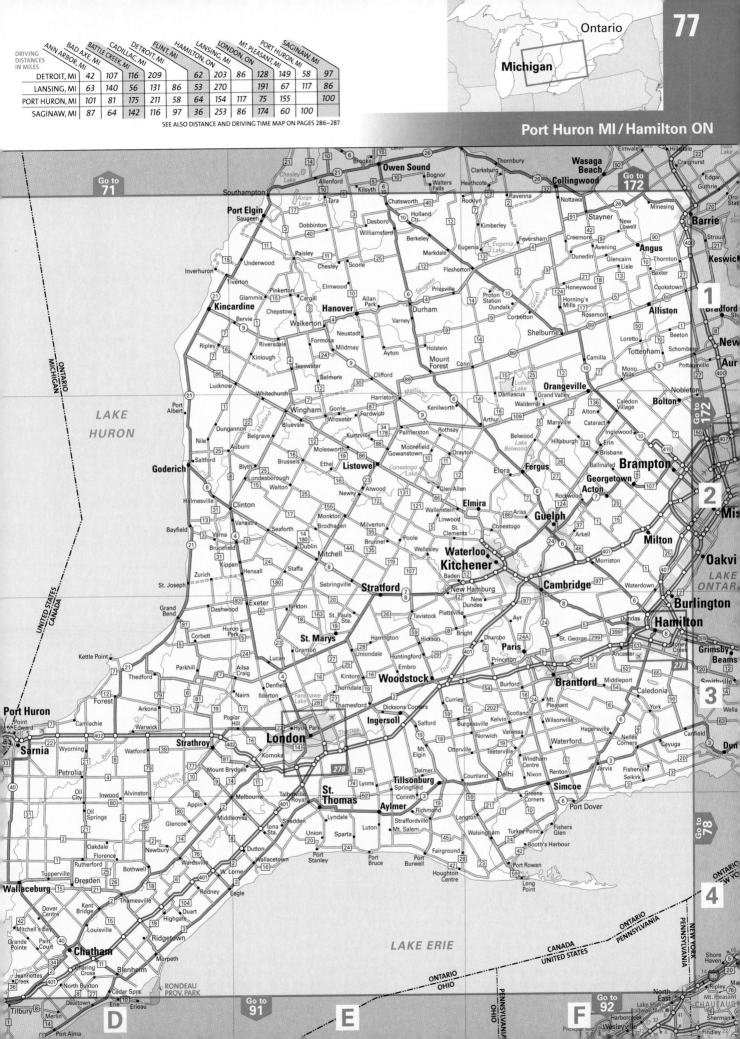

DRIVING DISTANCES IN MILES	ANN ARBOR, MI	BAD AXE, MI	BATTLE CREEK, MI	CADILLAC, MI	DETROIT, MI	FLINT, MI	HAMILTON, ON	LANSING, MI	LONDON, ON	MT. PLEASANT, MI	PORT HURON, MI	SAGINAW, MI
DETROIT, MI	42	107	116	209		62	203	86	128	149	58	97
LANSING, MI	63	140	56	131	86	53	270		191	67	117	86
PORT HURON, MI	101	81	175	211	58	64	154	117		75	155	100
SAGINAW, MI	87	64	142	116	97	36	253	86	174	60	100	

SEE ALSO DISTANCE AND DRIVING TIME MAP ON PAGES 286–287

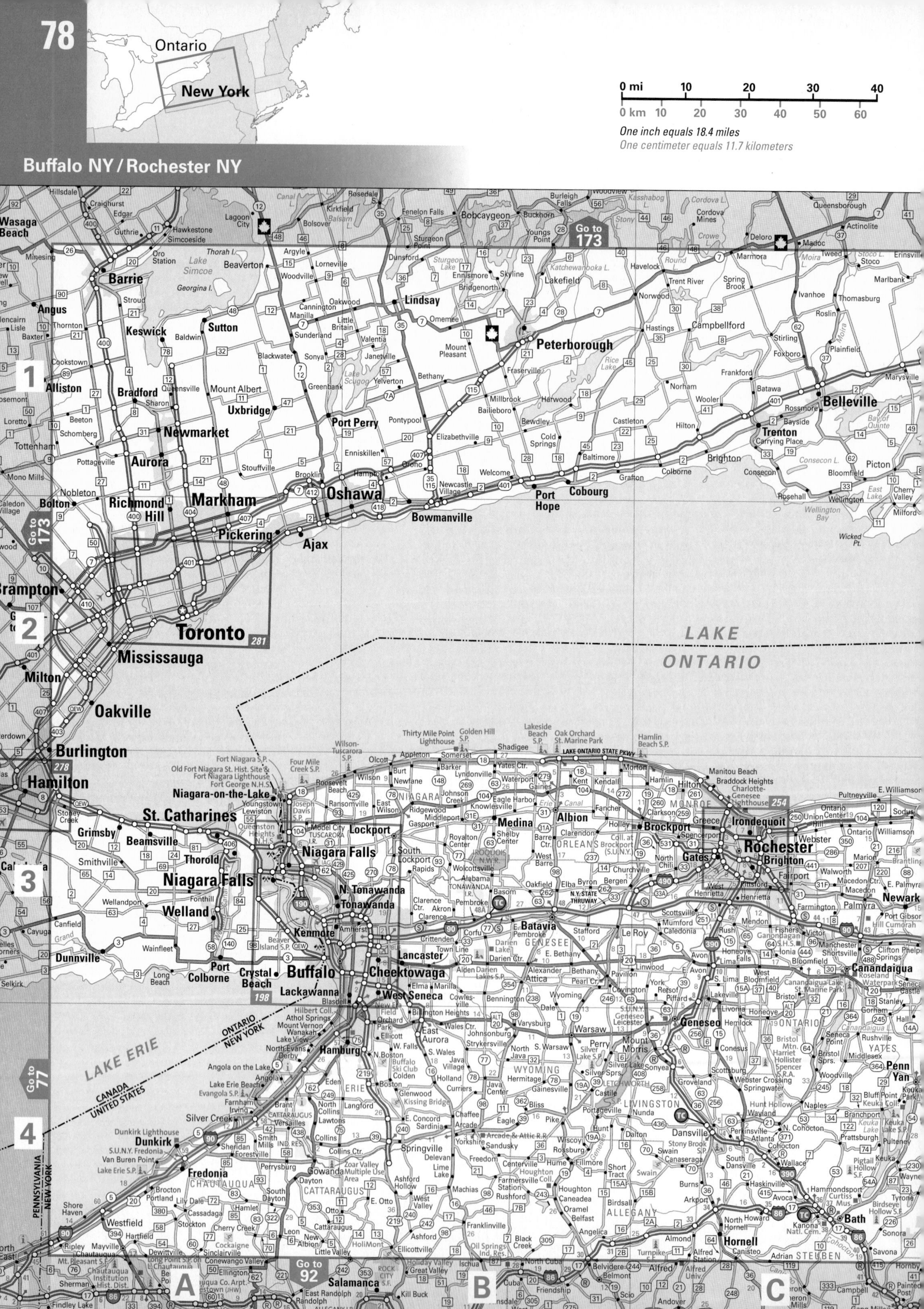

Ontario

New York

0 mi   10   20   30   40
0 km   10   20   30   40   50   60
One inch equals 18.4 miles
One centimeter equals 11.7 kilometers

LAKE ONTARIO

LAKE ERIE

Toronto
Mississauga
Markham
Oshawa
Pickering
Ajax
Bowmanville
Port Hope
Cobourg
Peterborough
Lindsay
Belleville
Trenton
Barrie
Newmarket
Aurora
Richmond Hill
Bolton
Brampton
Milton
Oakville
Burlington
Hamilton
St. Catharines
Niagara-on-the-Lake
Niagara Falls
Welland
Buffalo
Cheektowaga
West Seneca
Lackawanna
Kenmore
Tonawanda
N. Tonawanda
Lockport
Medina
Albion
Brockport
Rochester
Irondequoit
Brighton
Gates
Fairport
Canandaigua
Geneseo
Batavia
Le Roy
Dansville
Hornell
Bath
Dunkirk
Fredonia
Salamanca
Penn Yan
Newark
Grimsby
Beamsville
Thorold
Welland
Dunnville
Port Colborne
Crystal Beach
Hamburg
Springville
Arcade
Warsaw
Perry
Mount Morris

ONTARIO
NEW YORK

CANADA
UNITED STATES

PENNSYLVANIA
NEW YORK

Go to 173

Go to 173

Go to 77

Go to 92

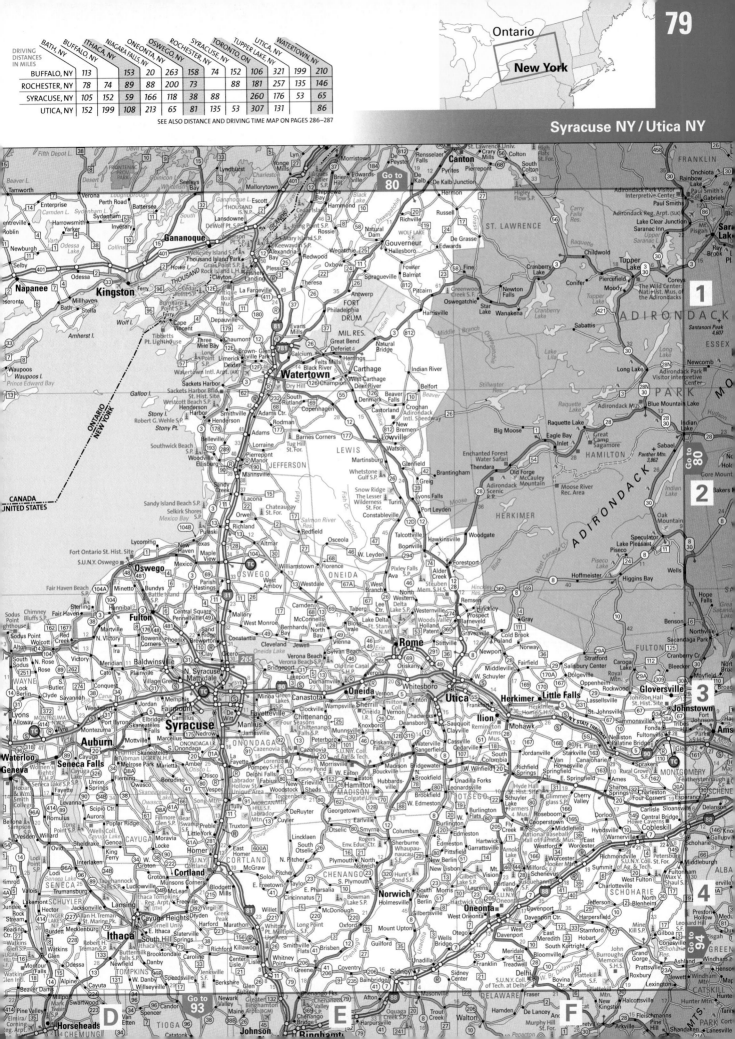

Ontario
New York

DRIVING DISTANCES IN MILES	BATH, NY	BUFFALO, NY	ITHACA, NY	NIAGARA FALLS, NY	ONEONTA, NY	OSWEGO, NY	ROCHESTER, NY	SYRACUSE, NY	TORONTO, ON	TUPPER LAKE, NY	UTICA, NY	WATERTOWN, NY
BUFFALO, NY	113		153	20	263	158	74	152	106	321	199	210
ROCHESTER, NY	78	74	89	88	200	73		88	181	257	135	146
SYRACUSE, NY	105	152	59	166	118	38	88		260	176	53	65
UTICA, NY	152	199	108	213	65	81	135	53	307	131		86

SEE ALSO DISTANCE AND DRIVING TIME MAP ON PAGES 286–287

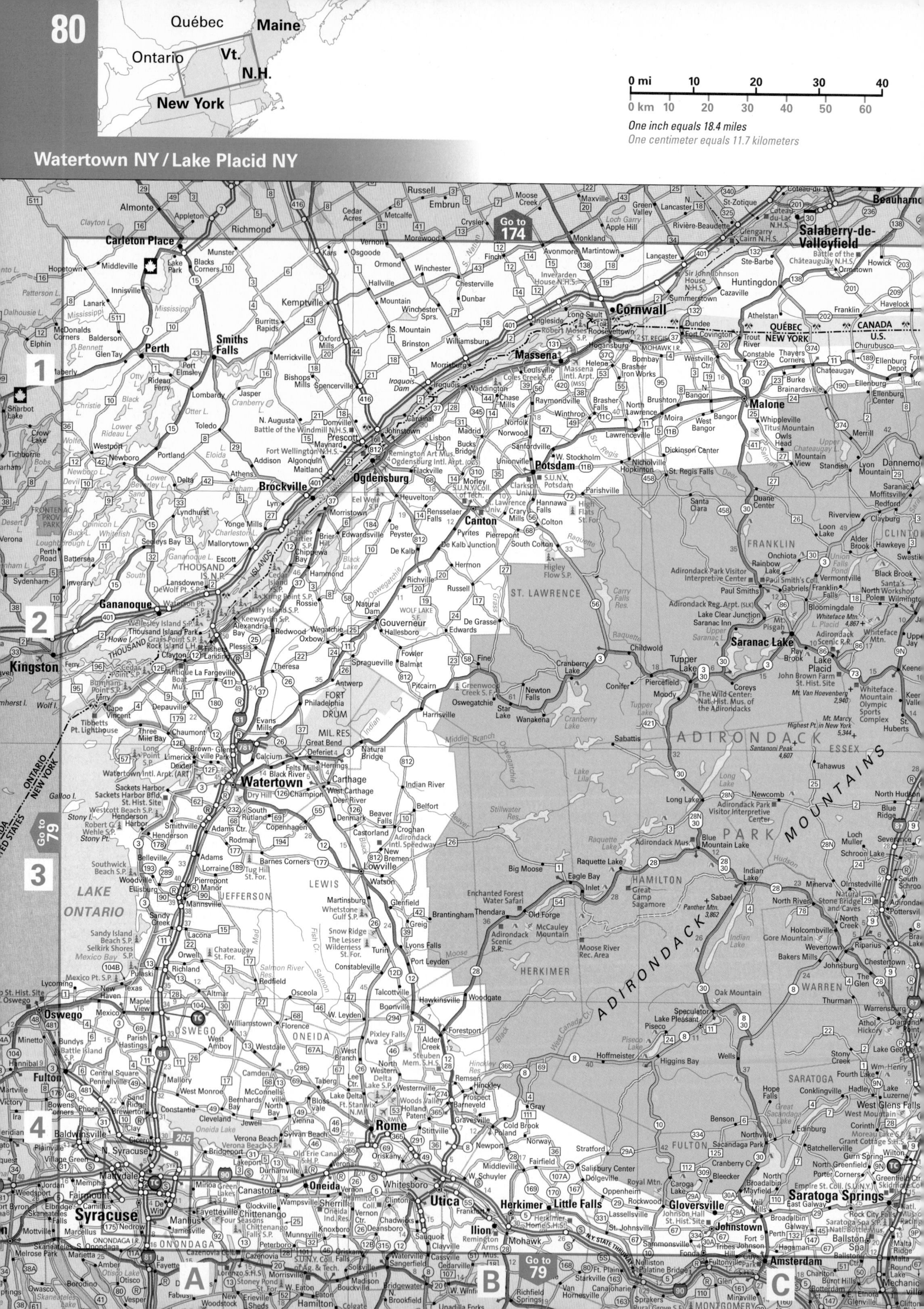
80
Québec
Maine
Ontario
Vt.
N.H.
New York
Watertown NY / Lake Placid NY
0 mi 10 20 30 40
0 km 10 20 30 40 50 60
One inch equals 18.4 miles
One centimeter equals 11.7 kilometers
Go to 174
Go to 79
1
2
3
4
A
B
C
Carleton Place
Almonte
Richmond
Smiths Falls
Perth
Kemptville
Russell
Embrun
Cornwall
Massena
Malone
Salaberry-de-Valleyfield
Huntingdon
Ogdensburg
Brockville
Prescott
Potsdam
Canton
Gananoque
Kingston
THOUSAND IS. N.P.
THOUSAND ISLANDS
Watertown
Gouverneur
FORT DRUM MIL. RES.
ST. LAWRENCE
FRANKLIN
Saranac Lake
Lake Placid
Tupper Lake
ADIRONDACK PARK
ADIRONDACK MOUNTAINS
ESSEX
HAMILTON
HERKIMER
WARREN
SARATOGA
FULTON
LAKE ONTARIO
JEFFERSON
LEWIS
OSWEGO
ONEIDA
ONONDAGA
Oswego
Fulton
Syracuse
Rome
Oneida
Utica
Herkimer
Little Falls
Gloversville
Johnstown
Amsterdam
Saratoga Springs
QUÉBEC
NEW YORK
CANADA
U.S.
ONTARIO
NEW YORK
Lowville
Old Forge
Long Lake
Blue Mountain Lake
Indian Lake
Speculator
Ilion
Mohawk
N.Y. STATE THRUWAY

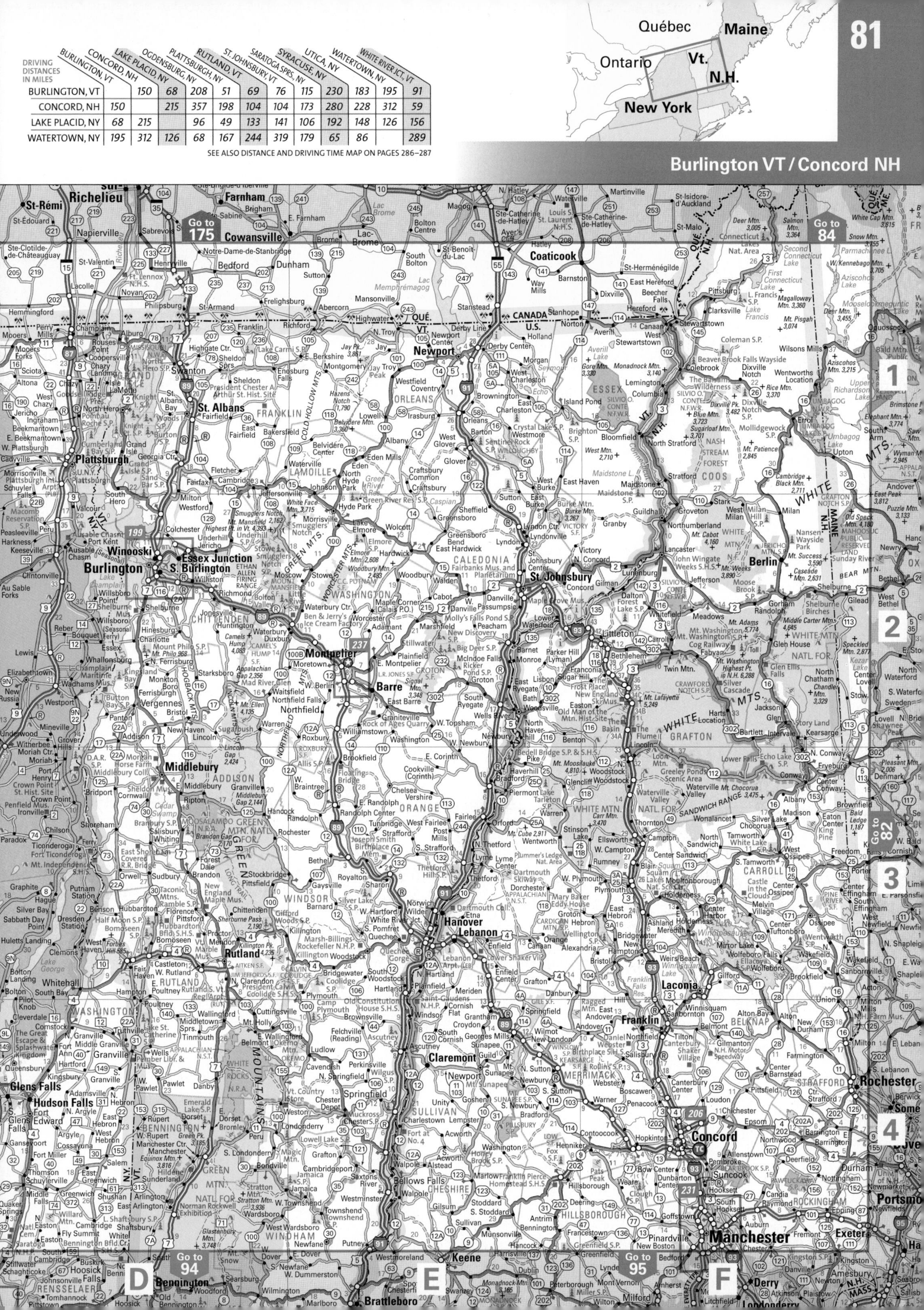

DRIVING DISTANCES IN MILES	BURLINGTON, VT	CONCORD, NH	LAKE PLACID, NY	OGDENSBURG, NY	PLATTSBURGH, NY	RUTLAND, VT	ST. JOHNSBURY, VT	SARATOGA SPRS., NY	SYRACUSE, NY	UTICA, NY	WATERTOWN, NY	WHITE RIVER JCT., VT
BURLINGTON, VT		150	68	208	51	69	76	115	230	183	195	91
CONCORD, NH	150		215	357	198	104	104	173	280	228	312	59
LAKE PLACID, NY	68	215		96	49	133	141	106	192	148	126	156
WATERTOWN, NY	195	312	126	68	167	244	319	179	65	86		289

SEE ALSO DISTANCE AND DRIVING TIME MAP ON PAGES 286–287

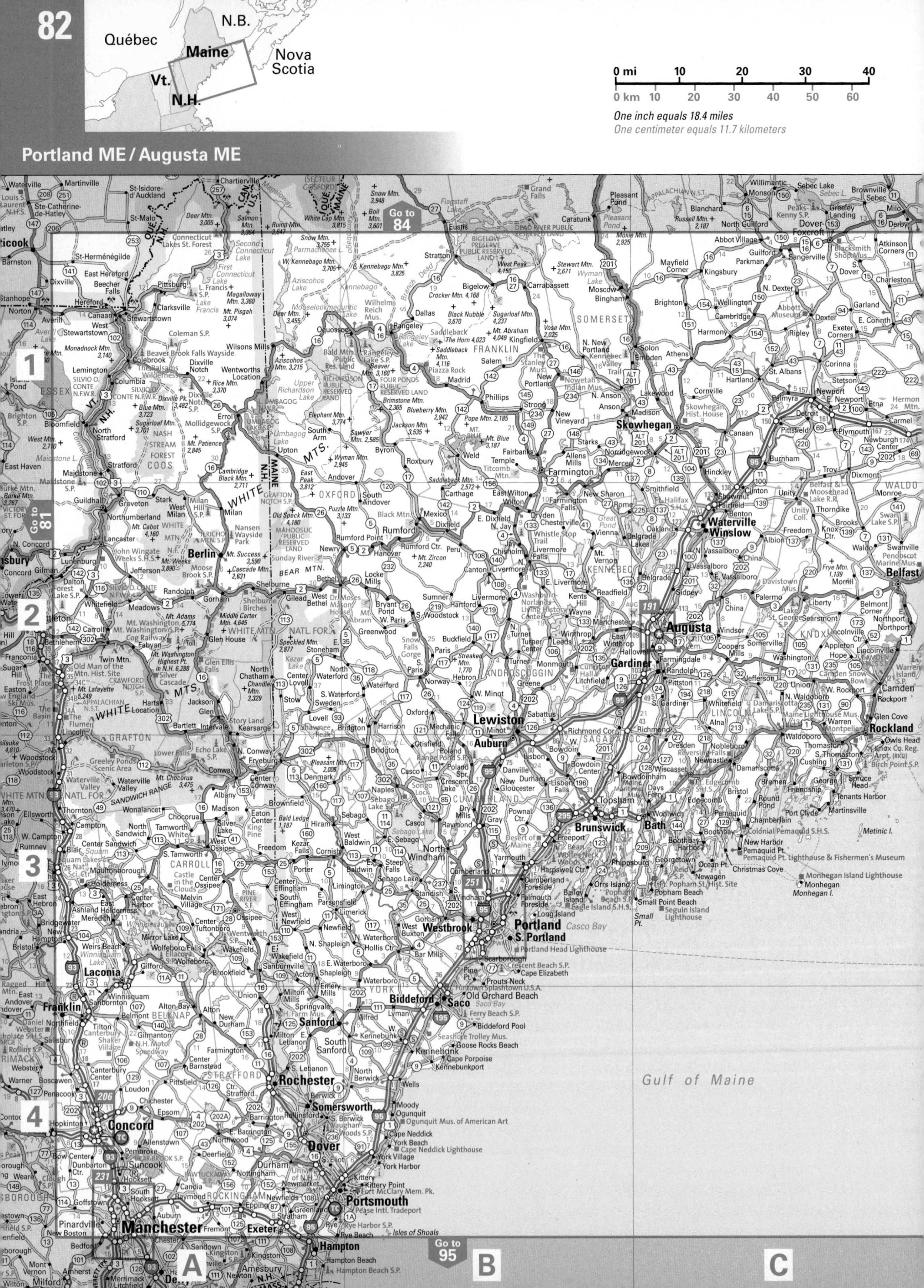

Québec
N.B.
Maine
Nova Scotia
Vt.
N.H.

0 mi   10   20   30   40
0 km 10   20   30   40   50   60
One inch equals 18.4 miles
One centimeter equals 11.7 kilometers

Gulf of Maine

DRIVING DISTANCES IN MILES

	AUGUSTA, ME	BANGOR, ME	BAR HARBOR, ME	BERLIN, NH	CALAIS, ME	CONCORD, NH	CONWAY, NH	LEWISTON, ME	MACHIAS, ME	PORTLAND, ME	PORTSMOUTH, NH	WATERVILLE, ME
AUGUSTA, ME		77	120	110	173	141	97	35	158	58	110	20
BANGOR, ME	77		45	160	112	214	170	108	83	131	184	56
BAR HARBOR, ME	120	45		204	112	257	214	151	71	175	227	100
PORTLAND, ME	58	131	175	93	228	83	62	36	213		53	84

SEE ALSO DISTANCE AND DRIVING TIME MAP ON PAGES 286–287

Québec · N.B. · Maine · Nova Scotia · Vt. · N.H.

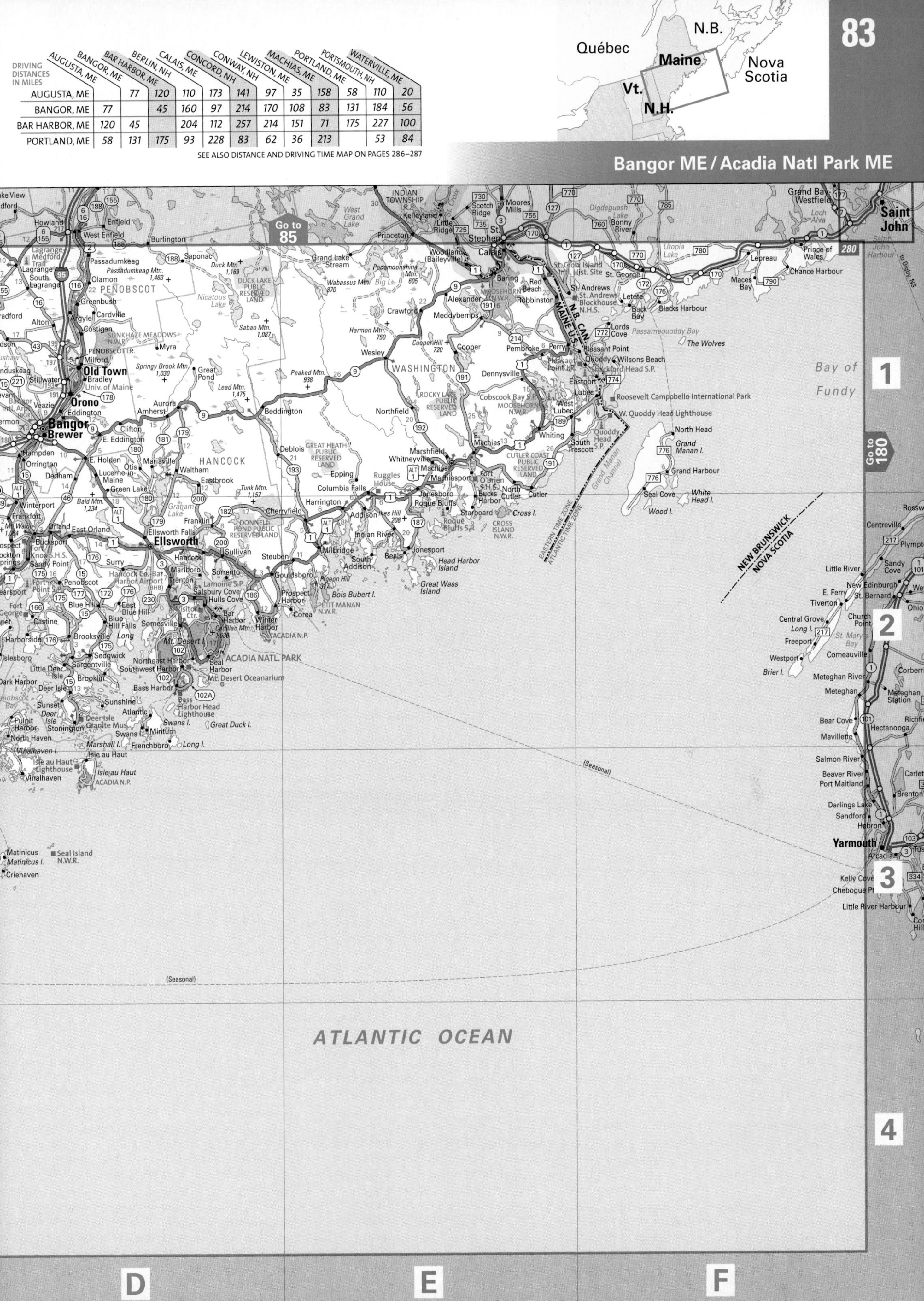

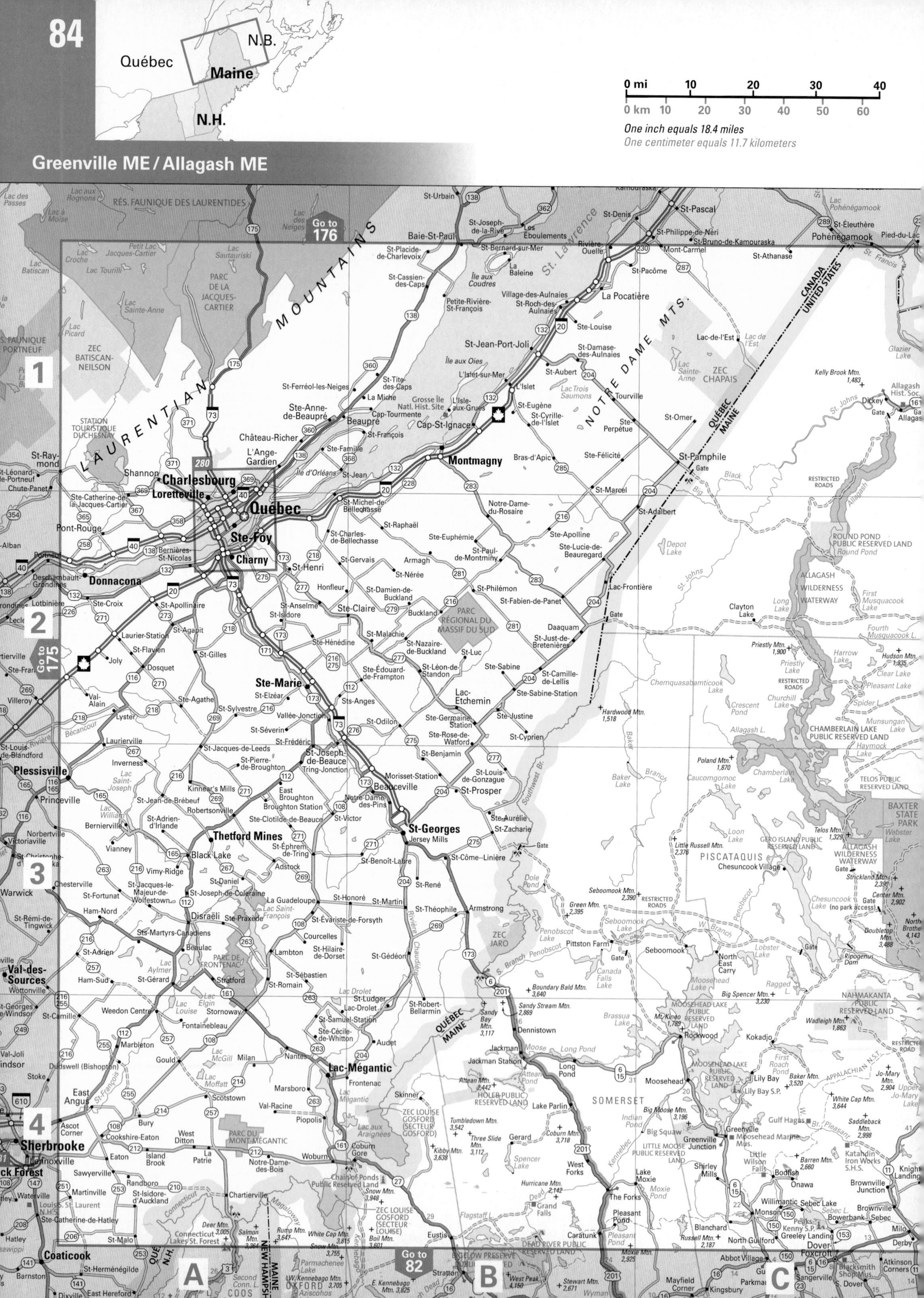

Québec
N.B.
Maine
N.H.

0 mi   10   20   30   40
0 km 10   20   30   40   50   60
One inch equals 18.4 miles
One centimeter equals 11.7 kilometers

DRIVING DISTANCES IN MILES	BANGOR, ME	CALAIS, ME	CARIBOU, ME	FREDERICTON, NB	GREENVILLE, ME	HOULTON, ME	JACKMAN, ME	LINCOLN, ME	MADAWASKA, ME	MILLINOCKET, ME	PRESQUE ISLE, ME	QUEBEC, QC
HOULTON, ME	122	91	55	73	155		204	83	102	73	42	286
LINCOLN, ME	51	77	135	114	83	83	132		174	35	122	231
MADAWASKA, ME	214	207	50	167	212	102	269	174		164	62	182
PRESQUE ISLE, ME	162	133	13	113	166	42	225	122	62	113		246

SEE ALSO DISTANCE AND DRIVING TIME MAP ON PAGES 286–287

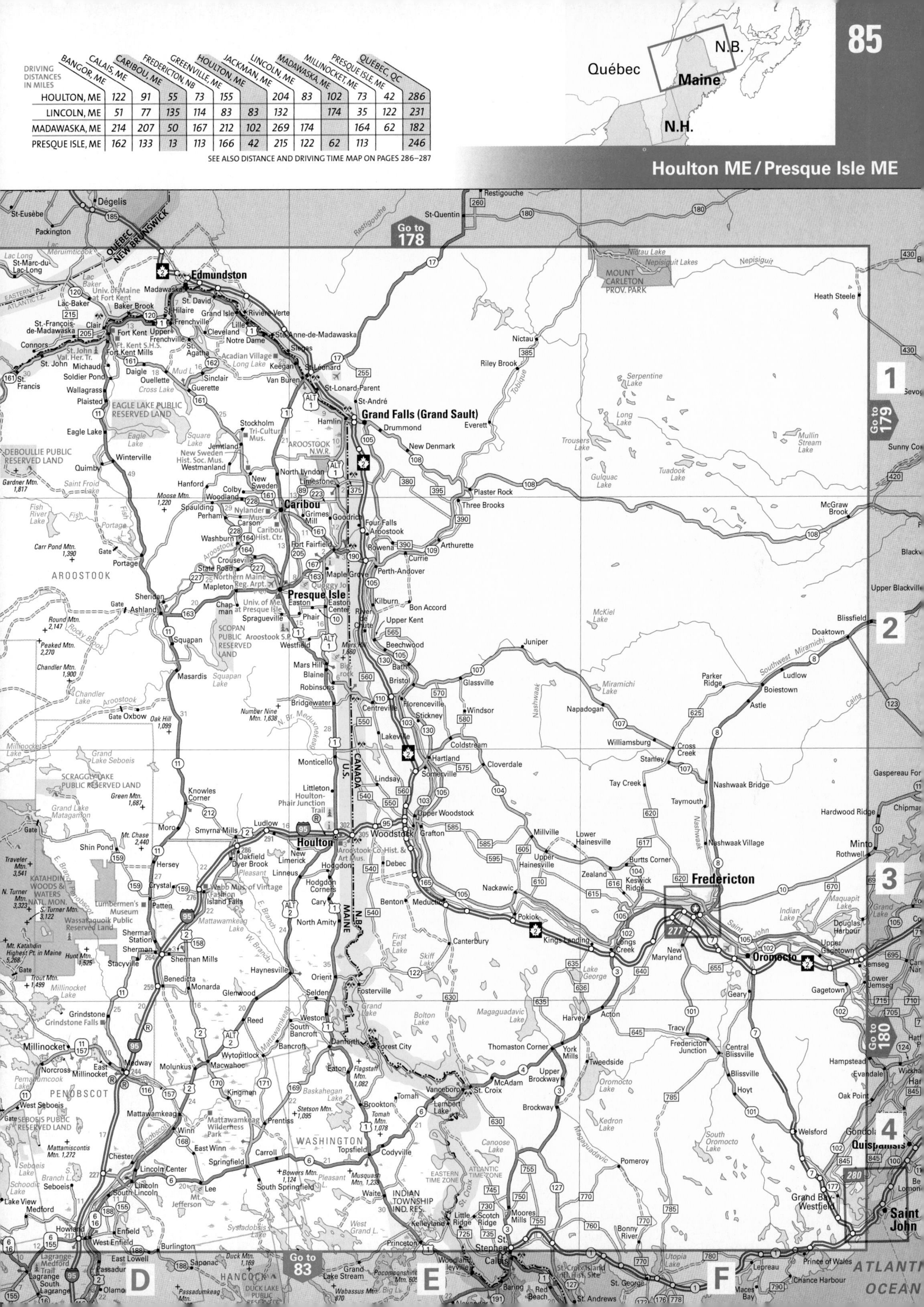

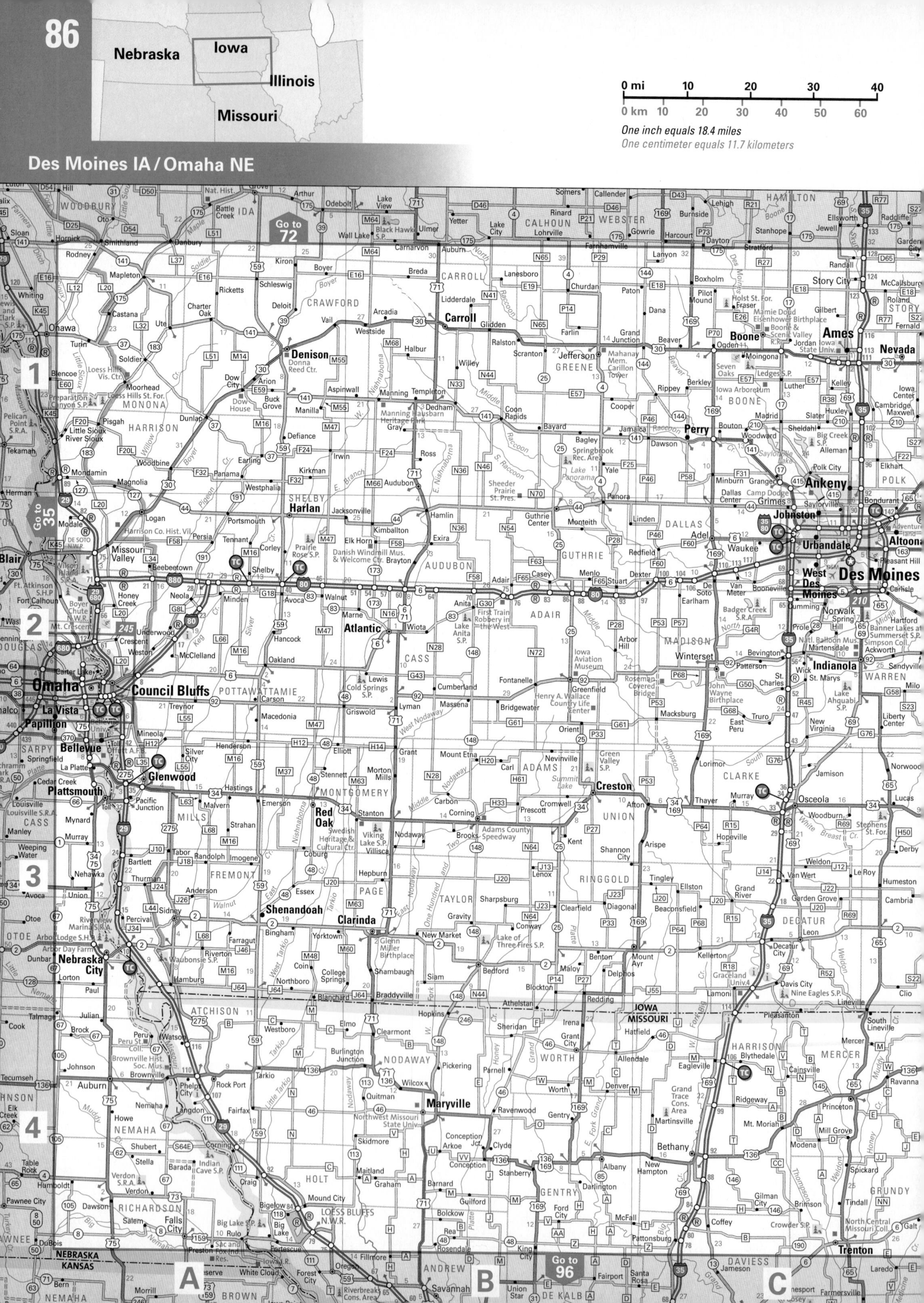

Nebraska Iowa
Illinois
Missouri

Des Moines IA / Omaha NE

0 mi 10 20 30 40
0 km 10 20 30 40 50 60
One inch equals 18.4 miles
One centimeter equals 11.7 kilometers

Nebraska   Iowa

Illinois

Missouri

DRIVING DISTANCES IN MILES	AMES, IA	BURLINGTON, IA	CARROLL, IA	CEDAR RAPIDS, IA	CRESTON, IA	DAVENPORT, IA	DES MOINES, IA	IOWA CITY, IA	KIRKSVILLE MO	MARYVILLE, MO	OMAHA, NE	OTTUMWA, IA
CEDAR RAPIDS, IA	108	106	173		211	87	129	28	170	276	266	111
DES MOINES, IA	34	157	90	129	81	171		113	170	145	146	136	86
IOWA CITY, IA	136	82	195	28	195	59	113		143	260	250	83
OMAHA, NE	171	328	97	266	98	308	136	250	275	112		221

SEE ALSO DISTANCE AND DRIVING TIME MAP ON PAGES 286–287

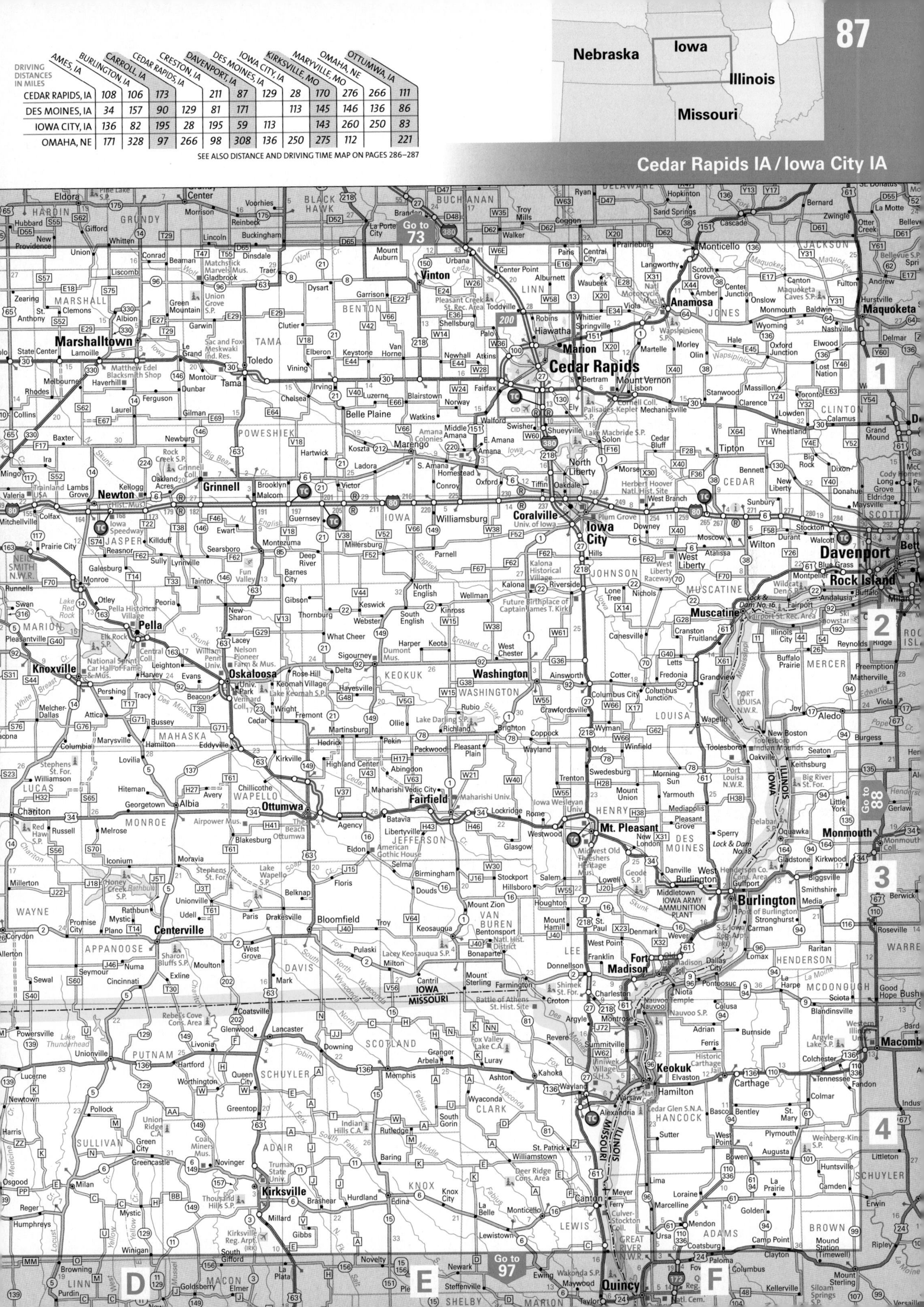

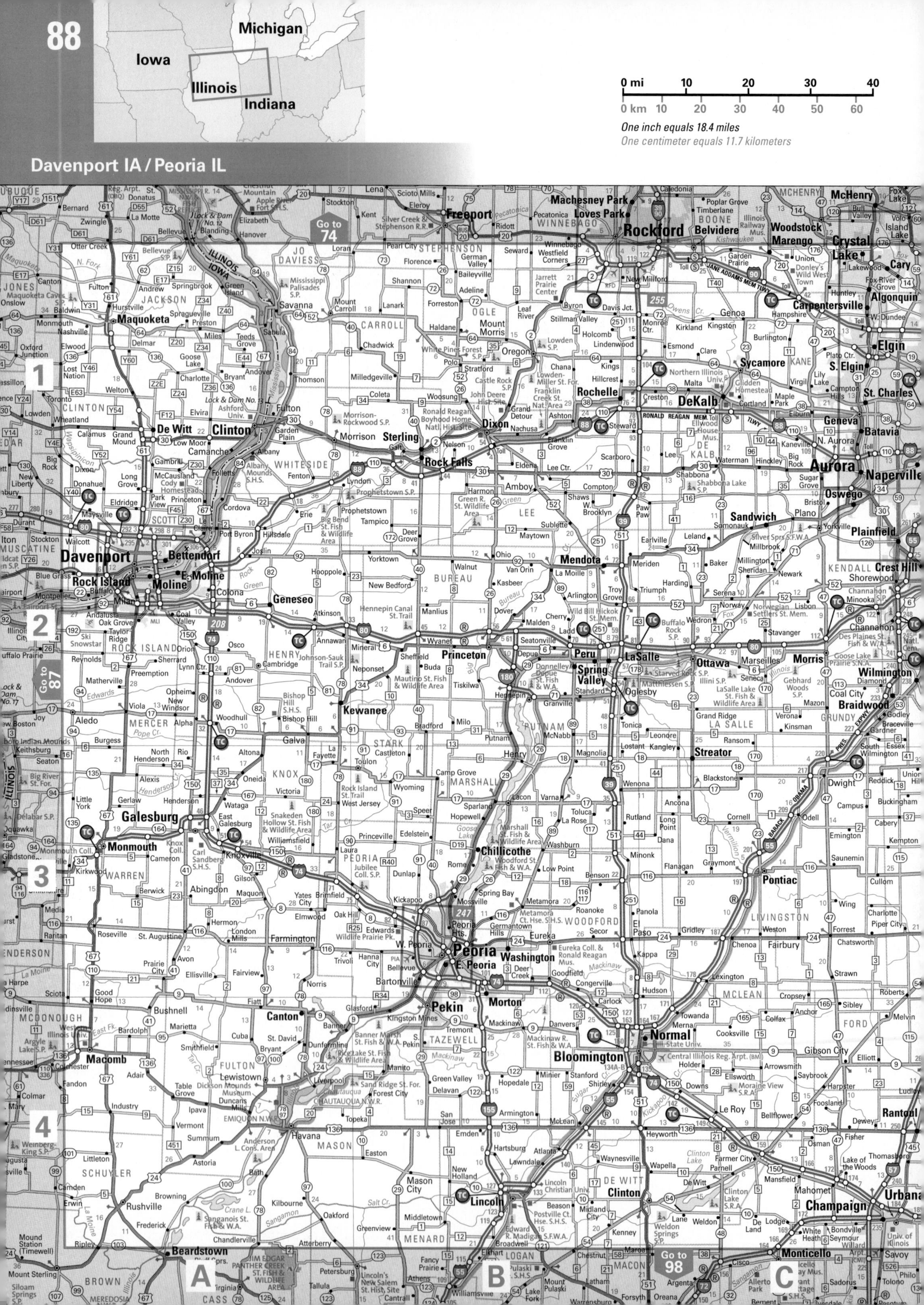
Michigan
Iowa
Illinois
Indiana
0 mi 10 20 30 40
0 km 10 20 30 40 50 60
One inch equals 18.4 miles
One centimeter equals 11.7 kilometers
Davenport
Rock Island
Moline
Bettendorf
Clinton
Rockford
Freeport
DeKalb
Aurora
Naperville
Peoria
Pekin
Bloomington
Normal
Champaign
Urbana
Galesburg
Macomb
Canton
Ottawa
LaSalle
Peru
Pontiac
Lincoln
Dixon
Sterling
Kewanee
Streator
Go to 74
Go to 87
Go to 98
A
B
C
1
2
3
4

DRIVING DISTANCES IN MILES

	BLOOMINGTON, IL	CHAMPAIGN, IL	CHICAGO, IL	DAVENPORT, IA	JOLIET, IL	KALAMAZOO, MI	KOKOMO, IN	LAFAYETTE, IN	LA SALLE, IL	PEORIA, IL	ROCKFORD, IL	SOUTH BEND, IN
CHAMPAIGN, IL	54		141	192	115	255	145	94	117	94	189	198
CHICAGO, IL	135	141		170	40	150	158	121	98	168	86	93
PEORIA, IL	41	94	168	99	132	291	235	184	63		135	234
SOUTH BEND, IN	201	198	93	248	105	76	86	104	164	234	183	

SEE ALSO DISTANCE AND DRIVING TIME MAP ON PAGES 286–287

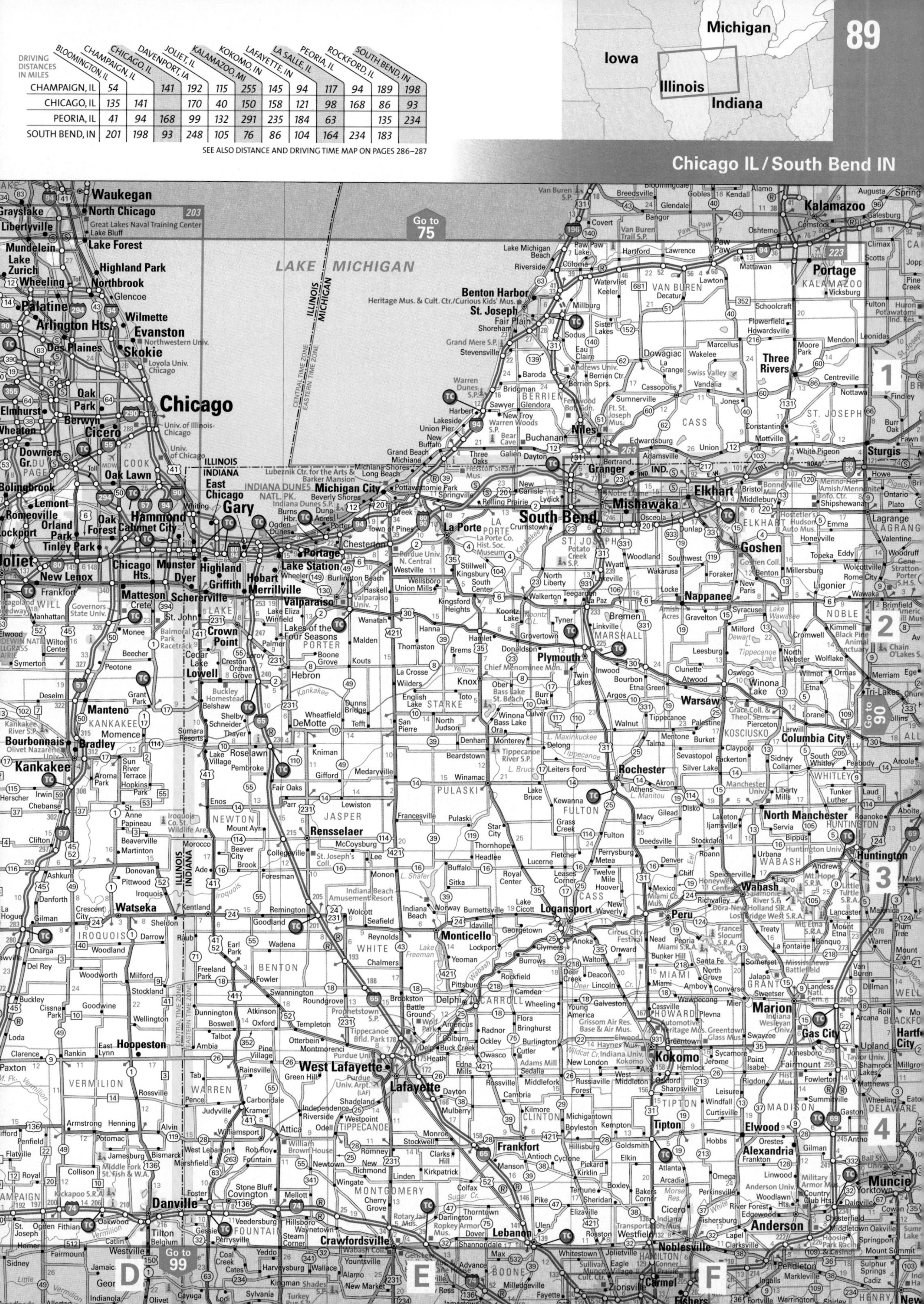

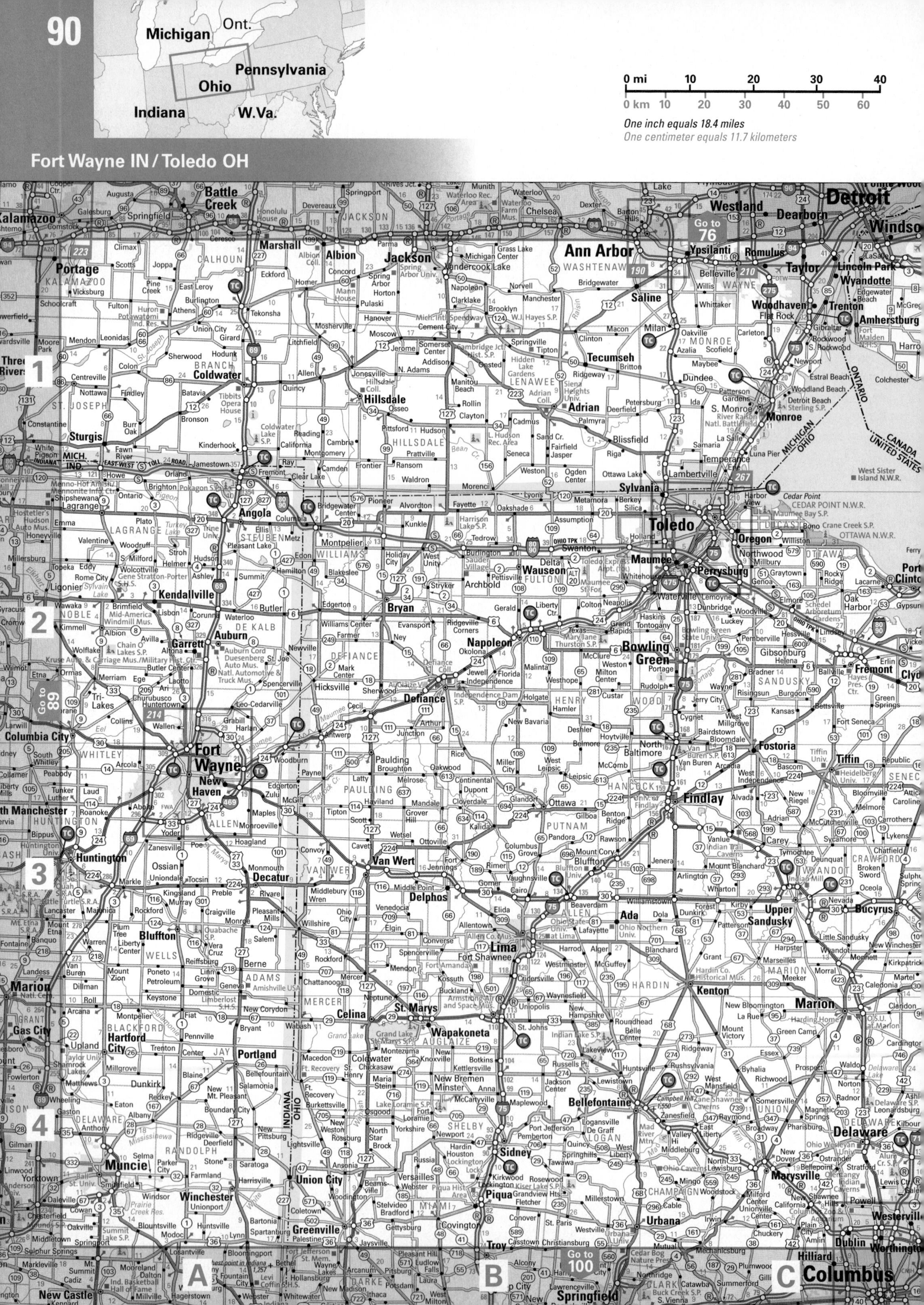
Michigan
Ont.
Pennsylvania
Ohio
Indiana
W.Va.
Fort Wayne IN / Toledo OH
0 mi 10 20 30 40
0 km 10 20 30 40 50 60
One inch equals 18.4 miles
One centimeter equals 11.7 kilometers
Go to 76
Go to 89
Go to 100
1
2
3
4
A
B
C
Detroit
Dearborn
Westland
Ann Arbor
Ypsilanti
Jackson
Battle Creek
Kalamazoo
Portage
Marshall
Albion
Coldwater
Hillsdale
Adrian
Tecumseh
Monroe
Sturgis
Toledo
Maumee
Perrysburg
Oregon
Sylvania
Angola
Kendallville
Auburn
Garrett
Bryan
Napoleon
Defiance
Bowling Green
Fremont
Fort Wayne
New Haven
Huntington
Decatur
Bluffton
Van Wert
Delphos
Lima
Findlay
Fostoria
Tiffin
Upper Sandusky
Bucyrus
Kenton
Marion
Celina
St. Marys
Wapakoneta
Sidney
Piqua
Troy
Urbana
Bellefontaine
Marysville
Delaware
Dublin
Columbus
Muncie
Portland
Winchester
Union City
Greenville
Springfield
New Castle
Hartford City
INDIANA
OHIO
MICHIGAN
ONTARIO
CANADA
UNITED STATES

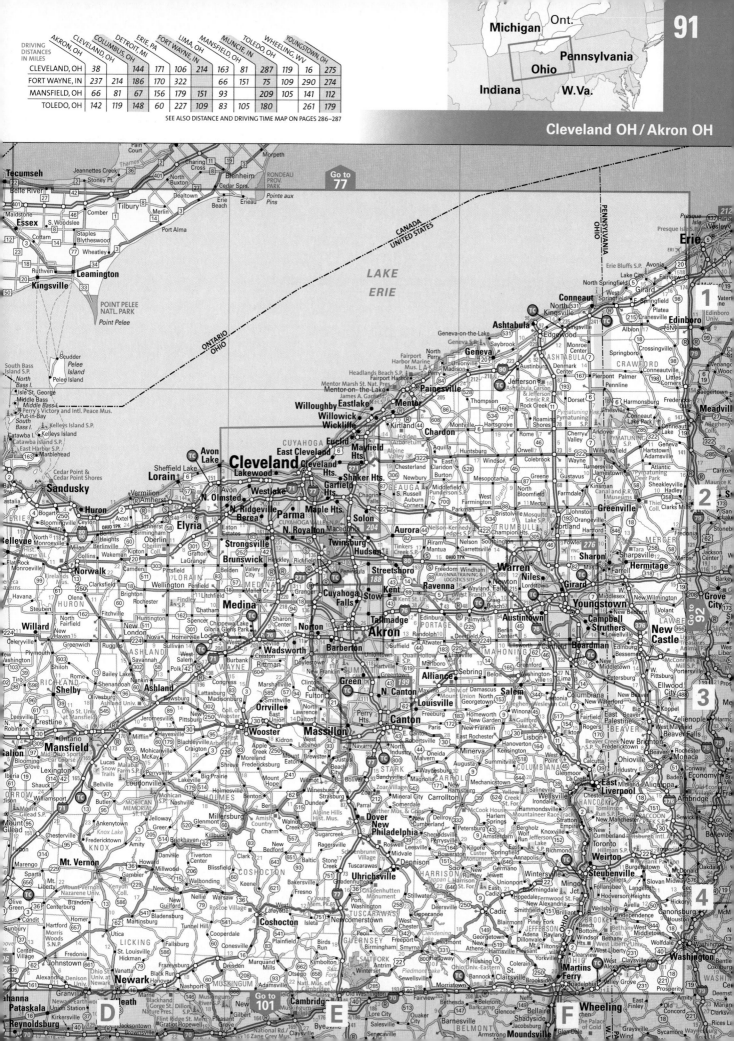

DRIVING DISTANCES IN MILES	AKRON, OH	CLEVELAND, OH	COLUMBUS, OH	DETROIT, MI	ERIE, PA	FORT WAYNE, IN	LIMA, OH	MANSFIELD, OH	MUNCIE, IN	TOLEDO, OH	WHEELING, WV	YOUNGSTOWN, OH
CLEVELAND, OH	38		144	171	106	214	163	81	287	119	16	275
FORT WAYNE, IN	237	214	186	170	322		66	151	75	109	290	274
MANSFIELD, OH	66	81	67	156	179	151	93		209	105	141	112
TOLEDO, OH	142	119	148	60	227	109	83	105	180		261	179

SEE ALSO DISTANCE AND DRIVING TIME MAP ON PAGES 286–287

New York

Pennsylvania New Jersey

0 mi 10 20 30 40

0 km 10 20 30 40 50 60

One inch equals 18.4 miles
One centimeter equals 11.7 kilometers

New York

Pennsylvania   New Jersey

DRIVING DISTANCES IN MILES	ALLENTOWN, PA	ALTOONA, PA	BINGHAMTON, NY	ELMIRA, NY	ERIE, PA	HARRISBURG, PA	JOHNSTOWN, PA	PITTSBURGH, PA	READING, PA	SCRANTON, PA	STATE COLLEGE, PA	WILLIAMSPORT, PA
ALLENTOWN, PA		218	132	188	361	82	217	284	37	76	165	116
HARRISBURG, PA	82	140	181	157	298		138	205	65	119	88	83
PITTSBURGH, PA	284	99	363	284	126	205	73		262	301	139	215
SCRANTON, PA	76	185	61	117	317	119	233	301	103		149	83

SEE ALSO DISTANCE AND DRIVING TIME MAP ON PAGES 286–287

Vt. N.H.
Massachusetts
New York
Rhode Island
Connecticut
Pa.
N.J.

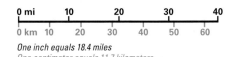

```
0 mi        10          20          30          40
0 km   10   20    30    40    50    60
```

One inch equals 18.4 miles
One centimeter equals 11.7 kilometers

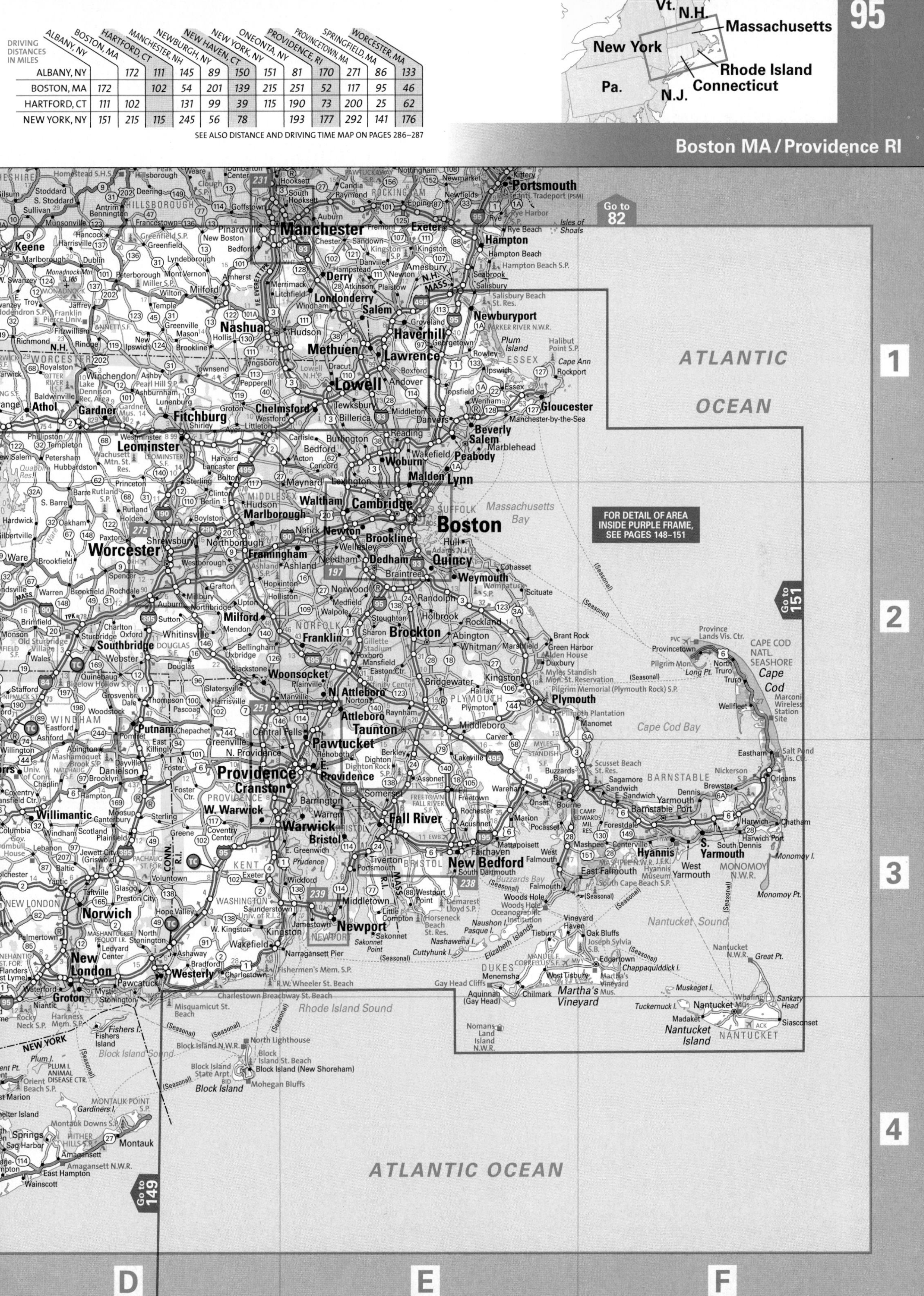

DRIVING DISTANCES IN MILES

	ALBANY, NY	BOSTON, MA	HARTFORD, CT	MANCHESTER, NH	NEWBURGH, NY	NEW HAVEN, CT	NEW YORK, NY	ONEONTA, NY	PROVIDENCE, RI	PROVINCETOWN, MA	SPRINGFIELD, MA	WORCESTER, MA
ALBANY, NY		172	111	145	89	150	151	81	170	271	86	133
BOSTON, MA	172		102	54	201	139	215	251	52	117	95	46
HARTFORD, CT	111	102		131	99	39	115	190	73	200	25	62
NEW YORK, NY	151	215	115	245	56	78		193	177	292	141	176

SEE ALSO DISTANCE AND DRIVING TIME MAP ON PAGES 286–287

Vt. N.H. Massachusetts
New York
Pa. Rhode Island
Connecticut
N.J.

Go to 82
Go to 151
Go to 149

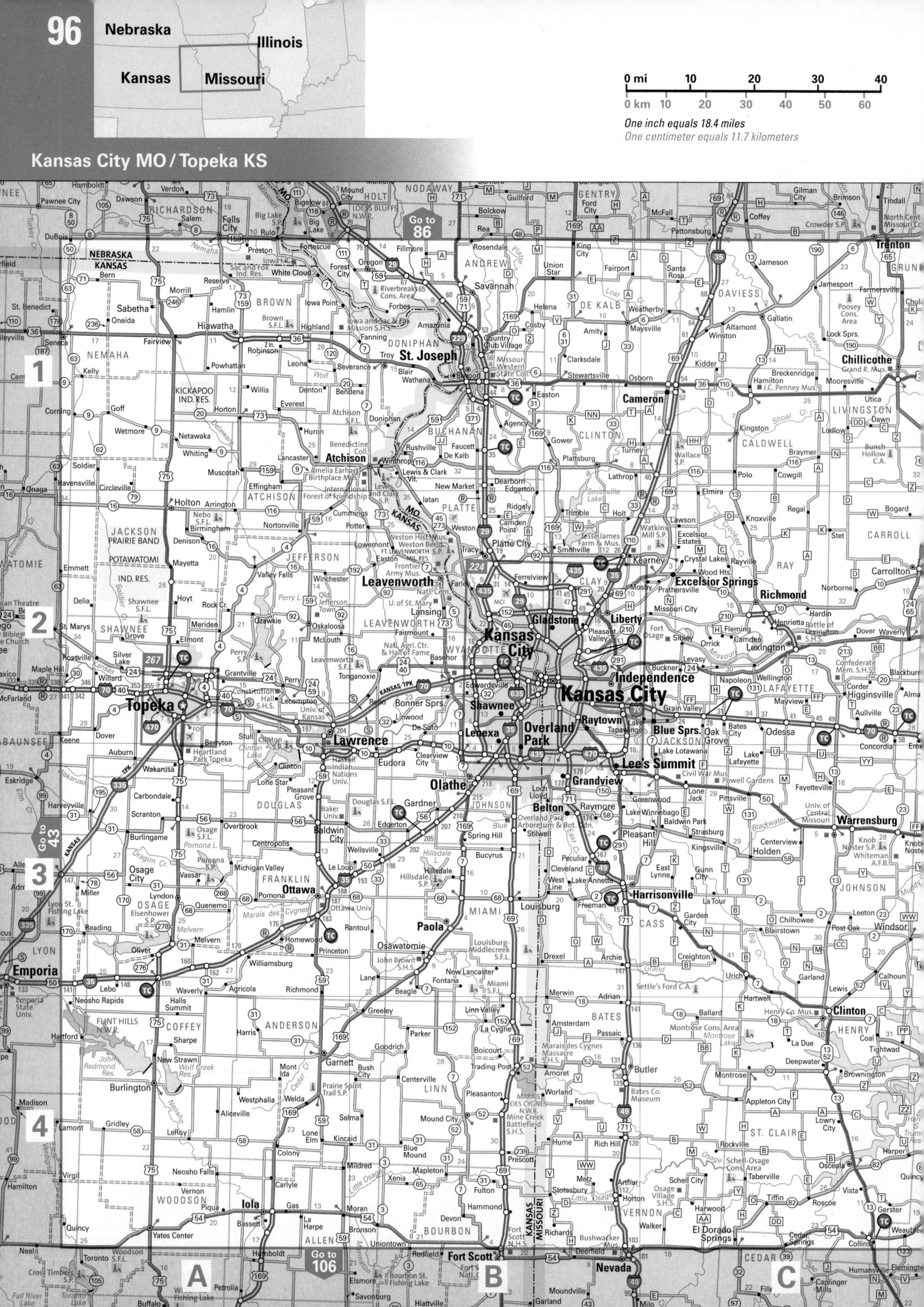
Nebraska
Illinois
Kansas
Missouri
Kansas City MO / Topeka KS
0 mi 10 20 30 40
0 km 10 20 30 40 50 60
One inch equals 18.4 miles
One centimeter equals 11.7 kilometers
Go to 86
Go to 43
Go to 106
NEBRASKA
KANSAS
MISSOURI
St. Joseph
Atchison
Leavenworth
Topeka
Lawrence
Kansas City
Independence
Overland Park
Olathe
Lee's Summit
Gladstone
Liberty
Excelsior Springs
Cameron
Chillicothe
Trenton
Richmond
Lexington
Warrensburg
Harrisonville
Belton
Grandview
Raytown
Blue Sprs.
Ottawa
Paola
Emporia
Burlington
Iola
Garnett
Fort Scott
Nevada
Butler
Clinton
Hiawatha
Sabetha
Holton
Osawatomie
Louisburg
Pleasant Hill
Odessa
Higginsville
Carrollton
Osceola
NEMAHA
BROWN
DONIPHAN
ATCHISON
JACKSON
JEFFERSON
LEAVENWORTH
WYANDOTTE
SHAWNEE
DOUGLAS
JOHNSON
OSAGE
FRANKLIN
MIAMI
COFFEY
ANDERSON
LINN
WOODSON
ALLEN
BOURBON
ANDREW
BUCHANAN
PLATTE
CLAY
CLINTON
DE KALB
DAVIESS
CALDWELL
RAY
CARROLL
LIVINGSTON
LAFAYETTE
CASS
BATES
HENRY
ST. CLAIR
VERNON
CEDAR
GENTRY
NODAWAY
HOLT
RICHARDSON
1
2
3
4
A
B
C

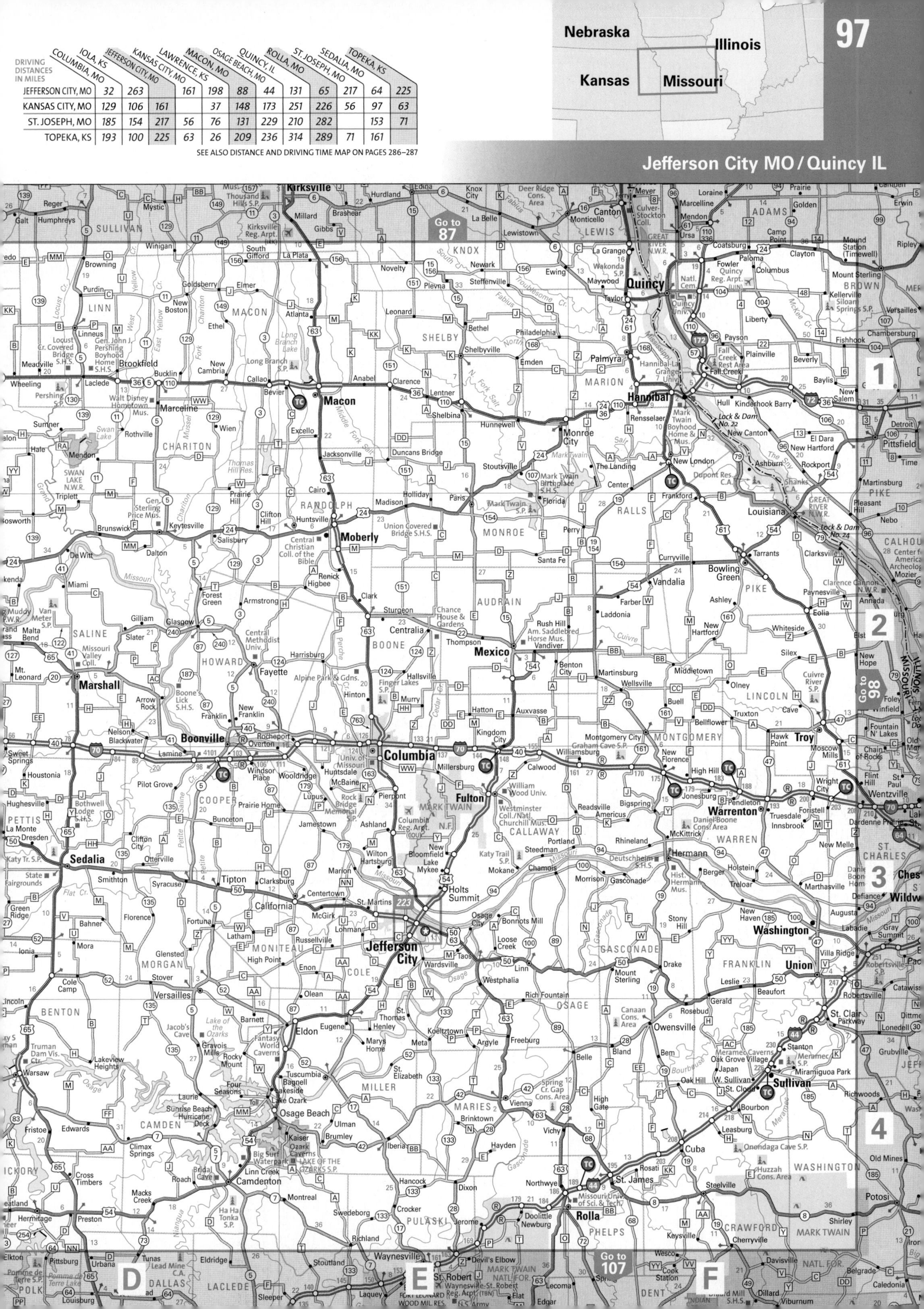

Nebraska
Illinois
Kansas
Missouri

DRIVING DISTANCES IN MILES	COLUMBIA, MO	IOLA, KS	JEFFERSON CITY, MO	KANSAS CITY, MO	LAWRENCE, KS	MACON, MO	OSAGE BEACH, MO	QUINCY, IL	ROLLA, MO	ST. JOSEPH, MO	SEDALIA, MO	TOPEKA, KS
JEFFERSON CITY, MO	32	263		161	198	88	44	131	65	217	64	225
KANSAS CITY, MO	129	106	161		37	148	173	251	226	56	97	63
ST. JOSEPH, MO	185	154	217	56		76	131	229	210	282		153	71
TOPEKA, KS	193	100	225	63	26	209	236	314	289	71	161	

SEE ALSO DISTANCE AND DRIVING TIME MAP ON PAGES 286–287

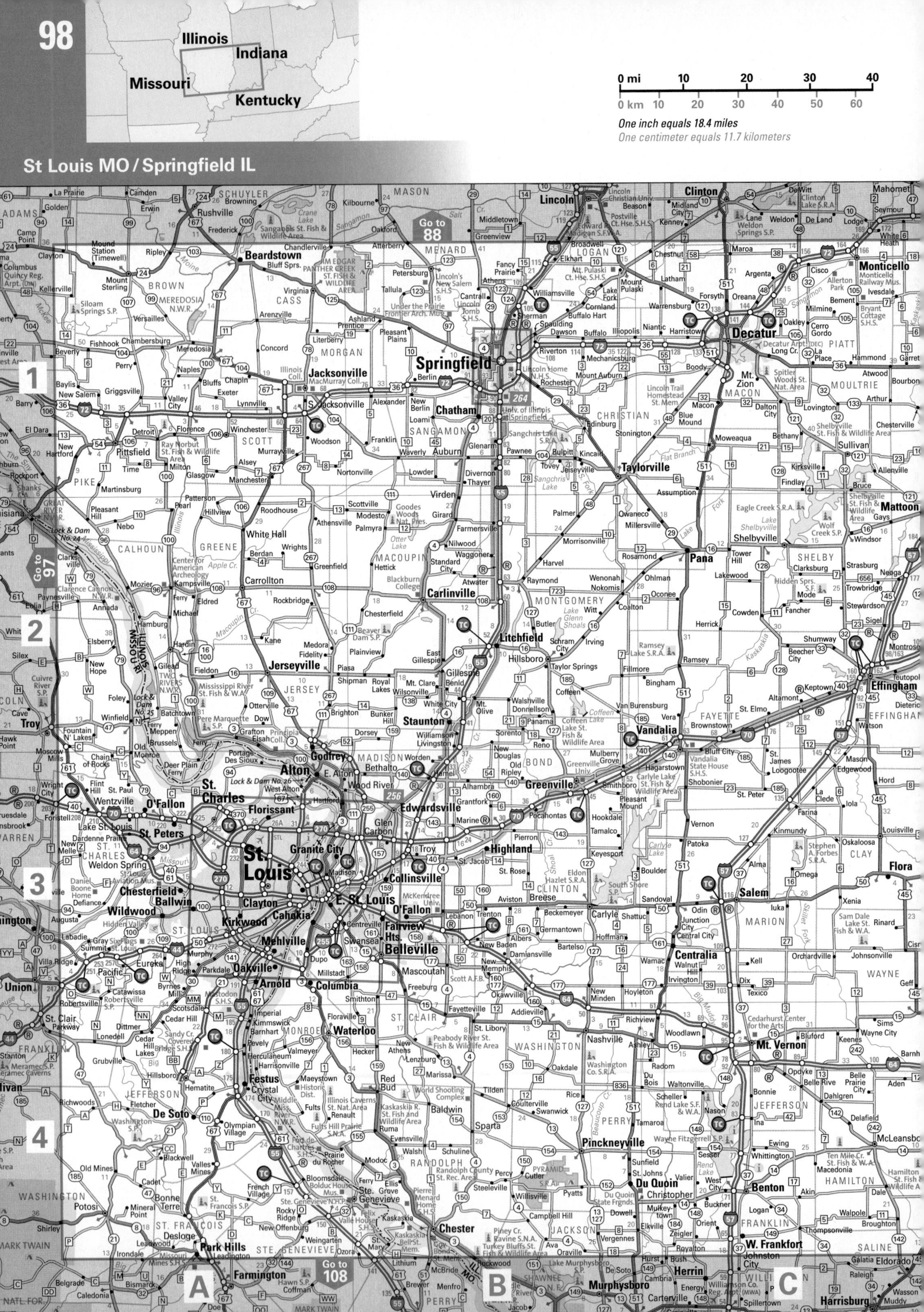

Illinois
Indiana
Missouri
Kentucky

0 mi   10   20   30   40
0 km 10   20   30   40   50   60
One inch equals 18.4 miles
One centimeter equals 11.7 kilometers

St Louis MO / Springfield IL

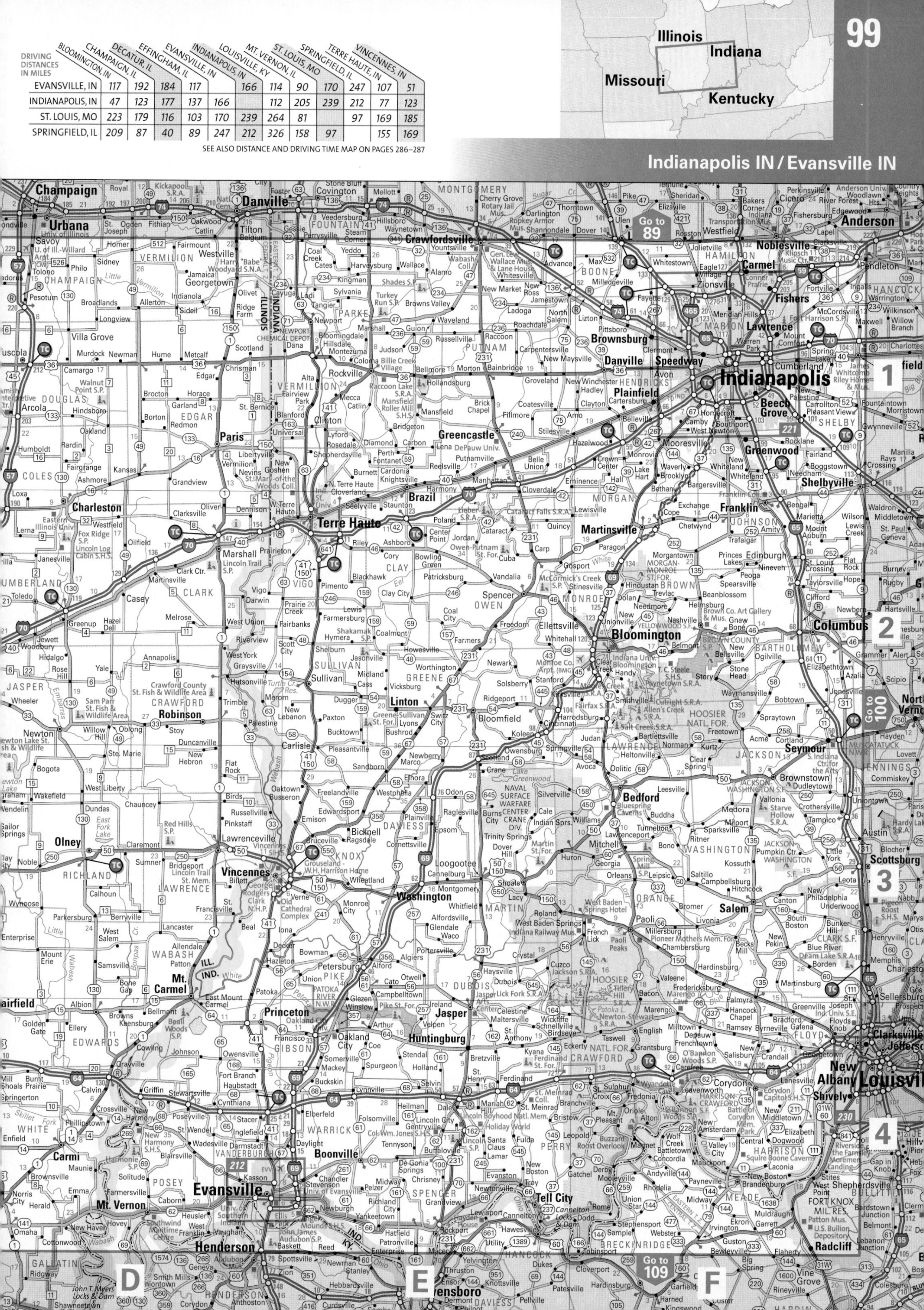

SEE ALSO DISTANCE AND DRIVING TIME MAP ON PAGES 286–287

DRIVING DISTANCES IN MILES	BLOOMINGTON, IN	CHAMPAIGN, IL	DECATUR, IL	EFFINGHAM, IL	EVANSVILLE, IN	INDIANAPOLIS, IN	LOUISVILLE, KY	MT. VERNON, IL	ST. LOUIS, MO	SPRINGFIELD IL	TERRE HAUTE, IN	VINCENNES, IN
EVANSVILLE, IN	117	192	184	117		166	114	90	170	247	107	51
INDIANAPOLIS, IN	47	123	177	137	166		112	205	239	212	77	123
ST. LOUIS, MO	223	179	116	103	170	239	264	81		97	169	185
SPRINGFIELD, IL	209	87	40	89	247	212	326	158	97		155	169

Ohio

Indiana   W. Va.

Kentucky

0 mi   10   20   30   40

0 km   10   20   30   40   50   60

One inch equals 18.4 miles
One centimeter equals 11.7 kilometers

Cincinnati OH / Louisville KY

Go to 90

Go to 99

Go to 110

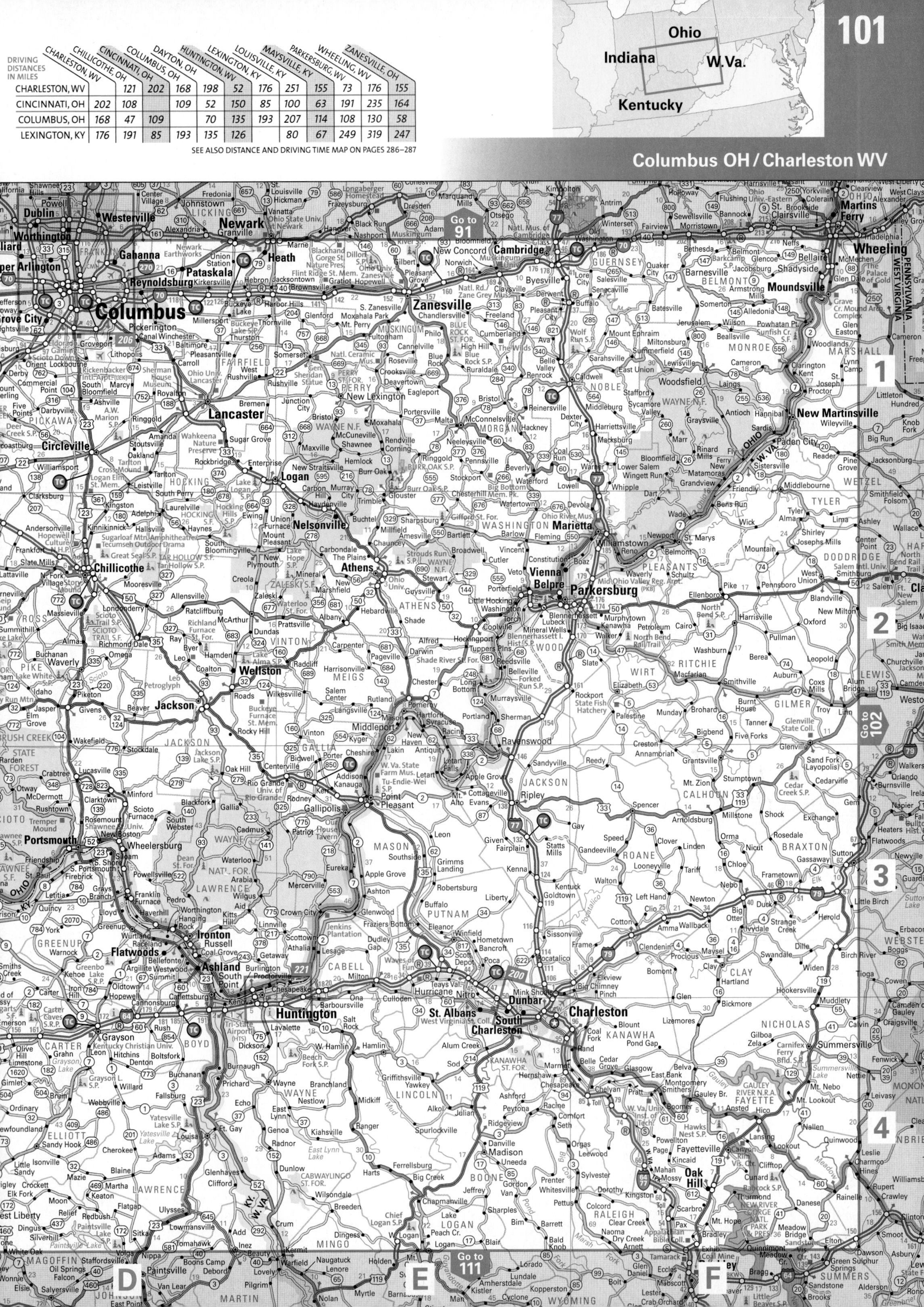

DRIVING
DISTANCES
IN MILES

	CHARLESTON, WV	CHILLICOTHE, OH	CINCINNATI, OH	COLUMBUS, OH	DAYTON, OH	HUNTINGTON, WV	LEXINGTON, KY	LOUISVILLE, KY	MAYSVILLE, KY	PARKERSBURG, WV	WHEELING, WV	ZANESVILLE, OH
CHARLESTON, WV		121	202	168	198	52	176	251	155	73	176	155
CINCINNATI, OH	202	108		109	52	150	85	100	63	191	235	164
COLUMBUS, OH	168	47	109		70	135	193	207	114	108	130	58
LEXINGTON, KY	176	191	85	193	135	126		80	67	249	319	247

SEE ALSO DISTANCE AND DRIVING TIME MAP ON PAGES 286–287

102

Pennsylvania
Ohio
Md. — Delaware
W.Va.
Virginia

Charlottesville VA / Morgantown WV

0 mi   10   20   30   40
0 km   10   20   30   40   50   60
One inch equals 18.4 miles
One centimeter equals 11.7 kilometers

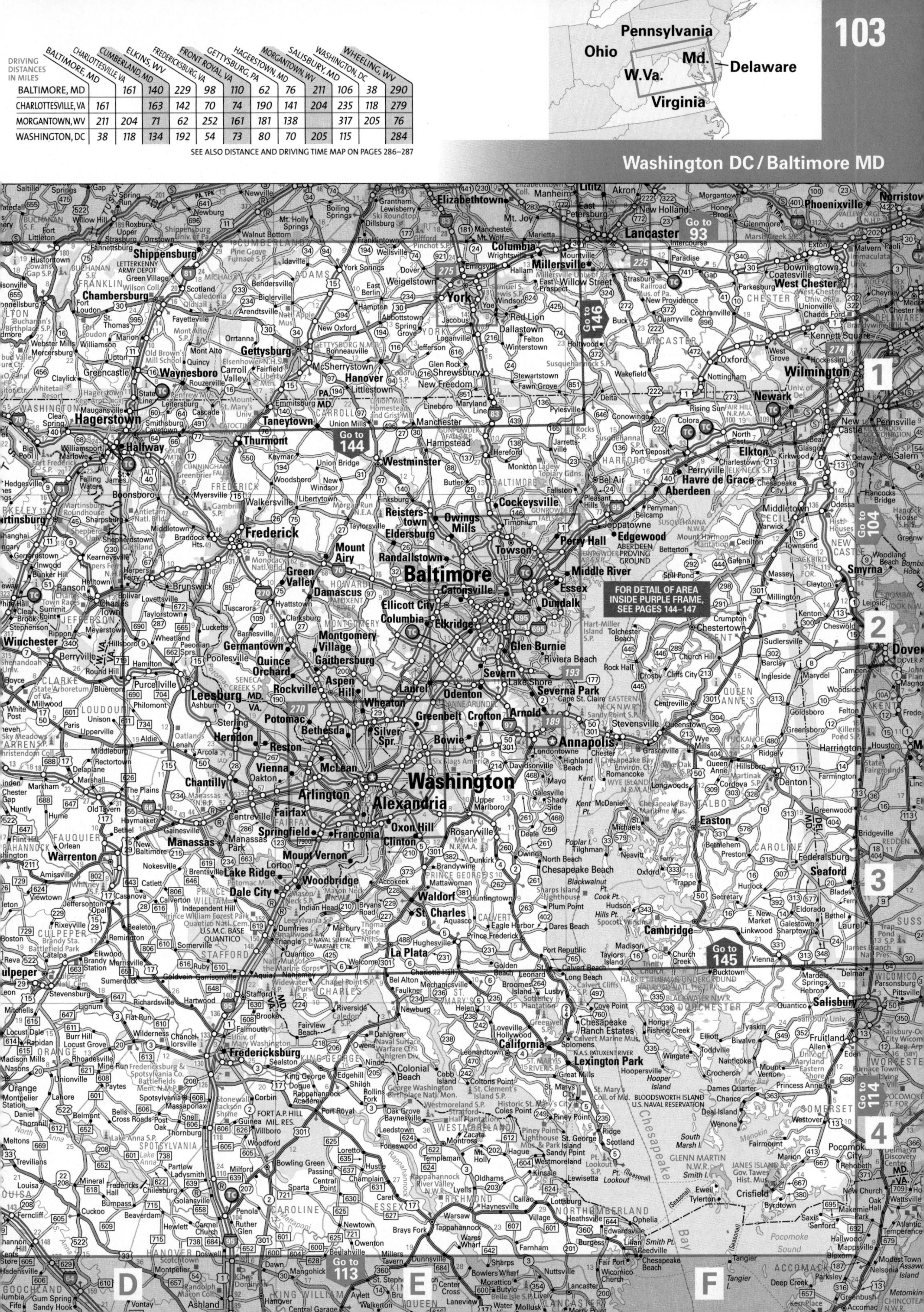

DRIVING DISTANCES IN MILES

	BALTIMORE, MD	CHARLOTTESVILLE, VA	CUMBERLAND, MD	ELKINS, WV	FREDERICKSBURG, VA	FRONT ROYAL, VA	GETTYSBURG, PA	HAGERSTOWN, MD	MORGANTOWN, WV	SALISBURY, MD	WASHINGTON, DC	WHEELING, WV
BALTIMORE, MD		161	140	229	98	110	62	76	211	106	38	290
CHARLOTTESVILLE, VA	161		163	142	70	74	190	141	204	235	118	279
MORGANTOWN, WV	211	204	71	62	252	161	181	138		317	205	76
WASHINGTON, DC	38	118	134	192	54	73	80	70	205	115		284

SEE ALSO DISTANCE AND DRIVING TIME MAP ON PAGES 286–287

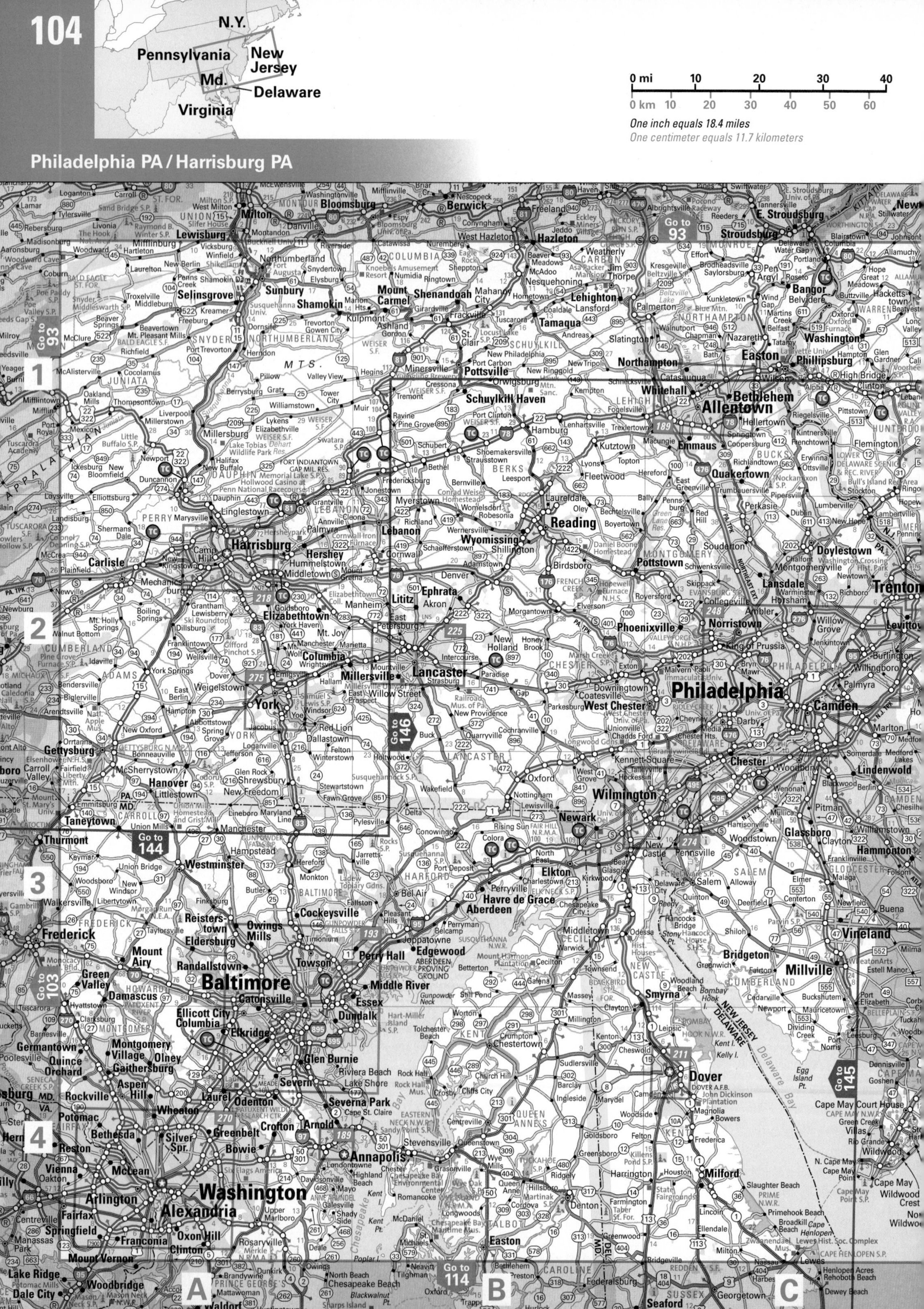

104
N.Y.
Pennsylvania
New Jersey
Md.
Delaware
Virginia
0 mi 10 20 30 40
0 km 10 20 30 40 50 60
One inch equals 18.4 miles
One centimeter equals 11.7 kilometers
Philadelphia PA / Harrisburg PA
Go to 93
Go to 146
Go to 144
Go to 103
Go to 114
Go to 145
1
2
3
4
A
B
C
Bloomsburg
Berwick
Hazleton
E. Stroudsburg
Stroudsburg
Lewisburg
Milton
Selinsgrove
Sunbury
Shamokin
Mount Carmel
Shenandoah
Lehighton
Tamaqua
Bangor
Easton
Phillipsburg
Washington
Pottsville
Schuylkill Haven
Allentown
Bethlehem
Whitehall
Emmaus
Quakertown
Northampton
Harrisburg
Carlisle
Hershey
Lebanon
Reading
Wyomissing
Pottstown
Doylestown
Trenton
Lansdale
Norristown
Phoenixville
King of Prussia
Philadelphia
Camden
Chester
Lancaster
Ephrata
Lititz
Elizabethtown
York
Gettysburg
Hanover
West Chester
Wilmington
Newark
Elkton
Dover
Smyrna
Milford
Vineland
Millville
Bridgeton
Glassboro
Baltimore
Towson
Westminster
Frederick
Columbia
Washington
Alexandria
Annapolis
Arlington
Bethesda
Rockville
Easton
Cape May Court House
Seaford
Georgetown
Havre de Grace
Aberdeen

DRIVING DISTANCES IN MILES	ALLENTOWN, PA	ATLANTIC CITY, NJ	BALTIMORE, MD	DOVER, DE	HARRISBURG, PA	LANCASTER, PA	NEWARK, NJ	NEW YORK, NY	PHILADELPHIA, PA	TRENTON, NJ	WASHINGTON, DC	WILMINGTON, DE
HARRISBURG, PA	82	171	83	126		44	154	165	109	135	123	102
NEW YORK, NY	84	125	192	160	165	165	11		91	55	228	120
PHILADELPHIA, PA	63	62	104	74	109	79	80	91		34	140	30
WASHINGTON, DC	188	186	38	94	123	123	218	228	140	179		110

SEE ALSO DISTANCE AND DRIVING TIME MAP ON PAGES 286–287

N.Y.
Pennsylvania
New Jersey
Md.
Delaware
Virginia

Go to 94

1

2

3

4

Go to 148

Go to 149

Go to 147

FOR DETAIL OF AREA INSIDE PURPLE FRAME, SEE PAGES 144–149

BONUS
Northeast Corridor coverage

ATLANTIC

OCEAN

D   E   F

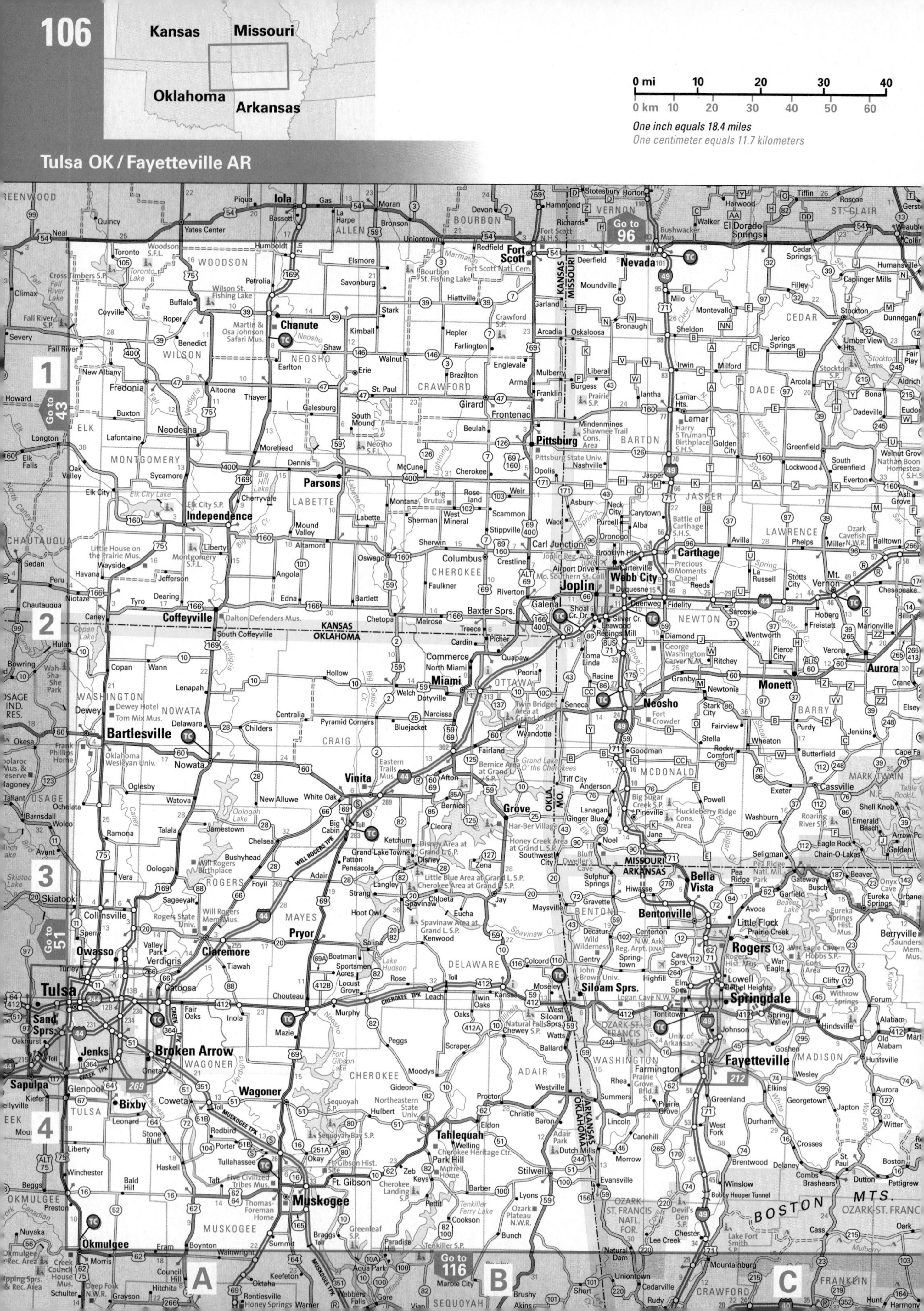

Kansas   Missouri

Oklahoma   Arkansas

0 mi   10   20   30   40
0 km   10   20   30   40   50   60
One inch equals 18.4 miles
One centimeter equals 11.7 kilometers

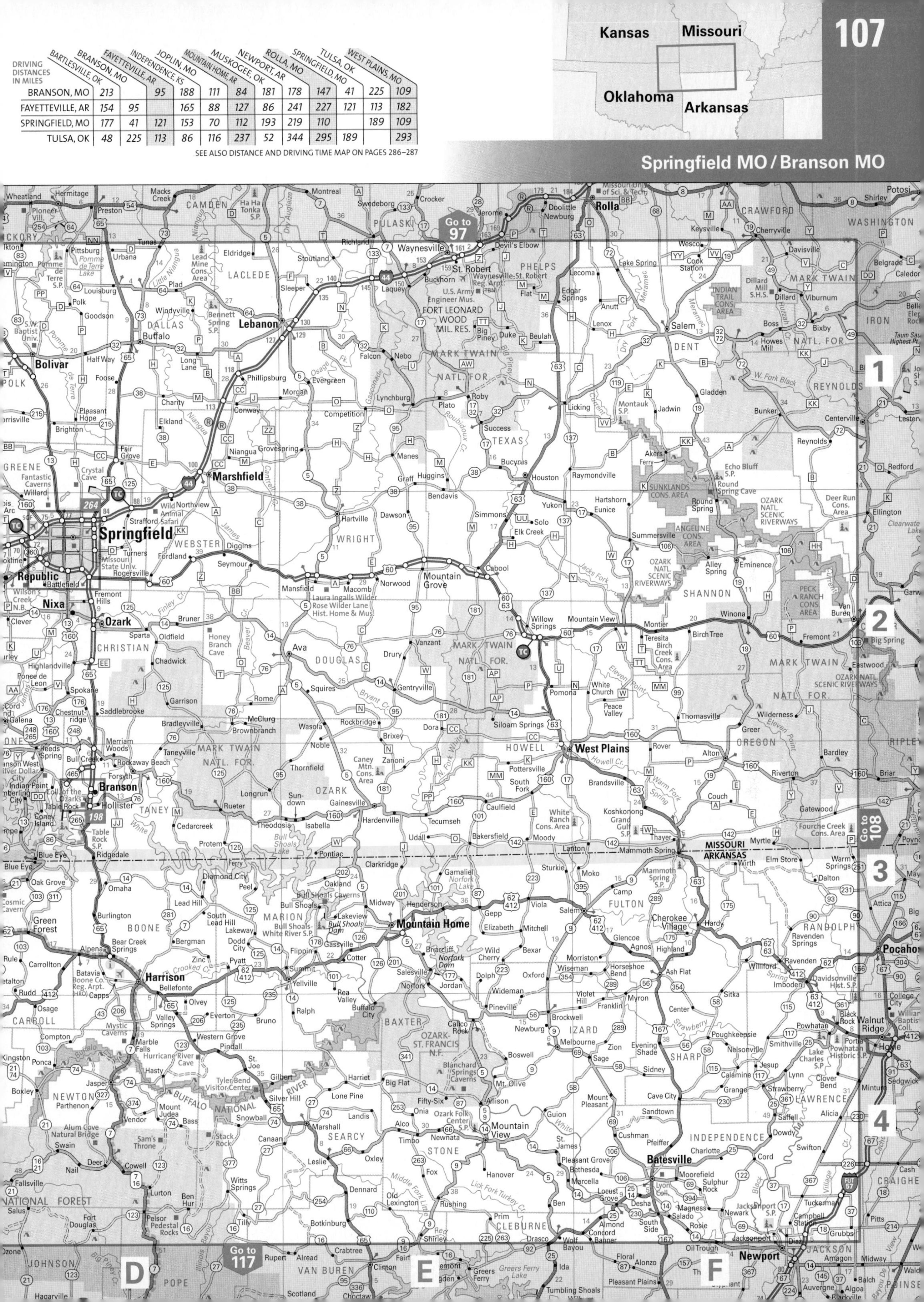

Kansas | Missouri
Oklahoma | Arkansas

DRIVING DISTANCES IN MILES	BARTLESVILLE, OK	BRANSON, MO	FAYETTEVILLE, AR	INDEPENDENCE, KS	JOPLIN, MO	MOUNTAIN HOME, AR	MUSKOGEE, OK	NEWPORT, AR	ROLLA, MO	SPRINGFIELD, MO	TULSA, OK	WEST PLAINS, MO
BRANSON, MO	213			95	188	111	84	181	178	147	41	225	109
FAYETTEVILLE, AR	154	95		165	88	127	86	241	227	121	113	182
SPRINGFIELD, MO	177	41	121	153	70	112	193	219	110	189	109
TULSA, OK	48	225	113	86	116	237	52	344	295	189	293

SEE ALSO DISTANCE AND DRIVING TIME MAP ON PAGES 286–287

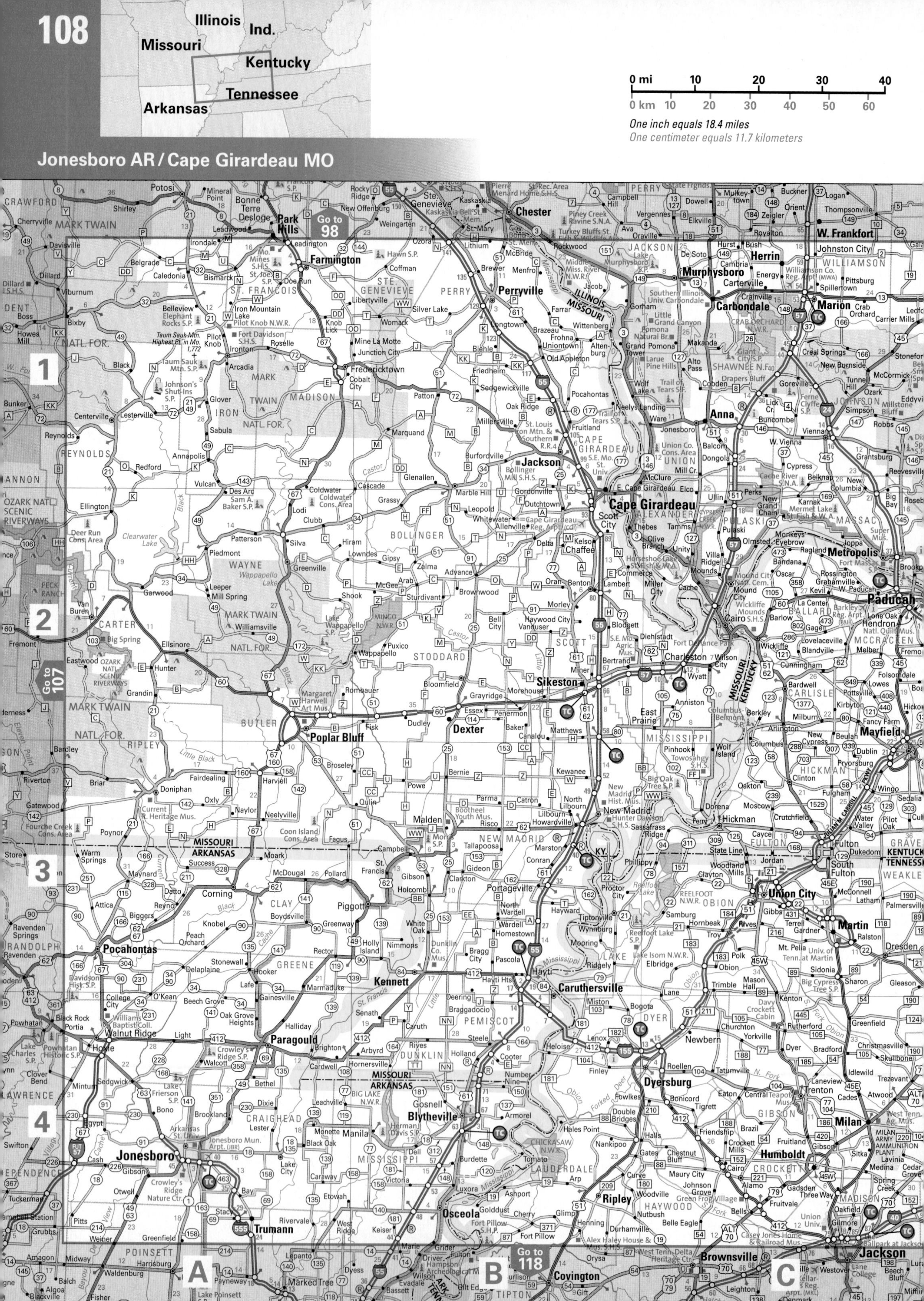

Illinois Ind.
Missouri
Kentucky
Tennessee
Arkansas

0 mi   10   20   30   40
0 km 10 20 30 40 50 60
One inch equals 18.4 miles
One centimeter equals 11.7 kilometers

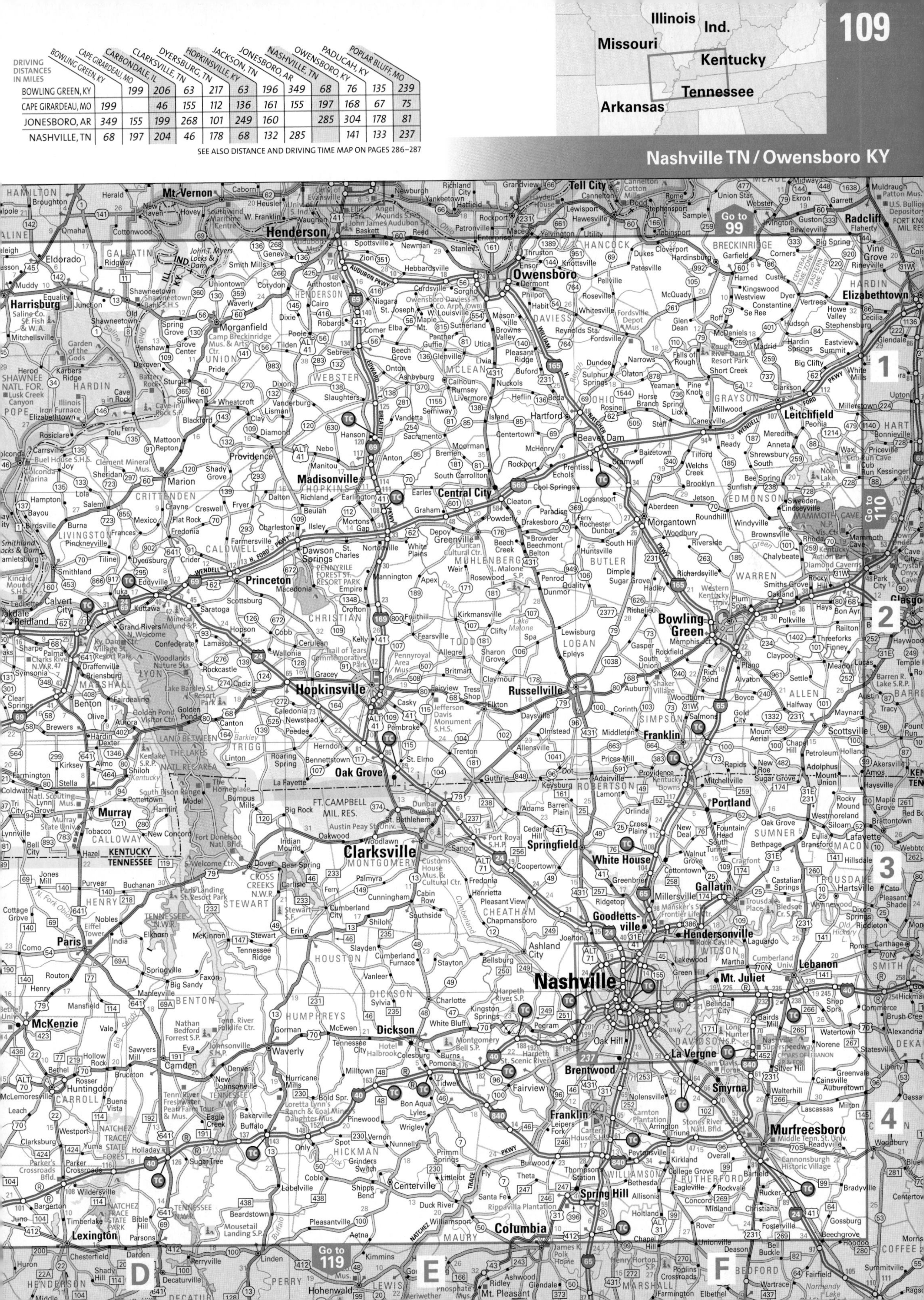

DRIVING DISTANCES IN MILES

	BOWLING GREEN, KY	CAPE GIRARDEAU, MO	CARBONDALE, IL	CLARKSVILLE, TN	DYERSBURG, TN	HOPKINSVILLE, KY	JACKSON, TN	JONESBORO, AR	NASHVILLE, TN	OWENSBORO, KY	PADUCAH, KY	POPLAR BLUFF, MO
BOWLING GREEN, KY		199	206	63	217	63	196	349	68	76	135	239
CAPE GIRARDEAU, MO	199		46	155	112	136	161	155	197	168	67	75
JONESBORO, AR	349	155	199	268	101	249	160		285	304	178	81
NASHVILLE, TN	68	197	204	46	178	68	132	285		141	133	237

SEE ALSO DISTANCE AND DRIVING TIME MAP ON PAGES 286–287

Knoxville TN / Richmond KY

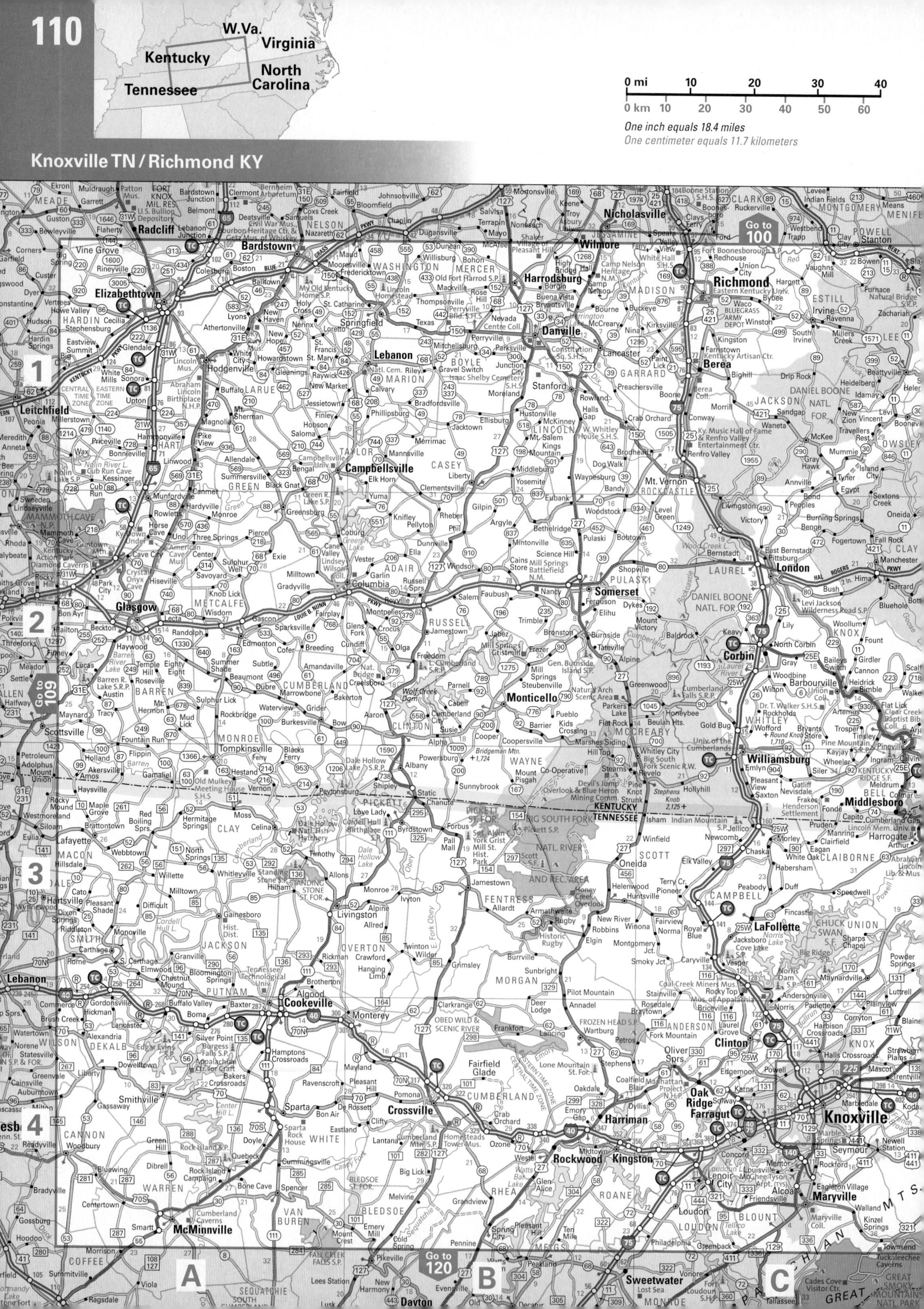
W.Va.
Virginia
Kentucky
North Carolina
Tennessee
0 mi 10 20 30 40
0 km 10 20 30 40 50 60
One inch equals 18.4 miles
One centimeter equals 11.7 kilometers
Go to 100
Go to 109
Go to 120
Richmond
Knoxville
Lexington
Danville
Somerset
London
Cookeville
Crossville
Oak Ridge
Maryville
Campbellsville
Columbia
Glasgow
Elizabethtown
Bardstown
Berea
Corbin
Williamsburg
Middlesboro
Harriman
Kingston
McMinnville
KENTUCKY
TENNESSEE
1
2
3
4
A
B
C

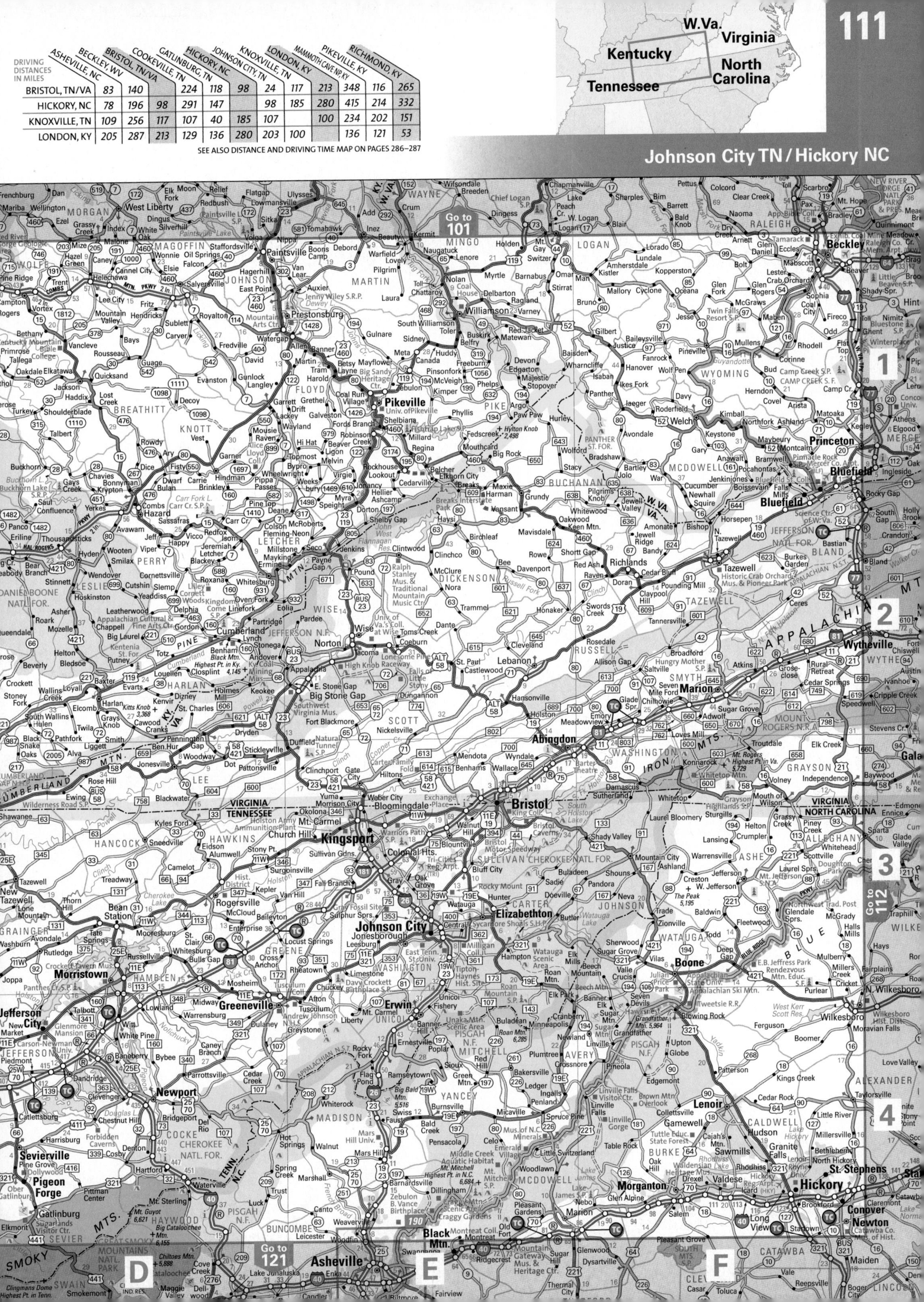

DRIVING DISTANCES IN MILES	ASHEVILLE, NC	BECKLEY, WV	BRISTOL, TN/VA	COOKEVILLE, TN	GATLINBURG, TN	HICKORY, NC	JOHNSON CITY, TN	KNOXVILLE, TN	LONDON, KY	MAMMOTH CAVE N.P., KY	PIKEVILLE, KY	RICHMOND, VA
BRISTOL, TN/VA	83	140		224	118	98	24	117	213	348	116	265
HICKORY, NC	78	196	98	291	147		98	185	280	415	214	332
KNOXVILLE, TN	109	256	117	107	40	185	107		100	234	202	151
LONDON, KY	205	287	213	129	136	280	203	100		136	121	53

SEE ALSO DISTANCE AND DRIVING TIME MAP ON PAGES 286–287

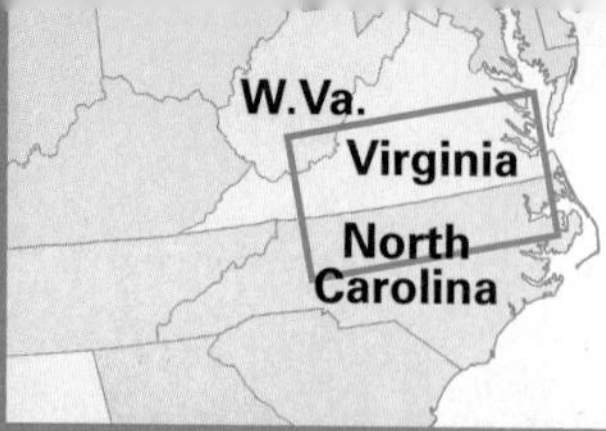

W.Va.
Virginia
North
Carolina

0 mi   10   20   30   40
0 km 10 20 30 40 50 60

One inch equals 18.4 miles
One centimeter equals 11.7 kilometers

Go to 102
Go to 111
Go to 122

DRIVING DISTANCES IN MILES

	DANVILLE, VA	GREENSBORO, NC	LYNCHBURG, VA	NORFOLK, VA	RALEIGH, NC	RICHMOND, VA	ROANOKE, VA	ROANOKE RAPIDS, NC	ROCKY MOUNT, NC	WILLIAMSBURG, VA	WINSTON-SALEM, NC	WYTHEVILLE, VA
GREENSBORO, NC	46		106	230	69	200	101	132	124	237	30	120
RALEIGH, NC	89	69	140	179		157	156	84	54	204	96	186
RICHMOND, VA	160	200	114	91	157		192	91	127	49	228	256
ROANOKE, VA	83	101	55	285	156	192		190	211	243	107	78

SEE ALSO DISTANCE AND DRIVING TIME MAP ON PAGES 286–287

Go to 103

Go to 114

Go to 115

Go to 123

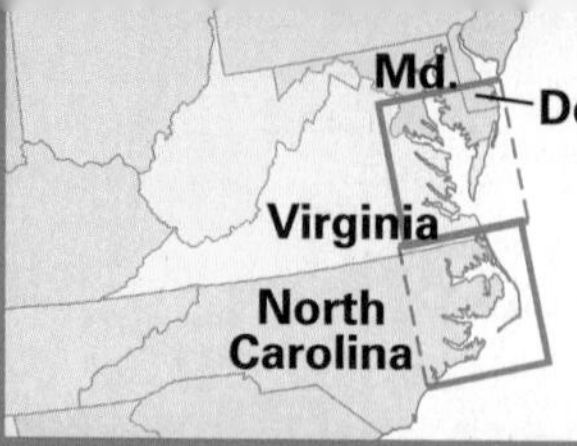

Md.— Delaware
Virginia
North Carolina

Norfolk VA / Ocean City MD

0 mi 10 20 30 40
0 km 10 20 30 40 50 60
One inch equals 18.4 miles
One centimeter equals 11.7 kilometers

FOR DETAIL OF AREA INSIDE PURPLE FRAME, SEE PAGES 144–145

Go to 104

Go to 103

Go to 144

Go to 145

Go to 113

Go to 115

ATLANTIC OCEAN

1
2
3
4

A
B
C

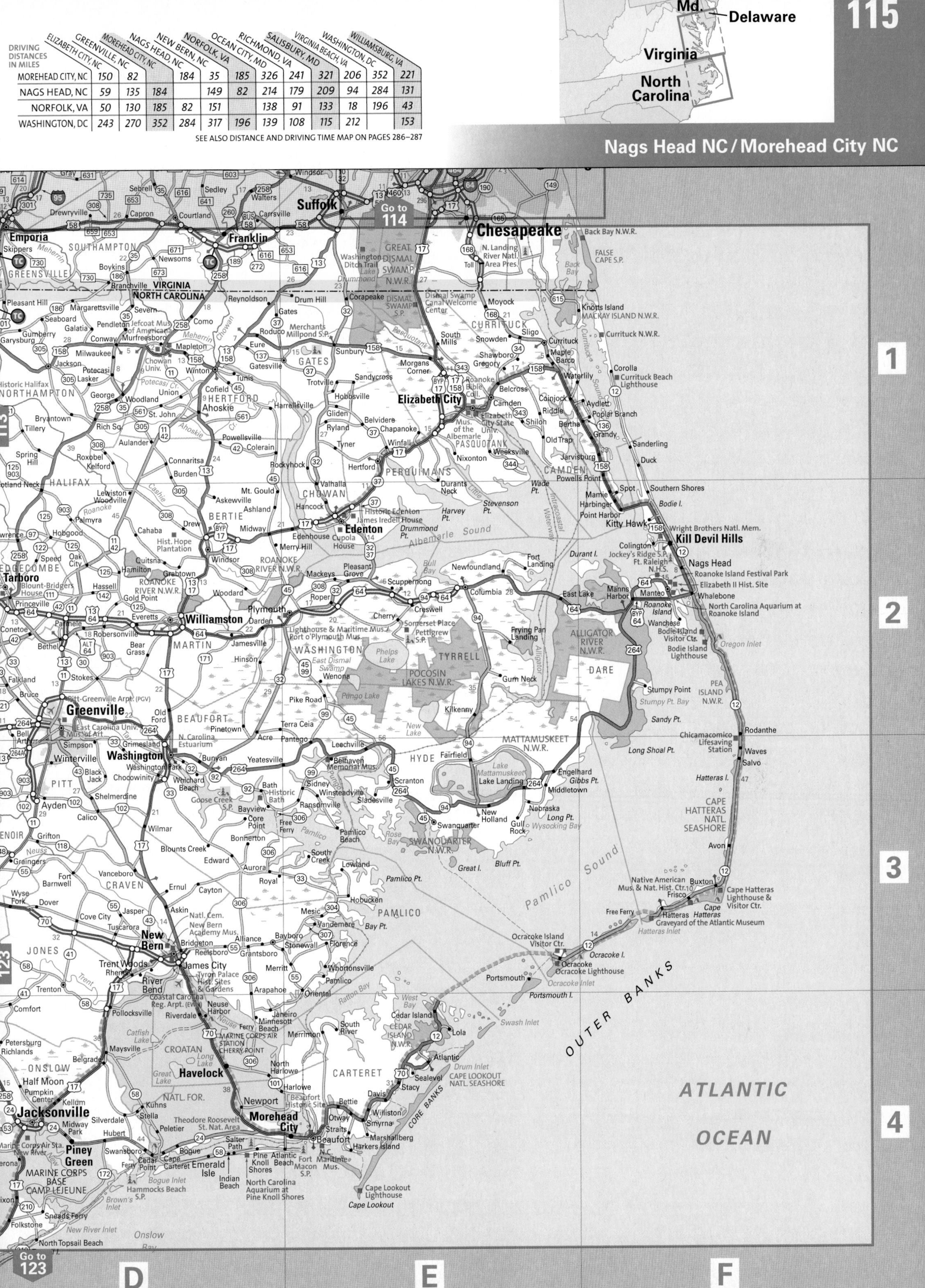

Md. — Delaware

Virginia

North Carolina

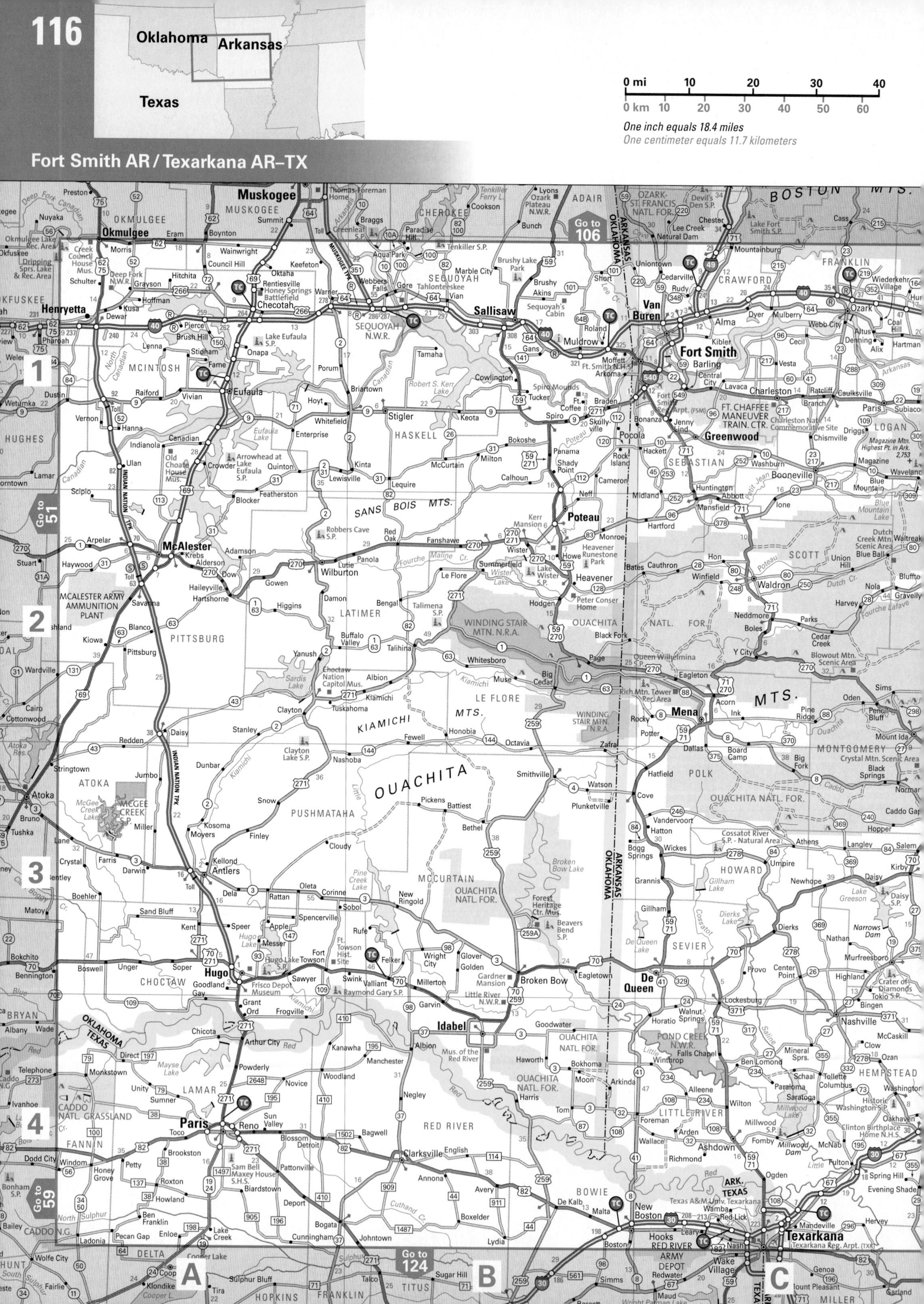

0 mi   10   20   30   40

0 km   10   20   30   40   50   60

One inch equals 18.4 miles
One centimeter equals 11.7 kilometers

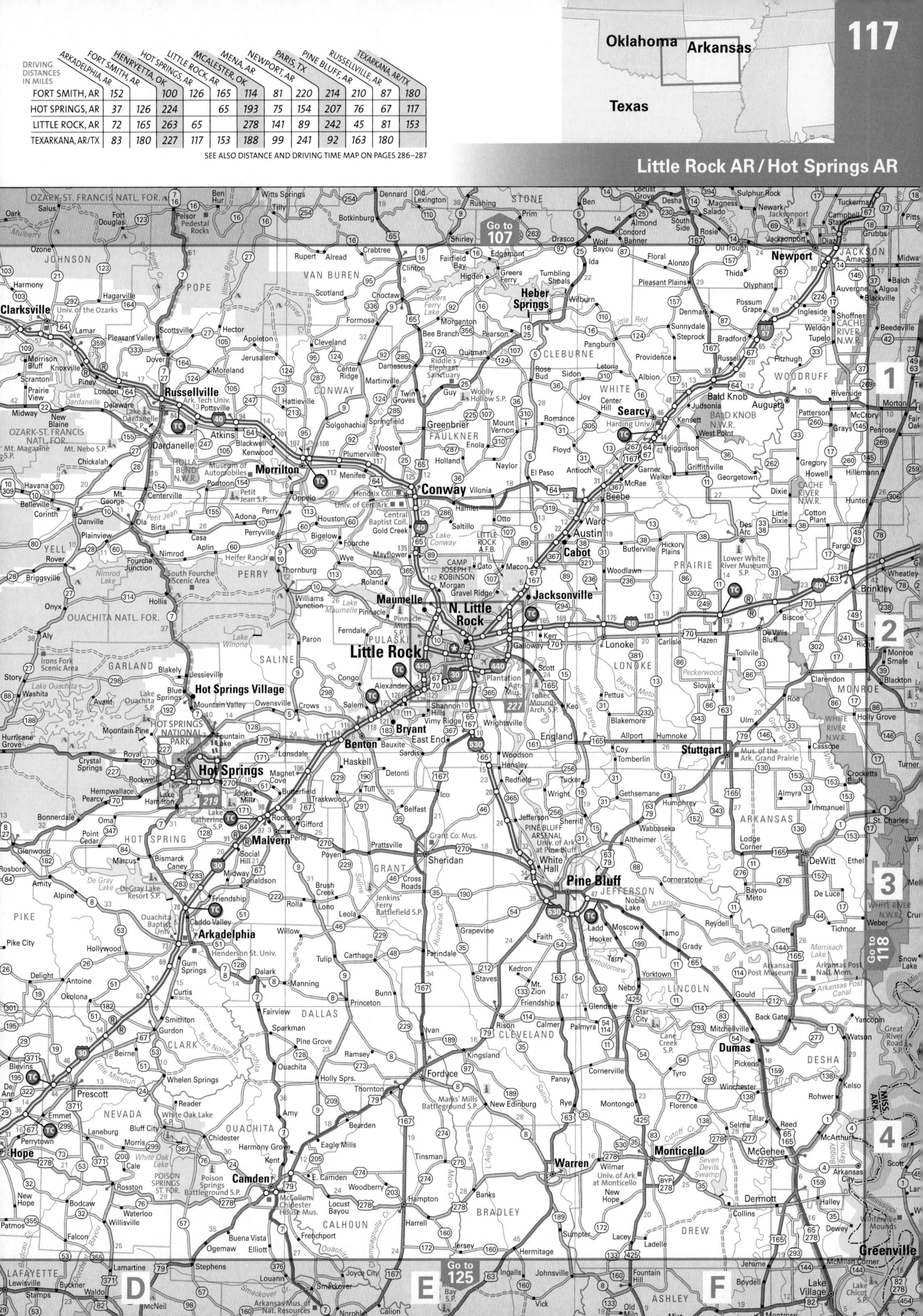

DRIVING DISTANCES IN MILES

	ARKADELPHIA, AR	FORT SMITH, AR	HENRYETTA, OK	HOT SPRINGS, AR	LITTLE ROCK, AR	MCALESTER, OK	MENA, AR	NEWPORT, AR	PARIS, TX	PINE BLUFF, AR	RUSSELLVILLE, AR	TEXARKANA, AR/TX
FORT SMITH, AR	152		100	126	165	114	81	220	214	210	87	180
HOT SPRINGS, AR	37	126	224		65	193	75	154	207	76	67	117
LITTLE ROCK, AR	72	165	263	65		278	141	89	242	45	81	153
TEXARKANA, AR/TX	83	180	227	117	153	188	99	241	92	163	180	

SEE ALSO DISTANCE AND DRIVING TIME MAP ON PAGES 286–287

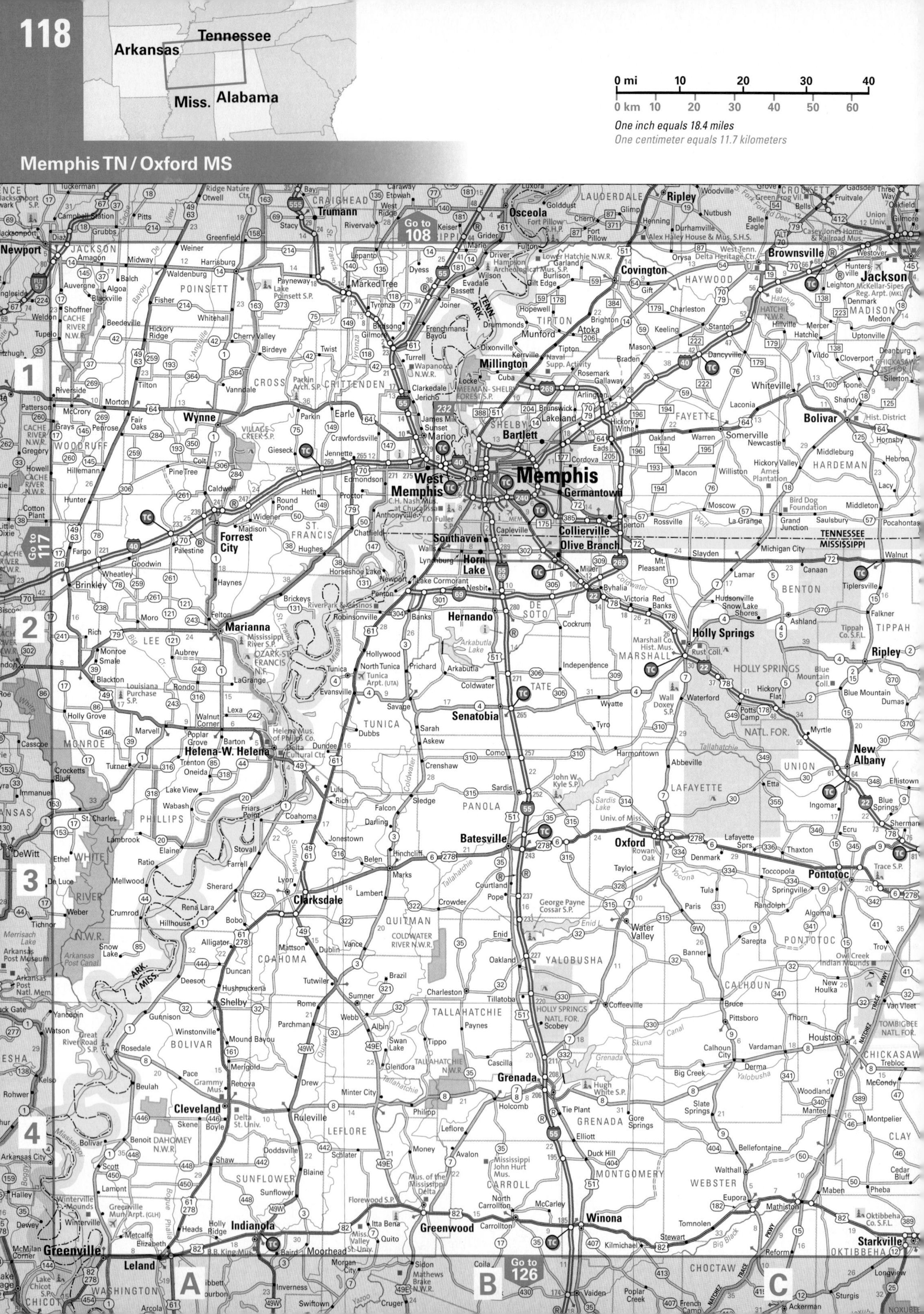

Arkansas Tennessee
Miss. Alabama

One inch equals 18.4 miles
One centimeter equals 11.7 kilometers

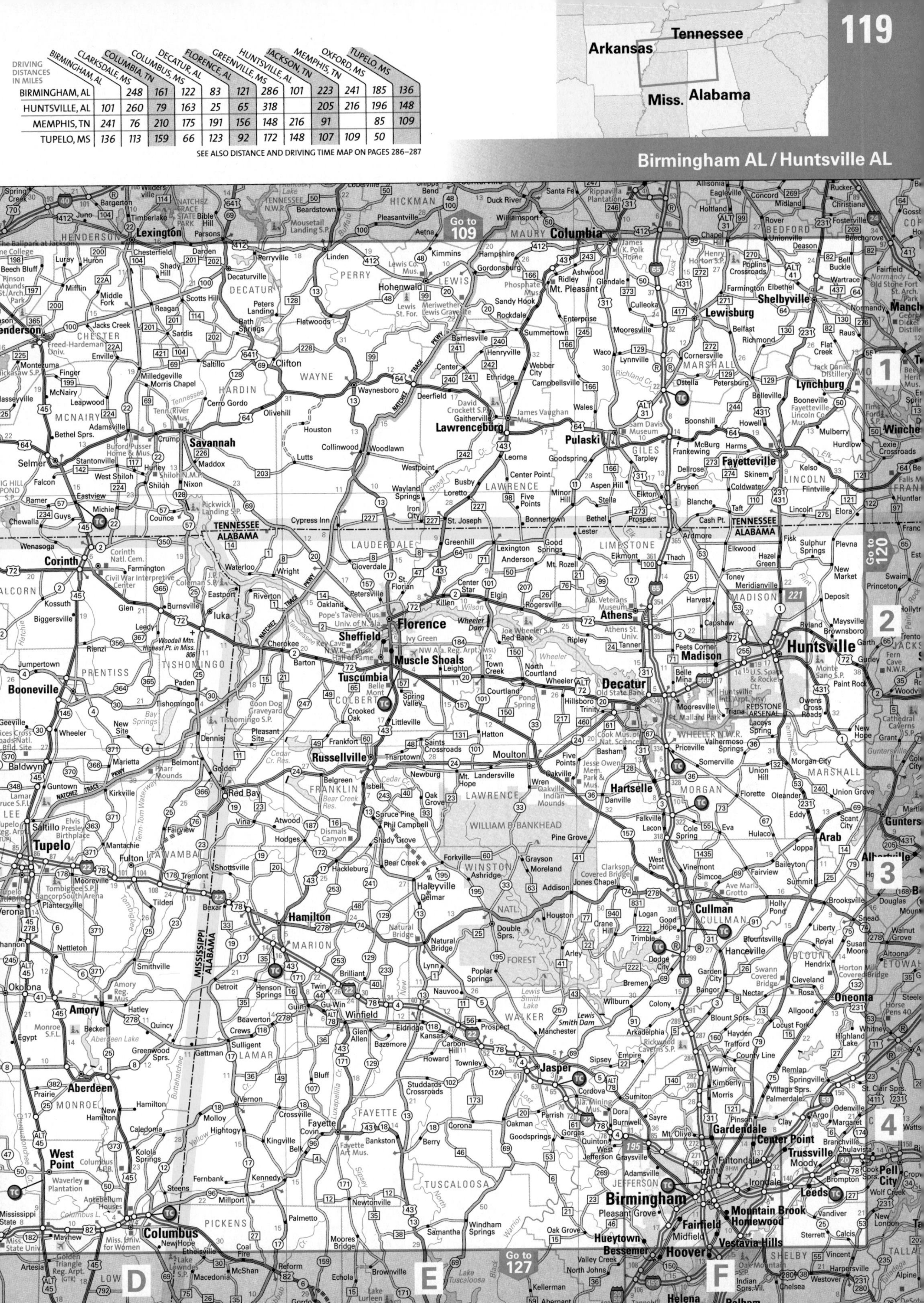

DRIVING DISTANCES IN MILES	CLARKSDALE, MS	COLUMBIA, TN	COLUMBUS, MS	DECATUR, AL	FLORENCE, AL	GREENVILLE, MS	HUNTSVILLE, AL	JACKSON, TN	MEMPHIS, TN	OXFORD, MS	TUPELO, MS
BIRMINGHAM, AL	248	161	122	83	121	286	101	223	241	185	136
HUNTSVILLE, AL	101	260	79	163	25	65	318		205	216	196	148
MEMPHIS, TN	241	76	210	175	191	156	148	216	91		85	109
TUPELO, MS	136	113	159	66	123	92	172	148	107	109	50	

SEE ALSO DISTANCE AND DRIVING TIME MAP ON PAGES 286–287

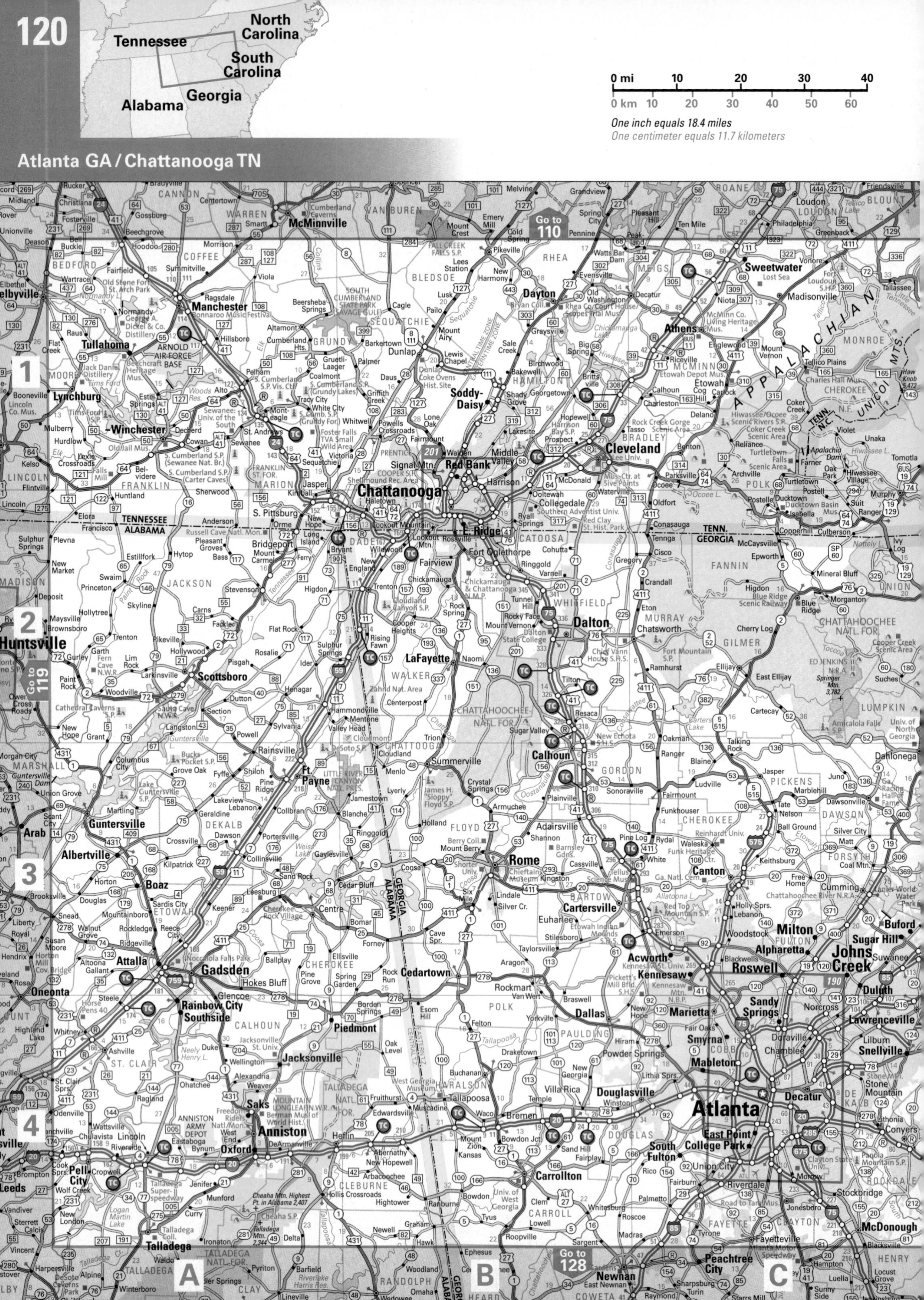
Tennessee
North Carolina
South Carolina
Alabama
Georgia
0 mi 10 20 30 40
0 km 10 20 30 40 50 60
One inch equals 18.4 miles
One centimeter equals 11.7 kilometers
Go to 110
Go to 119
Go to 128
1
2
3
4
A
B
C
McMinnville
Manchester
Tullahoma
Lynchburg
Winchester
Dayton
Sweetwater
Athens
Cleveland
Chattanooga
Red Bank
Soddy-Daisy
Huntsville
Scottsboro
Dalton
LaFayette
Calhoun
Ft. Payne
Guntersville
Albertville
Boaz
Rome
Cartersville
Canton
Gadsden
Attalla
Rainbow City
Southside
Cedartown
Dallas
Marietta
Kennesaw
Acworth
Roswell
Alpharetta
Milton
Johns Creek
Sandy Springs
Smyrna
Mableton
Douglasville
Atlanta
Decatur
East Point
College Park
South Fulton
Anniston
Oxford
Jacksonville
Piedmont
Carrollton
Talladega
Newnan
Peachtree City
McDonough
Duluth
Lawrenceville
Snellville
Buford
Sugar Hill
Dahlonega
Ellijay
Chatsworth
APPALACHIAN
CHATTAHOOCHEE NATL. FOR.
TENNESSEE
ALABAMA
TENN.
GEORGIA

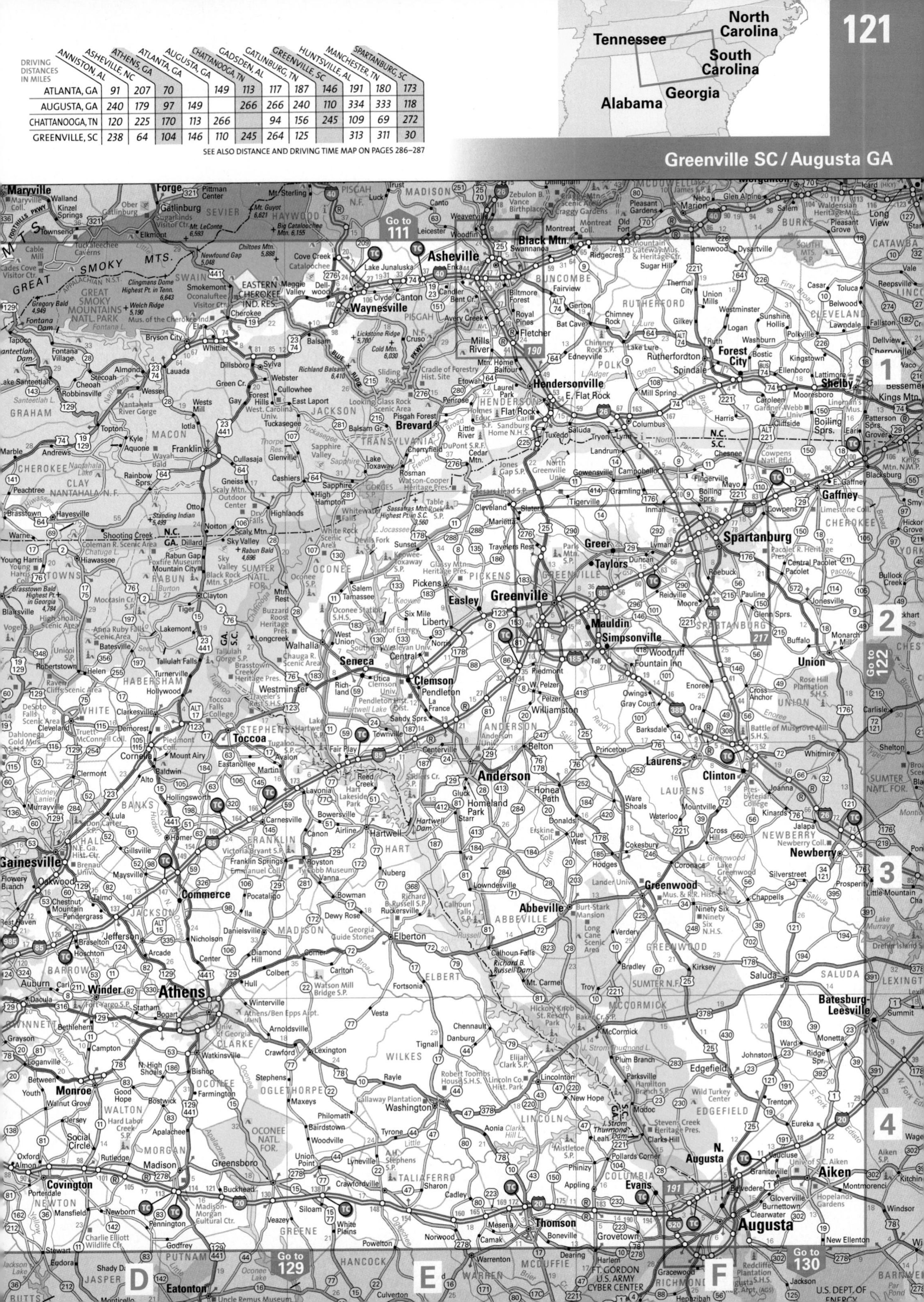

121

North Carolina
Tennessee
South Carolina
Alabama   Georgia

Greenville SC / Augusta GA

DRIVING DISTANCES IN MILES	ANNISTON, AL	ASHEVILLE, NC	ATHENS, GA	ATLANTA, GA	AUGUSTA, GA	CHATTANOOGA, TN	GADSDEN, AL	GATLINBURG, TN	GREENVILLE, SC	HUNTSVILLE, AL	MANCHESTER, TN	SPARTANBURG, SC
ATLANTA, GA	91	207	70		149	113	117	187	146	191	180	173
AUGUSTA, GA	240	179	97	149		266	266	240	110	334	333	118
CHATTANOOGA, TN	120	225	170	113	266		94	156	245	109	69	272
GREENVILLE, SC	238	64	104	146	110	245	264	125		313	311	30

SEE ALSO DISTANCE AND DRIVING TIME MAP ON PAGES 286–287

North Carolina
South Carolina

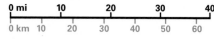

```
0 mi          10          20          30          40
0 km    10    20    30    40    50    60
One inch equals 18.4 miles
One centimeter equals 11.7 kilometers
```

Charlotte NC / Columbia SC

DRIVING DISTANCES IN MILES	CHARLOTTE, NC	COLUMBIA, SC	FAYETTEVILLE, NC	FLORENCE, SC	GOLDSBORO, NC	HICKORY, NC	LUMBERTON, NC	MOREHEAD CITY, NC	MYRTLE BEACH, SC	ROCK HILL, SC	SUMTER, SC	WILMINGTON, NC
CHARLOTTE, NC		91	139	107	208	47	128	298	173	26	115	205
COLUMBIA, SC	91		170	80	240	139	139	289	146	70	45	199
MYRTLE BEACH, SC	173	146	116	66	170	220	83	165		181	93	71
WILMINGTON, NC	205	199	92	120	100	292	77	95	71	220	158	

SEE ALSO DISTANCE AND DRIVING TIME MAP ON PAGES 286–287

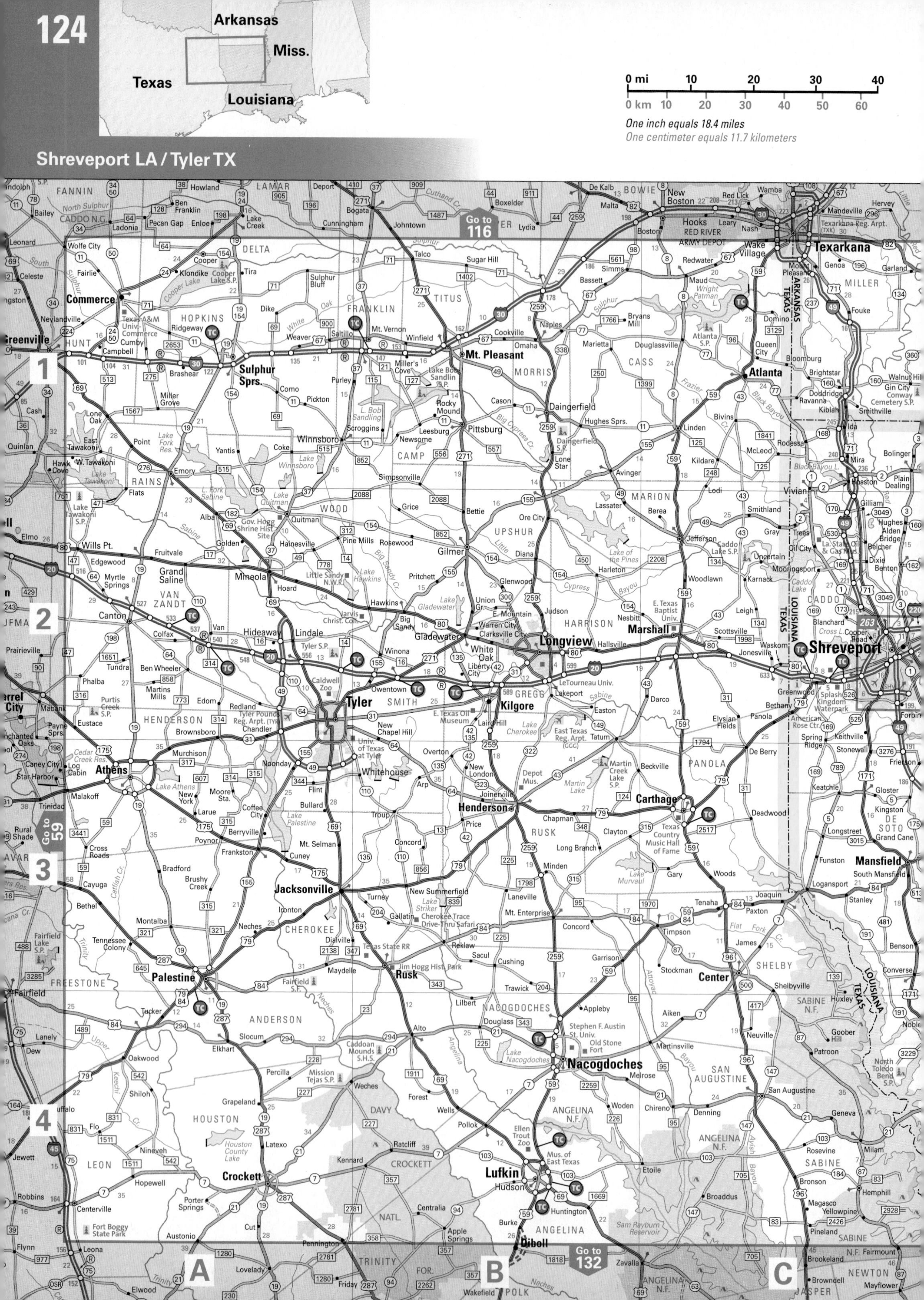

Arkansas

Miss.

Texas

Louisiana

One inch equals 18.4 miles
One centimeter equals 11.7 kilometers

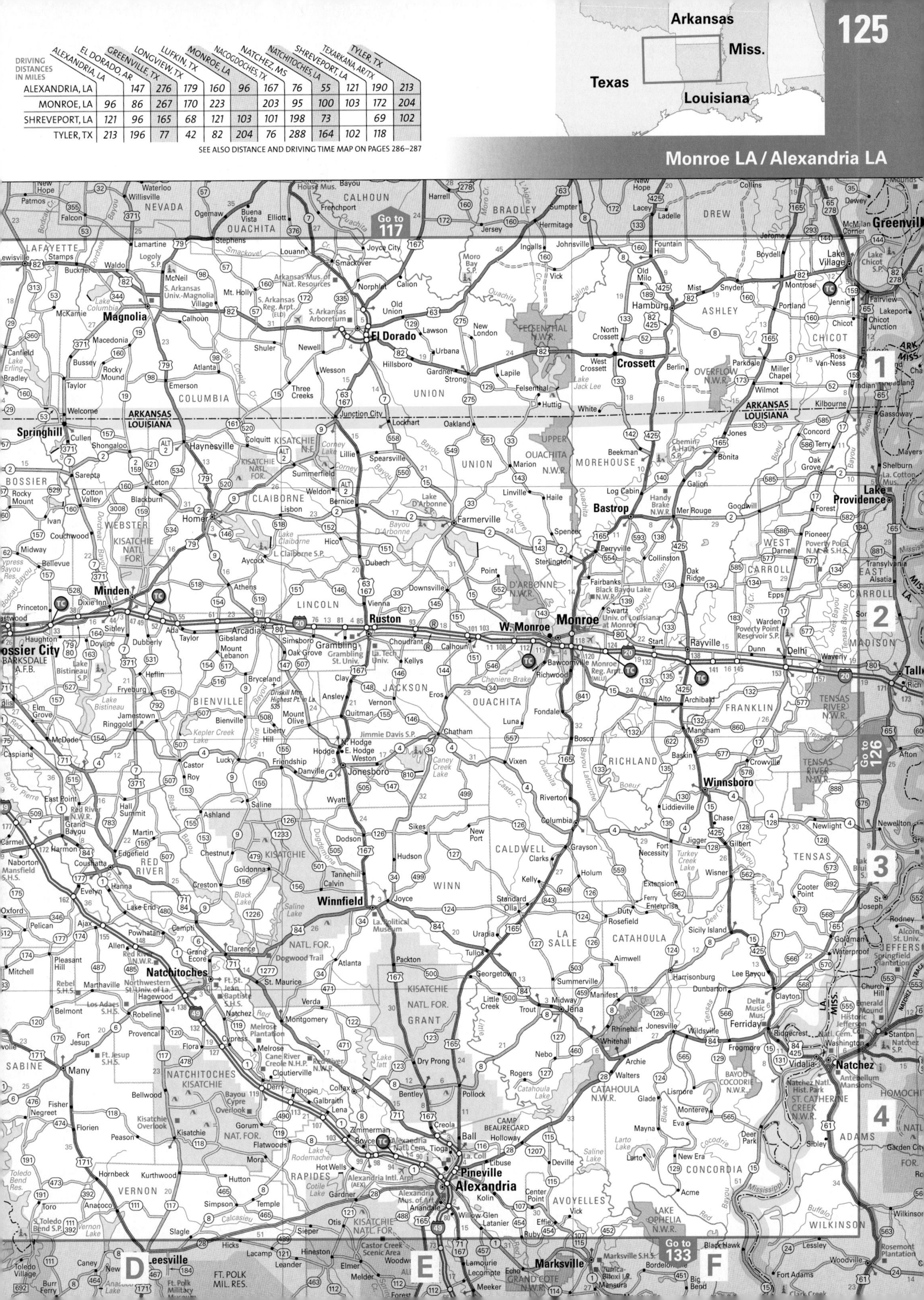

Arkansas
Miss.
Texas
Louisiana

DRIVING DISTANCES IN MILES	EL DORADO, AR	GREENVILLE, MS	LONGVIEW, TX	LUFKIN, TX	MONROE, LA	NACOGDOCHES, LA	NATCHEZ, MS	NATCHITOCHES, LA	SHREVEPORT, LA	TEXARKANA, AR/TX	TYLER, TX
ALEXANDRIA, LA	147	276	179	160	96	167	76	55	121	190	213
MONROE, LA	96	86	267	170	223		203	95	100	103	172	204
SHREVEPORT, LA	121	96	165	68	121	103	101	198	73		69	102
TYLER, TX	213	196	77	42	82	204	76	288	164	102	118	

SEE ALSO DISTANCE AND DRIVING TIME MAP ON PAGES 286–287

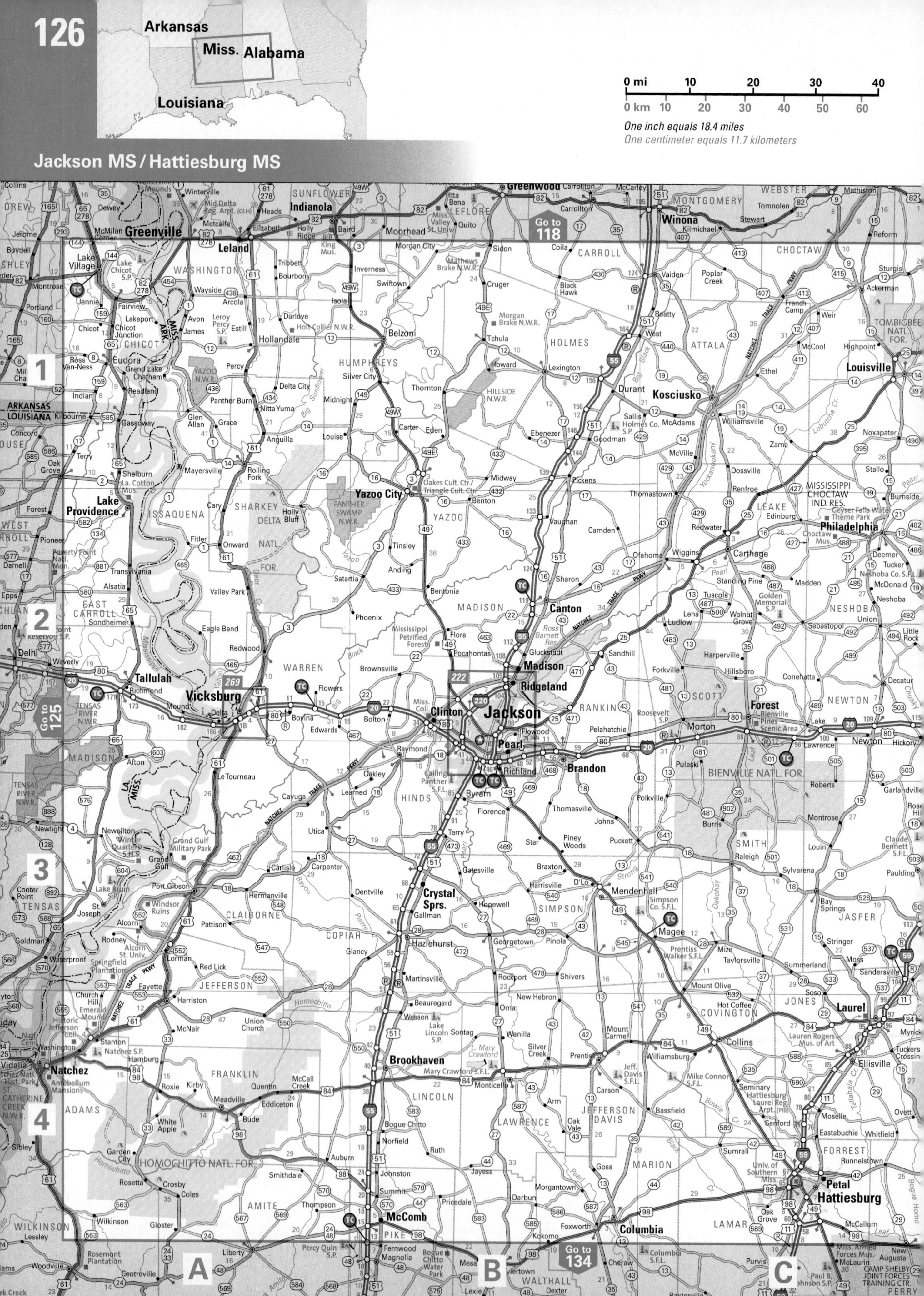

Arkansas

Miss. Alabama

Louisiana

0 mi   10   20   30   40
0 km 10 20 30 40 50 60
One inch equals 18.4 miles
One centimeter equals 11.7 kilometers

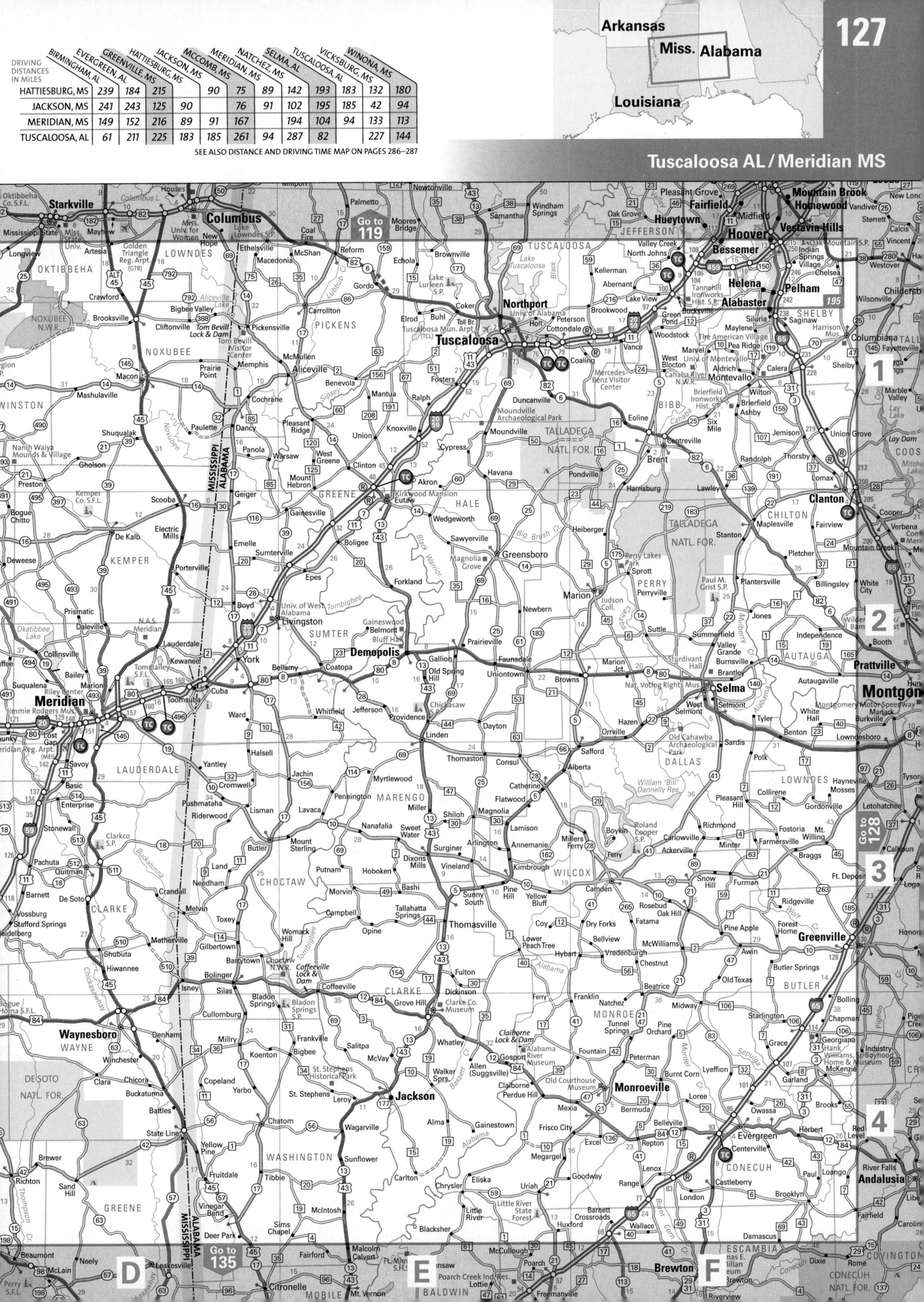

Arkansas

Miss. Alabama

Louisiana

DRIVING DISTANCES IN MILES	BIRMINGHAM, AL	EVERGREEN, AL	GREENVILLE, AL	HATTIESBURG, MS	JACKSON, MS	McCOMB, MS	MERIDIAN, MS	NATCHEZ, MS	SELMA, AL	TUSCALOOSA, AL	VICKSBURG, MS	WINONA, MS
HATTIESBURG, MS	239	184	215		90	75	89	142	193	183	132	180
JACKSON, MS	241	243	125	90		76	91	102	195	185	42	94
MERIDIAN, MS	149	152	216	89	91	167		194	104	94	133	113
TUSCALOOSA, AL	61	211	225	183	185	261	94	287	82		227	144

SEE ALSO DISTANCE AND DRIVING TIME MAP ON PAGES 286–287

Alabama   Georgia

0 mi   10   20   30   40
0 km 10 20 30 40 50 60
One inch equals 18.4 miles
One centimeter equals 11.7 kilometers

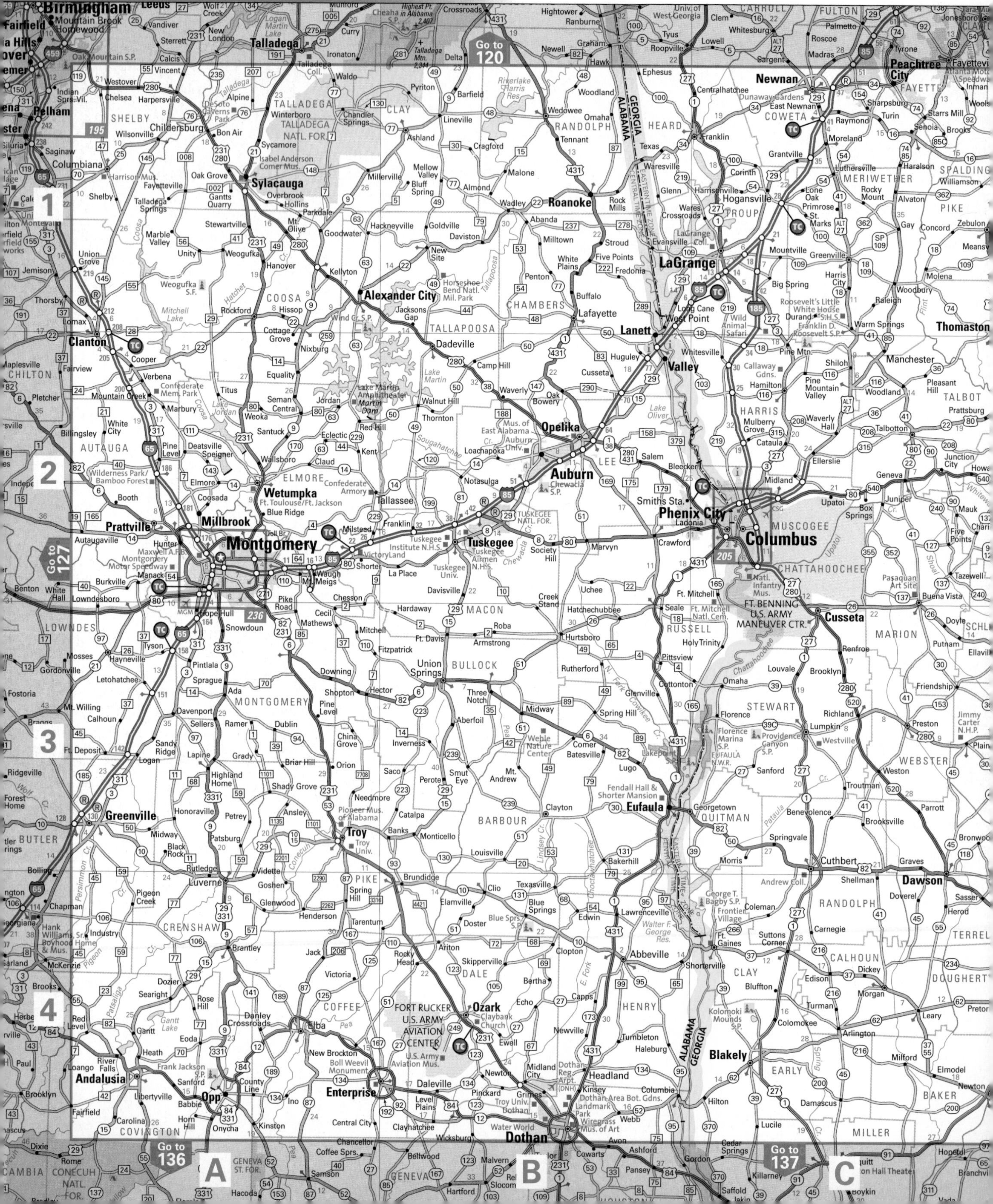

DRIVING DISTANCES IN MILES

	ALBANY, GA	ATLANTA, GA	AUBURN, AL	AUGUSTA, GA	BIRMINGHAM, GA	COLUMBUS, GA	DOTHAN, AL	LA GRANGE, GA	MACON, GA	MONTGOMERY, AL	TIFTON, GA	WAYCROSS, GA
ALBANY, GA		180	121	226	253	86	83	129	102	165	43	116
COLUMBUS, GA	86	106	34	249	167		97	46	95	79	135	208
MACON, GA	102	84	151	123	234	95	186	114		203	102	159
MONTGOMERY, AL	165	158	54	301	88	79	103	95	203		214	287

SEE ALSO DISTANCE AND DRIVING TIME MAP ON PAGES 286–287

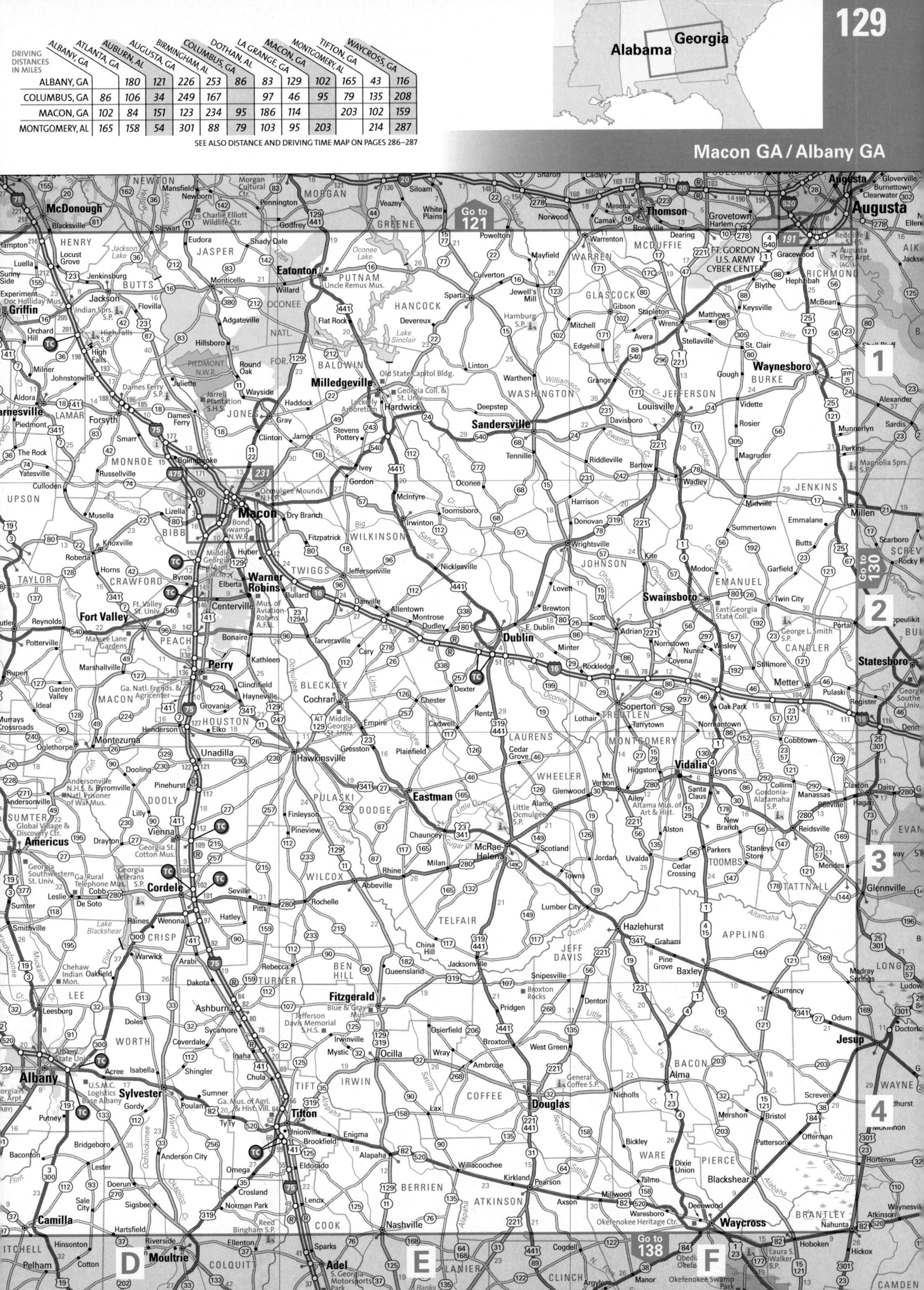

One inch equals 18.4 miles
One centimeter equals 11.7 kilometers

0 mi		10		20		30		40
0 km	10	20	30	40	50	60		

Savannah GA / Hilton Head Island SC

Go to 121

Go to 129

Go to 138

Go to 139

1

2

3

4

A

B

C

South Carolina
Georgia

DRIVING DISTANCES IN MILES	AUGUSTA, GA	BEAUFORT, SC	BRUNSWICK, GA	CHARLESTON, SC	GEORGETOWN, SC	HILTON HEAD I., SC	HINESVILLE, GA	ORANGEBURG, SC	SAVANNAH, GA	STATESBORO, GA	WALTERBORO, SC	WAYCROSS, GA
AUGUSTA, GA		126	194	142	181	127	157	74	135	81	111	184
CHARLESTON, SC	142	66	175		58	95	138	73	107	150	51	203
HILTON HEAD I., SC	127	32	113	95	157		75	116	35	88	64	141
SAVANNAH, GA	135	42	78	107	163	35	41	123		53	71	106

SEE ALSO DISTANCE AND DRIVING TIME MAP ON PAGES 286–287

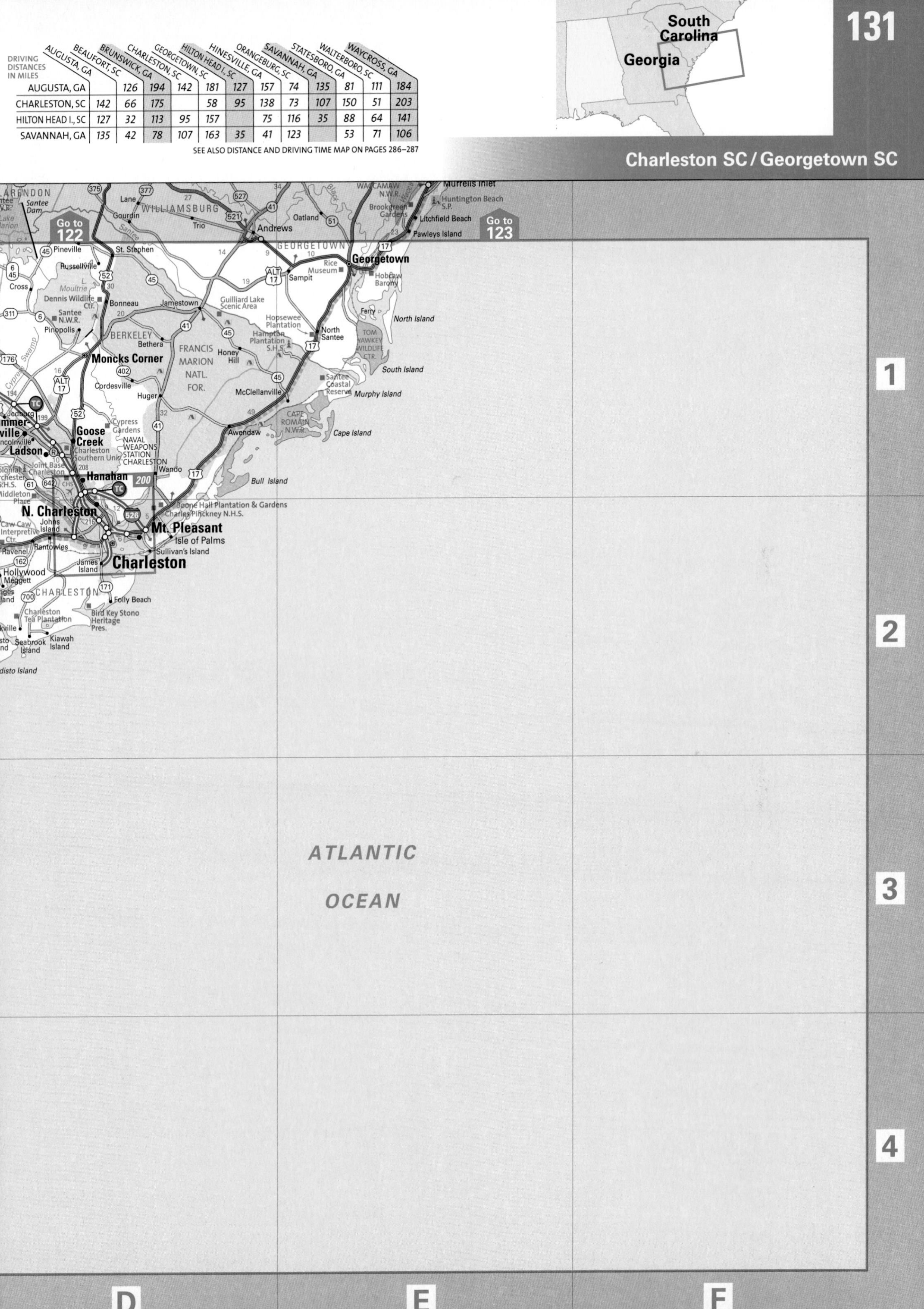

ATLANTIC

OCEAN

Go to 122
Go to 123

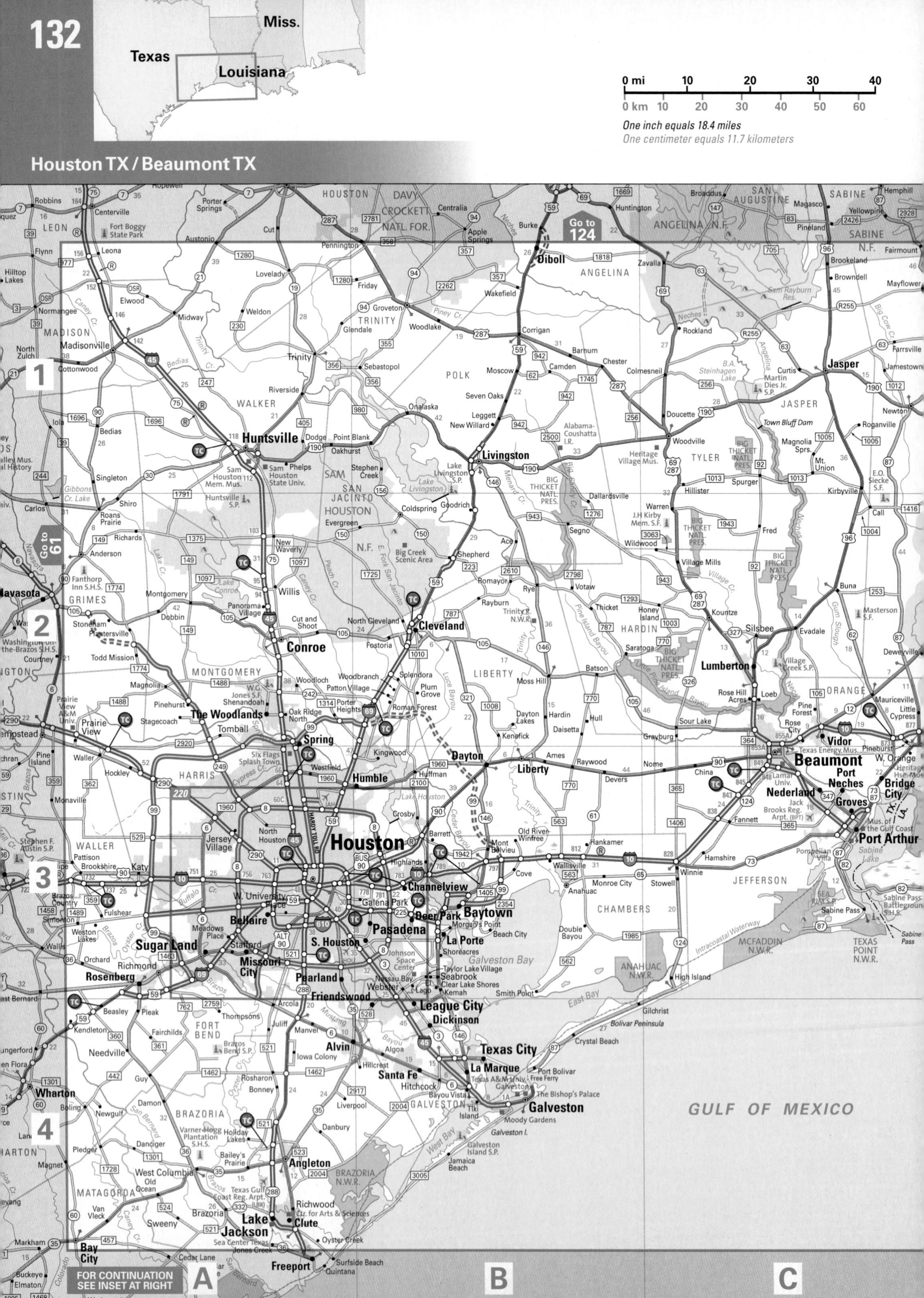

Miss.
Texas
Louisiana

0 mi   10   20   30   40
0 km 10 20 30 40 50 60
One inch equals 18.4 miles
One centimeter equals 11.7 kilometers

GULF OF MEXICO

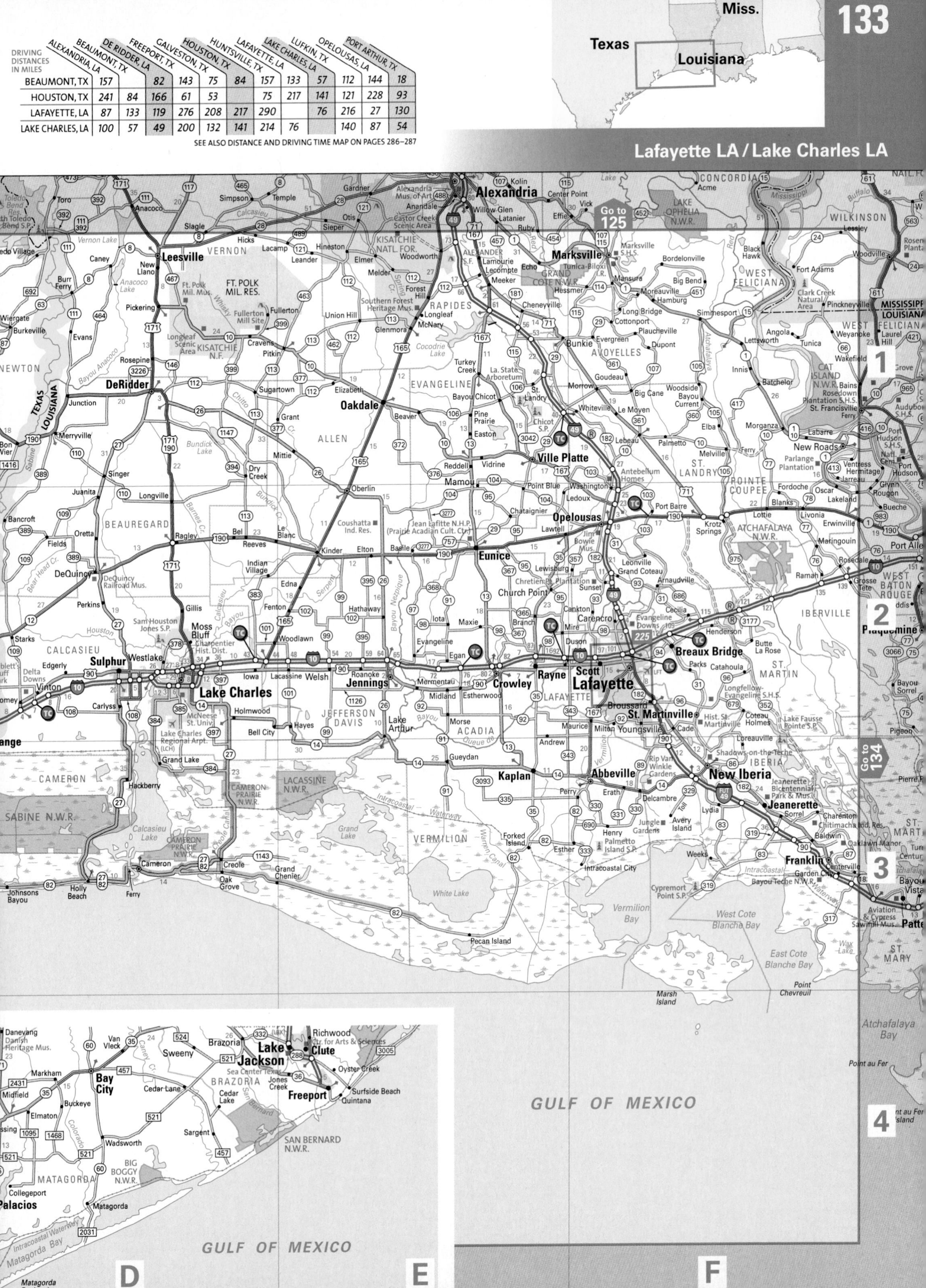

DRIVING DISTANCES IN MILES	ALEXANDRIA, LA	BEAUMONT, TX	DE RIDDER, LA	FREEPORT, TX	GALVESTON, TX	HOUSTON, TX	HUNTSVILLE, TX	LAFAYETTE, LA	LAKE CHARLES, LA	LUFKIN, TX	OPELOUSAS, LA	PORT ARTHUR, TX
BEAUMONT, TX	157		82	143	75	84	157	133	57	112	144	18
HOUSTON, TX	241	84	166	61	53		75	217	141	121	228	93
LAFAYETTE, LA	87	133	119	276	208	217	290		76	216	27	130
LAKE CHARLES, LA	100	57	49	200	132	141	214	76		140	87	54

SEE ALSO DISTANCE AND DRIVING TIME MAP ON PAGES 286–287

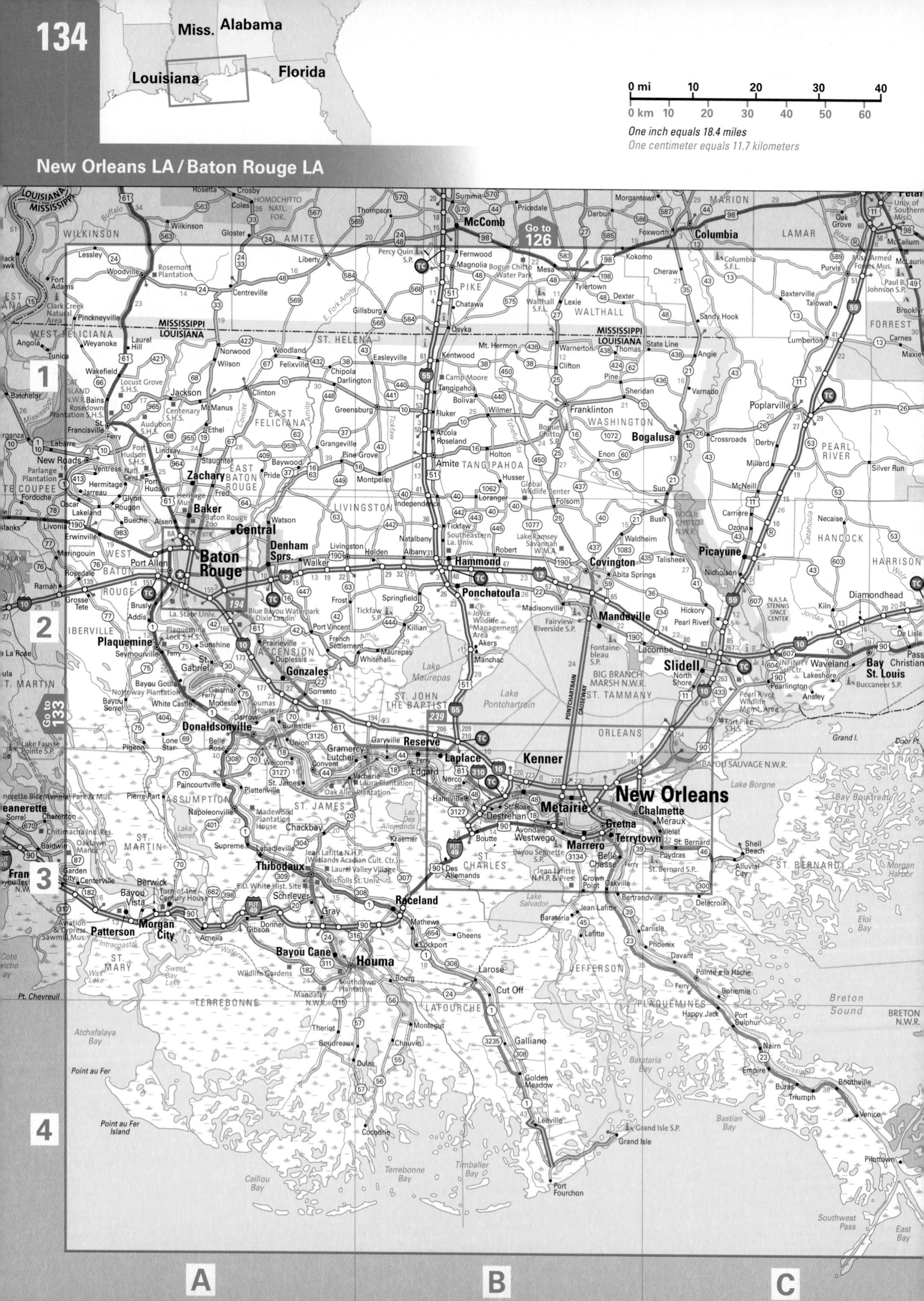

Miss. Alabama

Louisiana   Florida

0 mi   10   20   30   40
0 km   10   20   30   40   50   60
One inch equals 18.4 miles
One centimeter equals 11.7 kilometers

DRIVING DISTANCES IN MILES	BATON ROUGE, LA	BILOXI, MS	GULFPORT, MS	GULF SHORES, AL	HAMMOND, LA	HATTIESBURG, MS	HOUMA, LA	McCOMB, MS	MOBILE, AL	NEW ORLEANS, LA	PASCAGOULA, MS	PENSACOLA, FL
BATON ROUGE, LA		151	140	254	51	174	101	102	205	91	170	264
BILOXI, MS	151		12	110	106	82	148	161	61	93	20	120
MOBILE, AL	205	61	75	48	159	97	201	215		146	41	58
NEW ORLEANS, LA	91	93	81	195	57	115	57	111	146		112	205

SEE ALSO DISTANCE AND DRIVING TIME MAP ON PAGES 286–287

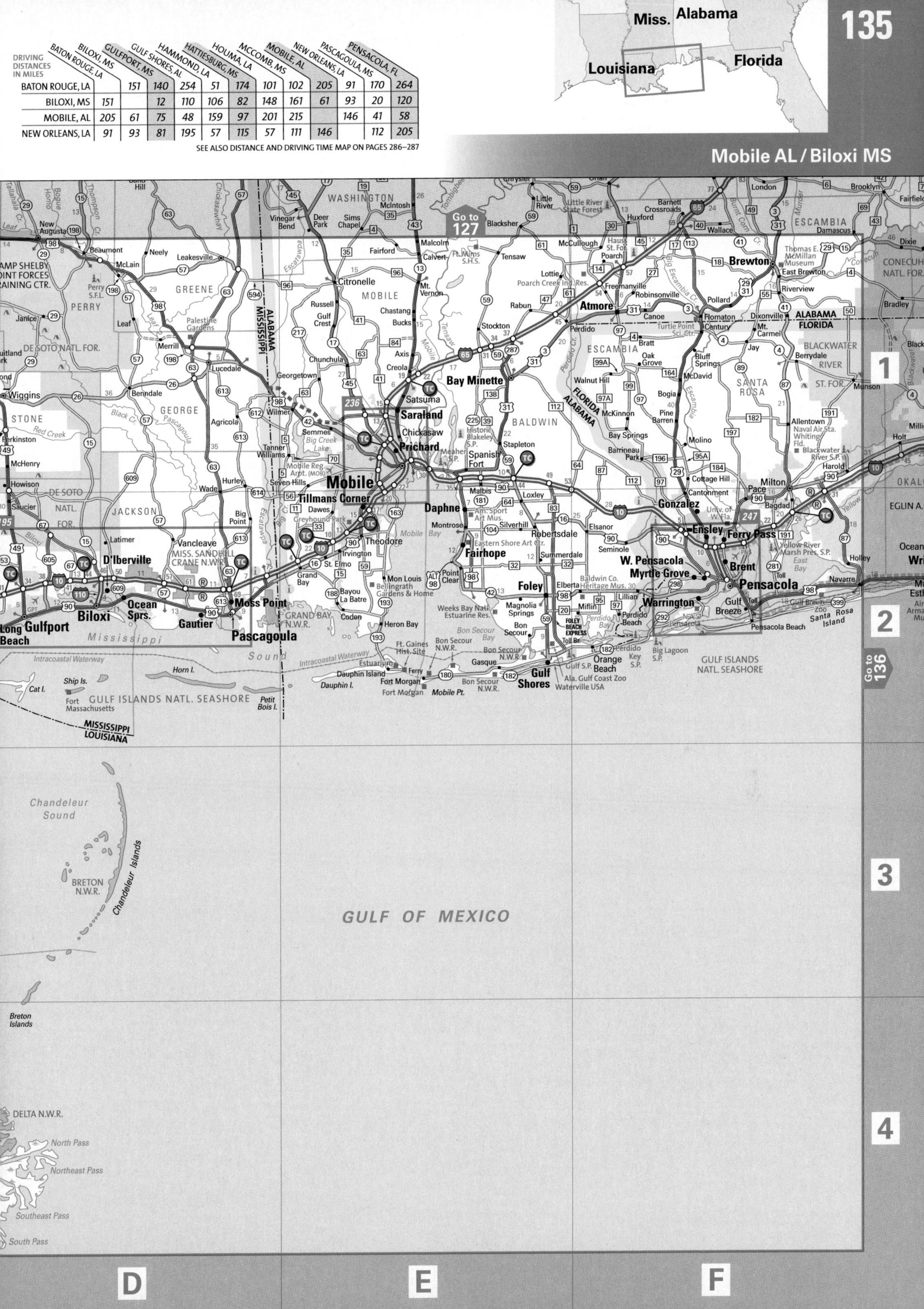

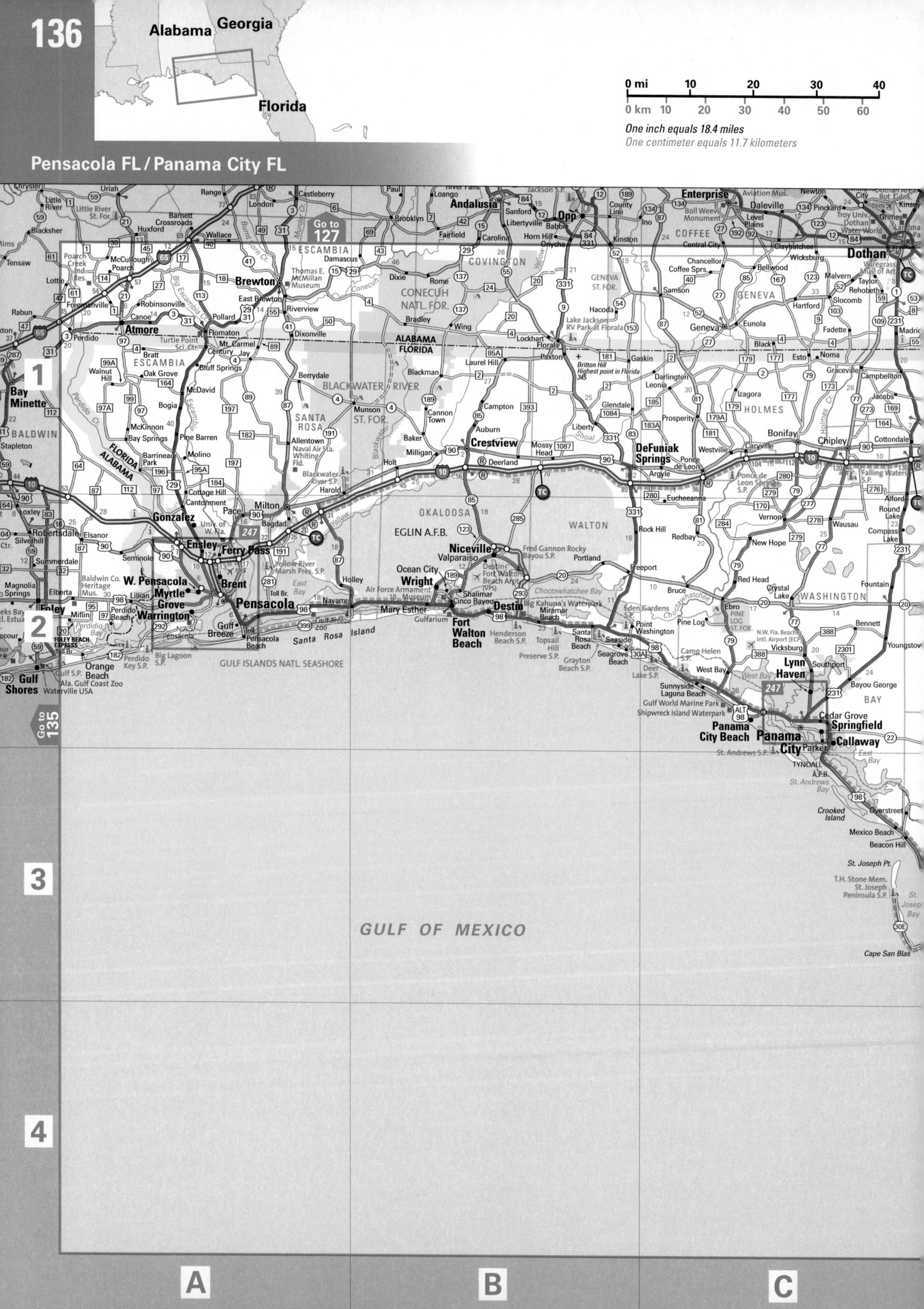
136
Pensacola FL / Panama City FL
Alabama
Georgia
Florida
0 mi 10 20 30 40
0 km 10 20 30 40 50 60
One inch equals 18.4 miles
One centimeter equals 11.7 kilometers
Go to 127
Go to 135
GULF OF MEXICO
GULF ISLANDS NATL. SEASHORE
BLACKWATER RIVER ST. FOR.
CONECUH NATL. FOR.
EGLIN A.F.B.
TYNDALL A.F.B.
ESCAMBIA
COVINGTON
COFFEE
GENEVA
HOLMES
WASHINGTON
WALTON
OKALOOSA
SANTA ROSA
BALDWIN
BAY
ALABAMA
FLORIDA
Andalusia
Opp
Enterprise
Dothan
Brewton
Atmore
Bay Minette
Crestview
DeFuniak Springs
Bonifay
Chipley
Milton
Pace
Gonzalez
Ensley
Ferry Pass
Brent
W. Pensacola
Myrtle Grove
Warrington
Pensacola
Gulf Breeze
Pensacola Beach
Santa Rosa Island
Niceville
Valparaiso
Wright
Fort Walton Beach
Destin
Mary Esther
Choctawhatchee Bay
Freeport
Seaside
Lynn Haven
Panama City Beach
Panama City
Springfield
Callaway
Mexico Beach
Cape San Blas
Foley
Gulf Shores
Orange Beach
Britton Hill
Highest point in Florida 345
A
B
C
1
2
3
4

Alabama Georgia

Florida

DRIVING DISTANCES IN MILES	BREWTON, AL	DE FUNIAK SPRS., FL	DOTHAN, AL	FT. WALTON BEACH, FL	MARIANNA, FL	MOBILE, AL	PANAMA CITY, FL	PENSACOLA, FL	PERRY, FL	TALLAHASSEE, FL	THOMASVILLE, GA	VALDOSTA, GA
PANAMA CITY, FL	143	65	82	64	61	160		102	160	104	134	186
PENSACOLA, FL	57	82	152	39	138	58	102		256	200	230	282
TALLAHASSEE, FL	201	123	110	166	68	247	104	200	52		35	85
VALDOSTA, GA	283	204	133	247	149	329	186	282	66	85	42	

SEE ALSO DISTANCE AND DRIVING TIME MAP ON PAGES 286–287

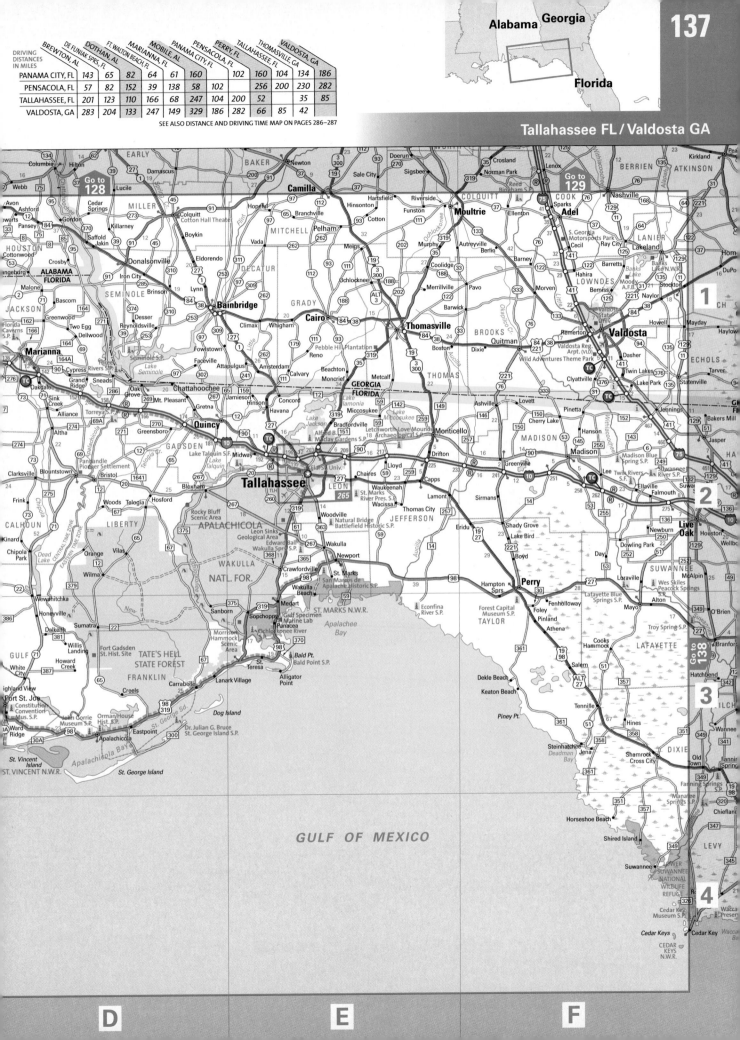

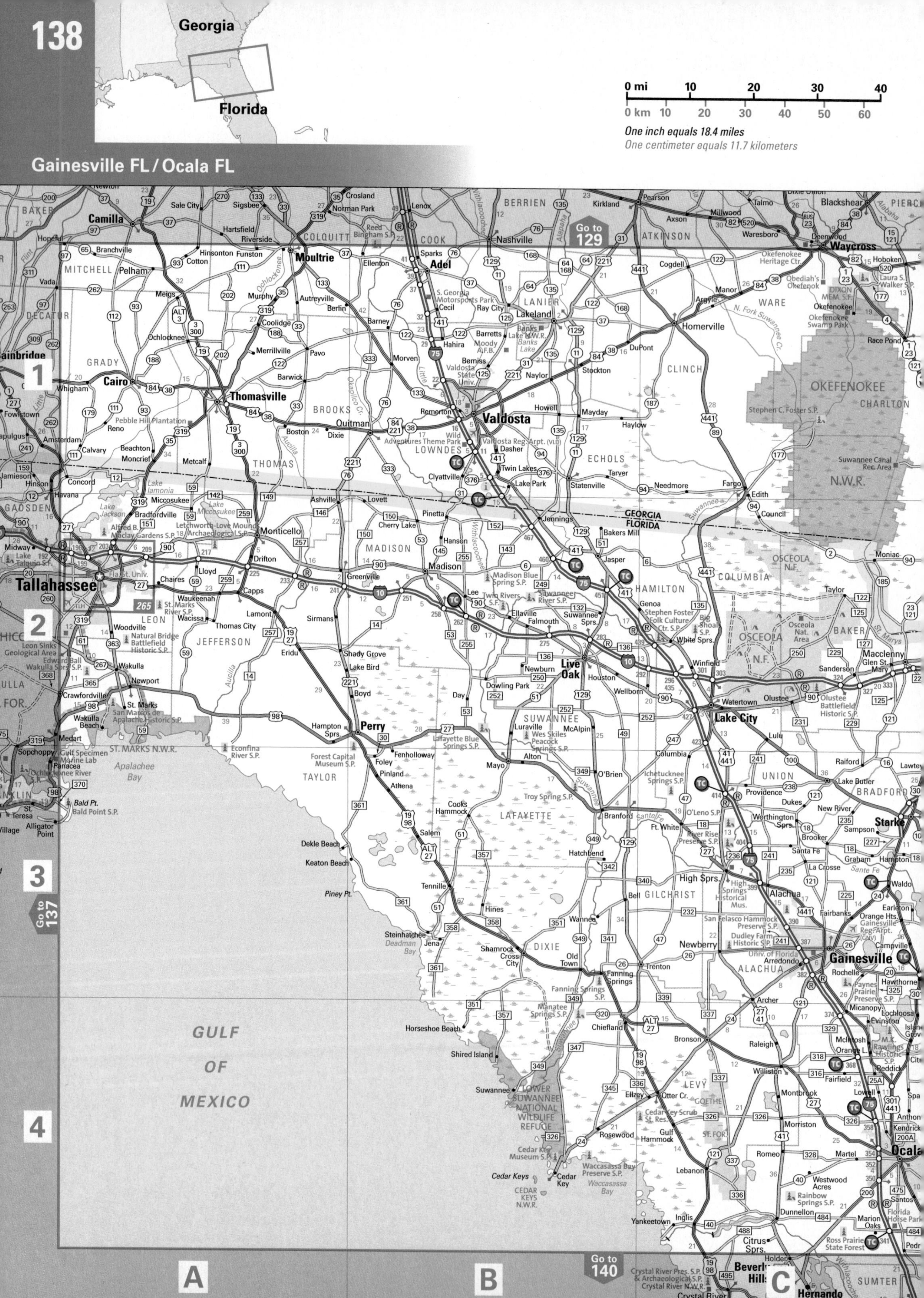

Georgia

Florida

One inch equals 18.4 miles
One centimeter equals 11.7 kilometers

GULF

OF

MEXICO

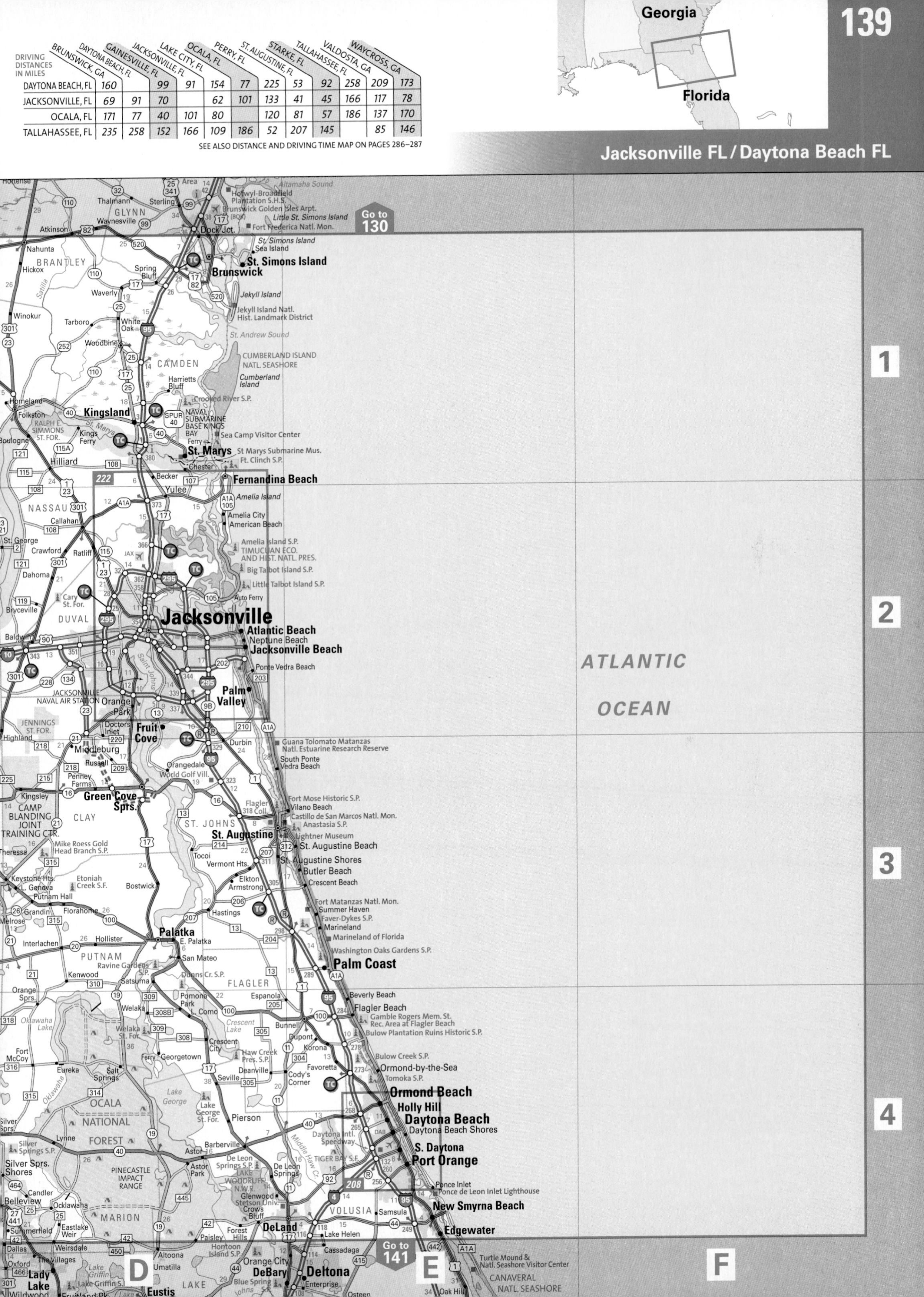

DRIVING DISTANCES IN MILES	BRUNSWICK, GA	DAYTONA BEACH, FL	GAINESVILLE, FL	JACKSONVILLE, FL	LAKE CITY, FL	OCALA, FL	PERRY, FL	ST. AUGUSTINE, FL	STARKE, FL	TALLAHASSEE, FL	VALDOSTA, GA	WAYCROSS, GA
DAYTONA BEACH, FL	160		99	91	154	77	225	53	92	258	209	173
JACKSONVILLE, FL	69	91	70		62	101	133	41	45	166	117	78
OCALA, FL	171	77	40	101	80		120	81	57	186	137	170
TALLAHASSEE, FL	235	258	152	166	109	186	52	207	145		85	146

SEE ALSO DISTANCE AND DRIVING TIME MAP ON PAGES 286–287

Georgia

Florida

Florida

0 mi 10 20 30 40
0 km 10 20 30 40 50 60
One inch equals 18.4 miles
One centimeter equals 11.7 kilometers

Go to 138
Go to 142

GULF

OF

MEXICO

Yankeetown · Inglis · Dunnellon · Marion Oaks · Belleview · Candler · Ocklawaha · MARION · FOREST

Citrus Sprs. · Crystal River Pres. S.P. & Archaeological S.P. · Crystal River N.W.R. · Crystal River · Beverly Hills · Hernando · Inverness · Homosassa Sprs. · SUMTER · Lady Lake · Wildwood · Leesburg · Tavares · Fruitland Pk. · Eustis · Mount Dora

Ellie Schiller Homosassa Springs Wildlife S.P. · Homosassa · Yulee Sugar Mill Ruins Historic S.P. · Homosassa Bay · Chassahowitzka · CHASSAHOWITZKA N.W.R. · CITRUS ST. FOR. · Floral City · Lake Panasoffkee · Sumterville · Coleman · Howey-in-the-Hills · Clermont · Minneola · Montverd

HERNANDO · McKethan Lake Rec Area · Nobleton · Bushnell · Dade Battlefield Historic S.P. · Center Hill · WITHLACOOCHEE ST. FOR. · Mascotte · Groveland · Bay Lake

Bayport · Weeki Wachee Gardens · Weeki Wachee Springs S.P. and Buccaneer Bay · Hernando Beach · Weeki Wachee · Brooksville · Spring Lake · Ridge Manor · Lacoochee · Pioneer Florida Museum

Spring Hill · Aripeka · Masaryktown · Blanton · St. Catherine · Webster

Hudson · Bayonet Point · Werner-Boyce Salt Springs S.P. · Port Richey · Jasmine Estates · New Port Richey · Trinity Coll. of Florida · Elfers · Holiday · PASCO · Gower's Corner · San Antonio · St. Leo Univ. · Wesley Chapel · Dade City · Zephyrhills · Withlacoochee · Berry · Eva · Colt Creek S.P.

Anclote Key Preserve S.P. · Tarpon Sprs. · Palm Harbor · Honeymoon Island S.P. · Caladesi Island S.P. · Odessa · Land O' Lakes · Lutz · Crystal Sprs. · Providence · Kathleen · Auburndale · Lake Alfred

Dunedin · Oldsmar · Temple Terrace · Tampa · Thonotosassa · Plant City · Lakeland · Winter Haven · Eagle Lake

Clearwater · Safety Harbor · PINELLAS · Belleair · Belleair Beach · Largo · Indian Rocks Beach · Seminole · Dover · Brandon · Medulla · Highland City · Lgoolne Florida

Redington Beach · Madeira Beach · Treasure Island · South Pasadena · Gulfport · Pinellas Park · St. Petersburg · Riverview · Mulberry · Bartow · Altura

Boyette · Pinecrest · Bradley Jct. · Homeland · Pembroke · Ft. Meade

St. Pete Beach · Ruskin · Sun City Center · HILLSBOROUGH · Balm · Brewster · POLK · Bowling Green

Fort De Soto S.P. · Egmont Key S.P. · Sun City · Wimauma · Little Manatee River St. Rec. Area · Baird · Ft. Green · Paynes Creek Historic S.P.

Parrish · Memphis · Palmetto · Bradenton · Anna Maria · Holmes Beach · Cortez · Bradenton Beach · Longboat Key · Oneco · Whitfield · Lake Manatee S.P. · MANATEE · HARDEE · Ona · Wauchula · Griffins Corner · Zolfo Sprs. · Gardner

Sarasota · Bee Ridge · Old Myakka · Verna · Wingate Creek S.P. · Solomon's Castle · Myakka City · Limestone · Pine Level · Brownsville

Ringling Mus. of Art · Siesta Key · Coral Cove · Vamo · Osprey · Oscar Scherer S.P. · MYAKKA RIVER S.P. · Sandy · SARASOTA · Arcadia · Nocatee · DE SOTO

Laurel · Nokomis · Venice · Hull · Ft. Ogden

South Venice · Venice Gardens · North Port · Murdock · Harbour Heights · Cleveland · Babcock · CHARLOTTE

Englewood · Englewood Beach · Grove City · Port Charlotte · Charlotte Harbor · Punta Gorda · Solana · Babcock Wilderness Adventures

Rotonda · Charlotte Harbor Pres. S.P. · Placida · Island Bay N.W.R. · Pirate Harbor

Don Pedro Island S.P. · Gasparilla Island · Gasparilla Island S.P. · Boca Grande · Charlotte Harbor

Old Port Boca Grande Lighthouse · Cayo Costa S.P. · Pine Island N.W.R. · Matlacha · Bokeelia · Pineland · Ft. Myers · Ft. Myers Shores · Fort Myers · LEE

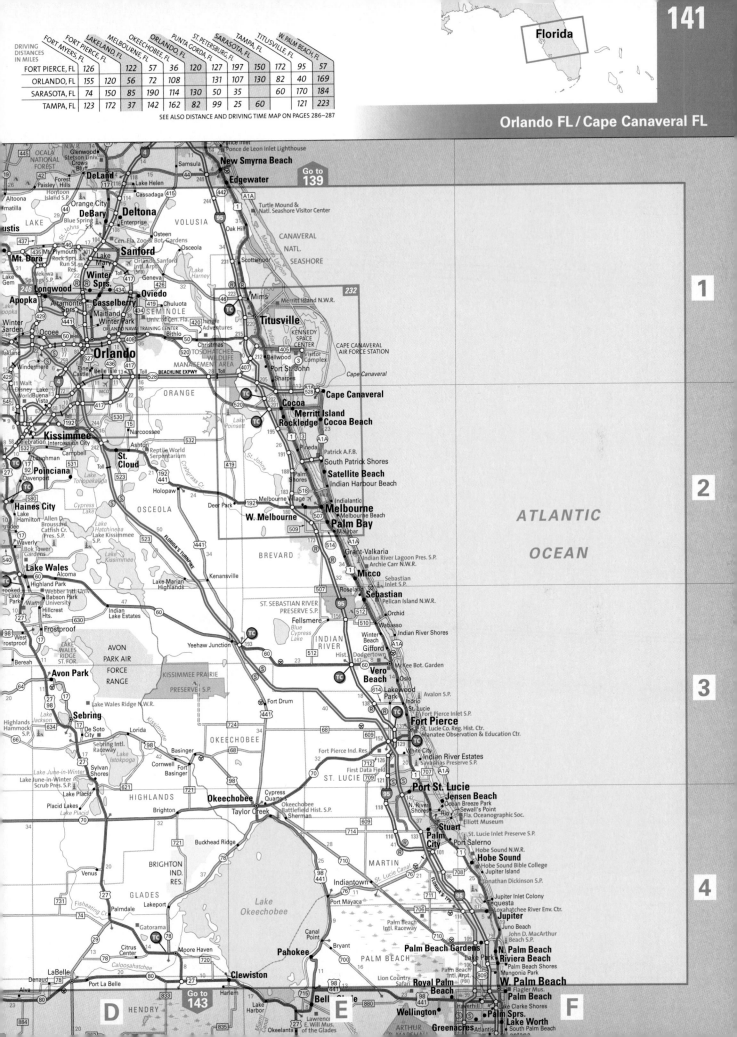

SEE ALSO DISTANCE AND DRIVING TIME MAP ON PAGES 286–287

DRIVING DISTANCES IN MILES	FORT MYERS, FL	FORT PIERCE, FL	LAKELAND, FL	MELBOURNE, FL	OKEECHOBEE, FL	ORLANDO, FL	PUNTA GORDA, FL	ST. PETERSBURG, FL	SARASOTA, FL	TAMPA, FL	TITUSVILLE, FL	W. PALM BEACH, FL
FORT PIERCE, FL	126		122	57	36	120	127	197	150	172	95	57
ORLANDO, FL	155	120	56	72	108		131	107	130	82	40	169
SARASOTA, FL	74	150	85	190	114	130	50	35		60	170	184
TAMPA, FL	123	172	37	142	162	82	99	25	60		121	223

Florida

Fort Myers FL / Key West FL

0 mi   10   20   30   40
0 km 10 20 30 40 50 60
One inch equals 18.4 miles
One centimeter equals 11.7 kilometers

1

Don Pedro Island S.P.
775
771
Placida
158
Charlotte Harbor Pres. S.P.
Babcock Wilderness Adventures
Gasparilla Island
765
41
23
75
31
Island Bay N.W.R.
Charlotte Harbor
Pirate Harbor 31
Go to 140
Gasparilla Island S.P.
Boca Grande
Old Port Boca Grande Lighthouse
Pine Island N.W.R.
Bokeelia
Pineland
765
80
78
143
TC
N. Ft. Myers
Tice
141
Ft. Myers Shore
Cayo Costa S.P.
Matlacha
767
78
Fort Myers
138
136
TC
Cape Coral
884
Ft. Myers Villa
82
Captiva I.
767
131 RSW
Captiva
Punta Rassa
Iona
128
San Carlos Park
LEE
St. James City
869
39
Sanibel
Toll
Ft. Myers Beach
865
Estero
123
Everglade Wonder Gardens
Sanibel I.
141
136
Lovers Key S.P.
116
Bonita Springs
75
214
Delnor-Wiggins Pass S.P.
865
84
Naples Park
111
95
Golden Gate
North Naples
Artis-Naples
31
107
Naples Zoo at Caribbean Gardens
Naples Municipal Arpt. (APF)
7
84
Naples
95
Naples Botanical Garden
E. Naples
Naples Manor
95
8

2

Marco Island
Marco Island
Marco I. Trolley Tours
Cape Romano

GULF

OF

MEXICO

3

4

DRY TORTUGAS NATL. PARK
Fort Jefferson
224
KEY WEST N.W.R.
Stock Island
1
Marquesas Keys
Key West
EYW
Naval Air Station Key West

A   B   C

DRIVING DISTANCES IN MILES

	BELLE GLADE, FL	BOCA RATON, FL	FLAMINGO, FL	FORT LAUDERDALE, FL	FORT MYERS, FL	HOMESTEAD, FL	KEY LARGO, FL	KEY WEST, FL	MARATHON, FL	MIAMI, FL	NAPLES, FL	W. PALM BEACH, FL
FORT MYERS, FL	84	155	227	139		174	195	308	260	155	36	125
KEY WEST, FL	235	211	181	190	308	133	113		48	168	273	234
MIAMI, FL	83	44	87	23	155	34	55	168	120		121	67
W. PALM BEACH, FL	41	28	153	48	125	100	121	234	186	67	144	

SEE ALSO DISTANCE AND DRIVING TIME MAP ON PAGES 286–287

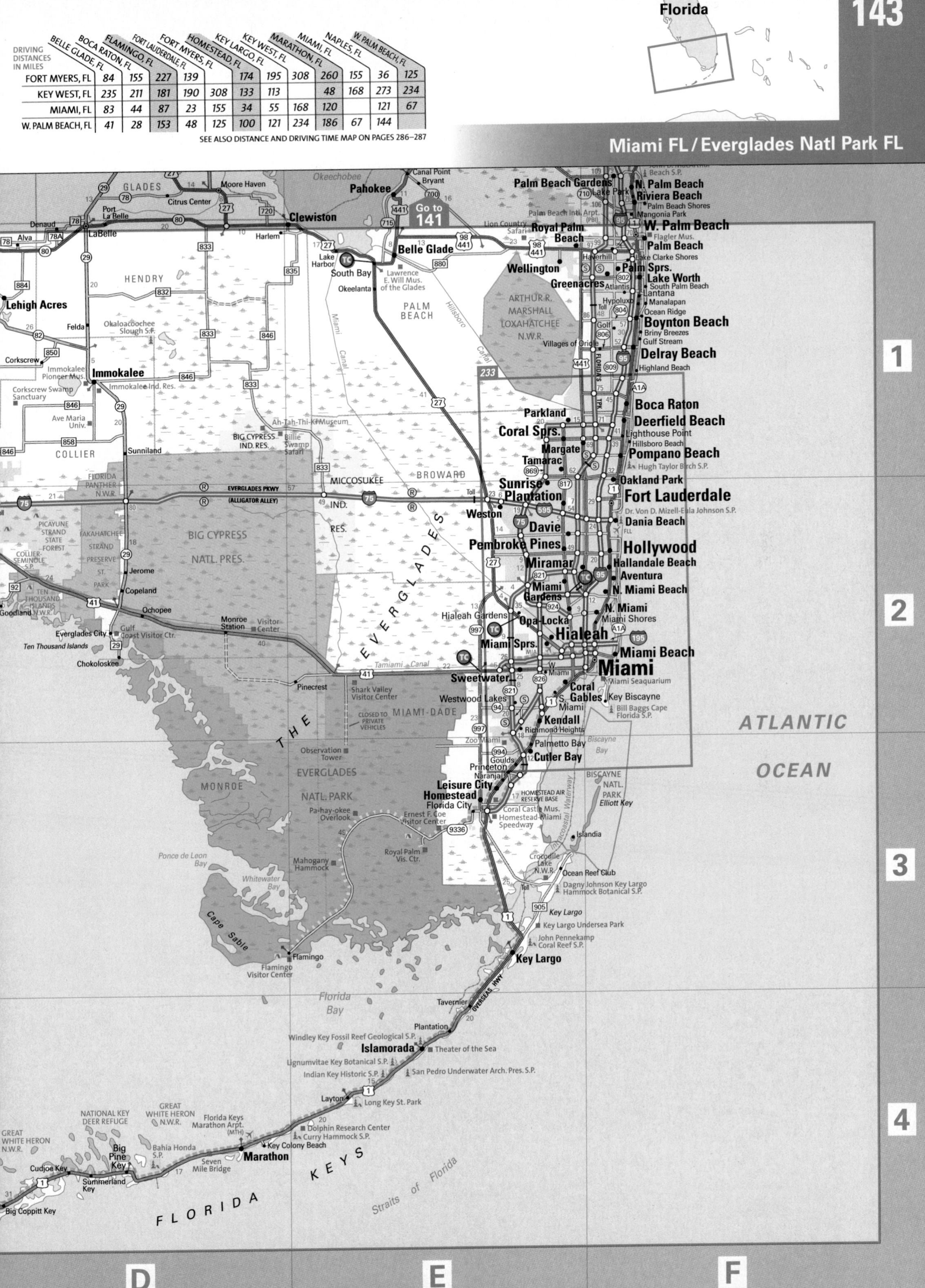

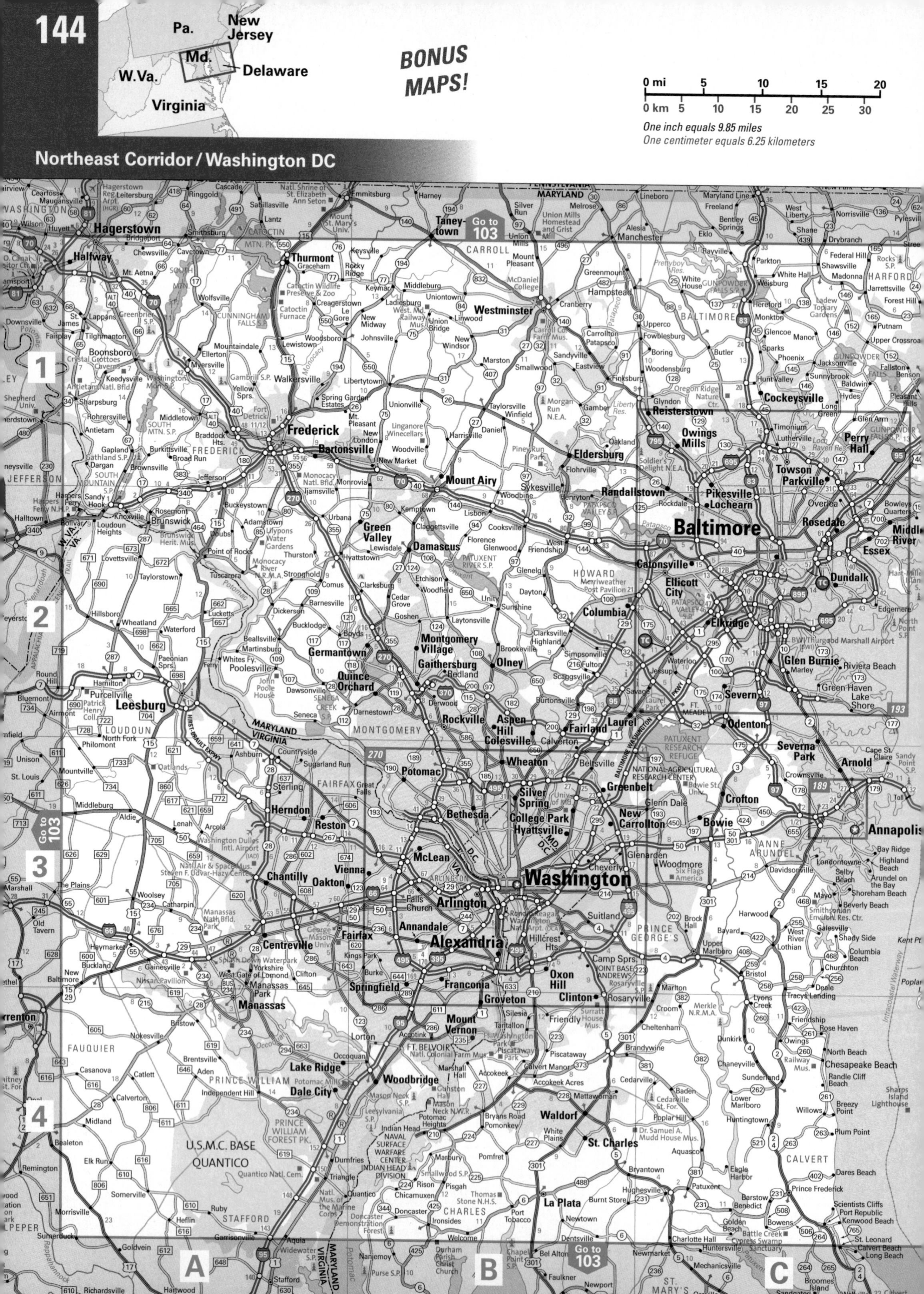

Pa. New Jersey
W.Va. Md. Delaware
Virginia

BONUS MAPS!

0 mi   5   10   15   20
0 km 5 10 15 20 25 30
One inch equals 9.85 miles
One centimeter equals 6.25 kilometers

Northeast Corridor / Washington DC

DRIVING DISTANCES IN MILES	ANNAPOLIS, MD	BALTIMORE, MD	CAMBRIDGE, MD	DOVER, DE	ELKTON, MD	FREDERICK, MD	HAGERSTOWN, MD	LEESBURG, VA	MANASSAS, VA	REHOBOTH BEACH, DE	VINELAND, NJ	WASHINGTON, DC
BALTIMORE, MD	25		78	98	58	51	76	71	67	111	109	38
DOVER, DE	62	98	64		40	135	160	135	131	43	77	94
FREDERICK, MD	73	51	128	135	106		28	25	61	161	158	44
WASHINGTON, DC	31	38	87	94	94	44	70	38	31	120	145	

SEE ALSO DISTANCE AND DRIVING TIME MAP ON PAGES 286-287

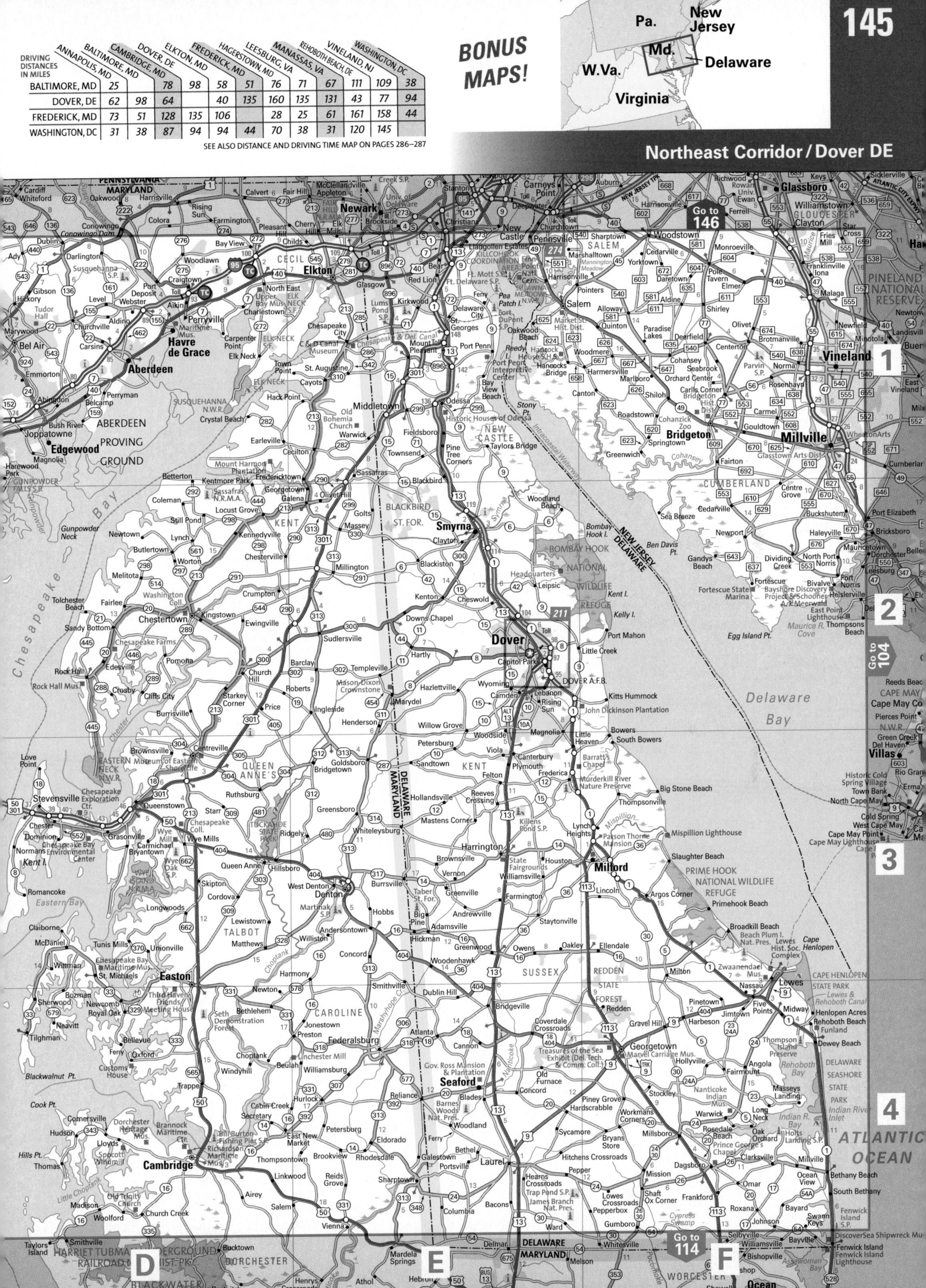

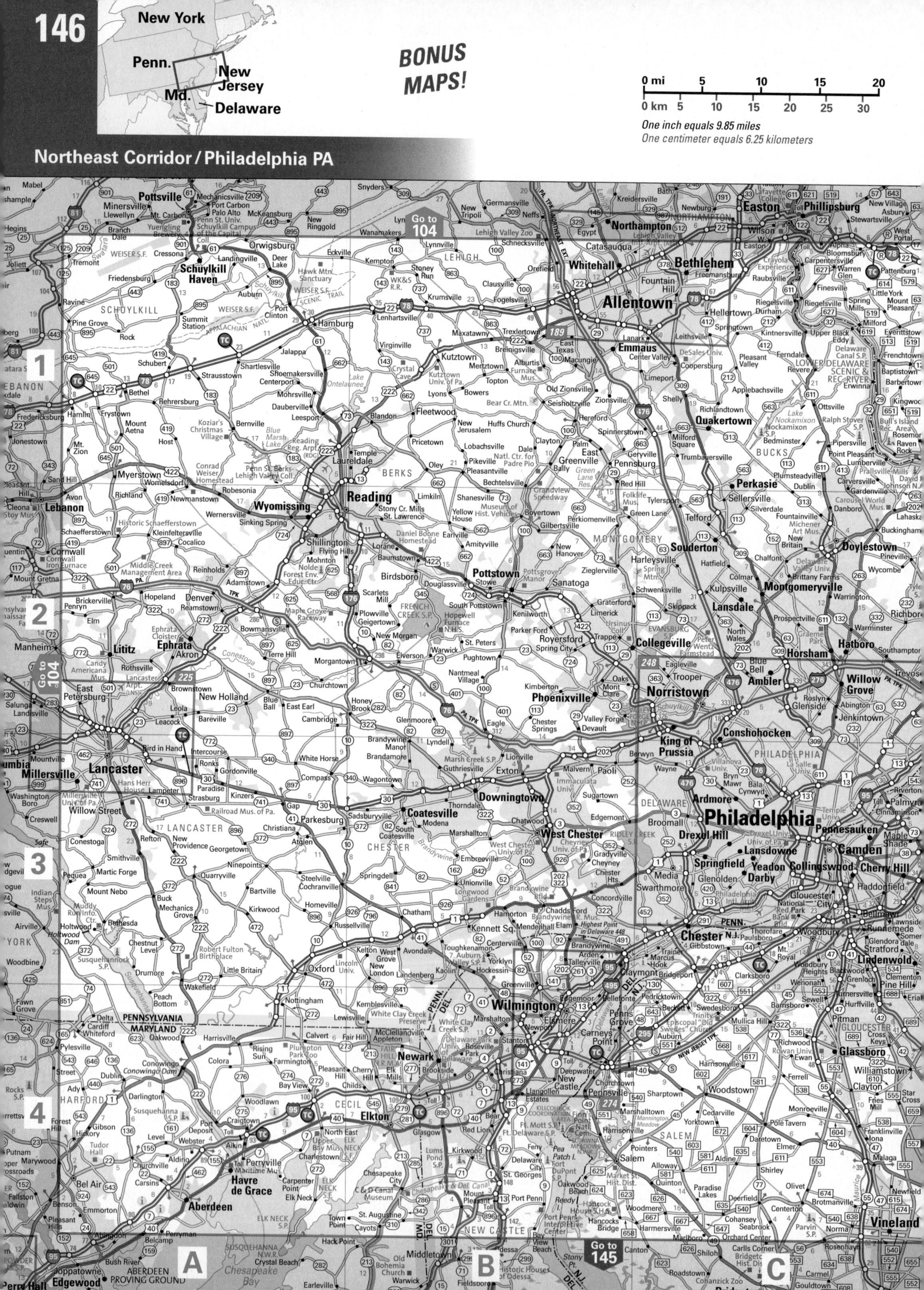

BONUS
MAPS!

New York

Penn.

New
Jersey

Md.
Delaware

0 mi   5   10   15   20
0 km   5   10   15   20   25   30
One inch equals 9.85 miles
One centimeter equals 6.25 kilometers

BONUS MAPS!

New York
Penn.
New Jersey
Md.
Delaware

DRIVING DISTANCES IN MILES	ALLENTOWN, PA	ATLANTIC CITY, NJ	ELKTON, MD	LANCASTER, PA	LONG BRANCH, NJ	NEW BRUNSWICK, NJ	NEW YORK, NY	PHILADELPHIA, PA	READING, PA	TOMS RIVER, NJ	TRENTON, NJ	WILMINGTON, DE
NEW YORK, NY	84	125	137	165	55	34		91	118	75	55	120
PHILADELPHIA, PA	63	62	50	79	77	55	91		63	58	34	30
TRENTON, NJ	66	77	88	105	53	22	55	34	89	48		68
WILMINGTON, DE	77	86	20	53	106	90	120	30	56	85	68	

SEE ALSO DISTANCE AND DRIVING TIME MAP ON PAGES 286–287

Go to 148

Go to 105

FOR CONTINUATION SEE INSET AT RIGHT

New York

ATLANTIC OCEAN

LONG ISLAND

1

2

3

4

D   E   F

New York
Pa.
Rhode Island
Conn.
New Jersey

BONUS MAPS!

0 mi   5   10   15   20
0 km   5   10   15   20   25   30
One inch equals 9.85 miles
One centimeter equals 6.25 kilometers

Go to 94

Go to 147

BONUS MAPS!

New York · Rhode Island · Pa. · Conn. · New Jersey

DRIVING DISTANCES IN MILES

	DANBURY, CT	BRIDGEPORT, CT	HARTFORD, CT	NEWARK, NJ	NEWBURGH, NY	NEW HAVEN, CT	NEW LONDON, CT	NEW YORK, NY	PATERSON, NJ	RIVERHEAD, NY	STAMFORD, CT	WATERBURY, CT
BRIDGEPORT, CT	31		56	69	73	19	64	60	71	115	21	33
NEWARK, NJ	69	79	125		66	88	134	11	18	88	48	108
NEW HAVEN, CT	19	35	39	88	78		46	78	89	133	40	30
NEW YORK, NY	60	69	115	11	56	78	124		16	78	38	99

SEE ALSO DISTANCE AND DRIVING TIME MAP ON PAGES 286–287

Massachusetts
Rhode Island
Connecticut

BONUS MAPS!

0 mi 5 10 15 20
0 km 5 10 15 20 25 30
One inch equals 9.85 miles
One centimeter equals 6.25 kilometers

Northeast Corridor / Hartford CT

Go to 94
Go to 95

1

Greenfield · Gardner · Fitchburg · Leominster · Chelmsford

Amherst · Northampton · Easthampton

WORCESTER · Worcester · Shrewsbury · Marlborough · Framingham · Natick

2

Holyoke · Chicopee · Westfield · West Springfield · Springfield · Agawam · Longmeadow

HAMPDEN · HAMPSHIRE · FRANKLIN

MASS. TURNPIKE · Sturbridge · Southbridge · Webster · Auburn · Milford · Franklin · Woonsocket

MASS. · CONN. · R.I.

Go to 94

3

Hartford · West Hartford · East Hartford · Manchester · Vernon · Storrs

TOLLAND · WINDHAM · Putnam · Danielson · Providence · North Providence · Pawtucket · Central Falls · Cranston

Wethersfield · Newington · New Britain · Willimantic · West Warwick · Warwick

4

Middletown · Meriden · Wallingford · Norwich · New London · Groton · Westerly · Wakefield · Kingston

MIDDLESEX · NEW LONDON · WASHINGTON · KENT

New Haven · North Haven · Guilford

Go to 149

Block Island Sound

A · B · C

DRIVING DISTANCES IN MILES	BOSTON, MA	GLOUCESTER, MA	HARTFORD, CT	HYANNIS, MA	NEW BEDFORD, MA	NEW LONDON, CT	NEWPORT, RI	PLYMOUTH, MA	PROVIDENCE, RI	PROVINCETOWN, MA	SPRINGFIELD, MA	WORCESTER, MA
BOSTON, MA		35	102	72	60	109	73	41	52	117	95	46
HARTFORD, CT	102	136		155	104	46	85	127	73	200	25	62
PROVIDENCE, RI	52	92	73	71	33	58	33	41		117	75	43
SPRINGFIELD, MA	95	129	25	148	127	71	111	120	75	193		55

SEE ALSO DISTANCE AND DRIVING TIME MAP ON PAGES 286–287

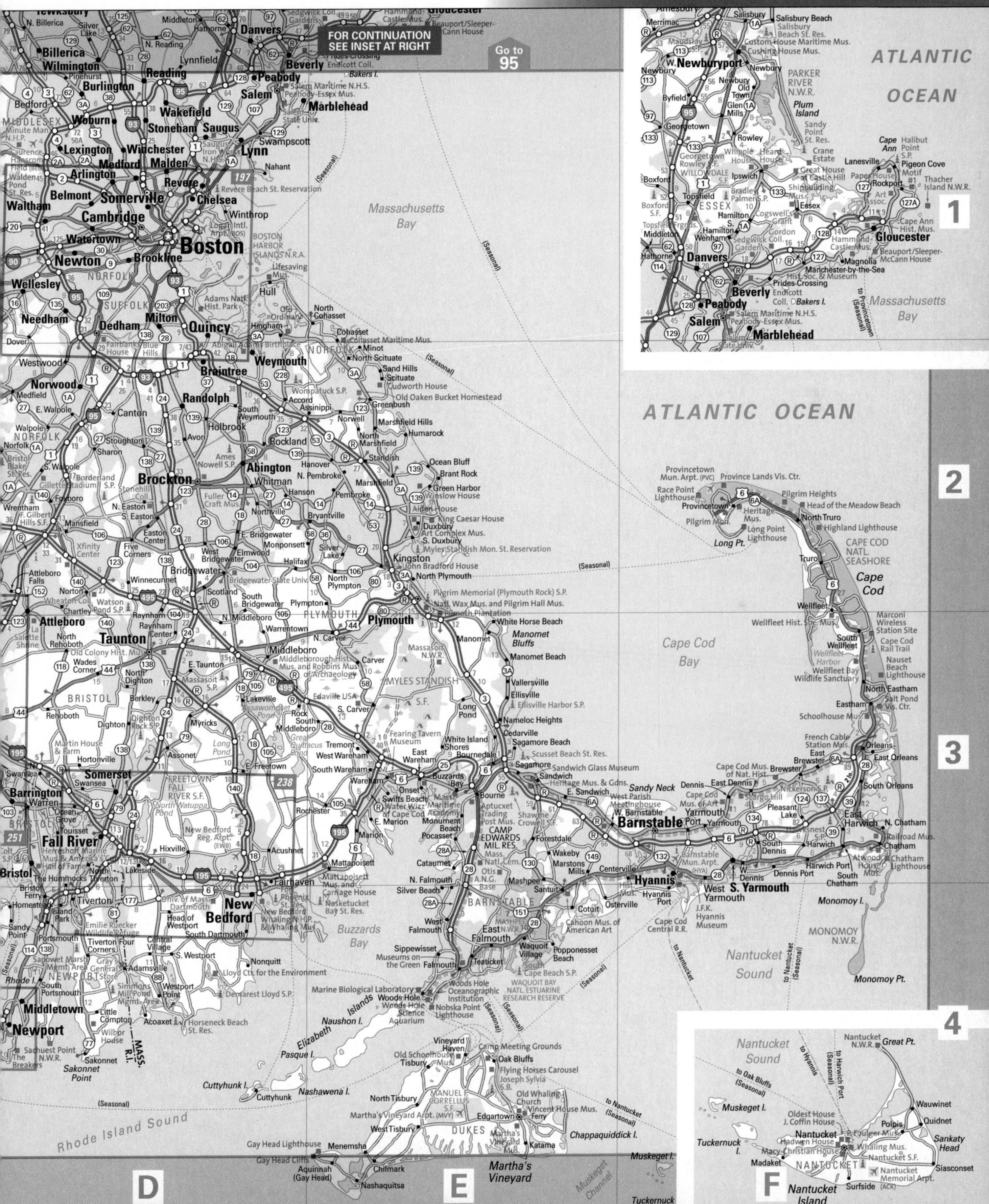

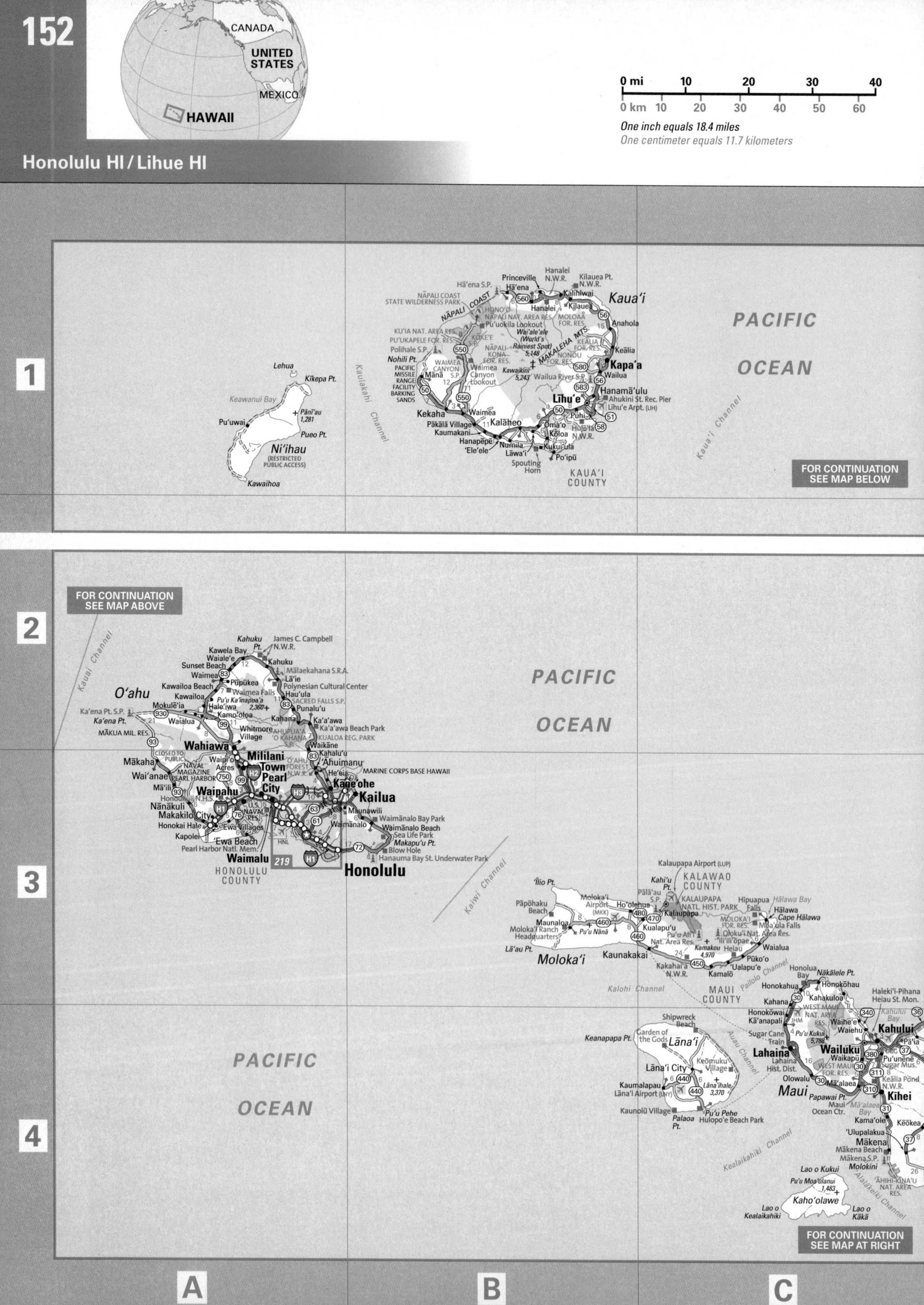

152
CANADA
UNITED STATES
MEXICO
HAWAII
Honolulu HI / Lihue HI
0 mi 10 20 30 40
0 km 10 20 30 40 50 60
One inch equals 18.4 miles
One centimeter equals 11.7 kilometers
1
2
3
4
A
B
C
PACIFIC OCEAN
Kaua'i
Princeville
Hanalei N.W.R.
Kilauea Pt. N.W.R.
Hā'ena S.P.
Hā'ena
Hanalei
Kalihiwai
Kilauea
NĀPALI COAST STATE WILDERNESS PARK
NĀPALI COAST
Pu'uokila Lookout
Wai'ale'ale (World's Rainiest Spot) 5,148
MAKALEHA MTS.
Anahola
Kealia
Kapa'a
Wailua
Polihale S.P.
Nohili Pt.
PACIFIC MISSILE RANGE FACILITY
BARKING SANDS
Mānā
Kawaikini 5,243
Wailua River S.P.
Hanamā'ulu
Ahukini St. Rec. Pier
Līhu'e
Līhu'e Arpt. (LIH)
Kekaha
Waimea
Kalāheo
Pākālā Village
Kaumakani
Hanapēpē
'Ele'ele
Numila
Lāwa'i
'Ōma'o
Kōloa
Kukui'ula
Po'ipū
Spouting Horn
KAUA'I COUNTY
Lehua
Kīkepa Pt.
Keawanui Bay
Pāni'au 1,281
Pu'uwai
Pueo Pt.
Ni'ihau (RESTRICTED PUBLIC ACCESS)
Kawaihoa
Kaulakahi Channel
Kaua'i Channel
FOR CONTINUATION SEE MAP BELOW
FOR CONTINUATION SEE MAP ABOVE
Kauai Channel
O'ahu
Kahuku Pt.
James C. Campbell N.W.R.
Kawela Bay
Waiale'e
Kahuku
Sunset Beach
Waimea
Mālaekahana S.R.A.
Pūpūkea
Lā'ie
Polynesian Cultural Center
Kawailoa Beach
Waimea Falls
Hau'ula
Kawailoa
Pu'u Ka'inapua'a 2,360
Hale'iwa
Punalu'u
Mokulē'ia
Ka'ena Pt. S.P.
Ka'ena Pt.
Waialua
Kamo'oloa
Kahana
Ka'a'awa
Ka'a'awa Beach Park
KUALOA REG. PARK
MĀKUA MIL. RES.
Whitmore Village
Wahiawā
Waikāne
Kahalu'u
Mililani Town
'Ahuimanu
Mākaha
Waipi'o Acres
He'eia
MARINE CORPS BASE HAWAII
Wai'anae
Pearl City
Kāne'ohe
Mā'ili
Waipahu
Kailua
Nānākuli
Makakilo City
Maunawili
Waimānalo Bay Park
Honokai Hale
Waimānalo
Waimānalo Beach
Kapolei
'Ewa Villages
Sea Life Park
'Ewa Beach
Makapu'u Pt.
Pearl Harbor Natl. Mem.
Blow Hole
Waimalu
Hanauma Bay St. Underwater Park
HONOLULU COUNTY
Honolulu
Kaiwi Channel
Kalaupapa Airport (LUP)
Kahi'u Pt.
KALAWAO COUNTY
'Īlio Pt.
Pālā'au S.P.
KALAUPAPA NATL. HIST. PARK
Hīpuapua Falls
Hālawa Bay
Moloka'i Airport (MKK)
Ho'olehua
Kalaupapa
Hālawa
Cape Hālawa
Pāpōhaku Beach
Maunaloa
Kualapu'u
Moa'ula Falls
Moloka'i Ranch Headquarters
Pu'u Nānā
Pu'u Ali'i Nat. Area Res.
Kamakou 4,970
Lā'au Pt.
Kaunakakai
Wailalua
Moloka'i
Kakahai'a N.W.R.
Kamalō
'Ualapu'e
Pūko'o
Kalohi Channel
Pailolo Channel
MAUI COUNTY
Honolua Bay
Nākālele Pt.
Honokōhau
Honokahua
Kahakuloa
Haleki'i-Pihana Heiau St. Mon.
Kahana
Shipwreck Beach
Honokōwai
Kā'anapali
Waihe'e
Waiehu
Kahului
Keanapapa Pt.
Garden of the Gods
Lāna'i
Sugar Cane Train
Pu'u Kukui 5,788
Pā'ia
Lahaina
Wailuku
Waikapū
Pu'unene
Lāna'i City
Keōmuku Village
Lahaina Hist. Dist.
Olowalu
Mā'alaea
Kealia Pond N.W.R.
Kaumalapau
Lāna'i Airport (LNY)
Lāna'ihale 3,370
Maui
Kīhei
Papawai Pt.
Maui Ocean Ctr.
Kaunolū Village
Pu'u Pehe
Hulopo'e Beach Park
Palaoa Pt.
Auau Channel
Kama'ole
'Ulupalakua
Kēōkea
Mākena
Mākena Beach
Mākena S.P.
Molokini
Kealaikahiki Channel
Lao o Kukui
Pu'u Moa'ulanui 1,483
'ĀHIHI-KINA'U NAT. AREA RES.
Kaho'olawe
Lao o Kealaikahiki
Lao o Kākā
Alalākeiki Channel
FOR CONTINUATION SEE MAP AT RIGHT

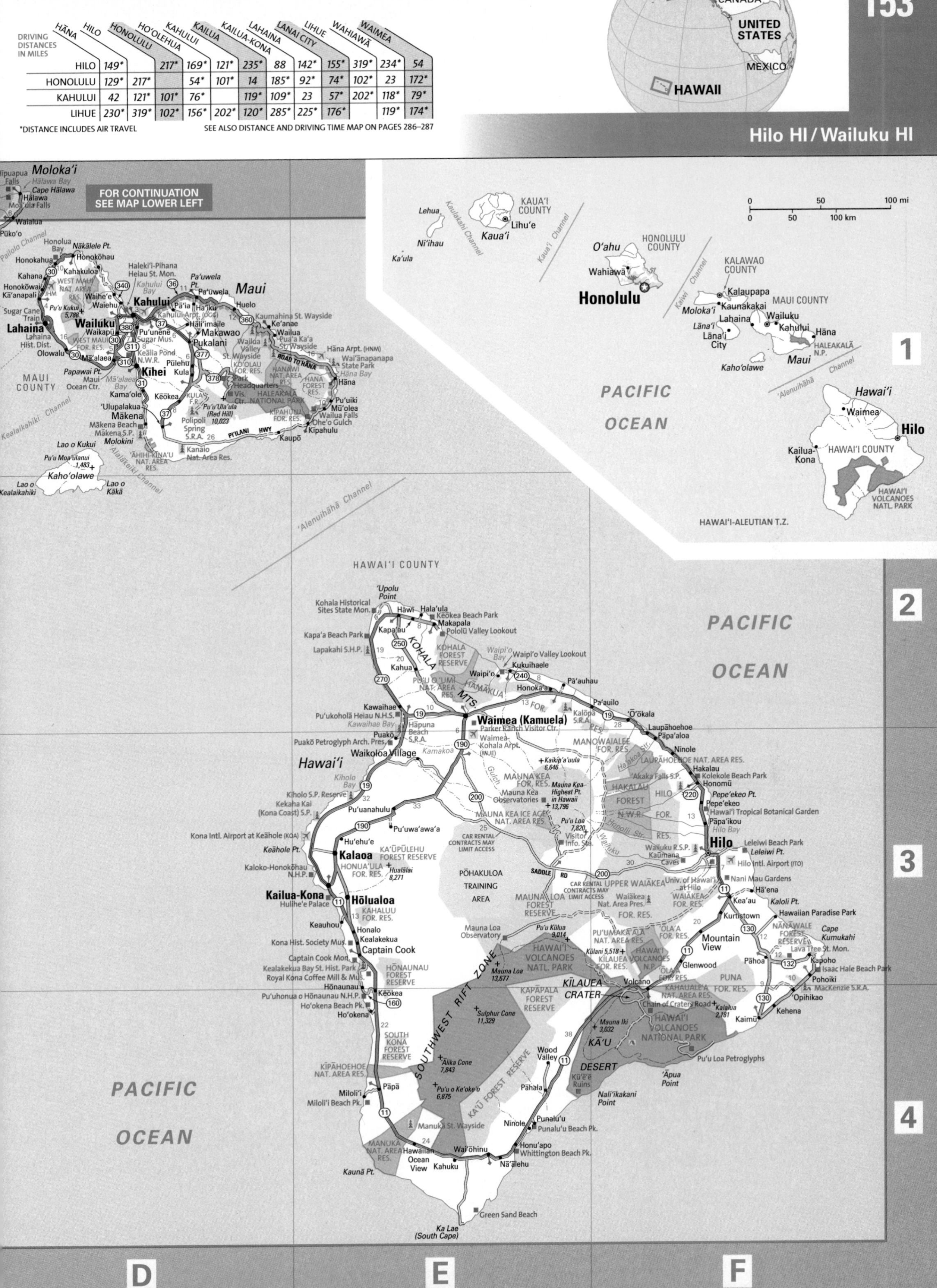

DRIVING DISTANCES IN MILES	HĀNA	HILO	HONOLULU	HO'OLEHUA	KAHULUI	KAILUA	KAILUA-KONA	LAHAINA	LANAI CITY	LIHUE	WAHIAWĀ	WAIMEA
HILO	149*		217*	169*	121*	235*	88	142*	155*	319*	234*	54
HONOLULU	129*	217*		54*	101*	14	185*	92*	74*	102*	23	172*
KAHULUI	42	121*	101*	76*		119*	109*	23	57*	202*	118*	79*
LIHUE	230*	319*	102*	156*	202*	120*	285*	225*	176*		119*	174*

*DISTANCE INCLUDES AIR TRAVEL

SEE ALSO DISTANCE AND DRIVING TIME MAP ON PAGES 286–287

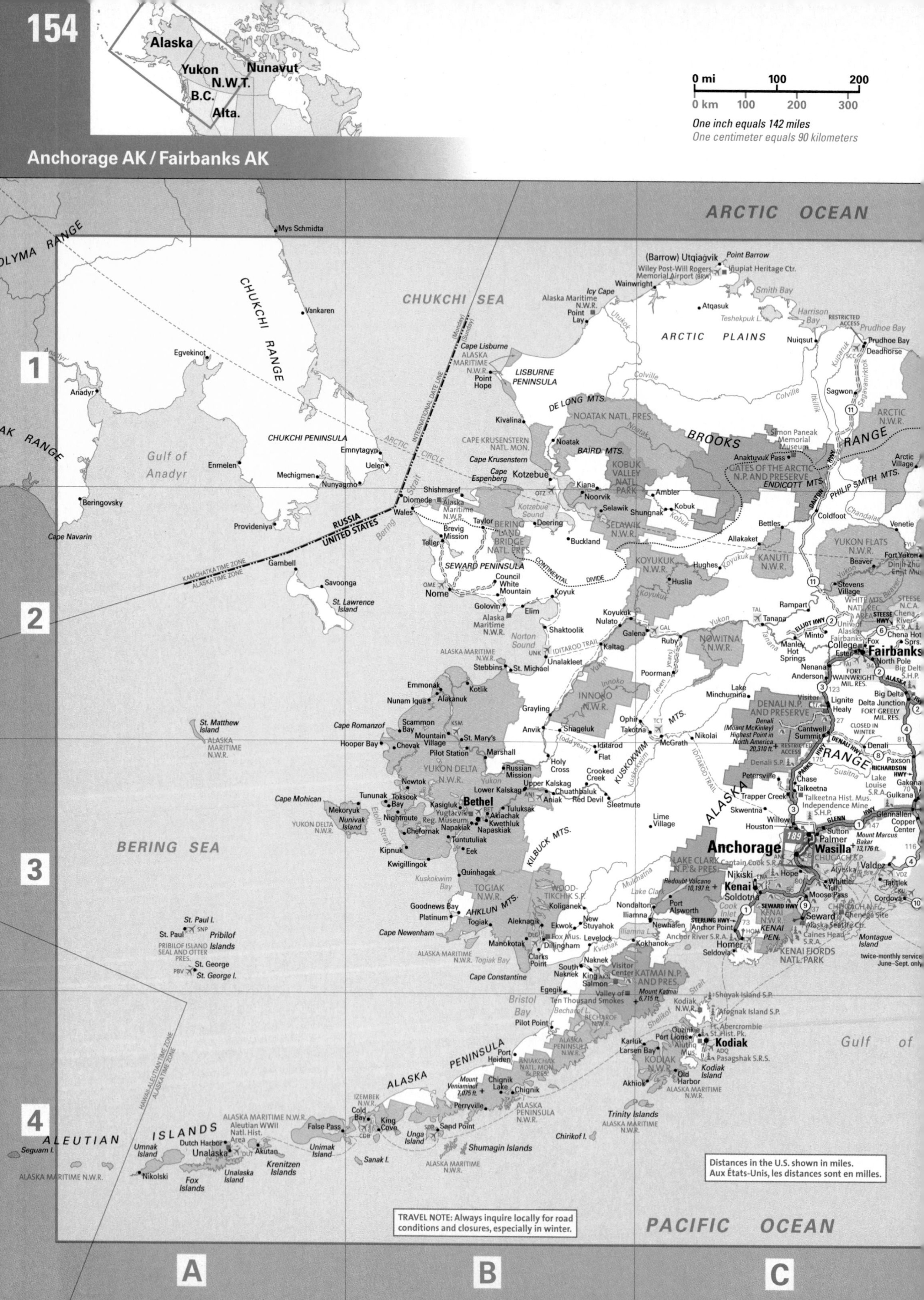

Alaska
Yukon
N.W.T. Nunavut
B.C.
Alta.

0 mi   100   200
0 km 100 200 300
One inch equals 142 miles
One centimeter equals 90 kilometers

ARCTIC OCEAN

OLYMA RANGE

CHUKCHI RANGE

CHUKCHI SEA

(Barrow) Utqiagvik
Point Barrow
Wiley Post-Will Rogers
Memorial Airport (BRW)
Iñupiat Heritage Ctr.
Wainwright
Icy Cape
Atqasuk
Smith Bay
Harrison Bay
RESTRICTED ACCESS
Prudhoe Bay
Point Lay
Alaska Maritime N.W.R.
Nuiqsut
Prudhoe Bay
Deadhorse
Sagwon

Mys Schmidta
Vankaren

ARCTIC PLAINS
Teshekpuk L.
Colville
Ikpikpuk
Kuparuk

Egvekinot
YAK RANGE
Anadyr

Cape Lisburne
ALASKA MARITIME N.W.R.
Point Hope
LISBURNE PENINSULA
DE LONG MTS.
NOATAK NATL. PRES.
BROOKS
Simon Paneak Memorial Museum
Colville
ARCTIC N.W.R.
RANGE

Kivalina
BAIRD MTS.
Anaktuvuk Pass
GATES OF THE ARCTIC N.P. AND PRESERVE
ENDICOTT MTS.
PHILIP SMITH MTS.
Arctic Village

Anadyr
CHUKCHI PENINSULA
ARCTIC CIRCLE
Noatak
Noatak
KOBUK VALLEY NATL. PARK
Ambler
Kobuk
Bettles
Coldfoot
Venetie

Gulf of Anadyr
Beringovsky
Enmelen
Mechigmen
Emnytagyp
Uelen
Kotzebue
Kiana
Noorvik
Selawik
Shungnak
SELAWIK N.W.R.
Hughes
Allakaket
YUKON FLATS N.W.R.
Beaver
Fort Yukon
Dinjii Zhu Enjit N.W.R.

Cape Krusenstern
Cape Espenberg
Kotzebue Sound
Deering
Buckland
KOYUKUK N.W.R.
Huslia
KANUTI N.W.R.
Stevens Village
WHITE MTS. N.R.A.
Chena River
Chena Hot Spr.

Cape Navarin
Providéniya
Nunyagmo
Shishmaref
Diomede
Wales
Brevig Mission
Teller
BERING LAND BRIDGE NATL. PRES.
Taylor
CONTINENTAL DIVIDE
Koyuk
Rampart
STEESE HWY
ELLIOT HWY
Univar
Tanana
Minto
Manley Hot Springs
Fairbanks
Ester
College
North Pole
Fox

RUSSIA
UNITED STATES
Gambell
KAMCHATKA TIME ZONE
ALASKA TIME ZONE
SEWARD PENINSULA
Brevig Mission
Council
White Mountain
Golovin
Elim
Koyukuk
Nulato
Galena
Ruby
Nenana
Anderson
FORT WAINWRIGHT MIL. RES.
Big Delta
Delta Junction

Savoonga
St. Lawrence Island
Nome
Shaktoolik
ALASKA MARITIME N.W.R.
Stebbins
St. Michael
Unalakleet
IDITAROD TRAIL
Kaltag
Poorman
Lake Minchumina
DENALI N.P. AND PRESERVE
Visitor Center
Lignite
Healy
Big Delta
FORT GREELY MIL. RES.
CLOSED IN WINTER

1

2

St. Matthew Island
ALASKA MARITIME N.W.R.
Emmonak
Nunam Iqua
Alakanuk
Kotlik
Grayling
Anvik
Shageluk
Ophir
Takotna
Flat
Nikolai
McGrath
Denali (Mount McKinley) Highest Point in North America 20,310 ft.
RESTRICTED ACCESS
Cantwell
Denali S.P.
Chase
Talkeetna
Cantwell
Denali
Paxson
RICHARDSON HWY
Gulkana

Cape Romanzof
Scammon Bay
Mountain Village
St. Mary's
Marshall
Holy Cross
Russian Mission
Upper Kalskag
Crooked Creek
Red Devil
Sleetmute
KUSKOKWIM MTS.
IDITAROD TRAIL
ALASKA RANGE
Petersville
Lake Louise S.R.A.
Glennallen
Copper Center

Hooper Bay
Chevak
Pilot Station
YUKON DELTA N.W.R.
Newtok
Lower Kalskag
Chuathbaluk
Aniak
Lime Village
Trapper Creek
Skwentna
Talkeetna Hist. Mus.
Independence Mine S.H.P.
Willow
Houston
Sutton
Mount Marcus Baker 13,176 ft.
CHUGACH S.P.

Cape Mohican
Mekoryuk
Nunivak Island
ALASKA MARITIME N.W.R.
Tununak
Toksook Bay
Nightmute
Chefornak
Kipnuk
Kwigillingok
Etolin Strait
Kasigluk
Yugtarvik Reg. Museum
Bethel
Napakiak
Napaskiak
Tuluksak
Akiachak
Kwethluk
Tuntutuliak
Eek
Quinhagak
Kuskokwim Bay
KILBUCK MTS.
TOGIAK N.W.R.
Anchorage
Wasilla
Palmer
GLENN HWY
Nikiski
Hope
SEWARD HWY
Kenai
Soldotna
Moose Pass
Whittier
Valdez
Tatitlek
CHUGACH N.F.
Cordova

3

BERING SEA

St. Paul I.
Pribilof
Islands
PRIBILOF ISLAND SEAL AND OTTER PRES.
St. George
St. George I.
St. Paul
Goodnews Bay
Platinum
Togiak
AHKLUN MTS.
Cape Newenham
WOOD-TIKCHIK S.P.
Koliganek
Aleknagik
New Stuyahok
Ekwok
Fox Mus.
Dillingham
Levelock
Newhalen
Nondalton
Iliamna
Port Alsworth
LAKE CLARK N.P. & PRES.
Lake Clark
Mulchatna
Redoubt Volcano 10,197 ft.
CAPTAIN COOK S.R.A.
STERLING HWY
Anchor Point
Homer
Seldovia
KENAI PEN.
KENAI N.W.R.
Chenega Site
Alaska SeaLife Ctr.
Caines Head S.R.A.
Montague Island
Seward
KENAI FJORDS NATL. PARK
twice-monthly service June–Sept. only

Manokotak
Clarks Point
South Naknek
Naknek
King Salmon
Visitor Center
Kohanok
KATMAI N.P. AND PRES.
Mount Katmai 6,715 ft.
Valley of Ten Thousand Smokes
Shuyak Island S.P.
Afognak Island S.P.
Kodiak N.W.R.
Ouzinkie
Port Lions
Kodiak
Ft. Abercrombie St. Hist. Pk.
Kodiak Island

Egegik
Bristol Bay
Becharof L.
BECHAROF N.W.R.
Pilot Point
Karluk
Larsen Bay
Alutiiq Mus.
KODIAK N.W.R.
Akhiok
Old Harbor
Pasagshak S.R.S.
ALASKA MARITIME N.W.R.

Cape Constantine

Gulf of

4

ALEUTIAN ISLANDS
HAWAII-ALEUTIAN TIME ZONE
ALASKA TIME ZONE
Seguam I.
Nikolski
Fox Islands
Unalaska Island
Dutch Harbor
Unalaska
Akutan
Krenitzen Islands
ALASKA MARITIME N.W.R.
Cold Bay
False Pass
King Cove
Unimak Island
Sand Point
Unga Island
Sanak I.
Shumagin Islands
Chirikof I.
Trinity Islands
IZEMBEK N.W.R.
ALASKA PENINSULA
Mount Veniaminof 7,075 ft.
Chignik Lake
Chignik
Perryville
Port Heiden
ANIAKCHAK NATL. MON.
ALASKA PENINSULA N.W.R.

ALASKA MARITIME N.W.R.

Distances in the U.S. shown in miles.
Aux États-Unis, les distances sont en milles.

TRAVEL NOTE: Always inquire locally for road conditions and closures, especially in winter.

PACIFIC OCEAN

A   **B**   **C**

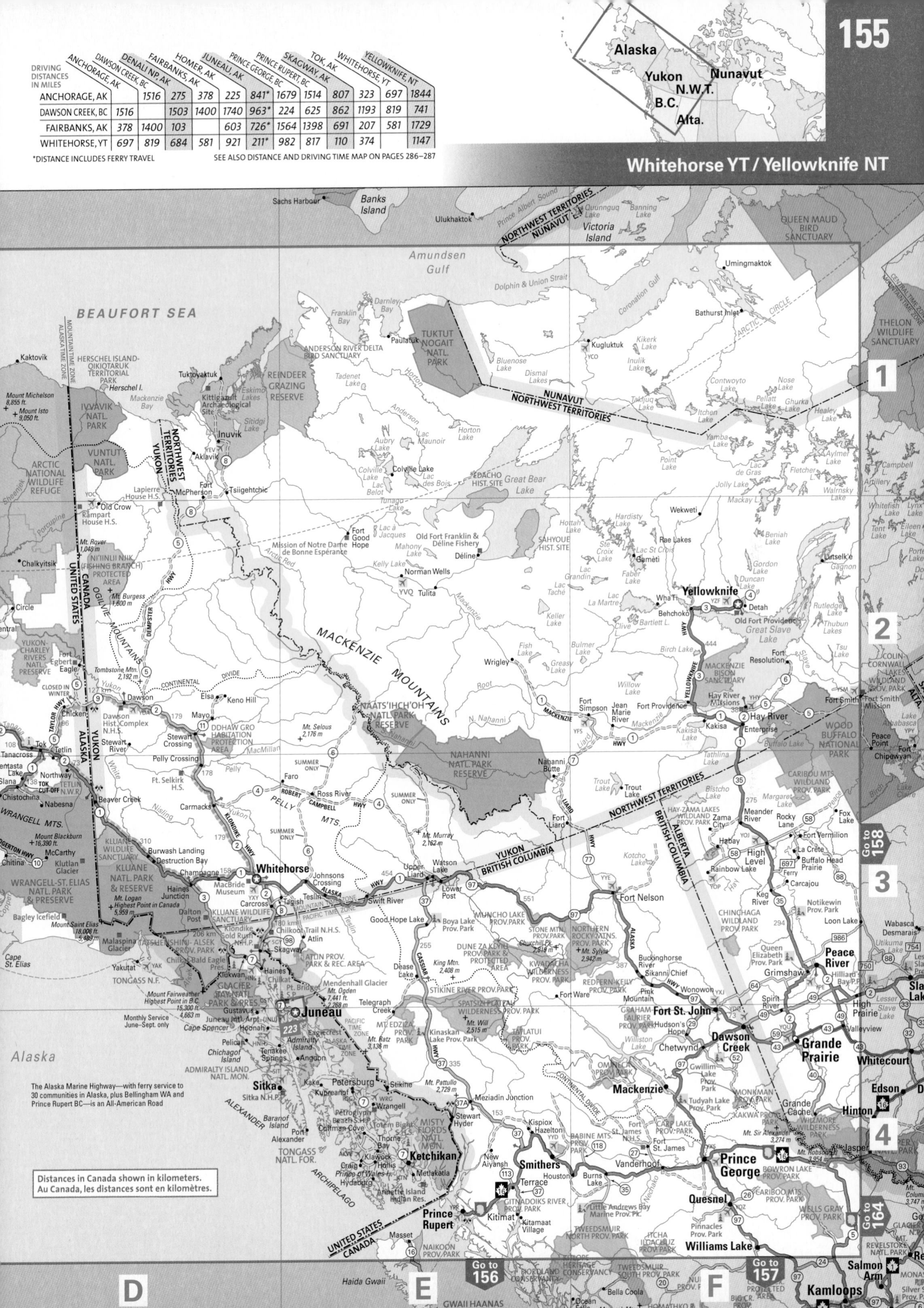

DRIVING DISTANCES IN MILES

	ANCHORAGE, AK	DAWSON CREEK, BC	DENALI NP, AK	FAIRBANKS, AK	HOMER, AK	JUNEAU, AK	PRINCE GEORGE, BC	PRINCE RUPERT, BC	SKAGWAY, AK	TOK, AK	WHITEHORSE, YT	YELLOWKNIFE, NT
ANCHORAGE, AK		1516	275	378	225	841*	1679	1514	807	323	697	1844
DAWSON CREEK, BC	1516		1503	1400	1740	963*	224	625	862	1193	819	741
FAIRBANKS, AK	378	1400	103		603	726*	1564	1398	691	207	585	1729
WHITEHORSE, YT	697	819	684	581	921	211*	982	817	110	374		1147

*DISTANCE INCLUDES FERRY TRAVEL   SEE ALSO DISTANCE AND DRIVING TIME MAP ON PAGES 286–287

Distances in Canada shown in kilometers.
Au Canada, les distances sont en kilomètres.

The Alaska Marine Highway—with ferry service to 30 communities in Alaska, plus Bellingham WA and Prince Rupert BC—is an All-American Road

Alaska

British Columbia   Alberta

0 mi   20   40   60
0 km 20   40   60   80
One inch equals 40.3 miles/Un pouce équivaut à 40.3 milles
One centimeter equals 25.4 km/Un cm équivaut à 25.4 km

Row 1 / Column A–B area

Coffman Cove
Mt. Pattullo 2,729 m
Meziadin Lake
Meziadin Junction
37A
Go to 155
Meziadin Lake Provincial Park
Stewart
Hyder
Nass L.
Motase Pk. 2,411 m
Bear Lake
SUSTUT PROVINCIAL PARK
CONTINENTAL DIVIDE
CASSIAR HWY
Heceta I.
Meyers Chuck
TONGASS
Cleveland Peninsula
Revillagigedo Island
MISTY FIORDS NATIONAL MONUMENT
Kinskuch Lake
SWAN LAKE-KISPIOX RIVER PROVINCIAL PARK
Shelagyote Pk. 2,466 m
AKW Thorne Bay
Klawock
Noyes I.
Craig Hollis Kasaan
Baker I.
NATIONAL
Lavender Pk. 2,323 m
Cranberry Junction
Kitwancool Lake
Cutoff Mtn. 1,649 m
Kisgegas Pk. 2,347 m
BABINE RIVER CORRIDOR PROVINCIAL PARK
Centre Pk. 1,990 m
Waterfall
Suemez I.
Prince of Wales Island
Ketchikan
Saxman
Alice Arm
Mt. Weber 2,007 m
37
65
73
Mt. Thomlinson 2,591 m
Mt. Lovell 1,995 m
Hydaburg
KTN Gravina Island
ANNETTE ISLAND IND. RES.
7
New Aiyansh
Gitwinksihlkw
Nass Camp
NISGA'A MEMORIAL LAVA BED PROVINCIAL PARK
Gitanyow Totem Poles
Gitwangals Battle Hill N.H.S.
Kispiox
New Hazelton
Hazelton
'Ksan Hist. Village & Mus.
Seeley Lake Prov. Pk.
Ross Lake Prov. Park
Fort Babine
Babine Lake
Smithers Landing Marine Prov. Park
Metlakatla
Sukkwan I.
Long I.
FOREST
Laxgalts'ap
Gingolx
Kitwanga
South Hazelton
Kitseguecla
Moricetown
Blunt Mtn. 2,286 m
BABINE MOUNTAINS PROV. PARK
Red Lake
Smithers Landing
Forrester I.
Dall I.
ALASKA MARITIME N.W.R.
Cordova Bay
Clarence Strait
Duke I.
Nass Bay
Nasoga Gulf
Alder Pk. 2,220 m
Oscar Pk. 2,304 m
Lava Lake
Cedarvale
113
16
SEVEN SISTERS PROV. PARK
Rosswood
37
Kitsumkalum Lake
Smithers Arpt. (YD)
Smithers
Telkwa
Granis
Red Lake Prov. Pk.

Row 2

ALASKA TIME ZONE / PACIFIC TIME ZONE
U.S. CANADA
Dixon Entrance
Chatham Sound
Dundas I.
Lax Kw'alaams
KHUTZEYMATEEN GRIZZLY BEAR SANCTUARY
Mt. Kenney 2,073 m
Heritage Park Mus.
Usk
Kleanza Creek Prov. Park
91
Ski Smithers
Tyhee Lake Provincial Park
257
118
Fulton L.
Masset Arpt. (ZMT)
Masset
Shames Mountain
Terrace
Eagle Pk. 2,093 m
Topley
Exchamsiks River Prov. Pk.
Y.C. Reg. Arpt.-Terrace-Kitimat (YXT)
Lakelse Lake Prov. Park
16
Graham Island
NAIKOON PROV. PARK
Mus. of Northern B.C.
Prudhomme Lake Prov. Park
Prince Rupert
Prince Rupert Arpt. (YPR)
North Pacific Hist. Fishing Village
Port Edward
Stephens I.
Diana Lake Prov. Park
Lakelse Lake
16
Houston
16
Ian Lake
Port Clements
Juskatla
Tlell
16
101
Porcher Island
Port Essington
Skeena
147
GITNADOIKS RIVER PROVINCIAL PARK
37
Khtada Lake
Kitimat
Kitamaat Village
McBride
Tagetochlain Lake
Noralee
Oona River
Kitkatla
McCauley I.
Pitt Island
Klewnuggit Inlet Marine Prov. Park
Morice Lake
Kidprice Lake
Nadina Lake
Wistaria Prov. Park
Little Andrews Bay Marine Prov. Park
Dotsa Lake

Row 3

Haida Gwaii (Queen Charlotte Islands)
Qay'llnagaay Heritage Center
Skidegate
Sandspit
Sandspit Arpt. (YZP)
Yakoun L.
Queen Charlotte
Alliford Bay
Moresby Camp
Sewell Inlet
Moresby Island
Hecate Strait
Banks Island
Lowe Inlet Marine Prov. Park
Union Passage Marine Prov. Park
Hartley Bay
Gribbell Island
Gil I.
Anchor Lake
Campania
Hawkesbury Island
Powell Pk. 2,012 m
Kemano
Nanika Lake
Tahtsa L.
Troitsa L.
Whtesail Lake
Tweedsmuir Pk. 2,182 m
Glatheli Lake
Michel Pk. 2,252 m
Fenton L.
GWAII HAANAS NATIONAL PARK RESERVE & HAIDA HERITAGE SITE
Aristazabal Island
Princess Royal Island
Green Inlet Marine Prov. Park
Mussel Inlet
Laredo Inlet
HUCHSDUWACHSDU NUYEM JEES/ KITLOPE HERITAGE CONSERVANCY
FIORDLAND CONSERVANCY
Surel L.
Pondosy L.
Eutsuk Lake
TWEEDSMUIR NORTH PROVINCIAL PARK
COAST
Oppy L.
Sigutlat L.
Kimsquit
Pooley I.
Price I.
Kynoch Inlet
Roderick
Klemtu
Swindle
Jackson Narrows Marine Prov. Park
Cascade Inlet
Dean
Kalone Pk. 2,557 m
Thunder Mtn. 2,681 m
Ocean Falls
Link Lake
Sir Alexander Mackenzie Provincial Park
Dean Channel
Firvale
Bella Coola
Hagensbo
20
MOUNTAINS

Row 4

PACIFIC OCEAN
Distances in Canada shown in kilometers.
Au Canada, les distances sont en kilomètres.
Oliver Cove Marine Prov. Park
Bella Bella
Shearwater
Codville Lagoon Marine Prov. Pk.
King I.
Mt. Saugstad 2,972 m
Goose I.
Hunter I.
Burke Channel
Namu
Rivers Inlet
Oweikeno Lake
HAKAI LUXVBALIS CONSERVANCY
Mt. Buxton 1,045 m
Calvert I.
Davsons Landing
Good Hope
Rivers Inlet
Draney Inlet
Penrose Island Marine Prov. Pk.
Smith Sound
Belize Inlet
Long L.

LANZ & COX ISLANDS PROV. PK.
Lanz I.
Cox I.
CAPE SCOTT PROV. PK.
Go to 162
Hope I.
Nigei I.
To Port Hardy
God's Pocket
Sullivan Bay
Seymour Inlet

A   B   C

1   2   3   4

Go to 155

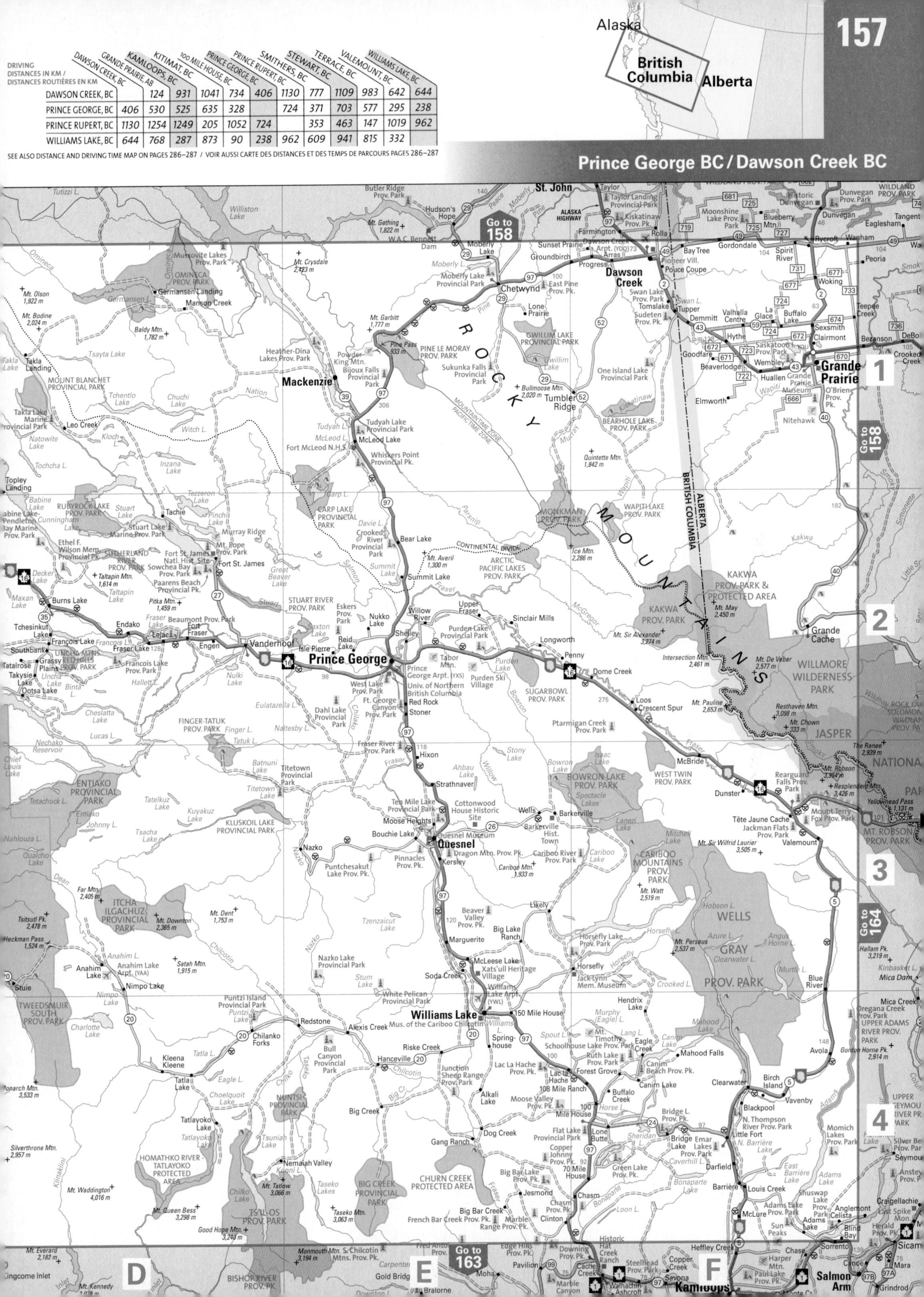

DRIVING DISTANCES IN KM / DISTANCES ROUTIÈRES EN KM

DAWSON CREEK, BC	GRANDE PRAIRIE, AB	KAMLOOPS, BC	KITIMAT, BC	100 MILE HOUSE, BC	PRINCE GEORGE, BC	PRINCE RUPERT, BC	SMITHERS, BC	STEWART, BC	TERRACE, BC	VALEMOUNT, BC	WILLIAMS LAKE, BC
DAWSON CREEK, BC	124	931	1041	734	406	1130	777	1109	983	642	644
PRINCE GEORGE, BC	406	530	525	635	328	724	371	703	577	295	238
PRINCE RUPERT, BC	1130	1254	1249	205	1052	724	353	463	147	1019	962
WILLIAMS LAKE, BC	644	768	287	873	90	238	962	609	941	815	332

SEE ALSO DISTANCE AND DRIVING TIME MAP ON PAGES 286–287 / VOIR AUSSI CARTE DES DISTANCES ET DES TEMPS DE PARCOURS PAGES 286–287

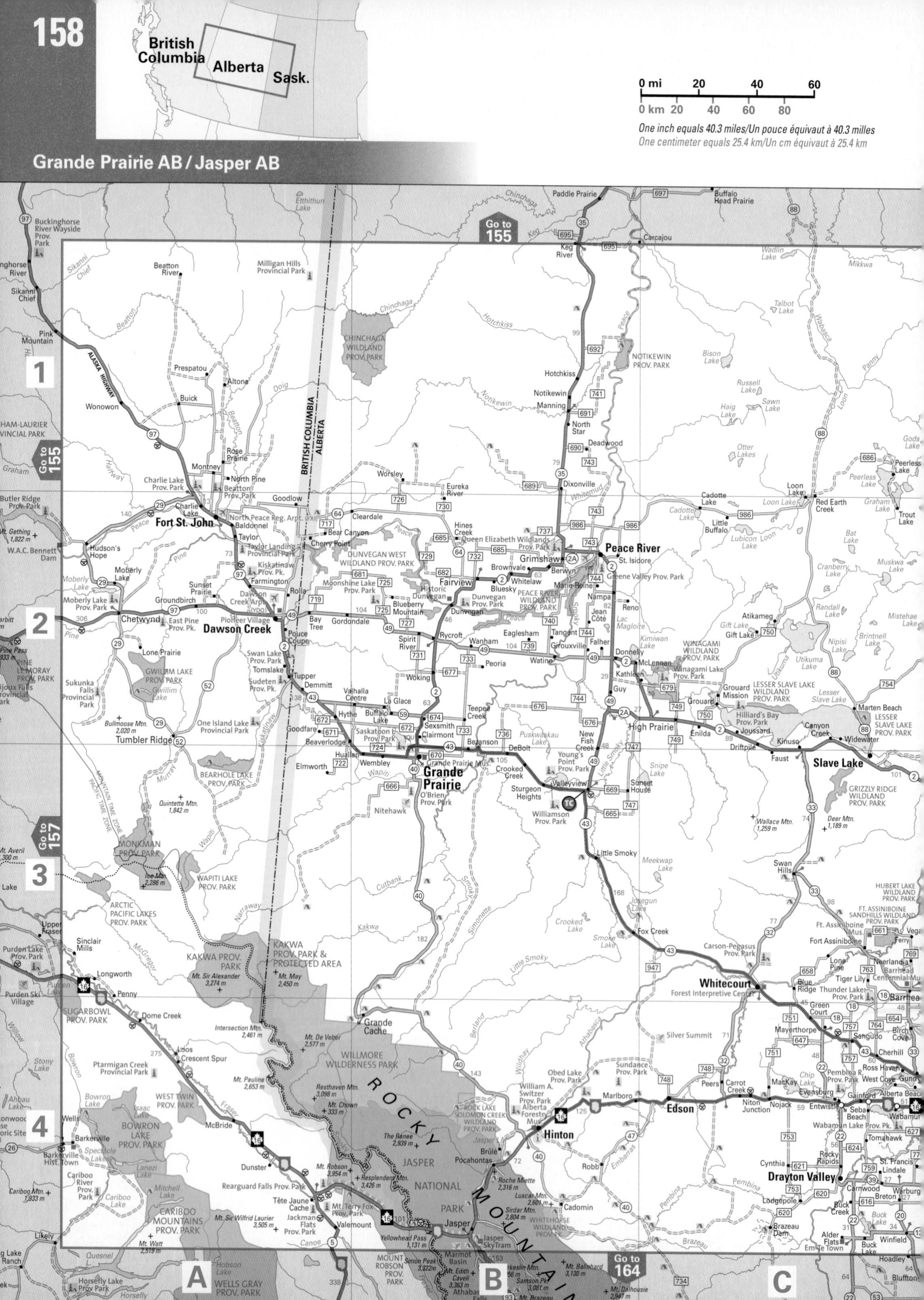

British Columbia   Alberta   Sask.

0 mi   20   40   60
0 km 20 40 60 80
One inch equals 40.3 miles/Un pouce équivaut à 40.3 milles
One centimeter equals 25.4 km/Un cm équivaut à 25.4 km

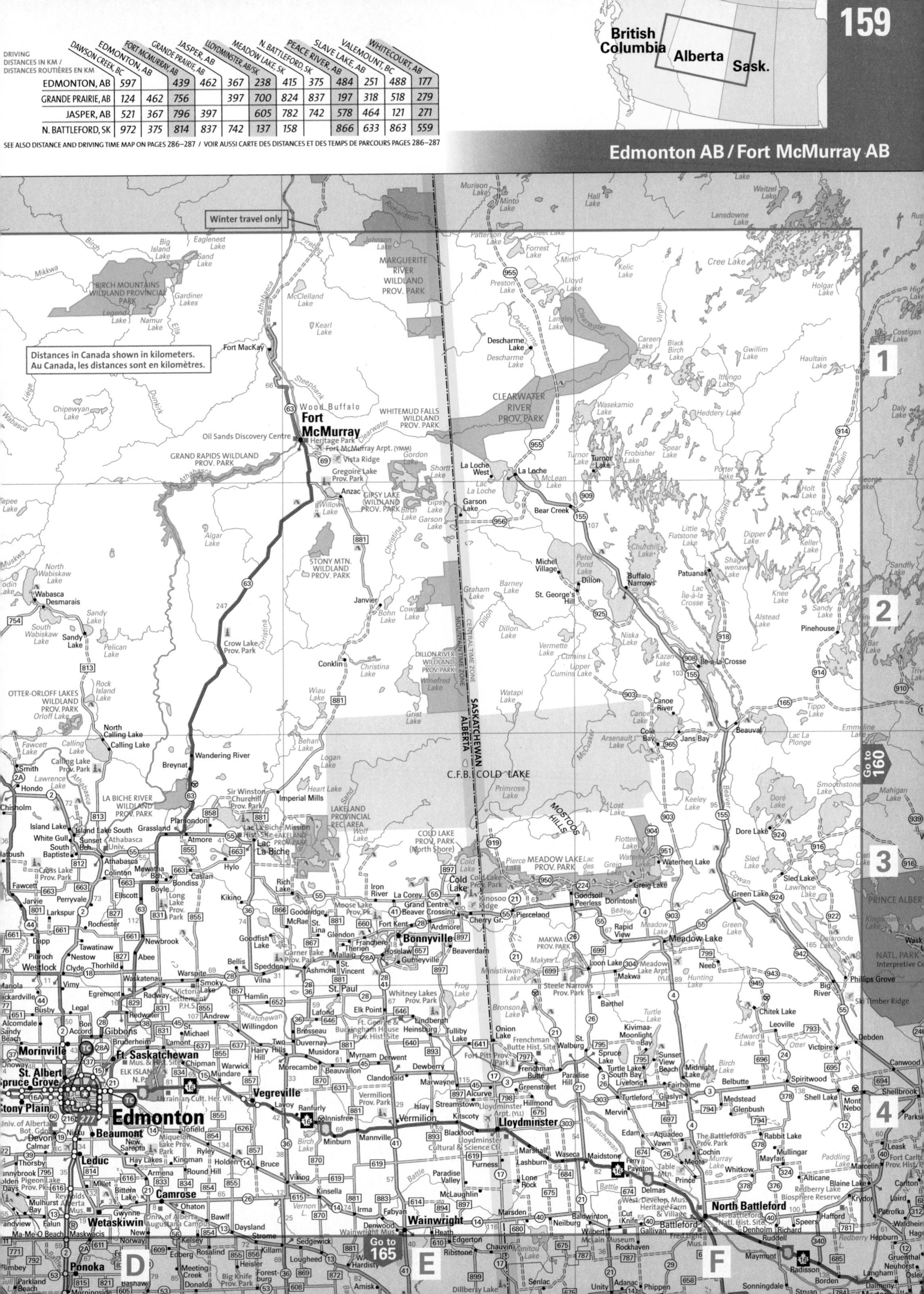

British Columbia Alberta Sask.

SEE ALSO DISTANCE AND DRIVING TIME MAP ON PAGES 286–287 / VOIR AUSSI CARTE DES DISTANCES ET DES TEMPS DE PARCOURS PAGES 286–287

DRIVING DISTANCES IN KM / DISTANCES ROUTIÈRES EN KM

	DAWSON CREEK, BC	EDMONTON, AB	FORT McMURRAY, AB	GRANDE PRAIRIE, AB	JASPER, AB	LLOYDMINSTER, AB/SK	MEADOW LAKE, SK	N. BATTLEFORD, SK	PEACE RIVER, AB	SLAVE LAKE, AB	VALEMOUNT, BC	WHITECOURT, AB
EDMONTON, AB	597		439	462	367	238	415	375	484	251	488	177
GRANDE PRAIRIE, AB	124	462	756		397	700	824	837	197	318	518	279
JASPER, AB	521	367	796	397		605	782	742	578	464	121	271
N. BATTLEFORD, SK	972	375	814	837	742	137	158		866	633	863	559

Distances in Canada shown in kilometers.
Au Canada, les distances sont en kilomètres.

Winter travel only

Go to 160

Go to 165

Edmonton ... Fort McMurray ... Grande Prairie ... Jasper ... Lloydminster ... North Battleford ... Wainwright ... Camrose ... Wetaskiwin ... Ponoka

Alberta | Sask. | Manitoba
Ontario

0 mi   20   40   60
0 km 20   40   60   80

One inch equals 40.3 miles/Un pouce équivaut à 40.3 miles
One centimeter equals 25.4 km/Un cm équivaut à 25.4 km

Go to 159
Go to 165
Go to 166

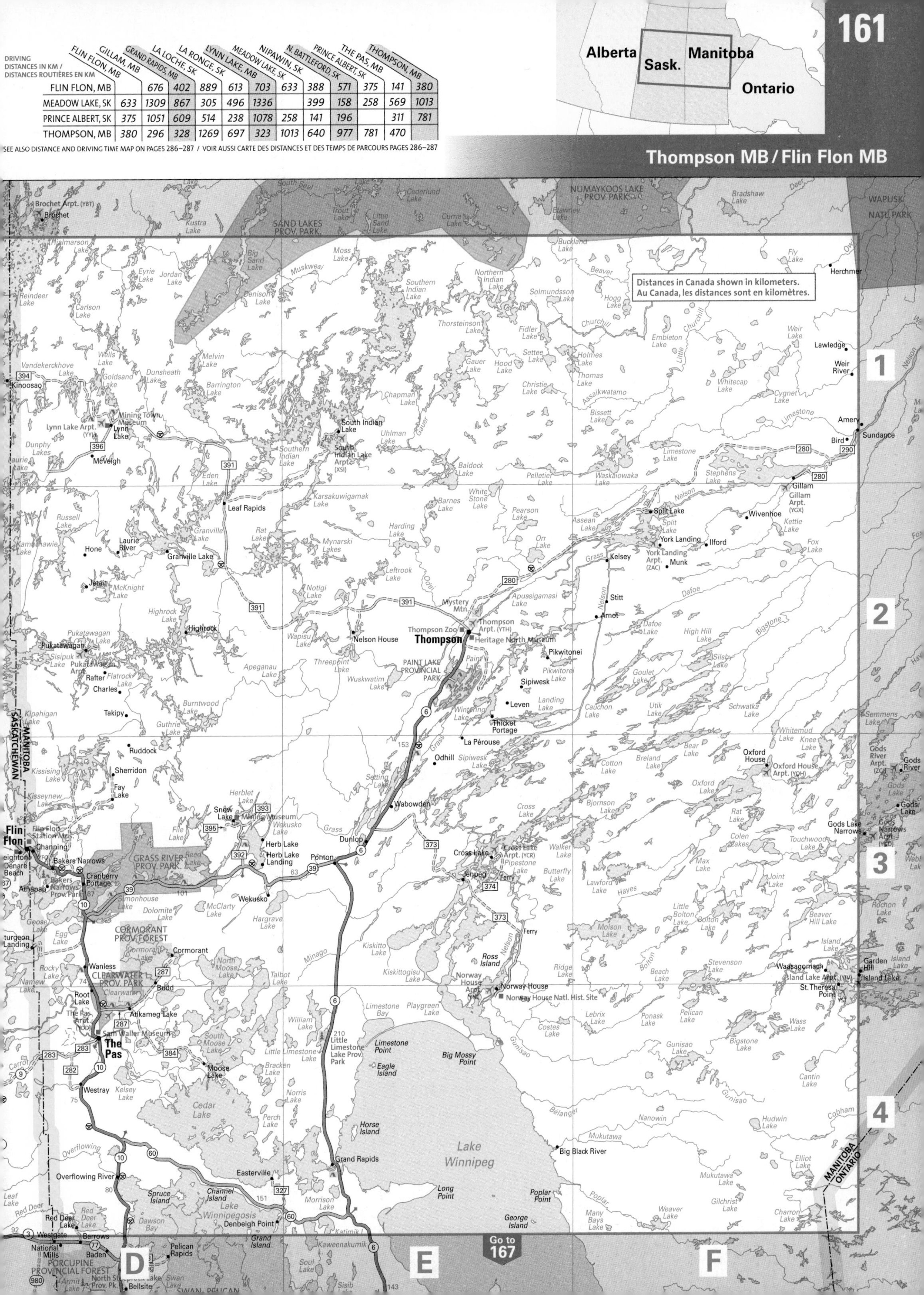

Alberta · Sask. · Manitoba · Ontario

DRIVING DISTANCES IN KM / DISTANCES ROUTIÈRES EN KM

	FLIN FLON, MB	GILLAM, MB	GRAND RAPIDS, MB	LA LOCHE, SK	LA RONGE, SK	LYNN LAKE, MB	MEADOW LAKE, SK	NIPAWIN, SK	N. BATTLEFORD, SK	PRINCE ALBERT, SK	THE PAS, MB	THOMPSON, MB
FLIN FLON, MB		676	402	889	613	703	633	388	571	375	141	380
MEADOW LAKE, SK	633	1309	867	305	496	1336		399	158	258	569	1013
PRINCE ALBERT, SK	375	1051	609	514	238	1078	258	141	196		311	781
THOMPSON, MB	380	296	328	1269	697	323	1013	640	977	781	470	

SEE ALSO DISTANCE AND DRIVING TIME MAP ON PAGES 286–287 / VOIR AUSSI CARTE DES DISTANCES ET DES TEMPS DE PARCOURS PAGES 286–287

Distances in Canada shown in kilometers.
Au Canada, les distances sont en kilomètres.

Go to 167

0 mi · 20 · 40
0 km · 20 · 40 · 60
One inch equals 25.4 miles/Un pouce équivaut à 25.4 milles
One cm equals 16.1 km/Un cm équivaut à 16.1 km

1
2
3
4

A **B** **C**

Go to 156

Go to 12

HOMATHKO RIVER TATLAYOKO PROTECTED AREA

Mt. Tatlow 3,066 m

Chilko Lake

Yohetta Lake

Mt. Queen Bess 3,298 m

TS'IL-OS PROV. PARK

Good Hope Mtn. 3,240 m

Long Lake

Belize Inlet

MacKenzie Sound

Mt. Everard 2,182 m

Costello Peak 1,713 m

Mt. Rodell 2,187 m

Mt. Grenville 3,109 m

Bishop

Monmouth Mtn. 3,194 m

BISHOP RIVER PROV. PARK

Queen Charlotte Strait

Hope I.

Nigei I.

God's Pocket Marine Prov. Pk.

Kingcome Inlet

Mt. Cridge 1,795 m

Southgate

Mt. Raleigh 3,078 m

UPPER LILLOOET PROV. PK.

Holberg

CAPE SCOTT PROV. PARK

William Lake

Port Hardy

Bear Cove

Port Hardy Arpt. (YZT)

Coal Harbour

Sullivan Bay

Broughton I.

Broughton Archipelago Marine Prov. Pk.

Simoom Sound

Tribune Ch.

Thompson Sound

Mt. Kennedy 2,028 m

Mt. Smith 2,299 m

Superb Mtn. 2,469 m

Mt. Gilbert 3,109 m

Toba Pk. 2,896 m

COAST MOUNTAINS

Holberg Inlet

Quatsino Prov. Park

Quatsino

Port McNeill

Sointula

Malcolm I.

Alert Bay

Cormorant Channel Marine Prov. Pk.

Gilford I.

Knight Inlet

Granite Pk. 2,048 m

Toba Inlet

CLENDINNING PROV. PK.

Winter Harbour

Quatsino Sound

Marble River Prov. Park

U'Mista Cult. Ctr.

Kokish

Telegraph Cove

Beaver Cove

Turnour I.

Minstrel Island

Cracroft Is.

Call Inlet

Port Neville

Loughborough Inlet

Phillips Arm

Bute Inlet

Lawn Point Prov. Pk.

Port Alice

Neroutsos Inlet

Victoria Lake

Nimpkish Lake

Nimpkish Lake Prov. Park

68

Bonanza Lake

Sayward

Hardwicke Island

Hardwicke I.

W. Thurlow I.

Blind Channel

Big Bay

Toba Inlet

CLENDINNING PROV. PK.

Brooks Bay

BROOKS PENINSULA PROV. PARK

Big Bunsby Marine Prov. Pk.

Checleset Bay

TAHSISH-KWOIS PROV. PARK

Tahsish Inlet

Woss

62

Mt. Cain

SCHOEN LAKE PROV. PARK

64

Hurston Bay Marine Prov. Pk.

Rock Bay

Rock Bay Marine Prov. Pk.

Sonora I.

Stuart Island

Octopus Is. Marine Prov. Pk.

Granite Bay

Quadra I.

Main Lake Prov. Pk.

Surge Narrows

Surge Narrows Prov. Pk.

Ha'thayim Marine Prov. Pk.

Walsh Cove Prov. Park

Princess Louisa Marine Prov. Pk.

Kyuquot

Zeballos

Woss Lake

Woss Lake Prov. Park

Vernon Lake

Victoria Pk. 2,163 m

Morton Lake Prov. Park

Mus. at Campbell River

Loveland Bay Prov. Park

Elk Falls Prov. Park

Heriot Bay

Quathiaski Cove

Kwagiulth Mus.

Whaletown

Mansons Landing Prov. Pk.

Refuge Cove

DESOLATION SOUND MARINE PROV. PK.

Okeover Arm Prov. Pk.

Inland Lake Prov. Pk.

Jervis Inlet

Kyuquot Sound

Rugged Point Marine Prov. Pk.

Catala Island Marine Prov. Pk.

Tahsis

Campbell River

Campbell River Arpt. (YBL)

Campbell River Prov. Park

Smelt Bay Prov. Pk.

Lund

Harmony Islands Marine Prov. Pk.

Esperanza Inlet

Nuchatlitz Prov. Park

Tahsis Inlet

Upper Campbell Lake

28

89

Saratoga Beach

Black Creek

Miracle Beach

Miracle Bch. Prov. Park

Mansons Landing

Powell River

Westview

28

Skookumchuc Narrows Prov. Pk.

Yuquot

Gold River

Buttle Lake

STRATHCONA

Mt. Washington

Merville

46

Little River

Lazo

Powell River Arpt. (YPW)

Blubber Bay

Van Anda

Texada Gillies Arpt. (YGB)

Saltery Bay

Saltery Bay Prov. Pk.

Nelson I.

Earls Cove

Spipiyus Prov. Pk.

Garden Bay Marine Pr. Pk.

Nootka Island

Nootka Sound

Sydney Inlet Prov. Park

Boat Basin

Sulphur Passage Prov. Park

PROV. PARK

19

Courtenay

Comox

Royston

Comox Valley Arpt. (YQQ)

Comox Bay

Texada I.

Gillies Bay

Sechelt Inlet

Irvines Landing

Madeira Park

Porpoise Bay Prov. Pk.

Sechelt

Cumberland

Sandy I. Marine Prov. Pk.

Union Bay

Denman I.

Fillongley Prov. Park

Jedediah Island Marine Prov. Pk.

Halfmoon Bay

Simson Prov. Pk.

HESQUIAT LAKE PROV. PARK

HESQUIAT PEN. PROV. PARK

Maquinna Marine Prov. Pk.

Stewardson Inlet

Herbert Inlet

Bedwell Sound

Great Central L.

92

Buckley Bay

Fanny Bay

Hornby I.

Rosewall Creek Prov. Park

False Bay

Lasqueti I.

Bowser

Squitty Bay Prov. Pk.

Sargeant Bay Prov. Pk.

Roberts Creek Prov. Pk.

Flores I.

Flores Island Prov. Park

Ahousat

Gibson Marine Prov. Pk.

Clayoquot Sound

Epper Passage Prov. Park

Dawley Passage Prov. Park

Clayoquot Plateau Prov. Park

Clayoquot Arm Prov. Park

Horne Lake Caves Prov. Pk.

Stamp River Prov. Pk.

Taylor Arm Prov. Pk.

Sproat Lake

MacMillan Prov. Park

47

Coombs

Qualicum Beach

XQU

French Creek

Parksville

Rathtrevor Beach Prov. Park

Nanoose Bay

35

Gabriola Island

Vargas Island Prov. Park

Whale Centre Museum

Tofino

Tofino Arpt. (YAZ)

34

4

Sproat L.

Port Alberni

Sproat Lake Prov. Park

Alberni Valley Museum

Errington

Little Qualicum Falls Prov. Pk.

Englishman River Falls Prov. Pk.

19

Nanaimo

Lantzville

19A

PACIFIC RIM NATIONAL PARK RESERVE (Long Beach Unit)

4

Kennedy L.

Alberni Inlet

Nahmint

Cedar

Hemer Prov. Pk.

Nanaimo Lakes (YCD)

Ucluelet

Kildonan

Green Cove

RESTRICTED ROAD

Cowichan Lake

Cassidy

52

Ladysmith

Barkley Sound

PACIFIC RIM NATIONAL PARK RESERVE (Broken Group Islands Unit)

Sarita

Youbou

Quw'utsun' Cult. Ctr.

Chemainus

N. Cowichan

30

18

Duncan

PACIFIC OCEAN

Bamfield

Hitchie Creek Prov. Park

Nitinat Lake

Gordon Bay Prov. Park

Honeymoon Bay

Mesachie L.

Lake Cowichan

Glenora

Cowichan River Prov. Pk.

PACIFIC RIM NATIONAL PARK RESERVE (West Coast Trail Unit)

Clo-oose

CARMANAH WALBRAN PROV. PARK

RESTRICTED ROAD

Port Renfrew

Sooke Lake

**Distances in Canada shown in kilometers.
Au Canada, les distances sont en kilomètres.**

Cape Flattery

Neah Bay

14

102

B.C. / WASH.

Juan de Fuca Prov. Park

River Jordan

French Beach Prov. Pk.

Milnes Landing

Sooke

Beechey Head

Strait of Juan de Fuca

MAKAH IND. RES.

112

Clallam Bay

Flattery Rocks N.W.R.

Cape Alava

Ozette Lake

OLYMPIC NATL. PARK

113

Sappho

112

Joyce

101

Sol Duc

OLYMPIC NATL. FOR.

110

Forks

OLYMPIC

19

30

36

101

DRIVING DISTANCES IN KM / DISTANCES ROUTIÈRES EN KM

	CAMPBELL RIVER, BC	KAMLOOPS, BC	KELOWNA, BC	MERRITT, BC	NANAIMO, BC	OSOYOOS, BC	PORT ALBERNI, BC	PORT HARDY, BC	SALMON ARM, BC	VANCOUVER, BC	VICTORIA, BC	WHISTLER, BC
KAMLOOPS, BC	512		163	87	363	231	441	750	108	355	393	475
NANAIMO, BC	153	363	403	279		404	82	391	471	23	113	104
VANCOUVER, BC	172	355	395	271	23	396	101	410	463		69	123
VICTORIA, BC	266	393	433	309	113	434	195	504	501	69		192

SEE ALSO DISTANCE AND DRIVING TIME MAP ON PAGES 286–287 / VOIR AUSSI CARTE DES DISTANCES ET DES TEMPS DE PARCOURS PAGES 286–287

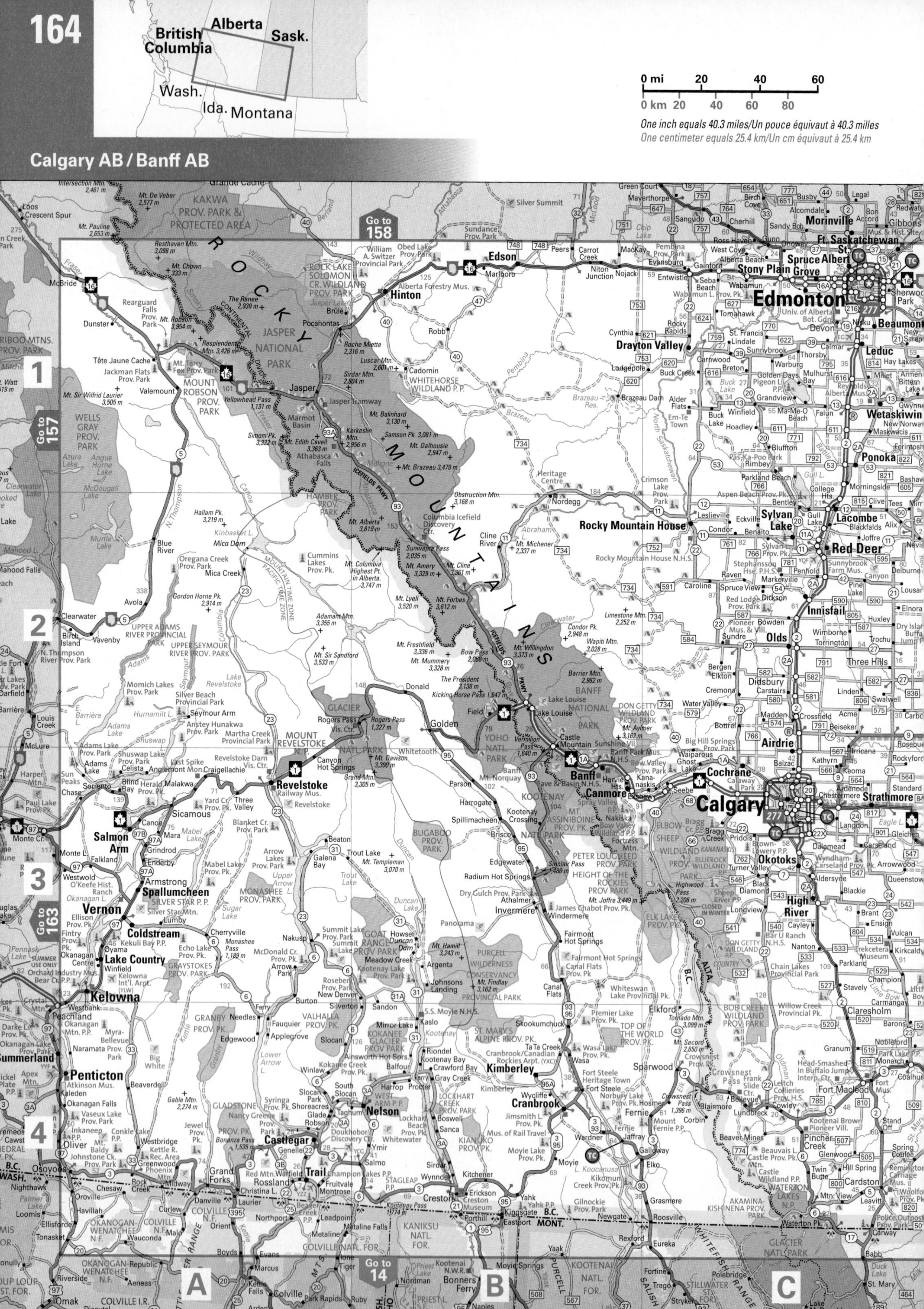

British Columbia | Alberta | Sask.
Wash. | Ida. | Montana

0 mi 20 40 60
0 km 20 40 60 80
One inch equals 40.3 miles/Un pouce équivaut à 40.3 milles
One centimeter equals 25.4 km/Un cm équivaut à 25.4 km

Go to 158
Go to 157
Go to 163
Go to 14

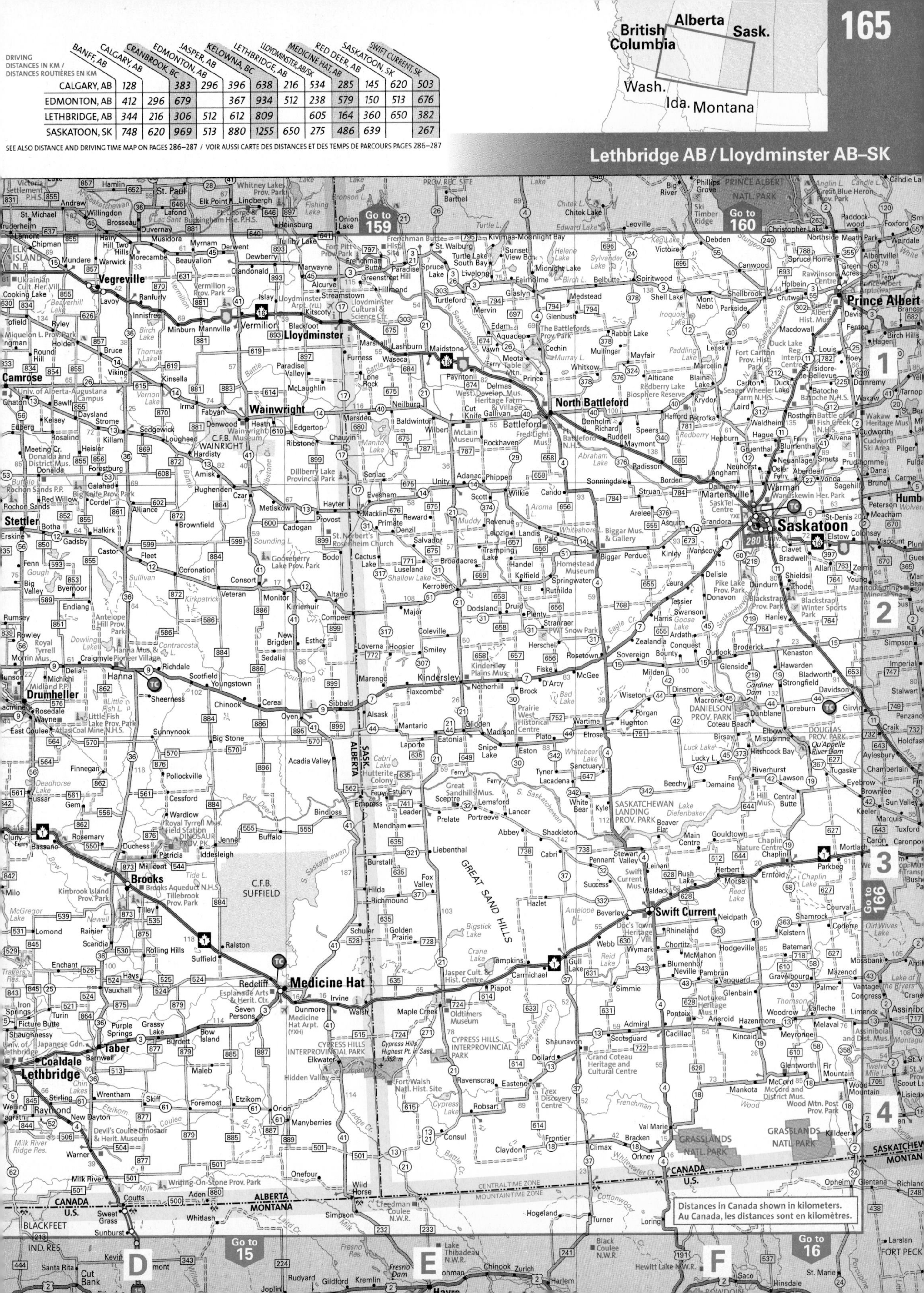

DRIVING DISTANCES IN KM / DISTANCES ROUTIÈRES EN KM

	BANFF, AB	CALGARY, AB	CRANBROOK, BC	EDMONTON, AB	JASPER, AB	KELOWNA, BC	LETHBRIDGE, AB	LLOYDMINSTER, AB/SK	MEDICINE HAT, AB	RED DEER, AB	SASKATOON, SK	SWIFT CURRENT, SK
CALGARY, AB	128		383	296	396	638	216	534	285	145	620	503
EDMONTON, AB	412	296	679		367	934	512	238	579	150	513	676
LETHBRIDGE, AB	344	216	306	512	612	809		605	164	360	650	382
SASKATOON, SK	748	620	969	513	880	1255	650	275	486	639		267

SEE ALSO DISTANCE AND DRIVING TIME MAP ON PAGES 286–287 / VOIR AUSSI CARTE DES DISTANCES ET DES TEMPS DE PARCOURS PAGES 286–287

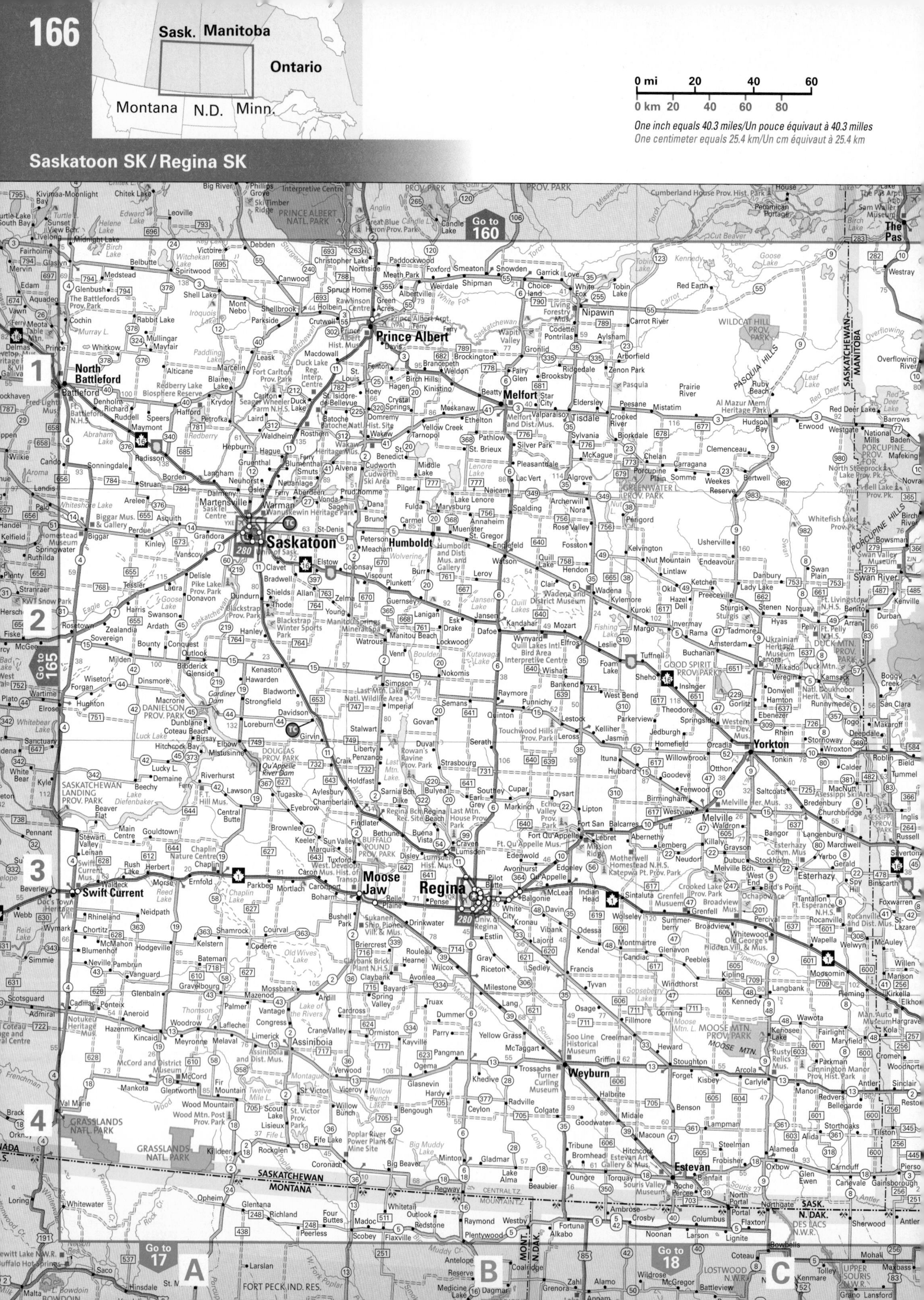

Sask. Manitoba

Ontario

Montana N.D. Minn.

0 mi   20   40   60
0 km 20   40   60   80
One inch equals 40.3 miles/Un pouce équivaut à 40.3 milles
One centimeter equals 25.4 km/Un cm équivaut à 25.4 km

Saskatoon SK / Regina SK

Sask. Manitoba
Ontario
Montana   N.D.   Minn.

DRIVING DISTANCES IN KM / DISTANCES ROUTIÈRES EN KM	BRANDON, MB	DAUPHIN, MB	GRAND RAPIDS, MB	MOOSE JAW, SK	PORTAGE LA PRAIRIE, MB	PRINCE ALBERT, SK	REGINA, SK	SASKATOON, SK	SWIFT CURRENT, SK	THE PAS, MB	WINNIPEG, MB	YORKTON, SK
BRANDON, MB		166	525	448	134	745	377	639	618	570	216	270
REGINA, SK	377	366	787	68	511	368		261	241	557	593	195
SASKATOON, SK	639	502	689	224	691	141	261		267	578	773	331
WINNIPEG, MB	216	322	430	664	82	819	593	773	834	611		442

SEE ALSO DISTANCE AND DRIVING TIME MAP ON PAGES 286–287 / VOIR AUSSI CARTE DES DISTANCES ET DES TEMPS DE PARCOURS PAGES 286–287

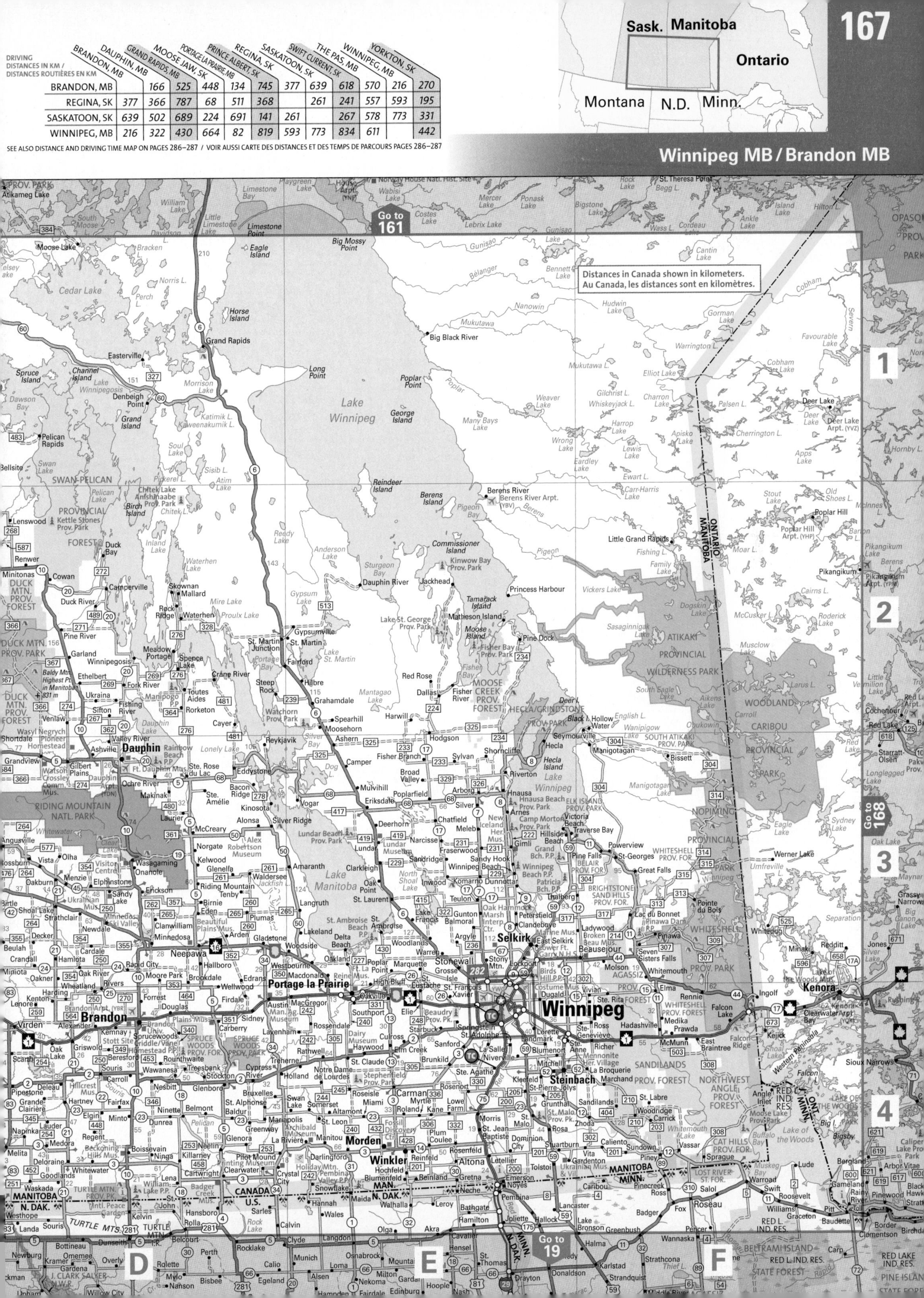

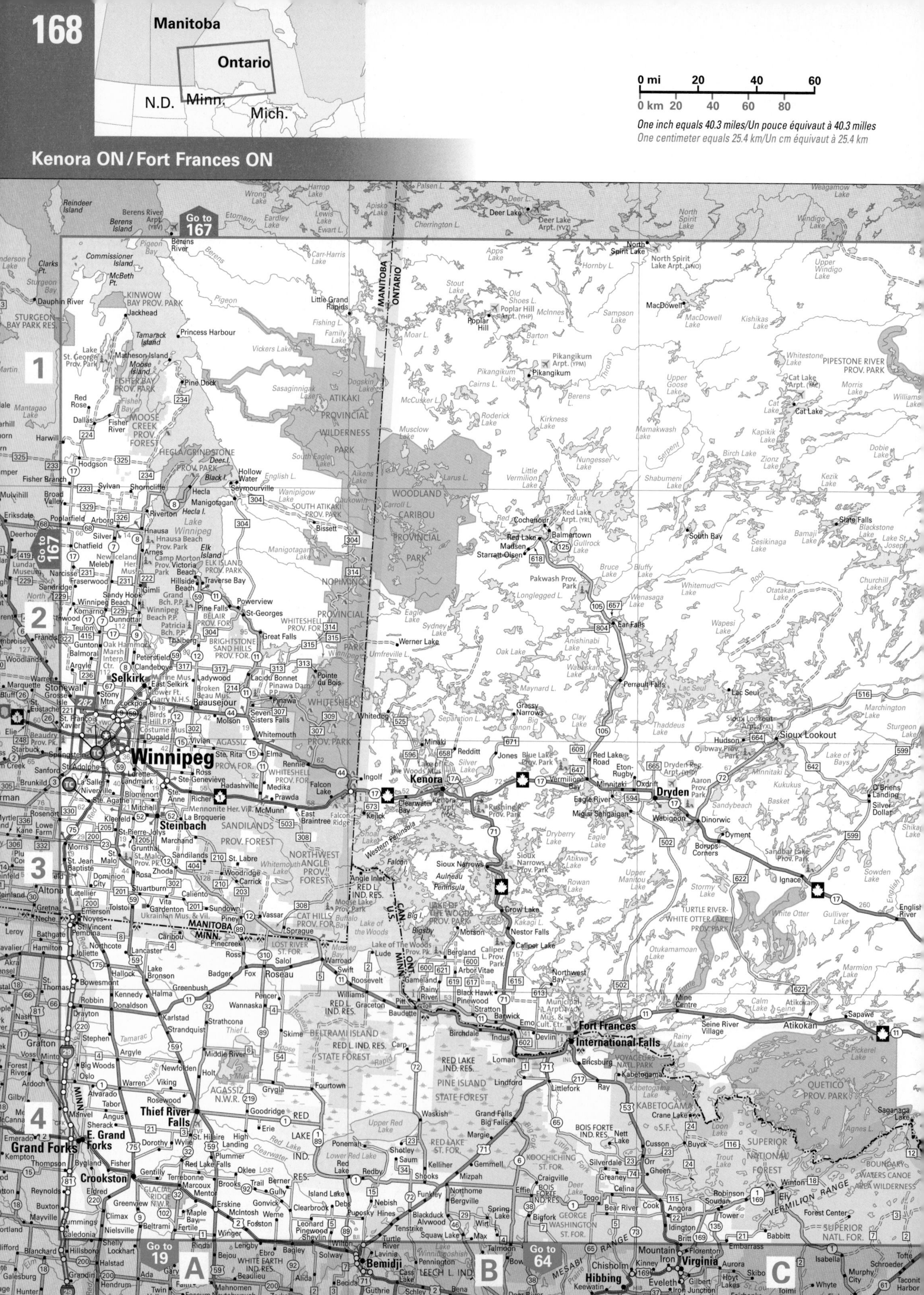
Manitoba
Ontario
N.D.
Minn.
Mich.
0 mi 20 40 60
0 km 20 40 60 80
One inch equals 40.3 miles/Un pouce équivaut à 40.3 milles
One centimeter equals 25.4 km/Un cm équivaut à 25.4 km
Go to 167
Go to 19
Go to 64
Winnipeg
Kenora
Dryden
Sioux Lookout
Fort Frances
International Falls
Red Lake
Steinbach
Selkirk
Thief River Falls
Grand Forks
Crookston
Bemidji
Hibbing
Virginia
ATIKAKI PROVINCIAL WILDERNESS PARK
WOODLAND CARIBOU PROVINCIAL PARK
QUETICO PROV. PARK
SUPERIOR NATIONAL FOREST
MANITOBA
ONTARIO
1
2
3
4
A
B
C

DRIVING DISTANCES IN KM / DISTANCES ROUTIÈRES EN KM

FROM	DRYDEN, ON	FORT FRANCES, ON	GERALDTON, ON	GRAND FORKS, ND	HEARST, ON	KENORA, ON	MARATHON, ON	NIPIGON, ON	STEINBACH, MB	THUNDER BAY, ON	WAWA, ON	WINNIPEG, MB
FORT FRANCES, ON	190		627	315	845	215	641	445	310	335	805	420
KENORA, ON	140	215	772	429	990		786	585	184	480	950	205
THUNDER BAY, ON	340	335	292		650	480	306	110	664		470	685
WINNIPEG, MB	345	420	977	228	1195	205	991	790	55	685	1155	

SEE ALSO DISTANCE AND DRIVING TIME MAP ON PAGES 286–287 / VOIR AUSSI CARTE DES DISTANCES ET DES TEMPS DE PARCOURS PAGES 286–287

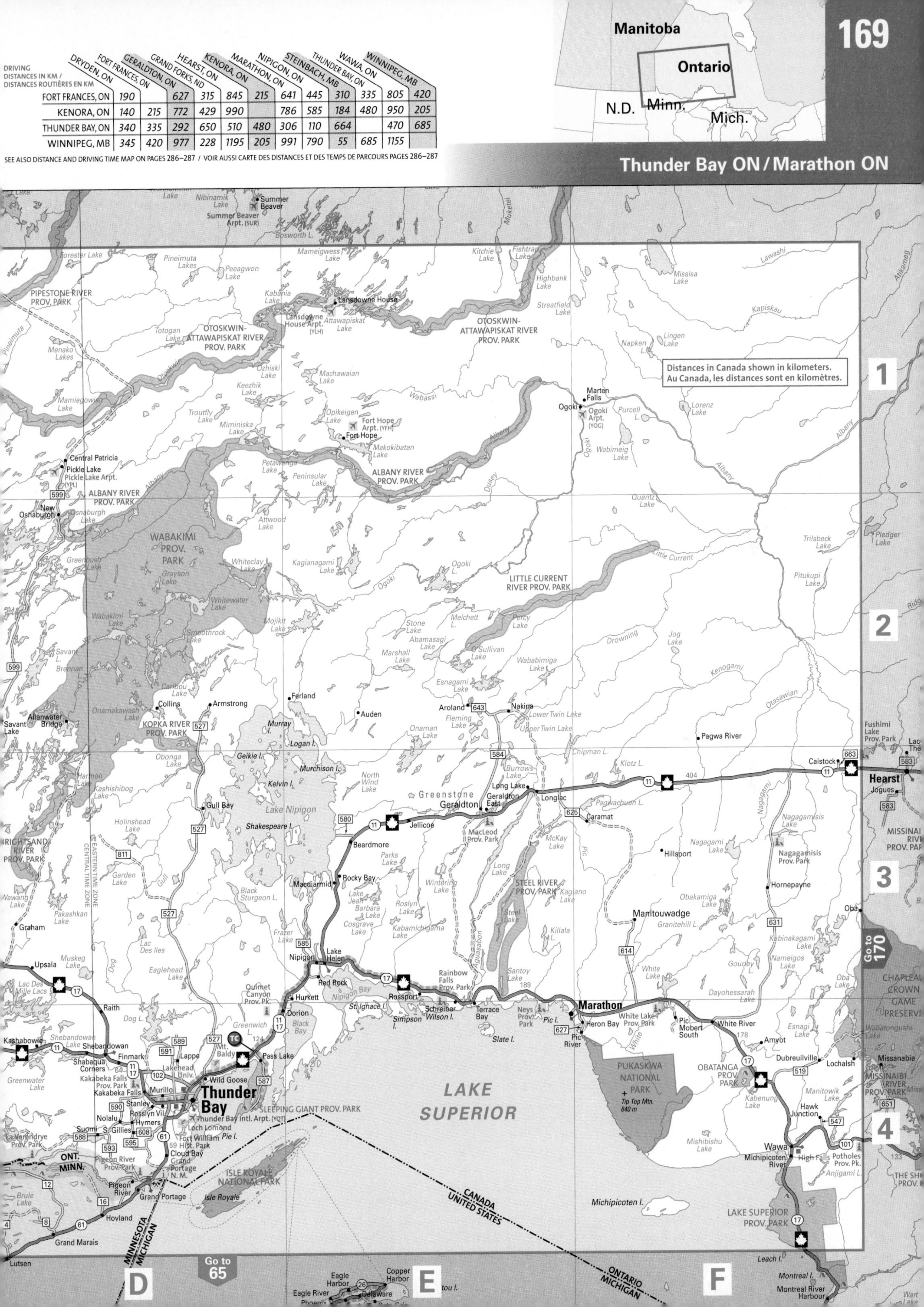

Distances in Canada shown in kilometers.
Au Canada, les distances sont en kilomètres.

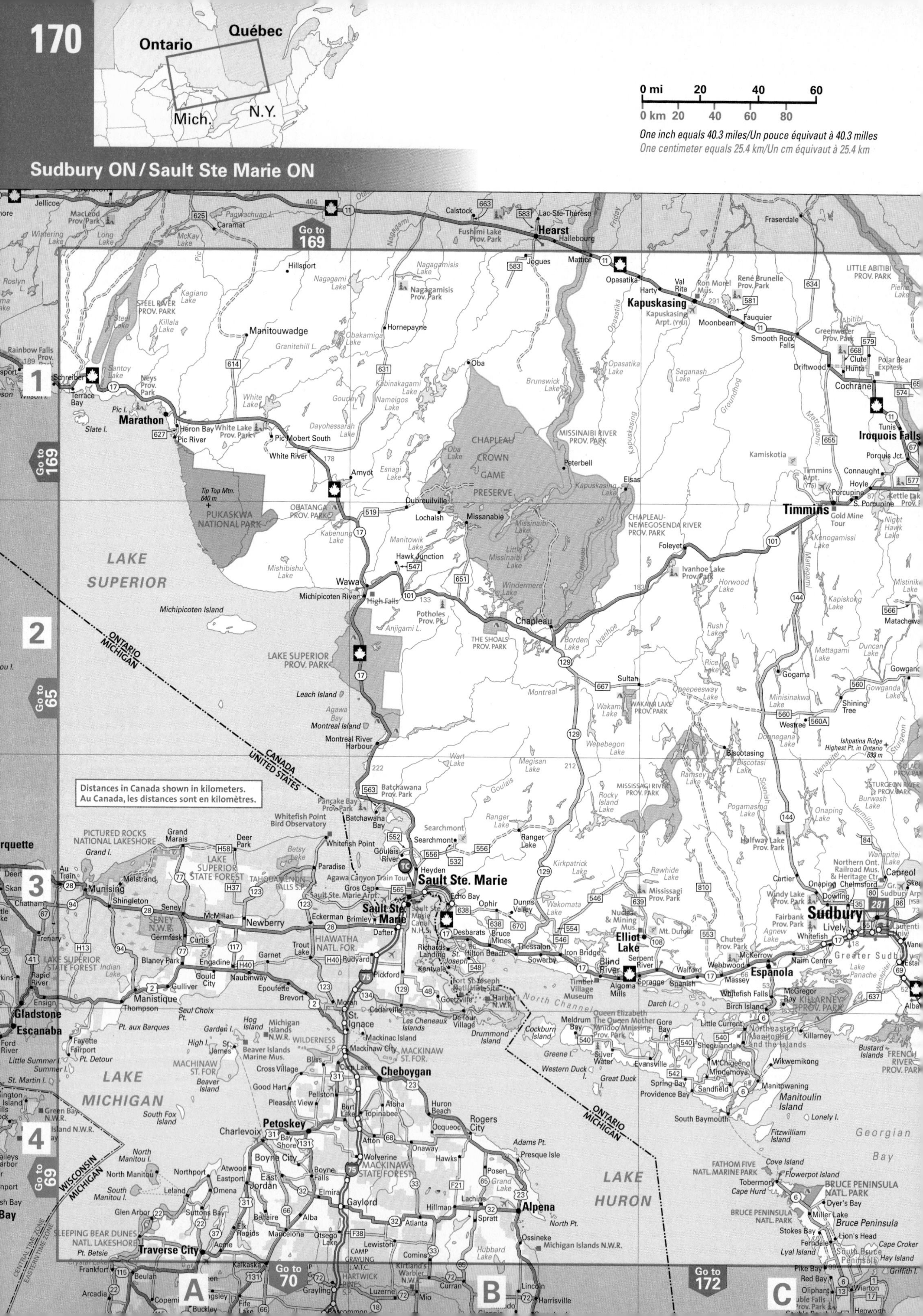

Ontario   Québec

Mich.   N.Y.

0 mi   20   40   60
0 km 20 40 60 80

One inch equals 40.3 miles/Un pouce équivaut à 40.3 milles
One centimeter equals 25.4 km/Un cm équivaut à 25.4 km

Distances in Canada shown in kilometers.
Au Canada, les distances sont en kilomètres.

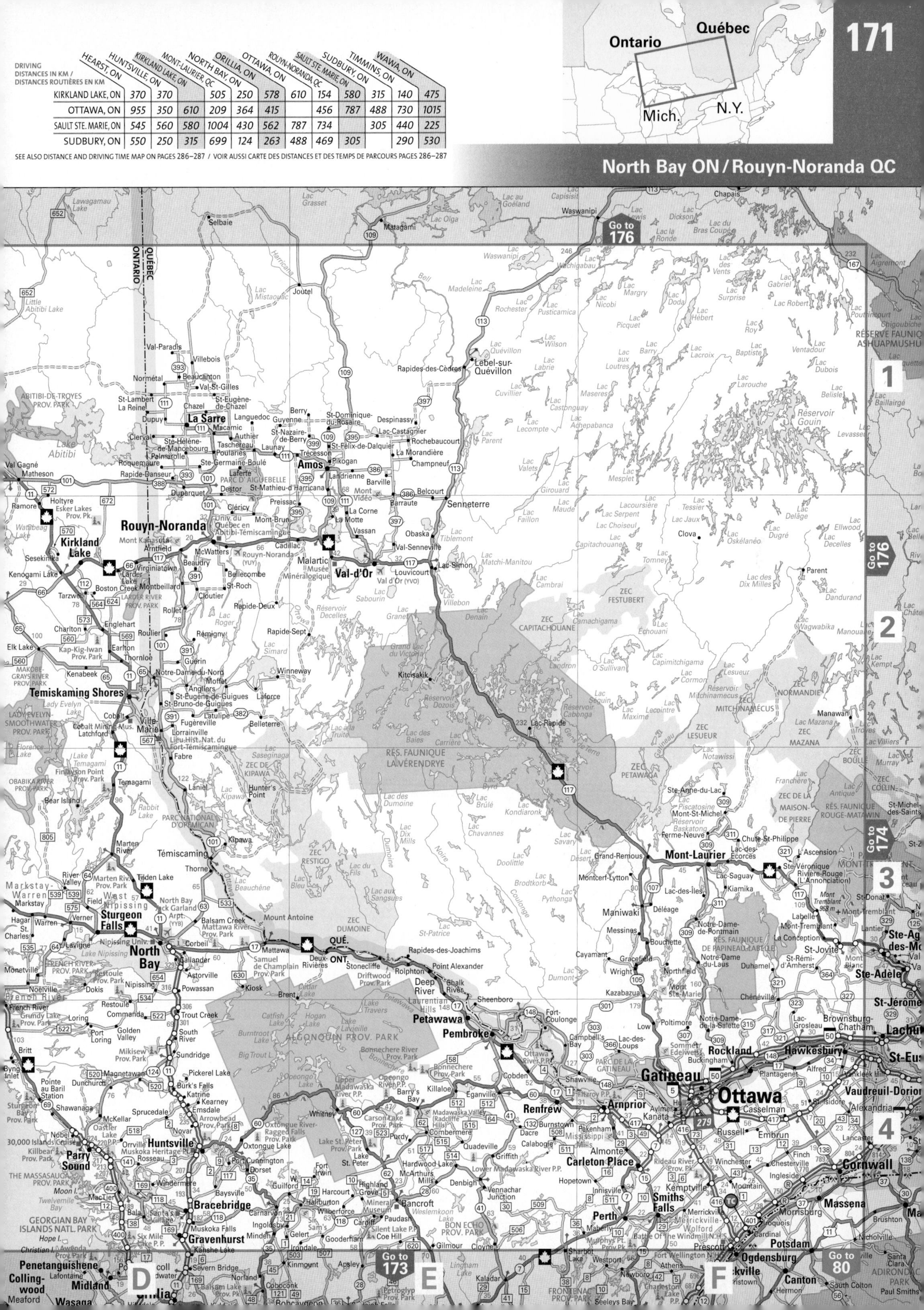

Ontario   Québec
Mich.   N.Y.

Go to 176
Go to 176
Go to 174
Go to 173
Go to 80

DRIVING DISTANCES IN KM / DISTANCES ROUTIÈRES EN KM

	HUNTSVILLE, ON	KIRKLAND LAKE, ON	MONT-LAURIER, QC	NORTH BAY, ON	ORILLIA, ON	OTTAWA, ON	ROUYN-NORANDA, QC	SAULT STE. MARIE, ON	SUDBURY, ON	TIMMINS, ON	WAWA, ON	HEARST, ON
KIRKLAND LAKE, ON	370	370		505	250	578	610	154	580	315	140	475
OTTAWA, ON	955	350	610	209	364		415		456	787	488	730	1015
SAULT STE. MARIE, ON	545	560	580	1004	430	562	787		734		305	440	225
SUDBURY, ON	550	250	315	699	124	263	488	469		305		290	530

SEE ALSO DISTANCE AND DRIVING TIME MAP ON PAGES 286–287 / VOIR AUSSI CARTE DES DISTANCES ET DES TEMPS DE PARCOURS PAGES 286–287

Ontario
Mich. N.Y.
Ohio Pa.

London ON / Windsor ON

0 mi 20 40
0 km 20 40 60
One inch equals 25.4 miles/Un pouce équivaut à 25.4 milles
One cm equals 16.1 km/Un cm équivaut à 16.1 km

Distances in Canada shown in kilometers.
Au Canada, les distances sont en kilomètres.

Go to 170

Go to 76

LAKE HURON

LAKE ERIE

Lake St. Clair

Saginaw Bay

Georgian Bay

ONTARIO / MICHIGAN

CANADA / UNITED STATES

MICHIGAN / OHIO

ONTARIO

OHIO / PENNSYLVANIA

Go to 90

Go to 91

1 2 3 4

A B C

DRIVING
DISTANCES IN KM /
Distances routières en km

	BARRIE, ON	HAMILTON, ON	KINGSTON, ON	KITCHENER, ON	LONDON, ON	NIAGARA FALLS, ON	ORILLIA, ON	OWEN SOUND, ON	PETERBOROUGH, ON	SARNIA, ON	TORONTO, ON	WINDSOR, ON
KINGSTON, ON	350	330		430	430	390	317	430	180	530	260	620
NIAGARA FALLS, ON	200	68	390	130	190		237	260	260	290	130	380
TORONTO, ON	90	70	260	105	185	130	127	190	135	280		370
WINDSOR, ON	430	310	620	285	190	380	467	390	490	160	370	

SEE ALSO DISTANCE AND DRIVING TIME MAP ON PAGES 286–287 / VOIR AUSSI CARTE DES DISTANCES ET DES TEMPS DE PARCOURS PAGES 286–287

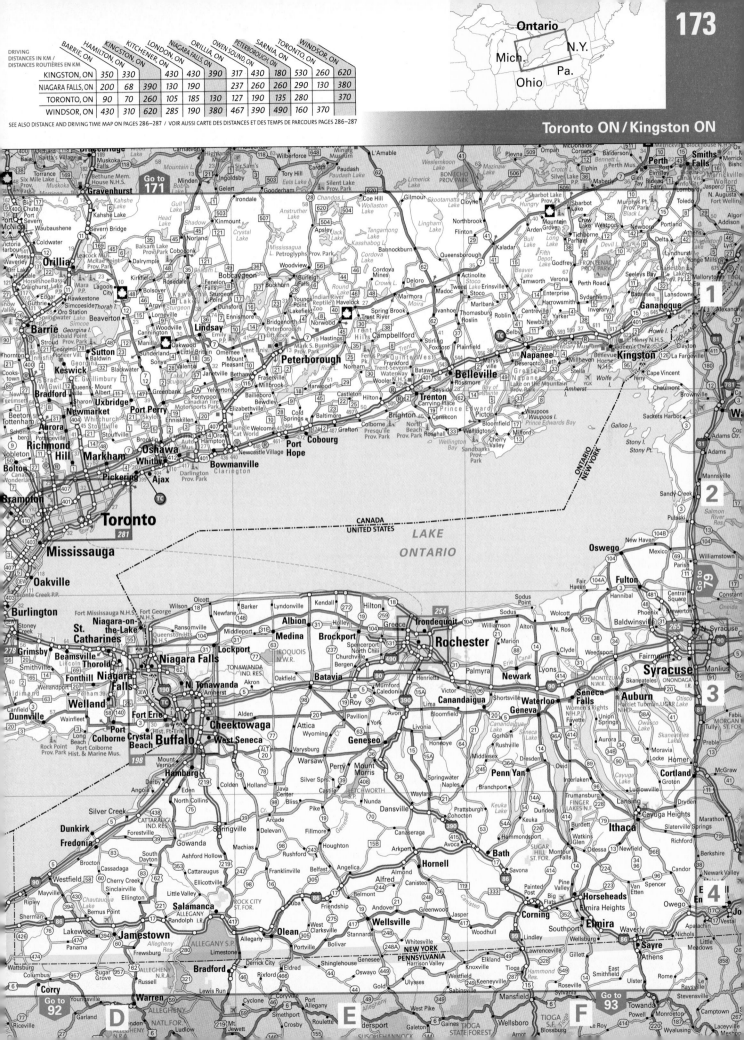

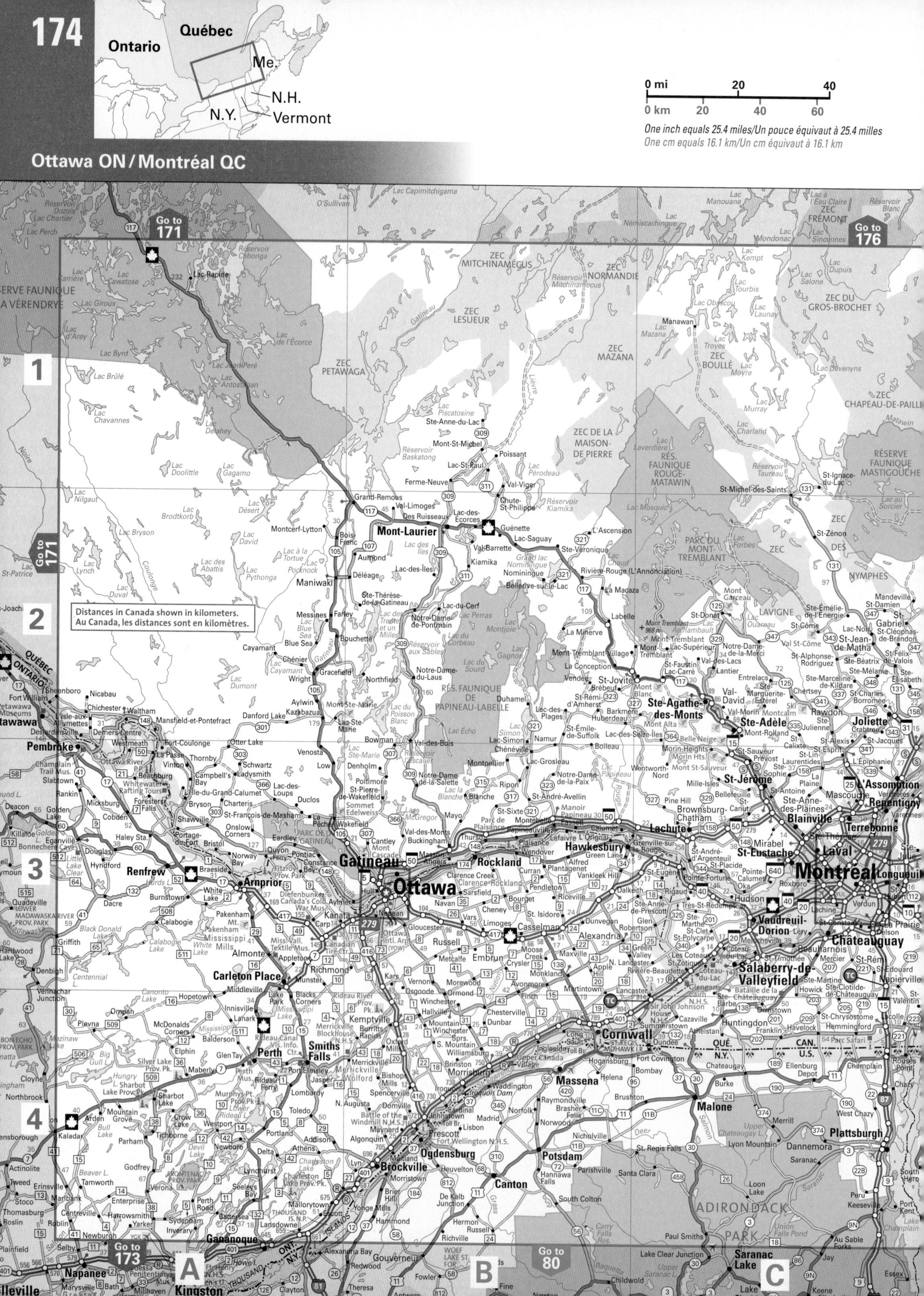

174

Ontario Québec

Me.

N.H.

N.Y. Vermont

Ottawa ON / Montréal QC

Go to 171

Go to 176

0 mi 20 40
0 km 20 40 60
One inch equals 25.4 miles/Un pouce équivaut à 25.4 milles
One cm equals 16.1 km/Un cm équivaut à 16.1 km

Distances in Canada shown in kilometers.
Au Canada, les distances sont en kilomètres.

Go to 173

Go to 80

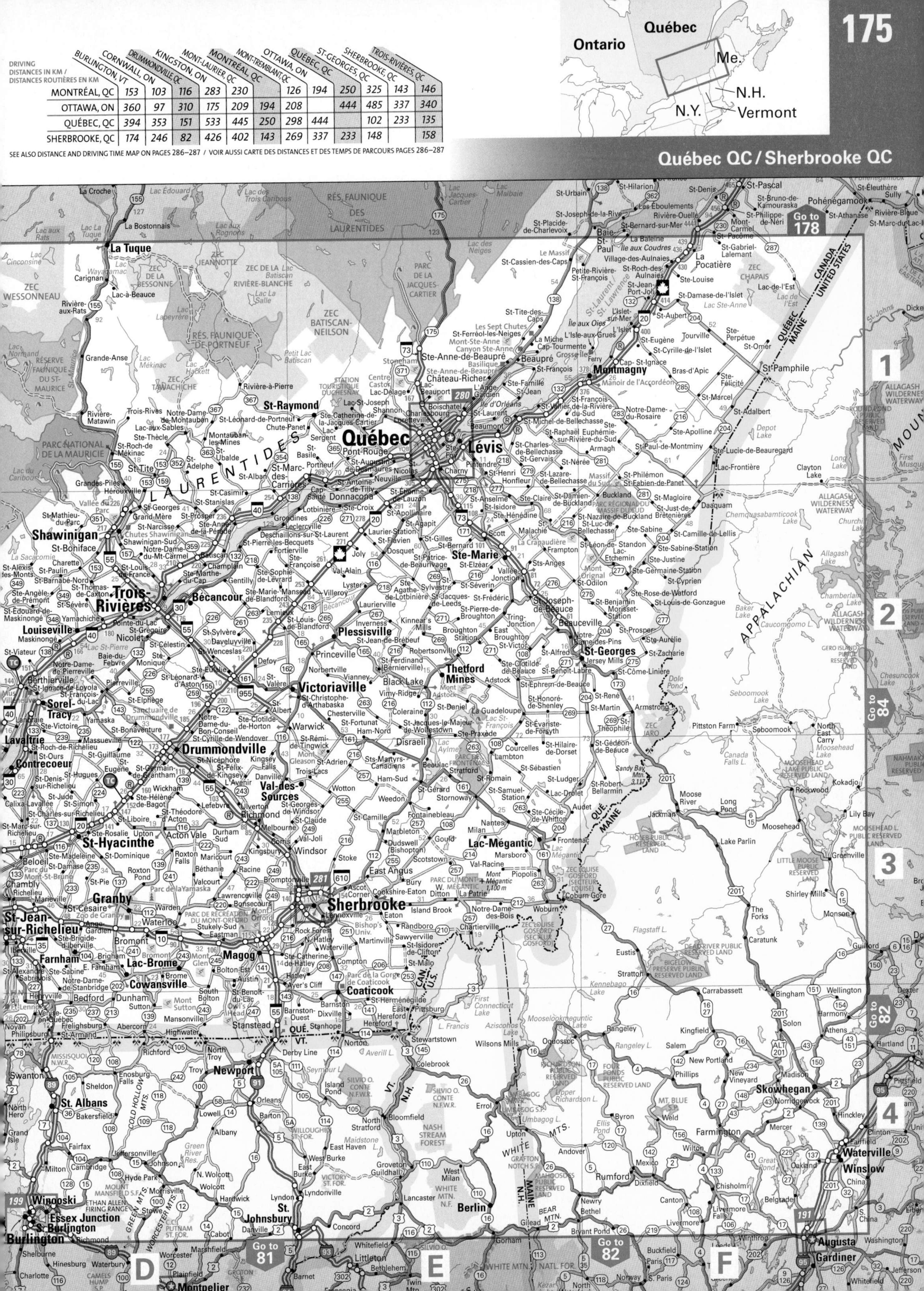

DRIVING DISTANCES IN KM / DISTANCES ROUTIÈRES EN KM	BURLINGTON, VT	CORNWALL, ON	DRUMMONDVILLE, QC	KINGSTON, ON	MONT-LAURIER, QC	MONTRÉAL, ON	MONT-TREMBLANT, QC	OTTAWA, ON	QUÉBEC, QC	ST-GEORGES, QC	SHERBROOKE, QC	TROIS-RIVIÈRES, QC
MONTRÉAL, QC	153	103	116	283	230		126	194	250	325	143	146
OTTAWA, ON	360	97	310	175	209	194	208		444	485	337	340
QUÉBEC, QC	394	353	151	533	445	250	298	444		102	233	135
SHERBROOKE, QC	174	246	82	426	402	143	269	337	233	148		158

SEE ALSO DISTANCE AND DRIVING TIME MAP ON PAGES 286–287 / VOIR AUSSI CARTE DES DISTANCES ET DES TEMPS DE PARCOURS PAGES 286–287

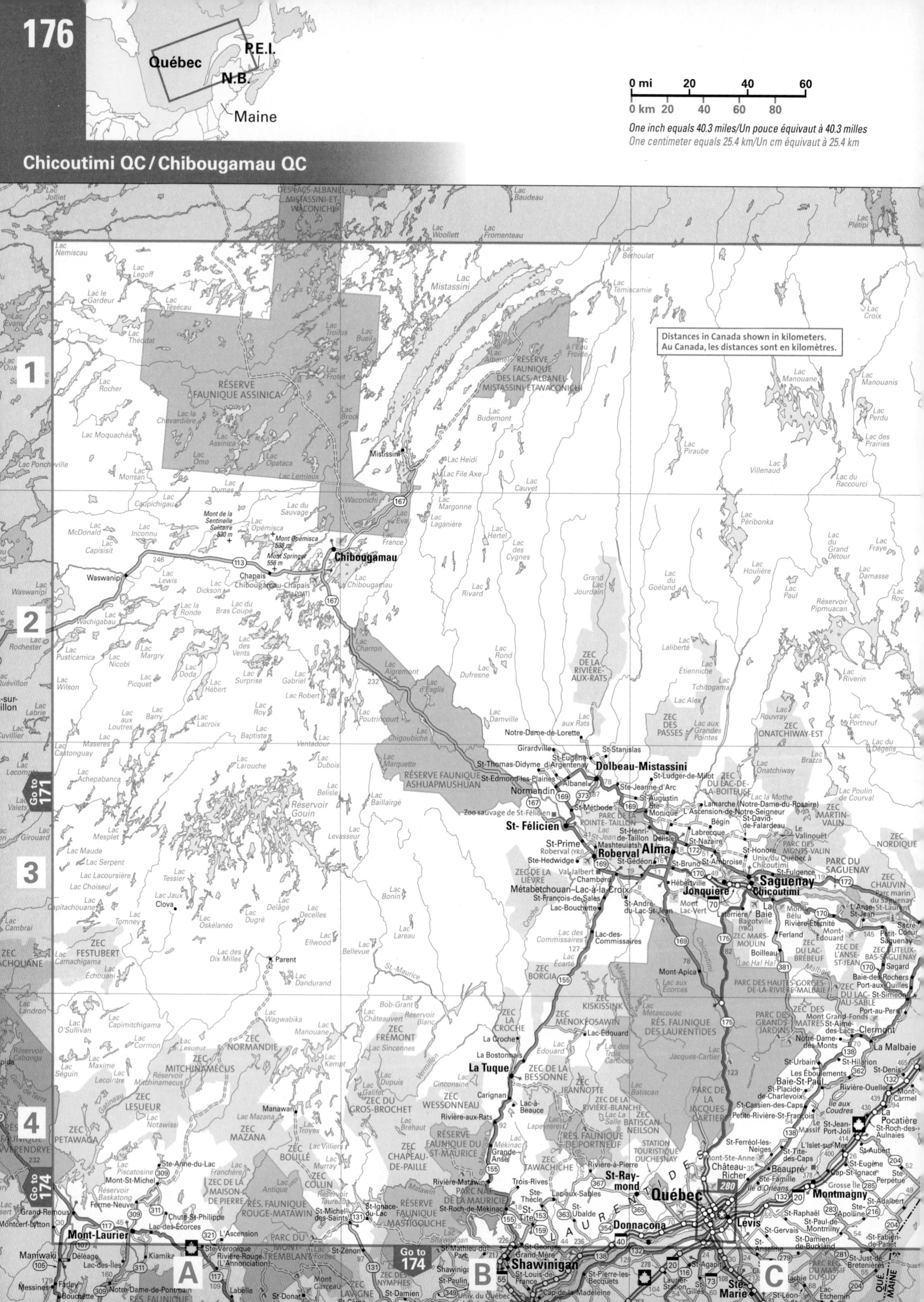
Québec
P.E.I.
N.B.
Maine
0 mi 20 40 60
0 km 20 40 60 80
One inch equals 40.3 miles/Un pouce équivaut à 40.3 milles
One centimeter equals 25.4 km/Un cm équivaut à 25.4 km
Distances in Canada shown in kilometers.
Au Canada, les distances sont en kilomètres.
Go to 171
Go to 174
Go to 174
1
2
3
4
A
B
C
Lac Mistassini
RÉSERVE FAUNIQUE ASSINICA
RÉSERVE FAUNIQUE DES LACS-ALBANEL-MISTASSINI-ET-WACONICHI
Mistissini
Chibougamau
Chapais
Waswanipi
Mont Opémisca 538 m
Mont Springer 556 m
Mont de la Sentinelle Solitaire 530 m
RÉSERVE FAUNIQUE ASHUAPMUSHUAN
Réservoir Gouin
Réservoir Pipmuacan
Dolbeau-Mistassini
Normandin
St-Félicien
Roberval
Alma
Saguenay
Jonquière
Chicoutimi
PARC DU SAGUENAY
RÉS. FAUNIQUE DES LAURENTIDES
PARC DE LA JACQUES CARTIER
La Tuque
Shawinigan
Québec
Lévis
Donnacona
Mont-Laurier
La Malbaie
Baie-St-Paul
Montmagny
Clova
Parent
Manawan
Trois-Rives
RÉSERVE FAUNIQUE MASTIGOUCHE
RÉS. FAUNIQUE ROUGE-MATAWIN
RÉSERVE FAUNIQUE DU ST-MAURICE
PARC NAT. DE LA MAURICIE
RÉS. FAUNIQUE DE PORTNEUF
ZEC FESTUBERT
ZEC NORMANDIE
ZEC MITCHINAMECUS
ZEC LESUEUR
ZEC PETAWAGA
ZEC MAZANA
ZEC BOULLÉ
ZEC COLLIN
ZEC WESSONNEAU
ZEC FRÉMONT
ZEC DU GROS-BROCHET
ZEC BORGIA
ZEC KISKISSINK
ZEC DE LA RIVIÈRE-AUX-RATS
ZEC DES PASSES
ZEC ONATCHIWAY-EST
LAURENTIDES
QUÉ. MAINE

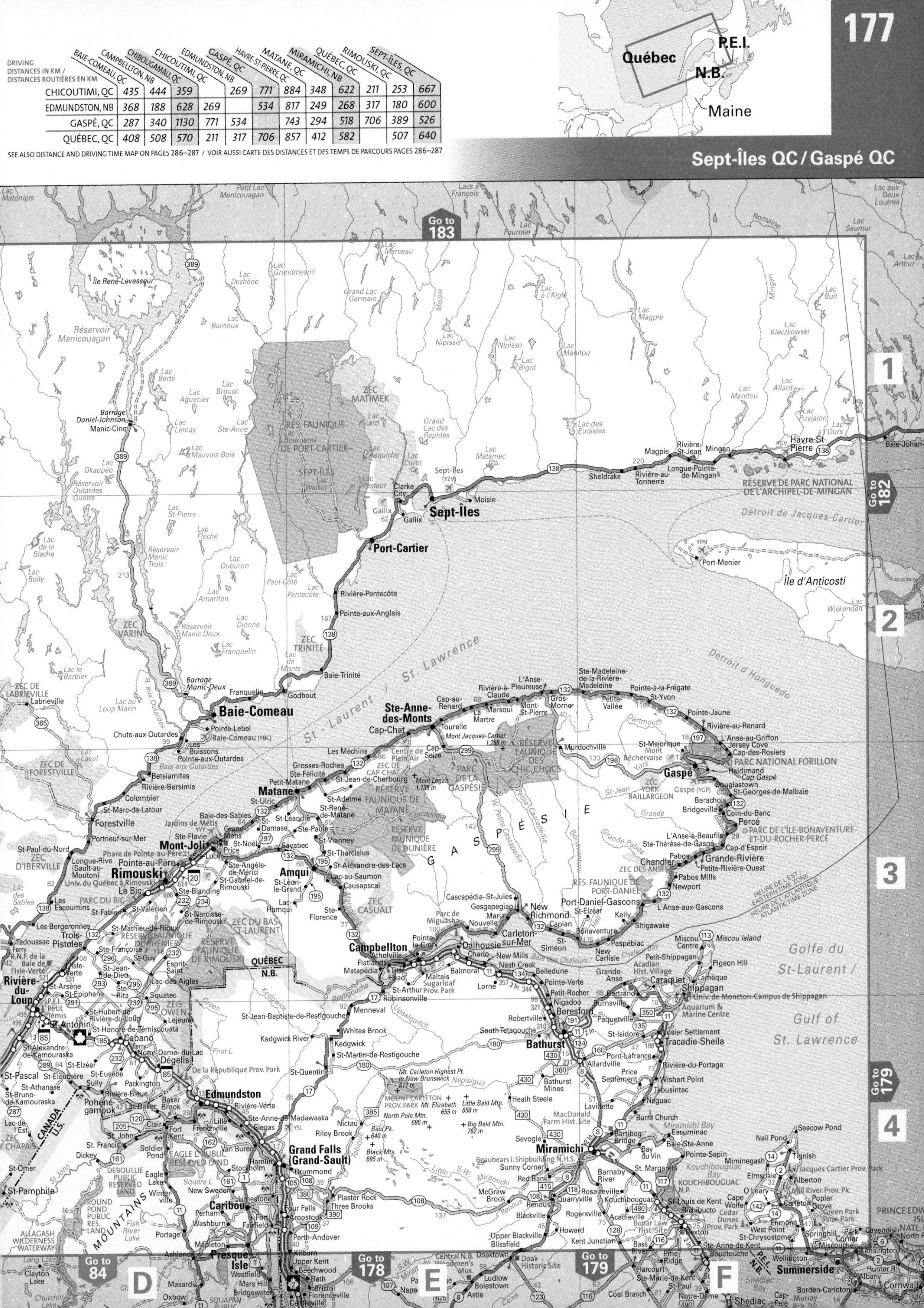

DRIVING DISTANCES IN KM / DISTANCES ROUTIÈRES EN KM

	BAIE-COMEAU, QC	CAMPBELLTON, NB	CHIBOUGAMAU, QC	EDMUNDSTON, QC	GASPÉ, QC	HAVRE-ST-PIERRE, QC	MATANE, QC	MIRAMICHI, NB	QUÉBEC, QC	RIMOUSKI, QC	SEPT-ÎLES, QC
CHICOUTIMI, QC	435	444	359		269	771	884	348	622	211	253	667
EDMUNDSTON, NB	368	188	628	269		534	817	249	268	317	180	600
GASPÉ, QC	287	340	1130	771	534		743	294	518	706	389	526
QUÉBEC, QC	408	508	570	211	317	706	857	412	582		507	640

SEE ALSO DISTANCE AND DRIVING TIME MAP ON PAGES 286–287 / VOIR AUSSI CARTE DES DISTANCES ET DES TEMPS DE PARCOURS PAGES 286–287

Québec
P.E.I.
N.B.
Maine

0 mi 20 40
0 km 20 40 60
One inch equals 25.4 miles/Un pouce équivaut à 25.4 milles
One cm equals 16.1 km/Un cm équivaut à 16.1 km

Go to 177
Go to 176
Go to 175
Go to 84
Go to 85
Go to 180

Baie-Comeau
Pointe-Lebel
Chute-aux-Outardes
Pointe-aux-Outardes
Les Buissons
Baie-Comeau (YGC)
Betsiamites
Rivière-Bersimis
Colombier
St-Marc-de-Latour
Forestville
Portneuf-sur-Mer
Pointe-à-Boisvert
St-Paul-du-Nord
Longue-Rive (Sault-au-Mouton)
Baie-des-Bacon
Les Escoumins
St-Laurent
Ste-Anne-des-Monts
Cap-Chat
La Martre
Rivière-à-Claude
Tourelle
Cap-au-Renard
Mont-St-Pierre
Marsoui
Cap-Seize
Mont Jacques-Cartier 1,268 m
Mont Logan 1,135 m
PARC DE LA GASPÉSIE
Les Méchins
Grosses-Roches
Matane
Petit-Matane
St-Adelme
St-Félicité
St-Jean-de-Cherbourg
St-Ulric
St-Luc-de-Matane
St-Léandre
St-René-de-Matane
RÉSERVE FAUNIQUE DE MATANE
RÉSERVE FAUNIQUE DE DUNIÈRE
GASPÉSIE
Baie-des-Sables
Métis-sur-Mer
Grand-Métis
Les Boules de Métis
Ste-Flavie
Ste-Luce
Mont-Joli
Price
Padoue
St-Donat
Ste-Angèle-de-Mérici
Mont-Comi
Rimouski
Rimouski-Est
Le Bic
Ste-Blandine
Mont-Lebel
St-Gabriel-de-Rimouski
Les Hauteurs
La Rédemption
St-Noël
Sayabec
Val-Brillant
Amqui
Lac Matapédia
St-Vianney
St-Paule
St-Damase
Mont-Castor
St-Léon-le-Grand
Lac-au-Saumon
Ste-Marguerite
St-Tharcisius
St-Alexandre-des-Lacs
Causapscal
St-Charles-Garnier
Lac-Humqui
Albertville
Ste-Florence
CASUALT
ZEC
Pointe-au-Père
Phare de Pointe-au-Père
Univ. du Québec à Rimouski
R.N.F. des Îles de l'Estuaire (Île Bicquette)
PARC DU BIC
St-Valérien
St-Narcisse-de-Rimouski
St-Fabien
St-Simon
Trois-Pistoles
St-Mathieu-de-Rioux
St-Eugène-de-Ladrière
St-Mathieu
RÉSERVE FAUNIQUE DUCHÉNIER
Lac des Baies
Esprit-Saint
Lac Mistigougèche
ZEC DU BAS-ST-LAURENT
QUÉBEC NEW BRUNSWICK
RÉSERVE FAUNIQUE DE RIMOUSKI
Cascapédia–St-Jules
Gesgapegiag
Maria
Nouvelle
New Richmond
Carleton-sur-Mer
Escuminac
Pointe-à-la-Croix
Parc de Miguasha
Point La Nim
Dalhousie Jct
Dalhousie
Eel River Crossing
Charlo
Heron I.
Campbellton
Atholville
Flatlands
Tide Head
Balmoral
Dundee
New Mills
Black Point
Nash Creek
Belledune
Matapédia
Mann Mtn.
Glencoe
Sugarloaf Prov. Park
Maltais
Lorne
Pointe-Verte
Dawsonville
St-Arthur
Robinsonville
Nicholas Denys
Robertville
North Tetagouche
South Tetagouche
Tetagouche
Menneval
Whites Brook
Kedgwick River
Kedgwick
St-Martin-de-Restigouche
St-Jean-Baptiste-de-Restigouche
L'Ascension-de-Patapédia
L'Ascension-de-Patapédia
St-François-d'Assise
Upsalquitch
Restigouche
St-Quentin
MOUNT CARLETON PROV. PARK
Mt. Carleton Highest Pt. in New Brunswick 817 m
Mt. Elizabeth 655 m
Little Bald Mtn. 658 m
Nepisiguit
Bathurst Mines
Heath Steele
Rivière-du-Loup
Notre-Dame-du-Portage
St-Antonin
Chemin-du-Lac
Cabano
St-Eugène-de-Ladrière
Ste-Françoise
St-Éloi
Isle-Verte
St-Médard
St-Jean-de-Dieu
Ste-Rita
St-Cyprien
St-Paul-de-la-Croix
Biencourt
Squatec
Lac-des-Aigles
St-Arsène
St-Épiphane
L'Anse-au-Persil
St-Modeste
St-François-Xavier-de-Viger
St-Hubert-de-Rivière-du-Loup
St-Pierre-de-Lamy
Lejeune
Auclair
ZEC OWEN
Lac Touladi
Lac Témiscouata
St-Honoré-de-Témiscouata
Ingall
Fort Ingall
Notre-Dame-des-Sept-Douleurs
Notre-Dame-des-Neiges
R.N.F. de la Baie de l'Isle-Verte
Vieille Chapelle
Tadoussac Ferry
Baie-Ste-Catherine
Parc marin du Saguenay–St-Laurent
Sacré-Coeur
ZEC NORDIQUE
ZEC D'IBERVILLE
ZEC DE FORESTVILLE
Portneuf
Lac des Sables
Petites-Bergeronnes
Les Bergeronnes
Port-au-Persil
St-André
Baie-des-Rochers
Île aux Lièvres
St-Georges-de-Cacouna
Ste-Hélène
St-Pacôme
St-Gabriel-Lalemant
La Pocatière
St-Alexandre-de-Kamouraska
St-Joseph-de-Kamouraska
St-Denis
St-Pascal
St-Bruno-de-Kamouraska
Mont-Carmel
St-Onésime
St-Athanase
St-Pacôme
Lac Pohénégamook
Pohénégamook
Sully
Pied-du-Lac
St-Éleuthère
St-Eusèbe
St-Juste-du-Lac
Notre-Dame-du-Lac
Dégelis
St-Marc-du-Lac-Long
St-Jean-de-la-Lande
Packington
Lac Touladi
St-Elzéar
Cabano
ZEC CHAPAIS
ZEC STE-ANNE
Lac-de-l'Est
Lac de l'Est
St-Omer
St-Pamphile
Lac-Frontière
Lucie-de-Beauregard
St-Adalbert
Ste-Lucie-de-Beauregard
De la République Prov. Park
Univ. de Moncton Campus d'Edmundston
Edmundston
Madawaska
St-Hilaire
Rivière-Verte
St-François-de-Madawaska
Baker Brook
Clair
Baker Lake
Frenchville
Grand Isle
Lille
Ste-Anne-de-Madawaska
St-Léonard (St-Léonard)
St-Léonard-Parent
St-André
Siegas
Van Buren
Connors
St. John
St. Francis
Dickey
Soldier Pond
Sinclair
Fort Kent
CANADA UNITED STATES
QUÉBEC MAINE
HEURE DE L'EST EASTERN TIME ZONE
HEURE DE L'ATLANTIQUE ATLANTIC TIME ZONE
Green
Kedgwick
Long L.
First L.
Grand Falls (Grand-Sault)
Grand Falls Gorge
Drummond
Everett
New Denmark
Riley Brook
Nictau
Little Bald Mtn.
North Pole Mtn. 686 m
Bald Pk. 640 m
Big Bald Mtn. 762 m
Black Mts. 695 m
Tobique
Sevogle
Sunny Corner
Red Bank
Quarryville
McGraw Brook
Renous
Blackville
Howard
Upper Blackville
Blissfield
Doaktown
Doak Historic Site
Central N.B. Woodmen's Mus.
Ludlow
Boiestown
Astle
Cains
Plaster Rock
Three Brooks
Caribou
Presque Isle
Washburn
Perham
New Sweden
Limestone
Fort Fairfield
Mapleton
Ashland
Masardis
Oxbow
Portage
Eagle Lake
Winterville
Square Lake
Stockholm
Hamlin
Van Buren
St-Léonard
Perth-Andover
Arthurette
Currie
Four Falls
Aroostook
Bon Accord
Kilburn
Beechwood
River de Chute
Upper Kent
Bath
Bristol
Florenceville
Stickney
Glassville
Windsor
Wilmot
Juniper
Napadogan
Parker Ridge
Williamsburg
Cross Creek
Stanley
Tay Creek
Nashwaak Bridge
Taymouth
Gasperau Forks
Cloverdale
Hartland Covered Bridge (World's Longest)
Coldstream
Hartland
Somerville
Upper Woodstock
Grafton
Woodstock
Millville
Lower Hainesville
Upper Hainesville
Zealand
Keswick Ridge
Nashwaak Village
Burtts Corner
Fredericton
Hardwood Ridge
Minto
Chipman
Cumberland Bay
Coles Island
Youngs Cove
MAINE
N.B.
Mars Hill
Westfield
Bridgewater
Centreville
Lakeville
Monticello
Littleton
Lindsay
Smyrna Mills
Houlton
Hodgdon
Linneus
Patten
Sherman Station
Island Falls
North Amity
Benton
Debec
Canterbury
Nackawic
Meductic
Pokiok
MOUNTAINS
APPALACHIAN
APPALACHIAN MOUNTAINS
ALLAGASH WILDERNESS WATERWAY
DEBOULLIE PUBLIC RESERVED LAND
EAGLE L. PUBLIC RESERVED LAND
ROUND POND PUBLIC RESERVED LAND
SQUAPAN PUBLIC RESERVED LAND
SCRAGGLY LAKE PUBLIC RESERVED LAND
GERO ISLAND PUBLIC RESERVED LAND
TELOS PUBLIC RESERVED LAND
KATAHDIN WOODS & WATERS NAT'L MON.
BAXTER STATE PARK
Fish River Lake
Portage L.
Rocky Brook
Musquacook Lake
Munsungan Lake
Millinocket Lake
Grand Lake Seboeis
Grand Lake Matagamon
Chesuncook Lake
Seboomook
Clayton Lake
Churchill Lake
Allagash Lake
Caucomgomoc L.
Umsaskis L.
Telos L.
North East Carry
Saint John
St. Lawrence
St. Laurent

DRIVING DISTANCES IN KM / DISTANCES ROUTIÈRES EN KM

	BATHURST, NB	BORDEN-CARLETON, PE	CAMPBELLTON, NB	CHARLOTTETOWN, PE	EDMUNDSTON, NB	FREDERICTON, NB	GASPÉ, QC	GRAND FALLS, NB	MATANE, QC	MIRAMICHI, NB	MONCTON, NB	RIMOUSKI, QC
CHARLOTTETOWN, PE	338	56	438		629	362	791	581	562	273	164	596
EDMUNDSTON, NB	189	428	188	638		279	534	57	249	268	447	180
MATANE, QC	262	506	168	562	249	553	294	331		346	487	95
MONCTON, NB	206	108	306	164	447	170	659	390	487	141		502

SEE ALSO DISTANCE AND DRIVING TIME MAP ON PAGES 286–287 / VOIR AUSSI CARTE DES DISTANCES ET DES TEMPS DE PARCOURS PAGES 286–287

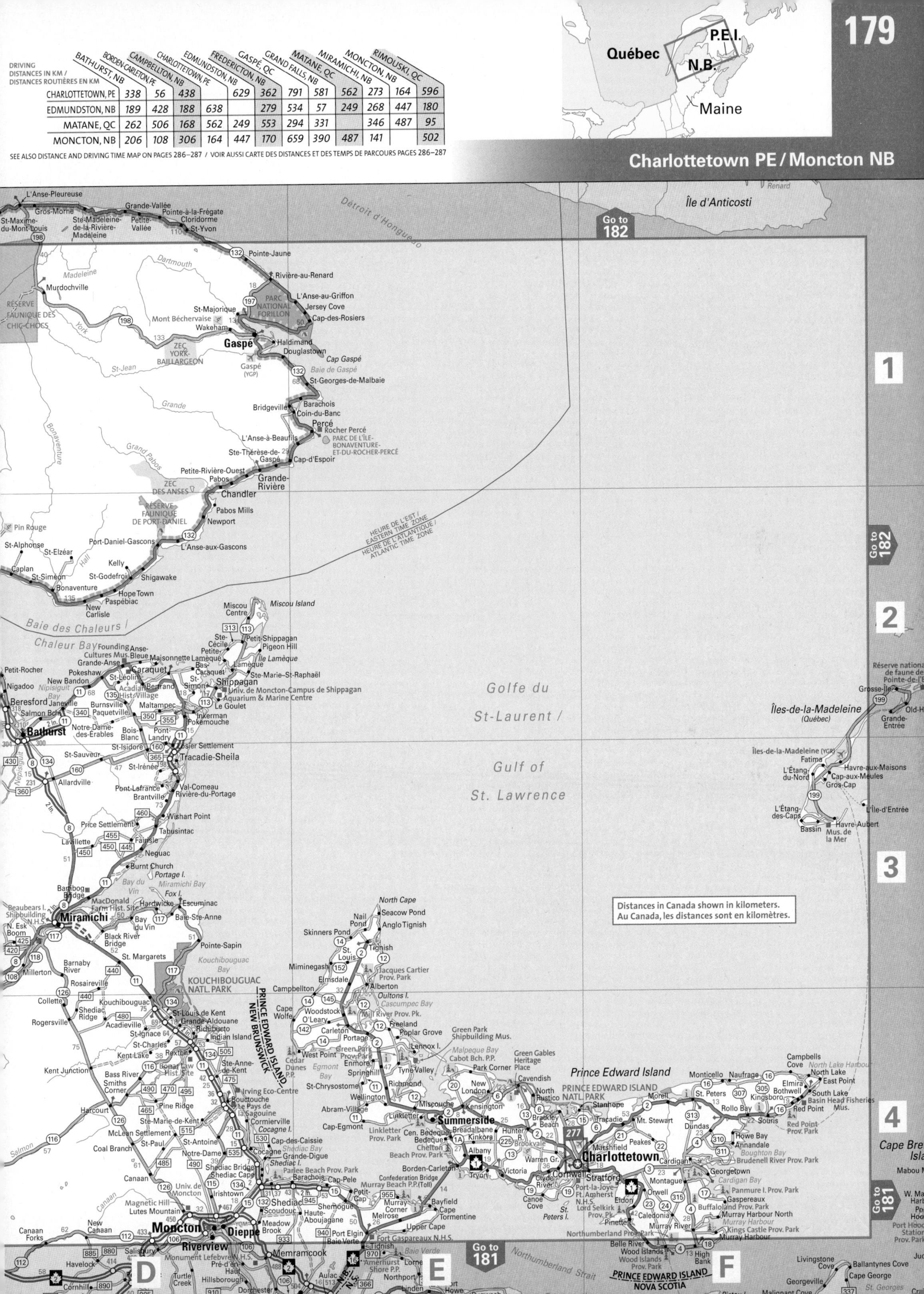

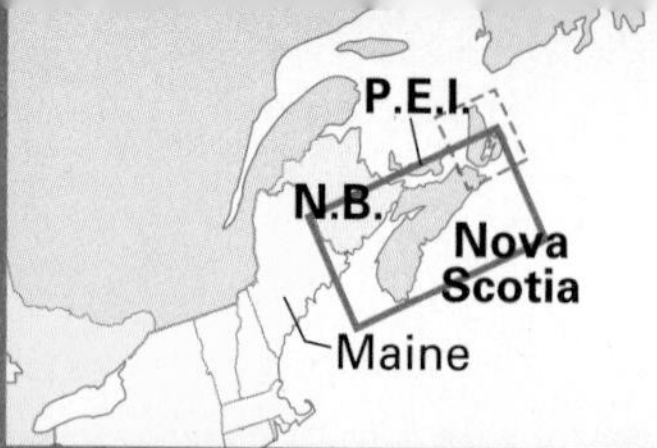

P.E.I.

N.B.

Nova Scotia

Maine

0 mi　　　　20　　　　40
0 km　　20　　　40　　60

One inch equals 25.4 miles/Un pouce équivaut à 25.4 milles
One cm equals 16.1 km/Un cm équivaut à 16.1 km

Go to 178

Go to 179

Go to 85

Go to 83

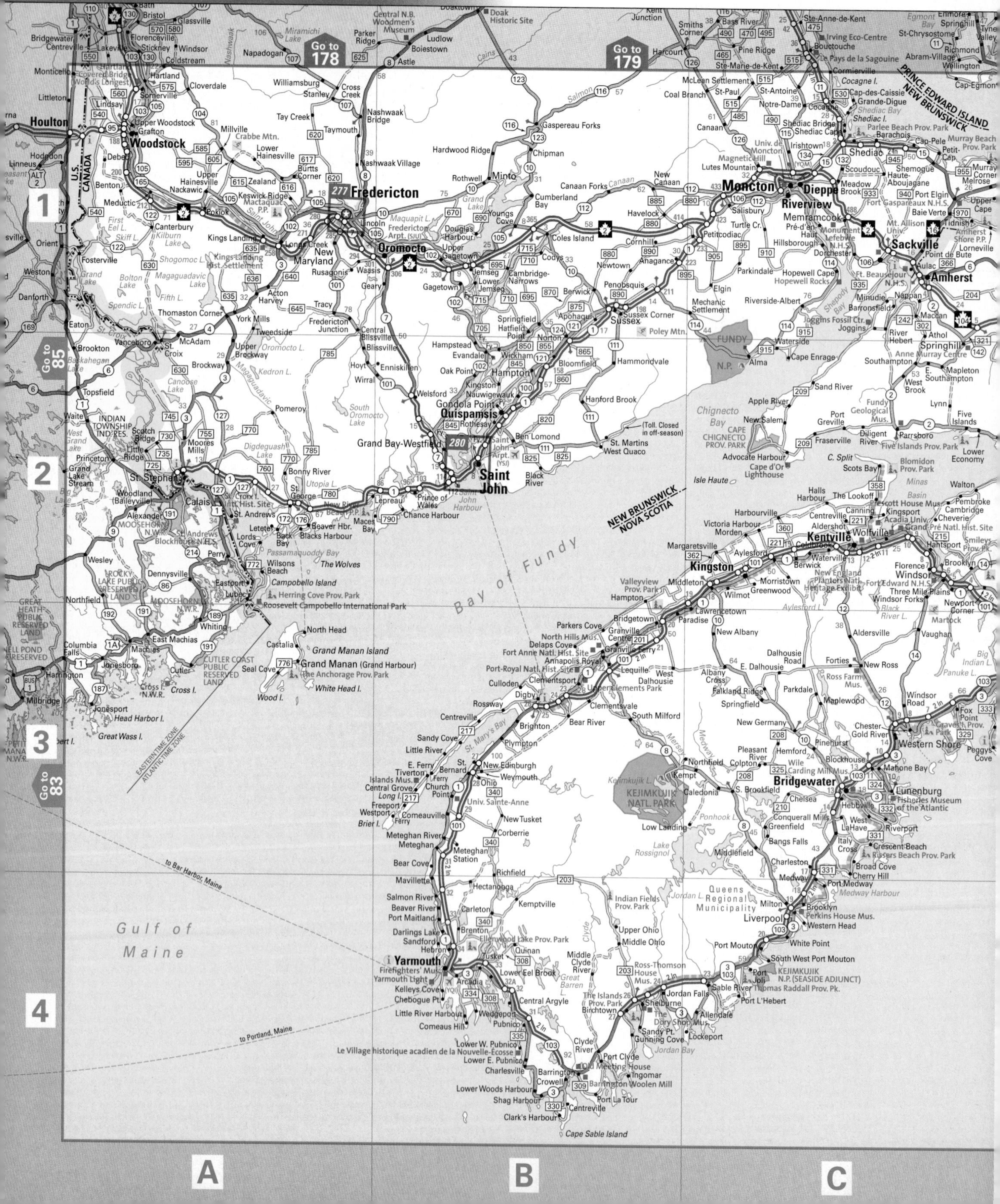

P.E.I
N.B.
Nova Scotia
Maine

DRIVING DISTANCES IN KM / DISTANCES ROUTIÈRES EN KM	CHARLOTTETOWN, PE	CHÉTICAMP, NS	DIGBY, NS	FREDERICTON, NB	HALIFAX, NS	MONCTON, NB	PORT HAWKESBURY, NS	SAINT JOHN, NB	ST. STEPHEN, NB	SYDNEY, NS	TRURO, NS	YARMOUTH, NS
HALIFAX, NS	322	425	235	462		260	265	410	515	415	89	339
MONCTON, NB	164	481	231	170	260		374	150	278	497	182	599
SAINT JOHN, NB	350	640	72	114	410	150	497		116	647	321	176
SYDNEY, NS	374	173	623	689	415	497	123	647			326	727

SEE ALSO DISTANCE AND DRIVING TIME MAP ON PAGES 286–287 / VOIR AUSSI CARTE DES DISTANCES ET DES TEMPS DE PARCOURS PAGES 286–287

Go to 182

FOR CONTINUATION SEE INSET LOWER RIGHT

Distances in Canada shown in kilometers.
Au Canada, les distances sont en kilomètres.

Nfld. & Lab.

P.E.I.

Québec

Nova Scotia

0 mi 20 40 60
0 km 20 40 60 80

One inch equals 40.3 miles/Un pouce équivaut à 40.3 milles
One centimeter equals 25.4 km/Un cm équivaut à 25.4 km

FOR CONTINUATION SEE INSET AT RIGHT
POUR CONTINUER VOIR À DROITE

Go to 177

Go to 179

Go to 181

1 **2** **3** **4**

A **B** **C**

RÉSERVE DE PARC NATIONAL DE L'ARCHIPEL-DE-MINGAN

Île d'Anticosti
PARC D'ANTICOSTI

Golfe du Saint-Laurent /
Gulf of St. Lawrence

Détroit de Jacques-Cartier

PARC NATIONAL DE FORILLON

Percé

Îles-de-la-Madeleine (Québec)

Réserve nationale de faune de la Pointe-de-l'Est

Île Brion

Prince Edward Island

PRINCE EDWARD ISLAND NATL. PARK

Charlottetown

Cape Breton Island

CAPE BRETON HIGHLANDS N.P.

White Hill Highest Pt. in Nova Scotia + 532 m

Corner Brook

Deer Lake

GROS MORNE N.P.

Gros Morne + 806 m

Stephenville

Channel-Port aux Basques

LONG RANGE

NEWFOUNDLAND & LABRADOR

NOVA SCOTIA

Cabot Strait

Distances in Canada shown in kilometers.
Au Canada, les distances sont en kilomètres.

SEE ALSO DISTANCE AND DRIVING TIME MAP ON PAGES 286–287 / VOIR AUSSI CARTE DES DISTANCES ET DES TEMPS DE PARCOURS PAGES 286–287

DRIVING DISTANCES IN KM / DISTANCES ROUTIÈRES EN KM	ARGENTIA, NL	BISHOP'S FALLS, NL	BONAVISTA, NL	CHAN.-PT. AUX BASQUES, NL	CORNER BROOK, NL	DEER LAKE, NL	GANDER, NL	GRAND FALLS-WINDSOR, NL	MARYSTOWN, NL	ST. ANTHONY, NL	ST. JOHN'S, NL	STEPHENVILLE, NL
BISHOP'S FALLS, NL	363		307	482	280	225	72	18	384	628	393	339
CHAN.-PT. AUX BASQUES, NL	845	482	789		202	257	554	464	866	875	875	151
CORNER BROOK, NL	643	280	587	202		55	352	262	664	458	673	59
ST. JOHN'S, NL	134	393	296	875	673	618	321	411	293	1021		732

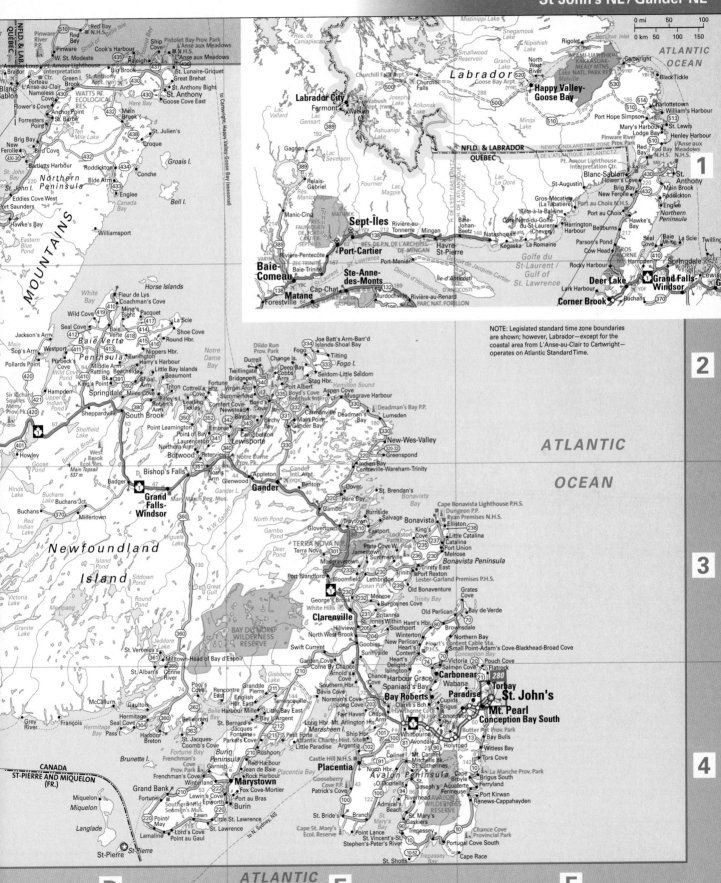

Ariz. N.M.
Texas
MEXICO

0 mi   50   100   150
0 km 50 100 150 200
One inch equals 83.75 miles/Una pulgada igual a 83.75 millas
One centimeter equals 53 km/Un centímetro igual a 53 km

1

San Diego
Tijuana
CALIFORNIA
El Centro
Phoenix
Go to 53
Go to 55
Casa Grande
ARIZONA
Rosarito
El Descanso
La Rumorosa Par. Nac.
Constitución
de 1857
Mexicali
San Luis Río Colorado
Safford
Francisco Zarco
Ojos Negros
Guadalupe Victoria
Riito
El Sauzal
Yuma
SAGUARO N.P.
SAGUARO NATL. PARK
Tucson
Isla de Todos Santos
La Bufadora
Ensenada
Maneadero
Lázaro Cárdenas
El Faro
Golfo de Santa Clara
RESERVA DE LA BIÓSFERA EL PINACATÉ Y GRAN DESIERTO DE ALTAR
Los Vidrios
Sonoyta
Nogales
Deming
Puerto Santo Tomás
Santo Tomás
Isla Montague
RESERVA DE LA BIÓSFERA ALTO GOLFO DE CALIFORNIA Y DELTA DEL RÍO COLORADO
UNITED STATES MÉXICO
División del Norte
El Sásabe
Nogales
Palomas Viejo
San Vicente
Puerto Peñasco
El Arenoso
Sáric
Naco
Agua Prieta
Douglas
Guadalupe Victoria
Colonet
Pico del Diablo 3,100 m
Punta Estrella
La Tubutama
Caborca
Imuris
Magdalena de Kino
Cananea
Fronteras
Esqueda
Ascensión
Janos
Fernández Leal
Villa Hidalgo
Parque Nacional Sierra de San Pedro Mártir
San Felipe
El Desemboque
Pitiquito
Atil
Santa Ana
Bacoachi
Casa Janos
Nuevo Casas Grandes
Vicente Guerrero
Lázaro Cárdenas
Puertecitos
Trincheras
Altar
El Claro
Cucurpe
Nacozari de García
Bavispe
Bacerac
Casas Grandes Juárez
Paquimé (ruinas)
Isla San Martín
San Quintín
Benjamín Hill
Querobabi
Arizpe
La Angostura
Villa Hidalgo
Galeana
Ricardo Flores Magón

2

El Rosario
Punta Baja
Cabo Tepoca
Opodepe
Aconchi
Cumpas
Huásabas
Buenaventura
Punta San Carlos
Cataviña
Punta Final
Cabo Lobos
Puerto Libertad
SONORA
Rayón
Carbó
Baviácora
Moctezuma
Ignacio Zaragoza
Las Varas
Punta Canoas
BAJA CALIFORNIA
Chapala
Isla Ángel de la Guarda
ÁREA DE PROTECCIÓN ISLAS DEL GOLFO DE CALIFORNIA
Cabo Tepopa
ÁREA DE PROTECCIÓN ISLAS DEL GOLFO DE CALIFORNIA
Ures
Mazocahui
Nacori Chico
Gómez Farías Santa Clara
Namiquipa
Punta María
Punta Prieta
La Gringa
Bahía de los Ángeles
Isla Tiburón
Punta de las Ánimas
Hermosillo
Miguel Alemán
San Pedro de la Cueva
Tepachi
Nicolás Bravo
Madera
Islas San Benito
Bahía Sebastián Vizcaíno
ÁREA DE PROTECCIÓN VALLE DE LOS CIRIOS
Kino Nuevo
Bahía Kino
La Colorada Pinturas Rupestres
Bacanora
Sahuaripa
Temósachi
Matachi
Isla Cedros
Santa Rosalita
Punta Baja Santa Eduwiges
La Misa
San Javier
Soyopa
Tonichi
Cd. Guerrero
Bachiniva
Isla Natividad
Punta Eugenia
Bahía de Tortugas
GUB
Guerrero Negro
Laguna Ojo de Liebre
El Arco
Misión Santa Gertrudis
Puerto San Franciquito
Punta San Carlos
Ortiz
Guaymas
Empalme
GYM
Suaqui Grande
Onavas
Yécora
Movas
Nuri
Cascada de Basaseachic
Yepachi
Basaseachi
Adolfo López Madero
Cuauhtémoc
Cusihuiriachi
Álvaro Obregón

3

Morro Hermoso
Volcán las Vírgenes 1,920 m
Santa Rosalía
San Carlos
Cabo Haro
Rosario
Par. Nac. Cascada de Basaseachic
Maguarichi
Basaseachi
Cajurichi
San Juanito
Punta San Pablo
RESERVA DE LA BIÓSFERA EL VIZCAÍNO
San Ignacio
Vicam
San Ignacio
Isla Lobos
Ciudad Obregón
Chinipas
San Rafael
Creel
Barranca del Cobre (Copper Canyon)
Bahía Asunción
Laguna San Ignacio
Punta Concepción
Mulegé
Potam
Pueblo Yaqui
Fundición
Navojoa
San Bernardo
Guazápares
Urique
Bocoyna
Carichi
Punta Abreojos
BAJA CALIFORNIA SUR
SIERRA DE LA GIGANTA
El Rosarito
Punta Púlpito
Villa Juárez
Bacobampo
Etchojoa
Bacabachi
Álamos
La Bufa
Temoris
Batopilas
OCCIDENTAL
La Purísima
Misión San Javier
Huatabampo
Punta Rosa Yávaros
Las Bocas
Choix
Morelos
Baborigame
Guachochi
Punta San Juanico
Comondú
Loreto
LTO
Isla Carmen
Puerto Escondido
Gustavo Díaz Ordaz
El Fuerte
Los Táscates
SINALOA
Santo Domingo
Isla Santa Catalina
Puerto Agua Verde
San Miguel Zapotitlán
Higuera de Zaragoza
Charay
San Blas
San José de Gracia
Guadalupe y Calvo
Puerto Adolfo López Mateos
Punta San Marcial
Los Mochis
Topolobampo
Constancia Naranjo
Sinaloa de Leyva
Leyva Solano
Guasave
Guamúchil
Santiago de los Caballeros
Badiraguato

4

OCÉANO PACÍFICO / PACIFIC OCEAN
Ciudad Insurgentes
Isla Magdalena
Ciudad Constitución
Isla San José
ÁREA DE PROTECCIÓN ISLAS DEL GOLFO DE CALIFORNIA
Bahía de CALIFORNIA
Isla Espíritu Santo
El Burrión
Tamazula
Mocorito
Las Glorias
Angostura
Tameapa
Pericos
Cabo San Lázaro
San Carlos
Puerto Cancún
Santa Rita
Puerto Cortés
Isla Santa Margarita
Ciudad Constitución
La Reforma
Presa A. López Mateos
Navolato
Culiacán
CUL
Altata
Villa Juárez
Costa Rica
Pichilingue
Isla Cerralvo
Península de Lucenilla
El Dorado
Quila
La Paz
San Pedro
Punta Arena
Los Planes
San Antonio
San Bartolo
El Triunfo
Buenavista
Península de Quevedo
Todos Santos
Santiago
El Pescadero
Cabo Pulmo
Parque Nacional Cabo Pulmo
Miraflores
La Cruz
Dimas
RESERVA DE LA BIÓSFERA SIERRA LA LAGUNA
Santa Rosa
San José del Cabo
Cabo Falso
Cabo San Lucas

Distances in Mexico shown in kilometers.
Distancias en México constan en kilómetros.

A   B   C

Ariz. N.M. Texas

DRIVING DISTANCES IN KM / DISTANCIAS DE MANEJO EN KM	CHIHUAHUA	CIUDAD JUÁREZ	CIUDAD VICTORIA	CULIACÁN	DURANGO	HERMOSILLO	MAZATLÁN	MÉXICO	MONTERREY	SAN LUIS POTOSÍ	TIJUANA	TORREÓN
CHIHUAHUA		385	1086	919	686	579	1209	1538	808	1155	1456	449
HERMOSILLO	579	795	1666	706	941		729	1810	1387	1416	884	1028
MONTERREY	808	1236	288	924	689	1387	901	892		509	2362	359
TORREÓN	449	834	637	914	266	1028	892	1089	359	706	1905	

SEE ALSO DISTANCE AND DRIVING TIME MAP ON PAGES 286–287 / CONSULTE, PARA DISTANCIAS Y TIEMPO DE MANEJO, EN LAS PÁGINAS 286–287

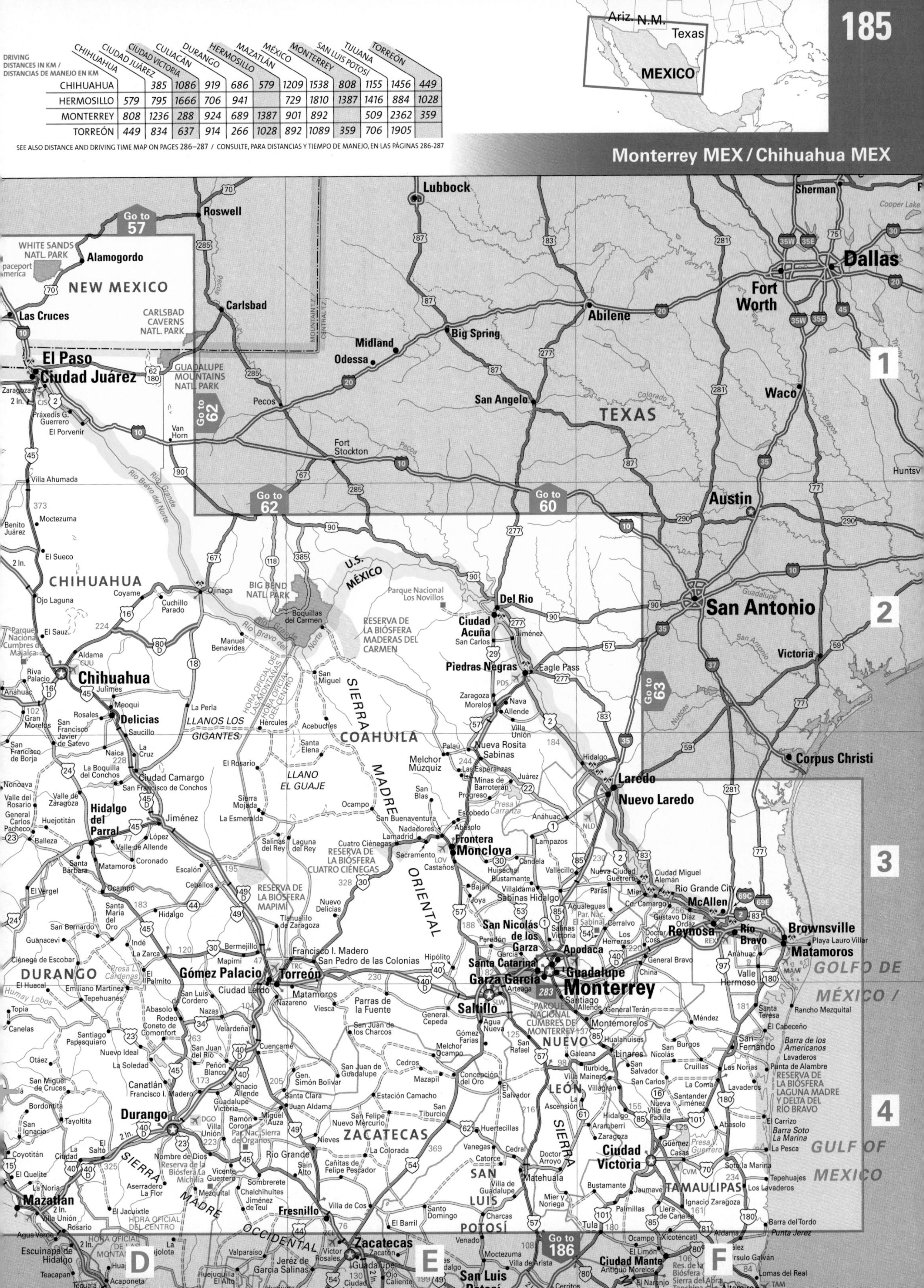

MEXICO

PUERTO RICO

México MEX / Guadalajara MEX

0 mi   50   100   150
0 km   50   100   150   200

One inch equals 83.75 miles/Una pulgada igual a 83.75 millas
One centimeter equals 53 km/Un centímetro igual a 53 km

Go to 185

Go to 184

DURANGO — Gómez Palacio, Torreón, Garza García, Guadalupe, **Monterrey**, Valle Hermoso

Saltillo, **NUEVO LEÓN**, Montemorelos, Linares, San Fernando

Mazatlán, Escuinapa de Hidalgo, **ZACATECAS**, SAN LUIS POTOSÍ, Ciudad Victoria, **TAMAULIPAS**

Tepic, **NAYARIT**, Aguascalientes, Zacatecas, **San Luis Potosí**, Ciudad Mante, **Tampico**, Ciudad Madero

Puerto Vallarta, **Zapopan**, **GUADALAJARA**, Tonalá, **León**, **GUANAJUATO**, Guanajuato, Querétaro, **Poza Rica**, **Xalapa**

JALISCO, La Piedad de Cabadas, Zamora de Hidalgo, Salamanca, San Juan del Río, **Pachuca**, Tulancingo

Colima, **COLIMA**, Manzanillo, Tecomán, Uruapan, **Morelia**, **MÉXICO**, Netzahualcóyoti, Tlaxcala, **PUEBLA**, **Córdoba**

Apatzingán, **MICHOACÁN**, Cuernavaca, Jiutepec, Cuautla, **MORELOS**, **PUEBLA**, Orizaba, Tehuacán

Lázaro Cárdenas, Ixtapa, Zihuatanejo, **GUERRERO**, Iguala, **Oaxaca**

Chilpancingo, **SIERRA MADRE DEL SUR**

Acapulco, Puerto Escondido

OCÉANO PACÍFICO / PACIFIC OCEAN

Distances in Mexico shown in kilometers.
Distancias en México constan en kilómetros.

A   B   C

1   2   3   4

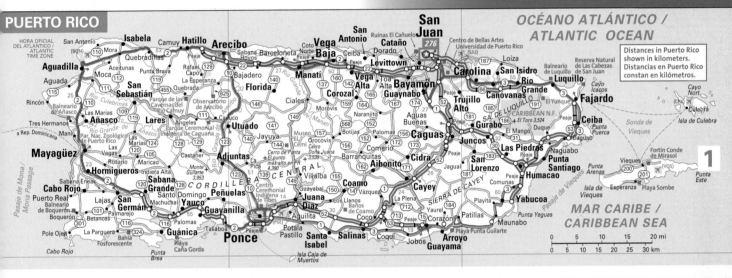

SEE ALSO DISTANCE AND DRIVING TIME MAP ON PAGES 286–287 / CONSULTE, PARA DISTANCIAS Y TIEMPO DE MANEJO, EN LAS PÁGINAS 286–287

DRIVING DISTANCES IN KM / DISTANCIAS DE MANEJO EN KM

	ACAPULCO	CANCÚN	CIUDAD VICTORIA	DURANGO	GUADALAJARA	MAZATLÁN	MÉRIDA	MÉXICO	PUEBLA	SAN LUIS POTOSÍ	TUXTLA GUTIÉRREZ	VERACRUZ
GUADALAJARA	897	2275	774	599		523	1904	578	691	336	1510	943
MÉRIDA	1777	321	1725	2182	1904	2408		1326	1282	1707	786	995
MÉXICO	422	1736	682	856	578	1081	1326		133	381	932	365
SAN LUIS POTOSÍ	834	2161	438	475	336	687	1707	381	496		1313	747

Figures after entries indicate page number and grid reference.

UNITED STATES

A

Abbeville AL 128 B4
Abbeville GA 129 E3
Abbeville LA 133 F3
Abbeville MS 118 C3
Abbeville SC 121 E3
Abbeville Co. SC 121 E3
Abbotsford WI 68 A4
Abbottstown PA 103 E1
Abercrombie ND 19 F4
Aberdeen ID 31 E1
Aberdeen MD 145 D1
Aberdeen MS 119 D4
Aberdeen NC 122 C1
Aberdeen OH 100 C3
Aberdeen SD 27 E2
Aberdeen WA 12 B4
Abernathy TX 58 A1
Abilene KS 43 E2
Abilene TX 58 C3
Abingdon IL 88 A3
Abingdon MD 145 D1
Abingdon VA 111 E3
Abington MA 151 D2
Abita Sprs. LA 134 B2
Absarokee MT 24 B2
Absecon NJ 147 F4
Acadia Par. LA 133 E2
Accokeek MD 144 B4
Accokeek Acres MD 144 B4
Accomac VA 114 C3
Accomack Co. VA 114 C3
Accord MA 151 D2
Accord NY 94 A3
Achille OK 59 F1
Achilles VA 113 F2
Ackerman MS 126 C1
Ackley IA 73 D4
Acme MI 69 F4
Acomita Lake NM 48 B3
Acton CA 52 C2
Acton MA 150 C1
Acushnet MA 151 D3
Acworth GA 120 C3
Ada MN 19 F3
Ada OH 90 B3
Ada OK 51 F4
Ada Co. ID 22 B4
Adair IA 86 B2
Adair OK 106 A3
Adair Co. IA 86 B2
Adair Co. KY 110 B2
Adair Co. MO 87 D4
Adair Co. OK 106 B4
Adairsville GA 120 B3
Adair Vil. OR 20 B3
Adairville KY 109 F3
Adams MA 94 C1
Adams MN 73 D2
Adams NE 35 F4
Adams NY 79 E2
Adams OR 21 F1
Adams TN 109 E3
Adams WI 74 A1
Adams Ctr. NY 79 E2
Adams Co. CO 41 F1
Adams Co. ID 22 B2
Adams Co. IL 87 F4
Adams Co. IN 90 A3
Adams Co. IA 86 B3
Adams Co. MS 126 A4
Adams Co. NE 35 D4
Adams Co. ND 26 A1
Adams Co. OH 100 C3
Adams Co. PA 103 E1
Adams Co. WA 13 F4
Adams Co. WI 74 A2
Adamston NJ 147 E3
Adamstown MD 144 A2
Adamstown PA 146 A2
Adamsville AL 119 F4
Adamsville RI 151 D4
Adamsville TN 119 D1
Addis LA 134 A2
Addison AL 119 E3
Addison IL 203 C4
Addison ME 83 E2
Addison MI 90 B1
Addison NY 93 D1
Addison TX 207 D1
Addison Co. VT 81 D3
Adel GA 137 F1
Adel IA 86 C2
Adelanto CA 53 D2
Adelphi MD 270 E1
Adelphia NJ 147 E2
Adena OH 91 F4
Adrian GA 129 F2
Adrian MI 90 B1
Adrian MN 72 A2
Adrian MO 96 B4
Advance IN 99 E1
Advance MO 108 B2
Adwolf VA 111 F2
Affton MO 256 B3
Afton IA 86 C3
Afton NY 93 F1
Afton OK 106 B3
Afton WY 31 F1
Agawam MA 150 A2
Agency IA 87 E3
Agency MO 96 B1
Agoura Hills CA 228 A2
Agua Dulce TX 63 E2
Agua Fria NM 49 D2
Aguilar CO 41 E4
Ahoskie NC 113 F3
Ahsahka ID 14 B4
Ahuimanu HI 152 A3
Aiken SC 121 F4
Aiken Co. SC 122 A4
Ainsworth IA 87 F2
Ainsworth NE 34 C1
Airmont NY 148 B3
Airport Drive MO 106 B2
Airway Hts. WA 13 F3
Aitkin MN 64 B4
Aitkin Co. MN 64 B4
Ajo AZ 54 B3
Ak-Chin Vil. AZ 54 C2
Akiachak AK 154 B3
Akins OK 116 B1
Akron AL 127 E1
Akron CO 41 F1
Akron IN 89 F3
Akron IA 35 F1
Akron MI 76 B2
Akron NY 78 B3

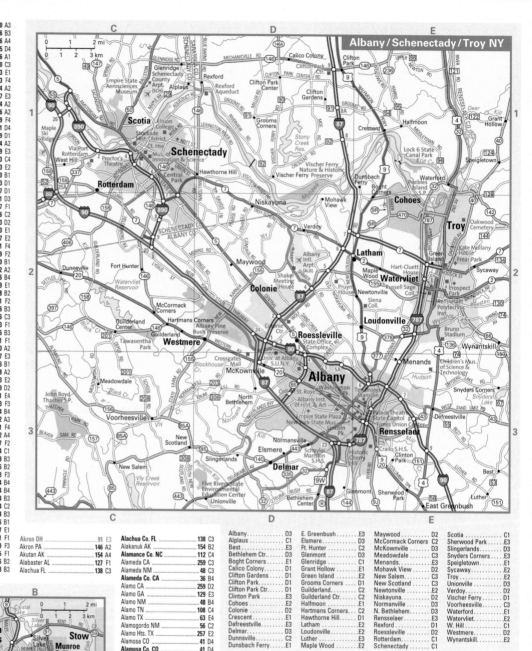

Albany D3
Alplaus C1
Best E3
Bethlehem Ctr. D3
Boght Corners E1
Calico Colony D1
Clifton Gardens D1
Clifton Park D1
Clifton Park Ctr. D1
Clinton Park E3
Cohoes E2
Colonie D2
Crescent E1
Defreestville E3
Delmar D3
Dunnsville C2
Dunsbach Ferry E1
E. Greenbush E3
Elsmere D3
Ft. Hunter C2
Glenmont D3
Glenridge C1
Grant Hollow E1
Green Island E2
Grooms Corners D1
Guilderland C2
Guilderland Ctr. C2
Halfmoon E1
Hartmans Corners C2
Hawthorne Hill D1
Latham E2
Loudonville E2
Luther E3
Maple Wood E2
Maywood D2
McCormack Corners C2
McKownville D3
Meadowdale C3
Menands E3
Mohawk View D2
New Salem C3
New Scotland C3
Newtonville E2
Niskayuna D2
Normanville D3
N. Bethlehem D3
Rensselaer E3
Rexford D1
Roessleville D2
Rotterdam C1
Schenectady C1
Scotia C1
Sherwood Park E3
Slingerlands D3
Snyders Corners E3
Speigletown E1
Sycaway E2
Troy E2
Unionville D3
Verdoy D2
Vischer Ferry D1
Voorheesville C3
Waterford E1
Watervliet E2
Westmere C2
W. Hill C1
Wynantskill E2

Akron OH 91 E3
Akron PA 146 A2
Akutan AK 154 A4
Alabaster AL 127 F1
Alachua FL 138 C3
Alachua Co. FL 138 C3
Alakanuk AK 154 B2
Alamance Co. NC 112 C4
Alameda CA 259 C3
Alameda NM 48 C3
Alameda Co. CA 36 B4
Alamo CA 259 D2
Alamo GA 129 E3
Alamo NM 48 B4
Alamo TN 108 C4
Alamo TX 63 E4
Alamogordo NM 56 C2
Alamo Hts. TX 257 E2
Alamosa CO 41 D4
Alamosa Co. CO 41 D4
Alanson MI 70 C3
Alapaha GA 129 E4
Alba MO 106 B2
Albany CA 259 C2
Albany GA 129 D4
Albany IL 88 A1
Albany IN 90 A4
Albany KY 110 B3
Albany LA 134 B2
Albany MN 66 B2
Albany MO 86 B4
Albany NY 94 B1
Albany OH 101 E2
Albany OR 20 B3
Albany TX 58 C2
Albany WI 74 B4
Albany Co. NY 94 B1
Albany Co. WY 33 E2
Albemarle NC 122 B1
Albemarle Co. VA 102 C4
Albers IL 98 B3
Albert City IA 72 B4
Albert Lea MN 72 C2
Alberton MT 15 D4
Albertville AL 120 A3
Albertville MN 66 C3
Albia IA 87 D3
Albin WY 33 F3
Albion ID 31 D2
Albion IL 99 D4
Albion IN 90 A2
Albion IA 87 D1
Albion MI 76 A4
Albion NE 35 E3
Albion NY 78 B3
Albion PA 91 F1
Albion WA 14 A4
Albuquerque NM 48 C3
Alburg VT 81 D1
Alburnett IA 87 E1
Alburtis PA 146 B1
Alcalde NM 49 D2
Alcester SD 35 F1
Alcoa TN 110 C4
Alcona Co. MI 71 D4
Alcorn MS 126 A3
Alcorn Co. MS 119 D2
Alda NE 35 D4
Aldan PA 248 B4
Alden IA 72 C4
Alden MN 72 C2
Alden NY 78 B3
Alderson WV 112 A1
Alderwood Manor WA 262 B2
Aldine TX 220 C1
Aledo IL 87 F2
Aledo TX 59 E2
Alex OK 51 E3
Alexander AR 117 E2
Alexander ND 17 F2
Alexander City AL 128 A1
Alexander Co. IL 108 C2
Alexander Co. NC 112 A4
Alexandria AL 120 A4
Alexandria IN 89 F4
Alexandria KY 100 B3
Alexandria LA 125 E4
Alexandria MN 66 B2
Alexandria SD 27 E4
Alexandria TN 110 A4
Alexandria VA 144 B3
Alexandria Bay NY 79 E1
Alexis IL 88 A3
Alfalfa Co. OK 51 D1
Alford FL 136 C1
Alfred ME 82 B4
Alfred NY 92 C1
Alger OH 90 B3
Alger Co. MI 69 E1
Algoa TX 132 B4
Algodones NM 48 C3
Algoma MS 118 C3
Algoma WI 69 D4
Algona IA 72 B3
Algona WA 262 B5
Algonac MI 76 C4
Algonquin IL 88 C1
Algood TN 110 A3
Alhambra CA 228 D2
Alhambra IL 98 B3
Alice TX 63 E2
Aliceville AL 127 E1
Ali Chuk AZ 54 B3
Aliquippa PA 91 F3
Aliso Viejo CA 229 G6
Allamakee Co. IA 73 F3
Allamuchy NJ 94 A4
Allardt TN 110 B3
Allegan MI 75 F4
Allegan Co. MI 75 F4
Allegany NY 92 C1
Allegany Co. MD 102 C1
Allegany Co. NY 78 C4
Alleghany Co. NC 111 F3
Alleghany Co. VA 102 A4
Allegheny Co. PA 92 A4
Allen NE 35 F2
Allen OK 51 F3
Allen SD 26 B4
Allen TX 59 F2
Allen Co. IN 90 A3
Allen Co. KS 96 A4
Allen Co. KY 109 F2
Allen Co. OH 90 B3
Allendale MI 75 F3
Allendale NJ 148 B3
Allendale SC 130 B1
Allendale Co. SC 130 B1
Allenhurst GA 130 B3
Allenhurst NJ 147 F2
Allen Par. LA 133 E1
Allen Park MI 210 B4
Allenspark CO 41 D1
Allenton RI 150 C4
Allenton WI 74 C2
Allentown NJ 147 D2
Allentown PA 146 B1
Allenwood NJ 147 E2
Allerton IA 87 D3

Akron OH

Akron A1
Barberton A2
Copley A1
Cuyahoga Falls B1
Fairlawn A1
Ghent A1
Lakemore B2
Mogadore B2
Montrose A1
Munroe Falls B1
Norton A2
Portage Lakes A2
Silver Lake B1
Stow B1
Tallmadge B1

Entries in **bold black** indicate counties or parishes.
Entries in **bold color** indicate cities with detailed inset maps.

Allgood AL ... 119 F4
Alliance NE ... 34 A2
Alliance NC ... 115 D3
Alliance OH ... 91 E3
Allison IA ... 73 D4
Allison Gap VA ... 111 F2
Alloway NJ ... 145 F1

Alpine CA ... 53 D4
Alpine NJ ... 148 B3
Alpine TX ... 62 B3
Alpine UT ... 31 F4
Alpine WY ... 31 F1
Alpine Co. CA ... 37 D3
Alsen LA ... 134 A2

Alton MO ... 107 F3
Alton NH ... 81 F4
Alton IL ... 88 A3
Altona NY ... 81 D1
Alton Bay NH ... 81 F4
Altoona AL ... 120 A3
Altoona IA ... 86 C2

Amber OK ... 51 E3
Amberley OH ... 204 B2
Ambler PA ... 146 C2
Amboy IL ... 88 B1
Amboy MN ... 72 C2
Amboy WA ... 20 C1
Amboy NY ... 148 C4

Amidon ND ... 18 A4
Amissville VA ... 103 D3
Amite LA ... 134 B1
Amite Co. MS ... 126 A1
Amity PA ... 117 D3
Amity OR ... 20 B2
Amityville NY ... 148 C4

Anahuac TX ... 132 B3
Anamoose ND ... 18 C2
Anamosa IA ... 87 F1
Anchorage AK ... 154 C3
Anchorage KY ... 230 F1
Anchor Pt. AK ... 154 C3
Anchorville MI ... 76 C4

Anderson Co. TN ... 110 C4
Anderson Co. TX ... 124 A4
Andersonville OH ... 101 D2
Andover CT ... 150 A3
Andover IL ... 88 A2
Andover KS ... 43 F4
Andover MA ... 95 E1
Andover MN ... 67 D3
Andover NJ ... 94 A4
Andover NY ... 92 C1
Andover OH ... 91 F2
Andrew Co. MO ... 96 B1
Andrews IN ... 89 F3
Andrews NC ... 121 D1
Andrews SC ... 122 C4
Andrews TX ... 57 F3
Andrews Co. TX ... 57 F3
Androscoggin Co. ME ... 82 B2
Aneta ND ... 19 E3
Aneth UT ... 40 A4
Angel Fire NM ... 49 D2
Angelica NY ... 78 B4
Angelina Co. TX ... 124 B4
Angels Camp CA ... 36 C3
Angier NC ... 123 D1
Angleton TX ... 132 A4
Angola IN ... 90 A2
Angola NY ... 78 A4
Angola on the Lake NY ... 78 A4
Angoon AK ... 155 E4
Anguilla MS ... 126 A1
Angwin CA ... 36 B3
Aniak AK ... 154 B3
Anita IA ... 86 C1
Ankeny IA ... 86 C1
Anmoore WV ... 102 A2
Anna IL ... 108 B1
Anna OH ... 90 B4
Anna TX ... 59 F1
Annabella UT ... 39 E2
Anna Maria FL ... 140 B3
Annandale MN ... 66 C3
Annandale NJ ... 147 D1
Annandale VA ... 144 B3
Annapolis MD ... 144 C3
Ann Arbor MI ... 76 B4
Anne Arundel Co. MD ... 144 C3
Annetta TX ... 59 E2
Anniston AL ... 120 A4
Annsville NY ... 148 B3
Annville KY ... 110 C1
Annville PA ... 93 E4
Anoka MN ... 67 D3

Amarillo TX

Allyn WA ... 12 C3
Alma AR ... 116 C1
Alma GA ... 129 F4
Alma KS ... 43 F2
Alma MI ... 76 A2
Alma NE ... 43 D1
Alma WI ... 73 E1
Almena KS ... 42 C1
Almena WI ... 67 E3
Almon GA ... 121 D4
Almont MI ... 76 C3
Aloe TX ... 61 E3
Aloha OR ... 20 B2
Alorton IL ... 256 C3
Alpaugh CA ... 45 D4
Alpena MI ... 71 D3
Alpena SD ... 27 E3
Alpena Co. MI ... 71 D4
Alpha IL ... 88 A2
Alpha NJ ... 146 C1
Alpharetta GA ... 120 C3

Alsip IL ... 203 D6
Alta IA ... 72 A4
Alta UT ... 31 F4
Alta WY ... 23 F4
Altadena CA ... 228 D1
Altamahaw NC ... 112 B4
Altamont IL ... 98 C2
Altamont KS ... 106 A2
Altamont NY ... 94 B1
Altamont OR ... 28 C2
Altamont TN ... 120 A1
Altamonte Sprs. FL ... 141 D1
Alta Vista KS ... 43 F2
Altavista VA ... 112 C2
Altha FL ... 137 D2
Altheimer AR ... 117 F3
Alto GA ... 121 D3
Alto TX ... 124 B4
Alton IL ... 98 A3
Alton KY ... 100 B4

Altoona KS ... 106 A1
Altoona PA ... 92 C4
Altoona WI ... 67 F4
Alturas CA ... 29 D3
Altus AR ... 116 C1
Altus OK ... 51 D4
Alum Creek WV ... 101 E4
Alva FL ... 143 D1
Alva OK ... 51 D1
Alvarado TX ... 59 E3
Alvin TX ... 132 B4
Alvord TX ... 59 E1
Ama LA ... 239 B2
Amado AZ ... 55 D4
Amador Co. CA ... 36 C3
Amagansett NY ... 149 E3
Amalga UT ... 31 E2
Amana IA ... 87 E1
Amanda OH ... 101 D1
Amawalk NY ... 148 B3

Amelia LA ... 134 A3
Amelia OH ... 100 B2
Amelia City FL ... 139 D2
Amelia Co. VA ... 113 D2
Amelia C.H. VA ... 113 D1
Amenia NY ... 94 B3
American Beach FL ... 139 D2
American Canyon CA ... 36 B3
American Falls ID ... 31 E1
American Fork UT ... 31 F4
Americus GA ... 129 D3
Americus KS ... 43 F3
Ames IA ... 86 C1
Ames TX ... 132 B3
Amesbury MA ... 95 E1
Amherst MA ... 150 A1
Amherst NH ... 95 D1
Amherst NY ... 78 B3
Amherst OH ... 91 D2
Amherst TX ... 57 F1
Amherst VA ... 112 C1
Amherst WI ... 74 B1
Amherst Co. VA ... 112 C1
Amherstdale WV ... 111 F1

Ammon ID ... 23 E4
Amory MS ... 119 D4
Amsterdam MT ... 23 F1
Amsterdam NY ... 94 A1
Amsterdam OH ... 91 F4
Anacoco LA ... 125 D4
Anaconda MT ... 23 D1
Anacortes WA ... 12 C2
Anadarko OK ... 51 E3
Anaheim CA ... 52 C3
Anahola HI ... 152 B1

Andale KS ... 43 E4
Andalusia AL ... 128 A4
Andalusia IL ... 87 F2
Anderson CA ... 28 C4
Anderson IN ... 89 F4
Anderson MO ... 106 B3
Anderson SC ... 121 E3
Anderson TX ... 61 E1
Anderson Co. KS ... 96 A4
Anderson Co. KY ... 100 A4
Anderson Co. SC ... 121 E2

Anchorage AK

Annapolis MD

Allentown / Bethlehem PA

Allentown ... A2
Balliettsville ... A1
Bethlehem ... B1
Bingen ... B2
Brodhead ... B1
Butztown ... B1
Catasauqua ... A1
Cementon ... A1
Cetronia ... A2
Coffeetown ... A1
Colesville ... B2
Coplay ... A1
Dorneyville ... A2
Egypt ... A1
Emmaus ... A2
Farmersville ... B1
Farmington ... A2
Fountain Hill ... B2
Freemansburg ... B1
Fullerton ... A1
Gauff Hill ... B2
Greenawalds ... A2
Guthsville ... A1
Hellertown ... B2
Hokendauqua ... A1
Ironton ... A1
Krocksville ... A2
Mechanicsville ... A1
Meyersville ... A1
Middletown ... B1
Northampton ... A1
N. Catasauqua ... A1
Ormrod ... A1
Ruchsville ... A1
Schererville ... B1
Schoenersville ... B1
Seidersville ... B2
Seiple ... A1
Steel City ... B1
Stetlersville ... A1
Stiles ... A1
Walbert ... A2
Weaversville ... A1
Wennersville ... A2
Wescosville ... A2
W. Catasauqua ... A1
Whitehall ... A1
Wydnor ... B2

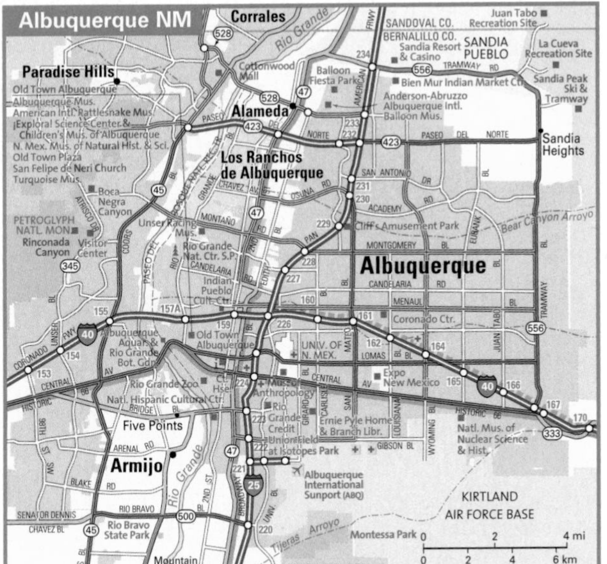

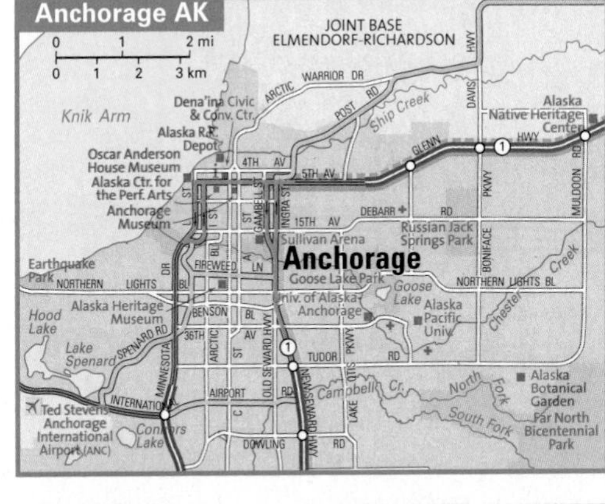

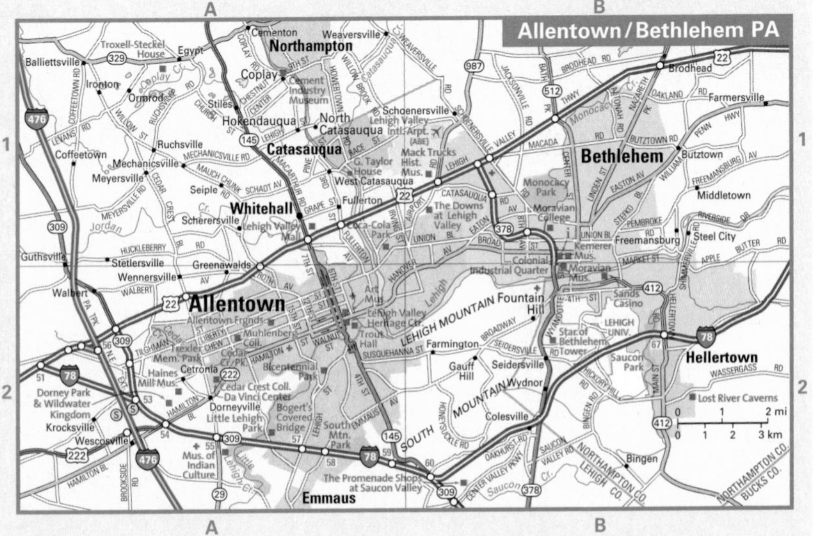

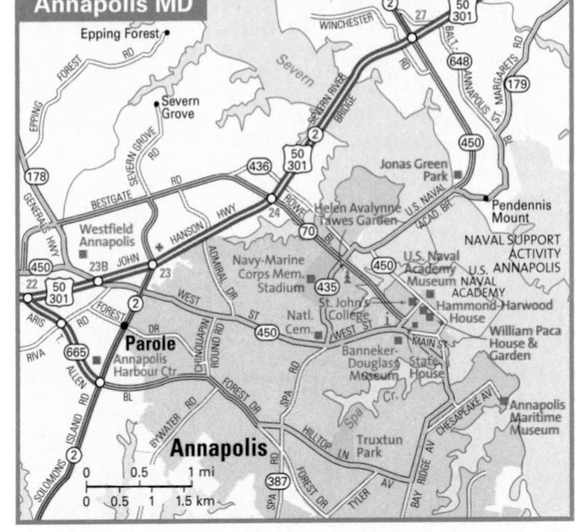

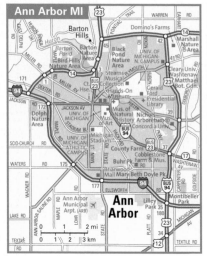

Ann Arbor MI

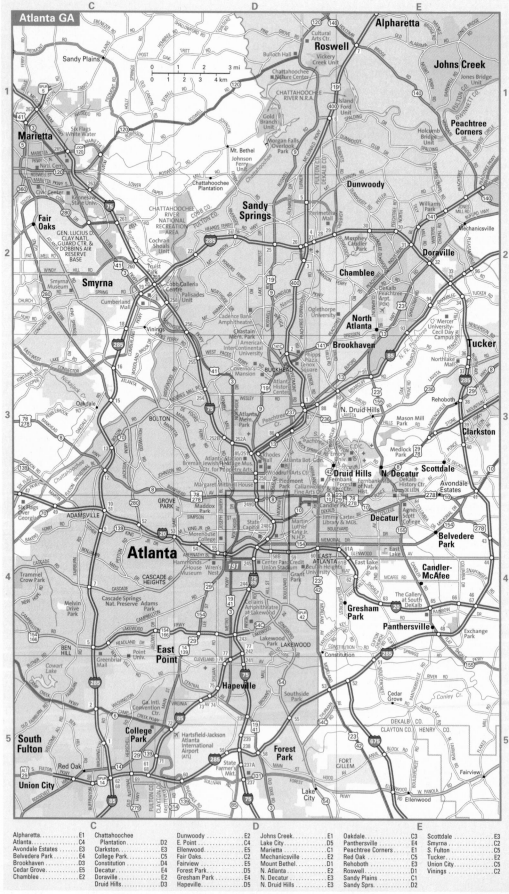

Atlanta GA

Anoka Co. MN	67 D3	Aplington IA	73 D4
Ansley NE	35 D3	Apollo PA	92 A4
Anson ME	82 B1	Apollo Beach FL	266 C3
Anson TX	58 C2	Apopka FL	141 D1
Anson Co. NC	122 B2	Appalachia VA	111 E2
Ansonia CT	149 D2	Appanoose Co. IA	87 D3
Ansonia OH	90 A4	Apple Creek OH	91 E3
Ansonville NC	122 B1	Applegate CA	36 C2
Ansted WV	101 F4	Appleton MN	27 F2
Antelope SD	26 C4	Appleton WI	74 C1
Antelope Acres CA	52 C1	Appleton City MO	96 C4
Antelope Co. NE	35 E2	Apple Valley CA	53 D2
Anthon IA	72 A4	Apple Valley MN	67 D3
Anthony FL	138 C4	Applewood CO	209 B3
Anthony KS	43 E4	Appling GA	121 F4
Anthony NM	56 C3	Appling Co. GA	129 F3
Anthony TX	56 C3	Appomattox VA	112 C1
Antigo WI	68 B3	Appomattox Co. VA	112 C1
Antioch CA	36 B3	Aptos CA	44 B2
Antioch IL	74 C4	Aquebogue NY	149 E3
Antlers OK	116 A3	Arab AL	119 F3
Anton TX	58 A1	Arabi LA	239 C1
Antonito CO	49 D1	Aragon GA	120 B3
Antrim NH	81 E4	Aransas Co. TX	61 F4
Antrim Co. MI	70 B3	Aransas Pass TX	63 F2
Antwerp NY	79 E1	Arapaho OK	51 D3
Antwerp OH	90 A2	Arapahoe NE	34 C4
Apache OK	51 D3	Arapahoe WY	32 B1
Apache Co. AZ	47 F3	Arapahoe Co. CO	41 E1
Apache Jct. AZ	54 C1	Arbuckle CA	36 B2
Apalachicola FL	137 D3	Arbutus MD	193 B3
Apalachin NY	93 E1	Arbyrd MO	108 B4
Apex NC	112 C4	Arcade CA	255 B2

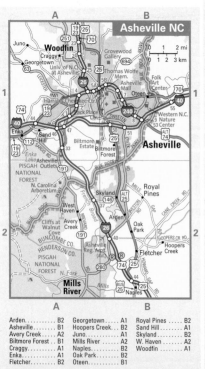

Asheville NC

Arden	B2	Georgetown	A1	Royal Pines	B2
Asheville	B1	Hoopers Creek	B2	Sand Hill	A1
Avery Creek	A2	Juno	A1	Skyland	B2
Biltmore Forest	B1	Mills River	A2	W. Haven	A2
Craggy	A1	Naples	B2	Woodfin	A1
Enka	A1	Oak Park	B2		
Fletcher	B2	Oteen	B1		

Alpharetta	E1	Chattahoochee		Dunwoody	E2	Johns Creek	E1	Oakdale	C3	Scottdale	E3
Atlanta	C4	Plantation	D2	E. Point	C4	Lake City	D5	Panthersville	E4	Smyrna	C2
Avondale Estates	E3	Clarkston	E3	Ellenwood	E5	Marietta	C1	Peachtree Corners	E1	S. Fulton	C5
Belvedere Park	E4	College Park	C5	Fair Oaks	C2	Mechanicsville	E2	Red Oak	C5	Tucker	E2
Brookhaven	D3	Constitution	D4	Fairview	E5	Mount Bethel	D1	Rehoboth	E3	Union City	C5
Cedar Grove	E5	Decatur	E4	Forest Park	D5	N. Atlanta	E2	Roswell	D1	Vinings	C2
Chamblee	E2	Doraville	E2	Gresham Park	E4	N. Decatur	E3	Sandy Plains	C1		
		Druid Hills	D3	Hapeville	D5	N. Druid Hills	E3	Sandy Sprs.	D2		

Entries in **bold black** indicate counties or parishes.
Entries in **bold color** indicate cities with detailed inset maps.

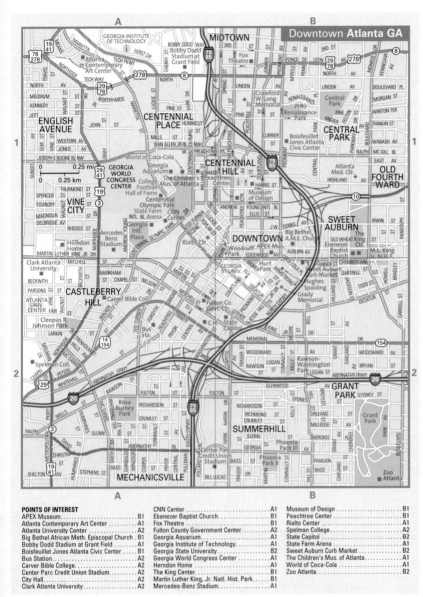

POINTS OF INTEREST

APEX Museum.... B1
Atlanta Contemporary Art Center.... A1
Atlanta University Center.... A2
Big Bethel African Meth. Episcopal Church.... B1
Bobby Dodd Stadium at Grant Field.... A1
Boisfeuillet Jones Atlanta Civic Center.... B1
Bus Station.... A2
Carver Bible College.... A2
Center Parc Credit Union Stadium.... A2
City Hall.... A2
Clark Atlanta University.... A2
CNN Center.... A1
Ebenezer Baptist Church.... B1
Fox Theatre.... B1
Fulton County Government Center.... A2
Georgia Aquarium.... A1
Georgia Institute of Technology.... A1
Georgia State University.... B2
Georgia World Congress Center.... A1
Herndon Home.... A1
The King Center.... B1
Martin Luther King, Jr. Natl. Hist. Park.... B1
Mercedes-Benz Stadium.... A1
Museum of Design.... B1
Peachtree Center.... B1
Rialto Center.... A1
Spelman College.... A2
State Capitol.... B2
State Farm Arena.... A1
Sweet Auburn Curb Market.... B2
The Children's Mus. of Atlanta.... A1
World of Coca-Cola.... A1
Zoo Atlanta.... B2

Arcade GA 121 D3
Arcade NY 78 B4
Arcadia CA 228 E2
Arcadia FL 140 C4
Arcadia IN 89 F4
Arcadia KS 106 B1
Arcadia LA 125 D2
Arcadia MO 108 A1
Arcadia OH 90 C3
Arcadia WI 73 E1
Arcadia Lakes SC 205 F1
Arcanum OH 100 B1
Arcata CA 28 A4
Archbald PA 93 F2
Archbold OH 90 B2
Archdale NC 112 B4
Archer FL 138 C3
Archer City TX 59 D1
Archer Co. TX 59 D1
Archie MO 96 B3
Archuleta Co. CO 40 C4
Arco ID 23 D4
Arcola IL 99 D1
Arcola MS 126 A1
Arcola TX 132 A4
Arden CA 255 B2
Arden DE 146 B3
Ardencroft DE 274 E1
Arden Hills MN 235 C1
Ardentown DE 274 E1
Ardmore AL 119 F2
Ardmore OK 51 F4
Ardmore PA 146 C3
Ardmore TN 119 F2
Ardonia NY 148 B1
Arena WI 74 A3
Arenac Co. MI 76 B1
Arendtsville PA 103 E1
Argenta IL 98 C1
Argentine MI 76 B4
Argo AL 119 F4
Argonia KS 43 E4
Argos IN 89 F2
Argos Corner DE 145 F3
Argyle MN 19 F2
Argyle TX 59 E2
Argyle WI 74 A4
Arimo ID 31 E1
Aripeka FL 140 B1
Ariton AL 128 B4
Arizola AZ 54 C2
Arizona City AZ 54 C2
Arkadelphia AR 117 D3
Arkansas City AR 117 F4
Arkansas City KS 51 E1
Arkansas Co. AR 117 F3
Arkoma OK 116 B1
Arkport NY 78 C4
Arlee MT 15 D3
Arlington GA 128 C4
Arlington IA 73 E4
Arlington KS 43 E4
Arlington KY 108 C2
Arlington MA 151 D1
Arlington MN 66 C4
Arlington NE 35 F3
Arlington NY 148 B1
Arlington OH 90 C3
Arlington OR 21 E1
Arlington SD 27 F3
Arlington TN 118 B1
Arlington TX 59 E2
Arlington VT 81 D4
Arlington VA 144 B3
Arlington WA 12 C2
Arlington Co. VA 144 B3
Arlington Hts. IL 89 D1
Arlington Hts. OH 204 B2
Arma KS 106 B1
Armada MI 76 C3
Armijo NM 48 C3
Armona CA 44 C3
Armonk NY 148 C2
Armour SD 27 E4
Armstrong IA 72 B2
Armstrong Co. PA 92 A3
Armstrong Co. TX 50 B3
Arnaudville LA 133 F2
Arnett OK 50 C2
Arnold CA 37 D3
Arnold MD 144 C3
Arnold MN 64 C4
Arnold MO 98 A3
Arnold NE 34 C3
Arnold PA 92 A4
Arnolds Park IA 72 A3
Aroma Park IL 89 D3
Aromas CA 44 B2
Aroostook Co. ME 85 D2
Arp TX 124 B3
Arredondo FL 138 C3
Arroyo Grande CA 52 A1
Arroyo Hondo NM 49 D1
Arroyo Seco NM 49 D1
Artesia CA 228 E4
Artesia MS 127 D1
Artesia NM 57 E2
Arthur IL 98 C1
Arthur NE 34 B3
Arthur ND 19 E3
Arthur TN 110 C3
Arthur Co. NE 34 B3
Arthurdale WV 102 B2
Arundel on the Bay MD 144 C3
Arundel Vil. MD 193 C4
Arvada CO 41 E1
Arvin CA 52 B1
Asbury IA 73 F4
Asbury Park NJ 147 F2
Ascension Par. LA 134 A2
Ascutney VT 81 E4
Asharoken NY 148 C3
Ashaway RI 150 C4
Ashburn GA 129 D4
Ashburn VA 144 A3
Ashburnham MA 95 D1
Ashdown AR 116 C4
Asheboro NC 112 B4
Ashe Co. NC 111 F3
Asherton TX 60 C4
Asheville NC 121 E1
Ashfield MA 94 C1
Ash Flat AR 107 F3
Ashford AL 137 D1
Ash Fork AZ 47 D3
Ash Grove MO 106 C1
Ashkum IL 89 D3
Ashland AL 128 B1
Ashland CA 259 D3
Ashland IL 98 B1
Ashland KS 42 C4
Ashland KY 101 D3
Ashland ME 85 D2
Ashland MA 150 C1
Ashland MS 118 C2
Ashland MO 97 E3
Ashland MT 25 D1
Ashland NE 35 F3
Ashland NH 81 F3
Ashland OH 91 D3
Ashland OR 28 C2
Ashland PA 93 E3
Ashland VA 113 E1
Ashland WI 65 D4
Ashland City TN 109 E3
Ashland Co. OH 91 D3
Ashland Co. WI 67 F1
Ashley IL 98 C4
Ashley IN 90 A2
Ashley MI 76 A3
Ashley ND 27 D1
Ashley PA 261 A2
Ashley Co. AR 125 F1
Ashmore IL 99 D1
Ashtabula OH 91 F1
Ashtabula Co. OH 91 F1
Ashton ID 23 F3
Ashton IL 88 B1
Ashton RI 150 C3
Ashuelot NH 94 C1
Ashville AL 120 A4
Ashville OH 101 D1
Ashwaubenon WI 68 C4
Asotin WA 14 B4
Asotin Co. WA 22 A1
Aspen CO 40 C2
Aspen Hill MD 144 B2
Aspen Park CO 209 A4
Aspermont TX 58 C2
Aspinwall PA 250 C1
Assaria KS 43 E3
Assinippi MA 151 E2
Assonet MA 151 D3
Assumption IL 98 C1
Assumption Par. LA 134 A3
Astatula FL 140 C1
Astor FL 139 D4
Astoria IL 88 A4
Astoria OR 20 B1
Atascadero CA 44 C4
Atascosa Co. TX 61 D3
Atchison KS 96 B1
Atchison Co. KS 96 A2
Atchison Co. MO 86 A4
Atco NJ 147 D4
Atglen PA 146 A3
Athena OR 21 F1
Athens AL 119 F2
Athens GA 121 D4
Athens IL 98 B1
Athens ME 82 C1
Athens MI 90 A1
Athens NY 94 B2
Athens OH 101 E2
Athens PA 93 E1
Athens TN 120 C1
Athens TX 124 A3
Athens WV 112 A1
Athens WI 68 A3
Athens Co. OH 101 E2
Atherton CA 259 C5
Athol ID 14 B2
Athol MA 95 D1
Atkins AR 117 D1
Atkins IA 87 E1
Atkins VA 111 F2
Atkinson IL 88 A2
Atkinson NE 35 D1
Atkinson NH 95 E1
Atkinson Co. GA 129 E4
Atlanta GA 120 C4
Atlanta IL 88 B4
Atlanta IN 89 F4
Atlanta MI 70 C4
Atlanta NY 78 C4
Atlanta TX 124 C1
Atlantic IA 86 B2
Atlantic Beach FL 139 D2
Atlantic Beach NY 147 F1
Atlantic Beach NC 115 D4
Atlantic City NJ 147 F4
Atlantic Co. NJ 147 D4
Atlantic Highlands NJ 147 E1
Atlantis FL 143 F1
Atmore AL 135 F1
Atoka OK 51 F4
Atoka TN 118 B1
Atoka Co. OK 51 F4
Attala Co. MS 126 C1
Attalla AL 120 A3
Attapulgus GA 137 E1
Attawaugan CT 150 B3
Attica IN 89 D4
Attica KS 43 E4
Attica MI 76 C3
Attica NY 78 B3
Attica OH 90 C3
Attleboro MA 151 D2
Atwater CA 36 C4
Atwater MN 66 B3
Atwater OH 91 E3
Atwood IL 98 C1
Atwood KS 42 B1
Atwood TN 108 C4
Auberry CA 45 D2
Aubrey TX 59 F2
Auburn AL 128 B2
Auburn CA 36 C2
Auburn GA 121 D3
Auburn IL 98 B1
Auburn IN 90 A2
Auburn KS 96 A3
Auburn KY 109 F2
Auburn ME 82 B3
Auburn MA 150 B2
Auburn MI 76 B2
Auburn NE 86 A4
Auburn NY 79 D3
Auburn PA 146 A1
Auburn WA 12 C3
Auburn WY 31 F1
Auburndale FL 140 C2
Auburndale WI 68 A4
Auburn Hills MI 210 B1
Audrain Co. MO 97 E2
Audubon IA 86 B1
Audubon NJ 248 D4
Audubon PA 248 A1
Audubon Co. IA 86 B2
Audubon Park KY 230 D2
Audubon Park NJ 248 D4
Auglaize Co. OH 90 B4
Au Gres MI 76 B1
Augusta AR 117 F1
Augusta GA 121 F4
Augusta IL 87 F4
Augusta KS 43 F4
Augusta KY 100 C3
Augusta ME 82 C2
Augusta MI 75 F4
Augusta MT 15 E3
Augusta WI 67 F4
Augusta Co. VA 102 B4

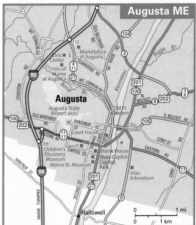

192
Aulander–Belmont

Figures after entries indicate page number and grid reference.

Aulander NC 113 E3
Ault CO 33 E4
Aumsville OR 20 B2
Aurelia IA 72 A4
Aurora CO 41 E1
Aurora IL 88 C1
Aurora IN 100 B2
Aurora MN 64 C3
Aurora MO 106 C2
Aurora NE 35 E4
Aurora NY 79 D4
Aurora NC 115 D3
Aurora OH 91 E2
Aurora OR 20 C2
Aurora SD 27 F3
Aurora TX 59 E2
Aurora UT 39 E2
Aurora Co. SD 27 D4
Au Sable MI 76 C1
Au Sable Forks NY 81 D2
Austin AR 117 E2
Austin IN 99 F3
Austin MN 73 D2
Austin NV 37 F1
Austin PA 92 C2
Austin TX 61 E1
Austin Co. TX 61 F2
Austintown OH 91 F3
Autauga Co. AL 127 F2
Autaugaville AL 127 F2
Auxvasse MO 97 E2
Ava IL 98 B4
Ava MO 107 E2
Avalon CA 52 C3
Avalon NJ 105 D4
Avalon PA 250 A1
Avawam KY 111 D2
Avella PA 91 F4
Avenal CA 44 C3
Avenel NJ 147 E1
Aventura FL 143 F2
Averill Park NY 94 B1
Avery CA 37 D3
Avery Co. NC 111 F4
Avery Creek NC 121 E1
Avilla IN 90 A2
Avis PA 93 D2
Aviston IL 98 B3
Avoca AR 106 C3
Avoca IA 86 A2
Avoca NY 78 C4
Avoca PA 261 C2
Avoca WI 74 A3
Avon AL 137 D1
Avon CO 40 C1
Avon CT 94 C3
Avon IL 88 A3
Avon IN 99 F1
Avon MN 66 C2
Avon NY 78 C3
Avon NC 115 F3
Avon OH 91 D2
Avon PA 146 A2
Avon SD 35 E1
Avon-by-the-Sea NJ 147 F2
Avondale AZ 54 C1
Avondale CO 41 E3
Avondale LA 134 B3
Avondale MO 224 C2
Avondale PA 146 B3
Avondale RI 149 F2
Avondale Estates GA 190 E3
Avonia PA 91 F1
Avon Lake OH 91 D2
Avonmore PA 92 A4
Avon Park FL 141 D3
Avoyelles Par. LA 125 F4
Awendaw SC 131 D1
Axtell KS 43 F1
Axtell NE 35 D4
Ayden NC 115 D3
Ayer MA 95 D1
Aynor SC 122 C3
Azalea Park FL 246 D2
Azle TX 59 E2
Aztec NM 48 B1
Azusa CA 228 E2

Austin TX

Bakersfield CA

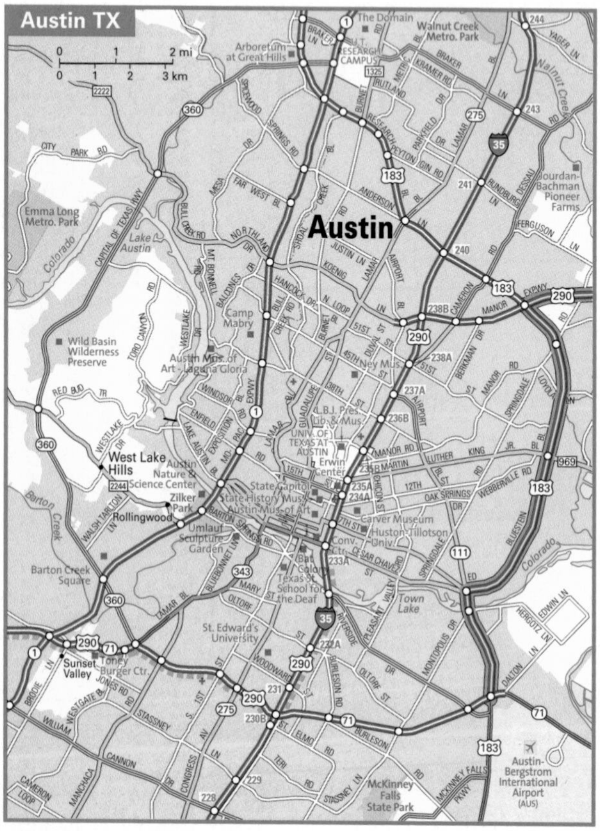

B

Babbie AL 128 A4
Babbitt MN 64 C3
Babson Park FL 141 D3
Babylon NY 148 C4
Baca Co. CO 42 A4
Bacon Co. GA 129 F4
Baconton GA 129 D4
Bad Axe MI 76 C2
Baden PA 92 A3
Badger IA 72 C4
Badin NC 122 B1
Bagdad AZ 46 C4
Bagdad FL 135 F2
Baggs WY 32 C3
Bagley MN 64 A3
Bahama NC 112 C4
Bailey NC 113 D4
Bailey Co. TX 49 F4
Bailey Island ME 82 B3
Bailey's Crossroads VA 270 B4
Bailey's Prairie TX 132 A4
Baileyton AL 119 F3
Baileyton TN 111 D3
Bainbridge GA 137 D1
Bainbridge IN 99 E1
Bainbridge NY 79 E4
Bainbridge OH 101 D2
Bainbridge Island WA 12 C3
Baird TX 58 C3
Baiting Hollow NY 149 E3
Baker LA 134 A2
Baker MT 17 F4
Baker City OR 21 F2
Baker Co. FL 138 C2
Baker Co. GA 128 C4
Baker Co. OR 21 F3
Bakersfield CA 45 D4
Bakersville NC 111 E4
Bala-Cynwyd PA 146 C3
Balaton MN 72 A1
Balch Sprs. TX 207 E3
Balcones Hts. TX 257 E2
Bald Knob AR 117 F1
Baldwin FL 139 D2
Baldwin GA 121 D3
Baldwin IL 98 B4
Baldwin LA 133 F3
Baldwin MD 144 C1
Baldwin MI 75 F2
Baldwin PA 250 C3
Baldwin WI 67 E4
Baldwin City KS 96 A3
Baldwin Co. AL 135 E1
Baldwin Co. GA 129 E1
Baldwin Harbor NY 147 F1
Baldwin Park CA 228 E2
Baldwinsville NY 79 D3
Baldwinville MA 95 D1
Baldwyn MS 119 D3
Balfour NC 121 E1
Bal Harbour FL 233 B3
Ball LA 125 E4
Ballantine MT 24 C1
Ballard UT 32 A4
Ballard Co. KY 108 C2
Ballentine SC 122 A3
Ball Ground GA 120 C3
Ballinger TX 58 C4
Ballouville CT 150 B3
Ballston Spa NY 80 C4
Ballville OH 90 C2
Ballwin MO 98 A3
Bally PA 146 B1
Balmorhea TX 62 B2
Balmville NY 148 B1
Balsam Lake WI 67 E3
Baltic CT 149 F1
Baltic OH 91 E4
Baltic SD 27 F4
Baltimore MD 144 C2
Baltimore OH 101 D1
Baltimore Co. MD 144 C1
Baltimore Highlands MD 193 C4
Bamberg SC 130 C1
Bamberg Co. SC 130 B1
Bancroft ID 31 E1
Bancroft IA 72 B3
Bancroft KY 230 F1
Bancroft MI 76 B3
Bancroft NE 35 F2
Bancroft WV 101 E3
Bandera TX 61 D2
Bandera Co. TX 60 C2
Bandon OR 28 A1
Bangor ME 83 D1
Bangor MI 75 E4
Bangor PA 93 F3
Bangor WI 73 F2
Bangs TX 59 D4
Banks OR 20 B1
Banks Co. GA 121 D3
Banner Co. NE 33 F3
Banner Elk NC 111 F4
Banner Hill TN 111 E4
Bannertown NC 112 A3
Banning CA 53 D2
Bannockburn IL 203 C2
Bannock Co. ID 31 E1
Banquete TX 63 F2
Bantam CT 94 C3
Baraboo WI 74 A2
Baraga MI 65 F4
Baraga Co. MI 65 F4
Barataria LA 134 B3
Barber Co. KS 43 D4
Barberton OH 91 E3
Barbour Co. AL 128 B3
Barbour Co. WV 102 A2
Barbourmeade KY 230 F1
Barboursville WV 101 E4
Barbourville KY 110 C2
Bardstown KY 110 A1
Bardwell KY 108 C2
Bardwell TX 59 F3
Bareville PA 146 A2
Bargersville IN 99 F1
Bar Harbor ME 83 D2
Barker NY 78 B3
Barling AR 116 C1
Barlow KY 108 C2
Bar Mills ME 82 B3
Barnegat NJ 147 E4
Barnegat Light NJ 147 E4
Barnegat Pines NJ 147 E3
Barnes Co. ND 19 D4
Barnesville GA 129 D1
Barnesville MN 19 F4
Barnesville OH 101 F1
Barneveld WI 74 A3
Barnhart MO 98 A4
Barnsboro NJ 146 C4
Barnsdall OK 51 F1
Barnstable MA 151 F3
Barnstable Co. MA 151 E4
Barnum MN 64 C4
Bar Nunn WY 33 D1
Barnwell SC 130 B1
Barnwell Co. SC 130 B1
Baroda MI 89 E1
Barrackville WV 102 A1
Barre MA 150 B1
Barre VT 81 E2
Barren Co. KY 110 A2
Barre Plains MA 150 B1
Barrett TX 132 B3
Barrington IL 203 B2
Barrington NH 81 F4
Barrington NJ 248 D4
Barrington RI 151 D3
Barrington Hills IL 203 A2
Barron WI 67 E3
Barron Co. WI 67 E3
Barrow AK 154 C1
Barrow Co. GA 121 D3
Barry IL 97 F1
Barry Co. MI 75 F4
Barry Co. MO 106 C2
Barstow CA 53 D1
Barstow MD 144 C4
Bartelso IL 98 B3
Bartholomew Co. IN 99 F2
Bartlesville OK 51 F1
Bartlett IL 203 A3
Bartlett NE 35 D2
Bartlett NH 81 F2
Bartlett TN 118 B1
Bartlett TX 61 E1
Barton MD 102 C1
Barton VT 81 E1
Barton Co. KS 43 D3
Barton Co. MO 106 B1
Bartonsville MD 144 A1
Bartonville IL 88 B3
Bartow FL 140 C2
Bartow Co. GA 120 B3
Barview OR 20 A4
Basalt CO 40 C2
Basalt ID 23 E4
Basehor KS 96 B2
Basile LA 133 E2
Basin MT 15 E4
Basin WY 24 C3
Basin City WA 13 E4
Baskett KY 99 E4
Basking Ridge NJ 148 A4
Bassett NE 35 D1
Bassett VA 112 B2
Bass Harbor ME 83 D2
Bass Lake IN 89 E2
Bastrop LA 125 F2
Bastrop TX 61 E2
Bastrop Co. TX 61 E2
Basye VA 102 C3
Batavia IL 88 C1
Batavia IA 87 E3
Batavia NY 78 B3
Batavia OH 100 B2
Batesburg-Leesville SC 122 A4
Bates Co. MO 96 B4
Batesville AR 107 F4
Batesville IN 100 A2
Batesville MS 118 B3
Batesville TX 60 C3
Bath ME 82 C3
Bath MI 76 A3
Bath NY 78 C4
Bath PA 93 F3
Bath Co. KY 100 C4
Bath Co. VA 102 B4
Baton Rouge LA 134 A2
Battle Creek IA 72 A4
Battle Creek MI 75 F4
Battle Creek NE 35 E2
Battlefield MO 107 D2
Battle Ground IN 89 E4
Battle Ground WA 20 C1
Battle Lake MN 19 F4
Battlement Mesa CO 40 B2
Battle Mtn. NV 30 A4
Baudette MN 64 A1
Baumstown PA 146 B2
Bauxite AR 117 E2
Bawcomville LA 125 E2
Baxley GA 129 F3
Baxter IA 87 D1
Baxter MN 64 A4
Baxter TN 110 A4
Baxter Co. AR 107 E4
Baxter Estates NY 241 G2
Baxter Sprs. KS 106 B2
Bay AR 108 A4
Bayard IA 86 B1
Bayard NE 33 F2
Bayard NM 55 F2
Bayboro NC 115 D3
Bay City MI 76 B2
Bay City OR 20 B2
Bay City TX 61 F3
Bay Co. FL 136 C2
Bay Co. MI 76 B2
Bayfield CO 40 C4
Bayfield WI 65 D4
Bayfield Co. WI 65 D4
Bay Harbor Islands FL 233 C4
Bay Head NJ 147 E3
Bay Hill FL 246 B3
Baylor Co. TX 59 D1
Bay Minette AL 135 E1
Bayonet Pt. FL 140 B2
Bayonne NJ 148 B4
Bayou Cane LA 134 A3
Bayou George FL 136 C2
Bayou Goula LA 134 A2
Bayou La Batre AL 135 E2
Bayou Vista LA 134 A3
Bayou Vista TX 132 B4
Bay Park NY 241 G5
Bay Pines FL 266 A3
Bay Pt. CA 259 D1
Bayport MN 67 D4
Bayport NY 149 D4
Bay Ridge MD 144 C3
Bay St. Louis MS 134 C2
Bay Shore NY 149 D4
Bayshore Gardens FL 266 B5
Bay Side NJ 147 E4
Bayside WI 234 D1
Bay Sprs. MS 126 C3
Baytown TX 132 B3
Bay View OH 91 D2
Bay Vil. OH 204 D2
Bayville NJ 147 E3
Bayville NY 148 C3
Beach ND 17 F4
Beach City OH 91 E3
Beach City TX 132 B3
Beach Haven NJ 147 E4
Beach Haven Gardens NJ 147 E4
Beach Haven Terrace NJ 147 E4
Beachwood NJ 147 E3
Beachwood OH 204 G2
Beacon IA 87 D2
Beacon NY 148 B1
Beacon Falls CT 149 D1
Beadle Co. SD 27 D3
Bealeton VA 103 D3
Beals ME 83 E2
Bean Sta. TN 111 D3
Bear DE 145 E1
Bear Creek AL 119 E3
Bearden AR 117 E4
Beardstown IL 98 A1
Bear Lake Co. ID 31 F2
Bear River City UT 31 E3
Beasley TX 132 A4
Beatrice AL 127 F4
Beatrice NE 35 F4
Beatty NV 45 F2
Beattyville KY 110 C1
Beatyestown NJ 94 A4
Beaufort NC 115 E4
Beaufort SC 130 C2
Beaufort Co. NC 113 F4
Beaufort Co. SC 130 C3
Beaumont CA 53 D2
Beaumont MS 135 D1
Beaumont TX 132 C3
Beaumont Place TX 220 D2
Beauregard Par. LA 133 D2
Beaver OK 50 C1
Beaver PA 91 F3
Beaver UT 39 D3
Beaver WV 111 F1
Beaver City NE 42 C1
Beaver Co. OK 50 C1
Beaver Co. PA 91 F3
Beaver Co. UT 39 D3
Beavercreek OH 100 C1
Beaver Crossing NE 35 E4
Beaverdale PA 92 B4
Beaver Dam KY 109 E1
Beaver Dam WI 74 B2
Beaver Falls PA 91 F3
Beaverhead Co. MT 23 D2
Beaver Meadows PA 93 E3
Beaver Sprs. PA 93 D3
Beaverton MI 76 A2
Beaverton OR 20 C2
Beavertown PA 93 D3
Bechtelsville PA 146 B1
Beckemeyer IL 98 B3
Becker MN 66 C3
Becker Co. MN 19 F3
Beckett NJ 146 C4
Beckham Co. OK 50 C3
Beckley WV 111 F1
Beckville TX 124 C3
Bedford IN 99 F3
Bedford IA 86 B3
Bedford KY 100 A3
Bedford MA 151 D1
Bedford NH 95 D1
Bedford NY 148 C2
Bedford OH 204 G3
Bedford PA 102 C1
Bedford TX 207 B2
Bedford VA 112 B1
Bedford Co. PA 92 C4
Bedford Co. TN 120 A1
Bedford Co. VA 112 B1
Bedford Hts. OH 204 G3
Bedford Hills NY 148 C2
Bedford Park IL 203 D5
Beebe AR 117 F2
Bee Cave TX 61 E1
Beech Bottom WV 91 F4
Beech Creek PA 93 D3
Beecher IL 89 D2
Beech Grove IN 99 F1
Beechwood Vil. KY 230 E1
Bee Co. TX 61 E4
Beemer NE 35 F2
Bee Ridge FL 140 B4
Beersheba Sprs. TN 120 A1
Beesleys Pt. NJ 147 F4
Beeville TX 61 E4
Beggs OK 51 F2
Bel Air MD 145 D1
Belcamp MD 145 D1
Belchertown MA 150 A1
Belcourt ND 18 C1
Belding MI 75 F3
Belen NM 48 C4
Belfair WA 12 C3
Belfast ME 82 C2
Belfast NY 78 B4
Belfast PA 93 F3
Belfield ND 18 A4
Belford NJ 147 E1
Belfry MT 24 B2
Belgium WI 75 D2
Belgrade MN 66 B3
Belgrade MT 23 F1
Belgrade Lakes ME 82 B2
Belhaven NC 115 E3
Belinda City TN 109 F4
Belington WV 102 A2
Belknap Co. NH 81 F4
Bell CA 228 D3
Bellair FL 222 C4
Bellaire MI 69 F4
Bellaire OH 101 F1
Bellaire TX 132 A3
Bellamy AL 127 E2
Bella Villa MO 256 B3
Bella Vista AR 106 C3
Bella Vista CA 28 C4
Bellbrook OH 100 C1
Bell Buckle TN 119 F1
Bell Co. KY 110 C3
Bell Co. TX 61 E1
Belle MO 97 F4
Belle WV 101 F4
Belleair FL 140 B2
Belleair Beach FL 140 B2
Belleair Bluffs FL 266 A2
Belle Ctr. OH 90 C4
Belle Chasse LA 134 B3
Bellefontaine OH 90 B4
Bellefontaine Neighbors MO 256 C1
Bellefonte AR 107 D3
Bellefonte DE 146 B4
Bellefonte KY 101 D3
Bellefonte PA 92 C3
Belle Fourche SD 25 F3
Belle Glade FL 143 E1
Belle Haven VA 114 B3
Belle Isle FL 141 D1
Bellemeade KY 230 F2
Belle Plaine IA 87 E1
Belle Plaine KS 43 E4
Belle Plaine MN 66 C4
Belle Rose LA 134 A3
Bellerose NY 241 G3
Bellerose Terrace NY 241 G3
Belle Terre NY 149 D3
Belle Vernon PA 92 A4
Belleview FL 139 D4
Belleville IL 98 B3
Belleville KS 43 E1
Belleville MI 90 C1
Belleville NJ 148 B4
Belleville PA 92 C4
Belleville WI 74 B3
Bellevue ID 22 C4
Bellevue IL 88 B3
Bellevue IA 74 A4
Bellevue KY 204 B3
Bellevue MI 76 A4
Bellevue NE 86 A2
Bellevue OH 204 B3
Bellevue PA 92 A4
Bellevue WA 12 C3
Bellevue WI 74 C1
Bellflower CA 228 D3
Bell Gardens CA 228 D3
Bellingham MA 150 C2
Bellingham WA 12 C1
Bellmawr NJ 146 C3
Bellmead TX 59 E4
Bellows Falls VT 81 E4
Bellport NY 149 D4
Bells TN 108 C4
Bells TX 59 F1
Bellview FL 247 A1
Bellville OH 91 D3
Bellville TX 61 F2
Bellwood IL 203 C4
Bellwood NE 35 E3
Bellwood PA 92 C4
Bellwood VA 254 B3
Belmar NJ 147 F2
Belmond IA 72 C3
Belmont CA 259 B5
Belmont MA 151 D1
Belmont MS 119 D3
Belmont NH 81 F4
Belmont NY 92 C1
Belmont NC 122 A1

Entries in **bold black** indicate counties or parishes.
Entries in **bold color** indicate cities with detailed inset maps.

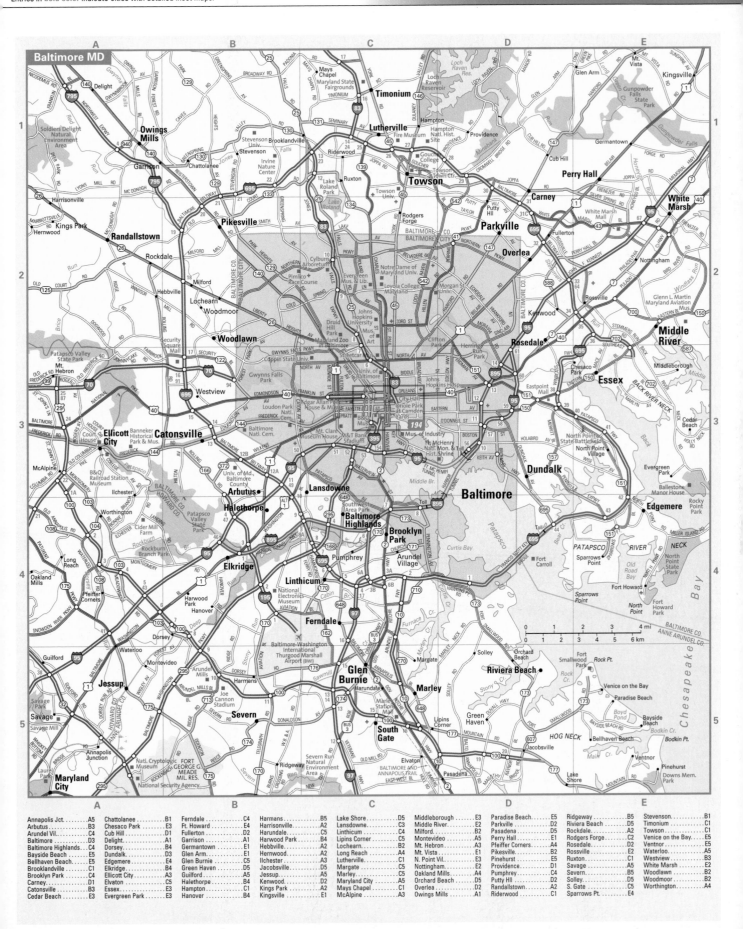

Annapolis Jct. A5
Arbutus B3
Arundel Vil. C4
Baltimore D3
Baltimore Highlands . . .C4
Bayside Beach E5
Bellhaven Beach E5
Brooklandville C1
Brooklyn Park C4
Carney D1
Catonsville B3
Cedar Beach E3
Chattolanee B1
Chesaco Park E3
Cub Hill D1
Delight A1
Dorsey B4
Dundalk D3
Edgemere E4
Elkridge B4
Ellicott City A3
Elvaton C5
Essex E3
Evergreen Park E3
Ferndale C4
Ft. Howard E4
Fullerton D2
Garrison A1
Germantown E1
Glen Arm E1
Glen Burnie C5
Green Haven D5
Guilford A5
Halethorpe B4
Hampton C1
Hanover B4
Harmans B5
Harrisonville A2
Harundale C5
Harwood Park B4
Hebbville A2
Hernwood A2
Ilchester A3
Jacobsville D5
Jessup A5
Kenwood D2
Kings Park A2
Kingsville E1
Lake Shore D5
Lansdowne C3
Linthicum C4
Lipins Corner C5
Lochearn B2
Long Reach A4
Lutherville C1
Margate C5
Marley C5
Maryland City A5
Mays Chapel C1
McAlpine A3
Middleborough E3
Middle River E2
Milford B2
Montevideo A5
Mt. Hebron A3
Mt. Vista E1
N. Point Vil. E3
Nottingham E2
Oakland Mills A4
Orchard Beach D5
Overlea D2
Owings Mills A1
Paradise Beach E5
Parkville D2
Pasadena D5
Perry Hall E1
Pfeiffer Corners A4
Pikesville B2
Pinehurst E5
Providence D1
Pumphrey C4
Putty Hll D2
Randallstown A2
Riderwood C1
Ridgeway B5
Riviera Beach D5
Rockdale A2
Rodgers Forge C2
Rosedale D2
Rossville E2
Ruxton C1
Savage A5
Severn B5
Solley D5
S. Gate C5
Sparrows Pt. E4
Stevenson B1
Timonium C1
Towson C1
Venice on the Bay E5
Ventnor E5
Waterloo A5
Westview B3
White Marsh E2
Woodlawn B2
Woodmoor B2
Worthington A4

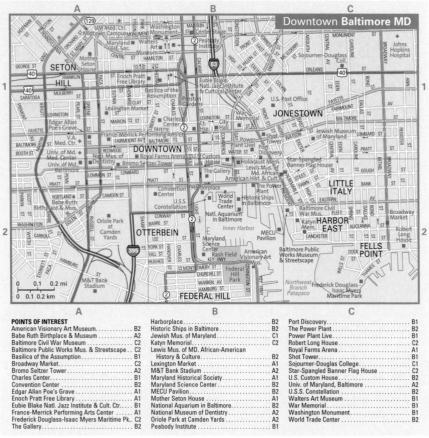

Figures after entries indicate page number and grid reference.

POINTS OF INTEREST

American Visionary Art Museum B2
Babe Ruth Birthplace & Museum A2
Baltimore Civil War Museum C2
Baltimore Public Works Mus. & Streetscape C2
Basilica of the Assumption B1
Broadway Market C2
Bromo Seltzer Tower A2
Charles Center B1
Convention Center B2
Edgar Allan Poe's Grave A1
Enoch Pratt Free Library A1
Eubie Blake Natl. Jazz Institute & Cult. Ctr. B1
France-Merrick Performing Arts Center A1
Frederick Douglass-Isaac Myers Maritime Pk. C2
The Gallery B2
Harborplace B2
Historic Ships in Baltimore B2
Jewish Mus. of Maryland C1
Katyn Memorial C2
Lewis Mus. of MD. African-American History & Culture B2
Lexington Market A1
M&T Bank Stadium A2
Maryland Historical Society A1
Maryland Science Center B2
MECU Pavilion B2
Mother Seton House A1
National Aquarium in Baltimore B2
National Museum of Dentistry A2
Oriole Park at Camden Yards A2
Peabody Institute B1
Port Discovery B1
The Power Plant B2
Power Plant Live B1
Robert Long House C2
Royal Farms Arena A1
Shot Tower B1
Sojourner-Douglas College C1
Star-Spangled Banner Flag House C2
U.S. Custom House B2
Univ. of Maryland, Baltimore A2
U.S.S. Constellation B2
Walters Art Museum B1
War Memorial B1
Washington Monument B1
World Trade Center B2

Belmont WV 101 F2
Belmont WI 74 A4
Belmont Corner ME 82 C2
Belmont Co. OH 101 F1
Bel-Nor MO 256 B2
Beloit KS 43 E1
Beloit OH 91 F3
Beloit WI 74 B4
Belpre OH 101 E2
Bel-Ridge MO 256 B2
Belt MT 15 F3
Belton KY 109 E2
Belton MO 96 B3
Belton SC 121 E3
Belton TX 59 E4
Beltrami Co. MN 64 A2
Beltsville MD 144 B3
Belvedere CA 259 B2
Belvedere SC 121 F4
Belvedere Park GA 190 E4
Belvidere IL 74 B4
Belvidere NJ 93 F3
Belwood NC 121 F1
Belzoni MS 126 B1
Bement IL 98 C1
Bemidji MN 64 A3
Bemiss GA 137 F1
Benavides TX 63 E2
Ben Avon PA 250 A1
Benbrook TX 207 A3
Bend OR 21 D3
Bendersville PA 103 E1
Benewah Co. ID 14 B3
Benham KY 111 D2
Ben Hill Co. GA 129 E3
Benicia CA 36 B3
Benjamin TX 58 C1
Benkelman NE 42 B1
Benld IL 98 B2
Ben Lomond CA 44 A2
Bennet NE 35 F4
Bennett CO 41 E1
Bennett Co. SD 26 B4
Bennettsville SC 122 C2
Bennington KS 43 E2
Bennington NE 35 F3
Bennington NH 81 E4
Bennington VT 94 C1
Bennington Co. VT 81 D4
Benoit MS 118 A4
Bensenville IL 203 C4
Bensley VA 113 E1
Benson AZ 55 D3
Benson MD 144 C1
Benson MN 66 A3
Benson NC 123 D1
Benson Co. ND 19 D2
Bent Co. CO 41 F3
Bent Creek NC 121 E1
Bentleyville OH 204 G3
Bentleyville PA 92 A4
Benton AR 117 E2
Benton IL 98 C4
Benton KS 43 F4
Benton KY 109 D2
Benton LA 124 C2
Benton ME 82 C2
Benton MO 108 B2
Benton PA 93 E2
Benton TN 120 C1
Benton WI 74 A4
Benton City WA 21 E1
Benton Co. AR 106 B3
Benton Co. IN 89 D3
Benton Co. IA 87 E1
Benton Co. MN 66 C2
Benton Co. MS 118 C2
Benton Co. MO 97 D4
Benton Co. OR 20 B3
Benton Co. TN 109 D4
Benton Co. WA 21 E1
Benton Harbor MI 89 E1
Bentonia MS 126 B2
Bentonville AR 106 C3
Benzie Co. MI 69 F4
Benzonia MI 69 E4
Berea KY 110 C1
Berea OH 91 E2
Berea SC 217 A2
Beresford SD 35 F1
Bergen NY 78 B3
Bergen Co. NJ 148 B3
Bergenfield NJ 148 B3
Bergholz OH 91 F4
Bergman AR 107 D3
Berino NM 56 C3
Berkeley CA 36 B4
Berkeley IL 203 C4
Berkeley MO 256 B1
Berkeley RI 150 C3
Berkeley Co. SC 131 D1
Berkeley Co. WV 103 D2
Berkeley Hts. NJ 148 A4
Berkeley Sprs. WV 102 C1
Berkley MA 151 D3
Berkley MI 210 B2
Berks Co. PA 146 B1
Berkshire CT 149 D2
Berkshire Co. MA 94 C2
Berlin CT 149 E1
Berlin GA 137 F1
Berlin MD 114 C2
Berlin MA 150 C1
Berlin NH 81 F2
Berlin NJ 147 D3
Berlin OH 91 E4
Berlin PA 102 C1
Berlin WI 74 B1
Berlin Hts. OH 91 D2
Bermuda Run NC 112 A4
Bernalillo NM 48 C3
Bernalillo Co. NM 48 C3
Bernardston MA 94 C1
Bernardsville NJ 148 A4
Berne IN 90 A3
Bernice LA 125 E2
Bernice OK 106 B3
Bernie MO 108 B3
Bernstadt KY 110 C2
Bernville PA 146 A1
Berrien Co. GA 129 E4
Berrien Co. MI 89 E1
Berrien Sprs. MI 89 E1
Berry AL 119 E4
Berryville AR 106 C3
Berryville TX 124 A3
Berryville VA 103 D2
Berthold ND 18 B2
Berthoud CO 33 E4
Bertie Co. NC 113 F4
Bertram IA 87 F1
Bertram TX 61 D1
Bertrand MI 89 F1
Bertrand MO 108 B2
Bertrand NE 35 D4
Berwick LA 134 A3
Berwick ME 82 A4
Berwick PA 93 E3
Berwyn IL 89 D1
Berwyn PA 146 B3
Berwyn Hts. MD 270 E2
Bessemer AL 127 F1
Bessemer MI 65 E4
Bessemer PA 91 F3
Bessemer City NC 122 A1
Bethalto IL 98 B3
Bethany CT 149 D1
Bethany IL 98 C1
Bethany MO 86 C4
Bethany OK 51 E3
Bethany WV 91 F4
Bethany Beach DE 145 F4
Bethel AK 154 B3
Bethel CT 148 C2
Bethel DE 145 E4
Bethel ME 82 B2
Bethel NC 113 E4
Bethel OH 100 C2
Bethel VT 81 E3
Bethel VA 103 D3
Bethel Acres OK 51 F3
Bethel Hts. AR 106 C3
Bethel Park PA 92 A4
Bethel Sprs. TN 119 D1
Bethesda MD 144 B3
Bethesda OH 101 F1
Bethlehem CT 149 D1
Bethlehem GA 121 D4
Bethlehem MD 145 D4
Bethlehem NH 81 F2
Bethlehem NC 111 F4
Bethlehem PA 146 C1
Bethlehem Ctr. NY 188 D3
Bethpage NY 148 C4
Betmar Acres FL 140 C2
Bettendorf IA 88 A2
Bettsville OH 90 C2
Beulah CO 41 E3
Beulah MI 69 E4
Beulah MS 118 A4
Beulah ND 18 B3
Beulaville NC 123 E2
Beverly MA 151 F1
Beverly NJ 147 D3
Beverly OH 101 E1
Beverly WV 102 B3
Beverly Beach FL 139 E4
Beverly Beach MD 144 C3
Beverly Hills CA 52 C2
Beverly Hills FL 140 B1
Beverly Hills MI 210 B2
Beverly Hills MO 256 B2
Beverly Shores IN 89 E2
Bevier MO 97 E1
Bevil Oaks TX 132 C2
Bevis OH 204 A1
Bexar Co. TX 61 D2
Bexley OH 206 C2
Bibb Co. AL 127 F1
Bibb Co. GA 129 D2
Bicknell IN 99 E3
Bicknell UT 39 E3
Biddeford ME 82 B4
Bienville Par. LA 125 D2
Big Bear City CA 53 D2
Big Bear Lake CA 53 D2
Big Beaver PA 91 F3
Big Bend WI 74 C3
Big Chimney WV 101 F3
Big Coppitt Key FL 143 D4
Big Delta AK 154 C2
Big Flats NY 93 D1
Bigfork MT 15 D2
Biggs CA 36 B2
Big Horn Co. MT 24 C2
Big Horn Co. WY 24 C3
Big Lake MN 66 C3
Big Lake TX 58 A4
Big Lake WA 12 C2
Biglerville PA 103 E1
Big Oak Flat CA 37 D4
Big Pine CA 37 E4
Big Pine Key FL 143 D4
Big Piney WY 32 A1
Big Rapids MI 75 F2
Big River CA 46 B4
Big Run PA 92 B3
Big Sandy MT 16 B2
Big Sandy TN 109 D3
Big Sandy TX 124 B2
Big Sky MT 23 F2
Big Spr. TX 58 A3
Big Sprs. NE 34 B3
Big Stone City SD 27 F2
Big Stone Co. MN 27 F2
Big Stone Gap VA 111 E2
Big Timber MT 24 A1
Big Water UT 47 D1
Big Wells TX 60 C4
Billerica MA 95 E1
Billings MO 106 C2
Billings MT 24 C1
Billings NY 148 B1
Billings OK 51 E1
Billings Co. ND 18 A3
Billington Hts. NY 78 B4
Biloxi MS 135 D2
Biltmore Forest NC 121 E1
Bingen PA 189 B2
Binger OK 51 D3
Bingham ME 82 B1
Bingham Co. ID 23 E4
Bingham Farms MI 210 B2
Binghamton NY 93 E1
Biola CA 44 C2
Birch Bay WA 12 C1
Birch Run MI 76 B3
Birch Tree MO 107 F2
Birchwood Vil. MN 235 E1
Bird City KS 42 B1
Bird Island MN 66 B4
Birdsboro PA 146 B2
Birmingham AL 119 F4
Birmingham MI 76 C4
Birnamwood WI 68 B4
Biron WI 74 A1
Bisbee AZ 55 E4
Biscayne Park FL 233 B4
Biscoe AR 117 F2
Biscoe NC 122 C1
Bishop CA 37 E4
Bishop TX 63 F2
Bishopville SC 122 B3
Bismarck MO 108 A1
Bismarck ND 18 C4
Bison SD 26 A2
Bithlo FL 141 D1
Bitter Sprs. AZ 47 D1
Biwabik MN 64 C3
Bixby OK 106 A4
Blackbird DE 145 E1
Black Canyon City AZ 47 D4
Black Creek NC 123 E1
Black Creek WI 68 C4
Black Diamond WA 12 C3
Blackduck MN 64 A3
Black Eagle MT 15 F3
Black Earth WI 74 A3
Blackfoot ID 31 E1
Blackford Co. IN 90 A4
Black Forest CO 41 E2
Blackhawk SD 26 A3
Black Hawk Co. IA 73 E4
Black Jack MO 256 B1
Black Lick PA 92 B4
Blacklick Estates OH 206 C3
Black Mtn. NC 121 E1
Black River NY 79 E1
Black River Falls WI 73 F1
Black Rock AR 107 F4
Black Rock NM 48 A3
Blacksburg SC 122 A1
Blacksburg VA 112 A2
Blackshear GA 129 F4
Blackstone MA 150 C2
Blackstone VA 113 D2
Blackville SC 130 B1
Blackwell OK 51 E1
Blackwells GA 120 C3
Blackwood NJ 146 C3
Bladenboro NC 123 D3
Bladen Co. NC 123 D2
Bladensburg MD 270 E3
Blades DE 145 E4
Blaine ME 85 E2
Blaine MN 67 D3
Blaine TN 110 C4
Blaine WA 12 C1
Blaine Co. ID 23 D4
Blaine Co. MT 16 B2
Blaine Co. NE 34 C2
Blaine Co. OK 51 D2
Blair NE 35 F3
Blair OK 51 D4
Blair WI 73 F1
Blair Co. PA 92 C4
Blairs VA 112 C3
Blairstown IA 87 E1
Blairstown NJ 93 F3
Blairsville GA 121 D2

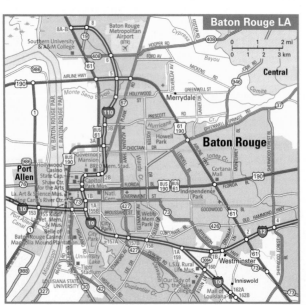

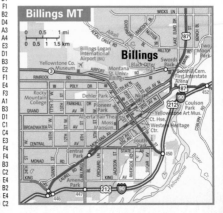

Entries in **bold black** indicate counties or parishes.
Entries in **bold color** indicate cities with detailed inset maps.

Blairsville PA 92 B4
Blakely GA 128 C4
Blakely PA 93 F2
Blakes VA 113 F1
Blanca CO 41 D4
Blanchard LA 124 C2
Blanchard OK 51 E3
Blanchard PA 93 D3
Blanchardville WI 74 A3
Blanchester OH 100 C2
Blanco TX 61 D2
Blanco Co. TX 61 D1
Bland MO 97 F4
Bland VA 112 A2
Bland Co. VA 111 F2
Blanding UT 40 A4
Blandinsville IL 87 F4
Blandon PA 146 B1
Blasdell NY 78 B3
Blauvelt NY 148 B3
Blawenburg NJ 147 D1
Blawnox PA 250 C1
Bleckley Co. GA 129 E2
Bledsoe Co. TN 110 B4
Blennerhassett WV 101 E2
Blessing TX 61 F3
Bliss ID 30 C1
Bliss Corner MA 238 C2
Blissfield MI 90 B1
Blocher IN 100 A3
Bloomdale OH 90 C2
Bloomer WI 67 F3
Bloomfield CT 150 A3
Bloomfield IN 99 E2
Bloomfield IA 87 E3
Bloomfield KY 100 A4
Bloomfield MO 108 B2
Bloomfield NE 35 E1
Bloomfield NJ 148 B4
Bloomfield NM 48 B1
Bloomfield NY 78 C3
Bloomfield WI 74 C4
Bloomfield Hills MI 210 B1
Bloomingburg OH 100 C1
Bloomingdale FL 266 D2
Bloomingdale IL 203 B3
Bloomingdale NJ 148 A3
Bloomingdale TN 111 E3
Blooming Grove NY 148 B1
Blooming Grove TX 59 F3
Blooming Prairie MN 73 D2
Bloomington CA 229 H2
Bloomington ID 31 F2
Bloomington IL 88 C4
Bloomington IN 99 F2
Bloomington MN 67 D4
Bloomington TX 61 F4
Bloomington WI 73 F3
Bloomsburg PA 93 E3
Bloomsbury NJ 146 C1
Bloomville OH 90 C3
Blossburg PA 93 D2
Blossom TX 116 A4
Blount Co. AL 119 F3
Blount Co. TN 110 C4
Blountstown FL 137 D2
Blountsville AL 119 F3
Blountville TN 111 E3
Blowing Rock NC 111 F4
Bloxom VA 114 C2
Blue Anchor NJ 147 D4
Blue Ash OH 100 B2
Blue Bell PA 146 C2
Blue Diamond NV 46 A2
Blue Earth MN 72 C2
Blue Earth Co. MN 72 C1
Bluefield VA 111 F2
Bluefield WV 111 F2
Blue Grass IA 87 F2
Blue Hill ME 83 D2
Blue Hill NE 35 D4
Blue Hills CT 150 A3
Blue Island IL 203 D6
Blue Lake CA 28 B4

Biloxi A2
D'Iberville B1
Escatawpa C1
Fontainebleau B2
Gautier C2
Gulfport A1
Helena C1
Latimer B1
Long Beach A2
Moss Pt. C2
New Hope A1
Ocean Sprs. B2
Pascagoula C2
Vancleave C1
Wortham A1

Birmingham AL

Adamsville D1
Alabaster E3
Bayview D1
Bessemer D3
Birmingham E1
Brighton D2
Brookside D1
Cardiff D1
Center Pt. F1
Chalkville F1
Chelsea F3
Concord D2
Edgewater D2
Fairfield D2
Forestdale E1
Fultondale E1
Gardendale E1
Graysville D1
Helena E3
Homewood E2
Hoover E3
Hueytown D2
Indian Sprs. Vil. E3
Irondale F1
Lipscomb D2
Maytown D1
McCalla D3
Midfield D2
Mtn. Brook F2
Mulga D1
Pelham E3
Pleasant Grove D2
Pleasant Hill D3
Republic E1
Shannon E2
Simmsville F3
Summit Farm D3
Sylvan Sprs. D2
Tarrant City E1
Trussville F1
Vestavia Hills E2
Watson E1

Blue Mound IL 98 C1
Blue Mound TX 207 A2
Blue Mounds WI 74 A3
Blue Mtn. MS 118 C2
Blue Pt. NY 149 D4
Blue Rapids KS 43 F1
Blue Ridge AL 128 A2
Blue Ridge GA 120 C2
Blue Ridge TX 59 F2
Blue Ridge VA 112 B1
Blue Ridge Manor KY 230 F2
Blue River CO 41 D2
Blue Sprs. MO 96 C2
Bluff UT 40 A4
Bluff City TN 111 E3
Bluffdale UT 31 E4
Bluffs IL 98 A1
Bluffton IN 90 A3
Bluffton OH 90 B3
Bluffton SC 130 C3
Bluford IL 98 C4
Blunt SD 26 C3
Blythe CA 53 F3
Blythe GA 129 F1
Blytheville AR 108 B4
Boalsburg PA 92 C3
Boardman OH 91 F3
Boardman OR 21 E1
Boardman Bridge CT 148 C1
Boaz AL 120 A3
Boaz WV 101 F2
Bobtown PA 102 A1
Boca Grande FL 140 C4
Boca Raton FL 143 F1
Bodega Bay CA 36 A3
Bodfish CA 45 E4
Boerne TX 61 D2
Bogalusa LA 134 C1
Bogart GA 121 D4
Bogata TX 116 A4
Boger City NC 122 A1
Bogota NJ 240 D1
Bogue NC 115 D4
Bogue Chitto MS 127 D2
Bohners Lake WI 74 C4
Boiling Spr. Lakes NC 123 E3
Boiling Sprs. NC 121 F1
Boiling Sprs. PA 93 D4
Boiling Sprs. SC 121 F2
Boise ID 22 B4
Boise City OK 50 A1
Boise Co. ID 22 C4
Bokchito OK 59 F1
Bokeelia FL 142 C1
Bokoshe OK 116 B1
Boley OK 51 F3
Boling TX 61 F3
Bolingbrook IL 89 D2
Bolivar MO 107 D1
Bolivar NY 92 C1
Bolivar OH 91 E3
Bolivar TN 118 C1
Bolivar WV 144 A2
Bolivar Co. MS 118 A4
Bolivia NC 123 E3
Bollinger Co. MO 108 B2
Bolton CT 150 A3
Bolton MS 126 B2
Bolton NC 123 D3
Bolton Landing NY 81 D3
Bon Air VA 113 E1
Bonaire GA 129 D2
Bonanza AR 116 C1
Bonanza OR 29 D2
Bonaparte IA 87 E3
Bond Co. IL 98 B3
Bondsville MA 150 A2
Bonduel WI 68 C4
Bondurant IA 86 C2
Bonesteel SD 35 D1
Bonham TX 59 F1
Bon Homme Co. SD 35 E1
Bonifay FL 136 C1
Bonita CA 258 C2
Bonita Sprs. FL 142 C1
Bonneauville PA 103 E1
Bonner MT 15 D4
Bonner Co. ID 14 B2
Bonners Ferry ID 14 B1
Bonner Sprs. KS 96 B2
Bonne Terre MO 98 A4
Bonnet Shores RI 150 C4
Bonneville Co. ID 23 F4
Bonney Lake WA 262 B5
Bonnieville KY 110 A1
Bono AR 108 A4
Bonsall CA 53 D3
Booker TX 50 B1
Boomer WV 101 F4
Boone CO 41 E3
Boone IA 86 C1
Boone NC 111 F3
Boone Co. AR 107 D3
Boone Co. IL 74 B4
Boone Co. IN 99 F1
Boone Co. IA 86 C1
Boone Co. KY 100 B2
Boone Co. MO 97 E2
Boone Co. NE 35 E3
Boone Co. WV 101 E4
Booneville AR 116 C1
Booneville KY 110 C1
Booneville MS 119 D2
Boonsboro MD 144 A1
Boonton NJ 148 A3
Boonville CA 36 A2
Boonville IN 99 E4
Boonville MO 97 D2
Boonville NY 79 E2
Boonville NC 112 A3
Boothbay ME 82 C3
Boothbay Harbor ME 82 C3
Boothville LA 134 C4
Bootjack CA 37 D4
Borden IN 99 F3
Borden Co. TX 58 B2
Bordentown NJ 147 D2
Borger TX 50 B2
Boron CA 52 C1
Borrego Sprs. CA 53 E3
Boscobel WI 73 F3
Bosque Co. TX 59 E3
Bosque Farms NM 48 C4
Bossier City LA 124 C2
Bossier Par. LA 125 D1
Boston GA 137 E1
Boston MA 151 D1
Boswell IN 89 D4
Boswell OK 59 F1
Boswell PA 92 B4
Botetourt Co. VA 112 B1
Bothell WA 12 C3
Botkins OH 90 B4
Botsford CT 149 D2
Bottineau ND 18 C1
Bottineau Co. ND 18 C1
Botto KY 110 C2
Boulder CO 41 E1
Boulder MT 23 E1
Boulder City NV 46 B2
Boulder Co. CO 41 D1
Boulder Creek CA 44 A2
Boundary Co. ID 14 B1
Bound Brook NJ 147 D1
Bountiful UT 31 E4
Bourbon IN 89 F2
Bourbon MO 97 F4
Bourbon Co. KS 96 B4
Bourbon Co. KY 100 B4
Bourbonnais IL 89 D2
Bourne MA 151 E3
Bouse AZ 54 A1
Boutte LA 134 B3
Bovey MN 64 B3
Bovill ID 14 B4
Bovina TX 49 F4
Bowbells ND 18 B1
Bow Ctr. NH 81 F4
Bowdle SD 27 D2
Bowdoin Ctr. ME 82 B3
Bowdoinham ME 82 B3
Bowdon GA 120 B4
Bowen IL 87 F4
Bowers DE 145 F3
Bowie AZ 55 E3

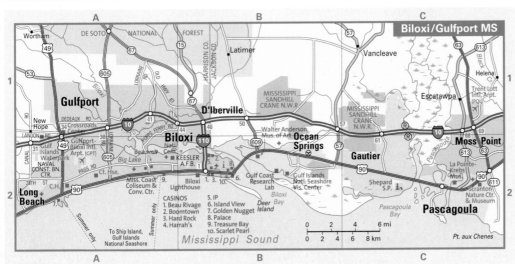

196
Bowie–Burien

Figures after entries indicate page number and grid reference.

Bowie MD 144 C3
Bowie TX 59 E1
Bowie Co. TX 116 B4
Bowleys Quarters MD 144 C2
Bowling Green FL 140 C3
Bowling Green KY 109 F2
Bowling Green MO 97 F2
Bowling Green OH 90 C2
Bowling Green VA 103 D4
Bowman GA 121 E3
Bowman ND 25 F1
Bowman SC 130 C1
Bowman Co. ND 25 F1
Bow Mar CO 209 B4
Boxborough MA 150 C1
Box Butte Co. NE 34 A2
Box Elder MT 16 B2
Box Elder SD 26 A3
Box Elder Co. UT 31 D3
Boxford MA 151 F1
Boyce LA 125 E4
Boyce VA 103 D2
Boyceville WI 67 E3
Boyd TX 59 E2
Boyd WI 67 F4
Boyd Co. KY 101 D4
Boyd Co. NE 35 D1
Boyden IA 35 F1
Boydton VA 113 D3
Boyertown PA 146 B2
Boyette FL 140 C3
Boykins VA 113 E3
Boyle MS 118 A4
Boyle Co. KY 110 B1
Boyne City MI 70 B3
Boynton Beach FL 143 F1
Boys Town NE 245 A2
Bozeman MT 23 F1
Braceville IL 88 C2
Bracken Co. KY 100 C3
Brackettville TX 60 B3
Bradbury CA 228 E2
Braddock PA 250 C2
Braddock Hts. MD 144 A1
Braddock Hills PA 250 C2
Bradenton FL 140 B3
Bradenton Beach FL 140 B3
Bradford AR 117 F1
Bradford IL 88 B2
Bradford NH 81 E4
Bradford OH 90 B4
Bradford PA 92 B1
Bradford RI 150 C4
Bradford TN 108 C4
Bradford VT 81 E3
Bradford Co. FL 138 C3
Bradford Co. PA 93 E2
Bradfordville FL 137 E2
Bradford Woods PA 92 A3
Bradley AR 125 D1
Bradley IL 89 D3
Bradley ME 83 D1
Bradley WV 101 F4
Bradley Beach NJ 147 F2
Bradley Co. AR 117 E4
Bradley Co. TN 120 C1
Bradley Jct. FL 140 C3
Bradner OH 90 C2
Brady TX 58 C4
Braham MN 67 D2
Braidwood IL 88 C2
Brainerd MN 64 B4
Braintree MA 151 D2
Bramwell WV 111 F1
Branch Co. MI 90 A1
Branchville AL 119 F4
Branchville NJ 94 A4
Branchville SC 130 C1
Brandenburg KY 99 F4
Brandon FL 140 C2
Brandon MS 126 B3
Brandon SD 27 F4
Brandon VT 81 D3
Brandon WI 74 C2
Brandywine MD 144 B4
Brandywine Manor PA 146 B3
Branford CT 149 D2
Branford FL 138 B3
Branson MO 107 D3
Brant Beach NJ 147 E4
Brantley AL 128 A4
Brantley Co. GA 129 F4
Brant Rock MA 151 E2
Braselton GA 121 D3
Brasher Falls NY 80 B1
Bratenahl OH 204 F1
Brattleboro VT 94 C1
Brawley CA 53 E4
Braxton Co. WV 101 F3
Bray OK 51 E4
Braymer MO 96 C1
Brazil IN 99 E1
Brazoria TX 132 A4
Brazoria Co. TX 132 A4
Brazos Co. TX 61 F1
Brea CA 229 F3
Breathitt Co. KY 111 D1
Breaux Bridge LA 133 F2
Breckenridge CO 41 D1
Breckenridge MI 76 A2
Breckenridge MN 27 F1
Breckenridge TX 59 D2
Breckenridge Hills MO 256 B2
Breckinridge Co. KY 99 F4
Brecksville OH 204 F3
Breese IL 98 B3
Breezy Pt. MD 144 C4
Breezy Pt. MN 64 B4
Breinigsville PA 146 B1
Bremen GA 120 B4
Bremen IN 89 F2
Bremen KY 109 E1
Bremen OH 101 D1
Bremer Co. IA 73 E3
Bremerton WA 12 C3
Bremond TX 59 F4
Brenham TX 61 F2
Brent AL 127 F1
Brent FL 135 F2
Brentsville VA 144 A4
Brentwood CA 36 B3
Brentwood MD 270 E2
Brentwood MO 256 B2
Brentwood NY 149 D4
Brentwood PA 250 B3
Brentwood TN 109 F4
Bressler PA 218 C2
Brevard NC 121 E1
Brevard Co. FL 141 E2
Brewer ME 83 D1
Brewerton NY 79 D3
Brewster MA 151 F3
Brewster MN 72 A2
Brewster NE 34 C2
Brewster NY 148 C2
Brewster OH 91 E3
Brewster WA 13 E2
Brewster Co. TX 62 C3
Brewster Hill NY 148 C1
Brewton AL 135 F1
Briar TX 59 E2
Briarcliff TX 61 D1
Briarcliffe Acres SC 123 D4
Briarcliff Manor NY 148 B2
Briar Creek PA 93 E3
Briarwood KY 230 F1
Briceville TN 110 C4
Brickerville PA 146 A2
Bridge City LA 239 B2
Bridge City TX 132 C3
Bridgehampton NY 149 F3
Bridgeport AL 120 A2
Bridgeport CA 37 E3
Bridgeport CT 149 D2
Bridgeport IL 99 D3
Bridgeport MD 144 A1
Bridgeport MI 76 B3
Bridgeport NE 34 A3
Bridgeport NY 79 E3
Bridgeport PA 248 A1
Bridgeport TX 59 E2
Bridgeport WA 13 E2
Bridgeport WV 102 A2
Bridger MT 24 B2
Bridgeton MO 256 B1
Bridgeton NJ 145 F1
Bridgetown OH 204 A2
Bridgeview IL 203 D5
Bridgeville DE 145 E4
Bridgeville PA 250 A3
Bridgewater MA 151 D2
Bridgewater NJ 147 D1
Bridgewater NY 79 E3
Bridgewater SD 27 E4
Bridgewater VA 102 C4
Bridgman MI 89 E1
Bridgton ME 82 B3
Brielle NJ 147 E2
Brier WA 262 B2
Brigantine NJ 147 F4
Brigham City UT 31 E3
Bright IN 100 B2
Brighton AL 195 D2
Brighton CO 41 E1
Brighton IL 98 A2
Brighton IA 87 E2
Brighton MI 76 B4
Brighton NY 78 C3
Brighton TN 118 B1
Brightwaters NY 149 D4
Brightwood VA 102 C3
Brilliant AL 119 E3
Brilliant OH 91 F4
Brillion WI 74 C1
Brimfield IL 88 B3
Brinckerhoff NY 148 B1
Brinkley AR 117 F2
Brinnon WA 12 C3
Brisbane CA 259 B3
Briscoe Co. TX 50 B4
Bristol CT 149 D1
Bristol FL 137 D2
Bristol IN 89 F1
Bristol NH 81 F3
Bristol PA 147 D2
Bristol RI 151 D3
Bristol SD 27 E2
Bristol TN 111 E3
Bristol VT 81 D2
Bristol VA 111 E3
Bristol WI 74 C4
Bristol Co. MA 151 D3
Bristol Co. RI 151 D3
Bristow OK 51 F2
Britt IA 72 C3
Brittany Farms PA 146 C2
Britton MI 90 B1
Britton SD 27 E1
Broadalbin NY 80 C4
Broad Brook CT 150 A3
Broadmoor CA 259 B3
Broadus MT 25 E2
Broadview IL 203 C4
Broadview Hts. OH 204 F3
Broadwater Co. MT 15 F4
Broadway NC 123 D1
Broadway VA 102 C3
Brock Hall MD 144 C3
Brockport NY 78 C3
Brockton MA 151 D2
Brockton MT 17 E2
Brockway PA 92 B2
Brocton NY 78 A4
Brodhead KY 110 C1
Brodhead WI 74 B4
Brodheadsville PA 93 F3
Brogden NC 123 E1
Broken Arrow OK 106 A4
Broken Bow NE 35 D3
Broken Bow OK 116 B3
Bromley KY 204 A3
Bronson FL 138 C4
Bronson MI 90 A1
Bronte TX 58 C3
Bronwood GA 128 C3
Bronx Co. NY 148 B4
Brook IN 89 D3
Brookdale SC 122 A4
Brooke VA 103 D4
Brooke Co. WV 91 F4
Brookfield CT 148 C1
Brookfield IL 203 C5
Brookfield MA 150 B2
Brookfield MO 97 D1
Brookfield OH 276 C1
Brookfield WI 234 B2
Brookfield Ctr. CT 148 C1
Brookhaven MS 126 B4
Brookhaven NY 149 D4
Brookhaven PA 248 A4
Brookings OR 28 A2
Brookings SD 27 F3
Brookings Co. SD 27 F3
Brookland AR 108 A4
Brooklandville MD 193 C1
Brooklawn NJ 248 C4
Brooklet GA 130 B2
Brookline MA 151 D1
Brookline NH 95 D1
Brooklyn CT 150 B3
Brooklyn IL 256 C2
Brooklyn IN 99 F1
Brooklyn IA 87 E1
Brooklyn MI 90 B1
Brooklyn OH 204 E2
Brooklyn WI 74 B3
Brooklyn Ctr. MN 235 B1
Brooklyn Hts. OH 204 F2
Brooklyn Park MD 193 C4
Brooklyn Park MN 235 B1
Brookneal VA 112 C2
Brook Park OH 204 E3
Brookport IL 108 C2
Brooks GA 128 C1
Brooks KY 100 A4
Brooks ME 82 C2
Brooks Co. GA 137 F1
Brooks Co. TX 63 E3
Brookshire TX 61 F2
Brookside AL 195 D1
Brookside DE 146 B4
Brookside OH 91 F4
Brookside Vil. TX 220 C4
Brookston IN 89 E3
Brooksville FL 140 C1
Brooksville KY 100 C3
Brooksville MS 127 D1
Brookville IN 100 A2
Brookville NY 148 C4
Brookville OH 100 B1
Brookville PA 92 B2
Brookwood AL 127 F1
Broomall PA 146 C3
Broome Co. NY 93 F1
Broomfield CO 41 E1
Broomfield Co. CO 41 E1
Brooten MN 66 B3
Broussard LA 133 F2
Broward Co. FL 143 E1
Browerville MN 66 B2
Brown City MI 76 C3
Brown Co. IL 87 F4
Brown Co. IN 99 F2
Brown Co. KS 96 A1
Brown Co. MN 72 B1
Brown Co. NE 34 C1
Brown Co. OH 100 C3
Brown Co. SD 27 E1
Brown Co. TX 59 D3
Brown Co. WI 74 C1
Brown Deer WI 234 C1
Brownfield TX 58 A2
Browning MT 15 E2
Brownsboro TX 124 A3
Brownsburg IN 99 F1
Brownsdale MN 73 D2
Browns Mills NJ 147 D3
Brownstown IL 98 C2
Brownstown IN 99 F3
Browns Valley MN 27 F1
Brownsville CA 36 C1
Brownsville KY 109 F2
Brownsville MN 73 F2
Brownsville OR 20 B3
Brownsville PA 102 B1
Brownsville TN 118 C1
Brownsville TX 63 F4
Brownsville WI 74 C2
Brownton MN 66 C4
Brownville NY 79 E1
Brownville Jct. ME 84 C4
Brownwood TX 59 D4
Broxton GA 129 E4
Broyhill Park VA 270 B4
Bruce MS 118 C3
Bruce SD 27 F3
Bruce WI 67 F3
Bruceton TN 109 D4
Bruceville-Eddy TX 59 E4
Brule Co. SD 27 D4
Brundidge AL 128 B4
Brunson SC 130 B1
Brunswick GA 139 D1
Brunswick ME 82 B3
Brunswick MD 144 A2
Brunswick MO 97 D2
Brunswick OH 91 E2
Brunswick Co. NC 123 E3
Brunswick Co. VA 113 D3
Brush CO 33 F4
Brush Prairie WA 20 C1
Brushy OK 116 B1
Brusly LA 134 A2
Bryan OH 90 B2
Bryan TX 61 F1
Bryan Co. GA 130 B3
Bryan Co. OK 59 F1
Bryans Road MD 144 B4
Bryant AR 117 E2
Bryant SD 27 E3
Bryantville MA 151 E2
Bryn Athyn PA 248 D1
Bryn Mawr PA 146 C3
Bryson TX 59 D2
Bryson City NC 121 D1
Buchanan GA 120 B4
Buchanan MI 89 E1
Buchanan NY 148 B2
Buchanan VA 112 B1
Buchanan Co. IA 73 E4
Buchanan Co. MO 96 B1
Buchanan Co. VA 111 F2
Buchanan Dam TX 61 D1
Buchtel OH 101 E2
Buckeye AZ 54 B1
Buckeye Lake OH 101 D1
Buckfield ME 82 B2
Buckhannon WV 102 A2
Buckhead Ridge FL 141 E4
Buckingham PA 146 C2
Buckingham VA 113 D1
Buckingham Co. VA 113 D1
Buckland AK 154 B2
Buckley IL 89 D4
Buckley MI 69 F4
Buckley WA 12 C3
Bucklin KS 42 C4
Bucklin MO 97 D1
Buckner KY 100 A4
Buckner MO 96 C2
Bucks Co. PA 146 C1
Bucksport ME 83 D2
Bucksport SC 123 D4
Bucoda WA 12 C4
Bucyrus OH 90 C3
Buda IL 88 B2
Buda TX 61 E2
Budd Lake NJ 94 A4
Bude MS 126 A4
Buellton CA 52 A2
Buena NJ 147 D4
Buena WA 13 D4
Buena Park CA 228 E3
Buena Ventura Lakes FL 246 C5
Buena Vista CO 41 D2
Buena Vista GA 128 C2
Buena Vista MI 76 B2
Buena Vista VA 112 C1
Buena Vista Co. IA 72 B4
Buffalo IN 89 E3
Buffalo IA 87 F2
Buffalo KY 110 A1
Buffalo MN 66 C3
Buffalo MO 107 D1
Buffalo NY 78 B3
Buffalo ND 19 E4
Buffalo OK 50 C1
Buffalo SC 121 F2
Buffalo SD 25 F1
Buffalo TX 59 F4
Buffalo WV 101 E3
Buffalo WY 25 D3
Buffalo Ctr. IA 72 C2
Buffalo City WI 73 E1
Buffalo Co. NE 35 D4
Buffalo Co. SD 27 D3
Buffalo Co. WI 67 E4
Buffalo Grove IL 203 C2
Buffalo Lake MN 66 B4
Buford GA 120 C3
Buhl ID 30 C1
Buhl MN 64 C3
Buhler KS 43 E3
Buies Creek NC 123 D1
Bullard TX 124 A3
Bullhead SD 26 C1
Bullhead City AZ 46 B3
Bullitt Co. KY 99 F4
Bulloch Co. GA 130 B2
Bullock Co. AL 128 B3
Bulls Gap TN 111 D3
Bull Shoals AR 107 E3
Bull Valley IL 74 C4
Bulverde TX 61 D2
Buna TX 132 C2
Buncombe Co. NC 111 E4
Bunker Hill IL 98 B2
Bunker Hill IN 89 F3
Bunker Hill OR 20 A4
Bunker Hill WV 103 D2
Bunker Hill Vil. TX 220 B2
Bunkerville NV 46 B1
Bunkie LA 133 E1
Bunnell FL 139 E4
Buras LA 134 C4
Burbank CA 52 C2
Burbank IL 203 D5
Burbank WA 21 E1
Burden KS 43 F4
Bureau Co. IL 88 B2
Burgaw NC 123 E2
Burgettstown PA 91 F4
Burgin KY 110 B1
Burien WA 12 C3

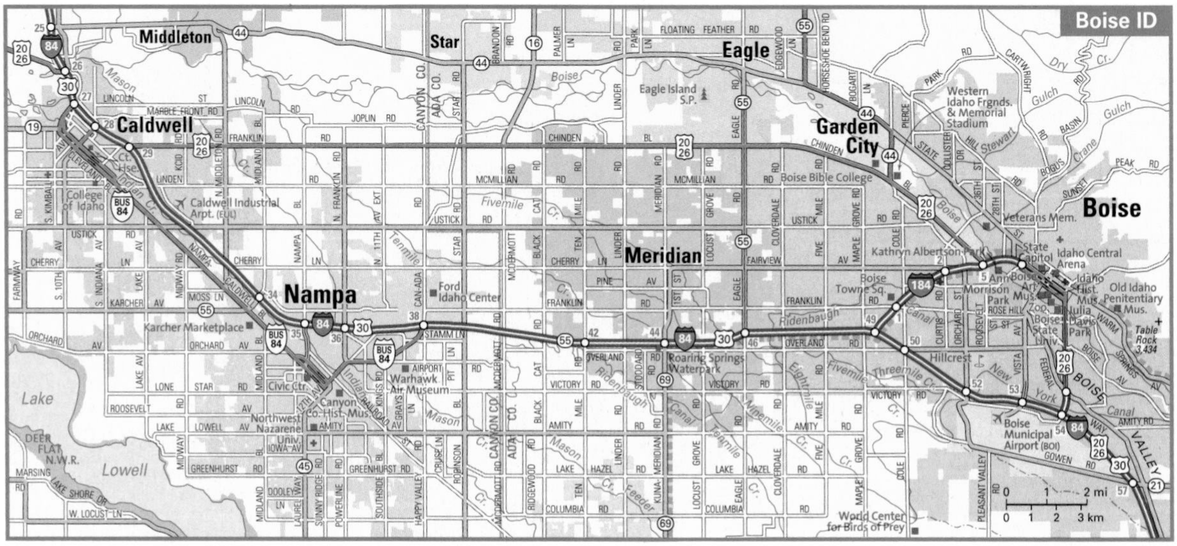
Boise ID
Middleton
Star
Eagle
Eagle Island S.P.
Caldwell
Garden City
Boise
Nampa
Meridian
Boise Bible College
Caldwell Industrial Arpt.
College of Idaho
Karcher Marketplace
Ford Idaho Center
Warhawk Air Museum
Roaring Springs Waterpark
Kathryn Albertson Park
Boise Towne Sq.
Idaho Central Arena
Hillcrest
Boise Municipal Airport (BOI)
World Center for Birds of Prey
Lake Lowell
Deer Flat N.W.R.
Table Rock 3,434
0 1 2 mi
0 1 2 3 km

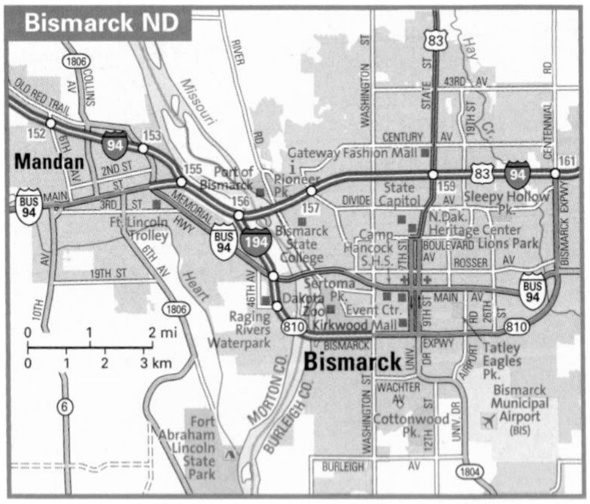
Bismarck ND
Mandan
Bismarck
Gateway Fashion Mall
State Capitol
Sleepy Hollow Pk.
Bismarck State College
Camp Hancock S.H.S.
Sertoma Pk.
Dakota Zoo
Raging Rivers Waterpark
Kirkwood Mall
Event Ctr.
Tatley Eagles Pk.
Bismarck Municipal Airport (BIS)
Cottonwood Pk.
Fort Abraham Lincoln State Park
Missouri
0 1 2 mi
0 1 2 3 km

Entries in **bold black** indicate counties or parishes.
Entries in **bold color** indicate cities with detailed inset maps.

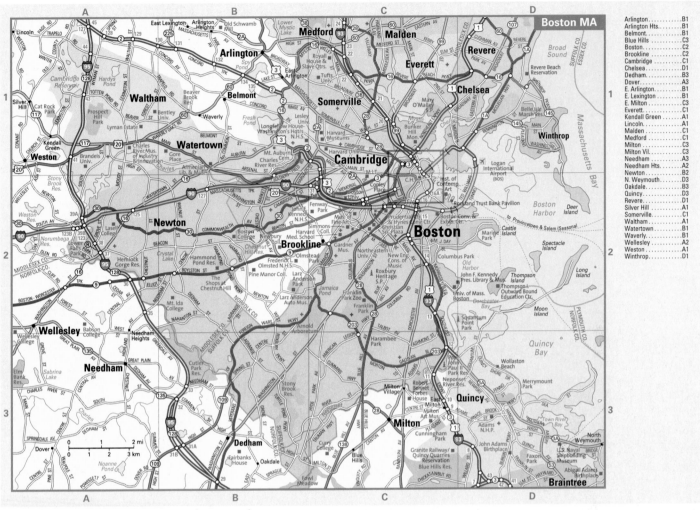

Boston MA

Arlington B1
Arlington Hts. B1
Belmont B1
Blue Hills C3
Boston C2
Brookline C2
Cambridge C1
Chelsea D1
Dedham B3
Dover A3
E. Arlington B1
E. Lexington B1
E. Milton C3
Everett C1
Kendall Green A1
Lincoln A1
Malden C1
Medford C1
Milton C3
Milton Vil. C3
Needham A3
Needham Hts. A2
Newton B2
N. Weymouth D3
Oakdale B3
Quincy D3
Revere D1
Silver Hill A1
Somerville C1
Waltham A1
Watertown B1
Waverly B1
Wellesley A2
Weston A1
Winthrop D1

Downtown Boston MA

POINTS OF INTEREST

200 Clarendon (Hancock Tower) E2	
Arlington Street Church E2	
Boch Center E2	
Boston Athenaeum E2	
Boston City Hall E2	
Boston Fire Museum F2	
Boston Massacre Monument E2	
Boston Massacre Site E2	
Boston Tea Party Ships & Museum F2	
Bunker Hill Pavilion F1	
Central Burying Ground E2	
Charles Street Meeting House E2	
Children's Museum F2	
Copp's Hill Burying Ground F1	
Custom House F2	
Emerson College E2	
Faneuil Hall F2	
Gibson House Museum E2	
Granary Burying Ground E2	
Harrison Gray Otis House E1	
Hatch Memorial Shell E1	
Hayden Mus. E1	
Hayden Planetarium E1	
JFK Federal Building F1	
King's Chapel F2	
Moakley Federal Courthouse F2	
Museum of Afro-American Hist. E1	
Museum of Science E1	
New England Aquarium F1	
North Station E1	
Old North Church F1	
Old South Meeting House E2	
Old State House F2	
Old West Church E1	
The Opera House E2	
Park Street Church E2	
Paul Revere House F1	
Paul Revere Mall F1	
Pierce Hichborn House F1	
Quincy Market F2	
St. Stephens Church F1	
Shaw Memorial E2	
South Station (Amtrak) F2	
State House E2	
Suffolk County Court House E2	
Suffolk Univ. E1	
TD Garden E1	
Thomas P. O'Neill Federal Building E1	
Trinity Church E2	
Tufts County Court House E2	
Tufts Medical School E2	
U.S.S. Constitution F1	

Burkburnett TX 59 D1	Burnsville MN 67 D4
Burke SD 35 D1	Burnsville MS 119 D2
Burke VA 144 B3	Burnsville NC 111 E4
Burke Co. GA 129 F1	Burnsville WV 102 A3
Burke Co. NC 111 F4	Burnt Hills NY 94 B1
Burke Co. ND 18 A1	Burr Oak MI 90 A1
Burkesville KY 110 A2	Burr Ridge IL 203 C5
Burkeville VA 113 D2	Burrton KS 43 E3
Burleigh Co. ND 18 C4	Burt IA 72 B3
Burleson TX 59 E3	Burt MI 76 B3
Burleson Co. TX 61 F1	**Burt Co. NE** 35 F2
Burley ID 31 D1	Burton MI 76 B3
Burley WA 262 A4	Burton OH 91 E2
Burlingame CA 259 B4	Burton SC 130 C2
Burlingame KS 96 A3	Burtonsville MD 144 B2
Burlingham NY 148 A1	Burwell NE 35 D2
Burlington CO 42 A2	Busby MT 25 D2
Burlington CT 94 C3	Bushnell FL 140 C1
Burlington IA 87 F3	Bushnell IL 88 A4
Burlington KS 96 A4	Bushyhead OK 106 A3
Burlington KY 100 B3	Butler AL 127 D3
Burlington MA 151 D1	Butler GA 129 D2
Burlington NJ 147 D2	Butler IN 90 A2
Burlington NC 112 C4	Butler KY 100 B3
Burlington ND 18 B2	Butler MO 96 B4
Burlington OH 101 D3	Butler NJ 148 A3
Burlington VT 81 D2	Butler OH 91 D4
Burlington WA 12 C2	Butler PA 92 A3
Burlington WI 74 C4	Butler WI 234 B1
Burlington WY 24 C3	Butler Beach FL 139 E3
Burlington Co. NJ 147 D3	**Butler Co. AL** 127 F3
Burlington Jct. MO 86 B4	**Butler Co. IA** 73 D4
Burlison TN 118 B1	**Butler Co. KS** 43 F4
Burnet TX 61 D1	**Butler Co. KY** 109 F2
Burnet Co. TX 61 D1	**Butler Co. MO** 108 A2
Burnett Co. WI 67 D2	**Butler Co. NE** 35 E3
Burnettown SC 121 E4	**Butler Co. OH** 100 B2
Burney CA 28 C4	**Butler Co. PA** 92 A3
Burnham IL 203 E6	Butner NC 112 C4
Burnham PA 93 D3	Butte MT 23 E1
Burning Sprs. KY 110 C2	Butte NE 35 D1
Burns OR 21 E4	**Butte Co. CA** 36 C1
Burns TN 109 E4	**Butte Co. ID** 23 D4
Burns WY 33 F3	**Butte Co. SD** 25 F2
Burns Flat OK 51 D3	Butte Falls OR 28 B3
Burns Harbor IN 89 E2	Butterfield MN 72 B1
Burnside KY 110 B2	Buttonwillow CA 45 D4

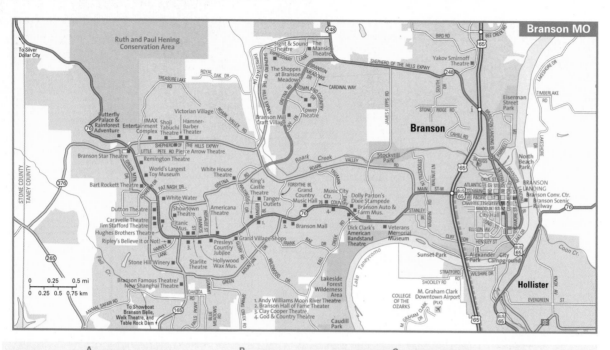

Figures after entries indicate page number and grid reference.

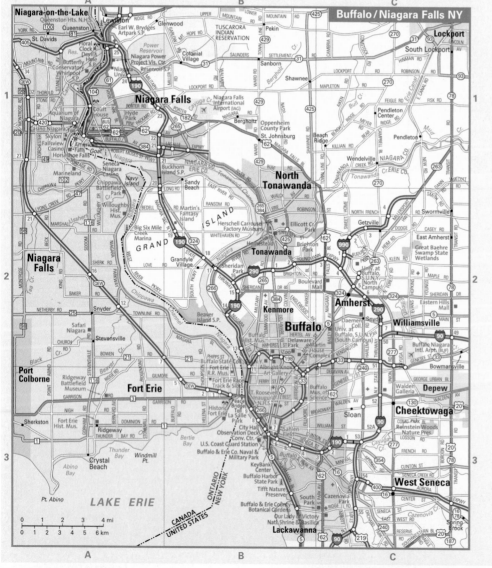

Buffalo / Niagara Falls NY

Amherst C2
Beach Ridge C1
Bergholtz B1
Bowmansville C2
Buffalo.............. B2
Cheektowaga........ C3
Colonial Vil. B1
Crystal Beach A3
Depew............... C3
E. Amherst C2
Ft. Erie.............. A3
Getzville C2
Glenwood........... A1
Grandyle Vil.......... B2
Kenmore............ B2
Lackawanna......... B3
Lewiston............ A1
Lockport C1
Niagara Falls, NY A1
Niagara Falls, ON A2
Niagara-on-the-Lake . A1
N. Tonawanda....... B1
Pekin................ B1
Pendleton........... C1
Pendleton Ctr. C1
Port Colborne........ A3
Queenston A1
Ridgeway A3
St. Davids........... A1
St. Johnsburg B1
Sanborn B1
Sandy Beach........ B1
Shawnee............ B1
Sherkston........... A3
Sloan............... C3
Snyder, NY.......... C2
Snyder, ON.......... A2
S. Lockport.......... C1
Spring Brook C3
Stevensville A2
Swormville C2
Tonawanda B2
Wendelville C1
W. Seneca C3
Williamsville......... C2

Butts Co. GA 129 D1
Buttzville NJ 93 F3
Buxton NC 115 F3
Buxton ND 19 E3
Buzzards Bay MA 151 E3
Byers CO 41 E1
Byers TX 59 D1
Byesville OH 101 E1
Byfield MA 151 F1
Byhalia MS 118 B2
Bylas AZ 55 E2
Byng OK 51 F3
Bynum AL 120 A4
Byram MS 126 B3
Byrdstown TN 110 B3
Byrnes Mill MO 98 A3
Byron CA 36 C4
Byron GA 129 D2
Byron IL 88 B1
Byron MI 76 B3
Byron MN 73 D1
Byron WY 24 C3
Byron Ctr. MI 75 F3

C

Cabarrus Co. NC 122 B1
Cabazon CA 53 D3
Cabell Co. WV 101 E3
Cabin John MD 270 B2
Cable WI 67 F1
Cabool MO 107 E2
Cabot AR 117 E2
Cabot VT 81 E2
Cache OK 51 D4
Cache Co. UT 31 F3
Cactus TX 50 A2
Cactus Flats AZ 55 E2
Caddo OK 51 F4
Caddo Co. OK 51 D3
Caddo Mills TX 59 F2
Caddo Par. LA 124 C2
Caddo Valley AR 117 D3
Cade LA 133 F2
Cadillac MI 75 F1
Cadiz KY 109 D2
Cadiz OH 91 F4
Cadott WI 67 F4
Cadyville NY 81 D1
Cahokia IL 98 A3
Cairo GA 137 E1
Cairo IL 108 C2
Cairo NE 35 D3
Cairo NY 94 B2
Cajah's Mtn. NC 111 F4
Calabasas CA 228 A2
Calabash NC 123 D4
Calais ME 83 E1
Calaveras Co. CA 36 C3
Calcasieu Par. LA 133 D2
Calcium NY 79 E1
Calcutta OH 91 F3
Caldwell AR 118 A1
Caldwell ID 22 B4
Caldwell KS 51 E1
Caldwell NJ 240 A2
Caldwell OH 101 F1
Caldwell TX 61 F1
Caldwell Co. KY 109 D2
Caldwell Co. MO 96 C1
Caldwell Co. NC 111 F4
Caldwell Co. TX 61 E2
Caldwell Par. LA 125 E3
Caledonia MI 75 F4
Caledonia MN 73 E2
Caledonia MS 119 D4
Caledonia NY 78 C3
Caledonia OH 90 C3
Caledonia Co. VT 81 E2
Calera AL 127 F1
Calera OK 59 F1
Calexico CA 53 E4
Calhan CO 41 E2
Calhoun GA 120 B3
Calhoun KY 109 E1
Calhoun MO 96 C3
Calhoun TN 120 C1
Calhoun City MS 118 C4
Calhoun Co. AL 120 A4
Calhoun Co. AR 117 E4
Calhoun Co. FL 137 D2
Calhoun Co. GA 128 C4
Calhoun Co. IL 98 A2
Calhoun Co. IA 72 B4
Calhoun Co. MI 90 A1
Calhoun Co. MS 118 C3
Calhoun Co. SC 122 B4
Calhoun Co. TX 61 F4
Calhoun Co. WV 101 F3
Calhoun Falls SC 121 E3
Calico Rock AR 107 E4
Caliente NV 38 C4
Califon NJ 104 C1
California MD 103 E4
California MO 97 E3
California PA 92 A4
California City CA 52 C1
Calimesa CA 229 K3
Calion AR 125 E1
Calipatria CA 53 E4
Calistoga CA 36 B3
Callahan FL 139 D2
Callahan Co. TX 58 C3
Callaway FL 136 C2

Entries in **bold black** indicate counties or parishes.
Entries in **bold color** indicate cities with detailed inset maps.

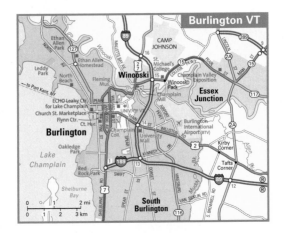

Canton OH

Cairo B1
Canton B1
Crystal Sprs. A1
Fairhope B1
Green A1
Hills and Dales A1
Louisville B1
Massillon A2
McDonaldsville A1
Meyers Lake B2
Middlebranch B1
N. Canton B1
Perry Hts. A2
Reedurban A2
Richville A2
Waco B2

Callaway NE 34 C3
Callaway Co. MO 97 E3
Calloway Co. KY 109 D3
Calmar IA 73 E3
Cal-Nev-Ari NV 46 B3
Calpella CA 36 A2
Calumet MI 65 F3
Calumet OK 51 E3
Calumet City IL 89 D2
Calumet Co. WI 74 C1
Calumet Park IL 203 E6
Calvert TX 61 F1
Calvert Beach MD 103 E3
Calvert City KY 109 D2
Calvert Co. MD 144 C4
Calvert Manor MD 144 B4
Calverton MD 144 B3
Calverton NY 149 E3
Calverton Park MO 256 B1
Camanche IA 88 A1
Camargo KY 100 C4
Camarillo CA 52 B2
Camas WA 20 C1
Camas Co. ID 22 C4
Cambria CA 44 B4
Cambria IL 108 C1
Cambria WI 74 B2
Cambria Co. PA 92 B4
Cambridge ID 22 B3
Cambridge IL 88 A2
Cambridge IA 86 C1
Cambridge MD 145 D4
Cambridge MA 151 D1
Cambridge MN 67 D3
Cambridge NE 34 C4
Cambridge NY 81 D4
Cambridge OH 101 E1
Cambridge VT 81 D1
Cambridge WI 74 B3
Cambridge City IN 100 A1
Cambridge Sprs. PA 92 A1
Camden AL 127 F3
Camden AR 117 D4
Camden DE 145 E2
Camden IN 89 E3
Camden ME 82 C2
Camden MI 90 A1
Camden NJ 146 C3
Camden NY 79 E3
Camden NC 115 E1
Camden OH 100 B1
Camden SC 122 B3
Camden TN 109 D4
Camden Co. GA 139 D1
Camden Co. MO 97 D4
Camden Co. NJ 147 D4
Camden Co. NC 115 E1
Camden Pt. MO 96 B2
Camdenton MO 97 D4
Cameron AZ 47 E2
Cameron LA 133 D3
Cameron MO 96 C1
Cameron SC 122 B4
Cameron TX 61 E1
Cameron WV 102 A1
Cameron WI 67 E3
Cameron Co. PA 92 C2
Cameron Co. TX 63 F4
Cameron Par. LA 133 D3
Camilla GA 129 D4
Camillus NY 79 D3
Camino CA 36 C2
Campbell CA 36 B4
Campbell FL 141 D2
Campbell MO 108 B3
Campbell OH 91 F3
Campbell TX 59 F2
Campbell Co. KY 100 B3
Campbell Co. SD 26 C1
Campbell Co. TN 110 C3
Campbell Co. VA 112 C2
Campbell Co. WY 25 E3
Campbell Hall NY 148 A1
Campbellsburg IN 99 F3
Campbellsburg KY 100 A3
Campbellsport WI 74 C2
Campbellsville KY 110 A1
Campbellton FL 136 C1
Camp Co. TX 124 B1
Camp Douglas WI 74 A1
Camp Hill AL 128 B2
Camp Hill PA 93 D4
Campion CO 33 E4
Campobello SC 121 F1
Camp Pt. IL 87 F4
Camp Sprs. MD 144 B3
Campti LA 125 D3
Campton KY 111 D1
Campton NH 81 F3
Camp Verde AZ 47 D4
Camp Wood TX 60 C2
Cana VA 112 A3
Canaan CT 94 B2
Canaan ME 82 C1
Canaan NH 81 E3
Canaan VT 81 F1
Canadian TX 50 C2
Canadian Co. OK 51 E3
Canajoharie NY 79 F3
Canal Fulton OH 91 E3
Canal Pt. FL 141 E4
Canal Winchester OH 101 D1
Canandaigua NY 78 C3
Canaseraga NY 78 C4
Canastota NY 79 E3
Canby MN 27 F3
Canby OR 20 C2
Candler Co. GA 129 F2
Cando ND 19 D2
Candor NY 93 E1
Candor NC 122 C1
Caney KS 51 F1
Caneyville KY 109 F1
Canfield OH 91 F3
Canisteo NY 78 C4
Canistota SD 27 E4
Cannelton IN 99 E4
Cannon Ball ND 18 C4
Cannon Beach OR 20 B1
Cannon Co. TN 110 A4
Cannondale CT 148 C2
Cannon Falls MN 67 D4
Cannonsburg KY 101 D4
Canon GA 121 E3
Canon City CO 41 E3
Canonsburg PA 92 A4
Canterbury DE 145 E3
Canton CT 94 C3
Canton GA 120 C3
Canton IL 88 A4
Canton KS 43 E3
Canton MA 151 D2
Canton MS 126 B2
Canton MO 87 F4
Canton NY 80 B2
Canton NC 121 E1
Canton OH 91 E3
Canton OK 51 D2
Canton PA 93 D2
Canton SD 27 F4
Canton TX 124 A2
Cantonment FL 135 F2
Cantua Creek CA 44 C3
Canute OK 51 D3
Canutillo TX 56 C3
Canyon TX 50 A3
Canyon City OR 21 F3
Canyon Co. ID 22 B4
Canyon Day AZ 55 E1
Canyon Lake CA 229 J5
Canyon Lake TX 61 D2
Canyonville OR 28 B1
Capac MI 76 C3
Cape Canaveral FL 141 E2
Cape Carteret NC 115 D4
Cape Charles VA 114 B3
Cape Coral FL 142 C1
Cape Cottage ME 251 B2
Cape Elizabeth ME 82 B3
Cape Girardeau MO 108 B1
Cape Girardeau Co. MO 108 B1
Cape May NJ 104 C4
Cape May Co. NJ 104 C4
Cape May C.H. NJ 104 C4
Cape Neddick ME 82 B4
Cape Porpoise ME 82 B4
Cape St. Claire MD 144 C3
Cape Vincent NY 79 D1
Capitan NM 57 D1
Capitola CA 44 B2
Capitol Hts. MD 270 E3
Capitol Park DE 145 E2
Capron IL 74 C4
Captain Cook HI 153 E3
Caraway AR 108 A4
Carbonado WA 12 C4
Carbon Cliff IL 208 C2
Carbon Co. MT 24 B2
Carbon Co. PA 93 F3
Carbon Co. UT 39 F1
Carbon Co. WY 33 D2
Carbondale CO 40 C2
Carbondale IL 108 C1
Carbondale KS 96 A3
Carbondale PA 93 F2
Carbon Hill AL 119 E4
Cardiff MD 146 A4
Cardiff NJ 147 F4
Cardington OH 90 C4
Cardwell MO 108 A4
Carefree AZ 54 C1
Carencro LA 133 F2
Carey ID 23 D4
Carey OH 90 C3
Caribou ME 85 D2
Caribou Co. ID 31 E1
Carleton MI 90 C1
Carlin NV 30 B4
Carlinville IL 98 B2
Carlisle AR 117 F2
Carlisle IN 99 E3
Carlisle IA 86 C2
Carlisle KY 100 C4
Carlisle MA 150 C1
Carlisle OH 100 B1
Carlisle PA 93 D4
Carlisle SC 122 A2
Carlisle Co. KY 108 C2
Carl Jct. MO 106 B2
Carlls Corner NJ 145 F1
Carlsbad CA 53 D4
Carlsbad NM 57 E3
Carlsborg WA 12 B2
Carlstadt NJ 240 C2
Carlton MN 64 C4
Carlton OR 20 B2
Carlton Co. MN 64 C4
Carlyle IL 98 B3
Carlyss LA 133 D2
Carmel IN 99 F1
Carmel ME 82 C1
Carmel NY 148 C1
Carmel-by-the-Sea CA 44 B3
Carmel Valley CA 44 B3
Carmen AZ 55 D4
Carmi IL 99 D4
Carmichael CA 255 C2
Carnation WA 12 C3
Carnegie OK 51 D3
Carnegie PA 250 A2
Carnesville GA 121 D3
Carney MD 193 D1
Carney OK 51 F2
Carneys Pt. NJ 146 B4
Caro MI 76 B2
Caroleen NC 121 F1
Carolina RI 150 C4
Carolina Beach NC 123 E3
Carolina Shores NC 123 D4
Caroline Co. MD 145 E4
Caroline Co. VA 103 E4
Carol Stream IL 203 B4
Carpendale WV 102 C1
Carpentersville IL 88 C1
Carpinteria CA 52 B2
Carrabelle FL 137 D3
Carrboro NC 112 C4
Carriere MS 134 C2
Carrier Mills IL 108 C1
Carrington ND 19 D3
Carrizo Sprs. TX 60 C4
Carrizozo NM 56 C1
Carroll IA 86 B1
Carroll Co. AR 107 D4
Carroll Co. GA 120 B4
Carroll Co. IL 88 B1
Carroll Co. IN 89 E4
Carroll Co. IA 86 B1
Carroll Co. KY 100 A3
Carroll Co. MD 144 B1
Carroll Co. MS 118 B4
Carroll Co. MO 96 C2
Carroll Co. NH 81 F3
Carroll Co. OH 91 E3
Carroll Co. TN 109 D4
Carroll Co. VA 112 A3
Carrollton AL 127 E1
Carrollton GA 120 B4
Carrollton IL 98 A2
Carrollton KY 100 A3
Carrollton MI 76 B2
Carrollton MS 118 B4
Carrollton MO 96 C2
Carrollton OH 91 F4
Carrollton TX 59 F2
Carrolltown PA 92 B4
Carroll Valley PA 103 D1
Carrollwood FL 266 C1
Carson CA 228 D4
Carson IA 86 A2
Carson ND 18 B4
Carson WA 20 C1
Carson City MI 76 A3
Carson City NV 37 D2
Carson Co. TX 50 B3
Carsonville MI 76 C2
Carter Co. KY 101 D4
Carter Co. MO 108 A2
Carter Co. MT 25 F2
Carter Co. OK 51 E4
Carter Co. TN 111 E3
Carteret NJ 147 E1
Carteret Co. NC 115 E4
Carter Lake IA 86 A2
Cartersville GA 120 B3
Carterville IL 108 C1
Carterville MO 106 B2
Carthage AR 117 E3
Carthage IL 87 F4
Carthage IN 100 A1
Carthage MS 126 C2
Carthage MO 106 C2
Carthage NY 79 E1
Carthage NC 122 C1
Carthage TN 110 A3
Carthage TX 124 C3
Caruthers CA 44 C3
Caruthersville MO 108 B4
Carver MA 151 E3
Carver MN 66 C4
Carver Co. MN 66 C4
Cary IL 88 C1
Cary MS 126 A2
Cary NC 112 C4
Caryville TN 110 C3
Casa Blanca AZ 54 C2
Casa Blanca NM 48 B3
Casa Grande AZ 54 C2
Cascade CO 41 E2
Cascade ID 22 B3
Cascade IA 73 F4
Cascade MD 103 D1
Cascade MT 15 F3
Cascade WI 74 C2
Cascade Co. MT 15 F3
Cascade Locks OR 20 C1
Casco ME 82 B3
Casco WI 69 D4
Caseville MI 76 C1
Casey IL 99 D2
Casey IA 86 B2
Casey Co. KY 110 B1
Caseyville IL 256 D2
Cashion OK 51 E2
Cashmere WA 13 D3
Cashton WI 73 F2
Casitas Sprs. CA 52 B2
Casper WY 33 D1
Caspian MI 68 C2
Cassadaga FL 141 D1
Cassadaga NY 78 A4
Cass City MI 76 C2
Cass Co. IL 98 A1
Cass Co. IN 89 F3
Cass Co. IA 86 B2
Cass Co. MI 89 F1
Cass Co. MN 64 B4
Cass Co. MO 96 C3
Cass Co. NE 35 F3
Cass Co. ND 19 E3
Cass Co. TX 124 C1
Casselberry FL 141 D1
Casselton ND 19 E4
Cassia Co. ID 31 D2
Cass Lake MN 64 A3
Cassopolis MI 89 F1
Cassville MO 106 C3
Cassville NJ 147 E2
Cassville WV 102 A1
Cassville WI 73 F4
Castaic CA 52 C2
Castalia OH 91 D2
Castanea PA 93 D3
Castile NY 78 B4
Castine ME 83 D2
Castleberry AL 127 F4
Castle Dale UT 39 F2
Castleford ID 30 C1
Castle Hayne NC 123 E3
Castle Hills TX 257 E2
Castle Rock CO 41 E2
Castle Rock WA 20 B1
Castle Shannon PA 250 B3
Castleton VT 81 D3
Castleton-on-Hudson NY 94 B1
Castle Valley UT 40 A3
Castlewood SD 27 F3
Castlewood VA 111 E2
Castro Co. TX 50 A4
Castro Valley CA 259 D3
Castroville CA 44 B2
Castroville TX 61 D3
Caswell Co. NC 112 C3
Catahoula Par. LA 125 F3
Catalina AZ 55 D3
Catasauqua PA 146 B1
Catawba NC 112 A4
Catawba SC 122 A2
Catawba Co. NC 122 A1
Catawba Island OH 91 D2
Catawissa PA 93 E3
Catharpin VA 144 A3
Cathcart WA 262 B2
Cathedral City CA 53 E3
Cathlamet WA 20 B1
Catlettsburg KY 101 D3
Catlin IL 89 D4
Cato NY 79 D3
Catonsville MD 144 C2
Catoosa OK 106 A3
Catoosa Co. GA 120 B2
Catron Co. NM 48 A4
Catskill NY 94 B2
Cattaraugus NY 78 A4
Cattaraugus Co. NY 78 A4
Cavalier ND 19 E1
Cavalier Co. ND 19 D1
Cave City AR 107 F4
Cave City KY 110 A2

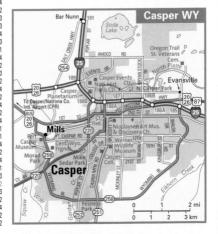

Figures after entries indicate page number and grid reference.

Cave Creek AZ 54 C1
Cave Jct. OR 28 B2
Cave Spr. GA 120 B3
Cave Spr. VA 112 B2
Cavetown MD 144 A1
Cawker City KS 43 D1
Cawood KY 111 D2
Cayce SC 122 A3
Cayucos CA 44 B4
Cayuga IN 99 E1
Cayuga NY 79 D3
Cayuga Co. NY 79 D4
Cayuga Hts. NY 79 D4
Cazenovia NY 79 E3
Cecil PA 92 A4
Cecil Co. MD 145 E1
Cecilia KY 110 A1
Cecilia LA 133 F2
Cecilton MD 145 E1
Cedar Bluff AL 120 A3
Cedar Bluff VA 111 F2
Cedar Bluffs NE 35 F3
Cedar Brook NJ 147 D4
Cedarburg WI 74 C3
Cedar City UT 39 D4
Cedar Co. IA 87 F1
Cedar Co. MO 106 C1
Cedar Co. NE 35 E1
Cedar Creek NE 35 F3
Cedar Crest NM 48 C3
Cedaredge CO 40 B2
Cedar Falls IA 73 D4
Cedar Fort UT 31 E4
Cedar Grove FL 136 C2
Cedar Grove MD 144 B2
Cedar Grove NJ 148 A3
Cedar Grove NM 48 C3
Cedar Grove WV 101 F4
Cedar Grove WI 75 D2
Cedar Hill MO 98 A4
Cedar Hill TX 207 C4
Cedar Hills OR 251 C2
Cedarhurst NY 241 G5
Cedar Key FL 138 B4
Cedar Lake IN 89 D2
Cedar Park TX 61 E1
Cedar Pt. NC 115 D4
Cedar Rapids IA 87 E1
Cedar Rapids NE 35 E3
Cedar Sprs. MI 75 F3
Cedartown GA 120 B3
Cedar Vale KS 51 F1
Cedarville AR 116 C1
Cedarville IL 74 B4
Cedarville NJ 145 F2
Cedarville OH 100 C1
Celebration FL 141 D1
Celeste TX 59 F2
Celina OH 90 B4
Celina TN 110 A3
Celina TX 59 F2
Celoron NY 92 B1
Cement OK 51 E3
Cement City MI 90 B1
Centennial CO 209 C4
Center CO 41 D4
Center MO 97 F1
Center NE 35 E1
Center ND 18 B3
Center TX 124 C3
Center Barnstead NH 81 F4

Centerbrook CT 149 E2
Centerburg OH 91 D4
Center City MN 67 D3
Centereach NY 149 D3
Centerfield UT 39 E2
Center Harbor NH 81 F3
Center Line MI 210 C2
Center Moriches NY 149 D4
Center Ossipee NH 81 F3
Center Pt. AL 119 F4
Center Pt. IA 87 E1
Center Pt. TX 61 D2
Centerport NY 148 C3
Centerton AR 106 C3
Centerton NJ 147 D3
Centertown KY 109 E1
Center Valley PA 146 C1
Centerville GA 129 D2
Centerville IN 100 B1
Centerville IA 87 D3
Centerville LA 133 F3
Centerville MA 151 F3
Centerville MO 108 A1
Centerville OH 100 B1
Centerville PA 92 A4
Centerville SC 121 E4
Centerville SD 35 F1
Centerville TN 109 E4
Centerville TX 124 A4
Centerville UT 31 E4
Central AZ 55 E2
Central SC 121 E2
Central TN 111 E3
Central Bridge NY 79 F4
Central City AR 116 C1
Central City CO 41 D1
Central City IL 98 C3
Central City IA 87 F1
Central City KY 109 E1
Central City NE 35 E3
Central City PA 92 B4
Central Falls RI 150 C3
Central High OK 51 E4
Central Islip NY 149 D4
Central Lake MI 69 F3
Central Park WA 12 B4
Central Pt. OR 28 B2
Central Square NY 79 D3
Central Valley (Woodbury) NY ... 148 B2
Central Vil. CT 150 B3
Central Vil. MA 151 D4
Centre AL 120 A3
Centre Co. PA 92 C3
Centre Hall PA 92 C3
Centreville AL 127 F1
Centreville IL 98 A3
Centreville MD 145 D3
Centreville MI 89 F1
Centreville MS 134 A1
Centreville VA 144 A3
Charleston AR 116 C1
Charleston IL 99 D2
Charleston ME 82 C1
Charleston MS 118 B3
Charleston MO 108 C2
Charleston TN 120 C1

Cerro Gordo Co. IA 73 D3
Chackbay LA 134 A3
Chadbourn NC 123 D3
Chadron NE 34 A1
Chaffee MO 108 B2
Chaffee Co. CO 41 D2
Chaffinville MA 150 B1
Chagrin Falls OH 91 E2
Chalco NE 35 F3
Chalfant PA 250 D2
Chalfont PA 146 C2
Challenge CA 36 C1
Challenge LA 36 C1
Challis ID 23 D3
Chalmers IN 89 E3
Chalmette LA 134 B3
Chama NM 48 C1
Chamberino NM 56 C3
Chamberlain SD 27 D4
Chamberlayne Farms VA ... 254 B3
Chambersburg PA 103 D1
Chambers Co. AL 128 B3
Chambers Co. TX 132 B3
Chamblee GA 120 C4
Chamisal NM 49 D2
Champaign IL 88 C4
Champaign Co. IL 88 C4
Champaign Co. OH 90 C4
Champion Hts. OH 91 F2
Champlain NY 81 D1
Chancellor SD 27 F4
Chandler AZ 54 C2
Chandler IN 99 E4
Chandler OK 51 F2
Chandler TX 124 A2
Chandler Hts. AZ 54 C2
Chandlerville IL 88 A4
Chanhassen MN 66 C2
Channahon IL 88 C2
Channel Lake IL 74 C4
Channelview TX 132 B3
Channing TX 50 A2
Chantilly VA 144 A3
Chanute KS 106 A1
Chaparral NM 56 C3
Chapel Hill NC 112 C4
Chapel Hill TN 109 F4
Chapin IL 98 A1
Chapin SC 122 A3
Chaplin KY 100 A4
Chapman KS 43 F2
Chapmanville WV 101 E4
Chappaqua NY 148 B3
Chappell NE 34 A3
Chardon OH 91 E2
Charenton LA 133 F3
Chariton IA 87 D3
Chariton Co. MO 97 D1
Charlack MO 256 B2
Charleroi PA 92 A4
Charles City IA 73 D3
Charles City VA 113 E1
Charles City Co. VA 113 E1
Charles Co. MD 144 B4
Charles Mix Co. SD 27 D4

Charleston UT 31 E4
Charleston WV 101 E4
Charleston Co. SC 131 D2
Charlestown IN 100 A3
Charlestown MD 145 D1
Charlestown NH 81 E4
Charlestown RI 150 C4
Charles Town WV 103 D2
Charlevoix MI 69 F3
Charlevoix Co. MI 70 B3
Charlotte MI 76 A4
Charlotte NC 122 A1
Charlotte TN 109 E4
Charlotte TX 61 D3
Charlotte Co. FL 140 C4
Charlotte Co. VA 113 D2
Charlotte C.H. VA 113 D2
Charlotte Hall MD 144 C4
Charlotte Harbor FL 140 C4
Charlottesville VA 102 C4
Charlton MA 150 B2
Charlton NY 94 B1
Charlton City MA 150 B2
Charlton Co. GA 138 C1
Charlton Depot MA 150 B2
Charter Oak CA 229 F2
Charter Oak IA 86 A1
Chartley MA 151 D2
Chase KS 43 D3
Chase City VA 113 D2
Chase Co. KS 43 F3
Chase Co. NE 34 B4
Chaska MN 66 C4
Chassahowitzka FL 140 B1
Chassell MI 65 F4
Chateaugay NY 80 C1
Chatcolet ID 72 E2
Chatfield MN 73 E1
Chatham MA 98 B1
Chatham LA 125 E2
Chatham MA 151 F3
Chatham NJ 148 A4
Chatham NY 94 B2
Chatham VA 112 C2
Chatham Co. GA 130 B3
Chatham Co. NC 112 C4
Chatom AL 127 D4
Chatsworth CA 228 C1
Chatsworth IL 88 C3
Chattahoochee FL 137 D1

Chattahoochee Co. GA 128 C2
Chattanooga OK 51 D4
Chattanooga TN 120 B2
Chattaroy WA 111 E1
Chatwood PA 146 B3
Chaumont NY 79 D1
Chauncey OH 101 E2
Chautauqua Co. KS 43 F4
Chautauqua Co. NY 78 A4
Chauvin LA 134 B4
Chaves Co. NM 57 E2
Chazy NY 81 D1
Cheatham Co. TN 109 E3
Cheat Lake WV 102 B1
Chebanse IL 89 D3
Cheboygan MI 70 C2
Cheboygan Co. MI 70 C3
Checotah OK 116 A1
Cheektowaga NY 78 B3
Chefornak AK 154 B3
Chehalis WA 12 B4
Chelan WA 13 E3
Chelan Co. WA 13 D2
Chelmsford MA 95 E1
Chelsea AL 127 F1
Chelsea MA 151 D1
Chelsea MI 76 B4
Chelsea NY 148 B1
Chelsea OK 106 A3
Chelsea VT 81 E3
Cheltenham MD 144 C4
Cheltenham PA 248 C2
Chelyan WV 101 F4
Chemung Co. NY 93 E1
Chenango Bridge NY 93 E1
Chenango Co. NY 79 E4
Chenequa WI 74 C3
Cheney KS 43 E4
Cheney WA 13 F3
Cheneyville LA 133 E1
Chenoa IL 88 C3
Chenoweth OR 21 D1
Chepachet RI 150 C3
Cheraw SC 122 C2
Cheriton VA 114 B3
Cherokee AL 119 D2
Cherokee IA 72 A4
Cherokee KS 106 B1
Cherokee OK 51 E1

Cherokee Co. AL 120 A3
Cherokee Co. GA 120 C3
Cherokee Co. IA 72 A3
Cherokee Co. KS 106 B2
Cherokee Co. NC 121 D1
Cherokee Co. OK 106 B4
Cherokee Co. SC 121 F2
Cherokee Co. TX 124 B2
Cherokee Forest SC 217 A1
Cherokee Vil. AR 107 F3
Cherry Co. NE 34 B1
Cherry Creek NY 78 A4
Cherryfield ME 83 E2
Cherry Grove OH 204 C3
Cherry Hill NJ 146 C3
Cherry Hills Vil. CO 209 C4
Cherryvale KS 106 A2
Cherry Valley AR 118 A1
Cherry Valley NY 79 F4
Cherryville NC 122 A1
Chesaning MI 76 B3
Chesapeake OH 101 D3
Chesapeake VA 113 F2
Chesapeake WV 101 F4
Chesapeake Beach MD 144 C4
Chesapeake City MD 145 E1
Chesapeake Ranch Estates MD 103 F4
Cheshire CT 149 D1
Cheshire MA 94 C1
Cheshire Co. NH 81 E4
Chesilhurst NJ 147 D4
Chesnee SC 121 F1
Chester CA 29 D4
Chester CT 149 E2
Chester IL 98 B4
Chester MD 145 D3
Chester MA 94 C2
Chester MT 15 F2
Chester NH 81 F4
Chester NJ 94 A4
Chester NY 148 A2
Chester PA 146 C3
Chester SC 122 A2
Chester VA 113 E1
Chester VT 81 E4
Chester WV 91 F3
Chester Co. PA 146 B3
Chester Co. SC 122 A2
Chester Co. TN 119 D1

Chester Depot VT 81 E4
Chesterfield IN 89 F4
Chesterfield MO 98 A3
Chesterfield SC 122 B2
Chesterfield VA 113 E1
Chesterfield Co. SC 122 B2
Chesterfield Co. VA 113 E1
Chester Hts. PA 146 B3
Chester Hill PA 92 C3
Chesterland OH 91 E2
Chesterton IN 89 E2
Chestertown MD 145 D2
Chestnut Hts. GA 121 D3
Chestnut Ridge NY 148 B3
Cheswick PA 250 D1
Cheswold DE 145 E2
Chetek WI 67 E3
Chetopa KS 106 B2
Chevak AK 154 B3
Cheverly MD 144 B3
Cheviot OH 100 B2
Chevy Chase MD 270 C2
Chevy Chase View MD 270 C1
Chewelah WA 13 F2
Cheyenne OK 50 C3
Cheyenne WY 33 E3
Cheyenne Co. CO 42 A2
Cheyenne Co. KS 42 B1
Cheyenne Co. NE 34 A3
Cheyenne Wells CO 42 A2
Cheyney PA 146 B3
Chicago IL 89 D1
Chicago Hts. IL 89 D2
Chicago Ridge IL 203 D5
Chichester NH 81 F4
Chickamauga GA 120 B2
Chickasaw AL 135 E1
Chickasaw Co. IA 73 E3
Chickasaw Co. MS 118 C4
Chickasha OK 51 E3
Chico CA 36 B1
Chico TX 59 E2
Chicopee MA 150 A2
Chicora PA 92 A3
Chicot Co. AR 125 F1
Chiefland FL 138 B4
Chilchinbito AZ 47 F1
Chilcoot CA 37 D1
Childersburg AL 128 A1
Childress TX 50 C4
Childress Co. TX 50 C4
Chilhowie VA 111 F2
Chillicothe IL 88 B3
Chillicothe MO 96 C1
Chillicothe OH 101 D2
Chillicothe TX 50 C4
Chillum MD 270 C2
Chiloquin OR 28 C1
Chilton WI 74 C1
Chilton Co. AL 127 F2
Chimayo NM 49 D2
China TX 132 C3
China Grove NC 122 B1
China Grove TX 61 D3
Chinchilla PA 261 E1
Chincoteague VA 114 C2
Chinle AZ 47 F2
Chino CA 229 G3
Chino Hills CA 229 G3
Chinook MT 16 B2
Chinook WA 20 B1
Chino Valley AZ 47 D4
Chipita Park CO 205 C1
Chipley FL 136 C1
Chippewa Co. MI 70 B1
Chippewa Co. MN 66 A3
Chippewa Co. WI 67 F3
Chippewa Falls WI 67 F4
Chippewa Lake OH 91 E3
Chisago City MN 67 D3
Chisago Co. MN 67 D3
Chisholm ME 82 B2
Chisholm MN 64 C3
Chittenango NY 79 E3
Chittenden VT 81 D3

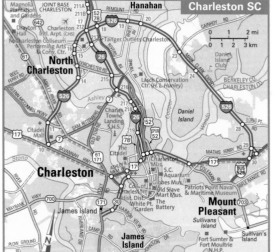

Charleston SC

Magnolia Plantation and Gardens · Joint Base Charleston · Hanahan · North Charleston · Charleston · Mount Pleasant · James Island

Cedar Rapids IA

Hiawatha · Marion · Cedar Rapids

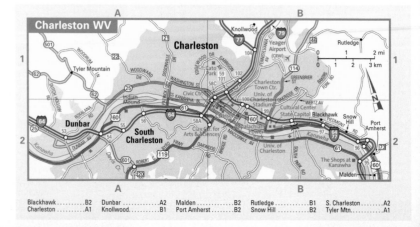

Charleston WV

Charleston · Knollwood · Rutledge · Tyler Mountain · Dunbar · South Charleston · Blackhawk · Snow Hill · Port Amherst · Malden

Blackhawk B2
Charleston A1
Dunbar A2
Knollwood B1
Malden B2
Port Amherst B2
Rutledge B1
Snow Hill B2
S. Charleston A2
Tyler Mtn. A1

Entries in **bold black** indicate counties or parishes.
Entries in **bold color** indicate cities with detailed inset maps.

Chittenden Co. VT	81 D2	Chubbuck ID	31 E1
Chocowinity NC	115 D3	Chugwater WY	33 E2
Choctaw NC	51 E3	Chuichu AZ	54 C2
Choctaw Co. AL	127 E3	Chula Vista CA	53 D4
Choctaw Co. MS	126 C1	Chuluota FL	141 D1
Choctaw Co. OK	116 A3	Church Hill MD	145 D2
Choteau MT	15 E3	Church Hill TN	111 E3
Choudrant LA	125 E2	Churchill OH	276 C2
Chouteau OK	106 A3	Churchill PA	250 D2
Chouteau Co. MT	15 F2	**Churchill Co. NV**	37 F1
Chowan Co. NC	113 F4	Church Pt. LA	133 E2
Chowchilla CA	44 C2	Church Rock NM	48 A3
Chrisman IL	99 D1	Churchton MD	144 C3
Chrisney IN	99 E4	Churchtown NJ	146 B4
Christiana PA	146 A3	Churchville MD	145 D1
Christian Co. IL	98 B1	Churchville NY	78 C3
Christian Co. KY	109 E2	Churubusco IN	90 A2
Christian Co. MO	107 D2	Cibecue AZ	55 D1
Christiansburg OH	90 B4	**Cibola Co. NM**	48 A4
Christiansburg VA	112 A2	Cibolo TX	257 F1
Christmas FL	141 D1	Cicero IL	89 D1
Christopher IL	98 C4	Cicero IN	89 F4
Chualar CA	44 B3	Cimarron KS	42 C4
		Claiborne Co. MS	126 A3

Cimarron NM	49 E1	**Claiborne Co. TN**	110 C3
Cimarron Co. OK	50 A1	**Claiborne Par. LA**	125 D2
Cincinnati OH	100 B2	Clairton PA	92 A4
Cinnaminson NJ	146 B3	Clallam Bay WA	12 B2
Circle MT	17 E3	**Clallam Co. WA**	12 B2
Circle Pines MN	235 C1	Clancy MT	15 E4
Circleville NY	148 A1	Clara City MN	66 B4
Circleville OH	101 D1	Clare MI	76 A2
Circleville UT	39 E3	**Clare Co. MI**	76 A1
Cisco TX	59 D3	**Clark Co. AR**	117 D4
Cisne IL	98 C3	**Clark Co. ID**	23 E3
Citra FL	138 C4	**Clark Co. IL**	99 D2
Citrus Co. FL	140 B1	**Clark Co. IN**	100 A3
Citrus Hts. CA	36 C3	**Clark Co. KS**	42 C4
Citrus Park FL	266 B1	**Clark Co. KY**	100 B4
Citrus Sprs. FL	138 C4	**Clark Co. MO**	87 E3
City View SC	217 A2	**Clark Co. NV**	46 A1
Clackamas OR	251 D3	**Clark Co. OH**	100 C1
Clackamas Co. OR	20 C2	**Clark Co. SD**	27 E2
Claflin KS	43 D3	**Clark Co. WA**	20 C1
Claiborne Co. MS	126 A3	**Clark Co. WI**	67 F4
		Clarkdale AZ	47 D4
		Clarendon TX	50 B3

Claiborne Co. TN	110 C3	**Clarendon Co. SC**	122 B4
Claiborne Par. LA	125 D2	Clarendon Hills IL	203 C5
Clairton PA	92 A4	Clarinda IA	86 B3
Clallam Bay WA	12 B2	Clarion IA	72 C4
Clallam Co. WA	12 B2	Clarion PA	92 B2
Clancy MT	15 E4	**Clarion Co. PA**	92 A3
Clara City MN	66 B4	Clarissa MN	66 B2
Clare MI	76 A2	Clark NJ	147 E1
Clare Co. MI	76 A1	Clark SD	27 E2
Clark Co. AR	117 D4	Clarkdale GA	190 B3
Clark Co. ID	23 E3	Clarksboro NJ	146 C3
Clark Co. IL	99 D2	Clarksburg MD	144 B2
Clark Co. IN	100 A3	Clarksburg WV	102 A2
Clark Co. KS	42 C4	Clarksdale MS	118 A3
Clark Co. KY	100 B4	Clarks Green PA	261 E1
Clark Co. MO	87 E3	Clarks Grove MN	72 C2
Clark Co. NV	46 A1	Clark Hill SC	89 E4
Clark Co. OH	100 C1	Clarkson KY	109 F1
Clark Co. SD	27 E2	Clarkson NE	35 F2
Clark Co. WA	20 C1	Clarks Summit PA	93 F2
Clark Co. WI	67 F4	Clarkston GA	190 E3
Clarkdale AZ	47 D4	Clarkston UT	31 E2
Clarendon TX	50 B3	Clarkston WA	14 B4
		Clarksville AR	117 D1
		Clarksville DE	145 F4

Clarendon Co. SC	122 B4	**Clarke Co. GA**	121 D4
Clarendon Hills IL	203 C5	**Clarke Co. IA**	86 C3
Clarinda IA	86 B3	**Clarke Co. MS**	127 D3
Clarion IA	72 C4	**Clarke Co. VA**	103 D2
Clarion PA	92 B2	Clarkesville GA	121 D2
Clarion Co. PA	92 A3	Clarkfield MN	66 A4
Clarissa MN	66 B2	Clark Fork ID	14 B2
Clark NJ	147 E1	Clarks LA	125 E3
Clark SD	27 E2	Clarksboro NJ	146 C3
Clarkdale GA	190 B3	Clarksburg MD	144 B2
Clarksboro NJ	146 C3	Clarksburg WV	102 A2
Clarksburg MD	144 B2	Clarksdale MS	118 A3
Clarksburg WV	102 A2	Clarks Green PA	261 E1
Clarksdale MS	118 A3	Clarks Grove MN	72 C2
Clarks Green PA	261 E1	Clark Hill SC	89 E4
Clarks Grove MN	72 C2	Clarkson KY	109 F1
Clark Hill SC	89 E4	Clarkson NE	35 F2
Clarkson KY	109 F1	Clarks Summit PA	93 F2
Clarkson NE	35 F2	Clarkston GA	190 E3
Clarks Summit PA	93 F2	Clarkston UT	31 E2
Clarkston GA	190 E3	Clarkston WA	14 B4
Clarkston UT	31 E2	Clarksville AR	117 D1
Clarkston WA	14 B4	Clarksville DE	145 F4
Clarksville AR	117 D1	
Clarksville DE	145 F4	**Clarke Co. AL**	127 E4

Clarke Co. GA	121 D4	Clay Co. KS	43 E2
Clarke Co. IA	86 C3	**Clay Co. KY**	110 C2
Clarke Co. MS	127 D3	**Clay Co. MN**	19 F4
Clarke Co. VA	103 D2	**Clay Co. MS**	118 C4
Clarkesville GA	121 D2	**Clay Co. MO**	96 B2
Clarkfield MN	66 A4	**Clay Co. NE**	35 E4
Clark Fork ID	14 B2	**Clay Co. NC**	121 D1
Clarks LA	125 E3	**Clay Co. SD**	35 F1
Clarksboro NJ	146 C3	**Clay Co. TN**	110 A3
Clarksburg MD	144 B2	**Clay Co. TX**	59 D1
Clarksburg WV	102 A2	**Clay Co. WV**	101 F3
Clarksdale MS	118 A3	Clayhatchee AL	128 B4
Clarks Green PA	261 E1	Claymont DE	146 B3
Clarks Grove MN	72 C2	Claypool AZ	55 D1
Clark Hill SC	89 E4	Claypool IN	89 F2
Clarkson KY	109 F1	Claypool Hill VA	111 F2
Clarkson NE	35 F2	Claysburg PA	92 C4
Clarks Summit PA	93 F2	Claysville PA	91 F4
Clarkston GA	190 E3	Clayton AL	128 B3
Clarkston UT	31 E2	Clayton CA	259 E2
Clarkston WA	14 B4	Clayton DE	145 E2
Clarksville AR	117 D1	Clayton GA	121 D2
Clarksville DE	145 F4	Clayton IL	87 F4
		Clayton IN	99 F1
Clarke Co. AL	127 E4	Clayton LA	125 F4
		Clayton MO	98 A3
		Clayton NJ	146 C3
		Clayton NM	49 F1
		Clayton NY	79 E1
		Clayton NC	113 D4
		Clayton OH	100 B1
		Clayton OK	116 A2
		Clayton Co. GA	120 C4
		Clayton Co. IA	73 E3
		Clearbrook MN	64 A3
		Clear Creek IN	99 F2
		Clear Creek Co. CO	41 D1
		Clearfield PA	92 C3
		Clearfield UT	31 E3
		Clearfield Co. PA	92 C3
		Clearlake CA	36 B2
		Clear Lake IA	72 C3
		Clear Lake SD	27 F2
		Clear Lake WA	12 C2
		Clear Lake WI	67 E3
		Clearlake Oaks CA	36 B2
		Clear Lake Shores TX	132 B3
		Clear Spr. MD	103 D1
		Clearview WV	91 F4
		Clearwater FL	140 B3
		Clearwater KS	43 E4
		Clearwater MN	66 C3
		Clearwater SC	121 F4
		Clearwater Co. ID	14 C4
		Clearwater Co. MN	64 A3
		Cleaton KY	109 E2
		Cleburne TX	59 E3
		Cleburne Co. AL	120 B4
		Cleburne Co. AR	107 E4
		Cle Elum WA	13 D3
		Clementon NJ	146 C3
		Clemmons NC	112 A4
		Clemson SC	121 E2
		Clendenin WV	101 F3
		Cleona PA	93 E4
		Cleora OK	106 B3
		Clermont FL	140 C1
		Clermont IN	99 F1
		Clermont IA	73 E3
		Clermont Co. OH	100 C2
		Cleveland AL	119 F3
		Cleveland FL	140 C4
		Cleveland GA	121 D2
		Cleveland MN	72 C1
		Cleveland MS	118 A4
		Cleveland MO	96 B3
		Cleveland NY	79 E3
		Cleveland NC	112 A4
		Cleveland OH	91 E2
		Cleveland OK	51 E2
		Cleveland TN	120 B1
		Cleveland TX	132 B2
		Cleveland UT	39 F2
		Cleveland WI	75 D2
		Cleveland Co. AR	117 E4
		Cleveland Co. NC	121 F1
		Cleveland Co. OK	51 E3
		Cleveland Hts. OH	91 E2
		Clever MO	107 D2
		Cleves OH	100 B2
		Clewiston FL	141 E4
		Cliffside NC	121 F1
		Cliffside Park NJ	148 B3
		Cliffwood Beach NJ	147 E1
		Clifton AZ	55 E2
		Clifton CO	40 B2
		Claverack NY	94 B2
		Clifton ID	31 E2
		Claxton GA	130 A3
		Clifton IL	89 D3
		Clay AL	119 F4
		Clifton KS	43 E1
		Clay KY	109 D1
		Clifton NJ	148 B3
		Clay WV	101 F3
		Clifton TN	119 D1
		Clay Ctr. KS	43 E2
		Clifton Forge VA	112 B1
		Clay Ctr. NE	35 E4
		Clifton Hts. PA	248 B3
		Clay City IL	99 D3
		Clifton Park NY	94 B1
		Clay City IN	99 E2
		Clifton Sprs. NY	78 C3
		Clay City KY	110 C1
		Climax MI	75 F4
		Claycomo MO	224 C2
		Clinchco VA	111 E2
		Clay Co. AL	128 B1
		Clinch Co. GA	138 C1
		Clay Co. AR	108 A3
		Clint TX	56 C4
		Clay Co. FL	139 D2
		Clinton AR	117 D1
		Clay Co. GA	128 C4
		Clinton CT	149 E2
		Clay Co. IL	98 C3
		Clinton IL	88 C4
		Clay Co. IN	99 E2
		Clinton IN	99 E1
		Clay Co. IA	72 B3

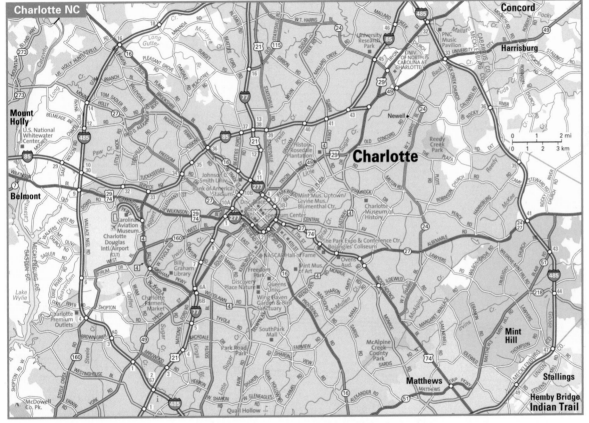

Charlotte NC

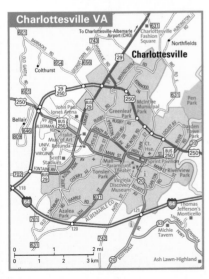

Charlottesville VA

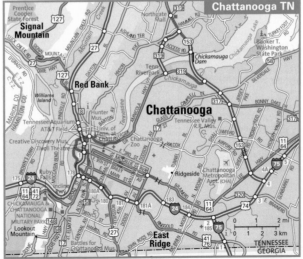

Chattanooga TN

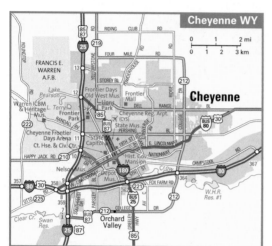

Cheyenne WY

Clinton IA 88 A1
Clinton KY 108 C3
Clinton LA 134 A1
Clinton ME 82 C2
Clinton MD 144 B4
Clinton MA 150 C1
Clinton MI 90 B1
Clinton MS 126 B2
Clinton MO 96 C4
Clinton MT 15 D4
Clinton NJ 147 D1
Clinton NY 79 E3
Clinton NC 123 E2
Clinton OH 91 E3
Clinton OK 51 D3
Clinton SC 121 F3
Clinton TN 110 C4
Clinton UT 244 A2
Clinton WA 12 C2
Clinton WI 74 B4
Clinton Co. IL 98 B3
Clinton Co. IN 89 E4
Clinton Co. IA 88 A1
Clinton Co. KY 110 B2
Clinton Co. MI 76 A3
Clinton Co. MO 96 B1
Clinton Co. NY 80 C2
Clinton Co. OH 100 C2
Clinton Co. PA 92 C2
Clintondale NY 148 B1
Clintonville WI 68 C4
Clintwood VA 111 F2
Clio AL 128 B4
Clio MI 76 B3
Clio SC 122 C2
Closter NJ 148 B3
Cloud Co. KS 43 E2
Cloudcroft NM 56 C2
Clover SC 122 A1
Cloverdale CA 36 A2
Cloverdale IN 99 E1
Cloverdale VA 112 B1
Cloverleaf TX 220 D1
Cloverport KY 109 F1
Clovis CA 44 C2
Clovis NM 49 F4
Clute TX 132 A4
Clyde KS 43 E1
Clyde NY 79 D3
Clyde NC 121 E1
Clyde OH 90 C2
Clyde TX 58 C3
Clyde Hill WA 262 B3
Clyde Park MT 23 F1
Clymer PA 92 B3
Coachella CA 53 E3
Coahoma TX 58 B3
Coahoma Co. MS 118 A4
Coal City IL 88 C2
Coal City WV 111 F1
Coal Co. OK 51 F4
Coal Creek CO 41 E3
Coaldale PA 93 E3
Coalfield WV 101 F4
Coalgate OK 51 F4
Coal Grove OH 101 D3
Coal Hill AR 116 C1
Coaling AL 127 F1
Coalmont TN 120 A1
Coal Mtn. GA 120 C3
Coal Run Vil. KY 111 E1
Coal Valley IL 88 A2
Coalville UT 31 F1
Coatesville IN 99 E1
Coatesville PA 146 B3
Coats NC 123 D1
Cobb CA 36 B2
Cobb Co. GA 120 C4

Cobb Island MD 103 E4
Cobden IL 108 C1
Cochise Co. AZ 55 E3
Cochiti NM 48 C3
Cochran Co. TX 57 F1
Cochranton PA 92 A2
Cochranville PA 146 B3
Cocke Co. TN 111 D4
Cockeysville MD 144 C1
Cockrell Hill TX 207 D2
Cocoa FL 141 E2
Cocoa Beach FL 141 E2
Cocoa West FL 232 A2
Coconino Co. AZ 47 D3
Coconut Creek FL 233 B1
Codington Co. SD 27 E2
Cody WY 24 B3
Coffee Co. AL 128 A4
Coffee Co. GA 129 E2
Coffee Co. TN 120 A1
Coffeen IL 98 B2
Coffeeville MS 118 B4
Coffeyville KS 106 A2
Coffey Co. KS 96 A4
Coggon IA 73 E4
Cohasset MA 151 E1
Cohasset MN 64 B3
Cohocton NY 78 C4
Cohoes NY 94 B1
Cohutta GA 120 B2
Cokato MN 66 C3
Cokeburg PA 92 A4
Coke Co. TX 58 B4
Coker AL 127 E1
Cokeville WY 31 F2
Colbert Co. AL 119 E2
Colbert GA 121 D3
Colbert OK 59 F1
Colby KS 42 B2
Colby WI 68 A4
Colchester CT 149 E1
Colchester IL 87 E4
Colchester VT 81 D2
Colcord OK 106 B3
Colden NY 78 B4
Cold Spr. KY 204 B3
Cold Spr. MN 66 C3
Cold Spr. NY 148 B1
Coldspring TX 132 B2
Coldwater KS 43 D4
Coldwater MI 90 A1
Coldwater MS 118 B3
Coldwater OH 90 A4
Cole OK 51 E3
Colebrook NH 81 F1
Cole Camp MO 97 D3
Cole Co. MO 97 E3
Coleman FL 140 C1
Coleman MI 76 A2
Coleman TX 58 C3
Coleman WI 68 C3
Coleman Co. TX 58 C3
Coleraine MN 64 B3
Coleridge NE 35 E1
Coles Co. IL 99 D1
Colesville MD 144 B2
Colfax CA 36 C2
Colfax IL 88 C4
Colfax IN 89 E4
Colfax IA 87 D2
Colfax LA 125 E4
Colfax WA 14 A4
Colfax WI 67 E3
Colfax Co. NE 35 E3
Colfax Co. NM 49 E1

Collbran CO 40 B2
College AK 154 C2
Collegedale TN 120 B2
College Park GA 120 C4
College Park MD 270 E1
College Place WA 21 F1
College Sta. TX 61 F1
Collegeville IN 89 E3
Collegeville PA 146 B2
Colleton Co. SC 130 B2
Colleyville TX 59 E2
Collier Co. FL 143 D1
Collierville TN 118 B2
Collin Co. TX 59 F2
Collingdale PA 248 B4
Collingswood NJ 146 C3
Collingsworth Co. TX 50 B3
Collins IA 87 D1
Collins MS 126 C4
Collins Park DE 274 D3
Collinsville AL 120 A3
Collinsville IL 98 B3
Collinsville MS 127 D2
Collinsville OK 106 A3
Collinsville TX 59 F1
Collinsville VA 112 B3
Collinwood TN 119 E1
Colma CA 259 B3
Colman SD 27 F4
Colmar PA 146 C2
Colmar Manor MD 270 E3
Colmesneil TX 132 C1
Colo IA 87 D1
Cologne MN 66 C4
Cologne NJ 147 D3
Coloma MI 89 F1
Coloma WI 74 B1
Colome SD 34 C1
Colon MI 90 A1
Colona IL 88 A2
Colonia NJ 147 E1
Colonial Beach VA 103 E4
Colonial Hts. TN 111 E4
Colonial Hts. VA 113 E2
Colonial Park PA 218 C1
Colonie NY 94 B1
Colony KS 96 A4
Colquitt Co. GA 137 F1
Colstrip MT 25 D1
Colton CA 229 J2
Colton SD 27 F4
Columbia AL 128 B4
Columbia IL 37 D3
Columbia CT 149 F1
Columbia IL 98 A3
Columbia KY 110 B2
Columbia LA 125 F3
Columbia MD 144 B2
Columbia MS 126 B4
Columbia MO 97 E3
Columbia NC 113 F4
Columbia PA 103 E1
Columbia SC 122 A3
Columbia TN 119 F1
Columbia Beach MD 144 C4
Columbia City IN 89 F2
Columbia City OR 20 C1
Columbia Co. AR 125 D1
Columbia Co. FL 138 C2

Collinsville IL 98 B3
Collinsville MS 127 D2
Collinsville OK 106 A3
Collinsville TX 59 F1
Collinsville VA 112 B3
Collinwood TN 119 E1
Colma CA 259 B3
Colman SD 27 F4
Colmar PA 146 C2
Colmar Manor MD 270 E3
Colmesneil TX 132 C1
Colo IA 87 D1
Cologne MN 66 C4
Cologne NJ 147 D3
Coloma MI 89 F1
Coloma WI 74 B1
Colome SD 34 C1
Colon MI 90 A1
Colona IL 88 A2
Colonia NJ 147 E1
Colonial Beach VA 103 E4
Colonial Hts. TN 111 E4
Colonial Hts. VA 113 E2
Colonial Park PA 218 C1
Colonie NY 94 B1
Colony KS 96 A4
Colquitt Co. GA 137 F1
Colstrip MT 25 D1
Colton CA 229 J2
Colton SD 27 F4
Columbia AL 128 B4
Columbia IL 37 D3
Columbia CT 149 F1
Columbia IL 98 A3
Columbia KY 110 B2
Columbia LA 125 F3
Columbia MD 144 B2
Columbia MS 126 B4
Columbia MO 97 E3
Columbia NC 113 F4
Columbia PA 103 E1
Columbia SC 122 A3
Columbia TN 119 F1
Columbia Beach MD 144 C4
Columbia City IN 89 F2
Columbia City OR 20 C1
Columbia Co. AR 125 D1
Columbia Co. FL 138 C2

Columbia Co. GA 121 F4
Columbia Co. NY 94 B2
Columbia Co. OR 20 B1
Columbia Co. PA 93 E3
Columbia Co. WA 13 F4
Columbia Co. WI 74 B3
Columbia Falls MT 15 D2
Columbia Hts. MN 235 C2
Columbiana AL 127 F1
Columbiana OH 91 F3
Columbiana Co. OH 91 F3
Columbiaville MI 76 B3
Columbiaville NY 94 B2
Columbine Valley CO 209 B4
Columbus IN 99 F2
Columbus KS 106 B2
Columbus MS 119 D4

CHICAGO MAP INDEX

Addison C4
Algonquin A2
Alsip D6
Arlington Hts. C2
Aurora A5
Bannockburn C1
Barrington A2
Barrington Hills A2
Bartlett A4
Batavia A4
Bedford Park D5
Bellwood C4
Bensenville C4
Berkeley C4
Berwyn C4
Bloomingdale B3
Blue Island D6
Bolingbrook B6
Bridgeview C4
Broadview C4
Brookfield C4
Buffalo Grove C2
Burbank C5
Burnham E6
Burr Ridge C4
Burtons Bridge A1
Calumet City E6
Calumet Park E6
Carol Stream B4
Carpentersville A2
Cary A1
Chicago E4
Chicago Ridge D5
Cicero D4
Clarendon Hills C5
Colfax C3
Countryside C5
Crest Hill B6
Crestwood D6
Crystal Lake A1
Darien C5
Deerfield C2
Deer Park B2
Des Plaines C3
Diamond Lake B1
Dixmoor D6
Dolton E6
Downers Grove B5
E. Dundee A2
Elgin A3
Elk Grove Vil. A3

Elmhurst C4
Elmwood Park D4
Evanston D3
Evergreen Park D5
Forest Lake B1
Forest Park D4
Forest View D5
Fox River Grove A2
Franklin Park C4
Geneva A4
Glencoe D2
Glendale Hts. B4
Glen Ellyn B4
Glenview D2
Golf D3
Grayslake B1
Green Oaks C1
Hanover Park B3
Harvey E6
Harwood Hts. D3
Hawthorn Woods B2
Hazel Crest E6
Hickory Hills D5
Highland Park D2
Highwood D2
Hillside C4
Hinsdale C5
Hodgkins C5
Hoffman Estates A3
Holiday Hills A1
Homer Glen C6
Hometown D5
Indian Creek B1
Indian Head Park C5
Inverness B2
Island Lake A1
Itasca B4
Ivanhoe B1
Justice C5
Kenilworth D2
Kildeer B2
Knollwood C1
La Grange C4
La Grange Park C4
Lake Barrington A2
Lake Bluff C1
Lake Forest C1
Lake in the Hills A2
Lakemoor A1
Lake Zurich B2
Lemont B6

Libertyville C1
Lincolnshire C2
Lincolnwood C2
Lisle B4
Lockport B6
Lombard B4
Long Grove B2
Lyons C4
Markham D6
Maywood D4
McCook C5
McHenry A1
Medinah B3
Melrose Park C4
Merrionette Park D6
Mettawa C2
Midlothian D6
Montgomery A5
Morton Grove D3
Mount Prospect C3
Mundelein B1
Naperville B5
Niles D3
Norridge D3
N. Aurora A5
N. Barrington B2
Northbrook D2
N. Chicago C1
Northfield D2
Northlake C4
N. Riverside D4
Oak Brook C4
Oakbrook Terrace C4
Oak Forest D6
Oak Lawn D5
Oak Park D4
Oakwood Hills A1
Orland Hills C6
Orland Park C6
Oswego A5
Palatine B2
Palos Hts. D5
Palos Hills D5
Palos Park C6
Park Ridge C3
Phoenix D6
Plainfield A6
Port Barrington A1
Posen D6
Prairie Grove A1
Prospect Hts. C2

Riverdale E6
River Forest D4
River Grove D4
Riverside D4
Riverwoods C2
Robbins D6
Rolling Meadows B3
Romeoville B6
Rondout C1
Roselle B3
Rosemont C3
St. Charles A4
Schaumburg B3
Schiller Park C3
Skokie D3
Sleepy Hollow A2
S. Barrington A2
S. Elgin A3
S. Holland E6
Stickney D5
Stone Park D4
Streamwood B3
Summit D5
Tinley Park D6
Tower Lakes B1
Trout Valley A1
Valley View C1
Vernon Hills C1
Villa Park B4
Volo B1
Warrenville A5
Wauconda B1
Wayne A4
Westchester C4
W. Chicago A4
W. Dundee A2
Western Sprs. C5
Westmont C5
Wheaton B4
Wheeling C2
Willowbrook C5
Willow Sprs. C5
Wilmette D2
Winfield B4
Winnetka D2
Wood Dale C3
Woodridge B5
Worth D6

POINTS OF INTEREST

875 N. Michigan Av.
(John Hancock Ctr.) B1
900 North Michigan Shops B1
Adler Planetarium &
Astronomy Museum C3
American Writers Museum B2
Art Institute of Chicago B2
Auditorium Building B2
Buckingham Fountain B2
Cadillac Palace Theatre B2
Centennial Fountain & Arc C1
Chicago Architecture Foundation .B2
Chicago Children's Museum C1
Chicago Cultural Center B2
Chicago Fire Marker A3
Chicago Mercantile Exchange ..A2
Chicago Stock Exchange B2
Chicago Theatre B2
Chicago Yacht Club C2
CIBC Theatre B2
City Hall B2
Civic Opera House A2
Cloud Gate B2
Credit Union 1 Arena A3
Crown Fountain B2
Daley Plaza B2
Dearborn Station B3
East-West University B3
The Field Museum C3
Ford Center for the Performing Arts .B2
Goodman Theatre B2
Harris Theater B2
Harold Washington Library Center .B2
Huntington Bank Pavilion at
Northerly Island C3
James R. Thompson Center B2
Jane Addams' Hull House Mus. .A3
John G. Shedd Aquarium C3
Merchandise Mart A2
Monadnock Building B2
Moody Bible Institute B1
Mus. of Broadcast Communications .B2
Mus. of Contemporary Art B1
Mus. of Contemporary Photography .B3
Navy Pier C1
Newberry Library B1
New Maxwell Street Market A3
Northwestern Univ. (Chi. Campus) .C1
Petrillo Band Shell B2
Pritzker Pavilion B2
The Shops at North Bridge B1
Soldier Field C3
Spertus Institute B3
Symphony Center B2
Tribune Tower B2
Trump Intl. Hotel & Tower B1
Union Station A2
Univ. of Illinois at Chicago A3
Water Tower B1
Water Tower Place B1
Willis Tower A2
Wrigley Building B1

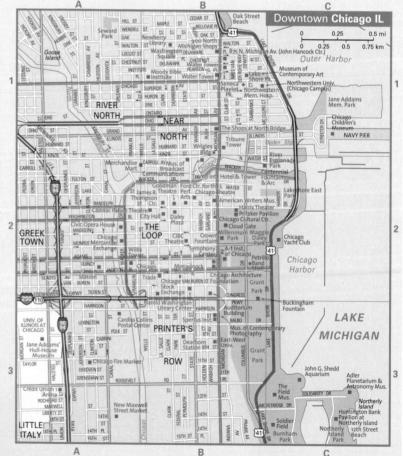

Downtown Chicago IL

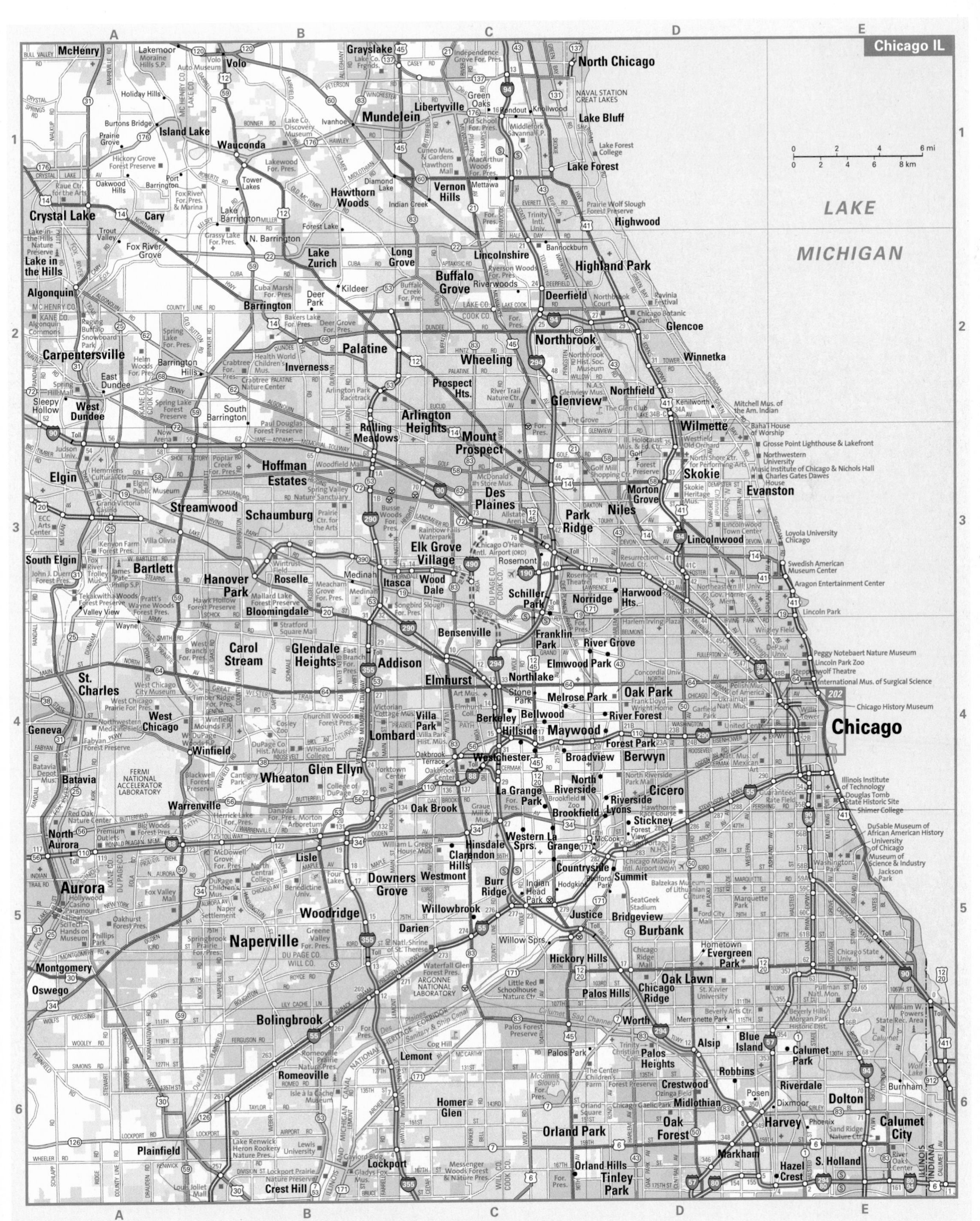

Chicago IL

Figures after entries indicate page number and grid reference.

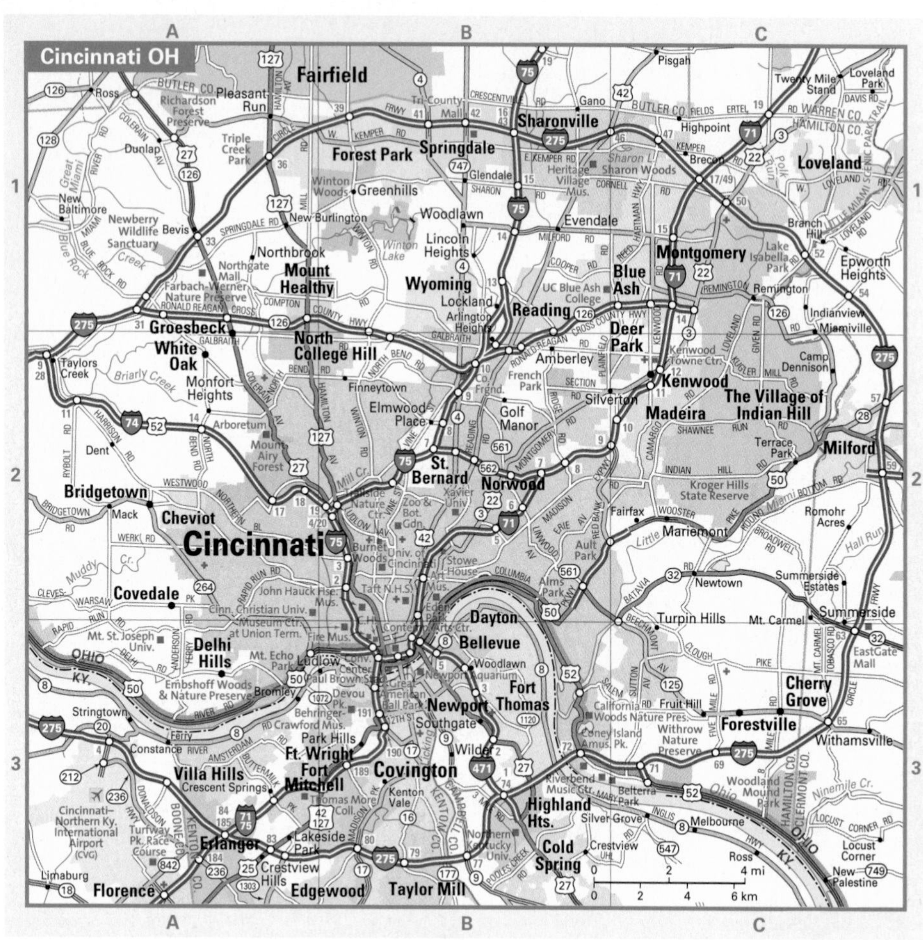

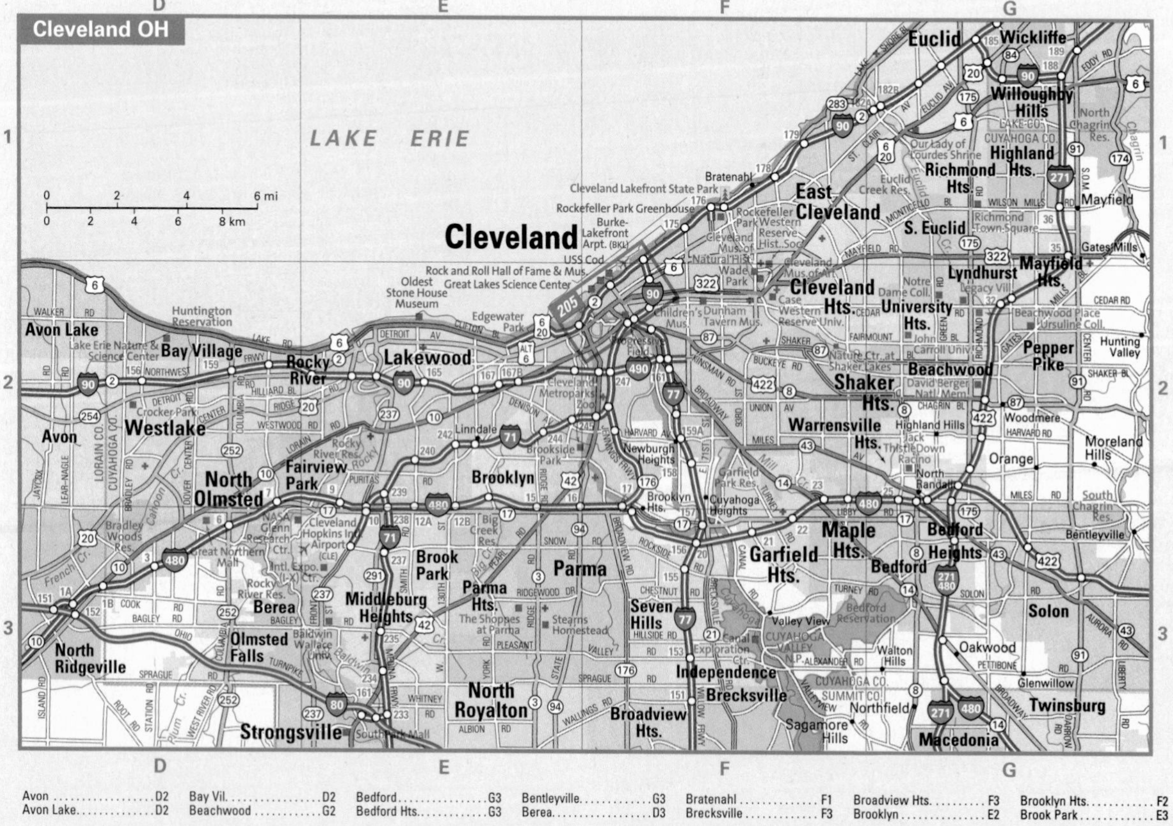

Entries in **bold black** indicate counties or parishes.
Entries in **bold color** indicate cities with detailed inset maps.

Concord NH 81 F4
Concord NC 122 B1
Concord TN 110 C4
Concord VA 112 C1
Concordia KS 43 E1
Concordia MO 96 C2
Concordia Par. LA 125 F4
Concrete WA 12 C2
Condon OR 21 E2
Conecuh Co. AL 127 F4
Conehatta MS 126 C2
Conejos CO 49 D1
Conejos Co. CO 41 D4
Conestoga PA 146 A3
Confluence PA 102 B1
Congers NY 148 B2
Congress AZ 46 C4
Conklin NY 93 F1
Conneaut OH 91 F1
Conneaut Lake PA 91 F2
Conneaut Lake Park PA 91 F2
Conneautville PA 91 F1
Connell WA 13 F4
Connellsville PA 102 B1
Connersville IN 100 A1
Conover NC 111 F4
Conovertown NJ 147 F4
Conrad IA 87 D1
Conrad MT 15 E2
Conroe TX 132 A2
Conshohocken PA 146 C2
Constantia NY 79 E3
Constantine MI 89 F1
Continental OH 90 B3
Contoocook NH 81 F4
Contra Costa Co. CA 36 B3
Convent LA 134 A3
Converse IN 89 F3
Converse LA 124 C3
Converse TX 257 F2
Converse Co. WY 33 E1
Convoy OH 90 A3
Conway AR 117 E1
Conway FL 246 C3
Conway MO 107 D1
Conway NH 81 F3
Conway NC 113 E3
Conway PA 91 F3
Conway SC 123 D4
Conway Co. AR 117 E1
Conway Sprs. KS 43 E4
Conyers GA 120 C4
Conyngham PA 93 E3
Cook MN 64 C3
Cook Co. GA 129 D4
Cook Co. IL 89 D1
Cook Co. MN 65 D2
Cooke Co. TX 59 E1
Cookeville TN 110 A4
Cooleemee NC 112 A4
Coolidge AZ 54 C2
Coolidge GA 137 E1
Coolidge TX 59 F4
Cool Valley MO 256 B1
Coon Rapids IA 86 B1
Coon Rapids MN 67 D3
Coon Valley WI 73 F2
Cooper TX 124 A1
Cooper City FL 233 A3
Cooper Co. MO 97 D3
Coopersburg PA 146 C1
Coopers Mills ME 82 C2
Cooperstown NY 79 F4
Cooperstown ND 19 E3
Coopersville MI 75 F3
Coopertown TN 109 E3
Coosa Co. AL 128 A1
Coosada AL 128 A2
Coos Bay OR 20 A4
Coos Co. NH 81 F1
Coos Co. OR 20 B4
Copalis Beach WA 12 B3
Copan OK 51 F1
Copenhagen NY 79 E2
Copiague NY 148 C4
Copiah Co. MS 126 A3
Coplay PA 189 A1
Copley OH 188 A1
Coppell TX 207 C1
Copperas Cove TX 59 E4
Copperhill TN 120 C2
Copperopolis CA 36 C3
Coquille OR 28 A1
Coral Gables FL 143 E2
Coral Hills MD 270 E4
Coral Sprs. FL 143 E1
Coralville IA 87 F2
Coram MT 15 D2
Coram NY 149 D3
Coraopolis PA 250 A1
Corbin KY 110 C2
Corcoran CA 45 D3
Corcoran MN 66 C3
Cordaville MA 150 C1
Cordele GA 129 D3
Cordova AL 119 E4
Cordova AK 154 C3
Cordova IL 88 A2
Cordova MD 145 D3
Cordova NC 122 C2
Cordova TN 118 B1
Corea ME 83 E2
Corfu NY 78 B3
Corinna ME 82 C1
Corinne UT 31 E3
Corinth MS 119 D2
Corinth NY 80 C4
Corinth TX 59 E2
Corn OK 51 D3
Cornelia GA 121 D3
Cornelius NC 122 A1
Cornelius OR 20 B2
Cornell WI 67 F3
Cornersville TN 119 F1
Cornfields AZ 47 F2
Corning AR 108 A3
Corning CA 36 B1
Corning IA 86 B3
Corning NY 93 D1
Corning OH 101 E1
Cornish ME 82 A3
Cornville AZ 47 D4
Cornwall PA 93 E4
Cornwall-on-Hudson NY 148 B1
Corona CA 53 D3
Coronado CA 53 D4
Corpus Christi TX 63 F2
Corrales NM 48 C3
Corralitos CA 44 B2
Correctionville IA 72 A4
Corrigan TX 132 B1
Corry PA 92 A1
Corryton TN 110 C4
Corsica SD 27 E4
Corsicana TX 59 F3

Columbia SC

Arcadia Lakes F1
Arthurtown F2
Cayce E2
Columbia F2
Denny Terrace E1
Dentsville F1
Dixiana E2
Forest Acres F1
Olympia E2
Pineridge E2
St. Andrews E1
Springdale E2
W. Columbia E2

Black Forest D1
Cascade C1
Chipita Park C1
Colorado Sprs. D1
Crystola C1
Fountain D2
Green Mtn. Falls C1
Manitou Sprs. C2
Security-Widefield D2
Stratmoor Hills D2

Cottondale AL 127 E1
Cottondale FL 136 C1
Cotton Plant AR 117 F2
Cottonport LA 133 F1
Cotton Valley LA 125 D2
Cottonwood AL 137 D1
Cottonwood AZ 47 D4
Cottonwood CA 28 C4
Cottonwood ID 22 B1
Cottonwood MN 66 A4
Cottonwood Co. MN 72 A1
Cottonwood Cove NV 46 B3
Cottonwood Falls KS 43 F3
Cottonwood Hts. UT 257 B3
Cottonwood Shores TX 61 D1
Cotuit MA 151 E4
Cotulla TX 60 C4
Coudersport PA 92 C1
Coulee City WA 13 E3
Coulee Dam WA 13 E2
Coulterville IL 98 B4
Council ID 22 B3
Council Bluffs IA 86 A2
Council Grove KS 43 F2
Country Club Hills MO 256 B1
Country Club Vil. MO 96 B1
Country Homes WA 14 A3
Country Knolls NY 94 B1
Countryside IL 203 C5
Countryside VA 144 A3
Coupeville WA 12 C2
Courtdale PA 261 B1
Courtland AL 119 E2
Courtland MN 72 B1
Courtland MS 118 B3
Courtland VA 113 E3
Courtney TX 61 F1
Coushatta LA 125 D3
Cove OR 21 F2
Covedale OH 204 A2
Covelo CA 36 A1
Coventry CT 150 A3
Coventry Ctr. RI 150 C3
Covert MI 75 E4
Covina CA 229 F2
Covington GA 121 D4
Covington IN 89 D4
Covington KY 100 B2
Covington LA 134 B2
Covington OH 90 B4
Covington OK 51 E2
Covington TN 118 B1
Covington VA 112 B1
Covington WA 262 B4
Covington Co. AL 128 A4
Covington Co. MS 126 C4
Cowan TN 120 A1
Cowan Hts. CA 229 F4
Coward SC 122 C4
Cowarts AL 137 D1
Cowden IL 98 C2
Cowen WV 102 A3
Coweta OK 106 A4
Coweta Co. GA 128 C1
Cowley WY 24 C2
Cowley Co. KS 43 F4
Cowlitz Co. WA 20 C1
Cowpens SC 121 F2
Coxsackie NY 94 B2
Cozad NE 34 C4
Crab Orchard KY 110 B1
Crab Orchard TN 110 B4
Crab Orchard WV 111 F1
Crafton PA 250 A2
Craig AK 155 E4
Craig CO 32 C4
Craig Beach OH 91 F3
Craig Co. OK 106 A2
Craig Co. VA 112 B1
Craighead Co. AR 108 A4
Craigmont ID 22 B1
Craigsville VA 102 B4
Craigsville WV 102 A3
Crainville IL 108 C1
Cramerton NC 122 A1
Cranbury NJ 147 D2
Crandall TX 59 F2
Crandon WI 68 B3
Crane MO 106 C2
Crane TX 58 A4
Crane Co. TX 57 F4
Cranesville PA 91 F1
Cranford NJ 147 E1
Cranston RI 150 C3
Craven Co. NC 115 D3
Crawford CO 40 C2
Crawford GA 121 E4
Crawford MS 127 D1
Crawford NE 33 F1
Crawford TX 59 E4
Crawford Co. AR 116 C1
Crawford Co. GA 129 D2
Crawford Co. IL 99 D2
Crawford Co. IN 99 F4
Crawford Co. IA 86 A1
Crawford Co. KS 106 B1
Crawford Co. MI 70 C4
Crawford Co. MO 97 F4
Crawford Co. OH 90 C3
Crawford Co. PA 91 F1
Crawford Co. WI 73 F3
Crawfordsville AR 118 B1
Crawfordsville IN 89 E4
Crawfordville FL 137 E2
Crawfordville GA 121 E4
Creal Sprs. IL 108 C1
Creede CO 40 C4
Creedmoor NC 112 C4
Creek Co. OK 51 F2
Creekside KY 230 F1
Creighton NE 35 E2
Crenshaw MS 118 B3
Crenshaw Co. AL 128 A4
Creola AL 135 E1
Cresaptown MD 102 C1
Crescent IA 86 A2
Crescent OK 51 E2
Crescent Beach FL 139 E3
Crescent City CA 28 A2
Crescent City FL 139 D4
Crescent City IL 89 D3
Crescent Sprs. KY 204 A3
Cresco IA 73 E2
Cresson PA 92 B4

POINTS OF INTEREST

Burke-Lakefront Airport B1
Cleveland Arcade A2
Cleveland Police Museum A1
Cleveland State University B2
Convention Center A1
FirstEnergy Stadium A1
Galleria at Erieview B1
Great Lakes Science Center A1
International Women's Air & Space Museum B1
Jacobs Pavilion at Nautica A1
Playhouse Square B2
Progressive Field A2
Rock and Roll Hall of Fame & Museum A1
Rocket Mortgage Fieldhouse A2
Tower City Center A2
U.S.S. Cod B1
West Side Market A2
William G. Mather Museum A1

Corson Co. SD 26 C1
Cortaro AZ 55 D3
Corte Madera CA 259 A2
Cortez CO 40 B4
Cortez FL 140 B3
Cortland IL 88 C1
Cortland NE 35 F4
Cortland NY 79 D4
Cortland OH 91 F2
Cortland Co. NY 79 E4
Corunna MI 76 B3
Corvallis MT 15 D4
Corvallis OR 20 B3
Corydon IN 99 F4
Corydon IA 87 D3
Corydon KY 109 E1
Coryell Co. TX 59 E4
Coshocton OH 91 E4
Coshocton Co. OH 91 E4
Cosmopolis WA 12 B4
Cosmos MN 66 B4
Costa Mesa CA 228 E5
Costilla Co. CO 41 E4
Cotati CA 36 B3
Coto de Caza CA 229 G5
Cottage City MD 270 E3
Cottage Grove MN 67 D4
Cottage Grove OR 20 B4
Cottage Grove WI 74 B3
Cottage Hill FL 135 F1
Cottageville SC 130 C1
Cottageville WV 101 E3
Cotter AR 107 E3
Cottle Co. TX 58 B1
Cotton Co. OK 51 D4

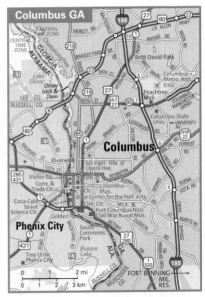

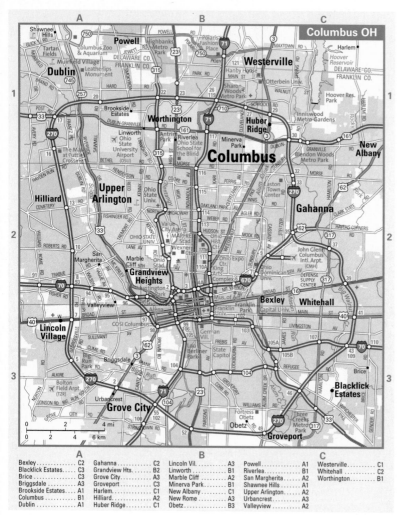

Columbus OH

Shawnee Hills · Powell · Dublin · Worthington · Westerville · Huber Ridge · New Albany · Columbus · Upper Arlington · Hilliard · Gahanna · Whitehall · Bexley · Grandview Heights · Lincoln Village · Briggsdale · Grove City · Obetz · Groveport · Blacklick Estates · Brice

Bexley	C2
Blacklick Estates	C3
Brice	C3
Briggsdale	A3
Brookside Estates	A1
Columbus	B1
Dublin	A1
Gahanna	C2
Grandview Hts.	B2
Grove City	A3
Groveport	C3
Harlem	C1
Hilliard	A2
Huber Ridge	C1
Lincoln Vil.	A3
Linworth	B1
Marble Cliff	A2
Minerva Park	B1
New Albany	C1
New Rome	A2
Obetz	B3
Powell	A1
Riverlea	B1
San Margherita	A2
Shawnee Hills	A1
Upper Arlington	A2
Urbancrest	A3
Valleyview	A2
Westerville	C1
Whitehall	C2
Worthington	B1

Cressona PA	146	A1
Crested Butte CO	40	C2
Crest Hill IL	89	D2
Crestline CA	53	D2
Crestline IL	89	D2
Crestline OH	91	D3
Creston IA	86	B3
Creston OH	91	E3
Crestview FL	136	B1
Crestview KY	204	B3
Crestview Hills KY	204	A3
Crestwood IL	203	D6
Crestwood KY	100	A4
Crestwood MO	256	B3
Crestwood Vil. NJ	147	E3
Creswell OR	20	B4
Crete IL	89	D2
Crete NE	35	F4
Creve Coeur MO	256	A2
Crewe VA	113	D2
Cricket NC	111	F4
Cridersville OH	90	B3
Crimora VA	102	C4
Cripple Creek CO	41	E2
Crisfield MD	103	F4
Crisp Co. GA	129	D3
Crittenden KY	100	B3
Crittenden Co. AR	118	B3
Crittenden Co. KY	109	D2
Crivitz WI	68	C3
Crocker MO	97	E4
Crockett CA	259	C1
Crockett TX	124	A4
Crockett Co. TN	108	C4
Crockett Co. TX	60	A1
Crofton KY	109	E2
Crofton MD	144	C3
Crofton NE	35	E1
Croghan NY	79	E2
Crompond NY	148	B2
Cromwell CT	149	E1
Crook Co. OR	21	D3
Crook Co. WY	25	F3
Crooked Lake Park FL	141	D3
Crooks SD	27	F3
Crookston MN	19	F3
Crooksville OH	101	E1
Crosby MN	64	B4
Crosby ND	18	A1
Crosby TX	132	B3
Crosby Co. TX	58	A1
Crosbyton TX	58	B1
Cross City FL	137	F3
Cross Co. AR	118	A1
Crossett AR	125	F1
Cross Hill SC	121	F3
Cross Keys NJ	146	C4
Crosslake MN	64	B4
Cross Plains TN	109	F3
Cross Plains TX	59	D3
Cross Plains WI	74	B3
Cross Roads TX	59	F2
Crossville AL	120	A3
Crossville IL	99	D4
Crossville TN	110	B4
Crosswicks NJ	147	D2
Croswell MI	76	C3
Crothersville IN	99	F3
Croton Falls NY	148	C2
Croton-on-Hudson NY	148	B2
Crow Agency MT	24	C1

Crowder MS	118	B3
Crowder OK	116	A1
Crowell TX	58	C1
Crowley LA	133	E2
Crowley TX	59	E2
Crowley Co. CO	41	F3
Crown Hts. NY	148	B1
Crown Pt. IN	89	D2
Crown Pt. LA	134	B3
Crownpoint NM	48	B2
Crown Pt. NY	81	D3
Crownsville MD	144	C3
Crow Wing Co. MN	66	C1
Croydon PA	248	E2
Crozet VA	102	C4
Cruger MS	126	B1
Crump TN	119	D1
Crystal MN	235	B2
Crystal NM	48	A2
Crystal Beach FL	266	A1
Crystal City MO	98	A4
Crystal City TX	60	C4
Crystal Falls MI	68	C2
Crystal Lake CT	150	A3
Crystal Lake IL	88	C1
Crystal Lakes OH	100	C1
Crystal River FL	140	B1
Crystal Sprs. FL	140	C2
Crystal Sprs. MS	126	B3
Cuba IL	88	A4
Cuba MO	97	F4
Cuba NM	48	C2
Cuba NY	92	C1
Cudahy CA	228	D3
Cudahy WI	75	D3
Cuddebackville NY	148	A1
Cudjoe Key FL	143	D4
Cuero TX	61	E3
Culberson NC	121	D1
Culberson Co. TX	57	E4
Culbertson MT	17	F2
Culbertson NE	34	C4
Culdesac ID	14	B4
Cullen LA	125	D1
Cullman AL	119	F3
Cullman Co. AL	119	F3
Culloden WV	101	F1
Cullowhee NC	121	D1
Culpeper VA	103	D3
Culpeper Co. VA	103	D3
Culver IN	89	E2
Culver OR	21	D3
Culver City CA	228	C3
Cumberland IN	99	F1
Cumberland KY	111	D2
Cumberland MD	102	C1
Cumberland NC	123	D2
Cumberland VA	113	D1
Cumberland WI	67	E3
Cumberland Ctr. ME	82	B3
Cumberland Co. IL	99	D3
Cumberland Co. KY	110	A2
Cumberland Co. ME	82	B3
Cumberland Co. NJ	145	E2
Cumberland Co. NC	123	D2
Cumberland Co. PA	103	D1
Cumberland Co. TN	110	B4
Cumberland Co. VA	113	D1
Cumberland Foreside ME	82	B3
Cumberland Hill RI	150	C2
Cumby TX	124	A1
Cuming Co. NE	35	F2
Cumming GA	120	C3
Cunningham KS	43	D4
Cupertino CA	36	B4
Curlew WA	266	A1
Currituck NC	115	E1
Currituck Co. NC	115	E1
Curry Co. NM	49	F4
Curry Co. OR	28	A2
Curtis NE	34	C4
Curwensville PA	92	B3
Cushing OK	51	F2
Cushing TX	124	B3
Cushman AR	107	F4
Cusseta GA	128	C3
Custer SD	25	F4
Custer Co. CO	41	E3
Custer Co. ID	23	D3
Custer Co. MT	25	E1
Custer Co. NE	34	C3
Custer Co. OK	51	D2
Custer Co. SD	25	F4
Cut and Shoot TX	132	A2
Cut Bank MT	15	E1
Cutchogue NY	149	E3
Cutler CA	45	D3
Cutler Bay FL	143	E3
Cutlerville MI	75	F3
Cut Off LA	134	B3
Cutten CA	28	A4
Cuyahoga Co. OH	91	E2
Cuyahoga Falls OH	91	E3
Cuyahoga Hts. OH	204	F2

Cygnet OH	90	C2
Cynthiana IN	99	D4
Cynthiana KY	100	B3
Cypress CA	228	E4
Cypress Quarters FL	141	E4
Cyril OK	51	E3

D

Dacono CO	41	E1
Dacula GA	121	D3
Dade City FL	140	C2
Dade Co. GA	120	B2
Dade Co. MO	106	C1
Dadeville AL	128	B2
Daggett CA	53	D1
Daggett Co. UT	32	A4
Dagsboro DE	145	F4
Dahlgren IL	103	E4
Dahlonega GA	120	C3
Daingerfield TX	124	B1
Daisetta TX	132	B2
Dakota City IA	72	C4
Dakota City NE	35	F2
Dakota Co. MN	67	D4
Dakota Co. NE	35	F2
Dale IN	99	E4
Dale City VA	144	A4
Dale Co. AL	128	B4
Daleville AL	128	B4
Daleville IN	89	F4
Daleville VA	112	B1
Dalhart TX	50	A2
Dallas GA	120	B4
Dallas NC	122	A1
Dallas OR	20	B2
Dallas PA	93	E2
Dallas TX	59	F2
Dallas Ctr. IA	86	C2
Dallas Co. AL	127	F3
Dallas Co. AR	117	E4
Dallas Co. IA	86	C2
Dallas Co. MO	107	D1
Dallas Co. TX	59	F2
Dallastown PA	103	E1
Dalton GA	120	B2
Dalton MA	94	C1
Dalton OH	91	E3
Dalton PA	93	F2
Dalton TX	98	C1
Dalton Gardens ID	14	B3
Dalworthington Gardens TX	207	F3
Daly City CA	36	B4
Dalzell SC	122	B3
Damariscotta ME	82	C3
Damascus MD	144	B2
Damascus OR	20	C2
Damascus VA	111	F3
Damon TX	132	A4
Dana IN	99	E1
Dana Pt. CA	52	C3
Danboro PA	146	C2
Danbury CT	148	C2
Danbury NC	112	B3
Danbury TX	132	A4
Dandridge TN	111	D4
Dane WI	74	B3
Dane Co. WI	74	B3
Danforth IL	89	D3
Dania Beach FL	143	F2
Daniel MD	144	B1
Daniels Co. MT	17	E1
Danielson CT	150	B3
Danielsville GA	121	D3
Dannemora NY	80	C1
Dansville NY	78	C4
Dante VA	111	E2
Danube MN	66	B4
Danvers IL	88	B4
Danvers MA	151	F1
Danville AR	117	D1
Danville CA	36	B4
Danville IL	89	D4
Danville IN	99	F1

Danville IA	87	F3
Danville KY	110	B1
Danville NH	95	E1
Danville OH	91	D4
Danville PA	93	E3
Danville VT	81	E2
Danville VA	112	C3
Danville WV	101	F4
Daphne AL	135	E2
Darby MT	23	D1
Darby PA	146	C3
Dardanelle AR	117	D1
Dardenne Prairie MO	98	A3
Dare Co. NC	115	F2
Dares Beach MD	144	C4
Darien CT	148	C3
Darien GA	130	B4
Darien IL	203	C5
Darien WI	74	C4
Darke Co. OH	100	B1
Darlington IN	89	E4
Darlington SC	122	C3
Darlington WI	74	A4
Darlington Co. SC	122	B3
Darmstadt IN	99	D4
Darnestown MD	144	B2
Darrington WA	12	C2
Dasher GA	137	F1
Dassel MN	66	C3
Dauphin PA	93	D4
Dauphin Co. PA	93	D4
Dauphin Island AL	135	D2
Davenport IA	88	A2
Davenport ND	19	E4
Davenport OK	51	F2
Davenport WA	13	F3
David City NE	35	F3
Davidson NC	122	A1
Davidson Co. NC	112	B4
Davidson Co. TN	109	F4
Davidsville PA	92	B4
Davie FL	143	F2
Davie Co. NC	112	A4
Daviess Co. IN	99	E3
Daviess Co. KY	109	E1
Daviess Co. MO	96	C1
Davis CA	36	B3
Davis IL	74	B4
Davis OK	51	F4
Davis WV	102	B2
Davisboro GA	129	F1
Davis Co. IA	87	E3
Davis Co. UT	31	E3
Davison Co. SD	27	E4
Davison MI	76	B3
Davison Co. SD	27	E4
Davy WV	111	F1
Dawes Co. NE	34	A1
Dawson GA	128	C3
Dawson MN	27	F2
Dawson TX	59	F3
Dawson Co. GA	120	C3
Dawson Co. MT	17	F3
Dawson Co. NE	35	D4
Dawson Co. TX	58	A2
Dawson Sprs. KY	109	E2
Dawsonville GA	120	C3
Day Co. SD	27	E2
Dayton ID	31	E2
Dayton IN	89	E4
Dayton IA	72	C4
Dayton KY	204	B2
Dayton MN	66	C3
Dayton NV	37	D2
Dayton NJ	147	D1
Dayton OH	100	B1
Dayton OR	20	B2
Dayton TN	120	B1
Dayton TX	132	B3
Dayton VA	102	C4
Dayton WA	13	F4
Dayton WY	24	C2
Daytona Beach FL	139	E4
Daytona Beach Shores FL	139	E4
Dayville CT	150	B3
Deadwood SD	25	F3
Deaf Smith Co. TX	49	F3
Deal NJ	147	E2
Deale MD	144	C3
Deal Island MD	103	F4
Dearborn MI	76	C4
Dearborn MO	96	B1
Dearborn Co. IN	100	B2
Dearborn Hts. MI	210	B3
Dearing KS	106	A2
DeArmanville AL	120	A4
Deary ID	14	B4
Deaver WY	24	B2
De Baca Co. NM	49	E4
DeBary FL	141	D1
De Beque CO	40	B2
Decatur AL	119	F2
Decatur AR	106	B3
Decatur GA	120	C4
Decatur IL	98	C1
Decatur IN	90	A3
Decatur MI	89	F1
Decatur MS	126	C3
Decatur NE	35	F2
Decatur TN	120	C1
Decatur TX	59	E2
Decatur Co. GA	137	E1
Decatur Co. IN	100	A2

Concord NH

Penacook · Concord · Bow Mills

Corpus Christi TX

Nueces Bay · Corpus Christi Intl. Arpt. (CRP) · Corpus Christi · Corpus Christi Bay · Texas A&M University Corpus Christi · N.A.S. Corpus Christi & Army Depot

Entries in **bold black** indicate counties or parishes.
Entries in **bold color** indicate cities with detailed inset maps.

Addison ... D1
Arlington ... C3
Avondale ... A1
Balch Sprs. ... E3
Bedford ... B2
Benbrook ... A3
Blue Mound ... A2
Carrollton ... D1
Cedar Hill ... C3
Cockrell Hill ... D2
Colleyville ... B1
Coppell ... C1
Crowley ... A3
Dallas ... D2
Dalworthington Gardens ... B3
De Soto ... D3
Duncanville ... D3
Edgecliff ... A3
Euless ... C2
Everman ... B3
Farmers Branch ... D1
Flower Mound ... C1
Forest Hill ... B3
Ft. Worth ... A2
Garland ... E1
Grand Prairie ... C3
Grapevine ... C1
Haltom City ... B2
Haslet ... A1
Highland Park ... D2
Hurst ... B2
Hutchins ... E3
Irving ... C2
Keller ... B1
Kennedale ... B3
Lakeview ... A1
Lake Worth ... A2
Lancaster ... D3
Lewisville ... C1
Mansfield ... B3
Mesquite ... E2
Murphy ... E1
Newark ... A1
N. Richland Hills ... B2
Pantego ... B3
Plano ... D1
Richardson ... E1
Richland Hills ... B2
River Oaks ... A2
Roanoke ... B1
Rowlett ... E1
Sachse ... E1
Saginaw ... A2
Sansom Park ... A2
Seagoville ... E3
Southlake ... B1
Sunnyvale ... E1
Trophy Club ... B1
University Park ... D2
Watauga ... B2
Westlake ... B1
Westover Hills ... A2
Westworth ... A2
White Settlement ... A2
Wilmer ... E3
Wylie ... E1

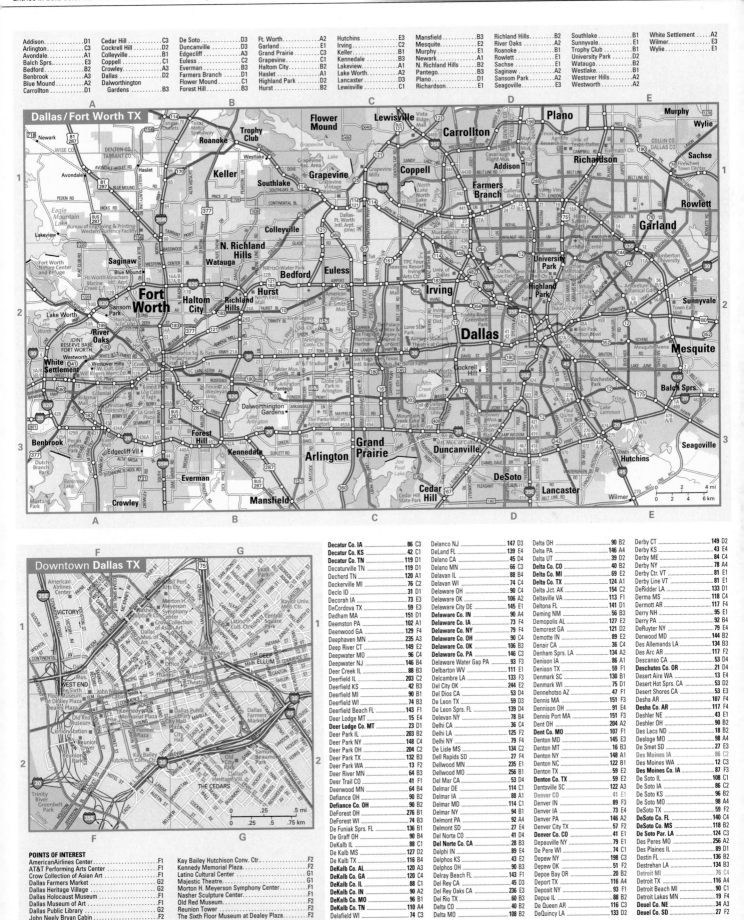

POINTS OF INTEREST

AmericanAirlines Center ... F1
AT&T Performing Arts Center ... F1
Crow Collection of Asian Art ... F1
Dallas Farmers Market ... G2
Dallas Heritage Village ... G2
Dallas Holocaust Museum ... F1
Dallas Museum of Art ... F1
Dallas Public Library ... G2
John Neely Bryan Cabin ... F2
Kay Bailey Hutchison Conv. Ctr. ... F2
Kennedy Memorial Plaza ... F2
Latino Cultural Center ... G1
Majestic Theatre ... G1
Morton H. Meyerson Symphony Center ... F1
Nasher Sculpture Center ... F1
Old Red Museum ... F2
Reunion Tower ... F2
The Sixth Floor Museum at Dealey Plaza ... F2

Decatur Co. IA ... 86 C3
Decatur Co. KS ... 42 C1
Decatur Co. TN ... 119 D1
Decaturville TN ... 119 D1
Decherd TN ... 120 A1
Deckerville MI ... 76 C2
Declo ID ... 31 D1
Decorah IA ... 73 E3
DeCordova TX ... 59 E3
Dedham MA ... 151 D1
Deemston PA ... 102 A1
Deenwood GA ... 129 F4
Deephaven MN ... 235 A3
Deep River CT ... 149 E2
Deepwater MO ... 96 C4
Deepwater NJ ... 146 B4
Deer Creek IL ... 88 B3
Deerfield IL ... 203 C2
Deerfield KS ... 42 B3
Deerfield MI ... 90 B1
Deerfield WI ... 74 B3
Deerfield Beach FL ... 143 F1
Deer Lodge MT ... 15 E4
Deer Lodge Co. MT ... 23 D1
Deer Park IL ... 203 B2
Deer Park NY ... 148 C4
Deer Park OH ... 204 C2
Deer Park TX ... 132 B3
Deer Park WA ... 13 F2
Deer River MN ... 64 B3
Deer Trail CO ... 41 F1
Deerwood MN ... 64 B4
Defiance OH ... 90 B2
Defiance Co. OH ... 90 B2
DeForest OH ... 276 B1
DeForest WI ... 74 B3
De Funiak Sprs. FL ... 136 B1
De Graff OH ... 90 B4
DeKalb IL ... 88 C1
De Kalb MS ... 127 D2
De Kalb TX ... 116 B4
DeKalb Co. AL ... 120 A3
DeKalb Co. GA ... 120 C4
DeKalb Co. IL ... 88 C1
DeKalb Co. IN ... 90 A2
DeKalb Co. MO ... 96 B1
DeKalb Co. TN ... 110 A4
Delafield WI ... 74 C3
Delanco NJ ... 147 D3
DeLand FL ... 139 E4
Delano CA ... 45 D4
Delano MN ... 66 C3
Delavan IL ... 88 B4
Delavan WI ... 74 C4
Delaware OH ... 90 C4
Delaware OK ... 106 A2
Delaware City DE ... 145 E1
Delaware Co. IN ... 90 A4
Delaware Co. IA ... 73 F4
Delaware Co. NY ... 79 F4
Delaware Co. OH ... 90 C4
Delaware Co. OK ... 106 B3
Delaware Co. PA ... 146 C3
Delaware Water Gap PA ... 93 F3
Delbarton WV ... 111 E1
Delcambre LA ... 133 F3
Del City OK ... 244 E2
Del Dios CA ... 53 D4
De Leon TX ... 59 D3
De Leon Sprs. FL ... 139 D4
Delevan NY ... 78 B4
Delhi CA ... 36 C4
Delhi LA ... 125 F2
Delhi NY ... 79 F4
De Lisle MS ... 134 C2
Dell Rapids SD ... 27 F4
Dellwood MN ... 235 E1
Dellwood MO ... 256 B1
Del Mar CA ... 53 D4
Delmar DE ... 114 C1
Delmar IA ... 88 A1
Delmar MD ... 114 C1
Delmar NY ... 94 B1
Delmont PA ... 92 A4
Delmont SD ... 27 E4
Del Norte CO ... 41 D4
Del Norte Co. CA ... 28 B3
Delphi IN ... 89 E4
Delphos KS ... 43 E2
Delphos OH ... 90 B3
Delray Beach FL ... 143 F1
Del Rey CA ... 45 D3
Del Rey Oaks CA ... 236 E3
Del Rio TX ... 60 B3
Delta CO ... 40 B2
Delta MO ... 108 B2
Delta OH ... 90 B2
Delta PA ... 146 A4
Delta UT ... 39 D2
Delta Co. CO ... 40 B2
Delta Co. MI ... 69 E2
Delta Co. TX ... 124 A1
Delta Jct. AK ... 154 C2
Deltaville VA ... 113 F1
Deltona FL ... 141 D1
Deming NM ... 56 B3
Demopolis AL ... 127 E2
Demorest GA ... 121 D2
Demotte IN ... 89 E2
Denair CA ... 36 C4
Denham Sprs. LA ... 134 A2
Denison IA ... 86 A1
Denison TX ... 59 F1
Denmark SC ... 130 B1
Denmark WI ... 75 D1
Dennehotso AZ ... 47 F1
Dennis MA ... 151 F3
Dennison OH ... 91 E4
Dennis Port MA ... 151 F3
Dent OH ... 204 A2
Dent Co. MO ... 107 F1
Denton MD ... 145 E3
Denton MT ... 16 B3
Denton NY ... 148 A1
Denton NC ... 122 B1
Denton TX ... 59 E2
Denton Co. TX ... 59 E2
Dentsville SC ... 122 A3
Denver CO ... 41 E1
Denver IN ... 89 F3
Denver IA ... 73 E4
Denver PA ... 146 A2
Denver City TX ... 57 F2
Denver Co. CO ... 41 E1
Depauville NY ... 79 E1
De Pere WI ... 74 C1
Depew NY ... 198 C3
Depew OK ... 51 F2
Depoe Bay OR ... 20 B2
Deport TX ... 116 A4
Deposit NY ... 93 F1
Depue IL ... 88 B2
De Queen AR ... 116 C3
DeQuincy LA ... 133 D2
Derby CT ... 149 D2
Derby KS ... 43 E4
Derby ME ... 84 C4
Derby NY ... 78 A4
Derby Ctr. VT ... 81 E1
Derby Line VT ... 81 E1
DeRidder LA ... 133 D1
Derma MS ... 118 C4
Dermott AR ... 117 F4
Derry NH ... 95 E1
Derry PA ... 92 B4
DeRuyter NY ... 79 E4
Derwood MD ... 144 B2
Des Allemands LA ... 134 B3
Des Arc AR ... 117 F2
Descanso CA ... 53 D4
Deschutes Co. OR ... 21 D4
Desert Aire WA ... 13 E4
Desert Hot Sprs. CA ... 53 D2
Desert Shores CA ... 53 E3
Desha AR ... 107 F4
Desha Co. AR ... 117 F4
Deshler NE ... 43 E1
Deshler OH ... 90 B2
Des Lacs ND ... 18 B2
Desloge MO ... 98 A4
De Smet SD ... 27 E3
Des Moines IA ... 86 C2
Des Moines WA ... 12 C3
Des Moines Co. IA ... 87 F3
De Soto IL ... 108 C1
De Soto IA ... 86 C2
De Soto KS ... 96 B2
De Soto MO ... 98 A4
DeSoto TX ... 59 F2
DeSoto Co. FL ... 140 C4
DeSoto Co. MS ... 118 B2
De Soto Par. LA ... 124 C3
Des Peres MO ... 256 A2
Des Plaines IL ... 89 D1
Destin FL ... 136 B2
Destrehan LA ... 134 B3
Detroit MI ... 76 C4
Detroit TX ... 116 A4
Detroit Beach MI ... 90 C1
Detroit Lakes MN ... 19 F4
Deuel Co. NE ... 34 A3
Deuel Co. SD ... 27 F2

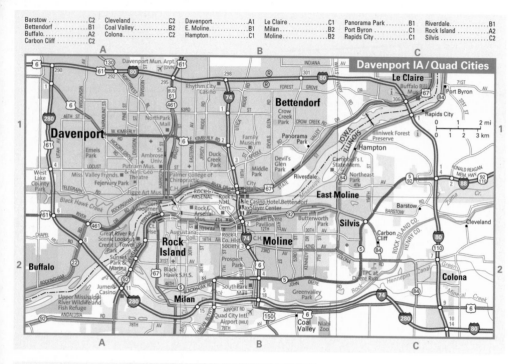

Figures after entries indicate page number and grid reference.

Barstow C2 · Bettendorf B1 · Buffalo A2 · Carbon Cliff C2 · Cleveland C2 · Coal Valley B2 · Colona C2 · Davenport A1 · E. Moline B1 · Hampton C1 · Le Claire C1 · Milan B2 · Moline B2 · Panorama Park B1 · Port Byron C1 · Rapids City C1 · Riverdale B1 · Rock Island A2 · Silvis C2

Dayton OH

Beavercreek E2 · Bellbrook E2 · Centerville E2 · Dayton E2 · Drexel D1 · Englewood D1 · Ft. McKinley D1 · Huber Hts. E1 · Kettering E2 · Little York E1 · Miamisburg D2 · Moraine D2 · Murlin Hts. D1 · Northridge D1 · Oakwood E2 · Riverside E1 · Shiloh D1 · Trotwood D1 · Vandalia E1 · W. Carrollton D2 · Woodbourne E2

Allandale G2 · Daytona Beach F1 · Daytona Beach Shores G2 · Holly Hill F1 · Ormond Beach F1 · Ponce Inlet G2 · Port Orange G2 · S. Daytona G2 · Wilbur-by-the-Sea G2

De Valls Bluff AR 117 F2
Deville LA 125 E4
Devils Lake ND 19 D2
Devine TX 61 D3
Devola OH 101 F2
Devon PA 248 A2
Dewar OK 116 A1
Dewey OK 51 F1
Dewey Beach DE 145 F4
Dewey Co. OK 51 D2
Dewey Co. SD 26 C2
Dewey-Humboldt AZ 47 D4
Deweyville TX 132 C2
Deweyville UT 31 E3
DeWitt AR 117 F3
De Witt IA 88 A1
DeWitt MI 76 A3
De Witt NE 35 F4
De Witt NY 79 E3
De Witt Co. IL 88 B4
DeWitt Co. TX 61 E3
Dexter GA 129 E2
Dexter IA 86 C2
Dexter ME 82 C1
Dexter MI 76 B4
Dexter MO 108 B2
Dexter NM 57 E2
Dexter NY 79 E1
Dexter OR 20 C4
Diablo CA 259 D2
Diamond IL 88 C2
Diamond MO 106 C2
Diamond Bar CA 229 F3
Diamond City AR 107 D3
Diamondhead MS 134 C2
Diamond Hill RI 150 C2
Diamond Sprs. CA 36 C2
Diamondville WY 31 F2
Diaz AR 107 F4
D'Iberville MS 135 D2
Diboll TX 132 B1
Dickens TX 58 B1
Dickens Co. TX 58 B1
Dickenson Co. VA 111 E2
Dickey Co. ND 27 D1
Dickeyville WI 73 F4
Dickinson ND 18 A4
Dickinson TX 132 B4
Dickinson Co. IA 72 B3
Dickinson Co. KS 43 E2
Dickinson Co. MI 69 D2
Dickson OK 51 F4
Dickson TN 109 E4
Dickson City PA 93 F2
Dickson Co. TN 109 E4
Dierks AR 116 C3
Dieterich IL 98 C2
Dighton KS 42 C3
Dighton MA 151 D3
Dike IA 73 D4
Dilkon AZ 47 F3
Dill City OK 51 D3
Dilley TX 60 C4
Dillingham AK 154 B3
Dillon CO 41 D1
Dillon MT 23 E2
Dillon SC 122 C3
Dillon Co. SC 122 C3
Dillonvale OH 91 F4
Dillsboro IN 100 A2
Dillsburg PA 93 D4
Dillwyn VA 113 D1
Dilworth MN 19 F4
Dimmit Co. TX 60 C4
Dimmitt TX 50 A4
Dimondale MI 76 A4
Dinosaur CO 32 B4
Dinuba CA 45 D3
Dinwiddie VA 113 E2
Dinwiddie Co. VA 113 E2
District Hts. MD 271 F4
Divernon IL 98 B1
Divide Co. ND 17 F1
Dixfield ME 82 B2
Dixie Co. FL 137 F3
Dixmoor IL 203 E6
Dixon CA 36 B3
Dixon IL 88 B1
Dixon KY 109 E1
Dixon MO 97 E4
Dixon MT 15 D3
Dixon Co. NE 35 F1
D'Lo MS 126 B3
Dobbins Hts. NC 122 C2
Dobbs Ferry NY 148 B3
Dobson NC 112 A3
Dock Jct. GA 139 D1
Doctor Phillips FL 246 B3
Doctors Inlet FL 139 D2
Doddridge Co. WV 102 A2
Dodge NE 35 F2
Dodge Ctr. MN 73 D1
Dodge City AL 119 F3
Dodge City KS 42 C4
Dodge Co. GA 129 E3
Dodge Co. MN 73 D1
Dodge Co. NE 35 F3
Dodge Co. WI 74 C2
Dodgeville WI 74 A3
Doerun GA 129 D4
Doland SD 27 E2
Dolan Sprs. AZ 46 B3
Dolgeville NY 79 F3
Dollar Bay MI 65 F3
Dolores CO 40 B4
Dolores Co. CO 40 B4
Dolton IL 203 E6
Doña Ana NM 56 B3
Dona Ana Co. NM 56 B3
Donald OR 20 B2
Donaldsonville LA 134 A2
Donalsonville GA 137 D1
Dongola IL 108 C1
Doniphan MO 108 A3
Doniphan NE 35 E4
Doniphan Co. KS 96 B1
Donley Co. TX 50 B3
Donna TX 63 E4
Donnellson IA 87 F3
Donora PA 92 A4
Doolittle MO 97 E4
Dooly Co. GA 129 D3
Doon IA 35 F1
Door Co. WI 69 D4
Dora AL 119 F4
Doraville GA 120 C4
Dorchester NE 35 F4
Dorchester WI 68 A4
Dorchester Co. MD 103 F4
Dorchester Co. SC 130 C1
Dormont PA 250 B3
Dorr MI 75 F4
Dorris CA 28 C2
Dorset VT 81 D4
Dorsey MD 193 B4
Dortches NC 113 D4
Dos Palos CA 44 C2
Dothan AL 128 B4
Double Sprs. AL 119 E3
Doubs MD 144 A2
Dougherty Co. GA 128 C4
Douglas AL 120 A3
Douglas AZ 55 E4
Douglas GA 129 E4
Douglas MA 150 C2
Douglas MI 75 E4
Douglas WY 33 E1
Douglas Co. CO 41 E2
Douglas Co. GA 120 C4
Douglas Co. IL 99 D1
Douglas Co. KS 96 A3
Douglas Co. MN 66 B2
Douglas Co. MO 107 E2
Douglas Co. NE 35 F3
Douglas Co. NV 37 D2
Douglas Co. OR 20 B4
Douglas Co. SD 27 E4
Douglas Co. WA 13 E3
Douglas Co. WI 64 C4
Douglass KS 43 F4
Douglass Hills KY 230 F2
Douglassville PA 146 B2
Douglasville GA 120 C4
Dousman WI 74 C3
Dove Creek CO 40 A4
Dover AR 117 D1
Dover DE 145 E2
Dover FL 140 C2
Dover ID 14 B2
Dover MA 151 D1
Dover NH 82 A4
Dover NJ 148 A3
Dover OH 91 E4
Dover PA 103 E1
Dover TN 109 D3
Dover-Foxcroft ME 82 C1
Dover Plains NY 94 B3
Dowagiac MI 89 F1
Dow City IA 86 A1
Dowling Park FL 137 F2
Downers Grove IL 89 D1
Downey CA 52 C2
Downey ID 31 E2
Downieville CA 36 C1
Downingtown PA 146 B3
Downs IL 88 C4
Downs KS 43 D1
Dows IA 72 C4
Doyle TN 110 A4
Doylestown OH 91 E3
Doylestown PA 146 C2
Doyline LA 125 D2
Drain OR 20 B4
Drake ND 18 C2
Drakesboro KY 109 E2
Drakes Branch VA 113 D2
Draper UT 31 E4
Dravosburg PA 250 C3
Drayton ND 19 E2
Dresden OH 91 D4
Dresden TN 108 C3
Dresser WI 67 D3
Drew MS 118 A4
Drew Co. AR 117 F4
Drexel MO 96 B3
Drexel NC 111 F4
Drexel OH 208 D1
Drexel Hill PA 146 C3
Driggs ID 23 F4
Dripping Sprs. TX 61 D2
Driscoll TX 63 F2
Druid Hills GA 190 D3
Drummond MT 15 E4
Drumright OK 51 F2
Dryden ME 82 B2
Dryden MI 76 C3
Dryden NY 79 D4
Dryden VA 111 D2
Dry Mills ME 82 B3
Dry Prong LA 125 E4
Dry Ridge KY 100 B3
Duarte CA 228 E2
Dubach LA 125 E2
Dublin CA 259 E3
Dublin GA 129 E2
Dublin IN 100 A1
Dublin MD 145 D1
Dublin OH 90 C4
Dublin PA 146 C2
Dublin TX 59 D3
Dublin VA 112 A2
Dubois ID 23 E3
DuBois PA 92 B3
Dubois WY 24 B4
Dubois Co. IN 99 E3
Duboistown PA 93 D2
Dubuque IA 73 F4
Dubuque Co. IA 73 F4
Duchesne UT 32 A4
Duchesne Co. UT 39 F1
Duck Hill MS 118 B4
Ducktown TN 120 C2
Ducor CA 45 D4
Dudley MA 150 B2
Dudleyville AZ 55 D2
Duenweg MO 106 B2
Due West SC 121 E3
Dufur OR 21 D2
Dugger IN 99 E2
Dukes Co. MA 151 E4

Entries in **bold black** indicate counties or parishes.
Entries in **bold color** indicate cities with detailed inset maps.

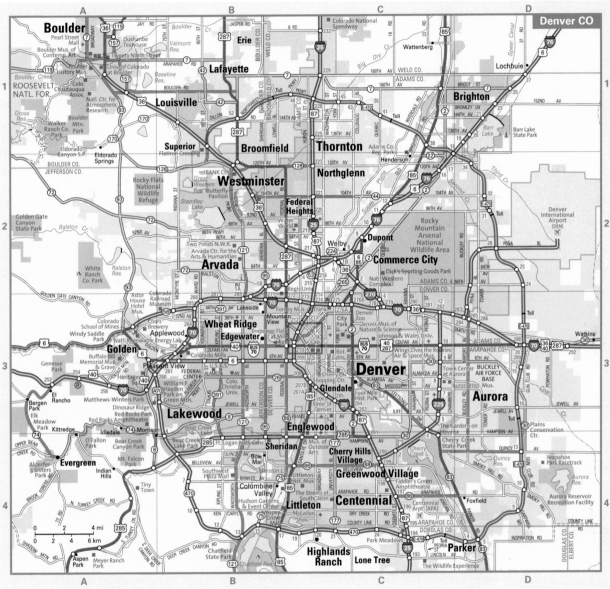

Denver CO

Place	Grid
Applewood	B3
Arvada	B2
Aspen Park	A4
Aurora	D3
Bergen Park	A3
Boulder	A1
Bow Mar	B4
Brighton	D1
Broomfield	B1
Centennial	C4
Cherry Hills Vil.	C4
Columbine Valley	B4
Commerce City	C2
Denver	C3
Dupont	C2
Edgewater	B3
Eldorado Sprs.	A1
El Rancho	A3
Englewood	C3
Erie	B1
Evergreen	A4
Federal Hts.	B2
Foxfield	D4
Glendale	C3
Golden	A3
Greenwood Vil.	C4
Henderson	C2
Highlands Ranch	C4
Idledale	A3
Indian Hills	A4
Kittredge	A4
Lafayette	B1
Lakeside	B3
Lakewood	B3
Littleton	B4
Lochbuie	D1
Lone Tree	C4
Louisville	B1
Morrison	A4
Mtn. View	B3
Northglenn	C2
Parker	D4
Pleasant View	B3
Sheridan	B4
Superior	B1
Thornton	C1
Watkins	D3
Wattenberg	C1
Welby	C2
Westminster	B2
Wheat Ridge	B3

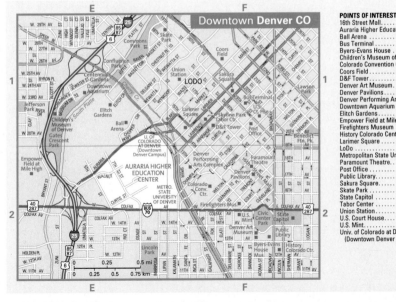

POINTS OF INTEREST

Point of interest	Grid
16th Street Mall	F2
Auraria Higher Education Center	E2
Ball Arena	E1
Bus Terminal	F1
Byers-Evans House	F2
Children's Museum of Denver	E1
Colorado Convention Center	F2
Coors Field	F1
D&F Tower	F1
Denver Art Museum	F2
Denver Pavilions	F2
Denver Performing Arts Complex	F2
Downtown Aquarium	E1
Elitch Gardens	E1
Empower Field at Mile High	E2
Firefighters Museum	F2
History Colorado Center	F2
Larimer Square	F1
LoDo	F1
Metropolitan State Univ. of Denver	E2
Paramount Theatre	F2
Post Office	F1
Public Library	F2
Sakura Square	F1
Skate Park	E1
State Capitol	F2
Tabor Center	F1
Union Station	F1
U.S. Court House	F1
U.S. Mint	F2
Univ. of Colorado at Denver (Downtown Denver Campus)	E2

Place	Page	Grid
Dulac LA	134	B4
Dulce NM	48	C1
Duluth GA	120	C3
Duluth MN	64	C4
Dumas AR	117	F4
Dumas MS	118	C2
Dumas TX	50	A2
Dumfries VA	144	A4
Dumont CO	41	D1
Dumont IA	73	D4
Dunbar PA	102	B1
Dunbar WV	101	E4
Duncan AZ	55	F2
Duncan MS	118	A3
Duncan OK	51	E4
Duncan SC	121	F2
Duncannon PA	93	D4
Duncansville PA	92	C4
Duncanville TX	59	F2
Dundalk MD	144	C2
Dundas MN	73	D1
Dundee FL	141	D2
Dundee MI	90	C1
Dundee NY	79	D4
Dundee OR	20	B2
Dundy Co. NE	42	B1
Dunean SC	217	A2
Dunedin FL	140	B2
Dunellen NJ	147	E1
Dunes City OR	20	A4
Dunkerton IA	73	E4
Dunkirk IN	90	A4
Dunkirk MD	144	C4
Dunkirk NY	78	A4
Dunkirk OH	90	C3
Dunklin Co. MO	108	B4
Dunlap IL	88	B3
Dunlap IN	89	F2
Dunlap IA	86	A1
Dunlap TN	120	B1
Dunleith DE	274	D2
Dunmore PA	93	F2
Dunn NC	123	D1
Dunn Co. ND	18	A3
Dunn Co. WI	67	E3
Dunnellon FL	138	C4
Dunn Loring VA	270	A3
Dunn's Corners RI	150	C4
Dunnstown PA	93	D3
Dunseith ND	18	C1
Dunsmuir CA	28	C3
Dunwoody GA	190	E2
DuPage Co. IL	89	D1
Duplin Co. NC	115	C4
Dupo IL	98	A3
Dupont CO	209	C2
Dupont PA	261	C2
DuPont WA	12	C3
Dupree SD	26	B2
Duquesne MO	106	B2
Duquesne PA	250	D3
Du Quoin IL	98	B4
Durand IL	74	B4
Durand MI	76	B3
Durand WI	67	E4
Durango CO	40	B4
Durant IA	87	F2
Durant MS	126	B1
Durant OK	59	F1
Durham CA	36	B1
Durham CT	149	E1
Durham NH	82	A4
Durham NC	112	C4
Durham OR	251	C3

Figures after entries indicate page number and grid reference.

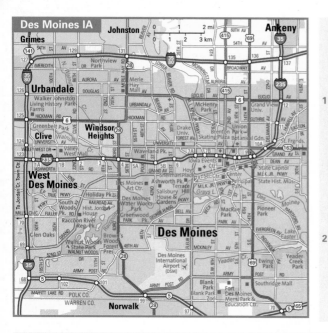

Des Moines IA

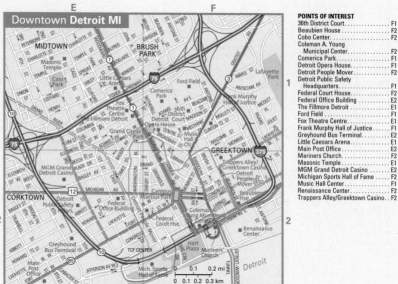

Downtown Detroit MI

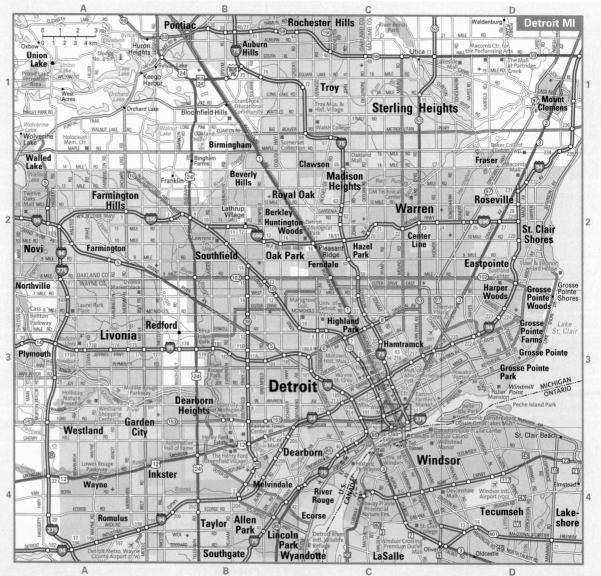

Detroit MI

Entries in **bold black** indicate counties or parishes.
Entries in **bold color** indicate cities with detailed inset maps.

Durham Co. NC 112 C4
Duryea PA 93 F2
Dushore PA 93 E2
Duson LA 133 E2
Dustin OK 51 F3
Dutchess Co. NY 148 C1
Dutch Neck NJ 147 D2
Dutton MT 15 F2
Duval Co. FL 139 D2
Duval Co. TX 63 E2
Duvall WA 12 C3

Duluth MN

Duxbury MA 151 E2
Duxbury VT 81 E2
Dwaar Kill NY 148 A1
Dwarf KY 111 D1
Dwight IL 88 C3
Dyer AR 116 C1
Dyer IN 89 D2
Dyer TN 108 C4
Dyer Co. TN 108 C4
Dyersburg TN 108 C4
Dyersville IA 73 F4
Dyess AR 118 B1
Dysart IA 87 E1

E

Eads CO 42 A3
Eagan MN 235 D4
Eagar AZ 48 A4
Eagle CO 40 C1
Eagle ID 22 B4
Eagle NE 35 F4
Eagle WI 74 C3
Eagle Bend MN 66 B1
Eagle Butte SD 26 B2
Eagle Co. CO 40 C1
Eagle Grove IA 72 C4
Eagle Lake FL 140 C2
Eagle Lake ME 85 D1
Eagle Lake MN 72 C1
Eagle Lake TX 61 F2
Eagle Mtn. UT 31 E4
Eagle Nest NM 49 D1
Eagle Pass TX 60 B4
Eagle Pt. OR 28 C2
Eagle River MI 65 F3
Eagle River WI 68 B2
Eagleton Vil. TN 110 C4
Eagleville PA 146 C2
Eagleville TN 109 F4
Earle AR 118 A1
Earlham IA 86 C2
Earlimart CA 45 D4
Earlington KY 109 E2
Earlsboro OK 51 F3
Earlville IL 88 C2
Earlville IA 73 F4
Earlville NY 79 E4
Earlville PA 146 B2
Early IA 72 A4
Early TX 59 D4
Early Co. GA 128 C4
Earlysville VA 102 C4
Earth TX 50 A4
Easley SC 121 E2
E. Alton IL 98 A3
E. Arcadia NC 123 E3
E. Arlington VT 81 D4
E. Atlantic Beach NY 241 G5
E. Aurora NY 78 B4
E. Bank WV 101 F4
E. Barre VT 81 E2
E. Barrington NH 81 F4
E. Baton Rouge Par. LA 134 A1
E. Bend NC 112 A3
E. Berlin PA 103 E1
E. Bernard TX 61 F2
E. Bernstadt KY 110 C2
E. Bethel MN 67 D3
E. Blackstone MA 150 C2
E. Brady PA 92 A3
E. Brewster MA 151 F3
E. Brewton AL 135 F1
E. Bridgewater MA 151 D2
E. Brookfield MA 150 B2
E. Brooklyn CT 150 B3
E. Brunswick NJ 147 E1
E. Butler PA 92 A3
E. Camden AR 117 E4
E. Canton OH 91 E3
E. Carbon UT 39 F1
E. Carroll Par. LA 126 A2
Eastchester NY 148 B3
E. Chicago IN 89 D2
E. Cleveland OH 91 E2
E. Dennis MA 151 F3
E. Douglas MA 150 C2
E. Dublin GA 129 E2
E. Dubuque IL 73 F4
E. Duke OK 50 C4
E. Dundee IL 203 A2
E. Ellijay GA 120 C2
E. End AR 117 E2
E. Falmouth MA 151 E4
E. Feliciana Par. LA 134 A1
E. Flat Rock NC 121 E1
E. Freehold NJ 147 E2
E. Freetown MA 151 D3
E. Gaffney SC 121 F1
E. Galesburg IL 88 A3
Eastgate WA 262 B3
E. Glacier Park MT 15 D2
E. Glastonbury CT 149 E1
E. Glenville NY 94 B1
E. Grand Forks MN 19 E2
E. Grand Rapids MI 215 B2
E. Greenbush NY 188 E3
E. Greenville PA 146 B1
E. Greenwich RI 150 C3
E. Gull Lake MN 64 A4
E. Haddam CT 149 E1
Eastham MA 151 F3
E. Hampton CT 149 E1
Easthampton MA 150 A1
E. Hampton NY 149 F3
E. Hanover NJ 148 A3
E. Hardwick VT 81 E2
E. Hartford CT 150 A3
E. Harwich MA 151 F3
E. Haven CT 149 D2
E. Helena MT 15 E4
E. Highland Park VA 254 B1
E. Holden ME 83 D1
E. Hope ID 14 B2
E. Ithaca NY 79 D4
E. Jordan MI 69 F3
Eastlake OH 91 E2
Eastland TX 59 D3
Eastland Co. TX 59 D3
E. Lansdowne PA 248 B3
E. Lansing MI 76 A4
E. Lebanon ME 82 A4
E. Liverpool OH 91 F3
E. Longmeadow MA 150 A2
E. Los Angeles CA 228 D3
Eastman GA 129 E3
E. Marion MA 151 E3
E. Marion NY 149 E2
E. McKeesport PA 250 D3
E. Meadow NY 148 C4
E. Middlebury VT 81 D3
E. Middletown NY 148 A1
E. Millcreek UT 257 B2
E. Millinocket ME 85 D4
E. Moline IL 88 A2
E. Montpelier VT 81 E2
E. Moriches NY 149 E4
E. Mtn. TX 124 B2
E. Naples FL 142 C2
E. Nassau NY 94 B1
E. Newark NJ 240 B3
E. Newnan GA 128 C1
E. Northport ME 82 C2
E. Northport NY 148 C3
E. Olympia WA 12 C4
Easton CA 44 C3
Easton CT 148 C2
Easton ME 85 E2
Easton MD 145 D3
Easton PA 93 F3
Easton TX 124 B2
E. Orange NJ 148 A4
E. Orleans MA 151 F3
Eastover NC 123 D1
Eastover SC 122 B4
E. Palatka FL 139 D3
E. Palestine OH 91 F3
E. Palo Alto CA 259 D5
E. Patchogue NY 149 D4
E. Peoria IL 88 B3
E. Petersburg PA 146 A2
E. Pittsburgh PA 250 D2
Eastpoint FL 137 D3
E. Point GA 120 C4
Eastpointe MI 210 D2
Eastport ME 83 F1
Eastport NY 149 E3
E. Poultney VT 81 D3
E. Prairie MO 108 C2
E. Prospect PA 103 E1
E. Providence RI 150 C3
E. Quincy CA 36 C1
E. Quogue NY 149 E3
E. Randolph NY 92 B1
E. Ridge TN 120 B2
E. Rochester NY 254 G2
E. Rockaway NY 147 F1
E. Rockingham NC 122 C2
E. Rutherford NJ 240 C2
E. St. Louis IL 98 A3
E. Sandwich MA 151 E3
E. Setauket NY 149 D3
E. Shoreham NY 149 D3
Eastsound WA 12 C1
E. Spencer NC 112 A4
E. Stroudsburg PA 93 F3
E. Swanzey NH 95 D1
E. Syracuse NY 265 B2
E. Tawakoni TX 59 F2
E. Tawas MI 76 B1
E. Texas PA 146 B1
E. Thermopolis WY 24 C4
E. Troy WI 74 C4
E. Vassalboro ME 82 C2
Eastview MD 144 B1
Eastview TN 119 D2
E. Village CT 149 D2
Eastville VA 114 B3
E. Wareham MA 151 E3
E. Washington PA 92 A4
E. Wenatchee WA 13 D3
E. Wilton ME 82 B2
E. Winthrop ME 82 B2
Eastwood LA 125 D2
E. York PA 275 F1
Eaton CO 33 E4
Eaton IN 90 A4
Eaton OH 100 B1
Eaton Co. MI 76 A4
Eaton Estates OH 91 D2
Eaton Park FL 266 E2
Eaton Rapids MI 76 A4
Eatons Neck NY 148 C3
Eatonton GA 129 E1
Eatontown NJ 147 E2
Eatonville FL 246 C1
Eatonville WA 12 C4
Eau Claire MI 89 F1
Eau Claire WI 67 F4
Eau Claire Co. WI 67 F4
Ebensburg PA 92 B4
Eccles WV 111 F1
Echo OR 21 E1
Echols Co. GA 138 B1
Eclectic AL 128 A2
Economy PA 92 A3
Ecorse MI 210 C4
Ecru MS 118 C3
Ector TX 59 F1
Ector Co. TX 57 F3
Edcouch TX 63 E4
Eddington ME 83 D1
Eddy Co. NM 57 E2
Eddy Co. ND 19 D3
Eddystone PA 248 A4
Eddyville IA 87 D2
Eddyville KY 109 D2
Eden ID 31 D1
Eden MD 103 F4
Eden NY 78 A4
Eden NC 112 B3
Eden TX 58 C4
Eden WI 74 C2
Eden WY 32 A2
Eden Prairie MN 235 A4
Edenton NC 113 F4
Eden Valley MN 66 B3
Edenville NY 148 A2
Edgar NE 35 E4
Edgar WI 68 A4
Edgar Co. IL 99 D1
Edgard LA 134 B3
Edgartown MA 151 E4
Edgecliff Vil. TX 207 A3
Edgecombe Co. NC 113 E4
Edgefield SC 121 F4
Edgefield Co. SC 121 F4
Edgeley ND 19 D4
Edgemere MD 144 C2
Edgemont SD 25 F4
Edgemoor DE 146 B4
Edgerton KS 96 B3
Edgerton MN 27 F4
Edgerton MO 96 B2
Edgerton OH 90 A2
Edgerton WI 74 B3
Edgerton WY 25 D4
Edgewater AL 195 D2
Edgewater CO 209 B3
Edgewater FL 139 E4
Edgewater NJ 240 D2
Edgewater Park NJ 147 D3
Edgewood FL 246 C3
Edgewood IN 89 F4
Edgewood IA 73 F4
Edgewood KY 204 B3
Edgewood MD 145 D1
Edgewood NM 48 C3
Edgewood OH 91 F1
Edgewood PA 250 C2
Edgewood TX 124 A2
Edgewood WA 262 B5
Edina MN 67 D4
Edina MO 87 E4
Edinboro PA 92 A1
Edinburg IL 98 B1
Edinburg NJ 147 D2
Edinburg ND 19 E2
Edinburg TX 63 E4
Edinburg VA 102 C3
Edinburgh IN 99 F2
Edison GA 128 C4
Edison NJ 147 E1
Edisto Beach SC 130 C2
Edmond OK 51 E2
Edmonds WA 12 C3
Edmondson AR 118 B1
Edmonson Co. KY 109 F2
Edmonston MD 270 E2
Edmonton KY 110 A2
Edmore MI 76 A2
Edmore ND 19 D2
Edmunds Co. SD 27 D2
Edmundson MO 256 B1
Edna KS 106 A2
Edna TX 61 F3
Edon OH 90 A2
Edwards CO 40 C1
Edwards MS 126 A2
Edwardsburg MI 89 F1
Edwards Co. IL 99 D4
Edwards Co. KS 43 D4
Edwards Co. TX 60 B2
Edwardsville IL 98 B3
Edwardsville KS 96 B2
Edwardsville PA 261 A1
Effingham IL 98 C2
Effingham KS 96 A1
Effingham Co. GA 130 B2
Effingham Co. IL 98 C2
Effort PA 93 F3
Egan SD 27 F3
Egg Harbor City NJ 147 D4
Egypt PA 189 A1
Ehrenberg AZ 53 F3
Ehrhardt SC 130 C1
Ekalaka MT 25 F1
Elaine AR 118 A3
Elam PA 146 B3
Elba AL 128 A4
Elba NY 78 B3
Elberfeld IN 99 E4
Elberta AL 135 F2
Elberta MI 69 E4
Elberta UT 39 E1
Elbert Co. CO 41 E2
Elbert Co. GA 121 E3
Elberton GA 121 E3
Elbow Lake MN 27 F1
Elbridge NY 79 D3
Elburn IL 88 C1
El Cajon CA 53 D4
El Campo TX 61 F3
El Cenizo TX 63 D2
El Centro CA 53 E4
El Cerrito CA 229 H4
El Cerrito CA 259 B2
Eldersburg MD 144 B1
Eldon IA 87 E3
Eldon MO 97 E4
Eldon OK 106 B4
Eldora IA 73 D4
El Dorado AR 125 E1
Eldorado IL 109 D1
El Dorado KS 43 F4
Eldorado OK 50 C4
Eldorado TX 60 B1
El Dorado Co. CA 36 C2
Eldorado Sprs. CO 209 A1
El Dorado Sprs. MO 96 C4
Eldred PA 92 C1
Eldridge IA 88 A2
Eleanor WV 101 E3
Electra TX 59 D1
Electric City WA 13 E2
Eleele HI 152 B1
Elephant Butte NM 56 B2
Eleva WI 67 F4
Elfers FL 140 B2
Elfrida AZ 55 E4
Elgin AZ 55 D4
Elgin IL 88 C1
Elgin IA 73 E3
Elgin MN 73 E1
Elgin NE 35 E2
Elgin ND 18 B4
Elgin OK 51 D4
Elgin OR 21 F1
Elgin SC 122 A3
Elgin SC 122 B2
Elgin TX 61 E1
El Granada CA 259 B5
Elida OH 90 B3
Elihu KY 110 B2
Elizabeth CO 41 E2
Elizabeth IL 74 A4
Elizabeth LA 133 E1
Elizabeth NJ 148 A4
Elizabeth PA 92 A4
Elizabeth WV 101 F2
Elizabeth City NC 113 F3
Elizabeth Lake CA 52 C2
Elizabethton TN 111 E3
Elizabethtown IL 109 D1
Elizabethtown KY 110 A1
Elizabethtown NY 81 D2
Elizabethtown NC 123 D2
Elizabethtown PA 93 E4
Elizabethville PA 93 D4
El Jebel CO 40 C2
Elkader IA 73 F3

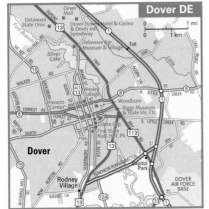

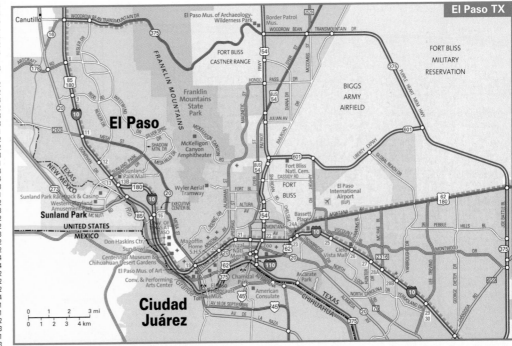

Figures after entries indicate page number and grid reference.

Elk City OK 50 C3
Elk Co. KS 43 F4
Elk Co. PA 92 B2
Elk Grove CA 36 C3
Elk Grove Vil. IL 203 C3
Elkhart IN 89 F2
Elkhart KS 50 A1
Elkhart TX 124 A4
Elkhart Co. IN 89 F2
Elkhart Lake WI 74 C2
Elkhorn CA 236 E2
Elk Horn IA 86 B2
Elkhorn WI 74 C4
Elkhorn City KY 111 E1
Elkin NC 112 A3
Elkins AR 106 C4
Elkins WV 102 A3
Elkland PA 93 D1
Elkmont AL 119 F2
Elk Mound WI 67 E4
Elko NV 30 B4
Elko Co. NV 30 C3
Elko New Market MN 67 D4
Elk Pt. SD 35 F1
Elk Rapids MI 69 F4
Elkridge MD 144 C2
Elk Ridge UT 39 E1
Elk River MN 66 C3
Elk Run Hts. IA 73 E4
Elkton KY 109 E2
Elkton MD 145 E1
Elkton MI 76 C2
Elkton SD 27 F3
Elkton TN 119 F2
Elkton VA 102 C3
Elkview WV 101 F3
Elkville IL 98 B4
El Lago TX 132 B3
Ellaville GA 129 D3
Ellenboro NC 121 F1
Ellenboro WV 101 F2
Ellendale DE 145 F3
Ellendale MN 72 C2
Ellendale ND 27 D1
Ellensburg WA 13 D4
Ellenton FL 266 B4
Ellenville NY 94 A3
Ellerbe NC 122 C2

Erie PA

Ellerslie MD 102 C1
Ellettsville IN 99 F2
Ellicott NY 78 B4
Ellicott City MD 144 C2
Ellijay GA 120 C2
Ellington CT 150 A3
Ellington MO 108 A2
Ellinwood KS 43 D3
Elliott Co. KY 101 D4
Ellis KS 42 C2
Ellis Co. KS 43 D2
Ellis Co. OK 50 C2
Ellis Co. TX 59 F3
Ellisport WA 262 A4
Elliston MT 15 E4
Elliston VA 112 B2
Ellisville MS 126 C4
Ellisville MO 256 A2
Elloree SC 122 B4
Ellsworth IA 72 C4
Ellsworth KS 43 E2
Ellsworth ME 83 D2
Ellsworth MI 69 F3
Ellsworth MN 27 F4
Ellsworth PA 92 A4
Ellsworth WI 67 E4
Ellsworth Co. KS 43 E3
Ellwood City PA 91 F3
Elma IA 73 D3
Elma NY 78 B3
Elma WA 12 B4
Elm City NC 113 D4
Elm Creek NE 35 D4
Elmendorf TX 61 D3
Elmer NJ 145 F1
Elm Grove WI 234 B2
Elmhurst IL 89 D1
Elmira NY 93 D1
El Mirage AZ 249 A1
Elmira Hts. NY 93 D1
Elm Mott TX 59 E4
Elmo UT 39 F2
Elmont NY 148 C4
Elmont VA 113 E1
El Monte CA 228 E2
Elmore MN 72 C2
Elmore OH 90 C2
Elmore City OK 51 E4
Elmore Co. AL 128 A2
Elmore Co. ID 22 B4
Elm Sprs. AR 106 C3
Elmville CT 150 B3
Elmwood IL 88 A3
Elmwood NE 35 F4
Elmwood WI 67 E4
Elmwood Park IL 203 D4
Elmwood Park NJ 240 C1
Elmwood Place OH 204 B2
Elnora IN 99 E3
Elnora NY 94 B1
Elon NC 112 C4
Eloy AZ 54 C2
El Paso IL 88 B3
El Paso TX 56 C4
El Paso Co. CO 41 E2
El Paso Co. TX 56 C4
El Portal FL 233 B4
El Prado NM 49 D1
El Reno OK 51 E3
El Rio CA 52 B2
El Rito NM 48 C2
Elroy WI 74 A2
Elsa TX 63 E4
Elsah IL 98 A2
Elsberry MO 98 A2
El Segundo CA 228 C3
Elsie MI 76 A3
Elsinore UT 39 E3
Elsmere DE 146 B4
Elsmere KY 100 B2
Elsmere NY 188 D3
El Sobrante CA 259 C1
Elton LA 133 E2
Elvaton MD 193 C5
Elverson PA 146 B2
Elwood IL 89 D2
Elwood IN 89 F4
Elwood KS 96 B1
Elwood NE 34 C4
Elwood NJ 147 D4
Elwood UT 31 E3
Ely IA 87 E1
Ely MN 64 C2
Ely NV 38 B2
Elyria OH 91 D2
Elysburg PA 93 E3
Elysian MN 72 C1
Emanuel Co. GA 129 F2
Emerado ND 19 E2
Emerald Isle NC 115 D4
Emerson GA 120 C3
Emerson NE 35 F2
Emerson NJ 148 B3
Emery SD 27 E4
Emery UT 39 E2
Emery Co. UT 39 F2
Emery Mills ME 82 A4
Emeryville CA 259 C2
Emigsville PA 103 E1
Emily MN 64 B4
Eminence KY 100 A4
Eminence MO 107 F2
Emlenton PA 92 A2
Emmaus PA 146 B1
Emmet AR 117 D4
Emmet Co. IA 72 B3
Emmet Co. MI 70 B3
Emmetsburg IA 72 B3
Emmett ID 22 B4
Emmitsburg MD 103 D1
Emmonak AK 154 B2
Emmons Co. ND 18 C4
Emmorton MD 145 D1
Emory TX 124 A1
Emory VA 111 F2
Empire CO 41 D1
Empire LA 134 C4
Empire NV 29 E4
Empire City OK 51 E4
Emporia KS 43 F3
Emporia VA 113 E3
Emporium PA 92 C2
Emsworth PA 250 A1
Encampment WY 33 D3
Encinal TX 60 C4
Encinitas CA 53 D4
Enderlin ND 19 E4
Endicott NY 93 E1
Endicott WA 13 F4
Endwell NY 93 E1
Energy IL 108 C1
Enfield CT 150 A2
Enfield IL 99 D4
Enfield NH 81 E3
Enfield NC 113 E4
Enfield Ctr. NH 81 E3
England AR 117 E2
Englewood CO 41 E1
Englewood FL 140 C4
Englewood NJ 148 B3
Englewood OH 100 B1
Englewood TN 120 C1
Englewood Beach FL 140 C4
Englewood Cliffs NJ 240 D1
English IN 99 F4
Englishtown NJ 147 E2
Enhaut PA 218 C2
Enid OK 51 E1
Enigma GA 129 E4
Enka NC 121 E1
Ennis MT 23 E2
Ennis TX 59 F3
Enoch UT 39 D4
Enochville NC 122 B1
Enola PA 218 A1
Enon OH 100 C1
Enoree SC 121 F2
Enosburg Falls VT 81 D1
Ensley FL 135 F2
Ensor KY 109 E1
Enterprise AL 128 B4
Enterprise KS 43 F2
Enterprise MS 127 D3
Enterprise OR 22 A2
Enterprise UT 38 C4
Enterprise WV 102 A2
Entiat WA 13 D3
Enumclaw WA 12 C3
Ephraim UT 39 E2
Ephrata PA 146 A2
Ephrata WA 13 E3
Epping NH 81 F4
Epps LA 125 F2
Epworth IA 73 F4
Epworth Hts. OH 204 C1
Equality IL 109 D1
Erath LA 133 F3
Erath Co. TX 59 D3
Erda UT 31 E4
Erial NJ 146 C4
Erick OK 50 C3
Erie CO 209 B1
Erie IL 88 A2
Erie KS 106 A1
Erie PA 92 A1
Erie Co. NY 78 B4
Erie Co. OH 91 D2
Erie Co. PA 92 A1
Erin TN 109 E3
Erlanger KY 100 B2
Erwin NC 123 D1
Erwin TN 111 E4
Erwinville LA 134 A2
Escalante UT 39 E4
Escalon CA 36 C4
Escambia Co. AL 136 A1
Escambia Co. FL 135 F1
Escanaba MI 69 D2
Escatawpa MS 195 C1
Escobares TX 63 D4
Escondido CA 53 D4
Esko MN 64 C4
Eskridge KS 43 F2
Esmeralda Co. NV 37 F4

Fargo ND

Española NM 49 D2
Espanong NJ 148 A3
Esparto CA 36 B2
Espy PA 93 E3
Essex CT 149 E2
Essex IA 86 A3
Essex MD 144 C2
Essex MA 151 F1
Essex MO 108 B2
Essex Co. MA 151 F1
Essex Co. NJ 148 A3
Essex Co. NY 80 C3
Essex Co. VT 81 E1
Essex Co. VA 103 E4
Essex Fells NJ 240 A2
Essex Jct. VT 81 D2
Essexville MI 76 B2
Estacada OR 20 C2
Estancia NM 49 D4
Estelle LA 239 C2
Estelline SD 27 F3
Estell Manor NJ 104 C3
Ester AK 154 C2
Estero FL 142 C1
Estes Park CO 33 E4
Estherville IA 72 B2
Estherwood LA 133 E2
Estill SC 130 B2
Estill Co. KY 110 C1
Estill Sprs. TN 120 A1
Estral Beach MI 90 C1
Ethan SD 27 E4
Ethel MS 126 C1
Ethete WY 32 B1
Ethridge TN 119 E1
Etna CA 28 B3
Etna PA 250 C1
Etna Green IN 89 F2
Etowah NC 121 E1
Etowah TN 120 C1
Etowah Co. AL 120 A3
Ettrick VA 113 E2
Ettrick WI 73 F1
Eubank KY 110 B2
Euclid OH 91 E2
Eudora AR 126 A1
Eudora KS 96 B3
Eufaula AL 128 B3
Eufaula OK 116 A1
Eugene OR 20 B4
Euharlee GA 120 B3
Euless TX 207 C2
Eunice LA 133 E2
Eunice NM 57 F3
Eupora MS 118 C4
Eureka CA 28 A4
Eureka IL 88 B3
Eureka KS 43 F4
Eureka MO 98 A3
Eureka MT 14 C1
Eureka NV 38 A1
Eureka SD 27 D1
Eureka UT 39 E1
Eureka Co. NV 30 B4
Eureka Mill SC 122 A2
Eureka Sprs. AR 106 C3
Eustace TX 59 F3
Eustis FL 140 C1
Eustis NE 34 C4
Eutaw AL 127 E2
Eva AL 119 F3
Evadale TX 132 C2
Evangeline Par. LA 133 E1
Evans CO 33 E4
Evans GA 121 F4
Evans WV 101 E3
Evans City PA 92 A3
Evans Co. GA 130 B3
Evansdale IA 73 E4
Evans Mills NY 79 E1
Evanston IL 89 D1
Evanston WY 31 F3
Evansville IL 98 B4
Evansville IN 99 D4
Evansville MN 66 A2
Evansville WI 74 B4
Evansville WY 33 D1
Evaro MT 15 D4
Evart MI 75 F1
Evarts KY 111 D2
Eveleth MN 64 C3
Evendale OH 204 B1
Evening Shade AR 107 F4
Everett MA 197 C1
Everett PA 102 C1
Everett WA 12 C2
Everglades City FL 143 D2
Evergreen AL 127 F4
Evergreen CO 41 D1
Evergreen MT 15 D2
Evergreen Park IL 203 D5
Everly IA 72 A3
Everman TX 207 B3
Everson PA 92 A4
Everson WA 12 C1
Evesboro NJ 147 D3
Ewa Beach HI 152 A3
Ewa Villages HI 152 A3
Ewing NE 35 E2
Ewing NJ 147 D2
Ewing VA 111 D3
Excel AL 127 F4
Excelsior Sprs. MO 96 C2
Exeter CA 45 D3
Exeter MO 106 C3
Exeter NE 35 E4

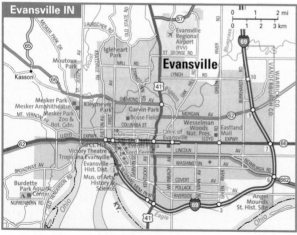

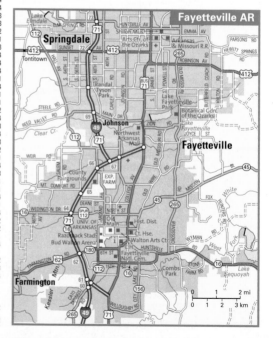

Entries in **bold black** indicate counties or parishes.
Entries in **bold color** indicate cities with detailed inset maps.

Exeter NH 82 A4
Exeter PA 261 C1
Exeter RI 150 C4
Exira IA 86 B2
Exmore VA 114 B3
Experiment GA 129 D1
Exton PA 146 B3
Eyota MN 73 E1

F

Fabens TX 56 C4
Factoryville PA 93 F2
Fairacres NM 56 B3
Fairbank IA 73 E4
Fairbanks AK 154 C2
Fairbanks FL 138 C3
Fairbanks ME 82 B1
Fair Bluff NC 123 D3
Fairborn OH 100 C1
Fairburn GA 120 C4
Fairbury IL 88 C3
Fairbury NE 43 E1
Fairchance PA 102 B1
Fairchild WI 67 F4
Fairchilds TX 132 A4
Fairfax CA 36 B3
Fairfax DE 274 E1
Fairfax IA 87 E1
Fairfax MN 66 B4
Fairfax MO 86 A4
Fairfax OH 204 C2
Fairfax OK 51 F1
Fairfax SC 130 B1
Fairfax VT 81 D1
Fairfax VA 144 A3
Fairfax Co. VA 144 A3
Fairfield AL 119 F4
Fairfield CA 36 B3
Fairfield CT 149 D2
Fairfield ID 22 C4
Fairfield IL 99 D4
Fairfield IA 87 E3
Fairfield ME 82 C2
Fairfield MT 15 E3
Fairfield NE 35 E4
Fairfield NJ 240 A1
Fairfield OH 100 B2
Fairfield TX 59 F4
Fairfield WA 14 B3
Fairfield Bay AR 117 E1
Fairfield Co. CT 149 D2
Fairfield Co. OH 101 D1
Fairfield Co. SC 122 A3
Fairfield Glade TN 110 B4
Fairgrove MI 76 B2
Fair Grove MO 107 D1
Fairhaven MA 151 D3
Fair Haven MI 76 C4
Fair Haven NJ 147 E2
Fair Haven NY 79 D3
Fair Haven VT 81 D3
Fairhope AL 135 E2
Fairland IN 99 F1
Fairland MD 144 B2
Fairland OK 106 B2
Fair Lawn NJ 148 B3
Fairlawn OH 188 A1
Fairlawn VA 112 A2
Fairlea WV 112 A1
Fairless Hills PA 147 D2
Fairmead CA 44 C2
Fairmont MN 72 B2
Fairmont NE 35 E4
Fairmont NC 123 D3
Fairmont WV 102 A2
Fairmont City IL 256 C2
Fairmount GA 120 C3
Fairmount IL 99 D1
Fairmount IN 89 F4
Fairmount MD 103 F4
Fairmount NY 79 D3
Fairmount ND 27 F1
Fairmount TN 120 B1
Fairmount Hts. MD 270 E3
Fair Oaks CA 255 C1
Fair Oaks GA 120 C4
Fair Oaks Ranch TX 61 D2
Fair Plain MI 89 E1
Fairplains NC 111 F3
Fairplay CO 41 D2
Fairport NY 78 C3
Fairport Harbor OH 91 E1
Fairton NJ 145 F1
Fairview AL 119 F3
Fairview GA 120 B2
Fairview MI 70 C4
Fairview MT 17 F2
Fairview NJ 148 B3
Fairview NC 121 E1
Fairview NC 122 B1
Fairview OK 51 D2
Fairview OR 20 C2
Fairview PA 91 F1
Fairview TN 109 E4
Fairview TX 59 F2
Fairview UT 39 E1
Fairview WV 102 A1
Fairview WY 31 F1
Fairview Hts. IL 98 B3
Fairview Park IN 99 E1
Fairview Park OH 204 D2
Fairview Shores FL 246 C1
Fairway KS 224 B3
Faison NC 123 E1
Faith NC 122 B1
Faith SD 26 B2
Falconer NY 92 B1
Falcon Hts. MN 235 C2
Falfurrias TX 63 E3
Falkville AL 119 F3
Fall Branch TN 111 E3
Fallbrook CA 53 D3
Fall City WA 12 C3
Fall Creek WI 67 F4
Falling Waters WV 103 D1
Fallon NV 37 E1
Fallon Co. MT 17 F4
Fall River MA 151 D3
Fall River WI 74 B2
Fall River Co. SD 33 F1
Fall River Mills CA 29 D3
Falls Church VA 144 B3
Falls City NE 86 A4
Falls City OR 20 B2
Falls City TX 61 E3
Falls Co. TX 59 F4
Falls Creek PA 92 B3
Fallston MD 144 C1
Fallston NC 122 A1
Falmouth KY 100 B3
Falmouth MA 151 E4
Falmouth VA 103 D4
Falmouth Foreside ME 82 B3
Fancy Farm KY 108 C2
Fannett TX 132 C3
Fannin Co. GA 120 C2
Fannin Co. TX 59 F1
Fanning Sprs. FL 138 B3
Fanwood NJ 147 E1
Fargo ND 19 F4
Far Hills NJ 148 A4
Faribault MN 73 D1
Faribault Co. MN 72 C2
Farley IA 73 F4
Farmer City IL 88 C4
Farmers Branch TX 207 D1
Farmersburg IN 99 E2
Farmers Mills NY 148 C1
Farmersville CA 45 D3
Farmersville IL 98 B2
Farmersville OH 100 B1
Farmersville PA 189 B1
Farmersville TX 59 F2
Farmerville LA 125 E2
Farmingdale ME 82 C2
Farmingdale NJ 147 E2
Farmingdale NY 148 C4
Farmington AR 106 C4
Farmington CT 94 C3
Farmington IL 88 A3
Farmington IA 87 E3
Farmington ME 82 B1
Farmington MI 210 A2
Farmington MN 67 D4
Farmington MS 119 D2
Farmington MO 108 A1
Farmington NH 81 F4
Farmington NM 48 B1
Farmington UT 31 E3
Farmington WV 102 A1
Farmington Hills MI 210 A2
Farmingville NY 149 D3
Farmland IN 90 A4
Farmville NC 115 C2
Farmville VA 113 D2
Farragut IA 86 A3
Farragut TN 110 C4
Farrell PA 91 F2
Farr West UT 244 A1
Farson WY 32 A2
Farwell MI 76 A2
Farwell TX 49 F4
Faulk Co. SD 27 D2
Faulkner Co. AR 117 E1
Faulkton SD 27 D2
Fauquier Co. VA 144 A4
Favoretta FL 139 E4
Fayette AL 119 E4
Fayette IA 73 E3
Fayette MS 126 A4
Fayette MO 97 D2
Fayette OH 90 B2
Fayette Co. AL 119 E4
Fayette Co. GA 120 C4
Fayette Co. IL 98 C2
Fayette Co. IN 100 A1
Fayette Co. IA 73 E4
Fayette Co. KY 100 B4
Fayette Co. OH 100 C1
Fayette Co. PA 102 B1
Fayette Co. TN 118 C1
Fayette Co. TX 61 E2
Fayette Co. WV 101 F4
Fayetteville AR 106 C4
Fayetteville GA 120 C4
Fayetteville NY 79 E3
Fayetteville NC 123 D2
Fayetteville PA 103 D1
Fayetteville TN 119 F1
Fayetteville WV 101 F4
Fearrington Vil. NC 112 C4
Feasterville PA 248 D1
Federal Hts. CO 209 B2
Federalsburg MD 145 E4
Federal Way WA 12 C3
Felicity OH 100 C3
Felida WA 20 C1
Fellowship NJ 147 D3
Fellsmere FL 141 E3
Felton CA 236 D1
Felton DE 145 E3
Fennimore WI 73 F3
Fennville MI 75 E4
Fenton MI 76 B4
Fenton MO 256 A3
Fentress Co. TN 110 B3
Fenwick Island DE 114 C1
Ferdinand IN 99 E4
Fergus Co. MT 16 B3
Fergus Falls MN 19 F4
Ferguson KY 110 B2
Ferguson MO 256 B1
Fernandina Beach FL 139 D1
Fernan Lake Vil. ID 14 B3
Ferndale CA 28 A4
Ferndale MD 193 C4
Ferndale MI 210 C2
Ferndale PA 146 C1
Ferndale WA 12 C1
Fernley NV 37 E1
Fern Park FL 246 C1
Ferrell NJ 146 C4
Ferrellsburg WV 101 E4
Ferrelview MO 96 B2
Ferriday LA 125 F4
Ferris TX 59 F3
Ferron UT 39 E2
Ferrum VA 112 B2
Ferry Co. WA 13 F2
Ferry Pass FL 135 F2
Ferrysburg MI 75 E3
Fertile MN 19 F3
Fessenden ND 18 C3
Festus MO 98 A4
Fieldale VA 112 B3
Fielding UT 31 E2
Fieldsboro NJ 147 D2
Fife WA 262 B5
Fife Lake MI 69 F4
Filer ID 30 C1
Fillmore CA 52 B2
Fillmore IN 99 E1
Fillmore UT 39 D2
Fillmore Co. MN 73 E2
Fillmore Co. NE 35 E4
Fincastle KY 230 F1
Fincastle VA 112 B1
Findlay IL 98 C1
Findlay OH 90 C3
Finley ND 19 E3
Finley WA 21 E1
Finney Co. KS 42 B3
Finneytown OH 204 B2
Fircrest WA 262 A5
Firebaugh CA 44 C2
Firth ID 23 E4
Firth NE 35 F4
Firthcliffe NY 148 B1
Fisher IL 88 C4
Fisher Co. TX 58 B2
Fishers IN 99 F1
Fishersville VA 102 C4
Fishkill NY 148 B1
Fishkill Plains NY 148 B1
Fiskdale MA 150 B2
Fitchburg MA 95 D1
Fitchburg WI 74 B3
Fitchville CT 149 F1
Fitzgerald GA 129 E4
Fitzwilliam NH 95 D1
Five Corners MA 151 D2
Flagler CO 41 F2
Flagler Beach FL 139 E4
Flagler Co. FL 139 D3
Flagstaff AZ 47 E3
Flagtown NJ 147 D1
Flanagan IL 88 C3
Flanders NY 149 E3
Flanders (E. Lyme) CT 149 F2
Flandreau SD 27 F3
Flasher ND 18 B4
Flathead Co. MT 14 C2
Flat Lick KY 110 C2
Flatonia TX 61 E2
Flat Rock MI 90 C1
Flat Rock NC 112 A3
Flat Rock NC 121 E1
Flatwoods KY 101 D3
Flatwoods WV 102 A3
Fleetwood PA 146 B1
Fleming CO 34 A4
Fleming Co. KY 100 C4
Fleming-Neon KY 111 E2
Flemingsburg KY 100 C3
Flemington NJ 147 D1
Flemington PA 93 D3
Fletcher NC 121 E1
Fletcher OK 51 D4
Flint MI 76 B3
Flint TX 124 A3
Flippin AR 107 E3
Flohrville MD 144 B1
Flomaton AL 135 F1
Floodwood MN 64 C4
Flora IL 98 C3
Flora IN 89 E4
Flora MS 126 B2
Florala AL 136 B1
Floral City FL 140 C1
Floral Park NY 241 G3
Flora Vista NM 48 B1
Flordell Hills MO 256 C1
Florence AL 119 E2
Florence AZ 54 C2
Florence CA 228 D3
Florence CO 41 E3
Florence KS 43 F3
Florence KY 100 B2
Florence MS 126 B3
Florence MT 15 D4
Florence NJ 147 D2
Florence OR 20 B4
Florence SC 122 C3
Florence SD 27 E2
Florence TX 61 E1
Florence WI 68 C2
Florence Co. SC 122 C3
Florence Co. WI 68 C2
Floresville TX 61 D3
Florham Park NJ 148 A4
Florida NY 148 A2
Florida City FL 143 E3
Florien LA 125 D4
Florin CA 36 C3
Florissant MO 98 A3
Flourtown PA 248 B1
Flovilla GA 129 D1
Flower Hill NY 241 G2
Flower Mound TX 207 C1
Flowery Branch GA 121 D3
Flowood MS 126 B3
Floyd VA 112 B2
Floydada TX 58 B1
Floyd Co. GA 120 B3
Floyd Co. IN 99 F4
Floyd Co. IA 73 D3
Floyd Co. KY 111 E1
Floyd Co. TX 50 B4
Floyd Co. VA 112 A2
Flushing MI 76 B3
Flushing OH 91 F4
Fluvanna Co. VA 113 D1
Flying Hills PA 146 A2
Foard Co. TX 58 C1
Fogelsville PA 146 B1
Folcroft PA 248 B4
Foley AL 135 E2
Foley MN 66 C2
Folkston GA 139 D1
Follansbee WV 91 F4
Folly Beach SC 131 D2
Folsom CA 36 C3
Folsom LA 134 B2
Folsom NJ 147 D4

Fayetteville NC

Flagstaff AZ

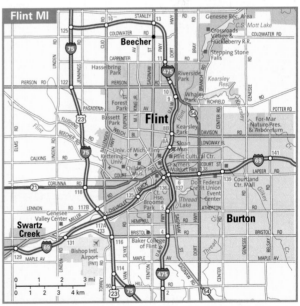

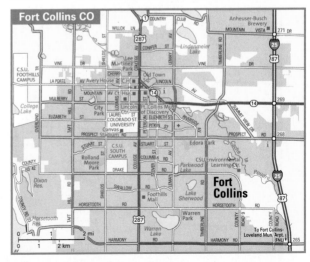

Figures after entries indicate page number and grid reference.

Folsom PA 248 A4
Fonda IA 72 B4
Fonda NY 79 F3
Fond du Lac WI 74 C2
Fond du Lac Co. WI 74 C2
Fontana CA 229 H2
Fontana WI 74 C4
Fontanelle IA 86 B2
Foothill Farms CA 255 C1
Footville WI 74 B4
Ford City CA 52 B1
Ford City PA 92 A3
Ford Co. IL 88 C4
Ford Co. KS 42 C4
Fordland MO 107 D2
Fordoche LA 133 F2
Fords NJ 240 A6
Fords Prairie WA 12 B4
Fordsville KY 109 F1
Fordville ND 19 E2
Fordyce AR 117 E4
Foreman AR 116 C4
Forest MS 126 C2
Forest OH 90 C3
Forest VA 112 C1
Forest Acres SC 205 F1
Forestbrook SC 123 D4
Forest City FL 246 B1
Forest City IA 72 C3
Forest City NC 121 F1
Forest City PA 93 F2
Forest Co. PA 92 B2
Forest Co. WI 68 C2
Forestdale AL 195 E1
Forestdale MA 151 E3
Forest Dale VT 81 D3
Forest Grove OR 20 B2
Forest Grove PA 250 A1
Forest Hts. MD 270 D5
Foresthill CA 36 C2
Forest Hill LA 133 E1
Forest Hill TX 59 E2
Forest Hills FL 139 D4
Forest Hills KY 230 F2
Forest Hills PA 250 C2
Forest Lake IL 203 B1
Forest Lake MN 67 D3
Forest Park GA 190 D5
Forest Park IL 203 D4
Forest Park OH 100 B2
Forest Park OK 244 E2
Forest View IL 203 D5
Forestville CA 36 A3
Forestville MD 271 F4
Forestville NY 78 A4
Forestville OH 100 B2
Forgan OK 50 C1
Forked River NJ 147 E3
Forkland AL 127 E2
Forks WA 12 A2
Forman ND 27 E1
Forney TX 59 F2
Forrest IL 88 C3
Forrest City AR 118 A2
Forrest Co. MS 126 C4
Forreston IL 88 B1
Forsyth GA 129 D1
Forsyth IL 98 C1
Forsyth MO 107 D3
Forsyth MT 25 D1
Forsyth Co. GA 120 C3
Forsyth Co. NC 112 A4
Ft. Ann NY 81 D4
Ft. Ashby WV 102 C2
Ft. Atkinson WI 74 B3
Ft. Belknap Agency MT 16 C2
Ft. Bend Co. TX 132 A4
Ft. Benton MT 15 F2
Ft. Bragg CA 36 A1
Ft. Branch IN 99 D4
Ft. Myers Beach FL 142 C1
Ft. Myers Shores FL 142 C1
Ft. Myers Villas FL 142 C1
Ft. Oglethorpe GA 120 B2
Ft. Payne AL 120 A3
Ft. Peck MT 17 D2
Ft. Pierce FL 141 E3
Ft. Pierre SD 26 C3
Ft. Pillow TN 108 B4
Ft. Plain NY 79 F3
Ft. Recovery OH 90 A4
Ft. Salonga NY 148 C3
Ft. Scott KS 106 B1
Ft. Shaw MT 15 F3
Ft. Shawnee OH 90 B3
Ft. Smith AR 116 C1
Ft. Stockton TX 62 C2
Ft. Sumner NM 49 E4
Ft. Thomas KY 204 B3
Ft. Thompson SD 27 D3
Fountain CO 41 E2
Fountain NC 113 E4
Fountain City IN 100 B1
Fountain City WI 73 E1
Fountain Co. IN 89 D4
Fountain Green UT 39 E1
Fountain Hill PA 146 C1
Fountain Hills AZ 54 C1
Fountain Inn SC 121 F2
Fountain Lake AR 117 D2
Fountain Valley CA 228 E5
Four Corners OR 20 B2
Four Corners TX 220 A3
Four Mile NJ 147 D3
Four Oaks NC 123 D1
Four Seasons MO 97 D4
Fowblesburg MD 144 C1
Fowler CA 44 C3
Fowler CO 41 F3
Fowler IN 89 D3
Frankfort IN 89 E4
Frankfort KS 43 F1
Frankfort KY 100 B4
Frankfort MI 69 E4
Frankfort NY 79 F3
Frankfort OH 101 D2
Franklin GA 128 C1
Franklin ID 31 E2
Franklin IL 98 B1
Franklin IN 99 F2
Franklin KY 109 F3
Franklin LA 133 F3
Franklin ME 83 D2
Franklin MA 150 C2
Franklin MI 210 B2
Franklin MN 66 B4
Franklin NE 43 D1
Franklin NH 81 F4
Franklin NJ 148 A2
Franklin NC 121 D1

Fort Myers FL

Bokeelia A1
Bonita Sprs. B2
Cape Coral A1
Captiva A2
Estero B2
Flamingo Bay A1
Ft. Myers B1
Ft. Myers Beach B2
Ft. Myers Shores B1
Ft. Myers Villas B1
Matlacha A1
N. Ft. Myers B1
Pine Island Ctr. A1
Pineland A1
Punta Rassa A2
St. James City A2
San Carlos Park B2
Sanibel A2
Tice B1
Truckland B2

Frankfort KY

Fresno CA

Fort Wayne IN

Ft. Bridger WY 32 A3
Ft. Calhoun NE 35 F3
Ft. Chiswell VA 112 A2
Ft. Cobb OK 51 D3
Ft. Collins CO 33 E4
Ft. Covington NY 80 C1
Ft. Davis TX 62 B2
Ft. Defiance AZ 48 A2
Ft. Deposit AL 128 A3
Ft. Dodge IA 72 C4
Ft. Dodge KS 42 C4
Ft. Duchesne UT 32 A4
Ft. Edward NY 81 D4
Ft. Fairfield ME 85 E2
Ft. Gaines GA 128 C4
Ft. Garland CO 41 D4
Ft. Gates TX 59 E4
Ft. Gay WV 101 D4
Ft. Gibson OK 106 A4
Ft. Grant AZ 55 E2
Ft. Hall ID 31 E1
Ft. Hancock TX 56 C4
Ft. Johnson NY 80 C4
Ft. Jones CA 28 B3
Ft. Kent ME 85 D1
Ft. Kent Mills ME 85 D1
Ft. Laramie WY 33 E2
Ft. Lauderdale FL 143 F2
Ft. Lawn SC 122 A2
Ft. Lee NJ 148 B3
Ft. Loramie OH 90 B4
Ft. Lupton CO 41 E1
Ft. Madison IA 87 F3
Ft. McKinley OH 208 D1
Ft. Meade FL 140 C3
Ft. Mill SC 122 A2
Ft. Mitchell KY 204 A3
Ft. Montgomery NY 148 B2
Ft. Morgan CO 33 F4
Ft. Myers FL 142 C1
Ft. Totten ND 19 D2
Ft. Towson OK 116 A3
Fortuna CA 28 A4
Ft. Valley GA 129 D2
Fortville IN 99 F1
Ft. Walton Beach FL 136 B2
Ft. Washakie WY 32 B1
Ft. Washington PA 248 C1
Ft. Wayne IN 90 A3
Ft. Wingate NM 48 A3
Ft. Worth TX 59 E2
Ft. Wright KY 204 B3
Ft. Yates ND 26 C1
Forty Fort PA 261 B1
Ft. Yukon AK 154 C2
Fossil OR 21 E2
Fosston MN 19 F3
Foster Ctr. RI 150 C3
Foster City CA 259 C4
Foster Co. ND 19 D3
Fostoria MI 76 C3
Fostoria OH 90 C3
Fouke AR 124 C1
Fowler KS 42 C4
Fowler MI 76 A3
Fowlerville MI 76 B4
Foxboro MA 151 D2
Fox Chapel PA 250 C1
Fox Chase KY 100 A4
Fox Crossing WI 74 C1
Foxfield CO 209 D4
Fox Island WA 262 A5
Fox Lake IL 74 C4
Fox Lake WI 74 B2
Fox Pt. WI 234 D1
Fox River Grove IL 88 C1
Frackville PA 93 E3
Framingham MA 150 C1
Francesville IN 89 E3
Francis UT 31 F4
Francisco IN 99 E4
Francis Creek WI 75 D1
Franconia VA 144 B3
Frankenmuth MI 76 B3
Frankford DE 145 F4
Frankfort IL 89 D2
Franklin OH 100 B1
Franklin PA 92 A2
Franklin TN 109 F4
Franklin TX 59 F4
Franklin VA 113 F3
Franklin WV 102 B3
Franklin WI 74 C3
Franklin Co. AL 119 E3
Franklin Co. AR 116 C1
Franklin Co. FL 137 D3
Franklin Co. GA 121 D3
Franklin Co. ID 31 F2
Franklin Co. IL 98 C4
Franklin Co. IN 100 A2
Franklin Co. IA 72 C4
Franklin Co. KS 96 A3
Franklin Co. KY 100 B4
Franklin Co. ME 82 B1
Franklin Co. MA 150 A1
Franklin Co. MS 126 A4
Franklin Co. MO 97 F3
Franklin Co. NE 43 D1
Franklin Co. NY 80 C2

Entries in **bold black** indicate counties or parishes.
Entries in **bold color** indicate cities with detailed inset maps.

Franklin Co. NC 113 D4
Franklin Co. OH 101 D1
Franklin Co. PA 103 D1
Franklin Co. TN 120 A1
Franklin Co. TX 124 B1
Franklin Co. VT 81 D1
Franklin Co. VA 112 B2
Franklin Co. WA 13 F4
Franklin Furnace OH 101 D3
Franklin Grove IL 88 B1
Franklin Par. LA 125 F2
Franklin Park IL 203 C4
Franklin Park PA 92 A3
Franklin Sprs. GA 121 E3
Franklin Square NY 241 G4
Franklinton LA 134 B1
Franklinton NC 113 D4
Franklinville NJ 145 F1
Franklinville NY 78 B4
Franklinville NC 112 B4
Frankston TX 124 A3
Frankton IN 89 F4
Frannie WY 24 B2
Fraser CO 41 D1
Fraser MI 210 D2
Frazee MN 19 F4
Frazer MT 17 E2
Frazeysburg OH 91 D4
Frazier Park CA 52 B1
Frederic WI 67 E2
Frederica DE 145 E3
Frederick CO 41 E1
Frederick MD 144 A1
Frederick OK 51 D4
Frederick SD 27 D1
Frederick Co. MD 144 A1
Frederick Co. VA 102 C2
Fredericksburg IA 73 E3
Fredericksburg PA 92 A2
Fredericksburg PA 93 E4
Fredericksburg TX 61 D2
Fredericksburg VA 103 D4
Fredericktown MO 108 A1
Fredericktown OH 91 D4
Fredonia AZ 47 D1
Fredonia KS 106 A1
Fredonia KY 109 D2
Fredonia NY 78 A4
Fredonia PA 91 F2
Fredonia WI 74 C2
Freeborn Co. MN 72 C2
Freeburg IL 98 B3
Freeburg PA 93 D3
Freedom CA 44 B2
Freedom WI 74 C1
Freehold NJ 147 E2
Freeland MI 76 B2
Freeland PA 93 E3
Freeland WA 262 A1
Freeman MO 96 B3
Freeman SD 27 E4
Freemansburg PA 146 C1
Freeport FL 136 B2
Freeport IL 74 B4
Freeport ME 82 B3
Freeport NY 147 F1
Freeport PA 92 A3
Freeport TX 133 E4
Freer TX 63 E2
Freestone Co. TX 59 F4
Freetown IN 99 F2
Freetown NY 149 F3
Freeville NY 79 D4
Freewood Acres NJ 147 E2
Fremont CA 36 B4
Fremont IN 90 A1
Fremont IA 87 E2
Fremont MI 75 F2
Fremont NE 35 F3
Fremont NH 81 F4
Fremont NC 123 E1
Fremont OH 90 C2
Fremont WI 74 B1
Fremont Co. CO 41 D3
Fremont Co. ID 23 F3
Fremont Co. IA 86 A3
Fremont Co. WY 32 C1
Fremont Hills MO 107 D2
Frenchburg KY 100 C4
French Camp CA 36 C4
French Lick IN 99 F3
French Settlement LA 134 A2
Frenchtown MT 15 D4
Frenchtown NJ 146 C1
Frenchville ME 85 D1
Fresno CA 44 C3
Fresno TX 220 B4
Fresno Co. CA 37 E4
Frewsburg NY 92 B1
Friant CA 44 C2
Friars Pt. MS 118 A3
Friday Harbor WA 12 B2
Fridley MN 67 D3
Friedens PA 102 C1
Friedensburg PA 146 A1
Friend NE 35 E4
Friendly MD 144 B4
Friendship ME 82 C3
Friendship NY 92 C1
Friendship TN 108 C4
Friendship WI 74 A1
Friendsville MD 102 B1
Friendsville TN 110 C4
Friendswood TX 132 B4
Fries VA 112 A3
Frio Co. TX 60 C3
Friona TX 49 F4
Frisco CO 41 D1
Frisco TX 59 F2
Frisco City AL 127 F4
Fritch TX 50 B2
Froid MT 17 F2
Fromberg MT 24 B2
Frontenac FL 232 A1
Frontenac KS 106 B1
Frontenac MO 256 B2
Frontier ND 19 F4
Frontier Co. NE 34 C4
Fronton TX 63 D4
Front Royal VA 102 C3
Frost TX 59 F3
Frostburg MD 102 C1
Frostproof FL 141 D3
Fruita CO 40 B2
Fruit Cove FL 139 D2
Fruit Hts. UT 31 E3
Fruit Hill OH 204 C3
Fruitland ID 22 A4
Fruitland IA 87 F2
Fruitland MD 103 F4
Fruitland NM 48 B1
Fruitland Park FL 140 C1
Fruitport MI 75 E3
Fruitville FL 266 C5
Fryeburg ME 81 F3
Fulda MN 72 A2
Fullerton CA 52 C3
Fullerton MD 193 D2
Fullerton NE 35 E3
Fulshear TX 132 A3
Fulton IL 88 A1
Fulton KY 108 C3
Fulton MD 144 B2
Fulton MS 119 D3
Fulton MO 97 E3
Fulton NY 79 D3
Fulton TX 61 E4
Fulton Co. AR 107 F3
Fulton Co. GA 120 C3
Fulton Co. IL 88 A4
Fulton Co. IN 89 F3
Fulton Co. KY 108 C3
Fulton Co. NY 79 F3
Fulton Co. OH 90 B2
Fulton Co. PA 103 D1
Fultondale AL 119 F4
Fultonville NY 79 F3
Fuquay-Varina NC 123 D1
Furnas Co. NE 42 C1
Fyffe AL 120 A3

G

Gabbs NV 37 F2
Gackle ND 19 D4
Gadsden AL 120 A3
Gadsden AZ 53 F4
Gadsden TN 108 C4
Gadsden Co. FL 137 D2
Gaffney SC 121 F2
Gage Co. NE 35 F4
Gahanna OH 101 D1
Gail TX 58 B2
Gainesboro TN 110 A3
Gaines Co. TX 57 F2
Gainesville FL 138 C3
Gainesville GA 121 D3
Gainesville MO 107 E3
Gainesville TX 59 E1
Gainesville VA 144 A3
Gaithersburg MD 144 B2
Galatia IL 108 C1
Galax VA 112 A3
Galena AK 154 C2
Galena IL 74 A4
Galena IN 99 F4
Galena KS 106 B2
Galena MO 107 D2
Galena Park TX 220 C3
Galesburg IL 88 A3
Galesburg MI 75 F4
Gales Ferry CT 149 F1
Galesville WI 73 F1
Galeton PA 92 C1
Galeville NY 265 A1
Galien MI 89 E1
Galilee RI 150 C4
Galion OH 91 D3
Galisteo NM 49 D3
Gallatin MO 96 C1
Gallatin TN 109 F3
Gallatin Co. IL 109 D1
Gallatin Co. KY 100 B3
Gallatin Co. MT 23 F2
Gallatin Gateway MT 23 F1
Galloway TN 118 B1
Gallia Co. OH 101 E3
Galliano LA 134 B4
Gallipolis OH 101 E3
Gallitzin PA 92 B4
Gallup NM 48 A3
Galt CA 36 C3
Galva IL 88 A2
Galva KS 43 E3
Galveston IN 89 F3
Galveston KY 111 E1
Galveston TX 132 B4
Galveston Co. TX 132 B4
Gamaliel KY 110 A3
Gambell AK 154 A2
Gamber MD 144 B1
Gambier OH 91 D4
Gamewell NC 111 F4
Ganado AZ 47 F2
Ganado TX 61 F3
Gang Mills NY 93 D1
Gann Valley SD 27 D3
Gansevoort NY 81 D4
Gantt SC 217 A2
Gap PA 146 A3
Garber OK 51 E1
Gardena CA 228 C4
Garden City AL 119 F3
Garden City CO 33 E4
Garden City GA 130 B3
Garden City ID 22 B4
Garden City KS 42 B3
Garden City MI 210 A3
Garden City MO 96 C3
Garden City NY 241 G3
Garden City SC 123 D4
Garden City TX 58 A3
Garden City UT 31 F2
Garden City South NY 241 G4
Garden Co. NE 34 A3
Gardendale AL 119 F4
Gardendale MI 76 C3
Gardendale TX 58 A3
Garden Grove CA 228 E4
Garden Home OR 251 C2
Garden Plain KS 43 E4
Garden Ridge TX 61 D2
Garden View PA 93 D2
Gardenville PA 146 C1
Gardiner ME 82 C2
Gardiner MT 23 F2
Gardiner NY 148 B1
Gardner IL 88 C2
Gardner KS 96 B3
Gardner MA 95 D1
Gardnertown NY 148 B1
Gardnerville NV 37 D2
Garfield AR 106 C3
Garfield NJ 148 B3
Garfield TX 61 E2
Garfield WA 14 B4
Garfield Co. CO 40 B1
Garfield Co. MT 17 D3
Garfield Co. NE 35 D2
Garfield Co. OK 51 E1
Garfield Co. UT 39 E3
Garfield Co. WA 14 A4
Garfield Hts. OH 91 E2
Garibaldi OR 20 B2
Garland NC 123 D2
Garland TX 59 F2
Garland UT 31 E2
Garland Co. AR 117 D2
Garnavillo IA 73 F3
Garner IA 72 C3
Garner KY 111 D1
Garner NC 113 D4
Garnett KS 96 A4
Garrard Co. KY 110 C1
Garretson SD 27 F4
Garrett IN 90 A2
Garrett Co. MD 102 B2
Garrett Park MD 270 C1
Garrettsville OH 91 F2
Garrison KY 101 D3
Garrison MD 193 A1
Garrison ND 18 B3
Garrison TX 124 B3
Garrisonville VA 144 A4
Garvin Co. OK 51 E4
Garwin IA 87 D1
Gary IN 89 D2
Gary SD 27 F2
Gary WV 111 F1
Garysburg NC 113 E3
Garyville LA 134 B3
Garza Co. TX 58 B2
Gas KS 96 A4
Gas City IN 89 F4
Gasconade Co. MO 97 F3
Gasport NY 78 B3
Gassaway WV 101 F3
Gassville AR 107 E3
Gaston IN 89 F4
Gaston NC 113 E3
Gaston OR 20 B2
Gaston SC 122 A4
Gaston Co. NC 122 A1
Gastonia NC 122 A1
Gate City VA 111 E3
Gates NY 78 C3
Gates OR 20 C3
Gates TN 108 B4
Gates Co. NC 113 F3
Gates Mills OH 204 G1
Gatesville NC 113 F3
Gatesville TX 59 E4
Gatlinburg TN 111 D4
Gauley Bridge WV 101 F4
Gautier MS 135 D2
Gayle Mill SC 122 A2
Gaylord MI 70 C3
Gaylord MN 66 C4
Gaylordsville CT 148 C1
Gays Mills WI 73 F3
Gayville SD 35 E1
Gearhart OR 20 B1
Geary OK 51 D3
Geary Co. KS 43 F2
Geauga Co. OH 91 E2
Geddes SD 35 D1
Geistown PA 92 B4
Gem Co. ID 22 B3
Genesee ID 14 B4
Genesee MI 76 B3
Genesee Co. MI 76 B3
Genesee Co. NY 78 B3
Geneseo IL 88 A2
Geneseo NY 78 C4
Geneva AL 136 C1
Geneva FL 141 D1
Geneva IL 88 C1
Geneva IN 90 A3
Geneva NE 35 E4
Geneva NY 79 D3
Geneva OH 91 F1
Geneva WA 12 C1
Geneva Co. AL 136 C1
Geneva-on-the-Lake OH 91 F1
Genoa IL 88 C1
Genoa NE 35 E3
Genoa OH 90 C2
Genoa City WI 74 C4
Genola UT 39 E1
Gentry AR 106 B3
Gentry Co. MO 86 B4
George IA 72 A2
George WA 13 E4
George Co. MS 135 D1
Georgetown CA 36 C2
Georgetown CO 41 D1
Georgetown CT 148 C2
Georgetown DE 145 F4
Georgetown GA 128 C3
Georgetown ID 31 F1
Georgetown IL 99 D1
Georgetown IN 99 F4
Germantown WI 74 C3
Germantown Hills IL 88 B3
Geronimo OK 51 D4
Geronimo TX 61 E2
Gerrardstown WV 103 D2
Gervais OR 20 B2
Gettysburg OH 90 B4
Gettysburg PA 103 E1
Gettysburg SD 26 C2
Geyserville CA 36 A2
Ghent KY 100 A3
Ghent NY 94 B2
Ghent OH 188 A1
Gholson TX 59 E4
Giants Neck CT 149 F2
Gibbon MN 66 B4
Gibbon NE 35 D4
Gibbsboro NJ 147 D3
Gibbstown NJ 146 C3
Gibraltar MI 90 C1
Gibsland LA 125 D2
Gibson GA 129 F1
Gibson MD 145 D1
Gibson NC 122 C2
Gibsonburg OH 90 C2
Gibson City IL 88 C4
Gibson Co. IN 99 E4
Gibson Co. TN 108 C4
Gibsonton FL 140 C3
Gibsonville NC 112 B4
Giddings TX 61 F2
Gideon MO 108 B3
Gifford FL 141 E3
Gifford IL 89 D4
Gig Harbor WA 12 C3
Gila Bend AZ 54 B2
Gila Co. AZ 55 D1
Gilbert AZ 54 C2
Gilbert IA 86 C1
Gilbert LA 125 F3
Gilbert MN 64 C3
Gilbert SC 122 A4
Gilmore City IA 72 B4
Gilpin Co. CO 41 D1
Gilroy CA 44 B2
Gilt Edge TN 118 B1
Ginger Blue MO 106 B3
Girard IL 98 B2
Girard KS 106 B1
Girard OH 91 F2
Girard PA 91 F1
Girardville PA 93 E3
Gisela AZ 47 E4
Glacier Co. MT 15 E1
Gladbrook IA 87 D1
Gladden AZ 54 B1
Glades Co. FL 141 D4
Glade Spr. VA 111 F2
Gladewater TX 124 B2
Gladstone MI 69 D2
Gladstone MO 96 B2
Gladstone ND 18 A4
Gladstone OR 251 D3
Gladwin MI 76 A1
Gladwin Co. MI 76 A1
Glandorf OH 90 B3
Glasco KS 43 E2
Glasco NY 94 B2
Glascock Co. GA 129 F1
Glasford IL 88 B4
Glasgow DE 145 E1
Glasgow KY 110 A2
Glasgow MO 97 D2
Glasgow MT 17 D2
Glasgow VA 112 C1
Glasgow WV 101 F4
Glasgow Vil. MO 256 C1
Glassboro NJ 146 C4
Glasscock Co. TX 58 A3
Glassmanor MD 270 D5
Glassport PA 250 C3
Glastonbury CT 150 A3
Gleason TN 108 C3
Glenaire MO 224 C2
Glen Allen AL 119 E4
Glen Allen VA 254 B1
Glen Alpine NC 111 F4
Glenarden MD 144 B3
Glenburn ND 18 B2
Glenburn PA 93 F2
Glen Burnie MD 144 C2
Glen Carbon IL 98 B3
Glencoe AL 120 A4
Glencoe IL 89 D1
Glencoe MN 66 C4
Glencoe OK 51 F2
Glen Cove ME 82 C2
Glen Cove NY 148 C3
Glendale AZ 54 C1
Glendale CA 52 C2
Glendale CO 209 C3
Glendale MO 256 B2
Glendale OH 204 B1
Glendale OR 28 B1
Glendale RI 150 C2
Glendale UT 39 D4
Glen Dale WV 101 F1
Glendale WI 234 C1
Glendale Hts. IL 203 B4
Glendive MT 17 F3
Glendo WY 33 E1
Glendora CA 229 F2
Glendora NJ 146 C3
Glen Elder KS 43 D1
Glen Ellen CA 36 B3
Glen Ellyn IL 203 B4
Glen Gardner NJ 104 C1
Glenham NY 148 B1
Glen Lyon PA 93 E2
Glen Mills MA 151 F1
Glenmoor OH 91 F3
Glenmora LA 133 E1
Glennallen AK 154 C3
Glenn Co. CA 36 B1
Glenn Dale MD 144 C3
Glenn Hts. TX 59 F3

Grand Rapids MI

Ada B2
Cascade B2
Comstock Park A1
E. Grand Rapids B2
Grand Rapids B1
Grandville A2
Jenison A2
Kentwood B2
Marne A1
Tallmadge A1
Walker A2
Wyoming A2

Georgetown KY 100 B4
Georgetown MA 151 F1
Georgetown OH 100 C3
Georgetown PA 146 A3
Georgetown PA 261 A2
Georgetown SC 131 E1
Georgetown TX 61 E1
Georgetown Co. SC 122 C4
George West TX 61 D4
Georgia Ctr. VT 81 D1
Georgiana AL 127 F4
Gerald MO 97 F3
Geraldine AL 120 A3
Geraldine MT 16 A3
Gerber CA 36 B1
Gering NE 33 F2
Gerlach NV 29 E4
Germania NJ 147 D4
Germantown IL 98 B3
Germantown MD 144 B2
Germantown NY 94 B2
Germantown OH 100 B1
Germantown TN 118 B1
Gilbert WV 111 F1
Gilbertsville PA 146 B2
Gilbertville IA 73 E4
Gilbertville MA 150 B1
Gilby ND 19 E2
Gilchrist Co. FL 138 C3
Gilcrest CO 33 E4
Giles Co. TN 119 F1
Giles Co. VA 112 A1
Gilford NH 81 F3
Gilford Park NJ 147 E3
Gillespie IL 98 B2
Gillespie Co. TX 61 D1
Gillett AR 117 F3
Gillett WI 68 C4
Gillette WY 25 E3
Gilliam Co. OR 21 D2
Gilman IL 89 D3
Gilman IA 87 D1
Gilman VT 81 F2
Gilmer TX 124 B2
Gilmer Co. GA 120 C2
Gilmer Co. WV 101 F2

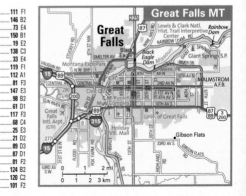

Figures after entries indicate page number and grid reference.

Glenns Ferry ID 30 C1
Glennville GA 130 A3
Glenolden PA 146 C3
Glenpool OK 51 F2
Glen Raven NC 112 C4
Glen Ridge NJ 240 B2
Glen Rock NJ 148 B3
Glen Rock PA 103 E1
Glenrock WY 33 D1
Glen Rose TX 59 E3
Glen St. Mary FL 138 C2
Glens Falls NY 81 D4
Glenside PA 146 C2
Glen Ullin ND 18 B4
Glenview IL 203 D2
Glenview KY 230 E1
Glenview Hills KY 230 E1
Glenville MN 73 D2
Glenville WV 101 F3
Glenwood AR 117 D3
Glenwood GA 129 F3
Glenwood IA 86 A3
Glenwood MD 144 B2
Glenwood MN 66 B2
Glenwood UT 39 E2
Glenwood City WI 67 E3
Glenwood Sprs. CO 40 C1
Glidden IA 86 B1
Glide OR 20 B4
Globe AZ 55 D1
Glorieta NM 49 D3
Gloster MS 126 A4
Gloucester MA 151 F1
Gloucester VA 113 F1
Gloucester City NJ 146 C3
Gloucester Co. NJ 146 C4
Gloucester Co. VA 113 F1
Gloucester Pt. VA 113 F2
Glouster OH 101 E2
Gloversville NY 79 F3
Gloverville SC 121 F4
Glyndon MD 144 C1
Glyndon MN 19 F4
Glynn Co. GA 130 B4
Gnadenhutten OH 91 E4
Gobles MI 75 F4
Goddard KS 43 E4
Godeffroy NY 148 A1
Godfrey IL 98 A2
Godley IL 88 C2
Godley TX 59 E3
Goessel KS 43 E3
Goffstown NH 81 F4
Gogebic Co. MI 65 E4
Golconda IL 109 D1
Golconda NV 30 A3
Gold Bar WA 12 C2
Gold Beach OR 28 A2
Golden CO 41 E1
Golden IL 87 F4
Golden Beach FL 233 C3
Golden Beach MD 144 C4
Golden Bridge NY 148 C2
Golden City MO 106 C1
Goldendale WA 21 D1
Golden Gate FL 142 C1
Golden Meadow LA 134 B4
Goldenrod FL 246 D1
Golden Valley MN 235 B2
Golden Valley Co. MT 16 B4
Golden Valley Co. ND 17 F3
Goldfield IA 72 C4
Goldfield NV 37 F4
Gold Hill OR 28 B2
Goldonna LA 125 D3
Goldsboro NC 123 E1
Goldsboro PA 93 D4
Goldsby OK 51 E3
Goldthwaite TX 59 D4
Goleta CA 52 B2
Golf Manor OH 204 B2
Goliad TX 61 E4
Goliad Co. TX 61 E3
Gonzales CA 44 B3
Gonzales LA 134 A2
Gonzales TX 61 E2
Gonzales Co. TX 61 E3
Gonzalez FL 135 F2
Goochland VA 113 D1
Goochland Co. VA 113 D1
Goodfield IL 88 B3
Good Hope AL 119 F3
Goodhue MN 73 D1
Goodhue Co. MN 73 D1
Gooding ID 30 C1
Gooding Co. ID 30 C1
Goodland IN 89 D3
Goodland KS 42 B2
Goodlettsville TN 109 F3
Goodman MS 126 B1
Goodman MO 106 B3
Goodrich MI 76 B3
Goodsprings NV 46 A2
Good Thunder MN 72 C1
Goodview MN 73 E1
Goodwater AL 128 A1
Goodwell OK 50 B1
Goodyear AZ 54 C1
Goose Creek SC 131 D1
Gordo AL 127 E1
Gordon AL 137 D1
Gordon GA 129 E1
Gordon NE 34 A1
Gordon PA 93 E3
Gordon Co. GA 120 B3
Gordonsville TN 110 A4
Gordonsville VA 102 C4
Gordonville PA 146 A3
Gore OK 116 B1
Goreville IL 108 C1
Gorham ME 82 B3
Gorham NH 81 F2
Gorham NY 78 C4
Gorman NC 112 C4
Gorman TX 59 D3
Goshen AR 106 C4
Goshen CA 45 D3
Goshen IN 89 F2
Goshen KY 100 A3
Goshen MD 144 B2
Goshen NY 148 A2
Goshen OR 20 B4
Goshen UT 39 E1
Goshen VA 102 B4
Goshen Co. WY 33 F2
Gosnell AR 108 B4
Gosper Co. NE 34 C4
Gosport IN 99 E2
Gotha FL 246 A2
Gothenburg NE 34 C4
Gould AR 117 F3
Goulding FL 247 B1
Goulds FL 143 E3
Gouldtown NJ 145 F1
Gouverneur NY 79 E1
Gove KS 42 C2
Gove Co. KS 42 C2
Gowanda NY 78 A4
Gower MO 96 B1
Gowrie IA 72 B4
Grabill IN 90 A2
Grace ID 31 F1
Graceville FL 136 C1
Graceville MN 27 F1
Grady AR 117 F3
Grady Co. GA 137 E1
Grady Co. OK 51 E4
Graettinger IA 72 B3
Graford TX 59 D2
Grafton IL 98 A2
Grafton MA 150 C2
Grafton ND 19 E2
Grafton OH 91 D2
Grafton WV 102 A2
Grafton WI 74 C3
Grafton Co. NH 81 F2
Graham KY 109 E2
Graham NC 112 C4
Graham TX 59 D2
Graham WA 12 C4
Graham Co. AZ 55 E2
Graham Co. KS 42 C2
Graham Co. NC 121 D1
Grainger Co. TN 111 D3
Grain Valley MO 96 C2
Grambling LA 125 E2
Gramercy LA 134 B3
Granada CO 42 A3
Granbury TX 59 E3
Granby CO 41 D1
Granby CT 94 C2
Granby MA 150 A1
Granby MO 106 C2
Grand Bay AL 135 E2
Grand Blanc MI 76 B3
Grand Canyon AZ 47 D2
Grand Coteau LA 133 F2
Grand Coulee WA 13 E2
Grand Co. CO 41 D1
Grand Co. UT 40 A2
Grandfield OK 51 D4
Grand Forks ND 19 E2
Grand Forks Co. ND 19 E3
Grand Haven MI 75 E3
Grandin NJ 147 D1
Grand Island NE 35 E4
Grand Isle LA 134 B4
Grand Isle VT 81 D1
Grand Isle Co. VT 81 D1
Grand Jct. CO 40 B2
Grand Jct. IA 86 C1
Grand Lake CO 33 D4
Grand Ledge MI 76 A4
Grand Marais MN 65 D3
Grand Meadow MN 73 D2
Grand Mound IA 88 A1
Grand Prairie TX 207 C3
Grand Rapids MI 75 F3
Grand Rapids MN 64 B3
Grand Rapids OH 90 B2
Grand Ridge FL 137 D1
Grand Rivers KY 109 D2
Grand Saline TX 124 A2
Grand Terrace CA 229 J3
Grand Tower IL 108 B1
Grand Traverse Co. MI 69 F4
Grandview CO 40 B4
Grand View ID 30 B1
Grandview IN 99 E4
Grandview IA 87 F2
Grandview MO 96 B3
Grandview TX 59 E3
Grandview WA 21 E1
Grandview Hts. OH 206 B2
Grandview Plaza KS 43 F2
Grandville MI 75 F3
Grandy NC 115 F1
Granger IN 89 F1
Granger IA 86 C1
Granger TX 61 E1
Granger WA 13 E4
Grangeville ID 22 B1
Granite OK 50 C3
Granite UT 257 B3
Granite City IL 98 A3
Granite Co. MT 15 D4
Granite Falls MN 66 A4
Granite Falls NC 111 F4
Granite Falls WA 12 C2
Granite Quarry NC 122 B1
Granite Shoals TX 61 D1
Granite Sprs. NY 148 B2
Graniteville SC 121 F4
Graniteville VT 81 E2
Grannis AR 116 C3
Grant AL 120 A2
Grant MI 75 F3
Grant MN 67 D3
Grant NE 34 B4
Grant City MO 86 B4
Grant Co. AR 117 E3
Grant Co. IN 89 F3
Grant Co. KS 42 B4
Grant Co. KY 100 B3
Grant Co. MN 27 F1
Grant Co. NE 34 B2
Grant Co. NM 55 F2
Grant Co. ND 18 B4
Grant Co. OK 51 E1
Grant Co. OR 21 F3
Grant Co. SD 27 F2
Grant Co. WA 13 E3
Grant Co. WV 102 B2
Grant Co. WI 73 F3
Grant Hollow NY 188 E1
Grant Par. LA 125 E4
Grant Park IL 89 D2
Grants NM 48 B3
Grantsburg WI 67 D2
Grantsdale MT 23 D1
Grants Pass OR 28 B2
Grantsville MD 102 B1
Grantsville UT 31 E4
Grantsville WV 101 F3
Grant Town WV 102 A1
Grantville GA 128 C1
Grantville PA 93 E4
Granville IL 88 B2
Granville NY 81 D4
Granville ND 18 C2
Granville OH 91 D4
Granville Co. NC 113 D3
Grapeland TX 124 A4
Grapeview WA 12 C3
Grapevine TX 59 E2
Grasonville MD 145 D3
Grass Lake MI 76 B4
Grass Valley CA 36 C2
Graterford PA 146 B2
Gratiot Co. MI 76 A3
Gratis OH 100 B1
Graton CA 36 A3
Gratz PA 93 E4
Gravel Ridge AR 117 E2
Graves Co. KY 108 C3
Gravette AR 106 B3
Grawn MI 69 F4
Gray GA 129 D1
Gray KY 110 C2
Gray LA 134 A3
Gray ME 82 B3
Gray TN 111 E3
Gray Co. KS 42 C4
Gray Co. TX 50 B3
Gray Court SC 121 F2
Grayland WA 12 B4
Grayling MI 70 C4
Graymoor-Devondale KY 230 E1
Grays Harbor Co. WA 12 B3
Grayslake IL 74 C4
Grayson GA 121 D4
Grayson KY 101 D4
Grayson LA 125 E3
Grayson Co. KY 109 F1
Grayson Co. TX 59 F1
Grayson Co. VA 111 F3
Gray Summit MO 98 A3
Graysville AL 119 F4
Graysville TN 120 B1
Grayville IL 99 D4
Greasewood AZ 47 F3
Great Barrington MA 94 B2
Great Bend KS 43 D3

Green Bay WI

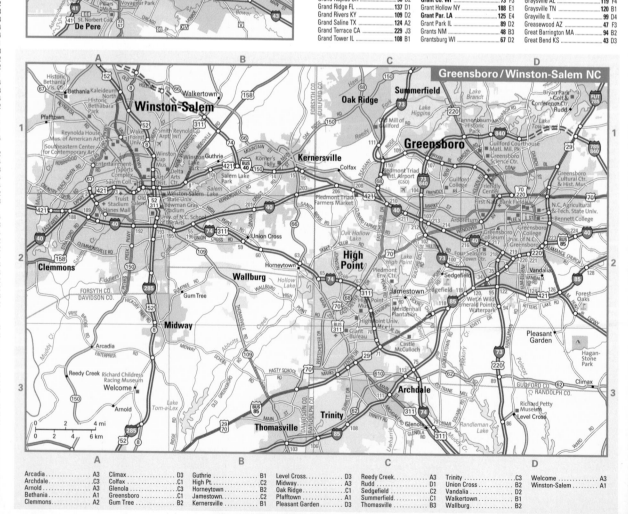

Arcadia A3
Archdale C3
Arnold A3
Bethania A1
Clemmons A2
Climax D3
Colfax C1
Glenola C3
Greensboro C1
Gum Tree B2
Guthrie B1
High Pt. C2
Horneytown B2
Jamestown C2
Kernersville B1
Level Cross D3
Midway C1
Oak Ridge C1
Pfafftown A1
Pleasant Garden D3
Reedy Creek A3
Rudd D1
Sedgefield C2
Summerfield C1
Thomasville B3
Trinity C3
Union Cross B2
Vandalia D2
Walkertown B1
Wallburg B2
Welcome A3
Winston-Salem A1

Entries in **bold black** indicate counties or parishes.
Entries in **bold color** indicate cities with detailed inset maps.

Great Bend NY 79 E1
Great Bend PA 93 F1
Great Falls MT 15 F3
Great Falls SC 122 A2
Great Falls VA 144 B3
Great Meadows NJ 94 A4
Great Mills MD 103 E4
Great Neck NY 148 B4
Great Neck Estates NY 241 G3
Great Neck Gardens NY 241 G2
Great Neck Plaza NY 241 G2
Great River NY 149 D4
Greece NY 78 C3
Greeley CO 33 E4
Greeley NE 35 D3
Greeley Co. KS 42 B3
Greeley Co. NE 35 D3
Greeleyville SC 122 B4
Green OH 91 E3
Green OR 28 B1
Greenacres CA 45 D4
Greenacres FL 143 F1
Greenback TN 110 C4
Green Bay WI 68 C4
Greenbelt MD 144 B3
Greenbrier AR 117 E1
Greenbrier TN 109 F3
Greenbrier Co. WV 102 A4
Greenbush MA 151 E2
Greenbush MN 19 F1
Greencastle IN 99 E1
Greencastle PA 103 D1
Green City MO 87 D4
Green Co. KY 110 A1
Green Co. WI 74 B4
Green Cove Sprs. FL 139 D3
Green Creek NJ 104 C4
Greendale IN 100 B2
Greendale MO 256 B2
Greendale WI 234 C3
Greene IA 73 D3
Greene ME 82 B2
Greene NY 79 E4
Greene Co. AL 127 E2
Greene Co. AR 108 A3
Greene Co. GA 121 E4
Greene Co. IL 98 A2
Greene Co. IN 99 E2
Greene Co. IA 86 B1
Greene Co. MS 127 D4
Greene Co. MO 107 D1
Greene Co. NY 94 A2
Greene Co. NC 115 C3
Greene Co. OH 100 C1
Greene Co. PA 102 A1
Greene Co. TN 111 D3
Greene Co. VA 102 C4
Greenevers NC 123 E2
Greeneville TN 111 D4
Greenfield CA 44 B3
Greenfield IL 98 A2
Greenfield IN 99 F1
Greenfield IA 86 B2
Greenfield MA 94 C1
Greenfield MO 106 C1
Greenfield NH 95 D1
Greenfield OH 100 C2
Greenfield TN 108 C4
Greenfield WI 234 C3
Green Forest AR 107 D3
Green Harbor MA 151 E2
Green Haven MD 144 C2
Green Haven NY 148 C1
Green Hill TN 109 F3
Greenhills OH 204 B1
Green Island NY 188 E2
Green Lake WI 74 B2
Green Lake Co. WI 74 B2
Greenland AR 106 C4
Greenland NH 82 A4
Green Lane PA 146 B2
Greenleaf ID 22 A4
Greenlee Co. AZ 55 E2
Greenmount MD 144 B1
Green Mtn. Falls CO 205 C1
Green Oaks IL 203 C1
Green Park MO 256 B3
Green Pond NJ 148 A3
Greenport NY 149 E3
Green River UT 39 F2
Green River WY 32 A3
Greensboro AL 127 E2
Greensboro FL 137 D2
Greensboro GA 121 D4
Greensboro MD 145 E3
Greensboro NC 112 B4
Greensboro Bend VT 81 E2
Greensburg IN 100 A2
Greensburg KS 43 D4
Greensburg KY 110 A2
Greensburg LA 134 B1
Greensburg PA 92 A4
Green Sprs. OH 90 C2
Greensville Co. VA 113 E2
Greentown IN 89 F4
Greentown OH 91 E3
Green Tree PA 250 B2
Greenup IL 99 D2
Greenup KY 101 D3
Greenup Co. KY 101 D3
Green Valley AZ 55 D3
Green Valley CA 52 C2
Green Valley IL 88 B4
Green Valley MD 144 B2
Greenview IL 88 B4
Green Vil. PA 103 D1
Greenville AL 128 A3
Greenville CA 36 C1
Greenville DE 146 B3
Greenville FL 137 F2
Greenville GA 128 C1
Greenville IL 98 B3
Greenville IN 99 F4
Greenville KY 109 E2
Greenville ME 84 C4
Greenville MI 75 F3
Greenville MS 126 A1
Greenville MO 108 A2
Greenville NH 95 D1
Greenville NY 94 B2
Greenville NC 115 D2
Greenville OH 90 A4
Greenville PA 91 F2
Greenville RI 150 C3
Greenville SC 121 E2
Greenville TX 59 F2
Greenville VA 102 B4
Greenville WI 74 C1
Greenville Co. SC 121 E2
Greenville Jct. ME 84 C4
Greenwich CT 148 C3
Greenwich NY 81 D4
Greenwich OH 91 D3
Greenwood AR 116 C1
Greenwood DE 145 E3
Greenwood FL 137 D1
Greenwood IN 99 F1
Greenwood LA 124 C2
Greenwood MS 118 B4
Greenwood MO 96 B3
Greenwood NE 35 F3
Greenwood SC 121 F3
Greenwood WI 68 A4
Greenwood Co. KS 43 F3
Greenwood Co. SC 121 F3
Greenwood Lake NY 148 A2
Greenwood Vil. CO 209 C4
Greer SC 121 F2
Greer Co. OK 50 C3
Greers Ferry AR 117 E1
Gregg Co. TX 124 B2
Gregory SD 35 D1
Gregory TX 63 F2
Gregory Co. SD 35 D1
Greilickville MI 69 F4
Grenada MS 118 B4
Grenada Co. MS 118 B4
Gresham OR 20 C2
Gresham WI 68 C4
Gresham Park GA 190 E4
Gretna FL 137 D2
Gretna LA 134 B3
Gretna NE 35 F3
Gretna VA 112 C2
Greybull WY 24 C3
Gridley CA 36 B2
Gridley IL 88 C3
Gridley KS 96 A4
Griffin GA 129 D1
Griffith IN 89 D2
Grifton NC 115 D3
Griggs Co. ND 19 D3
Griggsville IL 98 A1
Grimes AL 128 B4
Grimes IA 86 C2
Grimes Co. TX 132 A2
Grinnell IA 87 D1
Griswold IA 86 B2
Groesbeck OH 204 A2
Groesbeck TX 59 F4
Groom TX 50 B3
Grosse Pointe MI 210 D3
Grosse Pointe Farms MI 210 D3
Grosse Pointe Park MI 210 D3
Grosse Pointe Shores MI 210 D3
Grosse Pointe Woods MI 76 C4
Grosse Tete LA 133 F2
Grosvenor Dale CT 150 B2
Groton CT 149 F2
Groton MA 95 D1
Groton NY 79 D4
Groton SD 27 E2
Groton VT 81 E2
Groton Long Pt. CT 149 F2
Grottoes VA 102 C4
Grove OK 106 B3
Grove City FL 140 C4
Grove City MN 66 B3
Grove City OH 101 D1
Grove City PA 92 A2
Grove Hill AL 127 E4
Groveland CA 37 D4
Groveland FL 140 C1
Groveland MA 95 E1
Groveport OH 101 D1
Grover NC 122 A1
Grover Beach CA 52 A1
Groves TX 132 C3
Groveton NH 81 F2
Groveton TX 132 B1
Groveton VA 144 B4
Grovetown GA 121 F4
Grubbs AR 107 F4
Gruetli-Laager TN 120 A1
Grundy VA 111 E2
Grundy Ctr. IA 73 D4
Grundy Co. IL 88 C2
Grundy Co. IA 73 D4
Grundy Co. MO 86 C4
Grundy Co. TN 120 A1
Gruver TX 50 B2
Guadalupe AZ 249 C3
Guadalupe CA 52 A1
Guadalupe Co. NM 49 E4
Guadalupe Co. TX 61 E3
Guerneville CA 36 A3
Guernsey WY 33 E2
Guernsey Co. OH 91 E4
Gueydan LA 133 E3
Guilderland NY 188 C2
Guildhall VT 81 F2
Guilford CT 149 E2
Guilford ME 82 C1
Guilford MD 193 A5
Guilford Co. NC 112 B4
Guin AL 119 E4
Gulf Breeze FL 135 F2
Gulf Co. FL 137 D3
Gulfport FL 140 B3
Gulfport MS 135 D2
Gulf Shores AL 135 E2
Gulf Stream FL 143 F1
Gun Barrel City TX 59 F3
Gunnison CO 40 C3
Gunnison MS 118 A4
Gunnison UT 39 E2
Gunnison Co. CO 40 C2
Gunter TX 59 F1
Guntersville AL 120 A3
Guntown MS 119 D3
Gurdon AR 117 D4
Gurley AL 119 F2
Gurn Spr. NY 80 C4
Gustavus AK 155 D4
Gustine CA 36 C4
Guthrie KY 109 E3
Guthrie OK 51 E2
Guthrie TX 58 C1
Guthrie Ctr. IA 86 B2
Guthrie Co. IA 86 B2
Guthriesville PA 146 B3
Guttenberg IA 73 F4
Guttenberg NJ 240 D2
Guymon OK 50 B1
Guys TN 119 D2
Guyton GA 130 B2
Gwinn MI 69 D1
Gwinner ND 27 E1
Gwinnett Co. GA 121 D4
Gwynn VA 113 F1
Gypsum CO 40 C1
Gypsum KS 43 E2

H
Haakon Co. SD 26 B3
Habersham Co. GA 121 D2
Hacienda Hts. CA 228 E3
Hackberry LA 133 D3
Hackensack NJ 148 B3
Hackett AR 116 C1
Hackettstown NJ 94 A4
Hackleburg AL 119 E3
Haddam CT 149 E1
Haddonfield NJ 146 C3
Haddon Hts. NJ 248 D4
Hadley MA 150 A1
Hadley NY 80 C4
Hagaman NY 80 C4
Hagan GA 129 F3
Hagerhill KY 111 D1
Hagerman ID 30 C1
Hagerman NM 57 E2
Hagerstown IN 100 A1
Hagerstown MD 144 A1
Hahira GA 137 F1
Hahnville LA 134 B3
Haiku HI 153 D1
Hailey ID 22 C4
Haileyville OK 116 A2
Haines AK 155 D3
Haines OR 21 F2
Haines City FL 141 D2
Halaula HI 153 E2
Halawa HI 152 C3
Hale Ctr. TX 58 A1
Hale Co. AL 127 E2
Hale Co. TX 58 A1
Haledon NJ 148 B3
Haleiwa HI 152 A2
Hales Corners WI 74 C3
Haleyville AL 119 E3
Halfmoon NY 188 E1
Half Moon NC 115 D4
Half Moon Bay CA 36 B4
Halfway MD 144 A1
Halfway OR 22 A2
Halifax MA 151 D2
Halifax NC 113 E3
Halifax PA 93 D4
Halifax VA 112 C2
Halifax Co. NC 113 E4
Halifax Co. VA 112 C2
Haliimaile HI 153 D1
Hallam PA 103 E1
Hallandale Beach FL 143 F2
Hall Co. GA 121 D3
Hall Co. NE 35 D4
Hall Co. TX 50 B4
Hallettsville TX 61 F3
Halliday ND 18 A3
Hallock MN 19 E1
Hallowell ME 82 C2
Halls TN 108 C4
Hallsburg TX 59 F4
Halls Crossroads TN 110 C4
Halls Gap KY 110 B1
Hallstead PA 93 F1
Hallsville MO 97 E2
Hallsville TX 124 B2
Halsey OR 20 B3
Halstad MN 19 F3
Halstead KS 43 E3
Haltom City TX 207 B2
Hamblen Co. TN 111 D3
Hamburg AR 125 F1
Hamburg IA 86 A3
Hamburg MN 66 C4
Hamburg NJ 148 A2
Hamburg NY 78 B4
Hamburg PA 146 A1
Hamden CT 149 D2
Hamden OH 101 D2
Hamel IL 98 B3
Hamilton AL 119 D3
Hamilton GA 128 C2
Hamilton IL 87 F4
Hamilton IN 90 A2
Hamilton MI 75 F4
Hamilton MO 96 C1
Hamilton MT 23 D1
Hamilton NY 79 E3
Hamilton NC 113 E4
Hamilton OH 100 B2
Hamilton RI 150 C4
Hamilton TX 59 E4
Hamilton VA 144 A2
Hamilton City CA 36 B1
Hamilton Co. FL 138 C2
Hamilton Co. IL 98 C4
Hamilton Co. IN 99 F1
Hamilton Co. IA 72 C4
Hamilton Co. KS 42 A3
Hamilton Co. NE 35 E4
Hamilton Co. NY 79 F2
Hamilton Co. OH 100 B2
Hamilton Co. TN 120 B1
Hamilton Co. TX 59 D4
Hamilton Square NJ 147 D2
Ham Lake MN 67 D3
Hamler OH 90 B2
Hamlet IN 89 E2
Hamlet NC 122 C2
Hamlin TX 58 C2
Hamlin WV 101 E4
Hamlin Co. SD 27 E3
Hammon OK 50 C3
Hammond IL 98 C1
Hammond IN 89 D2
Hammond LA 134 B2
Hammond WI 67 E4
Hammondsport NY 78 C4
Hammondville AL 120 A2
Hammonton NJ 147 D4
Hamorton PA 146 B3
Hampden ME 83 D1
Hampden Co. MA 150 A2
Hampden Sydney VA 113 D2
Hampshire IL 88 C1
Hampshire Co. MA 94 C2
Hampshire Co. WV 102 C2
Hampstead MD 144 B1
Hampstead NH 95 E1
Hampton AR 117 E4
Hampton FL 138 C3
Hampton GA 129 D1
Hampton IL 208 C1
Hampton IA 73 D4
Hampton MD 193 C1
Hampton NE 35 E4
Hampton NH 95 E1
Hampton NJ 104 C1
Hampton PA 103 E1
Hampton SC 130 B2
Hampton TN 111 E3
Hampton VA 113 F2
Hampton Bays NY 149 E3
Hampton Beach NH 95 E1
Hampton Co. SC 130 B2
Hampton Park NY 149 E3
Hamtramck MI 210 C3
Hana HI 153 E1
Hanahan SC 131 D1
Hanamaulu HI 152 B1
Hanapepe HI 152 B1
Hanceville AL 119 F3
Hancock MD 102 C1
Hancock MI 65 F3
Hancock MN 66 A3
Hancock NH 81 E4
Hancock NY 93 F1
Hancock Co. GA 129 E1
Hancock Co. IL 87 F4
Hancock Co. IN 100 A1
Hancock Co. IA 72 C3
Hancock Co. KY 109 F1
Hancock Co. ME 83 D1
Hancock Co. MS 134 C2
Hancock Co. OH 90 B3
Hancock Co. TN 111 D3
Hancock Co. WV 91 F4
Hand Co. SD 27 D3
Hanford CA 45 D3
Hankinson ND 27 F1
Hanley Hills MO 256 B2
Hanna WY 33 D2
Hanna City IL 88 B3
Hannibal MO 97 F1
Hannibal NY 79 D3
Hanover CT 149 F1
Hanover IL 74 A4
Hanover IN 100 A3
Hanover KS 43 F1
Hanover MA 151 E2
Hanover MN 66 C3
Hanover NH 81 E3
Hanover NJ 148 A3
Hanover OH 91 D4
Hanover PA 103 E1
Hanover VA 113 E1
Hanover Co. VA 103 D4
Hanover Park IL 203 B3
Hansen ID 30 C1
Hansford Co. TX 50 B2
Hanson KY 109 E1
Hanson MA 151 D2
Hanson Co. SD 27 E4
Hapeville GA 190 D5
Happy TX 50 A4
Happy Camp CA 28 B2
Happy Valley OR 251 D2
Harahan LA 239 B2
Haralson Co. GA 120 B4
Harbert MI 89 E1
Harbeson DE 145 F4
Harbor OR 28 A2
Harbor Beach MI 76 C2
Harbor Bluffs FL 266 A2
Harbor Hills NY 241 G2
Harbor Hills OH 101 D1
Harbor Sprs. MI 70 B3
Harbour Hts. FL 140 C4
Hardee Co. FL 140 C3
Hardeeville SC 130 B3
Hardeman Co. TN 118 C1
Hardeman Co. TX 50 C4
Hardin IL 98 A2
Hardin KY 109 D2
Hardin MO 96 C2
Hardin MT 24 C1
Hardin TX 132 B2
Hardin Co. IL 109 D1
Hardin Co. IA 73 D4
Hardin Co. KY 110 A1
Hardin Co. OH 90 C3
Hardin Co. TN 119 D1
Hardin Co. TX 132 C2
Harding Co. NM 49 E2
Harding Co. SD 25 F1
Hardinsburg KY 109 F1
Hardwick GA 129 E1
Hardwick VT 81 E2
Hardy AR 107 F3
Hardy Co. WV 102 C2
Harewood Park MD 145 D1
Harford Co. MD 144 C1
Hargill TX 63 E4
Harker Hts. TX 59 E4
Harkers Island NC 115 E4
Harlan IA 86 A2
Harlan KY 111 D2
Harlan Co. KY 111 D2
Harlan Co. NE 35 D4
Harlem FL 141 D4
Harlem GA 129 F1
Harlem MT 16 C2
Harleysville PA 146 C2
Harleyville SC 130 C1
Harlingen TX 63 F4
Harlowton MT 16 B4
Harmon Co. OK 50 C4
Harmony IN 99 E1
Harmony MN 73 E2
Harmony NC 112 A4
Harmony PA 92 A3
Harmony RI 150 C3
Harnett Co. NC 123 D1
Harney Co. OR 21 E4
Harold KY 111 E1
Harper KS 43 E4
Harper TX 60 C1
Harper Co. KS 43 E4
Harper Co. OK 50 C1
Harpersville AL 128 A1
Harper Woods MI 210 D2
Harrah OK 51 E3
Harrah WA 13 D4
Harriman NY 148 B2
Harriman TN 110 B4
Harrington DE 145 E3
Harrington ME 83 E2
Harrington WA 13 F3
Harris MN 67 D3
Harrisburg AR 118 A1
Harrisburg IL 109 D1
Harrisburg NE 33 F3
Harrisburg NC 122 B1
Harrisburg OR 20 B3
Harrisburg PA 93 D4
Harrisburg SD 27 F4
Harris Co. GA 128 C2
Harris Co. TX 132 A3

Greenville / Spartanburg SC

Apalache B1
Arcadia C1
Berea A2
Cherokee Forest A1
Clifton D1
Conestee A2
Converse D1
Cowpens D1
Crescent C2
Delmar D1
Drayton D1
Duncan C1
Dunean A2
E. Gantt A2
Fairforest C1
Fairview B1
Gantt A2
Glendale D1
Glenn Sprs. D2
Greenville A2
Greer B1
Lake Forest A2
Lyman C1
Marietta A1
Mauldin B2
Moore C2
Paris A1
Pauline D2
Pelham B2
Reidville C2
Renfrew A1
Roebuck D2
Sans Souci A2
Saxon C1
Simpsonville B2
Spartanburg C1
Startex C1
Switzer C2
Taylors B1
Travelers Rest A1
Welcome A2
Wellford C1
White Stone D1
Whitney D1

Figures after entries indicate page number and grid reference.

Harrison AR 107 D3
Harrison GA 129 F2
Harrison ID 14 B3
Harrison ME 82 B2
Harrison MI 76 A1
Harrison NE 33 F1
Harrison NJ 148 B4
Harrison NY 148 C3
Harrison OH 100 B2
Harrison TN 120 B1
Harrisonburg LA 125 F3
Harrisonburg VA 102 C3
Harrison Co. IN 99 F4
Harrison Co. IA 86 A1
Harrison Co. KY 100 B3
Harrison Co. MS 134 C2
Harrison Co. MO 86 C4
Harrison Co. OH 91 E4
Harrison Co. TX 124 B2
Harrison Co. WV 102 A2

Bressler C2
Camp Hill A2
Colonial Park C1
Eberlys Mill B2
Edgemont B1
Enhaut C2
Enola A1
Estherton B1
Fair Acres B2
Good Hope A1
Green Lane Farms B2
Harrisburg B1
Highland Park B2
Highspire C2
Lawnton C1
Lemoyne B2
Marsh Run C2
Mechanicsburg A2
New Cumberland B2
Oakleigh C2
Oberlin C2
Paxtang B1
Paxtang Manor C1
Paxtonia C1
Penbrook B1
Progress B1
Reesers Summit B2
Rossmoyne A2
Rossmoyne Manor A2
Rutherford Hts. C1
Shiremanstown A2
Steelton B2
Summerdale A1
W. Enola A1
W. Fairview A1
White Hill A2
Wormleysburg B2

Harrisburg PA

Addison F2
Bloomfield E1
Blue Hills E1
Burnside F1
E. Hartford F1
Elmwood E2
Glastonbury F2
Griswoldville E2
Hartford E1
Hockanum F2
Kensington D3
New Britain D3
Newington E2
Rocky Hill F3
S. Glastonbury F3
S. Windsor F1
W. Hartford D2
Wethersfield E2
Wilson E1

Harrisonville MO 96 B3
Harristown IL 98 C1
Harrisville MD 146 A4
Harrisville MI 71 D4
Harrisville NH 95 D1
Harrisville NY 79 E1
Harrisville PA 92 A3
Harrisville RI 150 C2
Harrisville UT 31 E3
Harrisville WV 101 F2
Harrodsburg KY 110 B1
Harrogate TN 110 C3
Harrold SD 27 D3
Hart MI 75 E2
Hart TX 50 A4
Hart Co. GA 121 E3
Hart Co. KY 110 A2
Hartford AL 136 C1
Hartford AR 116 C2
Hartford CT 150 A3
Hartford IL 98 A3
Hartford IA 86 C2
Hartford KS 43 F3
Hartford KY 109 E1
Hartford MI 89 F1
Hartford SD 27 F4
Hartford WV 101 E2
Hartford WI 74 C3
Hartford City IN 90 A4
Hartford Co. CT 150 A3
Hartington NE 35 E1
Hartland ME 82 C1
Hartland VT 81 E3
Hartland WI 74 C3
Hartley IA 72 A3
Hartley Co. TX 50 A2
Hartly DE 145 E2
Hartman AR 116 C1
Harts WV 101 E4
Hartselle AL 119 F3
Hartshorne OK 116 A2
Hartsville SC 122 B3
Hartsville TN 109 F3
Hartville MO 107 E2
Hartville OH 91 E3
Hartwell GA 121 E3
Harvard IL 74 C4
Harvard MA 150 C1
Harvard NE 35 E4
Harvest AL 119 F2
Harvey IL 203 E6
Harvey LA 239 C2
Harvey MI 69 D1
Harvey ND 18 C3
Harvey Co. KS 43 E3
Harveysburg OH 100 C2
Harveys Lake PA 93 E2
Harwich MA 151 F3
Harwich Port MA 151 F3
Harwinton CT 94 C3
Harwood ND 19 F4
Harwood Hts. IL 203 D3
Hasbrouck Hts. NJ 240 C1
Haskell AR 117 E3
Haskell OK 106 A4
Haskell TX 58 C2
Haskell Co. KS 42 B4
Haskell Co. OK 116 B1
Haskell Co. TX 58 C2
Haskins OH 90 C2
Haslet TX 207 A1
Haslett MI 76 A4
Hastings FL 139 D3
Hastings MI 75 F4
Hastings MN 67 D4
Hastings NE 35 E4
Hastings PA 92 B3
Hatboro PA 146 C2
Hatch NM 56 B2
Hatfield AR 116 C3
Hatfield IN 99 E4
Hatfield MA 150 A1
Hatfield PA 146 C2
Hatley MS 119 D4
Hatteras NC 115 F3
Hattiesburg MS 126 C4
Hatton ND 19 E3
Haubstadt IN 99 D4
Haughton LA 125 D2
Hauppauge NY 149 D3
Hauser ID 14 B3
Hauula HI 152 A2
Havana FL 137 E2
Havana IL 88 A4
Havelock NC 115 D4
Haven KS 43 E4
Haverhill FL 143 F1
Haverhill MA 95 E1
Haverhill NH 81 E3
Haverstraw NY 148 B2
Havertown PA 248 B3
Haviland KS 43 D4
Havre MT 16 B2
Havre de Grace MD 145 D1
Hawaiian Gardens CA 228 E4
Hawaiian Ocean View HI 153 E4
Hawaiian Paradise Park HI 153 F3
Hawaii Co. HI 153 E2
Hawarden IA 35 F1
Hawesville KY 99 E4
Hawi HI 153 E2
Hawkins TX 124 B2
Hawkins Co. TN 111 D3

Hawkinsville GA 129 E3
Hawley MN 19 F4
Hawley PA 93 F2
Hawley TX 58 C2
Hawleyville CT 148 C1
Haw River NC 112 C4
Hawthorn PA 92 B3
Hawthorne CA 228 C3
Hawthorne FL 138 C3
Hawthorne NV 37 E3
Hawthorne NJ 148 B3
Hawthorne NY 148 B3
Hawthorn Woods IL 203 B1
Haxtun CO 34 A4
Hayden AL 119 F4
Hayden AZ 55 D2
Hayden CO 32 C4
Hayden ID 14 B3
Hayden Lake ID 14 B3
Haydenville MA 150 A1
Hayes LA 133 E2
Hayes Ctr. NE 34 B4
Hayes Co. NE 34 B4
Hayesville NC 121 D2
Hayesville OR 20 B2
Hayfield MN 73 D2
Hayfork CA 28 B4
Haymarket VA 144 A3
Haynesville LA 125 D1
Haynesville VA 103 E4
Hayneville AL 128 A3
Hays KS 43 D2
Hays MT 16 C2
Hays NC 112 A3
Hays Co. TX 61 D2
Hay Sprs. NE 34 A1
Haysville KS 43 E4
Hayti MO 108 B3
Hayti SD 27 F3
Hayti Hts. MO 108 B3
Hayward CA 36 B4
Hayward WI 67 F2
Haywood Co. NC 111 D4
Haywood Co. TN 108 C4
Hazard KY 111 D2
Hazardville CT 150 A2
Hazel KY 109 D3
Hazel Crest IL 203 E6
Hazel Green AL 119 F2
Hazel Green WI 74 A4
Hazel Park MI 210 C2
Hazelton ID 31 D1
Hazelton ND 18 C4
Hazelwood MO 256 B1
Hazen AR 117 F2
Hazen ND 18 B3
Hazlehurst GA 129 F3
Hazlehurst MS 126 B3
Hazleton IA 73 E4
Hazleton PA 93 E3
Hazlettville DE 145 E2
Headland AL 128 B4
Head of the Harbor NY 149 D3
Healdsburg CA 36 B3
Healdton OK 51 E4
Healy AK 154 C2
Heard Co. GA 128 B1
Hearne TX 61 F1
Heart Butte MT 15 E2
Heath OH 101 D1
Heathcote NJ 147 D1
Heath Sprs. SC 122 B2
Heathsville VA 103 E4
Heavener OK 116 B2
Hebbronville TX 63 E2
Hebbville MD 193 A2
Heber AZ 47 E4
Heber CA 53 E4
Heber City UT 31 F4
Heber Sprs. AR 117 E1
Hebron CT 149 E1
Hebron IL 74 C4
Hebron IN 89 E2
Hebron KY 100 B2
Hebron MD 103 F3
Hebron NE 43 E1

Hebron ND 18 B4
Hebron OH 101 D1
Hebron Estates KY 100 A4
Hecla SD 27 E1
Hector AR 117 D1
Hector MN 66 B4
Hedrick IA 87 E2
Hedwig Vil. TX 220 B2
Heeia HI 152 A3
Heflin AL 120 A4
Heidelberg MS 127 D3
Heidelberg PA 250 A3
Heilwood PA 92 B3
Helena AL 127 F1
Helena AR 118 A2
Helena GA 129 E3
Helena MS 195 C1
Helena MT 15 E4
Helena OK 51 D1
Helenwood TN 110 B3
Hellertown PA 146 C1
Helmetta NJ 147 E1
Helotes TX 61 D2
Helper UT 39 F1
Hemet CA 53 D3
Hemingford NE 34 A2
Hemingway SC 122 C4
Hemlock MI 76 B2
Hemphill TX 124 C4
Hemphill Co. TX 50 C2
Hempstead NY 148 C4
Hempstead TX 61 F2
Hempstead Co. AR 116 C4
Henagar AL 120 A2
Henderson KY 109 E1
Henderson LA 133 F2
Henderson MN 66 C4
Henderson NE 35 E4
Henderson NV 46 B2
Henderson NC 113 D3
Henderson TN 119 D1
Henderson TX 124 B3
Henderson Co. IL 87 F3
Henderson Co. KY 109 E1
Henderson Co. NC 121 E1
Henderson Co. TN 109 D4
Henderson Co. TX 124 A2
Hendersonville NC 121 E1
Hendersonville TN 109 F3
Hendricks MN 27 F3
Hendricks Co. IN 99 F1
Hendron KY 108 C2
Hendry Co. FL 143 D1
Henefer UT 31 F3
Henlopen Acres DE 145 F4
Hennepin IL 88 B2
Hennepin Co. MN 66 C4
Hennessey OK 51 E2
Henniker NH 81 F4
Henning MN 64 A4
Henning TN 108 B4
Henrico Co. VA 113 E1
Henrietta NY 78 C3
Henrietta TX 59 D1
Henry IL 88 B3
Henry SD 27 E2
Henry TN 109 D3
Henry Co. AL 128 B4
Henry Co. GA 129 D1
Henry Co. IL 88 A2
Henry Co. IN 100 A1
Henry Co. IA 87 F3
Henry Co. KY 100 A3
Henry Co. MO 96 C4
Henry Co. OH 90 B2
Henry Co. TN 109 D3
Henry Co. VA 112 B2
Henryetta OK 51 F3
Henryville IN 100 A3
Hephzibah GA 129 F1
Heppner OR 21 E2
Herculaneum MO 98 A4
Hercules CA 259 C1
Hereford PA 146 B1
Hereford TX 50 A4
Herington KS 43 F3

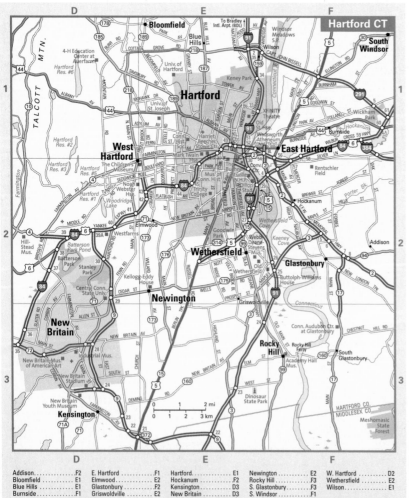

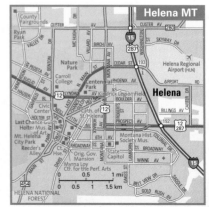

Entries in **bold black** indicate counties or parishes.
Entries in **bold color** indicate cities with detailed inset maps.

Herkimer NY 79 F3
Herkimer Co. NY 79 F2
Hermann MO 97 F3
Hermantown MN 64 C4
Herminie PA 92 A4
Hermiston OR 21 E1
Hermitage AR 117 E4
Hermitage MO 97 D4
Hermitage PA 91 F2
Hermon ME 83 D1
Hermosa CO 40 B4
Hermosa SD 26 A4
Hermosa Beach CA 228 C4
Hernandez NM 48 C2
Hernando FL 140 C1
Hernando MS 118 B2
Hickory MS 126 C2
Hickory NC 111 F4
Hickory Co. MO 97 D4
Hickory Flat MS 118 C2
Hickory Hills IL 203 D5
Hickory Withe TN 118 C1
Hicksville NY 148 C4
Hicksville OH 90 A2
Hico TX 59 E3
Hidalgo TX 63 E4
Hidalgo Co. NM 55 F4
Hidalgo Co. TX 63 E3
Hidden Hills CA 228 A2
Hiddenite NC 112 A4
Hideaway TX 124 A2
Higbee MO 97 E2
High Pt. FL 266 B2
High Pt. NC 112 B4
High Ridge MO 98 A3
High Rolls NM 56 C2
High Shoals NC 122 A1
Highspire PA 218 C2
High Sprs. FL 138 C3
Hightstown NJ 147 D2
Hightsville NC 275 A1
Highwood IL 203 D1
Hilbert WI 74 C1
Hilda SC 130 B1
Hildale UT 46 C1
Hiles WI 68 B2
Hillandale MD 270 E1
Hillburn NY 148 B2
Hillside NJ 148 A4
Hillside Lake NY 148 B1
Hillsville VA 112 A2
Hilltop MN 235 C1
Hillview KY 100 A4
Hilmar CA 36 C4
Hilo HI 153 F3
Hilshire Vil. TX 220 B2
Hilton NY 78 C3
Hilton Head Island SC 130 C3
Hinckley IL 88 C1
Hinckley MN 67 D2
Hinckley UT 39 D2
Hindman KY 111 D1
Hinds Co. MS 126 B3
Hines OR 21 E4
Hoke Co. NC 123 D2
Hokendauqua PA 189 A1
Hokes Bluff AL 120 A3
Holbrook AZ 47 F3
Holbrook MA 151 D2
Holbrook NY 149 D4
Holcomb KS 42 B3
Holcomb MO 108 B3
Holden MA 150 B1
Holden MO 96 C3
Holden UT 39 E2
Holden WV 111 E1
Holden Beach NC 123 E4
Holdenville OK 51 F3
Holdingford MN 66 B2
Holdrege NE 35 D4
Holgate OH 90 B2
Holiday FL 140 B2
Holiday Hills IL 203 A1
Holiday Lakes TX 132 A4
Holladay UT 257 B2
Holland AR 117 E1
Holland IN 99 E4
Holland MA 150 B2
Holland MI 75 E4
Holland NY 78 B4
Holland OH 90 C2
Holland TX 61 E1
Hollandale MS 126 A1
Holley FL 135 F2
Holley NY 78 B3
Holliday TX 59 D1
Hollidaysburg PA 92 C4
Hollins VA 112 B1
Hollis NH 95 D1
Hollis OK 50 C4
Hollis Ctr. ME 82 B3
Hollister CA 44 B2
Hollister MO 107 D3
Hollister NC 113 D3
Holliston MA 150 C2
Hollow Creek KY 230 E3
Hollow Rock TN 109 D4
Holly CO 42 A3
Holly MI 76 B4
Holly Grove AR 117 F2
Holly Hill FL 139 E4
Holly Hill SC 130 C1
Holly Park NJ 147 E3
Holly Pond AL 119 F3
Holly Ridge NC 115 C4
Holly Sprs. GA 120 C3
Holly Sprs. MS 118 C2
Holly Sprs. NC 112 C4
Hollyvilla KY 100 A4
Hollywood AL 120 A2
Hollywood FL 143 F2
Hollywood MD 103 E4
Hollywood SC 131 D2
Hollywood Park TX 61 D2
Holmdel NJ 147 E2
Holmen WI 73 F1
Holmes Beach FL 140 B3
Holmes Co. FL 136 C1
Holmes Co. MS 126 B1
Holmes Co. OH 91 D4
Holstein IA 72 A4
Holt AL 127 E1
Holt MI 76 A4
Holt Co. MO 86 A4
Holt Co. NE 35 D1
Holton KS 96 A2
Holts Summit MO 97 E3
Holtville CA 53 E4
Holualoa HI 153 E3
Holyoke CO 34 A4
Holyoke MA 150 A2
Holyrood KS 43 D3
Homecroft IN 99 F1
Homedale ID 22 A4
Home Gardens CA 229 H4
Homeland CA 229 K4
Homeland GA 139 D1
Homeland Park SC 121 E3
Homer AK 154 C3
Homer GA 121 D3
Homer IL 99 D1
Homer LA 125 D2
Homer MI 90 A1
Homer NE 35 F2
Homer NY 79 D4
Homer City PA 92 B4
Homer Glen IL 203 C6
Homerville GA 138 C1
Homestead FL 143 E3
Homestead PA 250 C2
Homestead Valley CA 259 A2
Hometown IL 203 D5
Hometown PA 93 E3
Hometown WV 101 E3
Homewood AL 119 F4
Hominy OK 51 F1
Homosassa FL 140 B1
Homosassa Sprs. FL 140 B1
Honaker VA 111 E2
Honalo HI 153 E3
Honaunau HI 153 E3
Hondo TX 60 C3
Honea Path SC 121 E3
Honeoye NY 78 C4
Honeoye Falls NY 78 C3
Honesdale PA 93 F2
Honey Brook PA 146 B2
Honey Grove TX 59 F1
Honeyville UT 31 E3
Honokaa HI 153 E2
Honokowai HI 153 D1
Honolulu HI 152 A3
Honolulu Co. HI 152 A3
Honomu HI 153 F3
Hood Co. TX 59 E3
Hood River OR 21 D1
Hood River Co. OR 20 C2
Hooker OK 50 B1
Hooker Co. NE 34 B2
Hooks TX 116 C4
Hooksett NH 81 F4
Hoonah AK 155 D4
Hooper NE 35 F3
Hooper UT 244 A2
Hooper Bay AK 154 B3
Hoopeston IL 89 D4
Hoople ND 19 E2
Hoosick Falls NY 94 B1
Hoover AL 127 F1
Hooverson Hts. WV 91 F4
Hooversville PA 92 B4
Hopatcong NJ 148 A3
Hope AR 117 D4
Hope IN 99 F2
Hope ND 19 E3
Hope RI 150 C3
Hopedale IL 88 B4
Hopedale MA 150 C2
Hopedale OH 91 F4
Hope Mills NC 123 D2
Hope Valley RI 150 C4
Hopewell NJ 147 D1
Hopewell TN 120 B1
Hopewell VA 113 E1
Hopewell Jct. NY 148 B1
Hopkins MI 75 F4
Hopkins MN 235 A3
Hopkins MO 86 B4
Hopkins Co. KY 109 E2
Hopkins Co. TX 124 A1
Hopkins Park IL 89 D3
Hopkinsville KY 109 E2
Hopkinton IA 73 F4
Hopkinton MA 150 C2
Hopkinton NH 81 F4
Hopwood PA 102 B1
Hoquiam WA 12 B4
Horace ND 19 E4
Horatio AR 116 C4
Horicon WI 74 C2

Honolulu HI

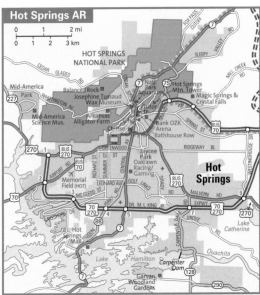

Hernando Beach FL 140 B1
Hernando Co. FL 140 B1
Herndon VA 144 A3
Heron Lake MN 72 A2
Herreid SD 26 C1
Herricks NY 241 G3
Herriman UT 31 E4
Herrin IL 108 C1
Herscher IL 89 D3
Hershey NE 34 B3
Hershey PA 93 E4
Hertford NC 113 F3
Hertford Co. NC 113 F3
Hesperia CA 53 D2
Hesperia MI 75 E2
Hessmer LA 133 F1
Hesston KS 43 E3
Hettinger ND 26 A1
Hettinger Co. ND 18 A4
Heuvelton NY 80 B2
Hewitt TX 59 E4
Hewitt WI 68 A4
Hewlett NY 241 G4
Hewlett Harbor NY 241 G5
Hewlett Neck NY 241 G5
Heyburn ID 31 D1
Heyworth IL 88 C4
Hialeah FL 143 E2
Hialeah Gardens FL 143 E2
Hiawassee GA 121 D2
Hiawatha IA 87 E1
Hiawatha KS 96 A1
Hibbing MN 64 B3
Hickman KY 108 C3
Hickman NE 35 F4
Hickman Co. KY 108 C3
Hickman Co. TN 109 E4
Higganum CT 149 E1
Higginsville MO 96 C2
High Bridge NJ 104 A1
Highgate Ctr. VT 81 D1
Highgrove CA 229 J3
Highland AR 107 F3
Highland CA 229 K2
Highland IL 98 B3
Highland IN 89 D2
Highland KS 96 A1
Highland MD 144 B2
Highland NY 94 B3
Highland UT 31 F4
Highland WI 74 A3
Highland Beach FL 143 F1
Highland City FL 140 C2
Highland Co. OH 100 C2
Highland Co. VA 102 B4
Highland Falls NY 148 B2
Highland Hts. KY 204 B3
Highland Hts. OH 204 G1
Highland Hills OH 204 G2
Highland Lakes NJ 148 A2
Highland Mills NY 148 B2
Highland Park IL 89 D1
Highland Park MI 210 C3
Highland Park NJ 147 E1
Highland Park PA 218 B2
Highland Park TX 207 D2
Highlands NJ 147 F1
Highlands NC 121 D2
Highlands TX 132 B3
Highlands Co. FL 141 D4
Highland Sprs. VA 254 C2
Highlands Ranch CO 209 C4
Highlandville MO 107 D2
Highmore SD 27 D3
Hill City KS 42 C2
Hill City MN 64 B4
Hill City SD 25 F4
Hill Country Vil. TX 257 E1
Hill Co. MT 16 A1
Hill Co. TX 59 E3
Hillcrest IL 88 B1
Hillcrest NY 148 B2
Hillcrest TX 132 B4
Hillcrest Hts. MD 144 B3
Hilliard FL 139 D1
Hilliard OH 101 D1
Hillman MI 70 C3
Hills IA 87 F2
Hills MN 27 F4
Hillsboro AL 119 E2
Hillsboro IL 98 B2
Hillsboro IN 89 E4
Hillsboro KS 43 E3
Hillsboro MO 98 A4
Hillsboro ND 19 E3
Hillsboro OH 100 C2
Hillsboro OR 20 B2
Hillsboro TX 59 E3
Hillsboro WI 74 A2
Hillsboro Beach FL 143 F1
Hillsborough CA 259 B4
Hillsborough NH 81 E4
Hillsborough NC 112 C4
Hillsborough Co. FL 140 C3
Hillsborough Co. NH 81 F4
Hillsdale IL 88 A2
Hillsdale MI 90 B1
Hillsdale MO 256 B2
Hillsdale NJ 148 B3
Hillsdale Co. MI 90 B1
Hillside IL 203 C4
Hinesburg VT 81 D2
Hinesville GA 130 B3
Hingham MA 151 D1
Hinsdale IL 203 C5
Hinsdale MA 94 C1
Hinsdale NH 94 C1
Hinsdale Co. CO 40 C4
Hinson FL 137 E2
Hinton IA 35 F1
Hinton OK 51 D3
Hinton WV 112 A1
Hiram GA 120 C4
Hiram OH 91 E2
Hitchcock TX 132 B4
Hitchcock Co. NE 34 B4
Hitchins KY 101 D4
Hobart IN 89 D2
Hobart OK 51 D3
Hobart WA 12 C3
Hobbs NM 57 F2
Hobe Sound FL 141 F4
Hoboken NJ 148 B4
Hobson MT 16 B4
Hockessin DE 146 B3
Hocking Co. OH 101 D1
Hockley Co. TX 58 A1
Hodge LA 125 E3
Hodgeman Co. KS 42 C3
Hodgenville KY 110 A1
Hodgkins IL 203 C5
Hoffman MN 66 A2
Hoffman NC 122 C2
Hoffman Estates IL 203 B3
Hogansville GA 128 C1
Hohenwald TN 119 E1
Hoisington KS 43 D3
Hokah MN 73 F2

Aldine C1	Channelview D2	Fresno B4	Houston................C2	Lynchburg D2	Pasadena D3	Spring Valley Village ...B2
Barrett D1	Cloverleaf D2	Friendswood D4	Humble C1	Magnolia Gardens ...C2	Pearland C4	Stafford B4
Beaumont Place D2	Crabb A4	Galena Park C3	Hunters Creek Vil. ...B2	Meadows Place A3	Piney Pt. Vil. B2	Sugar Land A3
Bellaire B3	Crosby D1	Hedwig Vil. B2	Jacinto City C2	Mission Bend A3	Satsuma A1	Webster D4
Booth A4	Cypress A1	Highlands D2	Jersey Vil. A1	Missouri City B4	Sheldon D2	W. University Place ...B3
Brookside Vil. C4	Deer Park D3	Hilshire Vil. B2	La Porte D3	Nassau Bay D4	S. Houston C3	
Bunker Hill Vil. B2	Four Corners A3	Houmont Park D2	League City D4	N. Houston B1	Southside Place B3	

Houston TX

POINTS OF INTEREST

Allen's Landing F1	
Alley Theatre F2	
Amtrak Station E1	
Bayou Music Center......................................E2	
Bayou Place..E2	
BBVA Stadium G2	
Bus Depot. E3	
City Hall E2	
Court House E2	
Downtown Aquarium....................................E1	
Federal Building E2	
George R. Brown Convention Center F2	
Heritage Society Complex.............................E2	
Hobby Center for the Performing Arts E2	
Houston Fire Museum....................................E3	
Jones Hall F2	
J.P. Morgan Chase Tower F2	
Library...F2	
Minute Maid Park..F1	
The Shops at Houston Center.........................F2	
Talento Bilingüe de Houston...........................G2	
Toyota Center...F2	
Univ. of Houston-Downtown...........................F1	
Wortham Theater Center................................E1	

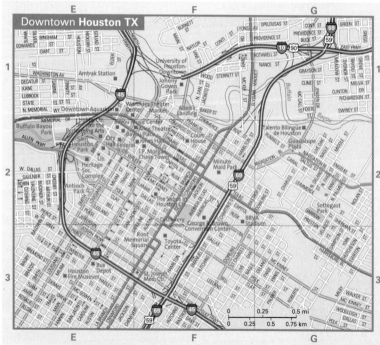

Downtown Houston TX

Horizon City TX 56 C4	Houston MO 107 E1	Howard KS 43 F4
Hornbeak TN 108 C3	Houston PA 92 A4	Howard PA 92 C3
Hornbeck LA 125 D4	Houston TX 132 A3	Howard SD 27 E4
Hornell NY 78 C4	Houston Acres KY 230 D1	Howard WI 68 C4
Hornersville MO 108 B4	Houston Co. AL 137 D1	Howard City MI 75 F2
Horn Lake MS 118 B2	Houston Co. GA 129 D2	Howard Co. AR 116 A3
Horry Co. SC 123 D3	Houston Co. MN 73 F2	Howard Co. IN 89 F4
Horse Cave KY 110 A2	Houston Co. TN 109 E3	Howard Co. IA 73 E3
Horseheads NY 93 D1	Houston Co. TX 124 A4	Howard Co. MD 144 B2
Horse Pasture VA 112 B3	Houtzdale PA 92 C3	Howard Co. MO 97 D2
Horseshoe Bay TX 61 D1	Hoven SD 27 D2	Howard Co. NE 35 D3
Horseshoe Bend AR .107 F3	Howard KS 43 F4	Howard Co. TX 58 B3
Horseshoe Bend ID ...22 B4	Howard PA 92 C3	Howard Lake MN 66 C3
Horsham PA 146 C2	Howard SD 27 E4	Howards Grove WI 75 D2
Horton KS 96 A1	Howard WI 68 C4	Howe IN 90 A1
Hortonville MA 151 D3	Howard City MI 75 F2	Howe OK 116 B2
Hortonville WI 74 C1	Howard Co. AR 116 A3	Howe TX 59 F1
Hoschton GA 121 D3	Howard Co. IN 89 F4	Howell MI 76 B4
Hosmer SD 27 D1	Howard Co. IA 73 E3	Howell Co. MO 107 E3
Hospers IA 35 F1	Howard Co. MD 144 B2	Howells NE 35 F3
Hotchkiss CO 40 B2	Howard Co. MO 97 D2	Howells NY 148 A1
Hotchkissville CT 149 D1	Howard Co. NE 35 D3	Howey-in-the-Hills FL .140 C1
Hotevilla-Bacavi AZ ...47 E2	Howard Co. TX 58 B3	Howland ME 85 D4
Hot Spr. Co. AR 117 D3	Howard Lake MN 66 C3	Hoxie AR 108 A4
Hot Sprs. AR 117 D3	Howards Grove WI 75 D2	Hoxie KS 42 C2
Hot Sprs. MT 14 C3	Howe IN 90 A1	Hoyt KS 96 A2
Hot Sprs. NC 111 D4	Howe OK 116 B2	Hoyt Lakes MN 64 C3
Hot Sprs. SD 25 F4	Howe TX 59 F1	Huachuca City AZ 55 D4
Hot Sprs. Co. WY 24 B4	Howell MI 76 B4	Hubbard IA 72 C4
Hot Sprs. Vil. AR 117 D2	Howell Co. MO 107 E3	Hubbard OH 276 C2
Hot Sulphur Sprs. CO .41 D1	Howells NE 35 F3	Hubbard OR 20 C2
Houck AZ 48 A3	Howells NY 148 A1	Hubbard TX 59 F3
Houghton MI 65 F3	Howey-in-the-Hills FL .140 C1	Hubbard Co. MN 64 A3
Houghton NY 78 B4	Howland ME 85 D4	Hubbard Lake MI 71 D4
Houghton Co. MI 65 F4	Hoxie AR 108 A4	Hubbell MI 65 F3
Houghton Lake MI 76 A1	Hoxie KS 42 C2	Huber Hts. OH 100 C1
Houlton ME 85 E3	Hoyt KS 96 A2	Huber Ridge OH 206 C1
Houma LA 134 A3	Hoyt Lakes MN 64 C3	Huddy KY 111 E1
Housatonic MA 94 B2	Huachuca City AZ 55 D4	Hudson CO 41 E1
Houston AK 154 C3	Hubbard IA 72 C4	Hudson FL 140 B2
Houston DE 145 E3	Hubbard OH 276 C2	Hudson IL 88 C3
Houston MN 73 E2	Hubbard OR 20 C2	Hudson IN 90 A2
Houston MS 118 C4	Hubbard TX 59 F3	Hudson IA 73 D4
	Hubbard Co. MN 64 A3	Hudson MA 150 C1
	Hubbard Lake MI 71 D4	Hudson MI 90 B1
	Hubbell MI 65 F3	Hudson NH 95 E1
	Huber Hts. OH 100 C1	Hudson NY 94 B3
	Huber Ridge OH 206 C1	Hudson NC 111 F4
	Huddy KY 111 E1	Hudson OH 91 E2
	Hudson CO 41 E1	Hudson SD 35 F1
	Hudson FL 140 B2	Hudson TX 124 B4
	Hudson IL 88 C3	Hudson WI 67 D4
	Hudson IN 90 A2	Hudson WY 32 B1
	Hudson IA 73 D4	Hudson Co. NJ 148 A3
	Hudson MA 150 C1	Hudson Falls NY 81 D4
	Hudson MI 90 B1	Hudsonville MI 75 F3
	Hudson NH 95 E1	Hudspeth Co. TX 57 D4
	Hudson NY 94 B3	Huerfano Co. CO 41 E4
		Hueytown AL 119 F4
		Huffs Church PA 146 B1
		Hughes AR 118 A2
		Hughes Co. OK 51 F3
		Hughes Co. SD 26 C3
		Hughes Sprs. TX 124 B1
		Hughestown PA 261 C2
		Hughesville MD 144 C4
		Hughesville PA 93 E2
		Hughson CA 36 C4
		Hugo CO 41 F2
		Hugo MN 67 D2
		Hugo OK 116 A3
		Hugoton KS 42 A4
		Huguenot NY 148 A1
		Huguley AL 128 B2
		Hulbert OK 106 B4
		Hulett WY 25 F3
		Hull IA 35 F1
		Hull MA 151 D1
		Hulmeville PA 147 D2
		Humansville MO 106 C1
		Humarock MA 151 E2
		Humble TX 132 B3
		Humboldt IA 72 B4
		Humboldt KS 106 A1
		Humboldt NE 43 F1
		Humboldt NV 29 E1
		Humboldt SD 27 F4
		Humboldt TN 108 C4
		Humboldt Co. CA 28 A4
		Humboldt Co. IA 72 B3
		Humboldt Co. NV 29 F3
		Humeston IA 86 C3
		Hummelstown PA 93 E4
		Humphrey AR 117 F3
		Humphrey NE 35 E3
		Humphreys Co. MS ...126 B1
		Humphreys Co. TN ...109 E4
		Hungerford TX 61 F3
		Hungry Horse MT 15 D2
		Hunt Co. TX 59 F2
		Hunter ND 19 E3
		Hunter TN 111 E3

Entries in **bold black** indicate counties or parishes.
Entries in **bold color** indicate cities with detailed inset maps.

Hunterdon Co. NJ 147 D1
Hunters Creek Vil. TX 220 B2
Hunters Pt. AZ 48 A3
Huntersville NC 122 A1
Huntertown IN 90 A2
Huntingburg IN 99 E4
Huntingdon PA 92 C4
Huntingdon TN 109 D4
Huntingdon Co. PA 92 C3
Huntington AR 116 C1
Huntington IN 89 F3
Huntington MA 94 C2
Huntington NY 148 C3
Huntington OR 22 A3
Huntington TX 124 B4
Huntington UT 39 F2
Huntington VA 270 C5
Huntington WV 101 D3
Huntington Bay NY 148 C3
Huntington Beach CA 52 C3
Huntington Co. IN 89 F3
Huntington Park CA 228 D3
Huntington Sta. NY 148 C3
Huntington Woods MI 210 B2
Huntingtown MD 144 C4
Hunting Valley OH 204 G2
Huntland TN 120 A2
Huntleigh MO 256 B2
Huntley IL 88 C1
Huntley MT 24 C1
Hunts Pt. WA 262 B3
Huntsville AL 119 F2
Huntsville AR 106 C4
Huntsville MO 97 E2
Huntsville TN 110 B3
Huntsville TX 132 A1
Huntsville UT 31 F3
Hurffville NJ 146 C4
Hurley MS 135 D1
Hurley NM 55 F2
Hurley NY 94 B2
Hurley SD 27 F4
Hurley WI 65 E4
Hurlock MD 145 E4
Huron CA 44 C3
Huron OH 91 D2
Huron SD 27 E3
Huron Co. MI 76 C2
Huron Co. OH 91 D3
Hurricane UT 39 D4
Hurricane WV 101 E3
Hurst IL 108 C1
Hurst TX 207 B2
Hurstbourne KY 230 F2
Hurstbourne Acres KY 230 F2
Hurt VA 112 C2
Hurtsboro AL 128 B3
Hustisford WI 74 C3
Hustonville KY 110 B1
Hutchins TX 207 E3
Hutchinson KS 43 E3
Hutchinson MN 66 C4
Hutchinson Co. SD 27 E4
Hutchinson Co. TX 50 B2
Hutsonville IL 99 D2
Huttig AR 125 E1
Hutto TX 61 E1
Huxley IA 86 C1
Hyannis MA 151 F3
Hyannis NE 34 B2
Hyannis Port MA 151 F4
Hyattsville MD 144 B3
Hyde PA 92 C3
Hyde Co. NC 113 F4
Hyde Co. SD 27 D3
Hyden KY 111 D2
Hyde Park NY 94 B3
Hyde Park UT 31 E2
Hyde Park VT 81 E2
Hydesville CA 28 A4
Hydetown PA 92 A2
Hydro OK 51 D3
Hymera IN 99 E2
Hyndman PA 102 C1
Hypoluxo FL 143 F1
Hyrum UT 31 E3
Hysham MT 25 D1

I

Iaeger WV 111 F1
Iberia MO 97 E4
Iberia Par. LA 133 F3
Iberville Par. LA 133 F2
Icard NC 111 F4
Ida MI 90 C1
Idabel OK 116 B4
Ida Co. IA 72 A4
Ida Grove IA 72 A4
Idaho City ID 22 B4
Idaho Co. ID 14 C4
Idaho Falls ID 23 E4
Idalou TX 58 A1
Ideal GA 129 D2
Ider AL 120 A2
Idyllwild CA 53 D3
Idylwood VA 270 B3
Ignacio CO 48 B1
Ilion NY 79 F3
Illiopolis IL 98 B1
Ilwaco WA 12 B4
Imboden AR 107 F3
Imlay NV 29 F4
Imlay City MI 76 C3
Immokalee FL 143 D1
Imperial CA 53 E4
Imperial MO 98 A4
Imperial NE 34 B4
Imperial PA 91 F4
Imperial Beach CA 53 D4
Imperial Co. CA 53 F4
Ina IL 98 C4
Incline Vil. NV 37 D2
Independence CA 45 E2
Independence IA 73 E4
Independence KS 106 A2
Independence KY 100 B3
Independence LA 134 B1
Independence MN 66 C4
Independence MO 96 B2
Independence OH 204 F3
Independence OR 20 B2
Independence VA 111 F3
Independence WI 73 E1
Independence Co. AR 107 F4
Independent Hill VA 144 A4
Indialantic FL 141 E2
Indiana PA 92 B3
Indiana Co. PA 92 B3
Indianapolis IN 99 F1
Indian Harbour Beach FL 141 E2
Indian Head MD 144 B4
Indian Head Park IL 203 C5
Indian Hills CO 209 A4
Indian Hills KY 230 E1
Indian Neck CT 149 D2
Indianola IA 86 C2
Indianola MS 118 A4
Indianola NE 34 C4
Indianola WA 262 A2
Indian Pt. MO 107 D3
Indian River MI 70 C3
Indian River Co. FL 141 E3
Indian River Estates FL 141 E3
Indian River Shores FL 141 E3
Indian Rocks Beach FL 140 B2
Indian Shores FL 266 A2
Indian Sprs. NV 46 A1
Indian Sprs. Vil. AL 127 F1
Indiantown FL 141 E4
Indian Trail NC 122 B2
Indian Wells CA 53 E3
Indio CA 53 E3
Indrio FL 141 E3
Industry CA 228 E3
Industry PA 91 F3
Inez KY 101 D4

Huntington WV

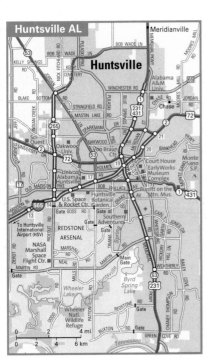

Indianapolis IN

Avon A3
Beech Grove C3
Camby A4
Carmel C1
Clermont A2
Crows Nest B2
Eagle Vil. B1
Fishers D1
Friendswood A4
Homecroft C4
Home Place C1
Indianapolis C2
Lawrence D2
Meridian Hills C1
N. Crows Nest B2
Plainfield A4
Rocky Ripple B2
Royalton A1
Southport C4
Speedway B3
Spring Hills B2
Warren Park D3
W. Newton A4
Williams Creek C1
Wynnedale B2
Zionsville A1

Figures after entries indicate page number and grid reference.

POINTS OF INTEREST

American Legion National Headquarters . . A1
Artsgarden . . . A2
Bankers Life Fieldhouse . . . B2
Canal & State Park Cultural District . . . A2
Circle Centre . . . A2
City Market . . . B2
Eiteljorg Museum . . . A2
Herron School of Art . . . A2
Indiana Avenue Cultural District . . . A1
Indiana Convention Center . . . A2
Indiana State Museum . . . A2
Indiana Univ./Purdue Univ. Indianapolis . . A1
Indiana War Memorial . . . A1
James Whitcomb Riley Home . . . B1
Lucas Oil Stadium . . . A2
Madame Walker Legacy Center . . . A1
Massachusetts Avenue Cultural District . . B1
Morris-Butler House . . . B1
NCAA Hall of Champions . . . A2
Old National Centre . . . B1
President Benjamin Harrison Home . . . B1
Scottish Rite Cathedral . . . A1
Soldiers & Sailors Monument . . . A2
State Capitol . . . A2
Victory Field . . . A2
White River State Park . . . A2
Zoo . . . A2

Iota LA ... 133 E2
Iowa LA ... 133 D2
Iowa City IA ... 87 F2
Iowa Colony TX ... 132 A4
Iowa Co. IA ... 87 E2
Iowa Co. WI ... 74 A3
Iowa Falls IA ... 73 D4
Iowa Park TX ... 59 D1
Ipswich MA ... 151 F1
Ipswich SD ... 27 D2
Iraan TX ... 60 A1
Iredell Co. NC ... 112 A4
Irene SD ... 35 E1
Ireton IA ... 35 F1
Irion Co. TX ... 58 B4
Irmo SC ... 122 A3
Iron City TN ... 119 E2
Iron Co. MI ... 68 C1
Iron Co. MO ... 108 A1
Iron Co. UT ... 39 D4
Iron Co. WI ... 68 A1
Irondale AL ... 119 F4
Irondequoit NY ... 78 C3
Iron Gate VA ... 112 B1
Iron Mtn. MI ... 68 C2
Iron Mtn. Lake MO ... 108 A1
Iron Ridge WI ... 74 C2
Iron River MI ... 68 C2
Ironton MN ... 64 B4
Ironton MO ... 108 A1
Ironton OH ... 101 D3
Ironwood MI ... 65 E4
Iroquois SD ... 27 E3
Iroquois Co. IL ... 89 D3
Irrigon OR ... 21 E1
Irvine CA ... 52 C3
Irvine KY ... 110 C1
Irving IL ... 98 B2
Irving TX ... 59 F2
Irvington IL ... 98 C3
Irvington KY ... 99 F4
Irvington NE ... 245 A1
Irvington NJ ... 148 A4
Irvington NY ... 148 B3
Irvington VA ... 113 F1
Irvona PA ... 92 B3
Irwin PA ... 92 A4
Irwin SC ... 122 B2
Irwin Co. GA ... 129 E4
Irwindale CA ... 228 E2
Irwinton GA ... 129 E2
Isabel SD ... 26 B2
Isabella Co. MI ... 76 A2
Isanti MN ... 67 D3
Isanti Co. MN ... 67 D2
Iselin NJ ... 147 E1
Ishpeming MI ... 65 F4
Islamorada FL ... 143 E4
Island KY ... 109 E1
Island City OR ... 21 F2
Island Co. WA ... 12 C2
Island Falls ME ... 85 D3
Island Hts. NJ ... 147 E3
Island Lake IL ... 74 C4
Island Park ID ... 23 F3
Island Park NY ... 147 F1
Island Pond VT ... 81 E1
Isla Vista CA ... 52 A2
Isle MN ... 67 D2
Isle of Hope GA ... 130 C3
Isle of Palms SC ... 131 D2
Isle of Wight VA ... 113 F2
Isle of Wight Co. VA ... 113 F2
Isleta NM ... 48 C3
Isleton CA ... 36 C3
Islip NY ... 149 D4
Isola MS ... 126 B1
Issaquah WA ... 12 C3
Issaquena Co. MS ... 126 A2
Italy TX ... 59 F3
Itasca IL ... 203 B3
Itasca TX ... 59 E3
Itasca Co. MN ... 64 B3
Itawamba Co. MS ... 119 D3
Ithaca MI ... 76 A3
Ithaca NY ... 79 D4
Itta Bena MS ... 118 B4
Iuka IL ... 98 C3
Iuka MS ... 119 D2
Iva SC ... 121 E3
Ivanhoe CA ... 45 D3
Ivanhoe MN ... 27 F3
Ivanhoe VA ... 112 A2
Ivey GA ... 129 E1
Ivins UT ... 38 C4
Ixonia WI ... 74 C3
Izard Co. AR ... 107 F4

J

Jacinto City TX ... 220 C2
Jack Co. TX ... 59 D2
Jackman ME ... 84 B4
Jackman Sta. ME ... 84 B4
Jackpot NV ... 30 C2
Jacksboro TN ... 110 C3
Jacksboro TX ... 59 D2
Jackson AL ... 127 E4
Jackson CA ... 36 C3
Jackson GA ... 129 D1
Jackson KY ... 111 D1
Jackson LA ... 134 A1
Jackson MI ... 76 A4
Jackson MN ... 72 B2
Jackson MS ... 126 B2
Jackson MO ... 108 B1
Jackson NC ... 113 E3
Jackson OH ... 101 D2
Jackson SC ... 130 B1
Jackson TN ... 118 C1
Jackson WI ... 74 C3
Jackson WY ... 23 F4
Jackson Ctr. OH ... 90 B4
Jackson Co. AL ... 120 A2
Jackson Co. AR ... 118 A1
Jackson Co. CO ... 33 D4
Jackson Co. FL ... 137 D1
Jackson Co. GA ... 121 D3
Jackson Co. IL ... 98 B4
Jackson Co. IN ... 99 F3
Jackson Co. IA ... 87 F1
Jackson Co. KS ... 96 A2
Jackson Co. KY ... 110 C1
Jackson Co. MI ... 76 A4
Jackson Co. MN ... 72 B2
Jackson Co. MS ... 135 D2
Jackson Co. MO ... 96 C3
Jackson Co. NC ... 121 E1
Jackson Co. OH ... 101 D3
Jackson Co. OK ... 50 C4
Jackson Co. OR ... 28 B1
Jackson Co. SD ... 26 B4
Jackson Co. TN ... 110 A3
Jackson Co. TX ... 61 F3
Jackson Co. WV ... 101 E3
Jackson Co. WI ... 67 F4
Jackson Par. LA ... 125 E2
Jacksons Gap AL ... 128 B1
Jacksonville AL ... 120 A4
Jacksonville AR ... 117 E2
Jacksonville FL ... 139 D2
Jacksonville IL ... 98 A1
Jacksonville MD ... 144 C1
Jacksonville NC ... 115 D4
Jacksonville OR ... 28 B2
Jacksonville PA ... 92 B4
Jacksonville TX ... 124 A3
Jacksonville VT ... 94 C1
Jacksonville Beach FL ... 139 D2
Jacobstown NJ ... 147 D2
Jacobus PA ... 103 E1

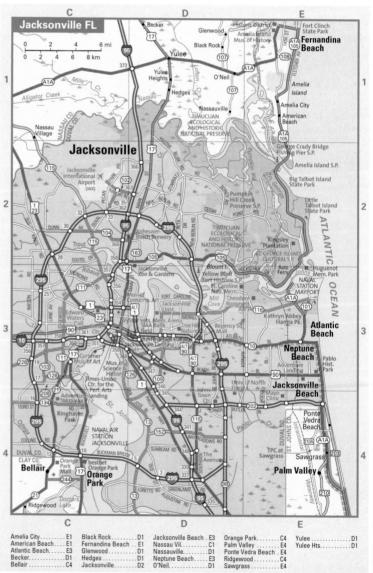

Inez TX ... 61 F3
Ingalls IN ... 99 F1
Ingham Co. MI ... 76 A4
Ingleside TX ... 63 F2
Ingleside on the Bay TX ... 63 F2
Inglewood CA ... 52 C2
Inglis FL ... 138 C4
Ingold NC ... 123 E2
Ingram PA ... 250 A2
Ingram TX ... 60 C2
Inkom ID ... 31 E1
Inkster MI ... 210 B4
Inman GA ... 128 C1
Inman KS ... 43 E3
Inman SC ... 121 F2
Inola OK ... 106 A4
Intercession City FL ... 141 D2
Interlachen FL ... 139 D3
Interlaken NJ ... 147 F2
Interlaken NY ... 79 D4
Interlochen MI ... 69 F4
International Falls MN ... 64 B2
Inver Grove Hts. MN ... 235 D4
Inverness CA ... 36 A3
Inverness FL ... 140 C1
Inverness IL ... 203 B2
Inverness MS ... 126 B1
Inwood FL ... 140 C2
Inwood IA ... 27 F4
Inwood NY ... 147 F1
Inwood WV ... 103 D2
Inyo Co. CA ... 37 F4
Inyokern CA ... 45 E4
Iola KS ... 96 A4
Iola WI ... 68 B4
Iona ID ... 23 E4
Ione CA ... 36 C3
Ione OR ... 21 E2
Ione WA ... 13 F1
Ionia MI ... 76 A3
Ionia Co. MI ... 75 F3
Iosco Co. MI ... 76 B1

Amelia City ... E1
American Beach ... E1
Atlantic Beach ... E3
Becker ... D1
Bellair ... C4
Black Rock ... D1
Fernandina Beach ... E1
Glenwood ... D1
Hedges ... D1
Jacksonville ... D2
Jacksonville Beach ... E3
Nassau Vil. ... C1
Nassauville ... D1
Neptune Beach ... E3
O'Neil ... D1
Orange Park ... C4
Palm Valley ... E4
Ponte Vedra Beach ... E4
Ridgewood ... C4
Sawgrass ... E4
Yulee ... D1
Yulee Hts. ... D1

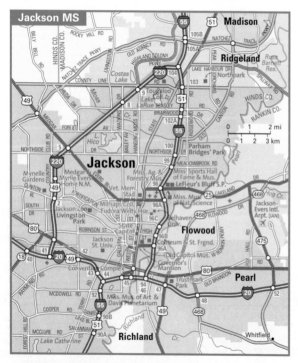

Entries in **bold black** indicate counties or parishes.
Entries in **bold color** indicate cities with detailed inset maps.

Jaffrey NH 95 D1
Jal NM 57 F3
Jamaica Beach TX 132 B4
Jamesburg NJ 147 E2
James City NC 115 D3
James City Co. VA 113 F1
Jamesport MO 96 C1
Jamesport NY 149 E3
Jamestown CA 37 D3
Jamestown IN 99 E1
Jamestown KS 43 E1
Jamestown KY 110 B2
Jamestown MI 75 F3
Jamestown NY 92 B1
Jamestown NC 112 B4
Jamestown ND 19 D4
Jamestown OH 100 C1
Jamestown PA 91 F2
Jamestown RI 150 C4
Jamestown TN 110 B3
James Town WY 32 A3
Jamesville NC 113 F4
Jamul CA 53 D4
Jane Lew WV 102 A2
Janesville CA 29 D4
Janesville IA 73 D4
Janesville MN 72 C1
Janesville WI 74 B4
Jarales NM 48 C4
Jarratt VA 113 E2
Jarrell TX 61 E1
Jarrettsville MD 144 C1
Jasmine Estates FL 140 B2
Jasonville IN 99 E2
Jasper AL 119 E4
Jasper AR 107 D4
Jasper FL 138 B2
Jasper GA 120 C3
Jasper IN 99 E4
Jasper MN 27 F4
Jasper MO 106 C1
Jasper OR 20 B4
Jasper TN 120 A2
Jasper TX 132 C1
Jasper Co. GA 129 D1
Jasper Co. IL 99 D2
Jasper Co. IN 89 E3
Jasper Co. IA 87 D2
Jasper Co. MS 126 C3
Jasper Co. MO 106 C2
Jasper Co. SC 130 C3
Jasper Co. TX 132 C1
Jay FL 135 F1
Jay ME 82 B2
Jay OK 106 B3
Jay Co. IN 90 A4
Jayton TX 58 B2
Jeanerette LA 133 F3
Jean Lafitte LA 134 B3
Jeannette PA 92 A4
Jeddito AZ 47 F2
Jeff Davis Co. GA 129 F3
Jeff Davis Co. TX 62 B2
Jefferson GA 121 D3
Jefferson IA 86 B1
Jefferson LA 239 B1
Jefferson MA 150 B1
Jefferson NC 111 F3
Jefferson OH 91 F1
Jefferson OR 20 B3
Jefferson PA 103 E1
Jefferson SC 122 B2
Jefferson SD 35 F1
Jefferson TX 124 C2
Jefferson WI 74 B3
Jefferson City MO 97 E3
Jefferson City MT 15 E4
Jefferson City TN 111 D4
Jefferson Co. AL 119 F4
Jefferson Co. AR 117 F3
Jefferson Co. CO 41 E1
Jefferson Co. FL 137 E2
Jefferson Co. GA 129 F1
Jefferson Co. ID 23 E4
Jefferson Co. IL 98 C4
Jefferson Co. IN 100 A3
Jefferson Co. IA 87 E3
Jefferson Co. KS 96 A2
Jefferson Co. KY 100 A4
Jefferson Co. MS 126 A3
Jefferson Co. MO 98 A4
Jefferson Co. MT 23 E1
Jefferson Co. NE 35 F4
Jefferson Co. NY 79 E2
Jefferson Co. OH 91 F4
Jefferson Co. OK 59 E1
Jefferson Co. OR 20 C3
Jefferson Co. PA 92 B2
Jefferson Co. TN 111 D4
Jefferson Co. TX 132 C3
Jefferson Co. WA 12 B3
Jefferson Co. WV 103 D2
Jefferson Co. WI 74 C3
Jefferson Davis Co. MS 126 B4
Jefferson Davis Par. LA 133 E2
Jefferson Hts. NY 94 B2
Jefferson Hills PA 92 A4
Jefferson Par. LA 134 B3
Jeffersontown KY 100 A4
Jefferson Valley NY 148 B2
Jeffersonville GA 129 E2
Jeffersonville IN 100 A4
Jeffersonville KY 100 C4
Jeffersonville OH 100 C1
Jeffersonville PA 248 A1
Jeffersonville VT 81 D1
Jellico TN 110 C3
Jemez Pueblo NM 48 C3
Jemez Sprs. NM 48 C2
Jemison AL 127 F1
Jena LA 125 E4
Jenison MI 75 F3
Jenkins KY 111 E2
Jenkins Co. GA 129 F2
Jenkintown PA 146 C2
Jenks OK 51 F2
Jennerstown PA 92 B4
Jennings FL 137 F2
Jennings LA 133 E2
Jennings MO 256 B1
Jennings Co. IN 100 A3
Jenny Lind AR 116 C1
Jensen Beach FL 141 E4
Jerauld Co. SD 27 D3
Jericho NY 148 C4
Jericho VT 81 D2
Jermyn PA 93 F2
Jerome AZ 47 D4
Jerome ID 30 C1
Jerome PA 92 B4
Jerome Co. ID 31 D1
Jersey City NJ 148 B4
Jersey Co. IL 98 A2
Jersey Shore PA 93 D2
Jersey Vil. TX 132 A3
Jerseyville IL 98 A2
Jerseyville NJ 147 E2
Jerusalem RI 150 C4
Jessamine Co. KY 100 B4
Jessup MD 144 C2
Jessup PA 93 F2
Jesup GA 130 A4
Jesup IA 73 E4
Jetmore KS 42 C3
Jewell IA 72 C4
Jewell KS 43 E1
Jewell Co. KS 43 E1
Jewett OH 91 F4
Jewett TX 59 F4
Jewett City (Griswold) CT 149 F1
Jim Hogg Co. TX 63 E3
Jim Thorpe PA 93 F3
Jim Wells Co. TX 63 E2
Joanna SC 121 F3
Joaquin TX 124 C3
Jo Daviess Co. IL 74 A4
John Day OR 21 F3
Johns Island SC 131 D2
Johnson AR 106 C4
Johnson VT 81 E2
Johnsonburg PA 92 B2
Johnson City KS 42 B4
Johnson City NY 93 E1
Johnson City OR 251 D3
Johnson City TN 111 E3
Johnson City TX 61 D1
Johnson Co. AR 117 D1
Johnson Co. GA 129 F2
Johnson Co. IL 108 C1
Johnson Co. IN 99 F2
Johnson Co. IA 87 F2
Johnson Co. KS 96 B3
Johnson Co. KY 111 D1
Johnson Co. MO 96 C3
Johnson Co. NE 35 F4
Johnson Co. TN 111 F3
Johnson Co. TX 59 E3
Johnson Co. WY 25 D4
Johnson Creek WI 74 C3
Johnsonville SC 122 C4
Johnston IA 86 C2
Johnston SC 121 F4
Johnston City IL 108 C1
Johnston Co. NC 113 D4
Johnston Co. OK 51 F4
Johnstown CO 33 E4
Johnstown NY 79 F3
Johnstown OH 91 D4
Johnstown PA 92 B4
Joiner AR 118 B1
Joliet IL 89 D2
Joliet MT 24 B2
Jollyville TX 61 E1
Jones OK 51 E3
Jonesboro AR 108 A4
Jonesboro GA 120 C4
Jonesboro IL 108 C1
Jonesboro IN 89 F4
Jonesboro LA 125 E3
Jonesborough TN 111 E3
Jonesburg MO 97 F3
Jones Co. GA 129 D1
Jones Co. IA 87 F1
Jones Co. MS 126 C4
Jones Co. NC 115 D3
Jones Co. SD 26 C4
Jones Co. TX 58 C2
Jones Creek TX 132 A4
Jonesport ME 83 E2
Jonestown MS 118 A3
Jonestown PA 93 E4
Jonestown TX 61 E1
Jonesville LA 125 F4
Jonesville MI 90 B1
Jonesville NC 112 A3
Jonesville SC 121 F2
Jonesville VT 81 D2
Jonesville VA 111 D3
Joplin MO 106 B2
Joplin MT 15 F2
Joppatowne MD 145 D1
Jordan MN 66 C4
Jordan MT 17 D3
Jordan NY 79 D3
Joseph OR 22 A2
Joseph City AZ 47 F3
Josephine TX 59 F2
Josephine Co. OR 28 B2
Joshua TX 59 E3
Joshua Tree CA 53 E2
Jourdanton TX 61 D3
Juab Co. UT 39 D1
Judith Basin Co. MT 16 A3
Judsonia AR 117 F1
Julesburg CO 34 A3
Juliaetta ID 14 B4
Julian CA 53 D4
Julian NC 112 B4
Jumpertown MS 119 D2
Junction TX 60 C1
Junction UT 39 E3
Junction City AR 125 E1
Junction City KS 43 F2
Junction City KY 110 B1
Junction City LA 125 E1
Junction City OH 101 E1
Junction City OR 20 B3
Juneau AK 155 E4
Juneau WI 74 C2
Juneau Co. WI 74 A1
Juniata NE 35 D4
Juniata Co. PA 93 D3
Junior WV 102 A2
Juno Beach FL 141 F4
Jupiter FL 141 F4
Jupiter Island FL 141 F4
Jurupa Valley CA 229 H3
Justice IL 203 D5
Justin TX 59 E2
Justus PA 261 E1

K

Kaaawa HI 152 A2
Kaanapali HI 153 D1
Kadoka SD 26 B4
Kahaluu HI 152 A3
Kahoka MO 87 E4
Kahuku HI 152 A2
Kahului HI 153 D1
Kaibab AZ 47 D1
Kaibito AZ 47 E1
Kailua HI 152 B3
Kailua-Kona HI 153 E3
Kake AK 155 E4
Kalaheo HI 152 B1
Kalama WA 20 C1
Kalamazoo MI 75 F4
Kalamazoo Co. MI 75 F4
Kalaoa HI 153 E3
Kalaupapa HI 152 C3
Kalawao Co. HI 152 C3
Kaleva MI 75 F1
Kalida OH 90 B3
Kalihiwai HI 152 B1
Kalispell MT 15 D2
Kalkaska MI 69 F4
Kalkaska Co. MI 70 B4
Kalona IA 87 E2
Kamas UT 31 F4
Kamiah ID 22 B1
Kanab UT 47 D1
Kanabec Co. MN 67 D2
Kanarraville UT 39 D4
Kanawha IA 72 C3
Kanawha WV 101 F2
Kanawha Co. WV 101 F4
Kandiyohi MN 66 B3
Kandiyohi Co. MN 66 B3
Kane PA 92 B2
Kane Co. IL 88 C1
Kane Co. UT 39 E4
Kaneohe HI 152 A3
Kankakee IL 89 D3
Kankakee Co. IL 89 D2
Kannapolis NC 122 B1
Kanopolis KS 43 E2
Kanosh UT 39 D2
Kansas IL 99 D1
Kansas OK 106 B3
Kansas City KS 96 B2
Kansas City MO 96 B2
Kapaa HI 152 B1
Kapaau HI 153 E2
Kaplan LA 133 E3
Karlstad MN 19 F2
Karnak IL 108 C2
Karnes City TX 61 E3
Karnes Co. TX 61 E3
Karns TN 110 C4
Kasigluk AK 154 B3
Kasota MN 72 C1
Kasson IN 99 D4
Kasson MN 73 D1
Kathleen FL 140 C2
Kathleen GA 129 D2
Katonah NY 148 C2
Katy TX 132 A3
Kauai Co. HI 152 B1
Kaufman TX 59 F2
Kaufman Co. TX 59 F3
Kaukauna WI 74 C1
Kaumakani HI 152 B1
Kaunakakai HI 152 C3
Kawkawlin MI 76 B2
Kaycee WY 25 D4
Kay Co. OK 51 E1
Kayenta AZ 47 F1
Kaysville UT 31 E3
Keaau HI 153 F3
Kealakekua HI 153 E3
Keams Canyon AZ 47 F2
Keansburg NJ 147 E1
Kearney MO 96 B2
Kearney NE 35 D4
Kearney Co. NE 35 D4
Kearneysville WV 103 D2
Kearns UT 257 A2
Kearny AZ 55 D2
Kearny NJ 148 B4
Kearny Co. KS 42 B3
Keauhou HI 153 E3
Keavy KY 110 C2
Kechi KS 43 E4
Keedysville MD 144 A1
Keegan ME 85 E1
Keego Harbor MI 210 A1
Keene NH 95 D1
Keene TX 59 E3
Keener NC 123 E2
Keenesburg CO 41 E1
Keeseville NY 81 D2
Keewatin MN 64 B3
Keiser AR 108 B4
Keith Co. NE 34 B3
Keithsburg IL 87 F3
Keizer OR 20 B2
Kekaha HI 152 B1
Keller TX 59 E2
Kellogg ID 14 B3
Kellogg IA 87 D1
Kellyville OK 51 F2
Kelseyville CA 36 B2
Kelso MO 108 B2
Kelso WA 20 B1
Kemah TX 132 B3
Kemblesville PA 146 B4
Kemmerer WY 31 F2
Kemp TX 59 F3
Kemper Co. MS 127 D2
Kempner TX 59 E4
Kenai AK 154 C3
Kenansville NC 123 E2
Kenbridge VA 113 D2
Kendall FL 143 E2
Kendall NY 78 B3
Kendall Co. IL 88 C2
Kendall Co. TX 61 D2
Kendall Park NJ 147 D1
Kendallville IN 90 A2
Kendrick FL 138 C4
Kendrick ID 14 B4
Kenedy TX 61 E3
Kenedy Co. TX 63 F3
Kenefick TX 132 B2
Kenesaw NE 35 D4
Kenilworth IL 203 D2
Kenilworth NJ 240 A4
Kenilworth PA 146 B2
Kenly NC 123 E1
Kenmare ND 18 B1
Kenmore NY 78 A3
Kenmore WA 262 B2
Kennebec SD 26 C4
Kennebec Co. ME 82 B2
Kennebunk ME 82 B4
Kennebunkport ME 82 B4
Kennedale TX 207 B3
Kennedy AL 119 D4
Kenner LA 134 B3
Kennesaw GA 120 C3
Kenneth City FL 266 A3
Kennett MO 108 B3
Kennett Square PA 146 B3
Kennewick WA 21 E1
Keno OR 28 C2
Kenosha WI 75 D4
Kenosha Co. WI 74 C4
Kenova WV 101 D4
Kensett AR 117 F1
Kensington CA 259 C2
Kensington CT 149 E1
Kensington KS 43 D1
Kensington MD 270 C1
Kensington NY 241 G2
Kensington Park FL 266 C5
Kent CT 94 B3
Kent OH 91 E3
Kent WA 12 C3
Kent City MI 75 F3
Kent Co. DE 145 E3
Kent Co. MD 145 D2
Kent Co. MI 75 F3
Kent Co. RI 150 C3
Kent Co. TX 58 B2
Kentfield CA 259 A1
Kentland IN 89 D3
Kenton DE 145 E2
Kenton KY 100 B3
Kenton OH 90 C3
Kenton TN 108 C3
Kenton Co. KY 100 B2
Kentwood LA 134 B1
Kentwood MI 75 F3
Kenvil NJ 148 A3
Kenwood MD 193 D2
Kenwood OH 204 C2
Kenwood Beach MD 144 C4
Kenyon MN 73 D1
Keokuk IA 87 F4
Keokuk Co. IA 87 E2
Keosauqua IA 87 E3
Keota IA 87 E2
Keota OK 116 B1
Kerens TX 59 F3
Kerhonkson NY 94 A3
Kerkhoven MN 66 B3
Kerman CA 44 C3
Kermit TX 57 F3
Kern Co. CA 45 D4
Kernersville NC 112 B4
Kernville CA 45 E4
Kerr Co. TX 60 C2
Kerrville TX 60 C2
Kersey CO 33 E4
Kershaw SC 122 B2
Kershaw Co. SC 122 B3
Keshena WI 68 C4
Ketchikan AK 155 E4
Ketchum ID 22 C4
Kettering OH 100 B1
Kettle Falls WA 13 F1
Kettleman City CA 44 C3
Kevil KY 108 C2
Kewanee IL 88 A2
Kewanna IN 89 E3
Kewaskum WI 74 C2
Kewaunee WI 75 D1
Kewaunee Co. WI 69 D4
Keweenaw Co. MI 65 F3
Keya Paha Co. NE 35 D1
Key Biscayne FL 143 F2
Key Colony Beach FL 143 D4
Keyes CA 36 C4
Key Largo FL 143 E3
Keyport NJ 147 E1
Keys OK 106 B4
Keyser WV 102 C2
Keystone CO 41 D1
Keystone IA 87 E1
Keystone SD 25 F4
Keystone WV 111 F1
Keystone Hts. FL 139 D3
Keysville VA 113 D2
Keytesville MO 97 D2
Key West FL 142 C4
Kezar Falls ME 82 A3
Kiamesha Lake NY 148 A1
Kiawah Island SC 131 D2
Kibler AR 116 C1
Kidder Co. ND 18 C4
Kiefer OK 51 F2

Jefferson City MO

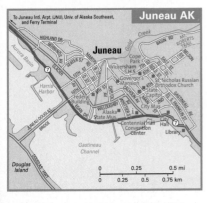

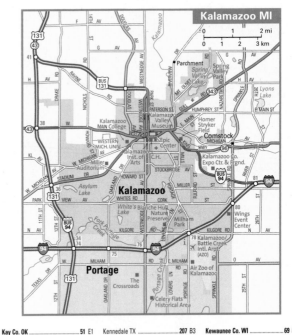

Figures after entries indicate page number and grid reference.

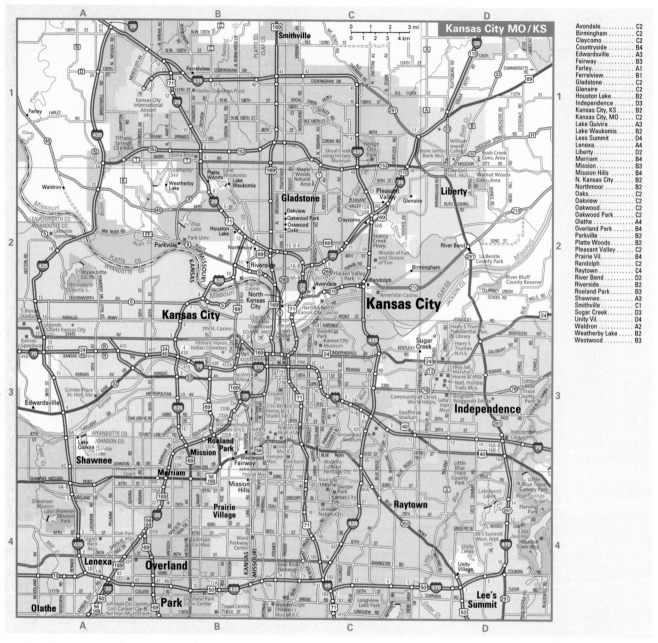

Kansas City MO/KS

Avondale C2
Birmingham C2
Claycomo C2
Countryside B4
Edwardsville......... A3
Fairway B3
Farley............... A1
Ferrelview........... B1
Gladstone C2
Glenaire C2
Houston Lake........ B2
Independence D3
Kansas City, KS...... B2
Kansas City, MO C2
Lake Quivira......... A3
Lake Waukomis...... B2
Lees Summit D4
Lenexa.............. A4
Liberty.............. D2
Merriam B4
Mission............. B3
Mission Hills B4
N. Kansas City....... B2
Northmoor B2
Oaks................ C2
Oakview C2
Oakwood............ C2
Oakwood Park....... C2
Olathe A4
Overland Park B4
Parkville B2
Platte Woods........ B2
Pleasant Valley C2
Prairie Vil............ B4
Randolph............ C2
Raytown C4
River Bend D2
Riverside............ B2
Roeland Park........ B3
Shawnee............ A3
Smithville C1
Sugar Creek......... D3
Unity Vil............. D4
Waldron A2
Weatherby Lake B2
Westwood B3

Kiel WI 74 C2
Kiester MN 72 C2
Kihei HI 153 D1
Kilauea HI 152 B1
Kilbourne LA 125 F1
Kildeer IL 203 B2
Kilgore TX 124 B2
Killbuck OH 91 E4
Killdeer ND 18 A3
Kill Devil Hills NC 115 F2
Killeen TX 59 E4
Killen AL 119 E2
Killian LA 134 B2
Killona LA 239 A1
Kilmarnock VA 113 F1
Kilmichael MS 118 C4
Kiln MS 134 C2
Kimball MN 66 C3
Kimball NE 33 F3
Kimball SD 27 D4
Kimball TN 120 A2
Kimball WV 111 F1
Kimball Co. NE 33 F3
Kimberling City MO 107 D3
Kimberly AL 119 F4
Kimberly ID 30 C1
Kimberly WI 74 C1
Kimberton PA 146 B2
Kimble Co. TX 60 C1
Kincaid IL 98 B1
Kinde MI 76 C1
Kinder LA 133 E2
Kinderhook NY 94 B2
Kindred ND 19 E4
King NC 112 A3
King WI 74 B1
King and Queen Co. VA 113 F1
King and Queen C.H. VA 113 F1
King City CA 44 B3
King City MO 86 B4
King City OR 251 C3
King Co. TX 58 C1
King Co. WA 12 C3
King Cove AK 154 B4
Kingfield ME 82 B1
Kingfisher OK 51 E2
Kingfisher Co. OK 51 E2
King George VA 103 E4
King George Co. VA 103 E4
Kingman AZ 46 B3
Kingman IN 99 E1
Kingman KS 43 E4
Kingman Co. KS 43 E4
King of Prussia PA 146 C2
King Salmon AK 154 B3
Kings Beach CA 37 D2
Kingsburg CA 45 D3
Kingsbury TX 61 E2
Kingsbury Co. SD 27 E3
Kings Co. CA 44 C3
Kings Co. NY 147 F1
Kingsford MI 68 C2
Kingsford Hts. IN 89 E2
Kingsland AR 117 E4
Kingsland GA 139 D1
Kingsland TX 61 D1
Kingsley IA 35 F1
Kingsley MI 69 F4
Kings Mtn. NC 122 A1
Kings Park NY 149 D3
Kings Pt. NY 148 B4
Kingsport TN 111 E3
Kingston GA 120 B3
Kingston ID 14 B3
Kingston IL 88 C1
Kingston KY 110 C1
Kingston MA 151 E2
Kingston MI 76 C2
Kingston MO 96 C1
Kingston NH 95 E1
Kingston NJ 147 D1
Kingston NY 94 B2
Kingston OH 101 D2
Kingston OK 59 F1
Kingston PA 93 E2
Kingston RI 150 C4
Kingston TN 110 B4
Kingston WA 12 C3
Kingston Sprs. TN 109 E4
Kingstown MD 145 D2
Kingstown NC 121 F1
Kingstree SC 122 C4
Kingsville MD 193 E1
Kingsville TX 63 F2
King William VA 113 E1
King William Co. VA 113 E1

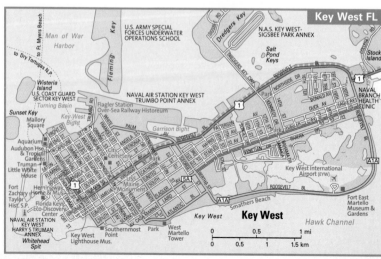

Entries in **bold black** indicate counties or parishes.
Entries in **bold color** indicate cities with detailed inset maps.

- Kingwood TX 132 B3
- Kingwood WV 102 B2
- Kinmundy IL 98 C3
- Kinnelon NJ 148 A3
- **Kinney Co. TX** 60 B3
- Kinsey AL 128 B4
- Kinsley KS 43 D4
- Kinsman OH 91 F2
- Kinston AL 128 A4
- Kinston NC 115 C3
- Kinzers PA 146 A3
- Kiowa CO 41 E2
- Kiowa KS 51 D1
- Kiowa OK 116 A2
- **Kiowa Co. CO** 42 A3
- **Kiowa Co. KS** 43 D4
- **Kiowa Co. OK** 51 D3
- Kipnuk AK 154 B3
- Kirby TX 61 D3
- Kirbyville TX 132 C1
- Kirkland IL 88 C1
- Kirkland WA 12 C3
- Kirklin IN 89 F4
- Kirksville MO 87 D4
- Kirkwood DE 145 E1
- Kirkwood IL 87 F3
- Kirkwood MO 98 A3
- Kirtland NM 48 B1
- Kirtland OH 91 E2
- Kiryas Joel NY 148 B2
- Kismet KS 42 B4
- Kissimmee FL 141 D2
- **Kit Carson Co. CO** 41 F1
- **Kitsap Co. WA** 12 C3
- Kittanning PA 92 A3
- Kittery ME 82 B4
- Kittery Pt. ME 82 B4
- Kittitas WA 13 D4
- **Kittitas Co. WA** 13 D3
- Kittredge CO 209 A4
- **Kittson Co. MN** 19 F1
- Kitty Hawk NC 115 F2
- Klamath CA 28 A3
- **Klamath Co. OR** 28 C2
- Klamath Falls OR 28 C2
- Klawock AK 155 E4
- **Kleberg Co. TX** 63 F2
- Klemme IA 72 C3
- Klickitat WA 21 D1
- **Klickitat Co. WA** 21 D1
- Knightdale NC 113 D4
- Knights FL 266 D1
- Knightsen CA 36 C3
- Knights Landing CA 36 B2
- Knightstown IN 100 A1
- Knightsville IN 99 E1
- Knippa TX 60 C3
- Knob Noster MO 96 C3
- Knollcrest CT 148 C1
- Knollwood CT 149 E2
- **Knott Co. KY** 111 D1
- Knox IN 89 E2
- Knox PA 92 A2
- Knox City TX 58 C1
- **Knox Co. IL** 88 A3
- **Knox Co. IN** 99 E3
- **Knox Co. KY** 110 C2
- **Knox Co. ME** 82 C2
- **Knox Co. MO** 87 E4
- **Knox Co. NE** 35 E1
- **Knox Co. OH** 91 D4
- **Knox Co. TN** 110 C4
- **Knox Co. TX** 58 C1
- Knoxville AR 117 D1
- Knoxville GA 129 D2
- Knoxville IL 88 A3
- Knoxville IA 87 D2
- Knoxville PA 93 D1
- **Knoxville TN** 110 C4
- Kodiak AK 154 C4
- Kohler WI 75 D2
- Kokomo IN 89 F4
- Kolin LA 125 E4
- Koloa HI 152 B1
- Komatke AZ 54 C2
- Konawa OK 51 F3
- **Koochiching Co. MN** 64 B2
- Koontz Lake IN 89 E2
- Kooskia ID 22 B1
- Kootenai ID 14 B2
- **Kootenai Co. ID** 14 B3
- Koppel PA 91 F3
- Kopperston WV 111 F1
- Kosciusko MS 126 C1
- **Kosciusko Co. IN** 89 F2
- **Kossuth Co. IA** 72 C3
- Kotlik AK 154 B2
- Kotzebue AK 154 B1
- Kountze TX 132 C2
- Kouts IN 89 E2
- Kreamer PA 93 D3
- Krebs OK 116 A2
- Kremmling CO 41 D1
- Kress TX 50 A4
- Krotz Sprs. LA 133 F2
- Krum TX 59 E2
- Kualapuu HI 152 C3
- Kulm ND 27 D1
- Kulpmont PA 93 E3
- Kulpsville PA 146 C2
- Kuna ID 22 B4
- Kure Beach NC 123 E3
- Kurtistown HI 153 F3
- Kuttawa KY 109 D2
- Kutztown PA 146 B1
- Kwethluk AK 154 B3
- Kykotsmovi Vil. AZ 47 E2
- Kyle SD 26 B4
- Kyle TX 61 E2

L

- Labadieville LA 134 A3
- La Barge WY 32 A2
- LaBelle FL 141 D4
- La Belle MO 87 E4
- **Labette Co. KS** 106 A2
- La Blanca TX 63 E4
- La Cañada Flintridge CA 228 D1
- Lac du Flambeau WI 68 A2
- La Center KY 108 C2
- La Center WA 20 C1
- Lacey WA 12 C4
- Laceys Spr. AL 119 F2
- La Cienega NM 48 C3
- Lackawanna NY 78 B3
- **Lackawanna Co. PA** 93 F2
- **Laclede Co. MO** 107 D1
- Lacombe LA 134 C2
- Lacon IL 88 B3
- Lacona NY 79 E2
- Laconia NH 81 F3
- La Conner WA 12 C2
- Lacoochee FL 140 C1
- LaCoste TX 61 D3
- **Lac qui Parle Co. MN** 27 F2
- La Crescent MN 73 F2
- La Crescenta CA 228 D1
- La Croft OH 91 F3
- La Crosse IN 89 E2
- La Crosse KS 43 D3
- La Crosse VA 113 D3
- La Crosse WI 73 F2
- **La Crosse Co. WI** 73 F2
- La Cygne KS 96 B4
- Ladd IL 88 B2
- Laddonia MO 97 F2
- Ladera Hts. CA 228 C3
- Ladoga IN 99 E1
- Ladonia AL 128 C2
- Ladonia TX 59 F1
- Ladson SC 131 D1
- Ladue MO 256 B2
- Lady Lake FL 140 C1
- Ladysmith VA 103 D4
- Ladysmith WI 67 F3
- La Farge WI 73 F2
- La Fargeville NY 79 E1
- Lafayette AL 128 B1
- Lafayette CA 259 D2
- Lafayette CO 41 E1
- LaFayette GA 120 B2
- Lafayette IN 89 E4
- **Lafayette LA** 133 F2
- Lafayette MN 72 B1
- Lafayette NJ 148 A3
- Lafayette OR 20 B2
- Lafayette TN 110 A3
- **Lafayette Co. AR** 125 D1
- **Lafayette Co. FL** 137 F3
- **Lafayette Co. MS** 118 C3
- **Lafayette Co. MO** 96 C2
- **Lafayette Co. WI** 74 A4
- **Lafayette Par. LA** 133 F2
- La Feria TX 63 F4
- Lafitte LA 134 B3
- Laflin PA 261 B2
- LaFollette TN 110 C3
- La Fontaine IN 89 F3
- **Lafourche Par. LA** 134 B4
- Lago Vista TX 61 E1
- La Grande OR 21 F2
- LaGrange GA 128 C1
- La Grange IL 203 C5
- Lagrange IN 90 A2
- La Grange KY 100 A3
- La Grange MO 97 F1
- La Grange NC 123 E1
- LaGrange OH 91 D2
- La Grange TX 61 F2
- La Grange WY 33 F3
- **LaGrange Co. IN** 90 A2
- La Grange Park IL 203 C4
- Lagrangeville NY 148 B1
- La Grulla TX 63 E4
- Laguna NM 48 B3
- Laguna Beach CA 52 C3
- Laguna Beach FL 136 C2
- Laguna Hts. TX 63 F4
- Laguna Hills CA 229 G5
- Laguna Niguel CA 229 G6
- Laguna Vista TX 63 F4
- Laguna Woods CA 229 G5
- Lagunitas CA 36 B3
- La Habra CA 228 E3
- La Habra Hts. CA 228 E3
- Lahaina HI 153 D1
- La Harpe IL 87 F3
- La Harpe KS 96 A4
- Lahoma OK 51 E2
- Laie HI 152 A2
- Laingsburg MI 76 A3
- La Jara CO 41 D4
- La Joya TX 63 E4
- La Junta CO 41 F3
- Lake MS 126 C2
- Lake Alfred FL 140 C2
- Lake Aluma OK 224 E2
- Lake Andes SD 35 D1
- Lake Ariel PA 93 F2
- Lake Arrowhead CA 53 D2
- Lake Arthur LA 133 E2
- Lake Arthur NM 57 E2
- Lake Barcroft VA 270 B4
- Lake Barrington IL 203 B1
- Lake Benton MN 27 F3
- Lake Bluff IL 75 D4
- Lake Butler FL 138 C3
- Lake Carmel NY 148 C1
- Lake Charles LA 133 D2
- Lake City AR 108 A4
- Lake City CO 40 C3
- Lake City FL 138 C2
- Lake City GA 190 D5
- Lake City IA 72 B4
- Lake City MI 75 F1

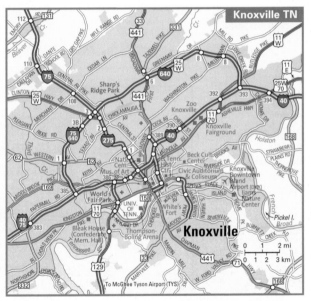

- Bird in Hand C2
- E. Petersburg A1
- Lancaster B2
- Landisville A1
- Leacock C1
- Leola C1
- Millersville A2
- Mountville A2
- Neffsville B1
- Rohrerstown A2
- Salunga A1
- Smoketown C2

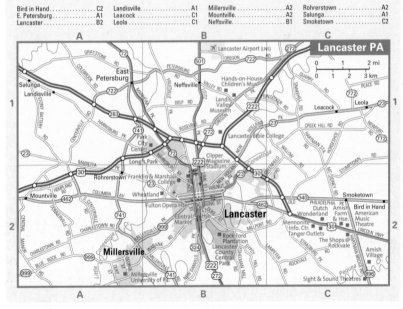

- Lake City MN 73 E1
- Lake City PA 91 F1
- Lake City SC 122 C4
- Lake City TX 61 E4
- Lake Clarke Shores FL 143 F1
- **Lake Co. CA** 36 B2
- **Lake Co. CO** 41 D2
- **Lake Co. FL** 141 D1
- **Lake Co. IL** 74 C4
- **Lake Co. IN** 89 D2
- **Lake Co. MI** 75 F1
- **Lake Co. MN** 65 D3
- **Lake Co. MT** 15 D3
- **Lake Co. OH** 91 E1
- **Lake Co. OR** 21 D4
- **Lake Co. SD** 27 F3
- **Lake Co. TN** 108 B3
- Lake Crystal MN 72 C1
- Lake Dallas TX 59 F2
- Lake Delton WI 74 A2
- Lake Elmo MN 235 E2
- Lake Elsinore CA 53 D3
- Lake Erie Beach NY 78 A4
- Lakefield MN 72 A2
- Lake Forest CA 229 G5
- Lake Forest IL 75 D4
- Lake Forest Park WA 262 B2
- Lake Geneva WI 74 C4
- Lake George NY 80 C4
- Lake Grove NY 149 D3
- Lake Hamilton AR 117 D3
- Lake Hamilton FL 141 D2
- Lake Havasu City AZ 46 B4
- Lakehead CA 28 C4
- Lake Helen FL 139 E4
- Lakehills TX 61 D2

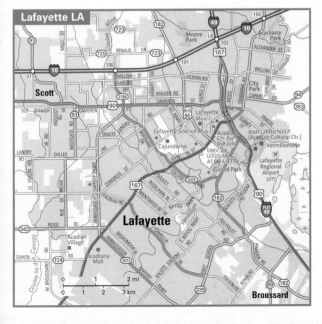

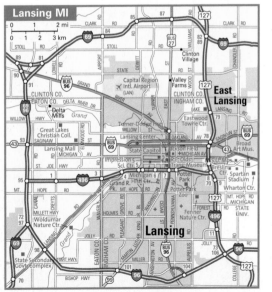

Figures after entries indicate page number and grid reference.

Lakehurst NJ 147 E3
Lake in the Hills IL 203 A2
Lake Isabella CA 45 E4
Lake Isabella MI 76 A2
Lake Jackson TX 132 A4
Lake Junaluska NC 121 F1
Lakeland FL 140 C2
Lakeland GA 137 F1
Lakeland MN 67 D4
Lakeland NY 265 A1
Lakeland TN 118 B1
Lakeland Vil. CA 229 J5
Lake Linden MI 65 F3
Lake Lotawana MO 96 C3
Lake Lure NC 121 F1
Lake Luzerne NY 80 C4
Lake Mary FL 141 D1
Lake Michigan Beach MI 89 E1
Lake Mills IA 72 C2
Lake Mills WI 74 B3
Lake Mohawk NJ 148 A3
Lake Mohegan NY 148 B2
Lakemont PA 92 C4
Lake Montezuma AZ 47 D4
Lakemoor IL 203 A1
Lakemore OH 188 B2
Lake Nebagamon WI 64 C3
Lake Norden SD 27 F3
Lake Odessa MI 75 F3
Lake of the Woods IL 88 C4
Lake of the Woods Co. MN 64 A1
Lake Orion MI 76 C4
Lake Oswego OR 20 C2
Lake Ozark MO 97 D3
Lake Panasoffkee FL 140 C1
Lake Park FL 141 F4
Lake Park GA 137 F1
Lake Park IA 72 A2
Lake Park MN 19 F4
Lake Peekskill NY 148 B2
Lake Placid FL 141 D3
Lake Placid NY 80 C2
Lake Pleasant NY 79 F2
Lake Pocotopaug CT 149 E1
Lakeport CA 36 A2
Lakeport MI 76 C3
Lakeport TX 124 B2
Lake Preston SD 27 E3
Lake Providence LA 126 A2
Lake Quivira KS 224 A3
Lake Ridge VA 144 A4
Lake St. Croix Beach MN 67 D4
Lake St. Louis MO 98 A3
Lakeshire MO 256 B3
Lake Shore MD 144 C2
Lake Shore MN 64 A4
Lakeside CA 53 D4
Lakeside CT 149 D1
Lakeside MT 15 D2
Lakeside OR 20 A4
Lakeside VA 113 E1
Lakeside City TX 59 D1
Lakeside Park KY 204 B3
Lakesite TN 120 B1
Lakes of the Four Seasons IN 89 D2
Lake Sta. IN 89 D2
Lake Stevens WA 12 C2
Lake Success NY 241 G3
Lake Summerset IL 74 B4
Lake Tanglewood TX 50 C2
Lake Tapawingo MO 96 C2
Laketon IN 89 F3
Lake View AL 127 F1
Lakeview AR 107 E3
Lake View AR 118 A3
Lakeview CA 229 K4
Lake View IA 72 B4
Lakeview MI 75 F2
Lake View NY 78 A4
Lakeview NY 241 G4
Lakeview OH 90 B4
Lakeview OR 29 D2
Lake View SC 122 C3
Lake Villa IL 74 C4
Lake Vil. AR 125 F1
Lake Vil. IN 89 D3
Lakeville CT 94 B2
Lakeville IN 89 F2
Lakeville MA 151 D3
Lakeville MN 67 D4
Lake Waccamaw NC 123 D3
Lake Wales FL 141 D2
Lake Waukomis MO 224 B2
Lakeway TX 61 E1
Lake Winnebago MO 96 C3
Lakewood CA 228 D4
Lakewood CO 41 E1
Lakewood IL 88 C1
Lakewood NJ 147 E2
Lakewood NY 92 B1
Lakewood OH 91 E2
Lakewood TN 109 F3
Lakewood WA 12 C3
Lakewood Club MI 75 E2
Lakewood Park FL 141 E3
Lakewood Park ND 19 D2
Lake Worth FL 143 F1
Lake Worth TX 207 A2
Lake Wylie SC 122 A1
Lake Zurich IL 89 D1
Lakin KS 42 B3
Lakota ND 19 D2
La Luz NM 56 C4

Lamar AR 117 D1
Lamar CO 42 A3
Lamar MO 106 C1
Lamar SC 122 B3
Lamar Co. AL 119 D4
Lamar Co. GA 129 D1
Lamar Co. MS 126 C4
Lamar Co. TX 116 A4
La Marque TX 132 B4
Lamb Co. TX 50 A4
Lambert MS 118 B3
Lamberton MN 72 A1
Lambertville MI 90 C1
Lambertville NJ 147 D2
Lame Deer MT 25 D1
La Mesa CA 53 D4
La Mesa NM 56 C3
Lamesa TX 58 A2
La Mirada CA 228 E3
La Moille IL 88 B2
Lamoille Co. VT 81 E1
Lamoni IA 86 C3
Lamont CA 45 D4
Lamont IA 73 E4
Lamont OK 51 E1
La Monte MO 97 D3
LaMoure ND 19 D4
LaMoure Co. ND 19 D4
Lampasas TX 59 D4
Lampasas Co. TX 59 D4
Lampeter PA 146 A3
Lanai City HI 152 C4
Lanare CA 44 C3
Lanark IL 88 B1
Lanark PA 146 C1
Lanark Vil. FL 137 D3
Lancaster CA 52 C2
Lancaster KY 110 B1
Lancaster MA 150 C1
Lancaster MO 87 D4
Lancaster NH 81 F2
Lancaster NY 78 B3
Lancaster OH 101 D1
Lancaster PA 146 A3
Lancaster SC 122 B2
Lancaster TX 59 F2
Lancaster VA 113 F1
Lancaster WI 73 F3
Lancaster Co. NE 35 F3
Lancaster Co. PA 146 A3
Lancaster Co. SC 122 B2
Lancaster Co. VA 113 F1
Lander WY 32 B1
Lander Co. NV 30 A4
Landfall MN 235 E3
Landis NC 122 B1
Landisville PA 225 A1
Land O' Lakes FL 140 B2
Landover MD 270 E3
Landover Hills MD 271 F2
Landrum SC 121 F1
Lane Co. KS 42 C3
Lane Co. OR 20 C4
Lanesboro MN 73 E2
Lanesboro PA 93 F1
Lanesborough MA 94 C1
Lanesville CT 148 C1
Lanesville IN 99 F4
Lanett AL 128 B2
Lapel IN 89 F4
La Pine OR 21 D4
Langdon ND 19 D1
Langdon Place KY 230 F1
Langford SD 27 E1
Langhorne PA 147 D2
Langlade Co. WI 68 B3
Langley OK 106 B3
Langley VA 270 B2
Langley WA 12 C2

Las Vegas NV (map)

Langley Park MD 270 D2
Langston OK 51 E2
Lanham MD 271 F2
Lanier Co. GA 137 F1
Lannon WI 234 A1
Lanoka Harbor NJ 147 E3
Lansdale PA 146 C2
Lansdowne MD 193 C3
Lansdowne PA 146 C3
L'Anse MI 65 F4
Lansford ND 18 B2
Lansford PA 93 E3
Lansing IA 73 F2
Lansing KS 96 B2
Lansing MI 76 A4
Lansing NY 79 D4
Lantana FL 143 F1
Laona WI 68 C3
La Palma CA 228 E4
La Paz IN 89 F2
La Paz Co. AZ 54 A1
Lapeer MI 76 C3
Lapeer Co. MI 76 C3
Lapel IN 89 F4
La Pine OR 21 D4
Laplace LA 134 B3
La Plata MD 144 B4
La Plata MO 87 D4
La Plata Co. CO 40 B4
Laporte CO 33 E4
La Porte IN 89 E2
Laporte PA 93 E2

La Porte TX 132 B3
La Porte City IA 73 E4
LaPorte Co. IN 89 E2
La Prairie MN 64 B3
La Pryor TX 60 C3
La Puente CA 228 E3
Lapwai ID 14 B4
La Quinta CA 53 E3
Laramie WY 33 E3
Laramie Co. WY 33 E3
Larchmont NY 241 F1
Larchwood IA 27 F4
Laredo TX 63 D2
Largo FL 140 B2
Largo MD 271 F2
Larimer Co. CO 33 E4
Larimore ND 19 E2
Larkspur CA 259 A1
Larksville PA 261 A1
Larned KS 43 D3
Larose LA 134 B3
La Rue OH 90 C4
Larue Co. KY 110 A1
La Sal UT 40 A3
La Salle CO 33 E4
LaSalle IL 88 B2
La Salle Co. IL 88 C2
La Salle Co. TX 60 C4
La Salle Par. LA 125 E2
Las Animas CO 41 F3
Las Animas Co. CO 41 F4
Lasara TX 63 E4
Las Cruces NM 56 C3
Las Lomas CA 236 E2
Lassen Co. CA 29 D4
Las Vegas NV 46 A2
Las Vegas NM 49 D3
Latah Co. ID 14 B4
Latham NY 188 E2
Lathrop CA 36 C4
Lathrop MO 96 B1
Lathrup Vil. MI 210 B2
Latimer IA 72 C4
Latimer Co. OK 116 B2
Laton CA 44 C3
Latrobe PA 92 A4
Latta OK 51 E4
Latta SC 122 C3
Lattingtown NY 148 B3
Lauderdale MN 235 C2
Lauderdale-by-the-Sea FL 233 C2
Lauderdale Co. AL 119 E2
Lauderdale Co. MS 127 D3
Lauderdale Co. TN 108 B4
Lauderdale Lakes FL 233 B2
Lauderhill FL 233 B2
Laughlin NV 46 B3
La Union NM 56 C3
Laura KY 111 E1
Laurel DE 145 E4
Laurel FL 140 B4
Laurel IN 100 A1
Laurel MD 144 B3
Laurel MS 126 C4
Laurel MT 24 B1
Laurel NE 35 F2

Laurel NY 149 E3
Laurel VA 113 E1
Laurel Bay SC 130 C2
Laurel Co. KY 110 C2
Laureldale NJ 147 D4
Laureldale PA 146 B1
Laurel Hill FL 136 B1
Laurel Hill NC 122 C2
Laurel Park NC 121 E1
Laurel Run PA 261 B1
Laurence Harbor NJ 147 E1
Laurens IA 72 B3
Laurens NY 79 F4
Laurens SC 121 F3
Laurens Co. GA 129 E3
Laurens Co. SC 121 F3
Laurinburg NC 122 C2
Laurium MI 65 F3
Lavaca AR 116 C1
Lavaca Co. TX 61 E3
Lava Hot Sprs. ID 31 F1
La Vale MD 102 C1
Lavalette WV 101 D4
Lavallette NJ 147 E3
La Vergne TN 109 F4
La Verkin UT 39 D4
La Verne CA 229 F2
Laverne OK 50 C1
La Vernia TX 61 D3
La Veta CO 41 E3
La Villa TX 63 E4
Lavina MT 24 B1
La Vista NE 35 F3
Lavonia GA 121 E3
Lawai HI 152 B1
Lawndale CA 228 C3
Lawndale NC 121 F1
Lawnside NJ 146 C3
Lawnton PA 218 C1
Lawrence KS 96 A2
Lawrence MA 151 E1
Lawrence MI 89 F1
Lawrence NY 147 E1
Lawrenceburg IN 100 B2
Lawrenceburg KY 100 B4
Lawrenceburg TN 119 E1
Lawrence Co. AL 119 E3
Lawrence Co. AR 107 F4

Las Vegas Strip NV (map)

POINTS OF INTEREST

Allegiant Stadium A3
Aria at CityCenter A3
Atomic Testing Museum B2
Bally's Las Vegas A2
Bellagio A2
Caesars Palace A2
Circus Circus B1
CityCenter A3
The Cosmopolitan A3
Encore at Wynn Las Vegas A1
Excalibur A3
Fashion Show Mall A2
Flamingo Las Vegas A2
Harrah's Las Vegas A2
High Roller (ferris wheel) A2
Las Vegas Convention Center B1
The LINQ A2
Luxor Las Vegas A3

Mandalay Bay A3
Mandarin Oriental A3
McCarran Intl. Airport B3
MGM Grand A3
The Mirage A2
New York-New York A3
Palace Station A1
The Palazzo A2
Paris-Las Vegas A2
Park MGM A3
Planet Hollywood A3
Resorts World Las Vegas A1
Showcase Mall A3
SLS Hotel B1
Stratosphere B1
T-Mobile Arena A3
Treasure Island A2
Tropicana A3
Trump International A2
Univ. of Nevada, Las Vegas B3
Vdara A2
The Venetian A2
Westgate Las Vegas Hotel & Casino . B1
Wynn Las Vegas A2

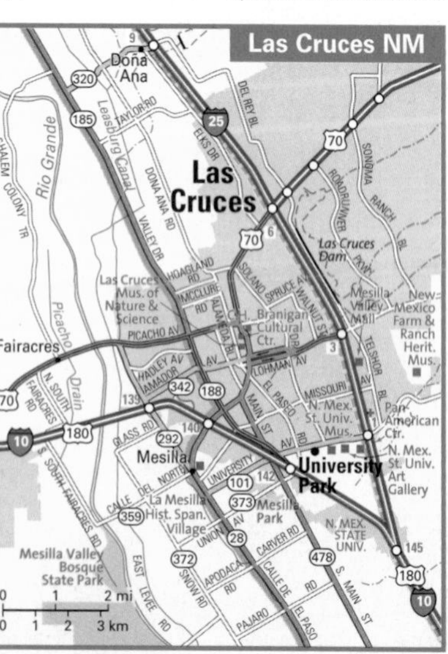
Las Cruces NM

Entries in **bold black** indicate counties or parishes.
Entries in **bold color** indicate cities with detailed inset maps.

Becknerville	C3	Faywood	A1	Keene	A3
Boonesboro	C3	Ford	C3	Lexington	B1
Clays Ferry	C3	Ft. Garrett	A2	Lisletown	C3
Clintonville	C1	Georgetown	A1	Locust Grove	C3
Colby	C2	Hootentown	A1	Midway	A1
E. Hickman	B3	Hutchison	C1	New Zion	B1

Nicholasville	A3	Pisgah	A2
Nugent Crossroads	A1	Troy	A3
Old Pine Grove	C2	Wallace	A1
Paris	C1	Wyandotte	C2
Pinckard	A3		
Pine Grove	C2		

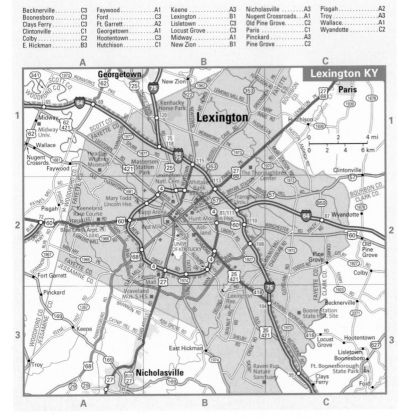

Lexington KY

Lincoln NE

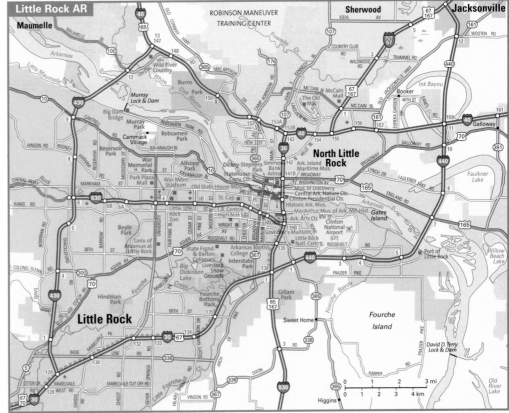

Little Rock AR

Le Claire IA	88	A2	Leland MI	69	F3
Lecompte LA	133	E1	Leland MS	126	A1
Lecompton KS	96	A2	Leland NC	123	E3
Ledbetter KY	109	D2	Le Mars IA	35	F1
Ledgewood NJ	148	A3	Lemay MO	256	B3
Ledyard Ctr. CT	149	F1	**Lemhi Co. ID**	23	D2
Lee MA	94	C2	Lemitar NM	48	C4
Leechburg PA	92	A3	Lemmon SD	26	B1
Lee Co. AL	128	B2	Lemmon Valley NV	37	D1
Lee Co. AR	118	A2	Lemon Grove CA	53	D4
Lee Co. FL	142	C1	Lemont IL	89	D2
Lee Co. GA	129	D4	Lemont PA	92	C3
Lee Co. IL	88	B2	Lemoore CA	44	C3
Lee Co. IA	87	F3	Lemoyne PA	218	B2
Lee Co. KY	110	C1	Lena IL	74	A4
Lee Co. MS	119	B3	**Lenawee Co. MI**	90	B1
Lee Co. NC	123	D1	Lenexa KS	96	B2
Lee Co. SC	122	B3	Lennon MI	76	B3
Lee Co. TX	61	F1	Lennox CA	228	C3
Lee Co. VA	111	D3	Lennox SD	27	F4
Leeds AL	119	F4	Lenoir NC	111	F4
Leeds ND	19	D2	Lenoir City TN	110	C3
Leeds UT	39	E4	**Lenoir Co. NC**	115	D3
Leelanau Co. MI	69	F4	Lenox GA	129	E4
Leesburg AL	120	A3	Lenox IA	86	B3
Leesburg FL	140	C1	Lenox MA	94	B2
Leesburg GA	129	D4	Lenwood CA	53	D1
Leesburg IN	89	F2	Lenzburg IL	98	B4
Leesburg NJ	145	E2	Leo-Cedarville IN	90	A2
Leesburg OH	100	C2	Leola AR	117	E3
Leesburg VA	144	A2	Leola PA	146	A2
Leesport PA	146	A1	Leola SD	27	D1
Lee's Summit MO	96	B3	Leominster MA	150	C1
Leesville LA	133	D1	Leon IA	86	C3
Leeton MO	96	C3	Leon KS	43	F4
Leetonia OH	91	F3	Leonard ND	19	E4
Leflore Co. MS	118	B4	Leonard TX	59	F1
Le Flore Co. OK	116	B2	Leonardo NJ	147	E1
Lefors TX	50	B3	Leonardtown MD	103	E4
Le Grand CA	37	D4	Leoni MI	76	B1
Le Grand IA	87	D3	**Leon Co. FL**	137	E2
Lehi UT	31	E4	**Leon Co. TX**	124	A4
Lehigh IA	72	C4	Leonia NJ	240	D1
Lehigh Acres FL	143	D1	Leon Valley TX	61	D2
Lehigh Co. PA	93	F3	Leonville LA	133	E2
Lehighton PA	93	F3	Leoti KS	42	B3
Leicester MA	150	B1	Lepanto AR	118	B1
Leigh NE	35	E3	Le Roy IL	88	C1
Leighton AL	119	E2	LeRoy KS	96	A4
Leipsic DE	145	E2	Le Roy MN	73	D2
Leipsic OH	90	B3	Le Roy NY	78	B3
Leisure City FL	143	E3	Leslie AR	107	E4

Le Sueur Co. MN	72	C1			
Letcher Co. KY	111	D2			
Leupp AZ	47	E3			
Levan UT	39	E1			
Levant ME	85	D4			
Levelland TX	57	F1			
Level Plains AL	128	B4			
Levittown NY	148	C4			
Levittown PA	147	D2			
Levy Co. FL	138	C4			
Lewes DE	145	F3			
Lewis KS	43	D3			
Lewis and Clark Co. MT	15	E3			
Lewisburg OH	100	B1			
Lewisburg PA	93	D3			
Lewisburg TN	119	F1			
Lewisburg WV	112	A1			
Lewis Co. ID	22	B1			
Lewis Co. KY	100	C3			
Lewis Co. MO	87	F1			
Lewis Co. NY	79	E2			
Lewis Co. TN	119	E1			
Lewis Co. WA	12	C4			
Lewis Co. WV	102	A2			
Lewisport KY	99	E4			
Lewis Run PA	92	B1			
Lewiston CA	28	B4			
Lewiston ID	14	B4			
Lewiston ME	82	B2			
Lewiston MI	70	C4			
Lewiston MN	73	E1			
Lewiston NY	78	A3			
Lewiston UT	31	E2			
Lewiston Woodville NC	113	E4			
Lewistown IL	88	A4			
Lewistown MD	144	A1			
Lewistown MO	87	F1			
Lewistown MT	16	B4			
Lewistown PA	93	D4			
Lewisville AR	125	D1			
Lewisville ID	23	E4			
Lewisville NC	112	A4			
Lewisville TX	59	F2			
Lexington AL	119	E2			
Lexington GA	121	E4			
Lexington IL	88	C1			
Lexington KY	100	B4			
Lexington MA	151	D1			
Lexington MI	76	C3			
Lexington MN	235	C1			
Lexington MS	126	B1			

Lawrence Co. IL	99	D3	**Lea Co. NM**	57	F2
Lawrence Co. IN	99	F3	Lead SD	25	F3
Lawrence Co. KY	101	D4	Leadville CO	41	D2
Lawrence Co. MS	126	B4	Leadwood MO	98	A4
Lawrence Co. MO	106	C2	League City TX	132	B4
Lawrence Co. OH	101	D3	**Leake Co. MS**	126	C2
Lawrence Co. PA	91	F3	Leakesville MS	135	D1
Lawrence Co. SD	25	F3	Leakey TX	60	C2
Lawrence Co. TN	119	E1	Lealman FL	266	B3
Lawrenceville GA	120	C4	Leander TX	61	E1
Lawrenceville IL	99	D3	Leary GA	128	C4
Lawrenceville NJ	147	D2	Leary TX	116	C4
Lawrenceville PA	93	D1	Leavenworth KS	96	B2
Lawrenceville VA	113	D2	Leavenworth WA	13	D3
Lawson MO	96	C2	**Leavenworth Co. KS**	96	B2
Lawtell LA	133	E2	Leavittsburg OH	276	A1
Lawtey FL	138	C3	Leawood MO	106	C2
Lawton IA	35	F1	Lebanon DE	145	E2
Lawton MI	89	F1	Lebanon IL	98	B3
Lawton OK	51	D4	Lebanon IN	89	E4
Laysville CT	149	F2	Lebanon KY	110	B1
Layton UT	31	E3	Lebanon MO	107	D2
Laytonville CA	36	A4	Lebanon NH	81	E3
Leachville AR	108	A4	Lebanon NJ	147	D1
Leacock PA	146	A2	Lebanon OH	100	B2

Lebanon OR	20	B3	Lebanon Jct. KY	100	A4
Lebanon PA	93	E4	Lebec CA	52	B1
Lebanon TN	109	F3	Leblanc TX	122	A2
Lebanon VA	111	E2	Lebo KS	96	A3
Lebanon OH	100	B2	Lecanto FL	140	B1
Lebanon Co. PA	93	E4	Le Center MN	72	C1

Leisuretowne NJ	147	D3	Leslie MI	76	A4
Leitchfield KY	109	F1	**Leslie Co. KY**	111	D2
Leitersburg MD	103	D1	Lesslie SC	122	A2
Leithsville PA	146	C1	Lester Prairie MN	66	C4
Leland IL	88	C1	Le Sueur MN	72	C1

Lexington MO	96	C2			
Lexington NE	34	C4			
Lexington NC	112	B4			
Lexington OH	91	D3			
Lexington OK	51	E3			

Figures after entries indicate page number and grid reference.

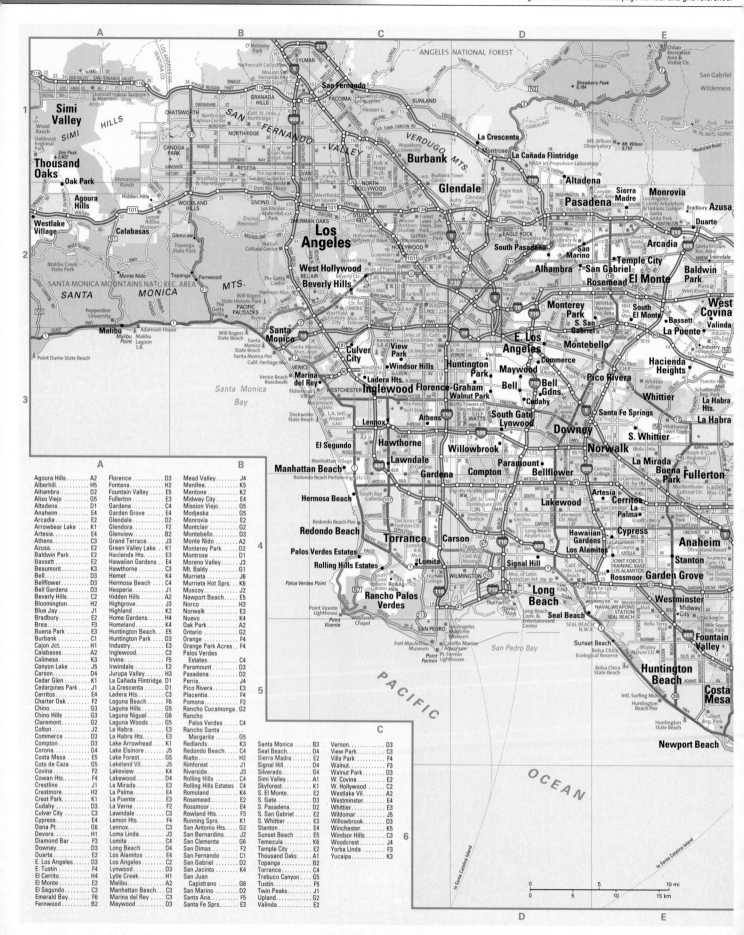

Place	Grid	Place	Grid	Place	Grid	Place	Grid
Agoura Hills	A2	Florence	D3	Mead Valley	J4	Santa Monica	B3
Alberhill	H5	Fontana	H2	Menifee	K5	Seal Beach	D4
Alhambra	D2	Fountain Valley	E5	Mentone	K2	Sierra Madre	D1
Aliso Viejo	G5	Fullerton	E3	Midway City	E4	Signal Hill	D4
Altadena	D1	Gardena	C4	Mission Viejo	G5	Silverado	G4
Anaheim	E4	Garden Grove	E4	Modjeska	G5	Simi Valley	A1
Arcadia	E2	Glendale	D2	Monclair	G2	Skyforest	K1
Arrowbear Lake	K1	Glendora	F2	Montebello	D3	S. El Monte	E2
Artesia	E4	Glenview	B2	Monte Nido	A2	S. Gate	D3
Athens	C3	Grand Terrace	J3	Monterey Park	D2	S. Pasadena	D2
Azusa	E2	Green Valley Lake	K1	Montrose	D1	S. San Gabriel	D2
Baldwin Park	E2	Hacienda Hts.	E3	Moreno Valley	J3	S. Whittier	E3
Bassett	E2	Hawaiian Gardens	E4	Mt. Baldy	G1	Stanton	E4
Beaumont	K3	Hawthorne	C3	Murrieta	J6	Sunset Beach	E5
Bell	D3	Hemet	K4	Murrieta Hot Sprs.	K6	Temecula	K6
Bellflower	D3	Hermosa Beach	C4	Muscoy	J2	Temple City	E2
Bell Gardens	D3	Hesperia	J1	Newport Beach	E5	Thousand Oaks	A1
Beverly Hills	C2	Hidden Hills	A2	Norco	H3	Topanga	B2
Bloomington	H2	Highgrove	J3	Norwalk	E3	Torrance	C4
Blue Jay	J1	Highland	K2	Nuevo	K4	Trabuco Canyon	G5
Bradbury	E2	Home Gardens	H4	Oak Park	A2	Tustin	F5
Brea	F3	Homeland	K4	Ontario	G2	Twin Peaks	J1
Buena Park	E3	Huntington Beach	D5	Orange	F4	Upland	G2
Burbank	C1	Huntington Park	D3	Orange Park Acres	F4	Valinda	E2
Cajon Jct.	H1	Industry	E3	Palos Verdes Estates	C4	Vernon	D3
Calabasas	A2	Inglewood	C3	Paramount	D3	View Park	C3
Calimesa	K3	Irvine	F5	Pasadena	D2	Villa Park	F4
Canyon Lake	J5	Irwindale	E2	Perris	J4	Walnut	F3
Carson	D4	Jurupa Valley	H3	Pico Rivera	E3	Walnut Park	D3
Cedar Glen	K1	La Cañada Flintridge	D1	Placentia	F4	W. Covina	E2
Cedarpines Park	J1	La Crescenta	D1	Pomona	F2	W. Hollywood	C2
Cerritos	E3	Ladera Hts.	C3	Rancho Cucamonga	G2	Westlake Vil.	A2
Charter Oak	F2	Laguna Beach	F6	Rancho Palos Verdes	C4	Westminster	E4
Chino	G3	Laguna Hills	G5	Rancho Santa Margarita	G5	Whittier	E3
Chino Hills	G3	Laguna Niguel	G6	Redlands	K3	Wildomar	J5
Claremont	G2	Laguna Woods	G5	Redondo Beach	C4	Willowbrook	D3
Colton	J2	La Habra	E3	Rialto	H2	Winchester	K5
Commerce	D3	La Habra Hts.	E3	Rimforest	J1	Windsor Hills	C3
Compton	D3	Lake Arrowhead	K1	Riverside	J3	Woodcrest	J3
Corona	G4	Lake Elsinore	J5	Rolling Hills	C4	Yorba Linda	F3
Costa Mesa	E5	Lake Forest	G5	Rolling Hills Estates	C4	Yucaipa	K3
Coto de Caza	G6	Lakeland Vil.	J5	Romoland	K4		
Covina	F2	Lakeview	K4	Rosemead	E2		
Cowan Hts.	F4	Lakewood	D4	Rossmoor	E4		
Crestline	J1	La Mirada	E3	Rowland Hts.	F3		
Crestmore	H2	La Palma	E4	Running Sprs.	K1		
Crest Park	K1	La Puente	E3	San Antonio Hts.	G2		
Cudahy	D3	La Verne	F2	San Bernardino	J2		
Culver City	C3	Lawndale	C4	San Clemente	G6		
Cypress	E4	Lemon Hts.	F4	San Dimas	F2		
Dana Pt.	G6	Lennox	C3	San Fernando	C1		
Devore	J2	Loma Linda	J3	San Gabriel	D2		
Diamond Bar	F3	Lomita	C4	San Jacinto	K4		
Downey	D3	Long Beach	D4	San Juan Capistrano	G6		
Duarte	E2	Los Alamitos	E4	San Marino	D2		
E. Los Angeles	D3	Los Angeles	C2	Santa Ana	F5		
E. Tustin	F4	Lynwood	D3	Santa Fe Sprs.	E3		
El Cerrito	H4	Lytle Creek	H1				
El Monte	E2	Malibu	A2				
El Segundo	C3	Manhattan Beach	C3				
Emerald Bay	F6	Marina del Rey	C3				
Fernwood	B2	Maywood	D3				

Entries in **bold black** indicate counties or parishes.
Entries in **bold color** indicate cities with detailed inset maps.

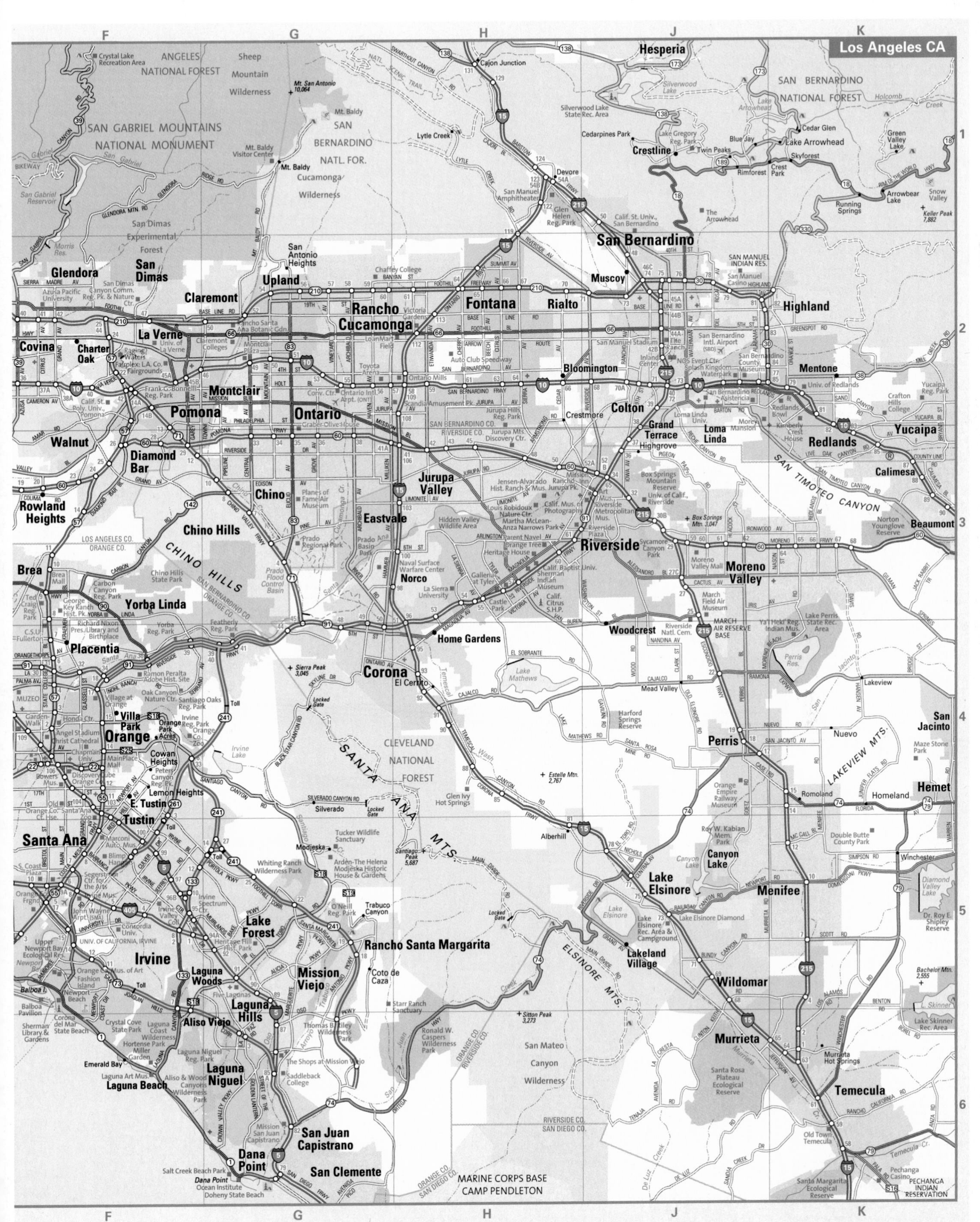

Los Angeles CA

Figures after entries indicate page number and grid reference.

POINTS OF INTEREST
Angels Flight A1
Bradbury Building A1
California Plaza A1
Cathedral of Our Lady of the Angels .. A1
Chinese American Museum B1
City Hall B1
City Market A2
Convention Center A2
Court House A1
Dodger Stadium B1
El Pueblo de Los Angeles Hist. Mon .. B1
Flower District A2
GRAMMY Museum A2
Institute of Contemporary Art B2
Japanese American Natl. Museum .. B1
Jewelry District A2
L.A. Center Studios A1
L.A. Live A2
Library A1
Los Angeles State Historical Park B1
Microsoft Theatre A2
Mt. St. Mary's University A2
Museum of Contemporary Art (MOCA) A1
Museum of Neon Art A2
Music Center A1
Post Office B1
STAPLES Center A2
The Geffen Contemporary at MOCA .. B1
Union Station B1
Walt Disney Concert Hall A1

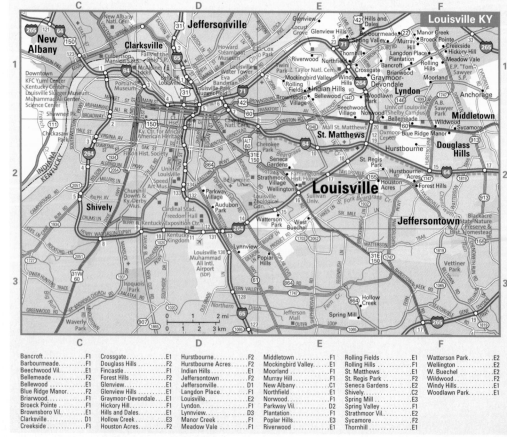

Downtown **Los Angeles CA**

Lexington SC 122 A3
Lexington TN 109 D4
Lexington TX 61 E1
Lexington VA 112 C1
Lexington Co. SC 122 A4
Lexington Park MD 103 F4
Libby MT 14 C2
Liberal KS 50 B1
Liberal MO 106 B1
Liberty IL 97 F1
Liberty IN 100 B1
Liberty KY 110 B1
Liberty ME 82 C2
Liberty MS 134 A1
Liberty MO 96 B2
Liberty NY 94 A3
Liberty NC 112 B4
Liberty PA 250 C3
Liberty SC 121 E2
Liberty TN 110 A4
Liberty TX 132 B3
Liberty Ctr. OH 90 B2
Liberty City TX 124 B2
Liberty Corner NJ 147 D1
Liberty Co. FL 137 D2
Liberty Co. GA 130 B3
Liberty Co. MT 15 F1
Liberty Co. TX 132 B2
Liberty Hill TX 61 E1
Liberty Lake WA 14 B3
Libertyville IL 74 C4
Licking MO 107 E1
Licking Co. OH 91 D4
Lidgerwood ND 27 E1
Lido Beach NY 147 F1
Lighthouse Pt. FL 143 F1
Ligonier IN 89 F2
Ligonier PA 92 B4
Lihue HI 152 B1
Lilbourn MO 108 B3
Lilburn GA 120 C4
Lillington NC 123 D1
Lilly PA 92 B4
Lily KY 110 C2
Lilydale MN 235 D3
Lily Lake IL 88 C1
Lima MT 23 E3
Lima NY 78 C3
Lima OH 90 B3
Lima PA 248 A4
Lime Lake NY 78 B4
Limeport PA 146 C1
Limerick ME 82 A3
Limerick PA 146 B2
Lime Sprs. IA 73 E2
Limestone ME 85 E1
Limestone Co. AL 119 F2
Limestone Co. TX 59 F4
Limon CO 41 F2
Lincoln AL 120 A4
Lincoln AR 106 B4
Lincoln CA 36 C2
Lincoln DE 145 F3
Lincoln ID 23 E4
Lincoln IL 88 B4
Lincoln KS 43 E2
Lincoln ME 85 D4
Lincoln MA 197 A1
Lincoln MO 97 D4
Lincoln MT 15 E4
Lincoln NE 35 F4
Lincoln NH 81 F3
Lincoln ND 18 C4
Lincoln Beach OR 20 B2
Lincoln City OR 20 B2
Lincoln Co. AR 117 F3
Lincoln Co. CO 41 F2
Lincoln Co. GA 121 E4
Lincoln Co. ID 31 D1
Lincoln Co. KS 43 E2
Lincoln Co. KY 110 B1
Lincoln Co. ME 82 C2
Lincoln Co. MN 27 F3
Lincoln Co. MS 126 B4
Lincoln Co. MO 97 F2
Lincoln Co. MT 14 C2
Lincoln Co. NE 34 C3
Lincoln Co. NV 38 B4
Lincoln Co. NM 49 D4
Lincoln Co. NC 122 A1
Lincoln Co. OK 51 F2
Lincoln Co. OR 20 B3
Lincoln Co. SD 35 F1
Lincoln Co. TN 119 F1
Lincoln Co. WA 13 F3
Lincoln Co. WV 101 E4
Lincoln Co. WI 68 A3
Lincoln Co. WY 32 A2
Lincolndale NY 148 C2
Lincoln Hts. OH 204 B1
Lincolnia VA 270 B4
Lincoln Par. LA 125 E2
Lincoln Park CO 41 E3
Lincoln Park MI 90 C1
Lincoln Park NJ 148 A3
Lincolnshire IL 203 C2
Lincolnton GA 121 E4
Lincolnton NC 122 A1
Lincoln Vil. OH 206 A3
Lincolnville SC 131 D1
Lincolnville Ctr. ME 82 C2
Lincolnwood IL 203 D3
Lincroft NJ 147 E2
Lind WA 13 F4
Linda CA 36 C2
Lindale GA 120 B3
Lindale TX 124 A2
Lindcove CA 45 D3
Linden AL 127 E2
Linden CA 36 C3
Linden IN 89 E4
Linden MI 76 B3
Linden NJ 147 E1
Linden TN 119 E1
Linden TX 124 C1
Linden WI 74 A3
Lindenhurst IL 74 C4
Lindenhurst NY 148 C4
Lindenwold NJ 146 C3
Lindon UT 31 F4
Lindsay CA 45 D3
Lindsay OK 51 E4
Lindsay TX 59 E1
Lindsborg KS 43 E3
Lindstrom MN 67 D3
Linesville PA 91 F2
Lineville AL 128 B1
Lingle WY 33 F2
Linglestown PA 93 D4
Linn KS 43 F1
Linn MO 97 E3
Linn TX 63 E3
Linn Co. IA 87 E1
Linn Co. KS 96 B4
Linn Co. MO 97 D1
Linn Co. OR 20 C3
Linneus MO 97 D1
Linn Valley KS 96 B4
Lino Lakes MN 235 D7
Linthicum MD 193 C4
Linton IN 99 E2
Linton ND 26 C1
Linwood IN 89 F4
Linwood KS 96 B2
Linwood MI 76 B2
Linwood NJ 147 F4
Lionville PA 146 B3
Lipscomb AL 195 D2
Lipscomb TX 50 C2
Lipscomb Co. TX 50 C2
Lisbon IA 87 F1
Lisbon ME 82 B3
Lisbon NH 81 E2
Lisbon ND 19 E4
Lisbon OH 91 F3
Lisbon Falls ME 82 B3
Lisle IL 203 B5
Lisman AL 127 D3
Litchfield CT 94 C3
Litchfield IL 98 B2
Litchfield ME 82 B2
Litchfield MI 90 A1
Litchfield MN 66 B3
Litchfield Co. CT 94 B3
Litchfield Park AZ 249 A2
Lithia Sprs. GA 120 C4
Lithonia GA 120 C4
Lithopolis OH 101 D1
Lititz PA 146 A2
Little Canada MN 235 D2
Little Chute WI 74 C1
Little Compton RI 151 D4
Little Creek DE 145 E2
Little Cypress TX 132 C2
Little Eagle SD 26 C1
Little Elm TX 59 F2
Little Falls MN 66 C2
Little Falls NJ 148 A3
Little Falls NY 79 F3
Little Ferry NJ 240 C2
Littlefield TX 58 A1
Little Flock AR 106 C3
Littlefork MN 64 B2
Little Heaven DE 145 E3
Little River KS 43 E3
Little River SC 123 D4
Little River-Academy TX 61 E1
Little River Co. AR 116 C4
Little Rock AR 117 E2
Littlerock CA 52 C2
Little Silver NJ 147 E2
Littlestown PA 103 E1
Littleton CO 41 E1
Littleton NH 81 F2
Littleton NC 113 D3
Little Valley NY 92 B1
Littleville AL 119 E2
Live Oak CA 36 C2
Live Oak CA 236 D1
Live Oak FL 138 B2
Live Oak TX 61 D2
Live Oak Co. TX 61 D4
Livermore CA 36 B4
Livermore KY 109 E1
Livermore Falls ME 82 B2
Liverpool NY 265 A1
Liverpool PA 93 D4
Livingston AL 127 D2
Livingston CA 36 C4
Livingston IL 98 B2
Livingston LA 134 A2
Livingston MT 23 F1
Livingston NJ 148 A4
Livingston TN 110 A3
Livingston TX 132 B1
Livingston WI 74 A3
Livingston Co. IL 88 C3
Livingston Co. KY 109 D2
Livingston Co. MI 76 B4
Livingston Co. MO 96 C1
Livingston Co. NY 78 C4
Livingston Manor NY 94 A2
Livingston Par. LA 134 B2
Livonia LA 133 F2
Livonia MI 76 B4
Livonia NY 78 C3
Llangollen Estates DE 145 E1
Llano TX 61 D1
Llano Co. TX 61 D1
Lloyd Harbor NY 148 C3
Loa UT 39 E3
Loami IL 98 B1
Lobelville TN 109 D4
Lochbuie CO 209 D1
Lochearn MD 144 C2
Loch Lynn Hts. MD 102 B2
Loch Sheldrake NY 94 A3
Lockeford CA 36 C3
Lockesburg AR 116 C4
Lockhart AL 136 B1
Lockhart FL 246 B1
Lockhart TX 61 E2
Lock Haven PA 93 D3
Lockland OH 204 B1
Lockney TX 50 B4
Lockport IL 89 D2
Lockport LA 134 B3
Lockport NY 78 B3
Lockwood MO 106 C1
Locust NC 122 B1
Locust Fork AL 119 F4
Locust Grove GA 129 D1
Locust Grove OK 106 B3
Locust Valley NY 148 C3
Lodge Grass MT 24 C2
Lodge Pole MT 16 C2
Lodi CA 36 C3
Lodi NJ 240 C1
Lodi OH 91 D3
Lodi WI 74 B3
Logan IA 86 A2
Logan KS 42 C1
Logan NM 49 F3
Logan OH 101 D1
Logan UT 31 E2
Logan WV 101 E4
Logan Co. AR 116 C1
Logan Co. CO 34 A4
Logan Co. IL 98 B1
Logan Co. KS 42 B2
Logan Co. KY 109 F2

Bancroft F1
Barbourmeade F1
Beechwood Vil. E1
Bellemeade F2
Bellewood E1
Blue Ridge Manor F2
Briarwood F1
Broeck Pointe F1
Brownsboro Vil. E1
Clarksville D1
Creekside F1
Crossgate E1
Douglass Hills F2
Fincastle F1
Forest Hills F2
Glenview E1
Glenview Hills E1
Graymoor-Devondale E1
Hickory Hill F1
Hills and Dales E1
Hollow Creek E3
Houston Acres F2
Hurstbourne F2
Hurstbourne Acres F2
Indian Hills E1
Jeffersontown F2
Jeffersonville D1
Langdon Place F1
Louisville E2
Lyndon F1
Lynnview D3
Manor Creek F1
Meadow Vale F1
Middletown F1
Mockingbird Valley E1
Moorland F1
Murray Hill F1
New Albany C1
Northfield E1
Norwood F1
Parkway Vil. D2
Plantation F1
Poplar Hills E3
Riverwood E1
Rolling Fields E1
Rolling Hills F1
St. Matthews F1
St. Regis Park F2
Seneca Gardens E2
Shively C2
Spring Mill E3
Spring Valley F1
Strathmoor Vil. E2
Sycamore F2
Thornhill E1
Watterson Park E2
Wellington E2
W. Buechel E2
Wildwood F2
Windy Hills E1
Woodlawn Park E1

Entries in **bold black** indicate counties or parishes.
Entries in **bold color** indicate cities with detailed inset maps.

Logan Co. NE 34 C3
Logan Co. ND 18 C4
Logan Co. OH 90 B4
Logan Co. OK 51 E2
Logan Co. WV 101 E4
Logandale NV 46 B1
Logansport IN 89 E3
Logansport LA 124 C3
Loganville GA 121 D4
Loganville PA 103 E1
Log Cabin TX 59 F3
Log Lane Vil. CO 33 F4
Loleta CA 28 A4
Lolita TX 61 F3
Lolo MT 15 D4
Loma Linda CA 229 J3
Long Beach MD 103 E3
Long Beach MS 135 D2
Long Beach NY 147 F1
Long Beach WA 12 B4
Longboat Key FL 140 B3
Long Branch NJ 147 F2
Long Co. GA 130 B3
Long Creek IL 98 C1
Long Green MD 144 C1
Long Grove IL 203 C2
Long Grove IA 88 A1
Long Lake MN 66 C4
Longmeadow MA 150 A2
Longmont CO 41 E1
Long Pond MA 151 E3
Longport NJ 147 F4
Loretto TN 119 E2
Loris SC 123 D3
Lorton VA 144 B4
Los Alamitos CA 228 E4
Los Alamos CA 52 A1
Los Alamos NM 48 C2
Los Alamos Co. NM 48 C2
Los Altos CA 36 B4
Los Altos Hills CA 259 C6
Los Angeles CA 52 C2
Los Angeles Co. CA 52 C2
Los Banos CA 44 B2
Los Chavez NM 48 C4
Los Fresnos TX 63 F4
Los Gatos CA 36 B4
Los Indios TX 63 F4

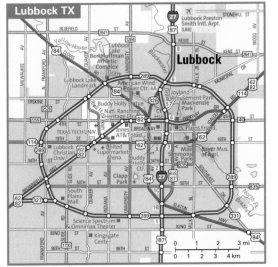

Loma Linda MO 106 B2
Loma Rica CA 36 C2
Lombard IL 203 B4
Lometa TX 59 D4
Lomira WI 74 C2
Lomita CA 228 C4
Lompoc CA 52 A2
Lonaconing MD 102 C1
London AR 117 D1
London KY 110 C2
London OH 100 C1
Londonderry NH 95 E1
Londonderry VT 81 D4
Londontowne MD 144 C3
Lone Grove OK 51 E4
Lone Jack MO 96 C3
Lone Oak KY 108 C2
Lone Oak TX 59 F2
Lone Pine CA 45 E3
Lone Rock WI 74 A3
Lone Star LA 239 A2
Lone Star TX 124 B1
Lone Tree CO 209 C4
Lone Tree IA 87 F2
Lone Wolf OK 51 D3
Long Beach CA 52 C3
Long Beach IN 89 E1
Long Prairie MN 66 B2
Longton KS 43 F4
Long Valley NJ 94 A4
Long View NC 111 F4
Longview TX 124 B2
Longview WA 20 B1
Longwood FL 141 D1
Lonoke AR 117 F2
Lonoke Co. AR 117 F2
Lonsdale MN 67 D4
Loogootee IN 99 E3
Lookout Mtn. GA 120 B2
Lookout Mtn. TN 120 B2
Loomis CA 36 C2
Loomis NE 35 D4
Lorain OH 91 D2
Lorain Co. OH 91 D2
Loraine TX 58 B3
Lorane PA 146 B2
Lordsburg NM 55 F3
Lordstown OH 91 F2
Loreauville LA 133 F3
Lorena TX 59 E4
Lorenzo TX 58 A1
Loretto KY 110 A1
Loretto MN 66 C3
Loretto PA 92 B4
Los Lunas NM 48 C4
Los Molinos CA 36 B1
Los Olivos CA 52 A2
Los Osos CA 44 B4
Los Padillas NM 48 C3
Los Ranchos de Albuquerque NM 48 C3
Lost Creek WV 102 A2
Lost Hills CA 44 C4
Lost Nation IA 87 F1
Lott TX 59 F4
Loudon TN 110 C4
Loudon Co. TN 110 C4
Loudonville NY 94 B1
Loudonville OH 91 D3
Loudoun Co. VA 144 A2
Loughman FL 141 D2
Louisa KY 101 D4
Louisa VA 103 D4
Louisa Co. IA 87 F2
Louisa Co. VA 103 D4
Louisburg KS 96 B3
Louisburg NC 113 D4
Louise TX 61 F3
Louisiana MO 97 F2
Louisville AL 128 B3
Louisville CO 41 E1

Louisville GA 129 F1
Louisville IL 98 C3
Louisville KY 100 A4
Louisville MS 126 C1
Louisville NE 35 F3
Louisville OH 91 E3
Louisville TN 110 C4
Loup City NE 35 D3
Loup Co. NE 35 D2
Love Co. OK 59 E1
Lovelady TX 132 A1
Loveland CO 33 E4
Loveland OH 100 B2
Loveland Park OH 204 C1
Lovell WY 24 C2
Lovelock NV 29 F4
Loves Park IL 74 B4
Lovettsville VA 144 A2
Loveville MD 103 E4
Lovilia IA 87 D3
Loving NM 57 E3
Loving Co. TX 57 E3
Lovingston VA 112 C1
Lovington IL 98 C1
Lovington NM 57 F2
Lowden IA 87 F1
Lowell AR 106 C3
Lowell IN 89 D2
Lowell MA 95 E1
Lowell MI 75 F3
Lowell NC 122 A1
Lowell OH 101 F1
Lowell OR 20 C4
Lowellville OH 91 F3
Lower Brule SD 27 D3
Lower Lake CA 36 B2
Lowesville NC 122 A1
Low Moor VA 112 B1
Lowndes Co. AL 127 F3
Lowndes Co. GA 137 F1
Lowndes Co. MS 127 D1
Lowry City MO 96 C4
Lowville NY 79 E2
Loxley AL 135 E2
Loyal WI 68 A4
Loyalhanna PA 92 B4
Loyall KY 111 D2
Loyalton CA 37 D1
Lubbock TX 58 A1
Lubbock Co. TX 58 A1
Lubec ME 83 F1
Lubeck WV 101 E2
Lucama NC 113 D4
Lucas KS 43 D2
Lucas OH 91 D3
Lucas TX 59 F2
Lucas Co. IA 87 D3
Lucas Co. OH 90 C2
Lucasville OH 101 D3
Luce Co. MI 69 F1
Lucedale MS 135 D1
Lucerne CA 36 B2
Lucerne WY 24 C4
Lucernemines PA 92 B4
Luck WI 67 E3
Luckey OH 90 C2
Ludington MI 75 E1
Ludingtonville NY 148 C1
Ludlow KY 204 A3
Ludlow MA 150 A2
Ludlow VT 81 E4
Ludowici GA 130 B4
Lufkin TX 124 B4
Lugoff SC 122 B3
Lukachukai AZ 48 A1
Lula GA 121 D3
Luling LA 239 A2
Luling TX 61 E2
Lumber City GA 129 F3
Lumberport WV 102 A2
Lumberton MS 134 C1
Lumberton NJ 147 D3
Lumberton NC 123 D2
Lumberton TX 132 C2
Lumpkin GA 128 C3
Lumpkin Co. GA 120 C2
Luna Co. NM 56 A3
Luna Pier MI 90 C1
Lunenburg MA 95 D1
Lunenburg VT 81 F2
Lunenburg VA 113 D2
Lunenburg Co. VA 113 D2
Lupton AZ 48 A3
Luray VA 102 C3
Lusby MD 103 F3
Lusk WY 33 E1
Lutcher LA 134 B3
Luther OK 51 E2
Luthersville GA 128 C1
Luttrell TN 110 C3
Lutz FL 140 B2
Luverne AL 128 A4
Luverne MN 27 F4
Luxemburg WI 69 D4
Luxora AR 108 B4
Luzerne PA 261 B1
Luzerne Co. PA 93 E3
Lycoming Co. PA 93 D2
Lydia LA 133 F3
Lydick IN 89 E2
Lyerly GA 120 B3
Lyford TX 63 F4
Lykens PA 93 E4
Lyle MN 73 D2
Lyle WA 21 D1
Lyman NE 33 F2
Lyman SC 121 F2
Lyman WA 12 C2
Lyman WY 32 A3
Lyman Co. SD 26 C4
Lynbrook NY 147 F1
Lynch KY 111 D2
Lynchburg MS 118 B2
Lynchburg OH 100 C2
Lynchburg SC 122 B3
Lynchburg TN 119 F1
Lynchburg VA 112 C1
Lynch Hts. DE 145 F3
Lynch Sta. VA 112 C2
Lyndell PA 146 B3
Lynden WA 12 C1
Lyndhurst NJ 240 C2
Lyndhurst OH 204 G2
Lyndhurst VA 102 C4
Lyndon KS 96 A3
Lyndon KY 230 F1
Lyndon NY 265 B2
Lyndon VT 81 E2
Lyndon Ctr. VT 81 E2
Lyndonville NY 78 B3
Lyndonville VT 81 E2
Lyndora PA 92 A3
Lynn AL 119 E3
Lynn IN 90 A4
Lynn MA 151 D1
Lynn Co. TX 58 A2
Lynn Haven FL 136 C2
Lynnview KY 230 D3
Lynnville IN 99 E4
Lynnwood WA 12 C3
Lynwood CA 228 D3
Lyon MS 118 A3
Lyon Co. IA 27 F4
Lyon Co. KS 43 F3
Lyon Co. KY 109 D2
Lyon Co. MN 72 A1
Lyon Co. NV 37 E2
Lyons CO 33 E4
Lyons GA 129 F3
Lyons IL 203 D5
Lyons IN 99 E2
Lyons KS 43 E3
Lyons MI 76 A3
Lyons NE 35 F2
Lyons NY 79 D3
Lyons OH 90 B2
Lyons OR 20 C3
Lyons Falls NY 79 E2
Lyons Plain CT 148 C2
Lytle TX 61 D3

M
Mabank TX 59 F3
Mabel MN 73 E2
Maben MS 118 C4
Mableton GA 120 C4
Mabscott WV 111 F1
Mabton WA 21 E1
Macclenny FL 138 C2
Macedon NY 78 C3
Macedonia OH 91 E2
Machesney Park IL 74 B4
Machias ME 83 E1
Machias NY 78 B4
Mack OH 204 A2
Mackay ID 23 D4
Mackinac Co. MI 70 B2
Mackinac Island MI 70 C2
Mackinaw IL 88 B4
Mackinaw City MI 70 C2
Macksville KS 43 D3
Macomb IL 88 A4
Macomb Co. MI 76 C4
Macon AR 117 E2
Macon GA 129 D2
Macon IL 98 C1
Macon MS 127 D1
Macon MO 97 E1
Macon Co. AL 128 B3
Macon Co. GA 129 D2
Macon Co. IL 98 C1
Macon Co. MO 97 D1
Macon Co. NC 121 D1
Macon Co. TN 110 A3
Macoupin Co. IL 98 B2
Macungie PA 146 B1
Macy NE 35 F2
Madawaska ME 85 D1
Maddock ND 19 D2

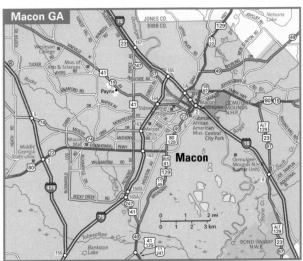

Fitchburg A2
Madison A1
Maple Bluff B1
McFarland B2
Middleton A1
Monona B2
Shorewood Hills A2
Sun Prairie B1
Waunakee A1

Madison WI

A B 1 2

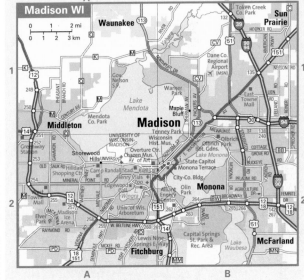

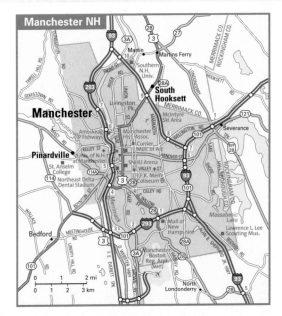

Figures after entries indicate page number and grid reference.

Madeira OH 204 C2
Madeira Beach FL 140 B3
Madelia MN 72 B1
Madera CA 44 C2
Madera Co. CA 44 C2
Madill OK 51 F4
Madison AL 119 F2
Madison AR 118 A2
Madison CT 149 E2
Madison FL 137 F2
Madison GA 121 D4
Madison IL 98 A3
Madison IN 100 A3
Madison KS 43 F3
Madison ME 82 B1
Madison MN 27 F2
Madison MS 126 B2
Madison MO 97 E2
Madison NE 35 E2
Madison NJ 148 A4
Madison NC 112 B3
Madison OH 91 F1
Madison SD 27 F3
Madison VA 102 C4
Madison WV 101 E4
Madison WI 74 B3
Madison Co. AL 119 F2
Madison Co. AR 106 C4
Madison Co. FL 137 F2
Madison Co. GA 121 E3
Madison Co. ID 23 F4
Madison Co. IL 98 B3
Madison Co. IN 89 F4
Madison Co. IA 86 C2
Madison Co. KY 110 C1
Madison Co. MS 126 B2
Madison Co. MO 108 A1
Madison Co. MT 23 E2
Madison Co. NE 35 E2
Madison Co. NY 79 E4
Madison Co. NC 111 E4
Madison Co. OH 100 C1
Madison Co. TN 108 C4
Madison Co. TX 61 F1
Madison Co. VA 102 C3
Madison Hts. MI 210 C2
Madison Hts. VA 112 C1
Madison Lake MN 72 C1
Madison Par. LA 126 A3
Madisonville KY 109 E1
Madisonville LA 134 B2
Madisonville TN 120 C1
Madisonville TX 61 F1
Madras OR 21 D3
Madrid IA 86 C1
Madrid NY 80 B1
Maeser UT 32 A4
Magalia CA 36 C1
Magazine AR 116 C1
Magdalena NM 48 B4
Magee MS 126 C3
Maggie Valley NC 121 E1
Magna UT 257 A2
Magnolia AR 125 D1
Magnolia DE 145 E2
Magnolia MS 134 B1
Magnolia NJ 248 D4
Magnolia NC 123 E2
Magnolia OH 91 E3
Magnolia TX 132 A2
Magoffin Co. KY 111 D1
Mahanoy City PA 93 E3
Mahaska Co. IA 87 D2
Mahnomen MN 19 F3
Mahnomen Co. MN 19 F3
Mahomet IL 88 C4
Mahoning Co. OH 91 F3
Mahopac NY 148 C2
Mahtomedi MN 235 E1
Mahwah NJ 148 B3
Maiden NC 122 A1
Maili HI 152 A3
Maine NY 93 E1
Maineville OH 100 B2
Maitland FL 141 D1
Maize KS 43 E4
Majestic KY 111 E1
Major Co. OK 51 D2
Makaha HI 152 A3
Makakilo City HI 152 A3
Makawao HI 153 D1
Makena HI 153 D1
Malabar FL 141 E2
Malad City ID 31 E2
Malaga CA 44 C3
Malaga NJ 145 F1
Malakoff TX 59 F3
Malcolm NE 35 F4
Malden MA 151 D1
Malden MO 108 B3
Malden WV 200 B2
Malheur Co. OR 22 A4
Malibu CA 52 B2
Malin OR 29 D2
Mallory WV 111 F1
Malone FL 137 D1
Malone NY 80 C1
Malone WA 12 B4
Malta ID 31 D2
Malta IL 88 C1
Malta MT 16 C2
Malta NY 94 B1
Malta OH 101 E1
Maltby WA 262 B2
Malvern AL 136 C1
Malvern AR 117 D3
Malvern IA 86 A3
Malvern OH 91 E3
Malvern PA 146 B3
Malverne NY 241 G4
Mamaroneck NY 148 C3
Mammoth AZ 55 D2
Mammoth Hot Sprs. WY 23 F2
Mammoth Lakes CA 37 E4
Mammoth Spr. AR 107 F3
Mamou LA 133 E2
Man WV 111 F1
Manahawkin NJ 147 E4
Manasquan NJ 147 E2
Manassa CO 41 D4
Manassas VA 144 A4
Manassas Park VA 144 A3
Manatee Co. FL 140 C3
Manawa WI 74 B1
Mancelona MI 70 B4
Manchaca TX 61 E2
Manchaug MA 150 C2
Manchester CT 150 A3
Manchester GA 128 C2
Manchester IA 73 F4
Manchester KY 110 C2
Manchester ME 82 B2
Manchester MD 103 E1
Manchester MI 90 B1
Manchester MO 256 A3
Manchester NH 81 F4
Manchester NY 78 C3
Manchester OH 100 C3
Manchester PA 93 E4
Manchester TN 120 A1
Manchester VT 81 D4
Manchester WA 262 A3
Manchester-by-the-Sea MA 151 F1
Manchester Ctr. VT 81 D4
Mancos CO 40 B4
Mandan ND 18 C4
Mandaree ND 18 A3
Manderson SD 26 A4
Mandeville AR 116 C4
Mandeville LA 134 B2
Mangham LA 125 F2
Mango FL 266 C2
Mangonia Park FL 141 F4
Mangum OK 50 C3
Manhasset NY 148 C4
Manhasset Hills NY 241 G3
Manhattan IL 89 D2
Manhattan KS 43 F2
Manhattan MT 23 F1
Manhattan Beach CA 228 C3
Manheim PA 93 E4
Manila AR 108 B4
Manila UT 32 A3
Manilla IA 86 A1
Manistee MI 75 E1
Manistee Co. MI 70 A4
Manistique MI 69 E2
Manito IL 88 B4
Manitou Beach MI 90 B1
Manitou Sprs. CO 41 E2
Manitowoc WI 75 D1
Manitowoc Co. WI 75 D1
Mankato KS 43 E1
Mankato MN 72 C1
Manlius NY 79 E3
Manly IA 73 D3
Mannford OK 51 F2
Manning IA 86 B1
Manning ND 18 A3
Manning SC 122 B4
Mannington WV 102 A1
Mannsville OK 51 F4
Manokotak AK 154 B3
Manomet MA 151 E3
Manor PA 92 A4
Manor TX 61 E1
Manorhaven NY 241 G2
Manorville NY 149 D3
Mansfield AR 116 C2
Mansfield IL 88 C4
Mansfield LA 124 C3
Mansfield MA 151 D2
Mansfield MO 107 E2
Mansfield OH 91 D3
Mansfield PA 93 D1
Mansfield TX 59 E3
Mansfield Ctr. CT 150 B3
Mansfield Four Corners CT 150 B3
Manson IA 72 B4
Manson WA 13 E2
Mansura LA 133 F1
Mantachie MS 119 D3
Manteca CA 36 C4
Manteno IL 89 D2
Manteo NC 115 F2
Manti UT 39 E2
Manton MI 75 F1
Mantorville MN 73 D1
Mantua OH 91 E2
Mantua UT 31 E3
Mantua VA 270 A4
Manvel ND 19 E2
Manvel TX 132 A4
Manville NJ 147 D1
Manville RI 150 C2
Many LA 125 D4
Many Farms AZ 47 F2
Manzanita OR 20 B1
Manzanola CO 41 F3
Maple Bluff WI 74 B3
Maple Grove MN 67 D3
Maple Hts. OH 91 E2
Maple Hill KS 43 F2
Maple Lake MN 66 C3
Maple Park IL 88 C1
Maple Plain MN 66 C4
Maple Rapids MI 76 A3
Maple Shade NJ 146 C3
Maplesville AL 127 F2

McAllen TX

Bellwood	A1	Indialantic	B3	Merritt Island	B2	Sharpes	A2
Bonaventure	B2	Indian Harbour Beach	B3	Mims	A1	S. Patrick Shores	B3
Cape Canaveral	B2	La Grange	A1	Palm Bay	B3	Titusville	A1
Cocoa	A2	Malabar	B3	Palm Shores	B3	Viera	A2
Cocoa Beach	B2	Melbourne	A3	Pineda	B2	W. Melbourne	B3
Cocoa West	A2	Melbourne Beach	B3	Port St. John	A1		
Frontenac	A1	Melbourne Vil.	B3	Rockledge	A2		
Georgiana	B2			Satellite Beach	B3		

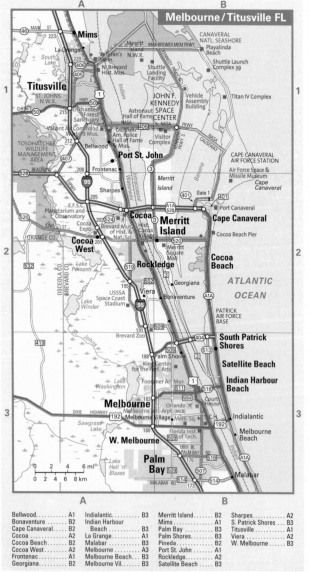

Entries in **bold black** indicate counties or parishes.
Entries in **bold color** indicate cities with detailed inset maps.

Mapleton IA	86 A1	Mapleton UT	39 E1
Mapleton ME	85 D2	Maple Valley WA	12 C3
Mapleton MN	72 C1	Maplewood MN	235 D2
Mapleton ND	19 E4	Maplewood MO	256 B2

Maplewood NJ ... 240 A3
Mappsville VA ... 114 C2
Maquoketa IA ... 88 A1
Marana AZ ... 55 D3

Marathon FL ... 143 D4
Marathon NY ... 79 E4
Marathon City WI ... 68 A4
Marathon Co. WI ... 68 A4

Marble MN ... 64 B3
Marble Cliff OH ... 206 A2
Marble Falls TX ... 61 D1
Marblehead MA ... 151 D1
Marblehead OH ... 91 D2
Marble Hill MO ... 108 B1
Marbleton WY ... 32 A1
Marbury MD ... 144 B4
Marceline MO ... 97 D1
Marcellus MI ... 89 F1
Marcellus NY ... 79 D3
Marco Island FL ... 142 C2
Marcus IA ... 72 A3
Marcus Hook PA ... 146 C3
Marengo IL ... 88 C1
Marengo IN ... 99 F4
Marengo IA ... 87 E1
Marengo Co. AL ... 127 E3
Marfa TX ... 62 B3
Margaret AL ... 119 F4
Margaretville NY ... 94 A2
Margate FL ... 143 E1
Margate City NJ ... 147 E4
Marianna AR ... 118 A2
Marianna FL ... 137 D1
Marianna PA ... 102 A1
Maricopa AZ ... 54 C2
Maricopa CA ... 52 B1
Maricopa Co. AZ ... 54 B1
Mariemont OH ... 204 C2
Maries Co. MO ... 97 E4
Marietta GA ... 120 C2
Marietta OH ... 101 F2
Marietta OK ... 59 E1
Marietta PA ... 93 E4
Marietta SC ... 121 E2
Marietta WA ... 12 C1
Marina CA ... 44 B3
Marina del Rey CA ... 228 C3
Marin Co. CA ... 36 B3
Marine IL ... 98 B3
Marine City MI ... 76 C4
Marine on St. Croix MN ... 67 D3
Marinette WI ... 69 D3
Marinette Co. WI ... 68 C3
Maringouin LA ... 133 F2
Marinwood CA ... 259 A1
Marion AL ... 127 F2
Marion AR ... 118 B1
Marion CT ... 149 C1
Marion IL ... 108 C1
Marion IN ... 89 F4
Marion IA ... 87 E1
Marion KS ... 43 E3
Marion KY ... 109 D1
Marion LA ... 125 E1
Marion MD ... 103 F4
Marion MA ... 151 E3
Marion MI ... 75 F1
Marion MS ... 127 D2
Marion NY ... 78 C3
Marion NC ... 111 E4
Marion OH ... 90 C4
Marion PA ... 103 D1
Marion SC ... 122 C3
Marion SD ... 27 F4
Marion VA ... 111 F2
Marion WI ... 68 B4
Marion Co. AL ... 119 E3

Marion Co. AR ... 107 E3
Marion Co. FL ... 139 D4
Marion Co. GA ... 128 C3
Marion Co. IL ... 98 C3
Marion Co. IN ... 99 F1
Marion Co. IA ... 87 D2
Marion Co. KS ... 43 E3
Marion Co. KY ... 110 B1
Marion Co. MS ... 126 C4
Marion Co. MO ... 97 F1
Marion Co. OH ... 90 C3
Marion Co. OR ... 20 C2
Marion Co. SC ... 122 C3
Marion Co. TN ... 120 A1
Marion Co. TX ... 124 C2
Marion Co. WV ... 102 A1
Marion Hts. PA ... 93 E3
Marionville MO ... 106 C2
Mariposa CA ... 37 D4
Mariposa Co. CA ... 37 D4
Marissa IL ... 98 B4
Marked Tree AR ... 118 B1
Markesan WI ... 74 B2
Markham IL ... 203 D6
Markham TX ... 61 F3
Markle IN ... 90 A3
Markleeville CA ... 37 D2
Marksville LA ... 133 F1
Mark MS ... 118 B3
Marlboro NY ... 147 E2
Marlboro NY ... 148 B1
Marlboro Co. SC ... 122 C3
Marlborough CT ... 149 E1
Marlborough MA ... 150 C1
Marlborough MO ... 256 B3
Marlborough NH ... 95 D1
Marlette MI ... 76 C3
Marley MD ... 144 C2
Marlin TX ... 59 F4
Marlinton WV ... 102 A4
Marlow OK ... 51 E4
Marlow Hts. MD ... 270 E4
Marlton MD ... 144 C3
Marlton NJ ... 147 D3
Maroa IL ... 98 C1
Marquette KS ... 43 E3
Marquette MI ... 69 D1
Marquette Co. MI ... 65 F4
Marquette Co. WI ... 74 B2
Marrero LA ... 134 B3
Mars PA ... 92 A3
Marseilles IL ... 88 C2
Marshall AR ... 107 E4
Marshall IL ... 99 D2
Marshall MI ... 76 A4
Marshall MN ... 72 A1
Marshall MO ... 97 D2
Marshall NC ... 111 E4
Marshall TX ... 124 C2
Marshall VA ... 103 D3
Marshall WI ... 74 B3
Marshallberg NC ... 115 E4
Marshall Co. AL ... 119 F3
Marshall Co. IL ... 88 B3

Marshall Co. IN ... 89 F2
Marshall Co. IA ... 87 D1
Marshall Co. KS ... 43 F1
Marshall Co. KY ... 109 D2
Marshall Co. MN ... 19 F2
Marshall Co. MS ... 118 C2
Marshall Co. OK ... 51 F1
Marshall Co. SD ... 27 E1
Marshall Co. TN ... 119 F1
Marshall Co. WV ... 102 A1
Marshalltown DE ... 146 B4
Marshallton PA ... 146 B3
Marshalltown IA ... 87 D1
Marshallville GA ... 129 D2
Marshallville OH ... 91 E3
Marshfield MA ... 151 E2
Marshfield MO ... 107 D1
Marshfield VT ... 81 E2
Marshfield Hills MA ... 151 E2
Mars Hill ME ... 85 E2
Mars Hill NC ... 111 E4
Marshville NC ... 122 B2
Marshing ID ... 22 A1
Marston MO ... 108 B3
Marstons Mills MA ... 151 F4
Mart TX ... 59 F4
Martha Lake WA ... 262 B2
Marthasville MO ... 97 F3
Martin KY ... 111 E1
Martin LA ... 125 D3
Martin TN ... 108 C3
Martin City MT ... 15 D2
Martin Co. FL ... 141 E4
Martin Co. IN ... 99 E3
Martin Co. KY ... 111 E1
Martin Co. MN ... 72 B2
Martin Co. NC ... 113 F4
Martin Co. TX ... 58 A3
Martindale TX ... 61 E2
Martinez CA ... 36 B3
Martin TN ... 108 C3
Martinsburg PA ... 92 C4
Martinsburg WV ... 103 D3
Martins Creek PA ... 93 F3
Martins Ferry OH ... 91 F4
Martinsville IL ... 99 D2
Martinsville IN ... 99 F2
Martinsville NJ ... 147 D1
Martinsville VA ... 112 B3
Marty SD ... 35 E1
Marvell AR ... 118 A2
Marvin NC ... 122 A2
Mary Esther FL ... 136 B2
Maryland City MD ... 193 A5
Maryland Hts. MO ... 256 A1
Marysvale UT ... 39 E3
Marysville CA ... 36 C2
Marysville KS ... 43 F1
Marysville MI ... 76 C3
Marysville OH ... 90 C4
Marysville PA ... 93 D4
Marysville WA ... 12 C2
Maryville IL ... 256 D1
Maryville MO ... 86 B4
Maryville TN ... 110 C4
Marywood MD ... 145 D1
Masaryktown FL ... 140 B1

Miami / Fort Lauderdale FL

Boca Raton
Coconut Creek
Parkland
Coral Springs
Deerfield Beach
Lighthouse Point
Margate
Pompano Beach
Tamarac
North Lauderdale
Lauderhill
Lauderdale Lakes
Oakland Park
Wilton Manors
Sunrise
Plantation
Fort Lauderdale
Weston
Davie
Dania Beach
Southwest Ranches
Cooper City
Hollywood
Pembroke Pines
West Park
Hallandale Beach
Miramar
Pembroke Park
Ojus
Aventura
Miami Gardens
North Miami Beach
North Miami
Miami Lakes
Opa-Locka
Hialeah Gardens
Hialeah
Miami Shores
Doral
Miami Springs
Miami
Miami Beach
Sweetwater
Westchester
West Miami
Westwood Lakes
South Miami
Kendale Lakes
Coral Gables
Key Biscayne
Kendall
Pinecrest
Richmond Hts.
Palmetto Bay
S. Miami Hts.
Goulds
Cutler Bay

ATLANTIC OCEAN

BISCAYNE NATIONAL PARK

Downtown Miami FL

OVERTOWN
DOWNTOWN
FINANCIAL DISTRICT

Aventura	B3	Golden Beach	C3	Lazy Lake	B2	Oakland Park	B2	S. Miami Hts.	A5
Bal Harbour	B3	Goulds	A5	Lighthouse Pt.	C1	Opa-Locka	B3	Southwest Ranches	A3
Bay Harbor Islands	C4	Hallandale Beach	C3	Margate	B1	Ojus	B3	Sunny Isles Beach	C3
Biscayne Park	B4	Hialeah	A4	Medley	A4	Palmetto Bay	A5	Sunrise	B2
Boca Raton	C1	Hialeah Gardens	A4	Miami	B4	Palm Springs North	B1	Surfside	C4
Coconut Creek	B1	Hillsboro Beach	C1	Miami Beach	C4	Parkland	B1	Sweetwater	A4
Cooper City	A3	Hollywood	B3	Miami Gardens	B3	Pembroke Park	B3	Tamarac	A2
Coral Gables	B5	Indian Creek	C4	Miami Lakes	A3	Pembroke Pines	A3	Virginia Gardens	A4
Coral Sprs.	A1	Kendale Lakes	A5	Miami Shores	B4	Perrine	A5	W. Miami	A4
Cutler Bay	A5	Kendall	A5	Miami Sprs.	A4	Pinecrest	A5	Westchester	A4
Dania Beach	B3	Key Biscayne	B5	Miramar	A3	Plantation	A2	Weston	A2
Davie	A2			N. Bay Vil.	B4	Pompano Beach	C1	West Park	B3
Deerfield Beach	C1	Lauderdale-by-the-Sea	C2	N. Lauderdale	B2	Richmond Hts.	A5	Westwood Lakes	A4
El Portal	B4	Lauderdale Lakes	B2	N. Miami	B3	Rockdale	A5	Wilton Manors	B2
Ft. Lauderdale	C2	Lauderhill	B2	N. Miami Beach	B3	S. Miami	A5		

POINTS OF INTEREST

AmericanAirlines Arena ... E1
Bayside Marketplace ... E2
Flagler Palm Cottage ... D2
Freedom Tower ... D1
Frost Museum of Science ... E1
HistoryMiami ... D2
James L. Knight Center ... D2
Jungle Island ... E1

Klipsch Amphitheater at Bayfront Park ... E2
Knight Concert Hall ... E1
Miami Children's Museum ... E1
Miami Herald Building ... E1
Miami Seaplane Base ... E1
Olympia Theater ... E2
PortMiami ... E2
Sanford & Dolores Ziff Ballet Opera House ... D1

Figures after entries indicate page number and grid reference.

Mascot TN ... 110 C4	Mason Co. MI ... 75 E1	Matador TX ... 58 B1	Mattawoman MD ... 144 B4	Maumelle AR ... 117 E2	Maxwell NM ... 49 E1
Mascotte FL ... 140 C1	Mason Co. TX ... 60 C1	Matagorda Co. TX ... 132 A4	Matteson IL ... 89 D2	Maunawili HI ... 152 B3	Maybee MI ... 90 C1
Mascoutah IL ... 98 B3	Mason Co. WA ... 12 B3	Matamoras PA ... 94 A3	Matthews IN ... 89 F4	Maupin OR ... 21 D2	Maybeury WV ... 111 F1
Mashpee MA ... 151 E3	Mason Co. WV ... 101 E3	Matawan NJ ... 147 E1	Matthews MO ... 108 B2	Maurertown VA ... 102 C3	Maybrook NY ... 148 B1
Mason MI ... 76 A4	Masontown PA ... 102 B1	Matewan WV ... 111 E1	Matthews NC ... 122 B1	Maurice LA ... 133 F2	Mayer AZ ... 47 D4
Mason NV ... 37 E2	Masontown WV ... 102 B1	Matherville IL ... 88 A2	Mattituck NY ... 149 E3	Mauriceville TX ... 132 C2	Mayer MN ... 66 C4
Mason NH ... 95 D1	Masonville KY ... 109 E1	Mathews LA ... 134 B3	Mattoon IL ... 98 C2	Maury City TN ... 108 C4	Mayersville MS ... 126 A1
Mason OH ... 100 B2	Masonville NJ ... 147 D3	Mathews VA ... 113 F1	Mattydale NY ... 79 D3	Maury Co. TN ... 109 E4	Mayesville SC ... 122 B3
Mason TN ... 118 C1	Massac Co. IL ... 108 C2	Mathis TX ... 61 E4	Matunuck RI ... 150 C4	Mauston WI ... 74 A2	Mayfield KY ... 108 C3
Mason TX ... 60 C1	Massapequa NY ... 148 C4	Mathiston MS ... 118 C4	Maud OH ... 100 B2	Maverick Co. TX ... 60 B3	Mayfield NY ... 80 C4
Mason WV ... 101 E2	Massapequa Park NY ... 148 C4	Matlacha FL ... 142 C1	Maud OK ... 51 F3	Mavisdale VA ... 111 E2	Mayfield OH ... 204 G1
Masonboro NC ... 123 E3	Massena NY ... 80 B1	Matmoret MS ... 91 E3	Maud TX ... 124 C1	Max ND ... 18 B3	Mayfield PA ... 93 F2
Mason City IL ... 88 B4	Massillon OH ... 91 E3	Mattapoisett MA ... 151 E3	Maugansville MD ... 103 D1	Max Meadows VA ... 112 A2	Mayfield UT ... 39 E2
Mason City IA ... 73 D3	Mastic NY ... 149 D4	Mattawa WA ... 13 E4	Maumee OH ... 90 C2	Maxton NC ... 122 C2	Mayfield Hts. OH ... 91 E2
Mason Co. IL ... 88 A4	Mastic Beach NY ... 149 D4	Mattawamkeag ME ... 85 D4		Maxwell CA ... 36 B2	Mayflower AR ... 117 E2
Mason Co. KY ... 100 C4	Masury OH ... 91 F2	Mattawan MI ... 89 F1		Maxwell IA ... 86 C1	

Maxwell NM ... 49 E1	McIntyre GA ... 129 E3	
Maybee MI ... 90 C1	McKean Co. PA ... 92 B1	

Milwaukee WI area index

Bayside ... D1	Elm Grove ... B2	Hales Corners ... B3	Pewaukee (city) ... A2	Sussex ... A1	Whitefish Bay ... D1
Brookfield ... B2	Fox Pt. ... D1	Lannon ... B1	Pewaukee (village) ... A2	Waukesha ... A2	
Brown Deer ... C1	Glendale ... C1	Menomonee Falls ... B1	River Hills ... D1	Wauwatosa ... C2	
Butler ... B1	Greendale ... C3	Milwaukee ... C2	St. Francis ... D3	W. Allis ... C3	
Cudahy ... D3	Greenfield ... C3	New Berlin ... B3	Shorewood ... D2	W. Milwaukee ... C3	

Milwaukee WI

Downtown Milwaukee WI

POINTS OF INTEREST

Amtrak/Intermodal Station ... F2
Betty Brinn Children's Museum ... G2
Broadway Theatre Center ... F2
Court House ... E1
Cudahy Gardens ... G2
Discovery World at Pier Wisconsin ... G2
Federal Plaza ... F2
Fiserv Forum ... F1
Grain Exchange ... F2
Haggerty Museum of Art ... E2
Harley-Davidson Museum ... F2
Helfaer Theatre ... E2
Historic Third Ward ... F2
Lakeshore State Park ... G2
Maier Festival Park ... G2
Marcus Ctr. for the Performing Arts ... F1
Marquette University ... E2
Miller High Life Theatre ... F1
Milwaukee Art Museum &
    War Memorial Center ... G1
Milwaukee County Hist. Society ... F1
Milwaukee Institute of Art & Design ... F2
Milwaukee Public Market ... F2
Milwaukee Public Museum ... F1
Milwaukee School of Engineering ... F1
Pabst Theater ... F1
Post Office ... F2
Potawatomi Hotel & Casino ... E2
St. Joan of Arc Chapel ... E2
State Office Building ... E2
UW-Milwaukee Panther Arena ... F1
Wisconsin Center ... F2
Wisconsin Conservatory of Music ... G1

Maxwell NM ... 49 E1	McIntyre GA ... 129 E3
Maybee MI ... 90 C1	McKean Co. PA ... 92 B1
Maybeury WV ... 111 F1	McKee KY ... 110 C1
Maybrook NY ... 148 B1	McKee City NJ ... 147 F4
Mayer AZ ... 47 D4	McKeesport PA ... 92 A4
Mayer MN ... 66 C4	McKees Rocks PA ... 250 B1
Mayersville MS ... 126 A1	McKenna WA ... 12 C4
Mayes Co. OK ... 106 A3	McKenney VA ... 113 E2
Mayesville SC ... 122 B3	McKenzie AL ... 127 F4
Mayfield KY ... 108 C3	McKenzie TN ... 109 D4
Mayfield NY ... 80 C4	McKenzie Co. ND ... 17 F2
Mayfield OH ... 204 G1	McKinley Co. NM ... 48 A3
Mayfield PA ... 93 F2	McKinleyville CA ... 28 A4
Mayfield UT ... 39 E2	McKinney TX ... 59 F2
Mayfield Hts. OH ... 91 E2	McKownville NY ... 188 D3
Mayflower AR ... 117 E2	McLain MS ... 135 D1
Maynard IA ... 73 E4	McLean IL ... 88 B4
Maynard MA ... 150 C1	McLean TX ... 50 B3
Maynardville TN ... 110 C3	McLean VA ... 144 B3
Mayo FL ... 137 F3	McLean Co. IL ... 88 C4
Mayo MD ... 144 C3	McLean Co. KY ... 109 E1
Mayo SC ... 121 F1	McLean Co. ND ... 18 B3
Mayodan NC ... 112 B3	McLeansboro IL ... 98 C3
Maypearl TX ... 59 F3	McLennan Co. TX ... 59 F4
Mays Chapel MD ... 193 C1	McLeod Co. MN ... 66 C4
Mays Landing NJ ... 105 D3	McLoud OK ... 51 E3
Maysville GA ... 121 D3	McLouth KS ... 96 A3
Maysville KY ... 100 C4	McMechen WV ... 101 F1
Maysville MO ... 96 B1	McMinn Co. TN ... 120 C1
Maysville NC ... 115 D4	McMinnville OR ... 20 B2
Maysville OK ... 51 E4	McMinnville TN ... 110 A4
Maytown AL ... 195 D1	McMullen Co. TX ... 61 D4
Mayville MI ... 76 C3	McMurray PA ... 92 A4
Mayville NY ... 78 A4	McNairy Co. TN ... 119 D1
Mayville ND ... 19 E3	McNary AZ ... 47 F4
Mayville WI ... 74 C2	McNeil AR ... 125 D1
Maywood CA ... 228 D3	McPherson KS ... 43 E3
Maywood IL ... 203 C4	McPherson Co. KS ... 43 E3
Maywood NJ ... 240 C1	McPherson Co. NE ... 34 B3
Maywood NY ... 188 D2	McPherson Co. SD ... 27 D1
Maywood Park OR ... 251 D2	McQueeney TX ... 61 D2
Mazeppa MN ... 73 D1	McRae AR ... 117 F1
Mazomanie WI ... 74 A3	McRae GA ... 129 E3
Mazon IL ... 88 C2	McRoberts KY ... 111 E2
McAdoo PA ... 93 E3	McSherrystown PA ... 103 E1
McAfee NJ ... 148 A2	McVeigh KY ... 111 E1
McAlester OK ... 116 A2	McVille ND ... 19 E3
McAlisterville PA ... 93 D3	Mead CO ... 33 E4
McAllen TX ... 63 E4	Mead NE ... 35 F3
McArthur OH ... 101 D2	Mead WA ... 14 A3
McBain MI ... 75 F1	Meade KS ... 42 C4
McBee SC ... 122 B3	Meade Co. KS ... 42 C4
McCall ID ... 22 B2	Meade Co. KY ... 99 F4
McCamey TX ... 58 A4	Meade Co. SD ... 26 A3
McCammon ID ... 31 E1	Meadow TX ... 58 A1
McCandless PA ... 92 A4	Meadowlakes TX ... 61 D1
McCaysville GA ... 120 C2	Meadows Place TX ... 132 A3
McClain Co. OK ... 51 E3	Meadow Vale KY ... 230 F1
McCleary WA ... 12 B4	Meadow Valley CA ... 36 C1
McClellandville DE ... 146 B4	Meadowview VA ... 111 F2
McClellanville SC ... 131 E1	Meadville MS ... 126 A4
McCloud CA ... 28 C3	Meadville PA ... 92 A2
McClure OH ... 90 B2	Meagher Co. MT ... 15 F4
McClure PA ... 93 D3	Mebane NC ... 112 C4
McClusky ND ... 18 C3	Mecca CA ... 53 E3
McColl SC ... 122 C2	Mechanic Falls ME ... 82 B2
McComb MS ... 126 B4	Mechanicsburg OH ... 90 C4
McComb OH ... 90 B3	Mechanicsburg PA ... 93 D4
McCone Co. MT ... 17 E3	Mechanicsville IA ... 87 F1
McConnellsburg PA ... 103 D1	Mechanicsville MD ... 103 E3
McConnelsville OH ... 101 E1	Mechanicsville VA ... 113 E1
McCook NE ... 42 C1	Mechanicville NY ... 94 B1
McCook Co. SD ... 27 E4	Mecklenburg Co. NC ... 122 B1
McCordsville IN ... 99 F1	Mecklenburg Co. VA ... 113 D2
McCormick Corners NY ... 188 C2	Mecosta Co. MI ... 75 F2
McCormick SC ... 121 F4	Medanales NM ... 48 C2
McCormick Co. SC ... 121 F4	Medaryville IN ... 89 E3
McCracken Co. KY ... 108 C2	Medfield MA ... 151 D2
McCreary Co. KY ... 110 C2	Medford MA ... 151 D1
McCrory AR ... 117 F1	Medford MN ... 73 D1
McCulloch Co. TX ... 58 C4	Medford NJ ... 147 D3
McCune KS ... 106 B1	Medford NY ... 149 D4
McCurtain OK ... 116 B3	Medford OK ... 51 E1
McCurtain Co. OK ... 116 B3	Medford OR ... 28 B2
McDermitt NV ... 30 A2	Medford WI ... 68 A3
McDonald OH ... 276 B2	Medford Lakes NJ ... 147 D3
McDonald PA ... 92 A4	Media PA ... 146 C3
McDonald Co. MO ... 106 C3	Mediapolis IA ... 87 F3
McDonough GA ... 120 C4	Medical Lake WA ... 13 F3
McDonough Co. IL ... 87 F3	Medicine Bow WY ... 33 D2
McDowell Co. NC ... 111 E4	Medicine Lake MT ... 17 F2
McDowell Co. WV ... 111 F1	Medicine Lodge KS ... 43 D4
McDuffie Co. GA ... 129 F1	Medina MN ... 66 C3
McEwen TN ... 109 E4	Medina NY ... 78 B3
McFarland CA ... 45 D4	Medina ND ... 19 D4
McFarland WI ... 74 B3	Medina OH ... 91 E3
McGaheysville VA ... 102 C4	Medina TN ... 108 C4
McGehee AR ... 117 F4	Medina WA ... 262 B3
McGill NV ... 38 B2	Medina Co. OH ... 91 E3
McGrath AK ... 154 C2	Medina Co. TX ... 60 C3
McGraw NY ... 79 E4	Medinah IL ... 203 B3
McGregor IA ... 73 F3	Medley FL ... 233 A4
McGregor TX ... 59 E4	Medina IN ... 99 F3
McHenry IL ... 74 C4	Medora ND ... 18 A4
McHenry KY ... 109 E1	Medulla FL ... 140 C2
McHenry Co. IL ... 74 C4	Medway ME ... 85 D4
McHenry Co. ND ... 18 C2	Medway MA ... 151 D2
McIntosh FL ... 138 C2	Medway NY ... —
McIntosh MN ... 19 F3	Meeker CO ... 40 B1
McIntosh SD ... 26 B1	Meeker OK ... 51 F3
McIntosh Co. GA ... 130 B4	Meeker Co. MN ... 66 B3
McIntosh Co. ND ... 27 D1	Menon WI ... 67 E2
McIntosh Co. OK ... 116 A1	Meeteetse WY ... 24 B3

Entries in **bold black** indicate counties or parishes.
Entries in **bold color** indicate cities with detailed inset maps.

Meggett SC 131 D2
Mehlville MO 98 A3
Meigs GA 137 E1
Meigs Co. OH 101 E2
Meigs Co. TN 110 B4
Meiners Oaks CA 52 B2
Melba ID 22 B4
Melbourne AR 107 E4
Melbourne FL 141 E2
Melbourne IA 87 D1
Melbourne KY 204 C3
Melbourne Beach FL 141 E2
Melbourne Vil. FL 141 E2
Melcher-Dallas IA 87 D2
Melfa VA 114 C3
Melissa TX 59 F2
Mellen WI 65 D4
Mellette SD 27 E2
Mellette Co. SD 26 C4
Melrose MN 66 B2
Melrose NM 49 F4
Melrose NY 94 B1
Melrose WI 73 F1
Melrose Park IL 203 C4
Melrose Park NY 79 D3
Melvern KS 96 A3
Melville LA 133 F1
Melvindale MI 210 B4
Memphis FL 140 B3
Memphis MI 76 C3
Memphis MO 87 E4
Memphis TN 118 B1
Memphis TX 50 B4
Memphis Jct. KY 109 F2
Mena AR 116 C2
Menahga MN 64 A4
Menan ID 23 E4
Menands NY 188 E3
Menard TX 60 C1
Menard Co. IL 88 B4
Menard Co. TX 60 C1
Menasha WI 74 C1
Mendenhall MS 126 B3
Mendenhall PA 146 B3
Mendham NJ 148 A4
Mendocino CA 36 A2
Mendocino Co. CA 36 A1
Mendon IL 87 F4
Mendon MA 150 C2
Mendon MI 89 F1
Mendon OH 90 B3
Mendon UT 31 E3
Mendota CA 44 C3
Mendota IL 88 B2
Mendota Hts. MN 235 D3
Menifee CA 53 D3
Menifee Co. KY 100 C4
Menlo GA 120 B3
Menlo Park CA 259 C5
Menno SD 27 E4
Menominee MI 69 D3
Menominee Co. MI 69 D3
Menominee Co. WI 68 C3
Menomonee Falls WI 74 C3
Menomonie WI 67 E4
Mentone AL 120 B2
Mentone CA 53 D2
Mentone IN 89 F2
Mentone TX 57 E4
Mentor OH 91 E2
Mentor TN 110 C4
Mentor-on-the-Lake OH 91 E1
Mequon WI 74 C3
Meraux LA 134 C3
Merced CA 37 D4
Merced Co. CA 44 C2
Mercedes TX 63 E4
Mercer PA 91 F2
Mercer Co. IL 87 F2
Mercer Co. KY 110 B1
Mercer Co. MO 86 C4
Mercer Co. NJ 147 D2
Mercer Co. ND 18 B3
Mercer Co. OH 90 A4
Mercer Co. PA 91 F2
Mercer Co. WV 112 A1
Mercer Island WA 262 B3
Mercersburg PA 103 D1
Mercerville NJ 147 D2
Merchantville NJ 248 D3
Meredith NH 81 F3
Meredosia IL 98 A1
Meriden CT 149 D1
Meriden KS 96 A2
Meridian ID 22 B4
Meridian MS 127 D2
Meridian PA 92 A3
Meridian TX 59 E3
Meridian Hills IN 99 F1
Meridianville AL 119 F2
Merigold MS 118 A4
Meriwether Co. GA 128 C1
Merkel TX 58 C3
Merlin OR 28 B1
Mermentau LA 133 E2
Merriam KS 224 B4
Merriam Woods MO 107 D3
Merrick NY 148 C4
Merrick Co. NE 35 E3
Merrifield VA 270 A3
Merrill IA 35 F1
Merrill MI 76 A2
Merrill OR 28 C2
Merrill WI 68 B3
Merrillan WI 73 F1
Merrillville IN 89 D2
Merrimac MA 151 F1
Merrimack NH 95 D1
Merrimack Co. NH 81 F4
Merrionette Park IL 203 D6
Merritt Island FL 141 E2
Mer Rouge LA 125 F2
Merrow CT 150 A3
Merryville LA 133 D1
Merton WI 74 C3
Mertzon TX 58 B4
Mertztown PA 146 B1
Mesa AZ 54 C1
Mesa WA 13 E4
Mesa Co. CO 40 B2
Mescalero NM 56 C2
Mesilla NM 56 C3
Mesita NM 48 B3
Mesquite NV 46 B1
Mesquite NM 56 C3
Mesquite TX 59 F2
Metairie LA 134 B3
Metamora IL 88 B3
Metamora MI 76 C3
Metamora OH 90 B2
Metcalfe MS 118 A4
Metcalfe Co. KY 110 A2
Methuen MA 95 E1
Metlakatla AK 155 E4
Metolius OR 21 D3
Metropolis IL 108 C2
Metter GA 129 F2
Metuchen NJ 147 E1
Metzger OR 251 C2
Mexia TX 59 F4
Mexico IN 89 F3
Mexico ME 82 B2
Mexico MO 97 E2
Mexico NY 79 D2
Mexico Beach FL 136 C3
Meyersdale PA 102 C1
Meyers Lake OH 199 B2
Miami AZ 55 D1
Miami FL 143 F2
Miami OK 106 B2
Miami TX 50 B2

Apple Valley C4
Arden Hills C1
Bald Eagle E1
Birchwood Vil. E1
Blaine C1
Bloomington B4
Brooklyn Ctr. B1
Brooklyn Park B1
Burnsville B4
Circle Pines C1
Columbia Hts. C2
Coon Rapids B1
Cottage Grove E4
Crystal B2
Deephaven A3
Dellwood E1
Eagan D4
Eden Prairie A4
Edina B3
Falcon Hts. C2
Fridley C1
Gem Lake D1
Golden Valley B2
Grant E1
Hilltop C1
Hopkins A3
Hugo E1
Inver Grove Hts. D4
Lake Elmo E2
Landfall E3
Lauderdale C2
Lexington C1
Lilydale D3
Lino Lakes D1
Little Canada D2
Mahtomedi E1
Maple Grove A1
Maplewood D2
Medicine Lake A2
Mendota C3
Mendota Hts. D3
Minneapolis B3
Minnetonka A3
Mounds View C1
New Brighton C1
New Hope B2
Newport D3
Nininger E4
N. Oaks D1
N. St. Paul D2
Oakdale E2
Osseo A1
Pine Sprs. E2
Plymouth A2
Richfield B3
Robbinsdale B2
Rosemount D4
Roseville C2
St. Anthony C2
St. Louis Park B2
St. Paul D2
St. Paul Park E4
Savage B4
Shakopee A4
Shoreview C1
S. St. Paul D3
Spring Lake Park C1
Sunfish Lake D3
Vadnais Hts. D1
Wayzata A2
W. St. Paul D3
White Bear Lake D1
Willernie E1
Withrow E1
Woodbury E3
Woodland A3

Minneapolis / St Paul MN

Figures after entries indicate page number and grid reference.

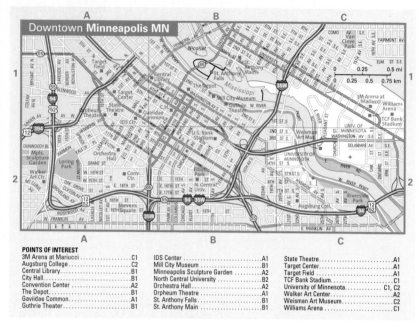

Downtown Minneapolis MN

POINTS OF INTEREST

3M Arena at Mariucci	C1	IDS Center A1	State Theatre A1
Augsburg College	C2	Mill City Museum B1	Target Center A1
Central Library	B1	Minneapolis Sculpture Garden A2	Target Field A1
City Hall	B1	North Central University B2	TCF Bank Stadium C1
Convention Center	A2	Orchestra Hall A2	University of Minnesota C1, C2
The Depot	B1	Orpheum Theatre A1	Walker Art Center A2
Gaviidae Common	B1	St. Anthony Falls B1	Weisman Art Museum C2
Guthrie Theater	B1	St. Anthony Main B1	Williams Arena C1

Milan IL	88 A2	Milbank SD	27 F2	Milford IL	89 D3
Milan IN	100 A2	Milbridge ME	83 E2	Milford IN	89 F2
Milan MI	90 C1	Miles TX	58 C4	Milford IA	72 A3
Milan MO	87 D4	Milesburg PA	92 C3	Milford KS	43 F2
Milan NM	48 B3	Miles City MT	17 E4	Milford ME	83 D1
Milan OH	91 D2	Milford CT	149 D2	Milford OH	193 B2
Milan TN	108 C4	Milford FL	143 F3	Milford MA	150 C2

Aptos	D1	Del Rey Oaks	E3	Monterey	D3	Salinas	E3
Aromas	E2	Elkhorn	E2	Moss Landing	E2	Sand City	E3
Ben Lomond	D1	Felton	D1	Mt. Hermon	D1	Santa Cruz	D1
Bolsa Knolls	E2	Freedom	E1	Opal Cliffs	D1	Scotts Valley	D1
Capitola	D1	Gabilan Acres	E2	Pacific Grove	D3	Seaside	E3
Carmel-by-the-Sea	D3	Gilroy	E1	Pajaro	E1	Soquel	D1
Carmel Highlands	D3	La Selva Beach	D1	Paradise Park	D1	Spreckels	D1
Carmel Valley	E3	Las Lomas	D1	Pebble Beach	D3	Twin Lakes	D1
Castroville	E1	Live Oak	D1	Prunedale	E2	Watsonville	E1
Corralitos	E2	Marina	E2	Rio del Mar	D1	Zayante	D1

Monterey Bay CA

Miami Beach FL	143 F2	Midlothian IL	203 D6
Miami Co. IN	89 F3	Midlothian TX	59 F3
Miami Co. KS	96 B3	Midlothian VA	113 E1
Miami Co. OH	90 B4	Midtown TN	110 B4
Miami-Dade Co. FL	143 E2	Midvale UT	257 B3
Miami Gardens FL	143 E2	Midway AL	128 B3
Miami Lakes FL	233 A3	Midway DE	145 F4
Miamisburg OH	100 B1	Midway FL	137 E2
Miami Shores FL	143 F2	Midway GA	130 B3
Miami Sprs. FL	143 E2	Midway KY	100 B4
Micanopy FL	138 C4	Midway LA	125 E4
Micaville NC	111 E4	Midway NM	57 E2
Micco FL	141 E2	Midway NC	112 B4
Michie TN	119 D2	Midway PA	91 F4
Michigan ND	19 E2	Midway TN	111 D4
Michigan Ctr. MI	90 B1	Midway UT	31 F1
Michigan City IN	89 E1	Midwest WY	25 D4
Middleboro MA	151 D3	Midwest City OK	51 E3
Middleburg WV	101 F2	Mifflin PA	93 D4
Middleburg FL	139 D3	Mifflinburg PA	93 D3
Middleburg PA	93 D3	Mifflin Co. PA	93 D3
Middleburg VA	144 A3	Mifflintown PA	93 D4
Middleburgh NY	79 F4	Mifflinville PA	93 E3
Middlebury Hts. OH	204 E3	Milaca MN	66 C2
Middlebury CT	149 D1	Milam TX	124 C4
Middlebury IN	89 F2	Milam Co. TX	61 F1
Middlebury VT	81 D3	Milan GA	129 E3
Middle Falls NY	81 D4	
Middlefield CT	149 E1	
Middlefield OH	91 F2	
Middle Haddam CT	149 E1	
Middle Island NY	149 D1	
Middle Pt. OH	90 B3	
Middleport NY	78 B3	
Middleport OH	101 E2	
Middle River MD	144 C4	
Middlesboro KY	110 C3	
Middlesex NJ	147 E1	
Middlesex NC	113 D4	
Middlesex Co. CT	149 E1	
Middlesex Co. MA	151 D1	
Middlesex Co. NJ	147 E2	
Middlesex Co. VA	113 F1	
Middleton ID	22 B4	
Middleton MA	151 E1	
Middleton TN	118 C2	
Middleton WI	74 B3	
Middletown CA	36 A2	
Middletown CT	149 E1	
Middletown DE	145 E1	
Middletown IN	89 F4	
Middletown IA	87 F3	
Middletown KY	100 A4	
Middletown MD	144 A4	
Middletown NY	148 A1	
Middletown OH	100 B1	
Middletown PA	93 D4	
Middletown PA	189 D1	
Middletown RI	151 D4	
Middletown VA	102 C2	
Middle Valley TN	120 B3	
Middleville MI	75 F4	
Middleville NY	79 F3	
Midfield AL	119 F4	
Midland MI	76 B2	
Midland NC	122 B1	
Midland PA	91 F3	
Midland TX	58 A3	
Midland WA	262 A5	
Midland City AL	128 B4	
Midland Co. MI	76 A2	
Midland Co. TX	58 A3	

Missoula MT

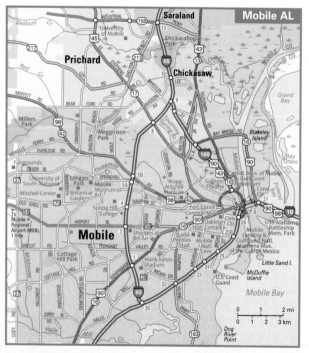

Mobile AL

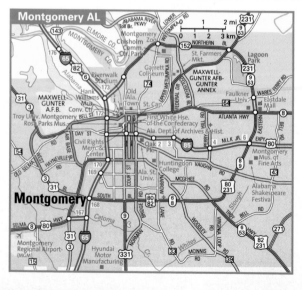

Montgomery AL

Entries in **bold black** indicate counties or parishes.
Entries in **bold color** indicate cities with detailed inset maps.

Milford MI 76 B4
Milford NE 35 F4
Milford NH 95 D1
Milford NJ 146 C1
Milford NY 79 F4
Milford OH 100 B2
Milford PA 94 A3
Milford TX 59 F3
Milford UT 39 D3
Milford Ctr. OH 90 C4
Milford Square PA 146 C1
Mililani Town HI 152 A3
Millard Co. UT 39 D2
Millbourne PA 248 B3
Millbrae CA 259 B4
Millbrook AL 128 A2
Millbrook NY 94 B3
Millburn NJ 240 A3
Millbury MA 150 C2
Millbury OH 90 C2
Mill City NV 29 F4
Mill City OR 20 C3
Mill Creek WA 12 C3
Mill Creek WV 102 A3
Milledgeville GA 129 E1
Milledgeville IL 88 B1
Mille Lacs Co. MN 66 C2
Millen GA 129 F2
Miller MO 106 C2
Miller SD 27 D3
Miller Co. AR 124 C1
Miller Co. GA 128 C4
Miller Co. MO 97 E4
Miller Place NY 149 D3
Millersburg IN 89 F2
Millersburg KY 100 B4
Millersburg OH 91 E4
Millersburg OR 20 B3
Millersburg PA 93 D4
Millers Creek NC 111 F3
Millers Falls MA 94 C1
Millersport OH 101 D1
Millerstown PA 93 D4
Millersville PA 146 A3
Millersville TN 109 F3
Millerton NY 94 B2
Mill Hall PA 93 D3
Milliken CO 33 E4
Millington MI 76 B3
Millington NJ 148 A4
Millington TN 118 B1
Millinocket ME 85 D4
Millis MA 150 C2
Mill Neck NY 148 C3
Millport AL 119 D4
Millry AL 127 D4
Mills WY 33 D1
Millsboro DE 145 F4
Mills Co. IA 86 A3
Mills Co. TX 59 D4
Millstadt IL 98 A3
Millstone KY 111 E2
Milltown IN 99 F4
Milltown NJ 147 E1
Milltown WI 67 E3
Millvale PA 250 B1
Mill Valley CA 36 B4
Millville CA 28 C4
Millville DE 145 F4
Millville NJ 145 F1
Millville OH 100 B2
Millville PA 93 E3
Millville UT 31 E3
Millwood NY 148 B2
Millwood WA 14 A3
Milner GA 129 D1
Milnor ND 27 E1
Milo IA 86 C2
Milo ME 84 C4
Milpitas CA 36 B4
Milroy IN 100 A2
Milroy PA 93 D3
Milton DE 145 F3
Milton FL 135 F1
Milton IN 100 A1
Milton IA 87 E3
Milton KY 100 A3
Milton MA 151 D1
Milton NH 81 F4
Milton NY 148 B1
Milton PA 93 D3
Milton VT 81 D1
Milton WA 262 B5
Milton WV 101 E3
Milton WI 74 B4
Milton-Freewater OR 21 F1
Miltonvale KS 43 E2
Milwaukee WI 74 C3
Milwaukee Co. WI 75 D3
Milwaukie OR 251 D2
Mimosa Park LA 239 A2
Mims FL 141 E1
Mina NV 37 F3
Minatare NE 33 F2
Minco OK 51 E3
Minden IA 86 A2
Minden LA 125 D2
Minden NE 35 D4
Minden NV 37 D2
Mineola NY 148 C4
Mineola TX 124 A2
Miner MO 108 B2
Mineral VA 103 D4
Mineral City OH 91 E4
Mineral Co. CO 40 C4
Mineral Co. MT 14 C3
Mineral Co. NV 37 E3
Mineral Co. WV 102 C2
Mineral Pt. WI 74 A3
Mineral Ridge OH 276 B2
Mineral Sprs. AR 116 C4
Mineral Sprs. NC 122 B2
Mineral Wells TX 59 E2
Mineral Wells WV 101 E2
Miner Co. SD 27 E3
Minersville PA 93 E3
Minersville UT 39 D3
Minerva OH 91 F3
Minerva Park OH 206 B1
Minetto NY 79 D2
Mineville NY 81 D2
Mingo Co. WV 101 E4
Mingo Jct. OH 91 F4
Minidoka Co. ID 31 D1
Minier IL 88 B4
Minneapolis KS 43 E2
Minneapolis MN 67 D4
Minnehaha Co. SD 27 F4
Minneola FL 140 C1
Minneola KS 42 C4
Minneota MN 27 F3
Minnesota Lake MN 72 C2
Minnetonka MN 235 A3
Minnewaukan ND 19 D2
Minoa NY 79 E3
Minocqua WI 68 B2
Minong WI 67 E2
Minonk IL 88 B3
Minooka IL 88 C2
Minor Hill TN 119 E2
Minot ME 82 B3
Minot MA 151 E2
Minot ND 18 B2
Minster OH 90 B4
Mint Hill NC 122 B1
Minto ND 19 E2
Minturn CO 41 D1
Mio MI 70 C4
Miramar FL 143 E2
Miramar Beach FL 136 B2
Misenheimer NC 122 B1
Mishawaka IN 89 F2
Mishicot WI 75 D1
Missaukee Co. MI 75 F1
Mission KS 224 B3
Mission OR 21 F1
Mission SD 26 C4
Mission TX 63 E4
Mission Bend TX 220 A3
Mission Hills KS 224 B4
Mission Viejo CA 52 C3
Mississippi Co. AR 108 B4
Mississippi Co. MO 108 C2
Mississippi State MS 119 D4
Missoula MT 15 D4
Missoula Co. MT 15 D4
Missouri City TX 132 A3
Missouri Valley IA 86 A2
Mitchell IN 99 F3
Mitchell NE 33 F2
Mitchell SD 27 E4
Mitchell Co. GA 137 E1
Mitchell Co. IA 73 D2
Mitchell Co. KS 43 E2
Mitchell Co. NC 111 E4
Mitchell Co. TX 58 B3
Mitchellville AR 117 F4
Mitchellville IA 87 D2
Mi-Wuk Vil. CA 37 D3
Moab UT 40 A3
Moapa NV 46 B1
Moberly MO 97 E2
Mobile AL 135 E1
Mobile Co. AL 135 E1
Mobridge SD 26 C2
Mocksville NC 112 A4
Moclips WA 12 B3
Modena NY 148 B1
Modena PA 146 B3
Modesto CA 36 C4
Modoc Co. CA 29 D3
Moenkopi AZ 47 E2
Moffat Co. CO 32 B4
Mogadore OH 188 B2
Mohall ND 18 B1
Mohave Co. AZ 46 B3
Mohave Valley AZ 46 B3
Mohawk MI 65 F3
Mohawk NY 79 F3
Mohegan CT 149 F1
Mohnton PA 146 A2
Mohrsville PA 146 A1
Mojave CA 52 C1
Mokelumne Hill CA 36 C3
Mokuleia HI 152 A2
Molalla OR 20 C2
Molena GA 128 C1
Moline IL 88 A2
Moline KS 43 F4
Moline Acres MO 256 C1
Molino FL 135 F1
Momence IL 89 D2
Mona UT 39 E1
Monaca PA 91 F3
Monahans TX 57 F4
Monarch Mill SC 121 F2
Moncks Corner SC 131 D1
Mondovi WI 67 E4
Monee IL 89 D2
Monessen PA 92 A4
Monett MO 106 C2
Monette AR 108 A4
Monfort Hts. OH 204 A2
Moniteau Co. MO 97 D3
Monmouth IL 88 A3
Monmouth ME 82 B2
Monmouth OR 20 B2
Monmouth Beach NJ 147 F2
Monmouth Co. NJ 147 E2
Monmouth Jct. NJ 147 D1
Mono Co. CA 37 E4
Monon IN 89 E3
Monona IA 73 F3
Monona WI 74 B3
Monona Co. IA 86 A1
Monongah WV 102 A2
Monongahela PA 92 A4
Monongalia Co. WV 102 A1
Monponsett MA 151 E2
Monroe CT 149 D2
Monroe GA 121 D4
Monroe IN 90 A3
Monroe IA 87 D2
Monroe LA 125 E2
Monroe MI 90 C1
Monroe NY 148 B2
Monroe NC 122 B2
Monroe OH 100 B2
Monroe OR 20 B3
Monroe UT 39 E3
Monroe VA 112 C1
Monroe WA 12 C3
Monroe WI 74 B4
Monroe City IN 99 E3
Monroe City MO 97 E1
Monroe Co. AL 127 F4
Monroe Co. AR 118 A2
Monroe Co. FL 143 D3
Monroe Co. GA 129 D1
Monroe Co. IL 98 A4
Monroe Co. IN 99 F2
Monroe Co. IA 87 D3
Monroe Co. KY 110 A2
Monroe Co. MI 90 C1
Monroe Co. MS 119 D4
Monroe Co. MO 97 E2
Monroe Co. NY 78 C3
Monroe Co. OH 101 F1
Monroe Co. PA 93 F3
Monroe Co. TN 120 C1
Monroe Co. WV 112 A1
Monroe Co. WI 73 F1
Monroeville AL 127 F4
Monroeville IN 90 A3
Monroeville OH 91 D2
Monroeville PA 92 A4
Monrovia CA 228 E2
Monrovia IN 99 F1
Monsey NY 148 B2
Monson MA 150 A2
Montague CA 28 C3
Montague MA 94 C1
Montague MI 75 E2
Montague TX 59 E1
Montague Co. TX 59 E1
Mont Alto PA 103 D1
Montana City MT 15 E4
Montara CA 259 A4
Montauk NY 149 F3
Mont Belvieu TX 132 B3
Montcalm WV 111 F1
Montcalm Co. MI 75 F2
Montclair CA 229 G2
Montclair NJ 148 A3
Mont Clare PA 146 B2
Monteagle TN 120 A1
Monte Alto TX 63 E4
Montebello CA 228 D3
Montecito CA 52 B2
Montegut LA 134 B4
Montello WI 74 B2
Monterey CA 44 B3
Monterey TN 110 B4
Monterey VA 102 B3
Monterey Co. CA 44 B3
Monterey Park CA 228 D2
Monte Rio CA 36 A3
Montesano WA 12 B4
Montevallo AL 127 F1
Montevideo MN 66 A4
Monte Vista CO 41 D4
Montezuma GA 129 D3

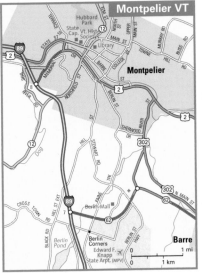

Atlantic Beach... B1
Briarcliffe Acres. B2
Brooksville...... A1
Cherry Grove Beach B1
Conway......... A3
Forestbrook A3
Myrtle Beach.... B2
Nixonville A2
N. Myrtle Beach . B1
Socastee........ A3
Springmaid Beach B3
Surfside Beach .. B3
Wampee......... A1

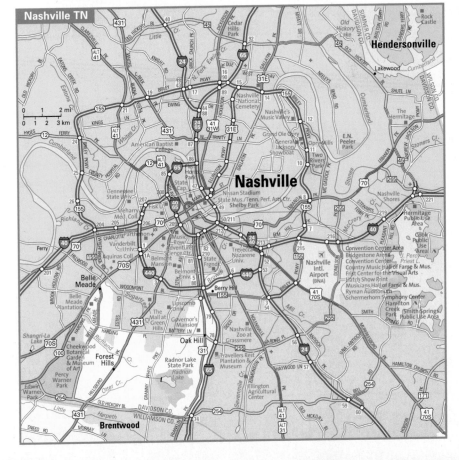

Figures after entries indicate page number and grid reference.

Montezuma IN ... 99 E1
Montezuma IA ... 87 D2
Montezuma KS ... 42 C4
Montezuma Co. CO ... 48 A1
Montezuma Creek UT ... 40 A4
Montfort WI ... 74 A3
Montgomery AL ... 128 A2
Montgomery IL ... 203 A5
Montgomery LA ... 125 D4
Montgomery MN ... 72 C1
Montgomery NY ... 148 A1
Montgomery OH ... 204 C1
Montgomery PA ... 93 D2
Montgomery WV ... 101 F4
Montgomery City MO ... 97 F2
Montgomery Co. AL ... 128 A3
Montgomery Co. AR ... 116 C3
Montgomery Co. GA ... 129 F3
Montgomery Co. IL ... 98 B2
Montgomery Co. IN ... 89 E4
Montgomery Co. IA ... 86 B3
Montgomery Co. KS ... 106 A1
Montgomery Co. KY ... 100 C4
Montgomery Co. MD ... 144 B2
Montgomery Co. MS ... 118 B4
Montgomery Co. MO ... 97 F2
Montgomery Co. NY ... 94 A1
Montgomery Co. NC ... 122 C1
Montgomery Co. OH ... 100 B1
Montgomery Co. PA ... 146 B2
Montgomery Co. TN ... 109 E3
Montgomery Co. TX ... 132 A2
Montgomery Co. VA ... 112 A2
Montgomery Vil. MD ... 144 B2
Montgomeryville PA ... 146 C2
Monticello AR ... 117 F4
Monticello FL ... 137 E2
Monticello GA ... 129 D1
Monticello IL ... 98 C1
Monticello IN ... 89 E3
Monticello IA ... 87 F1
Monticello KY ... 110 B2
Monticello MN ... 66 C3
Monticello MS ... 126 B4
Monticello MO ... 87 E4
Monticello NY ... 148 A1
Monticello UT ... 40 A4
Monticello WI ... 74 B4
Montmorency Co. MI ... 70 C4
Montour Co. PA ... 93 E3
Montour Falls NY ... 79 D4
Montoursville PA ... 93 D2
Montpelier ID ... 31 F2
Montpelier IN ... 90 A4
Montpelier OH ... 90 B2
Montpelier VT ... 81 E2
Montreal WI ... 65 E4
Montreat NC ... 111 E4
Montrose AR ... 125 F1
Montrose CA ... 228 D1
Montrose CO ... 40 B3
Montrose IA ... 87 F4
Montrose MI ... 76 B3
Montrose MN ... 66 C3
Montrose NY ... 148 B2
Montrose OH ... 188 A1
Montrose PA ... 93 E1
Montrose SD ... 27 F4
Montrose Co. CO ... 40 B3
Montross VA ... 103 E4
Montvale NJ ... 148 B3
Montverde FL ... 140 C1
Mont Vernon NH ... 95 D1
Montville NJ ... 148 A3
Montz LA ... 239 A1
Monument CO ... 41 E2
Monument Beach MA ... 151 E3
Moodus CT ... 149 E1
Moody AL ... 119 F4
Moody ME ... 82 B4
Moody TX ... 59 E4
Moody Co. SD ... 27 F3
Moonachie NJ ... 240 C2
Moorcroft WY ... 25 E3
Moore ID ... 23 D4
Moore MT ... 16 B4
Moore OK ... 51 E3
Moore TX ... 61 D3
Moore Co. NC ... 122 C1
Moore Co. TN ... 120 A1
Moore Co. TX ... 50 A2
Moorefield WV ... 102 C2
Moore Haven FL ... 141 D4
Mooreland OK ... 51 D1
Moores Hill IN ... 100 A2
Moorestown NJ ... 147 D3
Mooresville IN ... 99 F1
Mooresville NC ... 122 B1
Moorhead MN ... 19 F4
Moorhead MS ... 118 A4
Mooringsport LA ... 124 C2
Moorland KY ... 230 F1
Moorpark CA ... 52 B2
Moose Lake MN ... 64 C4
Moosic PA ... 261 D2
Moosup CT ... 150 B3
Mora MN ... 67 D2
Mora NM ... 49 D2
Mora Co. NM ... 49 D2
Morada CA ... 36 C3
Moraga CA ... 259 D2
Moraine OH ... 100 B1
Moran KS ... 96 A4
Moravia IA ... 87 D3
Moravia NY ... 79 D4
Moravian Falls NC ... 111 F4
Moreauville LA ... 133 F1
Morehead KY ... 100 C4
Morehead City NC ... 115 E4
Morehouse MO ... 108 B2
Morehouse Par. LA ... 125 F1
Moreland KY ... 110 B1
Moreland Hills OH ... 204 G2
Morenci AZ ... 55 E2
Morenci MI ... 90 B1
Moreno Valley CA ... 53 D3
Morgan GA ... 128 C4
Morgan MN ... 72 B1
Morgan UT ... 31 F3
Morgan City LA ... 134 A3
Morgan Co. AL ... 119 F3
Morgan Co. CO ... 33 F4
Morgan Co. GA ... 121 D4
Morgan Co. IL ... 98 A1
Morgan Co. IN ... 99 F2
Morgan Co. KY ... 100 C4
Morgan Co. MO ... 97 D3
Morgan Co. OH ... 101 E1
Morgan Co. TN ... 110 B3
Morgan Co. UT ... 31 F3
Morgan Co. WV ... 102 C1
Morganfield KY ... 109 D1
Morgan Hill CA ... 44 B2
Morgan's Pt. Resort TX ... 59 E4
Morganton NC ... 111 F4
Morgantown IN ... 99 F2
Morgantown KY ... 109 F2
Morgantown PA ... 146 B2
Morgantown WV ... 102 A1
Morganville NJ ... 147 E1
Morganza LA ... 133 F1
Moriarty NM ... 49 D3
Moriches NY ... 149 D4
Morley MI ... 75 F2
Morley MO ... 108 B2
Morningdale MA ... 275 D1
Morningside MD ... 271 F4
Morning Sun IA ... 87 F3
Moro OR ... 21 D2
Morocco IN ... 89 D3
Morongo Valley CA ... 53 D2
Moroni UT ... 39 E1
Morrice MI ... 76 B3
Morrill NE ... 33 F2
Morrill Co. NE ... 34 A2
Morrilton AR ... 117 E1
Morris AL ... 119 F4
Morris IL ... 88 C2
Morris MN ... 27 F1
Morris NY ... 79 E4
Morris OK ... 116 A1
Morris Co. KS ... 43 F3
Morris Co. NJ ... 94 A4
Morris Co. TX ... 124 B1
Morrison CO ... 209 A4
Morrison IL ... 88 A1
Morrison OK ... 51 F2
Morrison TN ... 120 A1
Morrison Co. MN ... 66 C2
Morrisonville IL ... 98 B2
Morrisonville NY ... 81 D1
Morris Plains NJ ... 148 A3
Morristown IN ... 100 A1
Morristown MN ... 72 C1
Morristown NJ ... 148 A4
Morristown TN ... 111 D3

New Bedford/Fall River MA

Acushnet ... C1
Bliss Corner ... C2
Braleys ... C1
Coury Hts. ... C1
Eagleville ... A2
Fairhaven ... C2
Fall River ... B1
Faunce Corner ... C1
Head of Westport ... B2
Hixville ... B1
Idlewood ... C2
Island Park ... A2
Lakeside ... B2
Long Plain ... C1
New Bedford ... C2
N. Dartmouth ... C2
N. Fairhaven ... C2
N. Tiverton ... A2
Ocean Grove ... A1
Sherwood Forest ... C1
Somerset ... A1
S. Dartmouth ... C2
S. Swansea ... A1
Summit Grove ... B2
Swansea ... A1
The Hummocks ... A2
Tiverton ... A2
Westport Factory ... B2

New Haven/Bridgeport CT

Ansonia ... F1
Aspetuck ... D1
Augerville ... H1
Branford ... H2
Bridgeport ... E2
Derby ... F1
E. Haven ... H2
Easton ... D1
Fairfield ... D2
Foxon ... H2
Greenfield Hill ... D2
Hamden ... H1
Long Hill ... E1
Lordship ... E2
Milford ... F2
Montowese ... H1
New Haven ... G2
Nichols ... E1
N. Haven ... H1
Orange ... F2
Oronoque ... F1
Shelton ... F1
Short Beach ... H2
Southport ... D2
Spring Glen ... H1
Stratfield ... D1
Stratford ... E2
Totoket ... H2
Trumbull ... E1
W. Haven ... G2
Whitneyville ... H1
Woodbridge ... G1

Entries in **bold black** indicate counties or parishes.
Entries in **bold color** indicate cities with detailed inset maps.

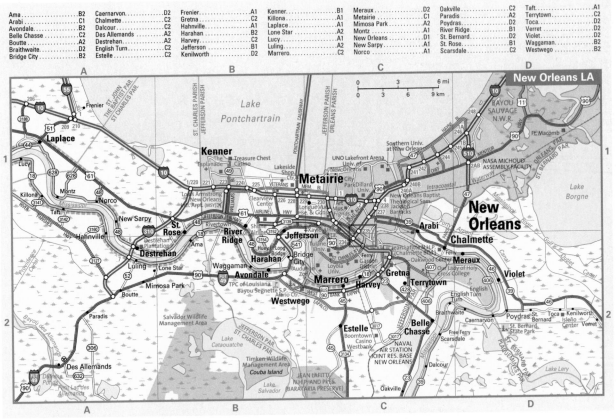

Ama	B2	Caernarvon	D2	Frenier	A1	Kenner	B1
Arabi	C1	Chalmette	C2	Gretna	C2	Killona	A1
Avondale	B2	Dalcour	C2	Hahnville	A2	Laplace	A1
Belle Chasse	C2	Des Allemands	A2	Harahan	B2	Lone Star	A2
Boutte	A2	Destrehan	A2	Harvey	C2	Lucy	A1
Braithwaite	D2	English Turn	C2	Jefferson	B1	Luling	A2
Bridge City	B2	Estelle	C2	Kenilworth	C2	Marrero	C2

Meraux	D2	Oakville	C2	Taft	A1
Metairie	C1	Paradis	A2	Terrytown	C2
Mimosa Park	A2	Poydras	D2	Toca	D2
Montz	A1	River Ridge	B1	Verret	D2
New Orleans	D1	St. Bernard	D2	Violet	D2
New Sarpy	A1	St. Rose	B1	Waggaman	B2
Norco	A1	Scarsdale	C2	Westwego	B2

New Orleans LA

Downtown New Orleans LA

POINTS OF INTEREST
Audubon Aquarium of the Americas	F2
Audubon Insectarium	F1
The Cabildo	E2
Ceasars Superdome	F2
Contemporary Arts Center	F2
Creole Queen	F2
Ernest N. Morial Convention Center	F1
French Quarter (Vieux Carré)	F1
Harrah's	F1
Jackson Square	F1
Jean Lafitte Natl. Hist. Park (Visitor Center)	F1
Louisiana's Civil War Museum at Confederate Memorial Hall	F2
M. Jackson Theatre for the Performing Arts	F1

National World War II Museum	F2
New Orleans Jazz N.H.P. Visitor Center	F1
Ogden Museum	F2
Old U.S. Mint	F2
One Canal Place	F2
Orpheum Theatre	F1
Pontalba Buildings	F2
The Presbytère	F2
Public Library	F2
Saenger Theatre	F1
St. Charles Avenue Streetcar	F1
St. Louis Cathedral	F2
Smoothie King Center	E2
Woldenberg Riverfront Park	F2

Morrisville NY	79 E3	Morse LA	133 E2	Morven NC	122 B2
Morrisville NC	112 C4	Morton IL	88 B3	Moscow ID	14 B4
Morrisville PA	102 A1	Morton MS	126 C2	Moscow ME	82 B1
Morrisville PA	147 D2	Morton PA	248 B4	Moscow PA	93 F2
Morrisville VT	81 E2	Morton TX	57 F1	Moscow TN	118 C2
Morrisville VA	144 A4	Morton WA	12 C4	Moscow Mills MO	97 F2
Morro Bay CA	44 B4	Moses Lake WA	13 E3	Moscow OK	51 D3
Morrow GA	120 C4	**Morton Co. KS**	42 A4	Mosheim TN	111 D3
Morrow OH	100 C2	**Morton Co. ND**	18 B4	Mosier OR	21 D1
Morrow Co. OH	91 D4	Mortons Grove IL	203 D3	Mosinee WI	68 B4
Morrow Co. OR	21 E2	Mortons Gap KY	109 E2	Mosquero NM	49 E2
		Morven GA	137 F1		

Moss Beach CA	259 A5	Mt. Airy NC	112 A3	Mt. Healthy OH	204 A1
Moss Bluff LA	133 D2	Mt. Angel OR	20 C2	Mt. Holly NJ	147 D3
Mosses AL	127 F3	Mt. Arlington NJ	148 A3	Mt. Holly NC	122 A1
Moss Pt. MS	135 D2	Mt. Ayr IA	86 C3	Mt. Holly Sprs. PA	93 D4
Mossville IL	88 B3	Mt. Bethel NJ	147 D1	Mt. Hope KS	43 E4
Mossyrock WA	12 C4	Mt. Calvary WI	74 C2	Mt. Hope WV	101 F4
Motley MN	64 A4	Mt. Carmel IL	99 D3	Mt. Horeb WI	74 A3
Motley Co. TX	50 B4	Mt. Carmel OH	204 C2	Mt. Ida AR	116 C2
Mott ND	18 A4	Mt. Carmel PA	93 E3	Mt. Ivy NY	148 B2
Moulton AL	119 E3	Mt. Carmel TN	111 E3	Mt. Jackson VA	92 B1
Moulton IA	87 D3	Mt. Carroll IL	88 A1	Mt. Jewett PA	92 C3
Moulton TX	61 E2	Mt. Clemens MI	76 C4	Mt. Joy PA	93 E4
Moultrie GA	137 E1	Mt. Cobb PA	93 F2	Mt. Juliet TN	109 F3
Moultrie Co. IL	98 C1	Mt. Crested Butte CO	40 C2	Mt. Kisco NY	148 B2
Mound MN	66 C4	Mt. Dora FL	141 D1	Mountlake Terrace WA	262 B2
Mound Bayou MS	118 A4	Mt. Enterprise TX	124 B3	Mt. Lebanon PA	92 A4
Mound City IL	108 C2	Mt. Ephraim NJ	248 C4	Mt. Morris IL	88 B1
Mound City KS	96 B4	Mt. Freedom NJ	148 A3	Mt. Morris MI	76 B3
Mound City MO	86 A4	Mt. Gay WV	101 E4	Mt. Morris NY	78 C4
Mound City SD	26 C1	Mt. Gilead NC	122 B1	Mt. Nebo PA	146 A3
Moundridge KS	43 E3	Mt. Gilead OH	91 D4	Mt. Olive AL	119 F4
Mounds IL	108 C2				
Mounds OK	51 F2				
Mounds View MN	235 C1				
Moundsville WV	101 F1				
Mound Valley KS	106 A3				
Moundville AL	127 E1				
Mt. Aetna MD	144 A1				
Mountainair NM	48 C4				
Mountainaire AZ	47 E3				
Mtn. Brook AL	119 F4				
Mountainburg AR	116 C1				
Mtn. City GA	121 D2				
Mtn. City TN	111 F3				
Mtn. City TX	61 E2				
Mtn. Grove MO	107 E2				
Mtn. Home AR	107 E3				
Mtn. Home ID	30 B1				
Mtn. Home PA	121 E1				
Mountainhome PA	93 F2				
Mtn. Iron MN	64 C3				
Mtn. Lake MN	72 B1				
Mtn. Lake Park MD	102 B2				
Mtn. Lakes NJ	148 A3				
Mtn. Pine AR	117 D2				
Mtn. Ranch CA	36 C3				
Mountainside NJ	148 A4				
Mtn. Top PA	93 E2				
Mtn. View AR	107 E4				
Mtn. View CA	259 D5				
Mtn. View CO	209 B3				
Mtn. View HI	153 F3				
Mtn. View MO	107 F2				
Mtn. View OK	51 D3				
Mtn. View WY	32 A3				
Mtn. Vil. AK	154 B2				
Mtn. Vil. CO	40 C2				
Mt. Airy GA	121 D2				
Mt. Airy MD	144 B1				

Mt. Olive IL	98 B2
Mt. Olive MS	126 C3
Mt. Olive NC	123 E1
Mt. Oliver PA	250 B2
Mt. Olivet KY	100 C3
Mt. Orab OH	100 C2
Mt. Pleasant AR	107 F4
Mt. Pleasant IA	87 F3
Mt. Pleasant MI	76 A2
Mt. Pleasant NC	122 B1
Mt. Pleasant PA	92 A4
Mt. Pleasant SC	131 D2
Mt. Pleasant TN	119 E1
Mt. Pleasant TX	124 B3
Mt. Pleasant UT	39 E1
Mt. Pleasant WI	75 D4
Mt. Plymouth FL	141 D1
Mt. Pocono PA	93 F2
Mt. Prospect IL	203 C3
Mt. Pulaski IL	98 B1
Mountrail Co. ND	18 A2
Mt. Rainier MD	270 C2
Mt. Royal NJ	146 C3
Mt. Savage MD	102 C2
Mt. Shasta CA	28 C3
Mt. Sidney VA	102 C4
Mt. Sinai NY	149 D3
Mt. Sterling IL	98 A1
Mt. Sterling KY	100 C4
Mt. Sterling OH	101 D1
Mt. Union PA	92 C4
Mt. Vernon AL	135 E1
Mt. Vernon GA	129 F3
Mt. Vernon IL	98 C4
Mt. Vernon IN	99 D4
Mt. Vernon IA	87 F1
Mt. Vernon KY	110 C1
Mt. Vernon MD	103 F4
Mt. Vernon MO	106 C2
Mt. Vernon NY	78 A4
Mt. Vernon NY	148 B3
Mt. Vernon OH	91 D4
Mt. Vernon OR	21 E3
Mt. Vernon SD	27 E3
Mt. Vernon TX	124 B1
Mt. Vernon VA	144 B4
Mt. Vernon WA	12 C2
Mt. Victory OH	90 C4
Mt. View RI	150 C4
Mountville PA	103 E1
Mt. Washington KY	100 A1
Mt. Wolf PA	93 E4
Mt. Zion GA	120 B4
Mt. Zion IL	98 C1
Moville IA	35 F1
Moweaqua IL	98 C1
Mower Co. MN	73 D2
Moxee WA	13 D4
Moyie Sprs. ID	14 B1
Mud Lake ID	23 E4
Muenster TX	59 E1
Muhlenberg Co. KY	109 E2
Muir MI	76 A3
Muir PA	93 E4
Mukilteo WA	12 C2
Mukwonago WI	74 C3
Mulberry AR	116 C1
Mulberry FL	140 C2
Mulberry IN	89 E4
Mulberry KS	106 B3
Mulberry NC	111 F3
Mulberry OH	100 B3
Mulberry Grove IL	98 B3
Muldraugh KY	99 F4
Muldrow OK	116 B1

Newport RI

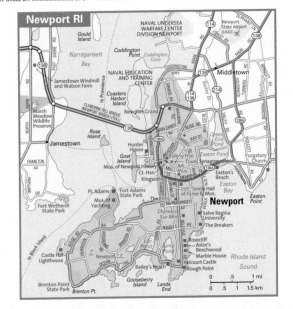

Newport

Figures after entries indicate page number and grid reference.

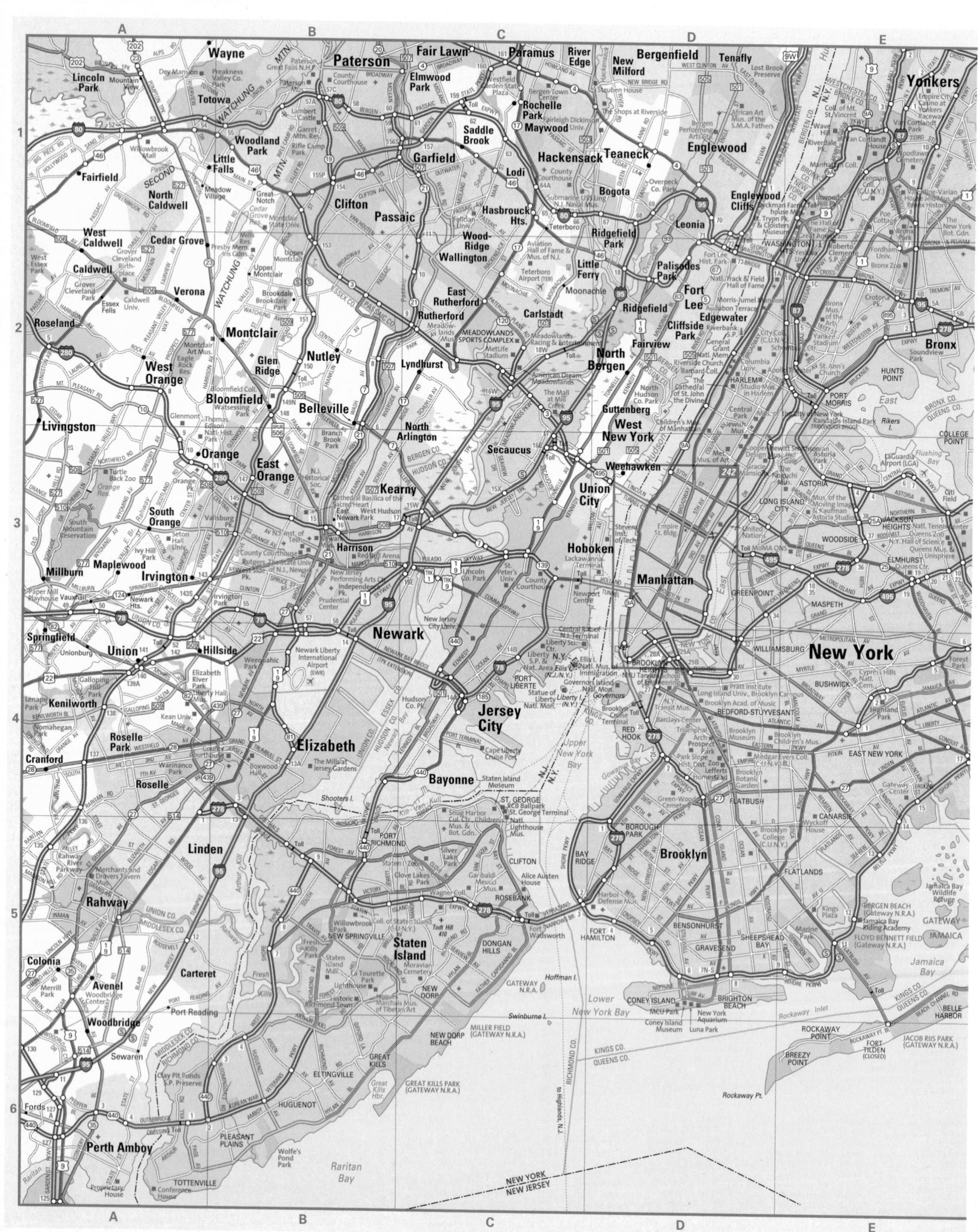

Entries in **bold black** indicate counties or parishes.
Entries in **bold color** indicate cities with detailed inset maps.

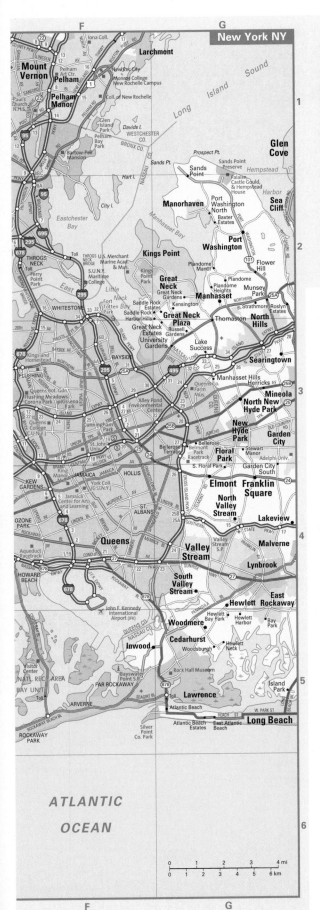

Atlantic Beach G5
Atlantic Beach Estates . . G5
Avenel A5
Baxter Estates G2
Bayonne C4
Bay Park G5
Bellerose G3
Bellerose Terrace G3
Belleville B2
Bergenfield D1
Bloomfield B2
Bogota D1
Brookdale B2
Caldwell A2
Carlstadt C2
Carteret A5
Cedar Grove A2
Cedarhurst G5
Cliffside Park D2
Clifton B1
Colonia A5
Cranford A4
E. Atlantic Beach G5
E. Newark B3
E. Orange B3
E. Rockaway G4
E. Rutherford C2
Edgewater D2
Elizabeth B4
Elmont G4
Elmwood Park C1
Englewood D1
Englewood Cliffs D1
Essex Fells A2
Fairfield A1
Fair Lawn C1
Fairview D2
Floral Park G3
Flower Hill G2
Fords A6
Ft. Lee D2
Franklin Square G4
Garden City G3
Garden City South G4
Garfield C1
Glen Cove G1
Glen Ridge B2
Great Neck G2
Great Neck Estates G3
Great Neck Gardens G2
Great Neck Plaza G2
Great Notch B1
Guttenberg D2
Hackensack C1
Harbor Hills G2
Harrison B3
Hasbrouck Hts. C1
Herricks G3
Hewlett G4
Hewlett Bay Park G5
Hewlett Harbor G5
Hewlett Neck G5
Hillside A4
Hoboken C3
Inwood F5
Irvington A3
Island Park G5
Jersey City C4
Kearny B3
Kenilworth A4
Kensington G2
Kings Pt. G2
Lake Success G3
Lakeview G4
Larchmont F1
Lawrence G5
Leonia D1
Lincoln Park A1
Linden A5
Little Falls A1
Little Ferry C2
Livingston A2
Lodi C1
Long Beach G5
Lynbrook G4
Lyndhurst C2
Malverne G4
Manhasset G2
Manhasset Hills G3
Manorhaven G2
Maplewood A3
Maywood C1
Meadow Vil. A1
Millburn A3
Mineola G3
Montclair B2
Moonachie C2
Mtn. View A1
Mt. Vernon F1
Munsey Park G2
Newark B4
Newark Hts. A3
New Hyde Park G3
New Milford D1
New York E4
N. Arlington C2
N. Bergen D2
N. Caldwell A1
N. Hills G3
N. New Hyde Park G3
N. Valley Stream G4
Nutley B2
Orange A3
Palisades Park D2
Paramus C1
Passaic B1
Paterson B1
Pelham F1
Pelham Manor F1
Perth Amboy A6
Plandome G2
Plandome Hts. G2
Plandome Manor G2
Port Reading A5
Port Washington G2
Port Washington North . . G2
Rahway A5
Ridgefield D2
Ridgefield Park D1
River Edge C1
Rochelle Park C1
Roseland A2
Roselle A4
Roselle Park A4
Roslyn Estates G2
Russell Gardens G3
Rutherford C2
Saddle Brook C1
Saddle Rock G2
Saddle Rock Estates G2
Sands Pt. G2
Sea Cliff G2
Searingtown G3
Secaucus C3
Sewaren A6
S. Floral Park G4
S. Orange A3
S. Valley Stream G4
Springfield A4
Stewart Manor G3
Strathmore G2
Teaneck D1
Tenafly D1
Teterboro C1
Thomaston G3
Totowa A1
Union A4
Unionburg A4
Union City C3
University Gardens G3
Upper Montclair B2
Valley Stream G4
Vauxhall A3
Verona A2
Wallington C2
Wayne A1
Weehawken D3
W. Caldwell A2
W. New York D2
W. Orange A2
Woodbridge A6
Woodland Park B1
Woodmere G5
Wood-Ridge C2
Woodsburgh G5
Yonkers E1

Muleshoe TX 49 F4
Mulga AL 195 D1
Mullan ID 14 C3
Mullen NE 34 B2
Mullens WV 111 F1
Mullica Hill NJ 146 C4
Mulliken MI 76 A4
Mullins SC 122 C3
Multnomah Co. OR 20 C2
Mulvane KS 43 E4
Muncie IN 90 A4
Muncy PA 93 D2
Munday TX 58 C1
Mundelein IL 74 C4
Munds Park AZ 47 E3
Munford AL 120 A4
Munford TN 118 B1
Munfordville KY 110 A2
Munhall PA 250 C3
Munich ND 19 D1
Munising MI 69 E1
Munroe Falls OH 188 B1
Munsey Park NY 241 G2
Munsons Corners NY 79 D4
Munster IN 89 D2
Murchison TX 124 A3
Murdo SD 26 C4
Murfreesboro AR 116 C3
Murfreesboro NC 113 E3
Murfreesboro TN 109 F4
Murphy ID 30 B1
Murphy MO 98 A3
Murphy NC 120 C2
Murphy TX 207 E1
Murphys CA 37 D3
Murphysboro IL 108 C1
Murray IA 86 C3
Murray KY 109 D3
Murray NE 86 A3
Murray UT 31 E4
Murray Co. GA 120 C2
Murray Co. MN 72 A1
Murray Co. OK 51 F4
Murray Hill KY 230 F1
Murrayville IL 98 A1
Murrells Inlet SC 123 D4
Murrieta CA 53 D3
Murrieta Hot Sprs. CA 229 K6
Murrysville PA 92 A4
Muscatine IA 87 F2
Muscatine Co. IA 87 F2
Muscle Shoals AL 119 E2
Muscoda WI 74 A3
Muscogee Co. GA 128 C2
Muscoy CA 229 J2
Muskego WI 74 C3
Muskegon MI 75 E3
Muskegon Co. MI 75 F3
Muskegon Hts. MI 75 E3
Muskingum Co. OH 91 E4
Muskogee OK 106 A4
Muskogee Co. OK 106 A4
Musselshell Co. MT 16 C4
Mustang OK 51 E3
Mustang Ridge TX 61 E2
Muttontown NY 148 C3
Myers Corner NY 148 B1
Myerstown PA 146 A1
Myersville MD 144 A1
Myricks MA 151 D3
Myrtle MS 118 C2
Myrtle Beach SC 123 D4
Myrtle Creek OR 28 B1
Myrtle Grove FL 135 F2
Myrtle Grove NC 123 E3
Myrtle Pt. OR 28 A1
Mystic CT 149 F2
Mystic IA 87 D3
Mystic Island NJ 147 E4
Myton UT 32 A4

N

Naalehu HI 153 E4
Naches WA 13 D4
Naco AZ 55 E4
Nacogdoches TX 124 B4
Nacogdoches Co. TX 124 B4
Nageezi NM 48 B2
Nags Head NC 115 F2
Nahant MA 151 D1
Nahunta GA 129 F4
Nain VA 102 C2
Naknek AK 154 B3
Nambe NM 49 D2
Nameloc Hts. MA 151 E3
Nampa ID 22 B4
Nanakuli HI 152 A3
Nance Co. NE 35 E3
Nanticoke PA 93 E2
Nantucket MA 151 F4
Nantucket Co. MA 151 F4
Nanty Glo PA 92 B4
Nanuet NY 148 B3
Napa CA 36 B3
Napa Co. CA 36 B2
Napanoch NY 94 A3
Napaskiak AK 154 B3
Napavine WA 12 B4
Naperville IL 88 C1
Naples FL 142 C2
Naples NY 78 C4
Naples TX 124 B1
Naples UT 32 A4
Naples Manor FL 142 C2
Naples Park FL 142 C1
Napoleon MI 90 B1
Napoleon ND 18 C4
Napoleon OH 90 B2
Napoleonville LA 134 A3
Nappanee IN 89 F2
Naranja FL 143 E3
Narberth PA 248 B3
Narragansett Pier RI 150 C4
Narrows VA 112 A1
Naschitti NM 48 A2
Nash TX 116 C4
Nash Co. NC 113 D4
Nashotah WI 74 C3
Nashua IA 73 D3
Nashua MT 17 D2
Nashua NH 95 D1
Nashville AR 116 C4
Nashville GA 129 E4
Nashville IL 98 B4
Nashville IN 99 F2
Nashville MI 76 A4
Nashville NC 113 D4
Nashville TN 109 F4
Nashwauk MN 64 B3
Nassau DE 145 F4
Nassau NY 94 B1
Nassau Bay TX 132 B3
Nassau Co. FL 139 D2
Nassau Co. NY 148 C4
Nassau Vil. FL 222 C1
Nassawadox VA 114 B3
Natalbany LA 134 B2
Natalia TX 61 D3
Natchez LA 125 D4
Natchez MS 125 F4
Natchitoches LA 125 D3
Natchitoches Par. LA 125 D4
Natick MA 150 C1
National City CA 258 B2
National Park NJ 146 C3
Natrona Co. WY 33 D1
Natrona Hts. PA 92 A3
Naturita CO 40 B3
Naugatuck CT 149 D1
Nauvoo IL 87 F4
Navajo NM 48 A2
Navajo Co. AZ 47 F3
Navarre OH 91 E3
Navarro Co. TX 59 F3
Navasota TX 61 F1
Navesink NJ 147 F1
Naylor MO 108 A3
Naytahwaush MN 19 F3
Nazareth KY 100 A4
Nazareth PA 93 F3
Nazlini AZ 47 F2
Neah Bay WA 12 A2
Neapolis OH 90 B2
Nebraska City NE 86 A3
Necedah WI 74 A1
Neche ND 19 E1
Nederland CO 41 D1
Nederland TX 132 C3
Nedrow NY 79 D3
Needham MA 151 D1
Needles CA 46 B4
Needville TX 132 A4
Neelyville MO 108 A3
Neenah WI 74 C1
Neffs OH 101 F1
Negaunee MI 65 F4
Neillsville WI 68 A4
Nekoosa WI 74 A1
Neligh NE 35 E2
Nelliston NY 79 F3
Nelson GA 120 C3
Nelson NE 35 E4
Nelson Co. KY 100 A4
Nelson Co. ND 19 E2
Nelson Co. VA 112 C1
Nelsonville NY 148 B1
Nelsonville OH 101 E2
Nemacolin PA 102 A1
Nemaha Co. KS 96 A1
Nemaha Co. NE 86 A4
Nenana AK 154 C2
Neodesha KS 106 A1
Neoga IL 98 C2
Neola IA 86 A2
Neola UT 32 A4
Neopit WI 68 C4
Neosho MO 106 B2
Neosho WI 74 C3
Neosho Co. KS 106 A1
Neotsu OR 20 B2
Nephi UT 39 E1
Neptune NJ 147 F2
Neptune Beach FL 139 D2
Neptune City NJ 147 F2
Nesbit MS 118 B2
Nesconset NY 149 D3
Nescopeck PA 93 E3
Neshoba Co. MS 126 C2
Nesquehoning PA 93 F3
Ness City KS 42 C3
Ness Co. KS 42 C3
Netarts OR 20 B2
Netcong NJ 94 A4
Nettleton MS 119 D3
Nevada IA 86 C1
Nevada MO 106 C1
Nevada OH 90 C3
Nevada City CA 36 C2
Nevada Co. AR 117 D4
Nevada Co. CA 36 C2
New Albany IN 99 F4
New Albany MS 118 C3
New Albin IA 73 F2
New Alexandria PA 92 A4
Newark AR 107 F4
Newark CA 259 D5
Newark DE 146 B4
Newark IL 88 C2
Newark NJ 148 B4
Newark NY 78 C3
Newark OH 91 D4
Newark TX 59 E2
Newark Valley NY 93 E1
New Athens IL 98 B4
New Auburn MN 66 C4
New Auburn WI 67 F3
New Augusta MS 126 C4
Newaygo MI 75 F2
Newaygo Co. MI 75 F2
New Baden IL 98 B3
New Baltimore MI 76 C4
New Baltimore NY 94 B1
New Baltimore VA 144 A3
New Beaver PA 91 F3
New Bedford MA 151 D4
Newberg OR 20 B2
New Berlin IL 98 B1
New Berlin NY 79 E4
New Berlin PA 93 D3
New Berlin WI 74 C3
New Bern NC 115 D3
Newbern TN 108 C4
Newberry FL 138 C3
Newberry MI 69 F1
Newberry SC 121 F3
Newberry Co. SC 121 F3
New Bethlehem PA 92 B3
New Bloomfield MO 97 E3
New Bloomfield PA 93 D4
Newborn GA 121 D4
New Boston IL 87 F2
New Boston NH 81 F4
New Boston OH 101 D3
New Boston TX 116 B4
New Braunfels TX 61 D2
New Bremen OH 90 B4
New Brighton MN 235 C1
New Brighton PA 91 F3
New Britain CT 149 E1
New Britain PA 146 C2
New Brockton AL 128 A4
New Brunswick NJ 147 E1
New Buffalo MI 89 E1
Newburg WV 102 B2
Newburg WI 74 C2
Newburgh IN 99 E4
Newburgh NY 148 B1
Newburgh Hts. OH 204 F2
Newbury VT 81 E2
Newburyport MA 151 F1
New Canaan CT 148 C2
New Carlisle IN 89 E1
New Carlisle OH 100 C1
New Carrollton MD 144 B3
New Castle CO 40 C1
New Castle DE 146 B4
New Castle IN 100 A1
New Castle KY 100 A3
Newcastle ME 82 C3
Newcastle OK 51 E3
New Castle PA 91 F3
Newcastle TX 59 D2
New Castle VA 112 B1
Newcastle WA 262 B3
Newcastle WY 25 F4
New Castle Co. DE 145 E1
New Chapel Hill TX 124 B3
New City NY 148 B2

Figures after entries indicate page number and grid reference.

Newcomb MD	145	D4
Newcomb NM	48	A2
Newcomerstown OH	91	E4
New Concord OH	101	E1
New Cordell OK	51	D3
New Cumberland PA	218	B2
New Cumberland WV	91	F4
Newdale ID	23	F4
New Deal TX	58	A1
New Durham NH	81	F4
New Eagle PA	92	A4
New Effington SD	27	F1
New Egypt NJ	147	D3
Newell IA	72	B4
Newell SD	25	F3
Newell WV	91	F3
New Ellenton SC	121	F4
Newellton LA	126	A3
New England ND	18	A4
New Era MI	75	E2
New Fairfield CT	148	C1
New Fairview TX	59	F4
Newfane NY	78	B3
Newfane VT	81	E4
Newfield NJ	145	F1
Newfield NY	79	D4
Newfields NH	82	A4
New Florence MO	97	F3
New Florence PA	92	B4
New Franklin MO	97	D2
New Franklin OH	91	E3
New Freedom PA	103	E1
New Glarus WI	74	B3
New Gloucester ME	82	B3
New Gretna NJ	147	E4
Newhall IA	87	E1
New Hamburg NY	148	B1
New Hampton IA	73	E3
New Hampton NY	148	A1
New Hanover PA	146	B2
New Hanover Co. NC	123	E3
New Harmony IN	99	D4
New Hartford CT	94	C2
New Hartford IA	73	D4
New Haven CT	149	D2
New Haven IN	90	A3
New Haven KY	110	A1
New Haven MI	76	C4
New Haven MO	97	F3
New Haven WV	101	E2
New Haven Co. CT	149	D1
New Hebron MS	126	B4
New Hempstead NY	148	B2
New Holland OH	101	D1
New Holland PA	146	A2
New Holstein WI	74	C1
New Hope AL	119	F2
New Hope GA	120	B4
New Hope MN	235	B2
New Hope MS	119	D4
New Hope NC	123	E1
New Hope PA	147	D2
New Hope TN	120	A2
New Hope VA	102	C4
New Houlka MS	118	C3
New Hyde Park NY	241	G3
New Iberia LA	133	F3
Newington CT	149	E1
New Ipswich NH	95	D1
New Jerusalem PA	146	B1
New Johnsonville TN	109	D4
New Kensington PA	92	A4
New Kent VA	113	F1
New Kent Co. VA	113	F1
Newkirk OK	51	E1
New Knoxville OH	90	B4
Newland NC	111	F4
New Lebanon OH	100	B1
New Leipzig ND	18	B4
New Lenox IL	89	D2
New Lexington OH	101	E1
New Lisbon WI	74	A2
New Llano LA	133	D1
New London CT	149	F2
New London IA	87	F3
New London MN	66	B3
New London MO	97	F2
New London NH	81	E4
New London OH	91	D3
New London PA	146	B3
New London TX	124	B3
New London WI	74	C1

POINTS OF INTEREST

601 Lexington Avenue	D2
African Burial Ground Natl. Mon.	B5
Algonquin Hotel	C2
Alvin Ailey American Dance Th.	C1
American Folk Art Museum	C1
American Standard Building	C2
Americas Society	D1
Appellate Division of the Supreme Court of New York	C3
Battery Park	A6
Bernard M. Baruch College of the City University of N.Y.	C3
Brookfield Place	A5
Carnegie Hall	C1
Castle Clinton Natl. Monument	A6
Central Park	D1
Central Park Zoo	D1
Chanin Building	D2
Chrysler Building	D2
City Hall	B5
Comcast Building	C2
ConEdison Building	C4
The Cooper Union	C4
Criminal Courts Building	B5
Cunard Building	A6
Daily News Building	D2
David Geffen Hall	C1
David H. Koch Theatre	C1
Empire State Building	C3
Fashion Institute of Technology & Museum	B3
Federal Hall National Memorial	A6
Federal Reserve Bank	A6
Flatiron Building	C3
Fordham University	C1
Foundation Building	C4
Fraunces Tavern	A6
French Building	C2
The Frick Collection	D1
Fuller Building	D1
General Assembly Building	D2
General Electric Building	D2
Grace Church	C4
Grand Central Terminal	D2
High Line Park	B2
Home Savings of America Building	C2
Hotel Chelsea	B3
Hunter College (C.U.N.Y.)	D1
Intrepid Sea, Air & Space Mus.	B1
Irish Hunger Memorial	A5
Italian American Museum	B4
Jacob Javits Convention Center	B2
Japan Society	D2
Jazz at Lincoln Center Frederick P. Rose Hall	C1
Jefferson Market Library	B4
John Jay College (C.U.N.Y.)	C1
Lever House	D2
Lincoln Center	C1
Lower East Side Tenement Mus. Natl. Hist. Site	C5
Lyceum Theatre	C2
Macdougal Alley	B4
Macy's	C2
Madame Tussauds–New York	C2
Madison Square Garden	B2
Manhattan Cruise Terminal	B1
Manhattan Mall	C2
Meatpacking District	A3
Merchant's House Museum	B4
Met Breuer	D1
Met Life Building	D2
Metropolitan Opera House	C1
Morgan Library & Museum	C2
Municipal Building	B5
Museum at Eldridge Street	B5
Museum of American Finance	A6
Museum of Arts & Design	C1
Museum of Chinese in America	B5
Museum of Jewish Heritage	A6
Museum of Modern Art	D2
Museum of Sex	C3
National Geographic Encounter	C2
National Museum of the American Indian	A6
Natl. Sept. 11 Mem. & Mus.	A5
New Mus. of Contemporary Art	B5
New York City Fire Museum	A4
New York Edition Hotel	C3
New York Life Insurance Company Building	C3
New York Mercantile Exchange	A5
The New York Public Library	C2
New York Stock Exchange	A6
New York Univ.	B4
New York Supreme & Co. Court	B5
Old New York Co. Court House	B5
One World Trade Ctr. (Freedom Tower)	A5
Pace University New York City Campus	B5
Paley Center for Media	D2
Paramount Building	C2
Pennsylvania Station	B2
Pier 17 Pavilion	B6
Plaza Hotel	D1
Port Authority Bus Terminal	B2
Public Theater	B4
Radio City Music Hall	C2
Rockefeller Center	C2
Roosevelt Island Aerial Tram	D2
Rubin Museum of Art	B3
St. Patrick's Cathedral	D2
St. Paul's Chapel	A6
Salmagundi Club	B4
Seagram Building	D2
Seaport Museum	B6
Secretariat Building	D2
Sheridan Square	B4
Skyscraper Museum	A6
Society of Illustrators	D1
South Street Seaport	B6
Stonewall National Monument	B4
The Oculus	A5
Theodore Roosevelt Birthplace Natl. Hist. Site	C3
Times Square	C2
Tisch Childrens Zoo	D1
Trinity Church	A6
Trump Tower	D1
Ukrainian Museum	C4
United Nations	D2
U.S. Court House	B5
Villard Houses	D2
Waldorf-Astoria	D2
Washington Arch	B4
Washington Square	B4
Whitney Mus. of American Art	A3
Wollman Rink	D1
Woolworth Building	A5
World Trade Center	A5

Manhattan **New York NY**

Entries in **bold black** indicate counties or parishes.
Entries in **bold color** indicate cities with detailed inset maps.

New London Co. CT 150 B4
New Lothrop MI 76 B3
New Madison OH 100 B1
New Madrid MO 108 B3
New Madrid Co. MO 108 B3
Newman CA 36 C4
Newman IL 99 D1
Newman Grove NE 35 E2
Newmanstown PA 146 A2
New Market AL 119 F2
New Market IN 99 E1
Newmarket NH 82 A4
New Market TN 111 D4
New Market VA 102 C3
New Martinsville WV 101 F1
New Matamoras OH 101 F1
New Meadows ID 22 B2
New Miami OH 100 B2
New Middletown OH 91 F3
New Milford CT 148 C1
New Milford NJ 240 D1
New Milford NY 148 A2
New Milford PA 93 F1
New Millford IL 88 B1
Newnan GA 128 C1
New Orleans LA 134 B3
New Oxford PA 103 E1
New Palestine IN 99 F1
New Paltz NY 94 B3
New Paris IN 89 F2
New Paris OH 100 B1
New Pekin IN 99 F3
New Philadelphia OH 91 E4
New Philadelphia PA 93 E3
New Plymouth ID 22 A4
Newport AR 117 F1
Newport DE 146 B4
Newport IN 99 E1
Newport KY 100 B2
Newport ME 82 C1
Newport MN 235 D3
Newport NH 81 E4
Newport NY 79 F3
Newport NC 115 D4
Newport OH 101 F2
Newport OR 20 B3
Newport PA 93 D4
Newport RI 151 D4
Newport TN 111 D4
Newport VT 81 E1
Newport WA 14 B2
Newport Beach CA 52 C3
Newport Ctr. VT 81 E1
Newport Co. RI 151 D4
Newport News VA 113 F2
New Port Richey FL 140 B2
New Prague MN 66 C4
New Preston CT 148 C1
New Providence NJ 148 A4
New Richland MN 72 C2
New Richmond OH 100 B3
New Richmond WI 67 E3
New River AZ 54 C1
New Roads LA 133 F1
New Rochelle NY 148 B3
New Rockford ND 19 D3
New Salem ND 18 B4
New Salem PA 102 B1
New Salem PA 275 E2
New Sarpy LA 239 A1
New Sharon IA 87 D2
New Site AL 128 B1
New Smyrna Beach FL 139 E4
New Stanton PA 92 A4
New Straitsville OH 101 E1
New Strawn KS 96 A4
New Stuyahok AK 154 B3
New Summerfield TX 124 B3
New Tazewell TN 111 D3
Newton AL 128 B4
Newton GA 128 C4
Newton IL 99 D2
Newton IA 87 D2
Newton KS 43 E3
Newton MA 151 D1
Newton MS 126 C2
Newton NH 95 E1
Newton NJ 94 A4
Newton NC 111 F4
Newton TX 132 C1
Newton UT 31 E2
Newton Co. AR 107 D4
Newton Co. GA 121 D4
Newton Co. IN 89 D3
Newton Co. MS 126 C2
Newton Co. MO 106 C2
Newton Co. TX 133 D1
Newton Falls OH 91 F2
Newton Grove NC 123 D1
Newtonville NJ 147 D4
Newtonville NY 188 E2
Newtown CT 148 C1
New Town ND 18 A2
Newtown OH 204 C2
Newtown PA 147 D2
New Ulm MN 72 B1
New Underwood SD 26 A3
New Vernon NJ 148 A4
New Vienna OH 100 C2
Newville AL 128 B4
Newville PA 93 D4
New Washington IN 100 A3
New Washington OH 91 D3
New Washoe City NV 37 D2
New Waterford OH 91 F3
New Waverly TX 132 A2
New Whiteland IN 99 F1
New Wilmington PA 91 F3
New Windsor IL 88 A2
New Windsor MD 144 B1
New Windsor NY 148 B1
New York NY 148 B4
New York Co. NY 148 B4
New York Mills MN 64 A4
Nezperce ID 22 B1
Nez Perce Co. ID 22 B1
Niagara WI 68 C2
Niagara Co. NY 78 B3
Niagara Falls NY 78 A3
Niantic CT 149 F2
Niantic IL 98 C1
Nibley UT 31 E3
Nice CA 36 B2
Niceville FL 136 B2
Nicholas Co. KY 100 C4
Nicholas Co. WV 101 F4
Nicholasville KY 100 B4
Nicholls GA 129 F4
Nichols NY 93 E1
Nichols Hills OK 244 D2
Nicholson GA 121 D3
Nicholson MS 134 C2
Nicholson PA 93 F2
Nickelsville VA 111 E2
Nickerson KS 43 E3
Nickerson NE 35 F3
Nicksville AZ 55 E4
Nicollet MN 72 C1
Nicollet Co. MN 72 B1
Nicoma Park OK 244 F2
Niederwald TX 61 E2
Nikiski AK 154 C3
Niland CA 53 E3
Niles IL 203 D3
Niles MI 89 F1
Niles OH 91 F2
Ninety Six SC 121 F3
Ninnekah OK 51 E3
Niobrara Co. WY 33 E1
Niota TN 120 C1
Nipomo CA 52 A1
Niskayuna NY 188 D2
Nisland SD 25 F3
Nissequogue NY 149 D3
Nisswa MN 64 A4
Nitro WV 101 E3
Niwot CO 41 E1
Nixa MO 107 D2
Nixon NV 37 D1
Nixon TX 61 E3
Noank CT 149 F2
Noatak AK 154 B1
Noble IL 99 D3
Noble OK 51 E3
Nobleboro ME 82 C3
Noble Co. IN 89 F2
Noble Co. OH 101 F1
Noble Co. OK 51 E2
Nobles Co. MN 72 A2
Noblesville IN 89 F4
Nocatee FL 140 C4
Nocona TX 59 E1
Nodaway Co. MO 86 B4
Noel MO 106 B3
Nogales AZ 55 D4
Nokesville VA 144 A4
Nokomis FL 140 B4
Nokomis IL 98 B2
Nolan Co. TX 58 B3
Nolanville TX 59 E4
Nolensville TN 109 F4
Nome AK 154 B2
Nome TX 132 C3
Nooksack WA 12 C1
Noonday TX 124 A3
Noorvik AK 154 B2
Nora Sprs. IA 73 D3
Norborne MO 96 C2
Norco CA 53 D2
Norco LA 134 B3
Norcross GA 120 C4
Norfolk CT 94 C2
Norfolk MA 151 D2
Norfolk NE 35 E2
Norfolk NY 80 B1
Norfolk VA 113 F2
Norfolk Co. MA 151 D2
Norfork AR 107 E3
Norlina NC 113 D3
Normal IL 88 C4
Norman AR 116 C3
Norman OK 51 E3
Norman Co. MN 19 F3
Normandy MO 256 B2
Normandy Park WA 262 B4
Normangee TX 59 F4
Norman Park GA 129 D4
Normans MD 145 D3
Norphlet AR 125 E1
Norridge IL 203 D3
Norridgewock ME 82 C1
Norris SC 121 E2
Norris TN 110 C4
Norris City IL 99 D4
Norristown PA 146 C2
North SC 122 A4
N. Acton MA 150 C1
N. Adams MA 94 C1
N. Adams MI 90 B1
N. Albany OR 20 B3
N. Amherst MA 150 A1
Northampton MA 150 A1
Northampton PA 93 F3
Northampton Co. NC 113 E3
Northampton Co. PA 93 F3
Northampton Co. VA 114 B3
N. Anson ME 82 B1
N. Apollo PA 92 A4

Norfolk VA / Hampton Roads

Bartlett A3
Battery Park A2
Carrollton A3
Chesapeake B4
Grafton A1
Hampton C2
Hobson A3
Kiptopeke E1
Newport News B2
Norfolk C3
Poquoson B1
Portsmouth B3
Rescue A2
Suffolk A4
Tabb A1
Virginia Beach E3

Figures after entries indicate page number and grid reference.

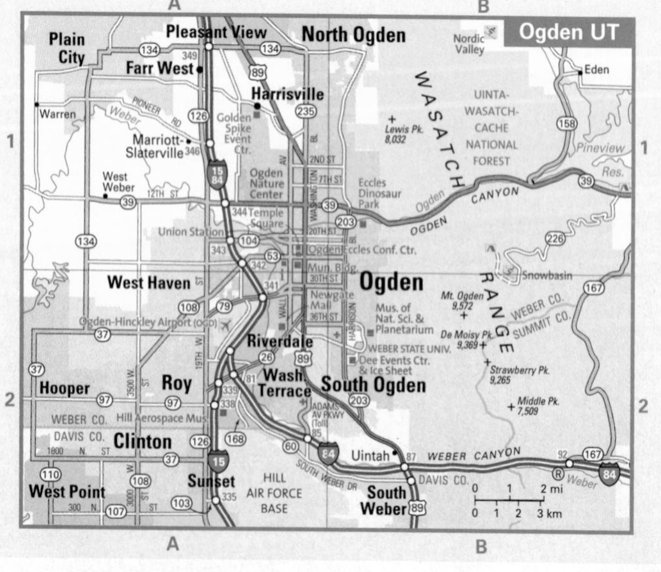

Entries in **bold black** indicate counties or parishes.
Entries in **bold color** indicate cities with detailed inset maps.

Norton VA 111 E2
Norton Co. KS 42 C1
Norton Shores MI 75 E3
Nortonville KS 96 A2
Nortonville KY 109 E2
Norwalk CA 52 C3
Norwalk CT 148 C2
Norwalk IA 86 C2
Norwalk OH 91 D2
Norwalk WI 73 F2
Norway IA 87 E1
Norway ME 82 B2
Norway MI 69 D2
Norwell MA 151 E2
Norwich CT 149 F1
Norwich KS 43 E4
Norwich NY 79 E4
Norwich VT 81 E3
Norwood CO 40 B3
Norwood KY 230 F1
Norwood MA 151 D2
Norwood MO 107 E2
Norwood NY 80 B1
Norwood NC 122 B1
Norwood OH 100 B2
Norwood PA 248 B4
Norwood Young America MN 66 C4
Notasulga AL 128 B2
Nottingham NH 81 F4
Nottoway VA 113 D2
Nottoway Co. VA 113 D2
Notus ID 22 B4
Novato CA 36 B3
Novi MI 76 B4
Novinger MO 87 D4
Nowata OK 106 A3
Nowata Co. OK 106 A2
Noxapater MS 126 C1
Noxon MT 14 C2
Noxubee Co. MS 127 D1
Noyack NY 149 E3
Nuangola PA 93 E3
Nuckolls Co. NE 35 E4
Nucla CO 40 B3
Nueces Co. TX 63 F2
Nuevo CA 53 D3
Nuiqsut AK 154 C1
Nunda NY 78 B4
Nunn CO 33 E4
Nutley NJ 148 B3
Nutter Fort WV 102 A2
Nyack NY 148 B3
Nye Co. NV 37 F3
Nyssa OR 22 A4

O

Oacoma SD 27 D4
Oak Bluffs MA 151 E4
Oakboro NC 122 B1
Oak Brook IL 203 C4
Oakbrook Terrace IL 203 C4
Oak City UT 39 D2
Oak Creek CO 32 C4
Oak Creek WI 74 C3
Oakdale CA 36 C4
Oakdale CT 149 F1
Oakdale KY 109 D2
Oakdale LA 133 E1
Oakdale MA 150 C1
Oakdale MN 235 E2
Oakdale NY 149 D4
Oakdale PA 92 A4
Oakes ND 27 E1
Oakesdale WA 14 A3
Oakfield ME 85 D3
Oakfield NY 78 B3
Oakfield WI 74 C2
Oak Forest IL 89 D2
Oak Grove AL 128 A1
Oak Grove IL 88 A2
Oak Grove KY 109 E3
Oak Grove LA 125 F1
Oak Grove MI 70 C4
Oak Grove MN 67 D3
Oak Grove MS 126 C4
Oak Grove OR 251 D3
Oak Grove SC 122 A3
Oak Grove TN 111 E3
Oak Grove Hts. AR 108 A4
Oak Grove Village MO 96 C2
Oak Harbor OH 90 C2
Oak Harbor WA 12 C2
Oak Hill FL 141 E1
Oak Hill OH 101 D3
Oak Hill WV 101 F4
Oak Hills IL 256 D2
Oakhurst CA 37 D4
Oakhurst NJ 147 F2
Oakhurst OK 51 F2
Oak Island NC 123 E4
Oakland CA 36 B4
Oakland FL 141 D1
Oakland IL 99 D1
Oakland IA 86 A2
Oakland ME 82 C2
Oakland MD 102 B1
Oakland MD 144 B1
Oakland MS 118 B3
Oakland MO 256 B3
Oakland NE 35 F2
Oakland NJ 148 A3
Oakland OK 51 F4
Oakland OR 20 B4
Oakland PA 93 F1
Oakland TN 118 C1
Oakland City IN 99 E4
Oakland Co. MI 76 B4
Oakland Park FL 143 F1
Oak Lawn IL 89 D1
Oakley ID 31 D2
Oakley KS 42 B2
Oakley UT 31 F4
Oaklyn NJ 248 D4
Oakman AL 119 E4
Oakmont PA 92 A4
Oak Orchard DE 145 F4
Oak Park CA 228 A2
Oak Park IL 89 D1
Oak Park MI 76 C4
Oak Park Hts. MN 67 D3
Oak Ridge NJ 148 A3
Oak Ridge NC 112 B4
Oakridge OR 20 C4
Oak Ridge TN 110 C4
Oak Ridge North TX 132 A2
Oak Shade NJ 147 D3
Oakton VA 144 A3
Oaktown IN 99 E3
Oak Trail Shores TX 59 E3
Oak View CA 52 B2
Oakville CT 149 D1
Oakville MO 98 A3
Oakville WA 12 B4
Oakwood GA 121 D3
Oakwood IL 89 D4
Oakwood OH 90 B3
Oakwood OH 204 G3
Oakwood OH 208 E2
Oakwood Beach NJ 145 E1
Oakwood Hills IL 203 A1
Oasis NV 30 C3
Oberlin KS 42 C1
Oberlin LA 133 E2
Oberlin OH 91 D2
Oberlin PA 218 C2
Obetz OH 206 B3
Obion TN 108 C3
Obion Co. TN 108 C3
Oblong IL 99 D2
O'Brien Co. IA 72 A3
Ocala FL 138 C4
Occidental CA 36 A3
Occoquan VA 144 B4
Oceana WV 111 F1
Oceana Co. MI 75 E2
Ocean Bluff MA 151 E2
Ocean Breeze Park FL 141 E4
Ocean City FL 136 B2
Ocean City MD 114 C1
Ocean City NJ 147 F4
Ocean Co. NJ 147 E3
Ocean Gate NJ 147 E3
Ocean Grove MA 151 D3
Ocean Grove NJ 147 F2
Oceano CA 52 A1
Ocean Park WA 12 B4
Ocean Pines MD 114 C1
Oceanport NJ 147 F2
Ocean Reef Club FL 143 E3
Ocean Ridge FL 143 F1
Ocean Shores WA 12 B4
Oceanside CA 53 D3
Oceanside NY 147 F1
Oceanside OR 20 B2
Ocean Sprs. MS 135 D2
Ocean View DE 145 F4
Ochelata OK 51 F1
Ocheyedan IA 72 A2
Ochiltree Co. TX 50 B2
Ochlocknee GA 137 E1
Ocilla GA 129 E4
Ocoee FL 141 D1
Oconee Co. GA 121 D4
Oconee Co. SC 121 E2
Oconomowoc WI 74 C3
Oconto WI 69 D4
Oconto Co. WI 68 C4
Oconto Falls WI 68 C4
Ocracoke NC 115 E3
Odebolt IA 72 A4
Odell IL 88 C3
Odell OR 20 C1
Odem TX 61 E4
Odenton MD 144 C2
Odenville AL 119 F4
Odessa DE 145 E1
Odessa FL 140 B2
Odessa MO 96 C2
Odessa NY 79 D4
Odessa TX 58 A3
Odessa WA 13 F3
Odin IL 98 C3
Odon IN 99 E3
O'Donnell TX 58 A2
Oelwein IA 73 E4
O'Fallon IL 98 B3
O'Fallon MO 98 A3
Ogallala NE 34 B3
Ogden IL 89 D4
Ogden IA 86 C1
Ogden KS 43 F2
Ogden NC 123 E3
Ogden UT 31 E3
Ogden Dunes IN 89 E2
Ogdensburg NJ 148 A3
Ogdensburg NY 80 B1
Ogemaw Co. MI 76 B1
Oglala SD 34 A1
Oglala Lakota Co. SD 26 A4
Ogle Co. IL 88 B1
Oglesby IL 88 B2
Oglethorpe GA 129 D3
Oglethorpe Co. GA 121 E4
Ogunquit ME 82 B4
Ohatchee AL 120 A4
Ohio City OH 90 B3
Ohio Co. IN 100 A2
Ohio Co. KY 109 F1
Ohio Co. WV 91 F4
Ohioville PA 91 F3
Oil City LA 124 C2
Oil City PA 92 A2
Oildale CA 45 D4
Oilton OK 51 F2
Ojai CA 52 B2
Okaloosa Co. FL 136 B2
Okanogan WA 13 E2
Okanogan Co. WA 13 E1
Okarche OK 51 E2
Okauchee WI 74 C3
Okawville IL 98 B3
Okay OK 106 A4
Okeechobee FL 141 E4
Okeechobee Co. FL 141 E3
Okeene OK 51 D2
Okemah OK 51 F3
Okemos MI 76 A4
Okfuskee Co. OK 51 F3
Oklahoma City OK 51 E3
Oklahoma Co. OK 51 E2
Okmulgee OK 51 F2
Okmulgee Co. OK 51 F2
Okoboji IA 72 A2
Okolona MS 119 D3
Oktibbeha Co. MS 118 C4
Ola AR 117 D2
Olanta SC 122 C4
Olathe CO 40 B3
Olathe KS 96 B3
Olcott NY 78 B3
Old Bennington VT 94 C1
Old Bridge NJ 147 E1
Oldenburg IN 100 A2
Old Field NY 149 D3
Old Forge NY 79 F2
Old Forge PA 93 F2
Old Fort NC 111 E4
Oldham SD 27 E3
Oldham Co. KY 100 A4
Oldham Co. TX 49 F3
Old Lyme CT 149 E2
Old Mystic CT 149 F2
Old Orchard Beach ME 82 B4
Old River-Winfree TX 132 B3
Old Saybrook CT 149 E2
Oldsmar FL 140 B2
Oldtown ID 14 B2
Old Town ME 83 D1
Old Zionsville PA 146 B1
Olean NY 92 C1
Oley PA 146 B1
Olin IA 87 F1
Olive Branch MS 118 B2
Olive Hill KY 101 D4
Olivehurst CA 36 C2
Oliver PA 102 B1
Oliver Co. ND 18 B4
Oliver Sprs. TN 110 C4
Olivet MI 76 A4
Olivet NJ 145 F1
Olivet SD 35 E1
Olivette MO 256 B2
Olivia MN 66 B4
Olla LA 125 E3
Olmos Park TX 257 E2
Olmsted Co. MN 73 E1
Olmsted Falls OH 204 D3
Olney IL 99 D3
Olney MD 144 B2
Olney TX 59 D1
Olney Sprs. CO 41 F3
Olpe KS 43 F3
Olton TX 50 A4
Olustee OK 50 C4
Olympia WA 12 B4
Olympian Vil. MO 98 A4
Olyphant PA 261 E2
Omaha NE 86 A2
Omaha TX 124 B1
Omak WA 13 E2
Omao HI 152 B1
Omega GA 129 D4
Omro WI 74 C1
Onaga KS 43 F1
Onalaska TX 132 B1
Onalaska WI 73 F2
Onamia MN 66 C2
Onancock VA 114 C3
Onarga IL 89 D3
Onawa IA 35 F2
Onaway ID 14 B4
Onaway MI 70 C3
Oneco FL 140 B3
Oneida IL 88 A3
Oneida NY 79 E3
Oneida TN 110 B3
Oneida WI 68 C4
Oneida Co. ID 31 E2
Oneida Co. NY 79 E2
Oneida Co. WI 68 B2
O'Neill NE 35 D2
Onekama MI 75 E1
Oneonta AL 119 F4
Oneonta NY 79 F4
Onida SD 26 C3
Onley VA 114 C3
Onondaga Co. NY 79 E3
Onset MA 151 E3
Onslow Co. NC 115 D4
Onsted MI 90 B1
Ontario CA 52 C2
Ontario OH 91 D3
Ontario OR 22 A4
Ontario Co. NY 78 C4
Ontonagon MI 65 E4
Ontonagon Co. MI 65 E4
Onyx CA 45 E4
Oolitic IN 99 F3
Oologah OK 106 A3
Ooltewah TN 120 B2
Oostburg WI 75 D2
Opal Cliffs CA 236 D1
Opa-Locka FL 143 E2
Opelika AL 128 B2
Opelousas LA 133 F2
Opp AL 128 A4
Oppelo AR 117 E1
Oquawka IL 87 F3
Oracle AZ 55 D2
Oracle Jct. AZ 55 D3
Oradell NJ 148 B3
Oran MO 108 B2
Orange CA 52 C3
Orange CT 149 D2
Orange MA 150 B1
Orange NJ 240 A3
Orange OH 204 G2
Orange TX 132 C2
Orange VA 103 D4
Orange Beach AL 135 F2
Orangeburg NY 148 B3
Orangeburg SC 122 A4
Orangeburg Co. SC 122 A4
Orange City FL 141 D1
Orange City IA 35 F1
Orange Co. CA 52 C3
Orange Co. FL 141 D1
Orange Co. IN 99 F3
Orange Co. NY 148 A2
Orange Co. NC 112 C4
Orange Co. TX 132 C2
Orange Co. VT 81 E3
Orange Co. VA 103 D4
Orange Cove CA 45 D3
Orange Grove TX 61 E4
Orange Lake FL 138 C4
Orange Lake NY 148 B1
Orange Park FL 139 D2
Orangeville IL 74 B4
Orangeville UT 39 F2
Orbisonia PA 92 C4
Orchard Beach MD 193 D5
Orchard City CO 40 B2
Orchard Lake MI 210 A1
Orchard Mesa CO 40 B2
Orchard Park NY 78 B4
Orchards WA 20 C1
Orcutt CA 52 A1
Ord NE 35 D3
Orderville UT 39 D4
Ordway CO 41 F3
Oreana IL 98 C1
Ore City TX 124 B2
Orefield PA 146 B1
Oregon IL 88 B1
Oregon MO 96 B1
Oregon OH 90 C2
Oregon WI 74 B3
Oregon City OR 20 C2
Oregon Co. MO 107 F3
Oreland PA 248 C1
Orem UT 31 F4
Orfordville WI 74 B4
Orient NY 149 F2
Oriental NC 115 E3
Orient Park FL 266 C2
Orinda CA 259 C2
Orion IL 88 A2
Oriskany NY 79 E3
Oriskany Falls NY 79 E3
Orland CA 36 B1
Orland ME 83 D2
Orland Hills IL 203 C6
Orlando FL 141 D1
Orland Park IL 89 D2
Orleans IN 99 F3
Orleans IA 72 B2
Orleans MA 151 F3
Orleans NE 43 D1
Orleans VT 81 E1
Orleans Co. NY 78 B3
Orleans Co. VT 81 E1
Orleans Par. LA 134 B2
Orlinda TN 109 F3
Orlovista FL 246 B2
Ormond Beach FL 139 E4
Ormond-by-the-Sea FL 139 E4
Orofino ID 14 B4
Orono ME 83 D1
Orono MN 66 C4
Oronoco MN 73 D1
Oronogo MO 106 B2
Orosi CA 45 D3
Oro Valley AZ 55 D3
Oroville CA 36 C1
Oroville WA 13 E1
Orrick MO 96 C2
Orrington ME 83 D1
Orrs Island ME 82 B3
Orrville OH 91 E3
Orting WA 12 C3
Ortonville MI 76 B3
Ortonville MN 27 F2
Orwell OH 91 F2
Orwigsburg PA 146 A1
Osage IA 73 D3
Osage WY 25 F4
Osage Beach MO 97 D4
Osage City KS 96 A3
Osage Co. KS 96 A3
Osage Co. MO 97 F4
Osage Co. OK 51 F1
Osakis MN 66 B2
Osawatomie KS 96 B3
Osborne KS 43 D2
Osborne Co. KS 43 D2
Osburn ID 14 B3
Oscawana Corners NY 148 B2
Osceola AR 108 B4
Osceola IN 89 F2
Osceola IA 86 C3
Osceola MO 96 C4
Osceola NE 35 E3
Osceola WI 67 D3
Osceola Co. FL 141 D2
Osceola Co. IA 72 A2
Osceola Co. MI 75 F1
Osceola Mills PA 92 C3
Oscoda MI 76 C1
Oscoda Co. MI 70 C4
Osgood IN 100 A2
Oshkosh NE 34 A3
Oshkosh WI 74 C1
Oskaloosa IA 87 D2
Oskaloosa KS 96 A2
Oslo FL 141 E3
Osmond NE 35 E2
Osprey FL 140 B4
Osseo MN 235 A1
Osseo WI 67 F4
Ossian IN 90 A3
Ossian IA 73 E3
Ossineke MI 71 D4
Ossining NY 148 B2
Ossipee NH 81 F3
Ossipee NC 112 B4
Osterville MA 151 E4
Oswego IL 88 C2
Oswego KS 106 B2
Oswego NY 79 D2
Oswego Co. NY 79 E2
Osyka MS 134 B1
Otego NY 79 F4
Otero Co. CO 41 F4

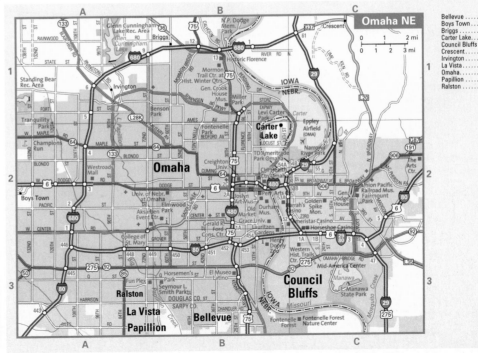

Olympia WA

Setchfield Lake
Budd Inlet
Bigelow L.
Percival Landing Park
Farmers Market
Bigelow House Museum
Capital Mall
Wash. Ctr. for the Perf. Arts
State Capitol
Capitol Lake
City Hall
Yashiro Japanese Garden
Court House
Watershed Park
Tumwater Hist. Pk.
Tumwater Falls Park
Ward Lake
Chambers Lake
LBA Park
Smith Lake
Tumwater Hill Park
Olympia
Lacey
Tumwater

Bellevue B3
Boys Town A2
Briggs B1
Carter Lake B2
Council Bluffs C3
Crescent C1
Irvington A1
La Vista A3
Omaha B2
Papillion A3
Ralston A3

Orlando FL

Entries in **bold black** indicate counties or parishes.
Entries in **bold color** indicate cities with detailed inset maps.

Palm Springs CA

Pensacola FL

Bellview A1
Brent B1
Brownsville B2
Ensley A1
Ferry Pass B1
Goulding B1
Gulf Breeze B2
Myrtle Grove A2
Pensacola...............B1
Pleasant Grove A2
Warrington..............A2
W. Pensacola A1

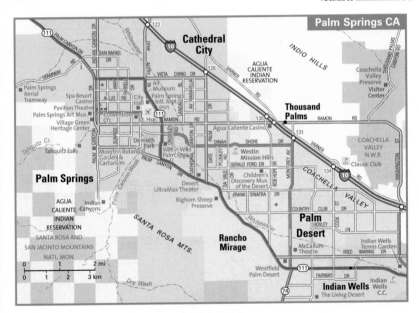

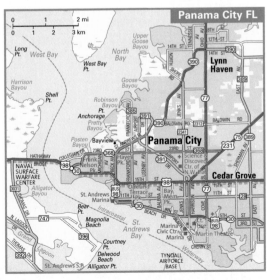

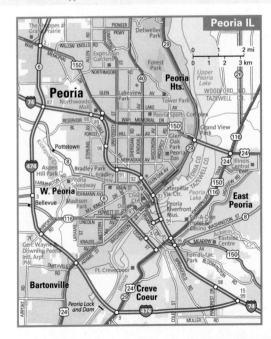

Palo IA 87 E1
Palo Alto CA 36 B4
Palo Alto Co. IA 72 B3
Palo Cedro CA 28 C4
Palo Pinto TX 59 D2
Palo Pinto Co. TX 59 D2
Palos Hts. IL 203 D6
Palos Hills IL 203 D5
Palos Park IL 203 D6
Palos Verdes Estates CA 228 C4
Palouse WA 14 B4
Pamlico Co. NC 115 E3
Pampa TX 50 B3
Pamplico SC 122 C3
Pana IL 98 C2
Panaca NV 38 C4
Panacea FL 137 E3
Panama OK 116 B1
Panama City FL 136 C2
Panama City Beach FL 136 C2
Pandora OH 90 B3
Pangburn AR 117 F1
Panguitch UT 39 D4
Panhandle TX 50 B3
Panola Co. MS 118 B3
Panola Co. TX 124 C3
Panora IA 86 B2
Panorama Vil. TX 132 A2
Pantano AZ 55 D3
Pantego TX 207 B3
Panthersville GA 190 E4
Paola KS 96 B3
Paoli IN 99 F3
Paoli OK 51 E4
Paoli PA 146 B3
Paonia CO 40 C2
Papaikou HI 153 F3
Papillion NE 35 F3
Parachute CO 40 B1
Paradis LA 239 A2
Paradise CA 36 C1
Paradise PA 146 A3
Paradise UT 31 E3
Paradise Hills NM 48 C3
Paradise Valley AZ 249 C2
Paragon IN 99 F2
Paragonah UT 39 D4
Paragould AR 108 A4
Paramount CA 228 D3
Paramus NJ 148 B3
Pardeeville WI 74 B2
Paris AR 116 C1
Paris ID 31 F2
Paris IL 99 D1
Paris KY 100 B4
Paris ME 82 B2
Paris MO 97 E2
Paris TN 109 D3
Paris TX 116 A4
Parish NY 79 D2
Parishville NY 80 B1
Park City KS 43 E4
Park City KY 110 A2
Park City MT 24 B1
Park City UT 31 F4
Park Co. CO 41 D2
Park Co. MT 23 F2
Park Co. WY 24 B3
Parke Co. IN 99 E1
Parker AZ 46 B4
Parker CO 41 E1
Parker FL 136 C2
Parker ID 23 E4
Parker PA 92 A3
Parker SD 27 F4
Parker City IN 90 A4
Parker Co. TX 59 E2
Parkersburg IA 73 D4
Parkersburg WV 101 E2
Parkers Prairie MN 66 B1
Parkertown NJ 147 E4
Parkesburg PA 146 A3
Park Falls WI 68 A2
Park Hill OK 106 B4
Park Hills KY 204 B3
Park Hills MO 98 A4
Parkin AR 118 A1
Parkland FL 143 E1
Parkland WA 12 C3
Park Lane CT 148 C1
Park Rapids MN 64 A4
Park Ridge IL 203 C3
Park Ridge NJ 148 B3
Park River ND 19 E2
Parks AZ 47 D3
Parks LA 133 F2
Parkside PA 248 A4
Parksley VA 114 C2
Parkston SD 27 E4
Park View IA 88 A1
Parkville MD 144 C1
Parkville MO 224 B2
Parkway Vil. KY 230 D2
Parlier CA 45 D3
Parma ID 22 A4
Parma MI 76 A4
Parma MO 108 B3
Parma OH 91 E2
Parma Hts. OH 204 E3
Parmelee SD 26 C4
Parmer Co. TX 49 F4
Parowan UT 39 D4
Parrish AL 119 E4
Parshall ND 18 B2
Parsons KS 106 A1
Parsons TN 109 D4
Parsons WV 102 B2
Pasadena CA 52 C2
Pasadena MD 193 D5
Pasadena TX 132 B3
Pascagoula MS 135 D2
Pasco WA 21 E1
Pascoag RI 150 C2
Pasco Co. FL 140 B2
Paso Robles CA 44 C4
Pasquotank Co. NC 115 E1
Passaic NJ 148 B3
Passaic Co. NJ 148 A3
Pass Christian MS 134 C2
Patagonia AZ 55 D4
Pataskala OH 101 D1
Patchogue NY 149 D4
Pateros WA 13 E2
Paterson NJ 148 B3
Patoka IL 98 C3
Patoka IN 99 D3
Patrick Co. VA 112 B3
Patrick Sprs. VA 112 B3
Patten ME 85 D3
Pattenburg NJ 146 C1
Patterson AR 117 F1
Patterson CA 36 C4
Patterson GA 129 F4
Patterson LA 134 A3
Patterson NY 148 C1
Patterson Gardens MI 90 C1
Patterson Sprs. NC 122 A1
Patton PA 92 B3
Patton Vil. TX 132 B2
Paul ID 31 D1
Paulden AZ 47 D3
Paulding MS 126 C3
Paulding OH 90 B3
Paulding Co. GA 120 B4
Paulding Co. OH 90 B3
Paullina IA 72 A3
Paulsboro NJ 146 C3

Figures after entries indicate page number and grid reference.

Abington........C1
Aldan..........B4
Ambler..........B1
Andalusia.......E2
Ardmore........B3
Aston..........A4
Audubon, NJ....D4
Audubon, PA....A1
Audubon Park...D4
Bala-Cynwyd....B3
Barren Hill.....B2
Barrington.....D4
Bellmawr.......D4
Bensalem.......E2
Bethayres.......D1
Beverly........E2
Blue Bell.......B1
Bridgeboro......E2
Bridgeport......A1
Brookhaven.....A4
Brooklawn......C4
Broomall........A3
Bryn Athyn......D1
Bryn Mawr.......B2
Camden.........D3
Centerton.......E3
Cheltenham.....C2
Cinnaminson....D3
Clifton Hts.....B3
Collingdale.....B4
Collingswood....D4
Colwyn.........B4
Conshohocken...B2
Croydon........E2
Darby..........B4
Delair..........D3
Delanco........E2
Delran.........E2
Devon..........A2
Dresher.........C1
Drexel Hill......B3
E. Lansdowne....B3
Eddystone.......A4
Edgemont.......A3
Edgewater Park..E2
Elkins Park......C2
Elwyn..........A4
Essington.......B4
Feasterville.....D1
Florida Park.....A3
Flourtown.......B1
Folcroft........B4
Folsom.........A4
Ft. Washington...C1
Gladwyne.......B2
Glenolden.......B4
Glen Riddle......A4
Glenside........C1
Gloucester City..C4
Gulph Mills......A2
Haddonfield.....D4
Haddon Hts......D4
Haverford.......B2
Havertown......B3
Hulmeville.......E1
Huntingdon Valley.........D1
Jeffersonville....A1
Jenkintown......C1
King of Prussia..A2
Lafayette Hill....B1
Lansdowne.......B3
Lima...........A4
Magnolia........D4
Manoa..........B3
Marple..........A3
Media..........A4
Melrose Park.....C2
Merchantville.....D3
Millbourne.......B3
Moorestown......E3
Morton..........B4
Mt. Ephraim.....C4
Narberth........B3
National Park....C4
Newportville.....E1
Newtown Square.........A3
Norristown.......B1
Norwood.........B4
Oakford.........E1
Oaklyn..........D4
Ogontz..........C2
Orchard View.....E2
Oreland.........C1
Palmyra.........D3
Parkside........A4
Penndel.........E1
Pennsauken.....D3
Penn Wynne.....B3
Philadelphia.....C2
Plymouth Meeting.......B1
Prospect Park...B4
Radnor..........A2
Rancocas........E2
Red Bank.......C4
Ridley Park......B4
Riverside........E2
Riverton.........D2
Rockledge.......D2
Rosemont........B2
Rose Tree.......A3
Rose Valley.....A4
Roslyn..........C1
Runnemede.....D4
Rutledge........B4
St. Davids......A2
Sharon Hill......B4
Springfield......B3
Swarthmore.....A4
Swedeland......B1
Swedesburg......A1
Town Estates....E2
Trevose.........D1
Trooper.........A1
Upland..........A4
Upper Darby.....B3
Village Green....A4
Villanova........A2
Wayne..........A2
W. Bristol.......E1
West Conshohocken..B2
Westmont.......D4
Westville........C4
Whitemarsh......B1
Willingboro......E2
Willow Grove....C1
Woodlyn........A4
Woodlynne......C4
Wyncote.........C1
Wynnewood......B3
Wyola...........A2
Yeadon.........B3

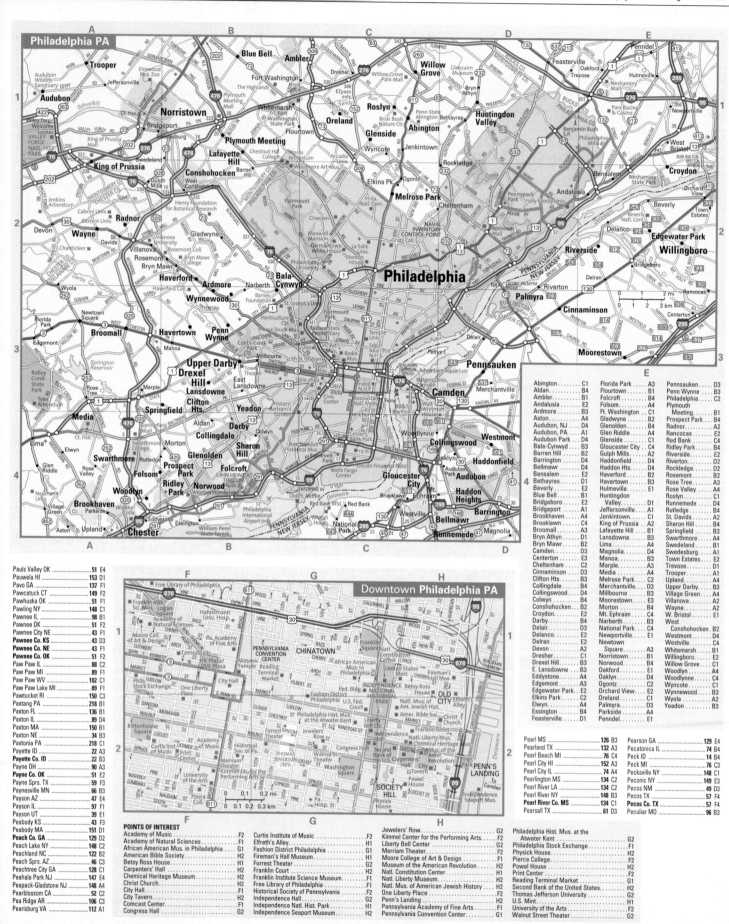

Pauls Valley OK 51 E4
Pauwela HI 153 D1
Pavo GA 137 F1
Pawcatuck CT 149 F2
Pawhuska OK 51 F1
Pawling NY 148 C1
Pawnee IL 98 B1
Pawnee OK 51 F2
Pawnee City NE 43 F1
Pawnee Co. KS 43 D3
Pawnee Co. NE 43 F1
Pawnee Co. OK 51 F2
Paw Paw IL 88 C2
Paw Paw MI 89 F1
Paw Paw WV 102 C1
Paw Paw Lake MI 89 F1
Pawtucket RI 150 C3
Paxtang PA 218 B1
Paxton FL 136 B1
Paxton IL 89 D4
Paxton MA 150 B1
Paxton NE 34 B3
Paxtonia PA 218 C1
Payette ID 22 A3
Payette Co. ID 22 B3
Payne OH 90 A3
Payne Co. OK 51 E2
Payne Sprs. TX 59 F3
Paynesville MN 66 B3
Payson AZ 47 E4
Payson IL 97 F1
Payson UT 39 E1
Peabody KS 43 F3
Peabody MA 151 D1
Peach Co. GA 129 D2
Peach Lake NY 148 C2
Peachland NC 122 B2
Peach Sprs. AZ 46 C3
Peachtree City GA 128 C1
Peahala Park NJ 147 E4
Peapack-Gladstone NJ 148 A4
Pearblossom CA 52 C2
Pea Ridge AR 106 C3
Pearisburg VA 112 A1

Pearl MS 126 B3
Pearland TX 132 A3
Pearl Beach MI 76 C4
Pearl City HI 152 A3
Pearl City IL 74 A4
Pearlington MS 134 C2
Pearl River LA 134 C2
Pearl River NY 148 B3
Pearl River Co. MS 134 C1
Pearsall TX 61 D3
Pearson GA 129 E4
Pecatonica IL 74 B4
Peck ID 14 B4
Peck MI 76 C3
Pecksville NY 148 C1
Peconic NY 149 E3
Pecos NM 49 D3
Pecos TX 57 F4
Pecos Co. TX 57 F4
Peculiar MO 96 B3

POINTS OF INTEREST

Academy of Music.......F2
Academy of Natural Sciences.......F1
African American Mus. in Philadelphia.......G1
American Bible Society.......H2
Betsy Ross House.......H1
Carpenters' Hall.......H2
Chemical Heritage Museum.......H2
Christ Church.......H2
City Hall.......F1
City Tavern.......H2
Comcast Center.......F1
Congress Hall.......G2
Curtis Institute of Music.......F2
Elfreth's Alley.......H1
Fashion District Philadelphia.......G1
Fireman's Hall Museum.......H1
Forrest Theater.......G2
Franklin Court.......H2
Franklin Institute Science Museum.......F1
Free Library of Philadelphia.......F1
Historical Society of Pennsylvania.......F2
Independence Hall.......G2
Independence Natl. Hist. Park.......H1
Independence Seaport Museum.......H2
Jewelers' Row.......G2
Kimmel Center for the Performing Arts.......F2
Liberty Bell Center.......G2
Merriam Theater.......F2
Moore College of Art & Design.......F1
Museum of the American Revolution.......H2
Natl. Constitution Center.......H1
Natl. Liberty Museum.......H2
Natl. Mus. of American Jewish History.......H2
One Liberty Place.......F2
Penn's Landing.......H2
Pennsylvania Academy of Fine Arts.......F1
Pennsylvania Convention Center.......G1
Philadelphia Hist. Mus. at the Atwater Kent.......G2
Philadelphia Stock Exchange.......F1
Physick House.......H2
Pierce College.......F2
Powel House.......H2
Print Center.......F2
Reading Terminal Market.......G1
Second Bank of the United States.......H2
Thomas Jefferson University.......G2
U.S. Mint.......H1
University of the Arts.......F2
Walnut Street Theater.......G2

Entries in **bold black** indicate counties or parishes.
Entries in **bold color** indicate cities with detailed inset maps.

Peebles OH 100 C3
Peekskill NY 148 B2
Pe Ell WA 12 B4
Peeples Valley AZ 47 D4
Peever SD 27 F2
Pegram TN 109 E4
Pekin IL 88 B4
Pelahatchie MS 126 B2
Peletier NC 115 D4
Pelham AL 127 F1
Pelham GA 137 E1
Pelham NH 95 E1
Pelham NY 148 B3
Pelham Manor NY 148 B3
Pelican Rapids MN 19 F4
Pelion SC 122 A4
Pella IA 87 D2
Pell City AL 120 A4
Pellston MI 70 C3
Pemberton NJ 147 D3
Pemberville OH 90 C2
Pembina ND 19 E1
Pembina Co. ND 19 E1
Pembroke GA 130 B3
Pembroke KY 109 E2
Pembroke ME 83 E1
Pembroke MA 151 E2
Pembroke NC 122 C2
Pembroke VA 112 A1
Pembroke Park FL 233 B3
Pembroke Pines FL 143 E2
Pemiscot Co. MO 108 B4
Pena Blanca NM 48 C3
Pen Argyl PA 93 F3
Peñasco NM 49 D2
Penbrook PA 218 B1
Pender NE 35 F2
Pender Co. NC 115 C4
Pendleton IN 99 F1
Pendleton MO 97 F3
Pendleton OR 21 F1
Pendleton SC 121 E2
Pendleton Co. KY 100 B3
Pendleton Co. WV 102 B3
Pend Oreille Co. WA 14 B2
Penhook VA 112 B2
Peninsula OH 91 E2
Penitas TX 63 E4
Penndel PA 147 D2
Penney Farms FL 139 D3
Penn Hills PA 92 A4
Pennington NJ 147 D2
Pennington Co. MN 19 F2
Pennington Co. SD 26 A4
Pennington Gap VA 111 D2
Pennock MN 66 B3
Pennsauken NJ 146 C3
Pennsboro WV 101 F2
Pennsburg PA 146 B1
Pennsbury Vil. PA 250 A2
Penns Creek PA 93 D3
Penns Grove NJ 146 B4
Pennsville NJ 145 E1
Pennville IN 90 A4
Penn Wynne PA 248 B3
Penn Yan NY 78 C4
Penobscot Co. ME 83 D1
Penrose CO 41 E3
Pensacola FL 135 F2
Pensacola Beach FL 135 F2
Pentwater MI 75 E2
Peoria AZ 54 C1
Peoria IL 88 B3
Peoria Co. IL 88 B3
Peoria Hts. IL 88 B3
Peosta IA 73 F4
Peotone IL 89 D2
Pepeekeo HI 153 F3
Pepin WI 73 E1
Pepin Co. WI 67 E4
Pepperell MA 95 D1
Pepper Pike OH 204 G2
Pequannock NJ 148 A3
Pequot Lakes MN 64 A4
Peralta NM 48 C4
Percy IL 98 B4
Perham MN 19 F4
Peridot AZ 55 D2
Perkasie PA 146 C1
Perkins OK 51 F2
Perkins Corner CT 150 B3
Perkins Co. NE 34 B4
Perkins Co. SD 26 B2
Perkinston MS 135 D1
Perkiomenville PA 146 B2
Perquimans Co. NC 113 F4
Perris CA 53 D3
Perry FL 137 F2
Perry GA 129 D2
Perry IA 86 C1
Perry KS 96 A2
Perry LA 133 F3
Perry MI 76 B3
Perry MO 97 F2
Perry NY 78 B4
Perry OH 91 E1
Perry OK 51 E2
Perry UT 31 E3
Perry Co. AL 127 F2
Perry Co. AR 117 D2
Perry Co. IL 98 B4
Perry Co. IN 99 E4
Perry Co. KY 111 D2

Avondale A2	Gilbert D3	Litchfield Park A2	Phoenix B1	Sun City A1	Youngtown A1
Chandler C3	Glendale A2	Maricopa Vil. A3	Queen Creek D3	Sun City West A1	
El Mirage A1	Goodyear A2	Mesa D2	Rio Verde D1	Surprise A1	
Ft. McDowell D1	Guadalupe C3	Paradise Valley C2	Santa Cruz B3	Tempe C3	
Fountain Hills D1	Komatke B3	Peoria A1	Scottsdale C1	Tolleson A2	

Downtown Phoenix AZ

POINTS OF INTEREST

Arizona Center F1	City Hall E2
Arizona Federal Theatre E2	Convention Center F2
Arizona Science Center F2	Heard Museum F1
Arizona State Capitol E2	Herberger Theater Center F2
Arizona State Fairgrounds E1	Heritage Square F2
Arizona State University Downtown F1	Orpheum Theatre E2
Arizona Veterans Memorial Coliseum E1	Phoenix Art Museum E1
Chase Field F2	Phoenix Suns Arena F2
Children's Museum F2	Symphony Hall F2

Perry Co. MS 135 D1
Perry Co. MO 108 B1
Perry Co. OH 101 E1
Perry Co. PA 93 D4
Perry Co. TN 119 E1
Perry Hall MD 144 C1
Perry Hts. OH 91 E3
Perryman MD 145 D1
Perryopolis PA 92 A4
Perrysburg OH 90 C2
Perrysville IN 89 D4
Perrysville OH 91 D3
Perryton TX 50 B2
Perryville AR 117 D2
Perryville KY 110 B1
Perryville MD 145 D1
Perryville MO 108 B1
Pershing Co. NV 29 F4
Person Co. NC 112 C3
Perth Amboy NJ 147 E1
Peru IL 88 B2
Peru IN 89 F3
Peru NE 86 A4
Peru NY 81 D2
Peshastin WA 13 D3
Peshtigo WI 69 D3

Petal MS 126 C4
Petaluma CA 36 B3
Peterborough NH 95 D1
Petersburg AK 155 E4
Petersburg IL 98 B1
Petersburg IN 99 E3
Petersburg KY 100 B2
Petersburg MI 90 C1
Petersburg NJ 148 A3
Petersburg PA 93 C4
Petersburg TN 119 F1
Petersburg TX 58 A1
Petersburg VA 113 E2
Petersburg WV 102 B2
Peterstown WV 112 A1
Petersville AL 119 E2
Petoskey MI 70 B3
Petroleum Co. MT 16 C3
Petrolia TX 59 D1
Petros TN 110 C4
Pettis Co. MO 97 D3
Pettit OK 106 B4
Pettus TX 61 E4
Pevely MO 98 A4
Pewamo MI 76 A3
Pewaukee (city) WI 234 A2
Pewaukee (village) WI 234 A2
Pewee Valley KY 100 A4
Pflugerville TX 61 E1
Pharr TX 63 E4
Phelan CA 53 D2
Phelps KY 111 E1
Phelps NY 78 C3
Phelps Co. MO 97 F4
Phelps Co. NE 35 D4
Phenix City AL 128 C2
Philadelphia MS 126 C2
Philadelphia NY 79 E1
Philadelphia PA 146 C3
Philadelphia TN 110 C4
Philadelphia Co. PA 146 C3
Phil Campbell AL 119 E3
Philip SD 26 B3
Philippi WV 102 A2
Philipsburg MT 15 D4
Philipsburg PA 92 C3
Phillips ME 82 B1
Phillips WI 68 A2
Phillipsburg KS 43 D1
Phillipsburg NJ 93 F3
Phillipsburg OH 100 B1
Phillips Co. AR 118 A3
Phillips Co. CO 34 A4
Phillips Co. KS 43 D1
Phillips Co. MT 16 C2
Philmont NY 94 B2
Philo IL 99 D1
Philo OH 101 E1
Philomath OR 20 B3
Philpot KY 109 E1
Phoenix AZ 54 C1
Phoenix IL 203 E6
Phoenix NY 79 D3
Phoenix OR 28 B2
Phoenixville PA 146 B2
Pia Oik AZ 54 B3
Piatt Co. IL 98 C1
Picacho AZ 54 C2
Picayune MS 134 C2
Picher OK 106 B2
Pickaway Co. OH 101 D1
Pickens MS 126 B1
Pickens SC 121 E2
Pickens Co. AL 119 D4
Pickens Co. GA 120 C3
Pickens Co. SC 121 E2
Pickensville AL 127 D1
Pickerington OH 101 D1
Pickett Co. TN 110 B3
Pico Rivera CA 228 E3
Picture Rocks PA 93 E2
Piedmont AL 120 A4
Piedmont CA 259 C2
Piedmont MO 108 A2
Piedmont OK 51 E2
Piedmont SC 121 E2
Piedmont SD 25 F3
Piedmont WV 102 B2
Pierce CO 33 E4

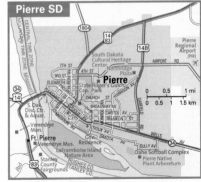

Figures after entries indicate page number and grid reference.

Pierce ID 14 C4	Pierce Co. ND 18 C2	Pierre Part LA 134 A3	Pigeon MI 76 C2	Pike Co. AR 117 D3	Pike Co. MS 126 B4	Piketon OH 101 E2
Pierce NE 35 E2	Pierce Co. WA 12 C4	Pierron IL 98 B3	Pigeon Cove MA 151 F1	Pike Co. GA 128 C1	Pike Co. MO 97 F2	Pikeville KY 111 E1
Pierce City MO 106 C2	Pierce Co. WI 67 E4	Pierson FL 139 D4	Pigeon Forge TN 111 D4	Pike Co. IL 98 A1	Pike Co. OH 101 D2	Pikeville NC 123 E1
Pierce Co. GA 129 F4	Pierceton IN 89 F2	Pierz MN 66 C2	Piggott AR 108 B3	Pike Co. IN 99 E3	Pike Co. PA 93 F2	Pikeville TN 120 B1
Pierce Co. NE 35 E2	Pierre SD 26 C3	Pigeon LA 134 A2	Pike Co. AL 128 A4	Pike Co. KY 111 E1	Pikesville MD 144 C1	Pilot Grove MO 97 D3

Acmetonia D1	Carnegie A2	Emsworth A1	Heidelberg A3	Munhall C3	Rennerdale A2	W. Homestead C2
Aspinwall C1	Castle Shannon B3	Etna C1	Homestead C2	N. Braddock C2	Rosslyn Farms A2	W. Mifflin C3
Avalon A1	Chalfant D2	Evergreen B1	Ingram A2	Oakmont D1	Sandy Creek C1	W. Park A1
Baldwin C3	Cheswick D1	Ewingsville A2	Kenmawr A1	Penn Hills D2	Sharpsburg C1	W. View B1
Bellevue B1	Churchill D2	Forest Grove A1	Kirwan Hts. A3	Pennsbury Vil. A2	Springdale D1	Whitaker C2
Ben Avon A1	Coraopolis A1	Forest Hills C2	Liberty C3	Perrysville B1	Stewartsville D1	Whitehall B3
Ben Avon Hts. A1	Crafton A2	Fox Chapel C1	McKeesport D3	Pitcairn D2	Swissvale C2	White Oak D3
Bethel Park B3	Cuddy A3	Glassport C3	McKees Rocks B1	Pittock A1	Sygan A3	Wilkinsburg C2
Blawnox C1	Dormont B3	Glenfield A1	Millvale B1	Pittsburgh B2	Thornburg A2	Wilmerding D3
Braddock C2	Dravosburg C3	Glen Osborne A1	Monroeville D2	Pleasant Hills C3	Trafford D2	
Braddock Hills C2	Duquesne D3	Glenshaw C1	Moon Run A3	Plum D1	Turtle Creek D2	
Brentwood B3	E. McKeesport D3	Green Tree B2	Morgan A3	Port Vue C3	Upper St. Clair A3	
Bridgeville A3	E. Pittsburgh D2	Groveton A1	Mt. Lebanon B3	Presto A3	Verona D1	
Broughton B3	Edgewood C2	Haysville A1	Mt. Oliver B2	Rankin C2	Wall D3	

Piketon OH 101 E2	Pine Island Ctr. FL 214 A1
Pikeville KY 111 E1	Pine Knoll Shores NC 115 D4
Pikeville NC 123 E1	Pine Knot KY 110 C3
Pikeville TN 120 B1	Pineland FL 142 C1
Pikesville MD 144 C1	Pineland TX 124 C4
Pilot Grove MO 97 D3	Pine Lawn MO 256 B2
Pilot Knob MO 108 A1	Pine Level NC 123 E1
Pilot Mtn. NC 112 A3	Pinellas Co. FL 140 B2
Pilot Pt. TX 59 F1	Pinellas Park FL 140 B3
Pilot Rock OR 21 F2	Pine Mtn. GA 128 C2
Pilot Sta. AK 154 B3	Pine Plains NY 94 B2
Pima AZ 55 E2	Pine Pt. ME 82 B3
Pima Co. AZ 54 C3	Pine Prairie LA 133 E1
Pimmit Hills VA 270 B3	Pine Ridge SC 122 A4
Pinardville NH 81 F4	Pine Ridge SD 34 A1
Pinal Co. AZ 55 D3	Pine River MN 64 A4
Pinch WV 101 F3	Pinesdale MT 15 D4
Pinckard AL 128 B4	Pinetop-Lakeside AZ 47 F4
Pinckney MI 76 B3	Pinetops NC 113 E4
Pinckneyville IL 98 B4	Pinetown DE 145 F4
Pinconning MI 76 B2	Pine Valley CA 53 D4
Pine AZ 47 E4	Pine Valley NY 93 D1
Pine Beach NJ 147 E3	Pineview GA 129 E3
Pine Bluff AR 117 E3	Pineville KY 110 C2
Pinebluff NC 122 C1	Pineville LA 125 E4
Pine Bluffs WY 33 F3	Pineville MO 106 B3
Pine Bush NY 148 A1	Pineville NC 122 A2
Pine Castle FL 141 D1	Pineville WV 111 F1
Pine City MN 67 D2	Pinewald NJ 147 E3
Pine Co. MN 64 C4	Pinewood SC 122 B4
Pinecrest FL 140 C5	Piney Green NC 115 D4
Pinecrest FL 233 A5	Piney Pt. MD 103 E3
Pineda FL 141 E4	Piney Pt. Vil. TX 220 B2
Pinedale WY 32 A1	Pink OK 51 E3
Pine Forest TX 132 C2	Pink Hill NC 123 E1
Pine Grove CA 36 C3	
Pine Grove PA 146 A1	
Pine Grove WV 101 F3	
Pine Grove Mills PA 92 C3	
Pine Haven WY 25 F3	
Pine Hill AL 127 E3	
Pine Hill NJ 146 C4	
Pine Hills FL 246 B2	
Pinehurst ID 14 C1	
Pinehurst MA 151 D1	
Pinehurst NC 122 C1	
Pinehurst TX 132 A2	
Pinehurst TX 132 C2	
Pine Island MN 73 D1	
Pine Island NY 148 A2	
Pine Island TX 61 F2	

POINTS OF INTEREST

Allegheny Center E1
The Andy Warhol Museum E1
Benedum Center F1
Block House E2
Bus Depot F1
Byham Theater F1
Carnegie Science Center E1
Chatham Center F2
City County Building F2
County Court House F2
David Lawrence Convention Center F1
Duquesne Incline E2
Duquesne University F2
Federal Building F1
Fort Pitt Museum E2
Gateway Center E1
Gateway Clipper Fleet E2
Heinz Field E1
Heinz Hall F1
Highmark Stadium E2
Monongahela Incline E2
Mr. Rogers Memorial E2
Mt. Washington Overlook E2
Penn Station F1
PNC Park E1
Point Park University E2
Point State Park E1
PPG Paints Arena F2
Robert Morris University F2
Senator John Heinz Hist. Center F1
Station Square E2

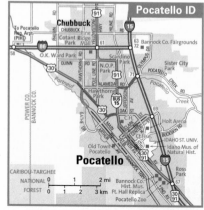

Entries in **bold black** indicate counties or parishes.
Entries in **bold color** indicate cities with detailed inset maps.

Pinnacle NC 112 A3
Pinole CA 259 C1
Pinon AZ 47 F2
Pinson AL 119 F4
Pioche NV 38 C3
Pioneer OH 90 B2
Pioneer Vil. KY 100 A4
Piper City IL 88 C3
Piperton TN 118 B2
Pipestone MN 27 F3
Pipestone Co. MN 27 F3
Piqua OH 90 B4
Pirtleville AZ 55 E4
Piru CA 52 B2
Piscataquis Co. ME 84 C3
Pisgah AL 120 A2
Pisgah Forest NC 121 E1
Pisinemo AZ 54 C3
Pismo Beach CA 52 A1
Pitcairn PA 250 D2
Pitkin Co. CO 40 C2
Pitman NJ 146 C4
Pitt Co. NC 113 E4
Pittman Ctr. TN 111 D4
Pittsboro IN 99 F1
Pittsboro MS 118 C4
Pittsboro NC 112 C4
Pittsburg CA 36 B3
Pittsburg IL 108 C1
Pittsburg KS 106 B1
Pittsburg TX 124 B1
Pittsburg Co. OK 116 A2
Pittsburgh PA 92 A4
Pittsfield IL 98 A1
Pittsfield ME 82 C1
Pittsfield MA 94 C1
Pittsfield NH 81 F4
Pittsford NY 78 C3
Pittsford VT 81 D3
Pittston ME 82 C2
Pittston PA 93 F2
Pittstown NY 94 B1
Pittsville MD 114 C1
Pittsville WI 74 A1
Pittsylvania Co. VA 112 C2
Piute Co. UT 39 E3
Pixley CA 45 D4
Placentia CA 229 F4
Placer Co. CA 36 C2
Placerville CA 36 C2
Placid Lakes FL 141 D4
Placitas NM 48 C3
Plain WI 74 A3
Plain City OH 90 C4
Plain City UT 31 E3
Plain Dealing LA 124 C1
Plainfield CT 149 F1
Plainfield IL 88 C2
Plainfield IN 99 F1
Plainfield NH 81 E3
Plainfield NJ 147 E1
Plainfield VT 81 E2
Plainfield WI 74 B1
Plains GA 128 C3
Plains KS 42 C4
Plains MT 14 C3
Plains PA 261 B2
Plains TX 57 F2
Plainsboro NJ 147 D2
Plainview AR 117 D2
Plainview MN 73 E1
Plainview NE 35 E2
Plainview NY 148 C4
Plainview TN 110 C4
Plainview TX 50 A4
Plainville CT 149 D1
Plainville IN 99 E3
Plainville KS 43 D2
Plainville MA 150 C2
Plainwell MI 75 F4
Plaistow NH 95 E1
Planada CA 37 D4
Plandome NY 148 C4
Plandome Hts. NY 241 G2
Plandome Manor NY 241 G2
Plankinton SD 27 E4
Plano IL 88 C2
Plano TX 59 F2
Plantation FL 143 E2
Plantation KY 230 F1
Plant City FL 140 C2
Plantersville MS 119 D3
Plantsville CT 149 D1
Plaquemine LA 134 A2
Plaquemines Par. LA 134 C4
Platte SD 27 D4
Platte City MO 96 B2
Platte Co. MO 96 B2
Platte Co. NE 35 E3
Platte Co. WY 33 E2
Plattekill NY 148 B1
Platteville CO 33 E4
Platteville WI 74 A4
Plattsburg MO 96 B1
Plattsburgh NY 81 D1
Plattsmouth NE 86 A3
Pleak TX 132 A4
Pleasantdale NY 94 B1
Pleasant Gap PA 92 C3
Pleasant Garden NC 112 B4
Pleasant Grove AL 119 F4
Pleasant Grove OH 101 E1
Pleasant Grove UT 31 F4
Pleasant Groves AL 120 A2
Pleasant Hill CA 259 D2
Pleasant Hill IL 97 F2
Pleasant Hill IA 86 C2
Pleasant Hill LA 125 D3
Pleasant Hill MO 96 C3
Pleasant Hill OH 90 B4
Pleasant Hill TN 110 B4
Pleasant Hills MD 144 C1
Pleasant Hills PA 250 C3
Pleasant Hope MO 107 D1
Pleasant Lake IN 90 A2
Pleasant Lake MA 151 F3
Pleasant Lake MI 76 A4
Pleasant Mills NJ 147 D4
Pleasanton CA 36 B4
Pleasanton KS 96 B4
Pleasanton TX 61 D3
Pleasant Plains IL 98 B1
Pleasant Plains NJ 147 E3
Pleasant Pt. ME 83 F1
Pleasant Prairie WI 74 C4
Pleasant Ridge MI 210 C2
Pleasant Run OH 204 A1
Pleasants Co. WV 101 F2
Pleasant Valley MO 96 B2
Pleasant Valley NY 94 B3
Pleasant Valley PA 146 C1
Pleasant Valley WV 102 A2
Pleasant View IN 99 F1
Pleasant View TN 109 E3
Pleasant View UT 31 E3
Pleasantville IA 87 D2
Pleasantville NJ 147 F4
Pleasantville NY 148 B2
Pleasantville OH 101 D1
Pleasantville PA 92 A2
Pleasure Beach CT 149 F2
Pleasureville KY 100 A4
Pleasureville PA 275 F1
Plentywood MT 17 F1
Plover WI 74 B1
Pluckemin NJ 147 D1
Plum PA 92 A4
Plumas Co. CA 36 C1
Plum City WI 67 E4
Plumerville AR 117 E1
Plum Grove TX 132 B2
Plummer ID 14 B3
Plum Pt. RI 150 C4
Plum Sprs. KY 109 F2
Plymouth CA 36 C3
Plymouth DE 145 E3
Plymouth IN 89 F2
Plymouth MA 151 E2
Plymouth MI 76 B4
Plymouth MN 67 D4
Plymouth NE 35 F4
Plymouth NH 81 F3
Plymouth NC 113 F4
Plymouth OH 91 D3
Plymouth PA 261 A1
Plymouth UT 31 E2
Plymouth WI 74 C2
Plymouth Co. IA 35 F1
Plymouth Co. MA 151 E3
Plymouth Meeting PA 248 B1
Plympton MA 151 E2
Poca WV 101 E3
Pocahontas AR 108 A3
Pocahontas IL 98 B3
Pocahontas IA 72 B4
Pocahontas VA 111 F1
Pocahontas Co. IA 72 B4
Pocahontas Co. WV 102 A4
Pocasset MA 151 E3
Pocatello ID 31 E1
Pocola OK 116 B1
Pocomoke City MD 114 C2
Pocono Pines PA 93 F3
Poestenkill NY 94 B1
Poinciana FL 141 D2
Poinsett Co. AR 118 A1
Point TX 124 A1
Pt. Arena CA 36 A2
Pt. Blank TX 132 B1
Pt. Clear AL 135 E2
Pt. Comfort TX 61 F4
Pointe a la Hache LA 134 C3
Pointe Coupee Par. LA 133 F2
Pt. Hope AK 154 B1
Pt. Judith RI 150 C4
Pt. Marion PA 102 B1
Pt. of Rocks MD 144 A2
Pt. Pleasant NJ 147 E2
Pt. Pleasant WV 101 E3
Pt. Pleasant Beach NJ 147 E2
Pt. Reyes Sta. CA 36 B3
Poipu HI 152 B1
Pojoaque NM 49 D2
Polacca AZ 47 F2
Poland OH 276 C3
Polk PA 92 A2
Polk City FL 140 C2

Portland ME

Cape Cottage B2
Cape Elizabeth B2
Cumberland Foreside B1
Eight Corners A2
Falmouth B1
Falmouth Foreside B1
Portland B2
S. Portland A2
Westbrook A1
W. Falmouth A1

Portland OR

Beaverton C2
Carver D3
Cedar Hills C2
Clackamas D3
Durham C3
Garden Home C2
Gladstone D3
Gresham D2
Happy Valley D2
Johnson City D3
King City C3
Lake Oswego C3
Maywood Park D2
Metzger C2
Milwaukie D2
Oak Grove D3
Oregon City D3
Portland D2
Raleigh Hills C2
Rivergrove C3
Tigard C3
Tualatin C3
Vancouver D1
W. Linn D3
W. Slope C2

Abbott Run F1
Albion E1
Arctic E3
Ashton E1
Attleboro F1
Barrington F3
Berkeley E1
Central Falls F1
Centredale E2
Cranston E3
E. Providence F2
Esmond E1
Georgiaville E1
Hughesdale E2
Johnston E2
Lime Rock E1
Lonsdale F1
N. Providence E2
Pawtucket F2
Phenix E3
Providence E2
Quidnick E3
Quinnville E1
Riverside F3
Rumford F2
Saylesville F1
Seekonk F2
Stillwater E1
Thornton E2
Valley Falls F1
Warwick F3
W. Barrington F3
W. Warwick E3

Figures after entries indicate page number and grid reference.

Polk City IA 86 C1
Polk Co. AR 116 C3
Polk Co. FL 140 C3
Polk Co. GA 120 B4
Polk Co. IA 86 C1
Polk Co. MN 19 F2
Polk Co. MO 107 D1
Polk Co. NE 35 E3
Polk Co. NC 121 F1
Polk Co. OR 20 B2
Polk Co. TN 120 C1
Polk Co. TX 132 B1
Polk Co. WI 67 E3
Polkton NC 122 B2
Polkville NC 121 F1
Pollock SD 26 C1
Pollock Pines CA 36 C2
Polo IL 88 B1
Polo MO 96 C1
Polson MT 15 D3
Pomeroy IA 72 B4
Pomeroy OH 101 E2
Pomeroy WA 13 F4
Pomona CA 52 C2
Pomona KS 96 A3
Pomona NJ 105 D3
Pomona NY 148 B2
Pomona Park FL 139 D4
Pomonkey MD 144 B4
Pompano Beach FL 143 F1
Pompton Lakes NJ 148 A3
Pompton Plains NJ 148 A3
Ponca NE 35 F1
Ponca City OK 51 E1
Ponce de Leon FL 136 C1
Ponce Inlet FL 139 E4
Poncha Sprs. CO 41 D3
Ponchatoula LA 134 B2
Pond Creek OK 51 E1
Pondera Co. MT 15 E2
Ponderay ID 14 B2
Ponderosa NM 48 C2
Ponemah MN 64 A2
Ponte Vedra Beach FL 139 D2
Pontiac IL 88 C3
Pontiac MI 76 C4
Pontoon Beach IL 256 D1
Pontotoc MS 118 C3
Pontotoc Co. MS 118 C3
Pontotoc Co. OK 51 F4
Pooler GA 130 B3
Poolesville MD 144 A2
Pope Co. AR 117 D1
Pope Co. IL 109 D1
Pope Co. MN 66 A3
Poplar CA 45 D3
Poplar MT 17 E2
Poplar WI 64 C4
Poplar Bluff MO 108 A2
Poplar Grove IL 74 B4
Poplar Hills KY 230 E3
Poplarville MS 134 C1
Poquetanuck CT 149 F1
Poquonock CT 150 A3
Poquonock Bridge CT 149 F2
Poquoson VA 113 F2
Poquott NY 149 D3
Porcupine SD 26 B4
Portage IN 89 E2
Portage MI 89 F1
Portage PA 92 B4
Portage WI 74 B2
Portage Co. OH 91 E3
Portage Co. WI 74 B1
Portage Lakes OH 188 A2
Portageville MO 108 B3
Portal GA 129 F2
Portales NM 49 F4
Port Allegany PA 92 C1
Port Allen LA 134 A2
Port Angeles WA 12 B2
Port Aransas TX 63 F2
Port Arthur TX 132 C3
Port Austin MI 76 C1
Port Barre LA 133 F2
Port Barrington IL 203 A1
Port Byron IL 88 A2
Port Byron NY 79 D3
Port Carbon PA 93 E3
Port Charlotte FL 140 C4
Port Chester NY 148 C3
Port Clinton OH 90 C2
Port Deposit MD 145 D1
Port Edwards WI 74 A1
Porter IN 89 E2
Porter OK 106 A4
Porter WA 12 B4
Porter Corners NY 80 C4
Porter Co. IN 89 E2
Porterdale GA 121 D4
Porter Hts. TX 132 A2
Porterville CA 45 D3
Port Ewen NY 94 B2
Port Gibson MS 126 A3
Port Hadlock WA 12 C2
Port Henry NY 81 D3
Port Hueneme CA 52 B2
Port Huron MI 77 D3
Portia AR 107 F4
Port Isabel TX 63 F4
Port Jefferson NY 149 D3
Port Jefferson Sta. NY 149 D3
Port Jervis NY 148 A2
Port La Belle FL 141 D4
Portland AR 125 F1
Portland CT 149 E1
Portland IN 90 A4
Portland ME 82 B3
Portland MI 76 A3
Portland ND 19 E3
Portland OR 20 C2
Portland PA 93 F3
Portland TN 109 F3
Portland TX 63 F2
Port Lavaca TX 61 F4
Port Leyden NY 79 E2
Port Ludlow WA 12 C2
Port Matilda PA 92 C3
Port Monmouth NJ 147 E1
Port Neches TX 132 C3
Port Norris NJ 145 F2
Portola CA 37 D1
Portola Valley CA 259 C6
Port Orange FL 139 E4
Port Orchard WA 12 C3
Port Orford OR 28 A1
Port Reading NJ 240 A5
Port Republic NJ 147 E4
Port Richey FL 140 B2
Port Royal PA 93 D4
Port Royal SC 130 C2
Port St. Joe FL 137 D3
Port St. John FL 141 E1
Port St. Lucie FL 141 E4
Port Salerno FL 141 E4
Port Sanilac MI 76 C2
Portsmouth NH 82 A4
Portsmouth OH 101 D3
Portsmouth RI 151 D4
Portsmouth VA 113 F2
Port Sulphur LA 134 C4
Port Townsend WA 12 C2
Portville NY 92 C1
Port Vincent LA 134 A2
Port Vue PA 250 C3
Port Washington NY 148 C3
Port Washington WI 75 D2
Port Washington North NY 241 G2
Port Wentworth GA 130 B3
Porum OK 116 A1
Posen IL 203 D6
Posey Co. IN 99 D4
Poseyville IN 99 D4
Post TX 58 B2
Post Falls ID 14 B3
Poston AZ 53 F2
Postville IA 73 E3
Poteau OK 116 B2
Poteet TX 61 D3
Poth TX 61 D3
Potlatch ID 14 B4
Potomac IL 89 D4
Potomac MD 144 B3
Potomac Hts. MD 144 B4
Potosi MO 98 A4
Potosi TX 58 C3
Potosi WI 73 F4
Potsdam NY 80 B1
Pottawatomie Co. KS 43 F2
Pottawatomie Co. OK 51 F3
Pottawattamie Co. IA 86 A2
Potter Co. PA 92 C2
Potter Co. SD 27 D2
Potter Co. TX 50 A3
Pottersville NY 80 C3
Potter Valley CA 36 A2
Potterville MI 76 A4
Pottsboro TX 59 F1
Potts Camp MS 118 C2
Pottstown PA 146 B2
Pottsville AR 117 D1
Pottsville PA 93 E3
Potwin KS 43 F3
Poughkeepsie NY 148 B1
Poughquag NY 148 C1
Poulan GA 129 D4
Poulsbo WA 12 C3
Poultney VT 81 D4
Pound VA 111 E2
Pound Ridge NY 148 C2
Poway CA 53 D4
Powderly KY 109 E2
Powder River Co. MT 25 E2
Powder Sprs. GA 120 C4
Powell AL 120 A2
Powell OH 90 C4
Powell TN 110 C4
Powell WY 24 B3
Powell Co. KY 100 C4
Powell Co. MT 15 D3
Powells Crossroads TN 120 B1
Powellton WV 101 F4
Power Co. ID 31 E1
Powers OR 28 A1
Powers Lake ND 18 A2
Powers Lake WI 74 C4
Poweshiek Co. IA 87 D1
Powhatan VA 113 D1
Powhatan Co. VA 113 E1
Powhatan Pt. OH 101 F1
Pownal VT 94 C1
Poydras LA 134 C3
Poynette WI 74 B2
Prague OK 51 F3
Prairie City IA 87 D2
Prairie City OR 21 F3
Prairie Co. AR 117 F2
Prairie Co. MT 17 E4
Prairie Creek AR 106 C3
Prairie du Chien WI 73 F3
Prairie du Rocher IL 98 A4
Prairie du Sac WI 74 A3
Prairie Grove AR 106 C4
Prairie Grove IL 203 A1
Prairie View TX 61 F2
Prairie Vil. KS 224 B4
Prairieville LA 134 A2
Pratt KS 43 D4
Pratt WV 101 F4
Pratt Co. KS 43 D4
Prattsburgh NY 78 C4
Prattville AL 128 A2
Preble Co. OH 100 B1
Premont TX 63 E2
Prentice WI 68 A3
Prentiss MS 126 B4
Prentiss Co. MS 119 D2
Prescott AZ 47 D4
Prescott AR 117 D4
Prescott WI 67 D4
Prescott Valley AZ 47 D4
Presho SD 26 C4
Presidential Lakes Estates NJ 147 D3
Presidio TX 62 B4
Presidio Co. TX 62 B3
Presque Isle ME 85 D2
Presque Isle Co. MI 70 C3
Preston GA 128 C3
Preston ID 31 E2
Preston IA 88 A1
Preston MD 145 E4
Preston MN 73 E2
Preston Co. WV 102 B2
Prestonsburg KY 111 E1
Pretty Prairie KS 43 E4
Price UT 39 F1
Price Co. WI 68 A2
Priceville AL 119 F3
Prichard AL 135 E1
Priest River ID 14 B2
Primghar IA 72 A3
Prince Edward Co. VA 113 D2
Prince Frederick MD 144 C4
Prince George VA 113 E2
Prince George Co. VA 113 E2
Prince George's Co. MD 144 C3
Princes Lakes IN 99 F2
Princess Anne MD 103 F4
Princeton FL 143 E3
Princeton IL 88 B2
Princeton IN 99 D4
Princeton IA 88 A2
Princeton KY 109 D2
Princeton MN 66 C3
Princeton MO 86 C4
Princeton NJ 147 D2
Princeton NC 123 E1
Princeton TX 59 F2
Princeton WV 111 F1
Princeton WI 74 B2
Princeton Jct. NJ 147 D2
Princeville HI 152 B1
Princeville IL 88 B3
Princeville NC 113 E4
Prince William Co. VA 144 A4
Prineville OR 21 D3
Pringle PA 261 B1
Prior Lake MN 67 D4
Proctor MN 64 C4
Proctor VT 81 D3
Proctorville OH 101 E3
Progreso TX 63 E4
Progress PA 218 B1
Progress Vil. FL 266 C2
Prophetstown IL 88 A2
Prospect CT 149 D1
Prospect KY 100 A4
Prospect OH 90 C4
Prospect PA 92 A3
Prospect Hts. IL 203 C2
Prospect Park PA 248 B4
Prosper TX 59 F2
Prosperity SC 122 A3
Prosser WA 21 E1
Protection KS 43 D4
Provencal LA 125 D4
Providence FL 140 C2
Providence KY 109 D1
Providence RI 150 C3
Providence UT 31 E3
Providence Co. RI 150 C3
Provincetown MA 151 F2
Provo UT 31 F4
Prowers Co. CO 42 A3
Prudenville MI 76 A1
Prue OK 51 F2
Prunedale CA 44 B2
Pruntytown WV 102 A2
Pryor MT 24 C2
Pryor OK 106 A3
Pueblo CO 41 E3
Pueblo Co. CO 41 E3
Pueblo Pintado NM 48 B2
Pueblo West CO 41 E3
Puhi HI 152 B1
Pukalani HI 153 D1
Pukwana SD 27 D4
Pulaski NY 79 D2
Pulaski TN 119 F1
Pulaski VA 112 A2
Pulaski WI 68 C4
Pulaski Co. AR 117 E2
Pulaski Co. GA 129 E3
Pulaski Co. IL 108 C2
Pulaski Co. IN 89 E3
Pulaski Co. KY 110 B2
Pulaski Co. MO 97 E4
Pulaski Co. VA 112 A2
Pullman MI 75 E4
Pullman WA 14 B4
Pumphrey MD 193 C4
Pumpkin Ctr. CA 45 D4
Pumpkin Ctr. NC 115 D4
Punaluu HI 152 A2
Punta Gorda FL 140 C4
Punta Rassa FL 142 C1
Punxsutawney PA 92 B3
Pupukea HI 152 A2
Purcell OK 51 E3
Purcellville VA 144 A2
Purdy MO 106 C2
Purdys NY 148 C2
Purvis MS 134 C1
Puryear TN 109 D3
Pushmataha Co. OK 116 A3
Putnam CT 150 B3
Putnam Co. FL 139 D3
Putnam Co. GA 129 E1
Putnam Co. IL 88 B2
Putnam Co. IN 99 E1
Putnam Co. MO 87 D4
Putnam Co. NY 148 B2
Putnam Co. OH 90 B3
Putnam Co. TN 110 A3
Putnam Co. WV 101 E3
Putnam Lake NY 148 C1
Putney GA 129 D4
Putney KY 111 D2
Putney VT 81 E4
Puxico MO 108 B2
Puyallup WA 12 C3
Pyatt AR 107 D3

Q

Quaker City OH 101 F1
Quaker Hill CT 149 F2
Quakertown PA 146 C1
Quanah TX 50 C4
Quantico VA 144 A4
Quapaw OK 106 B2
Quarryville CT 150 A3
Quarryville PA 146 A3
Quartz Hill CA 52 C2
Quartzsite AZ 54 A1
Quasqueton IA 73 E4
Quay Co. NM 49 F3
Quechee VT 81 E3
Queen Anne's Co. MD 145 D3
Queen City MO 87 D4
Queen City TX 124 C1
Queen Creek AZ 54 C2
Queens Co. NY 148 B4
Queenstown MD 145 D3
Quenemo KS 96 A3
Questa NM 49 D1
Quidnessett RI 150 C4
Quidnick RI 150 C3
Quilcene WA 12 C3
Quimby IA 72 A4
Quinby SC 122 C3
Quince Orchard MD 144 B2
Quincy CA 36 C1
Quincy FL 137 D2
Quincy IL 97 F1
Quincy MA 151 D1
Quincy MI 90 A1
Quincy OH 90 B4
Quincy PA 103 D1
Quincy WA 13 E3
Quinebaug CT 150 B2
Quinhagak AK 154 B3
Quinlan TX 59 F2
Quinnesec MI 68 C2
Quinter KS 42 C2
Quinton OK 116 A1
Quinwood WV 102 A4
Quitman AR 117 E1
Quitman GA 137 F1
Quitman MS 127 D3
Quitman TX 124 A2
Quitman Co. GA 128 C3

Elmwood Park B2
Franksville A1
Kenosha A3
Mount Pleasant A1
N. Bay B1
Pleasant Prairie A3
Racine B1
Sturtevant A2
Wind Pt. B1

Entries in **bold black** indicate counties or parishes.
Entries in **bold color** indicate cities with detailed inset maps.

Quitman Co. MS 118 B3
Quogue NY 149 E3

R

Rabun Co. GA 121 D2
Raceland KY 101 D3
Raceland LA 134 B3
Racine MN 73 D2
Racine OH 101 E2
Racine WV 101 E4
Racine WI 75 D4
Racine Co. WI 74 C4
Radcliff KY 99 F4
Radcliffe IA 72 C4
Radford VA 112 A2
Radium Sprs. NM 56 B3
Rancho Cordova CA 36 C3
Rancho Cucamonga CA 229 G2
Rancho Mirage CA 53 E3
Rancho Palos Verdes CA 228 C4
Rancho Santa Fe CA 53 D4
Rancho Santa Margarita CA 229 G5
Ranchos de Taos NM 49 D2
Rancocas NJ 147 D3
Rand WV 101 F4
Randall MN 66 B2
Randall Co. TX 50 A3
Randallstown MD 144 C1
Randle Cliff Beach MD 144 C4
Randleman NC 112 B4
Randlett OK 51 D4
Randolph ME 82 C2
Rapides Par. LA 125 E4
Rapids NY 78 B3
Rapids City IL 208 C1
Rappahannock Co. VA 103 D3
Raritan NJ 147 D1
Rathdrum ID 14 B3
Ratliff FL 139 D2
Raton NM 49 E1
Raubsville PA 146 C1
Ravalli Co. MT 23 D1
Raven VA 111 F2
Ravena NY 94 B1
Ravenden AR 107 F3
Ravenel SC 131 D2
Ravenna KY 110 C1
Ravenna MI 75 F3
Ravenna NE 35 D3
Ravenna OH 91 E3
Ravensdale WA 12 C3
Ravenswood WV 101 E3
Ravia OK 51 F4
Ravine PA 93 E4
Rawlings MD 102 C1
Rawlins WY 32 C2
Rawlins Co. KS 42 B1
Rawson OH 90 B3
Ray ND 18 A2
Ray City GA 137 F1
Ray Co. MO 96 C2
Raymond IL 98 B2
Raymond ME 82 B3
Raymond MN 66 B4
Raymond MS 126 B3
Raymond NH 81 F4
Raymond WA 12 B4
Raymondville TX 63 F4
Raymore MO 96 B3
Rayne LA 133 E2
Raynham MA 151 D2
Raynham Ctr. MA 151 D3
Raytown MO 96 B2
Rayville LA 125 F2
Readfield ME 82 B2
Reading MA 151 D1
Reading MI 90 A1
Reading OH 204 B1
Reading PA 146 A2
Readington NJ 147 D1
Readlyn IA 73 E4
Readsboro VT 94 C1
Reagan Co. TX 58 A4
Real Co. TX 60 C2
Reamstown PA 146 A2
Reardan WA 13 F3
Reaville NJ 147 D1
Rector AR 108 A3
Red Bank NJ 147 E2
Red Bank SC 122 A4
Red Bank TN 120 B1
Red Bay AL 119 D3
Red Bluff CA 36 B1
Red Boiling Sprs. TN 110 A3
Red Bud IL 98 B4
Redby MN 64 A2
Red Cloud NE 43 D1
Red Creek NY 79 D3
Reddick FL 138 C4
Redding CA 28 C4
Redding CT 148 C2
Redding Ridge CT 148 C2
Red Feather Lakes CO 33 E4
Redfield AR 117 E3
Redfield IA 86 C2
Redfield SD 27 D2
Redford MI 210 B3
Redford NY 80 C2
Redgranite WI 74 B1
Red Hill PA 146 B1
Red Hill SC 123 D4
Red Hook NY 94 B2
Redington Beach FL 140 B3
Redington Shores FL 266 A2
Red Jacket WV 111 E1
Redkey IN 90 A4
Red Lake MN 64 A2
Red Lake Co. MN 19 F2
Red Lake Falls MN 19 F2
Redland MD 144 B2
Redlands CA 53 D2
Red Level AL 128 A4
Red Lick TX 116 C4
Red Lion PA 103 E1
Red Lodge MT 24 B2
Red Mesa AZ 47 F1
Redmond OR 21 D3
Redmond UT 39 E2
Redmond WA 12 C3
Red Oak IA 86 A3
Red Oak NC 113 D4
Red Oak OK 116 B2
Red Oak TX 59 F3
Red Oaks Mill NY 148 B1
Redondo Beach CA 228 C4
Red River NM 49 D1
Red River Co. TX 116 B4
Red River Par. LA 125 D3
Red Sprs. NC 122 C2
Redwater MS 126 C2
Redwater TX 124 C1
Redway CA 36 A1
Red Willow Co. NE 42 C1
Red Wing MN 67 E4
Redwood NY 79 E1
Redwood City CA 36 B4
Redwood Co. MN 66 B4
Redwood Estates CA 36 B4
Redwood Falls MN 66 B4
Redwood Valley CA 36 A2
Reece City AL 120 A3
Reed City MI 75 F2
Reed Creek GA 121 E3
Reedley CA 45 D3
Reedsburg WI 74 A2
Reedsport OR 20 A4
Reedsville PA 93 D3
Reedsville WV 102 B1
Reedsville WI 74 C1
Reedville VA 103 F4
Reelsboro NC 115 D3
Reese MI 76 B2
Reeseville WI 74 B3
Reeves Co. TX 57 E4
Reeves Crossing DE 145 E3
Reform AL 127 E1
Refton PA 146 A3
Refugio TX 61 E4
Refugio Co. TX 61 E4
Regent ND 18 A4
Rehobeth AL 136 C1
Rehoboth MA 151 D3
Rehoboth NM 48 A3
Rehoboth Beach DE 145 F4
Reidland KY 109 D2
Reidsville GA 129 F3
Reidsville NC 112 B3
Reidville SC 121 F2
Reinbeck IA 73 D4
Reisterstown MD 144 C1
Reliance SD 27 D4
Reliance WY 32 B3
Remerton GA 137 F1
Remington IN 89 E3
Remington VA 103 D3
Remsen IA 35 F1
Remsen NY 79 F3
Remsenburg NY 149 E4
Reno NV 37 D1
Reno TX 59 E2
Reno TX 116 A4
Reno Co. KS 43 E4
Renova MS 118 A4
Renovo PA 92 C2
Rensselaer IN 89 E3
Rensselaer NY 94 B1
Rensselaer Co. NY 94 B1
Renton WA 12 C3
Renville MN 66 B4
Renville Co. MN 66 B4
Renville Co. ND 18 B1
Republic MI 65 F4
Republic MO 107 D2
Republic OH 90 C3
Republic PA 102 B1
Republic WA 13 F1
Republic Co. KS 43 E1
Resaca GA 120 B2
Reserve LA 134 B3

Raleigh / Durham / Chapel Hill NC

Apex B3
Bayleaf D2
Bethesda C2
Carrboro A2
Cary C3
Chapel Hill A2
Durham B2
Eno A1
Falls D2
Garner D3
Gorman C1
Green Level B3
Hillsborough A1
Leesville C2
Macedonia C3
Morrisville C3
Oak Grove C1
Raleigh D2
Redwood C1
Stony Hill D1

Radnor PA 248 A2
Raeford NC 122 C2
Ragland AL 120 A4
Rahway NJ 147 E1
Rainbow City AL 120 A4
Rainelle WV 101 F4
Rainier OR 20 B1
Rainier WA 12 C4
Rains SC 122 C3
Rains Co. TX 124 A1
Rainsville AL 120 A3
Raleigh MS 126 C3
Raleigh NC 113 D4
Raleigh Co. WV 101 F4
Raleigh Hills OR 251 C2
Ralls TX 58 B1
Ralls Co. MO 97 F2
Ralston NE 245 A3
Ralston WY 24 B3
Ramah NM 48 A3
Ramona CA 53 D4
Ramona OK 51 F1
Ramsay MI 65 E4
Ramseur NC 112 B4
Ramsey IL 98 C2
Ramsey MN 67 D3
Ramsey NJ 148 B3
Ramsey Co. MN 67 D3
Ramsey Co. ND 19 D2
Ranburne AL 120 B4
Ranchester WY 25 D2
Randolph MA 151 D2
Randolph NE 35 E2
Randolph NY 92 B1
Randolph UT 31 F3
Randolph VT 81 E3
Randolph WI 74 B2
Randolph Ctr. VT 81 E3
Randolph Co. AL 128 B1
Randolph Co. AR 107 F3
Randolph Co. GA 128 C4
Randolph Co. IL 98 B4
Randolph Co. IN 90 A4
Randolph Co. MO 97 E2
Randolph Co. NC 112 B4
Randolph Co. WV 102 B3
Randolph Hills MD 270 C1
Random Lake WI 74 C2
Rangeley ME 82 B1
Rangely CO 40 B1
Ranger TX 59 D3
Rankin IL 89 D4
Rankin PA 250 C2
Rankin TX 58 A4
Rankin Co. MS 126 B2
Ranlo NC 122 A1
Ransom Canyon TX 58 A1
Ransom Co. ND 19 E4
Ransomville NY 78 A3
Ranson WV 103 D2
Rantoul IL 88 C4
Rapid City SD 26 A3

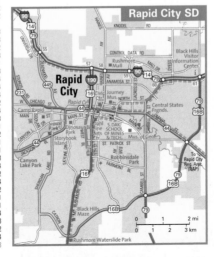

Figures after entries indicate page number and grid reference.

Atlee B1	Chamberlayne	Glen Allen B1	Mechanicsville ...C1	Rivermont C3
Bellwood B3	Farms B1	Greendale B1	Midlothian A2	Sandston C2
Bensley B3	Chester B3	Highland Sprs. ... C2	Newmans C1	Seven Pines C2
Bon Air A2	Chesterfield B3	Hunton C1	Old Cold Harbor... C1	Short Pump A1
Borkeys Store C1	E. Highland Park... B1	Lakeside B1	Pearsons Corner.. C1	Studley C1
Centralia B3	Fair Oaks C2	Laurel B1	Richmond B2	Varina C2

Reserve NM 55 F1	Richmond ME 82 C3	Ringoes NJ 147 A3
Reston VA 144 A3	Richmond MI 76 C4	Ringtown PA 93 E3
Revere MA 151 D1	Richmond MN 66 B2	Ringwood NJ 148 A2
Rexburg ID 23 E4	Richmond MO 96 C2	Rio FL 141 E4
Reyno AR 108 A3	Richmond TX 132 A3	Rio WI 74 B2
Reynolds GA 129 D2	Richmond UT 31 E2	Rio Arriba Co. NM 48 C1
Reynolds IN 89 E3	Richmond VT 81 D2	Rio Blanco Co. CO 40 B1
Reynolds ND 19 E3	Richmond VA 113 E1	Rio Bravo TX 63 D2
Reynoldsburg OH 101 D1	Richmond Co. GA 130 A1	Rio Dell CA 28 A4
Reynoldsville PA 92 B3	Richmond Co. NY 147 E1	Rio del Mar CA 236 D1
Rhea Co. TN 110 B4	Richmond Co. NC 122 C2	Rio Grande NJ 104 C4
Rhinebeck NY 94 B2	Richmond Co. VA 103 E4	Rio Grande OH 101 E3
Rhinelander WI 68 B2	Richmond Hts. FL 143 E2	Rio Grande City TX 63 E4
Rhome TX 59 E2	Richmond Hts. MO 256 B2	Rio Grande Co. CO 41 D4
Rialto CA 53 D2	Richmond Hts. OH 204 G1	Rio Hondo TX 63 F4
Rib Lake WI 68 A3	Richmond Hill GA 130 B3	Rio Linda CA 255 D1
Rice MN 66 C2	Richmondville NY 79 F4	Rio Rancho NM 48 C3
Rice TX 59 F3	Rich Square NC 113 E3	Rio Rico AZ 54 C1
Riceboro GA 130 B4	Richton MS 127 D4	Rio Verde AZ 54 C1
Rice City RI 150 C3	Richwood LA 125 C2	Rio Vista CA 36 B3
Rice Co. KS 43 E3	Richwood OH 90 C4	Rio Vista TX 59 E3
Rice Co. MN 72 C1	Richwood TX 132 A4	Ripley CA 53 F3
Rice Lake WI 67 E3	Richwood WV 102 A4	Ripley MS 118 C2
Riceville IA 73 D3	Riddle OR 28 B1	Ripley NY 78 A4
Riceville TN 120 C1	Ridge NY 149 D3	Ripley OH 100 C3
Richardson TX 207 E1	Ridgebury CT 148 A2	Ripley OK 51 F2
Richardson Co. NE 86 A4	Ridgebury NY 148 A2	Ripley TN 108 B4
Richardton ND 18 A4	Ridgecrest CA 45 E4	Ripley WV 101 E3
Richboro PA 146 C2	Ridge Farm IL 99 D1	Ripley Co. IN 100 A2
Rich Co. UT 31 F3	Ridgefield CT 148 C2	Ripley Co. MO 108 A3
Rich Creek VA 112 A1	Ridgefield NJ 240 D2	Ripon CA 36 C4
Richey MT 17 E3	Ridgefield WA 20 C1	Ripon WI 74 B2
Richfield ID 31 D1	Ridgefield Park NJ 240 D1	Ririe ID 23 E4
Richfield MN 235 B3	Ridgeland MS 126 B2	Rising Star TX 59 D3
Richfield NC 122 B1	Ridgeland SC 130 C2	Rising Sun DE 145 E2
Richfield OH 91 E2	Ridgely MD 145 E3	Rising Sun IN 100 B2
Richfield UT 39 E2	Ridgely TN 108 B3	Rising Sun MD 146 A4
Richfield Sprs. NY 79 F3	Ridge Manor FL 140 C1	Risingsun OH 90 C2
Richford VT 81 E1	Ridge Spr. SC 121 F4	Rison AR 117 E4
Richgrove CA 45 D4	Ridgetop TN 109 F3	Ritchie Co. WV 101 F2
Rich Hill MO 96 B4	Ridgeville IN 90 A4	Rittman OH 91 E3
Richland GA 128 C3	Ridgeville SC 130 C1	Ritzville WA 13 F3
Richland IN 87 E2	Ridgeway MO 86 C4	Riverbank CA 36 C4
Richland MI 75 F4	Ridgeway VA 112 B3	River Bend NC 115 D3
Richland MS 126 B3	Ridgeway WV 103 D2	River Bluff KY 100 A4
Richland MO 97 E4	Ridgeway WI 74 A3	Riverdale CA 44 C3
Richland NJ 147 D4	Ridgewood NJ 148 B3	Riverdale GA 203 D6
Richland PA 146 A2	Ridgway CO 40 B3	Riverdale IA 208 B1
Richland WA 13 E4	Ridgway IL 109 D1	Riverdale ND 18 B3
Richland Ctr. WI 74 A3	Ridgway PA 92 B2	Riverdale UT 244 A2
Richland Co. IL 99 D3	Ridley Park PA 248 B4	Riverdale Park MD 270 E2
Richland Co. MT 17 F2	Riegelsville PA 146 C1	River Edge NJ 240 C1
Richland Co. ND 19 E4	Riesel TX 59 F4	River Falls AL 128 A4
Richland Co. OH 91 D3	Rifle CO 40 B1	River Falls WI 67 D3
Richland Co. SC 122 B3	Rigby ID 23 E4	River Forest IL 203 D4
Richland Co. WI 74 A2	Riggins ID 22 B2	River Grove IL 203 D4
Richland Hills TX 207 B2	Riley KS 43 F2	Rivergrove OR 251 C3
Richland Par. LA 125 C2	Riley Co. KS 43 F2	Riverhead NY 149 E3
Richlands NC 115 D4	Rillito AZ 55 D3	River Hills WI 234 D1
Richlands VA 111 F2	Rimersburg PA 92 A3	River Oaks TX 207 A2
Richlandtown PA 146 C1	Rincon GA 130 B3	River Ridge LA 239 B1
Richmond CA 36 B3	Rindge NH 95 D1	River Rouge MI 210 C4
Richmond IL 74 C4	Rineyville KY 110 A1	Riverside AL 120 A4
Richmond IN 100 B1	Ringgold GA 120 B2	Riverside CA 53 D2
Richmond KS 96 A3	Ringgold LA 125 C2	Riverside IL 203 D4
Richmond KY 110 C1	Ringgold Co. IA 86 B3	Riverside IA 87 F2
Richmond LA 126 A2	Ringling OK 51 E4	Riverside MO 224 B2

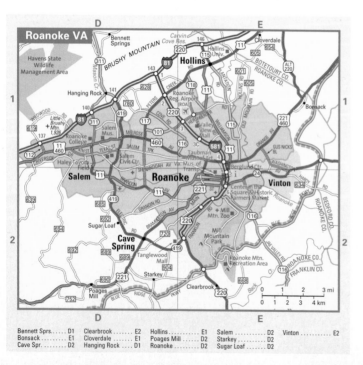

Bennett Sprs. D1	Clearbrook E2	Hollins E1	Salem D2	Vinton E2
Bonsack E1	Cloverdale E1	Poages Mill D2	Starkey D2	
Cave Spr. D2	Hanging Rock D1	Roanoke D2	Sugar Loaf D2	

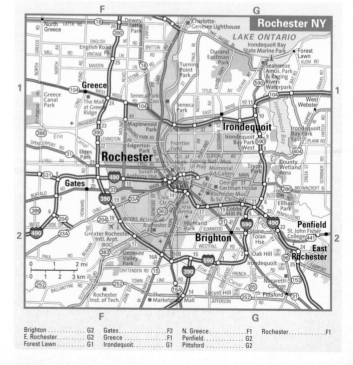

Brighton G2	Gates F2	N. Greece F1	Rochester F1
E. Rochester G2	Greece F1	Penfield G2	
Forest Lawn G1	Irondequoit G1	Pittsford G2	

Entries in **bold black** indicate counties or parishes.
Entries in **bold color** indicate cities with detailed inset maps.

Riverside NJ 147 D3
Riverside NY 149 E3
Riverside OH 100 C1
Riverside PA 93 E3
Riverside Co. CA 53 E3
Riverton IL 98 B1
Riverton KS 106 B2
Riverton NJ 146 C3
Riverton UT 31 E4
Riverton WY 32 B1
Riverview FL 140 C2
Riverview MO 256 C1
Riverwood KY 230 E1
Riverwoods IL 203 C2
Rives Jct. MI 76 A4
Rivesville WV 102 A1
Rockaway NJ 148 A3
Rockaway Beach MO 107 D3
Rockaway Beach OR 20 B1
Rockbridge Co. VA 102 B4
Rockcastle Co. KY 110 C2
Rock Co. MN 27 F4
Rock Co. NE 35 D2
Rock Co. WI 74 B4
Rock Creek MN 67 D2
Rock Creek OH 91 F2
Rockdale MD 144 C2
Rockdale TX 61 E1
Rockdale Co. GA 120 C4
Rockfall CT 149 E1
Rock Falls IL 88 B1
Rockford AL 128 A1
Rockwell City IA 72 B4
Rockwood MI 90 C1
Rockwood PA 102 B1
Rockwood TN 110 B4
Rocky Ford CO 41 F3
Rocky Hill CT 149 E1
Rocky Hill NJ 147 D1
Rocky Mount NC 113 E4
Rocky Mount VA 112 B2
Rocky Pt. NY 149 D3
Rocky Ridge UT 39 E1
Rocky Ripple IN 221 B2
Rocky River OH 204 E2
Rocky Top TN 110 C3
Rodeo CA 259 C1
Roebuck SC 121 F2
Roeland Park KS 224 B3
Roessleville NY 188 D2
Roff OK 51 F4
Roger Mills Co. OK 50 C2
Rogers AR 106 C3
Rogers MN 66 C3
Rogers TX 61 E1
Rogers City MI 71 D3
Rogers Co. OK 106 A3
Rogersville AL 119 E2
Rogersville MO 107 D2
Rogersville TN 111 D3
Rogue River OR 28 B2
Rohnert Park CA 36 B3
Roland IA 86 C1
Roland OK 116 B1
Rolesville NC 113 D4
Rolette ND 18 C1
Rolette Co. ND 18 C1
Rolfe IA 72 B3
Rolla KS 50 B1
Rolla MO 97 F4
Rolla ND 18 C1
Rolling Fields KY 230 E1
Rolling Fork MS 126 A1
Rolling Hills CA 228 C4
Rolling Hills KY 230 F1
Rolling Hills WY 33 D1
Rolling Hills Estates CA 228 C4
Rolling Meadows IL 203 B3
Rolling Prairie IN 89 E2
Rollingstone MN 73 E1
Rollinsford NH 82 A4
Roma TX 63 D4
Romancoke MD 145 D3
Roman Forest TX 132 B2
Rome GA 120 B3
Rome IL 88 B3
Rome NY 79 E3
Rome City IN 90 A2
Romeo CO 41 D4
Romeo MI 76 C4
Romeoville IL 89 D2
Romney WV 102 C2
Romoland CA 229 K4
Romulus MI 90 C1
Ronan MT 15 D3
Ronceverte WV 112 A1
Ronkonkoma NY 149 D3
Roodhouse IL 98 A2
Rooks Co. KS 43 D2
Roosevelt NJ 147 E2
Roosevelt UT 32 A4
Roosevelt Co. MT 17 E2
Roosevelt Co. NM 49 F4
Roosevelt Park MI 75 E3
Roper NC 113 F4
Ropesville TX 58 A1
Rosalia WA 14 A3
Rosamond CA 52 C1
Rosaryville MD 144 C4
Rosburg WA 12 B4
Roscoe IL 74 B4
Roscoe NY 94 A2
Roscoe SD 27 D2
Roscoe TX 58 B3
Roscommon MI 70 C4
Roscommon Co. MI 76 A1
Roseau MN 19 F1
Roseau Co. MN 19 F1
Roseboro NC 123 D2
Rose Bud AR 117 E1
Rosebud SD 34 C1
Rosebud TX 59 F4
Rosebud Co. MT 17 D4
Roseburg OR 28 B1
Rose City MI 76 B1
Rose City TX 132 C2
Rosedale IN 99 E1
Rosedale LA 133 F2
Rosedale MD 144 C2
Rosedale MS 118 A4
Rosedale Beach DE 145 F4
Rose Haven MD 144 C4
Rose Hill KS 43 F4
Rose Hill NC 123 E2
Rose Hill VA 111 D3
Rose Hill VA 270 C5
Roseland FL 141 E3
Roseland LA 134 B1
Roseland NJ 240 A2
Roselawn IN 89 D3
Roselle IL 203 B3
Roselle NJ 147 E1
Roselle Park NJ 147 E1
Rose Lodge OR 20 B2
Rosemead CA 228 E2
Rosemont CA 255 C3
Rosemont IL 203 C3
Rosemount MN 235 D4
Rosemount OH 101 D3
Rosenberg TX 132 A3
Rosendale NY 94 B3
Rosendale WI 74 C2
Rosenhayn NJ 145 F1
Rosepine LA 133 D1
Roseto PA 93 F3
Rose Valley PA 248 A4
Roseville CA 36 C2
Roseville IL 88 A3
Roseville MI 210 D2
Roseville MN 235 C2
Roseville OH 101 E1
Roseville Park DE 146 B4
Rosholt SD 27 F1
Rosiclare IL 109 D1
Roslyn PA 248 C1
Roslyn SD 27 E2
Roslyn WA 13 D3
Roslyn Estates NY 241 G2
Rosman NC 121 E1
Ross CA 259 A1
Ross OH 100 B2
Ross Co. OH 101 D2
Rossford OH 267 B2
Rossiter PA 92 B3
Rossmoor CA 228 E4
Rossmoor NJ 147 E2
Rossville GA 120 B2
Rossville IL 89 D4
Rossville IN 89 E4
Rossville KS 43 F2
Rossville MD 193 E2
Roswell GA 120 C3
Roswell NM 57 E1
Rotan TX 58 B2
Rothsay MN 19 F4
Rothschild WI 68 B4
Rothsville PA 146 A2
Rotonda FL 140 C4
Rotterdam NY 94 B1
Rotterdam Jct. NY 94 B1
Rougemont NC 112 C3
Rough Rock AZ 47 F1
Round Hill VA 103 D2
Round Lake NY 94 B1
Round Mtn. NV 37 F2
Round Pond ME 82 C3
Round Rock AZ 47 F1
Round Rock TX 61 E1
Roundup MT 16 C4
Rouses Pt. NY 81 D1
Routt Co. CO 32 C4
Rouzerville PA 103 D1
Rowan Co. KY 100 C4
Rowan Co. NC 112 A4
Rowland NC 122 C3
Rowland Hts. CA 229 F3
Rowlesburg WV 102 B2
Rowlett TX 207 E1
Rowley MA 151 F1
Roxana DE 145 F4
Roxboro NC 112 C3
Roxie MS 126 A4
Roxton TX 116 A4
Roy NM 49 E2
Roy UT 31 E3
Royal Ctr. IN 89 E3
Royal City WA 13 E4
Royal Oak MD 145 D4
Royal Oak MI 76 C4
Royal Palm Beach FL 143 E1
Royal Pines NC 121 E1
Royalton IL 98 C4
Royalton MN 66 C2
Royersford PA 146 B2
Royse City TX 59 F2
Royston GA 121 E3
Rubonia FL 266 B4
Ruch OR 28 B2
Rudyard MT 15 F2
Rugby ND 18 C2
Ruidoso NM 57 D2
Ruidoso Downs NM 57 D2
Rule TX 58 C2
Ruleville MS 118 A4
Rumford ME 82 B2
Rumson NJ 147 F2
Runaway Bay TX 59 E2
Runge TX 61 E3
Runnels Co. TX 58 C3
Runnemede NJ 146 C3
Running Sprs. CA 229 K1
Rupert ID 31 D1
Rupert WV 102 A4
Rural Hall NC 112 B3
Rural Retreat VA 111 F2
Rural Valley PA 92 B3
Rush City MN 67 D2
Rush Co. IN 100 A1
Rush Co. KS 43 D3
Rushford MN 73 E2
Rushford Vil. MN 73 E2
Rushmere VA 113 F2
Rush Sprs. OK 51 E4
Rush Valley UT 31 E4
Rushville IL 88 A4
Rushville IN 100 A1
Rushville NE 34 A1
Rushville NY 78 C4
Rusk TX 124 B3
Rusk Co. TX 124 B3
Rusk Co. WI 67 F3
Ruskin FL 140 B3
Russell IA 87 D3
Russell KS 43 D2
Russell KY 101 D3
Russell MA 94 C2
Russell PA 92 B1
Russell Co. AL 128 C3
Russell Co. KS 43 D2
Russell Co. KY 110 B2
Russell Co. VA 111 F2
Russell Gardens NY 241 G3
Russells Pt. OH 90 B4
Russell Sprs. KY 110 B2
Russellville AL 119 E3
Russellville AR 117 D1

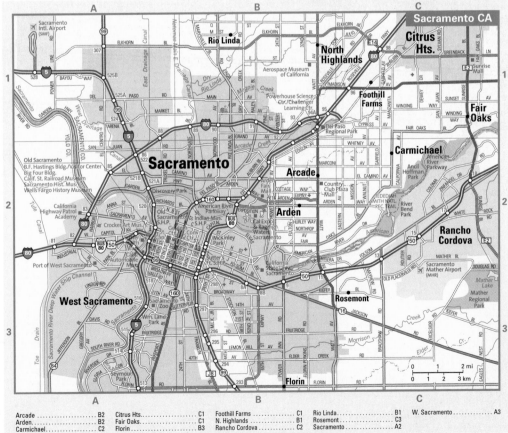

Rockford IL

Riviera Beach FL 141 F4
Riviera Beach MD 144 C2
Roachdale IN 99 E1
Roaming Shores OH 91 F2
Roane Co. TN 110 B4
Roane Co. WV 101 F3
Roan Mtn. TN 111 E3
Roanoke AL 128 B1
Roanoke IL 88 B3
Roanoke IN 90 A3
Roanoke TX 207 B1
Roanoke VA 112 B2
Roanoke Co. VA 112 B1
Roanoke Rapids NC 113 E3
Roaring Spr. PA 92 C4
Robards KY 109 E1
Robbins IL 203 D6
Robbins NC 122 C1
Robbinsdale MN 235 B2
Robbinsville NJ 147 D2
Robbinsville NC 121 D1
Robersonville NC 113 E4
Roberta GA 129 D2
Robert Lee TX 58 B3
Roberts ID 23 E4
Roberts WI 67 E4
Roberts Co. SD 27 F1
Roberts Co. TX 50 B2
Robertsdale AL 135 E2
Robertson Co. KY 100 C3
Robertson Co. TN 109 F3
Robertson Co. TX 61 F1
Robertsville NJ 147 E2
Robeson Co. NC 123 D2
Robesonia PA 146 A2
Robins IA 87 E1
Robinson IL 99 D2
Robinson TX 59 E4
Robstown TX 63 F2
Roby TX 58 B2
Rochdale MA 150 B2
Rochelle GA 129 E3
Rochelle IL 88 B1
Rochelle Park NJ 240 C1
Rochester IL 98 B1
Rochester IN 89 F3
Rochester MN 73 D1
Rochester NH 81 F4
Rochester NY 78 C3
Rochester PA 91 F3
Rochester VT 81 D3
Rochester WA 12 B4
Rochester WI 74 C4
Rochester Hills MI 76 C4
Rock MA 151 D3
Rockford IL 74 B4
Rockford IA 73 D3
Rockford MI 75 F3
Rockford MN 66 C3
Rockford OH 90 A3
Rockford TN 110 C4
Rockford WA 14 B3
Rock Hall MD 145 D2
Rock Hill MO 256 B2
Rock Hill NY 148 A1
Rock Hill SC 122 A2
Rockingham NC 122 C2
Rockingham Co. NH 81 F4
Rockingham Co. NC 112 B3
Rockingham Co. VA 102 C3
Rock Island IL 88 A2
Rock Island OK 116 B1
Rock Island WA 13 E3
Rock Island Co. IL 88 A2
Rockland ID 31 E1
Rockland ME 82 C2
Rockland MA 151 D2
Rockland WI 73 F1
Rockland Co. NY 148 B2
Rockledge AL 120 A3
Rockledge FL 141 E2
Rockledge PA 248 D2
Rocklin CA 36 C2
Rockmart GA 120 B3
Rock Mills AL 128 B1
Rock Pt. AZ 47 F1
Rockport AR 117 D3
Rockport IN 99 E4
Rockport KY 109 E1
Rockport ME 82 C2
Rockport MA 151 F1
Rock Port MO 86 A4
Rockport TX 61 E4
Rock Rapids IA 27 F4
Rock River WY 33 D2
Rocksprings TX 60 B2
Rock Sprs. WY 32 B3
Rockton IL 74 B4
Rockvale CO 41 E3
Rock Valley IA 35 F1
Rockville CT 150 A3
Rockville IN 99 E1
Rockville MD 144 B2
Rockville MN 66 C3
Rockville RI 150 C4
Rockwall TX 59 F2
Rockwall Co. TX 59 F2
Rockwell AR 117 D3
Rockwell IA 73 D3
Rockwell NC 122 B1

Arcade B2
Arden B2
Carmichael C2
Citrus Hts. C1
Fair Oaks C1
Florin B3
Foothill Farms C1
N. Highlands B1
Rancho Cordova C2
Rio Linda B1
Rosemont C3
Sacramento A2
W. Sacramento A3

Figures after entries indicate page number and grid reference.

Affton........B3
Alorton........C3
Ballwin........A2
Bella Villa........B3
Bellefontaine Neighbors..C1
Bellerive........B2
Belleville........D3
Bel-Nor........B2
Bel-Ridge........B2
Benevolent Hts........D3
Berkeley........B1
Beverly Hills........B2
Black Jack........B1
Breckenridge Hills........B2
Brentwood........B2
Bridgeton........B1
Brooklyn........C2
Cahokia........C3
Calverton Park........B1
Caseyville........D2
Cedar Park........D1
Centreville........C3
Champ........A1
Charlack........B2
Chesterfield........A2
Clayton........B2
Collinsville........D2
Columbia........C3
Concord........B3
Cool Valley........B1
Country Club Hills........B1
Country Life Acres........A2
Crestwood........B3
Creve Coeur........A2
Crystal Lake Park........B2
Dellwood........B1
Des Peres........A2
Dupo........C3
E. Carondelet........C3
E. St. Louis........C2
Edmundson........B1
Edwardsville........D1
Ellisville........A2
Fairmont City........C2
Fairview Hts........D2
Fenton........A3
Ferguson........B1
Flordell Hills........C1
Florissant........B1
Forest Acres........D2
Frontenac........B2
Glasgow Vil........C1
Glen Carbon........D1
Glendale........B2
Granite City........C1
Greendale........B2
Green Park........B3
Hanley Hills........B2
Hartford........D1
Hazelwood........B1
Hillsdale........B2
Hollywood Hts........D2
Huntleigh........B2
Imbs........C3
Jennings........B1
Kinloch........B1
Kirkwood........B3
Ladue........B2
Lakeshire........B3
Lemay........B3
Mackenzie........B3
Madison........C2
Manchester........A3
Maplewood........B2
Marlborough........B3
Maryland Hts........A1
Maryville........D1
Mattese........B3
Mehlville........B3
Mitchell........D1
Moline Acres........C1
Murphy........A3
Normandy........B2
N. Dupo........C3
Northwoods........B2
Oak Hills........D2
Oakland........B3
Oakville........B3
O'Fallon........D2
Olivette........B2
Overland........B2
Pagedale........B2
Parkdale........A3
Peerless Park........A3
Pine Lawn........B2
Poag........D1
Pontoon Beach........D1
Richmond Hts........B2
Riverview........C1
Robertson........B1
Rock Hill........B2
St. Ann........B1
St. Charles........A1
St. George........B3
St. John........B1
St. Louis........C2
St. Peters........A1
Sappington........B3
Sauget........C2
Shoveltown........B1
Shrewsbury........B3
Signal Hill........D3
S. Roxana........D1
Spanish Lake........C1
Sunset Hills........B3
Swansea........D3
Town and Country........A2
Twin Oaks........A3
University City........B2
Valley Park........A3
Venice........C2
Vinita Park........B2
Warson Woods........B2
Washington Park........D2
Webster Groves........B3
Wellston........B2
Westwood........A2
Wilbur Park........B3
Wildwood........A3
Winchester........A2
Woodson Terrace........B1

St Louis MO

Russellville KY 109 E2
Russellville MO 97 E3
Russellville TN 111 D3
Russiaville IN 89 F4
Rustburg VA 112 C2
Ruston LA 125 E2
Ruston WA 262 A5
Ruth NV 38 B2
Rutherford NJ 148 B3
Rutherford TN 108 C4
Rutherford Co. NC 121 F1
Rutherford Co. TN 109 F4
Rutherford Hts. PA 218 C1
Rutherfordton NC 121 F1
Ruthven IA 72 B3
Rutland MA 150 B1
Rutland ND 27 E1
Rutland VT 81 D3
Rutland Co. VT 81 D3
Rutledge AL 128 A4
Rutledge GA 121 D4
Rutledge PA 248 B4
Rutledge TN 111 D3
Ryall Sprs. TN 120 B2
Ryan OK 59 E1
Rye NH 82 A4
Rye NY 148 C3
Rye Beach NH 82 A4
Ryegate MT 16 B4
Ryland Hts. KY 100 B2

S

Sabattus ME 82 B2
Sabetha KS 96 A1
Sabina OH 100 C2
Sabinal TX 60 C3
Sabine Co. TX 124 C4
Sabine Par. LA 125 D4
Sabula IA 88 A1
Sacaton AZ 54 C2
Sac City IA 72 B4
Sac Co. IA 72 A4
Sachem Head CT 149 E2
Sachse TX 207 E1
Sackets Harbor NY 79 D1
Saco ME 82 B4
Saco MT 17 D2
Sacramento CA 36 C3
Sacramento KY 109 E1
Sacramento Co. CA 36 C3
Sacred Heart MN 66 B4
Saddle Brook NJ 240 C1
Saddle River NJ 148 B3
Saddle Rock NY 241 G2
Sadsburyville PA 146 B3
Saegertown PA 92 A1
Safety Harbor FL 140 B2
Safford AZ 55 E2
Sagadahoc Co. ME 82 B3
Sagamore MA 151 E3
Sagamore Beach MA 151 E3
Sagaponack NY 149 F3
Sag Harbor NY 149 F3
Saginaw MI 76 B2
Saginaw TX 207 A2
Saginaw Co. MI 76 B3
Sagle ID 14 B2
Saguache CO 41 D3
Saguache Co. CO 41 D3
Sahuarita AZ 55 D3
St. Albans VT 81 D1
St. Albans WV 101 E4
St. Albans Bay VT 81 D1
St. Andrew NY 148 B1
St. Andrews SC 205 E1
St. Ann MO 256 B1
St. Anne IL 89 D3
St. Ansgar IA 73 D2
St. Anthony ID 23 E4

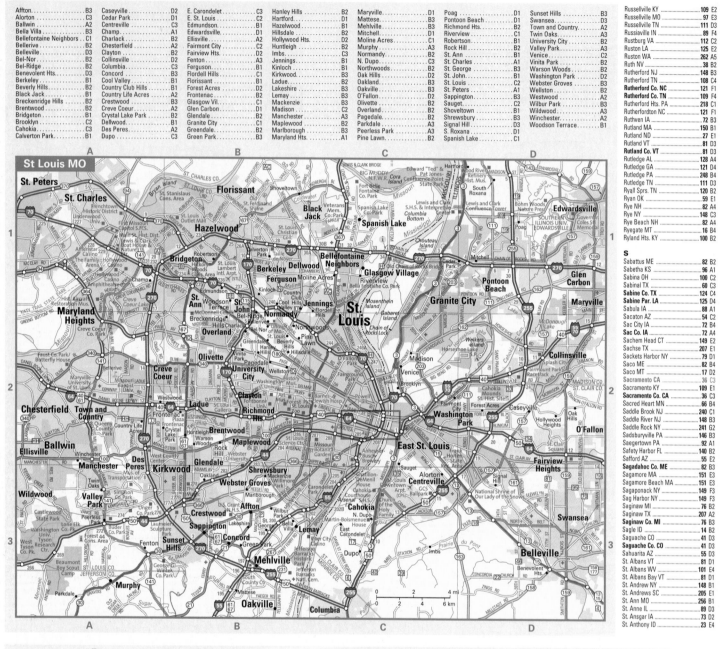

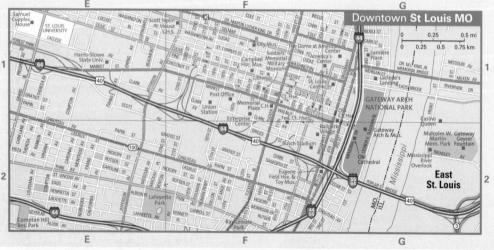

POINTS OF INTEREST

America's Center........G1
Ballpark Village........F2
Busch Stadium........F2
Campbell House Museum........F1
Casino Queen........G1
City Hall........F1
City Museum........F1
Court House........F1
Enterprise Center........F1
Eugene Field House & Toy Museum........F2
Federal Court House........F1
Gateway Arch & Museum........G2
Gateway Arch National Park........G1
Gateway Geyser Fountain........G2
Harris-Stowe State University........E1
Laclede's Landing........G1
Library........F1
Lumière Place........G1
Mississippi River Overlook........G2
Old Cathedral........G2
Old Court House........G1
Post Office........F1
St. Louis Centre........G1
St. Louis University........E1
Samuel Cupples House........E1
Scott Joplin House State Hist. Site........F1
Soldiers' Memorial Military Museum........F1
The Dome at America's Center........G1
Union Station........F1

Entries in **bold black** indicate counties or parishes.
Entries in **bold color** indicate cities with detailed inset maps.

St. Anthony MN	235	C2
St. Augusta MN	66	C3
St. Augustine FL	139	E3
St. Augustine Beach FL	139	E3
St. Augustine Shores FL	139	D3
St. Bernard LA	134	C3
St. Bernard OH	204	B2
St. Bernard Par. LA	134	C4
St. Bonifacius MN	66	C4
St. Charles IL	88	C1
St. Charles IA	86	C2
St. Charles MD	144	B4
St. Charles MI	76	B3
St. Charles MN	73	E1
St. Charles MO	98	A3
St. Charles Co. MO	98	A3
St. Charles Par. LA	134	B3

St. Clair MI	76	C3
St. Clair MN	72	C1
St. Clair MO	97	F4
St. Clair PA	93	E3
St. Clair Co. AL	120	A4
St. Clair Co. IL	98	B4
St. Clair Co. MI	76	C3
St. Clair Co. MO	96	C4
St. Clair Shores MI	76	C4
St. Clairsville OH	91	F4
St. Cloud FL	141	D2
St. Cloud MN	66	C3
St. Croix Co. WI	67	E3
St. Croix Falls WI	67	D3
St. David AZ	55	E3
St. David IL	88	A4
St. Edward NE	35	E3

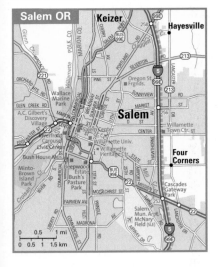

Salem OR

Alamo Hts.		E2
Balcones Hts.		F2
Bracken		F1
Buena Vista		E3
Castle Hills		E2
China Grove		F3
Cibolo		F1
Converse		F1
Garden Ridge		F1
Grey Forest		D1
Helotes		D1
Hill Country Vil.		E1
Hollywood Park		E1
Kirby		F2
Leon Valley		D2
Live Oak		F1
Macdona		D3
Olmos Park		E2
San Antonio		F3
Sayers		F1
Schertz		F1
Selma		F1
Shavano Park		E1
Southton		E3
Terrell Hills		E2
Universal City		F1
Von Ormy		D3
Windcrest		F2

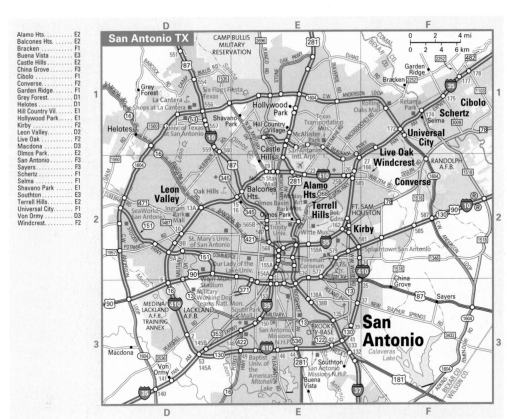

San Antonio TX

Salt Lake City UT

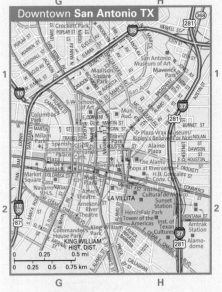

Downtown San Antonio TX

POINTS OF INTEREST

The Alamo	H2
Alamodome	H2
Amtrak Station	H2
Arneson River Theater	H2
Aztec Theatre	G2
Casa Navarro State Historic Site	G2
H.B. Gonzalez Convention Center	H2
HemisFair Park	H2
Institute of Texan Cultures	H2
Instituto Cultural de México	G2
Market Square	G2
Municipal Auditorium	H1
Plaza Wax Museum/Ripley's Believe It or Not!	H2
River Walk	H2
San Antonio Museum of Art	H1
San Fernando Cathedral	G2
Shops at Rivercenter	H2
Spanish Governor's Palace	G2
Sunset Station	H2
Southwest School of Art	G1
Tower of the Americas	H2

Alta		C3
Bountiful		B1
Brighton		C3
Copperton		A3
Cottonwood Hts.		B3

Draper		B3
E. Millcreek		B2
Granite		B2
Holladay		B2
Kearns		A2

Magna		A2
Midvale		B3
Millcreek		B2
Murray		B2
N. Salt Lake		B1

Riverton		A3
Salt Lake City		B1
Sandy		B3
Silver Fork		C3
S. Jordan		A3

S. Salt Lake		B2
Taylorsville		A2
W. Jordan		A3
W. Valley City		A2
Woods Cross		B1

Figures after entries indicate page number and grid reference.

Bonita C2
Chula Vista B3
Coronado A2
El Cajon C1
Imperial Beach B3
Lakeside C1
La Mesa C2
Lemon Grove C2
National City B2
San Diego C2
Santee C1
Spring Valley C2
Sunnyside C2
Tijuana, MX C3

POINTS OF INTEREST

Automotive Museum E1
Balboa Park E1
Balboa Stadium E1
Casa del Prado E1
Civic Center D2
Comic-Con Center for Popular Culture E1
Copley Symphony Hall E2
County Court House D2
Cruise Ship Terminal D2
Fleet & Industrial Supply Center D2
Fleet Science Center E1
Gaslamp Quarter & W. H. Davis House E2
House of Hospitality E1
Maritime Museum D2
Museum of Contemporary Art, San Diego D2
The New Children's Museum D2
The Old Globe Theatre E1
Petco Park E2
San Diego Air & Space Museum E1
San Diego Convention Center D2
San Diego International Airport D1
San Diego Museum of Art E1
San Diego Museum of Man E1
San Diego Natural History Museum E1
San Diego Zoo E1
Santa Fe Depot D2
Seaport Village D2
Spanish Village Art Center E1
Spreckels Organ Pavilion E1
Spreckels Theatre D2
Starlight Bowl E1
Timken Museum of Art E1
U.S. Court House D2
USS Midway Aircraft Carrier Museum D2
Veterans Museum & Memorial Center E1
Waterfront Park D1

Downtown San Diego CA

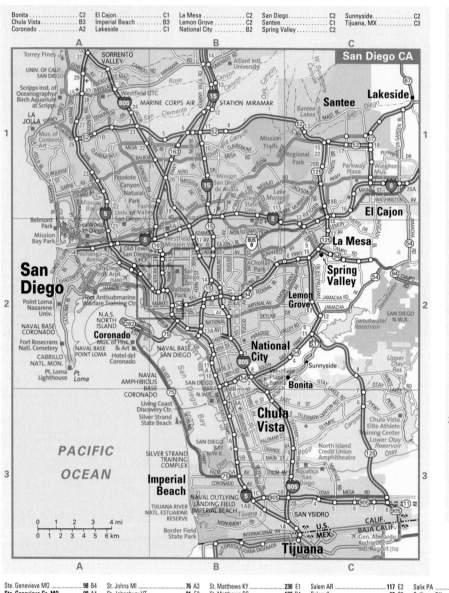

Ste. Genevieve MO 98 B4
Ste. Genevieve Co. MO 98 A4
St. Elmo IL 98 C2
St. Francis KS 42 B1
St. Francis MN 67 D3
St. Francis SD 34 C1
St. Francis WI 234 D3
St. Francis Co. AR 118 A2
St. Francisville IL 99 D3
St. Francisville LA 134 A1
St. Francois Co. MO 98 A4
St. Gabriel LA 134 A2
St. George KS 43 F2
St. George ME 82 C3
St. George MO 256 B3
St. George SC 130 C1
St. George UT 46 C1
St. Hedwig TX 61 D3
St. Helen MI 76 A1
St. Helena CA 36 B3
St. Helena Par. LA 134 A1
St. Helens OR 20 C1
St. Henry OH 90 A4
St. Ignace MI 70 C2
St. Ignatius MT 15 D3
St. Jacob IL 98 B3
St. James MD 144 A1
St. James MN 72 B1
St. James MO 97 F4
St. James NY 149 D3
St. James NC 123 E4
St. James City FL 142 C1
St. James Par. LA 134 A3
St. Jo TX 59 E1
St. John IN 89 D2
St. John KS 43 D3
St. John MO 256 B1
St. John ND 18 C1
St. John WA 13 F3
St. Johns AZ 48 A4
St. Johns MI 76 A3
St. Johnsbury VT 81 E2
St. Johnsbury Ctr. VT 81 E2
St. Johns Co. FL 139 D3
St. Johnsville NY 79 F3
St. John the Baptist Par. LA 134 B2
St. Joseph IL 89 D4
St. Joseph LA 126 A3
St. Joseph MI 89 E1
St. Joseph MN 66 C3
St. Joseph MO 96 B1
St. Joseph TN 119 E2
St. Joseph Co. IN 89 F2
St. Joseph Co. MI 89 F1
St. Landry Par. LA 133 F1
St. Lawrence PA 146 B2
St. Lawrence SD 27 D3
St. Lawrence Co. NY 79 F1
St. Leo FL 140 C2
St. Libory IL 98 B4
St. Louis MI 76 A2
St. Louis MO 98 A3
St. Louis Co. MN 64 C3
St. Louis Co. MO 98 A3
St. Louis Park MN 235 B2
St. Lucie FL 141 E3
St. Lucie Co. FL 141 E3
St. Maries ID 14 B3
St. Martin Par. LA 133 F2
St. Martins MO 97 E3
St. Martinville LA 133 F2
St. Mary Par. LA 134 A3
St. Mary's AK 154 B2
St. Marys GA 139 D1
St. Marys KS 43 F2
St. Marys OH 90 B4
St. Marys PA 92 B2
St. Marys WV 101 F2
St. Mary's City MD 103 F4
St. Mary's Co. MD 103 E3
St. Matthews KY 230 E1
St. Matthews SC 122 B4
St. Meinrad IN 99 E4
St. Michael MN 66 C3
St. Michaels AZ 48 A2
St. Michaels MD 145 D3
St. Nazianz WI 74 C1
St. Paris OH 90 B4
St. Paul AK 154 A3
St. Paul IN 100 A2
St. Paul KS 106 B1
St. Paul MN 67 D4
St. Paul MO 98 A3
St. Paul NE 35 D3
St. Paul OR 20 B2
St. Paul TX 59 F2
St. Paul TX 61 E4
St. Paul VA 111 E2
St. Paul Park MN 235 E4
St. Pauls NC 123 D2
St. Pete Beach FL 140 B3
St. Peter MN 72 C1
St. Peters MO 98 A3
St. Petersburg FL 140 B3
St. Regis MT 14 C3
St. Regis Falls NY 80 C1
St. Regis Park KY 230 F2
St. Robert MO 107 E1
St. Rose LA 134 B3
St. Simons Island GA 139 D1
St. Stephen MN 66 C2
St. Stephen SC 131 D1
St. Stephens NC 111 F4
St. Tammany Par. LA 134 B2
St. Thomas ND 19 E2
Saks AL 120 A4
Salado TX 61 E1
Salamanca NY 92 B1
Sale Creek TN 120 B1
Salem AR 107 F3
Salem AR 117 E2
Salem IL 98 C3
Salem IN 99 F3
Salem KY 109 D2
Salem MA 151 D1
Salem MO 107 F1
Salem NH 95 E1
Salem NJ 145 E1
Salem NM 56 B2
Salem NY 81 D4
Salem NC 111 F4
Salem OH 91 F3
Salem OR 20 B2
Salem SD 27 E4
Salem UT 39 E1
Salem VA 112 B2
Salem WV 102 A2
Salem Co. NJ 145 F1
Salem Lakes WI 74 C4
Salesville AR 107 E3
Salida CA 36 C4
Salida CO 41 D3
Salina KS 43 E2
Salina OK 106 B3
Salina UT 39 E2
Salinas CA 44 B3
Saline MI 90 B1
Saline Co. AR 117 D2
Saline Co. IL 98 C4
Saline Co. KS 43 E2
Saline Co. MO 97 D2
Saline Co. NE 35 E4
Salineville OH 91 F3
Salisbury CT 94 B2
Salisbury MD 114 C1
Salisbury MA 151 F1
Salisbury MO 97 D2
Salisbury NC 112 A4
Salisbury PA 102 B1
Salisbury Beach MA 151 F1
Salix PA 92 B4
Sallisaw OK 116 B1
Salmon ID 23 D2
Salome AZ 54 A1
Salsbury Cove ME 83 D2
Saltillo MS 119 D3
Salt Lake City UT 31 E4
Salt Lake Co. UT 31 E4
Salt Lick KY 100 C4
Salton City CA 53 E3
Saltsburg PA 92 A4
Salt Sprs. FL 139 D4
Saltville VA 111 F2
Saluda NC 121 E1
Saluda SC 121 F3
Saluda VA 113 F1
Saluda Co. SC 121 F3
Salunga PA 225 A1
Salyersville KY 111 D1
Sammamish WA 12 C3
Samoset FL 266 B4
Sampit SC 131 E1
Sampson Co. NC 123 D1
Samson AL 136 C1
Samsula FL 139 E4
San Andreas CA 36 C3
San Angelo TX 58 B4
San Anselmo CA 259 A1
San Antonio FL 140 C2
San Antonio TX 61 D3
San Antonio Hts. CA 229 G2
San Ardo CA 44 B3
Sanatoga PA 146 B2
Sanatorium MS 126 B3
San Augustine TX 124 C4
San Augustine Co. TX 124 C4

SAN FRANCISCO BAY MAP INDEX

Alameda C3
Alamo D2
Albany C2
Antioch E1
Ashland D3
Atherton C5
Bay Pt. D1
Belmont C5
Belvedere B2
Benicia C1
Berkeley C2
Brisbane B3
Broadmoor B3
Burlingame B4
Campbell E6
Canyon C2
Castro Valley D3
Clayton E2
Clyde D1
Colma B3
Concord D1
Corte Madera A2
Crockett C1
Cupertino D6
Daly City B3
Danville D2
Diablo D2
Dublin E3
E. Palo Alto C5
El Cerrito B2
El Granada B5
El Sobrante C1
Emeryville C2
Fairfax A1
Foster City C4
Fremont D5
Greenbrae A2
Half Moon Bay B5
Hayward D4
Hercules C1
Hillsborough B4
Homestead Valley A2
Ignacio A1
Kensington C2
Kentfield A2
Ladera C5
Lafayette D2
La Honda C6
Larkspur A2
Livermore E3
Los Altos D6
Los Altos Hills C6
Marinwood A1
Martinez D1
Menlo Park C5
Millbrae B4
Mill Valley A2
Milpitas E5
Montara A4
Moraga D2
Moss Beach A5
Mtn. View D5
Muir Beach A2
Newark D5
N. Fair Oaks C5
N. Richmond B2
Novato A1
Oakland C3
Orinda C2
Pacheco D1
Pacifica A4
Palo Alto D5
Pescadero B6
Piedmont C2
Pinole C1
Pittsburg E1
Pleasant Hill D2
Pleasanton E4
Port Costa C1
Portola Valley C6
Redwood City C5
Richmond B2
Rodeo C1
Ross A1
San Anselmo A1
San Bruno B4
San Carlos C5
San Francisco A3
San Gregorio B6
San Jose E6
San Leandro C3
San Lorenzo D4
San Mateo B4
San Pablo B1
San Quentin A2
San Rafael B1
San Ramon D3
Santa Clara D6
Santa Venetia A1
Saratoga D6
Sausalito B2
S. San Francisco B4
Stinson Beach A2
Sunnyvale D6
Sunol E4
Tamalpais Valley A2
Tara Hills B1
Tiburon B2
Union City D4
Vallejo C1
Vine Hill D1
Walnut Creek D2
Woodacre A1
Woodside C5

Entries in **bold black** indicate counties or parishes.
Entries in **bold color** indicate cities with detailed inset maps.

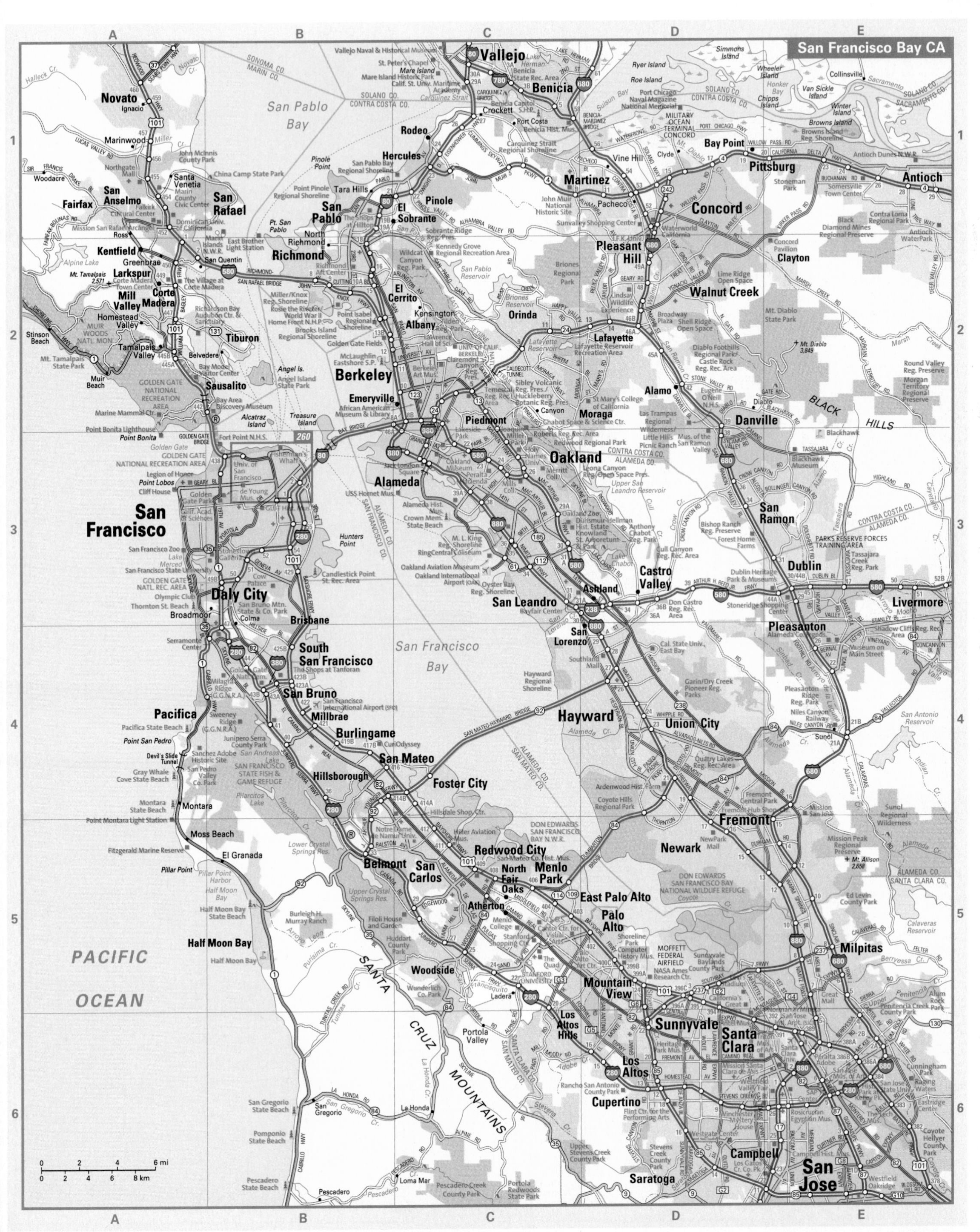

San Francisco Bay CA

Figures after entries indicate page number and grid reference.

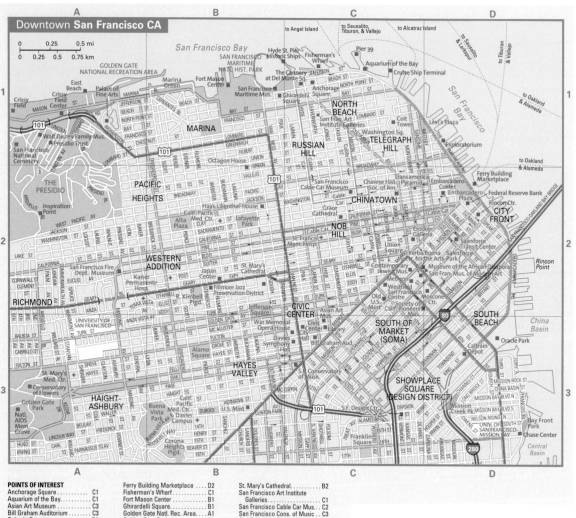

Downtown San Francisco CA

POINTS OF INTEREST

Anchorage Square C1
Aquarium of the Bay C1
Asian Art Museum C3
Bill Graham Auditorium C3
Caltrain Depot D3
The Cannery at Del Monte Square C1
Chase Center D3
Chinese Historical Society of America C2
City Hall C3
Coit Tower C1
Conservatory of Flowers A3
Contemporary Jewish Mus. C2
Crissy Field A1
Crissy Field Center A1
Crocker Galleria C2
Cruise Ship Terminal C1
Davies Symphony Hall C3
East Beach A1
Embarcadero Center D2
Exploratorium D1
Federal Reserve Bank D2
Fillmore Jazz Preservation District B2
Ferry Building Marketplace D2
Fisherman's Wharf C1
Fort Mason Center B1
Ghirardelli Square B1
Golden Gate Natl. Rec. Area A1
Golden Gate Park A3
Grace Cathedral C2
Haas-Lilienthal House B2
Hyde Street Pier Historic Ships C1
Inspiration Point A2
Japan Center B2
Levi's Plaza D1
Library C3
Metreon C2
Moscone Center D2
Museum of the African Diaspora D2
National AIDS Memorial Grove A3
Octagon House B2
Old U.S. Mint C2
Oracle Park D3
Palace of Fine Arts A1
Pier 39 .... C1
The Presidio A2
Presidio Trust A1
Rincon Center D2
St. Mary's Cathedral B2
San Francisco Art Institute Galleries C1
San Francisco Cable Car Mus. C2
San Francisco Cons. of Music C3
San Francisco Design Center C3
San Francisco Fire Dept. Mus. A2
San Francisco Maritime Mus. B1
San Francisco Maritime Natl. Hist. Park B1
San Francisco Museum of Modern Art D2
San Francisco Natl. Cemetery A1
Soc. of Calif. Pioneers Mus. C2
Transamerica Pyramid C2
Transbay Transit Center D2
U.S. Mint B3
Univ. of San Francisco A3
Univ. of San Francisco-Mission Bay D3
Walt Disney Family Mus. A1
War Memorial Opera House C3
Westfield San Francisco Centre C2
Yerba Buena Center for the Arts C2

San Benito TX 63 F4
San Benito Co. CA 44 B3
San Bernardino CA 53 D2
San Bernardino Co. CA 45 F4
Sanborn IA 72 A3
Sanborn Co. SD 27 E3
Sanbornville NH 81 F3
San Bruno CA 36 B4
San Carlos AZ 55 D2
San Carlos CA 259 C5
San Carlos Park FL 142 C1
San Clemente CA 52 C3
Sanders Co. MT 14 C3
Sanderson TX 62 C3
Sandersville GA 129 E1
Sandersville MS 126 C3
Sand Hills MA 151 E2
Sandia Park NM 48 C3
San Diego CA 53 D4
San Diego TX 63 E2
San Diego Co. CA 53 E4
San Dimas CA 229 F2
Sand Lake MI 75 F3
Sandoval IL 98 C3
Sandoval Co. NM 48 C2
Sandown NH 95 E1
Sand Pt. AK 154 B4
Sandpoint ID 14 B2
Sand Ridge NY 79 D3
Sand Rock AL 120 A3
Sands Pt. NY 241 G2
Sand Sprs. OK 51 F2
Sand Sprs. TX 58 B3
Sandston VA 113 E1
Sandstone MN 67 D2
Sandusky MI 76 C2
Sandusky OH 91 D2
Sandusky Co. OH 90 C2
Sandwich IL 88 C2
Sandwich MA 151 E3
Sandy OR 20 C2
Sandy PA 92 B3
Sandy UT 31 E4
Sandy Creek NY 79 E2
Sandy Hook KY 101 D4
Sandy Lake PA 92 A2
Sandy Sprs. GA 120 C4
Sandy Sprs. SC 121 E2
Sandy Valley NV 46 A2
Sandyville MD 144 B1
San Elizario TX 56 C4
San Felipe TX 61 F2
San Felipe Pueblo NM 48 C3
San Fernando CA 52 C2
Sanford CO 41 D4
Sanford FL 141 D1
Sanford ME 82 A4
Sanford MI 76 A2
Sanford NC 122 C1
San Francisco CA 36 B4
San Francisco Co. CA 36 B4
San Gabriel CA 228 D2
Sangamon Co. IL 98 B1
Sanger CA 45 D3
Sanger TX 59 E1
Sangerville ME 82 C1
Sanibel FL 142 C1

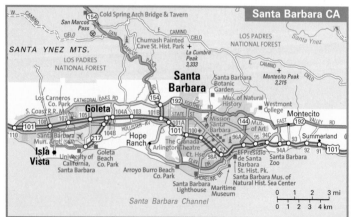

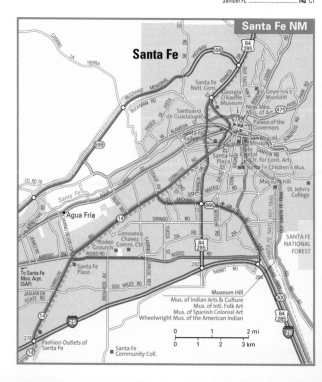

Entries in **bold black** indicate counties or parishes.
Entries in **bold color** indicate cities with detailed inset maps.

Sanilac Co. MI	76	C2
San Jacinto CA	53	D3
San Jacinto Co. TX	132	B1
San Joaquin CA	44	C3
San Joaquin Co. CA	36	C3
San Jon NM	49	F3
San Jose CA	36	B4
San Jose IL	88	B4
San Juan Bautista CA	44	B2
San Juan Capistrano CA	52	C3
San Juan Co. CO	40	C4
San Juan Co. NM	48	B1
San Juan Co. UT	39	F4
San Juan Co. WA	12	C2
Sankertown PA	92	B4
San Leandro CA	36	B4
San Lorenzo CA	259	D4
San Lucas CA	44	B3
San Luis AZ	53	F4
San Luis CO	41	D4
San Luis Obispo CA	44	C4
San Luis Obispo Co. CA	44	C4
San Manuel AZ	55	D2
San Marcos CA	53	D4
San Marcos TX	61	E2
San Marino CA	228	D2
San Martin CA	44	B2
San Mateo CA	36	B4
San Mateo FL	139	D3
San Mateo Co. CA	36	B4
San Miguel CA	44	C4
San Miguel NM	56	C3
San Miguel Co. CO	40	B3
San Miguel Co. NM	49	B3
Sanostee NM	48	A1
San Pablo CA	259	B1
San Patricio Co. TX	61	E4
San Perlita TX	63	F3
Sanpete Co. UT	39	E2
San Rafael CA	36	B3
San Ramon CA	36	B4
San Remo NY	149	D3
San Saba TX	59	D4
San Saba Co. TX	59	D4
Sansom Park TX	207	A1
Sans Souci SC	217	A2
Santa Ana CA	52	C3
Santa Ana Pueblo NM	48	C3
Santa Anna TX	58	C4
Santa Barbara CA	52	B2
Santa Barbara Co. CA	52	B1
Santa Clara CA	259	D6
Santa Clara NM	55	F2
Santa Clara OR	20	B3
Santa Clara UT	46	C1
Santa Clara Co. CA	36	C4
Santa Clarita CA	52	C2
Santa Claus IN	99	E4
Santa Cruz CA	44	A4
Santa Cruz NM	49	D2
Santa Cruz Co. AZ	55	D4
Santa Cruz Co. CA	44	A2
Santa Fe NM	49	D2
Santa Fe Co. NM	49	D3
Santa Margarita CA	44	C4
Santa Maria CA	52	A1
Santa Maria TX	63	F4
Santa Monica CA	52	C2
Santa Nella CA	44	B3
Santa Paula CA	52	B2
Santaquin UT	39	E1
Santa Rosa AZ	54	C3
Santa Rosa CA	36	B3
Santa Rosa NM	49	E3
Santa Rosa TX	63	F4
Santa Rosa Co. FL	135	F1
Santa Teresa NM	56	C3
Santa Venetia CA	259	A1
Santa Ynez CA	52	A2
Santee CA	53	D4
Santee SC	122	B4
Santo Domingo Pueblo NM	48	C3
San Ysidro NM	48	C3
Sappington MO	256	B3
Sapulpa OK	51	F2
Saraland AL	135	E1
Saranac MI	75	F3
Saranac Lake NY	80	C2
Sarasota FL	140	B3
Sarasota Co. FL	140	C4
Saratoga CA	36	B4
Saratoga WY	33	D3
Saratoga Co. NY	80	C3
Saratoga Sprs. NY	80	C4
Sarcoxie MO	106	C2
Sardinia OH	100	C2
Sardis GA	130	B1
Sardis MS	118	B3
Sardis TN	119	D1
Sardis City AL	120	A3
Sarepta LA	125	D1
Sargent GA	120	B4
Sargent NE	35	D3
Sargent Co. ND	27	E1
Sarita TX	63	F3
Sarpy Co. NE	35	F3
Sartell MN	66	C2
Satanta KS	42	B4
Satellite Beach FL	141	E2
Satsop WA	12	B4
Satsuma AL	135	E1
Satsuma FL	139	D3
Satus WA	21	E1
Saucier MS	135	D2
Saugatuck MI	75	E4
Saugerties NY	94	B2
Saugus MA	151	D1
Sauk City WI	74	A3
Sauk Co. WI	74	A3
Sauk Rapids MN	66	C2
Saukville WI	74	C2
Sault Ste. Marie MI	70	C1
Saunders Co. NE	35	F3
Saunderstown RI	150	C4
Sauquoit NY	79	E3
Sausalito CA	259	B2
Savage MD	144	C2
Savage MN	67	D4
Savanna IL	88	A1
Savanna OK	116	A2
Savannah GA	130	B3
Savannah MO	96	B1
Savannah TN	119	D1
Savona NY	78	C4
Savoonga AK	154	A2
Savoy IL	88	C4
Savoy TX	59	F1
Sawgrass FL	222	E4
Sawmill AZ	48	A3
Sawmills NC	111	F4
Sawyer ND	18	B2
Sawyer Co. WI	67	F2
Saxapahaw NC	112	C4
Saxis VA	103	F4
Saxon SC	217	C1
Saxonburg PA	92	A3
Saxton PA	92	C4
Saxtons River VT	81	E4
Saybrook IL	88	C3
Saybrook OH	91	F1
Saybrook Manor CT	149	E2
Saylorville IA	86	C2
Saylorsburg PA	93	F3
Sayre OK	50	C3
Sayre PA	93	E1
Sayreville NJ	147	E1
Sayville NY	149	D1
Scammon KS	106	B2
Scammon Bay AK	154	B2
Scandia KS	43	E1
Scanlon MN	64	C4
Scappoose OR	20	B1
Scarborough ME	82	B3
Scarbro WV	101	F4
Scarsdale NY	148	B3
Schaefferstown PA	146	A2
Schaghticoke NY	94	B1
Schaller IA	72	A4
Schaumburg IL	203	B3
Schenectady NY	94	B1
Schenectady Co. NY	94	B1
Schererville IN	89	D2
Schertz TX	257	F1
Schiller Park IL	203	C3
Schleicher Co. TX	58	B2
Schleswig IA	86	A1
Schley Co. GA	128	C3
Schnecksville PA	146	B1
Schofield WI	68	B4
Schoharie NY	94	A1
Schoharie Co. NY	79	F4
Schoolcraft MI	89	F1
Schoolcraft Co. MI	69	E1
Schoon Lake NY	80	C3
Schram City IL	98	B2
Schriever LA	134	A3
Schroon Lake NY	80	C3
Schulenburg TX	61	F2
Schuyler NE	35	F3
Schuyler Co. IL	88	A4
Schuyler Co. MO	87	E4
Schuyler Co. NY	79	D4
Schuyler Falls NY	81	D1
Schuylkill Co. PA	146	A1
Schuylkill Haven PA	146	A1
Schwenksville PA	146	B2
Science Hill KY	110	B2
Scio OH	91	F4
Scio OR	20	B3
Scioto Co. OH	101	D3
Scipio UT	39	E2
Scituate MA	151	E2
Scobey MT	17	E1
Scooba MS	127	D2
Scotch Plains NJ	148	A4
Scotchtown NY	148	A1
Scotia CA	28	A4
Scotia NY	94	B1
Scotland MA	151	D2
Scotland PA	103	D1
Scotland SD	35	E1
Scotland Co. MO	87	E4
Scotland Neck NC	113	E4
Scott LA	133	F2
Scott Co. AR	116	C2
Scott Co. IL	98	A1
Scott Co. IN	100	A3
Scott Co. IA	88	A2
Scott Co. KS	42	B3
Scott Co. KY	100	B4
Scott Co. MN	66	C4
Scott Co. MS	126	C2
Scott Co. MO	108	B2
Scott Co. TN	110	C3
Scott Co. VA	111	E2
Scottdale GA	190	E3
Scottdale PA	92	A4
Scott Depot WV	101	E3
Scottsbluff NE	33	F2
Scotts Bluff Co. NE	33	F2
Scottsboro AL	120	A2
Scottsburg IN	100	A3
Scottsdale AZ	54	C1
Scotts Hill TN	119	D1
Scotts Mills OR	20	C2
Scottsmoor FL	141	E1
Scotts Valley CA	44	A2
Scottsville KY	109	F2
Scottsville NY	78	C3
Scottsville VA	113	D1
Scottville MI	75	E1
Scranton IA	86	A3
Scranton KS	96	A3
Scranton ND	26	A1
Scranton PA	93	F2
Scranton SC	122	C4
Scraper OK	106	B4
Screven GA	129	F4
Screven Co. GA	130	B2
Scribner NE	35	F3
Scurry Co. TX	58	A3
Seaboard NC	113	E3
Sea Breeze NC	123	E3
Sea Bright NJ	147	F2
Seabrook MD	271	F2
Seabrook NH	95	E1
Seabrook NJ	145	F1
Seabrook TX	132	B3
Seabrook Island SC	131	D2
Sea Cliff NY	148	C3
Seadrift TX	61	F4
Seaford DE	145	E4

Savannah GA

(Inset map showing Savannah, Pooler, Port Wentworth, Garden City, Bloomingdale, Silk Hope, Thunderbolt, Whitemarsh Island, Isle of Hope, Oatland Island, Savannah/Hilton Head International Airport, Hunter Army Air Field, Savannah National Wildlife Refuge, Historic District, and Interstate routes 95, 16, 516, 204, US routes 17, 21, 80.)

Scranton / Wilkes-Barre PA

(Inset map showing Scranton, Wilkes-Barre, Dickson City, Dunmore, Olyphant, Blakely, Throop, Moosic, Old Forge, Taylor, Clarks Summit, Chinchilla, Nanticoke, Plymouth, Edwardsville, Kingston, Swoyersville, Exeter, West Pittston, Pittston, Avoca, Duryea, Dupont, Larksville, Luzerne, Forty Fort, and Interstate routes 81, 476, 84, 380.)

Ashley	A2
Avoca	C2
Avondale	A1
Blakely	E1
Breslau	A1
Browntown	C1
Buttonwood	A1
Chinchilla	E1
Clarks Green	E1
Clarks Summit	E1
Cork Lane	C2
Courtdale	B1
Curry Hill	A1
Dickson City	E1
Dundee	A1
Dunmore	E2
Dupont	C2
Duryea	C2
Edwardsville	A1
Exeter	B1
Forty Fort	B1
Georgetown	C1
Harding	C1
Hilldale	B1
Hudson	B2
Hughestown	C2
Inkerman	C1
Justus	E1
Kingston	B1
Laflin	C2
Larksville	A1
Laurel Run	B2
Lee Park	A1
Luzerne	B1
Midvale	B1
Milwaukee	D1
Moosic	D2
Mtn. Top	A2
Nanticoke	A1
Newtown	A2
Old Forge	D1
Olyphant	E2
Pittston	C1
Plains	B1
Plainsville	B1
Plymouth	A1
Preston	A1
Pringle	B1
Ransom	C1
Ridgewood	B2
Scranton	D2
Sugar Notch	A2
Swoyersville	B1
Taylor	D2
Throop	E2
Trucksville	B1
Warrior Run	A2
W. Pittston	C1
W. Wyoming	B1
Wilkes-Barre	B2
Wyoming	B1
Yatesville	C2

Figures after entries indicate page number and grid reference.

Seaford VA 113 F2
Seagate NC 123 E3
Sea Girt NJ 147 F2
Seagoville TX 59 F2
Seagraves TX 57 F2
Sea Isle City NJ 105 D4
Seal Beach CA 228 D4
Sealy TX 61 F2
Seaman OH 100 C3
Sea Ranch Lakes FL 233 C2
Searchlight NV 46 B3
Searcy AR 117 F1
Searcy Co. AR 107 E4
Searingtown NY 241 G3
Searsport ME 83 D2
Seaside CA 44 B3
Seaside OR 20 B1
Seaside Hts. NJ 147 E3
Seaside Park NJ 147 E3
SeaTac WA 12 C3
Seat Pleasant MD 271 F3
Seattle WA 12 C3
Sebago Lake ME 82 B3
Sebastian FL 141 E3
Sebastian TX 63 F4
Sebastian Co. AR 116 C1
Sebastopol CA 36 B3
Sebeka MN 64 A4
Sebewaing MI 76 B2
Sebree KY 109 E1
Sebring FL 141 D3
Sebring OH 91 F3
Secaucus NJ 240 C3
Second Mesa AZ 47 F2
Secretary MD 145 D4
Section AL 120 A2
Security CO 41 E2
Sedalia MO 97 D3
Sedalia NC 112 B4
Sedan KS 43 F4
Sedgefield NC 112 B4
Sedgwick KS 43 E3
Sedgwick Co. CO 34 A4
Sedgwick Co. KS 43 E4
Sedley VA 113 F2
Sedona AZ 47 D3
Sedro-Woolley WA 12 C2
Seeley CA 53 E4
Seeley Lake MT 15 D3
Seelyville IN 99 E2
Seffner FL 266 D2
Seguin TX 61 E2
Seiling OK 51 D2
Seisholtzville PA 146 B1
Selah WA 13 D4
Selawik AK 154 B2
Selby SD 26 C2
Selbyville DE 114 C1
Selden NY 149 D3
Selfridge ND 26 C1
Seligman AZ 46 C3
Seligman MO 106 C3
Selinsgrove PA 93 D3
Selkirk NY 94 B1
Sellersburg IN 100 A3
Sellersville PA 146 C2
Sells AZ 54 C3
Selma AL 127 F2
Selma CA 45 D3
Selma IN 90 A4
Selma NC 123 E1
Selma TX 257 F1
Selma VA 112 B1
Selmer TN 119 D1
Selmont AL 127 F2
Seminole FL 140 B2
Seminole OK 51 F3
Seminole TX 57 F2
Seminole Co. FL 141 D1
Seminole Co. GA 137 D1
Seminole Co. OK 51 F3
Senath MO 108 B4
Senatobia MS 118 B2
Seneca IL 88 C2
Seneca KS 43 F1
Seneca MO 106 B2
Seneca PA 92 A2
Seneca SC 121 E2
Seneca Co. NY 79 D4
Seneca Co. OH 90 C3
Seneca Falls NY 79 D3
Seneca Gardens KY 230 E2
Senoia GA 128 C1
Sentinel OK 51 D3
Sequatchie Co. TN 120 B1
Sequim WA 12 B2
Sequoyah Co. OK 116 B1
Sergeant Bluff IA 35 F2
Sergeantsville NJ 147 D1
Sesser IL 98 C4
Setauket NY 149 D3
Seth Ward TX 50 A4
Seven Corners VA 270 B4
Seven Fields PA 92 A3
Seven Hills OH 204 F3
Seven Lakes NC 122 C1
Seven Mile OH 100 B2
Seven Pts. TX 59 F3
Severance CO 33 E4
Severn MD 144 C2
Severna Park MD 144 C2

Seattle / Tacoma WA

Alderwood Manor B2
Algona B5
Arletta A5
Auburn B4
Bainbridge Island A3
Bay View A1
Beaux Arts B3
Bellevue B3
Bethel A4
Bonney Lake B5
Bothell B2
Bremerton A3
Brier B2
Brownsville A3
Burien B4
Burley A4
Burton A4
Cathcart B2
Clinton B1
Clyde Hill B3
Colby A3
Covington B4
Des Moines B4
Dockton A4
Eastgate B3
Edgewood B5
Edmonds B2
Ellisport A4
Everett B1
Federal Way B4
Fife B5
Fircrest A5
Fox Island A5
Freeland A1
Gig Harbor A4
Glendale B1
Hansville A1
Hunts Pt. B3
Indianola A2
Kenmore B2
Kent B4
Keyport A2
Kingston A2
Kirkland B3
Lake Forest Park B2
Lake Stevens B1
Lakewood A5
Langley A1
Lofall A2
Lynnwood B2
Maltby B2
Manchester A3
Martha Lake B2
Marysville B1
Maxwelton A1
McMillan B5
Medina B3
Mercer Island B3
Midland A5
Mill Creek B2
Milton B5
Mountlake Terrace B2
Mukilteo B1
Newcastle B3
Normandy Park B4
Olalla A4
Pacific B5
Parkland A5
Portage A4
Port Gamble A2
Port Orchard A3
Poulsbo A2
Purdy A4
Puyallup B5
Redmond B3
Redondo B4
Renton B4
Retsil A3
Rollingbay A3
Rosedale A4
Ruston A5
SeaTac B4
Seattle B2
Shine A2
Shoreline B2
Skyway B4
Snohomish B1
S. Colby A3
S. Hill B5
S. Prairie B5
Southworth A3
Steilacoom A5
Summit B5
Sumner B5
Suquamish A2
Tacoma A5
Tahlequah A4
Tracyton A3
Tukwila B4
Tulalip B1
University Place A5
Vashon A4
Vashon Hts. A3
Wauna A4
White Ctr. B4
Wollochet A5
Woodinville B2
Woodway A2
Yarrow Pt. B3

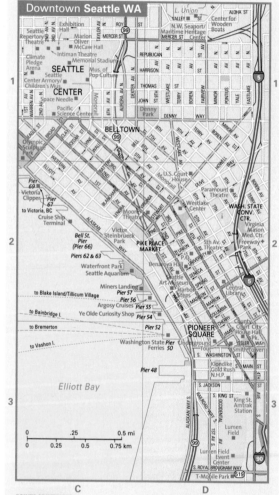

A B
1 2 3 4 5
0 2 4 mi
0 2 4 6 km

POINTS OF INTEREST

5th Avenue Theatre	D2	Olympic Sculpture Park	C1
Argosy Cruises	D2	Pacific Science Center	C1
Benaroya Hall	D2	Paramount Theatre	D2
Center for Wooden Boats	D1	Pike Place Market	D2
Central Library	D2	Post Office	D2
Climate Pledge Arena	C1	The Seattle Aquarium	C2
Cruise Ship Terminal	C2	Seattle Art Museum	D2
Exhibition Hall	C1	Seattle Center	C1
Harbor Steps	D2	Seattle Center Armory/Childrens Museum	C1
King Street Amtrak Station	D3	Seattle Repertory Theatre	C1
Klondike Gold Rush Natl. Hist. Park	D3	Smith Tower	D3
Lumen Field	D3	Space Needle	C1
Lumen Field Events Center	D3	T-Mobile Park	D3
Marion Oliver McCaw Hall	C1	Underground Tour	D3
Memorial Stadium	C1	Victoria Clipper	C2
Miners Landing	C2	Washington State Convention Center	D2
Monorail	C1, D2	Washington State Ferries	D3
Moore Theatre	D2	Westlake Center	D2
Museum of Pop Culture	C1	Ye Old Curiosity Shop	D2
Northwest Seaport/ Maritime Heritage Center	D1		

Entries in **bold black** indicate counties or parishes.
Entries in **bold color** indicate cities with detailed inset maps.

Sevier Co. AR 116 C3
Sevier Co. TN 111 D4
Sevier Co. UT 39 E2
Sevierville TN 111 D4
Seville OH 91 E3
Sewanee TN 120 A1
Seward AK 154 C3
Seward NE 35 F4
Seward Co. KS 42 B4
Seward Co. NE 35 E4
Sewaren NJ 240 A6
Sewell NJ 146 C4
Sewickley PA 92 A4
Seymour CT 149 D2
Seymour IN 99 F2
Seymour IA 87 D3
Seymour MO 107 D2
Seymour TN 110 C4
Seymour TX 58 C1
Seymour WI 68 C4
Seymourville LA 134 A2
Shabbona IL 88 C1
Shackelford Co. TX 58 C2
Shadeland IN 89 E4
Shady Cove OR 28 B1
Shady Pt. OK 116 B1
Shady Rest CT 148 C1
Shady Side MD 144 C3
Shadyside OH 101 F1
Shady Spr. WV 111 F1
Shafter CA 45 D4
Shaker Hts. OH 91 E2
Shakopee MN 66 C4
Shalimar FL 136 B2
Shallotte NC 123 D4
Shallowater TX 58 A1
Shamokin PA 93 E3
Shamokin Dam PA 93 D3
Shamrock TX 50 C3
Shandon CA 44 C4
Shannock RI 150 C4
Shannon GA 120 B3
Shannon IL 88 B1
Shannon MS 119 D3
Shannon Co. MO 107 F2
Shannon Hills AR 117 E2
Shannontown SC 122 B4
Sharkey Co. MS 126 A2
Sharon CT 94 B2
Sharon MA 151 D2
Sharon PA 91 F2
Sharon SC 122 A2
Sharon TN 108 C3
Sharon WI 74 C4
Sharon Hill PA 248 B4
Sharon Sprs. KS 42 B2
Sharon Sprs. NY 79 F4
Sharonville OH 100 B2
Sharp Co. AR 107 F4
Sharpes FL 141 E1
Sharpsburg MD 144 A1
Sharpsburg NC 113 E4
Sharpsburg PA 250 C1
Sharpsville IN 89 F4
Sharpsville PA 91 F2
Sharptown MD 145 E4
Shasta Co. CA 28 C3
Shasta Lake CA 28 C4
Shattuck OK 50 C2
Shavano Park TX 257 E1
Shaver Lake CA 45 D2
Shaw MS 118 A4
Shawanee TN 111 D3
Shawano WI 68 C4
Shawano Co. WI 68 C4
Shawnee KS 96 B2
Shawnee OH 101 E1
Shawnee OK 51 F3
Shawnee Co. KS 96 A2
Shawneetown IL 109 D1
Shawsville VA 112 B2
Sheboygan WI 75 D2
Sheboygan Co. WI 74 C2
Sheboygan Falls WI 75 D2
Sheep Sprs. NM 48 A2
Sheffield AL 119 E2
Sheffield IL 88 B2
Sheffield IA 73 D3
Sheffield MA 94 B2
Sheffield PA 92 B2
Sheffield Lake OH 91 D2
Shelbiana KY 111 E1
Shelbina MO 97 E1
Shelburn IN 99 E2
Shelburne VT 81 D2
Shelburne Falls MA 94 C1
Shelby IA 86 A2
Shelby MI 75 E2
Shelby MS 118 A4
Shelby MT 15 E2
Shelby NE 35 E3
Shelby NC 121 F1
Shelby OH 91 D3
Shelby Co. AL 127 F1
Shelby Co. IL 98 C2
Shelby Co. IN 99 F1
Shelby Co. IA 86 A1
Shelby Co. KY 100 A4
Shelby Co. MO 97 E1
Shelby Co. OH 90 B4
Shelby Co. TN 118 B1
Shelby Co. TX 124 C3
Shelbyville IL 98 C2
Shelbyville IN 99 F1
Shelbyville KY 100 A4
Shelbyville MO 97 E1
Shelbyville TN 119 F1
Sheldon IL 89 D3
Sheldon IA 35 F1
Sheldon MO 106 C1
Sheldon TX 220 D2
Shelley ID 23 E4
Shell Knob MO 106 C3
Shell Lake WI 67 E2
Shellman GA 128 C4
Shell Pt. SC 130 C2
Shell Rock IA 73 D4
Shellsburg IA 87 E1
Shelly PA 146 C1
Shelter Island NY 149 E3
Shelter Island Hts. NY 149 E3
Shelton CT 149 D2
Shelton NE 35 D4
Shelton WA 12 B3
Shenandoah IA 86 A3
Shenandoah PA 93 E3
Shenandoah TX 132 A2
Shenandoah VA 102 C3
Shenandoah Co. VA 102 C3
Shepherd MI 76 A2
Shepherd TX 132 B2
Shepherdstown WV 103 D2
Shepherdsville KY 100 A4
Sherando VA 102 C4
Sherborn MA 150 C1
Sherburn MN 72 B2
Sherburne NY 79 E4
Sherburne Co. MN 66 C3
Sheridan AR 117 E3
Sheridan CA 36 C2
Sheridan CO 209 B4
Sheridan IL 88 C2
Sheridan IN 89 F4
Sheridan MI 76 A3
Sheridan MT 23 E2
Sheridan OR 20 B2
Sheridan WY 25 D3
Sheridan Co. KS 42 C1
Sheridan Co. MT 17 E1
Sheridan Co. NE 34 A2
Sheridan Co. ND 18 C3
Sheridan Co. WY 25 D2
Sherman IL 98 B1
Sherman MS 118 C3
Sherman NY 92 A1
Sherman TX 59 F1
Sherman Co. KS 42 B2
Sherman Co. NE 35 D3
Sherman Co. OR 21 D2
Sherman Co. TX 50 A2
Sherrard IL 88 A2
Sherrill NY 79 E3
Sherrills Ford NC 112 A4
Sherwood ND 18 B1
Sherwood OH 90 B2
Sherwood OR 20 B2
Sherwood WI 74 C1
Sherwood Manor CT 150 A2
Sheyenne ND 19 D3
Shiawassee Co. MI 76 B4
Shickshinny PA 93 E3
Shidler OK 51 F1
Shields MI 76 B2
Shillington PA 146 A2
Shiloh NJ 145 F1
Shiloh OH 91 D3
Shiloh OH 208 D1
Shiloh PA 275 E1
Shiner TX 61 E3
Shinglehouse PA 92 C1
Shingle Sprs. CA 36 C3
Shingletown CA 28 C4
Shinnecock Hills NY 149 E3
Shinnston WV 102 A2
Shiocton WI 74 C1
Ship Bottom NJ 147 E4
Shipman IL 98 B2
Shippensburg PA 103 D1
Shiprock NM 48 A1
Shipshewana IN 89 F2
Shiremanstown PA 218 A2
Shirley IN 100 A1
Shirley MA 95 D1
Shirley NY 149 D4
Shishmaref AK 154 B2
Shively KY 99 F4
Shoals IN 99 E3
Shoemakersville PA 146 A1
Shokan NY 94 A2
Shongopovi AZ 47 E2
Shonto AZ 47 E1
Shore Acres NJ 147 E3
Shoreacres TX 132 B3
Shoreham MI 89 E1
Shoreham Beach MD 144 C3
Shoreline WA 12 C3
Shoreview MN 235 C1
Shorewood IL 88 C2
Shorewood MN 66 C4
Shorewood WI 234 D2
Shorewood Hills WI 231 A2
Short Beach CT 149 D2
Shortsville NY 78 C3
Shoshone ID 30 C1
Shoshone Co. ID 14 B3
Shoshoni WY 32 C1
Show Low AZ 47 F4
Shreve OH 91 D3
Shreveport LA 124 C2
Shrewsbury MA 150 C1
Shrewsbury MO 256 B3
Shrewsbury NJ 147 E2
Shrewsbury PA 103 E1
Shrub Oak NY 148 B2
Shubuta MS 127 D3
Shullsburg WI 74 A4
Shuqualak MS 127 D1
Sibley IA 72 A2
Sibley LA 125 D2
Sibley Co. MN 66 C4
Sicily Island LA 125 F3
Sicklerville NJ 147 D4
Sidell IL 99 D1
Sidman PA 92 B4
Sidney IL 99 D1
Sidney IA 86 A3
Sidney MT 17 F3
Sidney NE 34 A3
Sidney NY 79 E4
Sidney OH 90 B4
Sidon MS 126 B1
Sierra Blanca TX 57 D4
Sierra Co. CA 37 D1
Sierra Co. NM 56 B2
Sierra Madre CA 228 E2
Sierra Vista AZ 55 E4
Siesta Key FL 140 B4
Signal Hill CA 228 D4
Signal Mtn. TN 120 B1
Sigourney IA 87 E2
Sigurd UT 39 E2
Sikeston MO 108 B2
Silas AL 127 D3
Siler City NC 112 C4
Siletz OR 20 B3
Silica OH 90 C2
Siloam Sprs. AR 106 B3
Silsbee TX 132 C2
Silt CO 40 C1
Silters NY 94 B1
Silver Bay MN 65 D3
Silver Bow Co. MT 23 E1
Silver City NM 55 F2
Silver City NC 122 C2
Silver Cliff CO 41 D3
Silver Creek MO 106 B2
Silver Creek NE 35 E3
Silver Creek NY 78 A4
Silverdale PA 146 C2
Silverdale WA 12 C3
Silver Grove KY 100 B2
Silverhill AL 135 E2
Silver Hill MD 270 E4
Silver Lake IN 89 F3
Silver Lake KS 96 A2
Silver Lake MA 151 E2
Silver Lake MN 66 C4
Silver Lake NC 123 E3
Silver Lake OH 188 B1
Silver Ridge NJ 147 E3
Silver Spr. MD 144 B3
Silver Sprs. FL 139 D4
Silver Sprs. NV 37 E2
Silver Sprs. NY 78 B4
Silver Sprs. Shores FL 139 D4
Silverthorne CO 41 D1
Silverton CO 40 C4
Silverton NJ 147 E3
Silverton OH 204 B2
Silverton OR 20 C2
Silverton TX 50 B4
Silvis IL 208 C2
Simi Valley CA 52 B2
Simla CO 41 F2
Simmesport LA 133 F1
Simms MT 15 E3
Simonton TX 61 F2
Simpson LA 125 D4
Simpson Co. KY 109 F2
Simpson Co. MS 126 B3
Simpsonville KY 100 A4
Simpsonville MD 144 B2
Simpsonville SC 121 F2
Simsboro LA 125 E2
Simsbury CT 94 C3
Sinclair WY 32 C2
Sinclairville NY 78 A4
Sinking Spr. PA 146 A2
Sinton TX 61 E4
Sioux Ctr. IA 35 F1
Sioux City IA 35 F1
Sioux Co. IA 35 F1
Sioux Co. NE 33 F1
Sioux Co. ND 26 B1
Sioux Falls SD 27 F4
Sioux Rapids IA 72 A3
Sippewisset MA 151 E4
Sipsey AL 119 F4
Siren WI 67 E2
Siskiyou Co. CA 28 C3
Sisseton SD 27 F1
Sissonville WV 101 E3
Sister Bay WI 69 D3
Sister Lakes MI 89 F1
Sisters OR 21 D3
Sistersville WV 101 F1
Sitka AK 155 D4
Six Mile SC 121 E2
Skagit Co. WA 12 C2
Skagway AK 155 D3
Skamania Co. WA 12 C4
Skaneateles NY 79 D3
Skellytown TX 50 B3
Skiatook OK 51 F1
Skidaway Island GA 130 C3
Skidmore TX 61 E4
Skidway Lake MI 76 B1
Skippack PA 146 C2
Skokie IL 89 D1
Skowhegan ME 82 C1
Sky Lake FL 246 C3
Skyline AL 120 A2
Skyway WA 262 B4
Slater IA 86 C1
Slater MO 97 D2
Slater SC 121 E2
Slatersville RI 150 C2
Slatington PA 93 F3
Slaton TX 58 A1
Slaughter LA 134 A1
Slaughter Beach DE 145 F3
Slaughterville OK 51 E3
Slayton MN 72 A1
Sledge MS 118 B3
Sleepy Eye MN 72 B1
Sleepy Hollow IL 203 A2
Sleepy Hollow NY 148 B3
Slidell LA 134 C2
Sligo PA 92 A3
Slinger WI 74 C3
Slingerlands NY 188 D3
Slippery Rock PA 92 A3
Sloan IA 35 F2
Sloan NY 198 C3
Sloatsburg NY 148 B2
Slocomb AL 136 C1

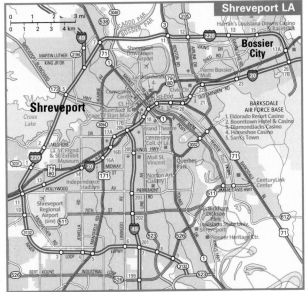

Shreveport LA

Sioux Falls SD

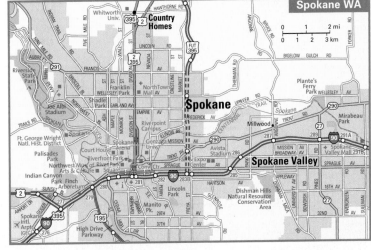

South Bend IN

Spokane WA

Figures after entries indicate page number and grid reference.

Slocum RI	150 C4	Smithton IL	98 B3	**Snohomish Co. WA**	12 C2	Solana FL	140 C4	Somers Pt. NJ	147 F4	Southampton PA	146 C2
Slope Co. ND	18 A4	Smithton MO	97 D3	Snook TX	61 F1	Solana Beach CA	53 D4	Somersworth NH	82 A4	**Southampton Co. VA**	113 E3
Smackover AR	125 E1	Smithtown NY	149 D3	Snoqualmie WA	12 C3	**Solano Co. CA**	36 B3	Somerton AZ	53 F4	S. Apopka FL	246 B1
Smallwood MD	144 B1	Smith Valley NV	37 D2	Snowflake AZ	47 F4	Soldiers Grove WI	73 F2	**Somervell Co. TX**	59 E3	Southaven MS	118 B2
Smallwood NY	94 A3	Smithville GA	129 D3	Snow Hill MD	114 C2	Soldotna AK	154 C3	Somerville MA	151 D1	S. Barrington IL	203 B2
Smelterville ID	14 B3	Smithville IN	99 F2	Snow Hill NC	115 C3	Soledad CA	44 B3	Somerville NJ	147 D1	S. Bay FL	143 E1
Smethport PA	92 C1	Smithville MS	119 D3	Snowmass Vil. CO	40 C2	Solomon AZ	55 E2	Somerville TN	118 C1	S. Belmar NJ	147 F2
Smith Ctr. KS	43 D1	Smithville MO	96 B2	Snow Shoe PA	92 C3	Solomon KS	43 E2	Somerville TX	61 F1	S. Beloit IL	74 B4
Smith Co. KS	43 D1	Smithville NJ	147 E4	Snyder OK	51 D4	Solomons MD	103 F4	Somis CA	52 B2	S. Bend IN	89 F2
Smith Co. MS	126 C3	Smithville OH	91 E3	Snyder TX	58 B2	Solon IA	87 F1	Somonauk IL	88 C2	S. Bend WA	12 B4
Smith Co. TN	110 A3	Smithville PA	146 A3	**Snyder Co. PA**	93 D3	Solon OH	91 E2	Sonoita AZ	55 D4	S. Berlin MA	150 C1
Smith Co. TX	124 B2	Smithville TN	110 A4	Soap Lake WA	13 E3	Solon Sprs. WI	64 C4	Sonoma CA	36 B3	S. Berwick ME	82 A4
Smithers WV	101 F4	Smithville TX	61 E2	Socastee SC	123 D4	Solvang CA	52 A2	**Sonoma Co. CA**	36 A2	S. Bethany DE	145 F4
Smithfield NC	123 E1	Smyrna DE	145 E2	Social Circle GA	121 D4	Solvay NY	265 A2	Sonora CA	37 D3	S. Bloomfield OH	101 D1
Smithfield OH	91 F3	Smyrna GA	120 C4	Society Hill SC	122 C3	Solway TN	110 C4	Sonora KY	110 A1	S. Boston VA	112 C3
Smithfield PA	102 B1	Smyrna TN	109 F4	Socorro NM	56 B1	Somerdale NJ	146 C3	Sonora TX	60 B1	S. Bound Brook NJ	147 D1
Smithfield UT	31 E2	Snead AL	119 D3	Socorro TX	56 C4	Somers CT	150 A2	Sopchoppy FL	137 E3	S. Bridgewater MA	151 D2
Smithfield VA	113 F2	Sneads FL	137 D1	**Socorro Co. NM**	48 C4	Somers MT	15 D2	Soperton GA	129 F2	Southbridge MA	150 B1
Smithland KY	109 D2	Sneads Ferry NC	115 D4	Soda Sprs. ID	31 F1	Somers NY	148 C2	Sophia WV	111 F1	S. Burlington VT	81 D2
Smithsburg MD	144 A1	Sneedville TN	111 D3	Soddy-Daisy TN	120 B1	Somers WI	74 C4	Soquel CA	236 D1	Southbury CT	149 D1
Smiths Grove KY	109 F2	Snellville GA	120 C4	Sodus NY	78 C3	Somerset KY	110 B2	Sorento IL	98 B2	S. Cairo NY	94 B2
Smiths Sta. AL	128 C2	Snohomish WA	12 C2	Sodus Pt. NY	79 D3	Somerset MD	270 C2	Sorrento LA	134 A2	S. Carthage TN	110 A3
						Somerset MA	151 D3	Soulsbyville CA	37 D3	S. Casco ME	82 B3
						Somerset NJ	147 E1	Sound Beach NY	149 D3	S. Charleston OH	100 C1
						Somerset OH	101 E1	Sound View CT	149 F2	S. Charleston WV	101 E4
						Somerset PA	102 B1	Sour Lake TX	132 C2	S. Chatham MA	151 F3
						Somerset TX	61 D3	S. Acton MA	150 C1	S. China ME	82 C2
						Somerset WI	67 D3	S. Amboy NJ	147 E1	S. Cle Elum WA	13 D3
						Somerset Co. ME	82 B1	S. Amherst MA	150 A1	S. Coatesville PA	146 B3
						Somerset Co. MD	103 F4	S. Amherst OH	91 D2	S. Coffeyville OK	106 A2
						Somerset Co. NJ	147 D1	Southampton NY	149 E3	S. Congaree SC	122 A4
						Somerset Co. PA	92 B4				

S. Connellsville PA	102 A3
S. Corning NY	93 D1
S. Dartmouth MA	151 D4
S. Dayton NY	78 A4
S. Daytona FL	139 E4
S. Deerfield MA	150 A1
S. Dennis MA	151 F3
S. Dos Palos CA	44 C2
S. Dover NY	148 C1
S. Duxbury MA	151 E2
S. Easton MA	151 D2
S. Elgin IL	88 C1
S. Eliot ME	82 A4
S. El Monte CA	228 E2
Southern Pines NC	122 C1
Southern Shores NC	115 F2
S. Euclid OH	204 G1
S. Fallsburg NY	94 A3
Southfield MI	76 B4
S. Floral Park NY	241 G4
S. Fork CO	40 C4
S. Fork PA	92 B4
S. Fulton TN	108 C3
S. Gastonia NC	122 A1
S. Gate CA	228 D3
Southgate KY	204 B3
S. Gate MD	193 C5
S. Glastonbury CT	149 E1
S. Glens Falls NY	81 D4
S. Greensburg PA	92 A4
S. Hadley MA	150 A1
S. Hadley Falls MA	150 A2
S. Haven KS	51 E1
S. Haven MI	75 E4
S. Heart ND	18 A4
S. Hill NY	79 D4
S. Hill VA	113 D3
S. Hill WA	262 B5
S. Holland IL	203 D4
S. Hooksett NH	81 F4
S. Houston TX	220 C3
S. Hutchinson KS	43 E3
Southington CT	149 D1
S. Jacksonville IL	98 A1
S. Jamesport NY	149 E3
S. Jordan UT	31 E4
S. Killingly CT	150 B3
Southlake TX	207 B1
S. Lake Tahoe CA	37 D2
S. Lancaster MA	150 C1
S. Lebanon ME	81 F4
S. Lebanon OH	100 B2
S. Lockport NY	78 B3
S. Lyon MI	76 B4
Southmayd TX	59 F1
S. Miami FL	143 E2
S. Miami Hts. FL	233 A5
S. Middleboro MA	151 E3
S. Mills NC	113 F3
S. Milwaukee WI	75 D3
S. Monroe MI	90 C1
Southmont NC	112 B4
S. Naknek AK	154 B3
S. Ogden UT	244 A2
Southold NY	149 E3
S. Orange NJ	240 A3
S. Orleans MA	151 F3
S. Padre Island TX	63 F4
S. Palm Beach FL	143 F1
S. Paris ME	82 B2
S. Pasadena CA	228 D2
S. Pasadena FL	140 B3

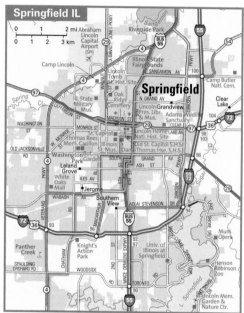

Springfield IL

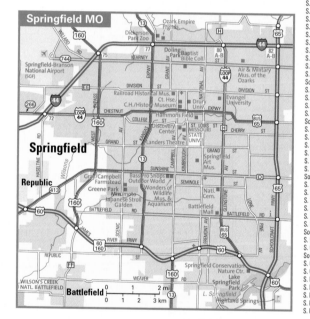

Springfield MO

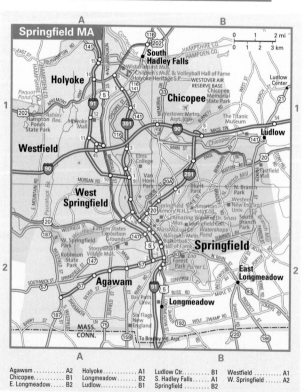

Springfield MA

Agawam	A2	Holyoke	A1	Ludlow Ctr.	B1	Westfield	A1
Chicopee	B1	Longmeadow	B2	S. Hadley Falls	A1	W. Springfield	A2
E. Longmeadow	B2	Ludlow	B1	Springfield	B2		

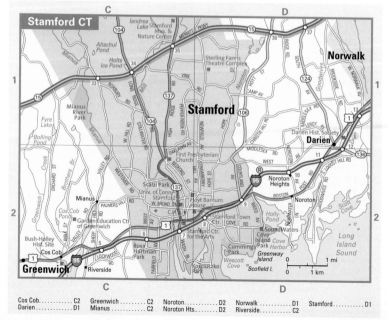

Stamford CT

Cos Cob	C2	Greenwich	C2	Noroton	D2	Norwalk	D1	Stamford	D1
Darien	D1	Mianus	C2	Noroton Hts.	D2	Riverside	C2		

Entries in **bold black** indicate counties or parishes.
Entries in **bold color** indicate cities with detailed inset maps.

S. Patrick Shores FL 141 E2
S. Pekin IL 88 B4
S. Pittsburg TN 120 A2
S. Plainfield NJ 147 E1
S. Point OH 101 D3
Southport FL 136 C2
Southport IN 99 F1
Southport NY 93 D1
Southport NC 123 E4
S. Portland ME 82 B3
S. Pottstown PA 146 B2
S. Range MI 65 F3
S. River NJ 147 E1
S. Rockwood MI 90 C1
S. Roxana IL 256 D1
S. Royalton VT 81 E3
S. Russell OH 91 E2
S. St. Paul MN 235 D3
S. Salt Lake UT 257 B2
S. Sanford ME 82 B2
S. San Francisco CA 259 B4
S. San Gabriel CA 228 E2
S. Shaftsbury VT 94 C1
S. Shore KY 101 D3
S. Shore SD 27 F2
Southside AL 120 A4
Southside Place TX 220 B3
S. Sioux City NE 35 F2
S. Toms River NJ 147 E3
S. Torrington WY 33 F2
S. Tucson AZ 55 D3
S. Valley Stream NY 241 G4
S. Venice FL 140 B4
S. Wallins KY 111 D2
S. Walpole MA 151 D2
S. Waverly PA 93 E1
S. Weber UT 244 B2
S. Webster OH 101 D3
S. Weldon NC 113 E3
Southwest City MO 106 B3
Southwest Harbor ME 83 D2
S. Westport MA 151 D4
S. Weymouth MA 151 D2
S. Whitley IN 89 F3
S. Whittier CA 228 E3
Southwick MA 150 A2
S. Williamson KY 111 E1
S. Williamsport PA 93 D2
S. Willington CT 150 A3
S. Wilmington IL 88 C2
S. Windham CT 149 F1
S. Windham ME 82 B3
S. Windsor CT 150 A3
Southwood Acres CT 150 A2
S. Woodstock CT 150 B3
S. Yarmouth MA 151 F3
S. Zanesville OH 101 E1
Spalding NE 35 E3
Spalding Co. GA 128 C1
Spanaway WA 12 C3
Spanish Fork UT 39 E1
Spanish Fort AL 135 E1
Spanish Lake MO 256 C1
Sparkman AR 117 D4
Sparks GA 137 F1
Sparks MD 144 C1
Sparks NV 37 D1
Sparrow Bush NY 94 A3
Sparta GA 129 E1
Sparta IL 98 B4
Sparta MI 75 F3
Sparta MO 107 D2
Sparta NJ 148 A3
Sparta NC 112 A3
Sparta TN 110 A4
Sparta WI 73 F1
Spartanburg SC 121 F2
Spartanburg Co. SC 121 F2
Spavinaw OK 106 B3
Spearfish SD 25 F3
Spearman TX 50 B2
Spearville KS 42 C4
Speedway IN 99 F1
Speigner AL 128 A2
Spencer IN 99 E2
Spencer IA 72 A3
Spencer MA 150 B1
Spencer NE 35 D1
Spencer NY 93 E1
Spencer NC 112 A4
Spencer OH 91 D3
Spencer OK 51 E3
Spencer TN 110 A4
Spencer WV 101 F3
Spencer WI 68 A4
Spencer Co. IN 99 E4
Spencer Co. KY 100 A4
Spencerport NY 78 C3
Spencerville OH 90 B3
Speonk NY 149 E3
Sperry OK 51 F2
Spiceland IN 100 A1
Spicer MN 66 B3
Spindale NC 121 F1
Spink Co. SD 27 E2
Spinnerstown PA 146 C1
Spirit Lake ID 14 B2
Spirit Lake IA 72 B2
Spiro OK 116 B1
Splendora TX 132 B2
Spofford NH 94 C1
Spokane WA 14 A3
Spokane Co. WA 14 B2
Spokane Valley WA 14 B3
Spooner WI 67 E2
Spotswood NJ 147 E1
Spotsylvania VA 103 D4
Spotsylvania Co. VA 103 D4
Spottsville KY 99 E4
Spout Sprs. NC 123 D1
Sprague WA 13 F3
Spreckels CA 236 E3
Spring TX 132 A2
Spring Arbor MI 90 B1
Springboro OH 100 B1
Spring City PA 146 B2
Spring City TN 110 B4
Spring City UT 39 E1
Spring Creek NV 30 B4
Springdale AR 106 C4
Springdale OH 204 B1
Springdale PA 250 D1
Springdale SC 205 E2
Springdale UT 39 D4
Springer NM 49 E2
Springer OK 51 E4
Springerville AZ 48 A4
Springfield CO 42 A4
Springfield FL 136 C2
Springfield GA 130 B2
Springfield IL 98 B1
Springfield KY 110 B1
Springfield LA 134 B2
Springfield MA 150 A2
Springfield MI 75 F4
Springfield MN 72 B1
Springfield MO 107 D2
Springfield NE 35 F3
Springfield NJ 148 A4
Springfield OH 100 C1
Springfield OR 20 B4
Springfield PA 146 C3
Springfield SC 122 A4
Springfield SD 35 E1
Springfield TN 109 F3
Springfield VT 81 E4
Springfield VA 144 B3
Spring Garden Estates MD 144 A1
Spring Glen UT 39 F1
Spring Green WI 74 A3
Spring Grove IL 74 C4
Spring Grove MN 73 E2
Spring Grove PA 103 E1
Spring Hill FL 140 B1
Spring Hill KS 96 B3
Springhill LA 125 D1
Spring Hill TN 109 E4
Spring Hope NC 113 D4
Spring Lake MI 75 E3
Spring Lake NJ 147 F2
Spring Lake NC 123 D1
Spring Lake Hts. NJ 147 E2
Spring Lake Park MN 235 C1
Spring Mill KY 230 E3
Springport MI 76 A4
Springs NY 149 F3
Springtown TX 59 E2
Springvale ME 82 A4
Spring Valley CA 53 D4
Spring Valley IL 88 B2
Spring Valley KY 230 F1
Spring Valley MN 73 D2
Spring Valley NY 148 B2
Spring Valley WI 67 E4
Spring Valley Vil. TX 220 B2
Springview NE 34 C1
Springville AL 119 F4
Springville CA 45 D3
Springville IA 87 F1
Springville NJ 147 D3
Springville NY 78 B4
Springville UT 39 E1
Springwater NY 78 C4
Spruce Pine NC 111 E4
Spry PA 275 F2
Spur TX 58 B1
Squaw Valley CA 45 D3
Staatsburg NY 94 B3
Stacy MN 67 D3
Stafford CT 150 B2
Stafford KS 43 D3
Stafford TX 132 A3
Stafford VA 103 D3
Stafford Co. KS 43 D3
Stafford Co. VA 144 A4
Stafford Sprs. CT 150 A2
Stallings NC 122 B1
Stamford CT 148 C3
Stamford NY 79 F4
Stamford TX 58 C2
Stamping Ground KY 100 B4
Stamps AR 125 D1
Stanardsville VA 102 C4
Stanberry MO 86 B4
Standing Pine MS 126 C2
Standish ME 82 B3
Standish MI 76 B1
Stanfield AZ 54 C2
Stanfield NC 122 B1
Stanfield OR 21 E1
Stanford IL 88 B4
Stanford KY 110 B1
Stanford MT 16 B3
Stanhope NJ 94 A4
Stanislaus Co. CA 36 C4
Stanley KY 109 E1
Stanley NC 122 A1
Stanley ND 18 A2
Stanley VA 102 C3
Stanley WI 67 F4
Stanley Co. SD 26 C3
Stanleytown VA 112 B2
Stanly Co. NC 122 B1
Stannards NY 92 C1
Stanton CA 228 E4
Stanton DE 146 B4
Stanton IA 86 B3
Stanton KY 110 C1
Stanton MI 76 A3
Stanton NE 35 E2
Stanton ND 18 B3
Stanton TN 118 C1
Stanton TX 58 A3
Stanton Co. KS 42 B4
Stanton Co. NE 35 E2
Stantonsburg NC 123 E1
Stanwood IA 87 F1
Stanwood WA 12 C2
Staples MN 64 A4
Stapleton NE 34 C3
Star ID 22 B4
Star NC 122 C1
Starbuck MN 66 A2
Star City AR 117 F4
Star City WV 102 A1
Star Cross NJ 145 F1
Stark Co. IL 88 B3
Stark Co. ND 18 A4
Stark Co. OH 91 E3
Starke FL 138 C3
Starke Co. IN 89 E2
Starkey VA 254 D2
Starks LA 133 D2
Starkville MS 118 C4
Star Lake NY 79 F1
Star Prairie WI 67 E3
Starr Co. TX 63 E3
Startex SC 217 C1
Startup WA 12 C2
Star Valley AZ 47 E4
Stateburg SC 122 B4
State Ctr. IA 87 D1
State College PA 92 C3
State Line MS 127 D4
Stateline NV 37 D2
State Line PA 103 D1
Statenville GA 137 F1
State Road NC 112 A3
Statesboro GA 130 B2
Statesville NC 112 A4
Statham GA 121 D4
Staunton IL 98 B2
Staunton IN 99 E2
Staunton VA 102 B4
Stayton OR 20 C3
Steamboat AZ 47 F2
Steamboat NV 37 D2
Steamboat Sprs. CO 33 D4
Stearns KY 110 B3
Stearns Co. MN 66 B3
Stebbins AK 154 B2
Stedman NC 123 D2
Steele AL 120 A4
Steele MO 108 B4
Steele ND 18 C4
Steele Co. MN 73 D1
Steele Co. ND 19 E3
Steeleville IL 98 B4
Steelton PA 218 B2
Steelville MO 97 F4
Steilacoom WA 12 C3
Steinhatchee FL 137 F3
Stephen MN 19 E2
Stephens AR 125 D1
Stephens City VA 102 C2
Stephens Co. GA 121 D2
Stephens Co. OK 51 E4
Stephens Co. TX 59 D2
Stephenson MI 69 D3
Stephenson VA 103 D2
Stephenson Co. IL 74 B4
Stephenville TX 59 D3
Sterling CO 34 A4
Sterling CT 150 B3
Sterling IL 88 B1
Sterling KS 43 E3
Sterling MA 150 C1
Sterling MI 76 B1
Sterling NE 35 F4
Sterling OK 51 E4
Sterling VA 144 A3
Sterling City TX 58 B3
Sterling Co. TX 58 B4
Sterling Forest NY 148 A2
Sterling Hts. MI 76 C4
Sterlington LA 125 E2
Stetsonville WI 68 A3
Steuben Co. IN 90 A2
Steuben Co. NY 78 C4
Steubenville KY 110 B2
Steubenville OH 91 F4
Stevens Co. KS 42 B4
Stevens Co. MN 27 F2
Stevens Co. WA 13 F2
Stevens Creek VA 112 A2
Stevenson AL 120 A2
Stevenson CT 149 D2
Stevenson WA 20 C1
Stevens Pt. WI 68 B4
Stevensville MD 145 D3
Stevensville MI 89 E1
Stevensville MT 15 D4
Stewardson IL 98 C2
Stewart MN 66 B4
Stewart Co. GA 128 C3
Stewart Co. TN 109 D3
Stewart Manor NY 241 G3
Stewartstown PA 103 E1
Stewartsville MO 96 B1
Stewartville MN 73 D2
Stickney IL 203 D5
Stickney SD 27 E4
Stigler OK 116 B1
Stillman Valley IL 88 B1
Stillmore GA 129 F2
Stillwater ME 83 D1
Stillwater MN 67 D3
Stillwater NY 94 B1
Stillwater OK 51 F2
Stillwater Co. MT 24 B1
Stilwell KS 96 B3
Stilwell OK 106 B4
Stimson Crossing WA 12 C2
Stinnett TX 50 B2
Stinson Beach CA 259 A2
Stites ID 22 B1
Stockbridge GA 120 C4
Stockbridge MA 94 B2
Stockbridge MI 76 B4
Stockbridge WI 74 C1
Stockdale TX 61 E3
Stock Island FL 142 C4
Stockton CA 36 C3
Stockton IL 74 A4
Stockton KS 43 D2
Stockton MN 73 E1
Stockton MO 106 C1

Syracuse NY

Bayberry A1
Collamer B1
DeWitt B2
E. Syracuse B2
Fairmount A2
Franklin Park B1
Galeville A1
Jamesville B2
Lakeland A1
Liverpool A1
Lyndon B2
Mattydale B1
Nedrow A2
N. Syracuse B1
Onondaga Hill A2
Solvay A2
Split Rock A2
Syracuse A2
Taunton A2
Westvale A2

Stockton CA

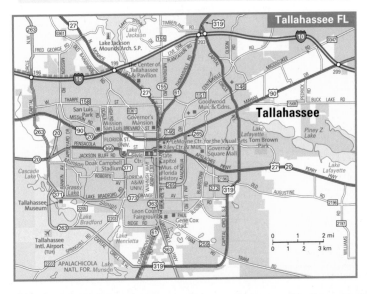

Figures after entries indicate page number and grid reference.

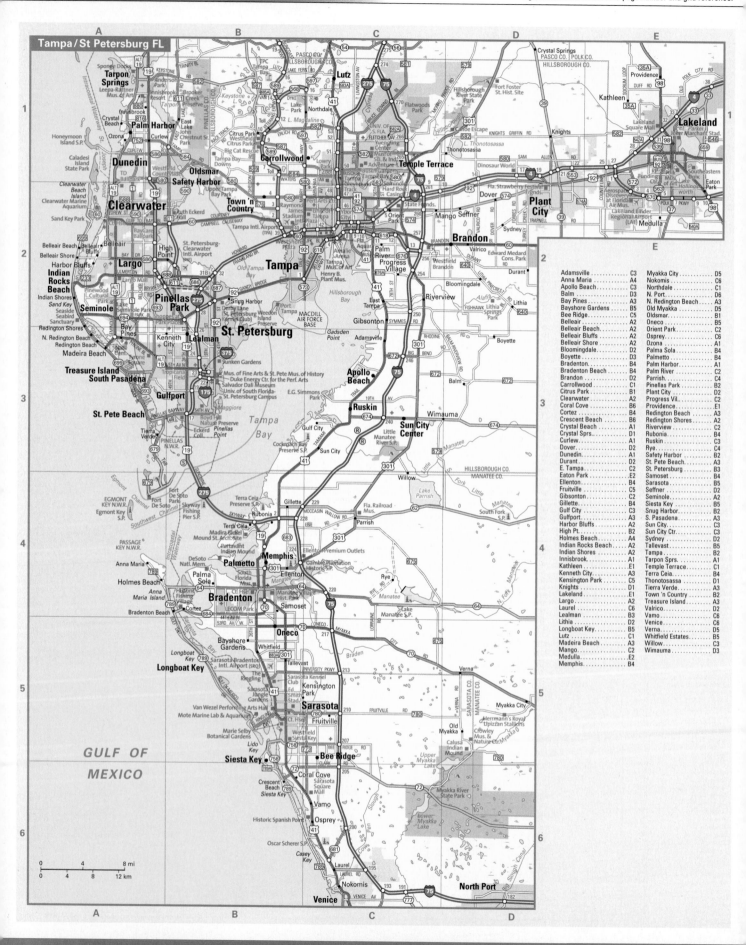

Tampa/St Petersburg FL

Location	Ref	Location	Ref
Adamsville	C3	Myakka City	D5
Anna Maria	A4	Nokomis	C6
Apollo Beach	C3	Northdale	C1
Balm	D3	N. Port	D6
Bay Pines	A3	N. Redington Beach	A3
Bayshore Gardens	B5	Old Myakka	D5
Bee Ridge	C5	Oldsmar	B1
Belleair	A2	Oneco	B5
Belleair Beach	A2	Orient Park	C2
Belleair Bluffs	A2	Osprey	C6
Belleair Shore	A2	Ozona	A1
Bloomingdale	D2	Palma Sola	B4
Boyette	D3	Palmetto	B4
Bradenton	B4	Palm Harbor	A1
Bradenton Beach	B4	Palm River	C2
Brandon	D2	Parrish	C4
Carrollwood	C1	Pinellas Park	B2
Citrus Park	B1	Plant City	D2
Clearwater	A2	Progress Vil.	C2
Coral Cove	B6	Providence	E1
Cortez	B4	Redington Beach	A3
Crescent Beach	C6	Redington Shores	A2
Crystal Beach	A1	Riverview	C2
Crystal Sprs.	D1	Rubonia	B4
Curlew	A1	Ruskin	C3
Dover	D2	Rye	C4
Dunedin	A1	Safety Harbor	B2
Durant	D2	St. Pete Beach	A3
E. Tampa	C2	St. Petersburg	B3
Eaton Park	E2	Samoset	B4
Ellenton	B4	Sarasota	B5
Fruitville	C5	Seffner	D2
Gibsonton	C2	Seminole	A2
Gillette	C3	Siesta Key	B5
Gulf City	C3	Snug Harbor	B2
Gulfport	A3	S. Pasadena	A3
Harbor Bluffs	A2	Sun City	C3
High Pt.	B2	Sun City Ctr.	C3
Holmes Beach	A4	Sydney	D2
Indian Rocks Beach	A2	Tallevast	B5
Indian Shores	A2	Tampa	B2
Innisbrook	A1	Tarpon Sprs.	A1
Kathleen	E1	Temple Terrace	C1
Kenneth City	A3	Terra Ceia	B4
Kensington Park	C5	Tierra Verde	A3
Knights	D1	Town 'n Country	B2
Lakeland	E1	Treasure Island	A3
Largo	A2	Valrico	D2
Laurel	C6	Vamo	C6
Lealman	B3	Venice	C6
Lithia	D2	Verna	D5
Longboat Key	B5	Whitfield Estates	B5
Lutz	C1	Willow	C3
Madeira Beach	A3	Wimauma	D3
Mango	C2		
Medulla	E2		
Memphis	B4		

Entries in **bold black** indicate counties or parishes.
Entries in **bold color** indicate cities with detailed inset maps.

Stockton NJ 146 C1
Stockton UT 31 E4
Stockton Sprs. ME 83 D2
Stockville NE 34 C4
Stoddard WI 73 F2
Stoddard Co. MO 108 B2
Stokes Co. NC 112 B3
Stokesdale NC 112 B3
Stoneboro PA 92 A2
Stone Co. AR 107 E4
Stone Co. MS 135 D1
Stone Co. MO 107 D3
Stonega VA 111 D2
Stoneham MA 151 D1
Stone Harbor NJ 104 C4
Stone Mtn. GA 120 C4
Stone Park IL 203 C4
Stone Ridge NY 94 B3
Stoneville NC 112 B3
Stonewall LA 124 C3
Stonewall MS 127 D3
Stonewall OK 51 F4
Stonewall Co. TX 58 B2
Stonewood WV 102 A2
Stoney Creek Mills PA 146 B2
Stonington CT 149 F2
Stonington IL 98 C1
Stonington ME 83 D2
Stony Brook NY 149 D3
Stony Creek CT 149 E2
Stony Pt. NY 148 B2
Stony Pt. NC 112 A4
Storey Co. NV 37 D2
Storm Lake IA 72 A4
Stormstown PA 92 C3
Storrs CT 150 B3
Story WY 25 D3
Story City IA 86 C1
Story Co. IA 86 C1
Stottville NY 94 B2
Stoughton MA 151 D2
Stoughton WI 74 B3
Stoutsville OH 101 D1
Stover MO 97 D3
Stow OH 91 E2
Stowe PA 146 B2
Stowe VT 81 E2
Stowell TX 132 C3
Strafford MO 107 D2
Strafford Co. NH 81 F4
Straitsville CT 149 D1
Strasburg CO 41 E1
Strasburg IL 98 C2
Strasburg ND 26 C1
Strasburg OH 91 E4
Strasburg PA 146 A3
Strasburg VA 102 C2
Stratford CA 44 C3
Stratford CT 149 D2
Stratford IA 72 C4
Stratford NJ 146 C3
Stratford OK 51 F4
Stratford TX 50 A2
Stratford WI 68 A4
Stratham NH 82 A4
Strathmoor Vil. KY 230 E2
Strathmore CA 45 D3
Strathmore NJ 147 E1
Stratmoor Hills CO 205 D2
Stratton CO 42 A2
Stratton ME 82 B1
Stratton NE 42 B1
Strawberry AZ 47 E4
Strawberry Pt. IA 73 E4
Strawn TX 59 D3
Streamwood IL 203 B3
Streator IL 88 C3
Streetsboro OH 91 E2
Stroh IN 90 A2
Stromsburg NE 35 E3
Strong AR 125 E1
Strong ME 82 B1
Strong City KS 43 F3
Stronghurst IL 87 F3
Strongsville OH 91 E2
Stroud OK 51 F2
Stroudsburg PA 93 F3
Strum WI 67 F4
Struthers OH 91 F3
Stryker OH 90 B2
Stuart FL 141 E4
Stuart IA 86 B2
Stuart NE 35 D1
Stuart VA 112 B3
Stuarts Draft VA 102 C4
Sturbridge MA 150 B2
Sturgeon MO 97 E2
Sturgeon Bay WI 69 D4
Sturgis KY 109 D1
Sturgis MI 90 A1
Sturgis SD 25 F3
Sturtevant WI 74 C4
Stutsman Co. ND 19 D3
Stuttgart AR 117 F3
Suamico WI 68 C4
Subiaco AR 116 C1
Sublette KS 42 B4
Sublette Co. WY 32 A1
Sublimity OR 20 C2
Succasunna NJ 148 A3
Sudan TX 57 F1
Sudbury MA 150 C1
Suffern NY 148 B2
Suffield CT 150 A2
Suffolk VA 113 F3
Suffolk Co. MA 151 D1
Suffolk Co. NY 149 D3
Sugar City ID 23 E4
Sugar Creek MO 224 D3
Sugarcreek OH 91 E4
Sugarcreek PA 92 A2
Sugar Grove IL 88 C1
Sugar Grove PA 92 B1
Sugar Grove VA 111 F2
Sugar Hill GA 120 C3
Sugar Land TX 132 A3
Sugarland Run VA 144 A3
Sugar Loaf NY 148 A2
Sugar Notch PA 261 A2
Suisun City CA 36 B3
Suitland MD 144 B3
Sulligent AL 119 D4
Sullivan IL 98 C1
Sullivan IN 99 E2
Sullivan MO 97 F4
Sullivan WI 74 C3
Sullivan City TX 63 E4
Sullivan Co. IN 99 E2
Sullivan Co. MO 87 D4
Sullivan Co. NH 81 E4
Sullivan Co. NY 94 A2
Sullivan Co. PA 93 E2
Sullivan Co. TN 111 E3
Sullivan's Island SC 131 D2
Sully IA 87 D2
Sully Co. SD 26 C3
Sulphur LA 133 D2
Sulphur OK 51 F4
Sulphur Rock AR 107 F4
Sulphur Sprs. AR 106 B3
Sulphur Sprs. TX 124 A1
Sultan WA 12 C3
Sumas WA 12 C1
Sumiton AL 119 F4
Summerdale AL 135 E2
Summerfield NC 112 B3
Summerland Key FL 143 D4
Summers Co. WV 112 A1
Summerside OH 204 C2
Summersville MO 107 F2
Summersville WV 101 F4
Summerton SC 122 B4
Summertown TN 119 E1
Summerville GA 120 B3
Summerville SC 131 D1
Summit AR 107 E3
Summit IL 203 D5
Summit KY 101 D3
Summit MS 126 B4
Summit NJ 148 A4
Summit SD 27 F2
Summit WA 262 B5
Summit Co. CO 41 D1
Summit Co. OH 91 E3
Summit Co. UT 31 F4
Summitville IN 89 F4
Sumner IL 99 D3
Sumner IA 73 E3
Sumner MS 118 B3
Sumner WA 12 C3
Sumner Co. KS 51 E1
Sumner Co. TN 109 F3
Sumrall MS 126 C4
Sumter SC 122 B4
Sumter Co. AL 127 E2
Sumter Co. FL 140 C1
Sumter Co. GA 129 D3
Sumter Co. SC 122 B4
Sun LA 134 C1
Sunapee NH 81 E4
Sunbright TN 110 B3
Sunburst MT 15 E1
Sunbury OH 91 D4
Sunbury PA 93 D3
Sun City AZ 54 C1
Sun City Ctr. FL 140 C3
Sun City West AZ 249 A1
Suncook NH 81 F4
Sundance WY 25 F3
Sunderland MD 144 C4
Sunderland MA 150 A1
Sundown TX 57 F1
Sunfield MI 76 A4
Sunfish Lake MN 235 D3
Sunflower MS 118 A4
Sunflower Co. MS 118 E4
Sun Lakes AZ 54 C2
Sunland Park NM 56 C4
Sunman IN 100 A2
Sunnybrook MD 144 C1
Sunny Isles Beach FL 233 C3
Sunnyside UT 39 F1
Sunnyside WA 13 E4
Sunnyvale CA 36 B4
Sunol CA 259 E4
Sun Prairie WI 74 B3
Sunray TX 50 A2
Sunrise FL 143 E1
Sunrise Beach Vil. TX 61 D1
Sunset LA 133 F2
Sunset UT 244 A2
Sunset Beach NC 123 D4
Sunset Hills MO 256 B3
Sun Valley ID 22 C4
Superior AZ 55 D2
Superior CO 209 B1
Superior MT 14 C3
Superior NE 43 E1
Superior WI 64 C4
Superior WY 32 B2
Supreme LA 134 A3
Suquamish WA 262 A2
Surf City NJ 147 E4
Surf City NC 123 E3
Surfside FL 233 C4
Surfside Beach SC 123 D4
Surfside Beach TX 133 E4
Surgoinsville TN 111 D3
Suring WI 68 C4
Surprise AZ 54 C1
Surrey ND 18 B2
Surry VA 113 F2
Surry Co. NC 112 A3
Surry Co. VA 113 F2
Susan VA 113 F1
Susan Moore AL 119 F3
Susanville CA 29 D4
Susquehanna PA 93 F1
Susquehanna Co. PA 93 E2
Sussex NJ 148 A2
Sussex VA 113 E2
Sussex WI 74 C3
Sussex Co. DE 145 F4
Sussex Co. NJ 148 A2
Sussex Co. VA 113 E2
Sutcliffe NV 37 D1
Sutherland IA 72 A3
Sutherland NE 34 B3
Sutherlin OR 20 B4
Sutter CA 36 B2
Sutter Co. CA 36 B2
Sutter Creek CA 36 C3
Sutton AK 154 C3
Sutton MA 150 C2
Sutton NE 35 E4
Sutton WV 101 F3
Sutton Co. TX 60 B1
Suttons Bay MI 69 F4
Suwanee GA 120 C3
Suwannee Co. FL 138 B2
Swain Co. NC 121 D1
Swainsboro GA 129 F2
Swampscott MA 151 D1
Swannanoa NC 121 E1
Swann Keys DE 145 F4
Swanquarter NC 115 E3
Swansboro NC 115 D4
Swansea IL 98 B3
Swansea SC 122 A4
Swanton OH 90 B2
Swanton VT 81 D1
Swan Valley ID 23 F4
Swarthmore PA 146 C3
Swartz LA 125 F2
Swartz Creek MI 76 B3
Swayzee IN 89 F4
Swea City IA 72 B2
Swedesboro NJ 146 C4
Sweeny TX 132 A4
Sweet Briar VA 112 C1
Sweet Grass Co. MT 24 A1
Sweet Home OR 20 C3
Sweetser IN 89 F3
Sweet Sprs. MO 97 D3
Sweetwater FL 143 E2
Sweetwater TN 120 C1
Sweetwater TX 58 B3
Sweetwater Co. WY 32 B2
Swepsonville NC 112 C4
Swift Co. MN 66 A3
Swifton AR 107 F4
Swifts Beach MA 151 E3
Swift Trail Jct. AZ 55 E2
Swiftwater PA 93 F3
Swink CO 41 F3
Swisher IA 87 E1
Swisher Co. TX 50 A4
Swissvale PA 250 C2
Switzer WV 111 E1
Switzerland Co. IN 100 B3
Swoyersville PA 93 E2
Sycamore GA 129 D4
Sycamore IL 88 C1
Sycamore OH 90 C3
Sycaway NY 188 E2
Sykesville MD 144 B1
Sykesville PA 92 B3
Sylacauga AL 128 A1
Sylva NC 121 D1
Sylvan Beach NY 79 E3
Sylvania AL 120 A2
Sylvania GA 130 B2
Sylvania OH 90 C2
Sylvan Lake MI 210 B1
Sylvan Lake NY 148 C1
Sylvan Shores FL 141 D3
Sylvan Sprs. AL 195 D2
Sylvester GA 129 D4
Symsonia KY 109 D2
Syosset NY 148 C3
Syracuse IN 89 F2
Syracuse KS 42 B3
Syracuse NE 35 F4
Syracuse NY 79 D3
Syracuse OH 101 E2
Syracuse UT 31 E3

T

Tabor IA 86 A3
Tabor SD 35 E1
Tabor City NC 123 D3
Tacna AZ 54 A2
Tacoma WA 12 C3
Taft CA 52 B1
Taft FL 246 C4
Taft TX 61 E4
Tahlequah OK 106 B4
Tahoe City CA 37 D2
Tahoka TX 58 A2
Taholah WA 12 A3
Takoma Park MD 270 D2
Talbot Co. GA 128 C2
Talbot Co. MD 145 D3
Talbott TN 111 D4
Talbotton GA 128 C2
Talco TX 124 B1
Talcottville CT 150 A3
Talent OR 28 B2
Taliaferro Co. GA 121 E4
Talihina OK 116 B2
Talkeetna AK 154 C3
Talladega AL 120 A4
Talladega Co. AL 128 A1
Tallahassee FL 137 E2
Tallahatchie Co. MS 118 B4
Tallapoosa GA 120 B4
Tallapoosa Co. AL 128 B1
Tallassee AL 128 A2
Tallevast FL 266 B5
Talleyville DE 146 B3
Tallmadge OH 91 E3
Tallula IL 98 B1
Tallulah LA 126 A2
Talmage CA 36 A2
Talmo GA 121 D3
Taloga OK 51 D2
Talty TX 59 F2
Tama IA 87 D1
Tama Co. IA 87 D1
Tamalpais Valley CA 259 A2
Tamaqua PA 93 E3
Tamarac FL 143 E1
Tamaroa IL 98 B4
Tamms IL 108 C2
Tampa FL 140 B2
Tampico IL 88 B2
Taney Co. MO 107 D3
Taneytown MD 103 E1
Tangelo Park FL 246 B3
Tangent OR 20 B3
Tangier VA 114 B2
Tangipahoa LA 134 B1
Tangipahoa Par. LA 134 B1
Tanner AL 119 F2
Tannersville PA 93 F3
Tanque Verde AZ 55 D3
Tantallon MD 144 B4
Taos MO 97 E3
Taos NM 49 D1
Taos Co. NM 49 D1
Tappahannock VA 103 E4
Tappan NY 148 B3
Tappen ND 18 C4
Tara Hills CA 259 B1
Tarboro NC 113 E4
Tarentum PA 92 A3
Tariffville CT 150 A3
Tarkiln RI 150 C2
Tarkio MO 86 A4
Tarpon Sprs. FL 140 B2
Tarrant AL 119 F4
Tarrant Co. TX 59 E2
Tarrytown NY 148 B3
Tasso TN 120 B1
Tatamy PA 93 F3
Tate Co. MS 118 B2
Tattnall Co. GA 129 F3
Tatum NM 57 F2
Tatum TX 124 B2
Taunton MA 151 D3
Tavares FL 140 C1
Tavernier FL 143 E4
Tawas City MI 76 B1
Taylor AL 136 C1
Taylor AZ 47 F4
Taylor AR 125 D1
Taylor MI 90 C1
Taylor NE 35 D2
Taylor PA 261 D1
Taylor TX 61 E1
Taylor Co. FL 137 F3
Taylor Co. GA 129 D2
Taylor Co. IA 86 B3
Taylor Co. KY 110 B1
Taylor Co. TX 58 C3
Taylor Co. WV 102 A2
Taylor Co. WI 67 F3
Taylor Creek FL 141 E4
Taylor Lake Vil. TX 132 B3
Taylor Mill KY 204 B3
Taylors SC 121 F2
Taylors Falls MN 67 D3
Taylor Sprs. IL 98 B2
Taylorsville IN 99 F2
Taylorsville KY 100 A4
Taylorsville MD 144 B1
Taylorsville MS 126 C3
Taylorsville NC 111 F4
Taylorsville UT 257 A2
Taylortown NJ 148 A3
Taylortown NC 122 C1
Taylorville IL 98 B1
Tazewell TN 111 D3
Tazewell VA 111 F2
Tazewell Co. IL 88 B4
Tazewell Co. VA 111 F2
Tchula MS 126 B1
Tea SD 27 F4
Teague TX 59 F4
Teaneck NJ 148 B3
Teaticket MA 151 E4
Teays Val. WV 101 E3
Tecumseh MI 90 B1
Tecumseh NE 35 F4
Tecumseh OK 51 F3
Teec Nos Pos AZ 48 A1
Tega Cay SC 122 A2
Tehachapi CA 52 C1
Tehama CA 36 B1
Tehama Co. CA 36 B1
Tekamah NE 35 F2
Tekoa WA 14 B3
Tekonsha MI 90 A1
Telfair Co. GA 129 E3
Telford PA 146 C2
Tell City IN 99 E4
Teller Co. CO 41 E2
Tellico Plains TN 120 C1
Telluride CO 40 B3
Temecula CA 53 D3
Tempe AZ 54 C1
Temperance MI 90 C1
Temple GA 120 B4
Temple OK 51 E4
Temple PA 146 B1
Temple TX 59 E4
Temple City CA 228 E2
Temple Hills MD 270 E5
Temple Terrace FL 140 C2
Templeton CA 44 C4
Templeton MA 95 D1
Tenafly NJ 148 B3
Tenaha TX 124 C3
Tenants Harbor ME 82 C3
Tenino WA 12 C4
Tennent NJ 147 E2
Tennessee Ridge TN 109 D3
Tennille GA 129 E1
Tensas Par. LA 125 F3
Ten Sleep WY 24 C3
Tequesta FL 141 F4
Terra Alta WV 102 B2
Terra Bella CA 45 D4
Terrace Hts. WA 13 D4
Terrace Park OH 204 C2
Terrebonne OR 21 D3
Terrebonne Par. LA 134 A4
Terre Haute IN 99 E2
Terre Hill PA 146 A2
Terrell TX 59 F2
Terrell Co. GA 128 C4
Terrell Co. TX 60 A2
Terrell Hills TX 257 E2
Terry MS 126 B3
Terry MT 17 E4
Terry Co. TX 57 F2
Terrytown LA 134 B3
Terrytown NE 33 F2
Terryville CT 149 D1
Terryville NY 149 D3
Tesuque NM 49 D2
Teton ID 23 F4
Teton Co. ID 23 F4
Teton Co. MT 15 E3
Teton Co. WY 24 A3
Tetonia ID 23 F4
Teutopolis IL 98 C2
Tewksbury MA 95 E1
Texarkana AR 116 C4
Texarkana TX 116 C4

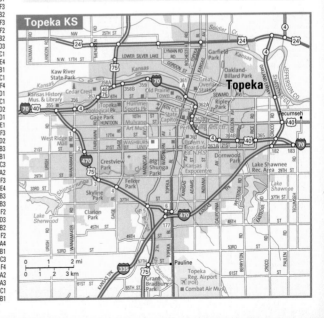

Figures after entries indicate page number and grid reference.

Texas MA	150 B2
Texas City TX	132 B4
Texas Co. MO	107 E1
Texas Co. OK	50 A1
Texhoma OK	50 A1
Texico NM	49 F4
Thatcher AZ	55 E2
Thaxton MS	118 C3
Thayer IL	98 B1
Thayer KS	106 A1
Thayer MO	107 F3
Thayer Co. NE	35 E4
Thayne WY	31 F1
The Colony TX	59 F2
The Dalles OR	21 D2
Thedford NE	34 C2
The Hills TX	61 E1
Theodore AL	135 E2
The Pinery CO	41 E1
The Plains OH	101 E2
Theresa NY	79 E1
Theresa WI	74 C2
Thermal CA	53 E3
Thermalito CA	36 C1
Thermopolis WY	24 C1
The Village OK	51 E3
The Vil. of Indian Hill OH	204 C3
The Woodlands TX	132 A2
Thibodaux LA	134 A3
Thief River Falls MN	19 F2
Thiells NY	148 B2
Thiensville WI	74 C3
Thomas OK	51 D2
Thomas WV	102 B2
Thomasboro IL	88 C4
Thomas Co. GA	137 E1
Thomas Co. KS	42 B2
Thomas Co. NE	34 C2
Thomaston CT	149 D1
Thomaston GA	128 C1
Thomaston ME	82 C3
Thomaston NY	241 G3
Thomasville AL	127 E3
Thomasville GA	137 E1
Thomasville NC	112 B4
Thompson IA	72 C2
Thompson ND	19 E3
Thompson Falls MT	14 C1
Thompson's Sta. TN	109 F4
Thompsontown PA	93 D4
Thompsonville CT	150 A2
Thompsonville IL	98 C4
Thompsonville MI	69 F4
Thomson GA	121 E4
Thomson IL	88 A1
Thonotosassa FL	140 C2
Thoreau NM	48 B3
Thorndale PA	146 B3
Thorndale TX	61 E1
Thorne Bay AK	155 E4
Thornton AR	117 E4
Thornton CA	36 C3
Thornton CO	41 E1
Thornton TX	59 F4
Thorntown IN	89 E4
Thornville OH	101 D1
Thornwood NY	148 B2
Thorofare NJ	146 C3
Thorp WI	67 F4
Thorsby AL	127 F1
Thousand Oaks CA	52 B2
Thousand Palms CA	53 E3
Thrall TX	61 E1
Three Bridges NJ	147 D1
Three Forks MT	23 F1
Three Oaks MI	89 E1
Three Pts. AZ	55 D3
Three Rivers CA	45 E3
Three Rivers MA	150 A2
Three Rivers MI	89 F1
Three Rivers TX	61 D4
Three Way TN	108 C4
Throckmorton TX	59 D2
Throckmorton Co. TX	59 D2
Throop PA	261 E2
Thurmont MD	144 A1
Thurston OH	101 D1
Thurston Co. NE	35 F2
Thurston Co. WA	12 C4
Tiana NY	149 E3
Tiburon CA	259 B2
Tice FL	142 C1
Tickfaw LA	134 B2
Ticonderoga NY	81 D3
Tidioute PA	92 B2
Tierra Amarilla NM	48 C1
Tierra Verde FL	266 A3
Tieton WA	13 D4
Tiffin IA	87 E1
Tiffin OH	90 C1
Tift Co. GA	129 E4
Tifton GA	129 E4
Tigard OR	20 C2
Tigerton WI	68 B4
Tignall GA	121 E4
Tijeras NM	48 C3
Tiki Island TX	132 B4
Tilden IL	98 B4
Tilden NE	35 E2
Tilden TX	61 D4
Tilghman MD	145 D4
Tillamook OR	20 B2
Tillamook Co. OR	20 B1

Tillman Co. OK	51 D4
Tillmans Corner AL	135 E2
Tillson NY	94 B3
Tilton IL	89 D4
Tilton NH	81 F4
Tiltonsville OH	91 F4
Timber Lake SD	26 C2
Timberlake VA	112 C1
Timberon NM	57 D2
Timberville VA	102 C3
Timmonsville SC	122 C3
Timpson TX	124 C3
Tinley Park IL	89 D2
Tinton Falls NJ	147 E2
Tioga LA	125 E4
Tioga ND	18 A2
Tioga PA	93 D1
Tioga TX	59 F1
Tioga Co. NY	93 E1
Tioga Co. PA	93 D1
Tionesta PA	92 A2
Tippah Co. MS	118 C2
Tipp City OH	100 B1
Tippecanoe Co. IN	89 E4
Tipton CA	45 D3
Tipton IN	89 E4
Tipton IA	87 F1
Tipton MO	97 D3
Tipton OK	51 D4
Tipton PA	92 C3
Tipton Co. IN	89 E4
Tipton Co. TN	118 B1
Tiptonville TN	108 B2
Tishomingo OK	51 F4
Tishomingo Co. MS	119 D2
Tiskilwa IL	88 B2
Titonka IA	72 C3
Titusville FL	141 E1
Titusville NJ	147 D2
Titusville PA	92 A2
Titus Co. TX	124 B1
Tiverton RI	151 D4
Tivoli NY	94 B2
Toano VA	113 F1
Toast NC	112 A3
Tobaccoville NC	112 A3
Toccoa GA	121 D2
Todd Co. KY	109 E2
Todd Co. MN	66 B1
Todd Co. SD	34 C1
Togiak AK	154 B3
Tohatchi NM	48 A2
Tok AK	155 D2
Toksook Bay AK	154 B3
Toledo IL	99 D2
Toledo IA	87 D1
Toledo OH	90 C2
Toledo OR	20 B3
Toledo WA	12 C4
Tolland CT	150 B1
Tolland Co. CT	149 E1
Tolles CT	149 D1
Tolleson AZ	249 A2
Tolono IL	99 D1
Toluca IL	88 B3
Tomah WI	74 A1
Tomahawk WI	68 B3
Tomball TX	132 A2
Tom Bean TX	59 F1
Tombstone AZ	55 E4
Tome NM	48 C4
Tom Green Co. TX	58 C4
Tomkins Cove NY	148 B2
Tompkins Co. NY	79 D4
Tompkinsville KY	110 A3
Toms River NJ	147 E3
Tonalea AZ	47 E2
Transylvania Co. NC	121 E1
Tonasket WA	13 E1
Tonawanda NY	78 A3
Tonganoxie KS	96 B2
Tonica IL	88 B2
Tonkawa OK	51 E1
Tontitown AR	106 C4
Tonopah NV	37 F3
Tool TX	59 F3
Toole Co. MT	15 F1
Tooele Co. UT	31 D4
Tooele UT	31 E4
Toombs Co. GA**	129 F3
Toomsboro GA	129 D2
Topeka IN	89 F2
Topeka KS	96 A2
Toppenish WA	13 D4
Topsfield MA	151 F1
Topsham ME	82 B3
Topton PA	146 B1
Toquerville UT	39 D4
Tornillo TX	56 C4
Toronto OH	91 F4
Toronto SD	27 F3
Torrance CA	52 C3
Torrance Co. NM	49 D4
Torreon NM	48 B2
Torreon NM	48 C4
Torrington CT	94 C3
Torrington WY	33 F2
Totowa NJ	240 A1
Toughkenamon PA	146 B3
Toulon IL	88 B3
Towaco NJ	148 A3
Towanda KS	43 F4
Towanda PA	93 E1
Towaoc CO	40 B4
Tower MN	64 C3
Tower City ND	19 E4

Tower City PA	93 E4
Tower Hill IL	98 C2
Tower Lakes IL	203 B1
Town and Country MO	256 A2
Town Creek AL	119 E2
Towner ND	18 C2
Towner Co. ND	19 D1
Town Line NY	78 B3
Town 'n Country FL	266 B2
Town of Pines IN	89 E2
Towns Co. GA	121 D2
Townsend DE	145 E1
Townsend MA	95 D1
Townsend MT	15 F4
Towson MD	144 C3
Tracy CA	36 C4
Tracy MN	72 A1
Tracy City TN	120 A1
Tracyton WA	262 A3
Trafalgar IN	99 F2
Trafford AL	119 F3
Trafford PA	250 D3
Trail Creek IN	89 E2
Traill Co. ND	19 E3
Trainer PA	146 C3
Tramway NC	122 C1
Tranquillity CA	44 C3
Trappe MD	145 D4
Trappe PA	146 C2
Trapper Creek AK	154 C3
Traskwood AR	117 E3
Travelers Rest SC	121 E2
Traver CA	45 D3
Traverse Co. MN	27 F1
Traverse City MI	69 F4
Travis Co. TX	61 E1
Treasure Co. MT	17 D4
Treasure Island FL	140 B3
Trego Co. KS	42 C2
Tremont IL	88 B4
Tremont PA	146 A1
Tremonton UT	31 E3
Trempealeau WI	73 F1
Trempealeau Co. WI	67 F4
Trent SD	27 F4
Trenton FL	138 C3
Trenton GA	120 B2
Trenton IL	98 B3
Trenton KY	109 E3
Trenton MI	90 C1
Trenton MO	86 C4
Trenton NE	42 A1
Trenton NJ	147 D2
Trenton NC	115 D3
Trenton OH	100 B2
Trenton TN	108 C4
Trenton TX	59 F1
Trenton UT	31 E2
Trent Woods NC	115 D3
Treutlen Co. GA**	129 F2
Trevorton PA	93 E3
Trevose PA	146 C2
Trexlertown PA	146 B1
Treynor IA	86 A2
Trezevant TN	108 C4

Triadelphia WV	91 F4
Triana AL	119 F2
Triangle VA	144 A4
Tribes Hill NY	94 A1
Tribune KS	42 B3
Tri-City OR	28 B1
Trigg Co. KY	109 D3
Tri-Lakes IN	90 A2
Trilby FL	140 C1
Trimble CO	40 B4
Trimble Co. KY	100 A3
Trimont MN	72 B2
Trinidad CO	41 E4
Trinidad TX	59 F3
Trinity AL	119 F2
Trinity NC	112 B4
Trinity TX	132 A1
Trinity Co. CA	28 B3
Trinity Co. TX	132 B1
Trion GA	120 B2
Tripoli IA	73 E4
Tripp SD	35 E1
Tripp Co. SD	26 C4
Triumph LA	134 C4
Trona CA	45 E4
Trooper PA	146 C2
Trophy Club TX	207 B1
Tropic UT	39 E4
Trotwood OH	100 B1
Troup TX	124 B3
Troup Co. GA	128 C1
Trousdale Co. TN**	109 F3
Trout Creek MT	14 C3
Troutdale OR	20 C2
Troutdale VA	111 F3
Trout Lake WA	21 D1
Troutman NC	112 A4
Trout Valley IL	203 A1
Troutville VA	112 B1
Trowbridge Park MI	69 D1
Troy AL	128 A3
Troy ID	14 B4
Troy IL	98 B3
Troy KS	96 B1
Troy MI	76 C4
Troy MO	97 F2
Troy MT	14 C2
Troy NH	95 D1
Troy NY	94 B1
Troy NC	122 C1
Troy OH	100 B1
Troy PA	93 D1
Troy TN	108 C3
Troy TX	59 E4
Troy VT	81 E1
Truckee CA	37 D2
Truman MN	72 B2
Trumann AR	108 A4
Trumansburg NY	79 D4
Trumbauersville PA	146 C1
Trumbull CT	149 D2
Trumbull Co. OH	91 F2
Trussville AL	119 F4
Truth or Consequences NM	56 B2
Tryon NE	34 B3
Tryon NC	121 D1

Bakersville	B1
Ewing	A1
Ewingville	A1
Fallsington	A2
Lawrenceville	B1
Lewisville	B1
Mercerville	B1
Morrisville	A2
Slackwood	B1
Trenton	B2
W. Trenton	A1
White Horse	B2

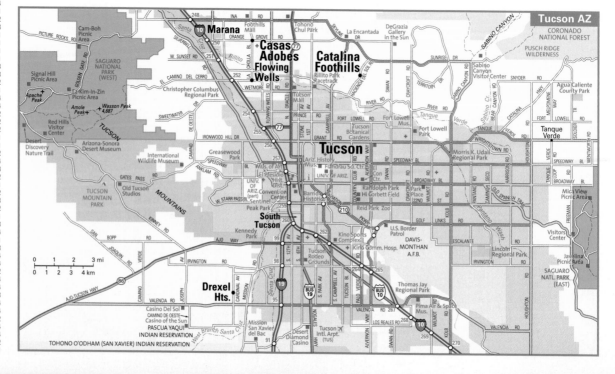

Entries in **bold black** indicate counties or parishes.
Entries in **bold color** indicate cities with detailed inset maps.

Tryon OK 51 F2
Tsaile AZ 48 A2
Tualatin OR 20 C2
Tubac AZ 55 D4
Tuba City AZ 47 E2
Tuckahoe NY 149 E3
Tucker MS 126 C2
Tucker Co. WV 102 B2
Tuckerman AR 107 F4
Tuckerton NJ 147 E4
Tucson AZ 55 D3
Tucumcari NM 49 F3
Tukwila WA 262 B4
Tulalip WA 262 B1
Tulare CA 45 D3
Tulare SD 27 E3
Tulare Co. CA 45 D3
Tularosa NM 56 C2
Tulelake CA 29 D2
Tulia TX 50 A4
Tullahoma TN 120 A1
Tullos LA 125 E3
Tully NY 79 E4
Tullytown PA 147 D2
Tulsa OK 51 F2
Tuscarora PA 93 E3
Tuscola IL 99 D1
Tuscola TX 58 C3
Tuscola Co. MI 76 C2
Tusculum TN 111 E4
Tuscumbia AL 119 E2
Tuscumbia MO 97 E4
Tuskegee AL 128 B2
Tustin CA 229 F5
Tuttle OK 51 E3
Tutwiler MS 118 A3
Tuxedo Park NY 148 B2
Twain Harte CA 37 D3
Twentynine Palms CA 46 A4
Twiggs Co. GA 129 E2
Twin Bridges MT 23 E2
Twin City GA 129 F2
Twin Falls ID 30 C1
Twin Falls Co. ID 30 C2
Twin Lake MI 75 E2
Twin Lakes CA 236 D1
Twin Lakes GA 137 F1
Twin Lakes NM 48 A2
Twin Lakes WI 74 C4
Twin Rivers NJ 147 E2
Uledi PA 102 B1
Ulen MN 19 F3
Ullin IL 108 C2
Ulm MT 15 F3
Ulster Co. NY 148 A1
Ulysses KS 42 B4
Ulysses PA 92 C1
Umatilla FL 141 D1
Umatilla OR 21 E1
Umatilla Co. OR 21 E2
Unadilla GA 129 D3
Unadilla NY 79 E4
Unalakleet AK 154 B2
Unalaska AK 154 A4
Uncasville CT 149 F1
Underhill VT 81 D2
Underwood IA 86 A2
Underwood ND 18 B3
Unicoi TN 111 E4
Unicoi Co. TN 111 E4
Union IL 88 C1
Union KY 100 B3
Union ME 82 C2
Union MS 126 C2
Union MO 97 F3
Union Co. TN 110 C3
Union Gap WA 13 D4
Union Grove WI 74 C4
Union Hall VA 112 B2
Union Lake MI 210 A1
Union Par. LA 125 E1
Union Park FL 246 D2
Union Pt. GA 121 E4
Union Sprs. AL 128 B3
Union Sprs. NY 79 D3
Uniontown AL 127 E2
Uniontown KY 109 D1
Uniontown OH 91 E3
Uniontown PA 102 B1
Unionville CT 94 C3
Unionville GA 129 E4
Unionville MI 76 B2
Unionville MO 87 D4
Unionville NV 29 F4
Unionville NY 148 A2
Unionville NC 122 B1
Unionville PA 146 B3
Unity ME 82 C2
Universal City TX 61 D2
University City MO 256 B2
Utah Co. UT 39 E1
Utica IN 100 A4
Utica MI 210 C1
Utica MS 126 A3
Utica NE 35 E4
Utica NY 79 E3
Utica OH 91 D4
Utica SC 121 E2
Uvalda GA 129 F3
Uvalde TX 60 C3
Uvalde Co. TX 60 C3
Uxbridge MA 150 C2

V

Vacaville CA 36 B3
Vader WA 12 B4
Vadito NM 49 D2
Vadnais Hts. MN 235 D1
Vado NM 56 C3
Vaiden MS 126 C1
Vail AZ 55 D3
Vail CO 41 D1
Vails Gate NY 148 B1
Valatie NY 94 B2
Valders WI 74 C1
Valdese NC 111 F4
Valdez AK 154 C3
Valdosta GA 137 F1
Vale OR 22 A4
Valencia NM 48 C4
Valencia Co. NM 48 C4
Valentine NE 34 C1
Valhalla NY 148 B3
Valier IL 98 C4
Valier MT 15 E2
Valinda CA 228 E2
Vallejo CA 36 B3
Vallersville MA 151 E3
Valley AL 128 B2
Valley NE 35 F3
Valley Brook OK 244 E3
Valley Ctr. CA 53 D3
Valley Ctr. KS 43 E4
Valley City ND 19 E4
Valley Cottage NY 148 B2
Valley Co. ID 22 C2
Valley Co. MT 17 D2
Valley Co. NE 35 D3
Valley Falls KS 96 A2
Valley Falls RI 150 C3
Valley Farms AZ 54 C2
Valley Forge PA 146 B2
Valley Grove WV 91 F4
Valley Head AL 120 A2
Valley Mills TX 59 E4
Valley Park MO 256 A3
Valley Sprs. CA 36 C3
Valley Sprs. SD 27 F4
Valley Stream NY 148 C4
Valley View OH 204 F3
Valleyview OH 206 A2
Valley View PA 93 E3
Valley View TX 59 E1
Valliant OK 116 B3
Valmeyer IL 98 A4
Valparaiso FL 136 B2
Valparaiso IN 89 E2
Valparaiso NE 35 F3
Valrico FL 266 D2
Val Verde CA 52 C2
Val Verde Co. TX 60 B2
Vamo FL 140 B4
Van TX 124 A2
Van Alstyne TX 59 F1
Van Buren AR 116 C1
Van Buren IN 89 F3
Van Buren ME 85 E1
Van Buren MO 107 F2
Van Buren Co. AR 117 E1
Van Buren Co. IA 87 E3
Van Buren Co. MI 75 F4
Van Buren Co. TN 110 A4
Vance AL 127 F1
Vanceboro NC 115 D3
Vanceburg KY 100 C3
Vance Co. NC 113 D3
Vancleave MS 135 D2
Vancouver WA 20 C1
Vandalia IL 98 C3
Vandalia MO 97 F2
Vandalia OH 100 B1
Vandenberg Vil. CA 52 A1
Vander NC 123 D2
Vanderbilt MI 70 C3
Vanderburgh Co. IN 99 D4
Vandercook Lake MI 90 B1
Vandergrift PA 92 A4
Vandling PA 93 F2
Van Etten NY 93 E1
Vanhiseville NJ 147 E2
Van Horn TX 57 D4
Van Horne IA 87 E1
Van Lear KY 111 E1
Vanlue OH 90 C3
Van Meter IA 86 C2
Vansant VA 111 E2
Van Vleck TX 132 A4
Van Wert OH 90 B3
Van Wert Co. OH 90 B3
Van Zandt Co. TX 124 A2
Vardaman MS 118 C4
Varnamtown NC 123 E4
Varnell GA 120 B2
Varnville SC 130 B2
Vashon WA 262 A4
Vashon Hts. WA 262 A3
Vass NC 122 C1
Vassalboro ME 82 C2
Vassar MI 76 B3
Vaughn MT 15 F3
Vaughn NM 49 D4
Veazie ME 83 D1
Veblen SD 27 E1
Veedersburg IN 89 D4
Vega TX 50 A3
Velma OK 51 E4
Velva ND 18 B2
Venango Co. PA 92 A2
Veneta OR 20 B3
Venice FL 140 B4
Venice IL 256 C2
Venice LA 134 C4
Venice Gardens FL 140 C4
Ventnor City NJ 147 F4
Ventura CA 52 B2
Ventura IA 72 C3
Ventura Co. CA 52 B2
Venus TX 59 E3
Verden OK 51 E3
Verdi NV 37 D1
Verdigre NE 35 E1
Vergennes VT 81 D2
Vermilion OH 91 D2
Vermilion Co. IL 89 D4
Vermilion Par. LA 133 E3
Vermillion SD 35 F1
Vermillion Co. IN 99 E1
Vermont IL 88 A4
Vermontville MI 76 A4
Vernal UT 32 A4
Verndale MN 64 A4
Vernon AL 119 D4
Vernon CT 150 A3
Vernon FL 136 C2
Vernon IN 100 A2
Vernon MI 76 B3
Vernon NY 79 E3
Vernon TX 51 D4
Vernon VT 94 C1
Vernon Co. MO 96 C4
Vernon Co. WI 73 F2
Vernon Hills IL 203 C1
Vernonia OR 20 B1
Vernon Par. LA 125 D4
Vernon Valley NJ 148 A2
Vero Beach FL 141 E3
Verona MS 119 D3
Verona MO 106 C2
Verona NJ 148 A3
Verona NC 115 D4

Tulsa OK

Bixby C3 | Broken Arrow C3 | Jenks B3 | Sand Sprs. A2 | Tiger C1
Bowden A3 | Catoosa C1 | Oakhurst A3 | Sapulpa A3 | Tulsa B2

Vicksburg MS

Waco TX

Tulsa Co. OK 106 A4
Tuluksak AK 154 B3
Tumacacori AZ 55 D4
Tunica MS 118 B2
Tunica Co. MS 118 B2
Tunkhannock PA 93 E2
Tunnel Hill GA 120 B2
Tuolumne CA 37 D3
Tuolumne Co. CA 37 D3
Tupelo MS 119 D3
Tupper Lake NY 79 F1
Turbeville SC 122 B4
Turbotville PA 93 D3
Turley NM 48 B1
Turley OK 51 F2
Turlock CA 36 C4
Turner ME 82 B2
Turner OR 20 B2
Turner Co. GA 129 D4
Turner Co. SD 27 F4
Turners Falls MA 94 C1
Turnersville NJ 146 C4
Turon KS 43 D4
Turpin Hills OH 204 C3
Turrell AR 118 B1
Turtle Creek PA 250 D2
Turtle Lake ND 18 C3
Turtle Lake WI 67 E3
Tusayan AZ 47 D2
Tuscaloosa AL 127 E1
Tuscaloosa Co. AL 119 E4
Tuscarawas OH 91 E4
Tuscarawas Co. OH 91 E4
Twinsburg OH 91 E2
Twin Valley MN 19 F3
Twisp WA 13 E2
Two Harbors MN 64 C4
Two Rivers WI 75 D1
Tybee Island GA 130 C3
Tye TX 58 C3
Tyler MN 27 F3
Tyler TX 124 A2
Tyler Co. TX 132 C1
Tyler Co. WV 101 F2
Tylersport PA 146 C2
Tylertown MS 134 B1
Tyndall SD 35 E1
Tyrone GA 120 C4
Tyrone NM 55 F2
Tyrone OK 50 B1
Tyrone PA 92 C3
Tyronza AR 118 B1
Tyrrell Co. NC 113 F4
Tysons VA 270 A3
Ty Ty GA 129 D4

U

Ubly MI 76 C2
Ucon ID 23 E4
Udall KS 43 F4
Uhrichsville OH 91 E4
Uinta Co. WY 31 F3
Uintah UT 244 B2
Uintah Co. UT 32 A4
Ukiah CA 36 A2
Ulah NC 122 C1
Union NH 81 F4
Union NJ 148 A4
Union OH 100 B1
Union OR 21 F2
Union SC 121 F2
Union WV 112 A1
Union Beach NJ 147 E1
Union Bridge MD 144 B1
Union City CA 259 D4
Union City GA 120 C4
Union City IN 90 A4
Union City MI 90 A1
Union City NJ 148 B4
Union City OH 90 A4
Union City OK 51 E3
Union City PA 92 A1
Union City TN 108 C3
Union Co. AR 125 E1
Union Co. FL 138 C3
Union Co. GA 120 C2
Union Co. IL 108 C1
Union Co. IN 100 B1
Union Co. IA 86 B3
Union Co. KY 109 D1
Union Co. MS 118 C3
Union Co. NJ 147 E1
Union Co. NM 49 F1
Union Co. NC 122 B2
Union Co. OH 90 C4
Union Co. OR 21 F2
Union Co. PA 93 D3
Union Co. SC 121 F2
Union Co. SD 35 F1
University Gardens NY 241 G3
University Hts. OH 204 G2
University Park IA 87 D2
University Park MD 270 E2
University Park NM 56 C3
University Park TX 207 D2
University Place WA 12 C3
Upland CA 229 G2
Upland IN 89 F4
Upland PA 248 A4
Upper Arlington OH 101 D1
Upper Darby PA 248 B3
Upper Lake CA 36 A2
Upper Marlboro MD 144 C3
Upper Saddle River NJ 148 B3
Upper Sandusky OH 90 C3
Upshur Co. TX 124 B2
Upshur Co. WV 102 A3
Upson Co. GA 129 D2
Upton KY 110 A1
Upton MA 150 C2
Upton WY 25 F3
Upton Co. TX 58 A4
Urania LA 125 E3
Urbana IL 88 C4
Urbana IA 87 E1
Urbana OH 90 B4
Urbancrest OH 206 A3
Urbandale IA 86 C2
Urbanna VA 113 F1
Urich MO 96 C3
Ursa IL 87 F4
Usquepaug RI 150 C4

Figures after entries indicate page number and grid reference.

Adelphi E1	Broyhill Park B4	Coral Hills E4	Garrett Park C1	Kings Park A5	McLean B2	Ravensworth A5	Spring Hill A2
Alexandria C5	Cabin John B2	Cottage City E3	Glassmanor D5	Knollwood E1	Merrifield A3	Ritchie F4	Suitland E4
Annandale B4	Calverton E1	Crystal City C4	Glenarden F3	Lake Barcroft B4	Morningside F4	Riverdale Hts. E2	Takoma Park D2
Arlington C3	Camp Sprs. E5	District Hts. F4	Glendale A2	Landover E3	Mt. Rainier E2	Riverdale Park E2	Temple Hills E5
Bailey's Crossroads .B4	Canterbury Woods .A4	Dodge Park F3	Glen Echo B2	Landover Hills F2	New Carrollton F2	Rosedale Estates .E5	Tysons A3
Ballston C3	Capitol Hts. E3	Dunn Loring A3	Glen Echo Hts. ...C2	Langley B2	N. Brentwood E2	Rose Hill C5	University Park E2
Barcroft C4	Cherrydale C3	E. Falls Church ...B3	Greenbelt F1	Langley Park E2	N. Chevy Chase ..C1	Rosslyn C3	Vienna A3
Belle Haven C5	Chesterbrook B3	Edmonston E2	Groveton C5	Lanham F2	N. Springfield A5	Seabrook F2	Virginia Hills C5
Belle View C5	Cheverly E3	Fairfax A4	Hillandale E1	Largo A5	Oaklawn E5	Seat Pleasant F3	Walker Mill F4
Beltsville E1	Chevy Chase C2	Fairmount Hts. E3	Hillcrest Hts. E5	Lewisdale E2	Oakview E1	Seven Corners ...B4	Washington D3
Berwyn Hts. E2	Chevy Chase View .C1	Falls Church B3	Huntington C5	Lincolnia B4	Oxon Hill D5	Shirlington C4	Westover B3
Bethesda C2	Chillum D2	Forest Hts. D5	Hyattsville E2	Luxmanor C1	Palmer Park F3	Silver Hill E4	W. Springfield A5
Bladensburg E3	Clarendon C3	Forestville F4	Idylwood B3	Mantua A4	Pimmit Hills B3	Silver Spr. D2	Wheaton D1
Bren Mar Park B5	College Park E1	Ft. Foote Vil. D5	Kensington C1	Marlow Hts. E4	Potomac A1	Somerset C2	White Oak D1
Brentwood E2	Colmar Manor E3	Franconia B5	Kentland F3	Martins Additions ..C2	Randolph Hills C1	Springfield B5	Woodyard F5

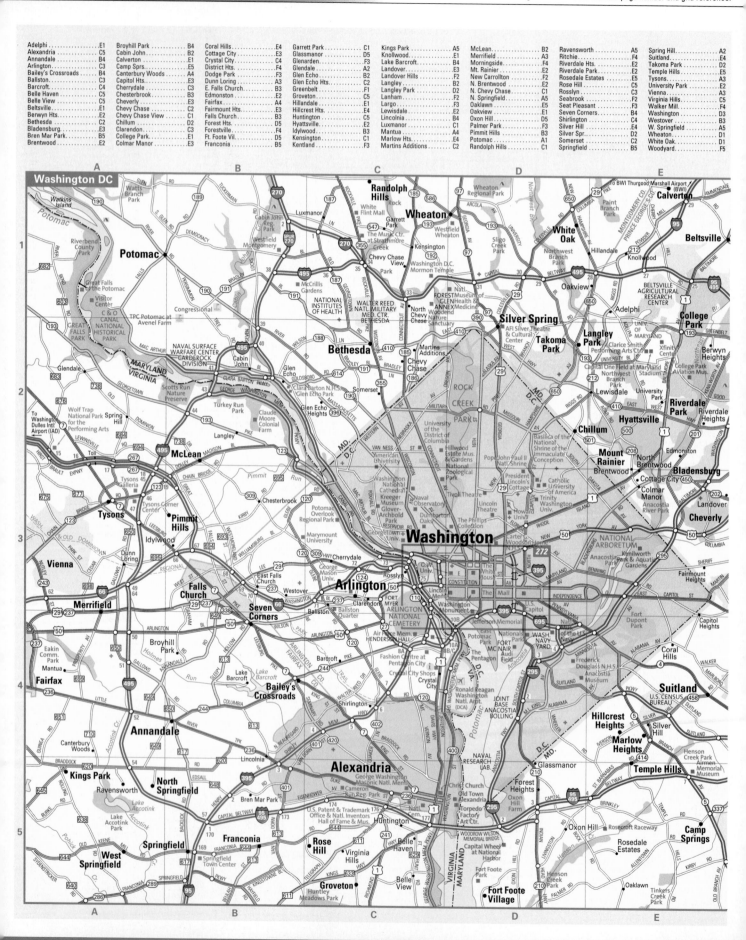

Washington DC

Entries in **bold black** indicate counties or parishes.
Entries in **bold color** indicate cities with detailed inset maps.

Verona PA 250 D1
Verona VA 102 C4
Verona WI 74 B3
Verplanck NY 148 B2
Versailles CT 149 F1
Versailles IN 100 A2
Versailles KY 100 B4
Versailles MO 97 D3
Versailles OH 90 B4
Vesper WI 68 A4
Vestal NY 93 E1
Vestal Ctr. NY 93 E1
Vestavia Hills AL 119 F4
Vevay IN 100 A3
Vian OK 116 B1
Viborg SD 35 F1
Viburnum MO 107 F1
Vici OK 51 D2
Vicksburg MI 89 F1
Vicksburg MS 126 A2
Victor CO 41 E2
Victor ID 23 F4
Victor IA 87 E1
Victor MT 15 D4
Victor NY 78 C3
Victoria KS 43 D2
Victoria MN 66 C4
Victoria TX 61 F3
Victoria VA 113 D2
Victoria Co. TX 61 F3

Victorville CA 53 D2
Victory Gardens NJ 148 A3
Vidalia GA 129 F3
Vidalia LA 125 F4
Vidor TX 132 C2
Vienna GA 129 D3
Vienna IL 108 C1
Vienna LA 125 E2
Vienna MO 97 E4
Vienna VA 144 B3
Vienna WV 101 E2
View Park CA 228 C3
Vigo Co. IN 99 E2
Vilano Beach FL 139 E3
Vilas Co. WI 68 B2
Village Green NY 79 D3
Village Green PA 248 A4
Villages of Oriole FL 143 F1
Villa Grove IL 99 D1
Villa Hills KY 204 A3
Villa Park CA 229 F4
Villa Park IL 203 C4
Villa Rica GA 120 B4
Villa Ridge MO 98 A3
Villas NJ 104 C4
Ville Platte LA 133 E1
Villisca IA 86 B3
Vilonia AR 117 E1
Vimy Ridge AR 117 E2
Vinalhaven ME 83 D3
Vincennes IN 99 D3
Vincent AL 128 A1
Vincent CA 52 C2
Vincentown NJ 147 D3
Vinco PA 92 B4
Vine Grove KY 110 A1
Vine Hill CA 259 D1
Vineland MN 66 C1
Vineland NJ 145 F1
Vinemont AL 119 F3
Vineyard Haven MA 151 E4
Vinings GA 190 C2
Vinita OK 106 B3
Vinita Park MO 256 B2
Vinton CA 37 D1
Vinton IA 87 E1
Vinton LA 133 D2
Vinton TX 56 C3
Vinton VA 112 B2
Vinton Co. OH 101 E2
Viola DE 145 E3
Viola IL 88 A2
Viola WI 73 F2
Violet LA 134 C3
Virden IL 98 B2
Virgin UT 39 D4
Virginia IL 98 A1
Virginia MN 64 C3
Virginia Beach VA 114 B4
Virginia City MT 23 E2
Virginia City NV 37 D2
Virginia Gardens FL 233 A4
Viroqua WI 73 F2
Visalia CA 45 D3
Vista CA 53 D3
Vivian LA 124 C1
Volcano HI 153 F4
Volga SD 27 F3
Volin SD 35 E1
Voluntown CT 149 F1
Volusia Co. FL 139 E4
Vonore TN 120 C1
Voorheesville NY 94 B1

W

Wabash IN 89 F3
Wabasha MN 73 E1
Wabasha Co. MN 73 E1
Wabash Co. IL 99 D3
Wabash Co. IN 89 F3
Wabasso FL 141 E3
Wabasso MN 72 A1
Wabaunsee Co. KS 43 F2
Waco TX 59 E4
Waconia MN 66 C4
Waddington NY 80 B1
Wade MS 135 D2
Wade NC 123 D1
Wadena MN 64 A4
Wadena Co. MN 64 A4
Wadesboro NC 122 B2
Wading River NY 149 D3
Wadley AL 128 B1
Wadley GA 129 F1
Wadsworth NV 37 D1
Wadsworth OH 91 E3
Waelder TX 61 E2
Wagener SC 122 A4
Waggaman LA 239 B2
Wagner SD 35 E1
Wagoner OK 106 A4
Wagoner Co. OK 106 A4
Wagon Mound NM 49 E2
Wagontown PA 146 B3
Wagram NC 122 C2
Wahiawa HI 152 A2
Wahkiakum Co. WA 12 B4
Wahoo NE 35 F3
Wahpeton ND 27 F1
Waialua HI 152 A2
Waianae HI 152 A3
Waiehu HI 153 D1
Waihee HI 153 D1
Waikane HI 152 A2
Waikapu HI 153 D1
Waikoloa Vil. HI 153 E3
Wailua HI 152 B1
Wailuku HI 153 D1
Waimalu HI 152 A3
Waimanalo HI 152 B3
Waimanalo Beach HI 152 B3
Waimea HI 152 B1
Waimea (Kamuela) HI 153 E2
Wainscott NY 149 F3
Wainwright AK 154 C1
Waipahu HI 152 A3
Waipio Acres HI 152 A3
Waite Park MN 66 C3
Waitsburg WA 13 F4
Waitsfield VT 81 D2
Wakarusa IN 89 F2
Wakeby MA 151 E3
Wake Co. NC 113 D4
WaKeeney KS 42 C2
Wakefield KS 43 F2
Wakefield MA 151 D1
Wakefield MI 65 E4
Wakefield NE 35 F2
Wakefield RI 150 C4
Wakefield VA 113 F2
Wake Forest NC 113 D4
Wakeman OH 91 D2
Wake Vil. TX 124 C1
Wakonda SD 35 F1
Wakulla Co. FL 137 E2
Walbridge OH 267 B2
Walcott IA 87 F2
Walden CO 33 D4
Walden NY 148 B1
Walden TN 120 B1
Waldo AR 125 D1
Waldo FL 138 C3
Waldoboro ME 82 C2
Waldo Co. ME 82 C2
Waldorf MD 144 B4
Waldport OR 20 B3
Waldron AR 116 C2
Waldron IN 100 A2
Waldron MI 90 B1
Wales MA 150 B2
Wales WI 74 C3
Waleska GA 120 C3
Walford IA 87 E1
Walhalla ND 19 E1
Walhalla SC 121 E2
Walker IA 73 E4
Walker LA 134 A2
Walker MI 75 F3
Walker MN 64 A3
Walker Co. AL 119 E4
Walker Co. GA 120 B2
Walker Co. TX 132 A1
Walker Mill MD 271 F4
Walkersville MD 144 A1
Walkerton IN 89 E2
Walkertown NC 112 B4
Walker Valley NY 148 A1
Walkerville MT 23 E1
Wall PA 250 D3
Wall SD 26 B3
Wallace ID 14 B3
Wallace NC 123 E2
Wallace VA 111 E3
Wallace Co. KS 42 B2
Walla Walla WA 21 F1
Walla Walla Co. WA 21 F1
Wallburg MI 112 B4
Walled Lake MI 210 A2
Waller TX 61 F2
Waller Co. TX 132 A3
Wallingford CT 149 D1
Wallingford VT 81 D4
Wallington NJ 148 B3
Wallis TX 61 F2
Wallkill NY 148 B1
Wall Lake IA 72 B4
Wallowa OR 22 A1
Wallowa Co. OR 22 A1
Walnut CA 229 F3
Walnut IL 88 B2
Walnut IA 86 A2
Walnut MS 118 C2
Walnut Cove NC 112 B3
Walnut Creek CA 36 B4
Walnut Creek NC 123 E1
Walnut Grove AL 120 A3
Walnut Grove CA 36 C3
Walnut Grove GA 121 D4
Walnut Grove MN 72 A1
Walnut Grove MS 126 C2
Walnut Grove MO 106 C1
Walnut Grove TN 109 F3
Walnut Hill TN 111 E3
Walnut Park CA 228 D3
Walnutport PA 93 F3
Walnut Ridge AR 108 A4
Walnut Sprs. TX 59 E3
Walpole MA 151 D2
Walpole NH 81 E4
Walsenburg CO 41 E4
Walsh CO 42 A4
Walsh Co. ND 19 E2
Walterboro SC 130 C1
Walterhill TN 109 F4
Walters OK 51 D4
Walthall MS 118 C4
Walthall Co. MS 134 B1
Waltham MA 151 D1
Walthill NE 35 F2
Walthourville GA 130 B3
Walton IN 89 F3
Walton KY 100 B3
Walton NY 93 F1
Walton Co. FL 136 B2
Walton Co. GA 121 D4
Walton Hills OH 204 G3
Walworth WI 74 C4
Walworth Co. SD 26 C2
Walworth Co. WI 74 C4
Wamac IL 98 C3
Wamego KS 43 F2
Wampsville NY 79 E3
Wamsutter WY 32 C3
Wanakah NY 78 A4
Wanamassa NJ 147 E2
Wanamingo MN 73 D1
Wanaque NJ 148 A3
Wanatah IN 89 E2
Wanblee SD 26 B4
Wanchese NC 115 F2
Wapakoneta OH 90 B4
Wapanucka OK 51 F4
Wapato WA 13 D4
Wapella IL 88 C4
Wapello IA 87 F2
Wapello Co. IA 87 D3
Waples TX 59 E3
Wappingers Falls NY 148 B1
War WV 111 F1
Ward AR 117 F2
Ward Co. ND 18 B2
Ward Co. TX 57 F4
Warden WA 13 E4
Wardner ID 14 B3
Wardsville MO 97 E3
Ware MA 150 B1
Ware Co. GA 129 F4
Wareham MA 151 E3
Ware Shoals SC 121 F3
Waretown NJ 147 E3
Warm Beach WA 12 C2
Warm Sprs. GA 128 C1
Warm Sprs. OR 21 D3
Warm Sprs. VA 102 B4
Warner NH 81 F4
Warner OK 116 A1
Warner SD 27 D2
Warner Robins GA 129 D2
Warr Acres OK 244 D2
Warren AR 117 E4
Warren IL 74 A4
Warren IN 90 A3
Warren ME 82 C2
Warren MA 150 B2
Warren MI 76 C4
Warren MN 19 F2
Warren OH 91 F2
Warren PA 92 B1
Warren RI 151 D3
Warren Co. GA 129 F1
Warren Co. IL 88 A3
Warren Co. IN 89 D4
Warren Co. IA 86 C2
Warren Co. KY 109 F2
Warren Co. MS 126 A2
Warren Co. MO 97 F3
Warren Co. NJ 93 F3
Warren Co. NY 80 C3
Warren Co. NC 113 D3
Warren Co. OH 100 C2
Warren Co. PA 92 B1
Warren Co. TN 110 A4
Warren Co. VA 103 D2
Warren Glen NJ 146 C1
Warren Park IN 99 F1
Warrensburg IL 98 C1
Warrensburg MO 96 C3
Warrensburg NY 80 C4
Warrensville PA 93 D2
Warrensville Hts. OH 204 G2
Warrenton GA 129 F1
Warrenton MO 97 F3
Warrenton NC 113 D3
Warrenton OR 20 B1
Warrenton VA 103 D3
Warrenville IL 203 A4
Warrick Co. IN 99 E4
Warrington FL 135 F2
Warrington PA 146 C2
Warrior AL 119 F4
Warrior Run PA 261 A2
Warroad MN 64 A1
Warsaw IL 87 F4
Warsaw IN 89 F2
Warsaw KY 100 B3
Warsaw MN 72 C1
Warsaw MO 97 D4
Warsaw NY 78 B4
Warsaw NC 123 E2
Warsaw OH 91 D4
Warsaw VA 103 E4
Warson Woods MO 256 B2
Wartburg TN 110 B4
Wartrace TN 120 A1
Warwick NY 148 A2
Warwick RI 150 C3
Wasatch Co. UT 31 F4
Wasco CA 45 D4
Wasco OR 21 D1
Wasco Co. OR 21 D2
Waseca MN 72 C1
Waseca Co. MN 72 C1
Washakie Co. WY 24 C4
Washburn IL 88 B3
Washburn IA 73 E4
Washburn ME 85 D2
Washburn ND 18 B3
Washburn WI 65 D4
Washburn Co. WI 67 E2
Washington CT 148 C1
Washington DC 144 B3
Washington GA 121 E4
Washington IL 88 B3
Washington IN 99 E3
Washington IA 87 E2
Washington KS 43 F1
Washington LA 133 F2
Washington MO 97 F3
Washington NJ 93 F3
Washington NC 115 D3
Washington OK 51 E3
Washington PA 91 F4
Washington UT 46 C1
Washington VT 81 E2
Washington VA 103 D3
Washington WV 101 E2
Washington Co. AL 127 E4
Washington Co. AR 106 B4
Washington Co. CO 34 A4
Washington Co. FL 136 C2
Washington Co. GA 129 E1
Washington Co. ID 22 A3
Washington Co. IL 98 B4
Washington Co. IN 99 F3
Washington Co. IA 87 E2
Washington Co. KS 43 E1
Washington Co. KY 110 B1
Washington Co. ME 83 E1
Washington Co. MD 103 D1
Washington Co. MN 67 D3
Washington Co. MS 126 A1
Washington Co. MO 97 F4
Washington Co. NE 35 F3
Washington Co. NY 81 D4
Washington Co. NC 113 F4
Washington Co. OH 101 E2
Washington Co. OK 106 A2
Washington Co. OR 20 B2
Washington Co. PA 92 A4
Washington Co. RI 150 C4
Washington Co. TN 111 E3
Washington Co. TX 61 F2
Washington Co. UT 38 C4
Washington Co. VT 81 E2
Washington Co. VA 111 F3
Washington Co. WI 74 C2
Washington C.H. OH 100 C1
Washington Crossing NJ 147 D2
Washington Crossing PA 147 D2
Washington Hts. NY 148 A1
Washington Par. LA 134 B1
Washington Park IL 256 D2
Washington Terrace UT 244 A2
Washingtonville NY 148 B1
Washingtonville OH 91 F3
Washita Co. OK 51 D3
Washoe Co. NV 29 E4
Washougal WA 20 C2
Washtenaw Co. MI 90 B1
Wasilla AK 154 C3
Waskom TX 124 C2
Wataga IL 88 A3
Watauga TN 111 E3
Watauga TX 207 B2
Watauga Co. NC 111 F3
Watchung NJ 147 E1
Waterboro ME 82 B3
Waterbury CT 149 D1
Waterbury VT 81 D2
Waterbury Ctr. VT 81 E2
Waterford CA 36 C4
Waterford CT 149 F2
Waterford MI 76 B4
Waterford NY 188 E1
Waterford PA 92 A1
Waterford WI 74 C4
Waterford Works NJ 147 D4
Waterloo IL 98 A4
Waterloo IN 90 A2
Waterloo IA 73 E4
Waterloo MD 144 C2
Waterloo NE 35 F3
Waterloo NY 79 D3
Waterloo WI 74 B3
Waterman IL 88 C1
Water Mill NY 149 E3
Waterproof LA 125 F3
Watertown CT 149 D1
Watertown FL 138 C2
Watertown MA 151 D1
Watertown MN 66 C4
Watertown NY 79 E1
Watertown SD 27 F2
Watertown TN 109 F4
Watertown WI 74 C3
Water Valley MS 118 B3
Waterville KS 43 F1
Waterville ME 82 C2
Waterville MN 72 C1
Waterville NY 79 E3
Waterville OH 90 C2
Waterville WA 13 E3
Watervliet MI 89 F1
Watervliet NY 188 E2
Watford City ND 18 A3
Wathena KS 96 B1
Watkins MN 66 C3
Watkins Glen NY 79 D4
Watkinsville GA 121 D4
Watonga OK 51 D2
Watonwan Co. MN 72 B1
Watseka IL 89 D3
Watson IL 98 C2
Watson LA 134 A2
Watsontown PA 93 D3
Watsonville CA 44 B2
Watterson Park KY 230 E2
Waubay SD 27 E2
Wauchula FL 140 C3
Wauconda IL 203 B1
Waukee IA 86 C2
Waukegan IL 75 D4
Waukesha WI 74 C3
Waukesha Co. WI 74 C3
Waukomis OK 51 E2
Waukon IA 73 E3
Waunakee WI 74 B3
Wauneta NE 34 B4
Waupaca WI 74 B1
Waupaca Co. WI 68 B4
Waupun WI 74 C2
Wauregan CT 150 B3
Waurika OK 51 E4
Wausa NE 35 E1
Wausau WI 68 B4
Wausaukee WI 68 C3
Wauseon OH 90 B2
Waushara Co. WI 74 B1
Wautoma WI 74 B1
Wauwatosa WI 234 C2
Wauzeka WI 73 F3
Waveland MS 134 C2
Waverly FL 141 D2
Waverly IL 98 B1
Waverly IA 73 D4
Waverly KS 96 A3
Waverly MN 66 C3
Waverly MO 96 C2
Waverly NE 35 F4
Waverly NY 93 E1
Waverly OH 101 D2
Waverly TN 109 D4
Waverly VA 113 E2
Waverly Hall GA 128 C2
Waxahachie TX 59 F3
Waxhaw NC 122 B2
Waycross GA 129 F4
Wayland IA 87 E2
Wayland MA 150 C1
Wayland MI 75 F4
Wayland NY 78 C4
Waymart PA 93 F2
Wayne IL 203 A4
Wayne MI 210 A4
Wayne NE 35 F2
Wayne NJ 148 A3
Wayne OH 90 C2
Wayne OK 51 E3
Wayne PA 146 C3
Wayne WV 101 D4
Wayne City IL 98 C4
Wayne Co. GA 130 A4
Wayne Co. IL 98 C3
Wayne Co. IN 100 A1
Wayne Co. IA 87 D3
Wayne Co. KY 110 B3
Wayne Co. MI 76 B4
Wayne Co. MS 127 D4
Wayne Co. MO 108 A2
Wayne Co. NE 35 F2
Wayne Co. NY 79 D3
Wayne Co. NC 123 E1
Wayne Co. OH 91 E3
Wayne Co. PA 93 F1
Wayne Co. TN 119 E1
Wayne Co. UT 39 F3
Wayne Co. WV 101 E4
Wayne Lakes OH 100 B1
Waynesboro GA 129 F1
Waynesboro MS 127 D4
Waynesboro PA 103 D1
Waynesboro TN 119 E1
Waynesboro VA 102 C4
Waynesburg OH 91 E3
Waynesburg PA 102 A1
Waynesfield OH 90 B4
Waynesville MO 107 E1
Waynesville NC 121 E1
Waynesville OH 100 C1
Waynetown IN 89 E4
Waynoka OK 51 D1
Wayzata MN 235 A2
Weakley Co. TN 108 C3
Weare NH 81 F4
Weatherby Lake MO 224 B2
Weatherford OK 51 D3
Weatherford TX 59 E2
Weatherly PA 93 F3
Weaubleau MO 96 C4
Weaver AL 120 A4
Weaverville CA 28 B4
Weaverville NC 111 E4
Webb AL 128 B4
Webb MS 118 B4
Webb City MO 106 B2

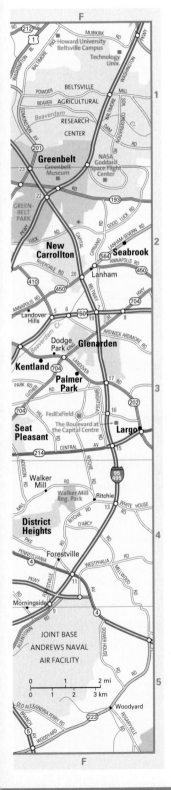

Figures after entries indicate page number and grid reference.

Webb Co. TX 60 C4
Webbers Falls OK 116 B1
Webberville MI 76 B4
Weber City VA 111 E3
Weber Co. UT 31 F3
Webster FL 140 C1
Webster MD 145 D1
Webster MA 150 B2
Webster NY 78 C3
Webster NC 121 D1
Webster SD 27 E2
Webster TX 132 B3
Webster WI 67 E2
Webster City IA 72 C4
Webster Co. GA 128 C3
Webster Co. IA 72 B4
Webster Co. KY 109 E1
Webster Co. MS 118 C4
Webster Co. MO 107 D2
Webster Co. NE 35 E4
Webster Co. WV 102 A3
Webster Groves MO 256 B3
Webster Par. LA 125 D2
Webster Sprs. WV 102 A3
Weddington NC 122 B2
Wedowee AL 128 B1
Weed CA 28 C3
Weedsport NY 79 D3
Weehawken NJ 148 B4
Weeki Wachee Gardens FL 140 B1
Weeping Water NE 35 F4
Weidman MI 76 A2
Weigelstown PA 103 E1
Weimar CA 36 C2
Weimar TX 61 F2
Weiner AR 108 A4
Weippe ID 14 B4
Weir KS 106 B2
Weir MS 126 C1
Weir TX 61 E1
Weirsdale FL 139 D4
Weirton WV 91 F4
Weiser ID 22 A3
Welaka FL 139 D4
Welby CO 209 C2
Welch OK 106 B2
Welch WV 111 F1
Welcome LA 134 A3
Welcome MN 72 B2
Welcome NC 112 B4
Welcome SC 217 A2
Weld Co. CO 33 F4
Weldon CA 45 E4
Weldon NC 113 E3
Weldon Spr. MO 98 A3
Weleetka OK 51 F3
Wellesley MA 151 D1
Wellfleet MA 151 F2
Wellford SC 217 C1
Welling OK 106 B4
Wellington CO 33 E4
Wellington FL 143 E1
Wellington KS 43 E4
Wellington KY 230 E2
Wellington MO 96 C2
Wellington OH 91 D2
Wellington TX 50 C4
Wellington UT 39 F1
Wellman IA 87 E2
Wells ME 82 B4
Wells MN 72 C2
Wells NV 30 C3
Wells TX 124 B4
Wells VT 81 D4
Wellsboro IN 89 E2
Wellsboro PA 93 D1
Wellsburg IA 73 D4
Wellsburg NY 93 D1
Wellsburg WV 91 F4
Wells Co. IN 90 A3
Wells Co. ND 18 C3
Wells River VT 81 E2
Wellston MO 256 B2
Wellston OH 101 D2
Wellston OK 51 F2
Wellsville KS 96 B3
Wellsville MO 97 F2
Wellsville NY 92 C1
Wellsville OH 91 F3
Wellsville UT 31 E3
Wellton AZ 54 A2
Welsh LA 133 E2
Wenatchee WA 13 D3
Wendell ID 30 C1
Wendell NC 113 D4
Wenden AZ 54 B1
Wendover UT 31 D4
Wenham MA 151 F1
Wenona IL 88 B3
Wenonah NJ 146 C3
Wentworth NC 112 B3
Wentzville MO 98 A3
Wernersville PA 146 A2
Weslaco TX 63 E4
Wesley Chapel FL 140 C2
Wesley Chapel NC 122 B2
Wesley Hills NY 148 B2
Wesleyville PA 92 A1
Wessington SD 27 D3
Wessington Sprs. SD 27 D3
Wesson MS 126 B4
West TX 59 E3
W. Alexandria OH 100 B1
W. Allis WI 74 C3
W. Alton MO 98 A3
W. Babylon NY 148 C4
W. Baden Sprs. IN 99 F3
W. Baraboo WI 74 A2
W. Barnstable MA 151 E3
W. Barrington RI 150 C3
W. Baton Rouge Par. LA 134 A2
W. Bend IA 72 B3
W. Bend WI 74 C2
W. Berlin NJ 147 D3
W. Blocton AL 127 F1
Westborough MA 150 C1

POINTS OF INTEREST

Arena Stage E4
Arlington Natl. Cemetery A4
Arthur M. Sackler Gallery E3
Art Museum of the Americas C2
Arts & Industries Building E3
Belmont-Paul Women's Equality National Monument C2
Blair House C2
Bureau of Engraving & Printing D3
Cathedral of St. Matthew the Apostle C1
Daughters of the American Revolution Constitution Hall C2
Decatur House C1
Dept. of Agriculture D3
Dept. of Commerce D2
Dept. of Education E3
Dept. of Energy E3
Dept. of Housing and Urban Development E3
Dept. of Justice E2
Dept. of Labor F2
Dept. of State C2
Dept. of the Interior C2
Dept. of the Treasury D2
Dept. of Transportation G4
Dept. of Veterans Affairs D1
District of Columbia Court House E2
District of Columbia War Memorial C3
Donald W. Reynolds Center for American Art & Portraiture E2
Dwight D. Eisenhower Memorial E3
The Ellipse D2
Environmental Protection Agency D2
Fish Wharf D4
Folger Shakespeare Library G3
Ford's Theatre Natl. Hist. Site E2
Franklin Delano Roosevelt Memorial C3
Freer Gallery of Art D3
Friendship Archway E1
Gallaudet Univ. G1
George Mason Memorial C4
Georgetown Univ. Law Center F2
George Washington Univ. C2
Government Publishing Office F1
Hirshhorn Mus. & Sculpture Garden E3
Ice Skating Rink E2
Internal Revenue Service E2
International Spy Museum E3
James Madison Building G3
J. Edgar Hoover FBI Building E2
John Adams Building G3
John Ericsson Memorial B3
John F. Kennedy Center for the Performing Arts B2
John F. Kennedy Gravesite A4
Judiciary Square E2
Korean War Veterans Memorial C3
Koshland Science Museum E2
Lafayette Square D1
Lansburgh Theatre E2
L'Enfant Plaza E3
Library of Congress G3
Lincoln Memorial B3
Lyndon B. Johnson Memorial Grove B4
The Mall E3
Marine Corps War Memorial (Iwo Jima Memorial) A3
Martin Luther King, Jr. Mem. Library E2
Martin Luther King, Jr. Natl. Memorial C3
Museum of the Bible E3
NASA E4
Natl. Air & Space Museum E3
The Natl. Archives E2
Natl. Building Museum E2
Natl. Gallery of Art East Building E3
Natl. Gallery of Art West Building E2
Natl. Geographic Society & Explorers Hall D1
Natl. Mus. of African Art E3
Natl. Mus. of African Amerian Hist. & Culture D3
Natl. Mus. of American Hist. E2
Natl. Mus. of Natural Hist. E2
Natl. Mus. of the American Indian E3
Natl. Mus. of Women in the Arts D1
Natl. Postal Museum F2
Natl. Theatre D2
Natl. WWI Memorial D2
Natl. WWII Memorial C3
Navy-Merchant Marine Memorial C4
The Netherlands Carillon A3
Octagon House C2
Old Stone House B1
Organization of American States C2
Reflecting Pool C3
Renwick Gallery C2
Ronald Reagan Building and Intl. Trade Center D2
Seabees of the U.S. Navy Memorial A3
The Shops at Georgetown Park A1
Sidney Harman Hall E2
Signers of the Declaration of Independence Memorial C3
Smithsonian Institution Building (The Castle) E3
The Supreme Court G3
Taft Memorial Carillon F2
Theodore Roosevelt Memorial A2
Thomas Jefferson Building G3
Thomas Jefferson Memorial D4
Union Station F2
United Spanish War Veterans Memorial A3
U.S. Botanic Garden F3
U.S. Capitol F3
U.S. Capitol Visitor Center F3
U.S. Claims Court D1
U.S. District Court House E2
U.S. Grant Memorial F3
U.S. Holocaust Memorial Museum D3
U.S. Navy Memorial & Naval Heritage Center E2
U.S. Postal Service Headquarters E3
Verizon Center E2
Vietnam Veterans Memorial C2
Vietnam Women's Memorial C3
Warner Theatre D2
Washington Convention Center E1
The Washington Design Center D1
Washington Harbour A1
Washington Monument D3
Washington Post D1
The White House D2
White House Visitor Center D2
Women in Military Service for America Memorial A4
Zero Milestone D2

Entries in **bold black** indicate counties or parishes.
Entries in **bold color** indicate cities with detailed inset maps.

W. Bountiful UT 31 E4
W. Bowdoin ME 82 B3
W. Boylston MA 150 C1
W. Branch IA 87 F2
W. Branch MI 76 B1
W. Bridgewater MA 151 D2
Westbrook CT 149 E2
Westbrook ME 82 B3
Westbrook MN 72 A1
W. Brookfield MA 150 B1
W. Buechel KY 230 E2
W. Burke VT 81 E1
W. Burlington IA 87 F3
Westbury NY 148 C4
W. Buxton ME 82 B3
Westby WI 73 F2
W. Caldwell NJ 240 A2
W. Carroll Par. LA 125 F2
W. Carrollton OH 100 B1
W. Carthage NY 79 E1
Westchester IL 203 C4
W. Chester PA 146 B3
Westchester Co. NY 148 B2
W. Chicago IL 203 A4
West City IL 98 C4
Westcliffe CO 41 D3
W. College Corner IN 100 B1
W. Columbia SC 205 E2
W. Columbia TX 132 A4
W. Concord MA 150 C1
W. Concord MN 73 D1
W. Conshohocken PA 248 B2
W. Covina CA 228 E2
W. Creek NJ 147 E4
W. Crossett AR 125 F1
W. Dennis MA 151 F3
W. Des Moines IA 86 C2
W. Dummerston VT 94 C1
W. Dundee IL 88 C1
W. Elmira NY 93 D1
W. End AL 120 A4
W. Enfield ME 85 D4
Westerly RI 150 B4
Western Grove AR 107 D4
Westernport MD 102 B2
Western Sprs. IL 203 C5
Westerville OH 90 C4
W. Fairlee VT 81 E3
W. Fairview PA 218 A1
W. Falmouth ME 251 A1
W. Falmouth MA 151 E4
W. Fargo ND 19 E4
W. Feliciana Par. LA 133 F1
Westfield IL 99 D2
Westfield IN 89 F4
Westfield MA 150 A2
Westfield NJ 147 E1
Westfield NY 78 A4
Westfield PA 93 D1
Westfield TX 132 A3
Westfield WI 74 B2
Westfield Ctr. OH 91 E3
W. Fork AR 106 C4
W. Frankfort IL 98 C4
W. Freehold NJ 147 E2
W. Friendship MD 144 B2
W. Gate of Lomond VA 144 A3
W. Glacier MT 15 D2
W. Glens Falls NY 80 C4
W. Grove PA 146 B3
W. Hamlin WV 101 E4
Westhampton NY 149 E3
Westhampton Beach NY 149 E4
W. Hartford CT 150 A3
W. Hartford VT 81 E3
W. Haven CT 149 D2
W. Haven UT 244 A1
W. Hazleton PA 93 E3
W. Helena AR 118 A2
W. Hollywood CA 228 C2
W. Homestead PA 250 C2
Westhope ND 18 B1
W. Hurley NY 94 B2
W. Islip NY 148 C4
W. Jefferson NC 111 F3
W. Jefferson OH 101 D1
W. Jordan UT 31 E4
W. Kennebunk ME 82 B4
W. Kingston RI 150 C4
W. Kittanning PA 92 A3
W. Lafayette IN 89 E4
W. Lafayette OH 91 E4
Westlake LA 133 D2
Westlake OH 91 E2
W. Lake Hills TX 61 E1
Westlake Vil. CA 52 B2
Westland MI 76 B4
W. Lebanon IN 89 D4
W. Leechburg PA 92 A3
Westley CA 36 C4
W. Liberty IA 87 F2
W. Liberty KY 101 D4
W. Liberty OH 90 B4
W. Liberty WV 91 F4
W. Linn OR 20 C2
W. Logan WV 101 E4
W. Long Branch NJ 147 F2
W. Mahopac NY 148 B2
W. Mansfield OH 90 C4
W. Mayfield PA 91 F3
W. Medway MA 150 C2
W. Melbourne FL 141 E2
W. Memphis AR 118 B1
Westmere NY 94 B1
W. Miami FL 143 E2
W. Middlesex PA 91 F2
W. Mifflin PA 250 C3
W. Milford NJ 148 A2
W. Milford WV 102 A2
W. Milton OH 100 B1
W. Milwaukee WI 234 C3
Westminster CA 228 E4
Westminster CO 41 E1
Westminster MD 144 B1
Westminster MA 95 D1
Westminster SC 121 E2
Westminster VT 81 E4
W. Monroe LA 125 E2
Westmont IL 203 C5
Westmont PA 92 B4
Westmoreland KS 43 F2
Westmoreland TN 109 F3
Westmoreland Co. PA 92 B4
Westmoreland Co. VA 103 E4
Westmorland CA 53 E4
W. Mystic CT 149 F2
W. Newton PA 92 A4
W. New York NJ 148 B4
W. Odessa TX 57 F3
W. Okoboji IA 72 A3
Weston CT 148 C2
Weston FL 143 E2
Weston ID 31 E2
Weston MO 96 B2
Weston NE 35 F3
Weston OH 90 B2
Weston OR 21 F1
Weston TX 59 F1
Weston WV 102 A2
Weston WI 68 B4
Weston Co. WY 25 F4
Weston Lakes TX 132 A3
Weston Mills NY 92 C1
W. Orange NJ 148 A4
W. Orange TX 132 C3
W. Ossipee NH 81 F3
Westover TN 118 C1
Westover Hills TX 207 A2
W. Palm Beach FL 143 F1
W. Paris ME 82 B2
W. Pelham MA 150 A1
W. Pelzer SC 121 E2
W. Pensacola FL 135 F2
W. Peoria IL 88 B3
Westphalia MI 76 A3
W. Pittston PA 261 C1
W. Plains MO 107 E3
W. Point CA 36 C3
W. Point GA 128 B1
Westpoint IN 89 E4
W. Point IA 87 F3
W. Point KY 99 F4
W. Point MS 119 D4
W. Point NE 35 F2
W. Point UT 31 E3
W. Point VA 113 F1
Westport CT 148 C2
Westport IN 100 A2
Westport KY 100 A3
Westport NY 81 D2
Westport OR 20 B1
Westport WA 12 B4
W. Portsmouth OH 101 D3
W. Redding CT 148 C2
W. Richland WA 13 E4
W. Rockport ME 82 C2
W. Rutland VT 81 D3
W. Sacramento CA 36 C3
W. St. Paul MN 235 D3
W. Salem IL 99 D3
W. Salem OH 91 D3
W. Salem WI 73 F2
W. Sand Lake NY 94 B1
W. Sayville NY 149 D4
W. Selmont AL 127 F2
W. Seneca NY 78 B3
W. Siloam Sprs. OK 106 B4
W. Slope OR 251 C2
W. Springfield MA 150 A2
W. Springfield VA 270 A5
W. Sterling MA 150 B1
W. Stockbridge MA 94 B2
W. Suffield CT 150 A2
W. Swanzey NH 95 D1
W. Tawakoni TX 59 F2
W. Terre Haute IN 99 E2
W. Topsham VT 81 E2
Westtown NY 148 A2
W. Townshend VT 81 E4
W. Union IA 73 E3
W. Union OH 100 C3
W. Union WV 101 F2
W. Unity OH 90 B2
W. University Place TX 132 A3
W. Upton MA 150 C2
Westvale NY 265 A2
W. Valley City UT 31 E4
W. View PA 250 B1
Westville IL 99 D1
Westville IN 89 E2
Westville NJ 248 C4
Westville OK 106 B4
W. Wareham MA 151 E3
W. Warren MA 150 B2
W. Warwick RI 150 C3
Westway TX 56 C3
Westwego LA 134 B3
W. Wendover NV 31 D4
W. Willington CT 150 A3
W. Winfield NY 79 F3
Westwood CA 29 D4
Westwood KS 224 B3
Westwood KY 101 D3
Westwood MA 151 D2
Westwood NJ 148 B3
Westwood Lakes FL 143 E2
Westworth Vil. TX 207 A2
W. Wyoming PA 261 B1
W. Yarmouth MA 151 F3
W. Yellowstone MT 23 F3
W. York PA 275 C1
Wethersfield CT 150 A3
Wetmore KS 96 A1
Wetumka OK 51 F3
Wetumpka AL 128 A2
Wetzel Co. WV 102 A1
Wewahitchka FL 137 D2
Wewoka OK 51 F3
Wexford Co. MI 69 F4
Weyauwega WI 74 B1
Weyers Cave VA 102 C4
Weymouth MA 151 D2
Wharton NJ 148 A3
Wharton OH 90 C3
Wharton TX 61 F3
Wharton Co. TX 61 F3
What Cheer IA 87 E2
Whatcom Co. WA 12 C1
Whately MA 150 A1
Wheatfield IN 89 E2
Wheatland CA 36 C2
Wheatland IN 99 E3
Wheatland IA 87 F1
Wheatland WY 33 E2
Wheatland Co. MT 16 B4
Wheatley AR 118 A2
Wheaton IL 89 D1
Wheaton MD 144 B3
Wheaton MN 27 F1
Wheaton MO 106 C2
Wheat Ridge CO 209 B3
Wheeler MS 119 D2

Downtown Washington DC

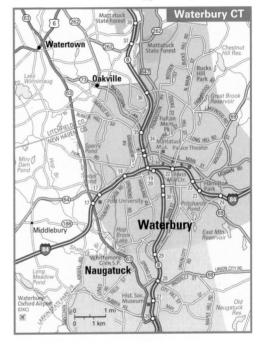

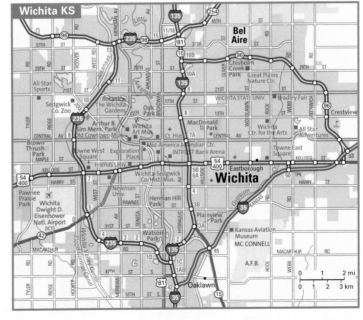

Figures after entries indicate page number and grid reference.

Wheeler OR 20 B1
Wheeler TX 50 C3
Wheeler Co. GA 129 E3
Wheeler Co. NE 35 D2
Wheeler Co. OR 21 E3
Wheeler Co. TX 50 C3
Wheelersburg OH 101 D3
Wheeling IL 89 D1
Wheeling WV 91 F4
Wheelwright KY 111 E1
Wheelwright MA 150 B1
Whigham GA 137 E1
Whippany NJ 148 A3
Whispering Pines NC 122 C1
Whitaker PA 250 C2
Whitakers NC 113 E4
White GA 120 C3
White SD 27 F3
White Bear Lake MN 235 D1
White Bird ID 22 B1
White Bluff TN 109 E4
White Castle LA 134 A2
White Ctr. WA 262 B4
White City FL 141 E3
White City KS 43 F2
White City OR 28 B2
White Cloud MI 75 F2
White Co. AR 117 F1
White Co. GA 121 D2
White Co. IL 99 D4
White Co. IN 89 E3
White Co. TN 110 A4
White Deer TX 50 B3
White Earth MN 19 F3
Whiteface TX 57 F1
Whitefield NH 81 F2
Whitefish MT 15 D2
Whitefish Bay WI 234 D1
Whiteford MD 146 A4
White Hall AL 127 F2
White Hall AR 117 E3
White Hall IL 98 A2
Whitehall MI 75 E2
Whitehall MT 23 E1
Whitehall NY 81 D3
Whitehall OH 206 C2
Whitehall PA 146 B1
Whitehall PA 250 B3
Whitehall VA 102 C4
White Hall VA 103 D2
White Hall WV 102 A2
Whitehall WI 73 F1
White Haven PA 93 F3
White Horse NJ 147 D2
White Horse PA 146 A3
White Horse Beach MA 151 E3
Whitehouse OH 90 B2
White House TN 109 F3
Whitehouse TX 124 B3
White House Sta. NJ 147 D1
White Island Shores MA 151 E3
White Lake NY 94 A3
White Lake NC 123 D2
White Lake SD 27 D4
Whiteland IN 99 F1
Whitelaw WI 75 D1
White Marsh MD 193 E2
White Marsh VA 113 F1
White Oak MD 270 D1
White Oak OH 204 A2
White Oak PA 92 A4
White Oak TX 124 B2
White Pigeon MI 89 F1
White Pine MI 65 E4
White Pine TN 111 D4
White Pine Co. NV 38 B1
White Plains KY 109 E2
White Plains MD 144 B4
White Plains NY 148 B3
White Plains NC 112 A3
Whiteriver AZ 55 E1
White River SD 26 C4
White River Jct. VT 81 E3
White Rock NM 48 C2
Whiterocks UT 32 A4
White Salmon WA 21 D1
Whitesboro NY 79 E3
Whitesboro TX 59 F1
Whitesburg GA 120 B4
Whitesburg KY 111 D2
White Settlement TX 207 A2
White Shield ND 18 B3
Whiteside Co. IL 88 A1
White Sprs. FL 138 C2
White Stone VA 113 F1
White Sulphur Sprs. MT 15 F4
White Sulphur Sprs. WV 112 B1
Whitesville KY 109 F1
Whitesville NY 92 C1
Whitesville WV 101 F4
White Swan WA 13 D4
Whiteville NC 123 D3
Whiteville TN 118 C1
Whitewater KS 43 E3
Whitewater WI 74 C3
Whitewood SD 25 F3
Whitewright TX 59 F1
Whitfield FL 140 B3
Whitfield Co. GA 120 B2
Whiting IN 89 D2
Whiting IA 35 F2
Whiting NJ 147 E3
Whiting WI 68 B4
Whitinsville MA 150 C2
Whitley City KY 110 C3
Whitley Co. IN 89 F3
Whitley Co. KY 110 C2
Whitman MA 151 D2
Whitman Co. WA 14 A4
Whitmire SC 121 F3
Whitmore Lake MI 76 B4
Whitmore Vil. HI 152 A2
Whitney TX 59 E3
Whitney Pt. NY 79 E4
Whitsett NC 112 B4
Whittemore IA 72 B3
Whittemore MI 76 B1
Whittier CA 52 C2
Whitwell TN 120 B1
Why AZ 54 B3
Wibaux MT 17 F4
Wibaux Co. MT 17 F4
Wichita KS 43 E4
Wichita Co. KS 42 B3
Wichita Co. TX 59 D1
Wichita Falls TX 59 D1
Wickenburg AZ 54 B1
Wickes AR 116 C3
Wickett TX 57 F4
Wickford RI 150 C4
Wickliffe KY 108 C2
Wickliffe OH 91 E2
Wicomico Church VA 113 F1
Wicomico Co. MD 114 C1
Widefield CO 205 D2
Wiggins CO 33 F4
Wiggins MS 135 D1
Wilbarger Co. TX 58 C1
Wilber NE 35 F4
Wilberforce OH 100 C1
Wilbraham MA 150 A2
Wilbur WA 13 F3
Wilbur Park MO 256 B3
Wilburton OK 116 A2
Wilcox NE 35 D4
Wilcox PA 92 B2
Wilcox Co. AL 127 F3
Wilcox Co. GA 129 E3
Wilder ID 22 A4
Wilder KY 204 B3
Wilder VT 81 E3
Wilderness VA 103 D4
Wildomar CA 53 D3
Wild Rose WI 74 B1
Wildwood FL 140 C1
Wildwood MO 98 A3
Wildwood NJ 104 C4
Wildwood TX 132 C2
Wildwood Crest NJ 104 C4
Wiley CO 42 A3
Wilhoit AZ 47 D4
Wilkes-Barre PA 93 E2
Wilkesboro NC 111 F4
Wilkes Co. GA 121 E4
Wilkes Co. NC 112 A3
Wilkeson WA 12 C3
Wilkin Co. MN 19 F4
Wilkinsburg PA 250 C2
Wilkinson Co. GA 129 E2
Wilkinson Co. MS 125 F4
Willacoochee GA 129 E4
Willacy Co. TX 63 F3
Willamina OR 20 B2
Willard MO 107 D2
Willard NM 49 D4
Willard OH 91 D3
Willard UT 31 E3
Willards MD 114 C1
Will Co. IL 89 D2
Willcox AZ 55 E3
Willernie MN 235 E1
Williams AZ 47 D3
Williams CA 36 B2
Williams IA 72 C4
Williams OR 28 B2
Williams Bay WI 74 C4
Williamsburg CO 41 E3
Williamsburg FL 246 B4
Williamsburg IA 87 E2
Williamsburg KS 96 A3
Williamsburg KY 110 C3
Williamsburg MA 150 A1
Williamsburg NM 56 B2
Williamsburg OH 100 C2
Williamsburg PA 92 C4
Williamsburg VA 113 F2
Williamsburg Co. SC 122 C4
Williams Co. ND 17 F2
Williams Co. OH 90 A2
Williams Creek IN 221 C1
Williamsfield IL 88 A3
Williamson NY 78 C3
Williamson WV 111 E1
Williamson Co. IL 108 C1
Williamson Co. TN 109 F4
Williamson Co. TX 61 E1
Williamsport IN 89 D4
Williamsport MD 103 D1
Williamsport OH 101 D1
Williamsport PA 93 D2
Williamston MI 76 A4
Williamston NC 113 E4
Williamston SC 121 E2
Williamstown KY 100 B3
Williamstown MA 94 C1
Williamstown NJ 146 C4
Williamstown NY 79 E2
Williamstown PA 93 E4
Williamstown VT 81 E2
Williamstown WV 101 F2
Williamsville DE 114 C1
Williamsville IL 98 B1
Williamsville MS 126 C1
Williamsville NY 198 C2
Willimantic CT 150 B3
Willingboro NJ 147 D3
Willis TX 132 A2
Willisburg KY 110 B1
Williston FL 138 C4
Williston MD 145 E3
Williston ND 17 F2
Williston OH 90 C2
Williston SC 130 B1
Williston TN 118 C1
Williston VT 81 D2
Willisville IL 98 B4
Willis Wharf VA 114 B3
Willits CA 36 A2
Willmar MN 66 B3
Willoughby OH 91 E2
Willoughby Hills OH 204 G1
Willow AK 154 C3
Willowbrook CA 228 D3
Willowbrook IL 203 C5
Willow City ND 18 C2
Willow Creek CA 28 B4
Willow Creek MT 23 E1
Willow Grove PA 146 C2
Willowick OH 91 E2
Willow Lake SD 27 E3
Willow Park TX 59 E2
Willows CA 36 B1
Willows MD 144 C4
Willow Sprs. IL 203 C5
Willow Sprs. MO 107 E2
Willow Street PA 146 A3
Willsboro NY 81 D2
Willshire OH 90 A3
Wills Pt. TX 59 F2
Willwood WY 24 B3
Wilmar AR 117 F4
Wilmer AL 135 E1
Wilmer TX 207 E3
Wilmerding PA 250 D3
Wilmette IL 89 D1
Wilmington DE 146 B4
Wilmington IL 88 C2
Wilmington NC 123 E3
Wilmington OH 100 C2
Wilmington VT 94 C1
Wilmington Island GA 130 C3
Wilmington Manor DE 274 D3
Wilmore KY 100 B4
Wilmot AR 125 F1
Wilmot SD 27 F2
Wilsall MT 23 F1
Wilson AR 118 B1
Wilson KS 43 D2
Wilson LA 134 A1
Wilson NY 78 B3
Wilson NC 113 D4
Wilson OK 51 E4
Wilson PA 93 F3
Wilson TX 58 A2
Wilson WY 23 F4
Wilson Co. KS 106 A1
Wilson Co. NC 113 E4
Wilson Co. TN 109 F3
Wilson Co. TX 61 E3
Wilson's Mills NC 123 D1
Wilsonville AL 128 A1
Wilsonville IL 98 B2
Wilsonville OR 20 C2
Wilton AL 127 F1
Wilton AR 116 C4
Wilton CA 36 C3
Wilton CT 148 C2
Wilton IA 87 F2
Wilton ME 82 B2
Wilton NH 95 D1
Wilton NY 80 C4
Wilton ND 18 C3
Wilton WI 73 F2
Wilton Manors FL 233 C2
Wimauma FL 140 C3
Wimberley TX 61 D2
Wimbledon ND 19 D3
Winamac IN 89 E3
Winchendon MA 95 D1
Winchester CA 53 D3
Winchester ID 22 B1
Winchester IL 98 A1
Winchester IN 90 A4
Winchester KS 96 A2
Winchester KY 100 B4
Winchester MA 151 D1
Winchester MO 256 A2
Winchester NH 94 C1
Winchester OH 100 C3
Winchester OK 51 F2
Winchester TN 120 A1
Winchester VA 103 D2
Winchester Bay OR 20 A4
Windber PA 92 B4
Windcrest TX 61 D2
Winder GA 121 D3
Windermere FL 141 D1
Windfall IN 89 F4
Wind Gap PA 93 F3
Windham CT 149 F1
Windham NH 95 E1
Windham OH 91 F2
Windham Co. CT 150 B3
Windham Co. VT 81 E4
Wind Lake WI 74 C3
Windom MN 72 B2
Window Rock AZ 48 A2
Wind Pt. WI 75 D4
Windsor CA 36 B3
Windsor CO 33 E4
Windsor CT 150 A3
Windsor IL 98 C2
Windsor MO 96 C3
Windsor NY 93 F1
Windsor NC 113 F4
Windsor PA 103 E1
Windsor VT 81 E4
Windsor VA 113 F2
Windsor WI 74 B3
Windsor Co. VT 81 E3
Windsor Hts. WV 91 F4
Windsor Hills CA 228 C3
Windsor Locks CT 150 A2
Windthorst TX 59 D1
Windy Hills KY 230 E1
Winfall NC 113 F3
Winfield AL 119 E4
Winfield IL 203 B4
Winfield IN 89 D2
Winfield IA 87 F3
Winfield KS 43 F4
Winfield MO 98 A2
Winfield TN 110 C3
Winfield TX 124 B1
Winfield WV 101 E3
Wingate NC 122 B2
Wingdale NY 148 C1
Wingo KY 108 C3
Winifred MT 16 B3
Wink TX 57 F4
Winkelman AZ 55 D2
Winkler Co. TX 57 F3
Winlock WA 12 B4
Winnebago IL 74 B4
Winnebago MN 72 C2
Winnebago NE 35 F2
Winnebago Co. IL 74 B4
Winnebago Co. IA 72 C2
Winnebago Co. WI 74 C1
Winneconne WI 74 C1
Winnecunnet MA 151 D2
Winnemucca NV 30 A3
Winner SD 26 C4
Winneshiek Co. IA 73 E3
Winnetka IL 203 D2
Winnett MT 16 C4
Winnfield LA 125 E3
Winnie TX 132 C3
Winnisquam NH 81 F4
Winn Par. LA 125 E3
Winnsboro LA 125 F3
Winnsboro SC 122 A3
Winnsboro TX 124 A1
Winnsboro Mills SC 122 A3
Winona MN 73 E1
Winona MS 118 B4
Winona MO 107 F2
Winona OH 91 F3
Winona TX 124 B2
Winona Co. MN 73 E1
Winona Lake IN 89 F2
Winooski VT 81 D2
Winside NE 35 E2
Winslow AZ 47 E3

Williamsburg VA

Five Forks A1
Gloucester Pt. C2
Hayes C1
Lackey C2
Newport News C2
Scotland A2
Wicomico C1
Williamsburg A1
Yorktown C2

Arden E1
Ardencroft E1
Ardentown E1
Bellefonte E1
Biddles Landing E3
Blue Ball E1
Carrcroft E1
Churchtown E3
Collins Park D3
Deepwater E3
Dunleith D2
Edgemoor E2
Elsmere D2
Fairfax E1
Greenville D1
Guyencourt D1
Hamilton Park E2
Hares Corner D3
Llangollen Estates D3
Minquadale D2
Montchanin D1
New Castle D3
Newport D2
Penns Grove E2
Pennsville E3
Rockland D1
Talleys Corner E1
Talleyville E1
Westover Hills D1
Wilmington E2
Wilmington Manor D3
Winterthur D1

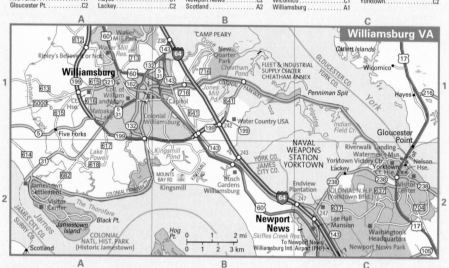

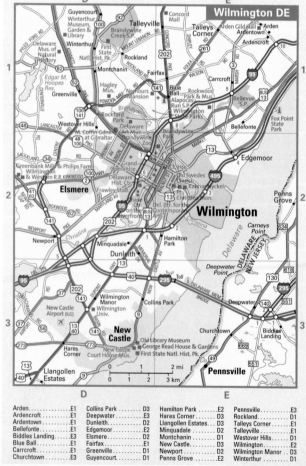

Entries in **bold black** indicate counties or parishes.
Entries in **bold color** indicate cities with detailed inset maps.

Winslow AR 106 C4
Winslow IN 99 E4
Winslow ME 82 C2
Winslow NJ 147 D4
Winsted CT 94 C2
Winsted MN 66 C4
Winston OR 28 B1
Winston Co. AL 119 E3
Winston Co. MS 127 D1
Winston-Salem NC 112 B4
Winstonville MS 118 A4
Winter Beach FL 141 E3
Winter Garden FL 141 D1
Winter Harbor ME 83 D2
Winterhaven CA 53 F4
Winter Haven FL 140 C2
Winter Park CO 41 D1
Winter Park FL 141 D1
Winterport ME 83 D2
Winters CA 36 B3
Winters TX 58 C3
Winterset IA 86 C2
Winter Sprs. FL 141 D1
Winterstown PA 103 E1
Wintersville OH 91 F4
Winterville GA 121 D4
Winterville NC 115 D3
Winthrop CT 149 E2
Winthrop IA 73 E4
Winthrop ME 82 B2
Winthrop MA 151 D1
Winthrop MN 66 C4
Winthrop NY 80 B1
Winthrop Harbor IL 75 D4
Winton CA 36 C4
Winton NC 113 F3
Wirt Co. WV 101 F2
Wiscasset ME 82 C3
Wisconsin Dells WI 74 A2
Wisconsin Rapids WI 74 A1
Wisdom MT 23 D1
Wise VA 111 E2
Wise Co. TX 59 E2
Wise Co. VA 111 E2
Wishek ND 27 D1
Wisner LA 125 F3
Wisner NE 35 F2
Wister OK 116 B2
Withamsville OH 204 C3
Withee WI 68 A4
Witherbee NY 81 D2
Witt IL 98 B2
Witt TN 111 D4
Wittenberg WI 68 B4
Wittmann AZ 54 B1
Wixom MI 76 B4
Woburn MA 151 D1
Wofford KY 110 C2
Wofford Hts. CA 45 E4
Wolcott CT 149 D1
Wolcott IN 89 E3
Wolcott NY 79 D3
Wolcottville IN 90 A2
Wolfdale PA 91 F4
Wolfeboro NH 81 F3
Wolfeboro Falls NH 81 F3
Wolfe City TX 59 F1
Wolfe Co. KY 111 D1
Wolfforth TX 58 A1
Wolf Lake MI 75 E3
Wolf Pt. MT 17 E2
Wolsey SD 27 E3
Wolverine Lake MI 210 A1
Womelsdorf PA 146 A2
Wonewoc WI 74 A2
Wonnie KY 111 D1
Woodacre CA 259 A1
Woodbine GA 139 D1
Woodbine IA 86 A1
Woodbine KY 110 C2
Woodbine MD 144 B2
Woodbine NJ 104 C4
Woodbourne NY 94 A3
Woodbourne OH 208 E2
Woodbranch TX 132 B2
Woodbridge CT 149 D2
Woodbridge NJ 147 E1
Woodbridge VA 144 B4
Woodburn IN 90 A3
Woodburn KY 109 F2
Woodburn OR 20 B2
Woodbury CT 149 D1
Woodbury GA 128 C1
Woodbury MN 67 D4
Woodbury NJ 146 C3
Woodbury TN 110 A4
Woodbury VT 81 E2
Woodbury Co. IA 35 F2
Woodbury Hts. NJ 146 C3
Wood Co. OH 90 C2
Wood Co. TX 124 A2
Wood Co. WV 101 E2
Wood Co. WI 68 A4
Woodcreek TX 61 D2
Woodcrest CA 229 J4
Wood Dale IL 203 C3
Woodfield MD 144 B2
Woodfin NC 111 E4
Woodford Co. IL 88 B3
Woodford Co. KY 100 B4
Woodhaven MI 90 C1
Wood Heights MO 96 C2
Woodhull IL 88 A2
Woodhull NY 93 D1
Woodinville NY 148 C1
Woodinville WA 12 C3
Woodlake CA 45 D3
Wood Lake MN 66 A4
Woodland CA 36 B3
Woodland GA 128 C2
Woodland MI 76 A4
Woodland MN 235 A3
Woodland NC 113 E3
Woodland WA 20 C1
Woodland (Baileyville) ME 83 E1
Woodland Beach MI 90 C1
Woodland Hills UT 39 E1
Woodland Park CO 41 E2
Woodland Park NJ 240 B1
Woodlawn IL 98 C4
Woodlawn KY 204 B3
Woodlawn MD 145 D1
Woodlawn MD 193 B2
Woodlawn OH 204 B1
Woodlawn VA 112 A3
Woodlawn Park KY 230 E1
Woodlyn PA 248 A4
Woodlynne NJ 248 C4
Woodmere NY 241 G5
Woodmere OH 204 G2
Woodmont CT 149 D2
Woodmore MD 144 C3
Woodport NJ 148 A3
Woodridge IL 203 B5
Wood-Ridge NJ 240 C2
Woodridge NY 94 A3
Wood River IL 98 A3
Wood River NE 35 D4
Woodruff SC 121 F2
Woodruff WI 68 B2
Woodruff Co. AR 117 F1
Woodsboro MD 144 A1
Woodsboro TX 61 E4
Woodsburgh NY 241 G5
Woods Co. OK 51 D1
Woods Cross UT 257 B1
Woodsfield OH 101 F1
Woods Hole MA 151 E4
Woodside CA 259 C5
Woodside DE 145 E2
Woodside MT 15 D4
Woods Landing WY 33 D3
Woodson AR 117 E3
Woodson IL 98 A1
Woodson Co. KS 96 A4
Woodson Terrace MO 256 B1
Woodstock AL 127 F1
Woodstock GA 120 C3
Woodstock IL 74 C4
Woodstock NY 94 B2
Woodstock VT 81 E3
Woodstock VA 102 C3
Woodstock Valley CT 150 B2
Woodstown NJ 145 F1
Woodsville NH 81 E2
Woodville AL 120 A2
Woodville CA 45 D3
Woodville FL 137 E2
Woodville GA 121 E4
Woodville MA 150 C2
Woodville MS 134 A1
Woodville OH 90 C2
Woodville TX 132 C1
Woodville WI 67 E4
Woodward IA 86 C1
Woodward OK 50 C1
Woodward Co. OK 51 D2
Woodway TX 59 E4
Woodway WA 262 A2
Woodworth LA 133 E1
Woody Creek CO 40 C2
Woonsocket RI 150 C2
Woonsocket SD 27 E3
Wooster AR 117 E1
Wooster OH 91 E3
Worcester MA 150 C1
Worcester NY 79 F4
Worcester VT 81 E2
Worcester Co. MD 114 C2
Worcester Co. MA 150 B1
Worden IL 98 B3
Worden MT 24 C1
Workmans Corners DE 145 F4
Worland WY 24 C4
Worley ID 14 B3
Wormleysburg PA 218 B2
Worth IL 203 D6
Wortham TX 59 F3
Worth Co. GA 129 D4
Worth Co. IA 73 D2
Worth Co. MO 86 B4
Worthing SD 27 F4
Worthington IN 99 E2
Worthington IA 73 F4
Worthington KY 101 D3
Worthington MN 72 A2
Worthington OH 90 C4
Worthington PA 92 A3
Wounded Knee SD 34 A1
Wrangell AK 155 E4
Wray CO 42 A1
Wrens GA 129 F1
Wrentham MA 151 D2
Wright FL 136 B2
Wright WY 25 E4
Wright City MO 97 F3
Wright City OK 116 B3
Wright Co. IA 72 C4
Wright Co. MN 66 C3
Wright Co. MO 107 E2
Wrightsboro NC 123 E3
Wrightstown NJ 147 D3
Wrightstown PA 147 D2
Wrightstown WI 74 C1
Wrightsville AR 117 E2
Wrightsville GA 129 E2
Wrightsville PA 103 E1
Wrightsville Beach NC 123 E3
Wrightwood CA 52 C2
Wrigley TN 109 E4
Wurtland KY 101 D3
Wurtsboro NY 148 A1
Wyalusing PA 93 E2
Wyandot Co. OH 90 C3
Wyandotte MI 90 C1
Wyandotte OK 106 B2
Wyandotte Co. KS 96 B2
Wyanet IL 88 B2
Wyckoff NJ 148 B3
Wycombe PA 146 C2
Wykoff MN 73 E2
Wylie TX 59 F2
Wymore NE 43 F1
Wynantskill NY 188 E2
Wyncote PA 248 C1
Wyndmere ND 27 F1
Wynne AR 118 A1
Wynnewood OK 51 E4
Wynona OK 51 F1
Wyocena WI 74 B2
Wyodak WY 25 E3
Wyola MT 24 C2
Wyoming DE 145 E2
Wyoming IL 88 B3
Wyoming IA 87 F1
Wyoming MI 75 F3
Wyoming MN 67 D3
Wyoming NY 78 B3
Wyoming OH 204 B1
Wyoming PA 261 B1
Wyoming RI 150 C4
Wyoming Co. NY 78 B4
Wyoming Co. PA 93 E2
Wyoming Co. WV 111 F1
Wyomissing PA 146 A2
Wythe Co. VA 112 A2

Auburn C2
Bramanville D2
Chaffinville C1
Cherry Valley C2
Dorothy Pond D2
E. Millbury D2
Edgemere D2
Leicester C2
Millbury D2
Morningdale D1
Pondville C2
Rochdale C2
Stoneville C2
Worcester C1

Belville A1
Hightsville A1
Masonboro B2
Ogden B1
Seagate B2
Wilmington A2
Wrightsboro A1
Wrightsville Beach B2

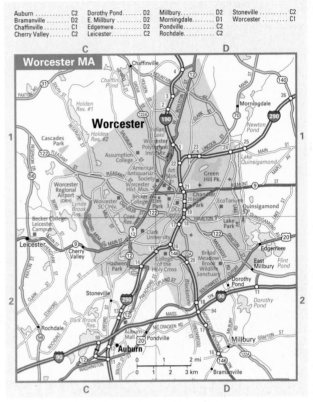

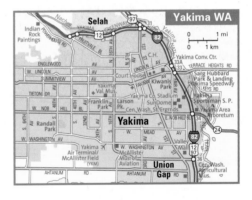

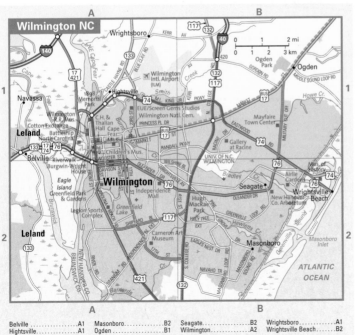

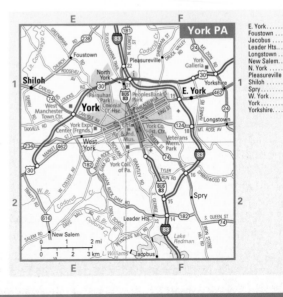

E. York F1
Foustown E1
Jacobus F2
Leader Hts. F2
Longstown F1
New Salem E2
N. York E1
Pleasureville F1
Shiloh E1
Spry F2
W. York E1
York E1
Yorkshire F1

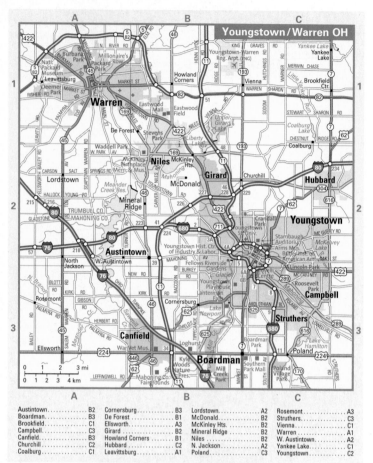

Figures after entries indicate page number and grid reference.

Austintown B2
Boardman B3
Brookfield C1
Campbell C3
Canfield B3
Churchill C2
Coalburg C1
Cornersburg B3
De Forest B1
Ellsworth A3
Girard B2
Howland Corners B1
Hubbard C2
Leavittsburg A1
Lordstown A2
McDonald B2
McKinley Hts. B2
Mineral Ridge B2
Niles B2
N. Jackson A2
Poland C3
Rosemont A3
Struthers C3
Vienna C1
Warren A1
W. Austintown A2
Yankee Lake C1
Youngstown C2

Yuma AZ

San Juan PR

Wytheville VA 112 A2

X

Xenia IL 98 C3
Xenia OH 100 C1

Y

Yachats OR 20 B3
Yacolt WA 20 C1
Yadkin Co. NC 112 A3
Yadkinville NC 112 A4
Yah-ta-hey NM 48 A2
Yakima WA 13 D4
Yakima Co. WA 13 D4
Yakutat AK 155 D3
Yalaha FL 140 C1
Yale MI 76 C3
Yale OK 51 F2
Yalesville CT 149 D1
Yalobusha Co. MS 118 B3
Yamhill OR 20 B2
Yamhill Co. OR 20 B2
Yampa CO 40 C1
Yancey Co. NC 111 E4
Yanceyville NC 112 C3
Yankeetown FL 138 C4
Yankton SD 35 E1
Yankton Co. SD 35 E1
Yaphank NY 149 D3
Yardley PA 147 D2
Yardville NJ 147 D2
Yarmouth ME 82 B3
Yarmouth MA 151 F3
Yarmouth Port MA 151 F3
Yarnell AZ 47 D4
Yarrow Pt. WA 262 B3
Yates Ctr. KS 96 A4
Yates City IL 88 A3
Yates Co. NY 78 C4
Yatesville GA 129 D1
Yatesville PA 261 C2
Yavapai Co. AZ 47 D4
Yazoo City MS 126 B2
Yazoo Co. MS 126 B2
Yeadon PA 146 C3
Yeagertown PA 93 D3
Yell Co. AR 117 D2
Yellow House PA 146 B2
Yellow Medicine Co. MN 66 A4
Yellow Sprs. MD 144 A1
Yellow Sprs. OH 100 C1
Yellowstone Co. MT 24 C1
Yellville AR 107 E3
Yelm WA 12 C4
Yemassee SC 130 C2
Yerington NV 37 E2
Yerkes KY 111 D2
Yermo CA 53 D1
Yoakum TX 61 E3
Yoakum Co. TX 57 F2
Yoder WY 33 F2
Yoe PA 103 E1
Yolo CA 36 B2
Yolo Co. CA 36 B2
Yoncalla OR 20 B4
Yonkers NY 148 B3
Yorba Linda CA 229 F3
York AL 127 D2
York NE 35 E4
York NY 78 C3
York PA 103 E1
York SC 122 A2
York Beach ME 82 B4
York Co. ME 82 B4
York Co. NE 35 E4
York Co. PA 103 E1
York Co. SC 122 A2
York Co. VA 113 F2
York Harbor ME 82 B4
York Haven PA 93 E4
Yorkshire NY 78 B4
Yorkshire VA 144 A3
York Sprs. PA 103 E1
Yorktown IN 89 F4
Yorktown NY 148 B2
Yorktown TX 61 E3
Yorktown VA 113 F2
Yorktown Hts. NY 148 B2
York Vil. ME 82 B4
Yorkville IL 88 C2
Yorkville OH 91 F4
Young AZ 47 E4
Young Co. TX 59 D2
Young Harris GA 121 D2
Youngstown NY 78 A3
Youngstown OH 91 F3
Youngstown PA 92 B4
Youngsville LA 133 F2
Youngsville NC 113 D4
Youngsville PA 92 B1
Youngtown AZ 249 A1
Youngwood PA 92 A4
Yountville CA 36 B3
Ypsilanti MI 90 C1
Yreka CA 28 C2
Yuba City CA 36 C2
Yuba Co. CA 36 C2
Yucaipa CA 53 D2
Yucca Valley CA 53 E2
Yukon OK 51 E3
Yulee FL 139 D2
Yuma AZ 53 F4
Yuma CO 42 A1
Yuma Co. AZ 54 A2
Yuma Co. CO 34 A4
Yutan NE 35 F3

Z

Zacata VA 103 E4
Zachary LA 134 A1
Zanesville IN 90 A3
Zanesville OH 101 E1
Zap ND 18 B3
Zapata TX 63 D3
Zapata Co. TX 63 D3
Zavala Co. TX 60 C3
Zavalla TX 132 C1
Zearing IA 87 D1
Zeb OK 106 B4
Zebulon GA 128 C1
Zebulon KY 111 E1
Zebulon NC 113 D4
Zeeland MI 75 F3
Zeigler IL 98 C4
Zelienople PA 92 A3
Zephyr Cove NV 37 D2
Zephyrhills FL 140 C2
Zia Pueblo NM 48 C3
Ziebach Co. SD 26 B2
Zillah WA 13 E4
Zimmerman MN 66 C3
Zion IL 75 D4
Zion KY 109 E1
Zion PA 92 C3
Zion Crossroads VA 102 C4
Zionsville IN 99 F1
Zolfo Sprs. FL 140 C3
Zumbrota MN 73 D1
Zuni Pueblo NM 48 A3
Zwolle LA 125 D4

PUERTO RICO

Aceitunas PR 187 D1
Adjuntas PR 187 D1
Aguada PR 187 D1
Aguadilla PR 187 D1
Aguas Buenas PR 187 E1
Aguilita PR 187 E1
Aibonito PR 187 E1
Añasco PR 187 D1
Arecibo PR 187 E1
Arroyo PR 187 E1
Bajadero PR 187 E1
Barceloneta PR 187 E1
Barranquitas PR 187 E1
Bayamón PR 187 E1
Betances PR 187 D1
Boquerón PR 187 D1
Cabo Rojo PR 187 D1
Caguas PR 187 E1
Camuy PR 187 D1
Canóvanas PR 187 F1
Carolina PR 187 F1
Cataño PR 187 E1
Cayey PR 187 E1
Cayuco PR 187 D1
Ceiba PR 187 F1
Ceiba PR 187 E1
Ciales PR 187 E1
Cidra PR 187 E1
Coamo PR 187 E1
Coco PR 187 E1
Comerío PR 187 E1
Comunas PR 187 F1
Coquí PR 187 E1
Corazón PR 187 E1
Corozal PR 187 E1
Coto Norte PR 187 E1
Daguao PR 187 F1
Dorado PR 187 E1
Duque PR 187 F1
El Mangó PR 187 F1
Esperanza PR 187 F1
Fajardo PR 187 F1
Florida PR 187 E1
Guánica PR 187 D1
Guayabal PR 187 E1
Guayama PR 187 E1
Guayanilla PR 187 D1
Guaynabo PR 187 E1
Gurabo PR 187 F1
Hatillo PR 187 D1
Hormigueros PR 187 D1
Humacao PR 187 F1
Isabela PR 187 D1
Jagual PR 187 E1
Jayuya PR 187 E1
Jobos PR 187 E1
Juana Diaz PR 187 E1
Juncos PR 187 F1
La Parguera PR 187 D1
La Plena PR 187 E1
Lajas PR 187 D1
Lares PR 187 D1
Las Marías PR 187 D1
Las Marías PR 187 D1
Las Piedras PR 187 F1
Levittown PR 187 E1
Loíza PR 187 F1
Los Llanos PR 187 E1
Luquillo PR 187 F1
Manatí PR 187 E1
Maricao PR 187 D1
Maunabo PR 187 F1
Mayagüez PR 187 D1
Moca PR 187 D1
Mora PR 187 D1
Morovis PR 187 E1
Naguabo PR 187 F1
Naranjito PR 187 E1
Orocovis PR 187 E1
Palmarejo PR 187 D1
Palomas PR 187 D1
Patillas PR 187 E1
Peñuelas PR 187 D1
Playita PR 187 F1
Pole Ojea PR 187 D1
Ponce PR 187 E1
Potala Pastillo PR 187 E1
Puerto Real PR 187 D1
Punta Santiago PR 187 F1
Quebrada PR 187 D1
Quebradillas PR 187 D1
Rafael Capó PR 187 D1
Rincón PR 187 D1
Río Grande PR 187 F1
Sabana Eneas PR 187 D1
Sabana Grande PR 187 D1
Sabana Hoyos PR 187 E1
Salinas PR 187 E1
San Antonio PR 187 E1
San Antonio PR 187 D1
San Germán PR 187 D1
San Isidro PR 187 F1
San Juan PR 187 E1
San Lorenzo PR 187 F1
San Sebastián PR 187 D1
Santa Isabel PR 187 E1
Santo Domingo PR 187 D1
Tallaboa PR 187 D1
Toa Alta PR 187 E1
Trujillo Alto PR 187 E1
Utuado PR 187 E1
Vázquez PR 187 E1
Vega Alta PR 187 E1
Vega Baja PR 187 E1
Vieques PR 187 F1
Villalba PR 187 E1
Yabucoa PR 187 F1
Yauco PR 187 D1
Yaurel PR 187 E1

Entries in **bold color** indicate cities with detailed inset maps.

CANADA

Abbotsford BC	163	D3
Aberdeen SK	165	F1
Acton ON	172	C2
Acton Vale QC	175	D3
Adstock QC	175	E2
Airdrie AB	164	C2
Air Ronge SK	160	B3

Beaumont AB	159	D4
Beaumont QC	175	E1
Beaupré QC	175	E1
Beausejour MB	167	F3
Beauval SK	159	F2
Beaverlodge AB	157	F1
Beaverton ON	173	D1
Bécancour QC	175	D2
Bedford NS	181	D3

Blenheim ON	172	B4
Blind Bay BC	163	F1
Blind River ON	170	B3
Blue Mts. ON	172	C1
Bluewater ON	172	B2
Blyth ON	172	B2
Bobcaygeon ON	173	E1
Bois-Blanc NB	179	D2
Boischatel QC	175	E1

Brockville ON	174	B4
Bromont QC	175	D3
Bromptonville QC	175	E3
Brooklin ON	173	D2
Brooklyn NS	180	C4
Brooks AB	165	D3
Brookside NS	181	D3
Brownsburg-Chatham QC	174	C3
Bruderheim AB	159	D4
Bruno SK	166	B2
Brussels ON	172	B2
Buchans NL	183	D3
Buckingham QC	174	B3
Buffalo Creek BC	157	F4
Buffalo Lake AB	157	F1
Buffalo Narrows SK	159	D2
Burford ON	172	C3
Burgeo NL	182	D3
Burin NL	183	E4
Burk's Falls ON	171	D4
Burlington ON	173	D3
Burnaby BC	163	D3
Burns Lake BC	157	E2
Burnt Islands NL	182	C4
Bury QC	175	E3
Cabano QC	178	A2
Cache Creek BC	163	E1
Caledon ON	172	C2
Caledon East ON	172	C2
Caledonia ON	172	C3
Caledon Vil. ON	172	C2
Calgary AB	164	C3
Calmar AB	159	D4
Cambridge NS	180	C3
Cambridge ON	172	C3
Cambridge-Narrows NB	180	C3
Campbellford ON	173	E1
Campbell River BC	162	B2
Campbellton NB	178	C2
Camperville MB	167	D2
Camrose AB	159	D4
Canal Flats BC	164	B3
Candle Lake SK	160	B4
Canmore AB	164	B3
Canning NS	180	C2
Cannington ON	173	D1
Canora SK	166	C2
Canso NS	181	F2
Cantley QC	174	B3
Cap-aux-Meules QC	179	D2
Cap-Chat QC	178	C1
Cap-de-la-Madeleine QC	175	D2
Cape Breton Reg. Mun. NS	181	F1
Cape St. George NL	182	C3
Cap-Pele NB	179	E4
Capreol ON	170	C3
Cap-St-Ignace QC	175	F1
Cap-Santé QC	175	E1
Caraquet NB	179	D2
Carberry MB	167	D4
Carbonear NL	183	E4
Cardigan PE	179	F4
Cardinal ON	174	B4
Cardston AB	164	C4
Carleton Place ON	174	A3
Carleton-St-Omer QC	178	C2
Carlisle ON	172	C2
Carlyle SK	166	C4
Carmacks YT	155	D3
Carman MB	167	E4
Carmanville NL	183	E3
Carndruff SK	166	C4
Caronport SK	166	A3
Carrot River SK	160	C4
Carseland AB	164	C3
Carstairs AB	164	C2
Cartwright MB	167	D4
Cartwright NL	183	F1
Casselman ON	174	B3
Cassidy BC	162	C3
Castlegar BC	164	A4
Castor AB	165	D2
Catalina NL	183	E3
Causapscal QC	178	B1
Cavendish PE	179	E4
Cawston BC	163	E3
Cayuga ON	172	C3
Cedar BC	162	C3
Central Saanich BC	163	D4
Centreville NS	180	C2
Centreville-Wareham-Trinity NL	183	E3
Chalk River ON	171	E4
Chambly QC	175	D3
Chambord QC	176	B3
Champlain QC	175	D2
Chandler QC	179	D2
Channel-Port aux Basques NL	182	C4
Chapais QC	176	A2
Chapleau ON	170	B2
Charlesbourg QC	175	E1
Charlie Lake BC	158	A2
Charlo NB	178	C2
Charlottetown PE	179	E4
Charny QC	175	E2
Chase BC	163	F1
Châteauguay QC	174	C3
Château-Richer QC	175	E1
Chatham ON	172	B4
Chatham-Kent ON	172	A4
Chemainus BC	162	C3
Chertsey QC	174	C2
Chesley ON	172	B1

Chester NS	180	C3
Chestermere AB	164	C3
Chesterville ON	174	B4
Chéticamp NS	181	E3
Chetwynd BC	157	E1
Chibougamau QC	176	A2
Chicoutimi QC	176	C3
Chilliwack BC	163	E3
Chipman NB	178	C4

Christina Lake BC	164	A4
Churchbridge SK	166	C3
Chute-aux-Outardes QC	177	D2
Clair NB	178	A3
Clairmont AB	157	F1
Clarence-Rockland ON	174	B3
Clarenville NL	183	E3
Claresholm AB	164	C4
Clarington ON	173	D2

Clarke's Beach NL	183	E4
Clark's Hbr. NS	180	B4
Clermont QC	176	C4
Clinton ON	172	B2
Clyde River PE	179	E4
Coaldale AB	165	D4
Coalhurst AB	165	D4
Coaticook QC	175	E3
Cobalt ON	171	D2

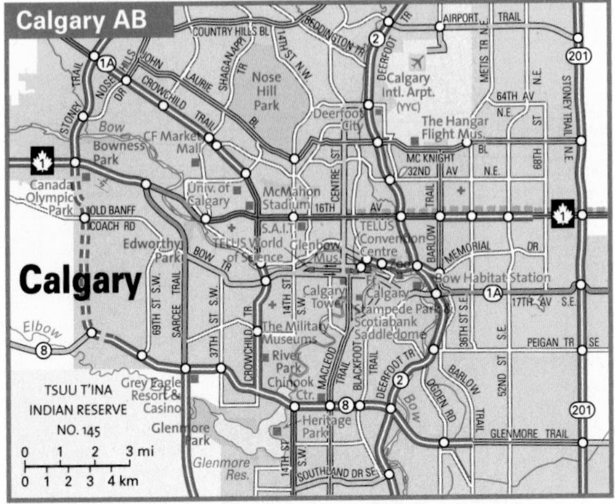

Calgary AB

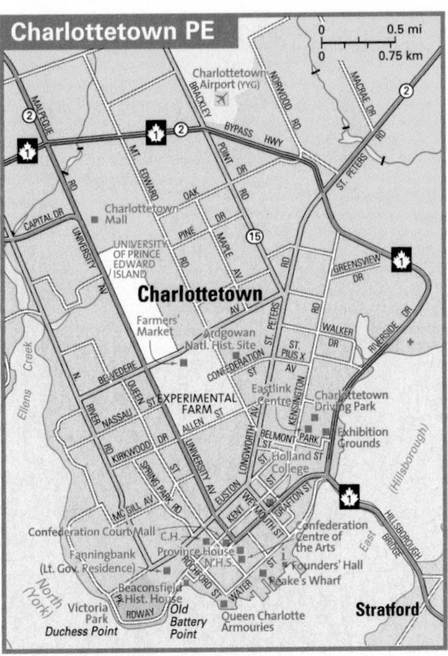

Edmonton AB

Fredericton NB

Ajax ON	173	D2
Aklavik NT	155	D1
Alban ON	170	C3
Albanel QC	176	B3
Alberta Beach AB	158	C4
Alberton PE	179	E3
Aldergrove BC	163	D3
Alexandria ON	174	B3
Alfred ON	174	B3
Alix AB	164	C2
Allan SK	165	F2
Alliston ON	172	C1
Alma QC	176	B3
Almonte ON	174	A3
Altona MB	167	E4
Amherst NS	180	C1
Amherstburg ON	172	A4
Amos QC	171	E1
Amqui QC	178	B1
Ange-Gardien QC	175	D3
Angus ON	172	C1
Annapolis Royal NS	180	B3
Antigonish NS	181	E1
Arborg MB	167	E3
Arcola SK	166	C4
Armagh QC	175	F1
Armstrong BC	164	A3
Arnold's Cove NL	183	E4
Arnprior ON	174	A3
Arthur ON	172	C2
Ascot Corner QC	175	E3
Ashcroft BC	163	E1
Asquith SK	165	F2
Assiniboia SK	166	A4
Athabasca AB	159	D3
Athens ON	174	B4
Atholville NB	178	C2
Atikokan ON	168	C2
Aurora ON	173	D2
Austin QC	175	D3
Avondale NL	183	E4
Ayer's Cliff QC	175	D3
Aylesford NS	180	C2
Aylmer ON	172	C3
Aylmer QC	174	B3
Ayr ON	172	C3
Baddeck NS	181	E1
Badger NL	183	D3
Baie-Comeau QC	177	D2
Baie-du-Febvre QC	175	D2
Baie-Ste-Anne NB	179	D3
Baie-St-Paul QC	176	C3
Baie Verte NL	183	D2
Balcarres SK	166	B3
Balgonie SK	166	B3
Balmoral NB	178	C2
Bancroft ON	171	E4
Banff AB	164	B3
Barraute QC	171	E2
Barrhead AB	158	C3
Barrie ON	173	D1
Barry's Bay ON	171	E4
Bas-Caraquet NB	179	D2
Bashaw AB	164	C1
Bassano AB	165	D3
Bathurst NB	179	D2
Battleford SK	159	F4
Bay Bulls NL	183	E4
Bayfield ON	172	B2
Bay Roberts NL	183	E4
Beachburg ON	174	A3
Beamsville ON	173	D3
Beauceville QC	175	E2
Beauharnois QC	174	C3

Bedford QC	175	D4
Beechville NS	181	D3
Beeton ON	173	D2
Behchokò NT	155	F2
Beiseker AB	164	C2
Bella Bella BC	156	C4
Belledune NB	178	C2
Bellefeuille QC	174	C3
Belleville ON	173	E1
Belmont QC	175	D3
Beloeil QC	175	D3
Benito MB	166	C2
Bentley AB	164	C2
Beresford NB	179	D2
Berthierville QC	175	D2
Bertrand NB	179	D2
Berwick NS	180	C2
Betsiamites QC	178	A1
Bible Hill NS	181	D2
Bienfait SK	166	C4
Biggar SK	165	F2
Big River SK	159	F3
Binscarth MB	166	C3
Birch Hills SK	160	B4
Birchy Bay NL	183	E3
Birtle MB	167	D3
Bishop's Falls NL	183	D3
Black Diamond AB	164	C3
Blackfalds AB	164	C2
Black Lake QC	175	E2
Blacks Hbr. NB	180	A2
Blackville NB	178	C4
Blaine Lake SK	160	B4
Blainville QC	174	C3
Blairmore AB	164	C4
Blanc-Sablon QC	183	D1

Boissevain MB	167	D4
Bolton ON	173	D2
Bon Accord AB	159	D4
Bonaventure QC	179	D2
Bonavista NL	183	E3
Bonnyville AB	159	E3
Borden-Carleton PE	179	E4
Bothwell ON	172	B3
Botwood NL	183	D2
Bouctouche NB	179	D3
Bourget ON	174	B3
Bowden AB	164	C2
Bowen Island BC	163	D3
Bow Island AB	165	D4
Bowmanville ON	173	D2
Bowser BC	162	C3
Bowsman MB	166	C2
Boyle AB	159	D3
Bracebridge ON	171	D4
Bradford ON	173	D2
Bradford-W. Gwillimbury ON	173	D1
Bragg Creek AB	164	C3
Brampton ON	173	D2
Brandon MB	167	D4
Brant ON	172	C3
Brantford ON	172	C3
Brantville NB	179	D3
Bridgenorth ON	173	E1
Bridgetown NS	180	B3
Bridgewater NS	180	C3
Brigham QC	175	D3
Brighton ON	173	E2
Brigus NL	183	E4
Bristol NB	178	B4
Broadview SK	166	C3
Brochet MB	161	D1

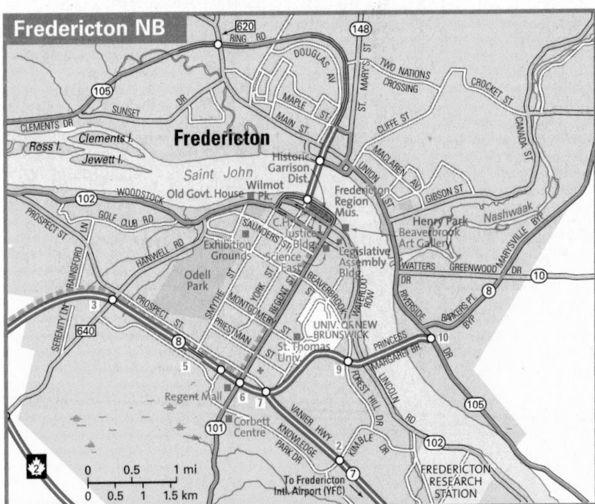

Charlottetown PE

Stratford

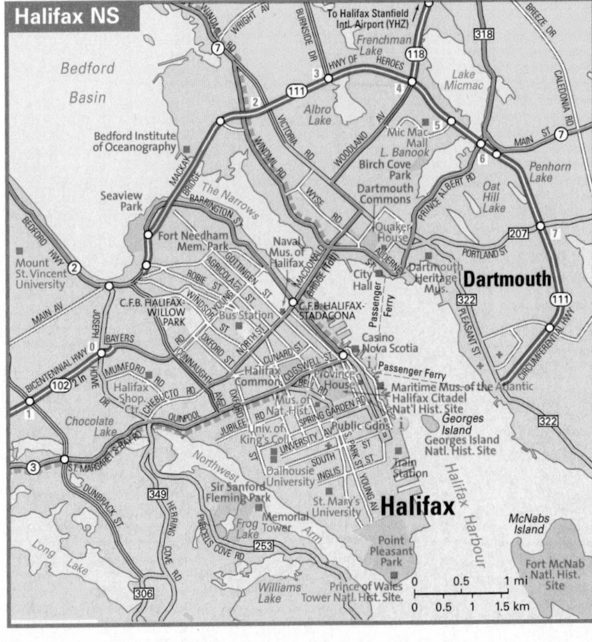

Halifax NS

Bedford Basin

Dartmouth

Halifax

Figures after entries indicate page number and grid reference.

Cobble Hill BC 163 D4
Cobourg ON 173 E2
Cocagne NB 179 D4
Cochrane AB 164 C3
Cochrane ON 170 C1
Colborne ON 173 E2
Colchester ON 172 A4
Coldbrook NS 180 C2
Cold Lake AB 159 E3
Coldstream BC 164 A3
Coleraine QC 175 E2
Collingwood ON 172 C1
Comox BC 162 C2
Compton QC 175 E3
Conception Bay South NL 183 F4
Conception Hbr. NL 183 E4
Constance Bay ON 174 A3
Contrecoeur QC 175 D3
Cookshire QC 175 E3
Cookstown ON 173 D1
Coombs BC 162 C3
Coquitlam BC 163 D3
Cormack NL 182 C2
Cormorant MB 161 D3
Corner Brook NL 182 C3
Cornwall ON 174 B4
Cornwall PE 179 E4
Coronach SK 166 A4
Coronation AB 165 D2
Coteau-du-Lac QC 174 C3
Côte-Nord-du-Golfe-du-St-Laurent QC 182 B1
Courtenay BC 162 C2
Cowansville QC 175 D3
Cowichan Bay BC 163 D4
Cox's Cove NL 182 C2
Crabtree QC 174 C2
Cranbrook BC 164 B4
Crane River MB 167 D2
Creemore ON 172 C1
Creighton SK 161 D3
Creston BC 164 B4
Crossfield AB 164 C3
Cross Lake MB 161 E3
Crowsnest Pass AB 164 C4
Crystal Beach ON 173 D3
Crystal City MB 167 D4
Cudworth SK 165 F1
Cumberland BC 162 C3
Cumberland House SK 160 C4
Cupar SK 166 B3
Cupids NL 183 E4
Cut Knife SK 159 F4
Dalhousie NB 178 C2
Dalmeny SK 165 F2
Danville QC 175 D3
Dartmouth NS 181 D3
Dauphin MB 167 D3
Davidson SK 165 F2
Dawson YT 155 D2
Dawson Creek BC 157 F1
Daysland AB 159 D4
Deep River ON 171 E3
Deer Lake NL 182 C2
Dégelis QC 178 A2
Delburne AB 164 C2
Déléage QC 174 B2
Delhi ON 172 C3
Déline NT 155 E1
Delisle QC 176 C3
Delisle SK 165 F2
Deloraine MB 167 D4
Delson QC 174 C3
Delta BC 163 D3
Denare Beach SK 161 D3
Denman Island BC 162 C3
Deschaillons-sur-St-Laurent QC 175 D2
Deschambault Lake SK 160 C3
Deseronto ON 173 F1
Des Ruisseaux QC 174 B2
Devon AB 159 D4
Didsbury AB 164 C2
Dieppe NB 179 D4
Digby NS 180 B3
Disraeli QC 175 E2
Doaktown NB 178 C4
Dolbeau-Mistassini QC 176 B3
Dominion NS 181 F1
Donnacona QC 175 E2
Dorchester NB 180 C1
Dover NL 183 E3
Drayton ON 172 C2
Drayton Valley AB 158 C4
Dresden ON 172 B4
Drumheller AB 165 D2
Drummond NB 178 B3
Drummondville QC 175 D3
Dryden ON 168 C3
Duchess AB 165 D3
Duck Bay MB 167 D2
Duck Lake SK 160 B4
Dudswell QC 175 E3
Duncan BC 162 C4
Dundalk ON 172 C1
Dundee NB 178 C2
Dundurn SK 165 F2
Dunham QC 175 D4
Dunnottar MB 167 E3
Dunnville ON 173 D3
Durham ON 172 C1
Dutton ON 172 B3
E. Angus QC 175 E3
E. Broughton QC 175 E2
Eastend SK 165 E4
E. Gwillimbury ON 173 D1
Eckville AB 164 C2
Edmonton AB 159 D4
Edmundston NB 178 B3
Edson AB 158 C4
Eel River Crossing NB 178 C2
Eganville ON 174 A3
Elkford BC 164 C4
Elkhorn MB 166 C4
Elk Pt. AB 159 E4
Elliot Lake ON 170 C3
Elmira ON 172 C2
Elmsdale NS 181 D2
Elmvale ON 172 C1
Elrose SK 165 F2
Embree NL 183 E2
Embrun ON 174 B3
Emerson MB 167 E4
Enderby BC 164 A3
Enfield NS 181 D2
Englee NL 183 D1
Englehart ON 171 D2
Entwistle AB 158 C4
Erickson MB 167 D3
Erin ON 172 C2
Errington BC 162 C3
Eskasoni NS 181 F1
Espanola ON 170 C3
Essex ON 172 A4
Esterhazy SK 166 C3
Estevan SK 166 C4
Eston SK 165 E3
Ethelbert MB 167 D2
Evansburg AB 158 C4
Everett ON 172 C1
Exeter ON 172 B3
Fairisle NB 179 D3
Fairview AB 158 B2
Falher AB 158 B2
Falkland BC 163 F1
Fall River NS 181 D3
Fanny Bay BC 162 C3
Farnham QC 175 D3
Faro YT 155 E3
Fatima QC 179 F3
Fenelon Falls ON 173 D1
Fergus ON 172 C2
Ferme-Neuve QC 174 B1
Fermont QC 183 E1
Fernie BC 164 C4
Ferryland NL 183 F4
Flatrock NL 183 F4
Flin Flon MB 161 D3
Florence NS 180 C2
Florenceville NB 178 B4
Foam Lake SK 166 B2
Fogo NL 183 E2
Forest ON 172 B3
Forestburg AB 165 D1
Forestville QC 178 A1
Ft. Chipewyan AB 155 F2
Fort-Coulonge QC 174 A3
Ft. Erie ON 173 D3
Ft. Frances ON 168 B4
Ft. Good Hope NT 155 E2
Ft. Liard NT 155 E3
Ft. Macleod AB 164 C4
Ft. McMurray AB 159 E1
Ft. McPherson NT 155 D1
Ft. Nelson BC 155 F3
Ft. Providence NT 155 E2
Ft. Qu'Appelle SK 166 B3
Ft. Resolution NT 155 F2
Ft. St. James BC 157 D2
Ft. St. John BC 158 A2
Ft. Saskatchewan AB 159 D4
Ft. Simpson NT 155 F2
Ft. Smith NT 155 F2
Fortune NL 183 D4
Ft. Vermilion AB 155 F3
Fox Creek AB 158 B3
Frampton QC 175 E2
Frankford ON 173 E1
Franklin QC 174 C4
Fraser Lake BC 157 D2
Fredericton NB 180 A1
Fredericton Jct. NB 180 A1
Frelighsburg QC 175 D4
French Creek BC 162 C3
French River ON 171 D3
Frontenac QC 175 E3
Fruitvale BC 164 A4
Gabriola Island BC 162 C3
Gagetown NB 180 B1
Gambo NL 183 E3
Gananoque ON 173 F1
Gander NL 183 E3
Garnish NL 183 D4
Gaspé QC 179 D1
Gatineau QC 174 B3
Genelle BC 164 A4
Gentilly QC 175 D2
Georgetown ON 172 C2
Georgetown PE 179 F4
Georgina ON 173 D1
Geraldton ON 169 E3
Gibbons AB 159 D4
Gibsons BC 163 D3
Gift Lake AB 158 C3
Gilbert Plains MB 167 D3
Gillam MB 161 F1
Gimli MB 167 E3
Girardville QC 176 B3
Glace Bay NS 181 F4
Gladstone MB 167 D3
Glenboro MB 167 D4
Glencoe ON 172 B3
Glenwood NL 183 E3
Glovertown NL 183 E3
Goderich ON 172 B2
Golden BC 164 B2
Gold River BC 162 B2
Gold River NS 180 C3
Gore Bay ON 170 C4
Granby QC 175 D3
Grand Bank NL 183 D4
Grand Bay-Westfield NB 180 B2
Grand Bend ON 172 B3
Grand Ctr. AB 159 E3
Grande-Anse NB 179 D2
Grande Cache AB 157 F2
Grande-Digue NB 179 D4
Grande Prairie AB 157 F1
Grande-Rivière QC 179 D1
Grande-Vallée QC 179 D1
Grand Falls (Grand-Sault) NB 178 B3
Grand Falls-Windsor NL 183 D3
Grand Forks BC 164 A4
Grand Manan NB 180 A3
Grand-Mère QC 175 D2
Grand Rapids MB 161 E4
Grand-Remous QC 174 B2
Grand Valley ON 172 C2
Grandview MB 167 D3
Gravelbourg SK 165 F3
Gravenhurst ON 171 D4
Greater Napanee ON 173 F1
Greater Sudbury ON 170 C3
Greenstone ON 169 E3
Greenwood BC 164 A4
Greenwood NS 180 C2
Grenfell SK 166 C3
Grenville-sur-la-Rouge QC 174 C3
Gretna MB 167 E4
Grimsby ON 173 D3
Grimshaw AB 158 B2
Grindrod BC 164 A3
Guelph ON 172 C2
Gull Lake SK 165 E3
Guysborough NS 181 E2
Hagersville ON 172 C3
Hague SK 165 F1
Haileybury ON 171 D2
Haines Jct. YT 155 D3
Haldimand ON 173 D3
Halifax NS 181 D3
Halton Hills ON 172 C2
Hamilton ON 172 C3
Hamiota MB 167 D3
Hammonds Plains Road NS 181 D3
Hampton NB 180 B2
Hanna AB 165 D2
Hanover ON 172 C1
Hantsport NS 180 C2
Happy Valley-Goose Bay NL 183 F1
Harbour Breton NL 183 D4
Harbour Grace NL 183 E4
Hardisty AB 165 D1
Hardwicke NB 179 D3
Hare Bay NL 183 E3
Harrison Hot Sprs. BC 163 E3
Harriston ON 172 C2
Harrow ON 172 A4
Hartland NB 178 B4
Hartney MB 167 D4
Hastings ON 173 E1
Haute-Aboujagane NB 179 E4
Havelock ON 173 E1
Havre-aux-Maisons QC 179 F3
Havre Boucher NS 181 E1
Havre-St-Pierre QC 177 F1
Hawkesbury ON 174 B3
Hay River NT 155 F2
Hearst ON 170 B1
Heart's Delight-Islington NL 183 E4
Hebbville NS 180 C3
Hébertville QC 176 C3
Henryville QC 175 D4
Hensall ON 172 B2
Herbert SK 165 F3
Hermitage NL 183 D4
Hérouxville QC 175 D1
Herring Cove NS 181 D3
Highlands BC 163 D4
High Level AB 155 F3
High Prairie AB 158 C2
High River AB 164 C3
Hillsborough NB 180 C1
Hillsburgh ON 172 C2
Hinton AB 158 B4
Holyrood NL 183 E4
Hope BC 163 E3
Hornby Island BC 162 C3
Hornepayne ON 169 F3
Houston BC 156 C2
Hudson QC 174 C3
Hudson Bay SK 160 C4
Hudson's Hope BC 158 A2
Hull QC 174 B3
Humber Arm South NL 182 C3
Humboldt SK 166 B2
Hunter River PE 179 E4
Huntingdon QC 174 C4
Huntsville ON 171 D4
Huron East ON 172 B2
Iberville QC 175 D3
Île-à-la-Crosse SK 159 F2
Indian Head SK 166 B3
Ingersoll ON 172 C3
Inkerman NB 179 D2
Innisfail AB 164 C2
Innisfil ON 173 D1
Inuvik NT 155 D1
Invermere BC 164 B3
Inverness NS 181 E1
Iqaluit NU 7
Irishtown-Summerside NL 182 C3
Iroquois ON 174 B4
Iroquois Falls ON 170 C1
Irricana AB 164 C2
Isle-aux Morts NL 182 C4
Ituna SK 166 B3
Jarvis ON 172 C3
Jasper AB 158 B4
Joe Batt's Arm-Barr'd Islands-Shoal Bay NL 183 E2
Joliette QC 174 C2
Jonquière QC 176 C3
Kaleden BC 163 F3
Kamloops BC 163 F1
Kamsack SK 166 C2
Kanata ON 174 A3
Kapuskasing ON 170 C1
Kars ON 174 B3
Kaslo BC 164 B4
Kawartha Lakes ON 173 D1
Kedgwick NB 178 B2
Kelowna BC 163 F2
Kelvington SK 166 B2
Kemptville ON 174 B4
Kenora ON 167 F4
Kensington PE 179 E4
Kent BC 163 E3
Kentville NS 180 C2
Keremeos BC 163 F3
Kerrobert SK 165 E2
Keswick ON 173 D1
Keswick Ridge NB 180 A1
Kikino AB 159 D3
Killam AB 165 D1
Killarney MB 167 D4
Kimberley BC 164 B4
Kincardine ON 172 B1
Kindersley SK 165 E2
Kingsey Falls QC 175 D3
King's Pt. NL 183 D2
Kingston NS 180 C2
Kingston ON 173 F1
Kingsville ON 172 A4
Kinistino SK 160 B4
Kipling SK 166 C3
Kippens NL 182 C3
Kirkland Lake ON 171 D2
Kitchener ON 172 C2
Kitimat BC 156 B2
Kitscoty AB 159 E4
Kugluktuk NU 155 F1
La Baie QC 176 C3
Labelle QC 174 B2
Labrador City NL 183 E1
Labrecque QC 176 C3
Lac-au-Saumon QC 178 B1
Lac-aux-Sables QC 175 D1
Lac-Beauport QC 175 E1
Lac-Bouchette QC 176 B3
Lac-Brome QC 175 D3
Lac-Drolet QC 175 E3
Lac du Bonnet MB 167 F3
Lac-Etchemin QC 175 F2
Lachine QC 174 C3
Lachute QC 174 C3
Lac La Biche AB 159 D3
Lac-Mégantic QC 175 E3
Lacolle QC 174 C4
Lacombe AB 164 C2
La Conception QC 174 B2
La Crête AB 155 F3
Lac-Supérieur QC 174 C2
Ladysmith BC 162 C3
La Guadeloupe QC 175 E2
Lake Country BC 163 F2
Lake Cowichan BC 162 C4
Lake Echo NS 181 D3
Lakefield ON 173 E1
Lake Louise AB 164 B2
Lakeshore ON 172 A4
La Loche SK 159 E1
La Malbaie QC 176 C4
Lambton QC 175 E3
Lambton Shores ON 172 B3
Lamèque NB 179 D2
La Minerve QC 174 B2
Lamont AB 159 D4
Lampman SK 166 C4
Lanark ON 174 A4
Landrienne QC 171 E1
Langdon AB 164 C3
L'Ange-Gardien QC 175 E1
Langenburg SK 166 C3
Langford BC 163 D4
Langham SK 165 F1
Langley BC 163 D3
Lanigan SK 166 B2
L'Annonciation QC 174 B2
Lanoraie QC 175 D2
L'Anse-St-Jean QC 176 C3
Lantz NS 181 D2
Lantzville BC 162 C3
La Pêche QC 174 A3
La Plaine QC 174 C3
La Pocatière QC 175 F1
Lappe ON 169 D4
La Prairie QC 174 C3
Lark Hbr. NL 182 C2
La Ronge SK 160 B3
LaSalle ON 172 A4
La Sarre QC 171 D1
L'Ascension-de-Notre-Seigneur QC 176 C3
La Scie NL 183 D2
Lashburn SK 159 E4
L'Assomption QC 174 C3
Laterrière QC 176 C3
La Tuque QC 175 D1
Laurentian Hills ON 171 E4
Laurier-Station QC 175 E2
Laurierville QC 175 E2
Laval QC 174 C3
Lavaltrie QC 175 D3
L'Avenir QC 175 D3
Lawn NL 183 D4
Lawrencetown NS 180 C2
Leader SK 165 E3
Leaf Rapids MB 161 D2
Leamington ON 172 A4
Lebel-sur-Quévillon QC 171 E1
Le Bic QC 178 A1
Leduc AB 159 D4
Legal AB 159 D4
Le Goulet NB 179 D2
Lennoxville QC 175 E3
L'Épiphanie QC 174 C3
Léry QC 174 C3
Les Coteaux QC 174 C3
Les Éboulements QC 176 C4
Les Escoumins QC 178 A1
Les Méchins QC 178 C1
L'Étang-du-Nord QC 179 F3
Lethbridge AB 165 D4
Lévis QC 175 E1
Lewisporte NL 183 E2
Lillooet BC 163 E1
Lincoln NB 180 A1
Lincoln ON 173 D3
Lindsay ON 173 D1
Lions Bay BC 163 D3
L'Islet QC 175 F1
L'Isle-Verte QC 178 A2
Listowel ON 172 C2
Little Current ON 170 C4
Lively ON 170 C3
Liverpool NS 180 C4
Lloydminster AB 159 E4
Lloydminster SK 159 E4
Lockeport NS 180 C4
Logan Lake BC 163 E1
London ON 172 B3
Longlac ON 169 E3

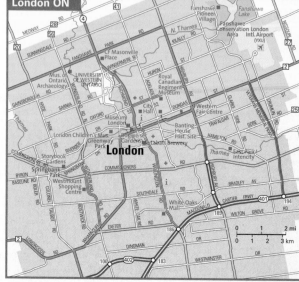

Entries in **bold color** indicate cities with detailed inset maps.

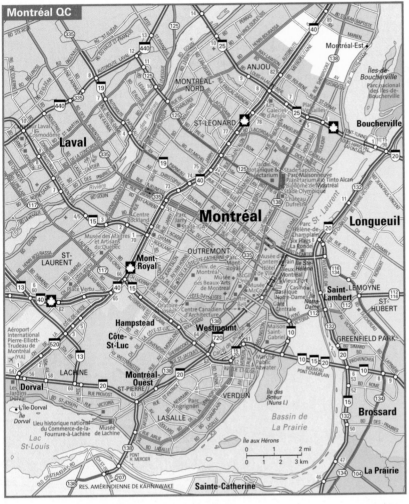

Longue-Rive QC 178 A1
Longueuil QC 174 C3
Loretteville QC 175 E1
L'Orignal ON 174 B3
Lorrainville QC 171 D2
Louisbourg NS 181 F4
Louiseville QC 175 D2
Lourdes NL 182 C3
Lucan ON 172 B3
Lucknow ON 172 B2
Lumby BC 164 A3
Lumsden NL 183 E2
Lumsden SK 166 B3
Lunenburg NS 180 C3
Luseland SK 165 E2
Lynn Lake MB 161 D1
Lyster QC 175 E2
Macamic QC 171 D1
MacGregor MB 167 E4
Mackenzie BC 157 E1
Macklin SK 165 E2
Madoc ON 173 E1
Magog QC 175 D3
Magrath AB 165 D4
Mahone Bay NS 180 C3
Maidstone SK 159 F4
Maisonnette NB 179 D2
Malartic QC 171 E2
Manawan QC 174 C1
Manigotagan MB 167 F3
Manitou MB 167 E4
Manitouwadge ON 169 F3
Maniwaki QC 174 A2
Manning AB 158 B1
Mannville AB 159 E4
Maple Creek SK 165 E4
Maple Ridge BC 163 D3
Marathon ON 169 E4
Maria QC 178 C2
Marieville QC 175 D3
Markdale ON 172 C1
Markham ON 173 D2
Markstay-Warren ON 171 D3
Marmora ON 173 E1
Marshall SK 159 E4
Martensville SK 165 F2
Marystown NL 183 E4
Mascouche QC 174 C3
Mashteuiatsh QC 176 B3
Maskinongé QC 175 D2
Masset BC 156 A2
Masson-Angers QC 174 B3
Matagami QC 171 E1
Matane QC 178 B1
Mattawa ON 171 D3
Maxville ON 174 B3
Mayerthorpe AB 158 C4
Mayo YT 155 D2
McAdam NB 180 A1
McBride BC 157 F3
McCreary MB 167 D3
McLennan AB 158 B2
McWatters QC 171 D2
Meadow Lake SK 159 F3
Meadows NL 182 C3
Meaford ON 172 C1
Medicine Hat AB 165 D4
Melfort SK 160 B4
Melita MB 167 D4
Melocheville QC 174 C3
Melville SK 166 C3
Memramcook NB 180 C1
Mercier QC 174 C3
Merrickville-Wolford ON 174 B4
Merritt BC 163 E2
Merville BC 162 C2
Messines QC 174 A2
Métabetchouan-Lac-à-la-Croix QC 176 C3
Metcalfe ON 174 B3
Metchosin BC 163 D4
Middleton NS 180 C2
Midland ON 172 C1
Mildmay ON 172 B2
Milestone SK 166 B4
Milk River AB 165 D4
Mill Bay BC 163 D4
Millbrook ON 173 E1
Mille-Isles QC 174 C3
Millet AB 159 D4
Milltown-Head of Bay d'Espoir NL 183 D3
Milton NS 180 C4
Milton ON 172 C2
Milverton ON 172 C2
Minitonas MB 167 D2
Minnedosa MB 167 D3
Minto NB 178 C4
Minto ON 172 C2
Mirabel QC 174 C3
Miracle Beach BC 162 B2
Miramichi NB 179 D3
Mira Road NS 181 F1
Miscou Ctr. NB 179 D2
Miscouche PE 179 E4
Mission BC 163 D3
Mississauga ON 173 D2
Mississippi Mills ON 174 A3
Mistissini QC 176 B1
Mitchell ON 172 B2
Moncton NB 179 D4
Mono ON 172 C2
Montague PE 179 F4
Mont-Carmel QC 176 C4
Mont-Joli QC 178 B1
Mont-Laurier QC 174 B2
Montmagny QC 175 F1
Montréal QC 174 C3
Montrose BC 164 A4
Moose Jaw SK 166 B3
Moose Lake MB 161 D4
Moosomin SK 166 C3
Morden MB 167 E4
Morin-Heights QC 174 C3
Morinville AB 159 D4
Morris MB 167 E4
Morrisburg ON 174 B4
Mt. Albert ON 173 D1
Mt. Brydges ON 172 B3
Mt. Forest ON 172 C2
Mt. Moriah NL 182 C3
Mt. Pearl NL 183 F4
Mt. Uniacke NS 181 D2
Mulgrave NS 181 E1
Mundare AB 159 D4
Munster ON 174 A3
Murdochville QC 179 D1
Murray Hbr. PE 179 F4
Murray River PE 179 F4
Musgrave Hbr. NL 183 E2
Musgravetown NL 183 E3
Nackawic NB 180 A1
Naicam SK 166 B2
Nakusp BC 164 A3
Nanaimo BC 162 C3
Nanoose Bay BC 162 C3
Nantes QC 175 E3
Nanton AB 164 C3
Napanee ON 173 F1
Napierville QC 174 C3
Naramata BC 163 F2
Nauwigewauk NB 180 B2
Neepawa MB 167 D3
Neguac NB 179 D3
Nelson BC 164 B4
Neuville QC 175 E1
New Aiyansh BC 156 B1
New Carlisle QC 179 D2
New Glasgow NS 181 D2
New Hamburg ON 172 C3
New Hazelton BC 156 C1
New Liskeard ON 171 D2
Newmarket ON 173 D2
New Maryland NB 180 A1
Newport QC 179 D2
New Richmond QC 178 C2
New Tecumseth ON 173 D2
New Victoria NS 181 F1
New Waterford NS 181 F1
New-Wes-Valley NL 183 E2
Niagara Falls ON 173 D3
Niagara-on-the-Lake ON 173 D3
Nicholas Denys NB 178 C2
Nicolet QC 175 D2
Nigadoo NB 179 D2
Nipawin SK 160 C4
Nipigon ON 169 E3
Niverville MB 167 E4
Nobleton ON 173 D2
Nominingue QC 174 B2
Norfolk ON 172 C3
Normandin QC 176 B3
Norman's Cove-Long Cove NL 183 E4
Norman Wells NT 155 E2
Norris Arm NL 183 D3
Norris Pt. NL 182 C2
N. Battleford SK 159 F4
N. Bay ON 171 D3
N. Cowichan BC 162 C4
Northeastern Manitoulin and the Islands ON 170 C4
N. Perth ON 172 C2
N. Rustico PE 179 E4
N. Saanich BC 163 D4
N. Sydney NS 181 F1
N. Tetagouche NB 178 C2
N. Vancouver BC 163 D3
Norton NB 180 B1
Norway House MB 161 E4
Norwich ON 172 C3
Norwood ON 173 E1
Notre Dame de Lourdes MB 167 E4
Notre-Dame-des-Érables NB 179 D2
Notre-Dame-des-Pins QC 175 E2
Notre-Dame-du-Bon-Conseil QC 175 D2
Notre-Dame-du-Lac QC 178 A2
Notre-Dame-du-Laus QC 174 B2
Notre-Dame-du-Mont-Carmel QC 175 D2
Notre-Dame-du-Nord QC 171 D2
Notre-Dame-du-Portage QC 178 A2
Nouvelle QC 178 C2
Noyan QC 175 D4
Oak Bay BC 163 D4
Oak Lake MB 167 D4
Oakville ON 173 D2
Oka QC 174 C3
Okanagan Falls BC 163 F3
Okotoks AB 164 C3
Old Perlican NL 183 E3
Olds AB 164 C2
O'Leary PE 179 E4
Oliver BC 163 F3
Omemee ON 173 E1
Onaping ON 170 C3
108 Mile Ranch BC 157 F4
150 Mile House BC 157 E4
100 Mile House BC 157 F4
Onoway AB 159 D4
Orangeville ON 172 C2
Orillia ON 173 D1
Ormstown QC 174 C4
Oromocto NB 180 B1
Orono ON 173 D2
Osgoode ON 174 B3
Oshawa ON 173 D2
Osler SK 165 F1
Osoyoos BC 163 F3
Ottawa ON 174 B3
Outlook SK 165 F2
Owen Sound ON 172 C1
Oxbow SK 166 C4
Oxford NS 181 D1
Oyen AB 165 E2
Pabos QC 179 D1
Pabos Mills QC 179 D2
Paisley ON 172 B1
Palmarolle QC 171 D1
Palmerston ON 172 C2
Papineauville QC 174 B3
Paquetville NB 179 D2
Paradise NL 183 F4
Paris ON 172 C3
Parkhill ON 172 B3
Parksville BC 162 C3
Parrsboro NS 180 C2
Parry Sound ON 171 D4
Pasadena NL 182 C3
Paspébiac QC 179 D2
Peace River AB 158 B2
Peachland BC 163 F2
Pelham ON 173 D3
Pelican Narrows SK 160 C3
Pelly Crossing YT 155 D3
Pemberton BC 163 D2
Pembroke ON 174 A3
Penetanguishene ON 172 C1
Penhold AB 164 C2
Pense SK 166 B3
Penticton BC 163 F3
Percé QC 179 E1
Perth ON 174 A4
Perth-Andover NB 178 B4
Petawawa ON 171 E4
Peterborough ON 173 E1
Peterview NL 183 D2
Petitcodiac NB 180 C1
Petit-Matane QC 178 B1
Petit-Rocher NB 179 D2
Petrolia ON 172 B3
Pickering ON 173 D2
Picton ON 173 F2
Pictou NS 181 D1
Picture Butte AB 165 D4
Pilot Butte SK 166 B3
Pilot Mound MB 167 D4
Pinawa MB 167 F3
Pincher Creek AB 164 C4
Pinehouse SK 159 F2
Pintendre QC 175 E1
Pitt Meadows BC 163 D3
Placentia NL 183 E4
Plantagenet ON 174 B3
Plaster Rock NB 178 B3
Plessisville QC 175 E2
Plum Coulee MB 167 E4
Plympton-Wyoming ON 172 B3
Pohénégamook QC 178 A3
Pointe-à-la-Croix QC 178 C2
Pointe-au-Père QC 178 B1
Pointe-aux-Outardes QC 178 B1
Pointe-Calumet QC 174 C3
Pointe-du-Lac QC 175 D2
Pt. Edward ON 172 A3
Pointe-Lebel QC 177 D2
Pointe-Sapin NB 179 D3
Pointe-Verte NB 178 C2
Pt. Leamington NL 183 D2
Ponoka AB 164 C1
Ponteix SK 165 F4
Pontiac QC 174 A3
Pont-Lafrance NB 179 D3
Pont-Landry NB 179 D2
Pont-Rouge QC 175 E1
Porcupine ON 170 C1
Porcupine Plain SK 166 C1
Portage la Prairie MB 167 E4
Port Alberni BC 162 C3
Port Alice BC 162 A1
Port au Choix NL 182 C1
Port au Port East NL 182 C3
Port-Cartier QC 177 E2
Port Colborne ON 173 D3
Port Coquitlam BC 163 D3
Port-Daniel-Gascons QC 179 D2
Port Dover ON 172 C3
Port Edward BC 156 B2
Port Elgin ON 172 B1
Port Hardy BC 162 A1
Port Hawkesbury NS 181 E1
Port Hope ON 173 E2
Port McNeill BC 162 A1
Portneuf QC 175 E1
Port Perry ON 173 D2
Port Saunders NL 183 D1
Port Stanley ON 172 B3
Pouce Coupe BC 157 F1
Pouch Cove NL 183 F4
Powassan ON 171 D3
Powell River BC 162 C2
Powerview MB 167 F3
Pré-d'en-Haut NB 180 C1

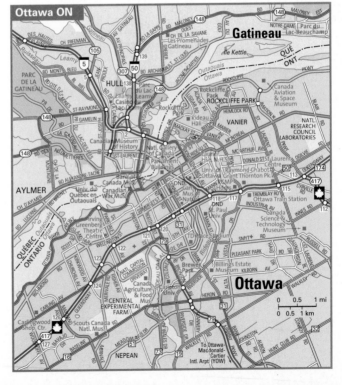

Figures after entries indicate page number and grid reference.

Preeceville SK 166 C2
Prescott ON 174 B4
Prévost QC 174 C3
Price QC 178 B1
Prince Albert SK 160 B4
Prince Edward ON 173 F2
Prince George BC 157 E2
Prince Rupert BC 156 B2
Princeton BC 163 F3
Princeville QC 175 E2
Provost AB 165 E2
Pugwash NS 181 D1
Qualicum Beach BC 162 C3
Qu'Appelle SK 166 B3

Regina SK 166 B3
Regina Beach SK 166 B3
Renfrew ON 174 A3
Renous NB 178 C3
Repentigny QC 174 C3
Reserve Mines NS 181 F1
Revelstoke BC 164 A3
Rexton NB 179 D4
Richelieu QC 175 D3
Richibucto NB 179 D4
Richmond BC 163 D3
Richmond ON 174 B3
Richmond QC 175 D3
Richmond Hill ON 173 D2

Roberval QC 176 B3
Roblin MB 166 C3
Robson BC 164 A4
Rocanville SK 166 C3
Rock Forest QC 175 E3
Rockland ON 174 B3
Rockwood ON 172 C2
Rocky Hbr. NL 182 C2
Rocky Mtn. House AB 164 C2
Roddickton NL 183 D1
Rodney ON 172 B4
Rogersville NB 179 D4
Rose Blanche-
Harbour Le Cou NL 182 C4

Rosetown SK 165 F2
Rossburn MB 167 D3
Rossland BC 164 A4
Ross River YT 155 E3
Rosthern SK 165 F1
Rothesay NB 180 B2
Rouyn-Noranda QC 171 D2
Roxboro QC 174 C3
Roxton Falls QC 175 D3
Roxton Pond QC 175 D3
Royston BC 162 C2
Rusagonis NB 180 A1
Russell MB 166 C3
Russell ON 174 B3

Saanich BC 163 D4
Sackville NB 180 C1
Sacré-Coeur QC 178 A2
St. Adolphe MB 167 E4
St-Agapit QC 175 E2
St-Aimé-des-Lacs QC 176 C4
St-Alban QC 175 D1
St. Alban's NL 183 D4
St. Albert AB 159 D4
St-Albert QC 175 D2
St-Alexandre QC 175 D3
St-Alexandre-
de-Kamouraska QC 178 A2
St-Alexis-des-Monts QC 175 D2
St-Alphonse-Rodriguez QC 174 C2
St-Ambroise QC 176 C3
St-André-Avellin QC 174 B3
St-André-d'Argenteuil QC 174 C3
St. Andrews NB 180 A2
St-Anselme QC 175 E2
St. Anthony NL 183 D1
St-Antoine NB 179 D4

St-Antoine QC 174 C3
St-Antoine-de-Tilly QC 175 E2
St-Antonin QC 178 A2
St-Apollinaire QC 175 E2
St-Armand QC 175 D4
St-Arsène QC 178 A2
St-Arthur NB 178 C2
St-Aubert QC 175 F1
St-Augustin-de-Desmaures QC 175 E1
St-Basile QC 175 E1
St-Benoît-Labre QC 175 E2
St-Bernard QC 175 E2
St. Bernard's-
Jacques Fontaine NL 183 E4
St-Boniface QC 175 D2
St-Brieux SK 166 B1
St-Bruno QC 176 C3
St-Bruno-de-Guigues QC 171 D2
St-Calixte QC 174 C2
St-Canut QC 174 C3
St-Casimir QC 175 D2
St. Catharines ON 173 D3

St-David-de-Falardeau QC 176 C3
St-Denis-sur-Richelieu QC 175 D3
St-Dominique QC 175 D3
St-Donat QC 174 C2
Ste-Adèle QC 174 C2
Ste-Agathe-de-Lotbinière QC 175 E2
Ste-Agathe-des-Monts QC 174 C2
Ste-Angèle-de-Mérici QC 178 B1
Ste. Anne MB 167 E4
Ste-Anne-de-Beaupré QC 175 E1
Ste-Anne de Kent NB 179 D4
Ste-Anne-de-la-Pérade QC 175 D2
Ste-Anne-de-Madawaska NB 178 B3
Ste-Anne-des-Monts QC 178 C1
Ste-Anne-des-Plaines QC 174 C3
Ste-Barbe QC 174 C3
Ste-Béatrix QC 174 C2
Ste-Blandine QC 178 B1
Ste-Brigide-d'Iberville QC 175 D3
Ste-Catherine-de-Hatley QC 175 D3
Ste-Catherine-de-la-
Jacques-Cartier QC 175 E1

Québec QC

Saskatoon SK

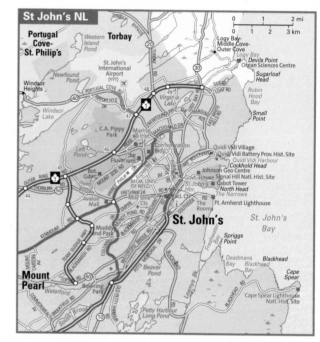

Québec QC 175 E1
Queens Reg. Mun. NS 180 C4
Quesnel BC 157 E3
Quinte West ON 173 E1
Quispamsis NB 180 B2
Racine QC 175 D3
Radium Hot Springs BC 164 B3
Radville SK 166 B4
Rainbow Lake AB 155 F3
Rainy River ON 167 F4
Ramea NL 182 C4
Rapid City MB 167 D3
Rawdon QC 174 C2
Raymond AB 165 D4
Raymore SK 166 B2
Redcliff AB 165 D3
Red Deer AB 164 C2
Red Lake ON 168 B2
Redvers SK 166 C4
Redwater AB 159 D4

Ridgetown ON 172 B4
Rigaud QC 174 C3
Rimbey AB 164 C1
Rimouski QC 178 A1
Rimouski-Est QC 178 A1
Ripon QC 174 B3
River Hebert NS 180 C1
Rivers MB 167 D4
Riverton MB 167 E3
Riverview NB 179 D4
Rivière-au-Renard QC 179 D1
Rivière-Beaudette QC 174 C3
Rivière-Bleue QC 178 A3
Rivière-du-Loup QC 178 A2
Rivière-Ouelle QC 176 C4
Rivière-Verte NB 178 B3
Robert's Arm NL 183 D2
Roberts Creek BC 163 D3
Robertsonville QC 175 E2
Robertville NB 178 C2

St-Césaire QC 175 D3
St-Charles NB 179 D4
St. Charles ON 171 D3
St-Charles-Borromée QC 174 C2
St-Charles-de-Bellechasse QC 175 E1
St-Charles-de-Mandeville QC 174 C2
St-Charles-sur-Richelieu QC 175 D3
St-Chrysostome QC 174 C4
St. Claude MB 167 E4
St-Claude QC 175 E3
St-Clet QC 174 C3
St-Côme QC 174 C2
St-Côme-Linière QC 175 F2
St-Constant QC 174 C3
St-Cyprien QC 178 A2
St-Cyrille-de-Wendover QC 175 D2
St-Damase QC 175 D3
St-Damien QC 174 C2
St-Damien-de-Buckland QC 175 E2

Ste-Cécile NB 179 D2
Ste-Claire QC 175 E2
Ste-Clotilde-de-
Châteauguay QC 174 C3
Ste-Clotilde-de-Horton QC 175 D2
Ste-Croix QC 175 E2
St-Édouard QC 174 C3
Ste-Élisabeth QC 174 C2
Ste-Émélie-de-l'Énergie QC 174 C2
Ste-Félicité QC 178 B1
Ste-Foy QC 175 E1
Ste-Hélène-de-Bagot QC 175 D3
Ste-Hénédine QC 175 E2
Ste-Jeanne-d'Arc QC 176 B3
Ste-Julie QC 174 C3
Ste-Justine QC 175 F2
Ste-Luce QC 178 B1
St-Elzéar QC 175 E2
Ste-Madeleine QC 175 D3

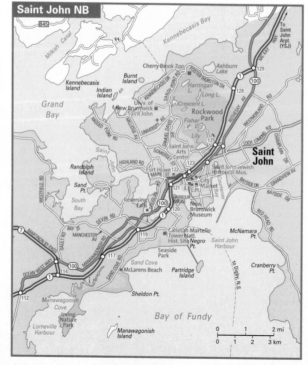

Entries in **bold color** indicate cities with detailed inset maps.

Ste-Marcelline de-Kildare QC ...174 C2		
Ste-Marguerite-Estérel QC ...174 C2		
Ste-Marie QC ...175 E2		
Ste-Marie-St-Raphaël NB ...179 D2		
Ste-Marthe-du-Cap QC ...175 D2		
Ste-Martine QC ...174 C3		
Ste-Mélanie QC ...174 C2		
Ste-Perpétue QC ...175 F1		
St-Éphrem-de-Beauce QC ...175 E2		
Ste-Rosalie QC ...175 D3		
Ste. Rose du Lac MB ...167 D3		
Ste-Sophie QC ...174 C3		
St-Esprit QC ...174 C3		
Ste-Thècle QC ...175 D1		
Ste-Thérèse QC ...174 C3		
Ste-Thérèse-de-Gaspé QC ...179 D1		
St-Étienne-de-Lauzon QC ...175 E2		
Ste-Eugène QC ...175 D3		
Ste-Eustache QC ...174 C3		
Ste-Véronique QC ...174 B2		
St-Fabien QC ...178 A1		
St-Faustin-Lac-Carré QC ...175 C3		
St-Félicien QC ...176 B3		
St-Félix-de-Kingsey QC ...175 D3		
St-Félix-de-Valois QC ...174 C3		
St-Ferdinand QC ...175 E2		
St-Ferréol-les-Neiges QC ...175 E1		
St-Flavien QC ...175 E2		
St-François-de-la- Rivière-du-Sud QC ...175 E1		
St-François-du-Lac QC ...175 D2		
St-Frédéric QC ...175 E2		
St-Fulgence QC ...176 C3		
St-Gabriel QC ...174 C2		
St-Gabriel-de-Rimouski QC ...178 B1		
St-Gédéon QC ...176 C3		
St-Gédéon-de-Beauce QC ...175 F3		
St-George NB ...180 C2		
St-George ON ...172 C3		
St. George's NL ...182 C3		
St-Georges QC ...175 F2		
St-Georges QC ...175 D2		
St-Georges-de-Cacouna QC ...178 A2		
St-Germain-de-Grantham QC ...175 D3		
St-Gervais QC ...175 E1		
St-Gilles QC ...175 E2		
St-Grégoire QC ...175 D2		
St-Guillaume QC ...175 D2		
St-Henri QC ...175 E1		
St-Hilarion QC ...176 C4		
St-Honoré QC ...176 C3	St-Hugues QC ...175 D3	St-Isidore NB ...179 D3
St-Honoré-de-Shenley QC ...175 E2	St-Hyacinthe QC ...175 D3	St-Isidore QC ...175 E2
St-Hubert QC ...174 C3	St-Ignace NB ...179 D4	St. Jacobs ON ...172 C2
St-Hubert-de- Rivière-du-Loup QC ...178 A2	St-Ignace-de-Loyola QC ...175 D2	St-Jacques QC ...174 C2
	St-Irénée NB ...179 D3	St-Jacques-Coomb's Cove NL ...183 D4
		St-Jean-de-Dieu QC ...178 A2
		St-Jean-de-Matha QC ...174 C2
		St-Jean-Port-Joli QC ...175 E1
		St-Jean-sur-Richelieu QC ...175 D3
		St-Jérôme QC ...174 C3
		Saint John NB ...180 B2
		St. John's NL ...183 F4
		St-Joseph-de-Beauce QC ...175 E2
		St-Jovite QC ...174 C2
		St-Jude QC ...175 D3
		St-Laurent QC ...175 E1
		St-Lawrence NL ...183 D4
		St-Lazare MB ...166 C3
		St-Lazare-de-Bellechasse QC ...175 E1
		St-Léolin NB ...179 D2
		St. Leonard NB ...178 B3
		St-Léonard-d'Aston QC ...175 D2
		St-Léon-de-Standon QC ...175 F2
		St-Léon-le-Grand QC ...175 B1
		St-Liboire QC ...175 D3
		St-Lin-Laurentides QC ...174 C3
		St-Louis-de-France QC ...175 D2
		St-Louis-de-Kent NB ...179 D4
		St-Ludger QC ...175 E3
		St-Lunaire-Griquet NL ...183 D1
		St-Malachie QC ...175 E2
		St-Marc-des-Carrières QC ...175 D1
		St-Marc-sur-Richelieu QC ...175 D3
		St-Martin QC ...175 F2
		St. Marys ON ...172 B3
		St-Mathieu-du-Parc QC ...175 D2
		St-Maxime-du-Mont-Louis QC ...179 D1
		St-Michel-de-Bellechasse QC ...175 E1
		St-Michel-des-Saints QC ...174 C1
		St-Narcisse QC ...175 D2
		St-Nazaire QC ...176 C3
		St-Nicéphore QC ...175 D3
		St-Nicolas QC ...175 E1
		St-Ours QC ...175 D3
		St-Pacôme QC ...175 E1
		St-Pamphile QC ...175 F1
		St-Pascal QC ...178 A2
		St-Patrice-de-Beaurivage QC ...175 E2
		St. Paul AB ...159 E4
		St-Paul QC ...175 D2
		St-Paulin QC ...175 D2
		St-Pie QC ...175 D3
		St-Pierre-Jolys MB ...167 E4
		St-Pierre-les-Becquets QC ...175 D2
		St-Placide QC ...174 C3
		St-Polycarpe QC ...174 C3
		St-Prime QC ...176 B3
		St-Prosper QC ...175 F2
		St-Quentin NB ...178 B3
		St-Raphaël QC ...175 E1
		St-Raymond QC ...175 E1
		St-Rémi QC ...174 C3
		St-Roch-de-Richelieu QC ...175 D3
		St-Sauveur NB ...179 D3

St-Sauveur-des-Monts QC ...174 C3	St-Victor QC ...175 E2	Sarnia ON ...172 A3	Sexsmith AB ...157 F1
St-Siméon QC ...179 D2	St-Walburg SK ...159 F4	Saskatoon SK ...165 F2	Shannon QC ...175 E1
St-Simon NB ...179 D2	St-Wenceslas QC ...175 D2	Saugeen Shores ON ...172 B1	Shaunavon SK ...165 F4
St-Stanislas QC ...175 D2	St-Zacharie QC ...175 F2	Sault Ste. Marie ON ...170 B3	Shawinigan QC ...175 D2
St. Stephen NB ...180 A2	St-Zénon QC ...174 C2	Sayabec QC ...178 B1	Shawinigan-Sud QC ...175 D2
St-Théodore-d'Acton QC ...175 D3	St-Zotique QC ...174 C3	Schomberg ON ...173 D2	Shawville QC ...174 A3
St. Thomas ON ...172 B3	Salaberry-de-Valleyfield QC ...174 C3	Scott QC ...175 E2	Shediac NB ...179 D4
St-Timothée QC ...174 C3	Salisbury NB ...180 C1	Scoudouc NB ...179 D4	Shediac Bridge NB ...179 D4
St-Tite QC ...175 D1	Salmo BC ...164 B4	Seaforth ON ...172 B2	Shediac Cape NB ...179 D4
St-Tite-des-Caps QC ...175 E1	Salmon Cove NL ...183 E4	Sechelt BC ...162 C3	Shelburne NS ...180 B4
St-Ubalde QC ...175 D1	Salmon Arm BC ...163 F1	Sedgewick AB ...165 D1	Shelburne ON ...172 C2
St-Ulric QC ...178 B1	Salmon River NS ...180 B4	Selkirk MB ...167 E3	Shellbrook SK ...160 B4
St-Urbain QC ...176 C4	Sandy Bay SK ...160 C2	Sennetere QC ...177 E2	Sherbrooke QC ...175 E3
St-Valère QC ...175 D2	Saratoga Beach BC ...162 B2	Sept-Îles QC ...177 E2	Sherwood Park AB ...164 C1

Toronto ON — map

Vaughan, Markham, SCARBOROUGH, NORTH YORK, YORK, EAST YORK, Toronto, ETOBICOKE, Mississauga

LAKE ONTARIO

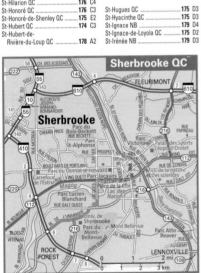

Sherbrooke QC — map

Sherbrooke, FLEURIMONT, ROCK FOREST, LENNOXVILLE

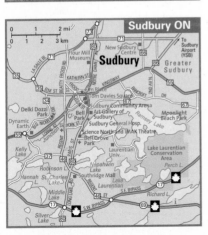

Sudbury ON — map

Sudbury, New Sudbury, Greater Sudbury

Downtown Toronto ON — map

LAKE ONTARIO

POINTS OF INTEREST

Art Gallery of Ontario ...A1	Hockey Hall of Fame ...B2	Royal Alexandra Theatre ...A1
Canadian Broadcasting Center ...A2	Jack Layton Ferry Terminal ...B2	Royerson University ...B1
CF Toronto Eaton Centre ...B1	MacKenzie House ...B1	Roy Thomson Hall ...A2
CN Tower ...A2	Massey Hall ...B1	Saint Lawrence Centre ...B2
Design Exchange ...B2	Metro Toronto Convention Ctr ...A2	Saint Lawrence Market ...B2
Ed Mirvish Theatre ...B1	Old City Hall ...B1	Scotiabank Arena ...B2
Four Seasons Centre for the Performing Arts ...A1	Princess of Wales Theatre ...A1	Sony Centre for the Perf. Arts ...B2
The Grange ...A1	Queen's Quay Terminal ...B2	Textile Museum of Canada ...A1
Harbourfront Centre ...A2	Redpath Sugar Museum ...B2	Toronto Stock Exchange ...A1
	Ripley's Aquarium ...A2	Union Station ...B2
	Rogers Centre ...A2	Yonge-Dundas Square ...B1

Figures after entries indicate page number and grid reference.

Shippagan NB 179 D2
Shoal Lake MB 167 D3
Shubenacadie NS 181 D2
Sicamous BC 164 A3
Sidney BC 163 D4
Silver Creek BC 163 F1
Simcoe ON 172 C3
Sioux Lookout ON 168 C2
Slave Lake AB 158 C3
Smithers BC 156 C2
Smiths Falls ON 174 A4
Smithville ON 173 D3
Smoky Lake AB 159 D3
Smooth Rock Falls ON 170 C1

Springdale NL 183 D2
Springhill NS 180 C1
Springside SK 166 C2
Sproat Lake BC 162 C3
Spruce Grove AB 159 D4
Squamish BC 163 D2
Stanstead QC 175 D4
Stayner ON 172 C1
Steinbach MB 167 E4
Stellarton NS 181 D2
Stephenville NL 182 C3
Stephenville Crossing NL 182 C3
Stettler AB 165 D2
Stewiacke NS 181 D2

Summerside PE 179 E4
Sundre AB 164 C2
Sundridge ON 171 D4
Sunny Corner NB 178 D3
Surrey BC 163 D3
Sussex NB 180 B1
Sussex Corner NB 180 B1
Sutton ON 173 D1
Sutton QC 175 D4
Swan Hills AB 158 C3
Swan River MB 166 C2
Swift Current SK 165 F3
Sydney NS 181 F1
Sydney Mines NS 181 F1

Thamesford ON 172 C3
Thamesville ON 172 B4
The Pas MB 161 D4
Thessalon ON 170 B3
Thetford Mines QC 175 D4
Thompson MB 161 E2
Thornbury ON 172 C1
Thorold ON 173 D3
Thorsby AB 159 D4
Three Hills AB 164 C2
Thunder Bay ON 169 D4
Thurso QC 174 B3
Tide Head NB 178 C2
Tignish PE 179 E3

Verdun QC 174 C3
Vermilion AB 159 E4
Vernon BC 164 A3
Victoria BC 163 D4
Victoria NL 183 E4
Victoriaville QC 175 D4
Viking AB 159 E4
Ville-Marie QC 171 D2
Virden MB 167 D4
Vulcan AB 164 C3

Wawa ON 169 F4
Wawanesa MB 167 D4
Wawota SK 166 C4
Wedgeport NS 180 B4
Weedon QC 175 E3
Welland ON 173 D3
Wellesley ON 172 C2
Wellington ON 173 E2
Wellington PE 179 E4
Wembley AB 157 F1
Wentworth-Nord QC 174 C3
Westbank BC 163 F2
Western Shore NS 180 C3
Westlock AB 159 D3

Wilkie SK 165 E2
Williams Lake BC 157 E4
Winchester ON 174 B4
Windermere BC 164 B3
Windsor NS 180 C2
Windsor ON 172 A4
Windsor QC 175 E3
Wingham ON 172 B3
Winkler MB 167 E4
Winnipeg MB 167 E4
Winnipeg Beach MB 167 E3
Winnipegosis MB 167 D2
Witless Bay NL 183 F4
Wolfville NS 180 C2

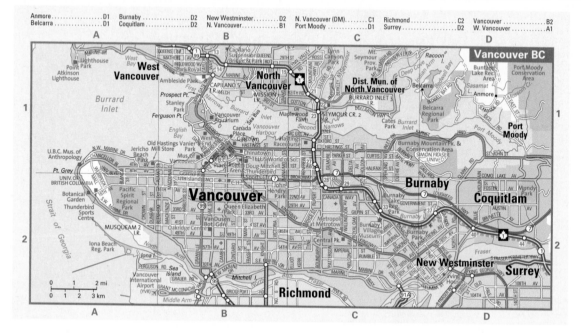

Anmore D1
Belcarra D1
Burnaby D2
Coquitlam D2
New Westminster D2
N. Vancouver B1
N. Vancouver (DM) C1
Port Moody D1
Richmond C2
Surrey D2
Vancouver B2
W. Vancouver A1

Snow Lake MB 161 D3
Somerset MB 167 E4
Sooke BC 162 C4
Sorel-Tracy QC 175 D2
Sorrento BC 163 F1
Souris MB 167 D4

Stirling AB 165 D4
Stirling ON 173 E1
Stoke QC 175 E4
Stonewall MB 167 E3
Stoney Pt. ON 172 A4
Stony Mtn. MB 167 E3

Sydney River NS 181 F1
Sylvan Lake AB 164 C2
Taber AB 165 D4
Tabusintac NB 179 D3
Tappen BC 163 F1
Tara ON 172 B1

Tilbury ON 172 A4
Tillsonburg ON 172 C3
Timberlea NS 181 D3
Timmins ON 170 C1
Tisdale SK 160 C4
Tofield AB 159 D4
Tofino BC 162 B3
Torbay NL 183 F4
Toronto ON 173 D2
Tottenham ON 173 D2
Tracadie-Sheila NB 179 D3
Trail BC 164 A4
Treherne MB 167 E4
Trent Hills ON 173 E1
Trenton NS 181 D2
Trenton ON 173 E2
Trepassey NL 183 F4
Tring-Jonction QC 175 E2
Triton NL 183 D2
Trochu AB 164 C2
Trois-Pistoles QC 178 A2
Trois-Rivières QC 175 D2
Truro NS 181 D2
Tuktoyaktuk NT 155 D1
Tumbler Ridge BC 157 F1
Turner Valley AB 164 C3
Tweed ON 173 E1
Twillingate NL 183 E2
Two Hills AB 159 E4
Ucluelet BC 162 B3
Union Bay BC 162 C3
Unity SK 165 E2
Upton QC 175 D3
Uxbridge ON 173 D2
Val-Comeau NB 179 D3
Valcourt QC 175 D3
Val-David QC 174 C2
Val-des-Monts QC 174 B3
Val-des-Sources QC 175 E3
Val-d'Or QC 171 E2
Valemount BC 157 F3
Val-Joli QC 175 E3
Vallée-Jonction QC 175 E2
Valleyview AB 158 B3
Val-Morin QC 174 C2
Val-Sennevile QC 171 E2
Vanderhoof BC 157 D2
Vankleek Hill ON 174 B3
Varennes QC 174 C3
Vaudreuil-Dorion QC 174 C3
Vauxhall AB 165 D4
Vegreville AB 159 D4
Venise-en-Québec QC 175 D4
Verchères QC 174 C3

Wadena SK 166 B2
Wainwright AB 159 E4
Wakaw SK 165 F1
Waldheim SK 165 F1
Walkerton ON 172 B1
Wallaceburg ON 172 A3
Warfield BC 164 A4
Warman SK 165 F2
Warwick QC 175 D3
Wasaga Beach ON 172 C1
Waterford ON 172 C3
Waterloo ON 172 C2
Waterloo QC 175 D3
Waterville NS 180 C2
Waterville QC 175 E3
Watford ON 172 B3
Watrous SK 166 B2
Watson Lake YT 155 E3
Waverley NS 181 D3

W. Lorne ON 172 B4
W. Nipissing ON 171 D3
W. Vancouver BC 163 D3
Westville NS 181 D2
Wetaskiwin AB 159 D4
Weyburn SK 166 B4

Wheatley ON 172 A4
Whistler BC 163 D2
Whitbourne NL 183 E4
Whitby ON 173 D2
Whitchurch-Stouffville ON 173 D2
White City SK 166 B3
Whitecourt AB 158 C3
Whitehorse YT 155 D3
White Rock BC 163 D3
Whitewood SK 166 C3
Wiarton ON 172 B1
Wickham QC 175 D3
Wikwemikong ON 170 C4

Wolseley SK 166 C3
Wood Buffalo AB 159 E1
Woodstock NB 178 B4
Woodstock ON 172 C3
Woodville ON 173 D2
Wotton QC 175 E3

Wright QC 174 A2
Wynyard SK 166 B2
Wyoming ON 172 B3
Yamachiche QC 175 D2
Yarmouth NS 180 B4
Yellowknife NT 155 F2
Yorkton SK 166 C3
Youbou BC 162 C3

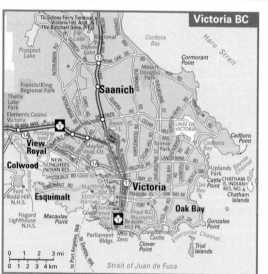

Souris PE 179 F4
Southampton ON 172 B1
S. Bruce Peninsula ON 172 B1
Southey SK 166 B3
S. Huron ON 172 B3
S. Indian Lake MB 161 E1
S. River ON 171 D4
Spallumcheen BC 164 A3
Spaniard's Bay NL 183 E4
Sparwood BC 164 C4
Spirit River AB 157 F1
Spiritwood SK 159 F4

Stony Plain AB 159 D4
Stouffville ON 173 D2
Stoughton SK 166 C4
Strasbourg SK 166 B3
Stratford ON 172 C2
Strathmore AB 164 C3
Strathroy ON 172 B3
Sturgeon Falls ON 171 D3
Sturgis SK 166 C2
Sudbury ON 170 C3
Summerford NL 183 D2
Summerland BC 163 F2

Tatamagouche NS 181 D2
Tavistock ON 172 C3
Taylor BC 158 A2
Tecumseh ON 172 A4
Teeswater ON 172 B2
Telkwa BC 156 C2
Temagami ON 171 D3
Témiscaming QC 171 D3
Terrace BC 156 C2
Terrace Bay ON 169 E4
Terrebonne QC 174 C3
Teulon MB 167 E3

Wadena SK 166 B2
Val-d'Or QC 171 E2

Warfield BC 164 A4
Warman SK 165 F2
Warwick QC 175 D3
Wasaga Beach ON 172 C1
Waterford ON 172 C3
Waterloo ON 172 C2
Waterloo QC 175 D3
Waterville NS 180 C2
Waterville QC 175 E3
Watford ON 172 B3
Watrous SK 166 B2
Watson Lake YT 155 E3
Waverley NS 181 D3

Entries in **bold color** indicate cities with detailed inset maps.

MEXICO

Acámbaro 186 B3
Acaponeta 186 A2
Acapulco 186 B4
Acayucan 187 D3
Actopan 186 C2
Agua Dulce 187 D3
Agua Prieta 184 C1
Aguascalientes 186 B2
Ajalpan 186 C3
Álamo 186 C2
Allende 185 E2
Altamira 186 C2
Alvarado 187 D3
Apan 186 C3
Apatzingán 186 B3
Apizaco 186 C3
Apodaca 185 E3
Arcelia 186 B3
Arriaga 187 D4
Atlixco 186 C3
Atoyac de Álvarez 186 B4
Autlán de Navarro 186 A2
Berriozábal 187 D4
Caborca 184 B1
Cabo San Lucas 184 C4
Calvillo 186 B2
Campeche 187 E2
Cananea 184 C1
Cancún 187 F2
Cárdenas 187 D3
Castaños 185 E3
Catemaco 187 D3
Celaya 186 B2
Cerro Azul 186 C2
Champotón 187 E3
Chapala 186 A2
Chetumal 187 F3
Chiapa 187 E4
Chihuahua 185 D2
Chilpancingo 186 C4
Cholula 186 C3
Cintalapa 187 D4
Cd. Acuña 185 E2
Cd. Altamirano 186 B3
Cd. Camargo 185 D3
Cd. Constitución 184 B4
Cd. del Carmen 187 E3
Cd. Guzmán 186 A3
Cd. Hidalgo 186 B3
Cd. Ixtepec 187 D4
Cd. Juárez 185 D1
Cd. Lerdo 185 D4
Cd. Madero 186 C2
Cd. Mante 186 C1
Cd. Mendoza 186 C3
Cd. Miguel Alemán 185 F3
Cd. Obregón 184 C3
Cd. Valles 186 C2
Cd. Victoria 185 F4
Coatepec 186 C3
Coatzacoalcos 187 D3
Colima 186 A3
Comalcalco 187 D3
Comitán de Domínguez 187 E4
Comonfort 186 B2
Córdoba 186 C3
Cosamaloapan 187 D3
Cosoleacaque 187 D3
Costa Rica 184 C4
Cozumel 187 F2
Cuauhtémoc 184 C2
Cuautla 186 C3
Cuernavaca 186 C3
Culiacán 184 C4
Delicias 185 D2
Dolores Hidalgo 186 B2
Durango 185 D4
Ébano 186 C2
Emiliano Zapata 187 E3
Empalme 184 B2
Ensenada 184 A1
Escárcega 187 E3
Escuinapa de Hidalgo 186 A1
Felipe Carrillo Puerto 187 F3
Francisco I. Madero 185 E3
Fresnillo 185 E4
Frontera 185 E3
Frontera 187 E3
Garza García 185 E3
Gómez Palacio 185 D3
Guadalajara 186 A2
Guadalupe 185 E3
Guadalupe 186 B1
Guamúchil 184 C4
Guanajuato 186 B2
Guasave 184 C3
Guaymas 184 B2
Hermosillo 184 B2
Hidalgo del Parral 185 D3
Huajuapan de León 186 C3
Huatabampo 184 C3
Huatusco 186 C3
Huauchinango 186 C2
Huejutla de Reyes 186 C2
Huetamo de Núñez 186 B3
Huimanguillo 187 D3
Huixtla 187 E4
Hunucmá 187 E2
Iguala 186 C3
Irapuato 186 B2
Ixmiquilpan 186 C2
Ixtlán del Río 186 A2
Izucar de Matamoros 186 C3
Jacona 186 B3
Jalostotitlán 186 B2
Jáltipan de Morelos 187 D3
Jérez de García Salinas 186 A1
Jiménez 185 D3
Jiutepec 186 C3
Juchitán de Zaragoza 187 D4
Kanasín 187 F2
La Barca 186 B2
Lagos de Moreno 186 B2
La Paz 184 B4
La Piedad de Cabadas 186 B2
Las Choapas 187 D3
Lázaro Cárdenas 186 B3
León 186 B2
Linares 185 F4
Loma Bonita 187 D3
Loreto 186 B2
Los Mochis 184 C3
Los Reyes de Salgado 186 B3
Macuspana 187 E3
Magdalena de Kino 184 B1
Manzanillo 186 A3
Martínez de la Torre 186 C2
Matamoros 185 E4
Matamoros 185 F3
Matehuala 185 E4
Matías Romero 187 D4
Mazatlán 185 D4
Melchor Múzquiz 185 E3
Meoqui 185 D2
Mérida 187 F2
Mexicali 184 A1
México 186 C3
Minatitlán 187 D3
Misantla 186 C3
Monclova 185 E3
Montemorelos 185 F4
Monterrey 185 E3
Morelia 186 B3
Moroleón 186 B2
Naranjos 186 C2
Navojoa 184 C3
Navolato 184 C4
Netzahualcóyotl 186 C3
Nogales 184 B1
Nueva Italia de Ruiz 186 B3
Nueva Rosita 185 E3
Nuevo Casas Grandes 184 C2
Nuevo Laredo 185 F3
Oaxaca 186 C4
Ocotlán 186 A2
Ocozocoautla 187 D4
Orizaba 186 C3
Pachuca 186 C2
Pánuco 186 C2
Papantla 186 C2
Paraíso 187 D3
Parras de la Fuente 185 E4
Pátzcuaro 186 B3
Perote 186 C3
Petatlán 186 B4
Piedras Negras 185 E2
Playa del Carmen 187 F2
Poza Rica 186 C2
Progreso 187 E2
Puebla 186 C3
Puerto Peñasco 184 B1
Puerto Vallarta 186 A2
Puruándiro 186 B2
Querétaro 186 B2
Reynosa 185 F3
Rincón de Romos 186 B2
Río Bravo 185 F3
Río Grande 185 E4
Río Verde 186 B2
Sabinas Hidalgo 185 E3
Sahuayo 186 B2
Salamanca 186 B2
Salina Cruz 187 D4
Saltillo 185 E4
Salvatierra 186 B2
San Andrés Tuxtla 187 D3
San Buenaventura 185 E3
San Cristóbal de las Casas 187 E4
San Felipe 186 B2
San Fernando 185 F4
San Francisco del Rincón 186 B2
San José del Cabo 184 C4
San Juan de los Lagos 186 B2
San Juan del Río 186 B2
San Luis de la Paz 186 B2
San Luis Potosí 186 B2
San Luis Río Colorado 184 A1
San Miguel de Allende 186 B2
San Nicolás de los Garza 185 E3
San Pedro de las Colonias 185 E3
Santa Catarina 185 E3
Santiago 185 E4
Santiago Papasquiaro 185 D4
Sayula 186 A3
Silao 186 B2
Sombrerete 185 D4
Tacámbaro de Codallos 186 B3
Tala 186 A2
Tamazunchale 186 C2
Tampico 186 C2
Tantoyuca 186 C2
Tapachula 187 E4
Taxco 186 B3
Teapa 187 E3
Tecamachalco 186 C3
Tecate 184 A1
Tecomán 186 A3
Tehuacán 186 C3
Tehuantepec 187 D4
Tejupilco de Hidalgo 186 B3
Teloloapan 186 B3
Tenancingo 186 B3
Tenosique 187 E3
Teocaltiche 186 B2
Tepatitlán 186 B2
Tepeji de Ocampo 186 C3
Tepic 186 A2
Tequila 186 A2
Tequisquiapan 186 B2
Tequixquiac 186 C3
Teziutlán 186 C3
Ticul 187 F2
Tierra Blanca 186 C3
Tijuana 184 A1
Tizayuca 186 C3
Tizimín 187 F2
Tlapa de Comonfort 186 C3
Tlapacoyan 186 C3
Tlaxcala 186 C3
Toluca 186 B3
Tonalá 186 A2
Tonalá 187 D4
Torreón 185 D3
Tres Valles 187 D3
Tulancingo 186 C2
Tuxpam 186 C2
Tuxpan 186 A2
Tuxpan 186 A3
Tuxtepec 187 D3
Tuxtla Gutiérrez 187 E4
Umán 187 E2
Uruapan 186 B3
Valladolid 187 F2
Valle de Santiago 186 B2
Valle Hermoso 185 F3
Veracruz 187 D3
Víctor Rosales 186 B1
Villa Flores 187 D4
Villahermosa 187 E3
Xalapa 186 C3
Xicotepec de Juárez 186 C2
Zacapu 186 B3
Zacatecas 186 B1
Zacatlán 186 C2
Zamora de Hidalgo 186 B3
Zapopan 186 A2
Zapotiltic 186 A3
Zihuatanejo 186 B3
Zitácuaro 186 B3
Zumpango 186 C3
Zumpango del Río 186 B3

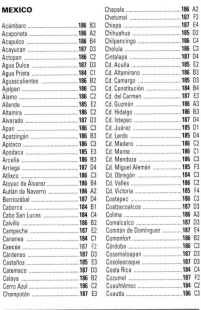

México MX

Acolman E1
Buenavista D1
Chalco E3
Chiautla E1
Chiconcuac E1
Chimalhuacán E2
Ciudad López Mateos C1
Coatlinchan E2
Cuajimalpa C3
Cuautitlán Izcalli C1
Dos RÌos C3
Ecatepec de Morelos D1
Ixtapaluca E3
Los Reyes E3
México D2
Magdalena Chichicaspa C2
Montecillo E2
Naucalpan C2
Netzahualcóyotl E2
Nexquipayac E1
San Bernardino E2
San Francisco Chimalpa C2
San Francisco Coacalco D1
San Lorenzo Acopilco C3
San Pedro Tepetitlán E1
San Salvador Atenco E1
San Vicente Chicoloapan E2
Santa Catarina E1
Santa Clara D1
Santo Tomás Chiconautla E1
Santiago Cuautlalpan E2
Santiago Tepatlaxco C2
Tepexpan E1
Tequisistlán E1
Texcoco E2
Tezoyuca E1
Tláhuac E3
Tlalnepantla C1
Tultitlán D1
Valle de Chalco E3
Villa Nicolás Romero C1
Xico E3
Xochimilco D3
Xometla E1

Colimilla B1
Coyula B1
El Aguacate B1
El Quince B2
El Vado B2
El Verde B2
Guadalajara A1
La Calerilla A2
La Punta B2
La Tijera A2
Las Pintitas B2
Los Gavilanes A2
Mascuala B1
Matatlán B1
Nuevo México A1
Puente Grande B2
San Antoni Juanacaxtle B2
San Francisco de la Soledad B2
San Agustín A2
San Sebastián El Grande A2
Santa Anita A2
Santa Cruz del Valle A2
Tlaquepaque A2
Tonalá B2
Zapopan A1

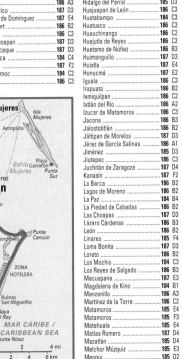

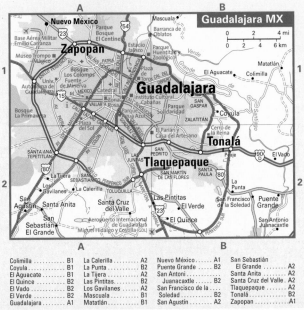

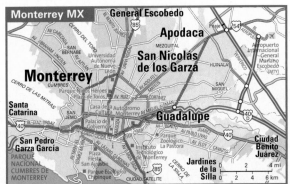

Miles

	Albuquerque, NM	Amarillo, TX	Anchorage, AK	Atlanta, GA	Baltimore, MD	Billings, MT	Birmingham, AL	Bismarck, ND	Boise, ID	Boston, MA	Buffalo, NY	Calgary, AB	Charleston, SC	Charleston, WV	Charlotte, NC	Cheyenne, WY	Chicago, IL	Cincinnati, OH	Cleveland, OH	Columbus, OH	Dallas, TX	Denver, CO	Des Moines, IA	Detroit, MI	El Paso, TX	Halifax, NS	Houston, TX	Indianapolis, IN	Jackson, MS	Jacksonville, FL	Kansas City, MO	Las Vegas, NV	Little Rock, AR	Los Angeles, CA	Louisville, KY
Albany, NY	2095	1811	4421	1010	333	2083	1093	1675	2526	172	292	2512	913	634	771	1789	832	730	484	621	1680	1833	1155	571	2326	877	1768	795	1331	1094	1282	2586	1354	2859	832
Albuquerque, NM		286	3563	1490	1902	991	1274	1333	966	2240	1808	1498	1793	1568	1649	538	1352	1409	1619	1476	754	438	1091	1608	263	2945	994	1298	1157	1837	894	578	900	806	1320
Amarillo, TX			3734	1206	1618	988	991	1398	1266	1957	1524	1669	1510	1285	1365	534	1069	1126	1335	1192	470	434	808	1324	438	2662	711	1014	874	1517	610	864	617	1092	1036
Anchorage, AK				4304	4297	2601	4253	2724	2745	4592	4133	2065	4495	4093	4348	3056	3584	3890	3935	3946	4087	3300	3421	3872	4002	4821	4328	3771	4294	4652	3547	3356	3929	3403	3886
Atlanta, GA					679	1889	150	1559	2218	1100	910	2395	317	503	238	1482	717	476	726	577	792	1403	967	735	1437	1805	800	531	386	344	801	2067	528	2237	419
Baltimore, MD						1959	795	1551	2401	422	370	2388	583	352	441	1665	708	521	377	420	1399	1690	1031	532	2045	1128	1470	600	1032	763	1087	2445	1072	2705	602
Billings, MT							1839	413	626	2254	1796	536	2157	1755	2012	455	1246	1552	1597	1608	1433	554	1007	1534	1255	2806	1673	1432	1836	2237	1088	965	1530	1239	1547
Birmingham, AL								1509	2170	1215	909	2346	466	578	389	1434	667	475	725	576	647	1356	919	734	1292	1921	678	481	241	494	753	1852	381	2092	369
Bismarck, ND									1039	1846	1388	794	1749	1347	1604	594	838	1144	1189	1200	1342	693	675	1126	1597	2398	1582	1024	1548	1906	801	1378	1183	1702	1139
Boise, ID										2697	2239	735	2520	2182	2375	737	1708	1969	2040	2036	1711	833	1369	1977	1206	3249	1952	1852	2115	2566	1376	760	1808	1033	1933
Boston, MA											462	2683	1003	741	861	1961	1003	862	654	760	1819	2004	1326	741	2465	714	1890	940	1453	1184	1427	2757	1493	3046	964
Buffalo, NY												2224	899	431	695	1502	545	442	197	333	1393	1546	868	277	2039	1167	1513	508	1134	1080	995	2299	1066	2572	545
Calgary, AB													2586	2184	2441	991	1675	1981	2026	2037	2114	1234	1512	1963	1936	2912	2355	1862	2385	2743	1638	1291	2020	1565	1977
Charleston, SC														468	204	1783	907	622	724	637	1109	1705	1204	879	1754	1708	1110	721	703	238	1102	2371	900	2554	610
Charleston, WV															265	1445	506	209	255	168	1072	1367	802	410	1718	1446	1192	320	816	649	764	2122	745	2374	251
Charlotte, NC																1637	761	476	520	433	1031	1559	1057	675	1677	1566	1041	575	625	385	956	2225	754	2453	464
Cheyenne, WY																	972	1233	1304	1300	979	100	633	1241	801	2513	1220	1115	1382	1829	640	843	1076	1116	1197
Chicago, IL																		302	346	359	936	1015	337	283	1543	1555	1108	184	750	1065	532	1768	662	2042	299
Cincinnati, OH																			253	105	958	1200	599	261	1605	1567	1079	116	700	803	597	1955	632	2215	106
Cleveland, OH																				144	1208	1347	669	171	1854	1359	1328	319	950	904	806	2100	882	2374	356
Columbus, OH																					1059	1266	665	192	1706	1465	1179	176	801	818	663	2021	733	2281	207
Dallas, TX																						887	752	1218	647	2524	241	913	406	1049	554	1331	327	1446	852
Denver, CO																							676	1284	701	2556	1127	1088	1290	1751	603	756	984	1029	1118
Des Moines, IA																								606	1283	1878	992	481	931	1315	194	1429	567	1703	595
Detroit, MI																									1799	1278	1338	318	960	1060	795	2037	891	2310	366
El Paso, TX																										3171	758	1489	1051	1642	1085	717	974	801	1499
Halifax, NS																											2595	1646	2158	1889	2133	3309	2198	3583	1669
Houston, TX																												839	445	884	795	1474	447	1558	972
Indianapolis, IN																													675	879	485	1843	587	2104	112
Jackson, MS																														598	747	1735	269	1851	594
Jacksonville, FL																															1148	2415	873	2441	766
Kansas City, MO																																1358	382	1632	516
Las Vegas, NV																																	1478	274	1874
Little Rock, AR																																		1706	526
Los Angeles, CA																																			2126

Kilometers

	Albany, NY	Albuquerque, NM	Amarillo, TX	Anchorage, AK	Atlanta, GA	Baltimore, MD	Billings, MT	Birmingham, AL	Bismarck, ND	Boise, ID	Boston, MA	Buffalo, NY	Calgary, AB	Charleston, SC	Charleston, WV	Charlotte, NC	Cheyenne, WY	Chicago, IL	Cincinnati, OH	Cleveland, OH	Columbus, OH	Dallas, TX	Denver, CO	Des Moines, IA	Detroit, MI	El Paso, TX	Halifax, NS	Houston, TX	Indianapolis, IN	Jackson, MS	Jacksonville, FL	Kansas City, MO	Las Vegas, NV	Little Rock, AR	Los Angeles, CA	Louisville, KY
Albuquerque, NM	3371																																			
Amarillo, TX	2914	460																																		
Anchorage, AK	7113	5733	6008																																	
Atlanta, GA	1625	2397	1940	6925																																
Baltimore, MD	536	3060	2603	6914	1093																															
Billings, MT	3352	1595	1590	4185	3039	3152																														
Birmingham, AL	1759	2050	1595	6843	241	1279	2959																													
Bismarck, ND	2695	2145	2249	4383	2508	2496	665	2428																												
Boise, ID	4064	1554	2037	4417	3569	3863	1007	3492	1672																											
Boston, MA	277	3604	3149	7389	1770	679	3627	1955	2970	4339																										
Buffalo, NY	470	2909	2452	6650	1464	595	2890	1463	2233	3603	743																									
Calgary, AB	4042	2410	2685	3323	3854	3842	862	3775	1278	1183	4317	3578																								
Charleston, SC	1469	2885	2430	7232	510	938	3471	750	2814	4055	1614	1446	4161																							
Charleston, WV	1020	2523	2068	6586	809	566	2824	930	2167	3511	1192	693	3514	753																						
Charlotte, NC	1241	2653	2196	6996	383	710	3237	626	2581	3821	1385	1118	3928	328	426																					
Cheyenne, WY	2879	866	859	4917	2385	2679	732	2307	956	1186	3155	2417	1595	2869	2325	2634																				
Chicago, IL	1339	2175	1720	5767	1154	1139	2005	1073	1348	2748	1614	877	2695	1459	814	1224	1564																			
Cincinnati, OH	1175	2267	1812	6259	766	838	2497	764	1841	3168	1387	711	3187	1001	336	766	1984	486																		
Cleveland, OH	779	2605	2148	6331	1168	607	2570	1167	1913	3282	1052	317	3260	1165	410	837	2098	557	407																	
Columbus, OH	999	2375	1918	6349	928	676	2587	927	1931	3276	1223	536	3278	1025	270	697	2092	578	169	232																
Dallas, TX	2703	1213	756	6576	1274	2251	2306	1041	2159	2753	2927	2241	3401	1784	1725	1659	1575	1506	1541	1944	1704															
Denver, CO	2949	705	698	5310	2257	2719	891	2182	1115	1340	3224	2488	1986	2743	2200	2508	161	1633	1931	2167	2037	1427														
Des Moines, IA	1858	1755	1300	5504	1556	1659	1620	1479	1086	2203	2134	1397	2433	1937	1290	1701	1018	542	964	1076	1070	1210	1088													
Detroit, MI	919	2587	2130	6230	1183	856	2468	1181	1812	3181	1192	446	3158	1414	660	1086	1997	455	420	275	309	1960	2066	975												
El Paso, TX	3743	423	705	6439	2312	3290	2019	2079	2570	1940	3966	3281	3115	2822	2764	2698	1289	2483	2582	2983	2745	1041	1128	2064	2895											
Halifax, NS	1411	4739	4283	7757	2904	1815	4515	3091	3858	5228	1149	1878	4685	2748	2327	2520	4043	2502	2521	2187	2357	4061	4113	3022	2056	5102										
Houston, TX	2845	1599	1144	6964	1287	2365	2692	1091	2545	3141	3041	2434	3789	1786	1918	1675	1963	1783	1736	2137	1897	388	1813	1596	2153	1220	4175									
Indianapolis, IN	1279	2088	1632	6068	854	965	2304	774	1648	2980	1512	817	2996	1160	515	925	1794	296	187	513	283	1469	1751	774	512	2396	2648	1350								
Jackson, MS	2142	1862	1406	6909	621	1660	2954	388	2491	3403	2338	1825	3837	1131	1313	1006	2224	1207	1126	1529	1289	653	2076	1498	1545	1691	3472	716	1086							
Jacksonville, FL	1760	2956	2441	7485	553	1228	3599	795	3067	4129	1905	1738	4413	383	1044	619	2943	1714	1292	1455	1316	1688	2817	2116	1706	2642	3039	1422	1414	962						
Kansas City, MO	2063	1438	981	5707	1289	1749	1751	1212	1289	2214	2296	1601	2636	1773	1229	1538	1030	856	961	1297	1067	891	970	312	1279	1746	3432	1279	780	1202	1847					
Las Vegas, NV	4161	930	1390	5400	3326	3934	1553	2980	2217	1223	4436	3699	2077	3815	3414	3580	1356	2845	3146	3379	3252	2142	1216	2299	3278	1154	5324	2372	2965	2792	3886	2185				
Little Rock, AR	2179	1448	993	6322	850	1725	2462	613	1903	2909	2402	1715	3250	1448	1199	1213	1731	1065	1017	1419	1179	526	1583	912	1434	1567	3537	719	944	433	1405	615	2378			
Los Angeles, CA	4600	1297	1757	5475	3599	4352	1994	3366	2739	1662	4901	4138	2518	4109	3820	3947	1796	3286	3564	3820	3670	2327	1656	2740	3717	1289	5765	2507	3385	2978	3928	2626	441	2745		
Louisville, KY	1339	2124	1667	6253	674	969	2489	594	1833	3110	1551	877	3181	981	404	747	1926	481	171	573	333	1371	1799	957	589	2412	2685	1564	180	956	1232	830	3015	846	3421	
Memphis, TN	1953	1662	1207	6570	626	1501	2615	388	2151	3144	2177	1492	3498	1223	975	988	1958	867	793	1194	956	750	1796	1158	1210	1789	3311	943	747	339	1179	862	2592	225	2959	621
México, MX	4520	2352	2051	8061	2821	3899	3641	2624	3952	3985	4574	4058	4737	3319	3541	3208	2911	3421	3360	3760	3522	1815	2750	3002	3776	1926	5709	1535	3287	2249	2956	2684	2846	2344	2981	3187
Miami, FL	2315	3467	2951	7997	1064	1784	4109	1307	3578	4639	2460	2293	4925	938	1599	1175	3455	2224	1836	2011	1871	2200	3329	2626	2254	3152	3595	1932	1924	1472	555	2359	4397	1915	4439	1744
Milwaukee, WI	1495	2294	1837	5651	1308	1295	1891	1228	1234	2813	1770	1033	2579	1614	967	1379	1628	143	640	713	730	1625	1697	608	611	2602	2658	1920	449	1344	1866	922	2909	1202	3350	634
Minneapolis, MN	2003	2154	1697	5110	1817	1804	1350	1736	693	2357	2280	1541	2039	2122	1477	1887	1418	658	1149	1223	1241	1607	1487	396	1121	2462	3168	1995	959	1852	2376	710	2698	1310	3139	1144
Mobile, AL	2162	2162	1780	7258	534	1630	3249	415	2840	3704	2306	1874	4187	1033	1347	920	2526	1485	1176	1578	1339	1028	2378	1794	1595	1981	1981	761	1186	301	660	1496	3092	735	3268	1006
Montréal, QC	370	3495	3038	6607	1997	907	3368	2074	2711	4079	504	639	3535	1842	1323	1614	2895	1353	1311	946	1167	2851	2965	1874	907	3802	1150	3044	1403	2436	2132	2187	4177	2327	4616	1480
Nashville, TN	1614	2008	1553	6534	389	1152	2652	312	2116	3179	1828	1152	3463	874	636	639	1995	763	452	854	615	1096	1870	1167	870	2137	2962	1289	462	681	948	899	2938	571	3305	282
New Orleans, LA	2317	2053	1598	7207	761	1837	3146	565	2790	3595	2515	2018	4135	1260	1490	1147	2417	1504	1319	1722	1482	845	2267	1797	1736	1799	3649	579	1329	298	895	1500	2983	732	3084	1149
New York, NY	243	3242	2785	7062	1398	309	3297	1585	2640	4008	346	644	3990	1244	829	1015	2824	1282	1023	750	861	2557	2895	1804	1001	3596	1480	2671	1150	1968	1533	1934	4106	2031	4537	1189
Oklahoma City, OK	2492	879	422	6245	1519	2179	1974	1173	1828	2423	2726	2031	3070	2008	1644	1773	1244	1298	1389	1726	1496	336	1096	879	1709	1186	3862	722	1210	985	2077	560	1809	571	2175	1245
Omaha, NE	2079	1566	1168	5409	1591	1879	1455	1514	991	1986	2354	1617	2338	2076	1532	1841	800	763	1184	1297	1290	1076	870	219	1195	1989	3242	1464	994	1504	2150	302	2082	917	2521	1133
Orlando, FL	1987	3112	2595	7641	708	1455	3754	951	3223	4283	2130	1965	4570	610	1271	845	3099	1868	1480	1681	1541	1844	2972	2270	1899	2796	3266	1577	1569	1117	227	2003	4042	1559	4084	1389
Ottawa, ON	486	3392	2936	6455	1866	842	3265	1971	2608	3977	665	536	3384	1780	1221	1483	2793	1252	1208	845	1064	2748	2862	1772	805	3701	1324	2941	1302	2333	2069	2085	4074	2224	4515	1377
Philadelphia, PA	359	3144	2689	7010	1258	167	3249	1443	2592	3961	516	666	3939	1102	730	874	2776	1236	927	703	763	2415	2806	1755	953	3455	1651	2529	1054	1826	1393	1836	4023	1891	4441	1091
Phoenix, AZ	4121	750	1212	5776	3006	3807	1929	2772	2674	1598	4354	3659	2454	3514	3274	3390	1615	2927	3018	3355	3125	1733	1455	2507	3337	695	5490	1911	2838	2385	3334	2188	459	2200	594	2874
Pittsburgh, PA	780	2687	2230	6526	1088	396	2766	1228	2109	3477	953	349	3455	1033	349	705	2293	751	470	219	306	2005	2349	1273	470	3046	2087	2198	595	1590	1323	1379	3564	1480	3984	634
Portland, ME	434	3762	3305	7546	1926	837	3784	2113	3128	4497	172	901	4475	1772	1350	1543	3313	1772	1545	1208	1381	3084	3382	2291	1348	4124	872	3199	1670	2494	2061	2454	4594	2558	5059	1709
Portland, OR	4753	2245	2727	3902	4259	4553	1430	4182	2093	695	5030	4291	1371	4743	4199	4508	1876	3438	3858	3973	3965	3443	2029	2893	3870	2843	5918	3831	3669	4093	4817	2904	1911	3599	1562	3800
Québec, QC	582	3734	3279	6846	2209	1120	3607	2314	2951	4320	624	879	3775	2055	1564	1826	3136	1595	1564	1187	1406	3091	3205	2114	1147	4043	940	3284	1644	2676	2344	2428	4417	2566	4858	1720
Raleigh, NC	1028	2867	2412	7157	637	497	3395	880	2739	4014	1173	1033	4085	449	504	254	2829	1385	840	914	776	1913	2703	1862	1165	2951	2307	1928	1028	1260	740	1733	3797	1430	4164	907
Rapid City, SD	2816	1353	1347	4795	2431	2616	610	2354	515	1496	3091	2354	1472	2935	2288	2700	491	1469	1961	2034	2051	1733	650	1012	1932	1778	3979	2121	1772	2346	2991	1142	1665	1759	2106	1955
Reno, NV	4420	1641	2101	4843	3926	4220	1545	3849	2208	692	4697	3958	2069	4410	3866	4175	1543	3105	3525	3640	3632	3110	1696	2560	3537	2116	5585	3334	3335	3760	4484	2571	711	3266	835	3467
Richmond, VA	776	3018	2563	7065	848	245	3303	1091	2647	4016	920	780	3994	689	518	465	2832	1290	853	758	832	2106	2716	1812	1009	3146	2055	2140	1031	1471	980	1746	3932	1582	4315	920
St. Louis, MO	1667	1691	1234	6113	883	1353	2158	806	1694	2619	1900	1205	3041	1368	824	1133	1435	473	563	901	671	1022	1376	702	883	1998	3036	1389	385	813	1442	405	2590	669	2986	425
Salt Lake City, UT	3578	1004	1551	4729	3083	3379	882	3006	1545	550	3854	3115	1406	3569	3025	3334	702	2262	2682	2796	2790	2269	854	1717	2695	1390	4742	2655	2492	2917	3643	1728	671	2425	1112	2624
San Antonio, TX	3142	1316	825	6833	1609	2689	2414	1413	2573	2833	3366	2679	3511	2108	2162	1997	1683	2043	1981	2383	2143	436	1522	1623	2397	895	4500	322	1908	1036	1744	1307	2047	965	2182	1810
San Diego, CA	4697	1327	1788	5673	3485	4383	2095	3252	2840	1763	4932	4235	2619	3995	3850	3870	1897	3387	3595	3921	3701	2212	1757	2841	3818	1175	5866	2393	3414	2864	3813	2727	542	2740	200	3450
San Francisco, CA	4769	1788	2248	4940	4212	4570	1892	3977	2814	1039	5044	4307	2409	4721	4216	4439	1892	3453	3873	3987	3981	2940	2045	2907	3886	1900	5932	3118	3685	3591	4541	2919	925	3237	619	3817
Seattle, WA	4664	2354	2837	3623	4352	4465	1313	4275	1977	805	4940	4203	1093	4784	4137	4549	1986	3318	3810	3883	3900	3553	2138	2932	3781	3128	5828	3940	3619	4203	4911	3012	2021	3709	1847	3804
Tampa, FL	2076	3136	2619	7664	732	1545	3778	975	3247	4307	2220	2053	4592	698	1360	935	3123	1892	1504	1772	1667	1868	2996	2294	1921	2821	3355	1601	1593	1141	315	2026	4064	1583	4108	1413
Toronto, ON	644	2962	2505	6595	1541	909	2835	1541	2179	3546	917	171	3524	1619	864	1290	2362	821	779	488	708	2319	2433	1342	375	3269	1681	2512	870	1903	1910	1654	3644	1794	4084	948
Vancouver, BC	4878	2570	3052	3430	4566	4679	1527	4491	2191	1018	5155	4417	899	4998	4352	4763	2201	3533	4024	4098	4116	3768	2354	3147	3995	3358	6043	4156	3834	4418	5126	3229	2237	3924	2077	4018
Washington, DC	594	3051	2594	6903	1023	61	3142	1220	2486	3854	737	618	3831	867	557	639	2669	1128	832	595	669	2191	2713	1649	846	3231	1873	2306	959	1603	1158	1743	3928	1667	4348	959
Wichita, KS	2367	1138	681	5921	1591	2053	1717	1348	1503	2166	2600	1905	2814	2077	1533	1842	986	1171	1263	1601	1371	591	838	628	1583	1445	3736	978	1084	1241	2151	309	2053	747	2434	1134
Winnipeg, MB	2730	2587	2285	4385	2542	2531	1324	2463	668	2336	3006	2269	1313	2850	2203	2615	1821	1384	1876	1948	1966	2193	1892	1121	1847	3010	3361	2581	1685	2526	3102	1324	3012	1939	3453	1870

Milles

Row headings (left column): Albany, NY · Albuquerque, NM · Amarillo, TX · Anchorage, AK · Atlanta, GA · Baltimore, MD · Billings, MT · Birmingham, AL · Bismarck, ND · Boise, ID · Boston, MA · Buffalo, NY · Calgary, AB · Charleston, SC · Charleston, WV · Charlotte, NC · Cheyenne, WY · Chicago, IL · Cincinnati, OH · Cleveland, OH · Columbus, OH · Dallas, TX · Denver, CO · Des Moines, IA · Detroit, MI · El Paso, TX · Halifax, NS · Houston, TX · Indianapolis, IN · Jackson, MS · Jacksonville, FL · Kansas City, MO · Las Vegas, NV · Little Rock, AR · Los Angeles, CA · Louisville, KY

Diagonal headings (column labels): Memphis, TN · México, MX · Miami, FL · Milwaukee, WI · Minneapolis, MN · Mobile, AL · Montréal, QC · Nashville, TN · New Orleans, LA · New York, NY · Oklahoma City, OK · Omaha, NE · Orlando, FL · Ottawa, ON · Philadelphia, PA · Phoenix, AZ · Pittsburgh, PA · Portland, ME · Portland, OR · Québec, QC · Raleigh, NC · Rapid City, SD · Reno, NV · Richmond, VA · St. Louis, MO · Salt Lake City, UT · San Antonio, TX · San Diego, CA · San Francisco, CA · Seattle, WA · Tampa, FL · Toronto, ON · Vancouver, BC · Washington, DC · Wichita, KS · Winnipeg, MB

Distances (miles) — upper block

City	Values (in column order: Memphis → Winnipeg)
Albany, NY	1214 2809 1439 929 1245 1344 230 1003 1440 151 1549 1292 1235 302 223 2561 485 270 2954 362 639 1750 2747 482 1036 2224 1953 2919 2964 2899 1290 400 3032 369 1471 1697
Albuquerque, NM	1033 1462 2155 1426 1339 1344 2172 2015 546 973 1934 2108 1954 1670 753 1386 2054 1695 2038 1499 837 1306 1593 767 964 513 1111 1397 1763 1628 1557 1897 1612 423 1420
Amarillo, TX	750 1275 1834 1142 1055 1106 1276 1888 965 993 1731 262 726 1613 1825 1671 753 1386 2054 1695 2038 1499 837 1306 1593 767 964 513 1111 2132 4290 3680 2725
Anchorage, AK	4083 5010 4970 3512 3176 4511 4106 4061 4479 4389 3881 3362 4749 4012 4357 3590 4056 4690 2425 4255 4448 2980 3010 4391 3799 2939 4247 3526 3070 2252 4763 4099 2132 4290 3680 2725
Atlanta, GA	389 1753 661 813 1129 332 1241 242 473 869 944 989 440 1160 782 1868 676 1197 2647 1373 396 1511 2440 527 549 1916 1000 2166 2618 2705 455 958 2838 636 989 1580
Baltimore, MD	933 2423 1109 805 1121 1013 564 716 1142 192 1354 1168 904 523 104 2366 246 520 2830 696 309 1626 2623 152 841 2100 1671 2724 2840 2775 960 565 2908 38 1276 1573
Billings, MT	1625 2263 2554 1175 839 2019 2093 1648 1955 2049 1227 904 2333 2029 2019 1199 1719 2352 889 2242 2110 379 960 2053 1341 548 1500 1302 1176 816 2348 1762 949 1953 1067 823
Birmingham, AL	241 1631 812 763 1079 258 1289 194 351 985 729 941 591 1225 897 1723 763 1313 2599 1438 547 1463 2392 678 501 1868 878 2021 2472 2657 606 958 2791 758 838 1531
Bismarck, ND	1337 2456 2224 767 431 1765 1685 1315 1734 1641 1136 616 2003 1621 1611 1662 1311 1944 1301 1834 1702 320 1372 1645 1053 960 1599 1765 1749 1223 2018 1354 1362 1545 934 415
Boise, ID	1954 2477 2883 1748 1465 2302 2535 1976 2234 2491 1506 1234 2662 2472 2462 993 2161 2795 432 2685 2495 930 430 2496 1628 342 1761 1096 646 500 2677 2204 633 2395 1346 1452
Boston, MA	1353 2843 1529 1100 1417 1433 313 1136 1563 215 1694 1463 1324 413 321 2706 592 107 3126 388 729 1921 2919 572 1181 2395 2092 3065 3135 3070 1380 570 3204 458 1616 1868
Buffalo, NY	927 2522 1425 642 958 1165 397 716 1254 400 1262 1005 1221 333 414 2274 217 560 2667 546 642 1463 2460 485 749 1936 1665 2632 2677 2612 1276 106 2745 384 1184 1410
Calgary, AB	2174 2944 3061 1603 1267 2602 2197 2152 2570 2480 1908 1453 2840 2103 2448 1525 2147 2781 852 2346 2539 915 1286 2482 1890 874 2182 1628 1497 2190 559 2381 1749 816
Charleston, SC	760 2063 583 1003 1319 642 1145 543 783 773 1248 1290 379 1106 685 2184 642 1101 2948 1277 279 1880 2741 681 850 2218 1344 2393 2620 2571 845 537 2705 346 953 1369
Charleston, WV	606 2201 994 601 918 837 822 395 926 515 1022 952 790 759 454 2035 217 839 2610 972 313 1422 2403 322 512 1880 1344 2393 2620 2571 581 802 2960 397 1145 1625
Charlotte, NC	614 1994 730 857 1173 572 1003 397 713 631 1102 1144 525 922 543 2107 438 959 2802 1135 158 1678 2595 289 704 2072 1241 2759 2827 581 802 2960 397 1145 1625
Cheyenne, WY	1217 1809 2147 1012 881 1570 1799 1240 1502 1755 773 497 1926 1736 1725 1004 1425 2059 1166 1949 1758 305 959 1760 892 436 1046 1179 1234 1941 1468 1368 1659 613 1132
Chicago, IL	539 2126 1382 89 409 923 841 474 935 797 807 474 1161 778 768 1819 467 1101 2137 991 861 913 1930 802 294 1406 1340 2105 2346 2368 935 484 2501 517 785 1166
Cincinnati, OH	493 2088 1141 398 714 731 815 281 820 636 863 736 920 751 576 1876 292 960 2398 972 522 1219 2191 530 350 1667 1231 2234 2407 2368 935 484 2501 517 785 1166
Cleveland, OH	742 2347 1250 443 760 981 588 531 1070 466 1073 806 1045 525 437 2085 136 751 2469 738 568 1264 2262 471 560 1738 1481 2437 2478 2413 1101 303 2547 370 995 1211
Columbus, OH	594 2189 1163 454 771 832 725 382 921 535 930 802 958 661 474 1942 190 858 2464 874 482 1275 2257 517 417 1734 1332 2300 2474 2424 1036 440 2558 416 852 1222
Dallas, TX	466 1128 1367 1010 999 639 1772 681 525 1589 209 669 1146 1708 1501 1077 1246 1917 2140 1921 1189 1077 1933 1309 635 1410 271 1375 1827 2208 1161 1441 2342 1362 367 1363
Denver, CO	1116 1709 2069 1055 924 1478 1843 1162 1409 1799 681 541 1847 1779 1744 904 1460 2102 1261 1992 1680 404 1067 1766 1126 436 1067 1009 1766 1807 1822 1426 834 1956 1025 390 697
Des Moines, IA	536 1896 1632 378 246 1115 1165 725 1117 1121 546 136 1411 1101 1091 1424 798 1451 1798 1314 1157 629 1591 1126 436 1067 1009 1766 1807 1822 1426 834 1956 1025 390 697
Detroit, MI	752 2347 1401 380 697 991 564 541 1079 622 1062 743 1180 500 592 2074 292 838 2405 713 724 1201 2198 627 549 1675 1490 2373 2415 2350 1194 233 2483 526 984 1148
El Paso, TX	1112 1197 1959 1617 1530 1231 2363 1328 1118 2235 737 1236 1738 2300 2147 432 1893 2563 1767 2513 1834 1105 1315 1955 1242 864 556 730 1181 1944 1753 2032 2008 898 1871
Halifax, NS	2058 3548 2234 1652 1969 1231 715 1841 2268 920 2400 2015 2030 823 1026 3412 1297 542 3678 584 1484 2371 1277 1882 1411 1311 2583 1433 608 1604
Houston, TX	586 954 1201 1193 1240 473 1892 801 360 1660 449 910 980 1828 1572 1188 1366 1988 2381 2041 1198 1318 2072 1330 863 1650 200 1487 1938 2449 995 1561 2583 1433 608 1604
Indianapolis, IN	464 2043 1196 279 596 732 872 287 826 715 752 618 975 809 655 1764 370 1038 2280 1022 639 1101 2073 641 239 1549 1186 2122 2290 2249 990 541 2383 596 674 1047
Jackson, MS	211 1398 915 835 1151 187 1514 423 185 1223 612 935 694 1450 1135 1482 988 1550 2544 1663 783 1458 2337 914 505 1813 644 1780 2232 2612 709 1183 2746 996 771 1570
Jacksonville, FL	733 1837 345 1160 1477 410 1325 589 556 953 1291 1336 141 1286 866 2072 822 1281 2994 1457 460 1859 2787 609 896 2264 1084 2370 2822 3052 196 1187 3186 720 1337 1928
Kansas City, MO	536 1668 1466 573 441 930 1359 559 932 1202 348 188 1245 1360 857 1525 1188 1560 1805 1509 1077 710 1598 1085 252 1074 812 1695 1814 1872 1259 1028 2007 1083 192 823
Las Vegas, NV	1611 1769 2733 1808 1677 1922 2596 1826 1834 2552 1124 1294 2512 2532 2500 285 2215 2855 1188 2745 2360 1035 442 2444 1610 417 1272 337 575 1256 2526 2265 1390 2441 1276 1872
Little Rock, AR	140 1457 1190 747 814 457 1446 355 455 1262 355 570 969 1382 1175 1367 920 1590 2237 1595 889 1093 2030 983 416 1507 600 1703 2012 2305 984 1115 2439 1036 464 1205
Los Angeles, CA	1839 1853 2759 2082 1951 2031 2869 2054 1917 2820 1352 1567 2538 2806 2760 369 2476 3144 971 3019 2588 1309 519 2682 1856 691 1356 124 381 1134 2553 2538 1297 2512 1513 2146
Louisville, KY	386 1981 1084 394 711 625 920 175 714 739 774 704 863 856 678 1786 394 1062 2369 1062 564 1215 2155 572 264 1631 1125 2144 2372 2364 878 589 2497 596 705 1162

Lower block (Kilomètres)

City	Values
Memphis, TN	1595 1051 624 940 395 1306 215 396 1123 487 724 830 1243 1035 1500 780 1451 2382 1456 749 1247 2175 843 294 1652 739 1841 2144 2440 845 975 2574 896 597 1359
México, MX	2154 2200 2113 1426 2900 1810 1313 2619 1323 1783 1933 2838 2525 1484 2375 2941 2819 3051 2151 2365 2367 2283 1825 2135 853 1683 2233 2996 1948 2570 3139 2386 1481 2477
Miami, FL	1478 1794 727 1671 907 874 1299 1609 1654 232 1631 1211 2390 1167 1627 3312 1803 805 3105 954 1214 2581 1401 2688 3140 3370 274 1522 3340 1065 1655 2246
Milwaukee, WI	337 1019 939 569 1020 894 880 514 1257 875 865 1892 564 1088 1986 842 1970 899 367 1446 1343 2145 2186 1991 1272 607 2124 749 769 789
Minneapolis, MN	1335 1255 886 1237 1211 793 383 1573 1192 1181 1805 881 1515 1727 1405 1273 606 1839 1216 621 1315 1257 2014 2055 1654 1588 924 1788 1115 637 452
Mobile, AL	1575 450 146 1203 799 1119 506 1481 1115 1662 1019 1531 2731 1707 730 1641 2545 861 688 2000 673 1960 2411 2799 521 1214 2933 970 958 1787
Montréal, QC	1094 1632 383 1625 1300 1466 121 454 2637 607 282 2963 155 871 1758 2756 714 1112 2232 2043 2931 2972 2907 1522 330 3040 1601 547 1337
Nashville, TN	539 906 750 747 686 1031 818 1715 569 1244 532 1256 2198 626 307 1615 954 2056 2298 2463 701 764 2597 679 748 1337
New Orleans, LA	1332 731 1121 653 1570 1245 1548 1108 1660 2663 1783 871 1643 2431 1002 690 1932 560 1846 2298 2731 668 1302 2865 1106 890 1755
New York, NY	1469 1258 1094 439 91 2481 367 313 2920 515 499 1716 2713 342 956 2189 1861 2839 2929 2864 1150 507 2998 228 1391 1665
Oklahoma City, OK	463 1388 1563 1408 1012 1124 1792 1934 1776 1237 871 1727 1331 505 1204 466 1370 1657 2002 1403 1295 2336 1350 161 1570
Omaha, NE	1433 1238 1228 1440 928 1541 1662 1451 1265 525 1455 1263 441 912 927 1630 1917 1448 971 1853 1162 307 638
Orlando, FL	1427 606 2169 963 1422 3091 1598 601 1955 2884 750 993 2360 1180 2467 2918 3149 63 1327 3283 860 1434 2025
Ottawa, ON	451 2575 545 382 2901 257 831 1696 2694 675 1050 2170 1981 2869 2910 2845 1483 268 2978 562 1485 1280
Philadelphia, PA	2420 306 419 2890 586 411 1686 2683 254 895 2160 1774 2779 2900 2835 1062 522 2968 140 1330 1633
Phoenix, AZ	2136 2804 1335 2788 2248 1308 883 2343 1517 651 987 358 750 1531 2184 2201 1655 2362 1173 2075
Pittsburgh, PA	690 2590 758 497 1386 2283 341 611 1859 1519 2494 2599 2534 1019 321 2668 240 1046 1332
Portland, ME	3223 264 827 2019 3016 670 1279 2493 2189 3162 3233 3168 1478 668 3301 556 1714 1966
Portland, OR	3114 2923 1268 578 2925 2057 771 2322 1093 638 170 3106 2633 313 2824 1775 1463
Québec, QC	1003 1908 2905 846 1261 2193 2080 3122 3057 1654 479 3190 732 1696 1523
Raleigh, NC	1777 2716 157 825 2193 1398 2563 2894 2926 656 820 3060 265 1266 1724
Rapid City, SD	1151 1720 963 628 1335 1372 1368 1195 1970 1429 1328 1620 712 792
Reno, NV	2718 1850 524 1870 621 755 2899 2426 898 2617 1568 1867
Richmond, VA	834 2194 1530 2684 2934 2869 805 660 3003 108 1274 1665
St. Louis, MO	1326 968 1835 2066 2125 1008 782 2259 837 441 1075
Salt Lake City, UT	1419 754 740 839 2375 1902 973 2094 1044 1455
San Antonio, TX	1285 1737 2275 1195 1714 2410 1635 624 1621
San Diego, CA	508 1271 2481 2601 1414 2720 1531 2193
San Francisco, CA	816 2933 2643 958 2834 1784 2193
Seattle, WA	3164 2577 140 2769 1843 1390
Tampa, FL	1383 3297 916 1448 2039
Toronto, ON	2711 563 1217 1375
Vancouver, BC	2902 1977 1375
Washington, DC	1272 1566
Wichita, KS	956
Winnipeg, MB	

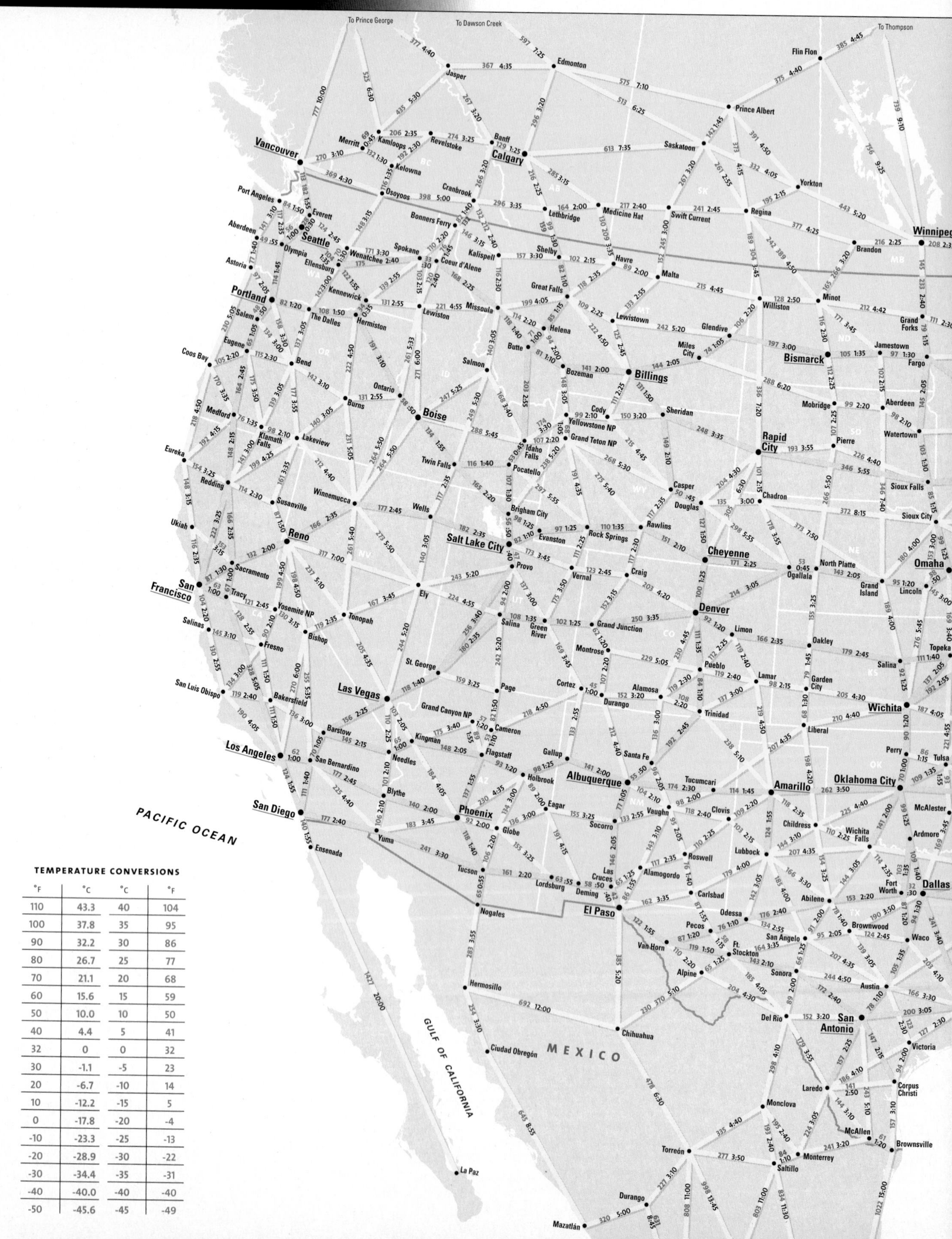

TEMPERATURE CONVERSIONS

°F	°C	°C	°F
110	43.3	40	104
100	37.8	35	95
90	32.2	30	86
80	26.7	25	77
70	21.1	20	68
60	15.6	15	59
50	10.0	10	50
40	4.4	5	41
32	0	0	32
30	-1.1	-5	23
20	-6.7	-10	14
10	-12.2	-15	5
0	-17.8	-20	-4
-10	-23.3	-25	-13
-20	-28.9	-30	-22
-30	-34.4	-35	-31
-40	-40.0	-40	-40
-50	-45.6	-45	-49

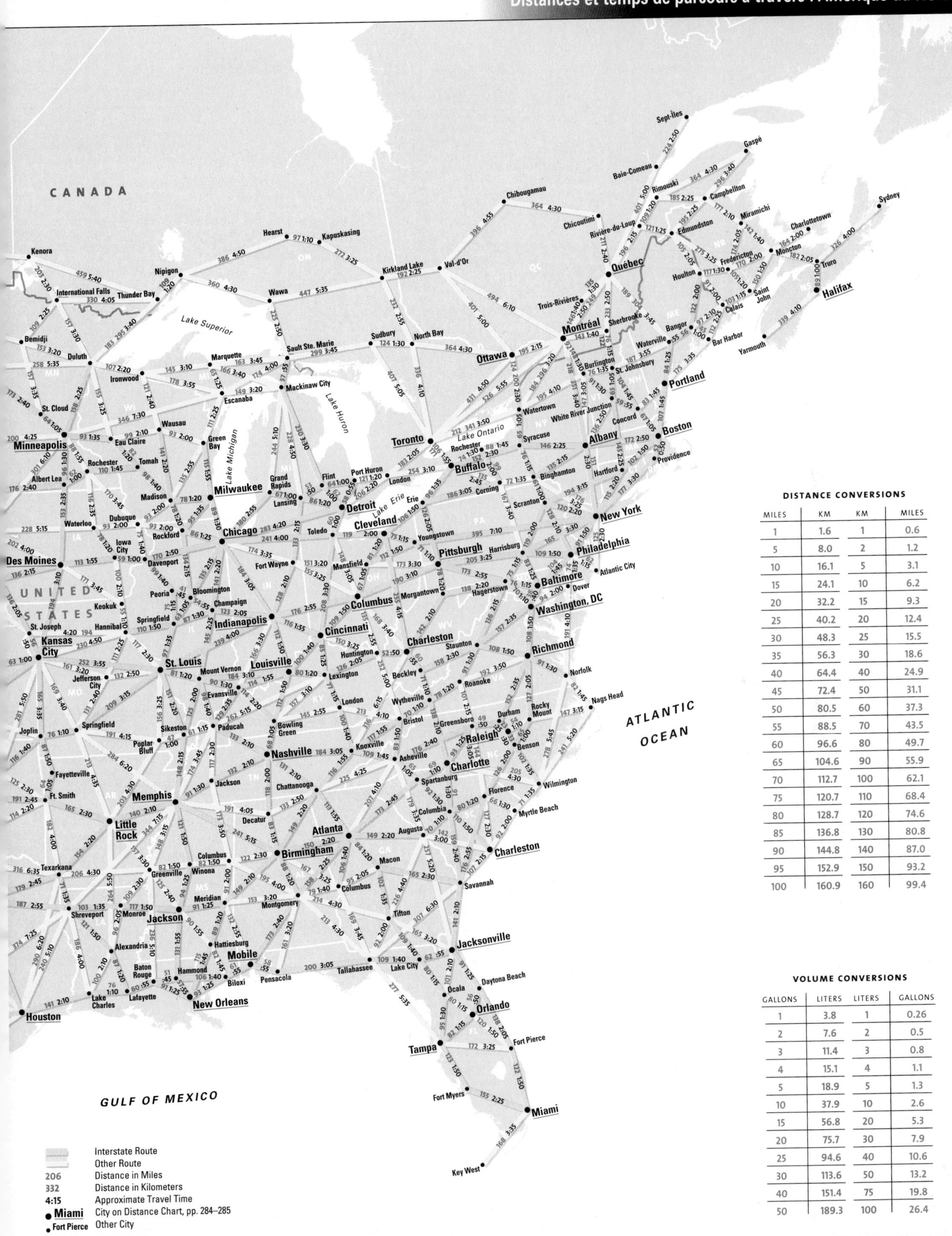

DISTANCE CONVERSIONS

MILES	KM	KM	MILES
1	1.6	1	0.6
5	8.0	2	1.2
10	16.1	5	3.1
15	24.1	10	6.2
20	32.2	15	9.3
25	40.2	20	12.4
30	48.3	25	15.5
35	56.3	30	18.6
40	64.4	40	24.9
45	72.4	50	31.1
50	80.5	60	37.3
55	88.5	70	43.5
60	96.6	80	49.7
65	104.6	90	55.9
70	112.7	100	62.1
75	120.7	110	68.4
80	128.7	120	74.6
85	136.8	130	80.8
90	144.8	140	87.0
95	152.9	150	93.2
100	160.9	160	99.4

VOLUME CONVERSIONS

GALLONS	LITERS	LITERS	GALLONS
1	3.8	1	0.26
2	7.6	2	0.5
3	11.4	3	0.8
4	15.1	4	1.1
5	18.9	5	1.3
10	37.9	10	2.6
15	56.8	20	5.3
20	75.7	30	7.9
25	94.6	40	10.6
30	113.6	50	13.2
40	151.4	75	19.8
50	189.3	100	26.4

Legend

	Interstate Route
	Other Route
206	Distance in Miles
332	Distance in Kilometers
4:15	Approximate Travel Time
● **Miami**	City on Distance Chart, pp. 284–285
• Fort Pierce	Other City

Distances and driving times may vary depending on actual

TOURISM INFORMATION

UNITED STATES

Alabama
@TweetHomeAla
www.alabama.travel

Alaska
@TravelAlaska
www.travelalaska.com

Arizona
@ArizonaTourism
www.visitarizona.com

Arkansas
@artourism
www.arkansas.com

California
@VisitCA
www.visitcalifornia.com

Colorado
@Colorado
www.colorado.com

Connecticut
@CTvisit
www.ctvisit.com

Delaware
@DelawareTourism
www.visitdelaware.com

District of Columbia
@washingtondc
www.washington.org

Florida
@VisitFlorida
www.visitflorida.com

Georgia
@ExploreGeorgia
www.exploregeorgia.org

Hawai'i
@gohawaii
www.gohawaii.com

Idaho
@visitidaho
www.visitidaho.org

Illinois
@enjoyillinois
www.enjoyillinois.com

Indiana
@visitindiana
www.visitindiana.com

Iowa
@Travel_Iowa
www.traveliowa.com

Kansas
@TravelKS
www.travelks.com

Kentucky
@KentuckyTourism
www.kentuckytourism.com

Louisiana
@LouisianaTravel
www.louisianatravel.com

Maine
@visitmaine
www.visitmaine.com

Maryland
@TravelMD
www.visitmaryland.org

Massachusetts
@VisitMA
www.visitma.com

Michigan
@PureMichigan
www.michigan.org

Minnesota
@ExploreMinn
www.exploreminnesota.com

Mississippi
@visitms
www.visitmississippi.org

Missouri
@VisitMO
www.visitmo.com

Montana
@visitmontana
www.visitmt.com

Nebraska
@NebraskaTourism
www.visitnebraska.com

Nevada
@TravelNevada
www.travelnevada.com

New Hampshire
@VisitNH
www.visitnh.gov

New Jersey
@Visit_NJ
www.visitnj.org

New Mexico
@NewMexico
www.newmexico.org

New York
@I_LOVE_NY
www.iloveny.com

North Carolina
@VisitNC
www.visitnc.com

North Dakota
@NorthDakota
www.ndtourism.com

Ohio
@OhioFindItHere
www.ohio.org

Oklahoma
@TravelOK
www.travelok.com

Oregon
@TravelOregon
www.traveloregon.com

Pennsylvania
@visitPA
www.visitpa.com

Rhode Island
@RITourism
www.visitrhodeisland.com

South Carolina
@Discover_SC
www.discoversouthcarolina.com

South Dakota
@southdakota
www.travelsouthdakota.com

Tennessee
@TNVacation
www.tnvacation.com

Texas
@TravelTexas
www.traveltexas.com

Utah
@VisitUtah
www.visitutah.com

Vermont
@VermontTourism
www.vermontvacation.com

Virginia
@VisitVirginia
www.virginia.org

Washington
@ExperienceWA
www.experiencewa.com

West Virginia
@WVtourism
www.wvtourism.com

Wisconsin
@TravelWI
www.travelwisconsin.com

Wyoming
@visitwyoming
www.travelwyoming.com

Puerto Rico
@discover_PR
www.discoverpuertorico.com

CANADA

Alberta
@TravelAlberta
www.travelalberta.com

British Columbia
@HelloBC
www.hellobc.com

Manitoba
@TravelManitoba
www.travelmanitoba.com

New Brunswick
@DestinationNB
www.tourismnewbrunswick.ca

Newfoundland & Labrador
@NLtweets
www.newfoundlandlabrador.com

Northwest Territories
@spectacularNWT
www.spectacularnwt.com

Nova Scotia
@VisitNovaScotia
www.novascotia.com

Nunavut
@TravelNunavut
www.travelnunavut.ca

Ontario
@OntarioTravel
www.ontariotravel.net

Prince Edward Island
@tourismpei
www.tourismpei.com

Québec
@TourismQuebec
www.bonjourquebec.com

Saskatchewan
@Saskatchewan
www.tourismsaskatchewan.com

Yukon
@TravelYukon
www.travelyukon.com

MEXICO

@VisitMex
www.visitmexico.com

BORDER CROSSING INFORMATION

TRAVEL ADVISORY

All U.S. citizens are now required to present a passport, passport card, or WHTI (Western Hemisphere Travel Initiative)-compliant document when entering the United States by air, sea or land. U.S. citizens traveling directly to or from Puerto Rico and the U.S. Virgin Islands are not required to have a passport. For more detailed information and updated schedules, please see http://travel.state.gov.

CANADA

Canadian law requires that all persons entering Canada carry both proof of citizenship and proof of identity. A valid U.S. passport, passport card or other WHTI-compliant document satisfies these requirements for U.S. citizens. U.S. citizens entering Canada from a third country must have a valid U.S. passport. A visa is not required for U.S. citizens to visit Canada for up to 180 days.

U.S. driver's licenses are valid in Canada. Drivers should be prepared to present proof of their vehicle's registration, ownership, and insurance.

UNITED STATES (FROM CANADA)

Canadian citizens are required to present valid WHTI-compliant documents when entering the United States by land or water. These documents include a passport or an Enhanced Driver's Licence/Enhanced Identification Card. Canadian citizens traveling by air to, through or from the United States must present a valid passport (see Travel Advisory). Visas are not required for customary tourist travel.

Canadian driver's licenses are valid in the U.S. for one year. Drivers should be prepared to present proof of their vehicle's registration, ownership, and insurance.

MEXICO

All persons entering Mexico need either a valid passport or their original birth certificate along with a valid photo ID such as a drivers license (U.S. citizens should bear in mind the requirements set by the U.S. government for re-entry to the U.S.). Visas are not required for stays of up to 180 days. Naturalized citizens and alien permanent residents should carry the appropriate official documentation. Individuals under the age of 18 traveling alone, with one parent, or with other adults must carry notarized parental/legal guardian authorization. All U.S. citizens visiting for up to 180 days must also procure a tourist card, obtainable from Mexican consulates, tourism offices, border crossing points, and airlines serving Mexico. However, tourist cards are not needed for visits shorter than 72 hours to areas within the Border Zone (extending approximately 25 km into Mexico).

U.S. driver's licenses are valid in Mexico. Visitors who wish to drive beyond the Baja California Peninsula or the Border Zone must obtain a temporary import permit for their vehicles. To acquire a permit, one must submit evidence of citizenship and of the vehicle's title and registration, as well as a valid driver's license. A processing fee must be paid. Permits are available at any Mexican Army Bank (Banjercito) located at border crossings or selected Mexican consulates. Mexican law also requires the posting of a refundable bond, via credit card or cash, at the Banjercito to guarantee the departure of the vehicle. Do not deal with any individual operating outside of official channels.

All visitors driving in Mexico should be aware that U.S. auto insurance policies are not valid and that buying short-term tourist insurance is mandatory. Many U.S. insurance companies sell Mexican auto insurance. American Automobile Association (for members only) and Sanborn's Mexico Insurance (800.638.9423) are popular companies with offices at most U.S. border crossings.

IMPORTANT WEB SITES

U.S. State Department,
www.travel.state.gov
U.S. Customs and Border Protection,
www.cbp.gov
Canada Border Services Agency,
www.cbsa-asfc.gc.ca
Citizenship and Immigration Canada,
www.cic.gc.ca
Mexican Ministry of Foreign Affairs,
www.gob.mx/sre
Mexican National Institute of Migration,
www.gob.mx/inm

COMMON ABBREVIATIONS

Abbr.	Meaning	Abbr.	Meaning
Arch.	Archaeological	N.H.S.	National Historic Site
Bfld.	Battlefield	N.H.P.	National Historical Park
Cons.	Conservation	N.M.P.	National Military Park
Ent.	Entrance	N.R.A.	National Recreation Area
Hist.	Historic(al)	Pk. Hqtrs.	Park Headquarters
Mem.	Memorial	Pres.	Preserve
Mon.	Monument	Prov.	Provincial
Mtn.	Mountain	Rec.	Recreation(al)
Mts.	Mountains	Res.	Reservation–Reserve
Mus.	Museum	S.H.S.	State Historic Site
Natl.	National	S.P.	State Park
Nat.	Natural	Sta.	Station
		Vis. Ctr.	Visitor Center

ALABAMA	PAGE	GRID	LATITUDE LONGITUDE
National Park & Rec. Areas			
Freedom Riders Natl. Mon.	120	A4	33.635108 -85.908448
Horseshoe Bend N.M.P.-Vis. Ctr.	128	B1	32.977130 -85.739600
Russell Cave Natl. Mon.-Main Road	120	A2	34.980220 -85.809650
Russell Cave Natl. Mon.-Vis. Ctr.	120	A2	34.980400 -85.809800
Tuskegee Airmen N.H.S.	128	B2	32.424942 -85.691052
Tuskegee Airmen N.H.S.-Pk. Hqtrs.	128	B2	32.428600 -85.708500
Tuskegee Institute N.H.S.	128	B2	32.428751 -85.704120
Tuskegee Institute N.H.S.-Pk. Hqtrs.	128	B2	32.428600 -85.708500
State Park & Rec. Areas			
Bladon Springs S.P.	127	E4	31.730920 -88.195580
Blue Springs S.P.	128	B4	31.661990 -85.508150
Bucks Pocket S.P.	120	A3	34.469560 -86.049080
Cathedral Caverns S.P.	120	A2	34.572299 -86.221499
Cheaha S.P.	120	A4	33.474490 -85.807260
Chewacla S.P.	128	B2	32.554520 -85.481920
Desoto S.P.	120	A3	34.495460 -85.618860
Frank Jackson S.P.	128	A4	31.291400 -86.255900
Gulf S.P.	135	F2	30.270490 -87.582130
Joe Wheeler S.P.	119	E2	34.793020 -87.379950
Lake Guntersville S.P.	120	A3	34.367530 -86.222850
Lake Jackson RV Park at Florala	136	B1	30.998590 -86.329980
Lake Lurleen S.P.	127	E1	33.295880 -87.676870
Lakepoint S.P.	128	C3	31.990320 -85.114970
Meaher S.P.	135	E1	30.669720 -87.936030
Monte Sano S.P.	119	F2	34.745220 -86.511650
Oak Mtn. S.P.	127	F1	33.324710 -86.758740
Paul M. Grist S.P.	127	F2	32.595380 -86.996080
Rickwood Caverns S.P.	119	F4	33.876870 -86.867230
Roland Cooper S.P.	127	F3	32.055350 -87.245330
Wind Creek S.P.	128	A1	32.856820 -85.946540

ALASKA	PAGE	GRID	LATITUDE LONGITUDE
National Park & Rec. Areas			
Admiralty Island Natl. Mon.	155	E4	57.618060 -134.161110
Aleutian WWII Natl. Hist. Area	154	A4	53.888889 -166.527222
Aniakchak Natl. Mon. & Pres.	154	B4	56.833333 -158.250556
Bering Land Bridge Natl. Pres.	154	B2	65.595320 -164.301800
Cape Krusenstern Natl. Mon.	154	B1	67.471630 -163.312300
Denali Natl. Park & Pres.-Denali Vis. Ctr.	154	C2	63.737000 -148.895000
Denali Natl. Park & Pres.-Eielson Vis. Ctr.	154	C2	63.440900 -150.239000
Gates of the Arctic Natl. Park & Pres.-Anaktuvuk Pass Ranger Sta.	154	C1	68.139900 -151.735400
Gates of the Arctic Natl. Park & Pres.-Arctic Interagency Vis. Ctr.	154	C1	67.253700 -150.187000
Gates of the Arctic Natl. Park & Pres.-Bettles Ranger Sta.	154	C1	66.912500 -151.667100
Gates of the Arctic Natl. Park & Pres.-Coldfoot Ranger Sta.	154	C1	67.253700 -150.187000
Glacier Bay Natl. Park & Pres.-Glacier Bay Lodge & Vis. Ctr.	155	D3	58.454900 -135.882600
Katmai Natl. Park & Pres.	154	C3	58.667030 -156.524600
Kenai Fjords Natl. Park-Vis. Ctr.	154	C3	60.105300 -149.435000
Klondike Gold Rush N.H.P.	155	D3	60.113550 -149.441342
Kobuk Valley Natl. Park	154	B1	67.073230 -159.839500
Lake Clark Natl. Park & Pres.	154	C3	60.471450 -154.576390
Misty Fiords Natl. Mon.	155	E4	55.472600 -130.429700
Noatak Natl. Pres.	154	C1	67.320740 -162.646370
White Mts. N.R.A.	154	C2	65.524300 -147.156400
Wrangell-Saint Elias Natl. Park & Pres.-Kennecott Vis. Ctr.	155	D3	61.485600 -142.881100
Wrangell-Saint Elias Natl. Park & Pres.-Wrangell-Saint Elias Vis. Ctr.	155	D3	61.964300 -145.317900
Yukon-Charley Rivers Natl. Pres.	155	D2	65.341680 -143.120650
State Park & Rec. Areas			
Afognak Island S.P.	154	C4	58.227100 -152.067300
Chilkat S.P.	155	D3	59.211111 -135.398056
Chugach S.P.	154	C3	61.037440 -149.780830
Denali S.P.	154	C3	62.734600 -150.199600
Point Bridget S.P.	155	E3	58.671225 -134.958801
Shuyak Island S.P.	154	C4	58.533100 -152.486100
Wood-Tikchik S.P.	154	B3	59.909600 -158.672000

ARIZONA	PAGE	GRID	LATITUDE LONGITUDE
National Park & Rec. Areas			
Agua Fria Natl. Mon.	47	D4	34.276490 -112.114350
Canyon de Chelly Natl. Mon.-Vis. Ctr.	48	A2	36.153200 -109.539000
Casa Grande Ruins Natl. Mon.-Ent. Sta.	54	C2	32.994700 -111.537000
Chiricahua Natl. Mon.-Main Road	55	E3	32.009250 -109.382230
Chiricahua Natl. Mon.-Ent. Sta.	55	E3	32.007500 -109.388900
Coronado Natl. Mem.-Vis. Ctr.	55	E4	31.346300 -110.254000
Fort Bowie N.H.S.-Vis. Ctr.	55	E3	32.146600 -109.435000
Glen Canyon N.R.A.-Ent. Sta.	47	E1	36.943300 -111.493600
Grand Canyon Natl. Park-East Ent.	47	D2	36.038800 -111.828000
Grand Canyon Natl. Park-North Ent.	47	D2	36.334900 -112.116000
Grand Canyon Natl. Park-South Ent.	47	D2	36.000100 -112.121600
Grand Canyon-Parashant Natl. Mon.	46	C2	36.452170 -113.724367
Ironwood Forest Natl. Mon.	54	C3	32.478380 -111.530220
Lake Mead N.R.A.-Boulder City Ent.	46	C2	36.020800 -114.796000
Lake Mead N.R.A.-Henderson Ent.	46	C2	36.105400 -114.901200
Lake Mead N.R.A.-Las Vegas–Rt 147 Ent.	46	C2	36.161000 -114.905100
Lake Mead N.R.A.-South Ent.	46	C2	35.225600 -114.551000
Montezuma Castle Natl. Mon.-Vis. Ctr.	47	D4	34.611600 -111.839000
Navajo Natl. Mon.-Betatakin Ruin	47	E1	36.683500 -110.541470
Navajo Natl. Mon.-Inscription House Ruin-Closed To Public	47	E1	36.661250 -110.775940
Navajo Natl. Mon.-Keet Seel Ruin	47	E1	36.683500 -110.541470
Navajo Natl. Mon.-Vis. Ctr.	47	E1	36.678200 -110.541000
Organ Pipe Cactus Natl. Mon.-Vis. Ctr.	54	B3	31.954800 -112.801000
Petrified Forest Natl. Park-North Ent.	47	F3	35.069600 -109.778000
Petrified Forest Natl. Park-South Ent.	47	F3	34.799600 -109.885000
Pipe Spring Natl. Mon.-Vis. Ctr.	47	D1	36.862500 -112.737000
Saguaro Natl. Park-East	55	D3	32.178430 -110.737990
Saguaro Natl. Park-Vis. Ctr.	55	D3	32.180200 -110.736000
Saguaro Natl. Park-West	55	D3	32.251660 -111.191660
Sonoran Desert Natl. Mon.	54	C2	33.001730 -112.421220
Sunset Crater Volcano Natl. Mon.-Vis. Ctr.	47	E3	35.368800 -111.543000
Tonto Natl. Mon.-Vis. Ctr.	55	D1	33.645200 -111.113000
Tumacácori N.H.P.-Vis. Ctr.	55	D4	31.567800 -111.051000
Tuzigoot Natl. Mon.-Pk. Hqtrs.	47	D4	34.561000 -111.853000
Vermilion Cliffs Natl. Mon.	47	D1	36.806389 -111.741111
Walnut Canyon Natl. Mon.-Walnut Canyon Vis. Ctr.	47	E3	35.171700 -111.509000
Wupatki Natl. Mon.-Vis. Ctr.	47	E3	35.520300 -111.372000
State Park & Rec. Areas			
Alamo Lake S.P.	46	C4	34.234270 -113.553220
Buckskin Mtn. S.P.	46	B4	34.255000 -114.134070
Catalina S.P.	55	D3	32.416760 -110.937500
Cattail Cove S.P.	46	B4	34.355075 -114.165877
Dead Horse Ranch S.P.	47	D4	34.748490 -112.022930
Homolovi S.P.	47	E3	35.023940 -110.630120
Kartchner Caverns S.P.	55	D3	31.840770 -110.342710
Lake Havasu S.P.	46	B4	34.473970 -114.345850
Lost Dutchman S.P.	54	C1	33.464920 -111.481350
Lyman Lake S.P.	48	A4	34.362870 -109.375370
Oracle S.P.	55	D2	32.610239 -110.740619
Patagonia Lake S.P.	55	D4	31.488970 -110.853790
Picacho Peak S.P.	54	C2	32.646340 -111.398090
Red Rock S.P.	47	D4	34.818920 -111.836700
Roper Lake S.P.	55	E2	32.758710 -109.709520
San Rafael State Nat. Area	55	D4	31.454275 -110.632850
Slide Rock S.P.	47	D3	34.944340 -111.752810
Tonto Nat. Bridge S.P.	47	E4	34.323400 -111.449460

ARKANSAS	PAGE	GRID	LATITUDE LONGITUDE
National Park & Rec. Areas			
Fort Smith N.H.S.-Main Road	116	B1	35.387480 -94.429660
Fort Smith N.H.S.-Vis. Ctr.	116	B1	35.385800 -94.429800
Hot Springs Natl. Park-Main Road	117	D2	34.511660 -93.053980
Hot Springs Natl. Park-Vis. Ctr.	117	D2	34.513800 -93.053400
Pea Ridge N.M.P.-Main Road	106	C3	36.442600 -94.025980
Pea Ridge N.M.P.-Vis. Ctr.	106	C3	36.443800 -94.025900
State Park & Rec. Areas			
Bull Shoals-White River S.P.	107	E3	36.365590 -92.557490
Conway Cemetery S.P.	124	C1	33.101909 -93.683161
Crater of Diamonds S.P.	116	C3	34.038610 -93.667630
Crowley's Ridge S.P.	108	A4	36.044840 -90.666770
Degray Lake Resort S.P.-North Ent.	117	D3	34.248870 -93.116880
Degray Lake Resort S.P.-South Ent.	117	D3	34.217390 -93.085820
Hampson Arch. Mus. S.P.	118	B1	35.568990 -90.041060
Historic Washington S.P.	116	C4	33.774005 -93.683235
Hobbs S.P.-Cons. Area	106	C3	36.244880 -93.972640
Jacksonport S.P.	107	F4	35.641440 -91.305350
Jenkins' Ferry Bfld. S.P.	117	E3	34.212070 -92.547490
Lake Charles S.P.	107	F4	36.066870 -91.132700
Lake Chicot S.P.	126	A1	33.373070 -91.194940
Lake Dardanelle S.P.	117	D1	35.251690 -93.213380
Lake Fort Smith S.P.	106	C4	35.654040 -94.150140
Lake Frierson S.P.	108	A4	35.985570 -90.717540
Lake Ouachita S.P.	117	D2	34.610990 -93.165520
Lake Poinsett S.P.	118	A1	35.535510 -90.688700
Louisiana Purchase S.P.	118	A2	35.150340 -90.734990
Lower White River Mus. S.P.	117	F2	34.977035 -91.495131
Mammoth Spring S.P.	107	F3	36.496010 -91.535960
Marks' Mills Battleground S.P.	117	E4	33.781085 -92.256427
Moro Bay S.P.	125	E1	33.298890 -92.348940
Mount Magazine S.P.	116	C1	35.149900 -93.563600
Mount Nebo S.P.	117	D1	35.224870 -93.229930
Ozark Folk Center S.P.	107	E4	35.883480 -92.116340
Parkin Arch. S.P.	118	A1	35.268607 -90.554809
Petit Jean S.P.	117	D1	35.128320 -92.898530
Poison Springs Battleground S.P.	117	D4	33.638340 -93.005250
Powhatan Hist. S.P.	107	F4	36.083234 -91.117858
Prairie Grove Bfld. S.P.	106	C4	35.983120 -94.305590
Toltec Mounds Arch. S.P.	117	E2	34.647370 -92.058510
Village Creek S.P.	118	A1	35.199650 -90.724540
White Oak Lake S.P.	117	D4	33.687490 -93.117240
Withrow Springs S.P.	106	C4	36.203800 -93.578200
Woolly Hollow S.P.	117	E1	35.286402 -92.285646

CALIFORNIA	PAGE	GRID	LATITUDE LONGITUDE
National Park & Rec. Areas			
Amboy Crater Natl. Nat. Landmark	53	E2	34.542196 -115.790920
Berryessa Snow Mountain Natl. Mon.	36	B2	38.902521 -123.411455
Carrizo Plain Natl. Mon.	52	B1	35.191000 -119.792000
Castle Mountains Natl. Mon.	53	F1	35.250563 -115.116773
Channel Islands Natl. Park	52	B2	34.248500 -119.267000
Death Valley Natl. Park-Furnace Creek Vis. Ctr.	45	F3	36.461800 -116.867000
Devils Postpile Natl. Mon.	37	E4	37.630330 -119.084300
Giant Sequoia Natl. Mon.-North Unit	45	D2	36.705501 -118.824821
Giant Sequoia Natl. Mon.-South Unit	45	E3	36.062389 -118.317784
Golden Gate N.R.A.-Marin Headlands	36	B4	37.830900 -122.525000
Golden Gate N.R.A.-Mott Vis. Ctr.	36	B4	37.799800 -122.460000
Joshua Tree Natl. Park-Indian Cove	53	E3	34.120000 -116.156000
Joshua Tree Natl. Park-North Ent.	53	E3	34.078300 -116.037000
Joshua Tree Natl. Park-West Ent.	53	E3	34.093600 -116.266000
Kings Canyon Natl. Park-East Ent.	45	D2	36.715870 -118.940420
Kings Canyon Natl. Park-West Ent.	45	D2	36.723720 -118.956490
Lassen Volcanic Natl. Park-Ent.	29	D4	40.537900 -121.571000
Lava Beds Natl. Mon.-Vis. Ctr.	29	D2	41.713900 -121.509000
Manzanar N.H.S.	45	E3	36.732260 -118.148500
Mojave Trails Natl. Mon.	53	E2	34.169528 -115.788162
Pinnacles Natl. Park-East Ent.	44	B3	36.483200 -121.162000
Pinnacles Natl. Park-West Ent.	44	B3	36.473300 -121.224400
Point Reyes Natl. Seashore-Bear Valley Vis. Ctr.	36	A3	38.043100 -122.799000
Point Reyes Natl. Seashore-Kenneth C. Patrick Vis. Ctr.	36	A3	38.027800 -122.961000
Point Reyes Natl. Seashore-Vis. Ctr.	36	A3	37.996500 -123.021000
Redwood Natl. Park-Kuchel Vis. Ctr.	28	A3	41.286800 -124.090900
Redwood Natl. Park-Prairie Creek Vis. Ctr.	28	A3	41.365300 -124.022000
Sand to Snow Natl. Mon.	53	D2	34.045197 -117.054096
San Gabriel Mountains Natl. Mon.	52	C2	34.286213 -117.884488
Santa Monica Mts. N.R.A.-Vis. Ctr.	52	B2	34.188600 -118.887000
Santa Rosa & San Jacinto Mts. Natl. Mon.	53	E3	33.755173 -116.729736
Sequoia Natl. Park-North Ent.	45	D3	36.647900 -118.826370
Sequoia Natl. Park-South Ent.	45	D3	36.487130 -118.836810
Shasta-Trinity N.R.A.	28	C4	40.633204 -122.601127
Trona Pinnacles Natl. Nature Landmark	45	F4	35.611944 -117.369444
Tule Lake Natl. Mon.	29	D2	41.969322 -121.567626
Whiskeytown-N.R.A.	28	C4	40.751500 -122.320580
Yosemite Natl. Park-Arch Rock Ent.	37	D3	37.687500 -119.730000
Yosemite Natl. Park-Big Oak Flat Ent.	37	D3	37.800800 -119.874000
Yosemite Natl. Park-South Ent.	37	D3	37.507000 -119.632000
Yosemite Natl. Park-Tioga Pass Ent.	37	D3	37.910700 -119.258000
State Park & Rec. Areas			
Ahjumawi Lava Springs S.P.	29	D3	41.107140 -121.468600
Anza-Borrego Desert S.P.	53	E4	33.256550 -116.399340
Big Basin Redwoods S.P.	44	A2	37.168380 -122.221530
Bothe-Napa Valley S.P.	36	B3	38.553410 -122.525640
Butano S.P.	44	A2	37.200660 -122.344140
Carlsbad State Beach	53	D3	33.147530 -117.345280
Castle Crags S.P.	28	C3	41.149280 -122.317480
China Camp S.P.	36	B3	38.003990 -122.466480
Clear Lake S.P.	36	B2	39.009780 -122.805400
Cuyamaca Rancho S.P.	53	D4	32.933790 -116.562560
Del Norte Coast Redwoods S.P.	28	A3	41.603280 -124.100130
Doheny State Beach	52	C3	33.463820 -117.688830
Donner Mem. S.P.	37	D2	39.323880 -120.228370
Ed Z'Berg Sugar Pine Point S.P.	37	D2	39.056290 -120.119200
Emerald Bay S.P.	37	D2	38.956710 -120.108850
Fremont Peak S.P.	44	B3	36.760340 -121.502670
Garrapata S.P.	44	B3	36.475310 -121.936280
Gaviota S.P.	52	A2	34.475250 -120.228590
Grizzly Creek Redwoods S.P.	28	B4	40.486630 -123.903520
Grover Hot Springs S.P.	37	D3	38.695230 -119.836760
Henry Cowell Redwoods S.P.	44	A2	37.044020 -122.070990
Henry W. Coe S.P.	44	B2	37.085600 -121.467340
Humboldt Lagoons S.P.	28	A3	41.284330 -124.089720
Humboldt Redwoods S.P.	28	A4	40.284740 -124.056950
Jedediah Smith Redwoods S.P.	28	A2	41.798190 -124.084030
Julia Pfeiffer Burns S.P.	44	B3	36.160700 -121.668210
Manchester S.P.	36	A2	38.980450 -123.703020
Marina State Beach	44	B3	36.683030 -121.809440
McGrath State Beach	52	B2	34.227270 -119.256460
Mendocino Headlands S.P.	36	A2	39.307570 -123.798910
Morro Bay S.P.	44	B4	35.354020 -120.843800
Morro Strand State Beach	44	B4	35.435390 -120.888060
Mount Diablo S.P.	36	B4	37.844210 -121.950200
Mount Tamalpais S.P.	36	B3	37.904290 -122.604040
Navarro River Redwoods S.P.	36	A2	39.175000 -123.676390

Park	Page	Grid	Latitude Longitude
Pacheco S.P.	44	B2	37.055650 -121.016250
Palomar Mtn. S.P.	53	D3	33.325340 -116.893330
Patrick's Point S.P.	28	A3	41.135690 -124.150500
Pfeiffer Big Sur S.P.	44	B3	36.250930 -121.786550
Placerita Canyon S.P.	52	C2	34.377530 -118.470290
Plumas-Eureka S.P.	36	C1	39.758360 -120.695360
Point Dume State Beach	52	B2	34.003110 -118.807250
Point Sal State Beach	52	A1	34.897760 -120.642760
Prairie Creek Redwoods S.P.	28	A3	41.355490 -124.073670
Red Rock Canyon S.P.	52	C1	35.359734 -117.978351
Russian Gulch S.P.	36	A2	39.330990 -123.805050
Saddleback Butte S.P.	52	C2	34.689820 -117.824340
Samuel P. Taylor S.P.	36	B3	38.004660 -122.708400
San Gregorio State Beach	36	B4	37.321490 -122.401640
San Onofre State Beach	53	D3	33.383380 -117.580790
Sonoma Coast State Beach	36	A3	38.441060 -123.122970
Sunset State Beach	44	B2	36.897780 -121.835450
The Forest of Nisene Marks S.P.	44	B2	37.042024 -121.856231
Tolowa Dunes S.P.	28	A2	41.825800 -124.187500
Trinidad State Beach	28	A3	41.061090 -124.142290
Van Damme S.P.	36	A2	39.273990 -123.790490
Westport-Union Landing State Beach	36	A1	39.658350 -123.784930
Wilder Ranch S.P.	44	A2	36.962160 -122.080850
Zmudowski State Beach	44	B2	36.845580 -121.804300

COLORADO	PAGE	GRID	LATITUDE LONGITUDE
National Park & Rec. Areas			
Arapaho N.R.A.	41	D1	40.197870 -105.869440
Bent's Old Fort N.H.S.	41	F3	38.045980 -103.431440
Black Canyon-Gunnison Natl. Park-North Ent.	40	C3	38.586890 -107.695940
Black Canyon-Gunnison Natl. Park-South Ent.	40	C3	38.553980 -107.686390
Browns Canyon Natl. Mon.	41	D2	38.753093 -105.973528
Canyons of the Ancients Natl. Mon.	40	A4	37.587880 -108.916890
Colorado Natl. Mon.-Northwest Ent.	40	B2	39.117620 -108.730910
Colorado Natl. Mon.-Southeast Ent.	40	B2	39.032860 -108.631460
Colorado Natl. Mon.-South Ent.	40	B2	39.021100 -108.659540
Colorado Natl. Mon.-Southwest Ent.	40	B2	39.055070 -108.742500
Curecanti N.R.A.-East Ent.	40	C3	38.515010 -107.020560
Curecanti N.R.A.-North Ent.	40	C3	38.463380 -107.419580
Curecanti N.R.A.-South Ent.	40	C3	38.473160 -107.076450
Curecanti N.R.A.-West Ent.	40	C3	38.444680 -107.341980
Dinosaur Natl. Mon.-East Ent.	32	B4	40.443120 -108.517790
Dinosaur Natl. Mon.-South Ent.	32	B4	40.243920 -108.973750
Florissant Fossil Beds Natl. Mon.	41	E2	38.937440 -105.283400
Great Sand Dunes Natl. Park-Ent. Sta.	41	D4	37.725000 -105.519000
Hovenweep Natl. Mon.-Cutthroat	40	A4	37.413000 -108.720240
Hovenweep Natl. Mon.-Hackberry	40	A4	37.398890 -109.036680
Hovenweep Natl. Mon.-Holly	40	A4	37.398890 -109.036680
Hovenweep Natl. Mon.-Horseshoe	40	A4	37.464610 -108.974680
Mesa Verde Natl. Park-Ent. Sta.	40	B4	37.331100 -108.416000
Rocky Mtn. Natl. Park-Beaver Meadows Ent.	33	E4	40.367300 -105.578000
Rocky Mtn. Natl. Park-Fall River Ent.	33	E4	40.404000 -105.590000
Rocky Mtn. Natl. Park-Grand Lake Ent.	33	E4	40.267300 -105.833000
Rocky Mtn. Natl. Park-Wild Basin Ent.	33	E4	40.219000 -105.534000
Sand Creek Massacre N.H.S.	42	A3	38.541250 -102.505910
Yucca House Natl. Mon.	40	B4	37.251678 -108.684911
State Park & Rec. Areas			
Barr Lake S.P.	41	E1	39.938160 -104.733470
Boyd Lake S.P.	33	E4	40.428990 -105.045400
Castlewood Canyon S.P.	41	E2	39.325860 -104.737640
Crawford S.P.	40	C3	38.708000 -107.617550
Eleven Mile S.P.	41	D2	38.948570 -105.526450
Golden Gate Canyon S.P.	41	D1	39.875560 -105.453650
Harvey Gap S.P.	40	C1	39.606210 -107.659010
Highline Lake S.P.	40	B2	39.270910 -108.835930
Jackson Lake S.P.	33	F4	40.409110 -104.070130
James M. Robb-Colorado River S.P.-Corn Lake	40	B2	39.062709 -108.455110
James M. Robb-Colorado River S.P.-Island Acres	40	B2	39.165709 -108.300610
John Martin Reservoir S.P.	42	A3	38.065390 -102.927110
Lake Pueblo S.P.	41	E3	38.258130 -104.719160
Lathrop S.P.	41	E4	37.602830 -104.833740
Lory S.P.	33	E4	40.593143 -105.185413
Mancos S.P.	40	B4	37.399890 -108.266750
Mueller S.P.	41	E2	38.884940 -105.157710
Navajo S.P.	48	B1	37.067800 -107.407599
North Sterling S.P.	34	A4	40.787740 -103.264990
Paonia S.P.	40	C2	38.980440 -107.342900
Pearl Lake S.P.	33	D4	40.790160 -106.894610
Ridgway S.P.	40	B3	38.229710 -107.729410
Rifle Falls S.P.	40	B1	39.695290 -107.701090
Rifle Gap S.P.	40	B1	39.627460 -107.762520
Roxborough S.P.	41	E2	39.451300 -105.070200
San Luis S.W.A.	41	D4	37.663130 -105.734480
Spinney Mtn. S.P.	41	D2	39.014760 -105.625880
Stagecoach S.P.	33	D4	40.286100 -106.866920
Staunton S.P.	41	D1	39.509959 -105.394411
Steamboat Lake S.P.	32	C4	40.805240 -106.943600
Sweitzer Lake S.P.	40	B2	38.712050 -108.042640
Sylvan Lake S.P.	40	C1	39.516710 -106.753170

Park	Page	Grid	Latitude Longitude
Trinidad Lake S.P.	49	E1	37.149700 -104.563650
Vega S.P.	40	B2	39.226890 -107.810250
Yampa River S.P.	32	C4	40.533190 -107.444483

CONNECTICUT	PAGE	GRID	LATITUDE LONGITUDE
National Park & Rec. Areas			
Weir Farm N.H.P.	148	C2	41.255890 -73.455980
State Park & Rec. Areas			
Bigelow Hollow S.P.	150	B2	41.991600 -72.134840
Bluff Point S.P.	149	F2	41.335800 -72.033520
Chatfield Hollow S.P.	150	A4	41.361400 -72.580190
Day Pond S.P.	150	A4	41.553432 -72.418419
Devil's Hopyard S.P.	150	A4	41.486529 -72.342462
Gay City S.P.	150	A3	41.716100 -72.434470
Gillette Castle S.P.	150	A4	41.430670 -72.427990
Hammonasset Beach S.P.	149	E2	41.273640 -72.562350
Haystack Mtn. S.P.	94	C2	42.002010 -73.209960
Hurd S.P.	150	A4	41.530650 -72.537650
John A. Minetto S.P.	94	C2	41.884020 -73.170280
Lake Waramaug S.P.	148	C1	41.706290 -73.382460
Mashamoquet Brook S.P.	150	B3	41.860320 -71.987230
Mount Riga S.P.	94	B2	42.028830 -73.428620
Putnam Mem. S.P.	148	C2	41.344200 -73.381500
Rocky Neck S.P.	149	F2	41.316920 -72.242690
Selden Neck S.P.	150	A4	41.287500 -72.331100
Silver Sands S.P.	149	D2	41.198410 -73.076180
Southford Falls S.P.	149	D1	41.455700 -73.166150
Squantz Pond S.P.	148	C1	41.508580 -73.471040
Stoddard Hill S.P.	150	B4	41.461900 -72.065500
Sunrise S.P.	149	E1	41.502642 -72.477201
Wadsworth Falls S.P.	150	A4	41.536080 -72.687380
West Rock Ridge S.P.	149	D2	41.347810 -72.968260

DELAWARE	PAGE	GRID	LATITUDE LONGITUDE
State Park & Rec. Areas			
Cape Henlopen S.P.	145	F3	38.782360 -75.103010
Delaware Seashore S.P.	145	F4	38.614420 -75.071540
Fenwick Island S.P.	145	F4	38.469740 -75.051550
Fort Delaware S.P.	145	E1	39.578700 -75.588320
Fort Dupont S.P.	145	E1	39.568930 -75.588590
Holts Landing S.P.	145	F4	38.584080 -75.128380
Killens Pond S.P.	145	E3	38.990320 -75.544920
Lums Pond S.P.	145	E1	39.570520 -75.733490
Trap Pond S.P.	145	E4	38.525860 -75.483170
White Clay Creek S.P.	146	B4	39.709810 -75.776560

FLORIDA	PAGE	GRID	LATITUDE LONGITUDE
National Park & Rec. Areas			
Biscayne Natl. Park-Dante Fascell Vis. Ctr.	143	F3	25.464400 -80.334900
Canaveral Natl. Seashore	141	E1	28.611410 -80.808390
Castillo de San Marcos Natl. Mon.	139	D3	29.897747 -81.311461
Dry Tortugas Natl. Park-Vis. Ctr.	142	B4	24.628500 -82.873400
Everglades Natl. Park-Ent.	143	E3	25.394400 -80.589300
Fort Matanzas Natl. Mon.	139	E3	29.715660 -81.234190
Gulf Islands Natl. Seashore	135	F2	30.362880 -87.139630
State Park & Rec. Areas			
Alafia River S.P.	140	C3	27.789920 -82.120830
Amelia Island S.P.	139	D2	30.543900 -81.449700
Anastasia S.P.	139	E3	29.874740 -81.285030
Anclote Key Pres. S.P.	140	B2	28.193070 -82.850660
Avalon S.P.	141	E3	27.542840 -80.318060
Bahia Honda S.P.	143	D4	24.659540 -81.277810
Bald Point S.P.	138	A3	29.902700 -84.408600
Big Lagoon S.P.	135	F2	30.322290 -87.401170
Big Shoals S.P.	138	C2	30.339115 -82.683182
Big Talbot Island S.P.	139	D2	30.460500 -81.421950
Blue Spring S.P.	141	D1	28.952270 -81.331300
Bulow Creek S.P.	139	E4	29.388000 -81.132399
Bulow Plantation Ruins Hist. S.P.	139	E4	29.433590 -81.144590
Caladesi Island S.P.	140	B2	28.059890 -82.813780
Cedar Key Mus. S.P.	138	B4	29.151172 -83.048299
Charlotte Harbor Pres. S.P.	140	C4	26.850691 -82.022026
Collier-Seminole S.P.	143	D2	25.991630 -81.591700
Crystal River Pres. S.P. & Arch. S.P.	140	B1	28.909530 -82.628680
Curry Hammock S.P.	143	E4	24.742640 -80.984793
Dade Bfld. Hist. S.P.	140	C1	28.654430 -82.124970
Deleon Springs S.P.	139	D4	29.131920 -81.360400
Delnor-Wiggins Pass S.P.	142	C1	26.272500 -81.826900
Dudley Farm Hist. S.P.	138	C3	29.649617 -82.630738
Eden Gardens S.P.	136	B2	30.361530 -86.125010
Egmont Key S.P.	140	B3	27.723490 -82.679390
Fakahatchee Strand Pres. S.P.	143	D2	25.961900 -81.364600
Faver-Dykes S.P.	139	E3	29.668050 -81.268030
Florida Caverns S.P.	137	D1	30.809160 -85.212270
Fort Clinch S.P.	139	D1	30.668010 -81.434300
Fort Cooper S.P.	140	C1	28.801300 -82.309200
Fort Pierce Inlet S.P.-East Ent.	141	E3	27.485160 -80.299430
Fort Pierce Inlet S.P.-West Ent.	141	E3	27.475930 -80.316980
Gasparilla Island S.P.	140	C4	26.718200 -82.261400
Grayton Beach S.P.	136	B2	30.328930 -86.155790
Henderson Beach S.P.	136	B2	30.387000 -86.447499
Highlands Hammock S.P.	141	D3	27.476554 -81.557148
Hontoon Island S.P.	141	D1	28.976680 -81.357690
Hugh Taylor Birch S.P.	143	F1	26.138220 -80.104450
Indian Key Hist. S.P.	143	E4	24.888056 -80.678056
John Gorrie Mus. S.P.	137	D3	29.725768 -84.983244
John Pennekamp Coral Reef S.P.	143	E3	25.127620 -80.409650
Jonathan Dickinson S.P.	141	F4	27.002920 -80.099980
Kissimmee Prairie Pres. S.P.	141	D3	27.538826 -81.022945
Lafayette Blue Springs S.P.	138	B2	30.115136 -83.229417
Lake Griffin S.P.	140	C1	28.857450 -81.902240
Lake Kissimmee S.P.	141	D2	27.971930 -81.380220
Lake Louisa S.P.	140	C1	28.460070 -81.751620
Lake Manatee S.P.	140	C3	27.475140 -82.336800
Little Talbot Island S.P.	139	D2	30.460500 -81.421950
Long Key S.P.	143	E4	24.821580 -80.819510
Lovers Key S.P.	142	C1	26.391000 -81.877800
Manatee Springs S.P.	138	B4	29.496230 -82.958630
Myakka River S.P.	140	C4	27.242670 -82.332240
Natural Bridge Bfld. Hist. S.P.	138	A2	30.284730 -84.152260
O'Leno S.P.	138	C3	29.809100 -82.550700
Olustee Bfld. Hist. S.P.	138	C2	30.214650 -82.428960
Oscar Scherer S.P.	140	B4	27.168840 -82.477360
Paynes Prairie Pres. S.P.	138	C3	29.520720 -82.300400
Perdido Key S.P.	135	F2	30.291480 -87.465360
Ponce De Leon Springs S.P.	136	C1	30.713260 -85.922490
Rainbow Springs S.P.	138	C4	29.103818 -82.438782
Ravine Gardens S.P.	139	D3	29.637490 -81.646830
River Rise Pres. S.P.	138	C3	29.859961 -82.605395
Saint Sebastian River Pres. S.P.	141	E3	27.815241 -80.513820
San Marcos de Apalache Hist. S.P.	138	A2	30.152890 -84.210030
Savannas Pres. S.P.	141	E3	27.245960 -80.250270
Sebastian Inlet S.P.	141	E2	27.870200 -80.453599
Silver River S.P.	139	D4	29.202550 -82.053610
Suwannee River S.P.	138	B2	30.389610 -83.157850
Three Rivers S.P.	137	D1	30.736800 -84.936500
Tomoka S.P.	139	E4	29.342210 -81.086200
Torreya S.P.	137	D2	30.553530 -84.946740
Troy Spring S.P.	138	B3	29.918000 -82.893300
Waccasassa Bay Pres. S.P.	138	B4	29.188100 -82.925500
Washington Oaks Gardens S.P.	139	E3	29.634670 -81.205500
Wekiwa Springs S.P.	141	D1	28.710490 -81.462810
Windley Key Fossil Reef Geological S.P.	143	E4	24.914100 -80.642800
Yulee Sugar Mill Ruins Hist. S.P.	140	B1	28.784730 -82.607370

GEORGIA	PAGE	GRID	LATITUDE LONGITUDE
National Park & Rec. Areas			
Chattahoochee River N.R.A.	120	C3	34.002910 -84.349180
Chickamauga & Chattanooga N.M.P.	120	B2	34.941430 -85.258790
Cumberland Island Natl. Seashore	139	D1	30.720300 -81.548760
Ed Jenkins N.R.A.	120	C2	34.682900 -84.198200
Fort Frederica Natl. Mon.	130	B4	31.219790 -81.386570
Fort Pulaski Natl. Mon.	130	C3	32.016520 -80.891680
Jimmy Carter N.H.P.	128	C3	32.034090 -84.401600
Kennesaw Mtn. Natl. Battlefied Park-Vis. Ctr.	120	C3	33.983000 -84.577900
Ocmulgee Mounds N.H.P.	129	D2	32.848560 -83.602140
State Park & Rec. Areas			
A.H. Stephens S.P.	121	E4	33.561998 -82.897677
Amicalola Falls S.P.	120	C2	34.558940 -84.248890
Black Rock Mtn. S.P.	121	D2	34.918150 -83.400310
Cloudland Canyon S.P.	120	B2	34.830430 -85.482040
Crooked River S.P.	139	D1	30.844840 -81.559350
Dames Ferry S.P	129	D1	33.043709 -83.758201
Don Carter S.P.	121	D3	34.387622 -83.746462
Elijah Clark S.P.	121	E4	33.854210 -82.391913
Florence Marina S.P.	128	C3	32.090988 -85.043263
Fort Mtn. S.P.	120	C2	34.763090 -84.689330
Fort Yargo S.P.	121	D4	33.984940 -83.733580
Franklin D. Roosevelt S.P.	128	C2	32.848670 -84.793230
General Coffee S.P.	129	E4	31.511490 -82.745360
George L. Smith S.P.	130	A2	32.570310 -82.103760
George T. Bagby S.P.	128	C4	31.739940 -85.074820
Georgia Veterans S.P.	129	D3	31.957951 -83.903787
Gordonia-Alatamaha S.P.	130	A3	32.081900 -82.123550
Hamburg S.P.	129	E1	33.208800 -82.774870
Hard Labor Creek S.P.	121	D4	33.677820 -83.593840
High Falls S.P.	129	D1	33.176590 -84.020280
Indian Springs S.P.	129	D1	33.247480 -83.921190
James H. "Sloppy" Floyd S.P.	120	B3	34.440260 -85.347580
Kolomoki Mounds S.P.	128	C4	31.468633 -84.9485331
Laura S. Walker S.P.	138	C1	31.143130 -82.212920
Little Ocmulgee S.P.	129	E3	32.100590 -82.886360
Magnolia Springs S.P.	130	A1	32.875760 -81.962560
Mistletoe S.P.	121	E4	33.638770 -82.390540
Moccasin Creek S.P.	121	D2	34.845160 -83.589140
Panola Mtn. S.P.	120	C4	33.622042 -84.173078
Providence Canyon S.P.	128	C3	32.068270 -84.929150
Red Top Mtn. S.P.	120	C3	34.145950 -84.720190
Reed Bingham S.P.	137	F1	31.161310 -83.538880
Richard B. Russell S.P.	121	E3	34.166778 -82.745691
Seminole S.P.	137	D1	30.811420 -84.873570
Skidaway Island S.P.	130	C3	31.947720 -81.052550
Stephen C. Foster S.P.	138	C1	30.827020 -82.361310

Tallulah Gorge S.P.	121	D2	34.736350 -83.391950
Tugaloo S.P.	121	E3	34.501940 -83.082320
Unicoi S.P.	121	D2	34.724620 -83.728170
Victoria Bryant S.P.	121	E3	34.299380 -83.158770
Vogel S.P.	121	D2	34.766190 -83.922000
Watson Mill Bridge S.P.	121	E3	34.041140 -83.126990

HAWAII	PAGE	GRID	LATITUDE LONGITUDE
National Park & Rec. Areas			
Haleakala Natl. Park-Main Road	153	D1	20.769130 -156.242850
Haleakala Natl. Park-Kipahulu Ent.	153	D1	20.662000 -156.045600
Haleakala Natl. Park-North Ent.	153	D1	20.769000 -156.243000
Hawaii Volcanoes Natl. Park-Ent.	153	F4	19.428700 -155.254500
Honouliuli N.H.S.	152	A3	21.354145 -158.090528
Kalaupapa N.H.P.	152	C3	21.174110 -157.002830
Pearl Harbor Natl. Mem.	152	A3	21.367603 -157.941052
State Park & Rec. Areas			
Ahupua'a 'O Kahana S.P.	152	A2	21.555210 -157.873260
Haena S.P.	152	B1	22.220930 -159.579600
Kaena Point S.P.	152	A2	21.551270 -158.244180
Kokee S.P.	152	B1	22.112580 -159.671050
Makena S.P.	153	D1	20.634030 -156.444180
Palaau S.P.	152	C3	21.174110 -157.002830
Polihale S.P.	152	B1	22.084480 -159.756700
Puaa Kaa State Wayside	153	D1	20.817560 -156.125800
Waianapanapa S.P.	153	E1	20.786230 -156.003010
Wailua River S.P.	152	B1	22.044180 -159.337250
Wailua Valley State Wayside	153	D1	20.840110 -156.139980
Wailuku River S.P.	153	F3	19.713340 -155.130490
Waimea Canyon S.P.	152	B1	22.031990 -159.671100

IDAHO	PAGE	GRID	LATITUDE LONGITUDE
National Park & Rec. Areas			
City of Rocks Natl. Res.	31	D2	42.078950 -113.677650
Craters of the Moon Natl. Mon. & Pres.	23	D4	43.462030 -113.559930
Hagerman Fossil Beds Natl. Mon.	30	C1	42.760980 -114.928220
Minidoka Natl. Hist. Site	31	D1	42.636944 -114.232222
Nez Perce N.H.P.-Clearwater Bfld.	22	B1	46.072600 -115.975400
Nez Perce N.H.P.-East Kamiah Site	22	B1	46.216600 -115.992400
Nez Perce N.H.P.-Vis. Ctr.	22	B1	46.446500 -116.817000
Nez Perce N.H.P.-White Bird Bfld.	22	B1	45.794400 -116.282000
Sawtooth N.R.A.	22	C3	44.211000 -114.946000
State Park & Rec. Areas			
Bear Lake S.P.	31	F2	42.026180 -111.257690
Bruneau Dunes S.P.	30	B1	42.910940 -115.713890
Castle Rocks S.P.	31	D2	42.135400 -113.670000
Dworshak S.P.	14	B4	46.577610 -116.327310
Eagle Island S.P.	22	B4	43.684510 -116.400300
Farragut S.P.	14	B2	47.952790 -116.602170
Harriman S.P.	23	F3	44.321000 -111.471200
Hells Gate S.P.	14	B4	46.380500 -117.044780
Henrys Lake S.P.	23	F3	44.620000 -111.373060
Heyburn S.P.	14	B3	47.353840 -116.748770
Lake Cascade S.P.	22	B3	44.520686 -116.046685
Lake Walcott S.P.	31	D1	42.674850 -113.482570
Land of the Yankee Fork S.P.	22	C3	44.475190 -114.208860
Lucky Peak S.P.	22	B4	43.530880 -116.055160
Massacre Rocks S.P.	31	D1	42.672200 -112.990800
McCroskey S.P.	14	B4	47.721080 -116.826310
Old Mission S.P.	14	B3	47.549420 -116.356940
Ponderosa S.P.	22	B2	44.926810 -116.083860
Priest Lake S.P.	14	B1	48.622082 -116.827798
Round Lake S.P.	14	B2	48.166110 -116.634230
Thousand Springs S.P.-Box Canyon	30	C1	42.709800 -114.791900
Thousand Springs S.P.-Malad Gorge	30	C1	42.864400 -114.854600
Thousand Springs S.P.-Niagara Springs	30	C1	42.662800 -114.672400
Three Island Crossing S.P.	30	C1	42.945280 -115.314850
Winchester Lake S.P.	22	B1	46.232280 -116.635570

ILLINOIS	PAGE	GRID	LATITUDE LONGITUDE
National Park & Rec. Areas			
Lincoln Home N.H.S.	98	B1	39.798120 -89.645150
Ronald Reagan Boyhood Home N.H.S.	88	B1	41.836700 -89.481100
State Park & Rec. Areas			
Apple River Canyon S.P.	74	A4	42.443990 -90.053280
Argyle Lake S.P.	87	F4	40.450680 -90.805080
Banner Marsh State Fish & Wildlife Area	88	B4	40.539600 -89.864500
Beall Woods S.P.	99	D4	38.351540 -87.836380
Beaver Dam S.P.	98	B2	39.214390 -89.959390
Big Bend State Fish & Wildlife Area	88	A2	41.634900 -90.044600
Buffalo Rock S.P.	88	C2	41.329720 -88.913090
Carlyle Lake State Fish & Wildlife Area	98	C3	38.768500 -89.193900
Castle Rock S.P.	88	B1	41.978230 -89.357040
Cave-In-Rock S.P.	109	D1	37.468010 -88.159950
Chain O'Lakes S.P.	74	C4	42.458390 -88.211950
Channahon S.P.	88	C2	41.415826 -88.223133
Coffeen Lake State Fish & Wildlife Area	98	B2	39.057000 -89.412400
Crawford County State Fish & Wildlife Area	99	D2	39.099800 -87.713100
Delabar S.P.	87	F3	40.957830 -90.939460
Des Plaines State Fish & Wildlife Area	88	C2	41.376600 -88.207400
Dixon Springs S.P.	108	C1	37.383600 -88.672830
Donnelley–Depue State Fish & Wildlife Area	88	B2	41.324000 -89.314100
Edward R. Madigan State Fish & Wildlife Area	88	B4	40.115280 -89.402240
Eldon Hazlet State Rec. Area	98	B3	38.667610 -89.327200
Ferne Clyffe S.P.	108	C1	37.532550 -88.966430
Fort Massac S.P.	108	C2	37.161720 -88.693850
Fox Ridge S.P.	99	D2	39.406020 -88.134810
Gebhard Woods S.P.	88	C2	41.357350 -88.440210
Giant City S.P.	108	C1	37.612250 -89.181790
Green River State Wildlife Area	88	B2	41.631600 -89.516500
Hamilton County State Fish & Wildlife Area	98	C4	38.065100 -88.404700
Hazel & Bill Rutherford Wildlife Prairie S.P.	88	B3	40.734180 -89.747270
Henderson County Cons. Area	87	F3	40.857505 -90.975005
Horseshoe Lake State Fish & Wildlife Area	108	C2	37.130465 -89.338505
Illini S.P.	88	C2	41.318770 -88.711070
Illinois Beach S.P.	75	D4	42.429920 -87.820150
Iroquois County State Wildlife Area	89	D3	40.994300 -87.598700
Jim Edgar Panther Creek State Fish & Wildlife Area	98	B1	40.011700 -90.177005
Johnson-Sauk Trail S.P.	88	A2	41.327510 -89.904850
Jubilee College S.P.	88	B3	40.844580 -89.827260
Kankakee River S.P.	89	D2	41.203400 -88.001880
Kaskaskia River State Fish & Wildlife Area	98	B4	38.229700 -89.879500
Kickapoo State Rec. Area	89	D4	40.138290 -87.737770
Lake Le Aqua-Na State Rec. Area	74	A4	42.422800 -89.823900
Lake Murphysboro S.P.	108	C1	37.771800 -89.382670
Lasalle Lake State Fish & Wildlife Area	88	C2	41.238400 -88.655500
Lincoln Trail S.P.	99	D2	39.346480 -87.696460
Lowden S.P.	88	B1	42.034860 -89.324950
Mackinaw River State Fish & Wildlife Area	88	B4	40.545801 -89.294301
Marshall State Fish & Wildlife Area	88	B3	41.007900 -89.410100
Matthiessen S.P.	88	C2	41.285010 -89.010050
Mautino State Fish & Wildlife Area	88	B2	41.323100 -89.718900
Middle Fork State Fish & Wildlife Area	89	D4	40.258300 -87.795900
Mississippi Palisades S.P.	88	A1	42.135820 -90.163300
Mississippi River State Fish & Wildlife Area	98	A2	38.991900 -90.542100
Morrison-Rockwood S.P.	88	A1	41.856350 -89.950120
Nauvoo S.P.	87	F4	40.543590 -91.386650
Newton Lake State Fish & Wildlife Area	99	D2	38.922400 -88.306700
Pere Marquette S.P.	98	A2	38.968110 -90.497430
Prophetstown S.P.	88	B2	41.672090 -89.920310
Pyramid State Rec. Area	98	B4	38.004110 -89.425680
Ray Norbut State Fish & Wildlife Area	98	A1	39.685000 -90.648500
Red Hills S.P.	99	D3	38.728850 -87.838660
Rend Lake State Fish & Wildlife Area	98	C4	38.043800 -88.988900
Rice Lake State Fish & Wildlife Area	88	A4	40.476785 -89.949205
Saline County State Fish & Wildlife Area	109	D1	37.691300 -88.379100
Sam Dale Lake State Fish & Wildlife Area	98	C3	38.536005 -88.565605
Sam Parr State Fish & Wildlife Area	99	D2	39.011022 -88.126955
Sanganois State Fish & Wildlife Area	88	A4	40.091605 -90.283205
Sangchris Lake State Rec. Area	98	B1	39.656830 -89.487940
Shabbona Lake S.P.	88	C1	41.732250 -88.864930
Shelbyville State Fish & Wildlife Area	98	C2	39.566300 -88.566200
Siloam Springs S.P.	97	F1	39.899340 -90.955050
Silver Springs State Fish & Wildlife Area.	88	C2	41.627500 -88.518550
Snakeden Hollow State Fish & Wildlife Area	88	A3	41.030200 -90.080100
South Shore S.P.	98	B3	38.610250 -89.314570
Starved Rock S.P.	88	C2	41.321750 -89.010850
Stephen A. Forbes State Rec. Area	98	C3	38.718140 -88.743250
Ten Mile Creek State Fish & Wildlife Area	98	C4	38.081200 -88.594200
Turkey Bluffs State Fish & Wildlife Area	98	B4	37.877200 -89.771100
Walnut Point S.P.	99	D1	39.705150 -88.030390
Wayne Fitzgerrell S.P.	98	C4	38.089250 -88.937010
Weinberg-King S.P.	87	F4	40.226830 -90.899700
Weldon Springs S.P.	88	C4	40.125080 -88.921400
White Pines Forest S.P.	88	B1	41.988730 -89.461590
Wolf Creek S.P.	98	C2	39.488310 -88.680370
Woodford State Fish & Wildlife Area	88	B3	40.878900 -89.444800

INDIANA	PAGE	GRID	LATITUDE LONGITUDE
National Park & Rec. Areas			
George Rodgers Clark N.H.P.	99	D3	38.677880 -87.535350
Indiana Dunes Natl. Park	89	D1	41.653160 -87.062630
Lincoln Boyhood Natl. Mem.	99	E4	38.116800 -86.997860
State Park & Rec. Areas			
Bass Lake State Beach	89	E2	41.220100 -86.580200
Brown County S.P.	99	F2	39.197170 -86.215830
Chain O' Lakes S.P.	90	A2	41.336000 -85.422950
Charlestown S.P.	100	A3	38.448300 -85.644700
Clifty Falls S.P.	100	A3	38.761220 -85.420720
Fort Harrison S.P.	99	F1	39.871921 -86.018859
Harmonie S.P.	99	D4	38.089210 -87.934080
Indiana Dunes S.P.	89	E2	41.651470 -87.062620
Lincoln S.P.	99	E4	38.118370 -86.980080
McCormick's Creek S.P.	99	E2	39.283340 -86.726680
O'Bannon Woods S.P.	99	F4	38.200600 -86.254678
Ouabache S.P.	90	A3	40.728090 -85.111060
Pokagon S.P.	90	A1	41.707960 -85.029320
Potato Creek S.P.	89	E2	41.534950 -86.360290
Prophetstown S.P.	89	E4	40.500211 -86.829548
Shades S.P.	99	E1	39.941630 -87.057670
Shakamak S.P.	99	E2	39.181800 -87.232200
Spring Mill S.P.	99	F3	38.723330 -86.418460
Summit Lake S.P.	100	A1	40.018680 -85.302720
Tippecanoe River S.P.	89	E3	41.117330 -86.602750
Turkey Run S.P.	99	E1	39.882010 -87.200550
Versailles S.P.	100	A2	39.063900 -85.205330
Whitewater Mem. S.P.	100	B1	39.611300 -84.942300

IOWA	PAGE	GRID	LATITUDE LONGITUDE
National Park & Rec. Areas			
Effigy Mounds Natl. Mon.	73	F3	43.089310 -91.192350
Herbert Hoover N.H.S.	87	F1	41.671390 -91.346640
State Park & Rec. Areas			
Ambrose A. Call S.P.	72	B3	43.049650 -94.243430
Backbone S.P.	73	E4	42.600730 -91.532700
Beeds Lake S.P.	73	D4	42.767209 -93.241705
Bellevue S.P.	88	A1	42.247870 -90.416920
Big Creek S.P.	86	C1	41.767799 -93.777615
Black Hawk S.P.	72	B4	42.302700 -95.048680
Clear Lake S.P.	72	C3	43.110281 -93.394441
Cold Springs S.P.	86	B2	41.289540 -95.083810
Elk Rock S.P.	87	D2	41.400470 -93.063050
Fort Defiance S.P.	72	B2	43.393260 -94.851290
Geode S.P.	87	F3	40.832500 -91.385000
George Wyth Mem. S.P.	73	E4	42.536980 -92.394210
Green Valley S.P.	86	B3	41.114490 -94.377270
Gull Point S.P.	72	A3	43.486153 -96.536551
Honey Creek S.P.	87	D3	40.863940 -92.939050
Lacey Keosauqua S.P.	87	E3	40.839296 -92.222861
Lake Ahquabi S.P.	86	C2	41.286710 -93.572690
Lake Anita S.P.	86	B2	41.434150 -94.762470
Lake Keomah S.P.	87	D2	41.286570 -92.541660
Lake Macbride S.P.	87	F1	41.803090 -91.570950
Lake of Three Fires S.P.	86	B3	40.716391 -94.691671
Lake Wapello S.P.	87	D3	40.824890 -92.570530
Ledges S.P.	86	C1	41.998970 -93.896110
Maquoketa Caves S.P.	87	F1	42.119890 -90.770950
McIntosh Woods S.P.	72	C3	43.132580 -93.457580
Mini-Wakan S.P.	72	B2	43.498460 -95.102320
Nine Eagles S.P.	86	C3	40.591250 -93.765130
Palisades-Kepler S.P.	87	F1	41.916880 -91.497050
Pikes Peak S.P.	73	F3	43.028215 -91.329671
Pikes Point S.P.	72	A2	43.415320 -95.162860
Pilot Knob S.P.	72	C3	43.255470 -93.574840
Prairie Rose S.P.	86	A2	41.601590 -95.210660
Preparation Canyon S.P.	86	A1	41.901570 -95.911670
Rice Lake S.P.	72	C2	43.401350 -93.502490
Rock Creek S.P.	87	D1	41.760580 -92.835410
Springbrook S.P.	86	B1	41.776390 -94.459440
Stone S.P.	35	F1	42.555460 -96.476050
Trappers Bay S.P.	72	A2	43.453630 -95.335510
Twin Lakes S.P.	72	B4	42.480180 -94.629860
Viking Lake S.P.	86	B3	40.973170 -95.053710
Wapsipinicon S.P.	87	F1	42.204448 -91.396368
Waubonsie S.P.	86	A3	40.677770 -95.683680
Wildcat Den S.P.	87	F2	41.467700 -90.869330

KANSAS	PAGE	GRID	LATITUDE LONGITUDE
National Park & Rec. Areas			
Fort Larned N.H.S.	43	D3	38.188740 -99.220620
Fort Scott N.H.S.	106	B1	37.843350 -94.704840
Monument Rocks Natl. Landmark	42	B2	38.790569 -100.762366
Nicodemus N.H.S.	42	C2	39.390833 -99.617500
State Park & Rec. Areas			
Atchison State Fishing Lake	96	B1	39.639010 -95.171830
Black Kettle State Fishing Lake	43	E3	38.229240 -97.509390
Bourbon State Fishing Lake	106	B1	37.793450 -95.069690
Brown State Fishing Lake	96	A1	39.847030 -95.373860
Cedar Bluff S.P.	42	C2	38.798230 -99.715060
Chase State Fishing Lake	43	F3	38.368480 -96.588000
Cheney S.P.	43	E4	37.732700 -97.844350
Clark State Fishing Lake	42	C4	37.391670 -99.784720
Clinton S.P.	96	A3	38.941970 -95.353960
Cowley State Fishing Lake	51	F1	37.104040 -96.795000
Crawford S.P.	106	B1	37.634320 -94.809820
Cross Timbers S.P.	106	A1	37.774514 -95.943431
Douglas State Fishing Lake	96	B3	38.796030 -95.165150
Eisenhower S.P.	96	A3	38.535720 -95.744270
El Dorado S.P.	43	F4	37.861420 -96.749460
Elk City S.P.	106	A2	37.251130 -95.774090
Fallriver S.P.	43	F4	37.653550 -96.043600
Glen Elder S.P.	43	D1	39.512160 -98.339140
Hain State Fishing Lake	42	C4	37.854250 -99.858020
Hamilton State Fishing Lake	42	B3	38.039090 -101.816940
Hillsdale S.P.	96	B3	38.660700 -94.894000
Kanopolis S.P.	43	E3	38.600340 -97.979500
Kingman State Fishing Lake	43	E4	37.651390 -98.306940
Kiowa State Fishing Lake	43	D4	37.612570 -99.299000
Leavenworth State Fishing Lake	96	B2	39.126970 -95.141700
Logan State Fishing Lake	42	B2	38.940280 -101.236940
Lovewell S.P.	43	E1	39.903310 -98.043090
Lyon State Fishing Lake	43	F3	38.546520 -96.058050
McPherson State Fishing Lake	43	E3	38.478667 -97.468267
Meade S.P.	42	C4	37.172220 -100.450000

Park	Page	Grid	Latitude Longitude
Miami State Fishing Lake	96	B3	38.422220 -94.785280
Milford S.P.	43	F2	39.104290 -96.895520
Mushroom Rock S.P.	43	E2	38.722222 -98.032222
Nebo State Fishing Lake	96	A2	39.447220 -95.595830
Neosho State Fishing Lake	106	B1	37.430570 -95.202550
Ottawa State Fishing Lake	43	E2	39.103040 -97.573060
Perry S.P.	96	A2	39.140210 -95.492480
Pomona S.P.	96	A3	38.652400 -95.600800
Pottawatomie State Fishing Lake No. 1	43	F1	39.470370 -96.407510
Pottawatomie State Fishing Lake No. 2	43	F2	39.228100 -96.533660
Prairie Dog S.P.	42	C1	39.811810 -99.963920
Prairie Spirit Trail S.P.	96	A4	38.280278 -95.242222
Rooks State Fishing Lake	43	D2	39.398290 -99.315020
Saline State Fishing Lake	43	E2	38.903159 -97.657510
Sand Hills S.P.	43	E3	38.116667 -97.833333
Scott S.P.	42	B2	38.684867 -100.922500
Shawnee State Fishing Lake	96	A2	39.206940 -95.804170
Tuttle Creek S.P.	43	F2	39.255560 -96.583330
Washington State Fishing Lake	43	E1	39.929780 -97.118830
Webster S.P.	43	D2	39.407840 -99.454550
Wilson State Fishing Lake	106	A1	38.910450 -98.497950
Wilson S.P.	43	D2	38.915000 -98.500000

KENTUCKY	PAGE	GRID	LATITUDE LONGITUDE
National Park & Rec. Areas			
Abraham Lincoln Birthplace N.H.P.	110	A1	37.532280 -85.733570
Camp Nelson Natl. Mon..	110	B1	37.761697 -84.779784
Land Between the Lakes N.R.A.	109	D2	36.776912 -88.059988
Mammoth Cave Natl. Park-Vis. Ctr.	109	F2	37.186800 -86.101300
Mill Springs Bfld. Natl. Mon.	110	B2	37.195931 -85.031625
State Park & Rec. Areas			
Barren River Lake State Resort Park	110	A2	36.853220 -86.053850
Blue Licks Bfld. State Resort Park	100	C3	38.434960 -83.991340
Buckhorn Lake State Resort Park	111	D1	37.312890 -83.423040
Carter Caves State Resort Park	101	D4	38.371470 -83.108510
Columbus-Belmont S.P.	108	C2	36.761990 -89.107000
Cumberland Falls State Resort Park	110	C2	36.834390 -84.350170
Fishtrap Lake S.P.	111	E1	37.432048 -82.417926
Fort Boonesborough S.P.	110	C1	37.899345 -84.270040
General Butler State Resort Park	100	A3	38.669950 -85.146050
Grayson Lake S.P.	101	D4	38.208630 -83.014910
Greenbo Lake State Resort Park	101	D3	38.479130 -82.867630
Green River Lake S.P.	110	A2	37.277440 -85.338730
Jenny Wiley State Resort Park	111	E1	37.697427 -82.726617
John James Audubon S.P.	99	D4	37.889250 -87.556510
Kentucky Dam Village State Resort Park	109	D2	36.996880 -88.285716
Kingdom Come S.P.	111	D2	36.981850 -82.982210
Lake Barkley State Resort Park	109	D2	36.809190 -87.928310
Lake Cumberland State Resort Park	110	B2	36.930320 -85.040960
Lake Malone S.P.	109	E2	37.076110 -87.038060
Levi Jackson Wilderness Road S.P.	110	C2	37.085250 -84.059250
Lincoln Homestead S.P.	110	B1	37.760080 -85.215930
My Old Kentucky Home S.P.	110	A1	37.808140 -85.458840
Natural Bridge State Resort Park	110	C1	37.777470 -83.676310
Nolin Lake S.P.	109	F1	37.297641 -86.212624
Old Fort Harrod S.P.	110	B1	37.762130 -84.845670
Pennyrile Forest State Resort Park	109	E2	37.057410 -87.649390
Pine Mtn. State Resort Park	110	C3	36.735270 -83.700790
Rough River Dam State Resort Park	109	F1	37.615410 -86.504410
Taylorsville Lake S.P.	100	A4	37.993990 -85.227813
Yatesville Lake S.P.	101	D4	38.093300 -82.617800

LOUISIANA	PAGE	GRID	LATITUDE LONGITUDE
National Park & Rec. Areas			
Cane River Creole N.H.P.	125	D4	31.739690 -93.083080
Jean Lafitte N.H.P. & Pres.-Chalmette Vis. Ctr.	134	A3	29.942100 -89.994400
Jean Lafitte N.H.P. & Pres.-French Quarter Vis. Ctr.	134	A3	29.954600 -90.065100
Jean Lafitte N.H.P.-Wetlands Acadian Cultural Center	134	A3	29.795969 -90.824480
Poverty Point Natl. Mon. & S.H.S.	125	F2	32.633370 -91.403880
State Park & Rec. Areas			
Bayou Segnette S.P.	134	B3	29.902720 -90.153800
Bogue Chitto S.P.	134	B1	30.774546 -90.168394
Chemin-A-Haut S.P.	125	F1	32.913460 -91.847550
Chicot S.P.	133	E1	30.829870 -92.276180
Cypremort Point S.P.	133	F3	29.731960 -91.840740
Fairview-Riverside S.P.	134	B2	30.408730 -90.140360
Fontainebleau S.P.	134	B2	30.345470 -90.022850
Grand Isle S.P.-Temp. Closed	134	B4	29.256640 -89.958480
Jimmie Davis S.P.	125	E3	32.265000 -92.540300
Lake Bistineau S.P.	125	D2	32.440250 -93.395910
Lake Bruin S.P.	126	A3	31.955370 -91.198080
Lake Claiborne S.P.	125	D2	32.713000 -92.923360
Lake D'Arbonne S.P.	125	E2	32.784850 -92.490310
Lake Fausse Pointe S.P.	133	F3	30.067820 -91.615790
North Toledo Bend S.P.	124	C4	31.558910 -93.732060
Palmetto Island S.P.	133	F3	29.862877 -92.144165
Poverty Point Reservoir S.P.	125	F2	32.540446 -91.421356
Saint Bernard S.P.	134	C3	29.864460 -89.899190
South Toledo Bend S.P.	125	D4	31.213889 -93.575000
Tickfaw S.P.	134	B2	30.382180 -90.631150

MAINE	PAGE	GRID	LATITUDE LONGITUDE
National Park & Rec. Areas			
Acadia Natl. Park-Park Loop Road	83	D2	44.338700 -68.183200
Acadia Natl. Park-Sieur de Monts Ent.	83	D2	44.360000 -68.205200
Acadia Natl. Park-Stanley Brook Ent.	83	D2	44.296300 -68.242000
Katahdin Woods & Waters Natl. Mon.	85	D3	45.883549 -68.737849
State Park & Rec. Areas			
Aroostook S.P.	85	E2	46.612720 -68.005840
Baxter S.P.	84	C3	45.950290 -69.049080
Camden Hills S.P.	82	C2	44.232050 -69.046530
Cobscook Bay S.P.	83	E1	44.855290 -67.171680
Damariscotta Lake S.P.	82	C2	44.200070 -69.452900
Ferry Beach S.P.	82	B4	43.482410 -70.391520
Lake Saint George S.P.	82	C2	44.398950 -69.345710
Lamoine S.P.	83	D2	44.456000 -68.298520
Mount Blue S.P.	82	B1	44.721780 -70.417080
Peaks-Kenny S.P.	84	C4	45.256680 -69.254600
Popham Beach S.P.	82	C3	43.738740 -69.795830
Rangeley Lake S.P.	82	B1	44.919550 -70.696950
Range Pond S.P.	82	B3	44.033540 -70.345080
Roque Bluffs S.P.	83	E2	44.614680 -67.479300
Saint Croix Island International Hist. Site	83	E1	45.128333 -67.133333
Sebago Lake S.P.	82	B3	43.916590 -70.570190
Shackford Head S.P.	83	F1	44.906191 -66.989979
Swan Lake S.P.	82	C2	44.568860 -68.981070
Vaughan Woods Mem. S.P.	82	A4	43.212680 -70.809320
Warren Island S.P.	82	C2	44.260445 -68.952255
Wolfes Neck Woods S.P.	82	B3	43.827190 -70.084460

MARYLAND	PAGE	GRID	LATITUDE LONGITUDE
National Park & Rec. Areas			
Assateague Island Natl. Seashore	114	C2	38.239580 -75.140410
Harriet Tubman Underground RR N.H.P.	103	F3	38.322307 -76.176243
Thomas Stone N.H.S.	144	B4	38.529700 -77.032370
State Park & Rec. Areas			
Assateague S.P.	114	C2	38.250170 -75.156270
Big Run S.P.	102	B1	39.545090 -79.137254
Catoctin Mtn. Park-Vis. Ctr.	144	A1	39.633100 -77.449700
Cunningham Falls S.P.	144	A1	39.625040 -77.458130
Deep Creek Lake S.P.	102	B1	39.512110 -79.300150
Elk Neck S.P.	145	D1	39.482890 -75.983630
Fort Frederick S.P.	103	D1	39.616050 -78.007060
Gambrill S.P.	144	A1	39.468330 -77.495730
Greenwell S.P.	103	E4	38.364930 -76.525260
Gunpowder Falls S.P.	144	C1	39.536710 -76.502800
Hart-Miller Island S.P.	144	C2	39.251219 -76.376903
Janes Island S.P.	103	F4	38.009810 -75.846380
Martinak S.P.	145	E3	38.862920 -75.837790
North Point S.P.	144	C2	39.221910 -76.431600
Patapsco Valley S.P.	144	B2	39.296580 -76.781500
Patuxent River S.P.	144	B2	39.280790 -77.129620
Pocomoke River S.P.	114	C2	38.135410 -75.494870
Point Lookout S.P.	103	F4	38.066190 -76.336550
Rocks S.P.	144	C1	39.630140 -76.418120
Rocky Gap S.P.	102	C1	39.698430 -78.651150
Rosaryville S.P.	144	C3	38.778450 -76.799260
Saint Clement's Island S.P.	103	E4	38.225200 -76.749690
Saint Mary's River S.P.	103	E4	38.262940 -76.525640
Sandy Point S.P.	144	C3	39.021750 -76.420280
Seneca Creek S.P.	144	A2	39.152200 -77.247710
Smallwood S.P.	144	B4	38.556509 -77.185257
South Mtn. S.P.	144	A1	39.540058 -77.607422
Susquehanna S.P.	145	D1	39.599840 -76.154590
Swallow Falls S.P.	102	B1	39.506550 -79.448750
Tuckahoe S.P.	145	D3	38.967120 -75.943410
Washington Mon. S.P.	144	A1	39.499810 -77.631890
Wye Oak S.P.	145	D3	38.939150 -76.080230

MASSACHUSETTS	PAGE	GRID	LATITUDE LONGITUDE
National Park & Rec. Areas			
Adams N.H.P.-Vis. Ctr.	151	D1	42.257000 -71.011200
Boston Harbor Island N.R.A.	151	D1	42.319705 -70.928555
Cape Cod Natl. Seashore	151	F2	41.835890 -69.973730
Lowell N.H.P.-Market Mills Vis. Ctr.	95	E1	42.644400 -71.312800
Minute Man N.H.P.-Minute Man Vis. Ctr.	151	D1	42.449000 -71.268700
Minute Man N.H.P.-North Bridge Vis. Ctr.	151	D1	42.470800 -71.352600
New Bedford Whaling N.H.P.	151	D4	41.635570 -70.924250
Salem Maritime N.H.S.	151	D1	42.521490 -70.886980
Saugus Iron Works N.H.S.	151	D1	42.468230 -71.009110
Waquoit Bay Natl. Estuarine Research Res.	151	E4	41.581300 -70.524800
State Park & Rec. Areas			
Ames Nowell S.P.	151	D2	42.113140 -70.975230
Ashland S.P.	150	C2	42.246380 -71.475560
Blackstone River & Canal Heritage S.P.	150	C2	42.099500 -71.618780
Borderland S.P.	151	D2	42.058560 -71.166330
Bradley Palmer S.P.	151	F1	42.652180 -70.911000
Callahan S.P.	150	C1	42.315140 -71.367710
Demarest Lloyd S.P.	151	D4	41.525790 -70.990530
Dighton Rock S.P.	151	D3	41.811230 -71.098440
Halibut Point S.P.	151	F1	42.686100 -70.631070
Hampton Ponds S.P.	150	A2	42.178350 -72.690030
Joseph Sylvia State Beach	151	E4	41.424140 -70.553870
Lake Wyola S.P.-Carroll Holmes Rec. Area	150	A1	42.500366 -72.430642
Moore S.P.	150	B1	42.312354 -71.954269
Mount Holyoke Range S.P.	150	A1	42.297270 -72.530890
Nickerson S.P.	151	F3	41.775550 -70.028290
Pilgrim Mem. (Plymouth Rock) S.P.	151	E2	41.958850 -70.662870
Red Bridge S.P.	150	A2	42.175500 -72.406600
Robinson S.P.	150	A2	42.081680 -72.658650
Rutland S.P.	150	B1	42.371470 -71.997680
Savoy Mtn. State Forest	94	C1	42.626540 -73.015580
Skinner S.P.	150	A1	42.304220 -72.598790
South Cape Beach S.P.	151	E4	41.554582 -70.508194
Wahconah Falls S.P.	94	C1	42.491430 -73.120790
Watson Pond S.P.	151	D2	41.956260 -71.116090
Wells S.P.	150	B2	42.142290 -72.042400
Whitehall S.P.	150	C2	42.227210 -71.584330
Wompatuck S.P.	151	D2	42.218770 -70.866600

MICHIGAN	PAGE	GRID	LATITUDE LONGITUDE
National Park & Rec. Areas			
Father Marquette Natl. Mem.	70	C2	45.853912 -84.728874
Grand Island N.R.A.	70	A1	46.500405 -86.657605
Isle Royale Natl. Park-Rock Harbor Vis. Ctr.	65	F2	48.145530 -88.482220
Isle Royale Natl. Park-Windigo Vis. Ctr.	65	F2	47.912700 -89.156990
Keweenaw N.H.P.	65	F3	47.242160 -88.448020
Pictured Rocks Natl. Lakeshore-East Ent.	70	A1	46.657450 -86.021160
Pictured Rocks Natl. Lakeshore-West Ent.	70	A1	46.474000 -86.553000
Sleeping Bear Dunes Natl. Lakeshore	70	A4	44.785210 -86.049690
State Park & Rec. Areas			
Albert E. Sleeper S.P.	76	C2	43.972880 -83.205530
Algonac S.P.	76	C4	42.654760 -82.514510
Aloha S.P.	70	C3	45.525850 -84.464390
Baraga S.P.	65	F4	46.762070 -88.499320
Bewabic S.P.	68	C2	46.094260 -88.422290
Brimley S.P.	70	C1	46.412970 -84.555040
Burt Lake S.P.	70	C3	45.401305 -84.619505
Cambridge Junction Hist. S.P.	90	B1	42.066990 -84.225550
Charles Mears S.P.	75	E2	43.781980 -86.439670
Cheboygan S.P.	70	C2	45.644860 -84.420440
Clear Lake S.P.	70	C3	45.127390 -84.173910
Coldwater Lake S.P.	90	A1	43.665975 -84.948703
Craig Lake S.P.	68	C1	46.538810 -88.127700
Duck Lake S.P.	75	E3	43.354880 -86.397560
F.J. Mclain S.P.	65	F3	47.239400 -88.587190
Fayette Hist. S.P.	70	A2	45.717200 -86.664600
Fisherman's Island S.P.	70	B3	45.307550 -85.301540
Fort Wilkins Hist. S.P.	65	F3	47.466780 -87.878240
Fred Meijer White Pine Trail S.P.	75	F2	44.222900 -85.426700
Grand Haven S.P.	75	E3	43.056100 -86.245990
Grand Mere S.P.	89	E1	41.995190 -86.538790
Harrisville S.P.	71	D4	44.649800 -83.293920
Hart-Montague Trail S.P.	75	E2	43.688800 -86.371900
Hartwick Pines S.P.	70	C4	44.744180 -84.648340
Holland S.P.	75	E4	42.780310 -86.201410
Indian Lake S.P.	70	A2	45.960420 -86.364400
Interlochen S.P.	70	B4	44.631370 -85.766630
J.W. Wells S.P.	69	D3	45.389070 -87.371360
Kal-Haven Trail S.P.	75	E4	42.324698 -85.667739
Keith J. Charters Traverse City S.P.	70	B4	44.748050 -85.553800
Lake Gogebic S.P.	68	B1	46.459950 -89.573110
Lakeport S.P.	76	C3	43.129120 -82.501820
Leelanau S.P.	70	B3	45.209320 -85.546220
Ludington S.P.	75	E1	44.031100 -86.505460
Mackinac Island S.P.	70	C2	45.849880 -84.617650
Mike Levine Lakelands Trail S.P.	76	B4	42.408249 -83.964043
Muskallonge Lake S.P.	70	B1	46.677100 -85.625210
Muskegon S.P.	75	E3	43.247900 -86.341480
Negwegon S.P.	71	D4	44.855020 -83.329240
Newaygo S.P.	75	F2	43.500600 -85.582260
North Higgins Lake S.P.	70	C4	44.515030 -84.753980
Onaway S.P.	70	C3	45.430530 -84.229020
Orchard Beach S.P.	75	E1	44.278860 -86.314480
Otsego Lake S.P.	70	C4	44.927770 -84.688980
P.H. Hoeft S.P.	70	C3	45.463700 -83.883560
P.J. Hoffmaster S.P.	75	E3	43.132870 -86.265460
Palms Book S.P.	70	A2	46.003280 -86.385130
Petoskey S.P.	70	B3	45.407950 -84.902160
Porcupine Mts. Wilderness S.P.	65	E4	46.816070 -89.621850
Port Crescent S.P.	76	C1	44.007570 -83.051290
Sanilac Petroglyphs Hist. S.P.	76	C2	43.649367 -83.018016
Saugatuck Dunes S.P.	75	E4	42.695990 -86.186840
Seven Lakes S.P.	76	B3	42.816750 -83.648120
Silver Lake S.P.	75	E2	43.663650 -86.492660
Sleepy Hollow S.P.	76	A3	42.925020 -84.408620
South Higgins Lake S.P.	76	A1	44.432818 -84.670299
Sterling S.P.	90	C1	41.921490 -83.342680
Straits S.P.	70	C2	45.858090 -84.720200
Tahquamenon Falls S.P.-East Ent.	70	B1	46.598030 -85.147890
Tahquamenon Falls S.P.-West Ent.	70	B1	46.564190 -85.292530
Tawas Point S.P.	76	B1	44.255820 -83.443050
Thompson's Harbor S.P.	71	D3	45.346705 -83.567431
Twin Lakes S.P.	65	E4	46.892210 -88.856560

Park	Page	Grid	Latitude Longitude
Van Buren S.P.	75	E4	42.333830 -86.304830
Van Buren Trail S.P.	89	F1	42.211405 -86.171105
Van Riper S.P.	68	C1	46.525260 -87.991150
Walter J. Hayes S.P.	90	B1	42.072830 -84.137820
Warren Dunes S.P.	89	E1	41.900980 -86.595260
Warren Woods S.P.	89	E1	41.840680 -86.631290
Wetzel Rec. Area	76	C4	42.596720 -82.825140
Wilderness S.P.-East Ent.	70	B2	45.748160 -84.853500
Wilderness S.P.-West Ent.	70	B2	45.679360 -84.964170
William Mitchell S.P.	75	F1	44.236880 -85.453990
Wilson S.P.	76	A1	44.029620 -84.806070
Young S.P.	70	B3	45.235240 -85.041450

MINNESOTA

MINNESOTA	PAGE	GRID	LATITUDE LONGITUDE
National Park & Rec. Areas			
Grand Portage Natl. Mon.	65	E2	47.996274 -89.734256
Pipestone Natl. Mon.	27	F3	44.013150 -96.325360
Voyageurs Natl. Park-Ash River Vis. Ctr.	64	C2	48.435600 -92.850300
Voyageurs Natl. Park-Kabetogama Lake Vis. Ctr.	64	C2	48.446100 -93.030100
Voyageurs Natl. Park-Rainy Lake Vis. Ctr.	64	C2	48.584400 -93.161500
State Park & Rec. Areas			
Afton S.P.	67	D4	44.847930 -92.791020
Banning S.P.	67	D2	46.179730 -92.855170
Bear Head Lake S.P.	64	C3	47.792720 -92.083720
Beaver Creek Valley S.P.	73	E2	43.636790 -91.573190
Blue Mounds S.P.	27	F4	43.714340 -96.183100
Buffalo River S.P.	19	F4	46.866260 -96.469980
Camden S.P.	27	F3	44.362880 -95.917480
Caribou Falls State Wayside	65	D3	47.463890 -91.030660
Carley S.P.	73	E1	44.116790 -92.169320
Cascade River S.P.	65	D3	47.712950 -90.497930
Charles A. Lindbergh S.P.	66	C2	45.959410 -94.387640
Crow Wing S.P.	66	C1	46.272630 -94.316400
Father Hennepin S.P.	66	C1	46.144520 -93.484260
Flandrau S.P.	72	B1	44.294360 -94.482020
Flood Bay State Wayside	64	C4	47.038500 -91.642540
Forestville Mystery Cave S.P.	73	E2	43.637520 -92.220270
Fort Ridgely S.P.	72	B1	44.454810 -94.718310
Franz Jevne S.P.	64	B2	48.641140 -94.058260
Frontenac S.P.	67	E4	44.525200 -92.338730
George H. Crosby Manitou S.P.	65	D3	47.478990 -91.123070
Glacial Lakes S.P.	66	A3	45.540550 -95.529600
Glendalough S.P.	19	F4	46.313314 -95.679290
Gooseberry Falls S.P.	65	D3	47.145430 -91.462380
Grand Portage S.P.	65	E2	47.999150 -89.598690
Great River Bluffs S.P.	73	E1	43.939100 -91.430050
Hayes Lake S.P.	19	F1	48.641070 -95.570600
Hill Annex Mine S.P.	64	B3	47.327490 -93.277520
Inspiration Peak State Wayside	66	A1	46.136880 -95.578650
Interstate S.P.	67	D3	45.391631 -92.664111
Itasca S.P.	64	A3	47.194490 -95.166740
Jay Cooke S.P.	64	C4	46.658790 -92.349200
John A. Latsch S.P.	73	E1	44.164720 -91.823860
Joseph R. Brown State Wayside	66	B4	44.750328 -95.324425
Judge C.R. Magney S.P.	65	E3	47.818090 -90.051230
Kilen Woods S.P.	72	B2	43.732140 -95.072220
Kodonce River State Wayside	65	E3	47.793930 -90.154140
Lac Qui Parle S.P.	27	F2	45.024680 -95.896580
Lake Bemidji S.P.	64	A3	47.536890 -94.832320
Lake Bronson S.P.	19	F1	48.730940 -96.630720
Lake Carlos S.P.	66	B2	46.000540 -95.334430
Lake Louise S.P.	73	D2	43.532620 -92.509250
Lake Maria S.P.	66	C3	45.304810 -93.935570
Lake Shetek S.P.	72	A1	44.105740 -95.699730
L.Vermilion-Soudan Underground Mine S.P.	64	C2	47.818130 -92.246090
Maplewood S.P.	19	F4	46.549910 -95.966720
McCarthy Beach S.P.	64	B3	47.674110 -93.027350
Mille Lacs Kathio S.P.	66	C2	46.160740 -93.758020
Minneopa S.P.	72	C1	44.162190 -94.110310
Minnesota Valley St. Rec. Area	66	C4	44.650309 -93.715927
Monson Lake S.P.	66	B3	45.321300 -95.270470
Moose Lake S.P.	64	C4	46.436360 -92.743090
Myre-Big Island S.P.	73	D2	43.623847 -93.289096
Nerstrand Big Woods S.P.	73	D1	44.327040 -93.111210
Old Mill S.P.	19	F2	48.369790 -96.569420
Ray Berglund State Wayside	65	D3	47.608200 -90.771930
Rice Lake S.P.	73	D1	44.095380 -93.063940
Saint Croix S.P.	67	D2	45.960615 -92.611630
Sakatah Lake S.P.	72	C1	44.218000 -93.509970
Sam Brown Mem. State Wayside	27	F1	45.596160 -96.841410
Savanna Portage S.P.	64	B4	46.819130 -93.176040
Scenic S.P.	64	B3	47.702450 -93.564710
Schoolcraft S.P.	64	B3	47.223040 -93.805320
Sibley S.P.	66	B3	45.318990 -95.011930
Split Rock Creek S.P.	27	F4	43.907240 -96.367970
Split Rock Lighthouse S.P.	65	D3	47.189800 -91.395010
Temperance River S.P.	65	D3	47.558780 -90.867930
Tettegouche S.P.	65	D3	47.337210 -91.200670
Upper Sioux Agency S.P.	66	B4	44.734540 -95.456460
Whitewater S.P.	73	E1	44.068880 -92.040100
Wild River S.P.	67	D3	45.524100 -92.754500
William O'Brien S.P.	67	D3	45.223900 -92.763500
Zippel Bay S.P.	64	A1	48.840630 -94.849950

MISSISSIPPI

MISSISSIPPI	PAGE	GRID	LATITUDE LONGITUDE
National Park & Rec. Areas			
Gulf Islands Natl. Seashore	135	D2	30.407200 -88.749220
Natchez N.H.P.-Vis. Reception Ctr.	125	F4	31.553900 -91.412400
State Park & Rec. Areas			
Bogue Homa State Fishing Lake	127	D4	31.703200 -89.026400
Calling Panther State Fishing Lake	126	B3	32.197100 -90.265100
Clarkco S.P.	127	D3	32.108500 -88.693970
Columbia State Fishing Lake	134	C1	31.183500 -89.738400
Florewood S.P.	118	B4	33.525120 -90.250362
George Payne Cossar S.P.	118	B3	34.122710 -89.882100
Golden Mem. S.P.	126	C2	32.568560 -89.407640
Great River Road S.P.	118	A4	33.851733 -91.027574
Hugh White S.P.	118	B4	33.796080 -89.743010
J.P. Coleman S.P.	119	D2	34.924254 -88.171706
Jeff Davis State Fishing Lake	126	B4	31.567700 -89.839800
John W. Kyle S.P.	118	B3	34.438060 -89.807500
Kemper County State Fishing Lake	127	D2	32.804167 -88.730556
Lake Lincoln S.P.	126	B4	31.684354 -90.337142
Legion S.P.	127	D1	33.148690 -89.042460
Leroy Percy S.P.	126	A1	33.160500 -90.938250
Mary Crawford State Fishing Lake	126	B4	31.574900 -90.154000
Monroe State Fishing Lake	119	D4	33.941500 -88.568700
Natchez S.P.	126	A4	31.589580 -91.220350
Neshoba County State Fishing Lake	126	C2	32.706200 -89.010500
Paul B. Johnson S.P.	134	C1	31.133800 -89.233910
Percy Quin S.P.	134	B1	31.189020 -90.510660
Perry State Fishing Lake	135	D1	31.132400 -88.899800
Prentiss Walker State Fishing Lake	126	C3	31.833200 -89.589500
Roosevelt S.P.	126	C2	32.321920 -89.664980
Simpson County State Fishing Lake	126	C3	31.913500 -89.794500
Tippah County State Fishing Lake	118	C2	34.794290 -88.950660
Tishomingo S.P.	119	D2	34.615670 -88.183390
Tom Bailey State Fishing Lake	127	D2	32.425030 -88.523069
Tombigbee S.P.	119	D3	34.231870 -88.628870
Trace S.P.	118	C3	34.260020 -88.886560
Wall Doxey S.P.	118	C2	34.660270 -89.459290
Walthall State Fishing Lake	134	B1	31.059184 -90.133939

MISSOURI

MISSOURI	PAGE	GRID	LATITUDE LONGITUDE
National Park & Rec. Areas			
George Washington Carver Natl. Mon.	106	C2	36.986160 -94.351890
Ozark Natl. Scenic Riverways	107	F2	37.281400 -91.408000
Ste. Genevieve Natl Hist. Park	98	A4	38.107373 -91.08916
State Park & Rec. Areas			
Bennett Spring S.P.	107	D1	37.725440 -92.856390
Big Lake S.P.	86	A4	40.092090 -95.347300
Big Oak Tree S.P.	108	C3	36.641990 -89.290180
Big Sugar Creek S.P.	106	C3	36.584106 -93.819122
Crowder S.P.	86	C4	40.082140 -93.669310
Cuivre River S.P.	97	F2	39.062380 -90.938640
Echo Bluff S.P.	107	F1	37.315893 -91.411322
Elephant Rocks S.P.	108	A1	37.652150 -90.690810
Finger Lakes S.P.	97	E2	39.075400 -92.314750
Graham Cave S.P.	97	F3	38.908850 -91.576090
Grand Gulf S.P.	107	F3	36.544100 -91.636370
Ha Ha Tonka S.P.	97	D4	37.975410 -92.762230
Harry S. Truman S.P.	97	D4	38.274650 -93.442390
Hawn S.P.	108	B1	37.833660 -90.241610
Johnson's Shut-Ins S.P.	108	A1	37.547920 -90.853020
Katy Trail S.P.	97	E3	38.975190 -92.750160
Knob Noster S.P.	96	C3	38.753020 -93.577440
Lake of the Ozarks S.P.	97	E4	38.133990 -92.564260
Lake Wappapello S.P.	108	A2	36.942210 -90.344400
Lewis & Clark S.P.	96	B1	39.538900 -95.052900
Long Branch S.P.	97	E1	39.767610 -92.526480
Mark Twain S.P.	97	E2	39.485270 -91.795340
Meramec S.P.	97	F4	38.215350 -91.123070
Montauk S.P.	107	F1	37.454710 -91.690970
Morris S.P.	108	B3	36.554166 -90.043220
Onondaga Cave S.P.	97	F4	38.064310 -91.230140
Pershing S.P.	97	D1	39.776270 -93.211130
Pomme de Terre S.P.	107	D1	37.874380 -93.318700
Roaring River S.P.	106	C3	36.590110 -93.834420
Robertsville S.P.	98	A3	38.429120 -90.818110
Saint Francois S.P.	98	A4	37.972900 -90.536210
Saint Joe S.P.	108	A1	37.824990 -90.537480
Sam A. Baker S.P.	108	A2	37.254530 -90.505080
Stockton S.P.	106	C1	37.622470 -93.753070
Table Rock S.P.	107	D3	36.583440 -93.309150
Taum Sauk Mtn. S.P.	108	A1	37.669500 -90.673400
Thousand Hills S.P.	87	D4	40.185160 -92.643070
Trail of Tears S.P.	108	B1	37.452880 -89.490760
Van Meter S.P.	97	D2	39.262590 -93.267210
Wakonda S.P.	97	F1	40.004250 -91.526060
Wallace S.P.	96	C1	39.660760 -94.213290
Washington S.P.	98	A4	38.085600 -90.685650
Watkins Mill S.P.	96	C2	39.383920 -94.265130
Weston Bend S.P.	96	B2	39.392960 -94.863430

MONTANA

MONTANA	PAGE	GRID	LATITUDE LONGITUDE
National Park & Rec. Areas			
Bighorn Canyon N.R.A.	24	C2	45.330090 -107.871650
Fort Benton Natl. Hist. Landmark	16	A2	47.823210 -110.661910
Glacier Natl. Park-Many Glacier Ent.	15	D1	48.827150 -113.551540
Glacier Natl. Park-St Mary Ent.	15	D1	48.747120 -113.439650
Glacier Natl. Park-Two Medicine Ent.	15	D1	48.494210 -113.262250
Glacier Natl. Park-West Ent.	15	D1	48.499890 -113.987190
Grant-Kohrs Ranch N.H.S.	15	E4	46.398900 -112.736680
Little Bighorn Bfld. Natl. Mon.	24	C1	45.570080 -107.434710
Natl. Bison Range	15	D3	47.371674 -114.262066
Rattlesnake N.R.A.	15	D4	47.040775 -113.933333
State Park & Rec. Areas			
Ackley Lake S.P.	16	B4	46.947220 -109.936110
Anaconda Smoke Stack S.P.	23	D1	46.111037 -112.969599
Bannack S.P.	23	D2	45.159170 -112.997780
Beaverhead Rock S.P.	23	E2	45.383330 -112.458330
Beavertail Hill S.P.	15	D4	46.721660 -113.576420
Big Arm S.P.	15	D3	47.815360 -114.307930
Black Sandy S.P.	15	E4	46.756940 -111.888890
Chief Plenty Coups S.P.	24	B2	45.429700 -108.532500
Clark's Lookout S.P.	23	E2	45.236110 -112.630560
Cooney S.P.	24	B2	45.435050 -109.225330
Council Grove S.P.	15	D4	46.912500 -114.150000
Finley Point S.P.	15	D3	47.763830 -114.078723
First Peoples Buffalo Jump S.P.	16	A3	47.494887 -111.525201
Fish Creek S.P.	14	C4	46.990214 -114.715914
Fort Owen S.P.	15	D4	46.519440 -114.095830
Frenchtown Pond S.P.	15	D3	47.039530 -114.259220
Granite Ghost Town S.P.	23	D1	46.319000 -113.257000
Greycliff Prairie Dog Town S.P.	24	B1	45.767600 -109.794180
Hell Creek S.P.	17	D3	47.620290 -106.884510
Lake Elmo S.P.	24	C1	45.845280 -108.481310
Lake Mary Ronan S.P.	15	D2	48.204020 -114.330340
Lewis & Clark Caverns S.P.	23	E1	45.821840 -111.848510
Logan S.P.	14	C2	48.204020 -114.330340
Lone Pine S.P.	15	D2	48.175580 -114.339560
Lost Creek S.P.	23	D1	46.203020 -112.993810
Madison Buffalo Jump S.P.	23	F1	45.665140 -111.062770
Makoshika S.P.	17	F4	47.090240 -104.709970
Medicine Rocks S.P.	25	F1	46.046460 -104.456740
Missouri Headwaters S.P.	23	F1	45.909129 -111.497411
Painted Rocks S.P.	22	C1	45.706650 -114.282530
Pictograph Cave S.P.	24	C1	45.737500 -108.430830
Pirogue Island S.P.	17	E4	46.440560 -105.816670
Placid Lake S.P.	15	D3	47.138040 -113.524960
Rosebud Bfld. S.P.	25	D2	45.208270 -106.944460
Salmon Lake S.P.	15	D4	47.042270 -113.390390
Sluice Boxes S.P.	16	A3	47.211400 -110.939660
Smith River S.P.	16	A4	46.721219 -111.173819
Spring Meadow Lake S.P.	15	E4	46.612220 -112.075000
Thompson Falls S.P.	14	C3	47.618060 -115.387500
Tongue River Reservoir S.P.	25	D2	45.093520 -106.804670
Tower Rock S.P.	15	E3	47.181000 -111.816000
Travelers' Rest S.P.	15	D4	46.751000 -114.089000
Wayfarers S.P.	15	D2	48.057400 -114.079550
West Shore S.P.	15	D2	47.948780 -114.189160
Whitefish Lake S.P.	15	D2	48.204020 -114.330340
Wild Horse Island S.P.	15	D3	47.844640 -114.279970
Yellow Bay S.P.	15	D2	47.874500 -114.027080

NEBRASKA

NEBRASKA	PAGE	GRID	LATITUDE LONGITUDE
National Park & Rec. Areas			
Agate Fossil Beds Natl. Mon.	33	F2	42.423860 -103.791120
Chimney Rock N.H.S.	33	F3	41.719650 -103.336070
Homestead N.H.P.	35	F4	40.296246 -96.858057
Pine Ridge N.R.A.	33	F1	42.625880 -103.205570
Scotts Bluff Natl. Mon.	33	F2	41.832380 -103.717550
State Park & Rec. Areas			
Chadron S.P.	34	A1	42.711540 -103.008500
Eugene T. Mahoney S.P.	35	F3	41.026387 -96.314180
Fort Robinson S.P.	33	F1	42.654050 -103.492100
Indian Cave S.P.	86	A4	40.263280 -95.586630
Platte River S.P.	35	F3	40.986840 -96.219290
Ponca S.P.	35	F1	42.600360 -96.714940
Smith Falls S.P.	34	C1	42.891670 -100.316670

NEVADA

NEVADA	PAGE	GRID	LATITUDE LONGITUDE
National Park & Rec. Areas			
Basin & Range Natl. Mon.	38	B3	37.931620 -115.350935
Devils Hole (Death Valley Natl. Park)	45	F3	36.423889 -116.305833
Gold Butte Natl. Mon.	46	B1	36.390553 -114.170000
Great Basin Natl. Park-Vis. Ctr.	38	C2	39.005600 -114.220000
Lake Mead N.R.A.-North Ent.	46	B2	36.161180 -114.905200
Lake Mead N.R.A.-South Ent.	46	B2	36.021230 -114.796340
Lake Mead N.R.A.-West Ent.	46	B2	36.105980 -114.900940
Spring Mts. N.R.A.	46	A1	36.245200 -115.233910
Tule Springs Fossil Beds Natl. Mon.	46	A1	36.324457 -115.293643
State Park & Rec. Areas			
Berlin-Ichthyosaur S.H.P.	37	F2	38.880300 -117.607930
Big Bend of the Colorado State Rec. Area	53	F1	35.116730 -114.640820

Park	Page	Grid	Latitude Longitude
Cathedral Gorge S.P.	38	C4	37.820280 -114.407890
Dayton S.P.-North Ent.	37	D2	39.253540 -119.587190
Echo Canyon S.P.	38	C4	38.195000 -114.512900
Kershaw-Ryan S.P.	38	C4	37.586380 -114.533260
Lake Tahoe-Nevada S.P.	37	D2	39.213670 -119.928300
Spring Mtn. Ranch S.P.	46	A2	36.073830 -115.443710
Spring Valley S.P.	38	C3	38.003920 -114.207570
Valley of Fire S.P.	46	B1	36.429710 -114.513590
Wild Horse State Rec. Area	30	B3	41.670739 -115.799805

NEW HAMPSHIRE	PAGE	GRID	LATITUDE LONGITUDE
National Park & Rec. Areas			
Saint-Gaudens N.H.P.	81	E4	43.501570 -72.362510
State Park & Rec. Areas			
Bear Brook S.P.	81	F4	43.133800 -71.366040
Cardigan Mountain S.P.	81	E3	43.647990 -71.949570
Crawford Notch S.P.	81	F2	44.181760 -71.398780
Echo Lake S.P.	81	F3	44.067430 -71.166000
Forest Lake S.P.	81	F2	44.354490 -71.673180
Hampton Beach S.P.	95	E1	42.898333 -70.812778
Kingston S.P.	95	E1	42.929020 -71.054680
Lake Tarleton S.P.	81	E3	43.975833 -71.963333
Miller S.P.	95	D1	42.861630 -71.878750
Monadnock S.P.	95	D1	42.845440 -72.086590
Mount Sunapee S.P.	81	E4	43.332120 -72.079800
Pawtuckaway S.P.	81	F4	43.082150 -71.152130
Pillsbury S.P.	81	E4	43.236860 -72.122830
Pisgah S.P.	94	C1	42.810310 -72.408340
Umbagog Lake S.P.	81	F1	44.712990 -71.072700
Wellington S.P.	81	F3	43.641280 -71.782980
Wentworth S.P.	81	F3	43.603056 -71.136389
White Lake S.P.	81	F3	43.830880 -71.218220
Winslow S.P.	81	E4	43.391730 -71.869540

NEW JERSEY	PAGE	GRID	LATITUDE LONGITUDE
National Park & Rec. Areas			
Delaware Water Gap N.R.A.	94	A4	40.970390 -75.128100
Gateway N.R.A.	147	F1	40.396420 -73.981160
Morristown N.H.P.	148	A4	40.744670 -74.565290
Thomas Edison N.H.P.	148	A4	40.787188 -74.256497
State Park & Rec. Areas			
Allaire S.P.	147	E2	40.153470 -74.111390
Allamuchy Mtn. S.P.	104	C1	40.921244 -74.782222
Barnegat Lighthouse S.P.	147	E4	39.762750 -74.107950
Cape May Point S.P.	104	C4	38.932950 -74.961010
Corson's Inlet S.P.	105	D4	39.216340 -74.647070
Delaware & Raritan Canal S.P.	147	D1	40.473230 -74.571100
Double Trouble S.P.	147	E3	39.900550 -74.225120
Farny S.P.	148	A3	40.997170 -74.459060
Fortescue State Marina	145	F2	39.243178 -75.176636
Fort Mott S.P.	146	B4	39.612100 -75.543430
Hacklebarney S.P.	105	D1	40.751170 -74.736590
High Point S.P.	148	A2	41.304800 -74.669650
Hopatcong S.P.	148	A3	40.911780 -74.667000
Island Beach S.P.	147	E3	39.905240 -74.081510
Liberty S.P.	148	B4	40.697330 -74.063870
Long Pond Ironworks S.P.	148	A2	41.140986 -74.309228
Monmouth Bfld. S.P.	147	E2	40.269340 -74.302800
Parvin S.P.	146	C4	39.524490 -75.160460
Pigeon Swamp S.P.	147	E1	40.394420 -74.487150
Princeton Bfld. S.P.	147	D2	40.332490 -74.675650
Rancocas S.P.	147	D3	39.990420 -74.837480
Ringwood S.P.	148	A2	41.127600 -74.260130
Swartswood S.P.	94	A4	41.081680 -74.813620
Voorhees S.P.	104	C1	40.695060 -74.887030
Washington Crossing S.P.	147	D2	40.296920 -74.866420
Washington Rock S.P.	148	A4	40.613580 -74.472860
Wawayanda S.P.	148	A2	41.199240 -74.392440

NEW MEXICO	PAGE	GRID	LATITUDE LONGITUDE
National Park & Rec. Areas			
Aztec Ruins Natl. Mon.	48	B1	36.833920 -108.000570
Bandelier Natl. Mon.	48	C2	35.780130 -106.264830
Capulin Mtn. Natl. Mon.	49	E1	36.781990 -103.986110
Carlsbad Caverns Natl. Park-Vis. Ctr.	57	E3	32.175400 -104.444000
Chaco Culture N.H.P.	48	B2	36.016190 -107.924060
Datil Well N.R.A.	48	B4	34.154130 -107.852610
El Malpais Natl. Cons. Area	48	B4	35.059720 -107.876400
El Morro Natl. Mon.	48	B3	35.043480 -108.346250
Fort Union Natl. Mon.	49	D2	35.904230 -105.010740
Gila Cliff Dwellings Natl. Mon.	56	A2	33.229540 -108.264630
Kasha-Katuwe Tent Rocks Natl. Mon.	48	C2	35.663200 -106.410800
Manhattan Project N.H.P.	48	C2	35.882455 -106.304212
Pecos N.H.P.	49	D3	35.578750 -105.762400
Petroglyph Natl. Mon.	48	C3	35.139490 -106.709670
Rio Grande Del Norte Natl. Mon.	49	D1	36.640260 -105.877033
Salinas Pueblo Missions Natl. Mon.	48	C4	34.520370 -106.241250
Salinas Pueblo Missions Natl. Mon.-Gran Quivira	49	D4	34.260000 -106.091000
White Sands Natl. Park	56	C2	32.820130 -106.272980
State Park & Rec. Areas			
Bluewater Lake S.P.	48	B3	35.302730 -108.106930
Bottomless Lakes S.P.	57	E2	33.316630 -104.332880
Brantley Lake S.P.	57	E3	32.571390 -104.366210
Caballo Lake S.P.	56	B2	32.911370 -107.313580
Cerrillos Hills S.P.	49	D3	35.446413 -106.098498
Cimarron Canyon S.P.	49	D1	36.537600 -105.221130
City of Rocks S.P.	56	A2	32.594860 -107.973850
Clayton Lake S.P.	49	F1	36.573070 -103.300690
Conchas Lake S.P.	49	E3	35.394760 -104.181790
Coronado S.P.	48	C3	35.329130 -106.557870
Coyote Creek S.P.	49	D2	36.188020 -105.233260
Eagle Nest S.P.	49	D1	36.542100 -105.261300
Elephant Butte Res. S.P.-South Ent.	56	B1	33.176180 -107.207460
El Vado Lake S.P.	48	C1	36.593710 -106.735790
Fenton Lake S.P.	48	C2	35.887230 -106.723170
Heron Lake S.P.	48	C1	36.693840 -106.654230
Hyde Mem. S.P.	49	D2	35.737890 -105.836540
Leasburg Dam S.P.	56	B3	32.492680 -106.922380
Living Desert Zoo & Gardens S.P.	57	E3	32.449839 -104.286341
Manzano Mtn. S.P.	48	C4	34.603880 -106.360960
Morphy Lake S.P.	49	D2	35.968660 -105.366600
Navajo Lake S.P.	48	B1	36.831950 -107.586950
Oasis S.P.	49	F4	34.259740 -103.334280
Oliver Lee Mem. S.P.	56	C2	32.744640 -105.934520
Pancho Villa S.P.	56	B4	31.828050 -107.641200
Percha Dam S.P.	56	B2	32.873610 -107.308100
Rockhound S.P.	56	B3	32.185550 -107.613090
Santa Rosa Lake S.P.	49	E3	34.987930 -104.658750
Smokey Bear Hist. S.P.	57	D1	33.545620 -105.573170
Storrie Lake S.P.	49	D2	35.655720 -105.231840
Sugarite Canyon S.P.	49	E1	36.944191 -104.381651
Sumner Lake S.P.	49	E4	34.607520 -104.389050
Ute Lake S.P.	49	F3	35.340630 -103.442500
Villanueva S.P.	49	D3	35.259530 -105.368970

NEW YORK	PAGE	GRID	LATITUDE LONGITUDE
National Park & Rec. Areas			
Eleanor Roosevelt N.H.S.	94	B3	41.763170 -73.902960
Fire Island Natl. Seashore	149	D4	40.735320 -72.866620
Fort Stanwix Natl. Mon.	79	E3	43.211930 -75.454740
Gateway N.R.A.	148	B4	40.581100 -73.887790
Home of F.D.R. N.H.S.	94	B3	41.767038 -73.938193
Sagamore Hill N.H.S.	148	C3	40.882480 -73.505550
Saratoga N.H.P.	81	D4	43.002690 -73.612110
Statue of Liberty Natl. Mon.	148	B4	40.689547 -74.044029
Thomas Cole N.H.S.	94	B2	42.225900 -73.861600
Van Buren N.H.S.	94	B2	42.370610 -73.701010
Vanderbilt Mansion N.H.S.	94	B3	41.796482 -73.942359
Women's Rights N.H.P.	79	D3	42.910580 -76.800260
State Park & Rec. Areas			
Adirondack Park	80	C2	43.455590 -73.695930
Allegany S.P.	92	B1	42.106480 -78.765940
Battle Island S.P.	79	D3	43.362780 -76.442150
Bear Mtn. S.P.	148	B2	41.278350 -73.970290
Beaver Island S.P.	78	A3	42.968170 -78.969560
Bowman Lake S.P.	79	E4	42.516970 -75.670400
Buttermilk Falls S.P.	79	D4	42.347410 -76.489130
Caleb Smith S.P. Pres.	149	D3	40.854190 -73.221190
Canandaigua Lake State Marine Park	78	C3	42.875964 -77.275600
Captree S.P.	149	D4	40.636640 -73.263210
Catskill Park	94	A2	42.050290 -74.288840
Cedar Point S.P.	79	D1	44.200670 -76.191000
Chenango Valley S.P.	93	E1	42.215040 -75.818020
Chittenango Falls S.P.	79	E3	42.981520 -75.845030
Clarence Fahnestock S.P.	148	B1	41.423620 -73.799560
Cold Spring Harbor S.P.	148	C3	40.867450 -73.461900
Connetquot River S.P. Pres.	149	D4	40.748070 -73.153510
Cumberland Bay S.P.	81	D1	44.725090 -73.421450
Darien Lakes S.P.	78	B3	42.908460 -78.433300
Delta Lake S.P.	79	E3	43.290030 -75.414910
Evangola S.P.	78	A4	42.604460 -79.105610
Fair Haven Beach S.P.	79	D3	43.320570 -76.696210
Fort Niagara S.P.	78	A3	43.261790 -79.061460
Four Mile Creek S.P.	78	A3	43.272530 -78.996270
Franny Reese S.P.	148	B1	41.704118 -73.956553
Gilbert Lake S.P.	79	F4	42.572720 -75.128170
Golden Hill S.P.	78	B2	43.365250 -78.489310
Goosepond Mtn. S.P.	148	A2	41.354460 -74.254470
Gov. Alfred E. Smith/Sunken Meadow S.P.	149	D3	40.911970 -73.262940
Green Lakes S.P.	79	E3	43.060000 -75.969030
Hamlin Beach S.P.	78	C2	43.361130 -77.944460
Harriman S.P.	148	B2	41.293010 -74.026560
Heckscher S.P.	149	D4	40.712860 -73.168480
Highland Lakes S.P.	148	A1	41.489806 -74.325085
Hither Hills S.P.	149	F3	41.007700 -72.014500
Hudson Highlands S.P.	148	B2	41.428060 -73.966740
Hudson River Islands S.P.	94	B2	42.318574 -73.778343
James Baird S.P.	148	B1	41.689100 -73.799390
Jones Beach S.P.	148	C4	40.595000 -73.521070
Keewaydin S.P.	79	E1	44.322390 -75.925740
Keuka Lake S.P.	78	C4	42.594280 -77.130360
Lake Erie S.P.	78	A4	42.419070 -79.434430
Lakeside Beach S.P.	78	B2	43.367090 -78.236040
Lake Superior S.P.	94	A3	41.658590 -74.86928
Letchworth S.P.	78	B4	42.693530 -77.96121
Lodi Point S.P.	79	D4	42.619210 -76.86398
Long Point S.P.	79	D1	44.026130 -76.21965
Mark Twain S.P.	93	D1	42.205200 -76.82379
Mary Island S.P.	79	E1	44.350460 -75.93040
Max V. Shaul S.P.	79	F4	42.546790 -74.41037
Minnewaska S.P. Pres.	148	A1	41.745910 -74.26837
Montauk Point S.P.	149	F3	41.065020 -71.88670
Moreau Lake S.P.	80	C4	43.226370 -73.70771
Oquaga Creek S.P.	93	F1	42.172320 -75.44284
Orient Beach S.P.	149	F2	41.154580 -72.24560
Pixley Falls S.P.	79	E2	43.401100 -75.34596
Point Au Roche S.P.	81	D1	44.779990 -73.41109
Robert Moses S.P.	148	C4	40.624930 -73.26190
Saratoga Spa S.P.	80	C4	43.056950 -73.80149
Selkirk Shores S.P.	79	D2	43.544300 -76.19151
Seneca Lake S.P.	79	D3	42.873410 -76.96094
Southwick Beach S.P.	79	D2	43.767270 -76.19623
Sterling Forest S.P.	148	A2	41.220200 -74.18721
Storm King S.P.	148	B2	41.432560 -73.98702
Taconic S.P.	94	B2	42.007680 -73.50840
Tallman Mtn. S.P.	148	B3	41.037270 -73.91592
Verona Beach S.P.	79	E3	43.179070 -75.72509
Waterson Point S.P.	79	E1	44.339030 -76.01058
Watkins Glen S.P.	79	D4	42.375896 -76.871078
Wellesley Island S.P.	79	E1	44.315970 -76.01948
Whetstone Gulf S.P.	79	E2	43.702310 -75.45912
Wildwood S.P.	149	D3	40.954230 -72.78847
Wilson-Tuscarora S.P.	78	B3	43.307080 -78.85450

NORTH CAROLINA	PAGE	GRID	LATITUDE LONGITUDE
National Park & Rec. Areas			
Cape Hatteras Natl. Seashore	115	F3	35.766700 -75.52664
Cape Lookout Natl. Seashore	115	E4	34.886110 -76.33122
Carl Sandburg Home N.H.S.	121	E1	35.270000 -82.450000
Fort Raleigh N.H.S.	115	F2	35.932360 -75.708500
Great Smoky Mts. Natl. Park-Cades Cove Vis. Ctr.	121	D1	35.585300 -83.842900
Great Smoky Mts. Natl. Park-Oconaluftee Vis. Ctr.	121	D1	35.515300 -83.305300
Great Smoky Mts. Natl. Park-Sugarlands Vis. Ctr.	121	D1	35.685600 -83.536700
State Park & Rec. Areas			
Carolina Beach S.P.	123	E3	34.045240 -77.903430
Cliffs of the Neuse S.P.	123	E1	35.232900 -77.898390
Crowders Mtn. S.P.	122	A1	35.212350 -81.292920
Dismal Swamp S.P.	113	F3	36.517470 -76.360720
Fort Macon S.P.	115	E4	34.697750 -76.699580
Goose Creek S.P.	123	F1	35.483140 -76.902290
Gorges S.P.	121	E1	35.108400 -82.943900
Hammocks Beach S.P.	123	F2	34.671810 -77.138720
Hanging Rock S.P.	112	B3	36.413030 -80.253950
Haw River S.P.	112	B3	36.249719 -79.755971
Jockey's Ridge S.P.	115	F2	35.961820 -75.626970
Jones Lake S.P.	123	D2	34.698900 -78.624990
Lake James S.P.	111	F4	35.728064 -81.901980
Lake Norman S.P.	112	A4	35.665780 -80.938410
Lake Waccamaw S.P.	123	D3	34.272650 -78.466040
Lumber River S.P.	123	D3	34.390831 -79.004145
Medoc Mtn. S.P.	113	D3	36.280410 -77.877820
Merchants Millpond S.P.	113	F3	36.450601 -76.692978
Morrow Mtn. S.P.	122	B1	35.370390 -80.102410
Mount Mitchell S.P.	111	E4	35.814600 -82.146100
Pettigrew S.P.	113	F4	35.789580 -76.406980
Pilot Mtn. S.P.	112	A3	36.345530 -80.478390
Raven Rock S.P.	123	D1	35.461520 -78.912660
Singletary Lake S.P.	123	D2	34.581570 -78.452070
South Mts. S.P.	121	F1	35.601190 -81.626700
Stone Mtn. S.P.	112	A3	36.374390 -81.018010

NORTH DAKOTA	PAGE	GRID	LATITUDE LONGITUDE
National Park & Rec. Areas			
Fort Union N.H.S.	17	F2	48.002390 -104.043560
Knife River N.H.S.	18	B3	47.336680 -101.387450
Theodore Roosevelt Natl. Park-Elkhorn Site	17	F3	47.226950 -103.622310
Theodore Roosevelt Natl. Park-North Unit	18	A3	47.600300 -103.261000
Theodore Roosevelt Natl. Park-South Unit	18	A4	46.915500 -103.527000
State Park & Rec. Areas			
Beaver Lake S.P.	18	C4	46.401260 -99.615860
Cross Ranch S.P.	18	B3	47.213530 -101.000180
Doyle Mem. S.P.	27	D1	46.204880 -99.482150
Fort Abercrombie S.P.	19	F4	46.444530 -96.718800
Fort Lincoln S.P.	18	B4	46.769420 -100.847860
Fort Ransom S.P.	19	E4	46.544100 -97.925570
Fort Stevenson S.P.	18	B3	47.596890 -101.420530
Grahams Island S.P.	19	D2	48.052500 -99.068300
Icelandic S.P.	19	E1	48.772620 -97.736990
Lake Metigoshe S.P.	18	C1	48.980640 -100.326710
Lake Sakakawea S.P.	18	B3	47.511020 -101.449350
Lewis & Clark S.P.	18	A2	48.115350 -103.241490
Little Missouri Bay S.P.	18	A3	47.550030 -102.738240
Pembina S.P.	19	E1	48.964720 -97.240500

urtle River S.P.	19	E2	47.931660 -97.505390
Vhitestone Bfld. S.P.	27	D1	46.169190 -98.857330

OHIO

OHIO	PAGE	GRID	LATITUDE LONGITUDE
National Park & Rec. Areas			
Charles Young Buffalo Soldiers Natl. Mon.	100	C1	39.689722,-83.891111
Cuyahoga Valley Natl. Park-Canal Vis. Ctr.	91	E2	41.372600 -81.613700
Cuyahoga Valley Natl. Park-Hunt Farm Vis. Info. Ctr.	91	E2	41.200900 -81.573100
Hopewell Culture N.H.P.	101	D2	39.298360 -82.917810
James A. Garfield N.H.S.	91	E2	41.663600 -81.351260
State Park & Rec. Areas			
A.W. Marion S.P.	101	D1	39.633730 -82.885720
Adams Lake S.P.	100	C3	38.812900 -83.519400
Alum Creek S.P.	90	C4	40.226870 -82.981320
Barkcamp S.P.	101	F1	40.047030 -81.031710
Beaver Creek S.P.	91	F3	40.726220 -80.613590
Blue Rock S.P.	101	E1	39.832780 -81.858370
Buck Creek S.P.	100	C1	39.946410 -83.729550
Buckeye Lake S.P.	101	D1	39.906540 -82.526270
Burr Oak S.P.	101	E1	39.527740 -82.023260
Caesar Creek S.P.	100	C1	39.515730 -84.041070
Catawba Island S.P.	91	D2	41.573530 -82.855780
Cowan Lake S.P.	100	C2	39.387600 -83.882970
Crane Creek S.P.	90	C2	41.603770 -83.192910
Deer Creek S.P.	101	D1	39.649260 -83.246340
Delaware S.P.	90	C4	40.377690 -83.071590
Dillon S.P.	101	E1	40.023600 -82.111910
East Fork S.P.	100	C2	39.002050 -84.151210
East Harbor S.P.	91	D2	41.540930 -82.820830
Findley S.P.	91	D3	41.122990 -82.219390
Forked Run S.P.	101	E2	39.085000 -81.770460
Geneva S.P.	91	F1	41.852760 -80.963280
Grand Lake Saint Marys S.P.	90	B4	40.549240 -84.436500
Guilford Lake S.P.	91	F3	40.796100 -80.893760
Harrison Lake S.P.	90	B2	41.637190 -84.361760
Headlands Beach S.P.	91	E1	41.752140 -81.294480
Hocking Hills S.P.	101	D2	39.494180 -82.611910
Hueston Woods S.P.	100	B1	39.573820 -84.715380
Independence Dam S.P.	90	B2	41.282470 -84.313500
Indian Lake S.P.	90	B4	40.510360 -83.842980
Jackson Lake S.P.	101	D3	38.902850 -82.596780
Jefferson Lake S.P.	91	F4	40.472050 -80.808930
John Bryan S.P.	100	C1	39.791020 -83.867790
Kelleys Island S.P.	91	D2	41.614080 -82.712110
Kiser Lake S.P.	90	B4	40.197650 -83.981740
Lake Alma S.P.	101	D2	39.153450 -82.516810
Lake Hope S.P.	101	E2	39.318500 -82.354920
Lake Logan S.P.	101	D1	39.536400 -82.460590
Lake Loramie S.P.	90	B4	40.359750 -84.359730
Lake White S.P.	101	D2	39.109160 -83.040330
Madison Lake S.P.	100	C1	39.866250 -83.374930
Malabar Farm S.P.	91	D3	40.649590 -82.398390
Mary Jane Thurston S.P.	90	B2	41.409630 -83.881320
Maumee Bay S.P.	90	C2	41.678020 -83.353360
Mohican S.P.	91	D4	40.609510 -82.257600
Mosquito Lake S.P.	91	F2	41.301940 -80.767990
Mount Gilead S.P.	91	D4	40.547820 -82.816770
Muskingum River S.P.	101	E1	40.044140 -81.978260
Nelson-Kennedy Ledges S.P.	91	F2	41.330090 -81.040190
Paint Creek S.P.	100	C2	39.228360 -83.374450
Pike Lake S.P.	101	D2	39.158270 -83.220950
Portage Lakes S.P.	91	E3	40.966260 -81.565190
Punderson S.P.	91	E2	41.461540 -81.219590
Pymatuning S.P.	91	F2	41.580110 -80.541530
Quail Hollow S.P.	91	E3	40.970200 -81.325100
Rocky Fork S.P.	100	C2	39.188310 -83.529730
Salt Fork S.P.	91	E4	40.081830 -81.460400
Scioto Trail S.P.	101	D2	39.223620 -82.931210
Shawnee S.P.	101	D3	38.747670 -83.211220
South Bass Island S.P.	91	D2	41.644690 -82.835950
Stonelick S.P.	100	C2	39.226160 -84.057210
Strouds Run S.P.	101	E2	39.334320 -82.017690
Sycamore S.P.	100	B1	39.803410 -84.373470
Tar Hollow S.P.	101	D2	39.353790 -82.780200
Tinkers Creek S.P.	91	E2	41.276180 -81.368910
Van Buren S.P.	90	C3	41.138290 -83.644940
West Branch S.P.	91	E3	41.133310 -81.189660
Wolf Run S.P.	101	F1	39.789770 -81.540180

OKLAHOMA

OKLAHOMA	PAGE	GRID	LATITUDE LONGITUDE
National Park & Rec. Areas			
Chickasaw N.R.A.	51	F4	34.497390 -96.970110
Washita Battlefield N.H.S.	50	C3	35.621151 -99.709854
Winding Stair Mtn. N.R.A.	116	B2	34.749705 -94.793055
State Park & Rec. Areas			
Alabaster Caverns S.P.	51	D1	36.697490 -99.149430
Arrowhead at Lake Eufaula S.P.	116	A1	35.168240 -95.639970
Beaver Dunes Park	50	B1	36.841129 -100.514988
Beavers Bend S.P.	116	B3	34.131792 -94.701382
Bernice Area at Grand Lake S.P.	106	B3	36.626670 -94.901670
Black Mesa S.P.	49	F1	36.855620 -102.885680
Boiling Springs S.P.	51	D1	36.452950 -99.298900
Brushy Lake Park	116	B1	35.543680 -94.817676
Cherokee Landing S.P.	106	B4	35.758890 -94.908610
Cherokee Area at Grand Lake S.P.	106	B3	36.480280 -95.050560
Clayton Lake S.P.	116	A2	34.549420 -95.308330
Disney Area at Grand Lake S.P.	116	B3	36.480260 -95.009130
Dripping Springs Lake and Rec. Are	51	F3	35.611437 -96.068911
Fort Cobb S.P.	51	D3	35.203720 -98.464990
Foss S.P.	51	D3	35.578510 -99.186830
Gloss Mtn. S.P.	51	D2	36.367190 -98.576460
Great Plains S.P.	51	D4	34.730340 -98.985690
Great Salt Plains S.P.	51	E1	36.753170 -98.149930
Greenleaf S.P.	106	A4	35.623260 -95.180950
Honey Creek Area at Grand Lake S.P.	106	B3	36.574060 -94.784370
Hugo Lake S.P.	116	A3	34.016384 -95.375061
Keystone S.P.	51	F2	36.137440 -96.264340
Little Blue Area at Grand Lake S.P.	116	B3	36.464053 -95.002535
Lake Eufaula S.P.	116	A1	35.427900 -95.546100
Lake Murray S.P.	51	F4	34.154880 -97.120950
Lake Texoma S.P.	59	F1	33.997590 -96.651310
Lake Thunderbird S.P.	51	E3	35.232320 -97.247550
Lake Wister S.P.	116	B2	34.948700 -94.710400
Little Sahara S.P.	51	D1	36.532900 -98.890870
McGee Creek S.P.	116	A3	34.302927 -95.875467
Natural Falls S.P.	106	B4	36.151900 -94.673300
Okmulgee Lake Rec. Area	51	F2	35.621900 -96.067700
Osage Hills S.P.	51	F1	36.757360 -96.176220
Quartz Mountain S.P.	50	C3	34.955790 -99.275244
Raymond Gary S.P.	116	A3	33.997580 -95.253860
Robbers Cave S.P.	116	A2	34.564650 -95.290393
Roman Nose S.P.	51	D2	35.929213 -98.42995
Sequoyah Bay S.P.	106	A4	35.886000 -95.276000
Sequoyah S.P.	106	A4	35.932960 -95.230650
Spavinaw Area at Grand Lake S.P.	106	B3	36.385890 -95.053290
Talimena S.P.	116	B2	34.788290 -94.950690
Tenkiller S.P.	116	B1	35.598000 -95.031100
Twin Bridges Area at Grand Lake S.P.	106	B2	36.804320 -94.757920
Wha-Sha-She Park	51	F1	36.926000 -96.091000
Winding Stair Mtn. N.R.A.-Cedar Lake	116	B2	34.778566 -94.693

OREGON

OREGON	PAGE	GRID	LATITUDE LONGITUDE
National Park & Rec. Areas			
Cascade-Siskiyou Natl. Mon.	28	C2	42.068300 -122.399940
Crater Lake Natl. Park-Annie Spring Ent. Sta.	28	C1	42.868700 -122.169000
Crater Lake Natl. Park-North Ent. Sta.	28	C1	43.086900 -122.116000
Hells Canyon N.R.A.-East Ent.	22	B1	45.500680 -116.806560
Hells Canyon N.R.A.-South Ent.	22	B1	44.903300 -116.957080
Hells Canyon N.R.A.-West Ent.	22	B1	45.176360 -117.040740
John Day Fossil Beds Natl. Mon.-Clarno Unit	21	D2	44.911250 -120.431780
John Day Fossil Beds Natl. Mon.-Painted Hills Unit	21	D3	44.661170 -120.254750
John Day Fossil Beds Natl. Mon.-Sheep Rock Unit	21	E3	44.555480 -119.645010
Lewis & Clark N.H.P.-Fort Clatsop	20	B1	46.138260 -123.876670
Lewis & Clark N.H.P.-Salt Works	20	B1	46.134551 -123.880420
Lewis & Clark N.H.P.-Sunset Beach	20	B1	46.099430 -123.936390
Newberry Natl. Volcanic Mon.	21	D4	43.716800 -121.376960
Oregon Caves Natl. Mon. & Pres.	28	B2	42.103910 -123.414300
Oregon Dunes N.R.A.-North Ent.	20	A4	43.885610 -124.120860
Oregon Dunes N.R.A.-South Ent.	20	A4	43.579470 -124.186490
State Park & Rec. Areas			
Ainsworth S.P.	20	C2	45.595720 -122.052980
Alfred A. Loeb S.P.	28	A2	42.113180 -124.188520
Beverly Beach S.P.	20	B3	44.726250 -124.057290
Bob Straub S.P.	20	B2	45.183160 -123.965160
Brian Booth S.P.	20	B3	44.518060 -124.075960
Bullards Beach S.P.	28	A1	43.150990 -124.395480
Cape Arago S.P.	20	A4	43.326140 -124.381770
Cape Blanco S.P.	28	A1	42.826660 -124.524640
Cape Lookout S.P.	20	B2	45.367667 -123.961127
Carl G. Washburne Mem. S.P.	20	A3	44.141990 -124.117490
Cascadia S.P.	20	C3	44.397100 -122.477480
Catherine Creek S.P.	22	A2	45.148890 -117.733990
Collier Mem. S.P.	28	C1	42.641810 -121.880630
Ecola S.P.	20	B1	45.916550 -123.967430
Elijah Bristow S.P.	20	C4	43.935470 -122.844270
Fort Columbia S.P.	20	B1	46.252580 -123.921500
Fort Stevens S.P.	20	B1	46.183200 -123.959940
Harris Beach S.P.	28	A2	42.067930 -124.305860
Hat Rock S.P.	21	F1	45.908260 -119.164510
Hilgard Junction S.P.	21	F2	45.342060 -118.236470
Humbug Mtn. S.P.	28	A1	42.686870 -124.445970
Illinois River Forks S.P.	28	B2	42.154870 -123.649870
Jessie M. Honeyman Mem. S.P.	20	A4	43.933440 -124.106440
L.L. Stub Stewart S.P.	20	B1	45.739050 -123.199461
Lake Owyhee S.P.	22	A4	43.638380 -117.229090
Lapine S.P.	21	D4	43.768452 -121.513399
Maryhill S.P.	21	D1	45.683060 -120.825830
Mayer S.P.	21	D1	45.682780 -121.301080
Milo Mciver S.P.	20	C2	45.306110 -122.372220
Molalla River S.P.	20	C2	45.294840 -122.696400
Nehalem Bay S.P.	20	B1	45.710000 -123.931470
Oswald West S.P.	20	B1	45.770000 -123.958610
Port Orford Heads S.P.	28	A1	42.739470 -124.509730
Prineville Reservoir S.P.	21	D3	44.144660 -120.737770
Rooster Rock S.P.	20	C2	45.546320 -122.236500
Shore Acres S.P.	20	A4	43.329940 -124.376510
Silver Falls S.P.	20	C2	44.853752 -122.662258
Smith Rock S.P.	21	D3	44.360540 -121.138400
South Beach S.P.	20	B3	44.598450 -124.059350
Starvation Creek S.P.	20	C1	45.688550 -121.690180
Sunset Bay S.P.	20	A4	43.339010 -124.353990
The Cove Palisades S.P.	21	D3	44.557460 -121.262110
Tumalo S.P.	21	D3	44.086760 -121.308730
Umpqua Lighthouse S.P.	20	A4	43.669610 -124.182830
Valley of the Rogue S.P.	28	B1	42.410770 -123.129310
Viento S.P.	20	C1	45.697240 -121.668310
Wallowa Lake S.P.	22	A2	45.280690 -117.208230
White River Falls S.P.	21	D2	45.166870 -121.087420
Willamette Mission S.P.	20	B2	45.080740 -123.031510
William M. Tugman S.P.	20	A4	43.623640 -124.181910

PENNSYLVANIA

PENNSYLVANIA	PAGE	GRID	LATITUDE LONGITUDE
National Park & Rec. Areas			
Allegheny N.R.A.	92	B1	41.943055 -78.867025
Allegheny Portage Railroad N.H.S.	92	B4	40.377020 -78.835870
Eisenhower N.H.S.	103	E1	39.818000 -77.232610
Flight 93 Natl. Mem.	92	B4	40.055200 -78.900900
Fort Necessity Natl. Bfld.	102	B1	39.816340 -79.584310
Friendship Hill N.H.S.	102	B1	39.777778 -79.929167
Gettysburg N.M.P.	103	E1	39.811600 -77.226100
Grey Towers N.H.S.	94	A3	41.325224 -74.871113
Hopewell Furnace N.H.S.	146	B2	40.206760 -75.773570
Johnstown Flood Natl. Mem.	92	B4	40.350710 -78.772480
Valley Forge N.H.P.	146	C2	40.102240 -75.422960
State Park & Rec. Areas			
Bald Eagle S.P.	92	C3	41.041960 -77.642780
Big Spring S.P.	92	C4	40.266850 -77.654410
Black Moshannon S.P.	92	C3	40.915190 -78.058570
Blue Knob S.P.	92	B4	40.265800 -78.584480
Buchanan's Birthplace S.P.	103	D1	39.872660 -77.953190
Caledonia S.P.	103	D1	39.905610 -77.478880
Chapman S.P.	92	B1	41.757850 -79.170350
Cherry Springs S.P.	92	C2	41.662778 -77.823056
Codorus S.P.	103	E1	39.783180 -76.908920
Colonel Denning S.P.	93	D4	40.281820 -77.416630
Colton Point S.P.	93	D2	41.711180 -77.465430
Cook Forest S.P.	92	B2	41.333790 -79.210440
Cowans Gap S.P.	103	D1	39.997980 -77.921530
Delaware Canal S.P.	146	C1	40.545565 -75.087831
Elk S.P.	92	B2	41.606100 -78.564780
Erie Bluffs S.P.	91	F1	42.008333 -80.410833
Evansburg S.P.	146	C2	40.197510 -75.407080
Frances Slocum S.P.	93	E2	41.347380 -75.893760
French Creek S.P.	146	B2	40.236580 -75.795660
Gouldsboro S.P.	93	F2	41.232250 -75.495730
Greenwood Furnace S.P.	92	C3	40.649610 -77.756090
Hickory Run S.P.	93	F3	41.035170 -75.736220
Hills Creek S.P.	93	D1	41.805190 -77.187600
Hyner Run S.P.	92	C2	41.359150 -77.623850
Kettle Creek S.P.	92	C2	41.377120 -77.930130
Keystone S.P.	92	A4	40.374250 -79.377830
Lackawanna S.P.	93	F2	41.575030 -75.711520
Laurel Hill S.P.	102	B1	39.984470 -79.234840
Laurel Mtn. S.P.	92	B4	40.179670 -79.131530
Laurel Ridge S.P.	92	B4	39.958400 -79.360160
Lehigh Gorge S.P.	93	F3	40.971900 -75.761840
Leonard Harrison S.P.	93	D2	41.698420 -77.450810
Little Buffalo S.P.	93	D4	40.454420 -77.169170
Little Pine S.P.	93	D2	41.371240 -77.360310
Lyman Run S.P.	92	C1	41.723650 -77.768470
Marsh Creek S.P.	146	B3	40.069360 -75.717320
Maurice K. Goddard S.P.	92	A2	41.428380 -80.145140
McConnells Mill S.P.	92	A3	40.963530 -80.168810
Memorial Lake S.P.	93	E4	40.424760 -76.590540
Mont Alto S.P.	103	D1	39.839130 -77.540630
Moraine S.P.	92	A3	40.940280 -80.098520
Nescopeck S.P.	93	E3	41.067100 -75.925300
Nockamixon S.P.	146	C1	40.463630 -75.242010
Ohiopyle S.P.	102	B1	39.865030 -79.504310
Oil Creek S.P.-East Ent.	92	A2	41.512130 -79.661810
Ole Bull S.P.	92	C2	41.543590 -77.709430
Parker Dam S.P.	92	C2	41.205140 -78.504310
Penn-Roosevelt S.P.	92	C3	40.726389 -77.702500
Pine Grove Furnace S.P.	103	D1	40.032910 -77.305070
Poe Paddy S.P.	93	D3	40.834150 -77.417380
Presque Isle S.P.	92	A1	42.114200 -80.153590
Prince Gallitzin S.P.	92	B3	40.669760 -78.575650
Promised Land S.P.	93	F2	41.313560 -75.210370
Pymatuning S.P.	91	F2	41.605440 -80.387840
Raccoon Creek S.P.	91	F4	40.503160 -80.424460
Ralph Stover S.P.	146	C1	40.440420 -75.106050
Raymond B. Winter S.P.	93	D3	40.992340 -77.200450

Ricketts Glen S.P.	93	E2	41.336190 -76.300420
Ryerson Station S.P.	102	A1	39.892310 -80.450030
S.B. Elliott S.P.	92	C3	41.112740 -78.526100
Salt Springs S.P.	93	E1	41.911090 -75.868720
Samuel S. Lewis S.P.	103	E1	39.996580 -76.550410
Shawnee S.P.	102	C1	40.038060 -78.645850
Shikellamy S.P.	93	D3	40.879390 -76.802950
Sinnemahoning S.P.	92	C2	41.450650 -78.055090
Susquehannock S.P.	146	A3	39.805770 -76.283410
Swatara S.P.	93	E4	40.481480 -76.551350
Tobyhanna S.P.	93	F2	41.214130 -75.384030
Trough Creek S.P.	92	C4	40.311620 -78.131820
Tyler S.P.	146	C2	40.233330 -74.951170
Warriors Path S.P.	92	C4	40.193330 -78.249880
Washington Crossing Hist. Park	104	C2	40.312256 -74.859711
Whipple Dam S.P.	92	C3	40.682250 -77.868410
Worlds End S.P.	93	E2	41.471880 -76.587060
Yellow Creek S.P.	92	B4	40.575830 -79.004420

RHODE ISLAND	PAGE	GRID	LATITUDE LONGITUDE
State Park & Rec. Areas			
Beavertail S.P.	150	C4	41.457030 -71.396950
Brenton Point S.P.	150	C4	41.450430 -71.355870
Burlingame S.P.	150	C4	41.361610 -71.701370
Charlestown Breachway S.B.	150	C4	41.356053 -71.640494
Colt S.P.	151	D3	41.684590 -71.288860
East Matunuck State Beach	150	C4	41.378350 -71.525630
Fishermen's Mem. S.P.	150	C4	41.380630 -71.488000
Fort Adams S.P.	150	C4	41.469150 -71.339990
Goddard Mem. S.P.	150	C3	41.651030 -71.442040
Haines Mem. S.P.	150	C3	41.752960 -71.348600
Misquamicut State Beach	95	D4	41.324510 -71.800670
Pulaski S.P. & Rec. Area	150	C3	41.950000 -71.766670
Rocky Point S.P.	150	C3	41.691482 -71.363654
R.W. Wheeler State Beach	150	C4	41.372620 -71.495530
Scarborough State Beach	150	C4	41.389770 -71.474260

SOUTH CAROLINA	PAGE	GRID	LATITUDE LONGITUDE
National Park & Rec. Areas			
Charles Pinckney N.H.S.	131	D2	32.847150 -79.824090
Congaree Natl. Park	122	A4	33.836100 -80.827660
Kings Mtn. N.M.P.	122	A1	35.140120 -81.386890
Ninety Six N.H.S.	121	F3	34.162740 -82.010980
Reconstruction Era N.H.P.	130	C2	32.432790 -80.670458
State Park & Rec. Areas			
Andrew Jackson S.P.	122	B2	34.839560 -80.810110
Barnwell S.P.	130	B1	33.329250 -81.300400
Calhoun Falls S.P.	121	E3	34.106792 -82.604200
Cheraw S.P.	122	C2	34.642370 -79.927640
Devils Fork S.P.	121	E2	34.952527 -82.946085
Edisto Beach S.P.	130	C2	32.505410 -80.310310
Givhans Ferry S.P.	130	C1	33.031640 -80.382150
Goodale S.P.	122	B3	34.281580 -80.525150
Hickory Knob State Resort Park	121	E4	33.884250 -82.416010
Huntington Beach S.P.	123	D4	33.502650 -79.081200
Jones Gap S.P.	121	E1	35.126360 -82.558350
Kings Mtn. S.P.	122	A1	35.113030 -81.394040
Lake Warren S.P.	130	B2	32.844830 -81.165070
Little Pee Dee S.P.	122	C3	34.331020 -79.282170
Myrtle Beach S.P.	123	D4	33.649210 -78.938600
Oconee S.P.	121	E2	34.867297 -83.106098
Paris Mtn. S.P.	121	E2	34.924970 -82.365540
Poinsett S.P.	122	B4	33.804360 -80.544920
Santee S.P.	122	B4	33.500200 -80.489820
Table Rock S.P.	121	E2	35.022050 -82.710700

SOUTH DAKOTA	PAGE	GRID	LATITUDE LONGITUDE
National Park & Rec. Areas			
Badlands Natl. Park-Interior Ent.	26	B4	43.741900 -101.957000
Badlands Natl. Park-Northeast Ent.	26	B4	43.792400 -101.906000
Badlands Natl. Park-Pinnacles Ent.	26	B4	43.885500 -102.238000
Jewel Cave Natl. Mon.	25	F4	43.736500 -103.819940
Minuteman Missile N.H.S.	26	B4	43.833931 -101.899685
Mount Rushmore Natl. Mem.	26	A4	43.886730 -103.440610
Wind Cave Natl. Park-Vis. Ctr.	26	A4	43.556100 -103.478000
State Park & Rec. Areas			
Bear Butte S.P.	26	A3	44.460580 -103.433750
Custer S.P.	26	A4	43.770310 -103.440130
Fisher Grove S.P.	27	E2	44.883340 -98.356640
Hartford Beach S.P.	27	F2	45.398870 -96.665260
Lake Herman S.P.	27	F4	43.993120 -97.159790
Newton Hills S.P.	35	F1	43.218860 -96.569700
Oakwood Lakes S.P.	27	F3	44.454310 -96.989490
Palisades S.P.	27	F4	43.687970 -96.511470
Roy Lake S.P.	27	E1	45.703360 -97.419650
Sica Hollow S.P.	27	E1	45.740690 -97.229150
Union Grove S.P.	35	F1	42.922630 -96.785530

TENNESSEE	PAGE	GRID	LATITUDE LONGITUDE
National Park & Rec. Areas			
Andrew Johnson N.H.S.	111	D4	36.157710 -82.836880
Big South Fork Natl. River & Rec. Area	110	B3	36.475400 -84.752100
Manhattan Project N.H.P.	37	D2	35.928419 -85.350923
State Park & Rec. Areas			
Big Hill Pond S.P.	119	D1	35.078890 -88.718860
Big Ridge S.P.	110	C3	36.241600 -83.929280
Bledsoe Creek S.P.	109	F3	36.378050 -86.356660
Cedars of Lebanon S.P. & Forest	109	F4	36.093930 -86.335620
Chickasaw S.P.	119	D1	35.393241 -88.772298
Cove Lake S.P.	110	C3	36.305830 -84.210750
Cumberland Mtn. S.P.	110	B4	35.898460 -84.995130
David Crockett S.P.	119	E1	35.242690 -87.354850
Davy Crockett Birthplace S.P.	111	E3	36.221980 -82.662770
Edgar Evins S.P.	110	A4	36.086050 -85.812460
Fall Creek Falls S.P.	120	B1	35.622200 -85.208000
Frozen Head S.P.-North Ent.	110	B4	36.122550 -84.433320
Frozen Head S.P.-South Ent.	110	B4	36.102180 -84.446970
Harpeth River S.P.	109	E4	36.079240 -86.956920
Harrison Bay S.P.	120	B1	35.175850 -85.115350
Henry Horton S.P.	119	F1	35.596510 -86.698690
Hiwassee–Ocoee Scenic Rivers S.P.	120	C1	35.224557 -84.504269
Indian Mtn. S.P.	110	C3	36.583050 -84.139900
Long Hunter S.P.	109	F4	36.094340 -86.557330
Meeman-Shelby Forest S.P.	118	B1	35.336800 -90.029010
Montgomery Bell S.P.	109	E4	36.106750 -87.268690
Mousetail Landing S.P.	109	D4	35.581900 -87.859100
Natchez Trace S.P.	109	D4	35.839580 -88.252820
Nathan Bedford Forrest S.P.	109	D4	36.087900 -87.979750
Norris Dam S.P.	110	C3	36.234560 -84.127020
Old Stone Fort State Arch. Park	120	A1	35.487270 -86.101330
Panther Creek S.P.	111	D3	36.212760 -83.412420
Paris Landing State Resort Park	109	D3	36.441760 -88.090180
Pickett S.P.	110	B3	36.537374 -84.802126
Pickwick Landing S.P.	119	D2	35.051790 -88.242650
Pinson Mounds State Arch. Park	119	D1	35.504130 -88.683020
Reelfoot Lake S.P.	108	B3	36.414410 -89.426880
Roan Mtn. S.P.	111	E4	36.161110 -82.097000
Rock Island S.P.	110	A4	35.810000 -85.641550
Standing Stone S.P.	110	A3	36.458910 -85.437690
T.O. Fuller S.P.	118	B2	35.057810 -90.113650
Tims Ford S.P.	120	A1	35.220999 -86.255889
Warriors Path S.P.	111	E5	36.504610 -82.481090

TEXAS	PAGE	GRID	LATITUDE LONGITUDE
National Park & Rec. Areas			
Alibates Flint Quarries Natl. Mon.	50	A3	35.571900 -101.633880
Amistad N.R.A.	60	B2	29.449920 -101.053170
Big Bend Natl. Park-North Ent.	62	C4	29.680900 -103.167000
Big Bend Natl. Park-West Ent.	62	C4	29.306600 -103.523000
Fort Davis N.H.S.	62	B2	30.604120 -103.886010
Guadalupe Mts. Natl. Park-Vis. Ctr.	57	D3	31.894300 -104.822000
Lyndon B. Johnson N.H.P.	61	D2	30.276020 -98.411990
Padre Island Natl. Seashore	63	F3	27.553470 -97.248370
Palo Alto Btld. N.H.P.	63	F4	26.011630 -97.481570
State Park & Rec. Areas			
Abilene S.P.	58	C3	32.241360 -99.879230
Atlanta S.P.	124	C1	33.229500 -94.249300
Balmorhea S.P.	62	B2	30.946270 -103.784890
Bastrop S.P.	61	E2	30.098960 -97.229090
Bentsen-Rio Grande Valley S.P.	63	E4	26.182530 -98.382360
Big Bend Ranch S.P.	62	B4	29.265070 -103.791910
Big Spring S.P.	58	A3	32.229650 -101.483090
Blanco S.P.	61	D2	30.093240 -98.423420
Bonham S.P.	59	F1	33.543100 -96.149640
Brazos Bend S.P.	132	A4	29.371480 -95.631890
Buescher S.P.	61	E2	30.073570 -97.176140
Caddo Lake S.P.	124	C2	32.684230 -94.177070
Caprock Canyons S.P. & Trailway	50	B4	34.406440 -101.048830
Choke Canyon S.P.-Calliham Unit	61	D4	28.460970 -98.356380
Choke Canyon S.P.-South Shore Unit	61	D4	28.467610 -98.239550
Cleburne S.P.	59	E3	32.265180 -97.560680
Colorado Bend S.P.	61	D1	31.062510 -98.504250
Cooper Lake S.P.	124	A1	33.305282 -95.648346
Copper Breaks S.P.	50	C4	34.113660 -99.747800
Daingerfield S.P.	124	B1	33.028720 -94.714510
Davis Mts. S.P.	62	B2	30.599520 -103.929220
Dinosaur Valley S.P.	59	E3	32.250020 -97.814620
Eisenhower S.P.	59	F1	33.822670 -96.616120
Fairfield Lake S.P.	59	F3	31.765910 -96.076220
Falcon S.P.	63	D3	26.583500 -99.144790
Fort Boggy S.P.	124	A4	31.189627 -95.986069
Fort Griffin S.H.S.	58	C2	32.924690 -99.219370
Fort Parker S.P.	59	F4	31.592650 -96.524370
Fort Richardson S.P. & Hist. Site	59	D2	33.206060 -98.164810
Franklin Mts. S.P.	56	C3	31.912060 -106.517140
Galveston Island S.P.	132	B4	29.196240 -94.956210
Garner S.P.	60	C2	29.600900 -99.744220
Goliad S.P. & Hist. Site	61	E4	28.655190 -97.383580
Goose Island S.P.	61	F4	28.134060 -96.984350
Guadalupe River S.P.	61	D2	29.849890 -98.509590
Hueco Tanks S.P. & Hist. Site	56	C3	31.926453 -106.042437
Huntsville S.P.	132	A2	30.638130 -95.511370
Inks Lake S.P.	61	D1	30.738290 -98.366450
Kickapoo Cavern S.P.	60	B2	29.610016 -100.452465
Lake Arrowhead S.P.	59	D1	33.759300 -98.396610
Lake Bob Sandlin S.P.	124	B1	33.054090 -95.101250
Lake Brownwood S.P.	59	D3	31.857370 -99.021280
Lake Casa Blanca International S.P.	63	D2	27.536739 -99.432449
Lake Colorado City S.P.	58	B3	32.313460 -100.92480
Lake Corpus Christi S.P.	61	E4	28.060360 -97.867690
Lake Livingston S.P.	132	B1	30.671300 -95.008200
Lake Mineral Wells S.P. & Trailway	59	E2	32.814570 -98.042270
Lake Somerville S.P. & Trailway	61	F1	30.315760 -96.625080
Lake Tawakoni S.P.	59	F2	32.841610 -95.990710
Lake Whitney S.P.	59	E3	31.924780 -97.356280
Lockhart S.P.	61	E2	29.857610 -97.697400
Longhorn Cavern S.P.	61	D1	30.686610 -98.351380
Lyndon B. Johnson S.P. & Hist. Site-Ranch Unit	61	D2	30.235180 -98.629100
Martin Creek Lake S.P.	124	B3	32.283090 -94.583470
Martin Dies Junior S.P.	132	C1	30.848980 -94.164720
Meridian S.P.	59	E3	31.892440 -97.695670
Mission Tejas S.P.	124	A4	31.546110 -95.234720
Monahans Sandhills S.P.	57	F4	31.634940 -102.81485
Mother Neff S.P.	59	E4	31.319150 -97.474210
Mustang Island S.P.	63	F2	27.677020 -97.173730
Old Tunnel S.P.	61	D2	30.101079 -98.820704
Palmetto S.P.	61	E2	29.597280 -97.584640
Palo Duro Canyon S.P.	50	B3	34.985710 -101.70319
Pedernales Falls S.P.	61	D1	30.273110 -98.256830
Possum Kingdom S.P.	59	D2	32.878970 -98.561740
Purtis Creek S.P.	124	A2	32.373340 -95.974530
Ray Roberts Lake S.P.	59	F1	33.444050 -96.925860
Sabine Pass Battleground S.H.S.	132	C3	29.726520 -93.878280
San Angelo S.P.	58	B4	31.491919 -100.54714
Sea Rim S.P.	132	C3	29.677900 -94.039900
Seminole Canyon S.P. & Hist. Site	60	A2	29.709000 -101.29848
South Llano River S.P.	60	C1	30.445430 -99.804610
Stephen F. Austin S.P.	61	F2	29.812030 -96.108200
Tyler S.P.	124	A2	32.481750 -95.281760
Village Creek S.P.	132	C2	30.250499 -94.178700

UTAH	PAGE	GRID	LATITUDE LONGITUDE
National Park & Rec. Areas			
Arches Natl. Park	40	A2	38.615570 -109.616920
Bears Ears Natl. Mon.	41	A3	37.703318 -109.919962
Bryce Canyon Natl. Park	39	E4	37.641700 -112.168000
Canyonlands Natl. Park-East Ent.	40	A3	38.168510 -109.750980
Canyonlands Natl. Park-Horseshoe Canyon Unit	39	F3	38.497740 -110.205960
Canyonlands Natl. Park-North Ent.	40	A3	38.490150 -109.807930
Canyonlands Natl. Park-West Ent.	40	A3	38.255440 -110.180050
Capitol Reef Natl. Park	39	E3	38.291020 -111.261410
Cedar Breaks Natl. Mon.-East Ent.	39	D4	37.655230 -112.811350
Cedar Breaks Natl. Mon.-North Ent.	39	D4	37.665730 -112.838130
Cedar Breaks Natl. Mon.-South Ent.	39	D4	37.598730 -112.850080
Glen Canyon N.R.A.	39	F4	38.255440 -110.180050
Golden Spike N.H.P.	31	E3	41.620482 -112.547471
Grand Staircase-Escalante Natl. Mon.	39	E4	37.420000 -111.550000
Natural Bridges Natl. Mon.	39	F4	37.608120 -109.966280
Rainbow Bridge Natl. Mon.	47	E1	37.110810 -110.406050
Zion Natl. Park-East Ent.	39	D4	37.235370 -112.864470
Zion Natl. Park-Main Ent.	39	D4	37.201970 -112.988380
State Park & Rec. Areas			
Anasazi S.P. Mus.	39	E3	37.922399 -111.425743
Antelope Island S.P.	31	E4	41.089290 -112.116490
Bear Lake (Rendezvous Beach) S.P.	31	F2	41.962200 -111.400320
Bear Lake S.P.	31	F2	41.965360 -111.399480
Camp Floyd S.P. Mus.	31	E4	40.258360 -112.097270
Coral Pink Sand Dunes S.P.	47	D1	37.036964 -112.731196
Dead Horse Point S.P.	40	A3	38.510220 -109.729460
Deer Creek S.P.	31	F4	40.452620 -111.477820
Edge of the Cedars S.P. Mus.	40	A4	37.629760 -109.491730
Escalante Petrified Forest S.P.	39	E4	37.783820 -111.630220
Fred Hayes S.P. at Starvation	32	A4	40.104100 -110.330900
Fremont Indian S.P. Mus.	39	D3	38.579537 -112.314773
Frontier Homestead S.P. Mus.	39	D4	37.688349 -113.061896
Goblin Valley S.P.	39	F3	38.580620 -110.712580
Goosenecks S.P.	40	A4	37.174730 -109.926950
Green River S.P.	39	F2	38.995500 -110.156910
Gunlock S.P.-North Ent.	38	C4	37.275970 -113.768780
Gunlock S.P.-South Ent.	38	C4	37.251490 -113.772820
Huntington S.P.	39	F2	39.315200 -110.977100
Hyrum Lake S.P.	31	E3	41.626220 -111.872170
Kodachrome Basin S.P.	39	E4	37.501670 -111.993610
Millsite S.P.	39	E2	39.099020 -111.184240
Otter Creek S.P.	39	E3	38.167430 -112.021570
Palisade S.P.	39	E2	39.195800 -111.691600
Piute S.P.	39	E3	38.322530 -112.204200
Quail Creek S.P.	39	D4	37.105000 -113.576600
Red Fleet S.P.	32	B4	40.553300 -109.518472
Rockport S.P.	31	F4	40.751890 -111.367410
Sand Hollow S.P.	46	C1	37.144830 -113.382139
Scofield S.P.	39	E1	39.708600 -110.921000
Snow Canyon S.P.-East Ent.	38	C4	37.212120 -113.630870
Snow Canyon S.P.-North Ent.	38	C4	37.256790 -113.632990
Snow Canyon S.P.-South Ent.	38	C4	37.183380 -113.645010

	PAGE	GRID	LATITUDE LONGITUDE
inaker S.P.-North Ent.	32	A4	40.534870 -109.522440
inaker S.P.-South Ent.	32	A4	40.504850 -109.528870
ritorial Statehouse S.P.	39	D2	38.985880 -112.353530
satch Mtn. S.P.	31	F4	40.477770 -111.519990
llard Bay S.P.-North Ent.	31	E3	41.418810 -112.052390
llard Bay S.P.-South Ent.	31	E3	41.350610 -112.069060
ba S.P.	39	E2	39.381240 -112.028360

VERMONT	PAGE	GRID	LATITUDE LONGITUDE
tional Park & Rec. Areas			
rsh-Billings-Rockefeller N.H.P.	81	E3	43.635833 -72.538333
osalamoo Natl. Rec. Area	81	D3	43.879457 -73.098532
ate Park & Rec. Areas			
is S.P.	81	E3	44.051150 -72.626440
anbury S.P.	81	D3	43.904250 -73.065370
rton Island S.P.	81	D1	44.779660 -73.180050
mp Plymouth S.P.	81	E4	43.475810 -72.694987
A.R. S.P.	81	D3	44.058850 -73.409210
erald Lake S.P.	81	D4	43.283790 -73.002250
f Moon S.P.	81	D3	43.699720 -73.223220
ngsland Bay S.P.	81	D2	44.226230 -73.277660
ke Saint Catherine S.P.	81	D4	43.483000 -73.202580
le River S.P.	81	D2	44.388940 -72.768360
lly Stark S.P.	94	C1	42.854920 -72.813790
rth Hero S.P.	81	D1	44.908210 -73.235110
cker Pond S.P.	81	E2	44.251467 -72.247550
llwater S.P.	81	E2	44.280200 -72.275060
wnshend S.P.	81	E4	43.041920 -72.691600
derhill S.P.	81	D2	44.528880 -72.843920
oodford S.P.	94	C1	42.894450 -73.037790
oods Island S.P.	81	D1	44.802500 -73.209283

VIRGINIA	PAGE	GRID	LATITUDE LONGITUDE
tional Park & Rec. Areas			
pomattox Court House N.H.P.	112	C1	37.377367 -78.795290
oker T. Washington Natl. Mon.	112	B2	37.120500 -79.733340
dar Creek & Belle Grove N.H.P.	102	C2	39.023500 -78.289000
lonial N.H.P.	114	A4	37.211390 -76.776730
mberland Gap N.H.P.-Vis. Ctr.	111	D3	36.602600 -83.695400
edericksburg & Spotsylvania Co. flds. Mem. N.M.P.	103	D4	38.254300 -77.451890
orge Washington Birthplace Natl. Mon.	114	A2	38.192353 -76.927192
anassas Natl. Bfld. Park	144	A3	38.806030 -77.572810
ount Rogers N.R.A.	111	F2	36.811360 -81.420130
enandoah Natl. Park-ront Royal North Ent.	102	C3	38.903300 -78.192400
enandoah Natl. Park-ockfish Gap South Ent.	102	C3	38.033900 -78.858900
enandoah Natl. Park-Swift Run Gap Ent.	102	C3	38.359100 -78.546700
enandoah Natl. Park-Thornton Gap Ent.	102	C3	38.662300 -78.320600
ate Park & Rec. Areas			
ar Creek Lake S.P.	113	D1	37.532970 -78.274890
le Isle S.P.	114	B2	37.774526 -76.599222
ippokes Plantation S.P.	114	A4	37.140400 -76.748590
aytor Lake S.P.	112	A2	37.057620 -80.622140
uthat S.P.	102	B4	37.914520 -79.796740
ry Stone S.P.	112	B2	36.791790 -80.117890
se Cape S.P.	115	F1	36.691370 -75.924410
st Landing S.P.	114	B4	36.915601 -76.057000
ayson Highlands S.P.	111	F3	36.611920 -81.489900
lliday Lake S.P.	113	D1	37.404610 -78.644920
ngry Mother S.P.	111	F2	36.880860 -81.525750
nes River S.P.	112	C1	37.540400 -78.839300
otopeke S.P.	114	B4	37.169292 -75.982919
ke Anna S.P.	103	D4	38.125850 -77.821690
ason Neck S.P.	103	E3	38.640740 -77.194400
tural Bridge S.P.	112	C1	37.633038 -79.543034
tural Tunnel S.P.	111	E3	36.707520 -82.744090
w River Trail S.P.	112	A2	36.870180 -80.868550
coneechee S.P.	113	D3	36.633330 -78.525420
cahontas S.P.	113	E1	37.366240 -77.573870
whatan S.P.	113	D1	37.678066 -77.925997
lor's Creek Bfld. Hist. S.P.	113	D1	37.298470 -78.229470
y Meadows S.P.	103	D2	38.988703 -77.968913
ith Mtn. Lake S.P.	112	B2	37.091110 -79.592110
in Lakes S.P.	113	D2	37.336900 -77.934100
estmoreland S.P.	103	E4	38.158690 -76.870120
k River S.P.	113	F1	37.414190 -76.713650

WASHINGTON	PAGE	GRID	LATITUDE LONGITUDE
tional Park & Rec. Areas			
lumbia River Gorge Natl. Scenic Area	21	D1	45.715322 -121.818667
rt Vancouver N.H.S.	20	C1	45.626940 -122.656310
nford Reach Natl. Mon.	13	E4	46.483333 -119.533333
ke Chelan N.R.A.	13	D2	48.309080 -120.657730
ke Roosevelt N.R.A.	13	F2	47.972680 -118.970580
wis & Clark N.H.P.-Discovery Trail	12	B4	46.370033 -124.053503
wis & Clark N.H.P.-Dismal Nitch	20	B1	46.249033 -123.862903
wis & Clark N.H.P.-Sta. Camp	20	B1	46.263111 -123.932571
nhattan Project N. H.P.	13	E4	46.316332 -119.301848
ount Baker N.R.A.	12	C1	48.714167 -121.805900
ount Rainier Natl. Park-Nisqually Ent.	12	C5	46.741400 -121.919040
ount Rainier Natl. Park-Stevens Can. Ent.	12	C7	46.754730 -121.557010
Mount Rainier Natl. Park-White River Ent.	12	C8	46.902040 -121.554340
Mount Saint Helens Natl. Mon.	12	C4	46.277590 -122.218820
North Cascades Natl. Park-Golden West	13	D1	48.308200 -120.655000
North Cascades Natl. Park-Northern Cascades Vis. Ctr.	13	D1	48.666100 -121.264000
Olympic Natl. Park-Vis. Ctr.	12	B2	48.096700 -123.428000
Olympic Natl. Park-Vis. Ctr.-Hoh Rain Forest	12	B2	47.860700 -123.935000
Olympic Natl. Park-Vis. Ctr.-Hurricane Ridge	12	B2	47.969200 -123.498000
Ross Lake N.R.A.	13	D1	48.674250 -121.244730
San Juan Island N.H.P.	12	B2	48.534580 -123.016250
San Juan Islands Natl. Mon.	12	C2	48.531944,-123.029167
Whitman Mission N.H.S.	21	F1	46.040910 -118.468110
State Park & Rec. Areas			
Alta Lake S.P.	13	E2	48.031990 -119.934710
Anderson Lake S.P.	12	C2	48.014590 -122.810680
Belfair S.P.	12	C3	47.430630 -122.881400
Birch Bay S.P.	12	C1	48.903210 -122.757880
Bogachiel S.P.	12	A2	47.894790 -124.362820
Bridgeport S.P.	13	E2	48.012549 -119.618571
Brooks Mem. S.P.	21	D1	45.950590 -120.664200
Camano Island S.P.	12	C2	48.131680 -122.503240
Cape Disappointment S.P.	20	B1	46.294210 -124.053610
Columbia Hills S.P.	21	D1	45.643030 -121.106410
Crawford S.P.	14	A1	48.992070 -117.370370
Curlew Lake S.P.	13	F1	48.719280 -118.661740
Deception Pass S.P.	12	C2	48.390970 -122.646880
Dosewallips S.P.	12	C3	47.687570 -122.899860
Fields Spring S.P.	22	A1	46.087520 -117.173650
Flaming Geyser S.P.	12	C3	47.280230 -122.041870
Fort Casey S.P.	12	C2	48.159760 -122.672410
Fort Columbia S.P.	20	B1	46.256833 -123.923070
Fort Simcoe S.P.	13	D4	46.345340 -120.823460
Fort Townsend S.P.	12	C2	48.078260 -122.805690
Ginkgo Petrified Forest S.P.	13	E4	46.949010 -119.997490
Goldendale Observatory S.P.	21	D1	45.837090 -120.815890
Grayland Beach S.P.	12	B4	46.792382 -124.097802
Ike Kinswa S.P.	12	C4	46.555780 -122.536570
Jarrell Cove S.P.	12	B3	47.285940 -122.881080
Joseph Whidbey S.P.	12	C2	48.308370 -122.713170
Kitsap Mem. S.P.	12	C3	47.816580 -122.646840
Lake Chelan S.P.	13	D2	47.869430 -120.191110
Lake Easton S.P.	13	D3	47.249380 -121.190920
Lake Wenatchee S.P.	13	D3	47.816340 -120.729780
Larrabee S.P.	12	C2	48.650620 -122.489810
Lewis & Clark S.P.	12	C4	46.525850 -122.817910
Lewis & Clark Trail S.P.	13	F4	46.287600 -118.073340
Lincoln Rock S.P.	13	D3	47.535490 -120.282280
Millersylvania S.P.	12	B4	46.909610 -122.905950
Moran S.P.	12	C1	48.657700 -122.859630
Mount Spokane S.P.	14	B2	47.899290 -117.124350
Nolte S.P.	12	C3	47.267320 -121.943420
Ocean City S.P.	12	B4	47.038520 -124.158130
Pacific Beach S.P.	12	A3	47.205980 -124.202220
Pacific Pines S.P.	12	B4	46.507610 -124.049150
Palouse Falls S.P.	13	F4	46.664030 -118.228660
Peace Arch S.P.	12	C1	49.000980 -122.751580
Pearrygin Lake S.P.	13	E2	48.496720 -120.146950
Peshastin Pinnacles S.P.	13	D3	47.578810 -120.613860
Potholes S.P.	13	E4	46.970780 -119.351180
Potlatch S.P.	12	B3	47.363000 -123.158140
Rainbow Falls S.P.	12	B4	46.631010 -123.237350
Rockport S.P.	12	C2	48.487920 -121.601870
Sacajawea S.P.	21	F1	46.210140 -119.046050
Scenic Beach S.P.	12	C3	47.649250 -122.845470
Seaquest S.P.	12	C4	46.295880 -122.820860
Sequim Bay S.P.	12	B2	48.040750 -123.030920
Shine Tidelands S.P.	12	C2	47.867990 -122.638700
Steamboat Rock S.P.	13	E2	47.828650 -119.134340
Sun Lakes-Dry Falls S.P.	13	E3	47.596540 -119.387760
Triton Cove S.P.	12	B3	47.609112 -122.986526
Twenty-Five Mile Creek S.P.	13	D2	47.992520 -120.263610
Twin Harbors S.P.	12	B4	46.858850 -124.104210
Wallace Falls S.P.	12	C2	47.865610 -121.680050
Wanapum Rec Area	13	E4	46.924760 -119.991690
Westport Light S.P.	12	B4	46.891700 -124.111630

WEST VIRGINIA	PAGE	GRID	LATITUDE LONGITUDE
National Park & Rec. Areas			
Bluestone Natl. Scenic River	112	A1	37.584300 -80.957900
Gauley River N.R.A.	101	F4	38.191800 -81.001920
Harpers Ferry N.H.P.	103	D2	39.318820 -77.759060
New River Gorge Natl. Park & Pres.	101	F4	37.875670 -81.077598
Spruce Knob Seneca Rocks N.R.A.	102	B3	38.681180 -79.544480
State Park & Rec. Areas			
Audra S.P.	102	A2	39.041110 -80.067500
Beartown S.P.	102	A4	38.051750 -80.275420
Blennerhassett Island Hist. S.P.	101	E2	39.273300 -81.644800
Bluestone S.P.	112	A1	37.623050 -80.934710
Cacapon Resort S.P.	102	C1	39.502980 -78.291330
Camp Creek S.P.	111	F1	37.508173 -81.132873
Carnifex Ferry Bfld. S.P.	101	F4	38.211290 -80.941850
Cass Scenic Railroad S.P.	102	A3	38.396520 -79.914280
Cedar Creek S.P.	101	F3	38.880780 -80.849420
Droop Mtn. Bfld. S.P.	102	A4	38.113200 -80.271670
Holly River S.P.	102	A3	38.653140 -80.382620
Little Beaver S.P.	112	A1	37.756570 -81.079780
Moncove Lake S.P.	112	B1	37.616950 -80.354730
Pinnacle Rock S.P.	111	F1	37.308190 -81.291430
Prickett's Fort S.P.	102	A1	39.514090 -80.099960
Tomlinson Run S.P.	91	F4	40.550660 -80.595950
Tygart Lake S.P.	102	A2	39.248160 -80.021060
Valley Falls S.P.	102	A2	39.392900 -80.070480
Watoga S.P.	102	A4	38.122510 -80.155660
Watters Smith Mem. S.P.	102	A2	39.174520 -80.414260

WISCONSIN	PAGE	GRID	LATITUDE LONGITUDE
National Park & Rec. Areas			
Apostle Islands Natl. Lakeshore	65	D4	46.812210 -90.820780
Saint Croix Natl. Scenic Riverway	67	E2	45.415700 -92.646270
State Park & Rec. Areas			
Amnicon Falls S.P.	64	C4	46.608210 -91.887850
Aztalan S.P.	74	B3	43.068310 -88.863750
Belmont Mound S.P.	74	A4	42.768611 -90.349444
Big Bay S.P.	65	D4	46.811030 -90.696960
Big Foot Beach S.P.	74	C4	42.567330 -88.436790
Blue Mound S.P.	74	A3	43.026990 -89.840740
Brunet Island S.P.	67	F3	45.176220 -91.161610
Buckhorn S.P.	74	A1	43.948280 -90.002130
Copper Culture S.P.	68	C4	44.887440 -87.897940
Copper Falls S.P.	65	D4	46.351710 -90.643670
Council Grounds S.P.	68	A3	45.184840 -89.734290
Devil's Lake S.P.	74	A2	43.429010 -89.734900
Governor Dodge S.P.	74	A3	43.019560 -90.141950
Governor Thompson S.P.	68	C3	45.326309 -88.219205
Harrington Beach S.P.	75	D2	43.499430 -87.811890
Hartman Creek S.P.	74	B1	44.318070 -89.194320
High Cliff S.P.	74	C1	44.166680 -88.291760
Interstate S.P.	67	D3	45.396410 -92.636580
Kinnickinnic S.P.	67	D4	44.837280 -92.733190
Kohler-Andrae S.P.	75	D2	43.672740 -87.719320
Lake Kegonsa S.P.	74	B3	42.978005 -89.230300
Lake Wissota S.P.	67	F4	44.980950 -91.313740
Merrick S.P.	73	E1	44.152740 -91.744120
Mill Bluff S.P.	74	A1	43.961610 -90.317980
Mirror Lake S.P.	74	A2	43.568770 -89.834930
Natural Bridge S.P.	74	A2	43.344930 -89.928290
Nelson Dewey S.P.	73	F4	42.743740 -91.037860
New Glarus Woods S.P.	74	B4	42.786830 -89.631980
Newport S.P.	69	D3	45.241470 -86.998830
Pattison S.P.	64	C4	46.535290 -92.121410
Peninsula S.P.	69	D3	45.133080 -87.213280
Perrot S.P.	73	F1	44.016350 -91.479670
Potawatomi S.P.	69	D4	44.849990 -87.407640
Rib Mtn. S.P.	68	B4	44.915800 -89.669360
Roche-A-Cri S.P.	74	A1	43.996120 -89.812370
Rock Island S.P.	69	E3	45.398990 -86.855970
Rocky Arbor S.P.	74	A2	43.647890 -89.808240
Straight Lake S.P.	67	E2	45.597399 -92.406609
Tower Hill S.P.	74	A3	43.147090 -90.043750
Whitefish Dunes S.P.	69	D4	44.928910 -87.182150
Wildcat Mtn. S.P.	74	A2	43.688870 -90.566800
Willow River S.P.	67	D3	45.017610 -92.672610
Wyalusing S.P.	73	F3	42.978770 -91.118560
Yellowstone Lake S.P.	74	A4	42.777360 -89.993540

WYOMING	PAGE	GRID	LATITUDE LONGITUDE
National Park & Rec. Areas			
Devils Tower Natl. Mon.	25	E3	44.586870 -104.706710
Flaming Gorge N.R.A.	32	A3	41.254860 -109.611400
Fort Laramie N.H.S.	33	E2	42.202530 -104.558590
Fossil Butte Natl. Mon.	31	F2	41.855370 -110.782340
Grand Teton Natl. Park-Granite Canyon Ent.	23	F4	43.597990 -110.801640
Grand Teton Natl. Park-Moose Ent.	23	F4	43.655860 -110.718350
Grand Teton Natl. Park-Moran Ent.	23	F4	43.843640 -110.511950
John D. Rockefeller Jr. Mem. Parkway	24	A3	44.108800 -110.685508
Medicine Wheel Natl. Hist. Landmark	24	C2	44.826200 -107.921717
Yellowstone Natl. Park-East Ent.	23	F3	44.489540 -110.001560
Yellowstone Natl. Park-North East Ent.	23	F3	45.006120 -109.991550
Yellowstone Natl. Park-North Ent.	23	F3	45.030110 -110.705460
Yellowstone Natl. Park-South Ent.	23	F3	44.134730 -110.666170
Yellowstone Natl. Park-West Ent.	23	F3	44.658720 -111.098970
State Park & Rec. Areas			
Bear River S.P.	31	F3	41.267257 -110.938030
Boysen S.P.	32	C1	43.270160 -108.115260
Buffalo Bill S.P.	24	B3	44.505020 -109.249540
Curt Gowdy S.P.	33	E3	41.175380 -105.243640
Edness K. Wilkins S.P.	33	D1	42.857220 -106.177370
Glendo S.P.	33	E1	42.476060 -104.998910
Guernsey S.P.	33	E2	42.287400 -104.763460
Hot Springs S.P.	24	C4	43.653980 -108.201790
Keyhole S.P.	25	E3	44.356490 -104.825810
Seminoe S.P.	33	D2	42.150350 -106.905870
Sinks Canyon S.P.	32	B1	42.752600 -108.804770

CANADA

ALBERTA

ALBERTA	PAGE	GRID	LATITUDE LONGITUDE
National Park & Rec. Areas			
Banff Natl. Park-Banff Vis. Ctr.	164	B2	51.177400 -115.570900
Banff Natl. Park-Lake Louise Vis. Ctr.	164	B2	51.425200 -116.178400
Banff Park Mus. N.H.S.	164	B3	51.174300 -115.571100
Bar U Ranch N.H.S.	164	C3	50.420300 -114.244400
Cave and Basin N.H.S.	164	B3	51.168300 -115.591400
Elk Island Natl. Park	159	D4	53.572500 -112.841900
Jasper Natl. Park-Icefield Center	164	A1	52.233500 -117.234800
Jasper Natl. Park-Jasper Information Center	164	A1	52.877300 -118.080900
Rocky Mtn. House N.H.S.	164	C2	52.377590 -114.931237
Waterton Lakes Natl. Park-Waterton Vis. Ctr.	164	C4	49.051400 -113.906300
Wood Buffalo Natl. Park-Fort Chipewyan Vis. Ctr.	155	F2	48.714100 -111.154300
Provincial Park & Rec. Areas			
Aspen Beach Prov. Park	164	C2	52.454530 -113.975750
Beauvais Lake Prov. Park	164	C4	49.409500 -114.117000
Big Hill Springs Prov. Park	164	C3	51.251670 -114.386940
Big Knife Prov. Park	165	D2	52.489720 -112.210560
Birch Mts. Wildland Prov. Park	159	D1	57.509400 -112.957000
Bluerock Wildland Prov. Park	164	C3	50.642300 -114.654000
Bob Creek Wildland Prov. Park	164	C4	49.973700 -114.286000
Bow Valley Prov. Park	164	C3	51.040400 -115.077000
Bow Valley Wildland Prov. Park	164	B3	51.032600 -115.259000
Brown-Lowery Prov. Park	164	C3	50.813900 -114.430600
Calling Lake Prov. Park	159	D3	55.179720 -113.272500
Caribou Mts. Wildland Prov. Park	155	F3	59.205600 -114.897000
Carson-Pegasus Prov. Park	158	C3	54.295800 -115.645000
Castle Wildland Prov. Park	164	C4	49.306456 -114.299287
Chain Lakes Prov. Park	164	C3	50.200000 -114.183330
Chinchaga Wildland Prov. Park	158	B1	57.163400 -119.582000
Cold Lake Prov. Park	159	E3	54.602400 -110.072000
Cold Lake Prov. Park-North Shore	159	E3	54.644800 -110.103600
Crimson Lake Prov. Park	164	C2	52.466900 -115.048000
Cross Lake Prov. Park	159	D3	54.649300 -113.791000
Crow Lake Prov. Park	159	D2	55.800456 -112.152014
Dillberry Lake Prov. Park	165	E1	52.570200 -110.030000
Dinosaur Prov. Park	165	D3	50.770100 -111.480000
Don Getty Wildland Prov. Park	164	B2	50.893000 -114.993000
Dry Island Buffalo Jump Prov. Park	164	C2	51.929500 -112.975000
Dunvegan Prov. Park	158	B2	55.923600 -118.594400
Dunvegan West Wildland Prov. Park	158	B2	56.088900 -119.297000
Elbow Sheep Wildland Prov. Park	164	C3	50.703500 -114.939000
Fort Assiniboine Sandhills Wildland Prov. Park	158	C3	54.387100 -114.608000
Garner Lake Prov. Park	159	D3	54.183420 -111.741000
Gipsy Lake Wildland Prov. Park	159	E2	56.493500 -110.386000
Gooseberry Lake Prov. Park	165	D2	52.116940 -110.759170
Grand Rapids Wildland Prov. Park	159	D1	56.484200 -112.343000
Greene Valley Prov. Park	158	B2	56.140900 -117.242000
Gregoire Lake Prov. Park	159	E1	56.485000 -111.182780
Grizzly Ridge Wildland Prov. Park	158	C3	55.137700 -115.049000
Hay-Zama Lakes Wildland Prov. Park	155	F3	58.774100 -119.016000
Hilliard's Bay Prov. Park	158	C2	55.502900 -116.001000
Hubert Lake Wildland Prov. Park	158	C3	54.554100 -114.244000
Kakwa Wildland Prov. Park	158	A3	54.034600 -119.810000
Kinbrook Island Prov. Park	165	D3	50.437189 -111.910595
La Biche River Wildland Prov. Park	159	D3	54.987000 -112.626000
Lakeland Prov. Park	159	E3	54.759300 -111.557000
Lakeland Prov. Rec. Area	159	E3	54.721800 -111.398000
Lesser Slave Lake Prov. Park	158	C2	55.448000 -114.817000
Lesser Slave Lake Wildland Prov. Park	158	C2	55.497700 -115.567000
Little Bow Prov. Park	164	C3	50.227930 -112.926590
Little Fish Lake Prov. Park	165	D2	51.374246 -112.200944
Long Lake Prov. Park	159	D3	54.439986 -112.763465
Marguerite River Wildland Prov. Park	159	E1	57.638400 -110.266000
Midland Prov. Park	165	D2	51.478295 -112.771085
Miquelon Lake Prov. Park	159	D4	53.246900 -112.874000
Moonshine Lake Prov. Park	158	B2	55.883800 -119.216000
Moose Lake Prov. Park	159	E3	54.272986 -110.931143
Notikewin Prov. Park	158	C1	57.218300 -117.148000
Obed Lake Prov. Park	158	B4	53.558200 -117.101000
O'Brien Prov. Park	158	B3	55.065242 -118.822285
Otter-Orloff Lakes Wildland Prov. Park	159	D2	55.364200 -113.551000
Park Lake Prov. Park	164	C4	49.806621 -112.924681
Peace River Wildland Prov. Park	158	B2	55.983200 -117.765000
Pembina River Prov. Park	158	C4	53.611859 -114.985313
Peter Lougheed Prov. Park	164	B3	50.684100 -115.184000
Pigeon Lake Prov. Park	164	C1	53.029547 -114.150507
Police Outpost Prov. Park	164	C4	49.004503 -113.464980
Queen Elizabeth Wildlands Prov. Park	158	B2	56.219128 -117.693540
Red Lodge Prov. Park	164	C2	51.947917 -114.243862
Rochon Sands Prov. Park	165	D2	52.461755 -112.892373
Rock Lake Solomon Creek Wildland Prov. Park	158	B4	53.413700 -118.118000
Saskatoon Island Prov. Park	158	B2	55.205201 -119.085401
Sheep River Prov. Park	164	C3	50.647300 -114.660000
Sir Winston Churchill Prov. Park	159	D3	54.832050 -111.976109
Spray Valley Prov. Park	164	B3	50.888700 -115.293000
Stony Mtn. Wildland Prov. Park	159	E2	56.211500 -111.244000
Sundance Prov. Park	158	B4	53.668700 -116.926000
Sylvan Lake Prov. Park	164	C2	52.315760 -114.092272
Thunder Lake Prov. Park	158	C3	54.131941 -114.725882
Tillebrook Prov. Park	165	D3	50.538593 -111.812268
Vermilion Prov. Park	159	E4	53.367679 -110.909771
Wabamun Lake Prov. Park	158	C4	53.565029 -114.441575
Whitehorse Wildland Prov. Park	164	B1	52.957900 -117.395000
Whitemud Falls Wildland Prov. Park	159	E1	56.703400 -110.084000
Whitney Lakes Prov. Park	159	E4	53.847100 -110.537000
William A. Switzer Prov. Park	158	B4	53.492000 -117.804000
Williamson Prov. Park	158	B3	55.081821 -117.560174
Willow Creek Prov. Park	164	C3	50.118067 -113.776021
Winagami Lake Prov. Park	158	C2	55.627500 -116.738000
Winagami Wildland Prov. Park	158	C2	55.611900 -116.635000
Woolford Prov. Park	164	C4	49.178498 -113.190438
Writing-On-Stone Prov. Park	165	D4	49.061400 -111.639000
Wyndham-Carseland Prov. Park	164	C3	50.827750 -113.436542
Young's Point Prov. Park	158	B3	55.148000 -117.572000

BRITISH COLUMBIA

BRITISH COLUMBIA	PAGE	GRID	LATITUDE LONGITUDE
National Park & Rec. Areas			
Chilkoot Trail N.H.S.	155	D3	59.756667 -134.960833
Fort Langley N.H.S.	163	D3	49.168056 -122.569167
Fort McLeod N.H.S.	157	E1	54.992384 -123.039629
Fort Saint James N.H.S.	157	D2	54.440278 -124.255556
Gitwangak Battle Hill N.H.S.	156	C1	55.119444 -128.018056
Glacier Natl. Park-Eastern Welcome Sta.	164	A2	51.511700 -117.442000
Glacier Natl. Park-Rogers Pass Discovery Center	164	A2	51.300600 -117.521500
Gulf Islands Natl. Park Res.	163	D4	48.769400 -123.210000
Gulf of Georgia Cannery N.H.S.	163	D3	49.124722 -123.199722
Gwaii Haanas Natl. Park Res. & Haida Heritage Site	156	A3	52.349722 -131.433056
Kootenay Natl. Park-Radium Hot Springs Vis. Ctr.	164	B3	50.619500 -116.069800
Kootenay Natl. Park-Vermilion Crossing Vis. Ctr.	164	B3	51.000000 -115.966000
Mount Revelstoke Natl. Park-Western Welcome Sta.	164	A2	51.042000 -117.983900
Pacific Rim Natl. Park Res.-Broken Group Islands	162	B3	48.891100 -125.300800
Pacific Rim Natl. Park Res.-Pacific Rim Vis. Ctr.	162	B3	48.992000 -125.587200
Pacific Rim Natl. Park Res.-West Coast Trail	162	C4	48.704800 -124.866100
Pacific Rim Natl. Park Res.-Wickaninnish Interpretive Center	162	B3	49.012700 -125.674200
Yoho Natl. Park-Field Vis. Ctr.	164	B2	51.397800 -116.492000
Provincial Park & Rec. Areas			
Akamina-Kishinena Prov. Park	164	C4	49.032700 -114.178000
Alexandra Bridge Prov. Park	163	E2	49.700000 -121.399722
Alice Lake Prov. Park	163	D2	49.783056 -123.116667
Allison Lake Prov. Park	163	F2	49.683056 -120.599722
Anstey Hunakwa Prov. Park	164	A2	51.140600 -118.924300
Arctic Pacific Lakes Prov. Park	157	E2	54.384400 -121.553000
Arrow Lakes Prov. Park	164	A3	49.883056 -118.065667
Arrowstone Prov. Park	163	E1	50.879900 -121.273000
Atlin Prov. Park	155	E3	59.165400 -133.914000
Babine Lake-Pendleton Bay Marine Prov. Park	157	D2	54.533000 -125.724800
Babine Lake-Smithers Landing Marine Prov. Park	156	C1	55.098400 -126.600000
Babine Mountains Prov. Park	156	C1	54.913100 -126.928000
Babine River Corridor Prov. Park	156	C1	55.577400 -127.032000
Bear Creek Prov. Park	163	F2	49.930556 -119.520556
Bearhole Lake Prov. Park	158	A3	55.043400 -120.568000
Beatton Prov. Park	158	A1	56.333056 -120.933056
Beaumont Prov. Park	157	D2	54.050000 -124.616667
Beaver Creek Prov. Park	164	A4	49.066667 -117.600000
Beaver Valley Prov. Park	157	E3	52.523583 -122.081938
Big Bar Lake Prov. Park	157	E4	51.316667 -121.816667
Big Bunsby Marine Prov. Park	162	A2	50.120800 -127.504200
Big Creek Prov. Park	157	E4	51.301500 -123.158000
Bijoux Falls Prov. Park	157	E1	55.300000 -122.666667
Birkenhead Lake Prov. Park	163	D1	50.577900 -122.737000
Bishop River Prov. Park	162	C1	50.912500 -124.038000
Blanket Creek Prov. Park	164	A3	50.833056 -118.083056
Bligh Island Marine Prov. Park	162	A2	49.633300 -126.553000
Bowron Lake Prov. Park	157	F3	53.174100 -121.012000
Boya Lake Prov. Park	155	E3	59.380500 -129.090000
Brandywine Falls Prov. Park	163	D2	50.033056 -123.116667
Bridal Veil Falls Prov. Park	163	E3	49.183056 -121.733056
Bridge Lake Prov. Park	157	F4	51.483056 -120.700000
Bromley Rock Prov. Park	163	F3	49.416667 -120.258056
Brooks Peninsula Prov. Park	162	A2	50.180300 -127.657000
Broughton Archipelago Marine Prov. Park	162	A1	50.687100 -126.663000
Bugaboo Prov. Park	164	B3	50.794700 -116.808000
Callaghan Lake Prov. Park	163	D2	50.206900 -123.189000
Bull Canyon Prov. Park	157	E4	52.091667 -123.374722
Canal Flats Prov. Park	164	B3	50.183056 -115.816667
Canim Beach Prov. Park	157	F4	51.816667 -120.872667
Cape Scott Prov. Park	162	A1	50.765900 -128.246000
Cariboo Mts. Prov. Park	157	F3	52.852600 -120.538000
Cariboo River Prov. Park	157	F3	52.873600 -121.2220
Carmanah Walbran Prov. Park	162	C4	48.654500 -124.6280
Carp Lake Prov. Park	157	E2	54.769400 -123.3870
Catala Island Marine Prov. Park	162	A2	49.835833 -127.0541
Cathedral Prov. Park	163	F3	49.069800 -120.1740
Champion Lakes Prov. Park	164	A4	49.184100 -117.6240
Charlie Lake Prov. Park	158	A1	56.316667 -120.9997
Chasm Prov. Park	157	F4	51.178900 -121.4380
Chilliwack Lake Prov. Park	163	E3	49.072200 -121.4360
Clayoquot Arm Prov. Park	162	B3	49.172800 -125.5600
Clayoquot Plateau Prov. Park	162	B3	49.225100 -125.4280
Clendinning Prov. Park	162	C1	50.429700 -123.7330
Codville Lagoon Marine Prov. Park	156	C4	52.060833 -127.8555
Conkle Lake Prov. Park	164	A4	49.166667 -119.1000
Coquihalla Canyon Prov. Park	163	E3	49.371944 -121.3666
Cormorant Channel Marine Prov. Park	162	A1	50.593500 -126.8509
Cowichan River Prov. Park	162	C4	48.780800 -123.9200
Crooked River Prov. Park	157	E2	54.466667 -122.6666
Crowsnest Prov. Park	164	C4	49.649722 -114.6997
Cummins Lakes Prov. Park	164	A2	52.104100 -118.0660
Cypress Prov. Park	163	D3	49.425800 -123.2090
Dahl Lake Prov. Park	157	E2	53.769900 -123.2930
Desolation Sound Marine Prov. Park	162	C2	50.101100 -124.7100
Diana Lake Prov. Park	156	B2	54.216667 -130.1666
Downing Prov. Park	163	E1	51.000000 -121.7830
Dry Gulch Prov. Park	164	B3	50.583056 -116.0330
Duffey Lake Prov. Park	163	D1	50.407500 -122.3370
Dune Za Keyih Prov. Park	155	E3	58.323000 -126.3550
Echo Lake Prov. Park	164	A3	50.199722 -118.7000
Edge Hills Prov. Park	163	E1	51.035900 -121.8710
Elk Falls Prov. Park	162	B2	50.041000 -125.3240
Elk Lakes Prov. Park	164	C3	50.480800 -115.0880
Ellison Prov. Park	164	A3	50.173333 -119.4330
Emory Creek Prov. Park	163	E3	49.516667 -121.4166
Eneas Lakes Prov. Park	163	F2	49.752400 -119.9360
Entiako Prov. Park	157	D3	53.221500 -125.4430
Epper Passage Prov. Park	162	B3	49.219167 -125.9497
Eskers Prov. Park	157	E2	54.081300 -123.2050
Ethel F. Wilson Mem. Prov. Park	157	D2	54.416667 -125.6830
Fillongley Prov. Park	162	C3	49.534100 -124.7552
Finger-Tatuk Prov. Park	157	D2	53.515600 -124.2260
Flat Lake Prov. Park	157	F4	51.499400 -121.5210
Flores Island Prov. Park	162	B3	49.291000 -126.1730
Francois Lake Prov. Park	157	D2	53.966667 -125.1666
French Beach Prov. Park	162	C4	48.383056 -123.9330
Garibaldi Prov. Park	163	D2	49.943200 -122.7510
Gibson Marine Prov. Park	162	B3	49.266667 -126.0666
Gitnadoiks River Prov. Park	156	B2	54.161700 -129.1620
Gladstone Prov. Park	164	A4	49.268900 -118.2690
God's Pocket Marine Prov. Park	162	A1	50.837200 -127.5620
Goldpan Prov. Park	163	E2	50.350000 -121.3830
Gordon Bay Prov. Park	162	C4	48.833056 -124.1997
Graham-Laurier Prov. Park	155	F4	56.594900 -123.4660
Graystokes Prov. Park	164	A3	49.986200 -118.8500
Green Inlet Marine Prov. Park	156	C3	52.918167 -128.4859
Green Lake Prov. Park	157	F4	51.400000 -121.1997
Hamber Prov. Park	164	A2	52.380300 -117.8820
Harmony Islands Marine Prov. Park	162	C2	49.862222 -124.0122
Ha'thayim Marine Prov. Park	162	C2	50.169400 -124.9550
Heather-Dina Lakes Prov. Park	157	E1	55.508300 -123.2850
Height of the Rockies Prov. Park	164	B3	50.488900 -115.2280
Herald Prov. Park	164	A3	50.788056 -119.2010
Hesquiat Lake Prov. Park	162	B3	49.500000 -126.3858
Hitchie Creek Prov. Park	162	C4	48.795556 -124.7375
Horne Lake Caves Prov. Park	162	C3	49.344167 -124.7555
Horsefly Lake Prov. Park	157	F3	52.383056 -121.3000
Inkaneep Prov. Park	163	F3	49.233056 -119.5330
Inland Lake Prov. Park	162	C2	49.953800 -124.4810
Itcha Ilgachuz Prov. Park	157	D3	52.711500 -124.9740
Jackman Flats Prov. Park	164	A1	52.950000 -119.4166
Jedediah Island Marine Prov. Park	162	C3	49.500000 -124.1997
Jewel Lake Prov. Park	164	A4	49.183056 -118.5997
Jimsmith Lake Prov. Park	164	B4	49.483056 -115.8330
Joffre Lakes Prov. Park	163	D2	50.344100 -122.4770
Johnstone Creek Prov. Park	164	A4	49.050000 -119.0497
Juan De Fuca Prov. Park	162	C4	48.489800 -124.2900
Junction Sheep Range Prov. Park	157	E4	51.801000 -122.4350
Juniper Beach Prov. Park	163	E1	50.785833 -121.0830
Kakwa Prov. Park & Protected Area	158	A3	54.057200 -120.2960
Kekuli Bay Prov. Park	164	A3	50.183056 -119.3402
Kentucky-Alleyne Prov. Park	163	F2	49.916667 -120.5666
Kianuko Prov. Park	164	B4	49.421600 -116.4560
Kikomun Creek Prov. Park	164	B4	49.233056 -115.2500
Kilby Prov. Park	163	E3	49.237500 -121.9608
Kinaskan Lake Prov. Park	155	E4	57.496100 -130.2340
Kiskatinaw Prov. Park	158	A2	55.950000 -120.5666
Kleanza Creek Prov. Park	156	C2	54.599722 -128.3997
Klewnuggit Inlet Marine Prov. Park	156	B2	53.688500 -129.6970
Kluskoil Lake Prov. Park	157	D3	53.202900 -123.8920
Kokanee Creek Prov. Park	164	B4	49.605722 -117.1330
Kokanee Glacier Prov. Park	164	B4	49.781800 -117.1360
Kootenay Lake Prov. Park	164	B3	50.085000 -116.9311

vadacha Wilderness Prov. Park	155	E3	57.820400 -125.058000
c Le Jeune Prov. Park	163	F1	50.483056 -120.483056
akelse Lake Prov. Park	156	C2	54.398900 -128.533000
awn Point Prov. Park	162	A1	50.333056 -127.966667
ockhart Beach Prov. Park	164	B4	49.516667 -116.783056
ockhart Creek Prov. Park	164	B4	49.497300 -116.705000
oveland Bay Prov. Park	162	B2	50.049722 -125.450000
owe Inlet Marine Prov. Park	156	B2	53.555556 -129.580278
acMillan Prov. Park	162	C3	49.283056 -124.666667
ain Lake Prov. Park	162	B2	50.210000 -125.215000
ansons Landing Prov. Park	162	C2	50.121500 -124.928300
aquinna Marine Prov. Park	162	B3	49.390500 -126.342000
arble River Prov. Park	162	A1	50.544300 -127.526000
artha Creek Prov. Park	164	A3	51.141667 -118.198122
cConnell Lake Prov. Park	163	F1	50.521944 -120.456667
cDonald Creek Prov. Park	164	A3	50.131056 -117.813667
ehatl Creek Prov. Park	163	E2	50.036100 -122.054000
oberly Lake Prov. Park	158	A2	55.800000 -121.700000
omich Lakes Prov. Park	164	A2	51.327200 -119.353000
onck Prov. Park	163	F2	50.178667 -120.533056
oose Valley Prov. Park	157	E4	51.649800 -121.648000
orton Lake Prov. Park	162	B2	50.116667 -125.483056
ount Assiniboine Prov. Park	164	B3	50.937400 -115.761000
ount Blanchet Prov. Park	157	D1	55.275500 -125.863000
ount Fernie Prov. Park	164	C4	49.483056 -115.099722
ount Pope Prov. Park	157	D2	54.490700 -124.331000
ount Robson Prov. Park	164	A1	52.927000 -118.831000
ount Seymour Prov. Park	163	D3	49.392400 -122.926000
ount Terry Fox Prov. Park	164	A1	52.940800 -119.254000
oyie Lake Prov. Park	164	B4	49.373333 -115.837222
yra-Bellevue Prov. Park	164	A4	49.752100 -119.374000
ahatlatch Prov. Park	163	E2	49.980200 -121.780000
aikoon Prov. Park	156	A2	53.863400 -131.889000
airn Falls Prov. Park	163	D2	50.283056 -122.833056
ancy Greene Prov. Park	164	A4	49.250000 -117.933056
ickel Plate Prov. Park	163	F3	49.399722 -119.949722
icolum River Prov. Park	163	E3	49.366667 -121.341667
impkish Lake Prov. Park	162	A2	50.337700 -127.005000
iskonlith Lake Prov. Park	163	F1	50.795556 -119.777778
orbury Lake Prov. Park	164	B4	49.533056 -115.483056
uchatlitz Prov. Park	162	A2	49.815700 -126.981000
ctopus Island Marine Prov. Park	162	B2	50.278400 -125.242100
kanagan Lake Prov. Park	163	F2	49.683056 -119.719867
kanagan Mtn. Prov. Park	163	F2	49.724600 -119.629000
keover Arm Prov. Park	162	C2	49.999722 -124.726667
ne Island Lake Prov. Park	158	A2	55.300000 -120.266667
aarens Beach Prov. Park	157	D2	54.416667 -124.399722
aul Lake Prov. Park	163	F1	50.741667 -120.120556
inecone Burke Prov. Park	163	D3	49.526200 -122.721000
orpoise Bay Prov. Park	162	C3	49.516667 -123.749722
orteau Cove Prov. Park	163	D3	49.549722 -123.233056
remier Lake Prov. Park	164	B4	49.900000 -115.650000
rincess Louisa Marine Prov. Park	162	C2	50.203722 -123.766667
tarmigan Creek Prov. Park	157	F2	53.487600 -120.880000
untchesakut Lake Prov. Park	157	E3	52.983056 -122.933056
urden Lake Prov. Park	157	E2	53.928000 -121.912000
uatsino Prov. Park	162	A1	50.491667 -127.816667
earguard Falls Prov. Park	157	F3	52.973333 -119.366667
edfern-Keily Prov. Park	155	F3	57.405600 -123.878000
oberts Creek Prov. Park	162	C3	49.433056 -123.666667
olley Lake Prov. Park	163	D3	49.250000 -122.400000
osebery Prov. Park	164	B3	50.033056 -117.400000
ubyrock Lake Prov. Park	157	D2	54.677100 -125.348000
uckle Prov. Park	163	D4	48.766667 -123.383056
ugged Point Marine Prov. Park	162	A2	49.963889 -127.238889
aint Mary's Alpine Prov. Park	164	B4	49.877000 -116.348000
andy Island Marine Prov. Park	162	C3	49.616667 -124.849722
choen Lake Prov. Park	162	B2	50.176500 -126.245000
choolhouse Lake Prov. Park	157	F4	51.883600 -120.993000
eeley Lake Prov. Park	156	C1	55.199722 -127.683056
even Sisters Prov. Park	156	C1	54.946900 -128.150000
ilver Beach Prov. Park	164	A2	51.240278 -118.955556
ilver Lake Prov. Park	163	E3	49.316667 -121.399722
ilver Star Prov. Park	164	A3	50.376900 -119.082000
imson Prov. Park	162	C3	49.479700 -123.962900
kihist Prov. Park	163	E2	50.249722 -121.500000
kookumchuck Narrows Prov. Park	162	C2	49.744700 -123.915500
melt Bay Prov. Park	162	C2	50.033056 -124.983056
owchea Bay Prov. Park	157	D2	54.419167 -124.448333
proat Lake Prov. Park	162	C3	49.300000 -124.916667
quitty Bay Prov. Park	162	C3	49.454167 -124.166667
tagleap Prov. Park	164	B4	49.058700 -117.048000
teelhead Prov. Park	163	E1	50.752778 -120.868056
temwinder Prov. Park	163	F3	49.366667 -120.133056
tone Mtn. Prov. Park	155	E3	58.588600 -124.757000
trathcona Prov. Park	162	B2	49.629300 -125.710000
tuart Lake Marine Prov. Park	157	D2	54.650000 -125.000000
ugarbowl Prov. Park	157	E2	53.801200 -121.589000
ukunka Falls Prov. Park	157	E1	55.316667 -121.700000
ulphur Passage Prov. Park	162	B3	49.412000 -126.094000
ummit Lake Prov. Park	164	A3	50.150000 -117.666667
urge Narrows Prov. Park	162	B2	50.233056 -125.149722
Sutherland River Prov. Park	157	D2	54.338300 -124.818000
Sydney Inlet Prov. Park	162	B3	49.480000 -126.283000
Syringa Prov. Park	164	A4	49.378000 -117.906000
Tahsish-Kwois Prov. Park	162	A2	50.189100 -127.161000
Tatlatui Prov. Park	155	E4	56.996200 -127.386000
Tatshenshini-Alsek Prov. Park	155	D3	59.595900 -137.443000
Taylor Arm Prov. Park	162	B3	49.283056 -125.049722
Ten Mile Lake Prov. Park	157	E3	53.066667 -122.450000
Thurston Bay Marine Prov. Park	162	B2	50.383056 -125.316667
Ts'il-os Prov. Park	157	D4	51.191700 -123.971000
Tudyah Lake Prov. Park	157	E1	55.066667 -123.033056
Tunkwa Prov. Park	163	E1	50.615200 -120.887000
Tyhee Lake Prov. Park	156	C2	54.700000 -127.033056
Union Passage Marine Prov. Park	156	B3	53.410900 -129.436000
Upper Adams River Prov. Park	164	A2	51.682700 -119.228000
Valhalla Prov. Park	164	A4	49.873700 -117.567000
Vargas Island Prov. Park	162	B3	49.174000 -126.031000
Vaseux Lake Prov. Park	164	A4	49.268200 -119.474000
Walsh Cove Prov. Park	162	C2	50.268056 -124.800000
Wasa Lake Prov. Park	164	B4	49.793056 -115.738056
West Arm Prov. Park	164	B4	49.507000 -117.118000
West Lake Prov. Park	157	E2	53.733056 -122.866667
Whiskers Point Prov. Park	157	E1	54.900000 -122.933056
White Pelican Prov. Park	157	E3	52.284000 -123.031000
Whiteswan Lake Prov. Park	164	B3	50.145300 -115.487000
Woss Lake Prov. Park	162	A2	50.060400 -126.626000
Yahk Provincial Park	164	B4	49.083056 -116.083056
Yard Creek Prov. Park	164	A3	50.899722 -118.799722

MANITOBA	PAGE	GRID	LATITUDE LONGITUDE
National Park & Rec. Areas			
Lower Fort Garry N.H.S.	167	E3	50.136850 -96.940569
Riding Mtn. Natl. Park-Deep Lake Ranger Sta.	167	D3	50.860300 -100.836600
Riding Mtn. Natl. Park-Lake Audy Ranger Sta.	167	D3	50.712900 -100.230600
Riding Mtn. Natl. Park-McKinnon Creek Ranger Sta.	167	D3	50.787100 -99.579500
Riding Mtn. Natl. Park-Moon Lake Ranger Sta.	167	D3	50.995900 -100.067200
Riding Mtn. Natl. Park-South Lake Ranger Sta.	167	D3	50.655200 -100.061600
Riding Mtn. Natl. Park-Sugarloaf Ranger Sta.	167	D3	50.985300 -100.742100
Riding Mtn. Natl. Park-Whirlpool Ranger Sta.	167	D3	50.683300 -99.553500
Provincial Park & Rec. Areas			
Asessippi Prov. Park	166	C3	50.966400 -101.379700
Atikaki Prov. Wilderness Park	167	F2	51.532200 -95.547000
Bakers Narrows Prov. Park	161	D3	54.671100 -101.675000
Beaudry Prov. Park	167	E4	49.853900 -97.473300
Bell Lake Prov. Park	166	C1	52.541700 -101.241400
Birds Hill Prov. Park	167	E3	50.028800 -96.893200
Camp Morton Prov. Park	167	E3	50.710000 -96.990300
Clearwater Lake Prov. Park	161	D3	54.096200 -101.162000
Criddle–Vane Homestead Prov. Park	167	D4	49.707600 -99.596600
Duck Mtn. Prov. Park	167	D2	51.715600 -101.112000
Elk Island Prov. Park	167	E3	50.758300 -96.536500
Grand Beach Prov. Park	167	E3	50.567900 -96.554900
Grass River Prov. Park	161	D3	54.655500 -101.092000
Hecla–Grindstone Prov. Park	167	E2	51.198300 -96.660200
Hnausa Beach Prov. Park	167	E3	50.900300 -96.992200
Kettle Stones Prov. Park	167	D2	52.359200 -100.595300
Lake Saint George Prov. Park	167	E2	51.719703 -97.406772
Lundar Beach Prov. Park	167	E3	50.724000 -98.273000
Manipogo Prov. Park	167	D2	51.517000 -99.550000
Nopiming Prov. Park	167	F3	50.665200 -95.305600
North Steeprock Lake Prov. Park	166	C1	52.611800 -101.380000
Paint Lake Prov. Park	161	E2	55.492100 -98.018000
Patricia Beach Prov. Park	167	E3	50.467300 -96.575300
Pembina Valley Prov. Park	167	E4	49.038500 -98.296400
Pinawa Dam Prov. Park	167	F3	50.145200 -95.945700
Rainbow Beach Prov. Park	167	D3	51.099400 -99.718400
Saint Ambroise Beach Prov. Park	167	E3	50.275500 -98.074300
Saint Malo Prov. Park	167	E4	49.321400 -96.930490
South Atikaki Prov. Park	167	F3	51.041400 -95.417600
Spruce Woods Prov. Park	167	D4	49.703100 -99.141900
Stephenfield Prov. Park	167	E4	49.523400 -98.300500
Turtle Mtn. Prov. Park	167	D4	49.041500 -100.216000
Watchorn Prov. Park	167	E2	51.293100 -98.598500
Whitefish Lake Prov. Park	166	C2	52.333900 -101.587100
Whiteshell Prov. Park	167	F3	50.140900 -95.584400
William Lake Prov. Park	167	D4	49.055000 -100.038800
Winnipeg Beach Prov. Park	167	E3	50.512300 -96.967000

NEW BRUNSWICK	PAGE	GRID	LATITUDE LONGITUDE
National Park & Rec. Areas			
Beaubears Island N.H.S.	179	D3	46.972778 -65.569444
Fort Beauséjour N.H.S.	180	C1	45.865278 -64.290278
Fort Gaspareaux N.H.S.	180	C1	46.040833 -64.072778
Fundy Natl. Park-Vis. Ctr.	180	C1	45.659500 -65.132600
Kouchibouguac Natl. Park-Vis. Ctr.	179	D3	46.773200 -65.004900
Monument Lefebvre N.H.S.	180	C1	45.979167 -64.567222
Roosevelt Campobello International Park	180	A2	44.849722 -66.949722
Saint Andrews Blockhouse N.H.S.	180	A2	45.076389 -67.063889
Saint Croix Island International Hist. Site	180	A2	45.127778 -67.133333
Provincial Park & Rec. Areas			
De la République Prov. Park	178	B3	47.442778 -68.395556
Herring Cove Prov. Park	180	A2	44.866667 -66.933056
Mactaquac Prov. Park	180	A1	45.959025 -66.892556
Mount Carleton Prov. Park	178	C3	47.392300 -66.835500
Murray Beach Prov. Park	180	C1	46.016667 -63.983056
New River Beach Prov. Park	180	A2	45.133056 -66.533056
Parlee Beach Prov. Park	180	C1	46.233056 -64.499722
Sugarloaf Prov. Park	178	C2	47.974000 -66.671900
The Anchorage Prov. Park	180	A3	44.649722 -66.800000

NEWFOUNDLAND & LABRADOR	PAGE	GRID	LATITUDE LONGITUDE
National Park & Rec. Areas			
Castle Hill N.H.S.	183	E4	47.251389 -53.971111
Gros Morne Natl. Park-Vis. Ctr.	182	C2	49.571500 -57.877900
Hawthorne Cottage N.H.S.	183	E4	47.543333 -53.210833
L'Anse aux Meadows N.H.S.	183	F1	51.595000 -55.532778
Port au Choix N.H.S.	182	C1	50.712222 -57.375278
Red Bay N.H.S.	183	F1	51.733056 -56.415556
Ryan Premises N.H.S.	183	E3	48.648056 -53.112500
Terra Nova Natl. Park-Information Center	183	E3	48.394900 -54.204000
Terra Nova Natl. Park-Saltons Vis. Ctr.	183	E3	48.580600 -53.958900
Provincial Park & Rec. Areas			
Barachois Pond Prov. Park	182	C3	48.477100 -58.256600
Blow Me Down Prov. Park	182	C2	49.090833 -58.364444
Butter Pot Prov. Park	183	F4	47.390900 -53.071300
Chance Cove Prov. Park	183	F4	46.776900 -53.045400
Codroy Valley Prov. Park	182	C4	47.833333 -59.337778
Deadman's Bay Prov. Park	183	E2	49.331389 -53.692500
Dildo Run Prov. Park	183	E2	49.535556 -54.721667
Dungeon Prov. Park	183	E3	48.666667 -53.083611
Frenchman's Cove Prov. Park	183	D4	47.209444 -55.401667
Gooseberry Cove Prov. Park	183	E4	47.068056 -54.087778
J.T. Cheeseman Prov. Park	182	C4	47.631111 -59.249444
La Manche Prov. Park	183	F4	47.175200 -52.901200
Lockston Path Prov. Park	183	E3	48.437778 -53.379722
Notre Dame Prov. Park	183	E2	49.115833 -55.086389
Pinware River Prov. Park	183	F1	51.631667 -56.704167
Sandbanks Prov. Park	182	C4	47.607222 -57.646944
Sir Richard Squires Mem. Prov. Park	183	D2	49.354000 -57.213400
The Arches Prov. Park	182	C2	50.113333 -57.663056

NORTHWEST TERRITORIES	PAGE	GRID	LATITUDE LONGITUDE
National Park & Rec. Areas			
Náátsʼihchʼoh Natl. Park Res.	155	E2	62.617399 -128.787113
Nahanni Natl. Park Res.	155	E3	61.083333 -123.600000
Tuktut Nogait Natl. Park	155	E1	69.283333 -123.016667

NOVA SCOTIA	PAGE	GRID	LATITUDE LONGITUDE
National Park & Rec. Areas			
Alexander Graham Bell N.H.S.	181	F1	46.102778 -60.745556
Cape Breton Highlands Natl. Park-East Ent.	182	B4	46.642800 -60.404200
Cape Breton Highlands Natl. Park-West Ent.	182	B4	46.647300 -60.950200
Fort Anne N.H.S.	180	B3	44.741667 -65.519167
Fort Edward N.H.S.	180	C2	44.995556 -64.135278
Fortress of Louisbourg N.H.S.	181	F1	45.900300 -59.995100
Grand-Pré N.H.S.	180	C2	45.108889 -64.311944
Grassy Island N.H.S.	181	F2	45.336667 -60.973611
Kejimkujik Natl. Park (Seaside Adjunct)	180	C4	43.865800 -64.836900
Kejimkujik Natl. Park and N.H.S.	180	B3	44.336700 -65.268200
Marconi N.H.S.	181	F4	46.211111 -59.952778
Port-Royal N.H.S.	180	B3	44.712500 -65.610556
Saint Peters Canal N.H.S.	181	F1	45.655556 -60.870556
York Redoubt N.H.S.	181	D3	44.596583 -63.552439
Provincial Park & Rec. Areas			
Amherst Shore Prov. Park	180	C1	45.961181 -63.879025
Battery Prov. Park	181	F1	45.657022 -60.866764
Beaver Mtn. Prov. Park	181	E2	45.567556 -62.153583
Blomidon Prov. Park	180	C2	45.255869 -64.352056
Boylston Prov. Park	181	E2	45.426839 -61.510603
Cape Chignecto Prov. Park	180	C2	45.375800 -64.891300
Caribou–Munroes Island Prov. Park	181	D1	45.721800 -62.656914
Ellenwood Lake Prov. Park	180	B4	43.929481 -66.005700
Five Islands Prov. Park	180	C2	45.407781 -64.021500
Graves Island Prov. Park	180	C3	44.565550 -64.218642
Laurie Prov. Park	181	D2	44.878175 -63.602194
Martinique Beach Prov. Park	181	D3	44.689911 -63.147567
Mira River Prov. Park	181	F1	46.026006 -60.037433
Porters Prov. Park	181	D3	44.691106 -63.308892
Rissers Beach Prov. Park	180	C3	44.232397 -64.423919
Salsman Prov. Park	181	E2	45.236856 -61.767150
Salt Springs Prov. Park	181	D2	45.545280 -62.878890
Shubenacadie Prov. Wildlife Park	181	D2	45.087222 -63.387500
Smileys Prov. Park	180	C2	45.013925 -63.961247
The Islands Prov. Park	180	B4	43.765503 -65.340347
Thomas Raddall Prov. Park	180	C4	43.844783 -64.919694
Valleyview Prov. Park	180	B2	44.875200 -65.316064
Wentworth Prov. Park	181	D2	45.627222 -63.567222
Whycocomagh Prov. Park	181	F1	45.968094 -61.109908

ONTARIO	PAGE	GRID	LATITUDE LONGITUDE
National Park & Rec. Areas			
Battle of the Windmill N.H.S.	174	B4	44.722778 -75.486944
Bell Homestead N.H.P.	172	C3	43.107946 -80.273060
Bellevue House N.H.S.	173	F1	44.220556 -76.506667
Bruce Peninsula Natl. Park	170	C4	45.189100 -81.485500
Fathom Five Natl. Marine Park	170	C4	45.304800 -81.727600
Fort George N.H.S.	173	D3	43.252778 -79.051111
Fort Henry N.H.S.	173	F1	44.230833 -76.459444
Fort Malden N.H.S.	172	A4	42.108056 -83.113889
Fort Mississauga N.H.S.	173	D3	43.260833 -79.076667
Fort Saint Joseph N.H.S.	170	B3	46.063889 -83.944167
Fort Wellington N.H.S.	174	B4	44.713889 -75.510833
Georgian Bay Islands Natl. Park-Welcome Center	171	D4	44.803900 -79.720400
Glengarry Cairn N.H.S.	174	C3	45.121667 -74.490278
Merrickville Blockhouse N.H.S.	174	B4	44.916667 -75.837500
Peterborough Lift Lock N.H.S.	173	E1	44.308056 -78.300556
Point Clark Lighthouse N.H.S.	172	B2	44.073056 -81.756667
Point Pelee Natl. Park-Park Ent. Kiosk	172	A4	41.987700 -82.549900
Point Pelee Natl. Park-Vis. Ctr.	172	A4	41.931700 -82.513500
Pukaskwa Natl. Park-Information Center	170	A2	48.700400 -86.197200
Queenston Heights N.H.S.	173	D3	43.158056 -79.052778
Sault Ste. Marie Canal N.H.S.	170	B3	46.511667 -84.355556
Sir John Johnson House N.H.S.	174	C4	45.144444 -74.580000
Southwold Earthworks N.H.S.	172	B3	42.677778 -81.351389
Thousand Islands Natl. Park-Vis. Ctr.	174	A4	44.452300 -75.860300
Trent-Severn Waterway N.H.S.	173	E1	44.137500 -77.590100
Woodside N.H.S.	172	C2	43.466667 -80.499722
Provincial Park & Rec. Areas			
Abitibi-De-Troyes Prov. Park	171	D1	48.786500 -80.066300
Albany River Prov. Park	169	E1	51.358200 -88.134000
Algonquin Prov. Park	171	E4	45.605300 -78.323900
Arrowhead Prov. Park	171	D4	45.391700 -79.197200
Awenda Prov. Park	172	C1	44.854400 -79.989800
Balsam Lake Prov. Park	173	D1	44.642000 -78.864000
Bass Lake Prov. Park	173	D1	44.602000 -79.475000
Batchawana Prov. Park	170	B3	46.941900 -84.587010
Blue Lake Prov. Park	168	B3	49.904200 -93.525600
Bon Echo Prov. Park	171	E4	44.905600 -77.246600
Bonnechere Prov. Park	171	E4	45.658400 -77.570800
Bonnechere River Prov. Park	171	E4	45.674400 -77.661500
Brightsand River Prov. Park	169	D3	49.936700 -90.265400
Bronte Creek Prov. Park	173	D2	43.410490 -79.767830
Caliper Lake Prov. Park	168	B3	49.061670 -93.912780
Carson Lake Prov. Park	171	E4	45.502780 -77.746390
Chapleau-Nemegosenda River Prov. Park	170	B2	48.262300 -83.035300
Charleston Lake Prov. Park	174	A4	44.515400 -76.013600
Chutes Prov. Park	170	C3	46.219510 -82.071480
Craigleith Prov. Park	172	C1	44.535000 -80.367000
Darlington Prov. Park	173	D2	43.875480 -78.778300
Devil's Glen Prov. Park	172	C1	44.361000 -80.207800
Driftwood Prov. Park	171	E3	46.179000 -77.843000
Earl Rowe Prov. Park	172	C1	44.150000 -79.898000
Emily Prov. Park	173	D1	44.340530 -78.532860
Esker Lakes Prov. Park	171	D2	48.290100 -79.906100
Fairbank Prov. Park	170	C3	46.468070 -81.440410
Ferris Prov. Park	173	E1	44.293000 -77.788000
Finlayson Point Prov. Park	171	D3	47.055000 -79.797000
Fitzroy Prov. Park	174	A3	45.482680 -76.209400
French River Prov. Park	171	D3	46.008600 -80.620900
Frontenac Prov. Park	174	A4	44.540500 -76.512700
Fushimi Lake Prov. Park	169	F3	49.824800 -83.913800
Greenwater Prov. Park	170	C1	49.215900 -81.291000
Grundy Lake Prov. Park	171	D4	45.939800 -80.530400
Halfway Lake Prov. Park	170	C3	46.905700 -81.650500
Inverhuron Prov. Park	172	B1	44.298000 -81.580000
Ivanhoe Lake Prov. Park	170	C2	47.957600 -82.742600
John E. Pearce Prov. Park	172	B4	42.617000 -81.444000
Kakabeka Falls Prov. Park	169	D4	48.403290 -89.624130
Kap-Kig-Iwan Prov. Park	171	D2	47.789960 -79.884990
Kettle Lakes Prov. Park	170	C1	48.569400 -80.865400
Killarney Prov. Park	170	C3	46.099400 -81.386900
Killbear Prov. Park	171	D4	45.346200 -80.191200
Kopka River Prov. Park	169	D2	50.006300 -89.493000
Lady Evelyn-Smoothwater Prov. Park	171	D2	47.368500 -80.489300
Lake of the Woods Prov. Park	168	B3	49.221200 -94.606000
Lake on the Mtn. Prov. Park	173	F1	44.039940 -77.056080
Lake Saint Peter Prov. Park	171	E4	45.322000 -78.024000
Lake Superior Prov. Park	170	A2	47.595200 -84.756500
Larder River Prov. Park	171	D2	47.936300 -79.642800
La Verendrye Prov. Park	169	D4	48.138300 -90.431300
Little Abitibi Prov. Park	170	C1	49.637900 -80.922900
Little Current River Prov. Park	169	E2	50.724100 -86.211000
Long Point Prov. Park	172	C4	42.565000 -80.306000
Lower Madawaska River Prov. Park	171	E4	45.236200 -77.289300
MacGregor Point Prov. Park	172	B1	44.403700 -81.465600
Macleod Prov. Park	169	E3	49.676190 -86.931000
Makobe-Grays River Prov. Park	171	D2	47.617200 -80.376300
Mara Prov. Park	173	D1	44.589000 -79.349000
Mark S. Burnham Prov. Park	173	E1	44.299900 -78.257000
Marten River Prov. Park	171	D3	46.729000 -79.807000
Mattawa River Prov. Park	171	D3	46.315000 -79.108400
McRae Point Prov. Park	173	D1	44.569000 -79.320000
Mikisew Prov. Park	171	D4	45.820000 -79.512000
Missinaibi River Prov. Park	170	B1	49.101400 -83.234700
Mississagi Prov. Park	170	C3	46.596500 -82.682500
Mississagi River Prov. Park	170	C3	47.012600 -82.632700
Murphys Point Prov. Park	174	A4	44.774300 -76.240700
Nagagamisis Prov. Park	169	F3	49.475700 -84.771000
Neys Prov. Park	169	E4	48.750500 -86.591900
North Beach Prov. Park	173	E2	43.951050 -77.522660
Oastler Lake Prov. Park	171	D4	45.309000 -79.964800
Obabika River Prov. Park	171	D3	47.221200 -80.262600
Obatanga Prov. Park	170	A2	48.323000 -85.093700
Ojibway Prov. Park	168	C3	49.990900 -92.144400
Opeongo River Prov. Park	171	E4	45.576256 -77.887363
Otoskwin-Attawapiskat River Prov. Park	169	D1	52.235700 -87.491300
Ottawa River Prov. Park	174	A3	45.741700 -76.779800
Ouimet Canyon Prov. Park	169	D4	48.773350 -88.667400
Oxtongue River-Ragged Falls Prov. Park	171	D4	45.366900 -78.914100
Pakwash Prov. Park	168	B2	50.749800 -93.551400
Pancake Bay Prov. Park	170	B3	46.967200 -84.661100
Petroglyphs Prov. Park	173	E1	44.618300 -78.041700
Pigeon River Prov. Park	169	D4	48.025041 -89.572294
Pinery Prov. Park	172	B3	43.257200 -81.834000
Pipestone River Prov. Park	169	D1	52.244300 -90.313500
Point Farms Prov. Park	172	B2	43.804000 -81.700000
Port Bruce Prov. Park	172	B3	42.664000 -81.027000
Port Burwell Prov. Park	172	C3	42.646000 -80.816000
Potholes Prov. Park	170	B2	47.958700 -84.294020
Presqu'Ile Prov. Park	173	E2	44.007000 -77.735000
Quetico Prov. Park	168	C4	48.404500 -91.498700
Rainbow Falls Prov. Park	169	E4	48.830090 -87.389580
Renè Brunelle Prov. Park	170	C1	49.453700 -82.147900
Restoule Prov. Park	171	D3	46.080400 -79.839800
Rideau River Prov. Park	174	B4	45.060000 -75.672000
Rock Point Prov. Park	173	D3	42.854000 -79.552000
Rondeau Prov. Park	172	B4	42.278200 -81.865100
Rushing River Prov. Park	168	B3	49.681850 -94.234890
Samuel de Champlain Prov. Park	171	D3	46.301900 -78.864100
Sandbanks Prov. Park	173	F2	43.910200 -77.267200
Sandbar Lake Prov. Park	168	C3	49.491000 -91.555700
Sauble Falls Prov. Park	172	B1	44.673170 -81.257350
Selkirk Prov. Park	172	C3	42.824000 -79.961000
Sharbot Lake Prov. Park	174	A4	44.775500 -76.724600
Sibbald Point Prov. Park	173	D1	44.322160 -79.325570
Silent Lake Prov. Park	171	E4	44.907500 -78.047200
Silver Lake Prov. Park	174	A4	44.829770 -76.574680
Sioux Narrows Prov. Park	168	B3	49.429570 -94.037260
Six Mile Lake Prov. Park	171	D4	44.819500 -79.733500
Sleeping Giant Prov. Park	169	D4	48.419300 -88.795500
Solace Prov. Park	170	C3	47.189200 -80.683500
Springwater Prov. Park	173	D1	44.443500 -79.748500
Steel River Prov. Park	169	E3	49.161900 -86.812600
Sturgeon Bay Prov. Park	171	D4	45.623400 -80.414100
Sturgeon River Prov. Park	170	C3	46.949800 -80.523900
The Massasauga Prov. Park	171	D4	45.203400 -80.044300
The Shoals Prov. Park	170	B2	47.884800 -83.808000
Turkey Point Prov. Park	172	C3	42.694000 -80.333150
Turtle River-White Otter Lake Prov. Park	168	C3	49.129700 -92.042300
Upper Madawaska River Prov. Park	171	E4	45.513700 -78.078700
Wabakimi Prov. Park	169	D2	50.719100 -89.448500
Wakami Lake Prov. Park	170	C2	47.489700 -82.842000
Wasaga Beach Prov. Park	172	C1	44.494000 -80.027100
Wheatley Prov. Park	172	A4	42.098000 -82.448800
White Lake Prov. Park	170	A1	48.603500 -85.880900
Windy Lake Prov. Park	170	C3	46.619820 -81.455980
Woodland Caribou Prov. Park	168	B2	51.096900 -94.744900

PRINCE EDWARD ISLAND	PAGE	GRID	LATITUDE LONGITUDE
National Park & Rec. Areas			
Port-la-Joye–Fort Amherst N.H.S.	179	E4	46.195278 -63.133611
Prince Edward Island Natl. Park-Brackley Vis. Ctr.	179	E4	46.406200 -63.196600
Prince Edward Island Natl. Park-Cavendish Vis. Ctr.	179	E4	46.492300 -63.379700
Provincial Park & Rec. Areas			
Brudenell River Prov. Park	179	F4	46.209583 -62.588556
Buffaloland Prov. Park	179	F4	46.092500 -62.617778
Cabot Beach Prov. Park	179	E4	46.557250 -63.704250
Cedar Dunes Prov. Park	177	F4	46.622222 -64.381944
Chelton Beach Prov. Park	179	E4	46.303944 -63.747167
Green Park Prov. Park	177	F4	46.590972 -63.890333
Jacques Cartier Prov. Park	177	F4	46.851222 -64.013000
Kings Castle Prov. Park	179	F4	46.019167 -62.567389
Linkletter Prov. Park	179	E4	46.402694 -63.850361
Lord Selkirk Prov. Park	179	F4	46.091889 -62.906000
Mill River Prov. Park	177	F4	46.749722 -64.166667
Northumberland Prov. Park	179	F4	45.966667 -62.716667
Panmure Island Prov. Park	179	F4	46.133056 -62.466667
Red Point Prov. Park	179	F4	46.366667 -62.133056
Wood Islands Prov. Park	181	D1	45.949722 -62.749722

QUÉBEC	PAGE	GRID	LATITUDE LONGITUDE
National Park & Rec. Areas			
Lieu Historique Natl. du Fort-Lennox	175	D4	45.120556 -73.26805
Lieu Historique Natl. du Fort-Témiscamingue	171	D2	47.295000 -79.45666
Parc Natl. de Forillon	179	D1	48.854300 -64.39630
Parc Natl. de la Mauricie-East Ent.	175	D1	46.752600 -72.79260
Parc Natl. de la Mauricie-South Ent.	175	D1	46.650000 -72.96920
Parc Natl. d'Opémican	171	D3	46.884041 -79.09660
Réserve de Parc Natl. de l'Archipel-de-Mingan	177	F1	50.237100 -63.60690
Provincial Park & Rec. Areas			
Parc d'Aiguebelle	171	D1	48.510300 -78.74580
Parc d'Anticosti	182	A2	49.463200 -62.81900
Parc de Frontenac	175	E3	45.848600 -71.18460
Parc de la Gaspésie	178	C1	48.941500 -66.21440
Parc de la Gatineau	174	A3	45.566667 -75.94972
Parc de la Jacques-Cartier	175	E1	47.317300 -71.34700
Parc de la Pointe-Taillon	176	C3	48.717300 -71.99360
Parc de la Yamaska	175	D3	45.429400 -72.60180
Parc de l'Île-Bonaventure-et-du-Rocher-Percé	179	E1	48.496389 -64.16194
Parc de Miguasha	178	C2	48.110556 -66.36944
Parc de Plaisance	174	B3	45.597900 -75.12360
Parc de Récréation du Mont-Orford	175	D3	45.344700 -72.21290
Parc des Grands-Jardins	176	C4	47.681300 -70.83690
Parc des Hautes-Gorges-de-la-Rivière-Malbaie	176	C3	47.918700 -70.49870
Parc des Monts-Valin	176	C3	48.598600 -70.82530
Parc du Bic	178	A1	48.355300 -68.79760
Parc du Mont-Mégantic	175	E3	45.450700 -71.16730
Parc du Mont-Saint-Bruno	175	D3	45.555278 -73.30972
Parc du Mont-Tremblant	174	C2	46.443000 -74.34460
Parc du Saguenay	176	C3	48.289900 -70.24340
Parc Marin du Saguenay-Saint-Laurent	178	A2	48.133056 -69.73305
Parc Régional du Massif du Sud	175	F2	46.581389 -70.46777

SASKATCHEWAN	PAGE	GRID	LATITUDE LONGITUDE
National Park & Rec. Areas			
Batoche N.H.S.	165	F1	52.752800 -106.1167
Battle of Fish Creek N.H.S.	165	F1	52.550000 -106.1803
Fort Battleford N.H.S.	165	E1	52.713800 -108.25960
Fort Espèrance N.H.S.	166	C3	50.451400 -101.7128
Fort Livingstone N.H.S.	166	C2	51.903880 -101.9606
Fort Pelly N.H.S.	166	C2	51.795900 -101.9518
Fort Walsh N.H.S.	165	E4	49.559100 -109.9017
Grasslands Natl. Park-East Block Vis. Ctr.	166	A4	49.370800 -106.38480
Grasslands Natl. Park-West Block Vis. Reception Ctr.	166	A4	49.203800 -107.7327
Prince Albert Natl. Park-Waskesiu Vis. Ctr.	160	B3	53.922500 -106.0818
Provincial Park & Rec. Areas			
Blackstrap Prov. Park	166	A2	51.755600 -106.4583
Buffalo Pound Prov. Park	166	B3	50.576200 -105.3610
Candle Lake Prov. Park	160	B4	53.845000 -105.25200
Cannington Manor Prov. Hist. Park	166	C4	49.712900 -102.0273
Clearwater River Prov. Park	159	E1	56.929300 -109.0430
Crooked Lake Prov. Park	166	C3	50.592200 -102.74140
Cumberland House Prov. Hist. Park	160	C4	53.948000 -102.4214
Cypress Hills Interprovincial Park	165	E4	49.632400 -109.80900
Danielson Prov. Park	166	A2	51.252200 -106.86600
Douglas Prov. Park	166	A3	51.025300 -106.4800
Echo Valley Prov. Park	166	B3	50.808500 -103.89190
Fort Carlton Prov. Park	166	A1	52.867100 -106.54270
Fort Pitt Prov. Park	165	E1	53.577000 -109.8063
Good Spirit Lake Prov. Park	166	C2	51.543500 -102.70700
Greenwater Lake Prov. Park	166	C1	52.532000 -103.4480
Katepwa Point Prov. Park	166	B3	50.693165 -103.62602
Lac La Ronge Prov. Park	160	C3	55.249200 -104.76900
Last Mtn. House Prov. Park	166	B3	50.722800 -104.8233
Makwa Lake Prov. Park	159	E3	54.016800 -109.23400
Meadow Lake Prov. Park	159	E3	54.501400 -109.07600
Moose Mtn. Prov. Park	166	C4	49.821300 -102.4240
Narrow Hills Prov. Park	160	C3	54.091300 -104.64300
Pike Lake Prov. Park	166	A2	51.893200 -106.81900
Rowan's Ravine Prov. Park	166	B3	50.995600 -105.17970
Saint Victor Prov. Park	166	A4	49.395300 -105.87320
Saskatchewan Landing Prov. Park	165	F3	50.664600 -107.99700
Steele Narrows Prov. Park	159	E3	54.025900 -109.31840
The Battlefords Prov. Park	165	E1	53.132500 -108.38130
Touchwood Hills Prov. Park	166	B2	51.306400 -104.01410
Wildcat Hill Prov. Park	166	C1	53.273946 -102.49282
Wood Mtn. Post Prov. Hist. Park	166	A4	49.320833 -106.37916

YUKON	PAGE	GRID	LATITUDE LONGITUDE
National Park & Rec. Areas			
Dawson Hist. Complex N.H.S.	155	D2	64.050000 -139.43333
Ivvavik Natl. Park	155	D1	69.519722 -139.52500
Kluane Natl. Park and Res.-North Vis. Ctr.	155	D3	60.991800 -138.52080
Kluane Natl. Park and Res.-South Vis. Ctr.	155	D3	60.752900 -137.51010
Vuntut Natl. Park	155	D1	68.306944 -140.04750
Provincial Park & Rec. Areas			
Herschel Island-Qikiqtaruk Territorial Park	155	D1	69.592100 -139.09240

continued from page 11

SOUTHEAST

Blue Ridge Parkway★★
574 miles/924 kilometers
Maps 102, 112, 111, 90, 121
From **Front Royal**, take US-340 S to begin **Skyline Drive★★**, the best-known feature of **Shenandoah NP★★**. The drive follows former Indian trails along the **Blue Ridge Parkway★★**. **Marys Rock Tunnel to Rockfish Entrance Station★★** passes the oldest rock in the park and **Big Meadows★**. The Drive ends at **Rockfish Gap** at I-64, but continue S on the Parkway. From Terrapin Hill Overlook, detour 6mi W on Rte. 130 to see **Natural Bridge★★**. Enter NC at **Cumberland Knob**, then pass **Blowing Rock★**, **Grandfather Mountain★★** and **Linville Falls★★**. Detour 4.8mi to **Mount Mitchell SP★** to drive to the top of the tallest mountain (6,684ft) E of the Mississippi. At mile 382, the **Folk Art Center** stocks high-quality regional crafts. Popular **Biltmore Estate★★** in **Asheville★** (North Exit of US-25, then 4mi N) includes formal **gardens★★**. The rugged stretch from **French Broad River to Cherokee** courses 17 tunnels within two national forests. **Looking Glass Rock★★** is breathtaking. The Parkway ends at **Cherokee**, gateway to **Great Smoky Mountains NP★★★** and home of Cherokee tribe members.

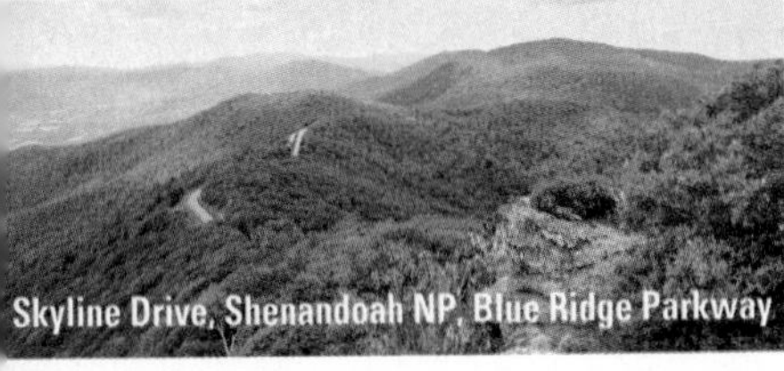
Skyline Drive, Shenandoah NP, Blue Ridge Parkway

Central Kentucky★★
379 miles/610 kilometers
Maps 230, 100, 214, 227, 110
From **Louisville★★**, home of the **Kentucky Derby★★★**, take I-64 E to **Frankfort**, the state capital. Continue E to **Lexington★★**, heart of **Bluegrass Country★★** with its rolling meadows and white-fenced horse farms. Stop at the **Kentucky Horse Park★★★** (4089 Iron Works Pkwy.) for the daily **Parade of Breeds**. Then head S on I-75 through Richmond to the craft center/college town of **Berea**. Return to Lexington and follow the Blue Grass Parkway SW to Exit 25. There, US-150 W leads to Bardstown, site of **My Old Kentucky Home SP★**, immortalized by Stephen Foster in what is now the state song. Drive S from Bardstown on US-31E past **Abraham Lincoln Birthplace NHS★**. Turn right onto Rte.

70 to Cave City, then take US-31W to Park City, gateway to **Mammoth Cave NP★★★**, which features the world's longest cave system. Return to Louisville via I-65 to end the tour.

Florida's Northeast Coast★★
174 miles/280 kilometers
Maps 222, 139, 141, 232
From **Jacksonville★**, drive E on Rte. 10 to **Atlantic Beach**, the most affluent of Jacksonville's beach towns. Head S on Rte. A1A through residential **Neptune Beach**, **Jacksonville Beach** and upscale **Ponte Vedra Beach** to reach **St. Augustine★★★**, the oldest city in the US and former capital of Spanish Florida. Farther S, car-racing mecca **Daytona Beach** is known for its **international speedway**. Take US-92 across the Intracoastal Waterway to US-1, heading S to **Titusville**. Take Rte. 402 across the Indian River to **Merritt Island NWR★★** to begin **Black Point Wildlife Drive★**. Return to **Titusville** and follow Rte. 405 to **Kennedy Space Center★★★**, one of Florida's top attractions, to end the tour.

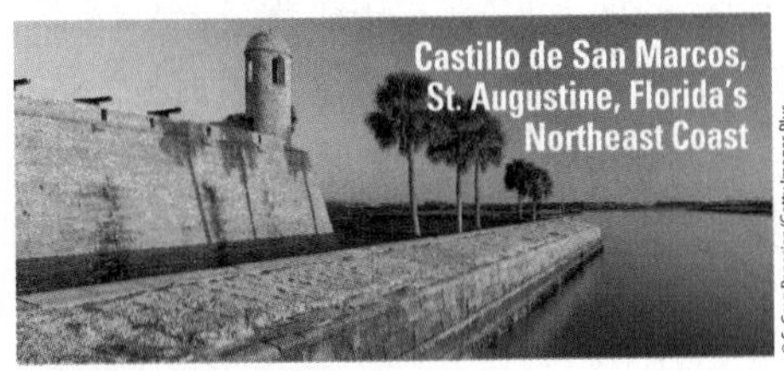
Castillo de San Marcos, St. Augustine, Florida's Northeast Coast

Florida Keys★★
168 miles/270 kilometers
Maps 143, 142
*Note: Green **mile-marker (MM)** posts, sometimes difficult to see, line US-1 (Overseas Hwy.), showing distances from Key West (MM 0). Most of the route is two-lane, and traffic can be heavy from December to April and on weekends. Allow 3hrs for the drive. Crossing 43 bridges and causeways (only one over land), the highway offers fine views of the Atlantic Ocean (E) and Florida Bay (W).*
Drive S from **Miami★★★** on US-1. Near **Key Largo★**, **John Pennekamp Coral Reef SP★★** habors tropical fish, coral and fine snorkeling waters. To the SW, **Islamorada** is known for **charter fishing**. At **Marathon** (MM 50), **Sombrero Beach** is a good swimming spot, but **Bahia Honda SP★★** (MM 36.8) is considered

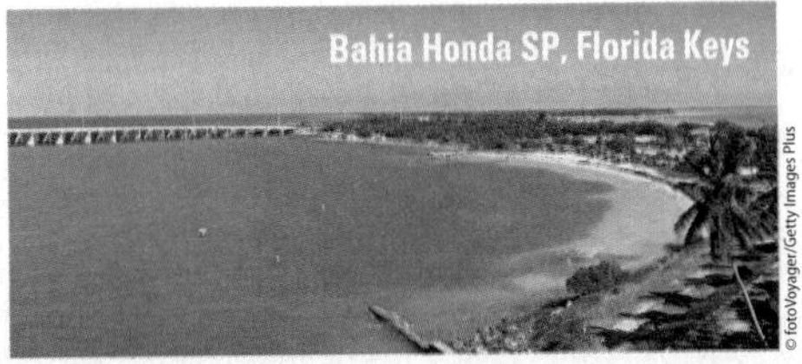
Bahia Honda SP, Florida Keys

the best **beach★★** in the Keys. Pass **National Key Deer Refuge★** (MM 30.5), haven to the 2ft-tall deer unique to the lower Keys. End at **Key West★★★**, joining others at **Mallory Square Dock** to view the **sunset★★**.

The Ozarks★
343 miles/552 kilometers
Maps 227, 117, 219, 107, 106
From the state capital of **Little Rock**, take I-30 SW to Exit 111, then US-70 W to Hot Springs. Drive N on Rte. 7/Central Ave. to **Hot Springs NP★★** to enjoy the therapeutic waters. Travel N on Rte. 7 across the Arkansas River to Russellville.
Continue on **Scenic Highway 7★** N through **Ozark National Forest** and across the **Buffalo National River** to Harrison. Take US-62/65 NW to Bear Creek Springs, continuing W on US-62 through **Eureka Springs★**, with its historic district, to **Pea Ridge NMP★**, a Civil War site. Return E on US-62 to the junction of Rte. 21 at Berryville. Travel N on Rte. 21 to Blue Eye, taking Rte. 86 E to US-65, which leads N to the entertainment hub of **Branson**, Missouri, to end the tour.

River Road Plantations★★
200 miles/323 kilometers
Maps 239, 134, 194
From **New Orleans★★★**, take US-90 W to Rte. 48 along the Mississippi River to Destrehan. **Destrehan★★** is considered the oldest plantation house in the Mississippi Valley. Continue NW on Rte. 48 to US-61 to Laplace to connect to Rte. 44. Head N past **San Francisco Plantation★**, built in 1856. At Burnside, take Rte. 75 N to St. Gabriel. En route, watch for **Houmas House★** (40136 Hwy. 942). Take Rte. 30 to **Baton Rouge★**, the state capital. Then drive S along the **West Bank★★** on Rte. 1 to White Castle, site of **Nottoway★**, the largest plantation home in the South. Continue to Donaldsonville, then turn onto Rte. 18. Travel E to Gretna, passing **Oak Alley★★** (no. 3645) and **Laura Plantation★★** (no. 2247) along the way. From Gretna, take US-90 to New Orleans, where the tour ends.

CANADA

Gaspésie, Québec★★★
933 kilometers/578 miles (loop)
Map 178, 179
Leave **Sainte-Flavie** via Rte. 132 NE, stopping to visit **Reford Gardens★★★** en route to **Matane**. After Cap-Chat, take Rte. 299 S to **Gaspésie Park★** for expansive **views★★**. Back

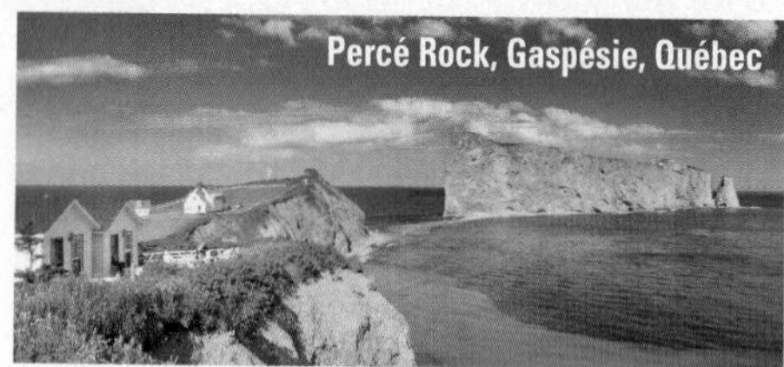
Percé Rock, Gaspésie, Québec

and **Neils Harbour★**. Rejoin Cabot Trail S, passing the resort area of the **Ingonishs**. Take the right fork after Indian Brook to reach St. Ann's, home of **Gaelic College★**, specializing in bagpipe and Highland dance classes. Rejoin Hwy. 105 to return to Baddeck.

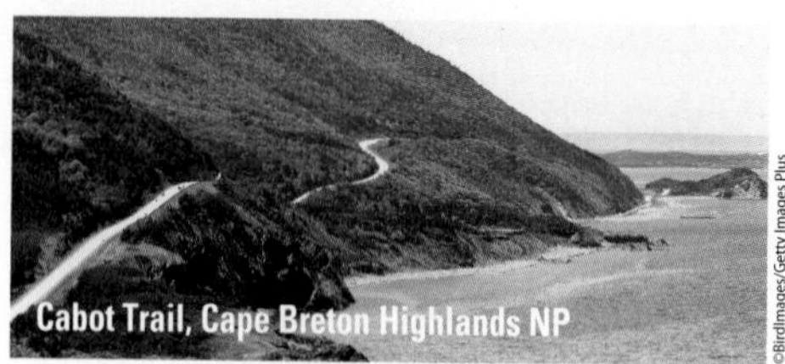
Cabot Trail, Cape Breton Highlands NP

on Rte. 132, follow the **Scenic Route from La Martre to Rivière-au-Renard★★**. Continue to **Cap-des-Rosiers**, entrance to majestic **Forillon NP★★**. Follow Rte. 132 along the coast through **Gaspé★**, the administrative center of the peninsula, to **Percé★★★**, a coastal village known for **Percé Rock★★**, a mammoth offshore rock wall. Drive SW on Rt. 132 through **Paspébiac** to **Carleton**, which offers a **panorama★★** from the summit of **Mont Saint-Joseph**. Farther SW, detour 6km/4mi S to see an array of fossils at **Parc de Miguasha★**. Back on Rte. 132, travel W to **Matapédia**, then follow Rte. 132 N, passing **Causapscal**—a departure point for salmon fishing expeditions—to end the tour at Sainte-Flavie.

North Shore Lake Superior★★

275 kilometers/171 miles   Map 169
From the port city of **Thunder Bay★★**—and nearby **Old Fort William★★**—drive the Trans-Canada Hwy. (Rte. 11/17) E to Rte. 587. Detour to **Sleeping Giant PP★**, which offers fine **views★** of the lake. Back along the Trans-Canada Hwy., **Amethyst Mine** (take E. Loon Rd.) is a rock hound's delight (fee). Farther NE, located 12km/8mi off the highway, **Ouimet Canyon★★** is a startling environment for the area. Just after the highway's Red Rock turnoff, watch for **Red Rock Cuesta**, a natural formation 210m/690ft high. Cross the Nipigon River and continue along **Nipigon Bay★★**, enjoying **views★★** of the rocky, conifer-covered islands. The **view★★** of **Kama Bay** through **Kama Rock Cut** is striking. Continue to **Schreiber** to end the tour.

Nova Scotia's Cabot Trail★★

338 kilometers/210 miles   Map 181
From **Baddeck★**, follow Hwy. 105 S to the junction with **Cabot Trail** to **North East Margaree★** in salmon-fishing country. Take this road NW to Margaree Harbour, then N to **Chéticamp**, an enclave of Acadian culture. Heading inland, the route enters **Cape Breton Highlands NP★★**, combining seashore and mountains. At Cape North, detour N around Aspy Bay to **Bay St. Lawrence★★**. Then head W to tiny **Capstick** for shoreline **views★**. Return S to Cape North, then drive E to South Harbour. Take the coast road, traveling S through the fishing villages of **New Haven**

Canadian Rockies★★★

467 kilometers/290 miles   Map 164
Note: Some roads in Yoho NP are closed to cars mid-Oct to June due to snow, but are open for skiing.
Leave Banff★★ by Hwy. 1, traveling W. After 5.5km/3.5mi, take **Bow Valley Parkway★** (Hwy. 1A) NW within **Banff NP★★★**. At Lake Louise Village, detour W to find **Lake Louise★★★**. Back on Hwy. 1, head N to the junction of Hwy. 93, turn W and follow Hwy. 1 past Kicking Horse Pass into **Yoho NP★★**. Continue through Field, and turn right onto the road N to **Emerald Lake★★★**. Return to the junction of Rte. 93 and Hwy. 1, heading N on Rte. 93 along the Icefields **Parkway★★★**. Pass **Crowfoot Glacier★★** and **Bow Lake★★** on the left. **Peyto Lake★★★** is reached by spur road. After **Parker Ridge★★**, massive **Athabasca Glacier★★★** looms on the left. Continue to **Jasper★** and **Jasper NP★★★**. From Jasper, turn left onto Hwy. 16 and head into **Mount Robson PP★★**, home to **Mount Robson★★★** (3,954m/12,972ft). End the tour at Tête Jaune Cache.

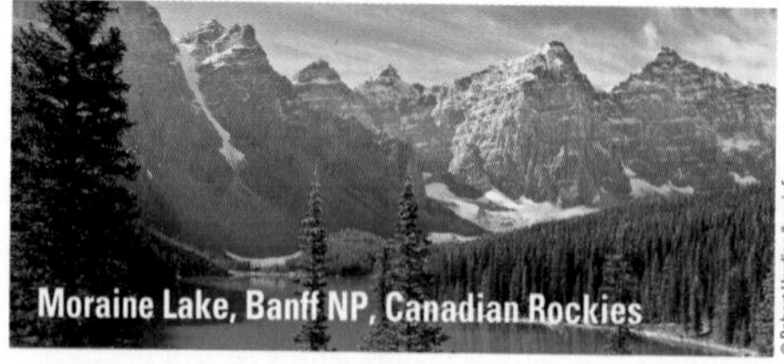
Moraine Lake, Banff NP, Canadian Rockies

Vancouver Island★★★

337 kilometers/209 miles
Maps 282, 163, 162
To enjoy a scenic drive that begins 11mi N of **Victoria★★★**, take Douglas St. N from Victoria to the Trans-Canada Highway (Hwy. 1) and follow **Malahat Drive★** (between Goldstream PP and Mill Bay Rd.) for 12mi. Continue N on Hwy. 1 past Duncan, **Chemainus★** —known for its murals—and Nanaimo to

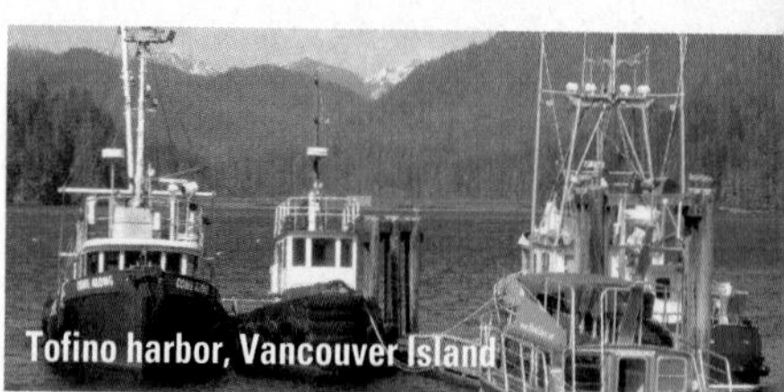
Tofino harbor, Vancouver Island

Parksville. Take winding Rte. 4 W (Pacific Rim Hwy.) passing **Englishman River Falls PP★** and **Cameron Lake**. Just beyond the lake, **Cathedral Grove★★** holds 800-year-old Douglas firs. The road descends to **Port Alberni**, departure point for cruises on Barkley Sound, and follows Sproat Lake before climbing Klitsa Mountain. The route leads to the Pacific along the Kennedy River. At the coast, turn left and drive SE to Ucluelet. Then head N to enter **Pacific Rim NPR★★★**. Continue to road's end at **Tofino★** to end the tour.

Yukon Circuit★★

1,485 kilometers/921 miles   Map 155
Note: Top of the World Highway is closed mid-Oct to mid-May due to snow.
From **Whitehorse★**, capital of Yukon Territory, drive N on the **Klondike Hwy.** (Rte. 2), crossing the Yukon River at **Carmacks**. After 196km/122mi, small islands divide the river into fast-flowing channels at **Five Finger Rapids★**. From Stewart Crossing, continue NW on Rte. 2 to **Dawson★★**, a historic frontier town. Ferry across the river and drive the **Top of the World Hwy.★★** (Rte. 9), with its **views★★★**, to the Alaska border. Rte. 9 joins Rte. 5, passing tiny **Chicken**, Alaska. At Tetlin Junction, head SE on Rte. 2, paralleling **Tetlin NWR**. Enter Canada and follow the **Alaska Highway★★** (Rte. 1) SE along **Kluane Lake★★** to **Haines Junction**, gateway to **Kluane NPR★★**, home of **Mount Logan**, Canada's highest peak (5,959m/19,550ft). Continue E to Rte. 2 to return to Whitehorse.

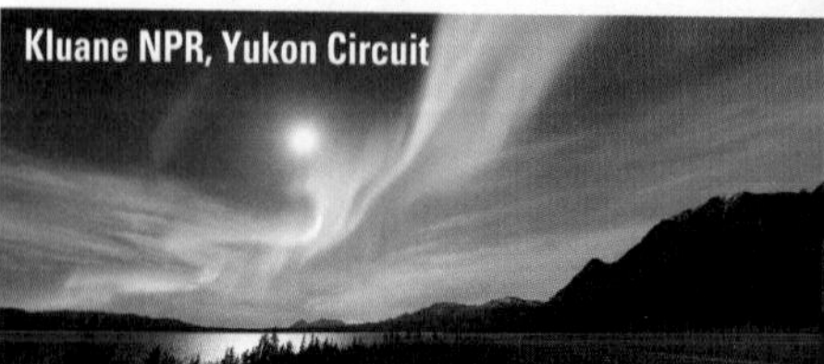
Kluane NPR, Yukon Circuit

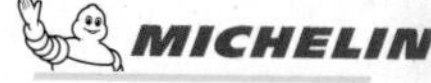

Notes

Notes

Édition 20.1 - 2022 – Éditeur : MICHELIN Éditions
Société par actions simplifiée au capital de 487 500 EUR
57 rue Gaston Tessier – 75019 Paris (France)
R.C.S. Paris 882 639 354 - DL : MAI 2022
Copyright © 2022 MICHELIN Éditions - Tous droits réservés
Printed by Transcontinental - Boucherville (Quebec) J4B 5Y2 - March 2022 - Printed in Canada

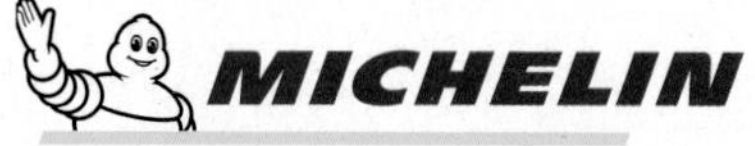